U0907145

2016
北京统计年鉴
Beijing Statistical Yearbook

© 中国统计出版社 2016
版权所有。未经许可，本书的任何部分不得以任何方式在世界任何地区以任何文字翻印、拷贝、仿制或转载。
© 2016 CHINA STATISTICS PRESS
All rights reserved. No part of the publication may be reproduced or transmitted in any form or by any means, electronic or mechanical, including photocopying, recording, or any information storage and retrieval system, without written permission from the publisher.

图书在版编目(CIP)数据

北京统计年鉴. 2016 : 汉英对照 / 北京市统计局，国家统计局北京调查总队编. -- 北京：中国统计出版社，2016.10

ISBN 978-7-5037-7816-2

Ⅰ. ①北 Ⅱ. ①北 ②国 Ⅲ. ①统计资料－北京市－2016－年鉴－汉、英 Ⅳ. ①C832.1-54

中国版本图书馆CIP数据核字(2016)第145281号

北京统计年鉴-2016

作　　者/北京市统计局 国家统计局北京调查总队
责任编辑/郭 栋 李 冲
封面设计/高 立
出版发行/中国统计出版社
通信地址/北京市丰台区西三环南路甲6号 邮政编码/100073
电　　话/邮购（010）63376909 书店（010）68783171
网　　址/http://www.zgtjcbs.com
印　　刷/北京联兴盛业印刷有限公司
经　　销/新华书店
开　　本/880mm×1230mm 1/16
字　　数/1200千字
印　　张/38.75印张 彩插/1.25印张
版　　别/2016年10月第1版
版　　次/2016年10月第1次印刷
定　　价/350.00元

本书附同版本CD-ROM一张，光盘内容以书面文字为准。
如有印装差错，由本社发行部调换。

2015年，面对错综复杂的外部环境和改革发展的艰巨任务，全市上下积极适应经济发展新常态，加快转变发展方式，扎实做好稳增长、促改革、调结构、惠民生各项工作，首都经济保持了平稳健康发展态势，为“十二五”划上圆满句号，同时为“十三五”顺利开局奠定了坚实基础。

In 2015, confronted with complicated external situation and the formidable task of reform and development, the whole city of Beijing actively adapted to the new normal of economic development, accelerated the transform of economic development mode and steadily completed the works on stabling growth, accelerating reform, restructuring and benefiting the people's livelihood. Beijing maintained a stable and sound momentum of economic development, successfully completed the 12th Five-Year Plan and laid a solid foundation for a smooth commencement of the 13th Five-Year Plan.

2015年的北京 Beijing in 2015

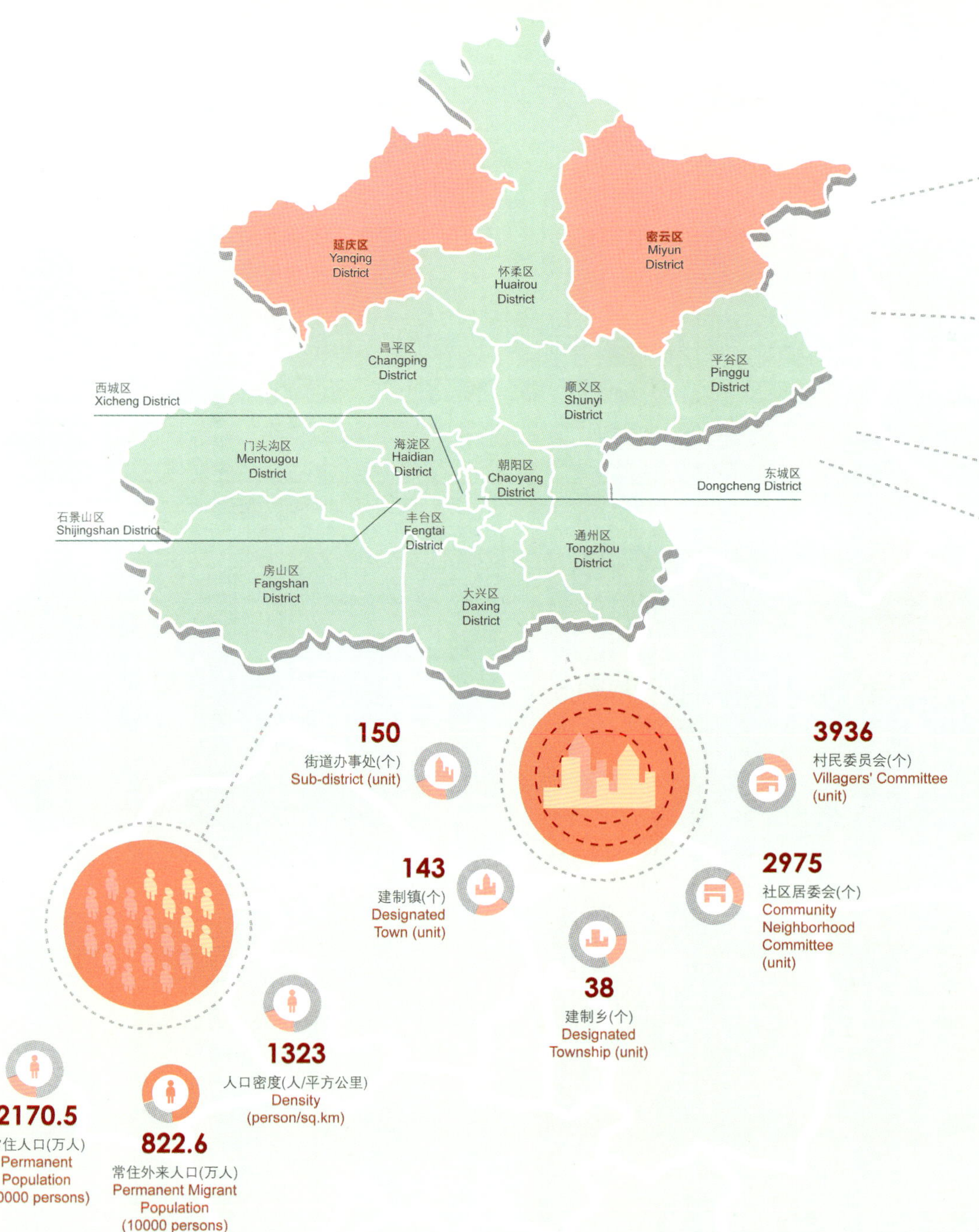

48.4
城市绿化覆盖率(%)
Urban Green Area Coverage (%)

16.0
人均公园绿地面积(平方米)
Per Capital Park Green Areas (square meter)

554
轨道交通运营线路长度(公里)
Length of Rail Transportation Lines in Operation (kilometer)

561.9
机动车保有量(万辆)
Number of Civil Motor Vehicles (10,000 units)

123.8
人均水资源(立方米/人)
Per-capita Water Resource(cu.m)

52859
城镇居民人均可支配收入(元)
Per Capita Annual Disposable Income of Urban Residents (yuan)

23014.6
地区生产总值(亿元)
Gross Domestic Product (100 million yuan)

106497
人均地区生产总值(元)
Per Capita Gross Domestic Product (USD)

20569
农村居民人均纯收入(元)
Per Capita Net Income of Rural Residents (yuan)

79.7
第三产业比重(%)
Percentage of Tertiary Industry (%)

101.8
居民消费价格指数(%)
Consumer Price Index (%)

4723.9
一般公共预算收入(亿元)
Local Public Budgetary Financial Revenue (100 million yuan)

7990.9
全社会固定资产投资额(亿元)
Total Investment in Fixed Assets (100 million yuan)

4.44
每千常住人口执业医师(人)
Number of Licensed Doctors per 1000 Permanent Population (person)

5.27
每千常住人口注册护士(人)
Number of Certified Nurses per 1000 Permanent Population (person)

10338.0
社会消费品零售总额(亿元)
Total Retail Sales of Consumer Goods (100 million yuan)

6.01
研究与试验发展(R&D)经费内部支出相当于地区生产总值比例(%)
Internal R&D Expenditure as Percentage of GDP (%)

3452.6
技术合同成交总额(亿元)
Total Amount of Technological Contracts Signed (100 million yuan)

41.0
万人发明专利申请数(件)
Number of Invention Patent Applications per 10,000 Persons (piece)

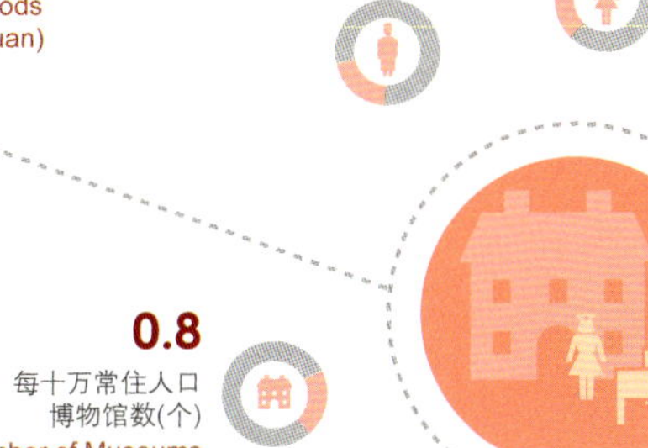

0.8
每十万常住人口博物馆数(个)
Number of Museums per 100000 Permanent Population (unit)

5.14
每千常住人口医院床位(张)
Number of Hospital Bed per 1000 permanent population (person)

6.9
每十万常住人口幼儿园数(个)
Number of Kindergartens per 100000 Permanent Population (unit)

14.3
平均每一专任教师负担小学生数(人)
Average Number of Students in Primary School Instructed by a Full-time Teacher (person)

北京一日 A Day in Beijing

每日创造
Daily Production

129420.8
一般公共预算收入(万元/日)
Local Public Budgeting Financial Revenue (10000 yuan/day)

157197.3
一般公共预算支出(万元/日)
Local Public Budgeting Financial Expenditure (10000 yuan/day)

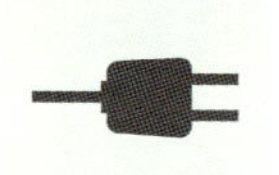

11435.2
发电量(万千瓦时/日)
Generating Capacity (10000 kWh/day)

6080
汽车生产量(辆/日)
Output of Motor Vehicles (unit/day)

261392
移动电话机生产量(台/日)
Output of Mobile Telephone (unit/day)

506
自来水综合生产能力(万立方米/日)
General Production Capacity of Tap Water (10,000 cu.m/day)

14219
显示器(台/日)
Display (unit/day)

3841.4
第一产业(万元/日)
Primary Industry (10000 yuan/day)

124455.9
第二产业(万元/日)
Secondary Industry (10000 yuan/day)

502239.5
第三产业(万元/日)
Tertiary Industry (10000 yuan/day)

630536.7
地区生产总值 (万元/日)
Gross Domestic Product (10000 yuan/day)

14976.9
海关出口总值(万美元/日)
Total Value of Export at Customs (USD 1000/day)

1112.3
公共电汽车客运量(万人次/日)
Passengers Carried by Buses and Trolley Buses (10000 person-times/day)

118356.2
国内旅游收入(万元/日)
Domestic Tourism Income (10000/day yuan/day)

910.6
轨道交通客运量(万人次/日)
Passengers Carried by Rail Transit (10000 person-times/day)

1261.6
旅游外汇收入(万美元/日)
Foreign Exchange Earnings from Tourism (USD 10000/day)

1.15
接待入境旅游人数(万人次/日)
Inbound Tourists (10000 persons /day)

19.7
民航客运量(万人次/日)
Civil Aviation Passenger Traffic (10000 person-times/day)

136.8
公路客运量(万人次/日)
Highway Passenger Traffic (10000 person-times/day)

35.1
铁路客运量(万人次/日)
Railway Passenger Traffic (10000 person-times/day)

2015 年 Year

❶ 人均地区生产总值(元/人)
Per Capita Gross Domestic Product (yuan/person)

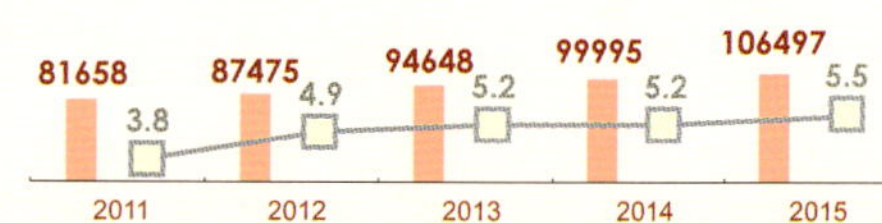

❷ 常住人口(万人)
Permanent Population (10000 persons)

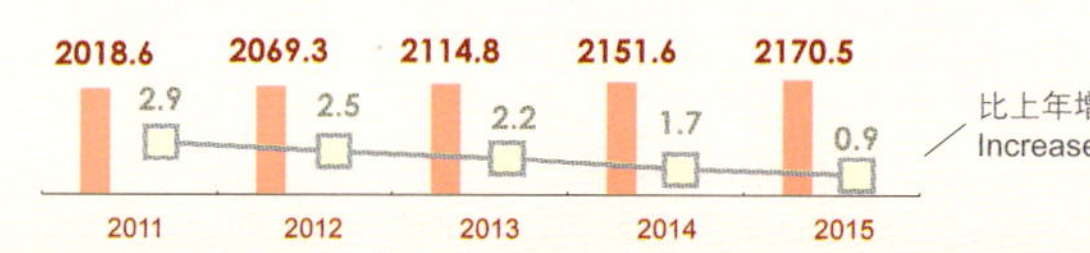

历史数据 Historical Data

每日生活 Daily Life

471
常住出生人口（人/日）
Birth Population (Permanent Population) (person/day)

293
常住死亡人口（人/日）
Death Population (Permanent Population) (person/day)

455
登记结婚对数（对/日）
Marriage Registered (couple/day)

225
离婚对数（对/日）
Registered Divorces (couple/day)

144.8
城镇居民人均可支配收入(元/日)
Per Capita Disposable Income of Urban Residents (yuan/day)

387.5
特快专递业务量（万件/日）
Business Volume of EMS (10000/day)

100.4
城镇居民人均消费性支出(元/日)
Per Capita Consumption Expenditures of Urban Residents (yuan/day)

53899.6
吃类商品(万元/日)
Food (10000 yuan/day)

20350.0
穿类商品(万元/日)
Clothing(10000 yuan/day)

196062.2
用类商品(万元/日)
Daily Supplies(10000 yuan/day)

12921.2
烧类商品(万元/日)
Fuel(10000 yuan/day)

283232.9
社会消费品零售总额 (万元/日)
Retail Sales of Consumer Goods (10000 yuan/day)

3145
机动车销售量（辆/日）
Sales of Automobiles (unit/day)

56.4
农村居民人均可支配收入(元/日)
Per Capita Net Income of Rural Residents (yuan/day)

2.17
生活垃圾清运量（万吨/日）
Domestic Waste Removed and Transported (10000 tons/day)

43.3
农村居民人均生活消费支出(元/日)
Per Capita Living Expenditures of Rural Residents (yuan/day)

4787.9
城乡居民生活用电量（万千瓦时/日）
Urban and Rural Residential Electricity Consumption (10000 kWh/day)

375.9
居民家庭用天然气（万立方米/日）
Natural Gas for Living Use (10000 cu.m/day)

139.5
居民家庭用自来水（万立方米/日）
Tap Water for Living Use (10000 cu.m/day)

5428
电影放映场次（场次/日）
Film Show Times (Times/day)

309.8
城镇单位在岗职工平均工资(元/日)
Average Wage of Fully Employed Staff and Workers in Urban Entities(yuan/day)

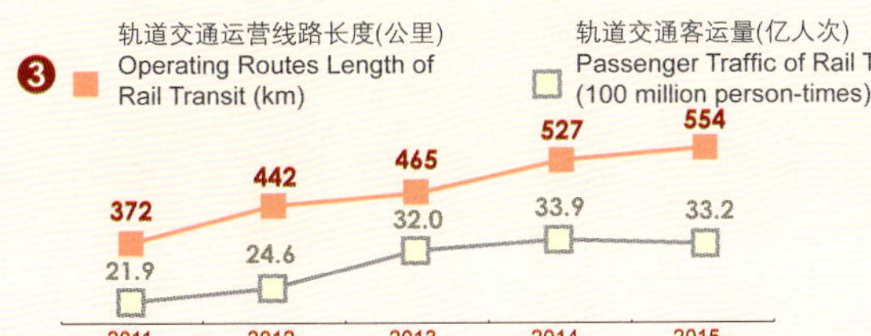

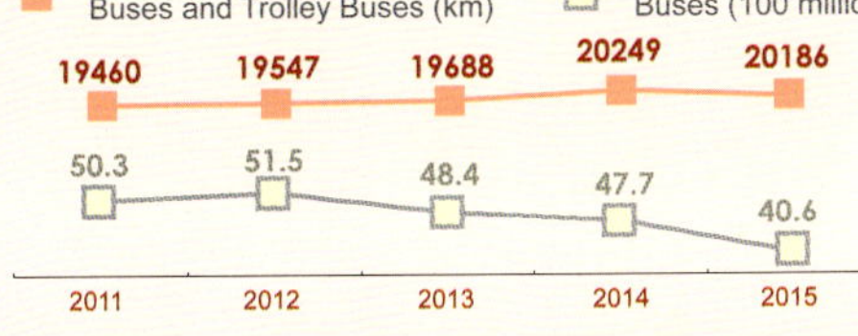

经济运行总体平稳 结构调整取得成效

Overall economic development was stable. The restructuring work delivered results.

地区生产总值增速运行在合理区间

The growth rate of GDP was within the reasonable range

地区生产总值(亿元)
Gross Domestic Product (100 million yuan)

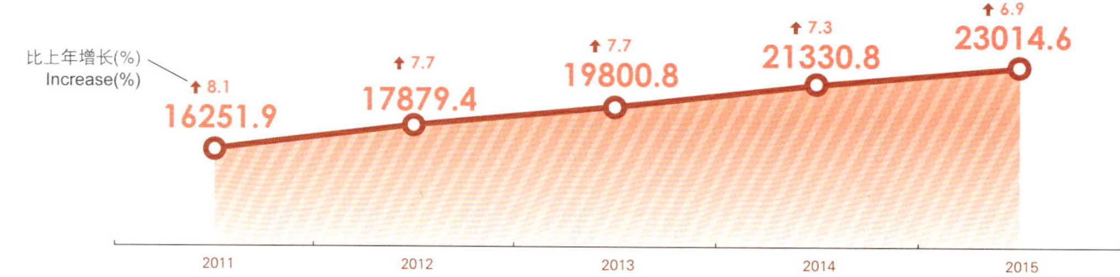

居民消费价格走势平稳

The CPI developed steadily

居民消费价格指数(%)
Consumer Price Index (%)

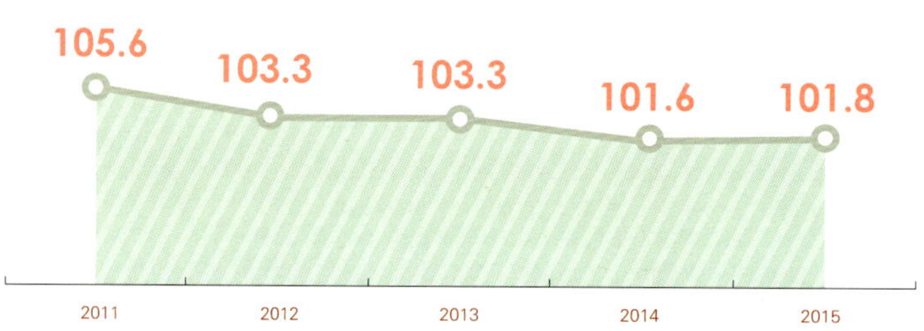

城镇登记失业率保持低位

The registered unemployed rate in urban area kept at a low level

城镇登记失业率(%)
Registered Unermployment Rate in Urban Area (%)

❶ 第三产业增加值占全市地区生产总值比重(%)
The percentage of tertiary industry in GDP (%)

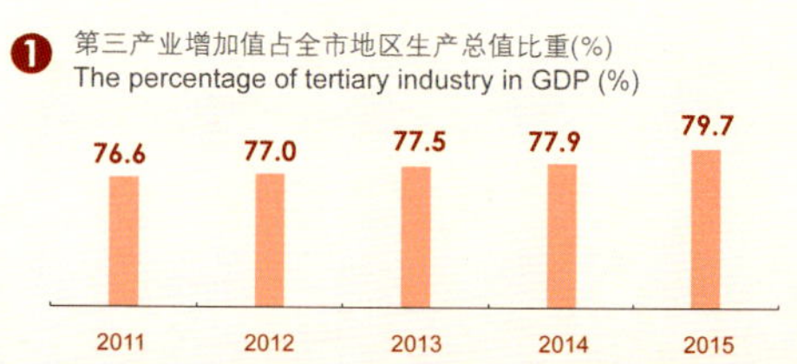

❷ 第三产业从业人员占全市从业人员比重(%)
The percentage of the tertiary industry in the employed persons(%)

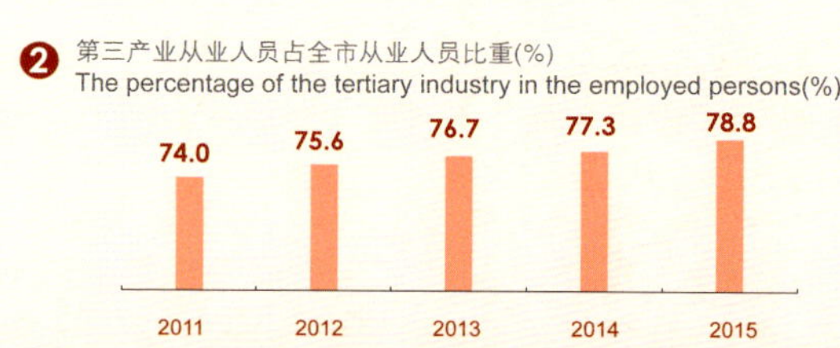

优势产业带动作用明显
Leading role of competitive industries was significant

生产性服务业增加值(亿元)
Added Value of Producer Services (100 million yuan)

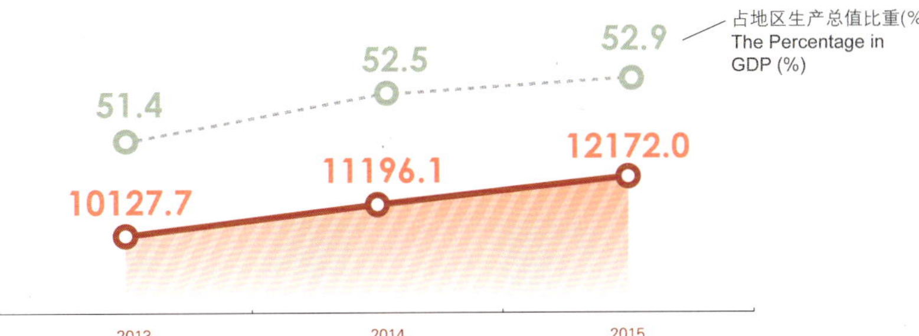

文化创意产业增加值(亿元)
Added Value of Cultural and Creative Industry (100 million yuan)

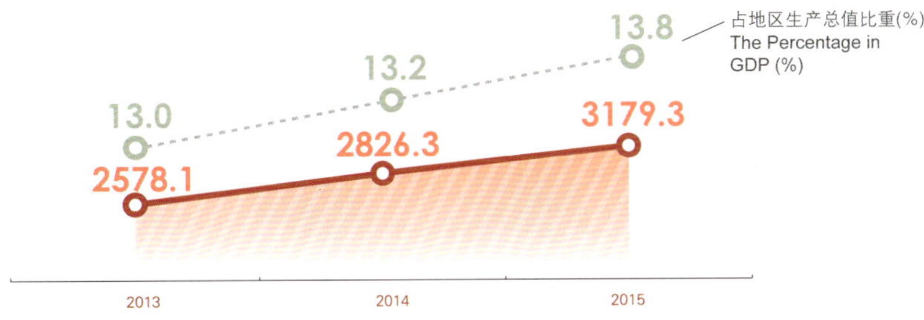

高技术产业增加值(亿元)
Added Value of High Technology Industry (100 million yuan)

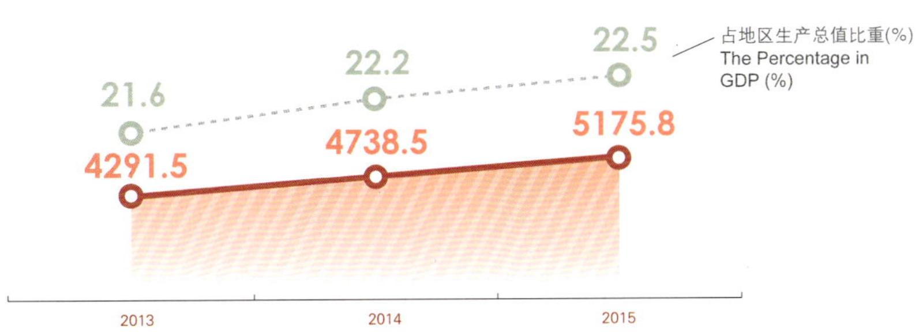

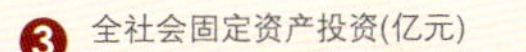

③ 全社会固定资产投资(亿元)
Total Investment in Fixed Assets (100 million yuan)

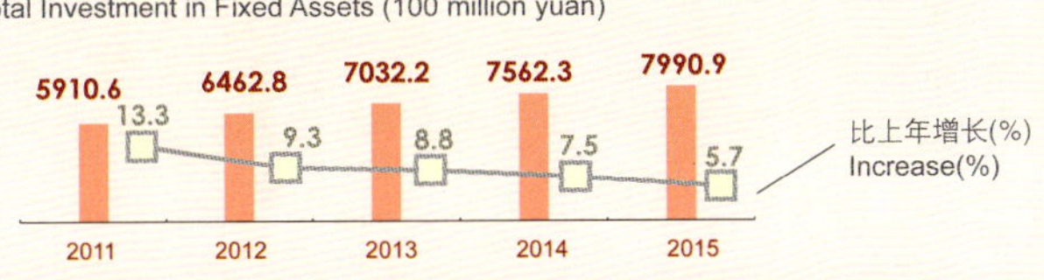

④ 社会消费品零售总额(亿元)
Total Retail Sales of Consumer Goods (100 million yuan)

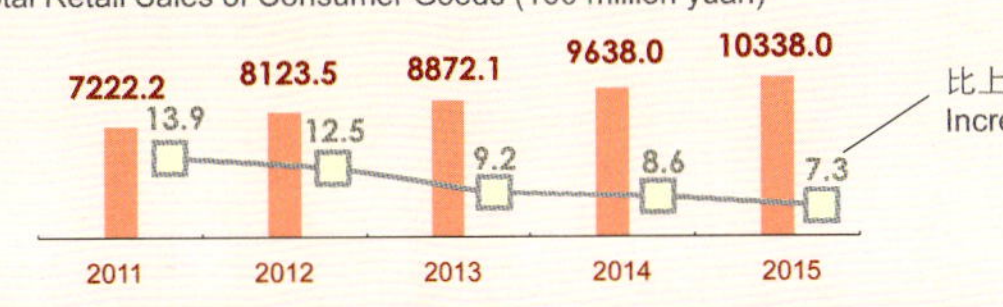

创新引领积蓄动能 科技投入与产出表现活跃

Innovation led in saving kinetic energy. S&T Input and output was active.

科技投入与产出持续增长
S&T input and output rose continuously

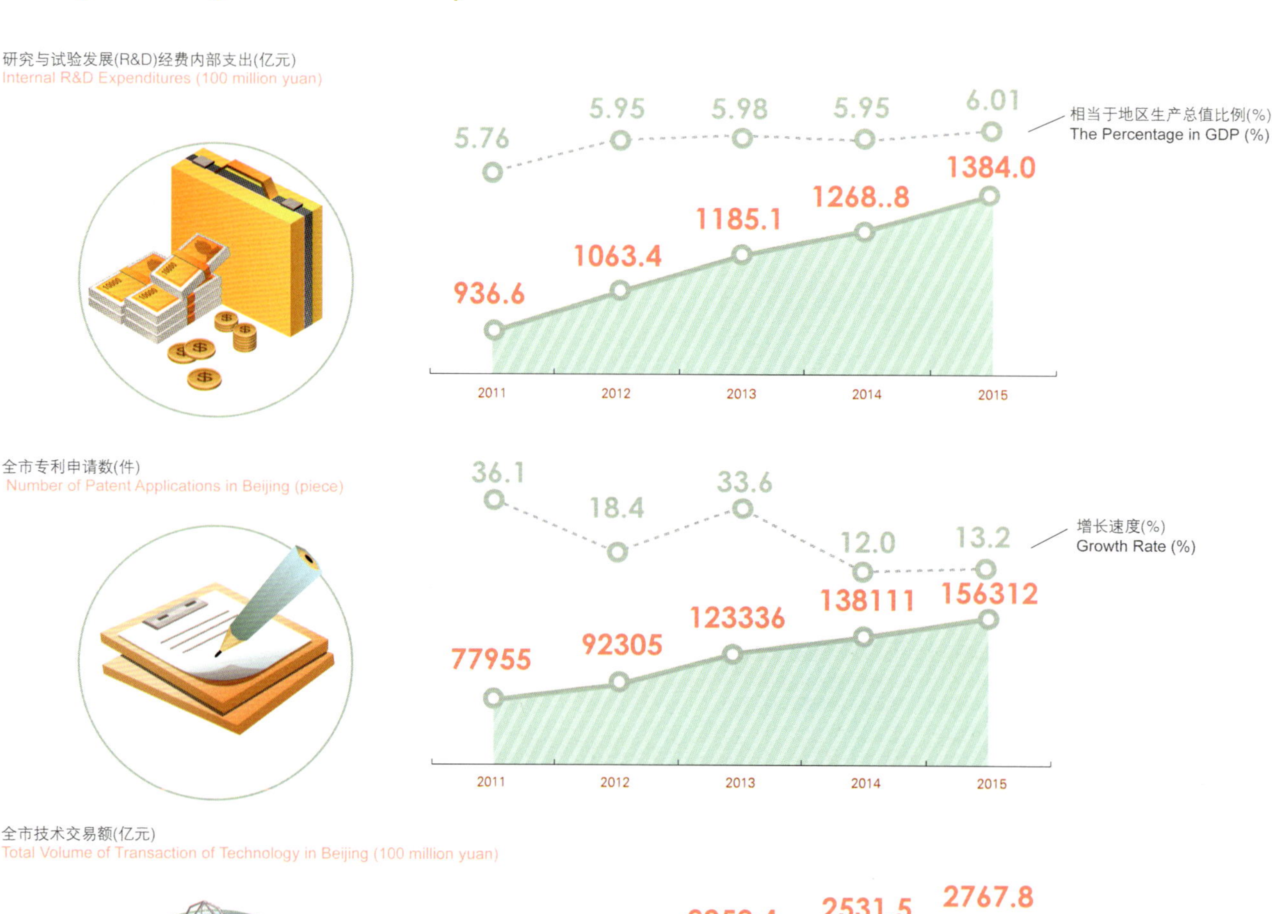

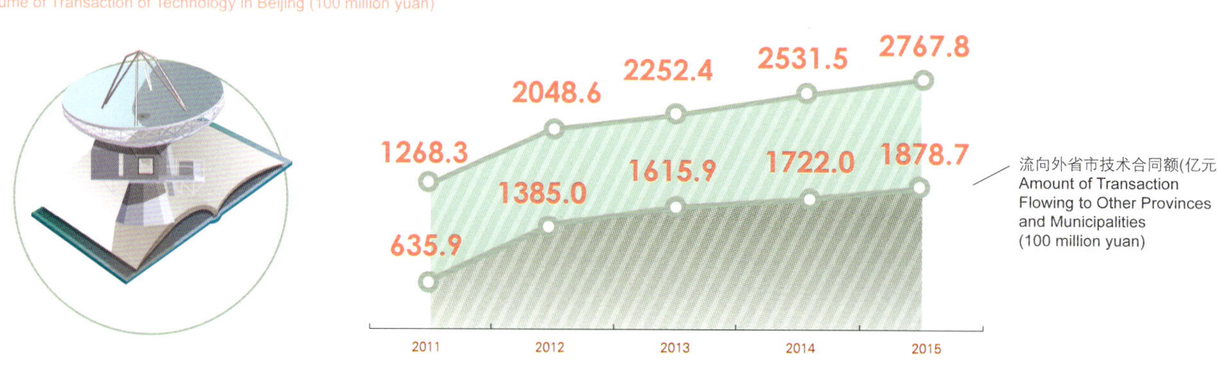

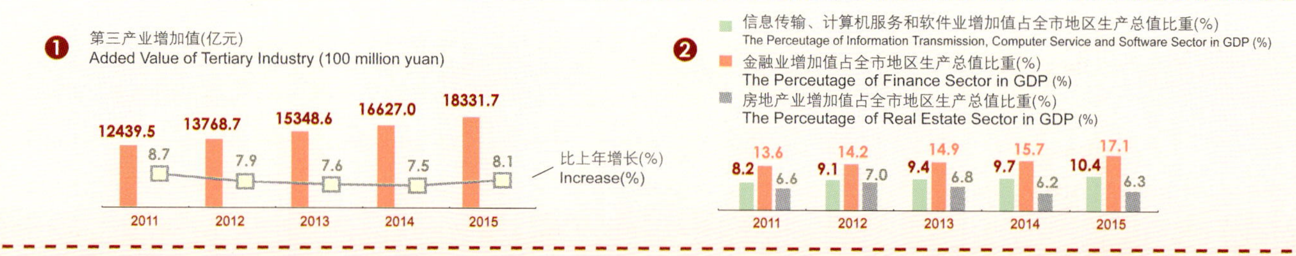

中关村示范区显现创新引领作用
Zhongguancun Science Park played a leading role in innovation

科技研发人员(万人)
R&D Personnel (10,000 persons)

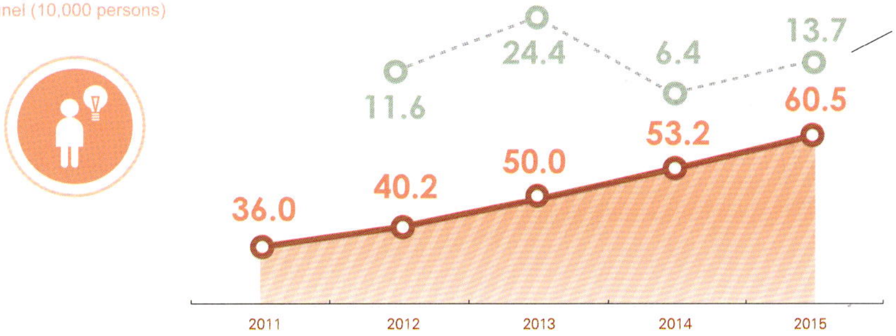

36.0
40.2
50.0
53.2
60.5
11.6
24.4
6.4
13.7
增长速度(%)
Growth Rate (%)
2011
2012
2013
2014
2015

拥有有效发明专利数(件)
Number of Valid Invention Patents (piece)

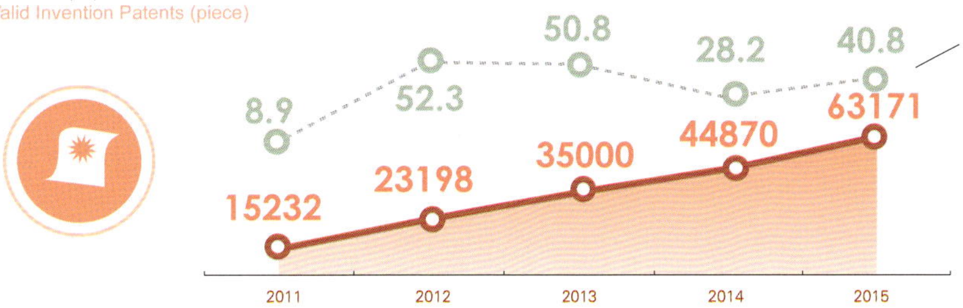

15232
23198
35000
44870
63171
8.9
52.3
50.8
28.2
40.8
增长速度(%)
Growth Rate (%)
2011
2012
2013
2014
2015

中关村示范区利润总额(亿元)
Total Profit of Zhongguancun Science Park (100 million yuan)

1533.9
1788.6
2264.8
3031.5
3404.5
18.0
16.6
26.6
33.9
12.3
增长速度(%)
Growth Rate (%)
2011
2012
2013
2014
2015

❸ 中关村国家自主创新示范区总收入(亿元)
Total Income of Zhongguancun Science Park (100 million yuan)

19646.0
2845.9
25025.0
3403.1
30497.4
4032.4
36057.6
4837.7
40811.9
6623.6
技术收入(亿元)
Technical Revenues
(100 million yuan)
2011
2012
2013
2014
2015

❹ 中关村国家自主创新示范区实缴税费总额(亿元)
Total Tax Paid of Zhongguancun Science Park (100 million yuan)

925.8
20.7
1445.8
56.2
1506.6
4.2
1857.6
23.3
2038.1
9.7
比上年增长(%)
Increase (%)
2011
2012
2013
2014
2015

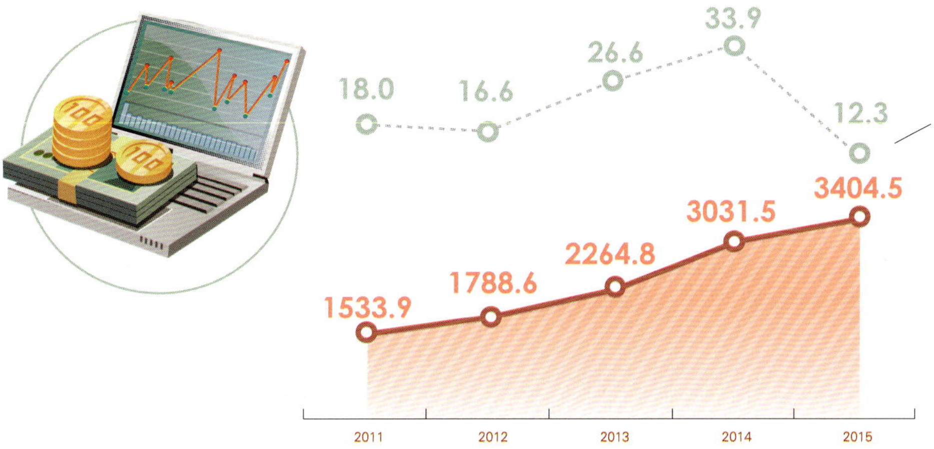

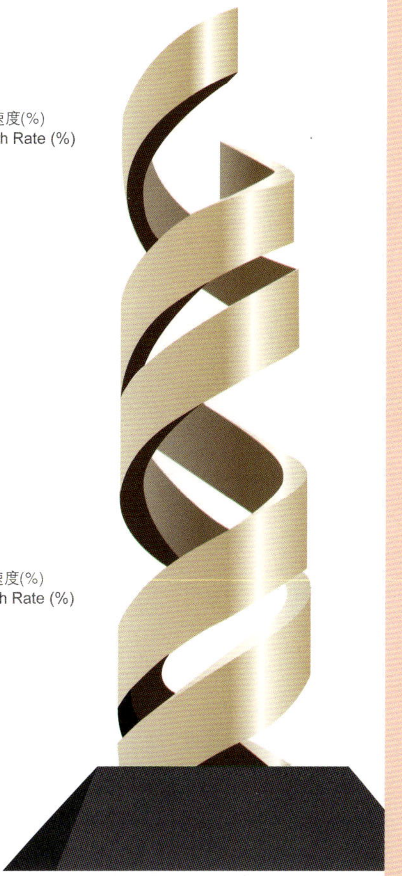

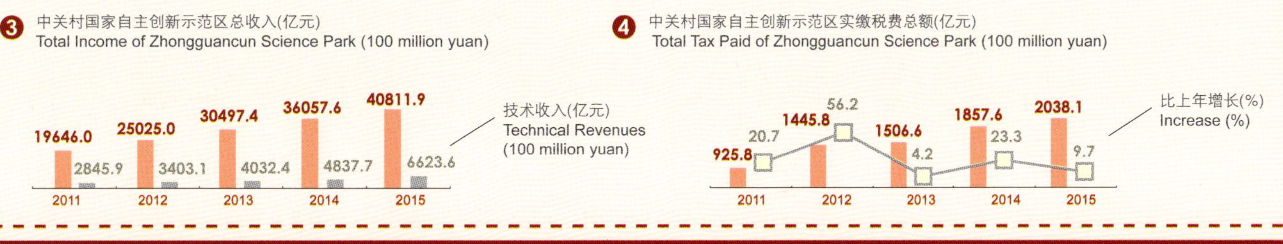

疏解促进协调发展 质量、效率共同提升

Function Dispersal promoted coordinated development. Improved both quality and efficiency.

产业疏解持续推进，“瘦身健体”成效明显
Industrial dispersal got significant results

商品交易市场数量(个)
Number of Commodity Transaction Markets (unit)

2013	2014	2015
821	728	719

商品交易市场总摊位数量(个)
Number of Booths in Commodity Transaction Markets (unit)

2013	2014	2015
274300	253087	243883

人口调控取得进展，增量增速实现双下降
Population regulation got reduction of growth amount and rate

常住人口增量(万人)
Annual Increment of Permanent Population (10,000 persons)

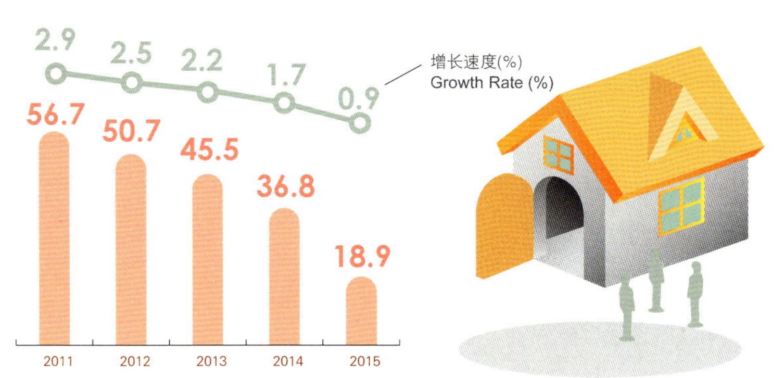

常住外来人口增量(万人)

Annual Increment of Permanent Migrant Population (10,000 persons)

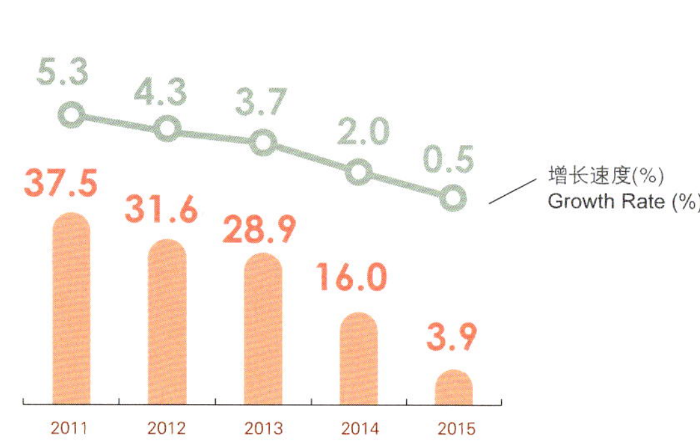

❶ 常住人口(万人)
Permanent Population (10,000 persons)
其中：常住外来人口(万人)
Including: Permanent Migrant Population (10,000 persons)

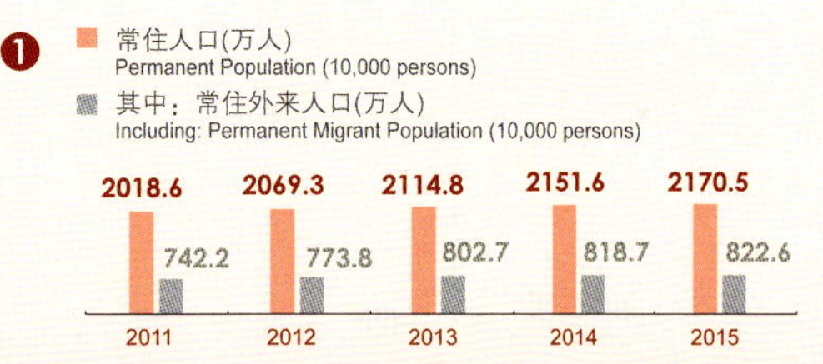

❷ 60岁及以上人口占常住人口比重(%)
The Percentage of Population over 60 Years Old in Permanent Population (%)
65岁及以上人口占常住人口比重(%)
The Percentage of Population over 65 Years Old in Permanent Population (%)

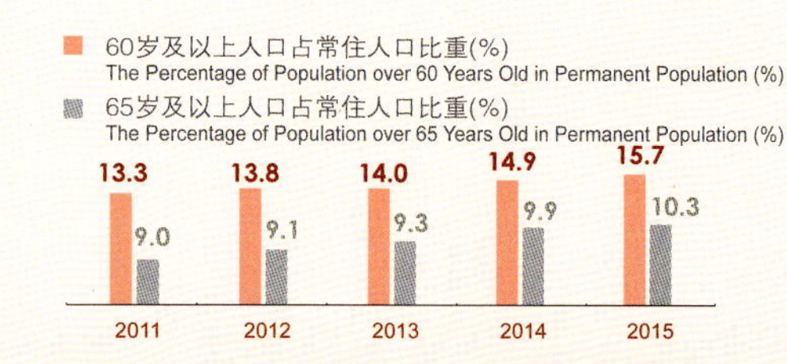

劳动生产率稳步提升，就业人口逐步向高端产业聚集
Overall labor productivity rose steadily, and the employment population gradually gathered towards the high-end industry

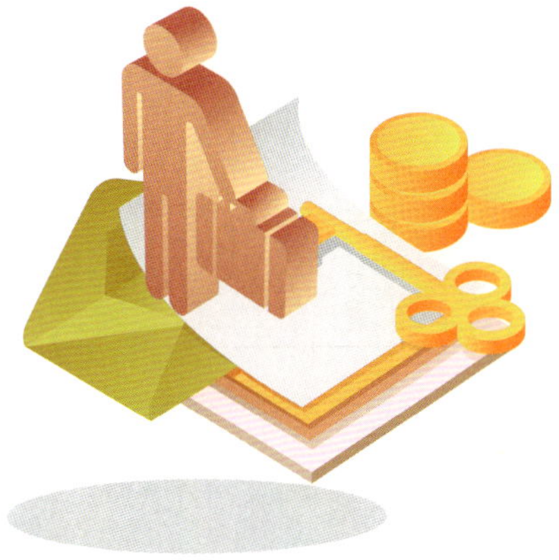

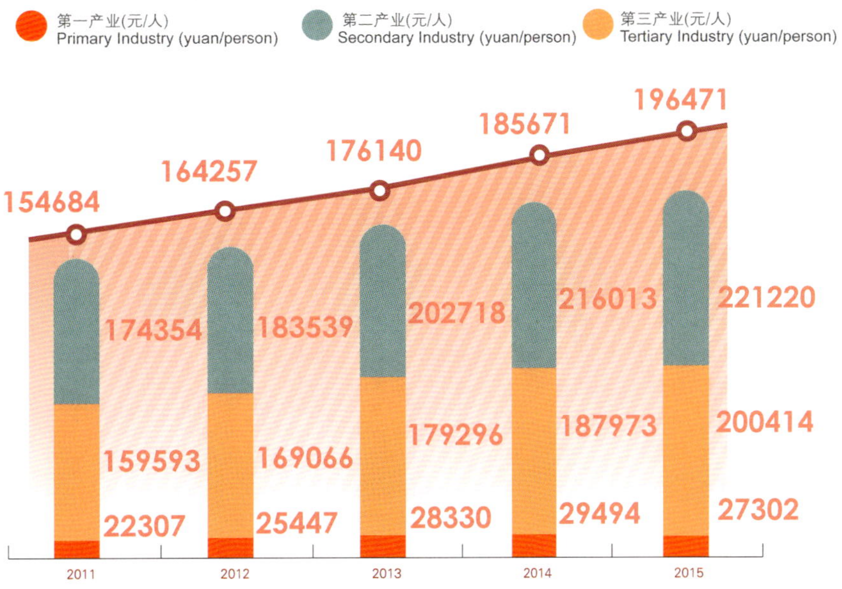

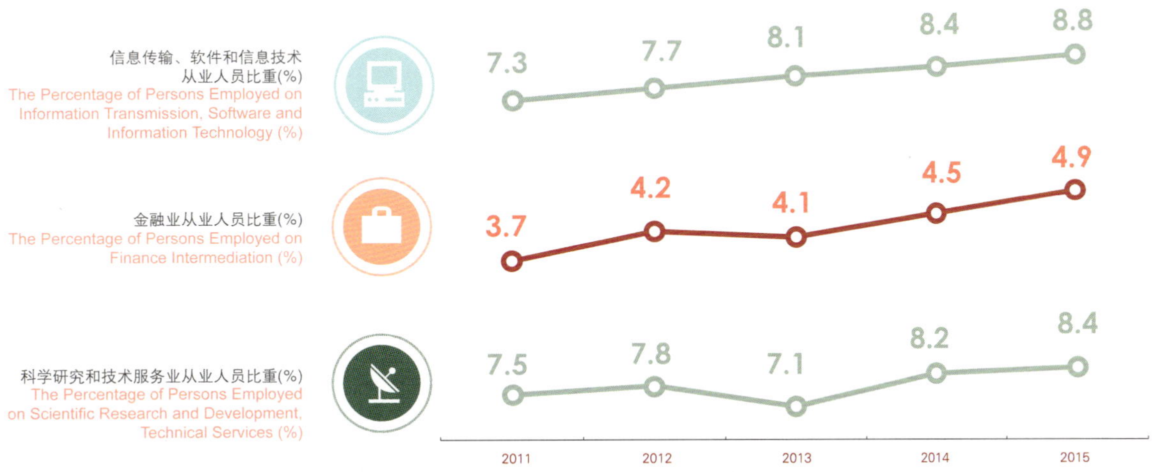

社会劳动生产率(元/人)
Overall Labor Productivity (yuan/person)
第一产业(元/人)
Primary Industry (yuan/person)
第二产业(元/人)
Secondary Industry (yuan/person)
第三产业(元/人)
Tertiary Industry (yuan/person)
154684
164257
176140
185671
196471
174354
183539
202718
216013
221220
159593
169066
179296
187973
200414
22307
25447
28330
29494
27302
2011
2012
2013
2014
2015

信息传输、软件和信息技术从业人员比重(%)
The Percentage of Persons Employed on Information Transmission, Software and Information Technology (%)
7.3
7.7
8.1
8.4
8.8
金融业从业人员比重(%)
The Percentage of Persons Employed on Finance Intermediation (%)
3.7
4.2
4.1
4.5
4.9
科学研究和技术服务业从业人员比重(%)
The Percentage of Persons Employed on Scientific Research and Development, Technical Services (%)
7.5
7.8
7.1
8.2
8.4
2011
2012
2013
2014
2015

❸ 全市从业人员年末人数(万人)
Number of Year-end Employed Persons in Beijing (10,000 persons)
其中：城镇单位从业人员(万人)
Including: Employed Persons in Urban Entities (10,000 persons)

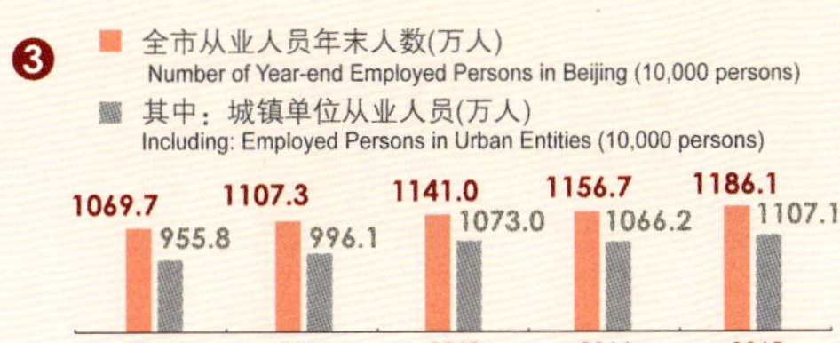

1069.7
955.8
1107.3
996.1
1141.0
1073.0
1156.7
1066.2
1186.1
1107.1
2011
2012
2013
2014
2015

❹ 城镇单位在岗职工平均工资(元)
Average wage of Fully Employed Staff and Workers in Urban Entities (yuan)

75834
15.5
85307
12.5
93997
10.2
103400
10.0
113073
9.4
比上年增长(%)
Increase (%)
2011
2012
2013
2014
2015

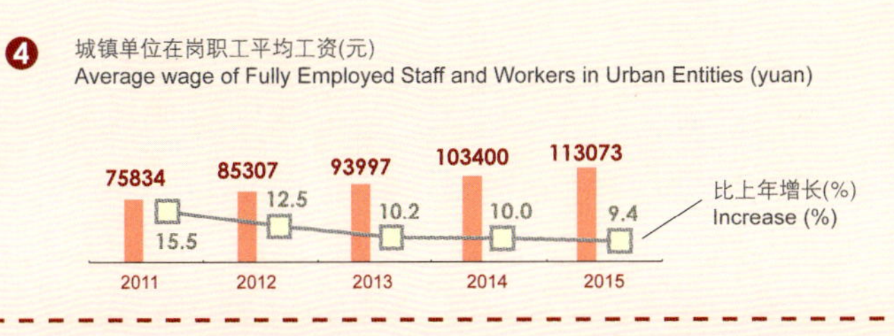

绿色低碳提质量 生态环境进一步改善

Improved the quality of green and low-carbon life. Further perfected the ecological environment.

能源品种结构继续优化
Continued to optimize the structure of energy species

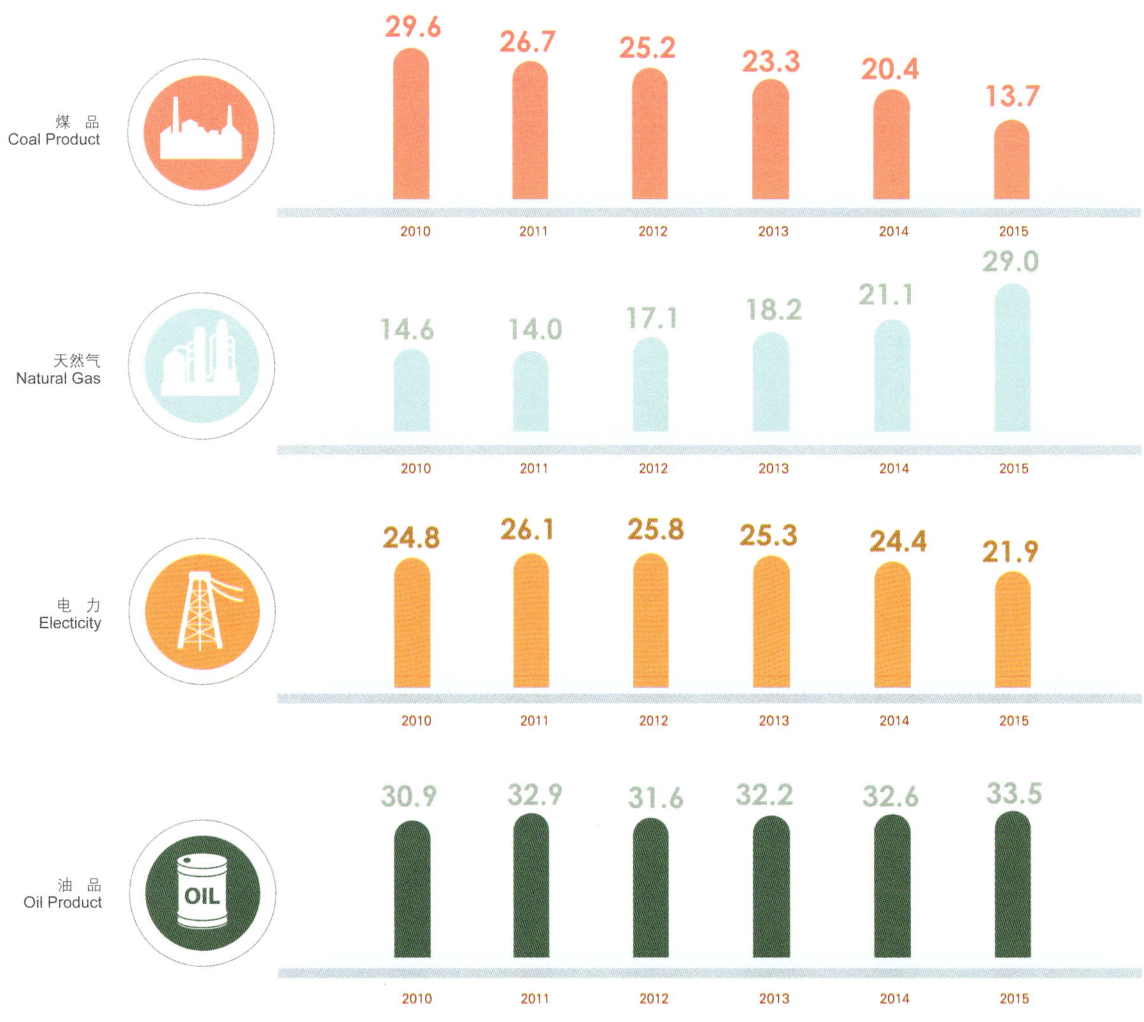

大气污染物浓度逐步降低
The concentration of atmospheric pollutants was gradually reduced

可吸入颗粒物年均浓度(微克/立方米)
Annual Concentration of Inspiratory Particulate Matter (μg/cu.m)

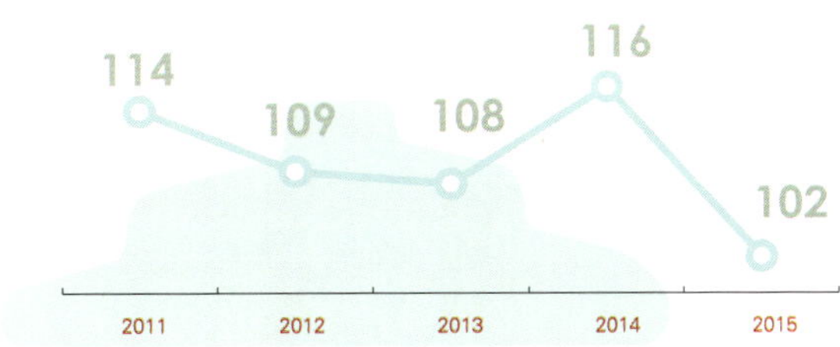

细颗粒物(PM2.5)年均浓度(微克/立方米)
Annual Concentration of PM2.5 (μg/m³)

绿化美化成果持续巩固
Continued to strengthen the afforestation and beautification achievements

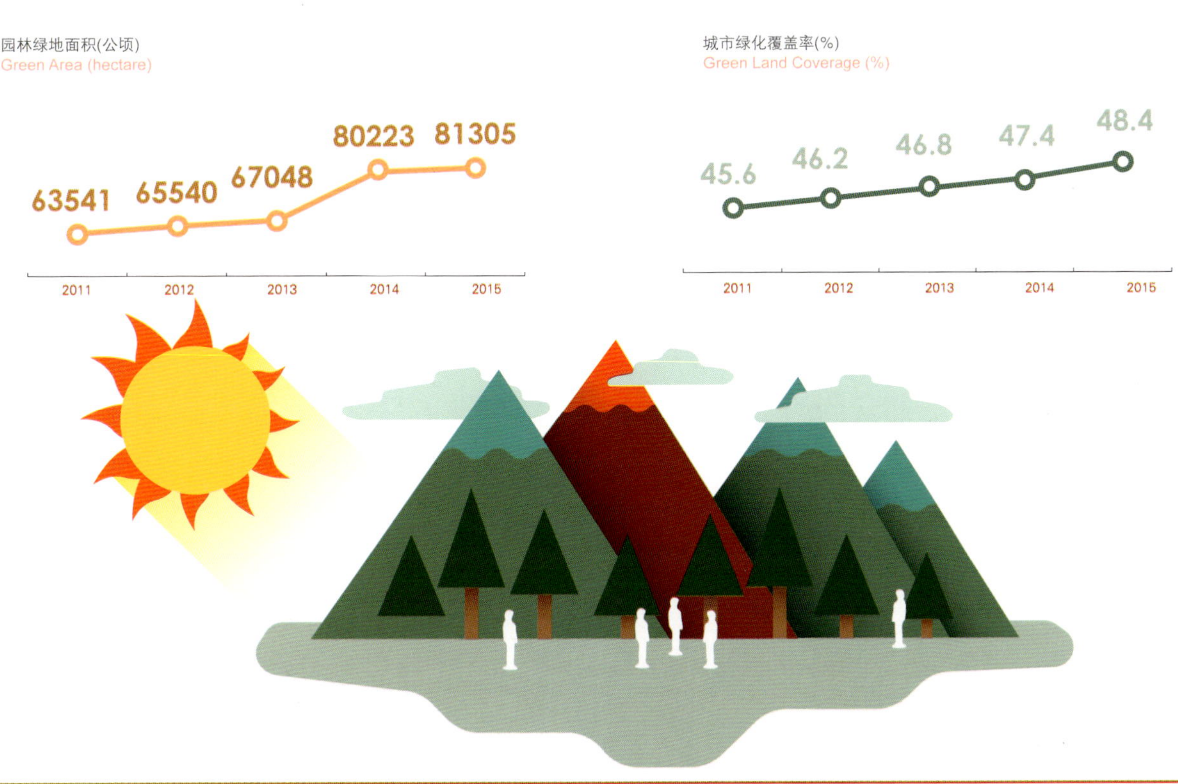

③ 化学需氧量（COD）排放量(万吨)
COD Emission Volume (10,000 tons)

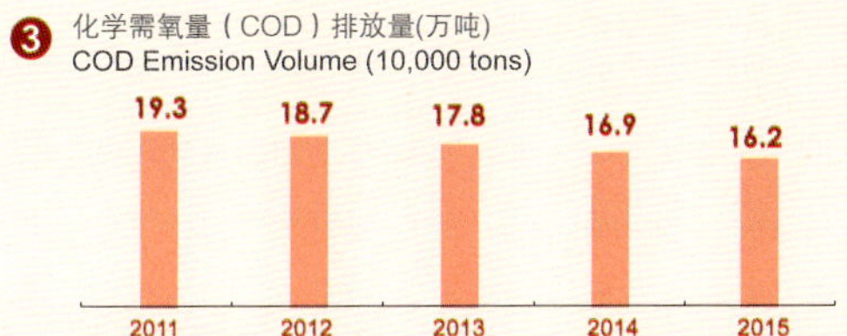

④ 二氧化硫(SO_2)排放量(万吨)
SO_2 Emission Volume (10,000 tons)

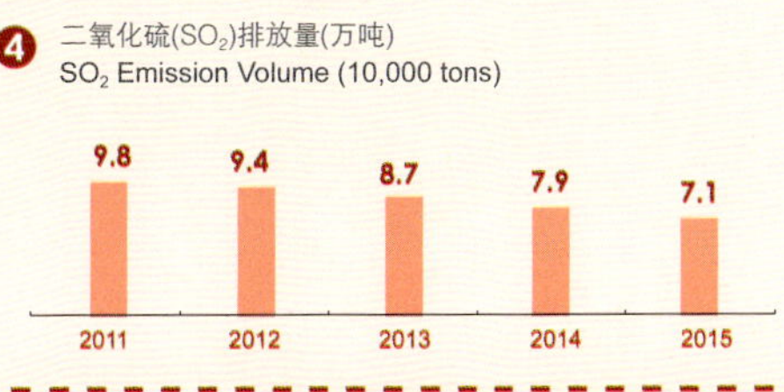

共享经济发展成果 城乡居民收支平稳增长

Shared the achievements of economic development. The revenue and expenditure of urban and rural residents grew steadily.

居民收入增长与经济增长同步
Synchronization of the residents' income growth and economic growth

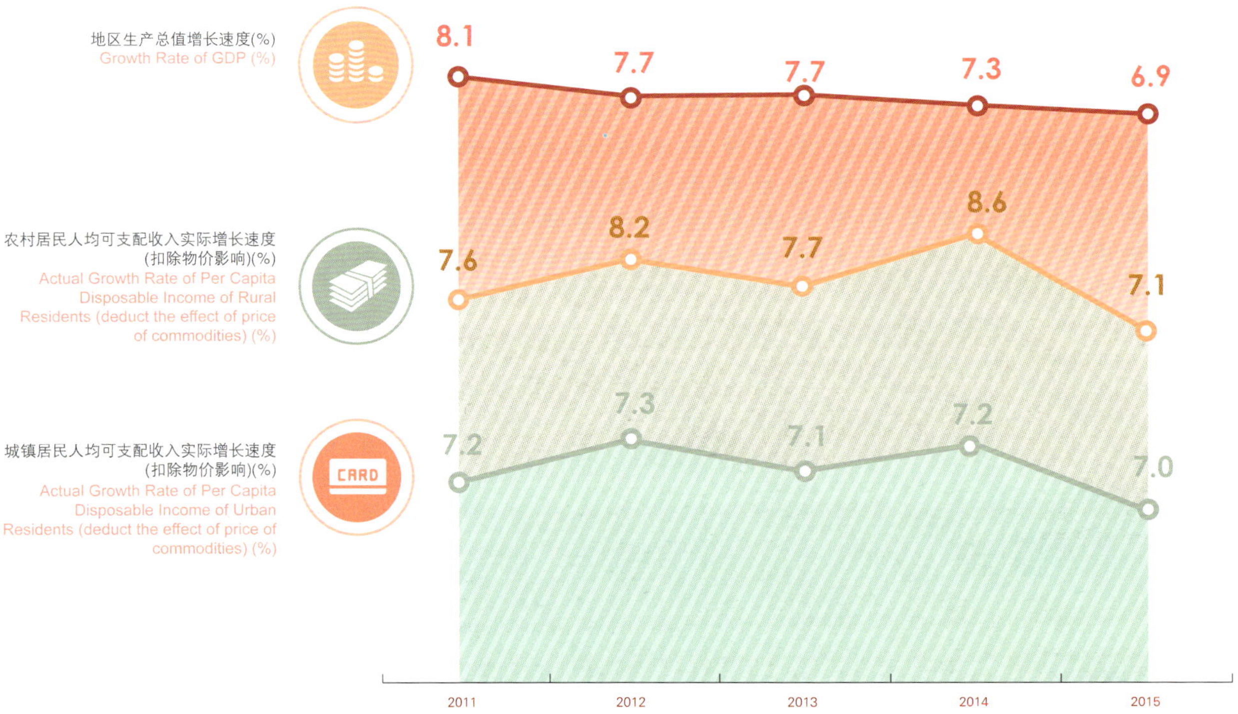

地区生产总值增长速度(%)
Growth Rate of GDP (%)
8.1
7.7
7.7
7.3
6.9
农村居民人均可支配收入实际增长速度(扣除物价影响)(%)
Actual Growth Rate of Per Capita Disposable Income of Rural Residents (deduct the effect of price of commodities) (%)
7.6
8.2
7.7
8.6
7.1
城镇居民人均可支配收入实际增长速度(扣除物价影响)(%)
Actual Growth Rate of Per Capita Disposable Income of Urban Residents (deduct the effect of price of commodities) (%)
CARD
7.2
7.3
7.1
7.2
7.0
2011
2012
2013
2014
2015

城乡居民消费水平逐步接近
The gap between the households consumption level in urban and that in rural areas was narrowed gradually

城镇居民 Urban Residents　农村居民 Rural Residents

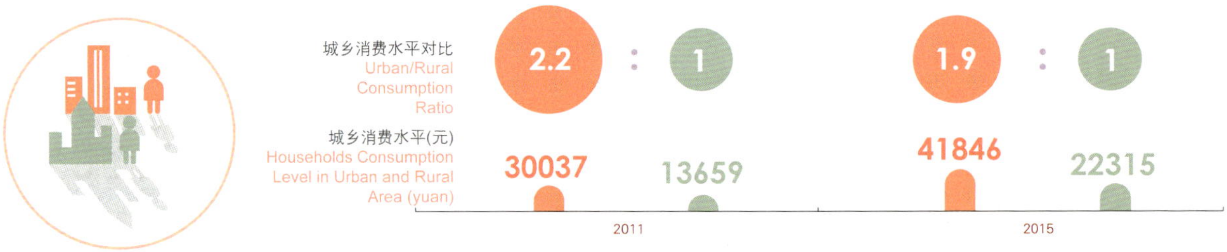

城乡消费水平对比
Urban/Rural Consumption Ratio
2.2 : 1
1.9 : 1
城乡消费水平(元)
Households Consumption Level in Urban and Rural Area (yuan)
30037
13659
41846
22315
2011
2015

❶ 城镇居民人均可支配收入(元)
Per Capita Disposable Income of Urban Residents (yuan)

32903
36469
40321
43910
52859
2011
2012
2013
2014
2015

❷ 农村居民人均可支配收入(元)
Per Capita Disposable Income of Rural Residents (yuan)

14736
16476
18337
20226
20569
2011
2012
2013
2014
2015

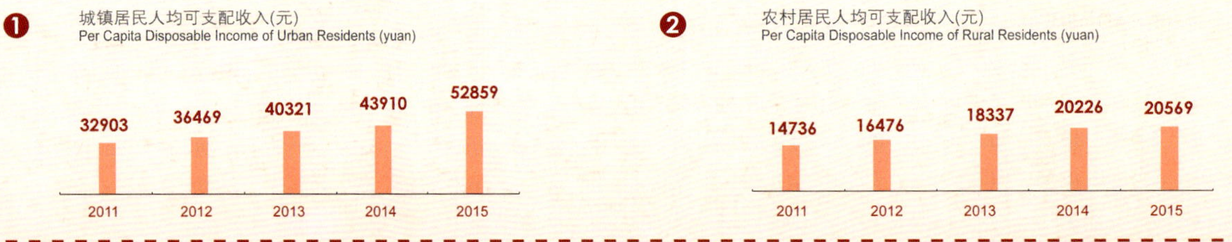

城乡居民消费支出稳步增加
Living expenditures of rural residents and urban residents were increasing steadily

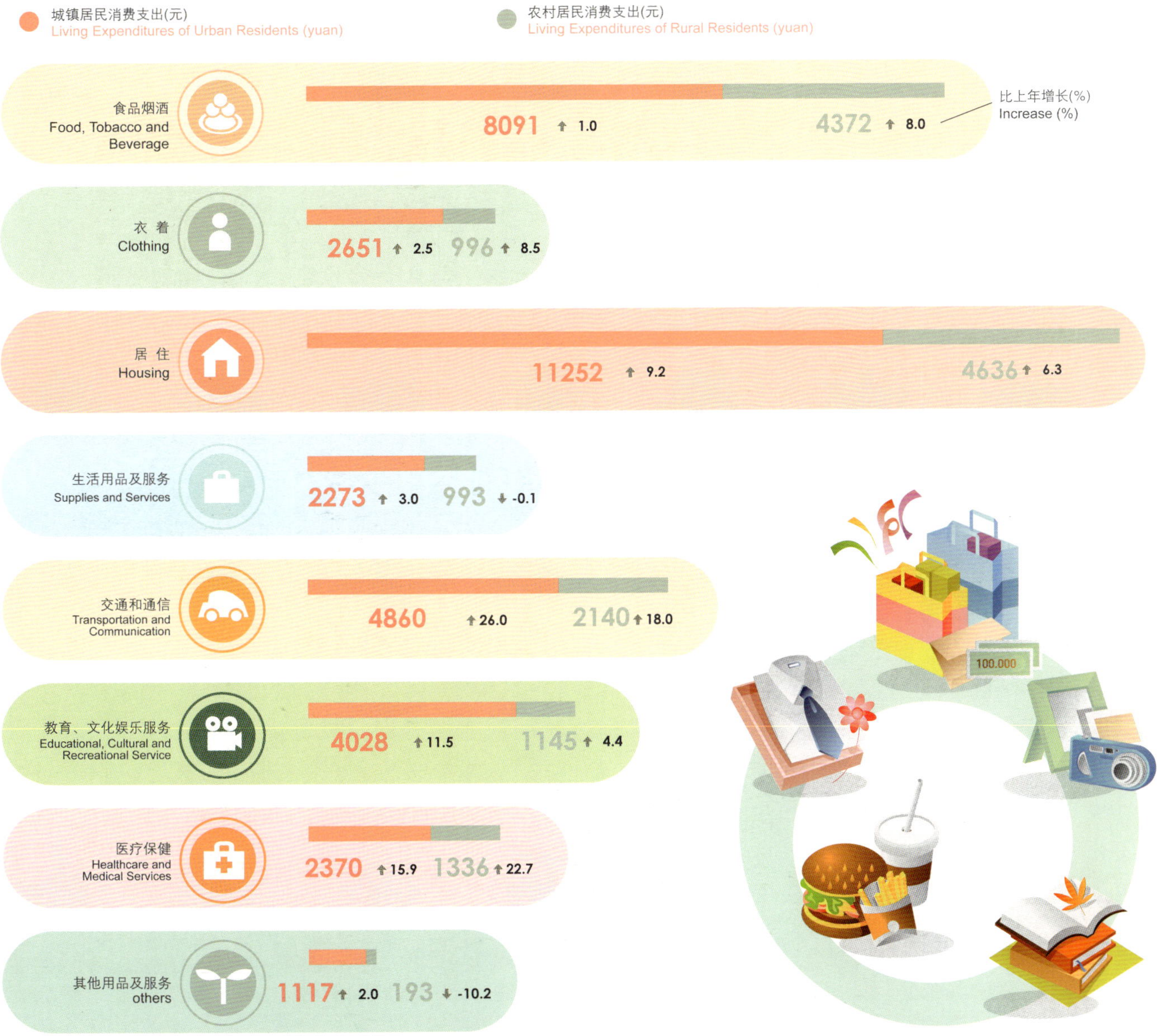

城镇居民消费支出(元) Living Expenditures of Urban Residents (yuan)
农村居民消费支出(元) Living Expenditures of Rural Residents (yuan)
比上年增长(%) Increase (%)

类别 Category	城镇居民消费支出(元)	比上年增长(%)	农村居民消费支出(元)	比上年增长(%)
食品烟酒 Food, Tobacco and Beverage	8091	↑ 1.0	4372	↑ 8.0
衣着 Clothing	2651	↑ 2.5	996	↑ 8.5
居住 Housing	11252	↑ 9.2	4636	↑ 6.3
生活用品及服务 Supplies and Services	2273	↑ 3.0	993	↓ -0.1
交通和通信 Transportation and Communication	4860	↑ 26.0	2140	↑ 18.0
教育、文化娱乐服务 Educational, Cultural and Recreational Service	4028	↑ 11.5	1145	↑ 4.4
医疗保健 Healthcare and Medical Services	2370	↑ 15.9	1336	↑ 22.7
其他用品及服务 others	1117	↑ 2.0	193	↓ -10.2

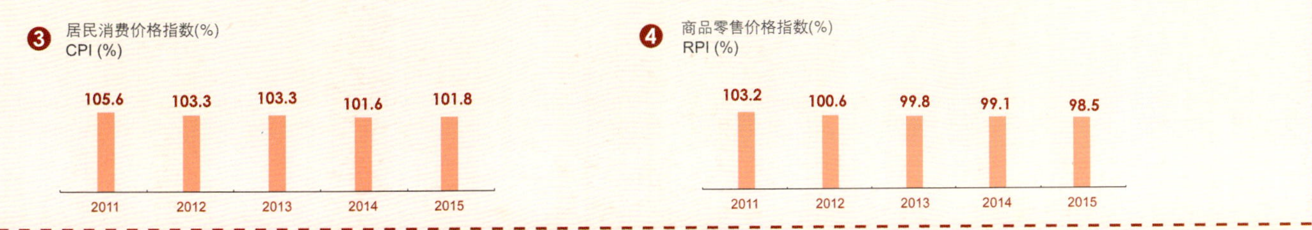

3 居民消费价格指数(%) CPI (%)

2011	2012	2013	2014	2015
105.6	103.3	103.3	101.6	101.8

4 商品零售价格指数(%) RPI (%)

2011	2012	2013	2014	2015
103.2	100.6	99.8	99.1	98.5

政策倾斜惠及民生 社会保障水平逐步提高

Preferential policies benefited the livelihood of the people and the social security level was improved gradually.

参加职工基本保险人数快速增长
Number of employed persons participating in basic social security insurance increased rapidly

	2014	2015
参加职工基本养老保险人数(万人) Employed Persons Participating in Basic Pension Insurance (10,000 persons)	1392.6	1424.2
参加职工基本医疗保险人数(万人) Employed Persons Participating in Basic Medical Care Insurance (10,000 persons)	1431.3	1475.7
参加失业保险人数(万人) Employed Persons Participating in Unemployment Insurance (10,000 persons)	1057.1	1082.3
参加工伤保险人数(万人) Employed Persons Participating in Work-related Injury Insurance (10,000 persons)	961.0	1020.1
参加生育保险人数(万人) Employed Persons Participating in Maternity Insurance (10,000 persons)	915.6	941.6

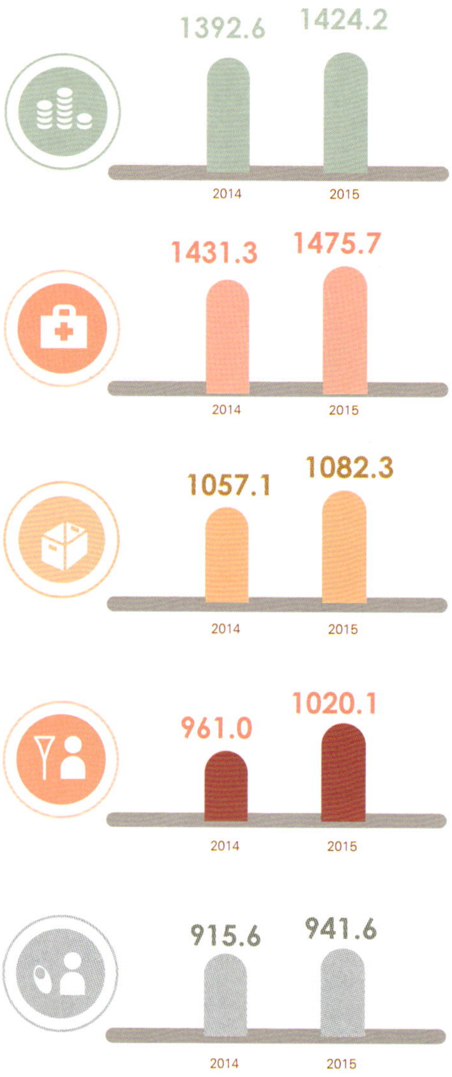

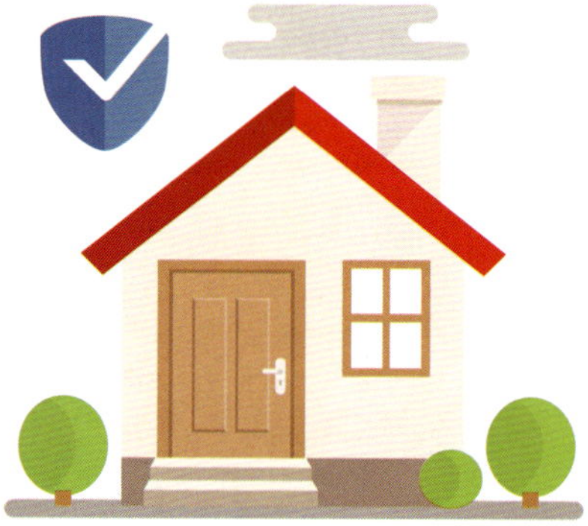

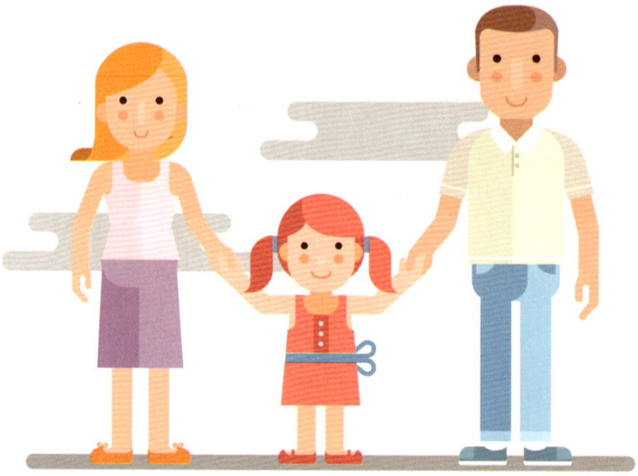

❶ 参加职工基本养老保险人数(万人)
Employed Persons Participating in Basic Pension Insurance (10,000 persons)

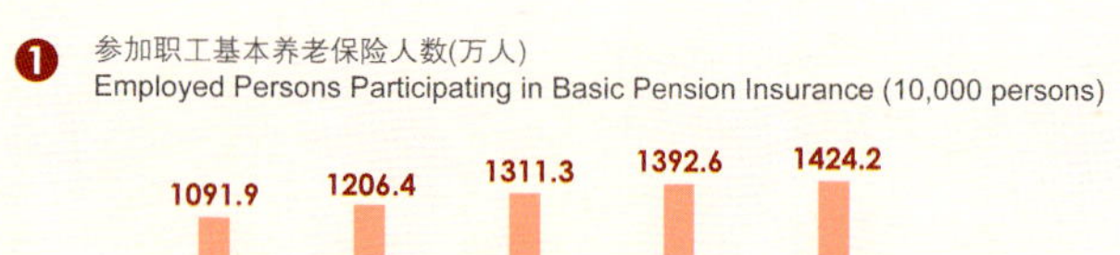

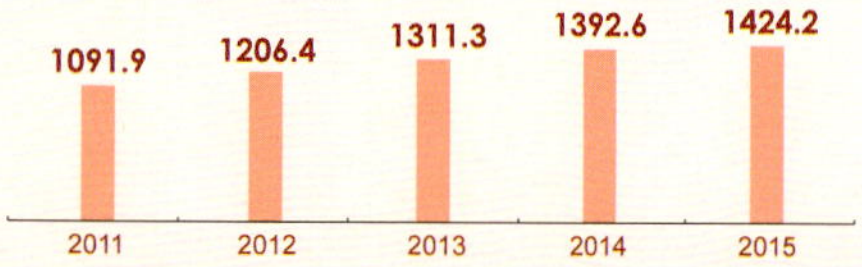

❷ 参加职工基本医疗保险人数(万人)
Employed Persons Participating in Basic Medical Care Insurance (10,000 persons)

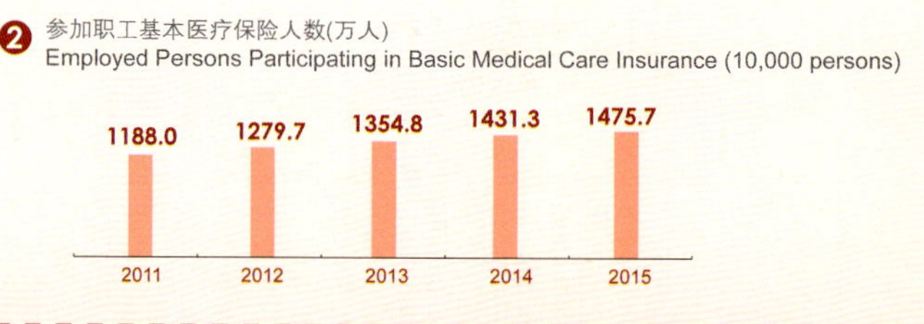

城乡居民保障范围逐步扩大
The guarantee range for urban and rural residents was enlarged gradually

城乡居民基本养老保险人数(万人)
Number of Rural and Urban Residents Participating in Basic Pension Insurance (10,000 persons)

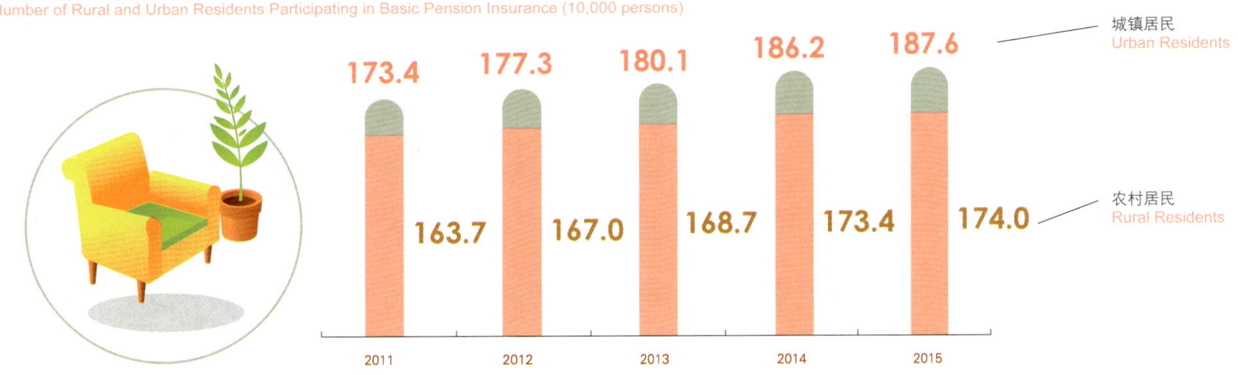

参加城镇居民基本医疗保险人数(万人)
Residents Participating in Basic Urban Medical Insurance (10,000 persons)

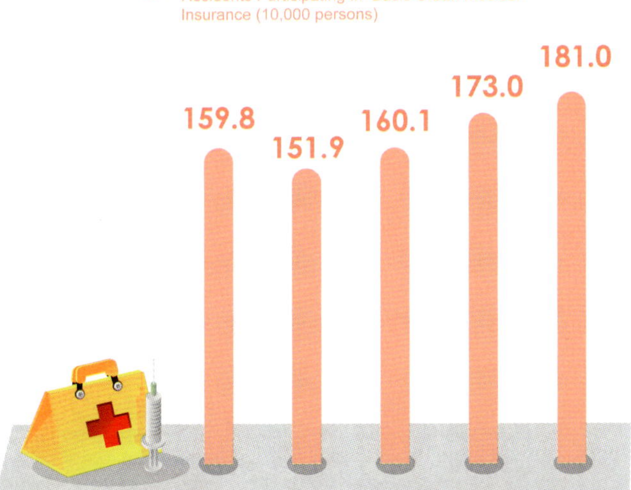

新型农村合作医疗参合率(%)
Percentage of Persons Participating in New-type Rural Cooperative Medicare(%)

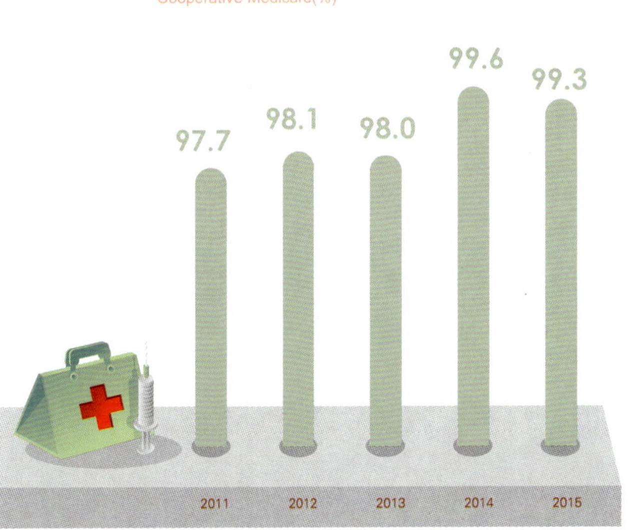

❸ 城市居民最低生活保障人数(万人)
Number of Persons Receiving Subsistence Allowances in Urban Areas (10,000 persons)

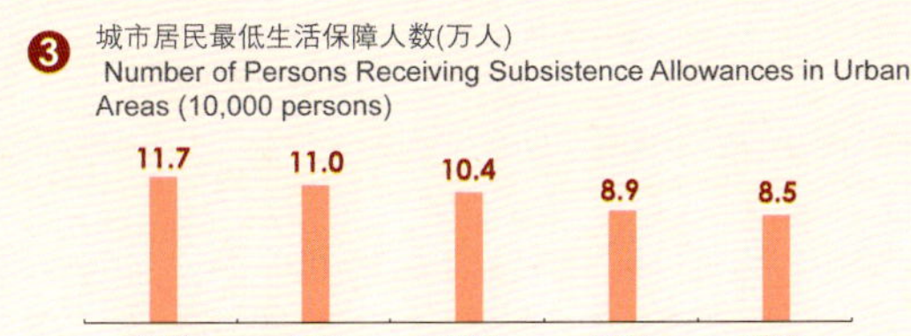

❹ 农村居民最低生活保障人数(万人)
Number of Persons Receiving Subsistence Allowances in Rural Areas (10,000 persons)

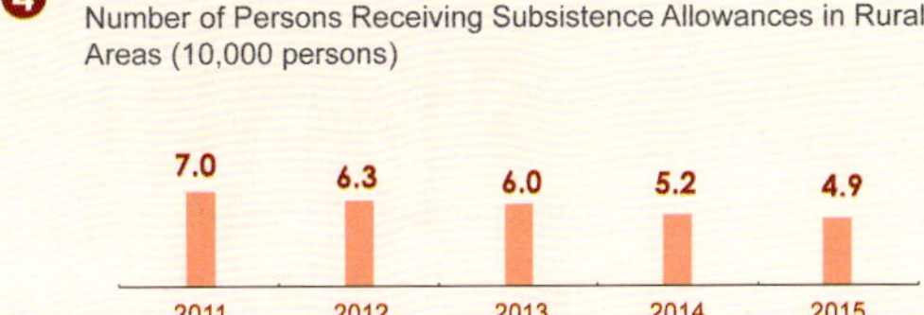

政策倾斜惠及民生 社会保障水平逐步提高

Preferential policies benefited the livelihood of the people and the social security level was improved gradually.

社会保障标准不断提高

The social security standard was improved step by step

北京市历年社会保障相关待遇标准
Historical Level on Social Welfare in Beijing

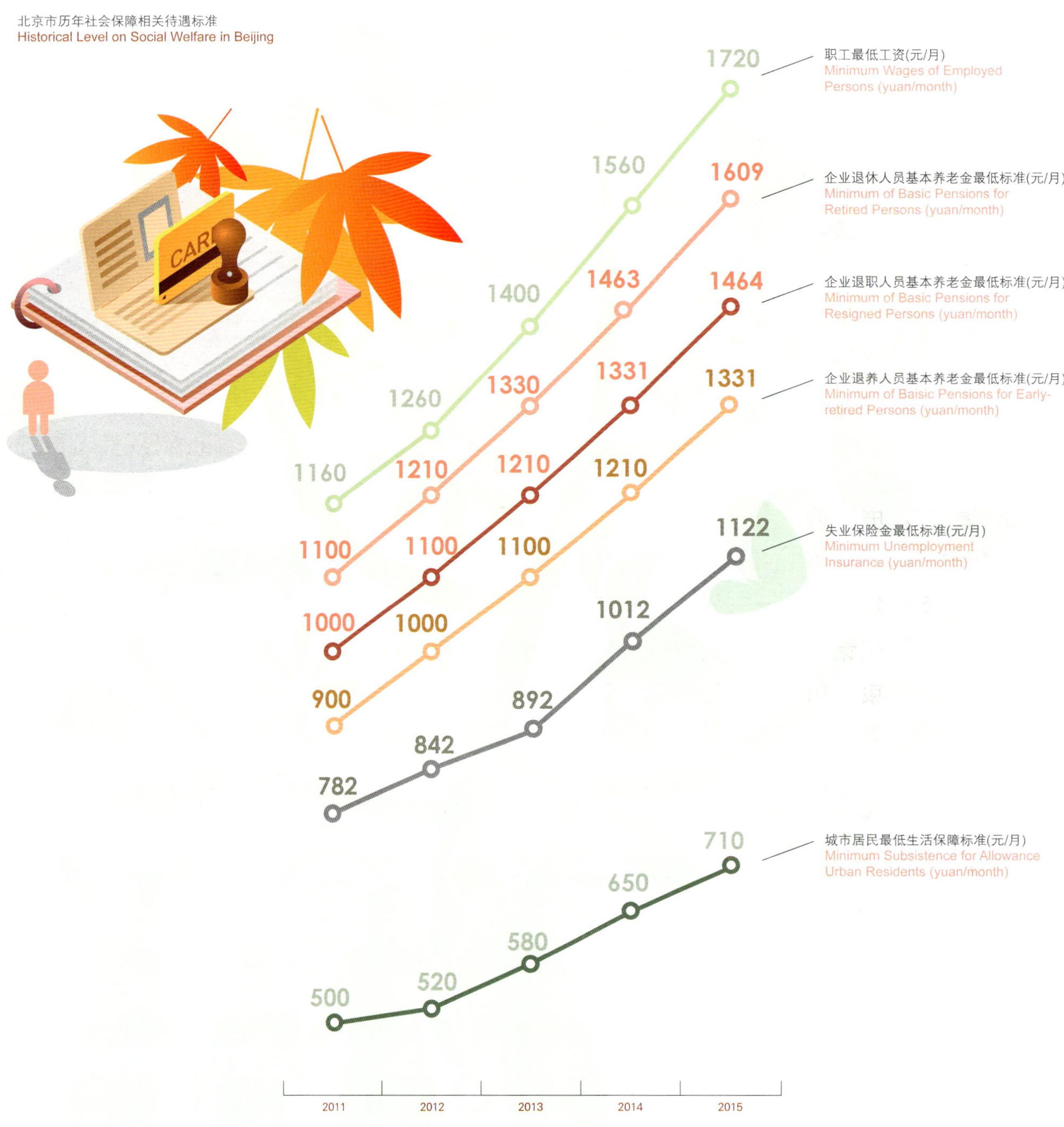

《北京统计年鉴—2016》
编辑委员会及编辑工作人员

编 委 会

主　　任： 蒋力歌　王尔淳

副 主 任：（以姓氏笔画为序）

王　军　卞　晶　孙晓冬　李　纲　李　萍　李文海　邬春仙　吴万标
陈泽星　庞江倩　郑　新　孟素洁　赵玉旺　袁海鹏　夏沁芳　钱　岩
魏小真

编辑委员：（以姓氏笔画为序）

王　滨　王乐强　王守琪　王铁梅　朱燕南　乔世勇　仲长远　刘　黎
刘宏义　李力红　何建红　沈　青　张　群　张铁军（核算处）张小洁
张培农　周　博　周锐（能源处）　徐世君　郭翰超　崔淑筠　颜　平

编辑工作人员

总 编 辑： 庞江倩

执行编辑： 石平平　刘红红

编辑人员： 徐　燕　李晓敏　杨　爽　周　静　吴寅洁　楚文杰　那　娜　李珊珊
张铭睿　肖京涛　代贵禄　于立平　周锐（核算处）　王玉涛　高　杨
束映川　张红阳　黄晨星　张春雷　孔　雷　王　玚　李　昂　胡中华
张立杰　孙稚锐　唐　蜜　付　梦　肖　楠　丁卓茹　李婷婷　李贝贝
于丽君　任全璐　崔　霞　许姝明　张国会　肖玉清　魏炬红　周俊玲
李玉娟　林　梅　姜　峰　李夏卿　郑　红　岳卫红　安　慧　王　鑫
王岚岚　陈　缇　王　斌　韩　康　徐剑琦　康　斌　李玉霞　刘明霞
郝小瑶　孟　醒　刘晓萌　周晓娜　茅振芳　赵　萍　雷　超　何　静
罗　勇　曹继东　周　兴　巩红卫　代朝勇　王冬苹　吴　寒　冷　冬
王志宇　齐　永　周　娟　刘国辉　孙萌萌　唐红燕　杜峥鸣　贾　薇
张　文　高　楠　樊　荣　任　虹　郑子濮　于　震　林　月　张国花
王军（数据中心）侯　蕊　陈　倩　高方圆　孙　倩　王义龙　杨莅群
解晓莉　张栋海

使用指南

《北京统计年鉴》是一部按年连续出版的大型统计资料。本年鉴通过大量的统计数据，真实地记录了北京市一年来经济社会发展变化情况，是国内外各界人士了解北京、认识北京的重要资料工具书。

一、关于框架结构

（一）总体结构

《北京统计年鉴》整体框架基本保持稳定，彩页内容以图文并茂的形式反映一年来本地区经济社会发展主要特点和亮点；统计表是年鉴的主体内容，主要包括综合，国民经济核算，人口与就业，能源、资源和环境，全社会固定资产投资和房地产开发，财政与税收，价格指数，人民生活，城市公用事业，农业及农村经济，工业，建筑业，交通运输邮电，批发和零售业、住宿和餐饮业，对外经济贸易，旅游业，金融和保险，教育、文化，科技，卫生、体育，社会福利、社区、政法及其他，第三产业，开发区等 23 个章节，从多行业、多领域客观反映全市经济和社会发展情况。

（二）章节结构

章节内结构：每一章节由简要说明、统计表和主要统计指标解释三部分组成。简要说明在每一章节首页，主要介绍该章节的主要内容、资料来源、统计范围、指标口径和历史数据调整方法；主要统计指标解释在每章节页尾，主要对本章节内所涉及的主要指标、计算方法等做简要解释；统计表是各章节的核心内容。

统计表排列：每一章节注重从反映该领域主要情况出发，编排统计表内容。统计表的排列顺序一般先是主要指标历史数据表，后为当年数据表。

二、关于使用要领

（一）年份

按照惯例，书名中标注的年份为出版年份，年鉴中统计表内最新数据则为上一年数据。例如，书名为《北京统计年鉴 2016》表示此本年鉴为 2016 年出版，年鉴中最新数据年份截至 2015 年。

统计表名中的“年份”大致会有三种标识方法，分别代表三种含义：一是“表格名称（****年-****年）”表示表内所列数据是包含了这两个年份之间的各年资料；二是统计表名中未显示年份，表示表内所列数据为当年和上年两年数据；三是“表格名称（****年）”表示表内所列数据仅为某一年资料。

（二）符号

统计表中常见符号如下:

#：表示总计中的其中项；有“#”号的分组指标表示总计的部分项目，无“#”号的分组指标则表示其中项之和等于总计。

‖：宾栏中的“‖”为分组符号，代表某个指标存在几种分组数据。

…：表示该数据不足该表最小计量单位数。

空格：表示该项指标数据不详或没有数据。

***：表示为使个体数据得以保密，该数据不予公布。

（三）文字说明

文字说明包括使用指南、目录、简要说明、指标解释和表下注解。使用指南在目录之前，是对年鉴整体框架进行介绍，对主要调整内容进行说明；简要说明在每一章节首页，主要介绍该章节的主要内容、资料来源、统计范围、指标口径和历史数据调整方法等；统计表下的注释则是对部分统计指标口径、方法、范围等内容的说明。

（四）数据

一般情况下，每一章节的前几张表均为该专业或该领域核心指标的历史数据。历史数据如果按年份连续反映在一张表内的，一般可以连续使用，但也需要留意表下的注释，以便对指标内涵有更详尽的了解；如果历史数据分成若干张表显示，则表示相关指标统计有过重大调整，需要分段反映。

此外，最新出版的年鉴上发布的部分历史数据会与以往年鉴上的数据有调整，存在差异，因此，在查询和使用历史数据时应以最新出版的年鉴为准。

（五）电子光盘

《北京统计年鉴》配有电子光盘，包括中文版和英文版两种语言的版本，辅助用户对数据进行加工处理。

（六）本年鉴中部分数据合计数或相对数由于计量单位取舍不同而产生的计算误差，均未作机械调整。

三、关于 2016 年版《北京统计年鉴》说明

与 2015 年版《北京统计年鉴》相比较，本年鉴在内容上主要做了如下调整：

1. 根据近年数据使用需求，在能源环境章节增加了“能源消费总量及构成情况”数据表，在工业章节增加了“工业企业战略性新兴产业总产值”数据表。

2. 根据国家统计局城乡居民调查一体化改革要求，2015 年按照改革新口径发布全市和分城乡的居民收支数据，在人民生活章节增加了 12 张反映全市居民收支情况的数据表，并在保持数据连续性的原则下，对原有城镇居民、农村居民收支情况表式进行修订，衔接新旧口径数据资料，方便读者准确使用数据。

3. 根据全国第三次经济普查结果，《北京统计年鉴 2015》对地区生产总值、社会消费品零售总额等历史数据进行同口径修订，《北京统计年鉴 2016》继续对能源、资源和环境章节中部分历史数据进行了同口径修订，以确保数据的可比性。具体修订内容包括：2005-2012 年的能源生产量、能源消费总量、万元地区生产总值能耗及下降率，以及 2010-2012 年的能源消费结构、能源消费弹性系数、平均每万元地区生产总值能源消费量、人均生活用能源、主要能源日均消费量数据等。

4. 2015 年经国务院批准，北京市撤销密云县、延庆县，设立密云区、延庆区，同时以原密云县的行政区域为密云区行政区域，以延庆县的行政区域为延庆区行政区域。本书对“撤县设区”称谓进行了统一规范使用。

5. 继续加强年鉴文字内容修订，方便读者了解数据变化情况。一是修订各章节简要说明内容，将各章节反映的数据内容、数据来源、统计标准以及数据历史变化等情况全面呈现；二是及时增减章节后的主要指标解释内容，根据当年指标变化等情况对各章节指标解释进行统一的修订、调整；三是注重表下注释内容的更新，准确反映当年数据口径内容调整变化情况，使读者了解当年数据变化，准确使用不同时期、不同专业的年度统计数据。

USER GUIDE

Beijing Statistical Yearbook is a large statistical book published continuously on a chronological basis. With a great deal of statistical data, this Yearbook gives a true reflection of the social and economic development and changes in Beijing over the past year. It serves as an important reference book for domestic and foreign personnel in all circles to understand and know Beijing.

I. Framework Structure

(I) Overall Structure

The overall structure of *Beijing Statistical Yearbook* remains basically stable. In color pages, main features and highlights about economic and social development of Beijing in this year have been presented with both illustration and pictures; statistical tables are the main part of this Yearbook, mainly including 23 chapters, i.e. General Survey; National Accounts; Population and Employment; Energy, Resources and Environmental Protection; Total Investment in Fixed Assets and Real Estate Development; Government Finance and Tax Revenues; Price Index; People's Livelihood; Public Utilities; Agriculture and Rural Economy; Industry; Construction; Transport, Post and Telecommunication Service; Wholesale and Retail Trade, Accomodation and Restaurants; Foreign Trade; Tourism; Finance and Insurance; Education and Culture; Science and Technology; Health Care and Sports; Social Welfare, Community, Plicies & Laws and Others; Tertiary Industry; and Development Zones 23 chapters in total, reflecting the economic and social development situation across the city through multiple industries and fields.

(II) Structure of Chapters

Internal structure of chapters: Each chapter is composed of the Brief Introduction, Statistical Tables and Explanatory Notes to Main Statistical Indicators. Brief Introduction appears on the first page of each chapter, mainly introducing the main content, source of data, statistical scope, indicator standards, method of adjustment to historical data in each chapter; Explanatory Notes to Main Statistical Indicators come on the last page of each chapter, mainly giving a brief explanation to the main indicators and calculation method, etc. involved in the chapter; Statistical Tables are the core content of each chapter.

Arrangement of statistical tables: In each chapter, statistical tables are arranged for the purpose of reflecting the main conditions in the field. Generally speaking, historical statistical tables come before current year statistical tables.

II. How to Use

(I) Years

Conventionally, the year indicated in the book is the year of publication. The latest data indicated in the statistical tables in this Yearbook are data in the previous years. For example, this book is titled *2016 Bejing Statistical Yearbook*, which means it will be published in 2016 while the lastest data in the book is by the end of 2015.

"Years" in the statistical tables are marked in three ways, each indicating a different meaning. Firstly, the statistical table is named "****** (AAAA- BBBB)", which refers to that the data listed in the table are those from the year of AAAA to BBBB; Secondly, the statistical table contains no years, indicating that the data listed in the table are those of current year and last year; Thirdly, the statistical table is named "****** (AAAA)", indicating that the data listed in the table are those of the year of AAAA.

(II) Symbols

Symbols in statistical tables include:

#: means that the item is included in the total. Grouped indicators marked with "#" are part of the total, while those without "#" mean that sum of inclded items equals to the total.

||: means that there are multiple ways of grouping the indicators.

…: means that the figure is less than the minimum measurement unit of the table.

Blank: mean that the figure is unknown or unavailable.

***: means that the figure is not disclosed for secrecy reasons.

(III) Explanations

Explanations include User Guide, Table of Contents, Brief Introduction, Explanatory Notes to Main Statistical Indicators and notes under the tables. User Guide appears before the Table of Contents, giving an introduction to the overall framework of this Yearbook, and explaining the main adjustments; Brief Introduction appears on the first page of each chapter, giving an introduction to the chapter's main content, source of data, statistical scope, standards of indicators, adjustment method of historical data, etc; Notes under the statistical tables make an explanation on standard of some indicators, method and scope, etc.

(IV) Data

In general cases, the first tables in each chapter contain historical data of core indicators in the area or field. Generally speaking, historical data that are shown in one table continuously by year can be used continuously. But it is also necessary to refer to the notes under the table in order to have a full understanding of the connation of indicators; historical data that are shown in several tables indicate that there were major adjustments to relevant indicators, and they need to be reflected by sections.

In addition, some of the historical data in the latest yearbook may have been adjusted over data in previous yearbooks. Therefore, please refer to the latest yearbook when enquiring or using historical data.

(V) Electronic CD-ROM

Beijing Statistical Yearbook is provided with a CD-ROM, which containes Chinese and English versions of this Yearbook. The CD-ROM helps users in working with and processing the data.

(VI) The sum of some statistics or some relative numbers in this Yearbook might have certain calculation errors because of the choice of different units of measurement. All the statistics have not undergone mechanical adjustment.

III. About 2016 *Beijing Statistical Yearbook*

Compared with 2015 *Beijing Statistical Yearbook*, the following adjustments have been mainly made:

1. According to the use demand of data in recent years, a data table of "Information on Total Energy Consumption and Compositions" is added in the chapter of Energy and Environment and a data table of "Total Output Value of Strategic Emerging Industries of Industrial Enterprises" in the chapter of Industry.

2. According to the requirements on the reform of integration of urban and rural residents survey of the National Bureau of Statistics, data of urban and rural residents' revenue and expenditure shall be issued in accordance with the new reform approach in 2015. Twelve data tables reflecting the revenue and expenditure of the residents in Beijing in the chapter of People's Life. The former table form of revenue and expenditure data of urban and rural residents is revised and the data under old and new approach are linked up to ensure that the readers can use the data accurately, follwing the principle of data continuity.

3. Certain historical data, such as gross regional domestic product and total retail sales of consumer goods under same approach were revised in the *2015 Beijing Statistical Yearbook* and part certain historical data in the chapter of Energy, Resources and Enviroment Protection under same approach were revised in the *2016 Beijing Statistical Yearbook* in accordance with the results of the Third Economic Census to guarantee the comparability of data. The specific revised content includes: the energy output, total energy consumption, total energy consumption per 10,000 yuan of GDP and decrease rate of 2005-2012, the energy consumption structure, elasticity coefficient energy consumption, energy consumption per 10,000 yuan of GDP, per-capita energy consumption for living, daily consumption of main energy varieties of 2010-2012, etc.

4. In 2015, Miyun County and Yanqing County were removed and replaced by Miyun District and Yanqing District and the former administrative region of Miyun County and Yanqing County were replaced by the administrative region of Miyun District and Yanqing District in Beijing separately according to the approval of the State Council. Certain titles related to "Removal of County and Establishment of District" are specified and used uniformly in the Yearbook.

5. Continue to strengthen the text revision work of the Yearbook to make it easier for readers to understand the data changes. 1) To revise the content of the overview part of each chapter, comprehensively reflecting the data content, data sources, statistical standards and the historical changes of data and so on; 2) To timely revise or adjust the explanation part of the major indicators attached after the body text in each chapter according to the changes of indicators and the content of indicators of that very year and so on; 3) To pay attention to updating the content of notes under the tables, accurately reflecting the changes and adjustments of the data approach of that very year to make readers understand the data changes and accurately use the annual statistical data in different periods and different sectors.

目　　录

Contents

一、综合

GENERAL SURVEY

二、国民经济核算
NATIONAL ACCOUNTS

三、人口与就业
POPULATION AND EMPLOYMENT

四、能源、资源和环境
ENERGY, RESOURCES AND ENVIRONMENT

五、全社会固定资产投资和房地产开发

TOTAL INVESTMENT IN FIXED ASSETS AND REAL ESTATE DEVELOPMENT

六、财政与税收

GOVERNMENT FINANCE AND TAX REVENUES

七、价格指数

PRICE INDEX

八、人民生活
PEOPLE’S LIFE

九、城市公用事业
PUBLIC UTILITIES

十、农业及农村经济
AGRICULTURE AND RURAL ECONOMY

十一、工业
INDUSTRY

十二、建筑业
CONSTRUCTION

十三、交通运输邮电
TRANSPORT, POST AND TELECOMMUNICATION SERVICES

十四、批发和零售业、住宿和餐饮业
WHOLESALE AND RETAIL TRADE, ACCOMMODATION AND RESTAURANTS

十五、对外经济贸易
FOREIGN ECONOMY AND TRADE

十六、旅游业
TOURISM

十七、金融和保险
FINANCE AND INSURANCE

十八、教育、文化
EDUCATION AND CULTURE

十九、科技
SCIENCE AND TECHNOLOGY

二十、卫生、体育
HEALTH CARE AND SPORTS

二十一、社会福利、社区、政法及其他
SOCIAL WELFARE, COMMUNITY, LAW AND OTHERS

二十二、第三产业
TERTIARY INDUSTRY

二十三、开发区
DEVELOPMENT ZONES

01

北京统计年鉴2016　BEIJING STATISTICAL YEARBOOK

综 合
GENERAL SURVEY

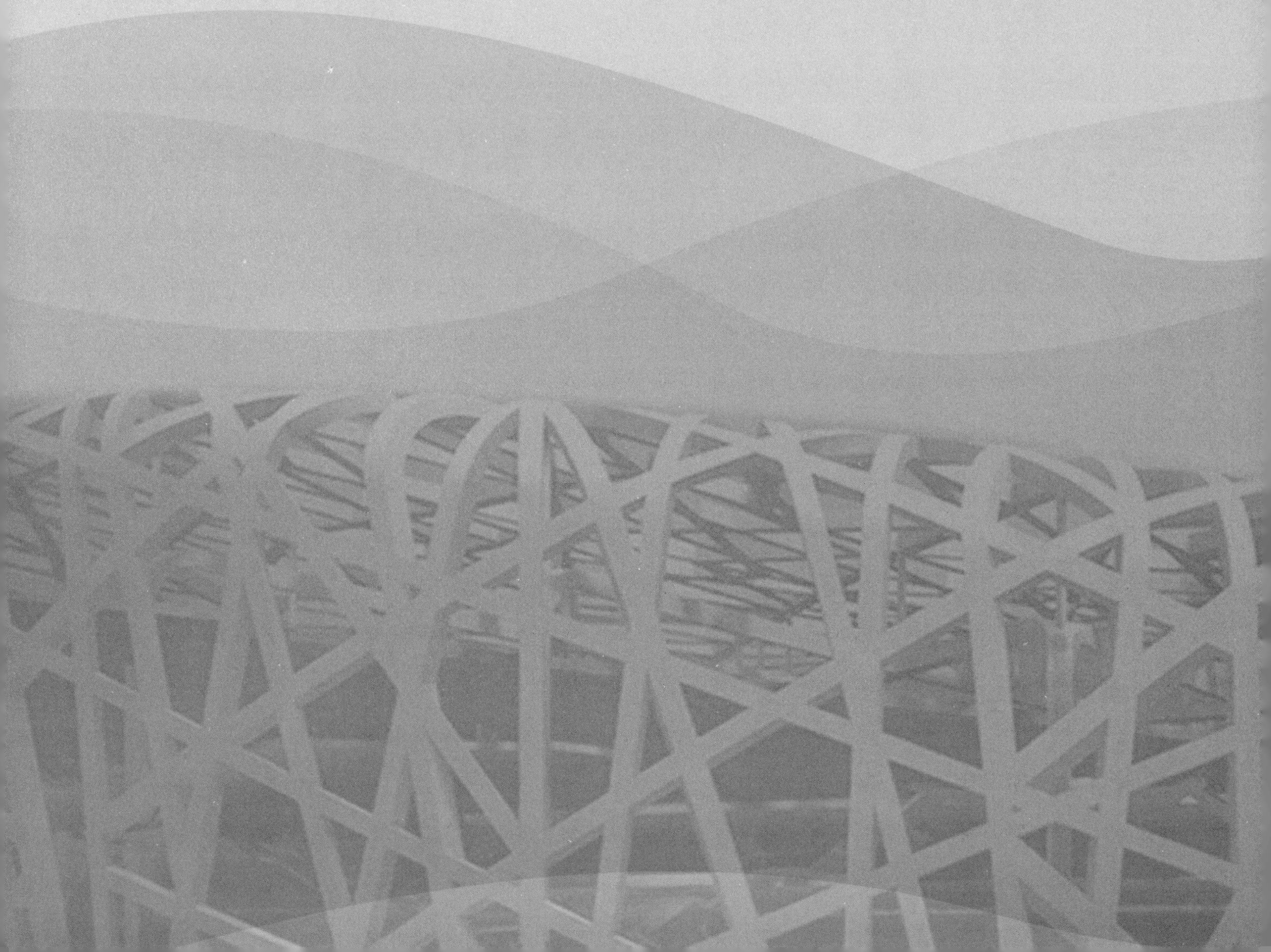

简要说明

一、本章资料的主要内容

本章主要包括北京市行政区划、法人及产业活动单位数、私营个体、非公经济、中小微型企业基本情况、全市社会经济发展的主要指标以及“十二五”时期监测指标等。

二、本章资料的数据来源

北京市行政区划情况来自北京市民政局；全市法人及产业活动单位情况来自北京市统计局；全市私营个体经济基本情况来自北京市工商行政管理局、北京市地方税务局、北京市国家税务局；非公经济数据和中小微型企业数据来自北京市统计局、国家统计局北京调查总队；全市社会经济主要指标及“十二五”时期主要监测指标资料由北京市统计局及国家统计局北京调查总队根据相关资料整理取得。

三、有关统计标准的变化说明

（一）《国民经济行业分类与代码》（GB/T 4754-2002版）与原（GB/T 4754-1994版）的主要框架结构变化：

增加的门类：a).信息传输、计算机服务和软件业 b).租赁和商务服务业 c).住宿和餐饮业 d).水利、环境和公共设施管理业 e).教育 f).国际组织

名称或范围进行调整的门类：a).农、林、牧、渔业 b).采矿业 c).制造业 d).交通运输、仓储和邮政业 e).批发和零售业 f).金融业 g).科学研究、技术服务和地质勘查业 h).居民服务和其他服务业 i).卫生、社会保障和社会福利业 j).文化、体育和娱乐业 k).公共管理和社会组织

取消的门类：a).地质勘查、水利管理 b).其它行业

（二）《国民经济行业分类》（GB/T 4754-2011版）与原（GB/T 4754-2002版）的主要框架结构变化：

门类名称调整：（1）“电力、燃气及水的生产和供应业”更名为“电力、热力、燃气及水生产和供应业”；（2）“信息传输、计算机服务和软件业”更名为“信息传输、软件和信息技术服务业”；（3）“科学研究、技术服务和地质勘查业”更名为“科学研究和技术服务业”；（4）“居民服务和其他服务业”更名为“居民服务、修理和其他服务业”；（5）“卫生、社会保障和社会福利业”更名为“卫生和社会工作”；（6）“公共管理和社会组织”更名为“公共管理、社会保障和社会组织”。

门类位次调整：（1）“批发和零售业”调至“建筑业”后面；（2）“住宿和餐饮业”调至“交通运输、仓储和邮政业”后面。

门类范围调整：A 农、林、牧、渔业；C 制造业；G 交通运输、仓储和邮政业；I 信息传输、软件和信息技术服务业；J 金融业；L 租赁和商务服务业；M 科学研究和技术服务业；O 居民服务、修理和其他服务业；P 教育；Q 卫生和社会工作；R 文化、体育和娱乐业；S 公共管理、社会保障和社会组织。

Brief Introduction

I. Main Content

Statistics in this chapter mainly show the basic information of administrative divisions of Beijing, number of corporate and industrial entities, non-public economy, small-, medium- and micro-sized enterprises,main indicators for social and economic development of the city, and monitoring indicators for the 12th Five-Year Plan, etc.

II. Source of Statistics

Statistics on administrative divisions of Beijing are from Beijing Municipal Bureau of Civil Affairs. Statistics on municipal corporate and industrial entities are from Beijing Municipal Bureau of Statistics. Statistics on private and self-employment economy in the city are from Beijing Administration for Industry and Commerce, Beijing Municipal Bureau of Local Tax and Beijing Municipal Bureau of State Tax. Statistics on non-public economy, small-, medium- and micro-sized enterprises are from National Bureau of Statistics Survey Office in Beijing and Beijing Municipal Bureau of Statistics. Statistics on social and economic indicators and main monitoring indicators for the 12th Five-Year Plan of the city are sorted out by Beijing Municipal Bureau of Statistics and National Bureau of Statistics Survey Office in Beijing on the basis of relevant statistics.

III. Adjustment to Historical Statistics According to New Industrial Standards

(I) Changes to the main framework of the *Classification and Codes of Sectors in National Economy* (GB/T 4754-2002) as compared with the previous version (GB/T 4754-1994):

Sectors added: a). information transmission, computer service and software, b). renting and leasing activities and business services, c). accommodation and restaurants, d). management of water conservancy, environment and public facilities, e). education, f). international organizations.

Sectors with name or range changed: a). agriculture, forestry, animal production and hunting, fishing, b). mining and quarrying, c). manufacturing, d). transport, storage and post, e). wholesale and retail trade, f). finance, g). scientific research, technical service, geological prospecting, h). resident service and other service, i). health care, social security, and social welfare, j). culture, sports and recreation, k). public administration and social organizations.

Sectors cancelled: a). geological prospecting, water conservancy management, b). other sectors.

（II）Compared with the previous (GB/T 4754-2002) version, the *Industrial Classification for National Economic Activities* (GB/T 4754-2011) mainly involves the following framework changes:

Changes to the name of category: (1) The "electric power, gas and water production and supply" is renamed "production and distribution of electricity,heating power, gas and water"; (2) the "information transmission, computer service and software" is renamed "information transmission, software and information technology services"; (3) the "scientific research, technical service and geological prospecting" is renamed "scientific research and development, technical services"; (4) the "resident service and other service" is renamed "resident services, repair and other services"; (5) the "health, social security and social welfare" is renamed "health care and social works"; (6) "public administration and social organization" is renamed "public administration, social security and social organizations".

Changes to the order of categories: (1) the "wholesale and retail trade" is put after the "construction"; (2) the "accommodation and restaurants" is put after the "transport, storage and post".

Changes to the scope of category: A. Agriculture, Forestry, Animal production and Hunting, Fishing; C. Manufacturing; G. Transport, Storage and Post; I. Information Transmission, Software and Information Technology Services; J. Finance; L. Renting and Leasing Activities and Business Services; M. Scientific Research and Development, Technical Service; O. Resident Services, Repair and Other Services; P. Education; Q. Health care and Social Works; R. Culture, Sports and Entertainment; S. Public Administration, Social Security and Social Organizations.

1-1 行政区划(2015年)
ADMINISTRATIVE DIVISIONS (2015)

单位：个 (unit)

地 区	District	街道办事处 Sub-district	建制镇 Designated Town	建制乡 Designated Township	社区居委会 Community Neighborhood Committee	村民委员会 Villagers' Committee
全 市	**Total**	**150**	**143**	**38**	**2975**	**3936**
首都功能核心区	**Core Functional Area of the Capital**	**32**			**443**	
东 城 区	Dongcheng District	17			182	
西 城 区	Xicheng District	15			261	
城市功能拓展区	**Urban Function Extension Area**	**71**	**9**	**22**	**1440**	**303**
朝 阳 区	Chaoyang District	24		19	409	154
丰 台 区	Fengtai District	16	2	3	308	65
石景山区	Shijingshan District	9			152	
海 淀 区	Haidian District	22	7		571	84
城市发展新区	**New Area of Urban Development**	**34**	**71**	**7**	**765**	**2188**
房 山 区	Fangshan District	8	14	6	133	459
通 州 区	Tongzhou District	4	10	1	111	475
顺 义 区	Shunyi District	6	19		114	426
昌 平 区	Changping District	8	14		220	301
大 兴 区	Daxing District	8	14		187	527
生态涵养发展区	**Ecological Conservation Area**	**13**	**63**	**9**	**327**	**1445**
门头沟区	Mentougou District	4	9		119	178
怀 柔 区	Huairou District	2	12	2	34	284
平 谷 区	Pinggu District	2	14	2	36	273
密 云 区	Miyun District	2	17	1	92	334
延 庆 区	Yanqing District	3	11	4	46	376

资料来源：北京市民政局。
Source: Beijing Municipal Bureau of Civil Affairs.

1-2 规模(限额)以上法人单位基本情况(2015年)
NUMBER OF LEGAL ENTITIES ABOVE DESIGNATED SIZE (2015)

单位：个 (unit)

项目	Item	法人单位数合计 Total Number of Legal Entities	单产业法人 Single-industry Legal Entities	多产业法人 Multi-industry Legal Entities
合计	**Total**	**39844**	**33885**	**5959**
按登记注册类型分组	**By Registration Type**			
内资	Domestically-invested Enterprises	36004	31057	4947
国有	State-owned Enterprises	6115	5397	718
集体	Collectively-owned Enterprises	614	539	75
股份合作	Joint-equity Cooperative Enterprises	380	326	54
联营	Associated Enterprises	25	21	4
有限责任公司	Limited Liability Companies	13834	11663	2171
股份有限公司	Companies Limited by Shares	1267	946	321
私营	Private Enterprises	13358	11774	1584
其他	Others	411	391	20
港澳台商投资	Hong Kong, Macao and Taiwan-invested Enterprises	1482	1108	374
与港澳台商合资经营	Joint Ventures	467	363	104
与港澳台商合作经营	Cooperative Enterprises	104	92	12
港澳台商独资	Solely-funded Enterprises	880	639	241
港澳台商投资股份有限公司	Companies Limited by Shares	30	13	17
其他港澳台商投资	Others	1	1	
外商投资	Foreign-invested Enterprises	2358	1720	638
中外合资经营	Joint Ventures	690	546	144
中外合作经营	Cooperative Enterprises	97	75	22
外资企业	Solely-funded Enterprises	1524	1071	453
外商投资股份有限公司	Companies Limited by Shares	38	21	17
其他外商投资	Others	9	7	2
按隶属关系分组	**By Affiliation**			
中央	Central	4403	3751	652
地方	Local	35441	30134	5307
按机构类型分组	**By Organization Type**			
企业	Enterprises	34542	29079	5463
事业单位	Institutions	3433	3196	237
机关	Government Agencies and Organizations	1144	942	202
社会团体	Social Organizations	245	199	46
其他机构	Others	480	469	11

注：本表为2015年年报规模(限额)以上法人单位数据。
Note: This table covers legal entities above designated size in the 2015 annual report.

1-3 国民经济各行业规模(限额)以上法人单位情况(2015年)
NUMBER OF LEGAL ENTITIES IN DIFFERENT SECTORS OF THE NATIONAL ECONOMY ABOVE DESIGNATED SIZE (2015)

单位：个 (unit)

行 业	Sector	法人单位数合计 Total Number of Legal Entities	单产业法人 Single-industry Legal Entities	多产业法人 Multi-industry Legal Entities
合 计	**Total**	**39844**	**33202**	**6642**
农、林、牧、渔业	**Agriculture, Forestry, Animal Production and Hunting, Fishing**			
采矿业	**Mining and Quarrying**	**19**	**13**	**6**
煤炭开采和洗选业	Mining and Washing of Coal	1		1
石油和天然气开采业	Extraction of Petroleum and Natural Gas	2		2
黑色金属矿采选业	Mining of Ferrous Metal Ores	7	6	1
有色金属矿采选业	Mining of Non-Ferrous Metal Ores			
非金属矿采选业	Mining and Processing of Nonmetal Ores	3	3	
开采辅助活动	Mining Support Service Activities	6	4	2
其他采矿业	Mining of Other Ores			
制造业	**Manufacturing**	**3417**	**2888**	**529**
农副食品加工业	Processing of Food from Agricultural Products	138	112	26
食品制造业	Manufacture of Foods	130	106	24
酒、饮料和精制茶制造业	Manufacture of Wine, Beverage and Refined Tea	43	30	13
烟草制品业	Manufacture of Cigarettes and Tobacco	1		1
纺织业	Manufacture of Textile	23	21	2
纺织服装、服饰业	Manufacture of Textile, Wearing Apparel and Ornament	128	93	35
皮革、毛皮、羽毛及其制品和制鞋业	Manufacture of Leather, Fur, Feather and Its Products, and Footwear	12	10	2
木材加工和木、竹、藤、棕、草制品业	Processing of Timbers, Manufacture of Wood, Bamboo, Rattan, Palm and Straw Products	16	14	2
家具制造业	Manufacture of Furniture	65	50	15
造纸和纸制品业	Manufacture of Paper and Paper Products	40	37	3
印刷和记录媒介复制业	Printing, Reproduction of Recording Media	113	104	9
文教、工美、体育和娱乐用品制造业	Manufacture of Articles for Culture, Education, Artwork, Sport and Entertainment Activities	34	28	6
石油加工、炼焦和核燃料加工业	Processing of Petroleum, Coking, Processing of Nucleus Fuels	20	17	3
化学原料和化学制品制造业	Manufacture of Chemical Raw Materials and Chemical Products	204	180	24
医药制造业	Manufacture of Medicines	201	170	31
化学纤维制造业	Manufacture of Chemical Fibres	2	2	
橡胶和塑料制品业	Manufacture of Rubber and Plastics Products	112	99	13
非金属矿物制品业	Manufacture of Non-metallic Mineral Products	237	204	33
黑色金属冶炼和压延加工业	Manufacture and Pressing of Ferrous Metals	23	22	1

注：1. 本表为2015年年报规模(限额)以上法人单位数据。
2. 本表行业划分执行2011年国民经济行业分类标准(GB/T 4754-2011)。

Note: a) This table covers legal entities above designated size in the 2015 annual report.
b) Sectors in this table are classified in accordance with the Standard for Classification of National Economic Sectors 2011 (GB/T 4754-2011).

1-3 续表 1 Continued 1

单位：个 (unit)

行业	Sector	法人单位数合计 Total Number of Legal Entities	单产业法人 Single-industry Legal Entities	多产业法人 Multi-industry Legal Entities
有色金属冶炼和压延加工业	Manufacture and Processing of Non-ferrous Metals	36	32	4
金属制品业	Manufacture of Fabricated Metal Products	203	177	26
通用设备制造业	Manufacture of General-Purpose Machinery	238	184	54
专用设备制造业	Manufacture of Special-Purpose Machinery	319	263	56
汽车制造业	Manufacture of Motor Vehicles	232	211	21
铁路、船舶、航空航天和其他运输设备制造业	Manufacture of Railway Locomotives, Building of Ships and Boats, Manufacture of Air and Spacecrafts and Other Transportation Equipments	74	67	7
电气机械和器材制造业	Manufacture of Electrical Machinery and Equipment	261	231	30
计算机、通信和其他电子设备制造业	Manufacture of Computers, Communication Equipment and Other Electronic Equipment	293	246	47
仪器仪表制造业	Manufacture of Measuring Instrument and Meter	163	131	32
其他制造业	Other Manufacturing	31	26	5
废弃资源综合利用业	Waste Rrecycling and Recovery	10	10	
金属制品、机械和设备修理业	Repair of Fabricated Metal Products, Machinery and Equipment	15	11	4
电力、热力、燃气及水生产和供应业	**Production and Distribution of Electricity, Heating Power, Gas and Water**	**112**	**89**	**23**
电力、热力生产和供应业	Production and Supply of Electric Power and Heat Power	68	56	12
燃气生产和供应业	Production and Distribution of Gas	21	16	5
水的生产和供应业	Production and Distribution of Water	23	17	6
建筑业	**Construction**	**3522**	**2812**	**710**
房屋建筑业	Construction of Building	658	412	246
土木工程建筑业	Civil Engineering Construction	585	441	144
建筑安装业	Construction Installation	863	734	129
建筑装饰和其他建筑业	Building Completion, Finishing and Other Construction	1416	1225	191
批发和零售业	**Wholesale and Retail Trade**	**6246**	**5082**	**1164**
批发业	Wholesale	4283	3673	610
零售业	Retail Trade	1963	1409	554
交通运输、仓储和邮政业	**Transport, Storage and Post**	**990**	**778**	**212**
铁路运输业	Transport via Railway	16	9	7
道路运输业	Transport via Road	480	407	73
水上运输业	Water Transport	5	3	2
航空运输业	Air Transport	22	15	7
管道运输业	Transport via Pipeline	2	2	
装卸搬运和运输代理业	Loading, Unloading, Portage and Other Transport Services	325	224	101
仓储业	Storage	110	99	11
邮政业	Post	30	19	11
住宿和餐饮业	**Accommodation and Restaurants**	**2395**	**1860**	**535**
住宿业	Accommodation	987	828	159
餐饮业	Restaurants	1408	1032	376
信息传输、软件和信息技术服务业	**Information Transmission, Software and Information Technology Services**	**2864**	**2328**	**536**
电信、广播电视和卫星传输服务	Telecommunications, Broadcasting, Television and Satellite Transmission Services	213	157	56
互联网和相关服务	Internet and Related Services	287	238	49
软件和信息技术服务业	Software and Information Technology Services	2364	1933	431

1-3 续表 2 Continued 2

单位：个 (unit)

行 业	Sector	法人单位数合计 Total Number of Legal Entities	单产业法人 Single-industry Legal Entities	多产业法人 Multi-industry Legal Entities
金融业	**Finance**	**1888**	**1608**	**280**
货币金融服务	Monetary Financial Services	505	421	84
资本市场服务	Capital Market Services	550	499	51
保险业	Insurance	398	295	103
其他金融业	Other Financial Services	435	393	42
房地产业	**Real Estate**	**4277**	**3653**	**624**
租赁和商务服务业	**Renting and Leasing Activities and Business Services**	**4837**	**4105**	**732**
租赁业	Renting and Leasing Activities	104	78	26
商务服务业	Business Services	4733	4027	706
科学研究和技术服务业	**Scientific Research and Development, Technical Services**	**3282**	**2824**	**458**
研究和试验发展	Research and Experimental Development	591	548	43
专业技术服务业	Professional Technique Services	1487	1200	287
科技推广和应用服务业	Technique Generalization and Application Services	1204	1076	128
水利、环境和公共设施管理业	**Management of Water Conservancy, Environment and Public Facilities**	**533**	**477**	**56**
水利管理业	Management of Water Conservancy	37	33	4
生态保护和环境治理业	Ecological Protection and Environmental Control	58	46	12
公共设施管理业	Management of Public Facilities	438	398	40
居民服务、修理和其他服务业	**Resident Services, Repair and Other Services**	**419**	**363**	**56**
居民服务业	Resident Services	138	109	29
机动车、电子产品和日用产品修理业	Repair of Motor Vehicles, Electronics and Household Appliances	134	115	19
其他服务业	Other Services	147	139	8
教育	**Education**	**1490**	**1367**	**123**
卫生和社会工作	**Health Care and Social Works**	**681**	**547**	**134**
卫生	Health Care	629	497	132
社会工作	Social Work Activities	52	50	2
文化、体育和娱乐业	**Culture, Sports and Entertainment**	**1197**	**1087**	**110**
新闻和出版业	Journalism and Publishing	475	427	48
广播、电视、电影和影视录音制作业	Radio Broadcasting, Television, Movies, Videos and Sound Recording	228	206	22
文化艺术业	Cultures and Arts	247	235	12
体育	Sports Activities	183	162	21
娱乐业	Entertainments	64	57	7
公共管理、社会保障和社会组织	**Public Administration, Social Security and Social Organizations**	**1675**	**1321**	**354**
中国共产党机关	Organs of Communist Party of China	48	41	7
国家机构	Organs of State	1266	988	278
人民政协、民主党派	Peole's Political Consultative Conference and Democratic Parties	25	24	1
社会保障	Social Security	10	10	
群众团体、社会团体和其他成员组织	Mass Communities, Social Organizations and Other Membership Organizations	286	221	65
基层群众自治组织	Grass Roots Self-Government Organization	40	37	3
国际组织	**International Organizations**			

1-4 规模(限额)以上企业法人单位情况(2015年)
NUMBER OF CORPORATE ENTERPRISES ABOVE DESIGNATED SIZE (2015)

单位：个 (unit)

项　　目	Item	法人单位合计 Total Number of Legal Entities
合　　计	**Total**	**34542**
按开业时间分	**By Openning Time**	
1949年以前	Before 1949	32
1950-1965	From 1950 to 1965	247
1966-1979	From 1966 to 1979	149
1980-1989	From 1980 to 1989	1332
1990年以后	After 1990	32782
按登记注册类型分	**By Registration Type**	
内资企业	Domestically-invested Enterprises	30706
国有企业	State-owned Enterprises	1498
集体企业	Collectively-owned Enterprises	531
股份合作企业	Joint-equity Cooperative Enterprises	373
联营企业	Associated Enterprises	20
有限责任公司	Limited Liability Companies	13830
股份有限公司	Companies Limited by Shares	1267
私营企业	Private Enterprises	13182
其他内资企业	Other Domestically-invested Enterprises	5
港澳台商投资企业	Hong Kong, Macao and Taiwan-invested Enterprises	1481
与港澳台商合资经营	Joint Ventures	467
与港澳台商合作经营	Cooperative Enterprises	104
港澳台商独资	Solely-funded Enterprises	879
港澳台商投资股份有限公司	Companies Limited by Shares	30
其他港澳台商投资	Others	1
外商投资企业	Foreign-invested Enterprises	2355
中外合资经营	Joint Ventures	690
中外合作经营	Cooperative Enterprises	95
外资企业	Solely-funded Enterprises	1523
外商投资股份有限公司	Companies Limited by Shares	38
其他外商投资	Other	9
按控股情况分	**By Share Holding Status**	
国有控股	State-owned Enterprises	7281
集体控股	Collectively-controlled Enterprises	1606
私人控股	Privately-controlled Enterprises	21519
港澳台商控股	Hong Kong, Macao and Taiwan-controlled Enterprises	1341
外商控股	Foreign-controlled Enterprises	2129
其　他	Others	666

注：本表为2015年年报规模(限额)以上企业法人单位数据。

Note: This table covers legal entities above designated size in the 2015 annual report.

1-5 全市私营个体经济基本情况
STATISTICS FOR PRIVATE AND INDIVIDUAL ECONOMY

单位：万元 (10000 yuan)

项 目	Item	私营 Private			个体 Individual		
		2015	2014	2015年为2014年% 2015 as % of 2014	2015	2014	2015年为2014年% 2015 as % of 2014
工商登记注册*	**Registered at Administration for Industry and Commerce**						
户 数 (户)	Number of Business Entities (unit)	1037789	848099	122.4	659357	653319	100.9
从业人员 (人)	Number of Employed Persons (person)	8485995	7255948	117.0	1031314	1029973	100.1
注册资本	Registered Capital	839869344	432893097	194.0	2266780	2180772	103.9
国税、地税入库	**Taxes Put into Local**						
税收合计	**and National Treasury**	**6653286**	**5753723**	**115.6**	**2447182**	**2015485**	**121.4**

注：*为期末时点数。

资料来源：北京市工商行政管理局、北京市地方税务局、北京市国家税务局。

Note: Figures with * indicate the accumulative figures at end of the year.

Source: Beijing Administration for Industry and Commerce, Beijing Municipal Bureau of Local Taxation, Beijing Municipal Bureau of State Taxation.

1-6 规模以上非公经济主要指标(2015年)
MAIN INDICATORS OF NON-PUBLIC SECTORS OF THE ECONOMY ABOVE DESIGNATED SIZE (2015)

项 目	Item	单位数 (个) Number of Enterprises (unit)	收入合计 (亿元) Total Income (100 million yuan)	利润总额 (亿元) Total Profits (100 million yuan)	应交税金合计 (亿元) Taxes Payable (100 million yuan)	从业人员平均人数 (万人) Average Number of Persons Employed (10000 persons)
合 计	**Total**	**25924**	**49811.3**	**4483.7**	**2302.0**	**376.1**
按登记注册类型分组	**Grouped by Registration Type**					
内 资	Domestic-funded	22349	27538.6	1748.5	1311.8	261.2
港澳台商投资	Hongkong, Macao and Taiwan-funded	1383	8376.3	533.1	331.5	47.1
外商投资	Foreign-funded	2192	13896.5	2202.1	658.6	67.8
按规模分	**Grouped by Size**					
#大型企业	Large-sized Enterprises	968	21035.7	2285.3	799.2	137.9
中小微型企业	Mini-, Small-, Mediume-sized Enterprises	22944	25155.1	1059.8	1044.1	214.3
中 型	Medium Size	5492	15007.0	753.4	665.0	120.7
小 型	Small Size	13177	9008.7	353.0	326.4	87.0
微 型	Mini Size	4275	1139.4	-46.6	52.7	6.6
按行业分组	**Grouped by Sector**					
#制造业	Manufacturing	2657	7809.3	460.9	369.4	59.5
建筑业	Construction	2723	2112.2	49.4	73.8	20.4
批发和零售业	Wholesale and Retail Trade	4906	20779.9	490.7	450.3	48.4
交通运输、仓储和邮政业	Transport, Storage and Post	705	956.8	44.9	23.7	17.5
住宿和餐饮业	Accommodation and Restaurants	1767	629.6	-7.0	43.7	24.9
信息传输、软件和信息技术服务业	Information Transmission,Software and Information Technology Services	2355	4760.3	1481.1	291.5	58.4
金融业	Finance	1294	2934.8	1080.0	424.3	12.7
房地产业	Real estate	2692	2260.6	226.7	308.2	26.8
租赁和商务服务业	Renting and Leasing Activities and Business Services	3531	4629.9	494.0	195.3	62.5
科学研究和技术服务业	Scientific Research and Development, Technical Services	1868	1448.6	80.0	69.6	21.3
水利、环境和公共设施管理业	Management of Water Conservancy, Environment and Public Facilities	169	198.8	17.3	9.4	2.2
居民服务、修理和其他服务业	Resident Services, Repair and Other Services	310	120.5	-1.3	7.4	7.0
教 育	Education	258	203.2	18.1	9.2	6.8
卫生和社会工作	Health Care and Social Works	177	111.9	0.3	1.7	2.9
文化、体育和娱乐业	Culture, Sports and Entertainment	375	235.9	10.3	12.7	3.0
公共管理和社会组织	Pulic Administration, Social Security and Social Organizations	105	229.7		0.8	0.4

注：1. 非公经济是指资产由我国私人、港澳台商、外商控股的“非公有控股”的企业法人单位，以及主要经费来源于私人、港澳台资和外资的非企业法人单位和个体工商户。私人、港澳台及外商控股是指由其绝对控股和相对控股的经济成分。本表不包含个体经营户数据。

2. 应交税金合计主要包括应交增值税、应交所得税、营业税金及附加和管理费用中的税金等。

3. 按规模分组中，各类型非公经济是指执行企业会计制度的非公企业数据，不包含执行事业会计制度的非公单位数据，因此，规模分组合计数不等于其他分组合计数。

4. 2015年，全市非公经济实现增加值8981亿元，其中第二产业增加值2075.8亿元，第三产业增加值6905.2亿元。

Note: a) Non-public economies mean enterprises as legal persons whose assets equity are held by non-public entities such as private, Hong Kong, Macao and Taiwan, and foreign businesses, as well as non-legal-person enterprises and self-employed entities whose main outlays come from private, Hong Kong, Macao and Taiwan, and foreign businesses. Economies with share held by private, Hong Kong, Macao and Taiwan, and foreign businesses mean economic elements with shares absolutely held by such businesses. This table excludes figures for self-employed entities.

b) Total Tax mainly includes payable VAT,payable income tax, business tax and surtax, and tax in management expenses, etc.

c) In the group by size, figures of various types of non-public sectors in the economy are those of non-public enterprises implementing enterprise accounting system, excluding those of non-public entities implementing public institution accounting system. Therefore, total amounts in the group by size are not equal to total amounts of other groups.

d) In 2015, non-public sectors of the economy in Beijing achieved added value of RMB 898.1 billion, of which the added value in the secondary industry reached RMB 207.58 billion and that in the tertiary industry hit RMB 690.52 billion.

1-7 规模以上中小微型企业主要指标(2015年)
MAIN INDICATORS OF MICRO- SMALL- AND MEDIUM-SIZED ENTERPRISES ABOVE DESIGNATED SIZE (2015)

项 目	Item	单位数 (个) Number of Enter-prises (unit)	收入合计 (亿元) Total Income (100 million yuan)	利润总额 (亿元) Total Profits (100 million yuan)	应交税金合计 (亿元) Taxes Payable (100 million yuan)	从业人员平均人数 (万人) Average Number of Persons Employed (10000 persons)
合 计	**Total**	**30262**	**47055.2**	**4320.6**	**2107.6**	**309.6**
按规模分	**Grouped by Size**					
中 型	Medium Size	8152	30545.5	2290.1	1468.9	181.7
小 型	Small Size	16700	13294.7	1244.4	531.5	113.8
微 型	Mini Size	5410	3215.0	786.2	107.3	14.2
按登记注册类型分	**Grouped by Registration Type**					
内 资	Domestic-funded	27200	39994.1	3812.3	1730.3	264.4
港澳台商投资	Hongkong, Macao and Taiwan-funded	1177	2481.8	143.8	128.1	18.3
外商投资	Foreign-funded	1885	4579.3	364.5	249.2	27.0
按行业分	**Grouped by Sector**					
#制造业	Manufacturing	3294	6777.5	449.1	369.5	62.1
建筑业	Construction	3185	2288.9	89.3	81.2	23.6
批发和零售业	Wholesale and Retail Trade	5861	22255.3	256.0	347.6	31.3
交通运输、仓储和邮政业	Transport, Storage and Post	928	943.9	47.4	202.3	15.5
住宿和餐饮业	Accommodation and Restaurants	2251	441.5	-21.2	32.0	19.8
信息传输、软件和信息技术服务业	Information Transmission,Software and Information Technology Services	2501	2519.0	625.1	107.4	31.6
房地产业	Real estate	3786	2981.1	484.6	459.9	25.8
租赁和商务服务业	Renting and Leasing Activities and Business Services	4472	5012.5	1996.9	323.7	64.6
科学研究和技术服务业	Scientific Research and Development, Technical Services	2400	2433.8	207.8	97.8	20.0
水利、环境和公共设施管理业	Management of Water Conservancy, Environment and Public Facilities	286	187.8	15.3	10.1	2.0
居民服务、修理和其他服务业	Resident Services, Repair and Other Services	317	95.1	1.0	5.7	3.2
卫生和社会工作	Health Care and Social Works	7	1.2	-0.1	…	0.1
文化、体育和娱乐业	Culture, Sports and Entertainment	859	657.7	76.2	40.9	6.8

注：1. 本表中的企业规模划型标准执行国家统计局《关于统计上大中小微型企业划分办法》(国统字〔2011〕75号)。按照国家统计局要求，铁路运输业、教育、卫生、自有房地产经营活动、金融业不划分规模，因此中小微数据不含这五个行业数据。

2. 行业划分执行2011年国民经济行业分类标准(GB/T 4754-2011)。

3. 2015年，全市中小微型企业实现增加值7055.1亿元，其中第二产业增加值1991.4亿元，第三产业增加值5063.7亿元。

Note: a) In this table, enterprise size is identified in accordance with the provisions stated in the Statistical Division Standards of Micro-, Small-, Medium- and Large-sized Enterprises released by the National Bureau of Statistics (G.T.Z. (2011) No. 75). According to requirements of National Bureau of Statistics, size division is unnecessary in sectors of railway transportation, education, health care, self-owned real estate operation and finance, so no data related to the five sectors is included in the table.

b) Sectors in this table are classified in accordance with the Standard for Classification of National Economic Sectors in 2011(GB/T 4754-2011).

c) In 2015, micro-, small- and medium-sized enterprises in Beijing achieved added value of RMB 705.51 billion, of which added value in the secondary industry reached RMB 199.14 billion and that in the tertiary industry reached RMB506.37 billion.

1-8 主要经济指标增长速度(1979-2015年)

单位：%

年 份 Year	地区生产总值比上年增长 YoY Growth Rate of Gross Domestic Product	全社会固定资产投资比上年增长 YoY Growth Rate of Fixed Asset Investment	房地产开发投资比上年增长 YoY Growth Rate of Real Estate Development Investment	一般公共预算收入比上年增长 YoY Growth Rate of Public Finance Budget Revenue	社会消费品零售总额比上年增长 YoY Growth Rate of Retail Sales of Consumer Goods	进出口总值比上年增长 YoY Growth Rate of Gross Value of Imports & Exports
1979	9.7	17.3			20.6	
1980	11.8	25.3			17.8	
1981	-0.5	10.2			12.6	
1982	7.4	5.5			6.6	
1983	16.4	32.9			14.6	
1984	17.4	29.2			22.5	16.3
1985	8.7	41.8			27.0	-8.6
1986	8.0	13.0			15.3	-6.0
1987	9.6	28.2			21.9	-12.7
1988	12.8	19.7			35.5	11.9
1989	4.4	-14.4			15.2	-4.3
1990	5.2	28.5			17.1	-17.4
1991	9.9	7.1	6.7		18.3	2.5
1992	11.3	38.5	40.4		23.2	3.1
1993	12.3	54.3	73.3		21.5	11.7
1994	13.7	58.1	70.4		25.4	3.5
1995	12.0	29.7	254.6		24.0	28.2
1996	9.0	4.2	-7.0		11.7	-20.8
1997	10.1	9.6	0.6		13.8	3.7
1998	9.5	20.2	14.3	20.0	13.7	0.4
1999	10.9	1.3	11.7	22.6	9.9	12.6
2000	11.8	10.8	23.9	22.7	9.9	43.8
2001	11.7	18.0	50.1	31.6	10.4	4.2
2002	11.5	18.5	26.2	25.9	9.5	2.0
2003	11.1	18.9	21.5	18.2	14.5	30.5
2004	14.1	17.2	22.5	29.7	14.4	38.1
2005	12.1	11.8	3.5	23.5	10.9	32.7
2006	13.0	19.3	12.8	21.5	13.2	25.9
2007	14.5	17.6	16.0	33.6	16.4	22.1
2008	9.1	-3.0	-4.4	23.1	21.1	40.8
2009	10.2	26.2	22.5	10.3	16.0	-20.9
2010	10.3	13.1	24.1	16.1	17.7	40.4
2011	8.1	13.3	10.1	27.7	13.9	29.1
2012	7.7	9.3	3.9	10.3	12.5	4.8
2013	7.7	8.8	10.5	10.4	9.2	5.4
2014	7.3	7.5	12.3	10.0	8.6	-3.4
2015	6.9	5.7	8.1	17.3	7.3	-23.1

注：1. 地区生产总值增长速度按可比口径计算。
2. 2015年财政部门对财政收支统计口径进行调整，地方公共财政预算收入更名为一般公共预算收入。
3. 农林牧渔业总产值增长速度按现价计算。
4. 2015年开始居民收支调查数据采用城乡一体化新口径，农村居民人均纯收入改为农村居民人均可支配收入，城镇居民人均可支配收入和农村居民人均可支配收入增长速度均按可比口径计算,表中实际增长速度是剔除物价影响因素后的增长速度。
5. 2009-2013年增长速度按第三次全国经济普查数据进行调整。

YOY GROWTH RATE OF MAIN INDICATORS (1979-2015)

(%)

农林牧渔业总产值比上年增长 YoY Growth Rate of Gross Output Value of Agriculture, Forestry, Animal Production and Hunting, Fishing	规模以上工业总产值比上年增长 YoY Growth Rate of Gross Output Value of Industrial Enterprises Above Designated Size	居民消费价格指数(上年=100) Consumer Price Index (Previous year=100)	城镇居民人均可支配收入 Per-capita Disposable Income of Urban Households		农村居民人均可支配收入 Per-capita Net Income of Rural Households	
			比上年名义增长 Nominal Growth Rate as Compared with That in the Last year	比上年实际增长 Real Growth Rate as Compared with That in the Last year	比上年名义增长 Normal Growth Rate as Compared with That in the Last year	比上年实际增长 Real Growth Rate as Compared with That in the Last year
7.0		101.8	13.6	11.6	11.1	10.9
16.3		106.0	20.8	14.0	23.2	22.1
4.2		101.3	2.5	1.2	17.2	17.1
12.8		101.8	9.1	7.2	19.1	17.3
16.7		100.5	5.2	4.7	20.7	20.9
13.3		102.2	17.5	15.0	27.9	25.7
16.7	17.4	117.6	30.8	11.3	16.7	14.5
8.5	3.8	106.8	17.6	10.1	6.2	3.7
22.4	15.2	108.6	10.7	1.9	11.3	6.5
52.9	27.9	120.4	21.6	1.0	16.0	3.1
14.8	21.6	117.2	11.1	-5.2	15.8	2.2
16.2	3.8	105.4	11.9	6.2	5.4	2.1
9.0	16.7	111.9	14.2	2.1	9.6	1.7
10.5	17.8	109.9	15.8	5.4	10.3	2.0
18.8	35.7	119.0	39.4	17.1	18.2	5.1
43.7	35.1	124.9	43.5	14.9	30.6	9.1
13.9	-5.3	117.3	24.0	5.7	32.5	6.3
2.7	6.5	111.6	17.3	5.1	11.1	4.8
0.9	14.4	105.3	13.5	7.8	5.6	5.1
2.5	7.0	102.4	8.4	5.9	7.1	6.7
3.3	12.1	100.6	8.4	7.8	7.1	7.2
4.4	30.2	103.5	12.7	8.9	8.6	7.3
7.2	15.1	103.1	11.9	8.5	12.5	8.7
5.6	10.7	98.2	13.5	15.6	11.5	12.3
5.2	21.8	100.2	11.4	11.2	10.5	11.5
4.5	30.0	101.0	12.6	11.5	10.4	9.2
1.9	21.2	101.5	12.9	11.2	9.6	8.1
0.4	18.2	100.9	13.2	12.2	9.7	8.7
13.4	17.5	102.4	13.9	11.2	10.9	8.2
11.6	7.9	105.1	12.4	7.0	12.4	6.5
3.6	6.0	98.5	8.1	9.7	11.5	13.4
4.1	24.1	102.4	8.7	6.2	10.6	8.1
10.7	5.9	105.6	13.2	7.2	13.6	7.6
9.0	7.5	103.3	10.8	7.3	11.8	8.2
6.6	11.4	103.3	10.6	7.1	11.3	7.7
-0.4	6.2	101.6	8.9	7.2	10.3	8.6
-12.3	-5.4	101.8	8.9	7.0	9.0	7.1

Note: a)The Growth Rate of Gross Domestic Product shall be calculated based on a comparable caliber.
Development Investment in 2011 are calculated at comparable basis.

b)In 2015, the financial sector adjusted the statistical caliber of financial revenue and expenditure, modified the "Local FinanceBudget Revenue" as "General Public Budget Revenue" and included 11 items of governmental fund income into "General Public Finance Budget Revenue".

c)The Growth Rate of Gross Output Value ofAgriculture, Forestry, Animal Husbandry and Fishery shall be calculated based on the current price.
census.

d)The new caliber under urban-rural integration have been adopted for calculation of data from residents' income survey since 2015. The "Net Per-capita Income of Rural Households" was modified as "Per-capita Disposable Income of Rural Households". The Growth Rate of Per-capita
Disposable Income of Urban Households and Per-capita Disposable Income of Rural Households is calculated based on a comparable caliber. The actual growth rate in the above form is the one with price influencing factors excluded.

e)The Growth Rate of Total Retail Sales of Society Consumer Goods from 2009 to 2013 have been adjusted in accordance with data from the Third National Economic Census.

1-9 主要年份国民经济和社会发展总量与速度指标

项目		Item		1990	1995
人口与就业		**Population and Employment**			
人口		**Population**			
年末全市常住人口	(万人)	Year-end Permanent Population	(10000 persons)	1086.0	1251.1
按性别分		By Sex			
男性人口		Male		545.0	627.0
女性人口		Female		541.0	624.1
按城乡分		By Urban Area and Rural Area			
城镇人口		Urban Population		798.0	946.2
乡村人口		Rural Population		288.0	304.9
年末户籍人口	(万人)	Year-end Registed Population	(10000 persons)	1032.2	1070.3
就业		**Employment**			
从业人员年末人数	(万人)	Year-end Employed Persons	(10000 persons)	627.1	665.3
#城镇单位在岗职工人数		On-the-job Staff and Workers		454.9	470.9
年末实有城镇登记失业人员	(万人)	Registered Unemployed Persons in Urban Areas at Year End	(10000 persons)	1.7	2.2
宏观经济		**Macro Economy**			
国民经济核算		**National Accounts**			
地区生产总值	(亿元)	Gross Domestic Product	(100 million yuan)	500.8	1507.7
第一产业		Primary Industry		43.7	72.2
第二产业		Secondary Industry		262.0	643.6
第三产业		Tertiary Industry		195.1	791.9
人均地区生产总值	(元/人)	Per Capita Gross Domestic Product	(yuan/person)	4635	12690
固定资产投资		**Fixed Asset Investment**			
全社会固定资产投资	(亿元)	Total Fixed Asset Investment	(100 million yuan)	179.2	841.5
#房地产开发投资		Real Estate Development		22.5	352.8
#国有单位		State-Owned Entities		154.2	514.2
全社会房屋施工面积	(万平方米)	Floor Space of Houses under Construction	(10000 sq.m)	2864.9	5524.3
全社会房屋竣工面积	(万平方米)	Floor Space of Houses Completed	(10000 sq.m)	1081.2	1530.2
财政		**Government Finance**			
地方财政收入	(亿元)	Local Finance Revenue	(100 million yuan)	74.0	115.3
#一般公共预算收入		Local Public Budgetary Revenue			
地方财政支出	(亿元)	Local Finance Expenditure	(100 million yuan)	66.5	154.4
#一般公共预算支出		Local Public Budgetary Expenditures			
价格指数(上年=100)		**Price Indices (Preceding Year=100)**			
居民消费价格指数	(%)	Consumer Price Index	(%)	105.4	117.3
商品零售价格指数	(%)	Retail Price Index	(%)	104.1	112.6
农产品生产价格指数	(%)	Farm Product Price Index	(%)	101.9	130.6
工业生产者出厂价格指数	(%)	Producer Price Index for Industrial Products	(%)	107.9	107.3
工业生产者购进价格指数	(%)	Purchase Price Index for Industrial Products	(%)	114.8	106.7
固定资产投资价格指数	(%)	Price Index of Investment in Fixed Asset	(%)		113.9
能源消费总量	**(万吨标准煤)**	**Total Energy Consumption**	**(10000 tons of SCE)**	**2709.7**	**3533.3**
产业		**Industry**			
农村经济		**Rural Economy**			
耕地面积	(万公顷)	Cultivated Areas	(10000 hectare)	41.3	39.4
农林牧渔业总产值(现价)	(亿元)	Gross Output Value of Agriculture, Forestry Animal Production and Hunting, Fishing (at current prices)	(100 million yuan)	70.2	164.4
主要农产品产量	(万吨)	Yield of Agricultural and Sideline Products	(10000 tons)		
粮食		Grain		264.6	259.8
蔬菜及食用菌		Vegetables and Edible Mushrooms		356.1	397.3
禽蛋		Poultry Eggs		25.8	28.5
牛奶		Milk		21.7	20.6
肉类		Meat		26.8	39.8

注：1. 地区生产总值绝对值按现价计算，发展速度按可比价格计算；2006-2010年人均地区生产总值根据第六次人口普查数据进行修正。自2013年开始，地区生产总值三次产业分组口径根据国家统计局规定调整,并对2012年以前三次产业数据进行相应调整。
2. 从2011年起，根据国家统计局相关规定，固定资产投资起点由50万元调整至500万元。

AGGREGATE INDICATORS AND SPEED INDICATORS ON NATIONAL ECONOMIC AND SOCIAL DEVELOPMENT IN KEY YEARS

总量指标 Aggregate Indicator					速度指标(%) Speed Indicator (%)					
					指 数(2015年为以下各年) Index (2015 as Percentage of the Following Year)					
2000	2005	2010	2014	2015	1990	1995	2000	2005	2010	2014
1363.6	1538.0	1961.9	2151.6	2170.5	199.9	173.5	159.2	141.1	110.6	100.9
710.9	778.7	1013.0	1106.5	1113.4	204.3	177.6	156.6	143.0	109.9	100.6
652.7	759.3	948.9	1045.1	1057.1	195.4	169.4	162.0	139.2	111.4	101.1
1057.4	1286.1	1686.4	1859.0	1877.7	235.3	198.4	177.6	146.0	111.3	101.0
306.2	251.9	275.5	292.6	292.8	101.7	96.0	95.6	116.2	106.3	100.1
1107.5	1180.7	1257.8	1333.4	1345.2	130.3	125.7	121.5	113.9	106.9	100.9
619.3	878.0	1031.6	1156.7	1186.1	189.1	178.3	191.5	135.1	115.0	102.5
434.2	448.4	587.7	708.8	724.8	159.3	153.9	166.9	161.6	123.3	102.3
3.3	10.6	7.7	8.8	9.2	548.5	418.3	275.9	86.7	118.5	104.4
3161.7	6969.5	14113.6	21330.8	23014.6	1244.9	711.7	436.8	246.8	143.8	106.9
77.3	86.2	122.7	159.0	140.2	117.6	112.6	105.1	102.4	95.7	89.2
1029.3	2017.2	3325.7	4544.8	4542.6	971.8	580.2	369.6	215.8	136.9	103.3
2055.1	4866.1	10665.2	16627.0	18331.7	1696.9	845.1	478.9	262.0	146.7	108.1
24127	45993	73856	99995	106497	621.1	390.7	264.7	173.0	132.8	105.5
1297.4	2827.2	5493.5	7562.3	7990.9						
522.1	1525.0	2901.1	3911.3	4226.3						
765.8	897.7	1907.3	2389.5	2529.2						
6995.9	14096.2	15572.1	21677.7	20009.1	698.4	362.2	286.0	141.9	128.5	92.3
2358.2	4679.2	3908.4	4967.5	4170.2	385.7	272.5	176.8	89.1	106.7	83.9
398.4	1007.4	3810.9	7214.5	6813.8	9206.6	5911.7	1710.3	676.4	178.8	94.4
345.0	919.2	2353.9	4027.2	4723.9			1369.2	513.9	200.7	117.3
490.3	1137.3	4065.0	7147.7	8080.7	12147.8	5233.6	1648.0	710.5	198.8	113.1
443.0	1058.3	2717.3	4524.7	5737.7			1295.2	542.2	211.2	126.8
103.5	101.5	102.4	101.6	101.8						
98.9	99.7	100.4	99.1	98.5						
95.0	102.9	106.5	99.7	99.8						
102.5	101.3	102.2	99.1	96.9						
100.0	111.4	110.5	98.8	93.7						
101.0	100.7	102.5	100.0	97.6						
4144.0	**5521.9**	**6954.1**	**6831.2**	**6852.6**	**252.9**	**193.9**	**165.4**	**124.1**	**98.5**	**100.3**
32.9	23.3	22.4	22.0							
188.6	239.3	328.0	420.1	368.2	524.6	224.0	195.2	153.9	112.3	87.7
144.2	94.9	115.7	63.9	62.6	23.7	24.1	43.4	66.0	54.1	98.0
466.3	373.1	303.0	236.2	205.1	57.6	51.6	44.0	55.0	67.7	86.9
16.0	16.0	15.1	19.7	19.6	75.9	68.7	122.4	122.4	129.7	99.6
30.3	64.2	64.1	59.5	57.2	263.4	277.7	188.8	89.1	89.3	96.2
50.5	53.3	46.3	39.3	36.4	135.8	91.6	72.1	68.3	78.7	92.6

Note: a) Absolute values on GDP are calculated at current prices, whereas growth rates are calculated at comparable prices.Per Capita Gross Domestic Product from 2006 to 2010 were adjusted according to the 6th population census.From 2013, The Gross Domestic Product of three industries were changed according to provisions of the National Bureau of Statistics, and the data on the three industries before 2012 was adjusted . Bureau of Statistics, and the data on the three industries before 2012 was adjusted .

b) From 2011, the starting point of fixed asset investment is changed from RMB 500,000 to RMB 5 million according to relevant regulations of National Bureau of Statistics.

1-9 续表 1

项　　目		Item		1990	1995
工　业		**Industry**			
工业增加值(现价，规模以上)	(亿元)	Added Value of Industry (at Current Prices, Above Designated Size)	(100 million yuan)		473.1
工业总产值(现价，规模以上)	(亿元)	Gross Output Value of Industry (at Current Prices, Above Designated Size)	(100 million yuan)	625.9	1493.3
轻工业		Light Industry		262.2	472.2
重工业		Heavy Industry		363.7	1021.1
工业企业主要经济指标(规模以上)		Main Indicators of Industrial Enterprises (Above Designated Size)			
资产总计	(亿元)	Total Asset	(100 million yuan)	498.3	2582.6
负债总额	(亿元)	Total Liability	(100 million yuan)		1528.8
主营业务收入	(亿元)	Revenue from Main Businesses	(100 million yuan)	610.5	1590.4
利润总额	(亿元)	Total Profit	(100 million yuan)	48.9	85.3
建　筑		**Construction**			
建筑业施工企业总产值	(亿元)	Gross Output Value	(100 million yuan)	94.7	426.6
建筑业施工企业年末从业人员	(万人)	Year-end Employed Persons	(10000 persons)	60.2	82.6
运　输		**Transport**			
货物周转量	(亿吨公里)	Total Freight Turnover	(100 million ton-km)	268.8	323.1
铁　路		Railway		206.7	239.3
公　路		Road		57.5	76.2
民　航		Civil Aviation		4.5	7.5
管　道		Pipeline		0.2	0.1
旅客周转量	(亿人公里)	Total Passenger Turnover	(100 million passenger-km)	119.8	207.7
邮　电		**Post and Telecommunication Services**			
邮电业务总量	(亿元)	Business Volume of Post and Telecommunications	(100 million yuan)	11.9	56.1
固定电话用户	(万户)	Fixed Telephone Subscribers	(10000 subscribers)	33.3	150.5
固定电话主线普及率	(线/百人)	Penetration Rate of Main Line	(lines/100 persons)	3.1	12.0
移动电话用户	(万户)	Mobile Telephone Subscribers	(10000 subscribers)	0.3	16.9
移动电话普及率	(户/百人)	Penetration Rate of Mobile Telephone	(sets/100 persons)	0.03	1.4
商　业		**Commerce**			
社会消费品零售总额	(亿元)	Retail Sales of Consumer Goods	(100 million yuan)	345.1	950.4
对外经济贸易和旅游		**Foreign Trade and Tourism**			
北京地区进出口总值	(亿美元)	Total Value of Imports and Exports	(USD 100 million)	236.4	370.4
进口值		Imports		192.3	267.9
出口值		Exports		44.1	102.5
实际利用外商直接投资额	(亿美元)	Paid-in Foreign Investment	(USD 100 million)	2.8	14.0
接待入境旅游者人数	(万人次)	Inbound Tourists	(10000 persons)	100.0	207.0
旅游外汇收入	(亿美元)	Foreign Exchange Earning from Tourism	(USD 100 million)	6.6	21.8
金融保险		**Finance and Insurance**			
金融机构(含外资)本外币存款余额	(亿元)	Deposits of Financial Institutions (Including Foreign Institutions)	(100 million yuan)		
金融机构(含外资)本外币贷款余额	(亿元)	Loans of Financial Institutions (Including Foreign Institutions)	(100 million yuan)		
原保险保费收入	(亿元)	Premiums Revenue	(100 million yuan)		

注：1．工业增加值按生产法计算。
2．邮电业务总量2000年及以前按1990年不变价格计算，2010年及以前按2000年不变价格计算,从2011年开始按2010年不变价格计算。
3．社会消费品零售额2010年数据根据第三次全国经济普查数据进行了修订。

1-9 Continued 1

总量指标 Aggregate Indicator					速度指标(%) Speed Indicator (%)					
					指 数(2015年为以下各年) Index (2014 as Percentage of the Following Year)					
2000	2005	2010	2014	2015	1990	1995	2000	2005	2010	2014
776.0	1627.0	2751.7	3612.0	3676.6						
2842.0	6946.2	13699.8	18452.9	17449.6	2787.9	1168.5	614.0	251.2	127.4	94.6
719.3	1164.9	2000.0	2568.0	2610.8	995.7	552.9	363.0	224.1	130.5	101.7
2122.7	5781.3	11699.8	15884.9	14838.8	4080.0	1453.2	699.1	256.7	126.8	93.4
4612.7	12829.8	22750.6	33557.0	38609.8	7748.3	1495.0	837.0	300.9	169.7	115.1
2676.4	4706.7	11548.1	17137.6	18102.4		1184.1	676.4	384.6	156.8	105.6
2821.4	7279.1	14807.1	19776.7	18864.9	3090.3	1186.2	668.6	259.2	127.4	95.4
127.1	413.5	1028.3	1515.8	1597.7	3264.9	1873.2	1257.2	386.4	155.4	105.4
812.5	1894.0	5196.0	8209.8	8436.7	8908.9	1977.7	1038.4	445.4	162.4	102.8
56.6	67.2	59.9	51.0	59.0	98.1	71.5	104.3	87.8	98.5	115.7
299.6	457.7	513.7	672.8	623.7	232.0	193.0	208.1	136.3	121.4	92.7
200.2	310.8	257.5	284.4	224.8	108.7	93.9	112.3	72.3	87.3	79.0
82.6	85.5	101.6	165.2	156.4	272.1	205.2	189.2	182.9	153.9	94.7
16.8	28.2	48.2	55.4	63.7	1426.3	850.0	379.9	226.2	132.0	115.1
0.04	33.3	106.4	167.9	178.9				537.8	168.2	106.5
314.0	838.1	1399.5	1602.7	1747.7	1458.8	841.4	556.6	208.5	124.9	109.0
214.7	413.0	1108.9	751.1	991.2						132.0
451.2	943.5	885.6	831.1	784.7	2356.8	521.3	173.9	83.2	88.6	94.4
33.1	61.3	45.1	38.6	36.2						
347.2	1459.8	2129.8	4076.2	4051.6			1166.9	277.5	190.2	99.4
25.5	94.9	108.6	189.4	186.7						
1658.7	2911.7	6340.3	9638.0	10338.0	2995.7	1087.8	623.3	355.1	163.1	107.3
494.0	1255.1	3016.6	4155.4	3194.2	1350.9	862.5	646.6	254.5	105.9	76.9
374.3	946.4	2462.2	3532.0	2647.5	1376.7	988.4	707.3	279.7	107.5	75.0
119.7	308.7	554.4	623.4	546.7	1238.6	533.3	456.7	177.1	98.6	87.7
24.6	35.3	63.6	90.4	130.0	4692.6	926.5	528.7	368.5	204.2	143.8
282.1	362.9	490.1	427.5	420.0	420.0	202.9	148.9	115.7	85.7	98.3
27.7	36.2	50.4	46.1	46.1	700.8	211.0	166.4	127.2	91.3	99.9
11526.0	28969.9	66584.6	100095.5	128573.0			1115.5	443.8	193.1	128.5
6407.9	15335.5	36479.6	53650.6	58559.4			913.9	381.9	160.5	109.1
93.4	498.2	966.5	1207.2	1403.9			1502.4	281.8	145.3	116.3

Note: a) Added value of industry is calculated with the production approach.

b) Business volumes of post and telecommunications before and in 2000 were calculated at 1990's constant price, those before and in 2000 were calculated at 2000's constant price, and those since 2011 were calculated at 2010's constant price.

c) Data of Retail Sales of Consumer Goods were revised according to the third national economic census in 2010.

1-9 续表 2

项目		Item		1990	1995
教育、文化、科技、卫生		**Education, Culture, Science and Technology and Health Care**			
教育		**Education**			
在校学生数	(万人)	Students Enrollment	(10000 persons)		238.0
专任教师数	(万人)	Full-time Teachers	(10000 persons)		17.7
文化		**Culture**			
公共图书馆总藏数	(万册、万件)	Collection of Public Libraries	(10000 volumes)	2205	2629
科技		**Science and Technology**			
研究与试验发展经费内部支	(亿元)	Internal R&D Expenditures	(100 million yuan)		
技术合同成交总额	(亿元)	Total Volume of Transaction of Technological Contracts Concluded	(100 million yuan)	20.3	41.2
专利授权量	(件)	Number of Patent Granted	(case)	2268	4025
卫生		**Health Care**			
卫生机构个数	(个)	Health Care Institutions	(unit)	4953	4955
卫生机构病床数	(万张)	Beds at Health Care Institutions	(10000 beds)	5.9	6.7
卫生技术人员数	(万人)	Medical Technical Personnel	(10000 persons)	11.2	11.6
#执业(助理)医师		Certified Doctors		5.1	5.4
注册护师(士)		Registered Nurses		3.5	3.7
生活与环境		**People's Living and Environment**			
婚姻		**Marriage and Divorce**			
登记结婚对数	(万对)	Number of Registered Marriages	(10000 couples)	9.30	8.55
离婚对数	(万对)	Number of Registered Divorces	(10000 couples)	1.47	2.02
居住		**Housing**			
城镇居民人均住房建筑面积	(平方米)	Per Capita Floor Space of Houses in Urban Area	(sq.m)		
农村居民人均住房面积	(平方米)	Per Capita Living Space of Rural Residents	(sq.m)	20.62	24.74
生活		**People's Life**			
城镇居民人均可支配收入	(元)	Per Capita Annual Disposable Income of Urban Residents	(yuan)	1787	5868
农村居民人均可支配收入	(元)	Per Capita Net Income of Rural Residents	(yuan)	1297	3209
工资		**Wages**			
城镇单位在岗职工工资总额	(亿元)	Total Wages of Fully Employed Staff and Workers in Urban Entities	(100 million yuan)	118.9	382.0
城镇单位在岗职工平均工资	(元)	Average Wages of Fully Employed Staff and Workers in Urban Entities	(yuan)	2653	8144
市政建设		**Municipal Facilities**			
全社会用电量	(亿千瓦时)	Electricity Consumption	(100 million kwh)	150.5	222.6
自来水销售总量	(亿立方米)	Total Sales Volume of Tap Water	(100 million cu.m)	5.3	6.8
居民燃气用户	(万户)	Households Gas Users	(10000 households)	176.1	219.8
城市公共交通客运量	(亿人次)	Passengers Carried by Urban Public Transport	(100 million person-times)	33.5	37.2
环境		**Environment**			
城市绿化覆盖率	(%)	Green Area Coverage	(%)	28.0	32.7
污水处理率	(%)	Sewage Treatment Rate	(%)	7.3	19.4

注：1. 北京地区用电量来源于北京市电力公司，2000年以前工业用电量不包含输配损失和发电企业自产自用电量。
2. 从2001年开始，有关职工的指标调整为在岗职工的指标。2007年及以前城镇单位在岗职工工资包括乡及乡以上独立核算法人单位，不包括乡镇企业、私营单位和个体工商户；2008年及以后包括乡镇企业。
3. 离婚对数包括在民政部门登记的对数和经法院调离和判离的对数。
4. 2010年及以前，本表中卫生机构数据都不包含村卫生室及驻京部队医院情况。2011年开始，包含村卫生室情况。2012年开始，卫生机构数、卫生技术人员数据中包含驻京部队医院，床位数不包含。
5. 2015年根据国家统计局城乡住户调查一体化工作要求，城乡住户调查样本、统计方法和指标口径有所变化，详见第八章“简要说明”。

1-9 Continued 2

总量指标 Aggregate Indicator					速度指标(%) Speed Indicator (%)					
					指 数(2015年为以下各年) Index (2015 as Percentage of the Following Year)					
2000	2005	2010	2014	2015	1990	1995	2000	2005	2010	2014
229.9	226.4	330.0	377.5	373.4		156.9	162.4	164.9	113.2	98.9
16.7	17.5	20.7	22.5	22.6		128.0	135.3	129.5	109.4	100.4
3020	3626	4613	5601	5943	269.5	226.1	196.8	163.9	128.8	106.1
155.7	379.5	821.8	1268.8	1384.0			888.9	364.7	168.4	109.1
140.3	434.4	1579.5	3136.0	3452.6	17032.9	8386.1	2461.0	794.8	218.6	110.1
5905	10100	33511	74661	94031	4146.0	2336.2	1592.4	931.0	280.6	125.9
6176	4818	6539	10265	10425	210.5	210.4	168.8	216.4	159.4	101.6
7.1	7.9	9.3	11.0	11.2	189.0	166.7	156.6	141.1	120.1	101.6
11.6	12.0	17.1	24.3	25.7	229.8	221.2	222.1	214.0	149.9	105.6
5.2	5.1	6.6	9.0	9.6	189.4	178.2	187.0	190.5	146.2	107.7
4.0	4.3	6.7	10.6	11.4	330.7	311.3	286.5	266.4	169.8	107.7
8.02	9.66	13.81	17.00	16.60	178.5	194.1	207.0	171.9	120.2	97.6
2.66	3.42	4.40	6.56	8.22	557.3	407.7	308.8	240.0	186.9	125.2
	22.03	28.94	31.54	31.69						
28.91	36.94	40.62	52.42	43.03						
10350	17653	29073	43910	52859						108.9
										109.0
4687	7860	13262	20226	20569						
695.5	1520.1	3789.1	7293.3	8225.2	6917.7	2153.2	1182.6	541.1	217.1	112.8
15726	34191	65683	103400	113073	4262.1	1388.4	719.0	330.7	172.1	109.4
384.4	570.5	809.9	937.0	952.7	633.1	428.0	247.8	167.0	117.6	101.7
7.5	7.2	8.9	10.3	10.4	197.2	153.1	137.9	145.2	116.6	100.5
291.9	462.6	634.2	846.0	885.7	503.0	403.0	303.4	191.5	139.7	104.7
40.7	51.8	69.0	81.6	73.8	220.6	198.7	181.6	142.6	107.0	90.5
36.5	42.0	45.0	47.4	48.4						
39.4	62.4	81.0	86.1	87.9						

Note: a) Figures on electricity consumption are provided by State Grid Beijing Electric Power Company. Before 2000, electricity consumption by industry excluded transmission and distribution losses and electricity generated and consumed by power generating enterprises.

b) From 2001, indicators related to the "staff and workers" have been changed to those of "fully employed staff and workers". In and before 2007, figures on wages of urban fully employed staff and workers in urban entities had been kept separate accounts at and above the township level, excluding township enterprises, private entities and self-employed operators; in and after 2008, such figures have included township enterprises.

c) Number of registered divorces includes those registered with civil affair authorities and those mediated and ruled in courts.

d) In and before 2010, figures on health centers were emerged with other health institutions such as community health service centers (stations). From 2011, health care institutions included village health centers. From 2012, figures of health care institutions and health care technical personnel have included military hospitals in Beijing, but beds are exclusive.

e) According to the work requirements to integration of urban and rural household survey of National bureau of statistics, there are some changes in survey samples of urban and rural household, statistic methods and indicator approaches. See Chapter VIII "Brief Introduction" for details.

1-10 主要年份国民经济和社会发展结构指标 STRUCTURAL INDICATORS ON NATIONAL ECONOMIC AND SOCIAL DEVELOPMENT IN KEY YEARS

单位：% (%)

项目	Item	1990	1995	2000	2005	2010	2014	2015
人口与就业	**Population and Employment**							
常住人口	**Permanent Population**							
按性别分	By Sex							
男	Male	50.2	50.1	52.1	50.6	51.6	51.4	51.3
女	Female	49.8	49.9	47.9	49.4	48.4	48.6	48.7
按城乡分	By Urban Area and Rural Area							
城 镇	Urban	73.5	75.6	77.5	83.6	86.0	86.4	86.5
乡 村	Rural	26.5	24.4	22.5	16.4	14.0	13.6	13.5
就 业	**Employment**							
从业人员年末人数	Year-end Employed Persons							
第一产业	Primary Industry	14.5	10.6	11.8	7.1	6.0	4.5	4.2
第二产业	Secondary Industry	44.9	40.7	33.6	26.3	19.6	18.2	17.0
第三产业	Tertiary Industry	40.6	48.7	54.6	66.6	74.4	77.3	78.8
宏观经济	**Macro Economy**							
国民经济核算	**National Accounts**							
地区生产总值	Gross Domestic Product							
第一产业	Primary Industry	8.7	4.8	2.4	1.2	0.9	0.7	0.6
第二产业	Secondary Industry	52.3	42.7	32.6	28.9	23.6	21.4	19.7
第三产业	Tertiary Industry	39.0	52.5	65.0	69.9	75.5	77.9	79.7
投 资	**Investment**							
全社会固定资产投资	Fixed Asset Investment							
城 镇	Urban	88.2	94.4	91.9	91.8	91.1	91.6	90.9
农 村	Rural	9.7	4.8	6.5	8.2	8.9	8.4	9.1
资金来源结构	Source of Capital							
国家预算内资金	State Budgetary Appropriation	25.3	7.7	7.4	2.8	1.2	1.6	1.7
国内贷款	Domestic Loans	16.7	13.4	26.0	23.2	26.6	27.8	22.2
利用外资	Foreign Investment	11.2	20.5	3.6	1.6	0.5	0.3	0.1
债券、自筹和其他资金	Securities, Fundraising and Other Investment	46.8	58.4	63.0	72.4	71.6	70.3	76.0
财 政	**Government Finance**							
地方一般公共预算收入主要税种	Main Taxes of Public Finance Budget Revenue							
#增值税	Value Added Tax			13.3	10.6	8.9	16.1	15.2
营业税	Business Tax			43.2	41.7	38.0	26.5	25.1
个人所得税	Private Income Tax			16.3	9.2	102.5	9.5	10.1
企业所得税	Corporate Income Tax			16.8	17.9	60.0	22.7	21.7
能源消费总量	**Energy Consumotion**							
第一产业	Primary Industry	3.9	3.4	2.5	1.6	1.4	1.3	1.2
第二产业	Secondary Industry	63.5	65.9	58.5	48.9	39.2	29.3	27.8
第三产业	Tertiary Industry	19.0	17.9	26.1	34.8	41.7	47.4	48.3
生活消费	Living Consumption	13.6	12.8	12.9	14.7	17.7	22.0	22.7

注：1. 自2012年开始，从业人员年末人数和能源消费总量三次产业分组口径根据国家统计局规定进行了调整。
2. 自2013年开始，地区生产总值三次产业分组口径根据国家统计局规定调整，并对2012年以前三次产业数据进行相应调整。

Note: a) From 2012, The grouping standards for Year-end Employed Persons and Energy Consumption of three industries were changed according to provisions of the National Bureau of Statistics.
b) From 2013, The Gross Domestic Product of three industries were changed according to provisions of the National Bureau of Statistics, and the data on the three industries before 2012 was adjusted .

1-10 续表 1 Continued 1

单位：% (%)

项 目	Item	1990	1995	2000	2005	2010	2014	2015
产 业	**Industry**							
农 业	**Agriculture**							
农林牧渔业产值结构	Structure of Gross Output Value of Agriculture							
农 业	Agriculture	55.6	52.8	46.7	38.0	47.0	36.9	42.0
林 业	Forestry	1.3	1.7	2.8	5.2	5.1	21.6	15.6
牧 业	Animal Production and Hunting	39.8	41.8	46.4	50.5	42.6	36.3	36.9
渔 业	Fishing	3.3	3.7	4.1	3.6	3.5	3.2	3.2
农林牧渔服务业	Service Activities for Agriculture, Forestry, Animal Production and Hunting, Fishing				2.7	1.8	2.0	2.3
工 业	**Industry**							
规模以上工业主要行业增加值结构	Structure of Added Value of Industry by Sector (Above Designated Size)							
#医药制造业	Manufacture of Medicines		1.6	3.6	3.0	5.6	7.8	8.2
汽车制造业	Manufacture of Motor Vehicles		9.4	3.7	8.7	16.6	20.1	21.8
计算机、通信和其他电子设备制造业	Manufacture of Computer, Communication Equipment and Other Electronic Equipment		9.9	24.7	16.7	8.7	8.4	7.7
电力、热力的生产和供应业	Production and Distribution of Electricity and Heating Power		7.0	6.4	11.8	14.9	18.9	18.0
建筑业	**Construction**							
建筑业总产值结构	Stucture of Gross Output Value of Construction							
#国有企业	State-owned Enterprises	68.7	69.1	44.8	27.4	6.3	3.5	3.0
集体企业	Collectively-owned Enterprises	31.3	26.4	21.7	4.7	2.0	1.6	1.2
港澳台商投资企业	Hong Kong, Macao and Taiwan-invested Enterprises		1.4	1.4	1.2	1.8	0.8	0.7
外商投资企业	Foreign-invested Enterprises		1.2	2.0	1.7	1.0	0.5	0.5
交通运输业	**Transport**							
货运量结构(按运输方式分)	Structure of Freignt (By Means of Transportation)							
铁 路	Railway	11.4	9.2	8.5	6.1	6.6	3.8	4.3
公 路	Road	87.5	90.4	91.2	92.4	85.1	86.1	82.0
民 航	Civil Aviation	0.04	0.05	0.1	0.2	0.5	0.5	0.7
管 道	Pipeline	1.0	0.3	0.2	1.2	7.7	9.6	13.0
客运量结构(按运输方式分)	Structure of Passenger (By Means of Transportation)							
铁 路	Railway	50.4	45.1	24.2	9.5	6.3	17.6	18.3
公 路	Road	46.7	47.7	70.7	85.3	89.7	73.0	71.4
民 航	Civil Aviation	2.9	7.2	5.1	5.2	4.0	9.4	10.3
国内贸易	**Domestic Trade**							
社会消费品零售总额结构	Structure Retail Sales of Consumer Goods							
吃类商品	Food	39.6	42.7	28.4	25.8	21.4	19.3	19.0
穿类商品	Clothing	13.2	14.6	12.0	9.7	8.8	8.1	7.2
用类商品	Daily Use Articles	44.8	40.8	56.2	56.5	62.4	66.5	69.2
烧类商品	Fuels	2.4	1.9	3.4	8.1	7.5	6.0	4.6
对外贸易	**Foreign Trade**							
地区出口商品结构	Structure of Export Commodities							
#一般贸易	General Trade		70.6	65.9	54.5	45.0	45.5	54.8
加工贸易	Processing Trade		21.3	29.6	39.6	42.1	35.9	28.0
地区进口商品结构	Structure of Import Commodities							
#一般贸易	General Trade		84.4	87.3	85.2	88.7	86.4	85.7
加工贸易	Processing Trade		5.2	3.5	8.2	5.9	7.1	7.7
国际旅游	**International Tourism**							
接待海外旅游人数结构	Structure of Inbound Tourist							
外国人	Foreigners	63.7	80.5	84.4	85.9	86.0	85.5	85.1
港澳台同胞	Compatriots from Hong Kong, Macao and Taiwan	34.6	17.6	15.6	14.1	14.0	14.5	14.9

1-10 续表 2 Continued 2

单位：% (%)

项　　目	Item	1990	1995	2000	2005	2010	2014	2015
教育、科技、文化、卫生	**Education, Science and Technology, Culture, Health Care**							
教　育	**Education**							
在校学生结构	Structure of Students Enrollment							
#高等教育	Higher Education	8.3	9.0	14.0	46.2	49.5	51.1	50.7
中等教育	Secondary Education	32.5	41.0	48.7	29.7	22.1	17.3	15.7
小学教育	Primary Education	59.0	49.6	36.8	16.9	19.8	21.8	22.8
专任教师结构	Structure of Full-time Teachers							
#高等教育	Higher Education	24.6	22.7	22.2	32.7	35.9	31.6	30.3
中等教育	Secondary Education	38.3	38.6	40.5	33.6	29.1	31.9	32.0
小学教育	Primary Education	36.7	37.9	36.8	25.3	23.9	22.0	22.1
科　技	**Science and Technology**							
研究与试验发展(R&D)人员折合全时当量结构	Structure of R&D Personnel							
基础研究	Basic Research				12.9	15.2	15.9	16.8
应用研究	Applied Research				29.8	27.1	24.1	25.1
试验发展	Experimental Development				57.3	57.7	60.0	58.1
研究与试验发展(R&D)经费内部支出结构	Structure of Full-time and Non-full Time R&D Personnel							
基础研究	Basic Research				10.1	11.6	12.6	13.8
应用研究	Applied Research				27.8	26.4	21.7	23.0
试验发展	Experimental Development				53.1	62.0	65.8	63.2
卫　生	**Health Care**							
卫生技术人员结构	Structure of Medical Personnel							
#执业(助理)医师	Certified Doctors	45.6	46.7	44.6	42.2	38.5	36.9	37.6
注册护士	Registered Nurses	31.0	31.7	34.5	35.8	39.3	43.7	44.6
生活与环境	**People's Livelihood and Environment**							
生　活	**People's Livelihood**							
城镇居民消费结构	Consumption Structure of Urban Residents							
#食品烟酒(恩格尔系数)	Food (Engel Coefficient)	54.2	48.5	36.3	31.8	32.1	30.8	22.1
衣　着	Clothing	14.8	15.1	8.9	8.9	10.4	10.4	7.2
医疗保健	Health Care and Medical Services	1.4	2.9	6.9	9.8	6.7	6.6	6.5
交通和通信	Transport and Communications	1.5	4.7	7.1	14.7	17.2	15.7	13.3
教育文化娱乐服务	Education, Cultural and Entertainment Services	11.5	10.2	15.1	16.5	14.6	14.9	11.0
农村居民消费结构	Consumption Structure of Rural Residents							
#食品烟酒(恩格尔系数)	Food (Engel Coefficient)	50.7	49.6	36.7	32.8	30.9	34.7	27.7
衣　着	Clothing	9.5	10.9	7.6	7.8	7.7	8.6	6.3
医疗保健	Health Care and Medical Services	3.8	4.8	8.0	9.0	8.9	8.9	8.5
交通和通信	Transport and Communications	1.7	4.1	6.3	11.0	13.1	10.9	13.5
教育文化娱乐服务	Education, Cultural and Entertainment Services	6.6	10.6	14.4	15.1	9.7	10.0	7.2
环　境	**Environment**							
林木绿化率	Green Area Coverage	28.3	36.3	42.0	50.5	53.0	58.4	59.0

1-11 国民经济和社会发展比例和效益指标
INDICATORS ON PROPORTIONS AND EFFICIENCY IN NATIONAL ECONOMIC AND SOCIAL DEVELOPMENT

项 目		Item		2015	2014
人口与就业		**Population and Employment**			
人 口		**Population**			
常住人口出生率	(‰)	Birth Rate of Permanent Population	(‰)	7.96	9.75
常住人口死亡率	(‰)	Death Rate of Permanent Population	(‰)	4.95	4.92
常住人口自然增长率	(‰)	Natural Growth Rate of Permanent Population	(‰)	3.01	4.83
就 业		**Employment**			
城镇登记失业率	(%)	Registered Unemployment Rate in Urban Areas	(%)	1.39	1.31
宏观经济		**Macro Economy**			
国民经济核算		**National Accounts**			
地区生产总值构成	(%)	Structure of Gross Domestic Product	(%)	100.0	100.0
第一产业		Primary Industry		0.6	0.7
第二产业		Secondary Industry		19.7	21.4
第三产业		Tertiary Industry		79.7	77.9
全社会劳动生产率	(元/人)	Overall Labor Productivity	(yuan/person)	196471	185671
第一产业		Primary Industry		27302	29494
第二产业		Secondary Industry		221220	216013
第三产业		Tertiary Industry		200414	187973
固定资产投资		**Fixed Asset Investment**			
全社会固定资产投资相当于		Proportion of Fixed Asset Investment			
地区生产总值比例	(%)	to Gross Domestic Product	(%)	34.72	35.45
能源消费		**Energy Consumption**			
能源消费弹性系数		Energy Consumption Elasticity Coefficient		0.05	0.22
电力消费弹性系数		Electricity Consumption Elasticity Coefficient		0.28	0.37
万元地区生产总值能耗	(吨标准煤)	Energy Consumption per 10000 yuan of GDP	(ton of SCE)	0.34	0.36
(可比价)		(Comparable Price)			
万元地区生产总值水耗	(立方米)	Water Consumption per 10000 yuan of GDP			
(现价)		(Current Price)	(cu.m)	16.60	17.58
产 业		**Industry**			
规模以上工业企业效益		**Efficiency of Industrial Enterprises**			
		Above Designated Size			
综合效益指数	(%)	General Efficiency Index	(%)	302.38	288.41
总资产贡献率	(%)	Total Asset Contribution Rate	(%)	6.79	8.23
资产保值增值率	(%)	Capital Maintenance and Appreciation Rate	(%)	124.95	112.32

1-11 续表 Continued

项目		Item		2015	2014
资产负债率	(%)	Asset-liability Ratio	(%)	46.89	51.07
流动资产周转率	(次)	Turnover Rate of Working Capital	(time)	1.27	1.48
成本费用利润率	(%)	Ratio of Profits to Total Industrial Cost	(%)	8.83	8.11
全员劳动生产率	(元/人)	Overall Labor Productivity	(yuan/person)	332913	309326
产品销售率	(%)	Ratio of Sales to Gross Output Value	(%)	99.02	98.78
建筑业		**Construction**			
产值竣工率	(%)	Rate of Buildings Completed (by Output Value)	(%)	50.8	49.4
面积竣工率	(%)	Rate of Buildings Completed (by Floor Space)	(%)	16.5	16.4
邮电通信业		**Post and Communications**			
移动电话普及率	(户/百人)	Penetration Rate of Mobile Phone	(sets/100 persons)	186.7	189.4
固定电话主线普及率	(线/百人)	Penetration Rate of Main Line of Fixed Telephone	(line/100 persons)	36.2	38.6
国内贸易		**Domestic Trade**			
人均社会消费品零售总额	(元)	Per Capita Retail Sales of Consumer Goods	(yuan)	47838	45181
教育、科技、文化、卫生		**Education, Science and Technology, Culture and Health Care**			
教 育		**Education**			
学龄儿童入学率	(%)	Enrollment Rate of Children at School-Age	(%)	100.0	100.0
平均每一专任教师负担学生数		Average Number of Students Instructed by a Full-time Teacher			
#普通中学	(人)	Ordinary Secondary Education	(person)	8.4	9.0
小学学校	(人)	Primary Education	(person)	14.3	14.4
科 技		**Science and Technology**			
研究与试验发展经费内部支出相当于地区生产总值比例	(%)	Internal R&D Expenditures as % of GDP	(%)	6.01	5.95
文 化		**Culture**			
每万人拥有公共图书馆	(个)	Public Libraries per 10,000 persons	(library)	0.01	0.01
每万人拥有博物馆	(个)	Museums per 10,000 persons	(museum)	0.08	0.08
卫 生		**Health Care**			
婴儿死亡率	(‰)	Infant Mortality Rate	(‰)	2.42	2.33
孕产妇死亡率	(1/10万)	Maternal Mortality Rate	(1/100,000)	8.69	7.19
平均每千人口拥有执业医师数(常住人口)	(人)	Certified Doctors per 1,000 Persons (Permanent Resident)	(person)	4.44	4.16
家庭、生活、环境、灾害		**Household, Livelihood, Environment and Accidents**			
家 庭		**Household**			
少儿抚养比(常住人口)	(%)	Child-age Dependency Rate (Permanent Population)	(%)	12.67	12.34
老年抚养比(常住人口)	(%)	Old-age Dependency Rate (Permanent Population)	(%)	12.89	12.30
生 活		**Livelihood**			
城镇与农村居民收入比例(以农村居民收入为1)		Ratio of Urban Residents' Income to Rural Residents' Income (Rural Residents' Income = 1)		2.57	2.17
城镇居民人均住房建筑面积	(平方米)	Per Capita Living Space for Urban Residents	(sq.m)	31.69	31.54
农村居民人均住房面积	(平方米)	Per Capita Living Space for Rural Residents	(sq.m)	43.03	52.42
环境、灾害		**Environment and Accidents**			
人均公园绿地面积	(平方米)	Per Capita Park and Green Area	(sq.m)	16.0	15.9
平均每起火灾直接经济损失	(元)	Average Direct Losses per Fire Accident	(yuan)	16195	15311
平均每起交通事故直接经济损失	(元)	Average Direct Losses per Traffic Accident	(yuan)	7918	9575
重点食品安全监测抽检合格率	(%)	Up-to-standard Rate of Key Foods Security Monitor Spot Checks	(%)	98.42	98.39
药品抽验合格率	(%)	Up-to-standard Rate of Druy Spot Checks	(%)	99.71	99.88

1-12 北京一日
A DAY IN BEIJING

项 目		Item		2015	2014
每天创造的财富		**Daily Production**			
地区生产总值	(万元)	Gross Domestic Product	(10000 yuan)	630536.7	584406.3
第一产业		Primary Industry		3841.4	4355.9
第二产业		Secondary Industry		124455.9	124515.1
第三产业		Tertiary Industry		502239.5	455535.3
#批发和零售业		Wholesale and retail trade		64447.7	66058.6
信息传输、软件和信息技术服务业		Information transmission,software and information technology services		65312.9	57038.4
金融业		Finance		107275.4	91992.1
科学研究和技术服务业		Scientific research and development, technical services		49880.3	45552.3
一般公共预算收入	(万元)	Local Public Finance Budget Revenue	(10000 yuan)	129420.8	110333.2
一般公共预算支出	(万元)	Local Public Finance Budget Expenditure	(10000 yuan)	157197.3	123963.5
发电量	(万千瓦时)	Electricity Generated	(10000 kWh)	11435.2	9275.9
汽车生产量	(辆)	Output of Motor Vehicles	(vehicle)	6080	5937
移动电话机生产量	(台)	Output of Mobile Telephones	(set)	261392	492701
每天收入与消费量		**Daily Income and Consumption**			
城镇居民人均可支配收入	(元)	Per Capita Disposable Income of Urban Residents	(yuan)	144.8	120.3
城镇居民人均消费性支出	(元)	Per Capita Living Expenditures of Urban Residents	(yuan)	100.4	76.7
农村居民人均可支配收入	(元)	Per Capita Net Income of Rural Residents	(yuan)	56.4	55.4
农村居民人均生活消费支出	(元)	Per Capita Living Expenditures of Rural Residents	(yuan)	43.3	39.8
城镇单位在岗职工平均工资	(元)	Average Wage of On-the-job Staff and Workers	(yuan)	309.8	283.3
社会消费品零售总额	(万元)	Retail Sales of Consumer Goods	(10000 yuan)	283232.9	264054.8
机动车销售量	(辆)	Sales of Motor Vehicles	(vehicle)	3145	3493
居民生活用电量	(万千瓦时)	Resident Electricity Use	(10000 kWh)	4787.9	4637.3
每天其他活动		**Other Daily Activities**			
地区出口值	(万美元)	Exports of Local Enterprises	(USD 10000)	14976.9	17078.3
旅游外汇收入	(万美元)	Foreign Exchange Earning from Tourism	(USD 10000)	1261.6	1262.4
国内旅游收入	(万元)	Domestic Tourism Earnings	(10000 yuan)	118356.2	109506.3
接待入境旅游人数	(人次)	Inbound Tourists	(person-time)	11506	11711
接待国内旅游者人数	(人次)	Domestic Tourists	(person-time)	735863	704717
市内公共交通客运量	(万人次)	Urban Public Transport Turnover	(10000 person-times)	2023.0	2235.2
每天人口和婚姻变动		**Daily Population and Marriage Changes**			
出生人口(常住人口)	(人)	Births (Permanent Residence)	(person)	471	570
死亡人口(常住人口)	(人)	Deaths (Permanent Residence)	(person)	293	288
登记结婚对数	(对)	Registered Marriages	(couple)	455	466
离婚对数	(对)	Divorces	(couple)	225	180

注：离婚对数包括在民政部门登记的对数和经法院调离和判离的对数。
Note: Divorces include those registered with civil affair authorities and those mediated and ruled in courts.

1-13 “十二五”时期经济社会发展主要监测指标
MAIN MONITORING INDICATORS OF SOCIAL AND ECONOMIC DEVELOPMENT IN THE TWELFTH FIVE-YEAR PLAN PERIOD

项目	Item	“十二五”时期监测发展目标 Target in the 12th Five-year Plan	2011	2012	2013	2014	2015
地区生产总值比上年增长 (%)	Growth Rate of GDP (%)	年均增长7.5%	8.1	7.7	7.7	7.3	6.9
第三产业占地区生产总值比重 (%)	Tertiary Industry as % of GDP (%)	达到78%以上	76.6	77.0	77.5	77.9	79.7
最终消费率 (%)	Final Consumption Rate (%)	达到60%	58.4	59.6	61.4	62.5	63.0
地方公共财政预算收入比上年增长 (%)	Growth Rate of Local Public Finance Budget Revenue (%)	年均增长9%	27.7	10.3	10.4	10.0	17.3
城镇居民人均可支配收入实际增长 (%)	Actual Growth Rate of Per-capita Disposable Income of Urban Residents (%)	年均实际增长8%	7.2	7.3	7.1	7.2	7.0
农村居民人均可支配收入实际增长 (%)	Actual Growth Rate of Per-capita Disposable Income of Rural Residents (%)	年均实际增长8%	7.6	8.2	7.7	8.6	7.1
城镇登记失业率 (%)	Urban Registered Unemployment Rate (%)	控制在3.5%以内	1.39	1.27	1.21	1.31	1.39
重点食品安全监测抽检合格率 (%)	Up-to-standard Rate of Key Foods Security	达到98%		95.29	96.94	98.39	98.42
药品抽验合格率 (%)	Up-to-standard Rate of Drug Spot Checks (%)	达到98%及以上	99.3	99.7	99.9	99.88	99.71
全社会研究与试验发展经费支出占地区生产总值的比例 (%)	R&D Expenditure as % of GDP (%)	达到5.5%以上	5.76	5.95	5.98	5.95	6.01
万元地区生产总值能耗降低 (%)	Decrease of Energy Consumption per 10000 yuan of GDP (%)	累计降低17%	6.95	4.75	4.88	5.29	6.13
万元地区生产总值水耗降低 (%)	Decrease of Water Consumption per 10000 yuan of GDP (%)	累计降低15%	5.49	7.38	5.87	3.93	4.65
林木绿化率 (%)	Green Area Coverage (%)	达到57%	54.0	55.5	57.4	58.4	59.0

注：2015年根据国家统计局要求对居民收支指标口径进行了调整，将农村居民人均纯收入统一改为农村居民人均可支配收入。

Note: According to national requirements, residents' income and expenses indicator caliber was adjusted in 2015, so that per capita net income of rural residents uniformly changed into per capita annual disposable income of rural residents.

主要统计指标解释

法人单位 指有权拥有资产、承担负债，并独立从事社会经济活动（或与其他单位进行交易）的组织。法人单位应同时具备以下条件：（1）依法成立，有自己的名称、组织机构和场所，能够独立承担民事责任；（2）独立拥有（或授权使用）资产或者经费，承担负债，有权与其他单位签订合同；（3）具有包括资产负债表在内的账户，或者能够根据需要编制账户。

单产业法人 指仅包含一个产业活动单位的法人单位，该法人单位同时也是一个产业活动单位。

多产业法人 指由两个及以上产业活动单位组成的法人单位，这些产业活动单位接受法人单位的管理和控制。

登记注册类型 企业法人或企业产业活动单位的登记注册类型，按其在工商行政管理机关登记注册的类型填写。如企业登记注册类型发生变化，但未及时到工商部门变更登记，企业应根据变化后的实际情况填写。其他法人和产业活动单位的登记注册类型，按其主要经费来源和管理方式，根据实际情况，比照《企业登记注册类型与代码》填写。

国有企业 指企业全部资产归国家所有，并按《中华人民共和国企业法人登记管理条例》规定登记注册的非公司制的经济组织。不包括有限责任公司中的国有独资公司。

集体企业 指企业资产归集体所有，并按《中华人民共和国企业法人登记管理条例》规定登记注册的经济组织。

股份合作企业 指以合作制为基础，由企业职工共同出资入股，吸收一定比例的社会资产投资组建，实行自主经营，自负盈亏，共同劳动，民主管理，按劳分配与按股分红相结合的一种集体经济组织。

联营企业 指两个及两个以上相同或不同所有制性质的企业法人或事业单位法人，按自愿、平等、互利的原则，共同投资组成的经济组织称为联营企业。联营企业包括国有联营企业、集体联营企业、国有与集体联营企业和其他联营企业。

有限责任公司 指根据《中华人民共和国公司登记管理条例》规定登记注册，由两个以上，五十个以下的股东共同出资，每个股东以其所认缴的出资额对公司承担有限责任，公司以其全部资产对其债务承担责任的经济组织。有限责任公司包括国有独资公司、其他有限责任公司。

私营企业 指由自然人投资设立或由自然人控股，以雇佣劳动为基础的营利性经济组织。包括按照《公司法》、《合伙企业法》、《私营企业暂行条例》、《个人独资企业法》规定登记注册的私营独资企业、私营合伙企业、私营有限责任公司、私营股份有限公司和个人独资企业。

其他企业 指上述类型之外的其他内资经济组织。

港澳台商投资企业 指港澳台地区投资者依照中华人民共和国有关涉外经济的法律、法规成立的企业，包括与港澳台商合资经营企业、与港澳台商合作经营企业、港澳台商独资经营企业、港澳台商投资股份有限公司、其他港澳台商投资企业。

外商投资企业 指外国企业或外国人依照中华人民共和国有关涉外经济的法律、法规成立的企业，包括中外合资经营企业、中外合作经营企业、外资企业、外商投资股份有限公司、其他外商投资企业。

非公经济 指资产由我国私人控股、港澳台商控股、外商控股的"非公有控股"的企业法人单位，以及主要经费来源于私人、港澳台资和外资的非企业法人单位和个体工商户。其中，私人、港澳台及外商控股是指由其绝对控股和相对控股的经济成分。

Explanatory Notes on Main Statistical Indicators

Legal Entity refers to any organization that has the right to own assets and bear liabilities, and conducts social and economic activities independently (or conducts transactions with other entities). A business entity shall meet all of such conditions as: (1) established in accordance with law, having its own name, organization and site, capable of assuming civil responsibilities independently; (2) independently owning and using (or using under authorization) assets or outlays, assuming liabilities, having the right to sign contracts with other entities; (3) maintaining accounts including balance sheet, or capable of preparing accounts as needed.

Single-industry Legal Entity refers any business entity conducting only one industrial activity. Such business entity is also an industrial activity entity.

Multi-industry Legal Entity refers to any business entity composed of two or more industrial activity entities which are managed and controlled by the business entity.

Registration type of an enterprise as legal person or as industrial activity entity shall be completed according to the type registered at the administration for industry and commerce. In the event of any change in registration type, and no registration alteration is made with administration for industry and commerce in good time, the registration type shall be completed according to the actual situation. Registration type for other legal persons and industrial activity entities shall be completed according to the main source of outlays and management manner, pursuant to the actual conditions, and by referring to the *Type of Enterprise Registration and Code*.

State-owned Enterprise refers to non-corporation economic organizations where the entire assets are owned by the state and which have registered in accordance with the *Regulation of the People's Republic of China on the Management of Registration of Corporate Enterprises*, excluding solely state-funded corporations in limited liability companies.

Collectively-owned Enterprise refer to economic organizations where the assets are owned collectively and which have registered in accordance with the *Regulation of the People's Republic of China on the Management of Registration of Corporate Enterprises*.

Joint-equity Cooperative Enterprise refers to a form of collective economic organizations based on cooperative system, where capitals come mainly from employees as their shares, with certain proportion of capital from the public, where production is organized on the basis of independent operation, independent accounting for profits and losses, joint work, democratic management, and where the distribution system integrates distribution according to work with distribution according to capital share.

Associated Enterprise refers to organizations established by two or more corporate legal persons or institutional legal persons of the same or different ownership, through joint investment on the basis of equality, voluntary participation and mutual benefits. They include state-owned associated enterprises, collectively-owned associated enterprises, state-collective associated enterprises and other associated enterprises.

Limited Liability Company refers to organizations established with investment from 2-50 shareholders and registered in accordance with the *Regulation of the People's Republic of China on the Management of Registration of Corporations*, each shareholder bearing limited liability to the corporation depending on its share of investment, and the corporation bearing liability to its debt to the maximum of its total assets. Limited liability companies include solely state-funded limited liability companies and other limited liability companies.

Private Enterprise refers to profit-making organizations established by natural persons or controlled by natural persons using employed labor. Private enterprises include solely private-funded enterprises, private partnership enterprises, private limited liability companies, private companies limited by shares, and private-funded enterprises registered in accordance with provisions in the *Corporation Law*, *Partnership Enterprises Law*, *Interim Regulations on Private Enterprises* and *Sole Proprietorship Enterprise Law*.

Other Enterprise refers to domestically funded organizations other than those mentioned above.

Hong Kong, Macao and Taiwan-invested Enterprise refers to enterprises established by investors from Hong Kong, Macao and Taiwan in accordance with laws and rules of the People's Republic of China on foreign-related businesses. They include joint ventures with investors from Hong Kong, Macao and Taiwan, cooperative enterprises with investors from Hong Kong, Macao and Taiwan, enterprises wholly funded by investors from Hong Kong, Macao and Taiwan, companies limited by shares and funded by investors from Hong Kong, Macao and Taiwan, and other enterprises funded by investors from Hong Kong, Macao and Taiwan.

Foreign-invested Enterprise refers to enterprises

established by foreign enterprises or foreigners in accordance with laws and regulations of the People's Republic of China on foreign-related businesses. They include Sino-foreign joint ventures, Sino-foreign cooperative enterprises, foreign wholly-funded enterprises, foreign-funded companies limited by shares, and other foreign-funded enterprises.

Non-public Economy means enterprises as business entities whose shares are controlled by "non-public entities" and whose assets are controlled by individuals, investors from Hong Kong, Macao and Taiwan, and foreign investors, along with enterprises not as business entities and self-employed operators whose main funds are from individuals, investors from Hong Kong, Macao and Taiwan, and foreign investors. Here, enterprises controlled by individuals, investors from Hong Kong, Macao and Taiwan, and foreign investors mean economic sectors with absolute or relative control by such companies.

02

北京统计年鉴2016　BEIJING STATISTICAL YEARBOOK

国民经济核算
NATIONAL ACCOUNTS

简 要 说 明

一、本章资料的主要内容

本章主要包括历年北京市地区生产总值、部分新兴产业增加值、各行业增加值、居民消费水平、全社会劳动生产率、三次产业的贡献率等资料。其中，地区生产总值是由北京市统计局根据统计资料、会计资料和部门财务资料采用不同方法核算的数据。

二、本章中关于历史数据调整的问题

本章中 1997-2008 年地区生产总值的数据及其分组资料，按照国家统一规定，根据“北京市第二次全国经济普查”和“北京市第二次全国农业普查”的数据结果进行了修正。

2006-2010 年人均地区生产总值数据根据全国第六次人口普查数据进行了修正。

2013 年数据为第三次全国经济普查数据。

三、有关统计标准的变化说明

（一）关于行业划分。根据国家统计局规定，执行《国民经济行业分类》GB/T 4754-2011 标准。

（二）关于三次产业划分。根据国家统计局《三次产业划分规定》(国统字[2012]108 号)，对三次产业的范围进行了调整。第一产业是指农、林、牧、渔业（不含农、林、牧、渔服务业）；第二产业是指采矿业（不含开采辅助活动），制造业（不含金属制品、机械和设备修理业），电力、热力、燃气及水生产和供应业，建筑业；第三产业是指除第一产业、第二产业以外的其他行业。

Brief Introduction

I. Main Content

Statistics in this chapter include the GDP of Beijing, added value of some emerging sectors, added value of different sectors, residents' consumption level, total productivity, contribution rate of three industries in previous years. Among them, the GDP of Beijing is calculated by Beijing Municipal Bureau of Statistics using different measures according to statistical data, accounting data and financial data of different sectors.

II. Adjustment to Historical Statistics

Figures of GDP 1997-2008 and grouping data have been corrected in accordance with the national uniform regulation and the results of “the 2nd National Economic Census in Beijing” and “the 2nd National Agricultural Census in Beijing”.

2006-2010 per-capita GDP figures were adjusted according to figures from the 6th national census.

The data of 2013 was adjusted to be the statistics for the 3rd National Economic Census.

Ⅲ. Explanation on Changes of Statistical Standards

(I) Industrial Classification. As regulated by National Bureau of Statistics, *Classification of National Economic Sectors* Standard GB/T 4754-2011 shall be adopted and accounting shall follow the standards.

(II) Classification of Three Industries. According to *Regulations on Three Industries Classification* (G.T.Z. [2012] No. 108) of National Bureau of Statistics, the scope of three industries has been adjusted. The primary industry refers to agriculture, forestry, animal production and hunting, fishing (excluding service activities for agriculture, forestry, animal production and hunting, fishing); secondary industry refers to mining and quarrying (excluding mining support service activities), manufacturing (excluding repair of fabricated metal products, machinery and equipment), production and distribution of electricity, heating power, gas and water and construction; the tertiary industry refers to others excluding the primary and secondary industries.

2-1 地区生产总值(1978-2015年)
GROSS DOMESTIC PRODUCT (1978-2015)

单位：亿元 (100 million yuan)

年份 Year	地区生产总值 Gross Domestic Product	按产业分组 By Three Industies			按行业分组 By Sector		人均地区生产总值(元/人) Per Capita Gross Domestic Product (yuan/person)	人均地区生产总值(美元/人) Per Capita Gross Domestic Product (USD/person)
		第一产业 Primary Industry	第二产业 Secondary Industry	第三产业 Tertiary Industry	#工业 Industry	#建筑业 Construction		
1978	108.8	5.6	77.2	26.0	70.2	7.2	1257	797
1979	120.1	5.2	85.0	29.9	77.4	7.8	1358	908
1980	139.1	6.1	95.6	37.4	86.9	8.9	1544	1009
1981-1985	**950.9**	**61.9**	**588.4**	**300.6**	**515.5**	**73.9**		
1981	139.2	6.6	92.3	40.3	82.7	9.8	1526	895
1982	154.9	10.2	99.6	45.1	89.3	10.5	1671	883
1983	183.1	12.7	112.5	57.9	98.8	13.9	1943	983
1984	216.6	14.7	130.5	71.4	114.0	16.7	2262	972
1985	257.1	17.7	153.5	85.9	130.7	23.0	2643	900
1986-1990	**1978.7**	**162.1**	**1082.5**	**734.1**	**917.3**	**167.0**		
1986	284.9	19.0	165.6	100.3	141.2	24.6	2836	821
1987	326.8	24.2	182.2	120.4	154.5	28.1	3150	846
1988	410.2	36.9	220.9	152.4	189.5	31.8	3892	1046
1989	456.0	38.3	251.8	165.9	212.8	39.4	4269	1134
1990	500.8	43.7	262.0	195.1	219.3	43.1	4635	969
1991-1995	**4847.2**	**286.4**	**2213.0**	**2347.8**	**1833.5**	**386.9**		
1991	598.9	45.5	290.5	262.9	255.6	35.9	5494	1032
1992	709.1	48.7	344.7	315.7	293.0	52.9	6458	1171
1993	886.2	53.2	418.2	414.8	339.2	80.4	8006	1389
1994	1145.3	66.8	516.0	562.5	417.9	99.7	10240	1188
1995	1507.7	72.2	643.6	791.9	527.8	118.0	12690	1520
1996-2000	**12084.0**	**378.6**	**4263.3**	**7442.1**	**3450.5**	**827.2**		
1996	1789.2	73.4	712.3	1003.5	576.2	138.5	14254	1714
1997	2077.1	75.5	779.2	1222.4	635.9	145.9	16621	2005
1998	2377.2	76.1	838.0	1463.1	670.4	170.2	19128	2310
1999	2678.8	76.3	904.5	1698.0	724.0	183.3	21407	2586
2000	3161.7	77.3	1029.3	2055.1	844.0	189.3	24127	2915
2001-2005	**26032.9**	**412.4**	**7727.9**	**17892.6**	**6446.2**	**1313.5**		
2001	3708.0	78.6	1137.1	2492.3	938.8	203.6	26980	3260
2002	4315.0	80.5	1245.7	2988.8	1021.2	228.8	30730	3713
2003	5007.2	81.8	1482.4	3443.0	1224.5	262.7	34777	4202
2004	6033.2	85.3	1845.5	4102.4	1554.7	298.9	40916	4943
2005	6969.5	86.2	2017.2	4866.1	1707.0	319.5	45993	5615
2006-2010	**55346.2**	**535.7**	**13394.6**	**41415.9**	**11103.4**	**2467.7**		
2006	8117.8	85.4	2177.9	5854.5	1821.8	369.6	51722	6488
2007	9846.8	99.4	2493.9	7253.5	2082.8	426.6	60096	7903
2008	11115.0	111.4	2592.9	8410.7	2131.7	494.7	64491	9286
2009	12153.0	116.8	2804.2	9232.0	2303.1	552.4	66940	9799
2010	14113.6	122.7	3325.7	10665.2	2764.0	624.4	73856	10910
2011-2015	**98277.5**	**741.3**	**21020.6**	**76515.6**	**17367.2**	**4164.8**		
2011	16251.9	134.4	3678.0	12439.5	3048.8	703.7	81658	12643
2012	17879.4	148.1	3962.6	13768.7	3294.3	765.0	87475	13857
2013	19800.8	159.6	4292.6	15348.6	3566.4	831.6	94648	15284
2014	21330.8	159.0	4544.8	16627.0	3746.8	902.7	99995	16278
2015	23014.6	140.2	4542.6	18331.7	3710.9	961.9	106497	17099

注：1. 本表数据按当年价格计算。2013年数据为第三次全国经济普查数据。
2. 2013年开始，地区生产总值行业划分执行《国民经济行业分类》GB/T 4754-2011标准。
3. 2013年开始，地区生产总值三次产业划分执行国家统计局《三次产业划分规定》(国统字[2012]108号)，并对本表1978-2012年以来三次产业数据进行相应调整。
4. 人均地区生产总值按年平均常住人口计算，2011年根据全国第六次人口普查数据对2006年至2010年人均地区生产总值进行了调整（下同）。

Note: a) Figures in this table are calculated at current year's prices.Data for 2013 were collected from the third national economic census.
b) Since 2013, GDP industrial classification has been subjected to Classification of National Economic Sectors Standard GB/T 4754-2011.
c) Since 2013, GDP three sector classification has been subject to Regulations on Three Industries Classification (G.T.Z. [2012] No. 108) issued by National Bureau of Statistics, according to which data on the three industries from 1978 to 2012 was adjusted in this table.
d) Per capita GDP is calculated at average permamnent population. In 2011,per capita GDP 2006-2010 were adjusted according to the 6th National Population Census (the same below).

2-2 地区生产总值指数(上年=100)(1978-2015年)
INDICES OF GROSS DOMESTIC PRODUCT (PRECEDING YEAR=100) (1978-2015)

单位：% (%)

年份 Year	地区生产总值 Gross Domestic Product	按产业分组 By Three Industies			按行业分组 By Sector		人均地区生产总值 Per Capita Gross Domestic Product
		第一产业 Primary Industry	第二产业 Secondary Industry	第三产业 Tertiary Industry	#工业 Industry	#建筑业 Construction	
1978	110.5	109.0	115.1	97.7	112.4	153.0	109.1
1979	109.7	105.0	109.2	113.2	110.1	108.4	107.4
1980	111.8	109.3	110.1	118.5	110.1	110.3	109.8
1981	99.5	109.1	96.3	106.0	95.3	106.4	98.3
1982	107.4	113.4	105.8	109.9	105.8	106.1	105.6
1983	116.4	107.5	113.6	124.2	111.5	132.3	114.5
1984	117.4	106.8	116.1	121.8	115.7	118.8	115.6
1985	108.7	106.3	111.0	104.4	109.1	124.7	106.9
1986	108.0	100.1	104.8	115.7	105.0	103.7	104.6
1987	109.6	113.4	105.6	116.7	105.5	106.3	106.1
1988	112.8	111.2	112.1	114.1	113.0	106.5	111.0
1989	104.4	101.1	108.9	97.3	108.4	112.2	103.1
1990	105.2	103.3	101.1	113.3	101.9	95.6	104.0
1991	109.9	103.7	107.5	114.5	112.6	81.6	108.9
1992	111.3	103.1	112.2	111.9	110.3	125.7	110.5
1993	112.3	103.2	113.0	113.1	110.5	128.5	111.4
1994	113.7	102.8	114.1	115.0	113.5	117.0	112.5
1995	112.0	92.0	107.7	120.5	107.7	107.6	105.4
1996	109.0	97.2	106.2	113.4	106.1	107.0	103.1
1997	110.1	102.9	108.1	113.2	108.7	105.1	110.6
1998	109.5	101.1	109.6	110.1	108.7	114.2	110.1
1999	110.9	102.8	112.0	110.6	112.8	108.0	110.1
2000	111.8	103.1	111.4	112.9	113.2	102.1	106.8
2001	111.7	103.7	109.5	113.1	110.2	106.6	106.5
2002	111.5	102.7	108.4	113.3	107.8	110.9	109.1
2003	111.1	98.9	112.0	111.2	112.2	110.7	108.3
2004	114.1	99.4	117.0	113.1	119.3	106.3	111.4
2005	112.1	98.1	110.1	113.4	110.9	106.3	109.1
2006	113.0	100.6	110.5	114.3	109.5	116.0	109.1
2007	114.5	102.2	112.7	115.4	113.1	110.9	109.7
2008	109.1	101.1	100.8	112.5	100.2	103.7	103.7
2009	110.2	104.6	110.4	110.2	108.8	118.5	104.6
2010	110.3	98.4	113.7	109.3	114.9	108.3	104.8
2011	108.1	100.9	106.7	108.7	107.5	102.9	103.8
2012	107.7	103.2	107.5	107.9	107.0	109.7	104.9
2013	107.7	103.0	108.1	107.6	107.8	109.7	105.2
2014	107.3	100.0	106.9	107.5	106.0	110.2	105.2
2015	106.9	89.2	103.3	108.1	101.0	113.2	105.5

注：1. 本表数据按可比价格计算。
2. 2013年数据为第三次全国经济普查数据。

Note: a) Statistics in this table are calculated at comparable prices.
b) Data for 2013 were collected from the third national economic census.

2-3 地区生产总值指数(1978年=100)(1978–2015年)
INDICES OF GROSS DOMESTIC PRODUCT (YEAR OF 1978=100) (1978-2015)

单位：%　　　　(%)

年份 Year	地区生产总值 Gross Domestic Product	按产业分组 By Three Industies			按行业分组 By Sector		人均地区生产总值 Per Capita Gross Domestic Product
		第一产业 Primary Industry	第二产业 Secondary Industry	第三产业 Tertiary Industry	#工业 Industry	#建筑业 Construction	
1978	100.0	100.0	100.0	100.0	100.0	100.0	100.0
1979	109.7	105.0	109.2	113.2	110.1	108.4	107.4
1980	122.6	114.8	120.2	134.1	121.2	119.6	117.9
1981	122.0	125.2	115.8	142.2	115.5	127.2	115.9
1982	131.1	142.0	122.5	156.3	122.2	135.0	122.4
1983	152.6	152.6	139.2	194.1	136.3	178.6	140.2
1984	179.1	163.0	161.6	236.4	157.7	212.1	162.0
1985	194.7	173.3	179.3	246.8	172.0	264.5	173.2
1986	210.3	173.5	187.9	285.5	180.6	274.3	181.2
1987	230.4	196.7	198.5	333.2	190.6	291.6	192.2
1988	259.9	218.7	222.5	380.2	215.3	310.6	213.4
1989	271.4	221.1	242.3	369.9	233.4	348.5	220.0
1990	285.5	228.4	244.9	419.2	237.9	333.1	228.8
1991	313.8	236.9	263.3	479.9	267.8	271.8	249.1
1992	349.2	244.2	295.4	537.0	295.4	341.7	275.3
1993	392.2	252.0	333.8	607.4	326.4	439.1	306.7
1994	445.9	259.1	380.9	698.5	370.5	513.7	345.0
1995	499.4	238.4	410.2	841.7	399.0	552.8	363.7
1996	544.3	231.7	435.7	954.5	423.4	591.5	374.9
1997	599.3	238.4	471.0	1080.5	460.2	621.7	414.6
1998	656.2	241.0	516.2	1189.6	500.2	710.0	456.5
1999	727.7	247.7	578.1	1315.7	564.2	766.8	502.8
2000	813.6	255.4	644.0	1485.4	638.7	782.9	536.8
2001	908.8	264.8	705.2	1680.0	703.8	834.6	571.7
2002	1013.3	271.9	764.4	1903.4	758.7	925.6	623.9
2003	1125.8	268.9	856.1	2115.9	851.3	1024.6	676.0
2004	1284.5	267.3	1001.6	2393.1	1015.6	1089.1	753.1
2005	1440.3	262.2	1102.8	2714.9	1126.3	1157.7	821.5
2006	1627.5	263.8	1218.6	3102.0	1233.3	1342.9	896.3
2007	1863.3	269.6	1373.4	3580.0	1394.9	1489.3	983.2
2008	2033.0	272.6	1384.4	4027.6	1397.7	1544.4	1019.6
2009	2240.4	285.2	1528.7	4437.6	1520.8	1829.4	1066.5
2010	2471.2	280.6	1738.1	4850.3	1747.4	1981.2	1117.7
2011	2671.4	283.1	1854.6	5272.3	1878.5	2038.7	1160.2
2012	2877.1	292.2	1993.7	5688.8	2010.0	2236.5	1217.0
2013	3098.6	301.0	2155.2	6121.1	2166.8	2453.4	1280.3
2014	3324.8	301.0	2303.9	6580.2	2296.8	2703.6	1346.9
2015	3554.2	268.5	2379.9	7113.2	2319.8	3060.5	1421.0

注：1. 本表数据按可比价格计算。
　　2. 2013年数据为第三次全国经济普查数据。

Note: a) Statistics in this table are calculated at comparable prices.
　　b) Data for 2013 were collected from the third national economic census.

2-4 地区生产总值构成(1978-2015年)
COMPOSITION OF GROSS DOMESTIC PRODUCT (1978-2015)

单位：% (%)

年 份 Year	地区生产总值 Gross Domestic Product	按产业分组 By Three Industies			按行业分组 By Sector	
		第一产业 Primary Industry	第二产业 Secondary Industry	第三产业 Tertiary Industry	#工业 Industry	#建筑业 Construction
1978	100.0	5.1	71.0	23.9	64.5	6.6
1979	100.0	4.3	70.8	24.9	64.4	6.5
1980	100.0	4.4	68.7	26.9	62.5	6.4
1981	100.0	4.7	66.3	29.0	59.4	7.1
1982	100.0	6.6	64.3	29.1	57.6	6.8
1983	100.0	6.9	61.4	31.7	53.9	7.6
1984	100.0	6.8	60.2	33.0	52.6	7.7
1985	100.0	6.9	59.7	33.4	50.8	9.0
1986	100.0	6.7	58.1	35.2	49.6	8.6
1987	100.0	7.4	55.8	36.8	47.3	8.6
1988	100.0	9.0	53.9	37.1	46.2	7.8
1989	100.0	8.4	55.2	36.4	46.7	8.6
1990	100.0	8.7	52.3	39.0	43.8	8.6
1991	100.0	7.6	48.5	43.9	42.7	6.0
1992	100.0	6.9	48.6	44.5	41.3	7.5
1993	100.0	6.0	47.2	46.8	38.3	9.0
1994	100.0	5.8	45.1	49.1	36.5	8.7
1995	100.0	4.8	42.7	52.5	35.0	7.8
1996	100.0	4.1	39.8	56.1	32.2	7.7
1997	100.0	3.6	37.5	58.9	30.6	7.0
1998	100.0	3.2	35.3	61.5	28.2	7.2
1999	100.0	2.8	33.8	63.4	27.0	6.9
2000	100.0	2.4	32.6	65.0	26.7	6.0
2001	100.0	2.1	30.7	67.2	25.3	5.5
2002	100.0	1.9	28.9	69.2	23.7	5.3
2003	100.0	1.6	29.6	68.8	24.5	5.2
2004	100.0	1.4	30.6	68.0	25.8	5.0
2005	100.0	1.2	28.9	69.9	24.5	4.6
2006	100.0	1.1	26.8	72.1	22.4	4.6
2007	100.0	1.0	25.3	73.7	21.2	4.3
2008	100.0	1.0	23.3	75.7	19.2	4.4
2009	100.0	1.0	23.1	75.9	19.0	4.5
2010	100.0	0.9	23.6	75.5	19.6	4.4
2011	100.0	0.8	22.6	76.6	18.8	4.3
2012	100.0	0.8	22.2	77.0	18.4	4.3
2013	100.0	0.8	21.7	77.5	18.0	4.2
2014	100.0	0.7	21.4	77.9	17.6	4.2
2015	100.0	0.6	19.7	79.7	16.1	4.2

注：1. 2013年数据为第三次全国经济普查数据。
2. 2013年开始，地区生产总值行业划分执行《国民经济行业分类》GB/T 4754-2011标准。
3. 2013年开始，地区生产总值三次产业划分执行国家统计局《三次产业划分规定》(国统字[2012]108号)，并对本表1978-2012年以来三次产业数据进行相应调整。

Note: a) Data for 2013 were collected from the third national economic census.
b) Since 2013, GDP industrial classification has been subjected to Classification of National Economic Sectors Standard GB/T 4757-2011.
c) Since 2013, GDP three sector classification has been subject to Regulations on Three Industries Classification (G.T.Z. [2012] No. 108) issued by National Bureau of Statistics, according to which data on the three industries from 1978 to 2012 was adjusted in this table.

2-5 地区生产总值指数(2000年=100)(2000−2015年)
INDICES OF GROSS DOMESTIC PRODUCT (YEAR OF 2000=100) (2000-2015)

单位：% (%)

年份 Year	地区生产总值 Gross Domestic Product	按产业分组 By Three Industies			按行业分组 By Sector		人均地区生产总值 Per Capita Gross Domestic Product
		第一产业 Primary Industry	第二产业 Secondary Industry	第三产业 Tertiary Industry	#工业 Industry	#建筑业 Construction	
2000	100.0	100.0	100.0	100.0	100.0	100.0	100.0
2001	111.7	103.7	109.5	113.1	110.2	106.6	106.5
2002	124.5	106.5	118.7	128.1	118.8	118.2	116.2
2003	138.3	105.3	132.9	142.4	133.3	130.8	125.9
2004	157.8	104.7	155.5	161.1	159.0	139.0	140.3
2005	176.9	102.7	171.2	182.8	176.3	147.8	153.0
2006	199.9	103.3	189.2	208.9	193.0	171.4	166.9
2007	228.9	105.6	213.2	241.1	218.3	190.1	183.1
2008	249.8	106.8	214.9	271.2	218.7	197.1	189.9
2009	275.3	111.7	237.3	298.8	238.0	233.5	198.6
2010	303.7	109.9	269.8	326.6	273.5	252.9	208.1
2011	328.3	110.9	287.9	355.0	294.0	260.2	216.0
2012	353.6	114.4	309.5	383.0	314.6	285.4	226.6
2013	380.8	117.8	334.6	412.1	339.1	313.1	238.4
2014	408.6	117.8	357.7	443.0	359.4	345.0	250.8
2015	436.8	105.1	369.5	478.9	363.0	390.5	264.6

注：1. 本表数据按可比价格计算。
2. 2013年数据为第三次全国经济普查数据。

Note: a) Statistics in this table are calculated at comparable prices.
b) Data for 2013 were collected from the third national economic census.

2-6 按行业分地区生产总值
GROSS DOMESTIC PRODUCT BY SECTOR

单位：亿元 (100 million yuan)

项　　目	Item	2015	2014
地区生产总值	**Gross Domestic Product**	**23014.6**	**21330.8**
按产业分组	**By there industies**		
第一产业	Primary Industry	140.2	159.0
第二产业	Secondary Industry	4542.6	4544.8
第三产业	Tertiary Industry	18331.7	16627.0
按行业分组	**By Sector**		
农、林、牧、渔业	Agriculture, Forestry, Animal Production and Hunting, Fishing	142.6	161.3
采矿业	Mining and Quarrying	149.6	176.2
制造业	Manufacturing	2811.2	2823.2
电力、热力、燃气及水生产和供应业	Production and Distribution of Electricity,Heating Power, Gas and Water	750.2	747.4
建筑业	Construction	961.9	902.7
批发和零售业	Wholesale and Retail Trade	2352.3	2411.1
交通运输、仓储和邮政业	Transport, Storage and Post	983.9	948.1
住宿和餐饮业	Accommodation and Restaurants	397.6	363.8
信息传输、软件和信息技术服务业	Information Transmission,Software and Information Technology Services	2383.9	2081.9
金融业	Finance	3926.3	3357.7
房地产业	Real Estate	1438.4	1329.2
租赁和商务服务业	Renting and Leasing Activities and Business Services	1766.8	1700.2
科学研究和技术服务业	Scientific Research and Development, Technical Services	1820.6	1662.7
水利、环境和公共设施管理业	Management of Water Conservancy, Environment and Public Facilities	180.5	136.0
居民服务、修理和其他服务业	Resident Services, Repair and Other Services	142.8	155.0
教　育	Education	965.5	859.0
卫生和社会工作	Health Care and Social Works	577.6	468.1
文化、体育和娱乐业	Culture, Sports and Entertainment	527.8	470.4
公共管理、社会保障和社会组织	Pulic Administration,Social Security and Social Organizations	735.3	576.8
国际组织	International Organizations		

注：本表数据按当年价格计算。
Note: Figures in this table are calculated at current year's prices.

2-7 按行业分地区生产总值指数(上年=100)
INDICES OF GROSE DOMESFIC PRODUCT BY SECTOR (PRECEDING YEAR=100)

单位：% (%)

项　目	Item	2015	2014
地区生产总值	**Gross Domestic Product**	**106.9**	**107.3**
按产业分组	**By Three Industies**		
第一产业	Primary Industry	89.2	100.0
第二产业	Secondary Industry	103.3	106.9
第三产业	Tertiary Industry	108.1	107.5
按行业分组	**By Sector**		
农、林、牧、渔业	Agriculture, Forestry, Animal Production and Hunting, Fishing	89.4	100.0
采矿业	Mining and Quarrying	93.1	98.2
制造业	Manufacturing	101.3	107.6
电力、热力、燃气及水生产和供应业	Production and Distribution of Electricity,Heating Power, Gas and Water	102.6	101.8
建筑业	Construction	113.2	110.2
批发和零售业	Wholesale and Retail Trade	98.6	105.0
交通运输、仓储和邮政业	Transport, Storage and Post	104.1	106.8
住宿和餐饮业	Accommodation and Restaurants	100.2	99.1
信息传输、软件和信息技术服务业	Information Transmission,Software and Information Technology Services	112.1	111.9
金融业	Finance	118.1	112.7
房地产业	Real Estate	104.2	97.8
租赁和商务服务业	Renting and Leasing Activities and Business Services	98.3	105.8
科学研究和技术服务业	Scientific Research and Development, Technical Services	114.1	111.1
水利、环境和公共设施管理业	Management of Water Conservancy, Environment and Public Facilities	113.3	111.4
居民服务、修理和其他服务业	Resident Services, Repair and Other Services	102.1	112.8
教　育	Education	111.8	109.7
卫生和社会工作	Health Care and Social Works	113.7	110.7
文化、体育和娱乐业	Culture, Sports and Entertainment	103.5	101.9
公共管理、社会保障和社会组织	Pulic Administration,Social Security and Social Organizations	108.6	97.4
国际组织	International Organizations		

注：本表数据按可比价格计算。
Note: Figures in this table are calculated at comparable prices.

2-8 部分新兴产业增加值
ADDED VALUE OF SOME EMERGING INDUSTRIES

单位：亿元 (100 million yuan)

项 目	Item	2015	2014
地区生产总值	**Gross Domestic Product**	**23014.6**	**21330.8**
文化创意产业	**Cultural and Creative Industry**	**3179.3**	**2826.3**
文化艺术	Culture and Arts	132.1	115.6
新闻出版	Journalism and Publishing	278.4	239.7
广播、电视、电影	Radio Broadcasting, Television and Movies	223.0	200.3
软件、网络及计算机服务	Software, Internet and Computer Services	1842.8	1605.2
广告会展	Advertising and Exhibitions	217.0	220.2
艺术品交易	Artwork Trading	64.3	56.2
设计服务	Design Service	132.0	127.7
旅游、休闲娱乐	Tourism, Leisure and Entertainment	107.2	99.7
其他辅助服务	Other Auxiliary Service	182.5	161.7
信息产业	**Information Industry**	**3449.3**	**3172.2**
电子信息设备制造	Manufacture of Electronic Information Equipment	356.7	398.8
电子信息设备销售和租赁	Sales and Renting of Electronic Information Equipment	312.3	339.3
电子信息传输服务	Electronic Information Transmission Service	948.6	833.8
计算机服务和软件业	Computer Service and Software	1435.3	1248.1
其他信息相关服务	Other Information-related Service	396.4	352.2
高技术产业	**High-tech Industry**	**5175.8**	**4738.5**
医药制造业	Manufacture of Medicines	275.6	269.3
航空、航天器及设备制造业	Manufacture of Aircrafts and Spacecrafts	56.9	58.8
电子及通信设备制造业	Manufacture of Electronic and Communication Equipment	249.5	294.2
计算机及办公设备制造业	Manufacture of Computers and Office Equipments	47.8	50.9
医疗仪器设备及仪器仪表制造业	Manufacture of Medical Equipments and Meters	134.1	126.4
信息化学品制造业	Information Chemical Manufacturing	0.8	1.6
信息服务	Inforamtion Service	2520.4	2194.8
电子商务服务	E-commerce Services	48.4	31.6
检验检测服务	Examination and Inspection Service	109.2	92.3
专业技术服务业的高技术服务	High-tech Service in Professional Technology Service Sector	726.6	702.1
研发与设计服务	Research and Design Service	539.6	485.4
科技成果转化服务	Transformation Service on Technological Achievements	323.2	291.3
知识产权及相关法律服务	Intellectual Property and Relevant Legal Services	107.1	112.1
环境监测及治理服务	Environmental Monitoring and Governance Service	36.5	27.7
现代制造业	**Modern Manufacturing Industry**	**1681.3**	**1744.6**
电子类	Electronics	272.4	325.6
机电类	Electromechanical	337.8	342.7
交通类	Transport	794.6	750.8
医药类	Pharmaceutical	301.3	293.5
其他类	Other	-24.9	32.0
现代服务业	**Modern Service Industry**	**13303.0**	**11820.0**
信息传输、软件和信息技术服务业	Information Transmission,Software and Information Technology Services	2383.9	2081.9
金融业	Finance	3926.3	3357.7
房地产业	Real Estate	1438.4	1329.2
商务服务业	Business Services	1673.2	1602.3
科学研究和技术服务业	Scientific Research and Development, Technical Services	1820.6	1662.7
环境管理业	Management of Environment	33.6	24.0
教 育	Education	965.5	859.0
卫 生	Health Care	533.7	432.8
文化、体育和娱乐业	Culture, Sports and Entertainment	527.8	470.4
生产性服务业	**Producer Services**	**12172.0**	**11196.1**
流通服务	Logistical Services	2274.5	2393.6
信息服务	Information Service	2383.9	2081.9
金融服务	Financial Service	3926.3	3357.7
商务服务	Business Service	1766.8	1700.2
科技服务	Scientific and Technological Services	1820.6	1662.7
信息服务业	**Inforamtion Service**	**2780.3**	**2434.1**
信息传输服务	Inforamtion Transmission Service	429.7	429.8
信息技术服务	Information Technology Service	1467.6	1274.9
信息内容服务	Information Content Service	883.1	729.4
物流业	**Logistics**	**779.0**	**790.2**
交通运输、邮政、仓储业	Transport, Post, Storage	607.3	615.9
流通加工、配送、包装业	Circulation and Processing, Delivery, Packaging	171.7	174.3

注：1. 本表数据按当年价格计算。
2. 新兴产业执行《国民经济行业分类》(GB/T4754-2011)标准。
3. 北京市从2013年开始执行国家高技术产业标准，包括高技术制造业和高技术服务业。

Note: a) Data in the table is calculated based on price in current year.
b) New emerging industries are subject to Classification of National Economic Sectors (GB/T4754-2011).
c) Beijing has implemented standards for national high-tech industries since 2013, industries on high-tech manufacturing and high-tech service are included.

2-9 收入法地区生产总值(1978-2015年)
GROSS DOMESTIC PRODUCT BY INCOME APPROACH (1978-2015)

单位：亿元 (100 million yuan)

年 份 Year	地区生产总值 Gross Domestic Product	劳动者报酬 Compensation for Labors	生产税净额 Net Taxes on Production	固定资产折旧 Depreciation of Fixed Assets	营业盈余 Operating Surplus
1978	108.8	37.1	16.5	11.5	43.7
1979	120.1	42.0	18.3	13.4	46.4
1980	139.1	48.9	21.0	15.4	53.8
1981-1985	**950.9**	**350.9**	**142.8**	**111.0**	**346.2**
1981	139.2	52.9	22.0	16.9	47.4
1982	154.9	57.4	23.2	17.7	56.6
1983	183.1	66.0	26.8	20.7	69.6
1984	216.6	79.1	31.8	25.4	80.3
1985	257.1	95.5	39.0	30.3	92.3
1986-1990	**1978.7**	**773.7**	**290.5**	**244.9**	**669.6**
1986	284.9	107.8	43.4	34.9	98.8
1987	326.8	125.4	48.0	40.9	112.5
1988	410.2	153.9	59.7	49.9	146.7
1989	456.0	179.3	66.5	57.1	153.1
1990	500.8	207.3	72.9	62.1	158.5
1991-1995	**4847.2**	**2102.6**	**717.3**	**608.1**	**1419.2**
1991	598.9	254.2	86.4	75.7	182.6
1992	709.1	304.7	103.3	89.5	211.6
1993	886.2	387.7	131.4	109.0	258.1
1994	1145.3	508.1	168.9	140.2	328.1
1995	1507.7	647.9	227.3	193.7	438.8
1996-2000	**12084.0**	**5112.5**	**1761.0**	**1664.8**	**3545.7**
1996	1789.2	760.9	264.9	236.9	526.5
1997	2077.1	880.1	302.6	275.0	619.4
1998	2377.2	1008.5	341.3	319.6	707.8
1999	2678.8	1135.3	388.1	375.3	780.1
2000	3161.7	1327.7	464.1	458.0	911.9
2001-2005	**26032.9**	**11244.4**	**3999.7**	**4091.6**	**6697.2**
2001	3708.0	1538.7	549.8	559.7	1059.8
2002	4315.0	1810.6	643.0	680.3	1181.1
2003	5007.2	2119.7	753.1	791.5	1342.9
2004	6033.2	2595.5	960.4	960.5	1516.8
2005	6969.5	3179.9	1093.4	1099.6	1596.6
2006-2010	**55346.2**	**26740.5**	**8959.8**	**7893.4**	**11752.5**
2006	8117.8	3657.3	1286.7	1268.3	1905.5
2007	9846.8	4405.8	1625.8	1383.0	2432.2
2008	11115.0	5615.8	1896.6	1608.4	1994.2
2009	12153.0	6141.6	1953.5	1707.7	2350.2
2010	14113.6	6920.0	2197.2	1926.0	3070.4
2011-2015	**98277.5**	**51149.3**	**15166.6**	**11908.5**	**20053.0**
2011	16251.9	7992.4	2566.1	2155.8	3537.6
2012	17879.4	9102.6	2894.6	2269.6	3612.6
2013	19800.8	10238.6	3179.8	2386.2	3996.2
2014	21330.8	11118.4	3227.4	2418.7	4566.3
2015	23014.6	12697.3	3298.7	2678.2	4340.4

注：2013年数据为第三次全国经济普查数据。
Note: Data for 2013 were collected from the third national economic census.

2-10 收入法地区生产总值(2015年)
GROSS DOMESTIC PRODUCT BY INCOME APPROACH (2015)

单位：亿元 (100 million yuan)

项 目	Item	地区生产总值 Gross Regional Product	劳动者报酬 Renumeration of Labor	生产税净额 Net Production Tax	固定资产折旧 Depreciation of Fixed Asset	营业盈余 Operating Surplus
地区生产总值	**Gross Domestic Product**	**23014.6**	**12697.3**	**3298.7**	**2678.2**	**4340.4**
按产业分组	**By Three Industies**					
第一产业	Primary Industry	140.2	123.8	1.1	15.3	0.01
第二产业	Secondary Industry	4542.6	1806.4	1004.1	727.6	1004.6
第三产业	Tertiary Industry	18331.7	10767.1	2293.5	1935.4	3335.8
按行业分组	**By Sector**					
农、林、牧、渔业	Agriculture, Forestry, Animal Production and Hunting, Fishing	142.6	125.3	1.4	15.9	0.01
采矿业	Mining and Quarrying	149.6	106.8	49.3	45.5	-52.0
制造业	Manufacturing	2811.2	1166.0	696.4	292.0	656.8
电力、热力、燃气及水生产和供应业	Production and Distribution of Electricity, Heating Power, Gas and Water	750.2	164.1	42.7	335.7	207.6
建筑业	Construction	961.9	450.3	252.4	62.2	197.1
批发和零售业	Wholesale and Retail Trade	2352.3	1223.2	768.0	145.5	215.7
交通运输、仓储和邮政业	Transport, Storage and Post	983.9	562.3	-89.7	246.3	265.0
住宿和餐饮业	Accommodation and Restaurants	397.6	311.5	73.6	49.2	-36.7
信息传输、软件和信息技术服务业	Information Transmission,Software and Information Technology Services	2383.9	1476.9	196.5	282.7	427.9
金融业	Finance	3926.3	1318.2	574.5	156.2	1877.3
房地产业	Real Estate	1438.4	421.2	356.2	372.2	288.9
租赁和商务服务业	Renting and Leasing Activities and Business Services	1766.8	1361.1	139.1	186.1	80.4
科学研究和技术服务业	Scientific Research and Development, Technical Services	1820.6	1350.3	170.9	191.2	108.3
水利、环境和公共设施管理业	Management of Water Conservancy, Environment and Public Facilities	180.5	128.8	8.8	20.0	23.0
居民服务、修理和其他服务业	Resident Services, Repair and Other Services	142.8	122.6	12.0	7.2	0.9
教 育	Education	965.5	828.4	18.0	94.3	24.8
卫生和社会工作	Health Care and Social Works	577.6	541.0	1.2	41.6	-6.2
文化、体育和娱乐业	Culture, Sports and Entertainment	527.8	388.8	22.8	54.7	61.6
公共管理、社会保障和社会组织	Pulic Administration,Social Security and Social Organizations	735.3	650.4	4.8	80.1	
国际组织	International Organizations					

2-11 支出法地区生产总值(1978-2015年)
GROSS DOMESTIC PRODUCT BY EXPENDITURE APPROACH (1978-2015)

单位：亿元 (100 million yuan)

年份 Year	地区生产总值 Gross Domestic Product	最终消费支出 Final Consumption Expenditure	居民消费 Households Consumption	政府消费 Government Consumption	资本形成总额 Gross Capital Formation	固定资本形成总额 Completed Fixed Assets	存货增加 Changes in Inventories	货物和服务净流出 Net Outflow of Goods and Services	最终消费率(消费率)(%) Final Consumption Rate (%)	资本形成率(投资率)(%) Capital Formation Rate (%)
1978	108.8	53.0	28.6	24.4	31.7	24.9	6.8	24.1	48.7	29.1
1979	120.1	55.4	31.5	23.9	37.0	29.1	7.9	27.7	46.1	30.8
1980	139.1	57.3	39.6	17.7	45.1	36.5	8.6	36.7	41.2	32.4
1981	139.2	61.8	44.2	17.6	50.5	40.2	10.3	26.9	44.4	36.3
1982	154.9	68.6	48.8	19.8	51.8	42.3	9.5	34.5	44.3	33.4
1983	183.1	77.6	54.6	23.0	62.9	56.1	6.8	42.6	42.4	34.4
1984	216.6	96.5	64.8	31.7	84.7	72.5	12.2	35.4	44.6	39.1
1985	257.1	127.1	88.7	38.4	150.6	102.7	47.9	-20.6	49.4	58.6
1986	284.9	161.1	109.9	51.2	178.8	116.0	62.8	-55.0	56.5	62.8
1987	326.8	181.5	124.3	57.2	201.2	148.6	52.6	-55.9	55.5	61.6
1988	410.2	222.6	161.9	60.7	251.1	177.7	73.4	-63.5	54.3	61.2
1989	456.0	244.0	176.1	67.9	271.5	151.9	119.6	-59.5	53.5	59.5
1990	500.8	269.7	194.1	75.6	296.5	195.0	101.5	-65.4	53.9	59.2
1991	598.9	302.6	225.7	76.9	327.3	208.8	118.5	-31.0	50.5	54.7
1992	709.1	341.5	260.7	80.8	414.6	289.0	125.6	-47.0	48.2	58.5
1993	886.2	445.6	354.9	90.7	535.0	445.5	89.5	-94.4	50.3	60.4
1994	1145.3	614.1	504.2	109.9	787.5	703.8	83.7	-256.3	53.6	68.8
1995	1507.7	844.2	672.8	171.4	1036.0	912.0	124.0	-372.5	56.0	68.7
1996	1789.2	1022.7	815.5	207.2	1034.8	949.6	85.2	-268.3	57.2	57.8
1997	2077.1	1215.5	927.0	288.5	1235.1	1040.1	195.0	-373.5	58.5	59.5
1998	2377.2	1335.5	988.5	347.0	1360.3	1249.4	110.9	-318.6	56.2	57.2
1999	2678.8	1510.4	1075.9	434.5	1533.9	1264.6	269.3	-365.5	56.4	57.3
2000	3161.7	1688.0	1155.8	532.2	1697.4	1400.4	297.0	-223.7	53.4	53.7
2001	3708.0	1911.7	1244.8	666.9	1936.5	1602.1	334.4	-140.2	51.6	52.2
2002	4315.0	2300.3	1528.0	772.3	2332.7	1951.9	380.8	-318.0	53.3	54.1
2003	5007.2	2636.5	1729.7	906.8	2737.8	2437.9	299.9	-367.1	52.7	54.7
2004	6033.2	3085.3	1979.5	1105.8	3167.5	2844.3	323.2	-219.6	51.1	52.5
2005	6969.5	3486.5	2221.8	1264.7	3580.9	3204.7	376.2	-97.9	50.0	51.4
2006	8117.8	4138.5	2587.6	1550.9	3936.7	3551.2	385.5	42.6	51.0	48.5
2007	9846.8	5108.7	3040.0	2068.7	4469.3	4022.6	446.7	268.8	51.9	45.4
2008	11115.0	6026.4	3466.5	2559.9	4722.9	3989.5	733.4	365.7	54.2	42.5
2009	12153.0	6930.4	3998.2	2932.2	5049.9	4435.0	614.9	172.7	57.0	41.6
2010	14113.6	8032.8	4774.0	3258.8	6059.7	5342.4	717.3	21.1	56.9	42.9
2011	16251.9	9488.2	5525.0	3963.2	6683.6	5953.9	729.7	80.1	58.4	41.1
2012	17879.4	10655.1	6203.3	4451.8	7409.6	7032.8	376.8	-185.3	59.6	41.4
2013	19800.8	12148.2	7099.9	5048.3	7989.6	7712.3	277.3	-337.0	61.4	40.3
2014	21330.8	13329.2	7691.6	5637.6	8309.4	7957.2	352.2	-307.8	62.5	39.0
2015	23014.6	14503.6	8471.4	6032.2	8490.0	8155.4	334.6	21.0	63.0	36.9

注：1. 2013年数据为第三次全国经济普查数据。
2. 2011年根据全国第六次人口普查数据对2006年-2010年的数据进行了调整。

Note: a) Data for 2013 were collected from the third national economic census.
b) In 2011,Figures for 2006-2010 are revised according to the results of the Sixth National Population Census.

2-12 支出法地区生产总值
GROSS DOMESTIC PRODUCT BY EXPENDITURE APPROACH

单位：亿元 (100 million yuan)

项 目	Item	2015	2014	2015年为2014年% 2015 as % of 2014
地区生产总值	**Gross Domestic Product**	**23014.6**	**21330.8**	**106.9**
最终消费支出	**Final Consumption Expenditure**	**14503.6**	**13329.2**	**107.5**
居民消费	Households Consumption	8471.4	7691.6	108.1
城镇居民	Urban Resident	7818.2	7094.6	108.2
农村居民	Rural Resident	653.2	597.0	107.1
政府消费	Government Consumption	6032.2	5637.6	106.7
资本形成总额	**Gross Capital Formation**	**8490.0**	**8309.4**	**103.6**
固定资本形成总额	Completed Fixed Asset	8155.4	7957.2	103.8
存货增加	Changes in Inventories	334.6	352.2	99.1
货物和服务净流出	**Net Outflow of Goods and Services**	**21.0**	**-307.8**	

注：发展速度按可比价格计算。
Note: Data for 2013 were collected from the third national economic census.

2-13 三大需求对地区生产总值增长的拉动(2001-2015年)
CONTRIBUTION OF THREE DEMANDS TO GROWTH OF GDP (2001-2015)

年 份 Year	最终消费支出 Final Consumption Expenditure		资本形成总额 Gross Capital Formation		货物和服务净流出 Net Outflow of Goods and Services	
	贡献率(%) Contribution Rate(%)	拉 动(百分点) Impetus (Percentage Points)	贡献率(%) Contribution Rate(%)	拉 动(百分点) Impetus (Percentage Points)	贡献率(%) Contribution Rate(%)	拉 动(百分点) Impetus (Percentage Points)
2001	32.4	3.8	43.2	5.1	24.4	2.8
2002	77.0	8.8	61.6	7.1	-38.6	-4.4
2003	40.7	4.5	66.3	7.4	-7.0	-0.8
2004	40.2	5.7	37.3	5.3	22.5	3.1
2005	37.2	4.5	45.7	5.5	17.1	2.1
2006	60.0	7.8	24.6	3.2	15.4	2.0
2007	61.1	8.9	21.0	3.0	17.9	2.6
2008	81.6	7.4	9.0	0.8	9.4	0.9
2009	76.4	7.8	39.0	4.0	-15.4	-1.6
2010	65.8	6.8	47.7	4.9	-13.5	-1.4
2011	83.4	6.8	12.7	1.0	3.9	0.3
2012	73.0	5.6	43.8	3.4	-16.8	-1.3
2013	68.4	5.3	37.3	2.9	-5.7	-0.5
2014	72.7	5.3	22.1	1.6	5.2	0.4
2015	67.0	4.7	20.7	1.4	12.3	0.8

注：1. 三大需求指支出法地区生产总值的三大构成项目，即最终消费支出、资本形成总额、货物和服务净流出。
2. 贡献率指三大需求增量与支出法地区生产总值增量之比。
3. 拉动百分点为地区生产总值增长速度与三大需求贡献率的乘积。
4. 本表数据按可比价格计算。
5. 根据全国第六次人口普查数据对2006年-2010年的数据进行了调整。2013年数据为第三次全国经济普查数据。

Note: a) Three demands of GDP by expenditure method are final consumption expenditure,gross capital formation and net outflow of goods and services.
b) Contribution rate of the three demands to GDP growth refers to the proportion of the increment of the each component of GDP by expenditure method to the increment of GDP.
c) Impetus of the three demands to GDP growth refers to the growth rate of GDP multiplied by the contribution share of the three demands.
d) Figures in this table are calculated at comparable prices.
e) Figures for 2006-2010 are revised according to the results of the Sixth National Population Census. Figures for 2013 were preliminary statistics.Data for 2013 were collected from the third national economic census.

2-14 居民消费水平(1978-2015年)
HOUSEHOLDS CONSUMPTION LEVEL (1978-2015)

年份 Year	居民消费水平(元) Level(yuan) 全市 All Households	城镇居民 Urban Households	农村居民 Rural Households	城乡消费水平对比(农村居民=1) Uban/Rural Consumption Ratio(Rural Households=1)	指数(1978年=100) Index(1978=100) 全市 All Households	城镇居民 Urban Households	农村居民 Rural Households	指数(上年=100) Index(Preceding=100) 全市 All Households	城镇居民 Urban Households	农村居民 Rural Households
1978	330	451	185	2.4	100.0	100.0	100.0	112.3	110.1	122.6
1979	356	464	221	2.1	117.5	114.5	120.8	117.5	114.5	120.8
1980	440	562	280	2.0	147.6	140.0	159.0	125.6	122.1	131.5
1981	485	590	338	1.7	160.3	144.8	189.4	108.6	103.6	119.2
1982	526	622	384	1.6	170.6	149.7	211.2	106.4	103.4	111.5
1983	579	674	432	1.6	175.4	151.2	222.6	102.8	101.0	105.4
1984	677	789	494	1.6	201.4	173.9	250.4	114.8	115.0	112.5
1985	912	1101	585	1.9	263.2	235.3	289.2	130.7	135.3	115.5
1986	1094	1284	749	1.7	312.9	272.0	365.8	118.9	115.6	126.5
1987	1198	1391	827	1.7	316.7	272.0	375.3	101.2	100.0	102.6
1988	1536	1779	1046	1.7	367.7	313.3	435.7	116.1	115.2	116.1
1989	1648	1874	1169	1.6	398.2	337.1	472.7	108.3	107.6	108.5
1990	1797	2045	1186	1.7	466.7	393.4	527.5	117.2	116.7	111.6
1991	2071	2330	1345	1.7	528.3	440.2	587.1	113.2	111.9	111.3
1992	2375	2696	1456	1.9	553.7	465.3	583.0	104.8	105.7	99.3
1993	3206	3743	1634	2.3	619.6	529.0	588.8	111.9	113.7	101.0
1994	4508	5307	2114	2.5	717.5	618.4	630.6	115.8	116.9	107.1
1995	5663	6497	3101	2.1	774.2	656.7	737.2	107.9	106.2	116.9
1996	6497	7477	3420	2.2	814.5	693.5	742.4	105.2	105.6	100.7
1997	7418	8594	3638	2.4	928.5	795.4	791.4	114.0	114.7	106.6
1998	7954	9195	3874	2.4	949.9	812.9	797.7	102.3	102.2	100.8
1999	8598	9916	4163	2.4	1025.9	876.3	855.1	108.0	107.8	107.2
2000	8820	10145	4277	2.4	1031.0	878.9	860.2	100.5	100.3	100.6
2001	9057	10301	4695	2.2	1026.9	865.7	915.3	99.6	98.5	106.4
2002	10882	12505	5020	2.5	1204.6	1026.7	952.8	117.3	118.6	104.1
2003	12014	13826	5275	2.6	1267.2	1082.1	954.7	105.2	105.4	100.2
2004	13425	15438	5713	2.7	1371.1	1169.8	1000.5	108.2	108.1	104.8
2005	14662	16478	6602	2.5	1442.4	1202.6	1105.6	105.2	102.8	110.5
2006	16487	18185	7580	2.4	1579.4	1292.8	1236.1	109.5	107.5	111.8
2007	18553	20320	8984	2.3	1691.5	1375.5	1389.4	107.1	106.4	112.4
2008	20113	21872	10375	2.1	1777.8	1436.0	1547.8	105.1	104.4	111.4
2009	22023	23812	11917	2.0	1928.9	1550.9	1742.8	108.5	108.0	112.6
2010	24982	26949	13392	2.0	2116.0	1696.7	1896.2	109.7	109.4	108.8
2011	27760	30037	13659	2.2	2243.0	1805.3	1835.5	106.0	106.4	96.8
2012	30350	32857	14664	2.2	2391.0	1922.6	1958.5	106.6	106.5	106.7
2013	33938	36375	18648	2.0	2548.8	2032.2	2326.7	106.6	105.7	118.8
2014	36057	38515	20506	1.9	2668.6	2119.6	2533.8	104.7	104.3	108.9
2015	39200	41846	22315	1.9	2846.9	2260.2	2699.4	106.7	106.6	106.5

注：1. 2013年数据为第三次全国经济普查数据。
2. 2011年根据全国第六次人口普查数据对2006年-2010年的数据进行了调整。

Note: a) Data for 2013 were collected from the third national economic census.
b) In 2011,Figures for 2006-2010 are revised according to the results of the Sixth National Population Census.

2-15 社会劳动生产率(1978-2015年)
OVERALL LABOR PRODUCTIVITY (1978-2015)

单位：元/人 (yuan/person)

年 份 Year	社会劳动生产率 Overall Labor Productivity	第一产业 Primary Industry	第二产业 Secondary Industry	第三产业 Tertiary Industry
1978	2504	444	4484	1911
1979	2626	421	4556	2033
1980	2914	510	4750	2391
1981	2795	561	4316	2420
1982	2959	878	4437	2467
1983	3368	1094	4799	2998
1984	3909	1287	5347	3646
1985	4580	1671	6040	4268
1986	5002	1932	6331	4783
1987	5669	2569	6917	5501
1988	7046	4084	8309	6745
1989	7742	4270	9432	7140
1990	8203	4810	9564	7941
1991	9498	5014	10351	10145
1992	11051	5556	12282	11549
1993	13878	7112	14909	14644
1994	17728	9660	18709	18682
1995	22679	10042	23697	24647
1996	26997	10259	26824	30815
1997	31567	10523	30102	37337
1998	37202	10681	34657	44887
1999	43179	10452	40909	52038
2000	51082	10488	48506	61705
2001	59414	10909	53624	73303
2002	65974	11599	55217	83242
2003	72437	12556	64298	87043
2004	77478	13736	80484	84186
2005	80475	13937	86967	85035
2006	90313	13943	95417	96078
2007	105743	16403	109985	112658
2008	115565	17982	119077	123306
2009	122807	18658	137799	127602
2010	139057	19854	165334	141824
2011	154684	22307	174354	159593
2012	164257	25447	183539	169066
2013	176140	28330	202718	179296
2014	185671	29494	216013	187973
2015	196471	27302	221220	200414

注：1. 本表数据按当年价格计算。2013年数据为第三次全国经济普查数据。
2. 2013年开始，地区生产总值三次产业划分执行国家统计局《三次产业划分规定》(国统字[2012]108号)，并对本表1978-2012年以来三次产业数据进行相应调整。

Note: a) Figures in this table are calculated at current year's prices.Data for 2013 were collected from the third national economic census.
b) Since 2013, GDP three sector classification has been subject to Regulations on Three Industries Classification (G.T.Z. [2012] No. 108) issued by National Bureau of Statistics, according to which data on the three industries from 1978 to 2012 was adjusted in this table.

2-16 三次产业贡献率(2001-2015年)
CONTRIBUTION RATE OF THREE INDUSTRIES TO THE INCREASE OF GDP (2001-2015)

单位：% (%)

年份 Year	地区生产总值 Gross Domestic Product	第一产业 Primary Industry	第二产业 Secondary Industry	第三产业 Tertiary Industry	#工业 Industry	#建筑业 Construction
2001	100.0	0.8	26.7	72.5	23.3	3.4
2002	100.0	0.5	23.4	76.1	18.0	5.4
2003	100.0	-0.2	33.4	66.8	28.0	5.4
2004	100.0	-0.1	37.9	62.2	35.4	2.5
2005	100.0	-0.3	26.9	73.4	24.1	2.8
2006	100.0	0.1	23.5	76.4	17.9	5.6
2007	100.0	0.2	24.9	74.9	21.4	3.5
2008	100.0	0.1	2.4	97.5	0.6	1.8
2009	100.0	0.4	26.5	73.1	18.6	7.9
2010	100.0	-0.1	34.4	65.7	30.7	3.7
2011	100.0	0.1	19.7	80.2	18.1	1.6
2012	100.0	0.3	22.9	76.8	17.6	5.3
2013	100.0	0.3	24.3	75.4	19.6	5.4
2014	100.0		21.7	78.3	16.0	6.1
2015	100.0	-1.1	10.9	90.2	2.7	8.6

注：1. 本表数据按可比价格计算。2013年数据为第三次全国经济普查数据。
2. 2013年开始，地区生产总值行业划分执行《国民经济行业分类》GB/T 4754-2011标准。
3. 2013年开始，地区生产总值三次产业划分执行国家统计局《三次产业划分规定》(国统字[2012]108号)。
4. 产业贡献率指各产业增加值增量与地区生产总值增量之比。

Note: a) Statistics in this table are calculated at comparable prices.Data for 2013 were collected from the third national economic census.
b) Since 2013, GDP industrial classification has been subjected to Classification of National Economic Sectors Standard GB/T 4754-2011.
c) Since 2013, GDP three sector classification has been subject to Regulations on Three Industries Classification (G.T.Z. [2012] No. 108) issued by National Bureau of Statistics.
d) Share of the contributions of the three industries to the increase of the GDP refers to the proportion of the increment of the value-added of each industry to the increment of GDP.

2-17 三次产业对地区生产总值增长的拉动(2001-2015年)
IMPETUS OF THREE INDUSTRIES TO GDP GROWTH (2001-2015)

单位：百分点 (Percentage Points)

年份 Year	地区生产总值 Gross Domestic Product	第一产业 Primary Industry	第二产业 Secondary Industry	第三产业 Tertiary Industry	#工业 Industry
2001	11.7	0.1	3.1	8.5	2.7
2002	11.5	0.1	2.7	8.7	2.1
2003	11.1	…	3.7	7.4	3.1
2004	14.1	…	5.3	8.8	5.0
2005	12.1	…	3.2	8.9	2.9
2006	13.0	…	3.1	9.9	2.3
2007	14.5	…	3.6	10.9	3.1
2008	9.1	…	0.2	8.9	0.1
2009	10.2	…	2.7	7.5	1.9
2010	10.3	…	3.5	6.8	3.2
2011	8.1	…	1.6	6.5	1.5
2012	7.7	…	1.8	5.9	1.4
2013	7.7	…	1.9	5.8	1.5
2014	7.3	…	1.6	5.7	1.2
2015	6.9	-0.1	0.8	6.2	0.2

注：1. 本表数据按可比价格计算。2013年数据为第三次全国经济普查数据。
2. 2013年开始，地区生产总值行业划分执行《国民经济行业分类》(GB/T 4754-2011)标准。
3. 2013年开始，地区生产总值三次产业划分执行国家统计局《三次产业划分规定》(国统字[2012]108号)。
4. 地区生产总值数据为其增速。三次产业拉动百分点为地区生产总值增长速度与各产业贡献率之乘积。

Note: a) Statistics in this table are calculated at comparable prices.Data for 2013 were collected from the third national economic census.
b) Since 2013, GDP industrial classification has been subjected to Classification of National Economic Sectors Standard (GB/T 4754-2011).
c) Since 2013, GDP three sector classification has been subject to Regulations on Three Industries Classification (G.T.Z. [2012] No. 108) issued by National Bureau of Statistics.
d) The data of GDP is that of its growth rate. Contribution of the three industries to GDP growth refers to the growth rate of GDP multiplied by the industrial shares.

主要统计指标解释

地区生产总值 是按市场价格计算的地区生产总值的简称。它是一个地区所有常住单位在一定时期内生产活动的最终成果。地区生产总值有三种表现形式，即价值形态、收入形态和产品形态。从价值形态看，它是所有常住单位在一定时期内所生产的全部货物和服务价值超过同期投入的全部非固定资产货物和服务价值的差额，即所有常住单位的增加值之和；从收入形态看，它是所有常住单位在一定时期内所创造并分配给常住单位和非常住单位的初次分配收入之和；从产品形态看，它是最终使用的货物和服务减去进口货物和服务。在实际核算中，地区生产总值的三种表现形态表现为三种计算方法，即生产法、收入法和支出法。三种方法分别从不同的方面反映地区生产总值及其构成。

三次产业 根据社会生产活动历史发展的顺序对产业结构的划分，产品直接取自自然界的部门称为第一产业，对初级产品进行再加工的部门称为第二产业，为生产和消费提供各种服务的部门称为第三产业。它是世界上通用的产业结构分类，但各国的划分不尽一致。我国 2011 年版国民经济行业分类标准：第一产业是指农、林、牧、渔业（不含农、林、牧、渔服务业）；第二产业是指采矿业（不含开采辅助活动），制造业（不含金属制品、机械和设备修理业），电力、热力、燃气及水生产和供应业，建筑业；第三产业是指除第一产业、第二产业以外的其他行业。

最终消费率(消费率)

$$最终消费率(消费率)=\frac{最终消费支出}{地区生产总值}\times 100\%$$

资本形成率(投资率)

$$资本形成率(投资率)=\frac{资本形成总额}{地区生产总值}\times 100\%$$

部分新兴产业统计划分标准

1.**文化创意产业** 北京市文化创意产业指以创作、创造、创新为根本手段，以文化内容和创意成果为核心价值，以知识产权实现或消费为交易特征，为社会公众提供文化体验的具有内在联系的行业集群。北京市文化创意产业标准是在《国民经济行业分类》(GB/T 4754-2011) 的基础上，根据文化创意活动的特点将行业分类中相关的类别重新进行的组合。适用于统计及政策管理中对文化创意相关活动的分类。内容上主要包括 9 大类，分别是文化艺术，新闻出版，广播、电视、电影，软件网络及计算机服务，广告会展，艺术品交易，设计服务，旅游、休闲娱乐，其他辅助服务。

2.**信息产业** 信息相关产业主要是指与电子信息相关联的各种活动的集合。信息产业标准是国家统计局在《国民经济行业分类》(GB/T 4754-2011) 的基础上，参考了联合国的《全部经济活动的国际标准产业分类》，并结合我国的实际情况制定的。北京市从 2004 年开始执行国家信息产业统计标准。

3.**高技术产业** 高技术产业主要是指与高技术产品相关联的各种活动的集合。高技术产业标准是国家统计局在《国民经济行业分类》(GB/T 4754-2011) 的基础上，根据高技术产业的特性，结合我国的实际情况制定的。北京市从 2013 年开始执行国家高技术产业统计标准。包括高技术制造业和高技术服务业。

4.**现代制造业** 现代制造业是指用现代科学技术武装起来的制造业，是现代科学技术与制造业相结合的产物。现代制造业是应用现代制造技术、现代生产组织系统和现代管理理念所进行的以现代集成制造为特征、知识密集为特色、高效制造为特点的技术含量高、附加值大、产业链长的产业组织体系。现代制造业产业标准是北京市统计局在《国民经济行业分类》(GB/T4754-2011) 的基础上，根据现代制造业的特性，将符合基本要求的行业归并，结合北京市的实际情况制定的。北京市从 2005 年开始执行现代制造业统计标准。

5.**现代服务业** 现代服务业是相对于传统服务业而言，是适应现代人和现代城市发展的需求，而产生和发展起来的具有高技术含量和高文化含量的服务业。现代服务业有新服务领域、新服务模式、高文化品位和高技术含量的特征。现代服务业标准是北京市统计局在《国民经济行业分类》(GB/T4754-2011) 的基础上，根据现代服务业的特性，将符合基本要求的行业归并，结合北京市的实际情况制定的。北京市从 2005 年开始执行现代服务业统计标准。

6. **生产性服务业** 指以市场化的中间投入服务为主导的行业，生产性服务业具有经营性和可贸易性的特点，不仅为制造业提供中间投入服务，也为第一产业和第三产业提供中间投入服务。北京市生产性服务业分类标准涉及《国民经济行业分类》(GB/T 4754-2011) 中交通运输、仓储和邮政业，信息传输、软件和信息技术服务业，批发和零售业，金融业，租赁和商务服务业，科学研究和技术服务业 6 个行业门类。根据业务活动特点将生产性服务业划分为流通服务、信息服务、金融服务、商务服务、科技服务五大类别。

7. **信息服务业** 指以信息资源为基础，利用现代信息技术，对信息进行生产、收集、处理、输送、存储、传播、使用并提供信息产品和服务的产业。本分类涉及《国民经济行业分类》(GB/T 4754-2011) 中信息传输、软件和信息技术服务业，文化、体育和娱乐业 2 个行业门类。根据信息服务业的概念和活动性质，将信息服务业划分为信息传输服务、信息技术服务和信息内容服务三大领域。

8. **物流业** 指为物品及其信息流动提供相关服务的经

济活动。按照国家发改委、国家统计局、中国物流与采购联合会联合制定的《社会物流统计核算与报表制度（试行方案)》中的相关规定，物流业统计范围为：在工商登记注册时企业（单位）名称中具有“物流”、“配送”、“快运”、“储运”、“货运”等物流功能，且业务经营范围以配送、流通加工、包装、仓储、运输等物流业务为主的单位。

Explanatory Notes on Main Statistical Indicators

Gross Regional Product (GRP) is calculated at market prices. It represents the final results of all resident units in an area from their productive activities over a given period of time. It is expressed from three different perspectives respectively, namely value, income, and product. GRP from the value perspective refers to the total value of all goods and services produced by all resident units during a certain period of time, minus the total value of input of goods and services of the nature of non-fixed assets; in other words, it is the sum of added value of all resident units. GRP from the income perspective is the sum of primary incomes created by all resident units and distributed to resident and non-resident units. GRP from the product perspective means the finally used goods and services minus the imported goods and services. In actual national accounting, gross regional product is calculated in three methods, namely production method, income method and expenditure method, which reflect the gross regional product and its composition from different angles.

Three Industries means the division of industrial structure according to the historical sequence of social productive activities. The sector which receives products directly from nature is called the primary industry. The sector which re-processes primary products is called the secondary industry. The sector which offers various services for production and consumption is called the tertiary industry. This is a universal classification of industrial structure. However, the classification of three industries may vary in different countries. As stated in China's standards on Classification of Sectors in National Economy Version 2011: The primary industry refers to agriculture, forestry, animal production and hunting, fishing (excluding service activities for agriculture, forestry, animal production and hunting, fishing); secondary industry refers to mining and quarrying (excluding mining support service activities), manufacturing (excluding repair of fabricated metal products, machinery and equipment), production and distribution of electricity, heating power, gas and water and construction; the tertiary industry refers to others excluding the primary and secondary industries.

Final Consumption Rate (Consumption Rate)

Final Consumption Rate (Consumption Rate) = Final Consumption / GRP × 100%

Capital Formation Rate (Investment Rate)

Capital Formation Rate (Investment Rate) = Total Capital Formation /GRP ×100%

Statistical Classification of Some New Industries

1. Cultural and Creative Industry The cultural and creative industry in Beijing refers to an internally correlated cluster of sectors with invention, creation and innovation as fundamental means, cultural content and creative fruits as core value, realization or consumption of intellectual property rights as transaction features, which provide cultural experience for the public. It is a new combination of related sectors in the industrial classification according to the characteristics of cultural and creative activities on the basis of Classification of Sectors in National Economy (GB/T 4754-2011). It consists of 9 sectors, namely culture & art; press & publishing; broadcasting, television and film; software, internet and computer services; advertising and exhibition; artwork trading; design services; tourism, leisure and recreation; and other auxiliary services.

2. Information Industry Information industry mainly means the set of activities related to electronic information. It is classified by the National Bureau of Statistics on the basis of Classification of Sectors in National Economy (GB/T 4754-2011) by referring to the International Standard Classification of Industries for All Economic Activities of the United Nations and combining the actual situation of China. The national statistical standard for information industry was implemented in 2004 in Beijing.

3. High-tech Industry High-tech industry mainly means the set of activities related to high-tech products. It is classified by the National Bureau of Statistics on the basis of Classification of Sectors in National Economy (GB/T 4754-2011), taking into consideration the features of high-tech industry and combining the actual situation of China. The national statistical standard for information industry was implemented in 2013 in Beijing.

4. Modern Manufacturing Modern manufacturing industry mainly means the manufacturing industry equipped with modern science and technology. Modern manufacturing is an industrial organization system with large content of technology, great added value and long industrial chain, with features of modern integrated manufacturing, intensive knowledge, efficient manufacturing, using modern manufacturing technologies, modern production organization system and modern management concepts. It is a combination of modern science, technology and manufacturing. It is classified by the Beijing Municipal Bureau of Statistics on the basis of Classification of Sectors in National Economy (GB/T 4754-2011), taking into consideration the features of modern manufacturing industry, merging the sectors meeting basic requirements and combining the actual situation of Beijing. The statistical standard for information industry was implemented in 2005 in Beijing.

5. Modern Service Modern service is in contrast with conventional service. It is a service sector with great content of high technology and great content of culture, which has emerged and developed to meet the need of modern people and modern cities' development. Modern service industry has new service fields, new service modes, high cultural taste and great content of high technology. It is classified by the Beijing Municipal Bureau of Statistics on the basis of Classification of Sectors in National Economy (GB/T 4754-2011), taking into consideration the features of modern service industry, merging the sectors meeting basic requirements and combining the actual situation of Beijing. The statistical standard for modern service industry was implemented in 2005 in Beijing.

6. **Producer Service** means the sector dominated by intermediate input services. Producer service is operational and tradable. It offers intermediate input services for manufacturing industry, and for the primary and tertiary industries. The classification standard for producer service in Beijing involves 6 sectors in Classification of Sectors in National Economy (GB/T 4754-2011), namely transportation, warehousing and post; information transmission, software and information technical service; wholesale and retail trade; finance; leasing and business service; and scientific research and technical service. According to features of business activities, producer service is divided into 5 categories, namely circulation service, information service, financial service, business service and technical service.

7. **Information Service** means the sector producing, collecting, processing, delivering, storing, transmitting and using information, and providing information products and services on the basis of information resources and by using modern information technology. Information service involves two sectors in the Classification of Sectors in National Economy (GB/T 4754-2011), namely information transmission, software and information technical service; and culture, sports and recreation. According to the definition and features of activities of information service, it is divided into three areas, namely information transmission service, information technical service and information content service.

8. **Logistics** means economic activities offering relevant services for goods and information movement. According to relevant provisions in the Statistical Calculation and Reporting System (Trial) for Social Logistics developed jointly by the State Development and Reform Commission, the National Bureau of Statistics, and China Federation of Logistics and Procurement, the statistical scope of logistics covers: companies specializing in delivery, circulation processing, package, storage, transport and other logistical service, with their names registered for industry and commerce containing such terms as “logistics”, “delivery”, “fast transport”, “storage and transport”, “cargo transport”, etc.

03

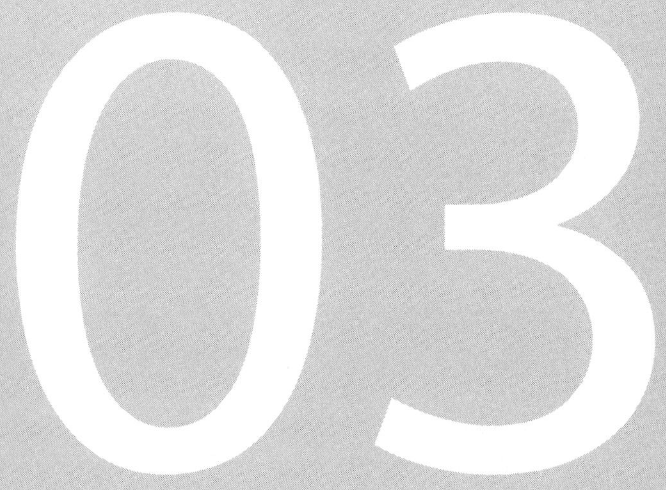

北京统计年鉴2016　　BEIJING STATISTICAL YEARBOOK

人口与就业
POPULATION AND EMPLOYMENT

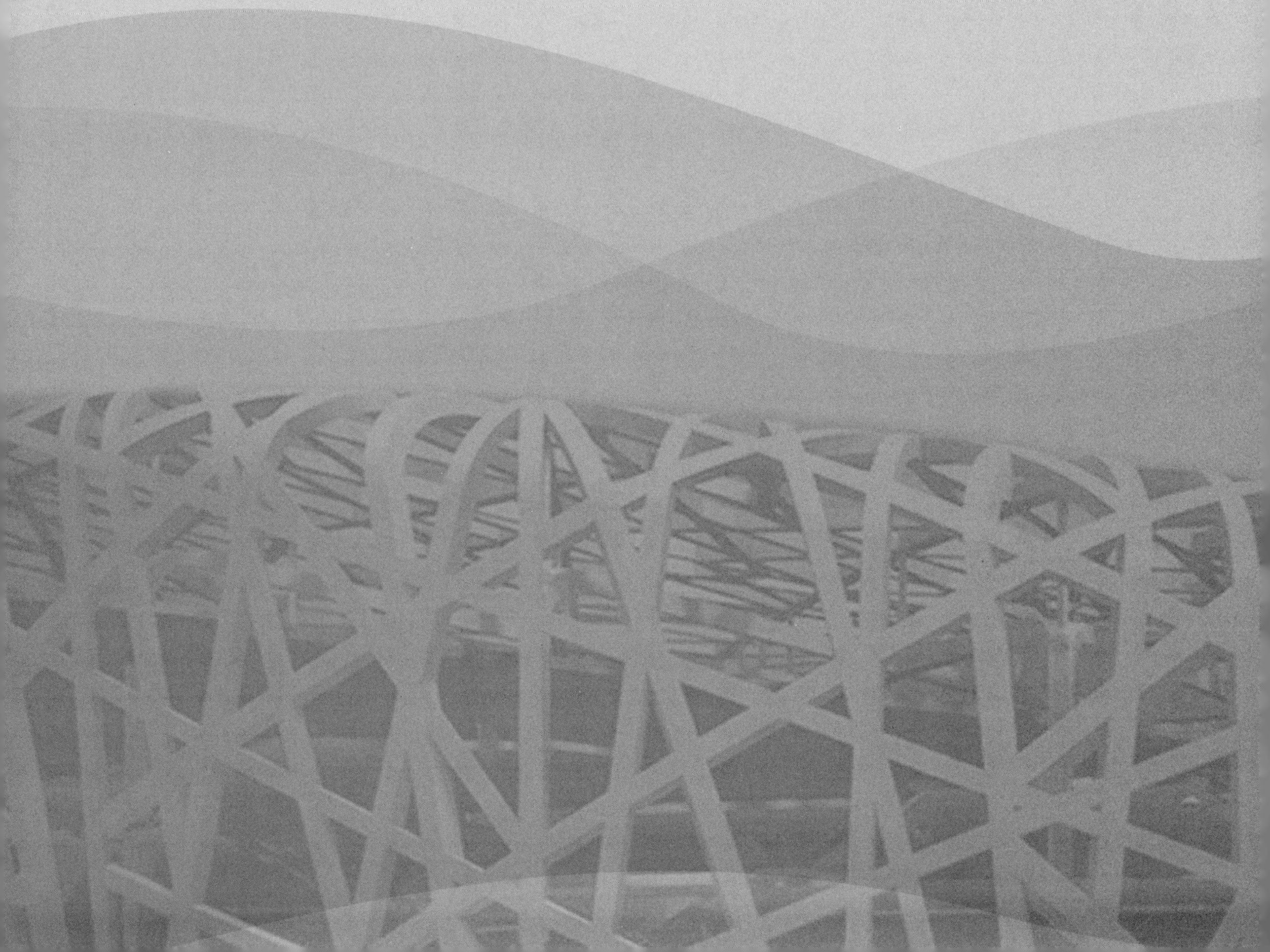

简要说明

一、本章资料的主要内容

本章人口部分包括历年北京市常住人口和户籍人口的分组资料；建国以来已开展的六次人口普查的北京市人口数据；1990 年以后的人口变动情况抽样调查数据。

本章劳动力部分包括北京市三次产业从业人员情况；法人单位从业人员及平均工资情况；城镇单位在岗职工人数及工资的分组情况；城镇登记失业情况等。

二、本章数据资料的来源

本章人口部分中，“户籍人口”数据来自于北京市公安局；“土地面积”数据来自于北京市国土资源局；计划生育情况来自于北京市卫生和计划生育委员会；其余资料均来自北京市统计局。

本章劳动力部分中，城镇登记失业情况由北京市人力资源和社会保障局提供，其他资料来源于北京市统计局。

三、有关统计标准的变化说明

（一）关于行业划分。根据国家统计局规定，自 2012 年开始执行《国民经济行业分类》（GB/T 4754-2011）标准。

（二）关于三次产业划分。根据国家统计局《三次产业划分规定》（国统字[2012]108 号），该规定对三次产业的范围进行了调整。其中第一产业是指农、林、牧、渔业（不含农、林、牧、渔服务业）；第二产业是指采矿业（不含开采辅助活动），制造业（不含金属制品、机械和设备修理业），电力、热力、燃气及水生产和供应业，建筑业；第三产业是指除第一产业、第二产业以外的其他行业。2012 年及以后开始执行此标准。

（三）关于统计上城乡划分标准

2008 年 7 月，国务院批复了国家统计局与民政部、住房城乡建设部、公安部、财政部、国土资源部、农业部共同制定的《关于统计上划分城乡的规定》（国函[2008]60 号文件和国家统计局令第 14 号），以后每年国家统计局都会出台《统计用区划代码和城乡分类代码》。本章中“城镇人口”和“乡村人口”的确定均执行当年的城乡分类标准。

Brief Introduction

I. Main Content

Population statistics in this chapter include classified data for permanent population and registered population in Beijing in previous years; statistics of population in Beijing from six national population censuses since the founding of the People's Republic of China; statistics from National Sample Survey on Population Changes after 1990.

Employment statistics in this chapter include information on employed persons in three industries in Beijing; employees and average wages in business entities; classified statistics for the number and wage of fully employed staff and workers in urban entities; registered unemployment in urban areas.

II. Source of Statistics

In the population section of this chapter, statistics on "registered population" are from Beijing Municipal Bureau of Public Security; statistics on "land area" are from Beijing Municipal Bureau of Land and Resources; family planning statistics are from Beijing Municipal Commission of Health and Family Planning; other statistics are from Beijing Municipal Bureau of Statistics.

In the employment section in this chapter, urban registered unemployment statistics are from Beijing Municipal Bureau of Human Resources and Social Security; other statistics are from Beijing Municipal Bureau of Statistics.

III. Changes in Relevant Statistical Standards

(I) Classification of Sectors. According to relevant provisions of the National Bureau of Statistics, the Standard for *Classification of National Economic Sectors* (GB/T 4754-2011) was implemented in 2012.

(II) Classification of Three Industries. According to the *Regulations on the Classification of the Three Industries (G.T.Z. [2012] No. 108)* issued by National Bureau of Statistics, the scope of three industries was changed. The primary industry refers to agriculture, forestry, animal production and hunting, fishing (excluding service for agriculture, forestry, animal production and hunting, fishing); the secondary industry refers to mining and quarrying (excluding mining support activities), manufacturing (excluding metal products, machinery and equipment repair), production and distribution of electricity, heating power, gas and water, and construction; the tertiary industry refers to sectors other than the primary and secondary industries. The *Regulations on the Classification of the Three Industries* (G.T.Z. [2012] No. 108) issued by National Bureau of Statistics came into effect in 2012.

(III) Urban-Rural Statistical Definition

In July 2008, the State Council approved the *Regulations on Urban-Rural Statistical Definition* (G.H. [2008] No. 60 and No. 14 Decree of National Bureau of Statistics) jointly developed by the National Bureau of Statistics, Ministry of Civil Affairs, Ministry of Housing and Urban-Rural Development, Ministry of Public Security, Ministry of Finance, Ministry of Land and Resources and Ministry of Agriculture. In the population section, new definition applies for the figures of "urban population" and "rural population".

3-1 六次人口普查人口基本情况
BASIC STATISTICS ON POPULATION CENSUS

项目		Item		1953	1964	1982	1990	2000	2010
常住人口	**（万人）**	**Permanent Population**	**(10000 persons)**	**276.8**	**759.7**	**923.1**	**1081.9**	**1356.9**	**1961.2**
按性别分		**By Sex**							
男		Male		159.8	391.1	467.1	559.3	707.4	1012.6
女		Female		117.0	368.6	456.0	522.6	649.5	948.6
性别比(女=100)		Sex Ratio (Female=100)		136.5	106.1	102.4	107.0	108.9	106.8
按城乡分		**By Urban Area and Rural Area**							
城镇人口		Urban Population		205.8	425.8	597.0	794.5	1052.2	1685.9
乡村人口		Rural Population		71.0	333.9	326.1	287.4	304.7	275.3
家庭户规模	**（人/户）**	**Average Family Size**	**(person/household)**			**3.7**	**3.2**	**2.9**	**2.5**
各年龄组人口比重	**(%)**	**Composition by Age Group**	**(%)**						
0-14		Age 0-14		30.1	41.5	22.4	20.2	13.6	8.6
15-59		Age 15-59		64.3	51.9	69.1	69.7	73.9	78.9
60岁及以上		Age 60 and Above		5.6	6.6	8.5	10.1	12.5	12.5
#65岁及以上		Age 65 and Above		3.3	4.1	5.6	6.3	8.4	8.7
总抚养比	**(%)**	**Gross Dependency Ratio**	**(%)**	**50.2**	**83.8**	**38.9**	**36.1**	**28.2**	**20.9**
老年抚养比		Old-age Dependency Ratio		5.0	7.5	7.8	8.6	10.8	10.5
少儿抚养比		Child Dependency Ratio		45.2	76.3	31.1	27.5	17.4	10.4
民族人口		**Population by Ethnic Group**							
汉　族	（万人）	Han Chinese	(10000 persons)	260.0	731.2	890.8	1040.5	1298.4	1881.1
占常住人口比重	(%)	Percentage in Permanent Populatioı	(%)	93.9	96.2	96.5	96.2	95.7	95.9
少数民族	（万人）	Ethnic Minority	(10000 persons)	16.8	28.5	32.3	41.4	58.5	80.1
占常住人口比重	(%)	Percentage in Permanent Populatioı	(%)	6.1	3.8	3.5	3.8	4.3	4.1
每十万人口拥有的各种受教育程度人口	**（人）**	**Population with Various Education Attainment Per 100000 Persons**	**(person)**						
大专及以上		Junior College and Above			4359	4866	9300	16839	31499
高中和中专		Senior Secondary/Secondary Technical School			4513	17646	18978	23165	21220
初　中		Junior Secondary School			11768	29086	30551	34380	31396
小　学		Primary School			31883	26197	22579	16963	9956
文盲人口及文盲率		**Illiterate Population and Illiteracy Rate**							
文盲人口	（万人）	Illiterate Population	(10000 persons)		168.9	114.7	94.3	57.8	33.3
文盲率	(%)	Illiteracy Rate	(%)		34.2	16.0	10.9	4.9	1.9
平均受教育年限	**（年）**	**Average Education Years**	**(year)**		**5.3**	**7.8**	**8.6**	**10.0**	**11.5**
平均预期寿命	**（岁）**	**Average Life Expectancy**	**(year old)**			**71.9**	**72.9**	**76.1**	**80.2**

注：1. 1964年的文盲人口数为12周岁及以上文盲和半文盲人口，1982年、1990年、2000年、2010年的文盲人口数为15周岁及以上文盲和半文盲人口。文盲率是指15周岁及以上人口中，文盲人口和半文盲人口所占比重。

2. 本表与表3-2相同的指标数据不同，是因为本表数据为普查时点数，表3-2为年末时点数。1953年普查时点为7月1日零时；1964年普查时点为7月1日零时；1982年普查时点为7月1日零时；1990年普查时点为7月1日零时；2000年普查时点为11月1日零时；2010年普查时点为11月1日零时。

Note: a) Statistics on illiterate population covered the illiterate and semi-illiterate people at 12 and above in 1964, and those at 15 and above in 1982, 1990, 2000, and 2010. Illiteracy rate means the share of illiterate and semi-illiterate people in the population at 15 and above.

b) This table has the same indicators but different figures from 3-2, because this table uses the data at the time point of the census, while 3-2 uses the year end as the time point. The time point of the census in 1953 was 12 o'clock midnight, July 1st; the time point in 1964 was 12 o'clock midnight, July 1st; the time point in 1982 was 12 o'clock midnight, July 1st; the time point in 1990 was 12 o'clock midnight,July 1st; the time point in 2000 was 12 o'clock midnight, November 1st; the time point in 2010 was 12 o'clock midnight, November 1st.

3-2 常住人口(1978-2015年)
PERMANENT POPULATION (1978-2015)

年 份 Year	常住人口(万人) Permanent Population (10000 persons)	# 常住外来人口 Permanent Migrant Population	按性别分 By Sex 男 Male	按性别分 By Sex 女 Female	按城乡分 By Urban Area and Rural Area 城镇人口 Urban Population	按城乡分 By Urban Area and Rural Area 乡村人口 Rural Population	常住人口出生率(‰) Birth Rate (‰)	常住人口死亡率(‰) Death Rate (‰)	常住人口自然增长率(‰) Natural Growth Rate (‰)
1978	871.5	21.8	443.2	428.3	479.0	392.5	12.93	6.12	6.81
1979	897.1	26.5	454.6	442.5	510.3	386.8	13.67	5.92	7.75
1980	904.3	18.6	457.8	446.5	521.1	383.2	15.56	6.30	9.26
1981	919.2	18.4	465.9	453.3	533.3	385.9	16.93	6.02	10.91
1982	935.0	17.2	474.0	461.0	544.0	391.0	20.04	5.68	14.36
1983	950.0	16.8	483.0	467.0	557.0	393.0	15.63	5.49	10.14
1984	965.0	19.8	491.0	474.0	570.0	395.0	16.74	5.53	11.21
1985	981.0	23.1	500.0	481.0	586.0	395.0	15.45	5.75	9.70
1986	1028.0	56.8	524.0	504.0	621.0	407.0	15.82	4.47	11.35
1987	1047.0	59.0	525.0	522.0	637.0	410.0	17.29	5.40	11.89
1988	1061.0	59.8	534.0	527.0	650.0	411.0	14.43	5.08	9.35
1989	1075.0	53.9	538.0	537.0	664.0	411.0	12.84	5.35	7.49
1990	1086.0	53.8	545.0	541.0	798.0	288.0	13.04	5.81	7.23
1991	1094.0	54.5	547.0	547.0	808.0	286.0	8.03	5.82	2.21
1992	1102.0	57.1	554.0	548.0	819.0	283.0	9.22	6.11	3.11
1993	1112.0	60.8	559.0	553.0	831.0	281.0	9.35	6.16	3.19
1994	1125.0	63.2	564.0	561.0	846.0	279.0	8.96	5.76	3.20
1995	1251.1	180.8	627.0	624.1	946.2	304.9	7.92	5.12	2.80
1996	1259.4	181.7	639.0	620.4	957.9	301.5	8.02	5.34	2.68
1997	1240.0	154.5	628.7	611.3	948.3	291.7	7.91	6.02	1.89
1998	1245.6	154.1	630.6	615.0	957.7	287.9	6.00	5.30	0.70
1999	1257.2	157.4	636.4	620.8	971.7	285.5	6.50	5.60	0.90
2000	1363.6	256.1	710.9	652.7	1057.4	306.2	6.20	5.30	0.90
2001	1385.1	262.8	722.1	663.0	1081.2	303.9	6.10	5.30	0.80
2002	1423.2	286.9	743.1	680.1	1118.0	305.2	6.60	5.73	0.87
2003	1456.4	307.6	761.2	695.2	1151.3	305.1	5.06	5.15	-0.09
2004	1492.7	329.8	779.9	712.8	1187.2	305.5	6.13	5.39	0.74
2005	1538.0	357.3	778.7	759.3	1286.1	251.9	6.29	5.20	1.09
2006	1601.0	403.4	817.6	783.4	1350.2	250.8	6.22	4.94	1.28
2007	1676.0	462.7	850.8	825.2	1416.2	259.8	8.16	4.83	3.33
2008	1771.0	541.1	900.2	870.8	1503.6	267.4	7.89	4.59	3.30
2009	1860.0	614.2	949.8	910.2	1581.1	278.9	7.66	4.33	3.33
2010	1961.9	704.7	1013.0	948.9	1686.4	275.5	7.27	4.29	2.98
2011	2018.6	742.2	1040.7	977.9	1740.7	277.9	8.29	4.27	4.02
2012	2069.3	773.8	1068.1	1001.2	1783.7	285.6	9.05	4.31	4.74
2013	2114.8	802.7	1090.7	1024.1	1825.1	289.7	8.93	4.52	4.41
2014	2151.6	818.7	1106.5	1045.1	1859.0	292.6	9.75	4.92	4.83
2015	2170.5	822.6	1113.4	1057.1	1877.7	292.8	7.96	4.95	3.01

注：1. 1978-1981年为户籍统计数，含暂住人口；1982-1989年数据是根据1982年、1990年两次人口普查数据调整的；1990年以后数据为人口变动情况抽样调查推算数,其中1995年、2005年为1%人口抽样调查推算数；2000年为第五次人口普查快速汇总推算数；2010年为第六次人口普查推算数。2006-2009年常住人口、出生率、死亡率等数据根据2010年人口普查数据进行了调整。

2. "按城乡分"栏包括的"城镇人口"和"乡村人口"，1978-1989年数据为户籍管理统计中的"非农业人口"和"农业人口"口径；1990-1999年数据是根据1990年、2000年两次人口普查数据调整的；2000年数据为国家统计局1999年发布的《关于统计上划分城乡的规定(试行)》中的"城镇人口"和"乡村人口"口径，2001-2005年数据为该口径的推算数；2006-2008年数据为国家统计局2006年发布的《关于统计上划分城乡的暂行规定》中的"城镇人口"和"乡村人口"口径的推算数；2009年以后数据为《国务院关于统计上划分城乡规定的批复》中的"城镇人口"和"乡村人口"口径的推算数。

Note: a) Statistics for 1978-1981 were figures of registered residents, including temporary residents; statistics for 1982-1989 were adjusted from population censuses in 1982 and 1990. Data after 1990 were estimated from sample surveys on population changes; data for 1995 and 2005 were estimated from sample surveys on 1% of the population. Data for 2000 were estimated from fast summarizing of the fifth population census. Data for 2010 were estimated from fast summarizing of the 6th population census. Data of permanant population, birth rate and death rate, etc. from 2006 to 2009 were adjusted from population census in 2010.

b) In classification by rural and urban areas, the "urban population" and "rural population" from 1978 to 1989 were non-agricultural population and agricultural population respectively in household registration. Data from 1990-1999 were adjusted from the population censuses conducted in 1990 and 2000, and those in 2000 were on the basis of statistical classification of rural and urban population stated in the Regulations on the Statistical Division of Rural and Urban Population (trial) issued by the State Statistical Bureau in 1999. Statistics from 2001 to 2005 were estimated on the same basis. Figures from 2006 to 2008 were the estimated figures of "urban population" and "rural population", of which the statistical range was provided in Provisional Regulations on Statistical Division of Rural and Urban Areas issued by the State Statistics Bureau in 2006. Figures after 2009 were the estimated figures of "urban population" and "ruralpopulation", of which the statistical range was provided in the Official Reply of the State Council Concerning the Statistical Division of Rural and Urban Areas.

3-3 常住人口总量(按区分)(2015年)
TOTAL NUMBER OF PERMANENT POPULATION (BY DISTRICT) (2015)

单位：万人 (10000 persons)

地 区	District	常住人口 Permanent Population	#常住外来人口 Permanent Migrant Population	城镇人口 Urban Population	乡村人口 Rural Population
全 市	**Total**	**2170.5**	**822.6**	**1877.7**	**292.8**
首都功能核心区	**Core Funtional Area of the Capital**	**220.3**	**51.7**	**220.3**	
东城区	Dongcheng District	90.5	20.7	90.5	
西城区	Xicheng District	129.8	31.0	129.8	
城市功能拓展区	**Urban Function Extension Area**	**1062.5**	**437.4**	**1051.1**	**11.4**
朝阳区	Chaoyang District	395.5	184.0	393.4	2.1
丰台区	Fengtai District	232.4	83.8	231.0	1.4
石景山区	Shijingshan District	65.2	21.0	65.2	
海淀区	Haidian District	369.4	148.6	361.5	7.9
城市发展新区	**New Area of Urban Development**	**696.9**	**302.2**	**488.1**	**208.8**
房山区	Fangshan District	104.6	27.4	74.0	30.6
通州区	Tongzhou District	137.8	55.9	88.2	49.6
顺义区	Shunyi District	102.0	40.2	55.4	46.6
昌平区	Changping District	196.3	102.6	159.6	36.7
大兴区	Daxing District	156.2	76.1	110.9	45.3
生态涵养发展区	**Ecological Conservation Area**	**190.8**	**31.3**	**118.2**	**72.6**
门头沟区	Mentougou District	30.8	4.8	26.7	4.1
怀柔区	Huairou District	38.4	10.5	25.5	12.9
平谷区	Pinggu District	42.3	5.3	23.3	19.0
密云区	Miyun District	47.9	7.1	26.6	21.3
延庆区	Yanqing District	31.4	3.6	16.1	15.3

注：本表数据为人口抽样调查推算数据，为年末数。
Note: Figures in this table are estimated figures from sample survey on population in the end of year.

3-4 常住人口密度(按区分)(2015年)
PERMANENT POPULATION DENSITY (BY DISTRICT) (2015)

地　区	District	土地面积(平方公里) Land Area (sq.km)	常住人口(万人) Permanent Population (10000 persons)	常住人口密度(人/平方公里) Permanent Population Density (person/sq.km)
全　市	**Total**	**16410.54**	**2170.5**	**1323**
首都功能核心区	**Capital Core Functional Area**	**92.39**	**220.3**	**23845**
东城区	Dongcheng District	41.86	90.5	21620
西城区	Xicheng District	50.53	129.8	25688
城市功能拓展区	**Urban Function Extension Area**	**1275.93**	**1062.5**	**8327**
朝阳区	Chaoyang District	455.08	395.5	8691
丰台区	Fengtai District	305.80	232.4	7600
石景山区	Shijingshan District	84.32	65.2	7732
海淀区	Haidian District	430.73	369.4	8576
城市发展新区	**Urban Development New Area**	**6295.57**	**696.9**	**1107**
房山区	Fangshan District	1989.54	104.6	526
通州区	Tongzhou District	906.28	137.8	1521
顺义区	Shunyi District	1019.89	102.0	1000
昌平区	Changping District	1343.54	196.3	1461
大兴区	Daxing District	1036.32	156.2	1507
生态涵养发展区	**Ecological Conservation Area**	**8746.65**	**190.8**	**218**
门头沟区	Mentougou District	1450.70	30.8	212
怀柔区	Huairou District	2122.62	38.4	181
平谷区	Pinggu District	950.13	42.3	445
密云区	Miyun District	2229.45	47.9	215
延庆区	Yanqing District	1993.75	31.4	157

注：本表常住人口数据为人口抽样调查数据推算数据，为年末数。
Note: Figures of permanent population in this table are estimated figures from the sample survey on population in the end of year.

3-5 常住人口自然变动(按区分)(2015年)
NATURAL CHANGE OF PERMANENT POPULATION (BY DISTRICT) (2015)

地区	District	出生人数(人) Number of Births (person)	死亡人数(人) Number of Deaths (person)	自然增加人数(人) Natural Increase of Population (person)	出生率(‰) Birth Rate (‰)	死亡率(‰) Death Rate (‰)	自然增长率(‰) Natural Growth Rate (‰)
全 市	**Total**	**172053**	**107039**	**65014**	**7.96**	**4.95**	**3.01**
首都功能核心区	**Capital Core Functional Area**	**16176**	**16349**	**-173**	**7.33**	**7.40**	**-0.07**
东城区	Dongcheng District	5765	7168	-1403	6.35	7.89	-1.54
西城区	Xicheng District	10411	9181	1230	8.01	7.06	0.95
城市功能拓展区	**Urban Function Extension Area**	**87462**	**41882**	**45580**	**8.26**	**3.96**	**4.30**
朝阳区	Chaoyang District	34523	13242	21281	8.76	3.36	5.40
丰台区	Fengtai District	17233	9666	7567	7.45	4.18	3.27
石景山区	Shijingshan District	4710	3772	938	7.24	5.79	1.45
海淀区	Haidian District	30996	15202	15794	8.41	4.12	4.29
城市发展新区	**Urban Development New Area**	**54702**	**34140**	**20562**	**7.92**	**4.94**	**2.98**
房山区	Fangshan District	8769	6660	2109	8.42	6.40	2.02
通州区	Tongzhou District	9992	6962	3030	7.31	5.09	2.22
顺义区	Shunyi District	10074	7388	2686	9.95	7.30	2.65
昌平区	Changping Ddistrict	11222	7718	3504	5.80	3.99	1.81
大兴区	Daxing District	14645	5412	9233	9.42	3.48	5.94
生态涵养发展区	**Ecological Conservation Area**	**13713**	**14668**	**-955**	**7.19**	**7.70**	**-0.51**
门头沟区	Mentougou District	1935	2134	-199	6.30	6.95	-0.65
怀柔区	Huairou District	3029	2884	145	7.91	7.53	0.38
平谷区	Pinggu District	3021	3405	-384	7.14	8.05	-0.91
密云区	Miyun District	3646	4094	-448	7.61	8.55	-0.94
延庆区	Yanqing District	2082	2151	-69	6.61	6.83	-0.22

注：本表数据为人口抽样调查推算数据。

Note: Figures in this table are estimated figures from the sample survey on population.

3-6 常住人口年龄构成(2015年)
PERMANENT POPULATION BY AGE COMPOSITION (2015)

年龄组 Age Group	常住人口数(万人) Permanent Population (10000 persons)	比重(%) Percentage (%)
合计 Total	**2170.5**	**100.0**
0-4	93.8	4.3
5-9	74.0	3.4
10-14	51.3	2.4
15-19	71.4	3.3
20-24	207.7	9.6
25-29	254.1	11.7
30-34	233.2	10.7
35-39	177.1	8.2
40-44	177.2	8.2
45-49	170.7	7.9
50-54	169.3	7.8
55-59	150.2	6.9
60-64	117.7	5.4
65-69	76.7	3.5
70-74	50.6	2.3
75-79	45.7	2.1
80-84	31.6	1.5
85岁及以上 85 and above	18.2	0.8

注：本表数据为人口抽样调查推算数据，为年末数。
Note: Figures in this table are estimated figures from the sample survey on population in the end of year.

3-7 常住人口受教育程度(2015年)
EDUCATION ATTAINMENT OF PERMANENT POPULATION (2015)

单位：人 (person)

项目	Item	调查人口合计 Total	男 Male	女 Female
6岁及以上人口	**Population at 6 and above**	**462380**	**232922**	**229458**
#小学	Primary School	55954	25588	30366
初中	Junior Secondary School	128560	68860	59700
普通高中	Senior Secondary School	68223	34340	33883
中职	Vocational School	34038	17898	16140
大学专科	Junior College	60295	30090	30205
大学本科	4-year Unversity Education	83897	42656	41241
研究生	Postgraduate	20659	10898	9761

注：本表数据为人口抽样调查样本数据。
Note: Figures in this table are sample figures from the sample survey on population.

3-8 常住人口家庭户规模(2015年)
FAMILY SIZE OF PERMANENT POPULATION (2015)

地区	Area	调查家庭总户数(户) Total Number of Households (household)	家庭户规模所占比重(%) Percentage of Various Sized Family (%)				
			一人户 One Person	二人户 Two Persons	三人户 Three Persons	四人户 Four Persons	五人及以上户 Five Persons and above
全市	**Total**	**177241**	**20.5**	**31.4**	**28.8**	**10.4**	**8.9**
城镇	Urban	144780	20.9	31.3	29.8	10.1	7.9
乡村	Rural	32461	18.8	31.8	24.1	12.0	13.3

注：本表数据为人口抽样调查样本数据。
Note: Figures in this table are sample figures from the sample survey on population.

3-9 户籍人口(1978-2015年)
REGISTERED POPULATION (1978-2015)

单位：万人 (10000 persons)

年 份 Year	户籍户数(万户) Registered Households (10000 households)	户籍人口 Registered Population	#60岁及以上人口 Population at 60 and above	按性别分 By Sex 男 Male	女 Female	按户籍性质分 By Type of Household Register 非农业户 Non-Agricultural	农业户 Agricultural	户籍人口出生人数 Births of Registered Population	户籍人口死亡人数 Deaths of Registered Population	户籍人口自然增加人数 Natural Increase of Registered Population
1978	205.5	849.7		432.1	417.5	467.0	382.6	10.9	5.2	5.7
1979	214.6	870.6		441.1	429.4	495.2	375.4	11.8	5.1	6.7
1980	223.2	885.7		448.4	437.3	510.4	375.3	13.7	5.5	8.2
1981	234.8	900.8		456.6	444.2	522.6	378.2	15.1	5.4	9.7
1982	245.0	917.8		465.5	452.3	534.0	383.8	18.2	5.2	13.1
1983	255.1	933.2		474.7	458.5	547.1	386.0	14.5	5.1	9.4
1984	263.1	945.2		481.2	464.0	558.1	387.0	13.2	5.1	8.1
1985	274.1	957.9		488.0	469.9	572.5	385.4	11.8	5.2	6.6
1986	284.6	971.2		495.5	475.7	586.8	384.4	12.9	5.2	7.8
1987	299.4	988.0		504.1	483.9	601.0	387.0	16.9	5.3	11.6
1988	310.8	1001.2		510.4	490.8	614.3	387.0	15.3	5.5	9.8
1989	322.5	1021.1		520.3	500.8	630.6	390.5	19.0	5.7	13.3
1990	335.0	1032.2		525.3	507.0	640.2	392.1	14.0	6.3	7.7
1991	343.1	1039.5		528.5	511.1	648.4	391.2	9.2	5.7	3.5
1992	349.3	1044.9		530.8	514.1	656.3	388.6	8.3	6.2	2.2
1993	354.6	1051.2		533.9	517.3	668.7	382.5	7.9	6.3	1.6
1994	360.3	1061.8		538.9	522.8	683.8	377.9	8.5	6.3	2.2
1995	365.7	1070.3		543.0	527.3	696.9	373.5	8.5	6.2	2.3
1996	370.9	1077.7		546.8	530.9	709.7	368.0	7.8	6.7	1.2
1997	375.7	1085.5		550.4	535.1	722.7	362.9	7.6	6.7	0.9
1998	383.4	1091.5		552.6	538.9	733.6	357.8	6.7	7.5	-0.8
1999	390.3	1099.8		556.7	543.1	747.2	352.6	6.3	6.2	0.1
2000	397.9	1107.5		560.1	547.4	760.7	346.8	7.2	7.8	-0.5
2001	405.3	1122.3		567.3	555.0	780.2	342.2	6.0	5.3	0.7
2002	416.3	1136.3		574.7	561.6	806.9	329.4	6.0	5.2	0.8
2003	427.6	1148.8		581.0	567.9	830.8	318.0	4.5	5.8	-1.3
2004	439.8	1162.9		587.2	575.7	854.7	308.2	6.6	6.2	0.4
2005	451.7	1180.7		596.0	584.7	880.2	300.5	7.5	7.0	0.5
2006	463.7	1197.6		604.2	593.4	905.4	292.2	7.7	5.1	2.6
2007	473.0	1213.3	210.3	612.0	601.3	929.0	284.3	9.9	5.2	4.8
2008	481.2	1229.9	218.6	620.0	609.9	950.7	279.2	10.6	5.1	5.5
2009	488.7	1245.8	228.7	627.5	618.9	971.9	273.9	10.9	6.2	4.7
2010	496.1	1257.8	237.2	632.8	625.0	989.5	268.3	10.2	9.1	1.1
2011	503.1	1277.9	250.5	642.4	635.6	1013.8	264.2	12.5	5.3	7.2
2012	509.2	1297.5	266.1	651.7	645.8	1039.3	258.2	14.5	5.7	8.8
2013	516.2	1316.3	283.2	660.4	655.9	1065.0	251.4	13.6	5.7	7.9
2014	522.6	1333.4	301.0	668.3	665.1	1089.8	243.6	17.2	7.6	9.6
2015	529.2	1345.2	318.0	673.3	671.9	1111.3	233.8	12.3	7.3	4.9

资料来源：北京市公安局。
Source: Beijing Municipal Bureau of Public Security.

3-10 户籍户数及人口数(按区分)(2015年)
REGISTERED HOUSEHOLDS AND POPULATION (BY DISTRICT) (2015)

地区	District	户籍户数及人口 Registered Households and Population					
		户数(万户) Households (10000 households)			人口数(万人) Population (10000 persons)		
		合计 Total	非农业户 Non-Agricultural	农业户 Agricultural	合计 Total	非农业户 Non-Agricultural	农业户 Agricultural
全市	**Total**	**529.2**	**425.4**	**103.8**	**1345.2**	**1111.3**	**233.8**
首都功能核心区	**Capital Core Functional Area**	**83.1**	**83.0**		**242.6**	**242.6**	
东城区	Dongcheng District	34.6	34.6		97.4	97.4	
西城区	Xicheng District	48.5	48.5		145.2	145.2	
城市功能拓展区	**Urban Function Extension Area**	**215.1**	**203.8**	**11.3**	**598.8**	**575.5**	**23.3**
朝阳区	Chaoyang District	81.0	76.2	4.8	207.4	197.6	9.9
丰台区	Fengtai District	47.0	42.8	4.2	113.7	104.9	8.7
石景山区	Shijingshan District	14.7	14.7		38.3	38.3	
海淀区	Haidian District	72.4	70.1	2.4	239.5	234.8	4.7
城市发展新区	**Urban Development New Area**	**153.7**	**96.8**	**56.8**	**339.0**	**206.6**	**132.4**
房山区	Fangshan District	37.8	22.9	15.0	79.9	47.4	32.5
通州区	Tongzhou District	35.4	22.6	12.7	71.8	43.9	27.8
顺义区	Shunyi District	27.0	16.4	10.6	61.5	36.1	25.4
昌平区	Changping District	26.6	18.2	8.4	59.5	41.6	17.9
大兴区	Daxing District	26.9	16.8	10.1	66.3	37.5	28.8
生态涵养发展区	**Ecological Conservation Area**	**77.4**	**41.8**	**35.6**	**164.7**	**86.6**	**78.2**
门头沟区	Mentougou District	12.1	9.4	2.7	24.9	20.1	4.8
怀柔区	Huairou District	13.6	6.6	7.0	28.2	13.5	14.7
平谷区	Pinggu District	17.0	9.6	7.5	40.1	21.6	18.5
密云区	Miyun District	20.7	9.4	11.3	43.3	18.6	24.7
延庆区	Yanqing District	14.0	6.9	7.2	28.2	12.8	15.4

资料来源：北京市公安局。
Source: Beijing Municipal Bureau of Public Security.

3-11 户籍人口年龄构成(2015年)
AGE COMPOSITION OF REGISTERED POPULATION (2015)

年龄组 Age Group	户籍人口(万人) Registered Population (10000 persons)			占人口比重(%) Percentage (%)		
	合计 Total	男 Male	女 Female	合计 Total	男 Male	女 Female
合 计 Total	**1345.2**	**673.3**	**671.9**	**100.0**	**50.1**	**49.9**
0-4	67.1	34.6	32.5	5.0	2.6	2.4
5-9	49.3	25.4	23.9	3.7	1.9	1.8
10-14	34.0	17.5	16.4	2.5	1.3	1.2
15-19	46.8	23.5	23.3	3.5	1.7	1.7
20-24	72.8	36.3	36.4	5.4	2.7	2.7
25-29	114.3	58.1	56.2	8.5	4.3	4.2
30-34	118.7	59.7	58.9	8.8	4.4	4.4
35-39	91.2	46.1	45.1	6.8	3.4	3.4
40-44	92.3	46.8	45.5	6.9	3.5	3.4
45-49	103.2	51.9	51.3	7.7	3.9	3.8
50-54	124.1	63.4	60.7	9.2	4.7	4.5
55-59	113.4	56.8	56.6	8.4	4.2	4.2
60-64	103.8	50.7	53.1	7.7	3.8	3.9
65-69	64.3	31.3	32.9	4.8	2.3	2.4
70-74	44.6	20.9	23.7	3.3	1.6	1.8
75-79	44.5	20.6	23.9	3.3	1.5	1.8
80-84	34.8	16.9	17.9	2.6	1.3	1.3
85-89	17.3	8.4	8.9	1.3	0.6	0.7
90岁及以上 90 and above	8.8	4.2	4.6	0.7	0.3	0.3

资料来源：北京市公安局。
Source: Beijing Municipal Bureau of Public Security.

3-12 户籍人口性别构成及性别比(按区分)(2015年)
SEX COMPOSITION AND SEX RATIO OF REGISTERED POPULATION (BY DISTRICT) (2015)

地区	District	户籍人口(万人) Registered Population (10000 persons)			性别比 (女=100) Sex Ratio (female=100)
		合计 Total	男 Male	女 Female	
全市	**Total**	**1345.2**	**673.3**	**671.9**	**100.2**
首都功能核心区	**Capital Core Functional Area**	**242.6**	**120.3**	**122.3**	**98.4**
东城区	Dongcheng District	97.4	48.0	49.4	97.1
西城区	Xicheng District	145.2	72.3	72.8	99.3
城市功能拓展区	**Urban Function Extension Area**	**598.8**	**301.0**	**297.8**	**101.1**
朝阳区	Chaoyang Dsitrict	207.4	103.8	103.6	100.2
丰台区	Fengtai District	113.7	57.5	56.1	102.6
石景山区	Shijingshan District	38.3	19.7	18.6	105.8
海淀区	Haidian District	239.5	120.0	119.5	100.4
城市发展新区	**Urban Development New Area**	**339.0**	**169.1**	**169.9**	**99.5**
房山区	Fangshan District	79.9	40.1	39.9	100.6
通州区	Tongzhou District	71.8	35.6	36.1	98.7
顺义区	Shunyi District	61.5	30.5	31.0	98.4
昌平区	Changping District	59.5	29.9	29.6	101.1
大兴区	Daxing District	66.3	33.0	33.3	99.0
生态涵养发展区	**Ecological Conservation Area**	**164.7**	**82.9**	**81.9**	**101.2**
门头沟区	Mentougou Dsitrict	24.9	12.7	12.2	104.1
怀柔区	Huairou District	28.2	14.1	14.1	100.1
平谷区	Pinggu District	40.1	20.1	19.9	101.2
密云区	Miyun District	43.3	21.7	21.7	99.9
延庆区	Yanqing District	28.2	14.2	14.0	101.7

资料来源：北京市公安局。
Source: Beijing Municipal Bureau of Public Security.

3-13 户籍人口变动情况
CHANGES OF REGISTERED POPULATION

单位：人 (person)

项　　目	Item	2015	2014
自然变动	**Natural Changes**		
自然增加	Natural Increase	49366	95725
非农业人口	Non-agricultural Population	60071	104363
农业人口	Agricultural Population	-10705	-8638
出　生	Births	122627	171690
非农业人口	Non-agricultural Population	112197	155866
农业人口	Agricultural Population	10430	15824
死　亡	Deaths	73261	75965
非农业人口	Non-agricultural Population	52126	51503
农业人口	Agricultural Population	21135	24462
机械变动	**Non-natural Changes**		
机械增加	Non-natural Increase	75497	74654
非农业人口	Non-agricultural Population	66282	65021
农业人口	Agricultural Population	9215	9633
市外迁入	Inflow	167506	166600
非农业人口	Non-agricultural Population	157074	155749
农业人口	Agricultural Population	10432	10851
迁往市外	Outflow	92009	91946
非农业人口	Non-agricultural Population	90792	90728
农业人口	Agricultural Population	1217	1218

资料来源：北京市公安局。
Source: Beijing Municipal Bureau of Public Security.

3-14 户籍人口自然变动情况(按区分)
NATURAL CHANGES OF REGISTERED POPULATION (BY DISTRICT)

单位：人 (person)

地 区	District	出生人数 Number of Births		死亡人数 Number of Deaths		自然增加人数 Number of Natural Increase	
		2015	2014	2015	2014	2015	2014
全 市	**Total**	**122627**	**171690**	**73261**	**75965**	**49366**	**95725**
首都功能核心区	**Capital Core Functional Area**	**22435**	**29789**	**22704**	**14508**	**-269**	**15281**
东城区	Dongcheng District	8814	11816	16645	6695	-7831	5121
西城区	Xicheng District	13621	17973	6059	7813	7562	10160
城市功能拓展区	**Urban Function Extension Area**	**54822**	**73037**	**21420**	**26690**	**33402**	**46347**
朝阳区	Chaoyang District	21146	27504	8020	10602	13126	16902
丰台区	Fengtai District	9672	13559	4905	6291	4767	7268
石景山区	Shijingshan District	3236	4512	1580	2543	1656	1969
海淀区	Haidian District	20768	27462	6915	7254	13853	20208
城市发展新区	**Urban Development New Area**	**33093**	**49850**	**18376**	**22664**	**14717**	**27186**
房山区	Fangshan District	6630	10395	4392	5388	2238	5007
通州区	Tongzhou District	7193	10294	4267	5527	2926	4767
顺义区	Shunyi District	5655	9399	3660	4023	1995	5376
昌平区	Changping District	6443	8883	2928	3959	3515	4924
大兴区	Daxing District	7172	10879	3129	3767	4043	7112
生态涵养发展区	**Ecological Conservation Area**	**12277**	**19014**	**10761**	**12103**	**1516**	**6911**
门头沟区	Mentougou District	1635	2465	1448	2165	187	300
怀柔区	Huairou District	2335	3493	1788	1836	547	1657
平谷区	Pinggu District	3157	4962	3030	3224	127	1738
密云区	Miyun District	3133	5047	2733	3095	400	1952
延庆区	Yanqing District	2017	3047	1762	1783	255	1264

资料来源：北京市公安局。
Source: Beijing Municipal Bureau of Public Security.

3-15 三次产业从业人员年末人数及构成(1978-2015年)
EMPLOYED PERSONS IN THREE INDUSTRIES AND THEIR COMPOSITION (1978-2015)

年 份 Year	从业人员年末人数 (万人) Year-end Employed Persons (10000 persons)				构 成(%) (合计=100) Composition (%) (Total=100)		
		第一产业 Primary Industry	第二产业 Secondary Industry	第三产业 Tertiary Industry	第一产业 Primary Industry	第二产业 Secondary Industry	第三产业 Tertiary Industry
1978	444.1	125.9	177.9	140.3	28.3	40.1	31.6
1979	470.5	121.4	195.2	153.9	25.8	41.5	32.7
1980	484.2	118.0	207.3	158.9	24.4	42.8	32.8
1981	511.7	117.2	220.4	174.1	22.9	43.1	34.0
1982	535.2	115.1	228.6	191.5	21.5	42.7	35.8
1983	552.0	117.1	240.2	194.7	21.2	43.5	35.3
1984	556.2	111.3	247.9	197.0	20.0	44.6	35.4
1985	566.5	100.6	260.4	205.5	17.7	46.0	36.3
1986	572.7	96.1	262.7	213.9	16.8	45.9	37.3
1987	580.2	92.3	264.1	223.8	15.9	45.5	38.6
1988	584.1	88.4	267.6	228.1	15.1	45.8	39.1
1989	593.9	91.0	266.3	236.6	15.3	44.9	39.8
1990	627.1	90.7	281.6	254.8	14.5	44.9	40.6
1991	634.0	90.8	279.7	263.5	14.3	44.1	41.6
1992	649.3	84.5	281.6	283.2	13.0	43.4	43.6
1993	627.8	65.1	279.4	283.3	10.4	44.5	45.1
1994	664.3	73.2	272.2	318.9	11.0	41.0	48.0
1995	665.3	70.6	271.0	323.7	10.6	40.7	48.7
1996	660.2	72.5	260.1	327.6	11.0	39.4	49.6
1997	655.8	71.0	257.6	327.2	10.8	39.2	50.0
1998	622.2	71.5	226.0	324.7	11.5	36.3	52.2
1999	618.6	74.5	216.2	327.9	12.1	34.9	53.0
2000	619.3	72.9	208.2	338.2	11.8	33.6	54.6
2001	628.9	71.2	215.9	341.8	11.3	34.3	54.4
2002	679.2	67.6	235.3	376.3	10.0	34.6	55.4
2003	703.3	62.7	225.8	414.8	8.9	32.1	59.0
2004	854.1	61.5	232.8	559.8	7.2	27.3	65.5
2005	878.0	62.2	231.1	584.7	7.1	26.3	66.6
2006	919.7	60.3	225.4	634.0	6.6	24.5	68.9
2007	942.7	60.9	228.1	653.7	6.5	24.2	69.3
2008	980.9	63.0	207.4	710.5	6.4	21.2	72.4
2009	998.3	62.2	199.6	736.5	6.2	20.0	73.8
2010	1031.6	61.4	202.7	767.5	6.0	19.6	74.4
2011	1069.7	59.1	219.2	791.4	5.5	20.5	74.0
2012	1107.3	57.3	212.6	837.4	5.2	19.2	75.6
2013	1141.0	55.4	210.9	874.7	4.8	18.5	76.7
2014	1156.7	52.4	209.9	894.4	4.5	18.2	77.3
2015	1186.1	50.3	200.8	935.0	4.2	17.0	78.8

注：1. 2010年及以前，劳务派遣人员按照“谁发工资谁统计”的原则进行统计。2011年以后，劳务派遣人员按照“谁用工谁统计”的原则进行统计。
2. 自2012年开始，三次产业划分执行国家统计局《三次产业划分规定》(国统字〔2012〕108号)。

Note: a) In 2010 and before, dispatched personnel of labor service were calculated by "wage payers". After 2011, dispatched personnel of labor service were calculated by "employers".
b) Since 2012, the three industries have been classified according to the Regulations on the Classification of the Three Industries (G.T.Z. [2012] No. 108) issued by National Bureau of Statistics.

3-16 按登记注册类型分从业人员年末人数(1978-2015年)
YEAR-END EMPLOYED PERSONS BY TYPE OF REGISTRATION (1978-2015)

单位：万人 (10000 persons)

年份 Year	合计 Total	#城镇 Urban	#国有单位 State-owned Enterprises	#集体单位 Collectively-owned Enterprises	#联营单位 Associated Enterprises	#有限责任公司 Limited Liability Companies	#股份有限公司 Companies Limited by Shares	#外商投资 Foreign-invested	#港澳台商投资 Hong Kong, Macao and Taiwan-invested	#私营 Private Enterprises	#个体 Individual Economy
1978	444.1	291.6	240.9	50.7							
1979	470.5	311.9	254.2	57.8							
1980	484.2	326.8	269.4	57.1							0.3
1981	511.7	345.2	283.1	61.3							
1982	535.2	361.1	293.0	67.1							
1983	552.0	373.8	303.4	68.5							
1984	556.2	377.6	302.5	71.6				1.3			
1985	566.5	392.6	308.1	72.6				1.6			2.5
1986	572.7	400.5	324.4	71.1				2.4			2.6
1987	580.2	408.3	331.8	70.7				2.8			3.1
1988	584.1	413.9	336.4	69.9	0.2			3.4			3.5
1989	593.9	424.0	343.8	67.4	3.4			3.7			5.6
1990	627.1	461.2	357.9	86.8	5.1			4.6			6.3
1991	634.0	477.2	367.8	89.0	0.5			7.7	0.2		7.2
1992	649.3	490.6	371.5	90.5	0.4			11.4	0.2		14.0
1993	627.8	481.4	362.3	79.7	2.8			11.0	6.4		14.0
1994	664.3	492.7	363.5	73.3	3.5			15.0	9.4		20.9
1995	665.3	492.7	358.2	72.1	3.7			17.4	10.0		21.9
1996	660.2	495.7	355.1	68.6	3.4			20.7	10.1		22.9
1997	655.8	498.7	354.7	68.5	3.2			21.2	10.2		21.2
1998	622.2	463.2	308.1	51.0	5.2	13.7	10.8	21.2	13.1		20.1
1999	618.6	456.1	287.6	49.7	4.8	24.0	12.2	20.6	13.5		23.7
2000	619.3	456.3	266.2	48.3	4.0	34.2	14.0	23.8	14.2		24.4
2001	628.9	464.2	246.3	45.8	4.1	50.6	17.3	22.4	12.9		24.8
2002	679.2	513.6	224.8	36.8	4.1	85.0	27.1	29.2	17.0	4.8	33.1
2003	703.3	533.7	212.8	30.1	3.8	102.3	33.4	31.5	17.3	5.2	37.2
2004	854.1	682.7	199.5	28.2	3.5	134.5	37.9	45.0	18.3	134.2	45.7
2005	878.0	694.0	195.0	23.8	2.4	149.4	36.4	49.6	21.7	131.2	57.2
2006	919.7	734.2	189.3	18.8	2.1	165.1	35.5	57.3	23.5	154.8	65.6
2007	942.7	745.4	189.3	17.3	1.9	179.5	38.7	69.3	28.8	133.8	67.2
2008	980.9	813.7	187.8	24.8	2.2	196.4	46.4	72.9	33.5	159.6	65.1
2009	998.3	856.6	185.7	24.3	0.9	215.7	58.4	71.2	36.6	172.2	67.5
2010	1031.6	905.4	189.0	22.7	0.9	228.2	64.7	74.9	42.4	193.5	65.3
2011	1069.7	955.8	188.8	20.1	0.7	243.0	75.9	90.1	50.6	210.6	59.3
2012	1107.3	996.1	188.3	19.8	0.7	261.6	83.2	92.7	54.3	227.9	50.8
2013	1141.0	1073.0	189.5	17.5	0.7	278.0	85.4	96.1	56.1	265.9	64.8
2014	1156.7	1066.2	188.6	18.8	0.5	290.6	86.2	94.5	58.7	254.6	55.7
2015	1186.1	1107.1	182.9	16.9	0.4	300.3	103.5	90.6	59.7	273.3	56.4

资料来源：表中2002-2013年私营从业人员数据来源于北京市工商行政管理局，2014-2015年数据根据劳动工资年报全面调查和抽样调查推算得到；个体从业人员数据来源于北京市工商行政管理局。

Source: Figures of employed persons in private enterprises from 2002 to 2013 in this table were from Beijing Administration for Industry and Commerce. Figures in 2014 were calculated based on comprehensive and sample surveys in annual report on employee salary; and figures on self-employed individuals were from Beijing Administration for Industry and Commerce.

3-17 全市法人单位从业人员年末人数和平均工资
YEAR-END EMPLOYED PERSONS IN LEGAL ENTITIES AND AVERAGE WAGES

项目	Item	从业人员年末人数（万人） Year-end Employed Persons (10000 persons)		从业人员平均工资（元） Average Wage (yuan)	
		2015	2014	2015	2014
合计	**Total**	**1050.7**	**1010.5**	**97616**	**89804**
按登记注册类型分	**By Registration Type**				
内资	Domestically-invested Enterprises	900.4	857.3	89949	82566
国有	State-owned Enterprises	182.9	188.6	115098	102538
集体	Collectively-owned Enterprises	16.9	18.8	49717	45500
股份合作	Joint-equity Cooperative Enterprises	5.2	6.6	43749	42134
联营	Associated Enterprises	0.4	0.5	71428	69300
有限责任公司	Limited Liability Companies	300.3	290.6	89353	82562
股份有限公司	Companies Limited by Shares	103.5	86.2	140491	140914
私营	Private Enterprises	273.3	254.6	58689	52902
其他	Others	17.9	11.4	55352	60536
港、澳、台商投资	Hong Kong, Macao and Taiwan-invested Enterprises	59.7	58.7	127552	114991
外商投资	Foreign-invested Enterprises	90.6	94.5	157966	139490
按国民经济行业分	**By Sector**				
农、林、牧、渔业	Agriculture, Forestry, Animal Production and Hunting, Fishing	5.1	4.2	47210	45877
采矿业	Mining and Quarrying	5.3	6.2	87853	90010
制造业	Manufacturing	119.0	129.9	80634	72672
电力、热力、燃气及水生产和供应业	Production and Distribution of Electricity, Heating Power, Gas and Water	8.6	8.6	125813	110032
建筑业	Construction	66.4	63.7	70625	67422
批发和零售业	Wholesale and Retail Trade	129.5	123.0	75843	73290
交通运输、仓储和邮政业	Transport, Storage and Post	66.8	66.6	77542	74259
住宿和餐饮业	Lodging and Catering Services	42.6	44.1	48497	45417
信息传输、软件和信息技术服务业	Information Transmission, Software and Information Technology Services	92.2	84.4	141333	128507
金融业	Financial Intermediation	50.9	45.9	240844	217409
房地产业	Real Estate	53.7	52.4	82760	73859
租赁和商务服务业	Leasing and Business Services	142.9	124.4	88683	85663
科学研究和技术服务业	Scientific Research and Development, Technical Services	88.5	82.7	110659	107430
水利、环境和公共设施管理业	Management of Water Conservancy, Environment and Public Facilities	12.4	11.8	69042	63375
居民服务、修理和其他服务业	Resident Service, Repair and Other Services	17.6	17.2	44740	42239
教育	Education	50.7	49.0	107713	96190
卫生和社会工作	Health Care and Social Works	28.8	26.9	135008	121326
文化、体育和娱乐业	Culture, Sports and Entertainment	23.0	22.8	113632	104626
公共管理、社会保障和社会组织	Public Management, Social Security and Social Organizations	46.7	46.7	91030	76226
国际组织	International Organizations				

注：行业划分执行2011年国民经济行业分类标准(GB/T 4754-2011)。
Note: Sectors in this table are classified in accordance with the Standard for Classification of National Economic Sectors 2011 (GB/T 4754-2011).

3-18 城镇单位在岗职工年末人数及工资总额(1978-2015年)
YEAR-END NUMBER AND WAGES OF FULLY EMPLOYED STAFF AND WORKERS IN URBAN ENTITIES (1978-2015)

年　份 Year	在岗职工年末人数(万人) Year-end Fully Employed Staff and Workers (10000 persons)	国有单位 State-owned	集体单位 Collectively-owned	其他单位 Others	在岗职工工资总额(亿元) Total Wages of Fully Employed Staff and Workers (100 million yuan)	国有单位 State-owned	集体单位 Collectively-owned	其他单位 Others
1978	291.6	240.9	50.7		18.7	16.2	2.5	
1979	311.9	254.2	57.7		22.4	19.4	3.0	
1980	326.5	269.4	57.1		26.9	23.3	3.6	
1981-1985					**183.7**	**153.7**	**29.6**	**0.4**
1981	344.4	283.1	61.3		28.3	24.2	4.1	
1982	360.1	293.0	67.1		30.5	25.9	4.6	
1983	371.9	303.4	68.5		33.8	28.5	5.3	
1984	375.4	302.5	71.6	1.3	40.4	33.7	6.6	0.1
1985	382.3	308.1	72.6	1.6	50.7	41.5	9.0	0.3
1986-1990					**421.1**	**349.7**	**64.4**	**7.0**
1986	397.9	324.4	71.1	2.4	58.0	48.5	9.1	0.4
1987	405.2	331.8	70.7	2.7	66.7	56.0	10.1	0.6
1988	410.4	336.4	69.9	4.1	81.2	68.1	12.1	1.0
1989	418.4	343.8	67.4	7.2	96.3	81.0	13.4	1.9
1990	454.9	357.9	86.8	10.2	118.9	96.1	19.7	3.1
1991-1995					**1198.1**	**950.3**	**156.6**	**91.2**
1991	470.0	367.8	89.0	13.2	132.2	106.1	21.5	4.6
1992	476.6	371.5	90.5	14.6	158.5	128.6	23.9	6.0
1993	467.3	362.3	79.6	25.4	218.9	176.6	28.5	13.8
1994	471.8	363.5	73.4	34.9	306.5	243.4	36.2	26.9
1995	470.9	358.2	72.1	40.6	382.0	295.6	46.5	39.9
1996-2000					**2825.4**	**1988.5**	**236.5**	**600.4**
1996	460.6	349.0	64.8	46.8	442.4	339.4	46.2	56.8
1997	465.3	348.7	65.0	51.6	514.8	383.6	53.8	77.4
1998	450.1	321.7	50.8	77.6	558.2	391.9	45.0	121.3
1999	438.0	303.0	49.6	85.4	614.5	420.0	44.8	149.7
2000	434.2	283.0	46.0	105.2	695.5	453.6	46.7	195.2
2001-2005					**5662.3**	**2872.7**	**184.6**	**2605.0**
2001	400.3	235.9	40.0	124.4	777.3	477.8	44.8	254.7
2002	434.2	212.6	32.7	188.9	950.9	508.8	40.0	402.1
2003	436.3	197.6	26.1	212.6	1098.9	565.5	35.0	498.4
2004	446.4	183.7	24.8	237.9	1315.1	625.7	34.0	655.4
2005	448.4	178.5	20.7	249.2	1520.1	694.9	30.8	794.4
2006-2010					**13890.4**	**4904.7**	**219.9**	**8765.8**
2006	453.1	172.9	16.4	263.8	1805.5	738.0	30.5	1037.0
2007	478.9	172.7	15.4	290.8	2194.3	862.4	31.2	1300.7
2008	526.1	171.0	22.7	332.4	2874.3	1008.8	48.2	1817.3
2009	560.4	170.9	22.4	367.1	3227.2	1074.3	53.3	2099.6
2010	587.7	175.1	21.1	391.5	3789.1	1221.2	56.7	2511.2
2011-2015					**32457.0**	**8671.8**	**367.1**	**23418.1**
2011	640.3	177.1	18.7	444.5	4778.6	1421.1	62.3	3295.2
2012	670.4	177.3	18.6	474.5	5657.9	1582.5	71.6	4003.8
2013	695.5	178.4	16.5	500.6	6502.0	1724.7	70.2	4707.1
2014	708.8	177.7	17.8	513.3	7293.3	1884.5	81.5	5327.3
2015	724.8	172.8	16.0	536.0	8225.2	2059.0	81.5	6084.7

注：1. 2007年及以前城镇单位是指乡及乡以上独立核算法人单位，不包括乡镇企业、私营单位和个体工商户。2008年及以后城镇单位是指不包括私营单位和个体工商户的独立核算法人单位(下表同)。

2. 表中2000年及以前数据为职工口径，职工包括在岗职工和不在岗职工(下表同)。

Note: a) Urban entities in and before 2007 referred to legal entities with independent accounting at and above township level, excluding township enterprises, private entities and self-employed businesses. Urban entities in and after 2008 referred to legal entities with independent accounting excluding private entities and self-employed businesses (the same to the follow s).

b) Figures before 2001 were counted by the statistical range of employees including on-the-job and off-the-job ones (the same to the follow tables).

3-19 城镇单位在岗职工平均工资(1978-2015年)
AVERAGE WAGES OF FULLY EMPLOYED STAFF AND WORKERS IN URBAN ENTITIES (1978-2015)

单位：元 (yuan)

年 份 Year	在岗职工平均工资 Average Wage of Fully Employed Staff and Workers	国有单位 State-owned Enterprises	集体单位 Collectively-owned Enterprises	其他单位 Others
1978	673	703	471	
1979	742	778	556	
1980	848	889	635	
1981	837	880	685	
1982	863	896	715	
1983	931	964	785	
1984	1086	1127	946	1170
1985	1343	1367	1231	1768
1986	1488	1530	1287	2080
1987	1670	1712	1449	2267
1988	2000	2048	1738	2661
1989	2312	2366	1992	2761
1990	2653	2713	2334	3243
1991	2877	2937	2504	3713
1992	3402	3500	2828	4289
1993	4780	4920	3834	5469
1994	6540	6695	5009	8179
1995	8144	8237	6516	10278
1996	9579	9645	7133	13851
1997	11019	10917	8259	15370
1998	12285	11971	8800	15989
1999	13778	13483	8928	17748
2000	15726	15483	9844	19165
2001	19155	19776	11063	20594
2002	21852	23754	11997	21432
2003	25312	28464	13580	23769
2004	29674	34009	13422	28026
2005	34191	39067	14695	32324
2006	40117	43298	17781	39513
2007	46507	50524	20379	45508
2008	54913	59361	20990	54983
2009	58140	63239	23553	57911
2010	65683	70320	26607	65755
2011	75834	81215	32469	75584
2012	85307	90456	38596	85234
2013	93997	97356	42482	94513
2014	103400	106097	45772	104473
2015	113073	119046	49969	113066

3-20 城镇单位在岗职工年末人数
YEAR-END NUMBER OF FULLY EMPLOYED STAFF AND WORKERS IN URBAN ENTITIES

单位：人 (person)

项 目	Item	2015	2014	2015年为2014年% 2015 as % of 2014
合 计	**Total**	**7247899**	**7087922**	**102.3**
按登记注册类型分	**By Registration Type**			
内 资	Domestically-invested Enterprises	5844677	5654074	103.4
国 有	State-owned Enterprises	1727534	1777188	97.2
集 体	Collectively-owned Enterprises	160286	177558	90.3
股份合作	Joint-equity Cooperative Enterprises	48550	61565	78.9
联 营	Associated Enterprises	3475	4174	83.3
有限责任公司	Limited Liability Companies	2816740	2750957	102.4
股份有限公司	Companies Limited By Shares	931042	787663	118.2
其他	Others	157050	94969	165.4
港、澳、台商投资	Hong Kong, Macao and Taiwan-invested Enterprises	561729	556049	101.0
外商投资	Foreign-invested Enterprises	841493	877799	95.9
按国民经济行业分	**By Sector**			
农、林、牧、渔业	Agriculture, Forestry, Animal Production and Hunting, Fishing	38024	31839	119.4
#农 业	Agriculture	14732	8991	163.9
采矿业	Mining and Quarrying	52733	60871	86.6
制造业	Manufacturing	898403	974278	92.2
电力、热力、燃气及水生产和供应业	Production and Distribution of Electricity, Heating Power, Gas and Water	80247	80364	99.9
建筑业	Construction	417942	428302	97.6
批发和零售业	Wholesale and Retail Trade	706228	679266	104.0
批发业	Wholesale	398156	380070	104.8
零售业	Retail Trade	308072	299196	103.0
交通运输、仓储和邮政业	Transport, Storage and Post	586448	589029	99.6
#铁路运输业	Transport via Railway	109304	110091	99.3
道路运输业	Transport via Road	284638	278198	102.3
邮政业	Post	66950	75790	88.3
住宿和餐饮业	Lodging and Catering Services	254728	261676	97.3
住宿业	Lodging	119626	126701	94.4
餐饮业	Catering Services	135102	134975	100.1
信息传输、软件和信息技术服务业	Information Transmission, Software and Information Technology Services	663216	597654	111.0
金融业	Financial Intermediation	374255	355455	105.3
房地产业	Real Estate	392353	381249	102.9
租赁和商务服务业	Leasing and Business Services	769553	676508	113.8
租赁业	Leasing	18688	18896	98.9
商务服务业	Business Services	750865	657612	114.2
科学研究和技术服务业	Scientific Research and Development, Technical Services	545017	554289	98.3
水利、环境和公共设施管理业	Management of Water Conservancy, Environment and Public Facilities	97439	94743	102.8
居民服务、修理和其他服务业	Resident Services, Repair and Other Services	83267	81363	102.3
#居民服务业	Resident Services	31230	27030	115.5
教 育	Education	429961	413158	104.1
卫生和社会工作	Health Care and Social Works	257088	239932	107.2
#卫 生	Health Care	244067	229295	106.4
文化、体育和娱乐业	Culture, Sports and Entertainment	171661	163532	105.0
#文化艺术业	Cultures and Arts	39014	31908	122.3
体 育	Sports Activities	21362	21595	98.9
公共管理、社会保障和社会组织	Public Management, Social Security and Social Organizations	429336	424414	101.2
国际组织	International Organizations			

注：行业划分执行2011年国民经济行业分类标准(GB/T 4754-2011)。
Note: Sectors in this table are classified in accordance with the Standard for Classification of National Economic Sectors 2011 (GB/T 4754-2011).

3-21 城镇单位在岗职工工资总额
TOTAL WAGES OF FULLY EMPLOYED STAFF AND WORKERS IN URBAN ENTITIES

单位：万元 (10000 yuan)

项目	Item	2015	2014	2015年为2014年% 2015 as % of 2014
合计	**Total**	**82252242**	**72933475**	**112.8**
按登记注册类型分	**By Registration Type**			
内资	Domestically-invested Enterprises	63050276	54893951	114.9
国有	State-owned Enterprises	20589795	18844866	109.3
集体	Collectively-owned Enterprises	815449	815114	100.0
股份合作	Joint-equity Cooperative Enterprises	210797	258467	81.6
联营	Associated Enterprises	24717	29717	83.2
有限责任公司	Limited Liability Companies	25325700	22844292	110.9
股份有限公司	Companies Limited By Shares	15265116	11555570	132.1
其他	Others	818702	545925	150.0
港、澳、台商投资	Hong Kong, Macao and Taiwan-invested Enterprises	7146947	6257128	114.2
外商投资	Foreign-invested Enterprises	12055019	11782396	102.3
按国民经济行业分	**By Sector**			
农、林、牧、渔业	Agriculture, Forestry, Animal Production and Hunting, Fishing	204769	161684	126.6
#农业	Agriculture	62568	40092	156.1
采矿业	Mining and Quarrying	496229	566759	87.6
制造业	Manufacturing	8054195	7787615	103.4
电力、热力、燃气及水生产和供应业	Production and Distribution of Electricity, Heating Power, Gas and Water	1028999	985803	104.4
建筑业	Construction	3566118	3298914	108.1
批发和零售业	Wholesale and Retail Trade	6785183	6215521	109.2
批发业	Wholesale	4796188	4382943	109.4
零售业	Retail Trade	1988995	1832578	108.5
交通运输、仓储和邮政业	Transport, Storage and Post	4816986	4534130	106.2
#铁路运输业	Transport via Railway	943273	929446	101.5
道路运输业	Transport via Road	1627636	1455206	111.8
邮政业	Post	601706	577940	104.1
住宿和餐饮业	Accommodation and Restaurants	1404336	1350865	104.0
住宿业	Accommodation	715018	703362	101.7
餐饮业	Restaurants	689318	647503	106.5
信息传输、软件和信息技术服务业	Information Transmission, Software and Information Technology Services	10457415	8628701	121.2
金融业	Finance	10457828	8857510	118.1
房地产业	Real Estate	3419712	3080021	111.0
租赁和商务服务业	Renting and Leasing Activities and Business Services	7953059	6739051	118.0
租赁业	Renting and Leasing Activities	156936	128322	122.3
商务服务业	Business Services	7796123	6610729	117.9
科学研究和技术服务业	Scientific Research and Development, Technical Services	7475107	6991615	106.9
水利、环境和公共设施管理业	Management of Water Conservancy, Environment and Public Facilities	717418	618061	116.1
居民服务、修理和其他服务业	Resident Services, Repair and Other Services	416799	378141	110.2
#居民服务业	Resident Services	155095	127828	121.3
教育	Education	4961049	4242184	116.9
卫生和社会工作	Health Care and Social Works	3609374	3023218	119.4
#卫生	Health Care	3531283	2962691	119.2
文化、体育和娱乐业	Culture, Sports and Entertainment	2288357	2038800	112.2
#文化艺术业	Cultures and Arts	380350	291910	130.3
体育	Sports Activities	180087	157765	114.1
公共管理、社会保障和社会组织	Public Management, Social Security and Social Organizations	4139309	3434882	120.5
国际组织	International Organizations			

注：行业划分执行2011年国民经济行业分类标准(GB/T 4754-2011)。
Note: Sectors in this table are classified in accordance with the Standard for Classification of National Economic Sectors 2011 (GB/T 4754-2011).

3-22 城镇单位在岗职工平均工资
AVERAGE WAGES OF FULLY EMPLOYED STAFF AND WORKERS IN URBAN ENTITIES

单位：元 (yuan)

项　　目	Item	2015	2014	2015年为2014年% 2015 as % of 2014
合　计	**Total**	**113073**	**103400**	**109.4**
按登记注册类型分	**By Registration Type**			
内　资	Domestically-invested Enterprises	106531	97602	109.1
国　有	State-owned Enterprises	119046	106097	112.2
集　体	Collectively-owed Enterprises	49969	45772	109.2
股份合作	Joint-equity Cooperative Enterprises	42692	41757	102.2
联　营	Associated Enterprises	70578	70004	100.8
有限责任公司	Limited Liability Companies	91233	83932	108.7
股份有限公司	Companies Limited By Shares	147294	146981	100.2
其　他	Others	50998	56947	89.6
港、澳、台商投资	Hong Kong, Macao and Taiwan-invested Enterprises	126537	113719	111.3
外商投资	Foreign-invested Enterprises	152406	134036	113.7
按国民经济行业分	**By Sector**			
农、林、牧、渔业	Agriculture, Forestry, Animal Production and Hunting, Fishing	51214	49798	102.8
#农　业	Agriculture	40761	43357	94.0
采矿业	Mining and Quarrying	88432	90485	97.7
制造业	Manufacturing	87581	79077	110.8
电力、热力、燃气及水生产和供应业	Production and Distribution of Electricity, Heating Power, Gas and Water	131438	113363	115.9
建筑业	Construction	84021	78069	107.6
批发和零售业	Wholesale and Retail Trade	94528	90717	104.2
批发业	Wholesale	119090	114033	104.4
零售业	Retail Trade	63131	60924	103.6
交通运输、仓储和邮政业	Transport, Storage and Post	81608	78294	104.2
#铁路运输业	Transport via Railway	86614	90381	95.8
道路运输业	Transport via Road	57364	53038	108.2
邮政业	Post	82963	74983	110.6
住宿和餐饮业	Accommodation and Restaurants	54731	51164	107.0
住宿业	Accommodation	59015	54638	108.0
餐饮业	Restaurants	50898	47858	106.4
信息传输、软件和信息技术服务业	Information Transmission, Software and Information Technology Service	158210	146996	107.6
金融业	Finance	285795	253148	112.9
房地产业	Real Estate	87044	80407	108.3
租赁和商务服务业	Renting and Leasing Activities and Business Services	104501	102437	102.0
租赁业	Renting and Leasing Activities	76918	66313	116.0
商务服务业	Business Services	105260	103532	101.7
科学研究和技术服务业	Scientific Research and Development, Technical Services	136687	127304	107.4
水利、环境和公共设施管理业	Management of Water Conservancy, Environment and Public Facilities	74242	66184	112.2
居民服务、修理和其他服务业	Resident Services, Repair and Other Services	49481	46320	106.8
#居民服务业	Resident Services	49241	46997	104.8
教　育	Education	115520	103198	111.9
卫生和社会工作	Health Care and Social Works	142971	128410	111.3
#卫　生	Health Care	147464	131786	111.9
文化、体育和娱乐业	Culture, Sports and Entertainment	132675	123807	107.2
#文化艺术业	Cultures and Arts	97398	91373	106.6
体　育	Sports Activities	83590	72194	115.8
公共管理、社会保障和社会组织	Pulic Management,Social Security and Social Organizations	96659	81288	118.9
国际组织	International Organizations			

注：行业划分执行2011年国民经济行业分类标准(GB/T 4754-2011)。
Note: Sectors in this table are classified in accordance with the Standard for Classification of National Economic Sectors 2011 (GB/T 4754-2011).

3-23 国民经济各行业城镇单位在岗职工平均工资(2015年)
AVERAGE WAGES OF URBAN ENTITIES FULLY EMPLOYED STAFF AND WORKERS IN DIFFERENT SECTORS OF NATIONAL ECONOMY (2015)

单位：元 (yuan)

项 目	Item	平均工资 Average Wages	国有单位 State-owned	集体单位 Collectively-Owned	其他单位 Others
合 计	**Total**	**113073**	**119046**	**49969**	**113066**
农、林、牧、渔业	**Agriculture, Forestry, Animal Production and Hunting,Fishing**	**51214**	**64228**	**34491**	**49658**
#农、林、牧、渔服务业	Service Activities for Agriculture, Forestry, Animal Production and Hunting, Fishing	94694	89268	41873	115891
采矿业	**Mining and Quarrying**	**88432**		**45659**	**88928**
煤炭开采和洗选业	Mining and Washing of Coal	72629			72629
石油和天然气开采业	Extraction of Petroleum and Natural Gas	133064			133064
黑色金属矿采选业	Mining and Processing of Ferrous Metal Ores	75366		47748	76064
有色金属矿采选业	Mining and Processing of Non-Ferrous Metal Ores				
非金属矿采选业	Mining and Processing of Nonmetal Ores	52319		28831	59476
开采辅助活动	Mining Support Service Activities	107647			107647
其他采矿业	Mining of Other Ores	116667			116667
制造业	**Manufacturing**	**87581**	**109027**	**42077**	**87611**
农副食品加工业	Processing of Food from Agricultural Products	61277	49981	28654	62353
食品制造业	Manufacture of Foods	70919	76447	27965	71005
酒、饮料和精制茶制造业	Manufacture of Wine, Beverage and Refined Tea	83075	86606	34067	82261
烟草制品业	Manufacture of Cigarettes and Tobacco	223585	223585		
纺织业	Manufacture of Textile	50815	43412	27497	51876
纺织服装、服饰业	Manufacture of Textile, Wearing Apparel and Ornament	49764	50624	38083	50407
皮革、毛皮、羽毛及其制品和制鞋业	Manufacture of Leather, Fur, Feather and Its Products, and Footwear	50377		95107	46461
木材加工和木、竹、藤、棕、草制品业	Processing of Timbers, Manufacture of Wood, Bamboo, Rattan, Palm and Straw Products	45119		29795	46043
家具制造业	Manufacture of Furniture	53062	55250	32038	53230
造纸和纸制品业	Manufacture of Paper and Paper Products	56149	41055	33904	59993
印刷和记录媒介复制业	Printing, Reproduction of Recording Media	68489	76835	58392	67578
文教、工美、体育和娱乐用品制造业	Manufacture of Articles for Culture, Education, Artwork, Sport and Entertainment Activities	56734	46760	47111	57483
石油加工、炼焦和核燃料加工业	Processing of Petroleum, Coking, Processing of Nucleus Fuels	91353	78193	27719	91662
化学原料和化学制品制造业	Manufacture of Chemical Raw Materials and Chemical Products	77262	99717	43648	76938
医药制造业	Manufacture of Medicines	133930	106950	44071	134957
化学纤维制造业	Manufacture of Chemical Fibers	54502			54502
橡胶和塑料制品业	Manufacture of Rubber and Plastics Products	54645	79825	46490	54927
非金属矿物制品业	Manufacture of Non-metallic Mineral Products	61708	59268	38851	62763
黑色金属冶炼和压延加工业	Manufacture and Pressing of Ferrous Metals	66557	69500	30564	67920

注：行业划分执行2011年国民经济行业分类标准(GB/T 4754-2011)。
Note: Sectors in this table are classified in accordance with the Standard for Classification of National Economic Sectors 2011 (GB/T 4754-2011).

3-23 续表 1 Continued 1

单位：元 (yuan)

行业	Sector	平均工资 Average Wages	国有单位 State-owned	集体单位 Collectively-Owned	其他单位 Others
有色金属冶炼和压延加工业	Manufacture and Pressing of Nonferrous Metals	73132	104540	30681	74405
金属制品业	Manufacture of Fabricated Metal Products	62527	49446	40812	64046
通用设备制造业	Manufacture of General-Purpose Machinery	86944	140388	36831	86850
专用设备制造业	Manufacture of Special-Purpose Machinery	92916	109765	43065	93042
汽车制造业	Manufacture of Motor Vehicles	89163	25389	42632	89375
铁路、船舶、航空航天和其他运输设备制造业	Manufacture of Railway Locomotives, Building of Ships and Boats, Manufacture of Air and Spacecrafts and Other Transportation Equipment	110991	147556	36629	95655
电气机械和器材制造业	Manufacture of Electrical Machinery and Equipment	96433	84227	38734	97562
计算机、通信和其他电子设备制造业	Manufacture of Computers, Communication Equipment and Other Electronic Equipment	106331	77644	45776	106768
仪器仪表制造业	Manufacture of Measuring Instruments and Meters	99595	83253	56895	100606
其他制造业	Other Manufacturing	109966	136173	31711	103348
废弃资源综合利用业	Waste Rrecycling and Recovery	64721	27000	30228	70699
金属制品、机械和设备修理业	Repair of Fabricated Metal Products, Machinery and Equipment	108887	59727	40599	110264
电力、热力、燃气及水生产和供应业	**Production and Distribution of Electricity, Heating Power, Gas and Water**	**131438**	**150491**	**42123**	**126792**
电力、热力生产和供应业	Production and Distribution of Electricity and Heating Power	145317	159816	43058	140766
燃气生产和供应业	Production and Distribution of Gas	111948	87792		115498
水的生产和供应业	Production and Distribution of Water	89544	92637	40064	90004
建筑业	**Construction**	**84021**	**90019**	**67391**	**84300**
房屋建筑业	Construction of Buildings	87531	76353	54981	90166
土木工程建筑业	Civil Engineering Construction	92493	107202	83097	90958
建筑安装业	Construction Installation	75402	50916	95693	74952
建筑装饰和其他建筑业	Building Completion, Finishing and Other Constructions	65386	81274	42318	65059
批发和零售业	**Wholesale and Retail Trade**	**94528**	**133450**	**55078**	**93560**
批发业	Wholesale	119090	164332	52430	117685
零售业	Retail Trade	63131	78218	56608	62784
交通运输、仓储和邮政业	**Transport, Storage and Post**	**81608**	**90353**	**31723**	**80350**
铁路运输业	Transport via Railway	86614	95702		66175
道路运输业	Transport via Road	57364	26970	22935	58206
水上运输业	Water Transport	196721			196708
航空运输业	Air Transport	166514	247183		166369
管道运输业	Transport via Pipeline	122080			122080
装卸搬运和运输代理业	Loading, Unloading, Portage and Other Transport Services	92982	85524	61520	94026
仓储业	Storage	66436	78865	34535	62915
邮政业	Post	82963	81333		83676
住宿和餐饮业	**Accommodation and Restaurants**	**54731**	**60211**	**47863**	**54062**
住宿业	Accommodation	59015	60379	52653	58930
餐饮业	Restaurants	50898	58450	34951	50988
信息传输、软件和信息技术服务业	**Information Transmission, Software and Information Technology Services**	**158210**	**146656**	**46491**	**158421**
电信、广播电视和卫星传输服务	Telecommunications, Broadcasting, Television and Satellite Transmission Services	164247	177224	47328	164086
互联网和相关服务	Internet and Related Services	140810	131195	22000	141044
软件和信息技术服务业	Software and Information Technology Services	160487	143285	46694	160733

3-23 续表 2 Continued 2

单位：元 (yuan)

行 业	Sector	平均工资 Average Wages	国有单位 State-owned	集体单位 Collectively-Owned	其他单位 Others
金融业	**Finance**	**285795**	**225831**	**38959**	**287530**
货币金融服务	Monetary Financial Services	275003	238994		276169
资本市场服务	Capital Market Services	467698	169179	57731	482510
保险业	Insurance	215304	271394		214613
其他金融业	Other Financial Services	237205	272890	33928	237525
房地产业	**Real Estate**	**87044**	**84338**	**47433**	**89239**
租赁和商务服务业	**Renting and Leasing Activities and Business Services**	**104501**	**90690**	**34729**	**114390**
租赁业	Renting and Leasing Activities	76918	92145	84235	76082
商务服务业	Business Services	105260	90685	33681	115761
科学研究和技术服务业	**Scientific Research and Development, Technical Services**	**136687**	**159269**	**78561**	**128455**
研究和试验发展	Research and Experimental Development	156765	161826	48445	147566
专业技术服务业	Professional Technique Services	133392	155474	94011	128692
科技推广和应用服务业	Technique Generalization and Application Services	125834	158244	68650	122503
水利、环境和公共设施管理业	**Management of Water Conservancy, Environment and Public Facilities**	**74242**	**76422**	**36279**	**73684**
水利管理业	Management of Water Conservancy	93627	94634	57718	94638
生态保护和环境治理业	Ecological Protection and Environmental Control	117449	104718		121246
公共设施管理业	Management of Public Facilities	68218	72776	34338	63458
居民服务、修理和其他服务业	**Resident Services, Repair and Other Services**	**49481**	**58250**	**35206**	**49204**
居民服务业	Resident Services	49241	55850	35681	48481
机动车、电子产品和日用产品修理业	Repair of Motor Vehicles, Electronics and Household Appliances	59191	66191	41018	60051
其他服务业	Other Services	43073	60683	30787	42127
教 育	**Education**	**115520**	**127303**	**74152**	**72676**
卫生和社会工作	**Health Care and Social Works**	**142971**	**158158**	**87596**	**78452**
卫 生	Health Care	147464	160741	96080	83720
社会工作	Social Works	60130	79579	35296	42944
文化、体育和娱乐业	**Culture, Sports and Entertainment**	**132675**	**154583**	**47353**	**102304**
新闻和出版业	Journalism and Publishing	151582	150202	78497	156408
广播、电视、电影和影视录音制作业	Radio Broadcasting, Television, Movies, Videos and Sound Recording	176276	218900	41719	110886
文化艺术业	Culture and Arts	97398	113953	42285	72378
体 育	Sports Activities	83590	113990	27340	71317
娱乐业	Entertainment	71497	94767	42637	69424
公共管理、社会保障和社会组织	**Public Management, Social Security and Social Organizations**	**96659**	**101072**	**69641**	**48362**
中国共产党机关	Organs of Communist Party of China	110766	110766		
国家机构	Organs of State	99748	99717	115737	126892
人民政协、民主党派	Peole's Political Consultative Conference and Democratic Parties	133788	133788		
社会保障	Social Security	92019	94602	42101	103929
群众团体、社会团体和其他成员组织	Mass Communities, Social Organizations and Other Membership Organizations	118342	121779	77502	115441
基层群众自治组织	Grass Roots Self-Government Organization	23397		22263	23398
国际组织	**International Organizations**				

3-24 城镇登记失业率和城镇新增就业人数(1979-2015年)
REGISTERED UNEMPLOYED RATE IN URBAN AREA AND NEWLY EMPLOYED PERSONS IN URBAN AREA (1979-2015)

单位：万人 (10000 persons)

年 份 Year	年末实有登记失业人员 Year-end Number of Actual Registed Unemployed Persons	城镇登记失业率(%) Registered Unemployment Rate in Urban Area	城镇新增就业人数 Newly Employed Persons in Urban Area
1979	4.96	1.60	
1980	8.67	1.60	
1981	8.36	1.28	
1982	7.03	1.62	
1983	4.20	1.09	
1984	2.03	0.54	
1985	1.61	0.40	
1986	1.25	0.30	
1987	2.24	0.45	
1988	1.58	0.40	
1989	1.71	0.40	
1990	1.67	0.30	
1991	1.92	0.40	
1992	1.72	0.36	
1993	1.92	0.41	
1994	1.91	0.41	
1995	2.19	0.46	
1996	2.80	0.58	
1997	3.29	0.73	
1998	2.95	0.66	
1999	2.80	0.62	
2000	3.32	0.76	
2001	5.19	1.18	
2002	6.02	1.35	
2003	6.96	1.43	
2004	6.46	1.30	
2005	10.57	2.11	31.50
2006	10.40	1.98	34.39
2007	10.63	1.84	40.71
2008	10.33	1.82	41.97
2009	8.16	1.44	42.44
2010	7.73	1.37	44.64
2011	7.89	1.39	44.69
2012	7.20	1.27	43.89
2013	6.81	1.21	42.87
2014	8.77	1.31	42.65
2015	9.16	1.39	42.62

注：2014年开始年末实有登记失业人员指标统计口径为全市口径，2014年以前为城镇口径。

资料来源：北京市人力资源和社会保障局。

Note: Since 2014, the year-end number of actual registered unemployed persons refers to the statistic of the whole city; while the number before 2014 refers to the statistic in urban and rural areas.

Source: Beijing Municipal Bureau of Human Resource and Social Security.

主要统计指标解释

户籍人口 指公民依照《中华人民共和国户口登记条例》已在其经常居住地的公安户籍管理机关登记了常住户口的人。

常住人口 指在某地区实际居住半年以上的人口。

常住外来人口 指不具有本市户籍户口，来自北京市行政区划以外的省、自治区、直辖市，且在京居住半年以上的人口。

出生率 指在一定时期内（通常为一年）出生人数与同期平均人数(或期中人数)之比，一般用千分比表示。计算公式:

$$出生率=\frac{年出生人数}{年平均人数}\times 1000‰$$

出生人数是指活产，即脱离母体时（不管怀孕月数），有过呼吸或其他生命现象的活婴儿总和。年平均人数是年初、年末人口数的平均数，也可用年中人口数代替。

死亡率 指在一定时期内（通常为一年）死亡人数与同期平均人数（或期中人数）之比，一般用千分比表示。计算公式:

$$死亡率=\frac{年死亡人数}{年平均人数}\times 1000‰$$

自然增长率 指在一定时期内（通常为一年）人口自然增加数（出生人数减死亡人数）与该时期内平均人数（或期中人数）之比，一般用千分比表示。计算公式:

$$自然增长率=\frac{年出生人数-年死亡人数}{年平均人数}\times 1000‰$$

人口自然增长率=人口出生率－人口死亡率

从业人员 指在各级国家机关、党政机关、社会团体及企业、事业单位中工作，取得工资或其他形式的劳动报酬的全部人员。包括：在岗职工、聘用的离退休人员以及在单位中工作的港澳台及外籍人员、兼职人员、借用的外单位人员和第二职业者。不包括本单位的不在岗职工。

在岗职工 指在本单位工作并由单位支付工资的人员，以及有工作岗位，但由于学习、病伤产假（六个月以内）等原因暂未工作，仍由单位支付工资的人员。

在岗职工工资总额 与“在岗职工”指标相对应，根据1990年1月1日的国家统计局令（一号）修订，指单位在报告期内直接支付给本单位在岗职工的劳动报酬总额。包括基础工资、职务工资、级别工资、工龄工资、计件工资、奖金、各种津贴和补贴、交通补贴、洗理费、书报费、旅游费、过节费、伙食补助、住房补贴、住房提租补贴、由单位从个人工资中直接为其代扣或代缴的个人所得税、房水电费以及住房公积金和社会保险基金个人缴纳部分等。

在岗职工平均工资 指企业、事业、机关等单位的在岗职工在一定时期内的人均劳动报酬。它表明一定时期在岗职工工资收入的高低程度，是反映在岗职工工资水平的主要指标。计算公式为:

$$在岗职工平均工资=\frac{报告期实际支付的全部在岗职工工资总额}{报告期全部在岗职工平均人数}$$

从业人员平均工资 指企业、事业、机关等单位的从业人员在一定时期内的人均劳动报酬。计算公式为:

$$从业人员平均工资=\frac{报告期实际支付的全部从业人员劳动报酬总额}{报告期全部从业人员平均人数}$$

期末实有登记失业人员 指报告期末实有的登记失业人员总数，包括城镇登记失业人员和城市化建设地区的登记失业农民（失地农民）。

城镇登记失业率 指城镇登记失业人数与城镇从业人数和城镇登记失业人数二者之和的比。计算公式如下:

$$城镇登记失业率=\frac{年末实有登记失业人数}{城镇从业人数+年末实有登记失业人数}\times 100\%$$

Explanatory Notes on Main Statistical Indicators

Registered Population refers to persons who have registered their permanent residence with the public security register authority of their habitual residence according to the Households Registration Regulations of PRC.

Permanent Population refers to persons actually living for more than half a year at a place.

Permanent Migrant Population refers to persons who have no permanent residence registration in Beijing, come from other provinces, autonomous regions and municipalities, and have stayed in Beijing for more than half a year.

Birth Rate refers to the ratio of the number of births to the average population (or mid-period population) during a certain period of time (usually a year), which is often expressed in ‰. The following formula is used:

Birth Rate = Annual Number of Births/Annual Average Number of Population×1,000‰

Number of births refers to live births i.e. the births when babies had shown any vital phenomena regardless of the length of pregnancy. Annual average number of population is the average of the number of population at the beginning of the year and that at the end of the year. Sometimes it is substituted with the mid-year population.

Death Rate refers to the ratio of the number of deaths to the average population (or mid-period population) during a certain period of time (usually a year), which is often expressed in ‰. The following formula is used:

Death Rate= Annual Number of Deaths/Annual Average Number of Population×1,000‰

Natural Growth Rate refers to the ratio of the natural growth of population (births minus deaths) to the average population (or mid-period population) during a certain period of time (usually a year), which is often expressed in ‰. The following formula is used:

Natural Growth Rate of Population = (Annual Number of Births - Annual Number of Deaths)/Annual Average Number of Population×1,000‰

Natural Growth Rate of Population = Birth Rate - Death Rate

Employed Persons refer to all persons working in government agencies, Party and political organs, social groups, enterprises and public institutions at all levels, and receiving wages or labor remuneration in other forms. They include: fully employed staff and workers, retired persons employed, persons from Hong Kong, Macao, Taiwan and foreign countries who are employed, part-time employees, employees transferred from other entities, and employees with a second job. They exclude employees that are not on the job in the entity.

Fully Employed Staff and Workers refer to persons working in the entity and paid by the entity, as well as persons having a job in the entity, but not working temporarily due to study, illness, injury or maternity leaves (less than 6 months) and other reasons, and still paid by the entity.

Total Wages of Full-time Staff and Workers corresponds to the indicator Full-time Staff and Workers. The indicator was revised in accordance with No. 1 Decree of the National Bureau of Statistics dated January 1, 1990, referring to the total wages directly paid by an entity to full-time staff and workers of the entity during the reporting period. It consists of basic wage, position-based wage, post wage, wage of a rank, piece rate wage, bonus, allowances and subsidies, traffic subsidy, washing and haircutting allowance, books and newspaper allowance, travel benefit, festival bonus, food subsidy, housing subsidy, subsidy for incremental house rent, as well as personal income tax, water and electricity fees and the personally payable portion of housing accumulation fund and social security fund withheld directly by the employer from the employee's wage.

Average Wage of Full-time Staff and Workers refers to the per-capita labor remuneration of full-time staff and workers in enterprises, public institutions and government agencies within a given period of time. It shows the level of wage income of fully employed staff and workers within a given period of time, serving as a main indicator reflecting the level of wage of fully employed staff and workers. The following formula is used:

Average Wage of Full-time Staff and Workers = Total Wages of Full-time Staff and Workers Actually Paid in the Reporting Period / Total Number of Full-time Staff and Workers in the Reporting Period

Average Wage of Employed Persons refers to the per-capita labor remuneration of employed persons in enterprises and government agencies within a given period of time. The following formula is used:

Average Wage of Employed Persons = Total Wages of All Employed Persons Actually Paid in the Reporting Period / Total Number of Employed Persons in the Reporting Period

Number of Actual Registered Unemployed Persons in Urban Area at Year-end refers to the actual number of unemployed persons registered at the year end (including all unemployed persons receiving unemployment insurance benefit).

Period-end Actual Registered Unemployed Persons refer to the total number of actual unemployed persons registered at the end period, including unemployed persons registered in urban regions and the unemployed peasants registered in urbanization regions (land-lost peasants).

Registered Unemployment Rate in Urban Area refers to the ratio of urban registered unemployed persons to the sum of urban staff and workers and urban registered unemployed persons. The following formula is used:

Registered Unemployment Rate in Urban Area =Number of Actual Registered Unemployed Persons at Year-end / (Urban Employed Persons + Number of Actual Registered Unemployed Persons at Year-end) × 100%

04

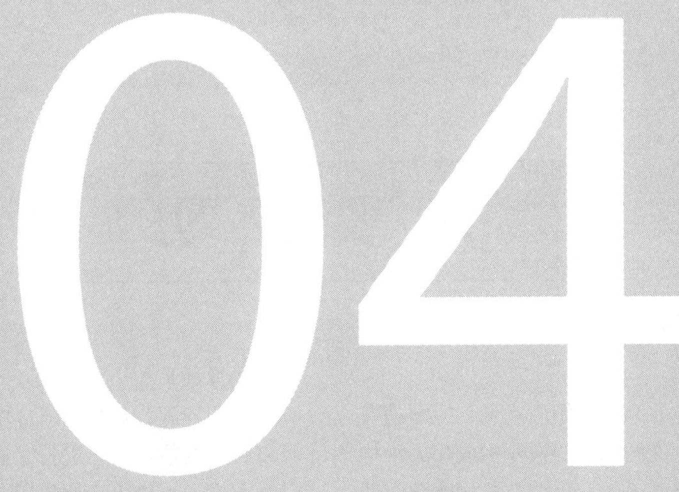

北京统计年鉴2016　BEIJING STATISTICAL YEARBOOK

能源、资源和环境
ENERGY, RESOURCES AND ENVIRONMENT

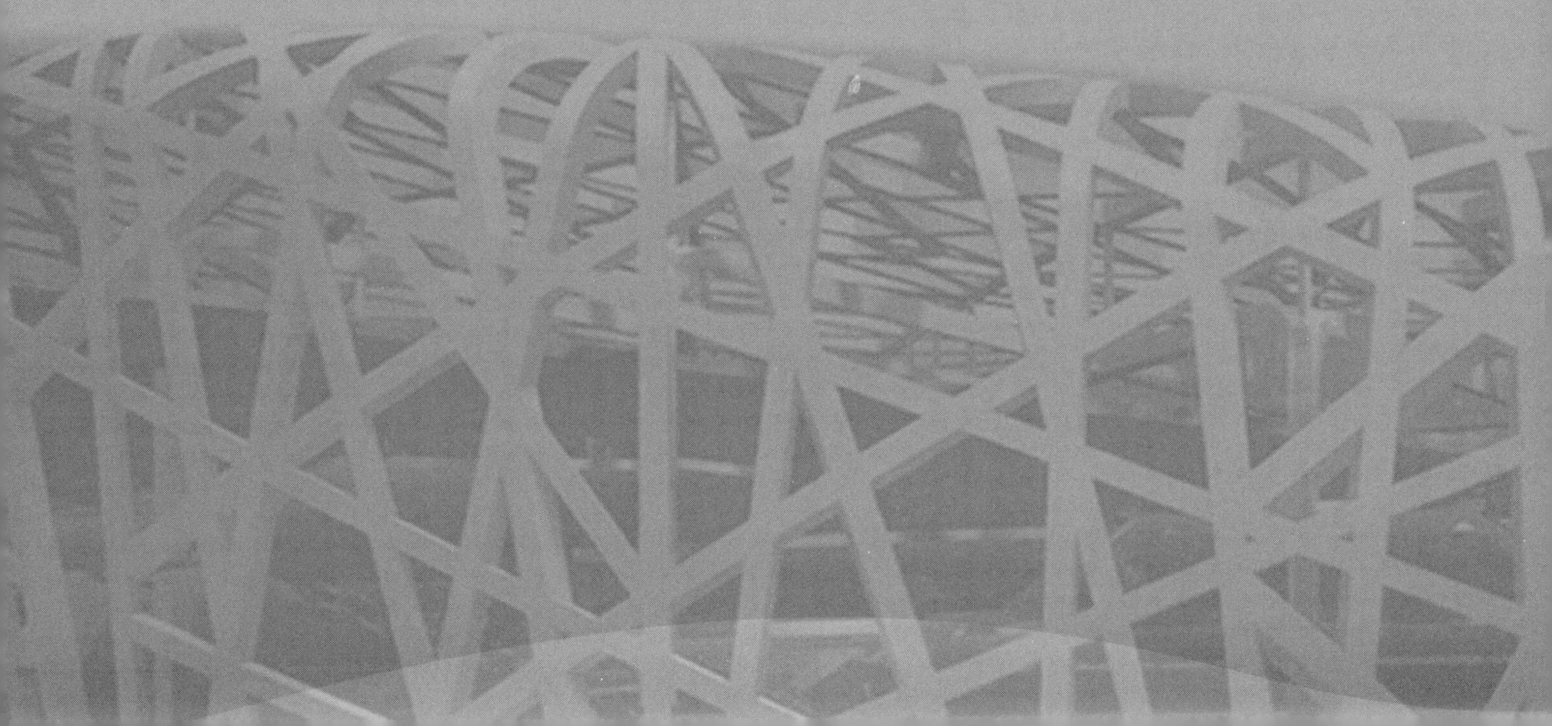

简要说明

一、本章资料的主要内容

本章包括的主要内容有：北京市能源生产量、能源消费量、万元地区生产总值能耗、能源消费的行业构成和品种构成、能源平衡表、能源消费弹性系数、人均及日均能源消费量和北京地区用电量情况；土地利用情况；气象情况、水资源情况、排水及节水情况；园林绿化及森林情况；大气环境、固体废物处置情况等环境保护资料。

二、本章资料的统计范围

本章能源部分统计范围为全社会口径。

三、本章资料的数据来源

本章能源部分由北京市统计局、国家统计局北京调查总队提供；土地利用情况由北京市国土资源局提供；气象资料由北京市气象局提供；水资源、排水及节水情况由北京市水务局提供；城市环境卫生由北京市市政市容管理委员会提供；环境保护资料由北京市环境保护局提供。

四、本章中关于历史数据调整的问题

本章中 2008 年能源消费数据为第二次经济普查数据，1995-2007 年的能源消费数据已根据北京市第二次全国经济普查的数据结果进行了修正。1997-2007 年的万元地区生产总值能耗及下降率、万元地区生产总值水耗及下降率、能源消费弹性系数、平均每万元地区生产总值能源消费量中使用的地区生产总值数据，已根据北京市第二次全国经济普查和北京市第二次全国农业普查的数据结果进行了修正。

2013 年能源消费数据为第三次全国经济普查数据。2005-2012 年的能源生产量、能源消费总量、万元地区生产总值能耗及下降率，以及 2010-2012 年的能源消费构成、能源消费弹性系数、平均每万元地区生产总值能源消费量、人均生活用能源、主要能源日均消费量数据已根据第三次全国经济普查的数据结果进行了修正。

本章中人均生活用能、人均水资源按年平均常住人口计算；同时，根据北京市第六次全国人口普查的数据结果对 2006-2010 年的人均指标数据进行了修正。

五、有关统计标准的变化说明

（一）关于行业划分。根据国家统计局规定，自 2012 年开始执行《国民经济行业分类》GB/T 4754-2011 标准。

（二）关于三次产业划分。根据国家统计局《三次产业划分规定》（国统字[2012]108 号），对三次产业的范围进行了调整。其中第一产业是指农、林、牧、渔业（不含农、林、牧、渔服务业）；第二产业是指采矿业（不含开采辅助活动），制造业（不含金属制品、机械和设备修理业），电力、热力、燃气及水生产和供应业，建筑业；第三产业是指除第一产业、第二产业以外的其他行业。自 2012 年开始执行此规定。

六、全市能源统计的内容及能源消费量的测算方法

全市能源统计主要内容包括第二、三产业限额以上法人单位能源消费情况全面调查；限额以下法人单位能源消费情况抽样调查；农业生产能源消费统计；居民生活能源消费情况抽样调查；能源供应部门的能源供应情况等。

从全市范围看，各能源品种的生产量、供应量和消费量存在平衡关系。因此，在进行生产和居民生活的能源消费量测算时，根据全市各能源品种的生产量、供应量和供应结构进行平衡修正。

Brief Introduction

I. Main Content

This chapter consists of statistics for volume of energy production and energy consumption in Beijing, energy consumption in regions with RMB 10,000 GDP, energy consumption by sector and by type, energy balance sheet, energy consumption elasticity coefficient, per-capita and daily energy consumption and electricity consumption in Beijing; land utilization; meteorology, water resources, water drainage and water saving; landscaping and forest; atmospheric environment, solid waste disposal and other environmental protection data.

II. Scope of Statistics

In this chapter, statistics on energy cover the entire society.

III. Source of Statistics

Energy statistics are from Beijing Municipal Bureau of Statistics, and the NBS Survey Office in Beijing; statistics on land utilization are from Beijing Municipal Bureau of Land and Resources; meteorology statistics are from Beijing Meteorological Service; water resources, water drainage and water saving statistics are from Beijing Water Authority; urban environment and sanitation statistics are from Beijing Municipal Commission of City Administration and Environment; other statistics on environmental protection are from Beijing Municipal Environmental Protection Bureau.

IV. Adjustment to Historical Statistics

Total energy consumption figures of 2008 in this chapter are the results from the "second economic census". Statistics on total energy consumption from 1995 to 2007 are corrected based on the second national economic census in Beijing. Figures of GDP of Beijing used in the 1997-2007 energy consumption and decrease rate in regions with RMB 10,000 GDP, water consumption and decrease rate in regions with RMB 10,000 GDP, energy consumption elasticity coefficient, and energy consumption in regions with per RMB 10,000 GDP by different energy have been corrected in accordance with results from the second economic census and the second agricultural census.

Energy consumption figures of 2013 are the results from the 3rd national economic census. Figures of energy production, total energy consumption, energy consumption and decrease rate in regions with RMB 10,000 GDP in the 2005-2012, as well as the energy consumption structure, energy consumption elasticity coefficient, energy consumption in regions with per RMB 10,000 GDP by different energy, per-capita energy consumption for living and average daily consumption of primary energy in the 2010-2012 have been corrected in accordance with results from the third national economic census.

In this chapter, the per-capita energy consumption for living and per-capita water resources are calculated by average permanent population; at the same time, per-capita index figures from 2006 to 2010 have been corrected in accordance with the sixth national population census.

V. Changes in Relevant Statistical Standards

(I) Classification of Sectors. According to relevant provisions of the National Bureau of Statistics of the People's Republic of China, the *Classification of National Economic Sectors* (Standard GB/T 4754-2011) came into effect in 2012.

(II) Classification of Three Industries. According to the *Regulations on Three Industries Classification* (G.T.Z. [2012] No. 108) of National Bureau of Statistics, the scope of three industries has been adjusted. The primary industry refers to agriculture, forestry, animal production and hunting, fishing (excluding service activities for agriculture, forestry, animal production and hunting, fishing); secondary industry refers to mining and quarrying (excluding mining support service activities), manufacturing (excluding repair of fabricated metal products, machinery and equipment), production and distribution of electricity, heating power, gas and water and construction; the tertiary industry refers to others excluding the primary and secondary industries. The Provisions of the National Bureau of Statistics on *Regulations on Three Industries Classification* (G.T.Z. [2012] No. 108) came into effect in 2012.

VI. Content of Energy Statistics in Beijing and Calculation Method of Energy Consumption

Energy statistics in Beijing include complete survey on energy consumption in entities above designated size in the secondary and tertiary industries; sample survey on energy consumption in entities below designated size; statistics on energy consumption in agricultural production; sample survey on energy consumption in residents' living and energy supply in energy supply departments, etc.

In terms of the whole city, the volume of production, supply and consumption shall be balanced among all types of energy. Therefore, in the calculation of energy consumption in production and residents' living by using the above-mentioned method, a balanced correction shall be made according to the volume of production, supply and supply structure of all types of energy in the city.

4-1 能源生产量(2005-2015年)
ENERGY PRODUCTION (2005-2015)

项目		Item		2005	2006	2007	2008	2009	2010
一次能源	**(万吨标准煤)**	**Primary Energy**	**(10000 tons of SCE)**	**679.5**	**460.6**	**466.1**	**414.2**	**475.7**	**499.9**
#原煤	(万吨)	Raw Coal	(10000 tons)	945.2	642.1	648.8	578.5	641.3	500.1
二次能源	**(万吨标准煤)**	**Secondary Energy**	**(10000 tons of SCE)**	**2772.6**	**2632.9**	**2767.9**	**3104.9**	**3146.9**	**3418.3**
#汽油	(万吨)	Gasoline	(10000 tons)	142.2	145.6	160.4	202.3	242.1	247.7
煤油	(万吨)	Kerosene	(10000 tons)	12.4	11.6	36.4	85.2	111.6	116.1
柴油	(万吨)	Diesel Oil	(10000 tons)	154.7	167.1	244.7	354.8	314.8	314.5
燃料油	(万吨)	Fuel Oil	(10000 tons)	64.5	57.9	36.7	28.6	28.0	33.7
液化石油气	(万吨)	Liquefied Petroleum Gas	(10000 tons)	47.3	23.0	41.0	42.9	28.8	29.0
热力	(万百万千焦)	Heat	(10 billion kilo-joules)	11335.7	12181.6	12686.9	13650.5	14226.1	15345.0
电力	(亿千瓦时)	Electricity	(100 million kwh)	209.8	209.7	224.2	244.7	241.9	262.0

4-1 续表 Continued

项目		Item		2011	2012	2013	2014	2015
一次能源	**(万吨标准煤)**	**Primary Energy**	**(10000 tons of SCE)**	**500.3**	**507.2**	**541.7**	**514.0**	**545.6**
#原煤	(万吨)	Raw Coal	(10000 tons)	500.1	493.1	500.1	457.5	450.1
二次能源	**(万吨标准煤)**	**Secondary Energy**	**(10000 tons of SCE)**	**3080.9**	**3155.5**	**3019.0**	**3333.2**	**3476.8**
#汽油	(万吨)	Gasoline	(10000 tons)	245.3	255.2	223.9	287.4	296.3
煤油	(万吨)	Kerosene	(10000 tons)	126.4	132.9	99.4	152.3	160.0
柴油	(万吨)	Diesel Oil	(10000 tons)	309.3	274.5	194.7	219.8	180.4
燃料油	(万吨)	Fuel Oil	(10000 tons)	21.3	18.4	16.9	4.7	1.4
液化石油气	(万吨)	Liquefied Petroleum Gas	(10000 tons)	27.2	31.9	28.1	32.1	34.0
热力	(万百万千焦)	Heat	(10 billion kilo-joules)	14795.5	15400.5	14893.6	15055.4	15819.7
电力	(亿千瓦时)	Electricity	(100 million kwh)	256.1	283.3	326.7	351.6	412.5

注：2013年数据为第三次全国经济普查数据。2005-2012年数据根据第三次经济普查的数据结果进行了修正。

Note: Data for 2013 were collected from the third national economic census.Data for 2005-2012 were revised acording to the third national economic census.

4-2 能源消费总量及构成情况(2010-2015年)
PRIMARY ENERGY CONSUMPTION AND ITS COMPOSITION(2010-2015)

年 份 Year	能源消费总量 (万吨标准煤) Total Energy Consumption (10000 tons of SCE)	占能源消费总量的比重 (%) As Percentage of Primary Energy Production (%)				
		煤 品 Coal	油 品 Petroleum	天然气 Natural Gas	电 力 Primary Electricity	其他能源 Primary Electricity
2010	6359.5	29.6	30.9	14.6	24.8	0.1
2011	6397.3	26.7	32.9	14.0	26.1	0.3
2012	6564.1	25.2	31.6	17.1	25.8	0.3
2013	6723.9	23.3	32.2	18.2	25.3	1.0
2014	6831.2	20.4	32.6	21.1	24.4	1.5
2015	6852.6	13.7	33.5	29.0	21.9	1.9

注：2013年数据为第三次全国经济普查数据。2010-2012年数据根据第三次全国经济普查的数据结果进行了修正。

Note: Data for 2013 were collected from the third national economic census.Data for 2010-2012 were revised acording to the third national economic census.

4-3 能源消费总量及万元地区生产总值能耗(1980-2015年)
TOTAL ENERGY CONSUMPTION AND ENERGY CONSUMPTION PER 10000 YUAN OF GDP (1980-2015)

单位：万吨标准煤 (10000 tons of SCE)

年 份 Year	能源消费总量 Total Energy Consumption	第一产业 Primary Industry	第二产业 Secondary Industry	第三产业 Tertiary Industry	生 活 消 费 Residential Consumption	万元地区生产总值能耗（吨标准煤） Energy Consumption per 10000 yuan of GDP (ton of SCE)	万元地区生产总值能耗下降率(%) Decrease Rate of Energy Consumption per 10000 yuan GDP(%)
1980	1907.7	66.8	1400.3	297.6	143.0	13.715	
1981	1902.6	53.3	1339.4	334.9	175.0	13.668	-0.23
1982	1920.4	55.7	1346.2	338.0	180.5	12.398	6.02
1983	1984.7	73.4	1379.4	313.6	218.3	10.839	11.22
1984	2144.1	85.8	1470.9	347.3	240.1	9.899	7.98
1985	2211.4	90.7	1488.3	351.6	280.8	8.601	5.12
1986	2400.0	95.7	1612.0	380.4	311.9	8.424	-0.49
1987	2475.8	89.0	1647.8	424.7	314.3	7.576	5.88
1988	2612.6	111.7	1748.1	412.2	340.6	6.369	6.45
1989	2653.2	114.4	1735.9	427.0	375.9	5.818	2.73
1990	2709.7	105.7	1720.1	515.3	368.6	5.411	2.92
1991	2872.0	126.7	1807.6	542.0	395.7	4.795	3.56
1992	2987.5	143.6	1888.1	552.4	403.4	4.213	6.54
1993	3264.6	133.6	2150.9	561.0	419.1	3.684	2.69
1994	3385.9	143.6	2234.1	574.8	433.4	2.956	8.78
1995	3533.3	120.4	2328.4	632.7	451.8	2.344	6.83
1996	3734.5	110.8	2477.0	698.1	448.6	2.087	2.75
1997	3719.2	95.7	2369.6	799.8	454.1	1.792	9.55
1998	3808.1	96.2	2400.5	856.4	455.0	1.603	6.49
1999	3906.6	86.9	2370.7	971.8	477.2	1.459	7.49
2000	4144.0	104.8	2424.8	1080.9	533.5	1.311	5.12
2001	4229.2	105.4	2366.6	1196.2	561.0	1.198	8.62
2002	4436.1	103.0	2414.6	1334.5	584.0	1.127	5.93
2003	4648.2	99.9	2476.7	1391.0	680.6	1.062	5.73
2004	5139.6	85.6	2664.2	1638.0	751.8	1.029	3.09
2005	5049.8	85.4	2363.7	1771.7	829.0	0.902 (0.725)	4.17
2006	5399.3	91.1	2421.2	1962.8	924.2	0.686	5.37
2007	5747.7	95.1	2434.6	2198.4	1019.6	0.637	7.02
2008	5786.2	95.2	2215.6	2394.3	1081.1	0.588	7.74
2009	6008.6	97.1	2206.5	2527.3	1177.7	0.554	5.76
2010	6359.5	98.5	2364.1	2654.4	1242.5	0.532 (0.451)	4.04
2011	6397.3	98.3	2160.1	2818.9	1320.0	0.419	6.95
2012	6564.1	98.1	2082.1	2967.0	1416.9	0.399	4.75
2013	6723.9	97.3	2079.2	3109.1	1438.3	0.380	4.88
2014	6831.2	91.7	1998.4	3236.5	1504.6	0.360	5.29
2015	6852.6	84.6	1902.7	3312.6	1552.7	0.338 (0.298)	6.13

注：1. 本表能源消费量指标按等价值计算,万元地区生产总值能耗下降率按可比价格计算。
2. 2000年及以前万元地区生产总值能耗按当年价格计算；2000年以后按可比价格计算，可比价格每五年调整一次基期，更换基期年份计算两个可比价数据，括号内数据按新基期价格计算。
3. 2013年数据为第三次全国经济普查数据。2005-2012年数据根据第三次全国经济普查的数据结果进行了修正。

Note: a) Enery consumption in this table is at equivalent prices. Reduction rate of Energy Consumption per 10000 yuan of GDP is calculated at comparable prices.
b) Energy consumption per 10000 yuan of GDP before 2000 was calculated at the price of that year; figures after 2000 were calculated at comparable prices. The base period of comparable prices is changed every five years. Two figures at comparable prices were calculated for the year in which the base period is changed. Figures in brackets were calculated at the price of new base period.
c) Data for 2013 were collected from the third national economic census.Data for 2005-2012 were revised acording to the third national economic census.

4-4 按行业分能源消费总量
TOTAL ENERGY CONSUMPTION BY SECTOR

单位：万吨标准煤 (10000 tons of SCE)

项　　目	Item	2015	2014
能源消费总量	**Total Energy Consumption**	**6852.6**	**6831.2**
按产业分组	**By There Industies**		
第一产业	Primary Industry	84.6	91.7
第二产业	Secondary Industry	1902.7	1998.4
第三产业	Tertiary Industry	3312.6	3236.5
生活消费	Residential Consumption	1552.7	1504.6
按行业分组	**By Sector**		
#采矿业	Mining and Quarrying	17.2	22.2
制造业	Manufacturing	1292.5	1332.8
电力、热力、燃气及水生产和供应业	Production and Distribution of Electricity, Heating Pewer, Gas and Water	474.7	518.5
建筑业	Construction	118.3	124.9
批发和零售业	Wholesale and Retail Trade	198.5	194.2
交通运输、仓储和邮政业	Transport, Storage and Post	1249.4	1204.2
住宿和餐饮业	Accommodation and Restaurants	299.1	292.0
信息传输、软件和信息技术服务业	Information Transmission,Software and Information Technology Services	164.9	148.4
金融业	Finance	66.8	68.4
房地产业	Real Estate	376.9	374.9
租赁和商务服务业	Renting and Leasing Activities and Business Services	195.5	210.5
科学研究和技术服务业	Scientific Research and Development, Technical Services	170.9	159.8
水利、环境和公共设施管理业	Management of Water Conservancy, Environment and Public Facilities	60.3	61.5
居民服务、修理和其他服务业	Resident Services, Repair and Other Services	30.3	32.7
教　育	Education	228.7	220.5
卫生和社会工作	Healtlcare and Social Works	84.1	84.7
文化、体育和娱乐业	Culture, Sports and Entertainment	72.2	65.4
公共管理、社会保障和社会组织	Public Administration, Social Security and Social Organizations	115.0	119.3

注：1. 行业划分执行《国民经济行业分类》(GB/T 4754—2011)标准(下同)。
2. 2012年开始执行国家统计局《三次产业划分规定》，具体调整内容见本章简要说明(下同)。

Note: a) Sectors in this table are classified in accordance with Standard for Classification of National Economic Sectors (GB/T 4754-2011) (the same below).
b) From 2012, Classification of Three Industires released by National Bureau of Statistics became effective. See brief introduction to this chapter for detailed changes (the same below).

4-5 按三次产业分万元地区生产总值能耗及能耗下降率(2001–2015年)
ENERGY CONSUMPTION PER 10000 YUAN OF GDP AND DECREASE RATE BY THREE INDUSTRIES (2001-2015)

单位：吨标准煤 (ton of SCE)

年 份	万元地区生产总值能耗	按产业分组 By Three Industies			按主要行业分组 By Sector	
Year	Energy Consumption per 10000 yuan of GDP	第一产业 Primary Industry	第二产业 Secondary Industry	第三产业 Tertiary Industry	#工 业 Industry	#交通运输、仓储和邮政业 Transport, Storage and Post
2001	1.198	1.282	2.091	0.516	2.460	1.633
2002	1.127	1.220	1.968	0.508	2.318	1.675
2003	1.062	1.196	1.803	0.476	2.114	1.564
2004	1.029	1.031	1.658	0.496	1.898	1.929
2005	0.902	1.049	1.336	0.473	1.527	1.757
	(0.725)	(0.963)	(1.166)	(0.365)	(1.333)	(1.244)
2006	0.686	1.021	1.081	0.354	1.249	1.476
2007	0.637	1.044	0.965	0.343	1.108	1.588
2008	0.588	1.034	0.871	0.332	0.998	1.802
2009	0.554	1.008	0.785	0.319	0.902	1.801
2010	0.532	1.039	0.740	0.306	0.839	1.739
	(0.451)	(0.792)	(0.698)	(0.250)	(0.804)	(1.371)
2011	0.419	0.783	0.598	0.245	0.683	1.362
2012	0.399	0.757	0.536	0.239	0.616	1.336
2013	0.380	0.740	0.509	0.230	0.569	1.325
2014	0.360	0.697	0.458	0.223	0.516	1.304
2015	0.338	0.721	0.422	0.211	0.486	1.300
	(0.298)	(0.603)	(0.419)	(0.181)	(0.481)	(1.270)

注：1. 万元地区生产总值能耗按可比价格计算，可比价格每五年调整一次基期，更换基期年份计算两个可比价数据，括号内数据是按新基期价格计算。

2. 2013年数据为第三次全国经济普查数据。2005–2012年数据根据第三次经济普查的数据结果进行了修正。

Note: a) Energy consumption per 10000 yuan of GDP were calculated at comparable prices. The base period of comparable prices is changed every five years. Two figures at comparable prices were calculated for the year in which the base period is changed. Figures in brackets were calculated at the price of new base period.

b) Data for 2013 were collected from the third national economic census.Data for 2005-2012 were revised acording to the third national economic census.

4-5 续表 Continued

单位：% (%)

年 份 Year	万元地区生产总值能耗下降率 Decrease Rate of Energy Consumption per 10000 yuan GDP	按产业分组 By Three Industies			按主要行业分组 By Sector	
		第一产业 Primary Industry	第二产业 Secondary Industry	第三产业 Tertiary Industry	#工 业 Industry	#交通运输、仓储和邮政业 Transport, Storage and Post
2001	8.62	2.98	10.90	2.13	11.91	-14.90
2002	5.93	4.83	5.88	1.56	5.75	-2.60
2003	5.73	1.96	8.39	6.23	8.80	6.66
2004	3.09	13.79	8.04	-4.08	10.22	-23.40
2005	4.17	-2.80	7.89	-3.25	8.07	-2.24
2006	5.37	-6.08	7.31	3.04	6.32	-18.63
2007	7.02	-2.21	10.79	2.95	11.24	-7.63
2008	7.74	0.98	9.71	3.19	9.93	-13.43
2009	5.76	2.45	9.81	4.20	9.68	0.07
2010	4.04	-3.05	5.79	3.89	6.92	3.41
2011	6.95	1.07	14.35	2.31	15.07	0.64
2012	4.75	3.29	10.32	2.42	9.83	1.87
2013	4.88	3.87	7.50	2.90	7.72	0.36
2014	5.29	5.76	10.06	3.14	9.43	1.60
2015	6.13	-3.41	7.80	5.33	5.67	0.31

注：表内万元地区生产总值能耗下降率按可比价格计算。

Note: Energy consumption per 10000 yuan of GDP decrease rate is at comparable prices.

4-6 电力平衡表
ELECTRICITY BALANCE

单位：亿千瓦时 (100 million kwh)

项　　目	Item	2015	2014
可供本地区消费的能源量	**Total Energy Available for Local Consumption**	**541.44**	**577.77**
加工转换投入(-)产出(+)量	**Input(-) or Output(+) in Processing and Conversion**	**412.53**	**351.57**
火力发电	Thermal Power	412.53	351.57
供　热	Heating		
煤炭洗选	Washing of Coal		
炼　焦	Coking		
炼油及煤制油	Oil Refining and Coal to Liquid		
#油品再投入量(-)	Oil Product Re-input(-)		
制　气	Gas Production		
#焦炭再投入量(-)	Coke Re-input(-)		
煤制品加工	Coal Product Processing		
回收能	**Energy Recycled**		
损失量	**Losses**	**61.29**	**59.94**
#运输和输配损失	In Transportation and Transmission	61.29	59.94
终端消费量	**End-use Energy Consumption**	**889.96**	**873.47**
第一产业	Primary Industry	18.50	18.56
第二产业	Secondary Industry	249.65	260.77
工业	Industry	228.89	238.38
#用作原料、材料	Use as Materials		
建筑业	Construction	20.76	22.38
第三产业	Tertiary Industry	447.05	424.88
生活消费	Residential Consumption	174.76	169.26
城镇	Urban	149.61	145.74
乡村	Rural	25.15	23.52
平衡差额	Balance	2.72	-4.07
消费量合计	**Total Energy Consumption**	**951.25**	**933.41**

4-7 综合能源平衡表(标准量)
COMPREHENSIVE ENERGY BALANCE (STANDARD VOLUME)

单位：万吨标准煤 (10000 tons of SCE)

项　　目	Item	2015	2014
可供本地区消费的能源量	**Total Energy Available for Consumption**	**6860.13**	**6818.29**
加工转换投入(-)产出(+)量	**Input(-) or Output(+) in Processing and Conversion**	**-73.90**	**-83.45**
火力发电	Thermal Power		
供　热	Heating	-81.24	-94.52
煤炭洗选	Washing of Coal	-0.02	-0.11
炼　焦	Coking		
炼油及煤制油	Oil Refining and Coal to Liquid	345.18	300.81
#油品再投入量(-)	Oil Product Re-input(-)	-353.95	-308.12
制　气	Gas Production		
#焦炭再投入量(-)	Coke Re-input(-)		
煤制品加工	Coal Product Processing	-0.26	-0.34
回收能	**Energy Recycled**	**16.39**	**18.83**
损失量	**Losses**	**217.64**	**233.66**
#运输和输配损失	In Transportation and Transmission	171.13	172.11
终端消费量	**End-use Energy Consumption**	**6561.01**	**6514.12**
第一产业	Primary Industry	84.56	91.69
第二产业	Secondary Industry	1611.18	1681.25
工 业	Industry	1492.88	1556.40
#用作原料、材料	Use as Materials	285.64	279.86
建筑业	Construction	118.30	124.85
第三产业	Tertiary Industry	3312.56	3236.55
生活消费	Residential Consumption	1552.71	1504.63
城　镇	Urban	1297.69	1248.07
乡　村	Rural	255.02	256.56
平衡差额	Balance	7.58	-12.94
消费量合计	**Total Energy Consumption**	**6852.55**	**6831.23**

4-8 能源平衡表(实物量简表)(2015年)
ENERGY BALANCE (PHYSICAL VOLUME) (SIMPLE EDITION) (2015)

单位：万吨 (10000 tons)

项目	Item	原煤 Coal	洗精煤 Washed Coal	其他洗煤 Other Washed Coal	煤制品 Coal Products	煤矸石 Coal Slack	焦炭 Coke	焦炉煤气(亿立方米) Coking Gas (100 million cu.m)
可供本地区消费的能源量	**Total Energy Available for Local Consumption**	**1153.57**	**6.76**	**0.03**	**4.82**		**0.44**	
加工转换投入(-)产出(+)量	**Input(-) or Output(+) in Procesing and Conversion**	**-507.85**	**-6.72**		**-0.97**			
火力发电	Thermal Power	-157.58			-3.66			
供 热	Heating	-347.24			-9.57			
煤炭洗选	Washing of Coal	-3.03	1.95					
炼 焦	Coking							
炼油及煤制油	Oil Refining and Coal to Liquid							
#油品再投入量(-)	Oil Product Re-input(-)							
制 气	Gas Production							
#焦炭再投入量(-)	Coke Re-input(-)							
煤制品加工	Coal Product Processing		-8.67		12.26			
回收能	**Energy Recycled**							
损失量	**Losses**							
#运输和输配损失	In Transportation and Transmission							
终端消费量	**End-use Energy Consumption**	**645.72**	**0.04**	**0.03**	**3.85**		**0.44**	
第一产业	Primary Industry	30.50						
第二产业	Secondary Industry	163.87	0.01		0.47		0.43	
工 业	Industry	158.14	0.01		0.13		0.43	
#用作原料、材料	Use as Materials	0.18						
建筑业	Construction	5.73			0.34			
第三产业	Tertiary Industry	178.33	0.03	0.03	3.38		0.01	
生活消费	Residential Consumption	273.02						
城 镇	Urban	101.21						
乡 村	Rural	171.81						
平衡差额	Balance							
消费量合计	**Total Energy Consumption**	**1153.57**	**8.71**	**0.03**	**17.08**		**0.44**	

4-8 续表 1 Continued 1

单位：万吨 (10000 tons)

项 目	Item	高炉煤气（亿立方米）Blast Furnace Gas (100 million cu.m)	转炉煤气（亿立方米）Converter Gas (100 million cu.m)	其它煤气（亿立方米）Other Gas (100 million cu.m)	其它焦化产品 Other Carbonized Products	原油 Crude Oil	汽油 Gaso-line	煤油 Kero-sene
可供本地区消费的能源量	**Total Energy Available for Local Consumption**					**991.55**	**166.43**	**384.39**
加工转换投入(-)产出(+)量	**Input(-) or Output(+) in Procesing and Conversion**					**-989.85**	**296.32**	**160.00**
火力发电	Thermal Power							
供 热	Heating							
煤炭洗选	Washing of Coal							
炼 焦	Coking							
炼油及煤制油	Oil Refining and Coal to Liquid					-989.85	296.32	160.00
#油品再投入量(-)	Re-inputs of Oil Products							
制 气	Gas Production							
#焦炭再投入量(-)	Coke Re-input(-)							
煤制品加工	Coal Product Processing							
回收能	**Energy Recycled**							
损失量	**Losses**					**1.69**		
#运输和输配损失	In Transportation and Transmission							
终端消费量	**Final Consumption Industry**						**462.75**	**544.38**
第一产业	Primary Industry						4.09	
第二产业	Secondary Industry						27.03	0.06
工 业	Industry						19.44	0.06
#用作原料、材料	Use in Materials						0.04	0.01
建筑业	Construction						7.59	
第三产业	Tertiary Industry						125.09	544.32
生活消费	Residential Consumption						306.54	
城 镇	Urban						306.54	
乡 村	Rural							
平衡差额	Balance							
消费量合计	**Total Energy Consumption**					**991.54**	**462.75**	**544.38**

4-8 续表 2 Continued 2

单位：万吨 (10000 tons)

项 目	Item	柴 油 Diesel Oil	燃料油 Fuel Oil	石脑油 Naphtha	润滑油 Grease Oil	石 蜡 Oilfin	溶剂油 Solvent Oil	石油沥青 Oil Asphalt	石油焦 Petroleum Coal
可供本地区消费的能源量	**Total Energy Available for Local Consumption**	**2.00**	**3.92**	**22.75**	**0.97**	**-8.50**	**0.09**	**2.73**	**-19.59**
加工转换投入(-)产出(+)量	**Input(-) or Output(+) in Procesing and Conversion**	**178.87**	**1.10**	**19.08**		**8.73**		**12.27**	**19.31**
火力发电	Thermal Power	-0.40							-5.24
供 热	Heating	-1.09	-0.30						-14.25
煤炭洗选	Washing of Coal								
炼 焦	Coking								
炼油及煤制油	Oil Refining and Coal to Liquid	180.35	1.40	133.79		8.73		12.27	38.80
#油品再投入量(-)	Oil Product Re-input(-)			-114.71					
制 气	Gas Production								
#焦炭再投入量(-)	Coke Re-input(-)								
煤制品加工	Coal Product Processing								
回收能	**Energy Recycled**								
损失量	**Losses**								
#运输和输配损失	In Transportation and Transmission								
终端消费量	**End-use Energy Consumption**	**180.87**	**4.61**	**41.84**	**0.97**	**0.23**	**0.09**	**15.00**	**0.01**
第一产业	Primary Industry	3.32							
第二产业	Secondary Industry	40.69	2.69	41.84	0.97	0.23	0.09	15.00	0.01
工 业	Industry	15.01	2.69	41.84	0.97	0.23	0.09	15.00	0.01
#用作原料、材料	Use in Materials	0.17		41.84	0.97	0.23	0.09	15.00	
建筑业	Construction	25.68							
第三产业	Tertiary Industry	136.87	1.92						
生活消费	Residential Consumption								
城 镇	Urban								
乡 村	Rural								
平衡差额	Balance		0.41						-0.29
消费量合计	**Total Energy Consumption**	**182.35**	**4.91**	**156.55**	**0.97**	**0.23**	**0.09**	**15.00**	**19.50**

4-8 续表 3 Continued 3

单位：万吨 (10000 tons)

项　目	Item	液化石油气 Liquefied Petroleum Gas	炼厂干气 Refinery Gas	其它石油制品 Other Petroleum Products	天然气(亿立方米) Natural Gas (100 million cu.m)	液化天然气 Liquefied Natural Gas	热力(万百万千焦) Heat (10000 million kilo-joule)	电力(亿千瓦时) Electricity (100 million kwh)	其它能源(万吨标准煤) Others (10000 tons of SCE)
可供本地区消费的能源量	**Total Energy Available for Local Consumption**	**17.11**		**20.01**	**145.36**	**10.91**	**983.66**	**541.44**	**94.05**
加工转换投入(-)产出(+)量	**Input(-) or Output(+) in Procesing and Conversion**	**33.89**	**74.71**	**148.65**	**-86.25**		**15819.74**	**412.53**	**-33.19**
火力发电	Thermal Power		-0.18	-1.48	-60.52			412.53	-49.58
供　热	Heating	-0.15	-1.46	-8.49	-25.73		15819.74		
煤炭洗选	Washing of Coal								
炼　焦	Coking								
炼油及煤制油	Oil Refining and Coal to Liquid	34.04	76.35	310.19					
#油品再投入量(-)	Oil Product Re-input(-)			-151.57					
制　气	Gas Production								
#焦炭再投入量(-)	Coke Re-input(-)								
煤制品加工	Coal Product Processing								
回收能	**Energy Recycled**								**16.39**
损失量	**Losses**				**3.71**			**61.29**	
#运输和输配损失	In Transportation and Transmission							61.29	
终端消费量	**Final Consumption Industry**	**50.99**	**74.78**	**168.65**	**55.42**	**10.91**	**16803.40**	**889.96**	**60.86**
第一产业	Primary Industry	0.06			0.01			18.50	
第二产业	Secondary Industry	2.08	74.78	168.65	11.84	0.25	3898.67	249.65	7.73
工　业	Industry	1.80	74.78	168.65	11.68	0.25	3764.09	228.89	7.32
#用作原料、材料	Use in Materials	0.13	18.04	141.56					
建筑业	Construction	0.28			0.16		134.57	20.76	0.40
第三产业	Tertiary Industry	23.79			29.80	10.66	8681.73	447.05	35.91
生活消费	Residential Consumption	25.05			13.76		4223.00	174.76	17.22
城　镇	Urban	15.55			13.71		4223.00	149.61	
乡　村	Rural	9.50			0.05			25.15	17.22
平衡差额	Balance		-0.07		-0.01			2.72	
消费量合计	**Total Energy Consumption**	**51.15**	**76.41**	**330.20**	**145.37**	**10.91**	**16803.40**	**951.25**	**110.44**

4-9 能源平衡表(标准量简表)(2015年)
ENERGY BALANCE (STANDARD VOLUME) (SIMPLE EDITION) (2015)

单位：万吨标准煤 (10000 tons of SCE)

项目	Item	合计 Total	原煤 Coal	洗精煤 Washed Coal	其他洗煤 Other Washed Coal	煤制品 Coal Products	煤矸石 Coal Slack	焦炭 Coke	焦炉煤气 Coking Gas
可供本地区消费的能源量	**Total Energy Available for Local Consumption**	**6860.13**	**928.21**	**6.34**	**0.01**	**2.67**		**0.42**	
加工转换投入(-)产出(+)量	**Input(-) or Output(+) in Processing and Transformation**	**-73.90**	**-412.61**	**-6.29**		**-0.36**			
火力发电	Thermal Power		-148.02			-2.30			
供热	Heating	-81.24	-262.64			-6.01			
煤炭洗选	Washing of Coal	-0.02	-1.95	1.92					
炼焦	Coking								
炼油及煤制油	Oil Refining and Coal to Liquid	345.18							
#油品再投入量(-)	Oil Product Re-input(-)	-353.95							
制气	Gas Production								
#焦炭再投入量(-)	Coke Re-input(-)								
煤制品加工	Coal Product Processing	-0.26		-8.22		7.96			
回收能	**Energy Recycled**	**16.39**							
损失量	**Losses**	**217.64**							
#运输和输配损失	In Transportation and Transmission	171.13							
终端消费量	**Final Consumption Industry**	**6561.01**	**515.60**	**0.04**	**0.01**	**2.31**		**0.43**	
第一产业	Primary Industry	84.56	21.85						
第二产业	Secondary Industry	1611.18	117.96	0.01		0.28		0.42	
工业	Industry	1492.88	113.80	0.01		0.08		0.42	
#用作原料、材料	Use as Materials	285.64	0.09						
建筑业	Construction	118.30	4.16			0.21			
第三产业	Tertiary Industry	3312.56	129.66	0.03	0.01	2.03		0.01	
生活消费	Residential Consumption	1552.71	246.12						
城镇	Urban	1297.69	95.42						
乡村	Rural	255.02	150.70						
平衡差额	Balance	7.58						-0.01	
消费量合计	**Total Energy Consumption**	**6852.55**							

4-9 续表 1 Continued 1

单位：万吨标准煤 (10000 tons of SCE)

项 目	Item	高炉煤气（亿立方米）Furnace Gas (100 million cu.m)	转炉煤气（亿立方米）Converter Gas (100 million cu.m)	其它煤气 Other Gas	其它焦化产品 Other Carbonized Products	原油 Crude Oil	汽油 Gaso-line	煤油 Kero-sene
可供本地区消费的能源量	**Total Energy Available for Local Consumption**					**1416.52**	**244.89**	**565.59**
加工转换投入(-)产出(+)量	**Input(-) or Output(+) in Proce-ssing and Transformation**					**-1414.10**	**436.01**	**235.42**
火力发电	Thermal Power							
供 热	Heating							
煤炭洗选	Washing of Coal							
炼 焦	Coking							
炼油及煤制油	Oil Refining and Coal to Liquid					-1414.10	436.01	235.42
#油品再投入量(-)	Oil Product Re-input(-)							
制 气	Gas Production							
#焦炭再投入量(-)	Coke Re-input(-)							
煤制品加工	Coal Product Processing							
回收能	**Energy Recycled**							
损失量	**Losses**					**2.41**		
#运输和输配损失	In Transportation and Transmission							
终端消费量	**Final Consumption Industry**						**680.90**	**801.01**
第一产业	Primary Industry						6.01	
第二产业	Secondary Industry						39.77	0.09
工 业	Industry						28.60	0.09
#用作原料、材料	Use as Materials						0.06	0.02
建筑业	Construction						11.17	
第三产业	Tertiary Industry						184.07	800.92
生活消费	Residential Consumption						451.05	
城 镇	Urban						451.05	
乡 村	Rural							
平衡差额	Balance					0.01		
消费量合计	**Total Energy Consumption**							

4-9 续表 2 Continued 2

单位：万吨标准煤 (10000 tons of SCE)

项 目	Item	柴 油 Diesel Oil	燃料油 Fuel Oil	石脑油 Naphtha	润滑油 Grease Oil	石 蜡 Oilfin	溶剂油 Solvent Oil	石油沥青 Oil Asphalt	石油焦 Petroleum Coal
可供本地区消费的能源量	**Total Energy Available for Local Consumption**	**2.91**	**5.60**	**34.13**	**1.37**	**-11.60**	**0.14**	**3.63**	**-22.01**
加工转换投入(-)产出(+)量	**Input(-) or Output(+) in Proce -ssing and Transformation**	**260.63**	**1.57**	**28.63**		**11.91**		**16.33**	**21.71**
火力发电	Thermal Power	-0.58							-5.88
供 热	Heating	-1.58	-0.43						-15.99
煤炭洗选	Washing of Coal								
炼 焦	Coking								
炼油及煤制油	Oil Refining and Coal to Liquid	262.79	2.00	200.69		11.91		16.33	43.58
#油品再投入量(-)	Oil Product Re-input(-)			-172.07					
制 气	Gas Production								
#焦炭再投入量(-)	Coke Re-input(-)								
煤制品加工	Coal Product Processing								
回收能	**Energy Recycled**								
损失量	**Losses**								
#运输和输配损失	In Transportation and Transmission								
终端消费量	**Final Consumption Industry**	**263.54**	**6.59**	**62.75**	**1.37**	**0.31**	**0.14**	**19.96**	**0.01**
第一产业	Primary Industry	4.83							
第二产业	Secondary Industry	59.28	3.84	62.75	1.37	0.31	0.14	19.96	0.01
工 业	Industry	21.87	3.84	62.75	1.37	0.31	0.14	19.96	0.01
#用作原料、材料	Use as Materials	0.25		62.75	1.37	0.31	0.14	19.96	
建筑业	Construction	37.42							
第三产业	Tertiary Industry	199.43	2.75						
生活消费	Residential Consumption								
城 镇	Urban								
乡 村	Rural								
平衡差额	Balance		0.59						-0.31
消费量合计	**Total Energy Consumption**								

4-9 续表 3 Continued 3

单位：万吨标准煤 (10000 tons of SCE)

项　目	Item	液化石油气 Liquefied Petroleum Gas	炼厂干气 Refinery Gas	其它石油制品 Other Petroleum Products	天然气 Natural Gas (100 million cu.m)	液化天然气 Liquefied Natural Gas	热力 Heat	电力 Electricity	其它能源 Others
可供本地区消费的能源量	**Total Energy Available for Local Consumption**	**29.33**		**28.01**	**1965.51**	**19.17**	**33.54**	**1511.69**	**94.05**
加工转换投入(-)产出(+)量	**Input(-) or Output(+) in Processing and Transformation**	**58.09**	**117.39**	**177.06**	**-1263.33**		**539.45**	**1151.77**	**-33.19**
火力发电	Thermal Power		-0.29	-1.97	-943.14			1151.77	-49.58
供　热	Heating	-0.26	-2.29	-11.31	-320.18		539.45		
煤炭洗选	Washing of Coal								
炼　焦	Coking								
炼油及煤制油	Oil Refining and Coal to Liquid	58.35	119.97	372.23					
#油品再投入量(-)	Oil Product Re-input(-)			-181.89					
制　气	Gas Production								
#焦炭再投入量(-)	Coke Re-input(-)								
煤制品加工	Coal Product Processing								
回收能	**Energy Recycled**								**16.39**
损失量	**Losses**				**44.09**			**171.13**	
#运输和输配损失	In Transportation and Transmission							171.13	
终端消费量	**Final Consumption Industry**	**87.42**	**117.50**	**205.07**	**658.26**	**19.18**	**573.00**	**2484.75**	**60.86**
第一产业	Primary Industry	0.11			0.09			51.66	
第二产业	Secondary Industry	3.57	117.50	205.07	140.70	0.44	132.94	697.02	7.73
工　业	Industry	3.09	117.50	205.07	138.78	0.44	128.36	639.06	7.32
#用作原料、材料	Use as Materials	0.22	28.34	172.13					
建筑业	Construction	0.48			1.92		4.59	57.96	0.40
第三产业	Tertiary Industry	40.79			354.04	18.74	296.05	1248.15	35.91
生活消费	Residential Consumption	42.95			163.43		144.00	487.92	17.22
城 镇	Urban	26.67			162.84		144.00	417.70	
乡 村	Rural	16.28			0.59			70.22	17.22
平衡差额	Balance		-0.11		-0.17	-0.01		7.58	
消费量合计	**Total Energy Consumption**								

4-10 分行业能源消费总量和主要能源品种消费量(2015年)

单位：万吨

项　目	Item	能源消费总量(万吨标准煤) Total Energy Consumption (10000 tons of SCE)	煤　炭 Coal
合　计	**Total**	**6852.55**	**1165.18**
农、林、牧、渔业	Agriculture, Forestry, Animal Production and Hunting, Fishing	84.56	30.50
采矿业	Mining and Quarrying	17.26	1.83
煤炭开采和洗选业	Mining and Washing of Coal	4.76	0.83
石油和天然气开采业	Extraction of Petroleum and Natural Gas	0.02	
黑色金属矿采选业	Mining of Ferrous Metal Ores	11.49	0.94
有色金属矿采选业	Mining of Non-ferrous Metal Ores	0.01	
非金属矿采选业	Mining and Processing of Nonmetal Ores	0.84	0.06
开采辅助活动	Mining Support Service Activities	0.14	
其他采矿业	Mining of Other Ores n.e.c		
制造业	Manufacturing	1292.49	142.71
农副食品加工业	Processing of Food from Agricultural Products	23.52	8.22
食品制造业	Manufacture of Foods	29.87	4.66
酒、饮料和精制茶制造业	Manufacture of Wine, Beverage and Refined Tea	27.28	14.55
烟草制品业	Manufacture of Cigarettes and Tobacco	***	
纺织业	Manufacture of Textile	4.48	1.81
纺织服装、服饰业	Manufacture of Textile Wearing Apparel and Ornament	13.35	4.77
皮革、毛皮、羽毛及其制品和制鞋业	Manufacture of Leather, Fur, Feather and Its Products, and Footwear	1.14	0.14
木材加工和木、竹、藤、棕、草制品业	Processing of Timbers, Manufacture of Wood, Bamboo, Rattan, Palm, and Straw Products	4.78	0.34
家具制造业	Manufacture of Furniture	7.73	1.05
造纸和纸制品业	Manufacture of Paper and Paper Products	10.99	3.23
印刷和记录媒介复制业	Printing, Reproduction of Recording Media	23.92	1.40
文教、工美、体育和娱乐用品制造业	Manufacture of Articles for Culture, Education, Artwork, Sport and Entertainment Activities	4.30	0.75
石油加工、炼焦和核燃料加工业	Processing of Petroleum, Coking, Processing of Nucleus Fuel	478.19	0.48
化学原料和化学制品制造业	Manufacture of Chemical Raw Materials and Chemical Products	114.51	3.67
医药制造业	Manufacture of Medicines	35.04	5.11
化学纤维制造业	Manufacture of Chemical Fibers	1.34	0.01
橡胶和塑料制品业	Manufacture of Rubber and Plastics Products	23.92	2.25
非金属矿物制品业	Manufacture of Non-Metallic Mineral Products	132.73	72.18

注：各行业能源消费总量为各行业终端消费量与各行业分摊的损失量和加工转换损失量之和，不等于分品种能源消费量(标准煤)的合计。

CONSUMPTION OF TOTAL ENERGY AND MAIN ENERGY VARIETIES BY SECTOR (2015)

(10000 tons)

焦 炭 Coke	汽 油 Gasoline	煤 油 Kerosene	柴 油 Diesel Oil	燃料油 Fuel Oil	液 化 石油气 Liquefied Petroleum Gas	天然气 (亿立方米) Natural Gas (100 million cu.m)	热 力 (万百万千焦) Heat (10 billion kilo-joule)	电 力 (亿千瓦时) Electricity (100 million kwh)
0.44	**462.76**	**544.38**	**182.35**	**4.91**	**51.15**	**145.37**	**16803.40**	**951.25**
	4.09		3.32		0.06	0.01		18.50
	0.10		1.07		0.03	0.01	7.16	4.95
	0.02		0.05		0.02		1.84	1.40
	0.01							0.01
	0.04		0.73		0.01	0.01	5.03	3.38
	0.01		0.28				0.14	0.13
	0.02		0.01				0.15	0.03
0.43	18.29	0.06	13.50	2.69	1.71	11.15	3574.39	170.48
	0.46		0.30		0.06	0.22	52.78	4.26
	0.56		0.56		0.12	0.59	77.96	5.30
	0.28		0.25		0.01	0.26	53.54	3.99
						***		***
	0.17		0.02		0.01	0.03	4.85	0.85
	0.80		0.13		0.03	0.05	35.36	2.29
	0.07		0.01		0.01		3.45	0.27
	0.25		0.10		0.01		0.46	1.25
	0.61		0.11	0.01	0.03	0.03	11.55	1.81
	0.38		0.19	0.01	0.02	0.15	7.69	2.05
	1.14		0.20		0.03	0.19	58.11	5.89
	0.24		0.06		0.01	0.02	16.60	0.88
	0.09		0.14		0.36	2.73	1245.79	16.57
	0.90		0.62	0.07	0.10	0.39	866.27	13.68
	0.51		0.25		0.04	0.57	146.59	6.66
	0.02					0.03		0.32
	0.68		0.24		0.21	0.20	36.84	6.07
	1.11		6.81	2.60	0.08	0.83	33.69	16.18

Note: Total energy consumption in each sector is the end consumption of each sector plus losses shared by each sector and losses from processing in each sector, but not equal to sum of consumption (SCE equivalent) of all sorts of energy.

4-10 续表

单位：万吨

项　目	Item	能源消费总量（万吨标准煤）Total Energy Consumption (10000 tons of SCE)	煤　炭 Coal
黑色金属冶炼及压延加工业	Manufacture and Pressing of Ferrous Metals	22.78	0.37
有色金属冶炼及压延加工业	Manufacture and Pressing of Non-Ferrous Metals	5.10	0.12
金属制品业	Manufacture of Fabricated Metal Products	32.46	3.83
通用设备制造业	Manufacture of General-purpose Machinery	29.36	2.48
专用设备制造业	Manufacture of Special-purpose Machinery	22.49	2.00
汽车制造业	Manufacture of Motor Vehicles	109.47	0.86
铁路、船舶、航空航天和其他运输设备制造业	Manufacture of Railway Locomotives, Building of Ships and Boats, Manufacture of Air and Spacecrafts and Other Transportation Equipment	15.23	4.54
电气机械和器材制造业	Manufacture of Electrical Machinery and Equipment	20.30	1.50
计算机、通讯和其他电子设备制造业	Manufacture of Computer, Communication Equipment and Other Electronic Equipment	78.35	0.55
仪器仪表制造业	Manufacture of Measuring Instruments and Meters	8.26	0.36
其他制造业	Other Manufacturing	4.82	1.08
废弃资源综合利用业	Waste recycling and recovery	0.89	0.09
金属制品、机械和设备修理业	Repair of Fabricated Metal Products, Machinery and Equipment	3.85	0.31
电力、燃气及水的生产和供应业	Production and Distribution of Electricity, Gas and Water	474.67	529.28
电力、热力生产和供应业	Production and Supply of Electric Power and Heat Power	390.06	528.96
燃气生产和供应业	Production and Distribution of Gas	48.24	0.01
水的生产和供应业	Production and Distribution of Water	36.37	0.31
建筑业	Construction	118.30	6.08
批发和零售业	Wholesale and Retail Trade	198.51	6.97
交通运输、仓储和邮政业	Transport, Storage and Post	1249.37	12.36
住宿和餐饮业	Accommodation and Restaurants	299.09	19.62
信息传输、软件和信息技术服务业	Information transmission,software and information technology services	164.88	0.79
金融业	Finance	66.81	0.80
房地产业	Real Estate Trade	376.88	47.19
租赁和商务服务业	Renting and Leasing Activities and Business Services	195.50	24.27
科学研究和技术服务业	Scientific Research and Development, Technical Services	170.88	12.85
水利、环境和公共设施管理业	Water, Environment and Municipal Engineering Conservancy	60.32	4.86
居民服务、修理和其他服务业	Resident services, repair and other services	30.29	11.00
教　育	Education	228.74	18.28
卫生和社会工作	Healthcare and Social Works	84.06	8.06
文化、体育和娱乐业	Culture, Sports and Entertainment	72.22	1.94
公共管理、社会保障和社会组织	Public Administration, Social Security and Social Organizations	115.01	12.77
生活消费	Residential Consumption	1552.71	273.02
城　镇	Urban	1297.69	101.21
乡　村	Rural	255.02	171.81

4-10 Continued

(10000 tons)

焦炭 Coke	汽油 Gasoline	煤油 Kerosene	柴油 Diesel Oil	燃料油 Fuel Oil	液化石油气 Liquefied Petroleum Gas	天然气(亿立方米) Natural Gas (100 million cu.m)	热力(万百万千焦) Heat (10 billion kilo-joule)	电力(亿千瓦时) Electricity (100 million kwh)
0.42	0.13		0.18		0.01	0.80	1.27	4.30
	0.11		0.04		0.02	0.02	11.92	1.45
	1.62		0.40		0.19	0.34	62.69	7.21
	1.41	0.01	0.40		0.12	0.16	130.42	6.44
	1.37		0.22		0.04	0.14	122.78	4.55
	2.30		1.16		0.09	2.67	141.85	23.61
0.01	0.24		0.19		0.01	0.06	111.11	2.78
	1.10		0.11		0.05	0.10	85.34	4.43
	0.77		0.42		0.01	0.24	167.98	24.17
	0.67	0.01	0.04		0.01	0.06	57.72	1.51
	0.10		0.11		0.01	0.02	24.98	0.74
	0.03		0.02		0.01	0.02	0.84	0.19
	0.17	0.04	0.22		0.01	0.12	3.96	0.51
	1.04		1.92	0.30	0.22	90.48	182.55	114.76
	0.60		1.75	0.30	0.20	86.29	149.41	101.98
	0.25		0.07			4.11	8.56	0.85
	0.19		0.10		0.02	0.08	24.58	11.93
	7.59		25.68		0.28	0.16	134.57	20.76
	24.89		3.86	0.01	0.49	0.73	708.26	42.07
	44.65	543.78	118.00	1.79	0.38	2.11	594.20	47.31
0.01	1.59		0.56	0.02	20.42	6.52	645.62	51.10
	4.87		0.25		0.05	0.21	299.63	51.22
	2.55		0.16		0.03	0.14	339.58	17.47
	4.44		0.71		0.16	8.53	1205.27	67.11
	13.23		5.19	0.01	0.38	1.97	780.18	35.14
	12.07	0.54	0.81	0.06	0.34	2.02	794.18	31.85
	2.24		3.79	0.01	0.14	0.54	42.91	13.94
	1.76		0.57	0.01	0.10	0.27	79.32	4.51
	3.26		1.53		0.43	4.27	1564.07	33.52
	0.91		0.23		0.25	1.19	442.16	15.61
	1.86		0.37		0.11	0.56	362.68	17.02
	6.79		0.83	0.01	0.52	0.74	823.67	19.17
	306.54				25.05	13.76	4223.00	174.76
	306.54				15.55	13.71	4223.00	149.61
					9.50	0.05		25.15

4-11 能源消费弹性系数(2000-2015年)
ELASTICITY COEFFICIENT OF ENERGY CONSUMPTION (2000-2015)

项 目 Item	能源消费比上年增长 (%) Growth of Energy Consumption over the Previous Year	电力消费比上年增长(%) Growth of Electricity Consumption over the Previous Year	地区生产总值比上年增长(%) Growth of Gross Domestic Product(GDP) over the Previous Year	能源消费弹性系数 Elasticity Coefficient of Energy Consumption	电力消费弹性系数 Elasticity Coefficient of Electricity Consumption
2000	6.08	9.53	11.8	0.51	0.81
2001	2.06	5.68	11.7	0.18	0.49
2002	4.89	9.54	11.5	0.43	0.83
2003	4.78	5.71	11.1	0.43	0.51
2004	10.57	10.60	14.1	0.75	0.75
2005	7.44	11.16	12.1	0.61	0.92
2006	6.92	9.16	13.0	0.53	0.71
2007	6.45	9.06	14.5	0.45	0.63
2008	0.67	4.90	9.1	0.07	0.54
2009	3.84	7.15	10.2	0.38	0.70
2010	5.84	9.49	10.3	0.57	0.92
2011	0.59	2.21	8.1	0.07	0.27
2012	2.61	5.91	7.7	0.34	0.77
2013	2.44	4.42	7.7	0.32	0.57
2014	1.60	2.72	7.3	0.22	0.37
2015	0.31	1.91	6.9	0.05	0.28

注：1. 地区生产总值增长速度按可比价计算。
2. 2013年数据为第三次全国经济普查数据。2005-2012年电力数据根据第三次全国经济普查的数据结果进行了修正。

Note: a) The groth rates of GDP are calculated at comparable prices.
b) Data for 2013 were collected from the third national economic census.Data for 2005-2012 were revised acording to the third national economic census.

4-12 平均每万元地区生产总值能源消费量(2010-2015年)
ENERGY CONSUMPTION PER 10000 YUAN OF GROSS DOMESTIC PRODUCT (2010-2015)

项 目 Item	能源总消费量 (吨标准煤) Total (ton of SCE)	煤 炭 (吨) Coal (ton)	电 力 (千瓦时) Electricity (kwh)	石 油 (吨) Petroleum (ton)
2010	0.53	0.21	672.13	0.11
	(0.45)	(0.18)	(569.60)	(0.10)
2011	0.42	0.15	538.34	0.09
2012	0.40	0.13	529.22	0.09
2013	0.38	0.11	513.11	0.08
2014	0.36	0.09	491.30	0.08
2015	0.34	0.06	468.52	0.08
	(0.30)	(0.05)	(413.32)	(0.07)

注：1. 本表中每万元地区生产总值能源消费量按可比价格计算，可比价格每五年调整一次基期，更换基期年份计算两个可比价格数据，括号内数据是按新基期价格计算。
2. 2013年数据为第三次全国经济普查数据。2010-2012年数据根据第三次全国经济普查的数据结果进行了修正。

Note: a) Energy consumption per 10000 yuan of GDP were calculated at comparable prices. The base period of comparable prices is changed every five years. Two figures at comparable prices were calculated for the year in which the base period is changed. Figures in brackets were calculated at the price of new base period.
b) Data for 2013 were collected from the third national economic census.Data for 2010-2012 were revised acording to the third national economic census.

4-13 人均生活用能源(2010-2015年) PER CAPITA ENERGY CONSUMPTION FOR NON-PRODUCTIVE PURPOSE (2010-2015)

年份 Year	合计 (千克标准煤) Total (kg of SCE)	煤炭 (千克) Coal (kg)	电力 (千瓦时) Electricity (kwh)	液化石油气 (千克) Liquefied Petroleum Gas(kg)	天然气 (立方米) Natural Gas (cu.m)	汽油 (升) Gasoline (liter)
2010	650.2	173.6	729.1	11.3	53.1	164.9
2011	663.2	167.1	727.2	10.7	52.7	167.6
2012	693.2	159.0	791.8	9.3	56.5	174.4
2013	687.5	147.7	750.6	9.9	57.1	180.7
2014	705.3	137.6	793.5	11.0	59.6	182.5
2015	718.5	126.3	808.7	11.6	63.7	194.3

注：1. 本表人均生活用能源按常住人口年平均数计算。2006-2010年数据根据全国第六次人口普查进行了修正。
2. 2013年数据为第三次全国经济普查数据。2010-2012年数据根据第三次全国经济普查的数据结果进行了修正。

Note: a) Per-capita energy consumption for non-productive prupose is calculated by average permanent population. Figures for 2006-2010 have been revised in accordance with the 6th national population census.

b) Data for 2013 were collected from the third national economic census.Data for 2010-2012 were revised acording to the third national economic census.

4-14 主要能源日均消费量(2010-2015年) DAILY CONSUMPTION OF MAIN ENERGY VARIETIES(2010-2015)

年份 Year	合计 (万吨标准煤) Total (10000 tons of SCE)	煤炭 (吨) Coal (ton)	原油 (吨) Crude Oil (ton)	汽油 (吨) Gasoline (ton)	煤油 (吨) Kerosene (ton)	柴油 (吨) Diesel Oil (ton)	燃料油 (吨) Fuel Oil (ton)	电力 (万千瓦时) Electricity (10000 kwh)	天然气 (万立方米) Natural Gas (10000 cu.m)
2010	17.4	69315.4	30175.6	9935.4	10757.0	5333.0	442.3	22024.9	2048.9
2011	17.5	62056.8	29778.2	10418.6	11503.7	5366.2	340.3	22512.5	2014.0
2012	18.0	59714.8	29072.1	11116.6	12146.1	5166.4	302.4	23842.3	2522.4
2013	18.4	55321.3	23860.7	11605.7	13070.1	5312.2	227.3	24896.0	2707.2
2014	18.7	47576.5	28345.6	12071.7	13906.3	5382.5	154.3	25572.9	3115.0
2015	18.8	31922.7	27165.5	12678.2	14914.6	4995.9	134.5	26061.7	3982.9

注： 2013年数据为第三次全国经济普查数据。2010-2012年数据根据第三次全国经济普查的数据结果进行了修正。

Note: Data for 2013 were collected from the third national economic census.Data for 2010-2012 were revised acording to the third national economic census.

4-15 全社会用电量情况(1978-2015年)
TOTAL ELECTRICITY CONSUMPTION IN BEIJING (1978-2015)

单位：万千瓦时 (10000 kwh)

年份 Year	全社会用电量 Electricity Consumption	第一产业 Primary Industry	第二产业 Secondary Industry	工业 Industry	建筑业 Construction	第三产业 Tertiary Industry	城乡居民生活用电 Residential Electricity Consumption	城市 Urban	乡村 Rural
1978	735000	48993	570621	570621		94555	20831	11022	9809
1979	802317	52134	620262	620262		107437	22484	11495	10989
1980	854638	65283	648496	648496		116947	23912	12441	11471
1981	867153	80027	643976	643976		121883	21267	9452	11815
1982	925700	104842	657060	657060		139403	24395	10820	13575
1983	956293	92601	687937	687937		151290	24465	12320	12145
1984	1029420	105234	716653	716653		177455	30078	16025	14053
1985	1106255	111110	746324	746324		210622	38199	22479	15720
1986	1181155	105688	851519	835725	15794	175090	48858	31008	17850
1987	1285023	77909	923797	899760	24037	224747	58570	35063	23507
1988	1378574	83809	970885	943383	27502	248446	75434	48624	26810
1989	1421817	100151	979216	949629	29587	258067	84383	56120	28263
1990	1504785	93049	1014037	986356	27681	302775	94924	65262	29662
1991	1613977	93256	1061207	1032064	29143	348769	110745	77575	33170
1992	1759611	101985	1155514	1123835	31679	375874	126238	88621	37617
1993	1924978	107010	1243115	1206001	37114	429835	145018	103579	41439
1994	2054504	101134	1307898	1262961	44937	479679	165791	119025	46766
1995	2225922	102099	1403864	1341398	62466	538936	181022	130897	50125
1996	2443709	111904	1496968	1422590	74378	617286	217551	158474	59077
1997	2636078	120444	1529201	1449129	80072	721774	264659	196641	68018
1998	2762080	108267	1548485	1457149	91336	811283	294045	220543	73502
1999	2972629	121242	1581977	1478523	103454	912834	356576	276642	79934
2000	3844266	130865	2172604	2066892	105712	1064322	476475	385396	91079
2001	3999415	131811	2105819	1978673	127146	1222471	539314	439058	100256
2002	4399637	137370	2293735	2145292	148443	1342490	626042	517386	108656
2003	4676056	107372	2418419	2250525	167894	1447344	702921	574623	128298
2004	5131804	104234	2593504	2391414	202090	1628731	805335	647474	157861
2005	5705364	114308	2795753	2605832	189921	1906093	889210	706405	182805
2006	6115719	122550	2943550	2744127	199423	2090888	958731	768884	189847
2007	6670089	133557	3091374	2881807	209567	2378399	1066759	862604	204155
2008	6897189	136065	2943893	2763399	180494	2654140	1163091	949878	213213
2009	7391465	157310	3027974	2853018	174956	2918229	1287952	982720	305232
2010	8099029	168992	3278682	3081364	197319	3258009	1393346	951811	441535
2011	8217055	170368	3109174	2894464	214708	3490143	1447370	945588	501782
2012	8742835	181391	3209078	2980645	228430	3734022	1618344	1370932	247412
2013	9131113	185749	3345854	3110626	235229	4029145	1570365	1347401	222964
2014	9370485	185633	3352904	3129060	223846	4139319	1692629	1457398	235231
2015	9527169	185031	3238220	3030638	207583	4356332	1747586	1496078	251508

注：1. 1985年以前农、林、牧、渔和水利业用电量中，只包含农业排灌、农副业和社队企业的用电量。
2. 1980年以前的城市居民用电量以全市市政用电量的 1/10计算。
3. 2000年以前工业用电量不包含输配损失和发电企业自产自用电量。

资料来源：北京市电力公司。

Note: a) Before 1985, electricity consumption by agriculture, forestry, animal production and hunting, fishing and water conservancy only included the electricity consumption by farming irrigation, agricultural and sideline products, and village enterprises.
b) Before 1980, electricity consumption by urban residents was one-tenth of the total electricity consumption by municipal administration in Beijing.
c) Before 2000, electricity consumption by industry excluded transmission and distribution losses and electricity generated and consumed by power generating enterprises.

Source: Beijing Electric Power Corporation.

4-16 主要土地利用状况(2009-2014年)
LAND UTILIZATION (2009-2014)

单位：公顷 (hectare)

年份 Year	耕地面积 Arable Land	园地面积 Garden Plot	林地面积 Forest Land	草地面积 Grass Land	城镇村及工矿用地面积 Land for Urban, Rural,Industrial and Mining Use	交通运输用地面积 Land for Transportation	水域及水利设施用地面积 Water Areas and Land for Water Conservancy Facilities
2009	227170.43	141617.22	743696.19	84843.14	284791.79	44446.42	80235.85
2010	223779.38	139298.50	742018.50	85827.05	290782.01	45335.78	79774.99
2011	221956.16	138072.99	740730.87	85651.69	295116.72	45452.68	79380.05
2012	220856.16	137117.72	739633.48	85491.29	297758.79	46327.98	79088.32
2013	221157.28	135573.37	738036.45	85348.82	300847.83	46626.41	78739.52
2014	219948.76	135103.71	737542.89	85139.49	302939.17	47006.28	78378.65

注：表中2009年数据为第二次全国土地调查数据，2010-2014年为各年土地变更调查数据。
资料来源：北京市国土资源局。
Note: Statistics for 2009 were from the 2nd National Land Survey, and statistics for 2010-2014 were survey data of land changed.
Source: Beijing Municipal Bureau of Land Resources.

4-17 水资源情况(2001-2015年)

单位：亿立方米

项　目	Item	2001	2002	2003	2004
全年水资源总量	**Total Volume of Water Resource in the Year**	**19.2**	**16.1**	**18.4**	**21.4**
地表水资源量	Volume of Surface Water Resource	7.8	5.3	6.1	8.2
地下水资源量	Volume of Underground Water Resource	15.7	14.7	14.8	16.5
人均水资源(立方米)	**Per-capita Water Resource(cu.m)**	**139.7**	**114.7**	**127.8**	**145.1**
全年供水(用水)总量	**Total Volume of Water Supplied (Consumed) in the Year**	**38.9**	**34.6**	**35.8**	**34.6**
按来源分	By Source				
地表水	Surface Water	11.7	10.4	8.3	5.7
地下水	Underground Water	27.2	24.2	25.4	26.8
再生水	Recycled Water			2.1	2.0
南水北调	Water Transit from South to North				
应急供水	Emergent Water Supply				
按用途分	By Purpose				
农业用水	Water Used by Agriculture	17.4	15.5	13.8	13.5
工业用水	Water Used by Industry	9.2	7.5	8.4	7.7
生活用水	Domestic Water	12.0	10.8	13.0	12.8
环境用水	Water for the Environment	0.3	0.8	0.6	0.6
万元地区生产总值水耗(立方米)	**Water Consumption per 10000 yuan GDP (cu.m)**	**104.91**	**80.19**	**71.50**	**57.35**
万元地区生产总值水耗下降率(%)	**Decrease Rate of Water Consumption per 10000 yuan GDP (%)**	**13.79**	**20.22**	**6.91**	**15.29**

注：1. 万元地区生产总值水耗按现价计算，下降率按可比价计算，如按可比价计算，2015年万元地区生产总值水耗为18.81立方米。
2. 本表人均水资源按常住人口年平均数计算。2006-2010年数据根据全国第六次人口普查进行了修正。
3. 2013年万元地区生产总值水耗及下降率数据为第三次全国经济普查数据。

资料来源：除人均数据和万元地区生产总值水耗以外其它数据来自北京市水务局。

STATISTICS FOR WATER RESOURCES (2001-2015)

(100 million cu.m)

2005	2006	2007	2008	2009	2010	2011	2012	2013	2014	2015
23.2	**22.1**	**23.8**	**34.2**	**21.8**	**23.1**	**26.8**	**39.5**	**24.8**	**20.3**	**26.8**
7.6	6.7	7.6	12.8	6.8	7.2	9.2	18.0	9.4	6.5	9.3
15.6	15.4	16.2	21.4	15.1	15.9	17.6	21.6	15.4	13.8	17.4
153.1	**140.6**	**145.3**	**198.5**	**120.3**	**120.8**	**134.7**	**193.3**	**118.6**	**94.9**	**123.8**
34.5	**34.3**	**34.8**	**35.1**	**35.5**	**35.2**	**36.0**	**35.9**	**36.4**	**37.5**	**38.2**
6.4	5.7	5.0	4.7	3.8	3.9	4.8	4.4	3.9	7.7	2.2
23.1	22.2	21.6	20.5	19.7	19.1	18.8	18.3	17.9	17.5	16.7
2.6	3.6	5.0	6.0	6.5	6.8	7.0	7.5	8.0	8.6	9.5
			0.7	2.6	2.6	2.6	2.8	3.5	0.8	7.6
2.5	2.8	3.2	3.2	2.9	2.9	2.7	2.9	3.0	2.8	2.3
13.2	12.8	12.4	12.0	12.0	11.4	10.9	9.3	9.1	8.2	6.5
6.8	6.2	5.8	5.2	5.2	5.1	5.0	4.9	5.1	5.1	3.9
13.4	13.7	13.9	14.7	14.7	14.8	15.6	16.0	16.2	17.0	17.5
1.1	1.6	2.7	3.2	3.6	4.0	4.5	5.7	5.9	7.2	10.4
49.50	**42.25**	**35.34**	**31.58**	**29.92**	**24.94**	**22.13**	**20.07**	**18.37**	**17.58**	**16.60**
11.07	**12.01**	**11.38**	**7.56**	**8.12**	**10.14**	**5.49**	**7.38**	**5.87**	**3.93**	**4.65**

Note: a) Water consumption per 10000 yuan GDP is at current prices,and decrease rate is at comparable prices.Caculated at comparable prices, the water consumption per 10000 yuan GDP in 2015 is 18.81 cubic metres.

b) Per-capita water resource are calculated by average permanent population.Per-capita figures 2006-2010 have been corrected in accordance with the Sixth Population Census.

c) Water consumption per 10000 yuan GDP and Decrease Rate of Water Consumption for 2013 is were collected from the third national economic census.

Source: Except for per-capita figures and water consumption per 10000 yuan GDP,other figures are from Beijing Water Authority.

4-18 气象情况(1978-2015年)
METEOROLOGY (1978-2015)

年 份 Year	降水量 (毫米) Precipitation (mm)	平均气温(℃) Average Temperature (℃)	最高 Highest	最低 Lowest	日照时数(时) Hours of Sunshine (hours)	平均风速(米/秒) Average Wind Speed (meter/second)	平均气压(百帕) Average Air Pressure (100 pa)	大风日数(日) Days of Strong Wind (day)	雨日数(日) Days of Rain (day)
1978	664.8	11.6	37.5	-14.4	2865.4	2.6	1012.8	35	64
1979	718.4	11.1	35.9	-15.4	2667.4	2.5	1012.2	33	63
1980	380.7	11.0	35.1	-15.4	2920.8	2.5	1012.7	29	83
1981	393.2	12.3	38.1	-14.0	2803.9	2.5	1010.8	15	92
1982	544.4	12.8	37.3	-14.3	2825.1	2.6	1010.5	26	92
1983	489.9	13.0	37.2	-15.0	2844.3	2.4	1010.3	29	100
1984	488.8	11.9	36.1	-14.9	2767.6	2.4	1010.6	18	90
1985	721.0	11.5	35.1	-15.2	2511.9	2.2	1010.4	12	104
1986	665.3	12.1	38.5	-15.4	2804.1	2.3	1010.7	21	96
1987	683.9	12.3	36.1	-15.5	2631.9	2.4	1010.3	23	102
1988	673.3	12.7	38.1	-13.2	2558.1	2.4	1010.8	17	96
1989	442.2	13.2	35.8	-11.0	2626.2	1.9	1011.1	3	78
1990	697.3	12.7	37.5	-14.8	2325.0	1.9	1010.6	12	113
1991	747.9	12.5	35.7	-12.6	2536.6	2.1	1010.8	8	98
1992	541.5	12.8	37.5	-8.7	2712.5	2.2	1011.0	6	100
1993	506.7	13.0	35.8	-13.0	2669.8	2.6	1010.8	12	91
1994	813.2	13.7	37.2	-11.5	2470.5	2.5	1010.1	9	92
1995	572.5	13.3	35.0	-9.2	2519.1	2.6	1010.3	16	89
1996	700.9	12.7	36.0	-10.0	2418.7	2.6	1011.0	16	103
1997	430.9	13.1	38.2	-14.0	2596.5	2.5	1012.9	11	76
1998	731.7	13.1	37.2	-14.2	2420.7	2.3	1012.5	10	93
1999	266.9	13.1	41.9	-12.2	2594.0	2.4	1012.5	7	86
2000	371.1	12.8	39.4	-15.0	2667.2	2.5	1012.7	10	83
2001	338.9	12.9	39.6	-17.0	2611.7	2.4	1012.9	10	78
2002	370.4	13.2	41.1	-12.8	2588.4	2.3	1012.7	15	84
2003	444.9	12.9	37.6	-15.0	2260.2	2.5	1013.3	6	93
2004	483.5	13.5	38.9	-12.9	2515.4	2.4	1012.6	12	94
2005	410.7	13.2	38.9	-11.5	2576.1	2.4	1012.8	5	79
2006	318.0	13.4	37.3	-14.7	2192.7	2.2	1012.5	5	86
2007	483.9	14.0	37.3	-11.7	2351.1	2.2	1012.6	5	78
2008	626.3	13.4	36.3	-13.5	2391.4	2.2	1012.6	8	100
2009	480.6	13.3	39.6	-12.2	2511.8	2.2	1011.9	15	86
2010	522.5	12.6	40.6	-16.7	2382.9	2.3	1012.2	14	88
2011	720.6	13.4	35.9	-11.6	2485.7	2.2	1013.2	3	82
2012	733.2	12.9	38.0	-13.7	2450.2	2.2	1012.2	3	85
2013	578.9	12.8	38.2	-14.1	2371.1	2.1	1012.2	3	71
2014	461.5	14.1	41.1	-11.2	2344.1	2.1	1013.0	8	77
2015	458.6	13.7	38.9	-9.2	2420.2	2.1	1013.2	7	99

资料来源：北京市气象局。
Source: Beijing Municipal Bureau of Meteorology.

4-19 气 象(2015年)
METEOROLOGY (2015)

月 份 Month	降水量 (毫米) Precipitation (mm)	平均气温(℃) Average Temperature (℃)	日照时数(时) Hours of Sunshine (hours)	平均风速(米/秒) Average Wind Speed (meter/second)	平均气压(百帕) Average Air Pressure (100 pa)	大风日数(日) Days of Strong Wind (day)	雨日数(日) Days of Rain (day)
全 年 Total	**458.6**	**13.7**	**2420.2**	**2.1**	**1013.2**	**7**	**99**
1	0.4	-0.6	198.2	2.1	1024.1		
2	11.2	1.3	179.8	2.3	1020.7	2	
3	7.7	8.8	250.4	2.5	1017.2		1
4	34.5	15.5	237.9	2.7	1011.3	2	7
5	35.0	21.5	276.3	2.6	1003.8	1	10
6	42.2	24.9	200.9	2.3	1000.6	1	19
7	107.4	26.8	209.9	1.9	1001.4		17
8	82.6	26.7	248.2	1.8	1003.6		15
9	87.2	21.0	192.1	1.8	1011.6		14
10	19.0	14.7	223.8	2.0	1016.0	1	6
11	29.6	3.6	59.3	1.8	1023.7		9
12	1.8	0.2	143.4	1.8	1024.3		1

注：1. 无霜期225天。
2. 年极端最高气温38.9℃，出现日期7月13日。
3. 年极端最低气温-9.2℃，出现日期2月8日和2月9日。

资料来源：北京市气象局。

Note: a) Annual frost-free period is225 days.
b) Annual utmost highest air temperature is 38.9℃, seen on the 13th of July.
c) Annual utmost lowest air temperature is -9.2℃, seen on the 8th of February and 9th of February.

Source: Beijing Municipal Bureau of Meteorology.

4-20 污水处理及环境卫生(1978-2015年)
SEWAGE DISPOSAL AND ENVIRONMENTAL SANITATION (1978-2015)

年份 Year	污水管道长度(公里) Length of Sewage Pipes (km)	污水处理能力(万立方米/日) Sewage Treatment Capacity (10000 cu.m/day)	污水处理率(%) Sewage Treatment Rate (%)	再生水利用量(万立方米) Volume of Recycled Water Used (10000 cu.m)	生活垃圾无害化处理能力(吨/日) Harmless Disposal Capacity of Domestic Waste (ton/day)	生活垃圾产生量(万吨) Output of Domestic Garbage (10000 tons)	生活垃圾清运量(万吨) Domestic Waste Removed and Transported (10000 tons)	生活垃圾无害化处理率(%) Rate of Harmless Disposal of Domestic Waste (%)	粪便清运量(万吨) Excrement Removed and Transported (10000 tons)
1978	290	23.2	7.6				107.20		88.9
1979	309	23.2	10.2				128.00		89.4
1980	334	23.2	9.4				147.00		95.1
1981	347	25.2	10.8				174.00		97.6
1982	365	25.2	10.9				204.70		99.3
1983	411	25.2	10.2				221.40		99.5
1984	568	25.2	10.0				235.40		98.8
1985	706	25.2	10.0				248.10		142.2
1986	747	26.4	8.9				274.40		167.5
1987	805	26.4	7.7				298.30		181.0
1988	770	26.4	7.4				319.90		190.0
1989	860	26.4	6.6				337.00		196.0
1990	904	30.4	7.3				384.10		210.0
1991	968	30.4	6.6				397.10		210.3
1992	1036	4.5	1.2				430.90		216.0
1993	1064	4.5	3.1				446.30		220.6
1994	1122	24.5	9.6				467.20		238.1
1995	1065	58.5	19.4				483.90		258.4
1996	1597	58.5	21.2				483.00		268.0
1997	1635	58.5	22.0				490.00		279.0
1998	1712	58.5	22.5				495.10		295.6
1999	1754	58.5	25.0				505.00		298.0
2000	1852	128.5	39.4		6550		295.56	56.4	274.0
2001	2163	143.5	42.0		6750		309.27	82.2	301.0
2002	2658	180.6	45.0		8750		321.35	86.4	311.7
2003	2903	215.0	50.1		9400		361.36	91.3	268.0
2004	2909	255.0	53.9		10050	495.46	405.86	93.8	175.0
2005	2521	324.0	62.4	23816	10350	536.93	454.59	96.0	171.7
2006	3398	331.0	73.2	36088	10350	585.13	538.32	92.5	175.7
2007	4357	348.0	76.2	49501	10350	619.49	600.93	95.7	189.1
2008	4458	329.4	78.9	60000	12148	672.82	656.61	97.7	206.8
2009	4495	356.0	80.3	64999	13680	669.13	656.12	98.2	211.2
2010	4479	365.0	81.0	68014	16680	634.86	632.98	96.9	194.4
2011	4765	369.4	82.0	71012	16930	634.35	634.35	98.2	207.5
2012	5735	388.5	83.0	75003	17530	648.31	648.31	99.1	207.2
2013	6363	393.0	84.6	80108	21971	671.69	671.69	99.3	220.7
2014	6536	425.0	86.1	86620	21971	733.84	733.84	99.6	216.1
2015	7157	439.5	87.9	94826	27321	790.33	790.33	99.8	204.7

注：1. 污水处理能力等指标1992年及以后为污水无害化处理情况，1992年以前为污水简易处理情况。
2. 生活垃圾无害化处理率按清运量计算。

资料来源：北京市水务局、北京市市政市容管理委员会。

Note: a) Disposal capacity and other indicators in and after 1992 were about harmless disposal, and those before 1992 were about simple disposal.
b) The harmless disposal rate of domestic waste is calculated with the volume of waste cleared and transported.

Source: Beijing Water Authority，Beijing Municipal Commission of City Administration and Environment.

4-21 排水及节水
WATER DRAINAGE AND SAVING

项目		Item		2015	2014
排水		**Water Drainage**			
污水处理能力	(万立方米/日)	Sewage Treatment Capacity	(10000 cu.m/day)	439.5	425.0
#二三级	(万立方米/日)	Grade-II and III Treatment	(10000 cu.m/day)	439.5	425.0
污水年处理量	(万立方米)	Annual Treatment Volume of Sewage	(10000 cu.m)	144453	139107
#污水厂	(万立方米)	Treated by Sewage Treatment Plants	(10000 cu.m)	140413	136531
#二三级	(万立方米)	Grade-II and III Treatment	(10000 cu.m)	140413	136531
污水处理率	(%)	Sewage Treatment Rate	(%)	87.9	86.1
#集中处理率	(%)	Rate of Concentrated Treatment	(%)	87.9	86.1
污水排放总量	(万立方米)	Total Volume of Sewage Drainage	(10000 cu.m)	164217	161548
排水管道长度	(公里)	Length of Drainage Pipelines	(km)	15528	14290
污水管	(公里)	Sewage Pipes	(km)	7157	6536
雨水管	(公里)	Rain Pipes	(km)	6139	5555
雨污合流管	(公里)	Rain-sewage Sewer	(km)	2232	2198
再生水利用量	(万立方米)	Volume of Recycled Water Used	(10000 cu.m)	94826	86620
节水		**Water Saving**			
节水量	(万立方米)	Volume Saved	(10000 cu.m)	9878	12024
节水措施	(项)	Water Saving Measures Implemented	(unit)	137	127

资料来源：北京市水务局。
Source: Beijing Water Authority.

4-22 环境卫生
MUNICIPAL ENVIRONMENT AND SANITATION

项目		Item		2015	2014
工作量		**Work Load**			
清扫街道面积	(万平方米／日)	Area of Cleaned Streets	(10000 sq.m/day)	15122	15104
生活垃圾无害化处理能力	(吨/日)	Harmless Disposal Capacity of Domestic Waste	(ton/day)	27321	21971
生活垃圾产生量	(万吨)	Output of Domestic Waste	(10000 tons)	790.3	733.8
生活垃圾清运量	(万吨)	Domestic Waste Removed and Transported	(10000 tons)	790.3	733.8
生活垃圾无害化处理量	(万吨)	Volume of Harmless Disposal of Domestic Waste	(10000 tons)	788.7	730.8
生活垃圾无害化处理率	(%)	Rate of Harmless Disposal of Domestic Waste	(%)	99.8	99.6
(按清运量计算)		(Calculated by Volume of Waste Cleared and Transported)			
餐余垃圾处理量	(万吨)	Kitchen Waste Removed and Transported	(10000 tons)	27.3	24.3
粪便清运量	(万吨)	Excrement Removed and Transported	(10000 tons)	204.7	216.1
环卫机械数量	**(辆)**	**Number of Environmental Sanitation Machinery**	**(unit)**	**10747**	**10255**
环卫设施		**Environmental Sanitation Facilities**			
公共厕所	(座)	Public Lavatories	(unit)	5401	5429

资料来源：北京市市政市容管理委员会。
Source: Beijing Municipal Commission of City Administration and Environment.

4-23 环境保护(2000-2015年) ENVIRONMENTAL PROTECTION (2000-2015)

年份 Year	可吸入颗粒物年日均值(毫克/立方米) Daily Average of Inspiratory Particulate Matter in the Year (mg/cu.m)	二氧化硫年日均值(毫克/立方米) Daily Average of Sulfur Dioxide in the Year (mg/cu.m)	二氧化氮年日均值(毫克/立方米) Daily Average of Nitrogen Dioxide (mg/cu.m)	化学需氧量(COD)排放量(万吨) COD Emission Volume (10000 tons)	二氧化硫(SO_2)排放量(万吨) SO_2 Emission Volume (10000 tons)	区域环境噪声平均值(分贝) Average Value of Noises in Regional Environment (db)	道路交通干线噪声平均值(分贝) Average Value of Noises in Road Transportation (db)
2000	0.162	0.071	0.071	17.9	22.4	53.9	71.0
2001	0.165	0.064	0.071	17.0	20.1	53.9	69.6
2002	0.166	0.067	0.076	15.3	19.2	53.5	69.5
2003	0.141	0.061	0.072	13.4	18.3	53.6	69.7
2004	0.149	0.055	0.071	13.0	19.1	53.8	69.6
2005	0.142	0.050	0.066	11.6	19.1	53.2	69.5
2006	0.161	0.053	0.066	11.0	17.6	53.9	69.7
2007	0.148	0.047	0.066	10.7	15.2	54.0	69.9
2008	0.122	0.036	0.049	10.1	12.3	53.6	69.6
2009	0.121	0.034	0.053	9.9	11.9	54.1	69.7
2010	0.121	0.032	0.057	9.2	11.5	54.1	70.0
2011	0.114	0.028	0.055	19.3	9.8	53.7	69.6
2012	0.109	0.028	0.052	18.7	9.4	54.0	69.2
2013	0.108	0.027	0.056	17.8	8.7	53.9	69.1
2014	0.116	0.022	0.057	16.9	7.9	53.6	69.1
2015	0.102	0.014	0.050	16.2	7.1	53.3	69.2

注：化学需氧量(COD)排放量和二氧化硫排放量(SO_2)指标自2011年起调整统计口径和核算方法。

资料来源：北京市环境保护局。

Note: From 2011, statistical standard and calculation method are adjusted for COD emission volume and SO2 emission volume.

Source: Beijing Municipal Bureau of Environmental Protection.

4-24 环境保护
ENVIRONMENTAL PROTECTION

项目		Item		2015	2014
水环境		**Water Environment**			
废水排放总量	(万吨)	Total Discharge of Sewage	(10000 tons)	151733.34	150713.57
#工业废水排放量		Industrial Waste Water Discharge Volume		8978.08	9174.35
化学需氧量(COD)排放量	(吨)	COD Emission Volume	(ton)	161536	168840
#工业废水中COD排放量		Emission of COD in Industrial Waster Water		4738	6050
氨氮排放量	(吨)	Ammonia Nitrogen Discharge	(ton)	16491	18951
#工业废水中氨氮排放量		Ammonia Nitrogen Discharge in Industrial Waster Water		307	328
大气环境		**Atmosphere Environment**			
二氧化硫(SO_2)排放量	(吨)	SO_2 Emission Volume	(ton)	71172	78906
#工业二氧化硫排放量		Emission of Industrial SO_2		22070	40347
氮氧化物排放量	(吨)	Smoke and Dust Emission	(ton)	137627	150955
#工业氮氧化物排放量		Emission of Industrial Smoke and Dust		26864	64400
烟(粉)尘排放量	(吨)	Smoke and Dust Emission	(ton)	49387	57372
#工业烟(粉)尘排放量		Emission of Industrial Smoke and Dust		12987	22710
固体废物		**Solid Waste**			
一般工业固体废物产生量	(万吨)	General Industrial Solid Waste Generated	(10000 tons)	709.86	1020.76
一般工业固体废物综合利用量	(万吨)	General Industrial Solid Waste Recycled	(10000 tons)	591.56	894.98
一般工业固体废物处置量	(万吨)	General Industrial Solid Waste Disposed	(10000 tons)	118.41	125.92
危险废物产生量	(吨)	Hazardous Wastes Generated	(ton)	149939	148278
危险废物综合利用量	(吨)	Hazardous Wastes Recycled	(ton)	75886	82056
危险废物处置量	(吨)	Hazardous Wastes Disposed	(ton)	73728	66071
生态环境		**Ecological Environment**			
自然保护区个数	(个)	Number of Nature Reserves	(unit)	20	20
#国家级自然保护区		State-level Nature Reserves		2	2
自然保护区面积	(万公顷)	Area of Nature Reserves	(10000 hectares)	13.79	13.79

数据来源：北京市环境保护局。
Source: Beijing Municipal Bureau of Environmental Protection.

4-25 园林绿化及森林情况(1978-2015年)

年 份 Year	年末公园绿地面积 (公顷) Green Land and Park (year-end) (hectare)	人均公园绿地面积 (平方米/人) Per Capita Green Land and Park (sq.m/person)	城市绿化覆盖率 (%) Green Land Coverage (%)	林木绿化率 (%) Forest Coverage (%)	年末园林绿地面积 (公顷) Green Area (year-end) (hectare)
1978	2693	5.07	22.30		
1979	2693	5.07	22.30		
1980	2746	5.14	20.10	16.6	
1981	2751	5.14	20.10	16.6	
1982	2779	5.14	20.10	16.6	
1983	2823	5.14	20.10	16.6	
1984	2878	5.14	20.10	16.6	
1985	3263	4.94	22.10	16.6	
1986	3606	5.07	22.86	16.6	
1987	3570	5.07	22.90	16.6	
1988	4074	5.80	25.00	16.6	
1989	6910	6.00	26.00	16.6	
1990	7110	6.14	28.00	28.3	
1991	4279	6.41	28.43	28.3	
1992	4213	6.65	30.33	28.3	
1993	4452	7.76	31.33	28.3	
1994	5221	7.89	32.39	28.3	
1995	5017	7.48	32.68	36.3	
1996	5147	7.54	33.24	36.3	
1997	5408	7.80	34.22	36.3	
1998	6351	9.00	35.60	36.3	
1999	6457	9.10	36.30	36.3	
2000	7140	9.66	36.50	42.0	26680
2001	7554	10.07	38.78	44.0	30224
2002	7907	10.66	40.57	45.5	32572
2003	9115	11.43	40.87	47.5	38475
2004	10446	11.45	41.91	49.5	36755
2005	11365	12.00	42.00	50.5	38877
2006	11788	12.00	42.50	51.0	45495
2007	12101	12.60	43.00	51.6	46320
2008	12316	13.60	43.50	52.1	46993
2009	18070	14.50	44.40	52.6	61695
2010	19020	15.00	45.00	53.0	62672
2011	19728	15.30	45.60	54.0	63541
2012	21178	15.50	46.20	55.5	65540
2013	22215	15.70	46.80	57.4	67048
2014	28798	15.90	47.40	58.4	80223
2015	29503	16.00	48.40	59.0	81305

资料来源：北京市园林绿化局。

STATISTICS FOR LANDSCAPING AND FORESTS (1978-2015)

森林面积 (公顷) Forest Area (hectare)	森林覆盖率 (%) Forest Coverage Rate (%)	活立木蓄积量 (万立方米) Total Stock of Standing Trees (10000 cu.m)	森林蓄积量 (万立方米) Forest Stock (10000 cu.m)	森林火灾次数 (次) Number of Forest Fires (unit)	森林火灾经济损失 (万元) Economic Loss of Forest Fires (10000 yuan)
619243.2		1521.4	1295.3	9	11.4
626006.3	35.9	1521.4	1295.3	13	96.7
636565.7	36.5	1559.5	1368.9	8	28.1
641368.3	36.5	1574.0	1394.4		
658914.1	36.7	1810.3	1406.2	2	…
666050.7	37.0	1854.7	1435.4	4	1.4
673411.8	37.6	1899.4	1468.7	3	1.7
691341.1	38.6	1943.3	1499.0	1	
716456.1	40.1	1993.4	1536.8		
734530.6	41.0	2109.1	1669.9	1	
744956.1	41.6	2149.3	1701.1	3	29.7

Source: Beijing Municipal Bureau of Landscape and Forestry.

主要统计指标解释

能源生产量 能源生产量是反映能源生产规模、构成、生产成果的重要指标。按能源的成因分为一次能源（亦称天然能源）生产量和二次能源（亦称人工能源）生产量。

一次能源生产量 指报告期内生产一次能源的企业将自然界现存的能源资源经过开采而产出的合格产品，主要包括原煤、原油、天然气、水电等。

二次能源生产量 指报告期内将一次能源经过各种加工转换设备生产出的另一种形式的各种合格的能源产品。如火电、热力、洗煤、焦炭、各种石油制品、焦炉煤气、其他煤气等。

能源消费总量 指一定地域（行政或地理区域）内，国民经济各行业和居民家庭在一定时期所消费的各种能源的总和。能源消费总量包括终端能源消费量、能源加工转换损失量、能源运输和管理过程的损失量三部分。

能源消费总量（等价值） 是电力、热力按等价热值计算的能源消费总量。等价热值是能源统计中经常使用的一个热值概念，是指加工转换产出的某种二次能源所投入的一次能源的量，即获得一个度量单位的某种二次能源所消耗的以热值表示的一次能源。

能源加工转换投入产出量 能源具有由一种能量形式转换为另一种能量形式及耗用过程中可用一种能源替代另一种能源的特征。为提高能源的利用价值和效率，对能源进行加工、转换，产出适合生产和生活需要的更高级的能源产品。在加工转换投入(-)产出(+)量中，“-”表示能源加工转换的投入量，“+”表示二次能源的产出量。

投入量 是指为生产二次能源产品，所投入到能源加工转换设备的各种能源数量。在表中以负数表示。

产出量 是指各种能源（一次能源或少量再投入的二次能源）经过加工转换后，产出的各种二次能源产品（包括不作为能源使用的副产品，联产品）数量。

加工转换损失量 是指在能源加工、转换过程中损失的能量（能源），即能源加工、转换过程中投入的能源和产出的二次能源之间的差额。

损失量 指能源在经营管理和生产、输送、分配、储存等过程中发生的损失以及由于自然因素等原因造成的损失数量。不包括加工转换损失量。

终端消费量 是指能源消费环节的最后一个环节的能源消费，包括直接用作燃料、原材料和动力的各种能源的消费。它们的消费过程体现了能源消费的终止，不会再重新作为能源投入使用。终端消费量不包括用于能源加工转换投入量、加工转换损失量和损失量。

能源消费弹性系数 指能源消费总量增长率与地区生产总值增长率的比值。

电力消费弹性系数 指电力消费量增长率与地区生产总值增长率的比值。

平均每万元地区生产总值能源消费量 能源总消费量或分品种能源消费量与地区生产总值之比。

人均生活用能量 指用于生活消费的各种能源数量与人口总数之比。

日均能源消费量 指各品种能源消费量与当年实际天数之比。

垃圾无害化处理能力 指垃圾无害化处理场（厂）按工艺设计每天所能处理生活垃圾的数量。垃圾无害化处理场（厂）必须是按照有关技术、环境、卫生标准和规范进行设计、建设、运行、维护和管理的各种生活垃圾处理设施，主要包括卫生填埋场、堆肥厂和焚烧厂等。

水资源总量 指降水形成的地表和地下水总量，不包括过境水量。

排水管道长度 指所有排水总管、干管、支管、检查井及连接井进出口等长度之和。计算时应按单管计算，即在同一条街道上如有两条或两条以上并排的排水管道时，应按每条排水管道的长度相加计算。

污水处理能力 指污水处理厂（或处理装置）每昼夜处理污水量的设计能力。

按污水处理的程度，一般可分为一级处理、二级处理和三级处理。

一级处理是以沉淀为主体的处理工艺。指去除污水中的漂浮物和悬浮物的净化过程，主要为沉淀。

二级处理是以生物处理为主体的处理工艺。指污水经一级处理后，用生物处理方法继续除去污水中胶体和溶解性有机物的净化过程。

三级处理也称高级处理或深度处理。指进一步去除二级处理不能完全去除的污水中的污染物的处理工艺。

污水处理量 指污水处理厂和处理装置实际处理的污水量。包括物理处理量、生物处理量和化学处理量。

污水处理率 指污水处理量与污水排放总量的比率。计算公式:

$$\text{污水处理率} = \frac{\text{污水处理量}}{\text{污水排放总量}} \times 100\%$$

生活垃圾清运量 指报告期内收集和运送到各垃圾处理场（厂）的垃圾的数量。

粪便清运量 指报告期内收集和运送到各粪便处理场

（厂）的粪便的数量。

生活垃圾无害化处理量 指报告期内简易处理场和各种垃圾无害化处理场（厂）处理垃圾的总量。垃圾简易处理量指垃圾简易填埋场所处理的垃圾总量。垃圾无害化处理量指垃圾无害化处理场（厂）所处理的垃圾总量。

生活垃圾无害化处理率 指报告期垃圾无害化处理量与垃圾产生量的比率。计算公式:

$$垃圾无害化处理率 = \frac{垃圾无害化处理量}{垃圾产生量} \times 100\%$$

在统计时，如果生活垃圾产生量不易取得，可用清运量代替。

化学需氧量（COD）排放量 指工业废水中 COD 排放量与生活污水中 COD 排放量之和。指用化学氧化剂氧化水中有机污染物时所需的氧量。COD 值越高，表示水中有机污染物污染越重。

二氧化硫（SO_2）排放量 指报告期内工业 SO_2 排放量与生活 SO_2 排放量之和。

工业固体废物综合利用量 指报告期内企业通过回收、加工、循环、交换等方式，从固体废物中提取或者使其转化为可以利用的资源、能源和其他原材料的固体废物量（包括当年利用的往年工业固体废物贮存量）。如用做农业肥料、生产建筑材料、筑路等。

公园绿地 指向公众开放，以游憩为主要功能，兼具生态、美化、防灾等作用，其绿地率达到 65%以上，配有多种乔灌木及地被植物，有一定设施和艺术布局的绿地。包括公园、社区公园、街旁绿地、其他公园绿地。人均公园绿地面积计算口径为户籍非农业人口。

绿化覆盖率 指报告期末区域内绿化覆盖面积与区域面积的比率。

计算公式:

$$绿化覆盖率 = \frac{区域内绿化覆盖面积}{区域面积} \times 100\%$$

森林面积 指由乔木树种构成，郁闭度 0.20 以上(含 0.20)的林地或冠幅宽度 10 米以上的林带的面积，即有林地面积。它是反映森林资源总面积的重要指标。森林面积包括天然起源和人工起源的针叶林面积、阔叶林面积、针阔混交林面积和竹林面积。

活立木蓄积量 指一定范围土地上全部树木蓄积的总量，包括森林蓄积、疏林蓄积、散生木蓄积和四旁树蓄积。

森林蓄积量 指一定森林面积上存在着的林木树干部分的总材积，以立方米为计量单位。

森林火灾次数 指发生在城市市区外的一切森林、林木和林地的火灾次数，包括森林火警、一般灾害、重大灾害和特大灾害。

Explanatory Notes on Main Statistical Indicators

Energy Production is an important indicator reflecting the size, composition and results of energy production. By the cause of formation, it consists of the production of primary energy (also known as natural energy) and that of secondary energy (also known as artificial energy).

Production of Primary Energy means up-to-grade products produced by primary energy producers in the reporting period through extraction of existing energy in the nature, mainly including raw coal, crude oil, natural gas, hydroelectricity, etc.

Production of Secondary Energy means various up-to-grade energy products in another form that are made from primary energy with various processing and converting equipment in the reporting period, including thermal power, heating power, washed coal, coke, various petroleum products, coke oven gas and other gases, etc.

Total Energy Consumption means the total consumption of various energies by national economic sectors and resident households in a specific region (administrative or geographic). Total energy consumption can be divided into three parts: end-use energy consumption, loss during energy processing and conversion and loss during energy transport and management.

Total Energy Consumption (in Equivalent Caloricity) means the total consumption of electric power and heating power calculated in equivalent caloricity. Equivalent caloricity is a caloricity concept frequently used in statistics of energy. It means the quantity of primary energy input for a secondary energy produced through processing and conversion, i.e. the primary energy in terms of caloricity which is consumed to produce one measuring unit of a secondary energy.

Input and Output of Energy Processing and Conversion One form of energy can be converted into another form of energy. And in consumption, one sort of energy can be replaced with another. In order to improve the energy use value and efficiency, energy is processed and converted to produce energy products at higher levels which are suitable for productive and living needs. In the processing and conversion input (-) and output (+), "-" means the input for energy processing and conversion. And "+" means the output from energy processing and conversion.

Input means the volume of energy put into the energy processing and converting equipment in order to produce secondary energy products.

Output means the volume of secondary energy products (including byproducts and multi-products that cannot be used as energy) from processing and conversion of energy sources (primary energy or a small amount of secondary energy re-input).

Loss during Processing and Conversion means the energy lost in the processing and conversion of energy, namely the difference between the energy input and the secondary energy output during energy processing and conversion.

Energy Loss means the loss of energy during operation, management, production, transportation, distribution and storage, as well as the loss due to natural factors and other reasons. It excludes the loss during processing and conversion.

End-use Energy Consumption means the energy consumption in the last section of energy consumption, including the consumption of various energy sources used as fuel, raw materials and power. Such consumption represents the end of energy consumption, and the energy will not be put into use again as energy. End-use energy consumption does not include the input for energy processing and conversion, loss during the processing and conversion of energy, and energy loss.

Elasticity Coefficient of Energy Consumption means the ratio of growth rate of total energy consumption to the growth rate of GDP.

Elasticity Coefficient of Electric Power Consumption means the ratio of growth rate of electric power consumption to the growth rate of GDP.

Average Energy Consumption per RMB 10000 of GDP means the ratio of total energy consumption or energy consumption by variety to GDP.

Per-capital Energy Consumption by Households means the ratio of quantity of energy consumed by households to the total population.

Daily Energy Consumption means the ratio of energy consumption to the actual days in the same year.

Harmless Disposal Capacity of Waste means the daily quantity of domestic waste that can be disposed at harmless disposal facilities (sites) according to the process designed. Harmless disposal facilities (sites) must be domestic waste disposal facilities, including landfills, manure yards, incineration facilities and so on, which are designed, built, operated and managed in accordance with relevant technological, environmental, and sanitary standards and criterion.

Total Water Resources means the total volume of surface water and underground water caused by rainfall, excluding passing-by water.

Length of Sewage Pipes means the total length of all main drainage pipes, trunk pipes, branch pipes, access manholes, and connector well entrances and exits, and so on. The length of single pipes shall be included, i.e. if there are two or more drainage pipes parallel on a street, the length of every pipe shall be included.

Sewage Treatment Capacity means the designed capacity of sewage disposal day and night for a sewage disposal plant (or facility).

In terms of extent, sewage disposal consists of primary disposal, secondary disposal and tertiary disposal.

Primary Disposal is a disposal process focusing on precipitation. It means a purification process removing the floating and suspended substances in sewage, mostly precipitation.

Secondary Disposal is a disposal process focusing on biological disposal. It means a purification process further removing the colloids and resolvable organic substances in sewage after the process of primary disposal.

Tertiary Disposal is also known as senior or deep disposal. It means a disposal process further removing any pollutants that cannot be removed completely in the process of secondary disposal.

Volume of Sewage Treated means the volume of sewage actually disposed by sewage disposal plants and facilities, consisting of physical volume, biological volume and chemical volume of waste water disposed.

Sewage Treatment Rate means the ratio of sewage disposed to the total discharge of sewage. The formula is:

Sewage Disposal Rate = Volume of Sewage Disposed / Total Discharge of Sewage × 100%

Domestic Waste Removed and Transported means the quantity of waste collected and transported to waste treatment sites (plants) in the reporting period.

Excrement Removed and Transported means the quantity of excrement collected and transported to waste treatment sites (plants) in the reporting period.

Volume of Harmless Disposal of Domestic Waste means the total volume of waste disposed by simple disposal sites and harmless waste disposal sits (plants) in the reporting period. Simple disposal of waste means the total volume of waste by simple landfills. Harmless waste disposal means the total volume of waste disposed by harmless waste disposal sites (plants).

Rate of Harmless Disposal of Domestic Waste means the ratio of harmless waste disposal to the waste produced in the reporting period. The formula is:

Rate of Harmless Disposal of Domestic Waste = Harmless Waste Disposal / Waste Produced × 100%

In practical statistics, if it is hard to get figures on the volume of domestic waste produced, the volume removed and transported may be used.

COD Emission Volume means the sum of COD emission in industrial sewage and in domestic waste water. It means the amount of oxygen required when chemical oxidants are used to oxidize organic pollutants in water. A higher value of COD corresponds to more serious pollution by organic pollutants.

SO_2 Emission Volume means the sum of industrial SO_2 emission and domestic SO_2 emission in the reporting period.

Industrial Solid Waste Utilized means the volume of solid wastes from which useful materials can be extracted or which can be converted into usable resources, energy or other materials by means of reclamation, processing, recycling and exchange (including utilizing in the year the stocks of industrial solid wastes of the previous year). Examples of such utilizations include fertilizers, building materials and road materials.

Green Land and Parks means the green land open to the public, with main function of recreation, together with ecological, landscaping and disaster preventing functions, and with more than 65% green coverage, provided with multiple arbors, shrubs and ground-cover plants, along with certain facilities and artistic layouts. They include parks, community parks, street-side green land and other green land in gardens. Per capita area of green land is calculated on the basis of non-agricultural household population.

Green Land Coverage means the ratio of area of green land in a region to the total area of the region in the reporting period. The formula is:

Green Land Coverage = Area of Green Land in a Region / Total Area of the Region × 100%

Forest Area means the area of forest where arbor trees grow with canopy density above 0.2 (and at 0.2) or forest area with crown width more than 10m, i.e. the area of land with forest. It is an important indicator reflecting the total area of forest resources. Forest Area includes the area of coniferous forest, broad leaf forest, mixed coniferous-broad-leaf forest and bamboo forest from both natural and artificial origins.

Total Stock of Standing Trees mean the total stock of all trees on specific area of land, including trees in forest, trees in sparse forest, scattered trees and trees planted by the side of villages, farm houses and along roads and rivers.

Forest Stock means the total volume of timber of forest tree trunks growing on specific area of forest, which are measured in cubic meters.

Number of Forest Fires means the number of all fires occurring in forests, woods, woodlands outside the urban districts, including forest fires, general fires, severe fires and fire disasters.

北京统计年鉴2016　BEIJING STATISTICAL YEARBOOK

全社会固定资产投资和房地产开发

TOTAL INVESTMENT IN FIXED ASSETS AND REAL ESTATE DEVELOPMENT

简要说明

一、本章资料的主要内容

本章资料包括历年北京市全社会固定资产投资、房地产开发的主要分组数据、保障性安居工程建设等情况。

二、本章资料的统计范围

1996 年及以前固定资产投资统计起点为 5 万元以上，1996 年以后调整为 50 万元及以上，从 2011 年开始调整为 500 万元及以上。

三、有关统计标准的变化说明

（一）关于行业划分。根据国家统计局规定，自 2012 年开始执行《国民经济行业分类》（GB/T 4754-2011）标准。

（二）关于三次产业划分。根据国家统计局《三次产业划分规定》（国统字[2012]108 号），该规定对三次产业的范围进行了调整。其中第一产业是指农、林、牧、渔业（不含农、林、牧、渔服务业）；第二产业是指采矿业（不含开采辅助活动），制造业（不含金属制品、机械和设备修理业），电力、热力、燃气及水生产和供应业，建筑业；第三产业是指除第一产业、第二产业以外的其他行业。自 2012 年开始执行此规定。

四、本章资料的数据来源

本章资料来源于北京市统计局、国家统计局北京调查总队。

五、本章的统计调查方法

除农户固定资产投资统计采用抽样调查方法外，其他均为全面调查。

Brief Introduction

I. Main Content

Statistics in this chapter include figures on fixed assets investment in Beijing and its main grouped figures as well as figures on government-subsidized housing projects.

II. Scope of Statistics

Before and in 1996, the threshold of fixed assets statistics was over RMB 50,000; after 1996, it was increased to RMB 500,000 and above; since 2011, the figure has been set at RMB 5 million and above.

III. Changes in Relevant Statistical Standards

(I) Classification of Sectors. According to relevant provisions of the National Bureau of Statistics, the Standard for Classification of National Economic Sectors (GB/T 4754-2011) came into effect in 2012.

(II) Classification of Three Industries. According to the Regulations on the Classification of the Three Industries (G.T.Z. [2012] No. 108) issued by National Bureau of Statistics, the scope of three industries has been adjusted. The primary industry refers to agriculture, forestry, animal production and hunting, fishing (excluding services for a agriculture, forestry, animal production and hunting, fishing); the secondary industry refers to mining (excluding mining support activities), manufacturing (excluding metal products, machinery and equipment repair), production and distribution of electricity, heating power, gas and water, and construction; the tertiary industry refers to sectors other than the primary and secondary industries. The Regulations on the Classification of the Three Industries (G.T.Z. [2012] No. 108) issued by National Bureau of Statistics came into effect in 2012.

IV. Source of Statistics

Statistics in this chapter are from the Beijing Municipal Bureau of Statistics and NBS Survey Office in Beijing.

V. Method of Statistical Survey

Sample survey is used for the statistics on investment of rural households in fixed assets. For other statistics, the complete survey is conducted.

5-1 全社会固定资产投资和增长速度情况(1978-2015年)
TOTAL INVESTMENT IN FIXED ASSETS AND GROWTH RATE (1978-2015)

单位：亿元 (100 million yuan)

年份 Year	全社会固定资产投资 Total Investment in Fixed Assets	城镇固定资产投资 Investment in Urban Fixed Assets	#房地产开发投资 Investment in Real Estate Development	农村固定资产投资 Investment in Rural Fixed Assets	#基础设施投资 Infrastructure Investment	#建筑安装投资 Construction and Installation Investment	新增固定资产 Incremental Fixed Assets
1978	22.6	22.6			5.4		16.9
1979	26.5	26.5			5.8		21.2
1980	33.2	33.2			6.0		23.2
1981-1985	**286.8**	**234.4**		**50.8**	**40.6**		**184.4**
1981	36.6	31.4		5.2	5.8		30.9
1982	38.6	34.5		4.1	6.1		26.3
1983	51.3	38.5		12.8	6.7		32.5
1984	66.3	52.2		14.1	8.8		47.1
1985	94.0	77.8		14.6	13.2		47.6
1986-1990	**724.1**	**634.9**	**22.5**	**76.5**	**117.9**		**417.4**
1986	106.2	94.5		10.4	14.5		58.5
1987	136.2	121.4		12.7	22.1		79.9
1988	163.0	138.7		21.3	23.2		77.3
1989	139.5	122.2		14.7	26.5		79.6
1990	179.2	158.1	22.5	17.4	31.6		122.1
1991-1995	**2358.7**	**2181.5**	**568.4**	**154.1**	**494.9**	**1297.1**	**1229.1**
1991	192.0	168.4	24.0	21.0	35.2	107.3	139.0
1992	266.0	234.7	33.7	27.2	58.8	136.2	157.8
1993	410.4	376.6	58.4	30.0	91.4	232.0	201.6
1994	648.8	607.4	99.5	35.7	153.4	362.6	356.0
1995	841.5	794.4	352.8	40.2	156.1	459.0	374.7
1996-2000	**5461.7**	**5063.8**	**1979.5**	**322.7**	**1382.1**	**3069.5**	**4051.2**
1996	876.9	825.6	328.2	43.6	188.8	515.8	592.5
1997	961.2	912.4	330.3	40.6	218.3	546.2	637.9
1998	1155.6	1060.3	377.4	75.8	320.4	626.9	759.3
1999	1170.6	1072.9	421.5	78.2	302.7	679.1	949.5
2000	1297.4	1192.6	522.1	84.5	351.9	701.5	1112.0
2001-2005	**10857.4**	**10033.6**	**5974.0**	**755.4**	**2260.0**	**5926.2**	**6897.4**
2001	1530.5	1417.1	783.8	93.7	356.4	801.6	1177.0
2002	1814.3	1688.2	989.4	102.5	411.9	964.9	1251.0
2003	2157.1	1999.9	1202.5	132.1	417.8	1151.3	1165.9
2004	2528.3	2333.0	1473.3	195.3	463.2	1438.9	1455.1
2005	2827.2	2595.4	1525.0	231.8	610.7	1569.5	1848.4
2006-2010	**21538.5**	**19678.6**	**10863.2**	**1859.9**	**6137.3**	**9860.6**	**11666.8**
2006	3371.5	3086.3	1719.9	285.2	935.3	1836.0	1972.1
2007	3966.6	3656.7	1995.8	309.9	1175.8	2117.9	2004.9
2008	3848.5	3554.8	1908.7	293.7	1160.7	1798.8	2666.8
2009	4858.4	4378.2	2337.7	480.2	1462.0	1983.0	2457.2
2010	5493.5	5002.6	2901.1	490.9	1403.5	2124.9	2565.8
	(5218.3)						
2011-2015	**34958.8**	**31863.2**	**17810.7**	**3095.7**	**9167.7**	**15608.7**	**15996.7**
2011	5910.6	5463.9	3036.3	446.7	1400.2	2585.3	2382.0
2012	6462.8	5853.1	3153.4	609.8	1789.2	3076.6	2570.4
2013	7032.2	6352.6	3483.4	679.6	1785.7	3482.2	3163.8
2014	7562.3	6926.6	3911.3	635.7	2018.1	3468.1	3887.3
2015	7990.9	7267.0	4226.3	723.9	2174.5	2996.5	3993.2

注：1. 根据国家统计局有关规定，从2004年起，全社会固定资产投资中不包括零星购置投资。
2. 2004年起,新增固定资产、基础设施投资、建筑安装投资中包含农村投资。
3. 根据国家统计局有关规定，2011年起投资统计起点调整为500万元，为便于比较，2010年的相应数据也作了调整，未加括号的为原口径数，括号内为调整后的数据，当年固定资产投资增长速度及“十二五”时期平均增长速度均按可比口径计算。

Note: a) According to related regulations of National Bureau of Statistics, since 2004, total investment in fixed assets has not included investment in acquiring minor items.
b) Since 2004, rural investment has been counted in incremental fixed assets, infrastructure investment, construction and installation investment.
c) Since 2011, the statistical threshold of investment has been adjusted to RMB 5 million according to the related regulations of National Bureau of Statistics. For comparison, relevant figures in 2010 were adjusted accordingly. Figures with no brackets are based on the former standard. Figures in brackets are data after adjustment. Growth rates of fixed assets investment in respective years are calculated in comparable terms.

5-1 续表 Continued

单位：% (%)

年份 Year	全社会固定资产投资比上年增长 Growth rate of Total Investment in Fixed Assets	城镇固定资产投资 Growth rate of Investment in Urban Fixed Assets	#房地产开发投资 Growth rate of Investment in Real Estate Development	农村固定资产投资 Growth rate of Investment in Rural Fixed Assets	#基础设施投资 Growth rate of Infrastructure Investment	#建筑安装投资 Growth rate of Construction and Installation Investment
1978						
1979	17.3	17.3			7.4	
1980	25.3	25.3			3.4	
1981-1985	**18.8**	**11.7**			**10.3**	
1981	10.2	-5.4			-3.3	
1982	5.5	9.9		-21.2	5.2	
1983	32.9	11.6		212.2	9.8	
1984	29.2	35.6		10.2	31.3	
1985	41.8	49.0		3.5	50.0	
1986-1990	**14.8**	**16.8**		**1.5**	**20.0**	
1986	13.0	21.5		-28.8	9.8	
1987	28.2	28.5		22.1	52.4	
1988	19.7	14.3		67.7	5.0	
1989	-14.4	-11.9		-31.0	14.2	
1990	28.5	29.4		18.4	19.2	
1991-1995	**34.2**	**36.0**	**59.9**	**19.7**	**40.8**	
1991	7.1	6.5	6.7	20.7	11.4	
1992	38.5	39.4	40.4	29.5	67.0	26.9
1993	54.3	60.5	73.3	10.3	55.4	70.3
1994	58.1	61.3	70.4	19.0	67.8	56.3
1995	29.7	30.8	254.6	12.6	1.8	26.6
1996-2000	**8.9**	**8.2**	**3.9**	**16.2**	**19.7**	**9.9**
1996	4.2	3.9	-7.0	8.5	20.9	12.4
1997	9.6	10.5	0.6	-6.9	15.6	5.9
1998	20.2	16.2	14.3	86.7	46.8	14.8
1999	1.3	1.2	11.7	3.2	-5.5	8.3
2000	10.8	11.2	23.9	8.1	16.3	3.3
2001-2005	**17.7**	**17.9**	**29.0**	**20.1**	**8.5**	**18.0**
2001	18.0	18.8	50.1	10.9	1.3	14.3
2002	18.5	19.1	26.2	9.4	15.6	20.4
2003	18.9	18.5	21.5	28.9	1.4	19.3
2004	17.2	16.7	22.5	47.8	10.9	25.0
2005	11.8	11.2	3.5	18.7	31.8	9.1
2006-2010	**14.4**	**14.2**	**12.0**	**16.2**	**24.2**	**7.7**
2006	19.3	18.9	12.8	23.0	53.2	17.0
2007	17.6	18.5	16.0	8.7	25.7	15.4
2008	-3.0	-2.8	-4.4	-5.2	-1.3	-15.1
2009	26.2	23.2	22.5	63.5	26.0	10.2
2010	13.1	14.3	24.1	2.2	-4.0	7.2
2011-2015	**9.9**	**9.9**	**8.7**	**10.1**	**9.0**	**13.3**
2011	13.3	14.8	10.1	-2.9	0.3	22.4
2012	9.3	7.1	3.9	36.5	27.8	19.0
2013	8.8	8.5	10.5	11.5	-0.2	13.2
2014	7.5	9.0	12.3	-6.5	13.0	-0.4
2015	5.7	4.9	8.1	13.9	7.7	-13.6

5-2 按登记注册类型分全社会固定资产投资(1978-2015年) TOTAL INVESTMENT IN FIXED ASSETS BY REGISTRATION TYPE (1978-2015)

单位：亿元 (100 million yuan)

年 份 Year	全社会固定资产投资 Total Investment in Fixed Assets	国 有 State-owned	集 体 Collectively-owned	股份制 Joint-stock	港澳台商 Hong Kong, Macao and Taiwan	外 商 Foreign	私营个体 Private	其 他 Others
1978	22.6							
1979	26.5							
1980	33.2							
1981-1985	**286.8**	**223.8**	**22.6**				**40.4**	
1981	36.6	30.1	1.3				5.2	
1982	38.6	33.0	1.5				4.1	
1983	51.3	37.1	1.4				12.8	
1984	66.3	50.0	2.2				14.1	
1985	94.0	73.6	16.2				4.2	
1986-1990	**724.1**	**609.6**	**83.1**				**31.4**	
1986	106.2	88.7	13.3				4.2	
1987	136.2	115.8	15.2				5.2	
1988	163.0	133.2	21.4				8.4	
1989	139.5	117.7	15.1				6.7	
1990	179.2	154.2	18.1				6.9	
1991-1995	**2358.7**	**1764.2**	**188.7**				**24.8**	
1991	192.0	165.0	20.2				6.8	
1992	266.0	230.1	27.3				8.6	
1993	410.4	340.1	37.4				2.0	
1994	648.8	514.8	44.6				3.1	
1995	841.5	514.2	59.2				4.3	
1996-2000	**5461.7**	**3380.8**	**261.8**				**155.3**	
1996	876.9	545.7	57.6				4.8	
1997	961.2	605.7	54.7				4.0	
1998	1155.6	727.9	48.7				30.9	
1999	1170.6	735.7	55.8				36.1	
2000	1297.4	765.8	45.0				79.5	
2001-2005	**10857.4**	**3922.4**	**303.3**				**809.4**	
2001	1530.5	752.6	45.8				110.9	
2002	1814.3	771.5	53.9				150.6	
2003	2157.1	745.1	62.4				201.3	
2004	2528.3	755.5	69.5	1063.8	204.5	198.8	176.4	59.8
2005	2827.2	897.7	71.7	1211.8	164.1	274.1	170.2	37.6
2006-2010	**21538.5**	**8162.9**	**398.0**	**9206.8**	**903.8**	**1480.8**	**1121.2**	**265.0**
2006	3371.5	1207.2	69.3	1384.5	180.9	315.9	174.9	38.8
2007	3966.6	1343.0	80.4	1679.0	236.4	378.9	209.0	39.9
2008	3848.5	1388.6	66.8	1688.5	145.3	274.9	242.2	42.2
2009	4858.4	2316.8	68.9	1728.5	172.2	273.0	233.0	66.0
2010	5493.5	1907.3	112.6	2726.3	169.0	238.1	262.1	78.1
2011-2015	**34958.8**	**11452.2**	**635.5**	**17733.9**	**1525.3**	**1468.8**	**1707.3**	**435.7**
2011	5910.6	1903.3	99.4	3053.2	224.1	266.8	278.4	85.4
2012	6462.8	2248.2	106.8	3280.9	208.8	300.2	231.7	86.1
2013	7032.2	2382.0	151.4	3318.4	464.2	321.7	317.0	77.5
2014	7562.3	2389.5	151.4	3944.0	380.7	255.9	366.1	74.7
2015	7990.9	2529.2	126.5	4137.4	247.5	324.2	514.1	112.0

注：1. 根据国家统计局有关规定，从2004年起，全社会固定资产投资中不包括零星购置投资。
2. 国有包括登记注册类型为国有、国有联营及国有独资公司的单位。
3. 集体包括登记注册类型为集体和集体联营的单位。

Note: a) According to related regulations of National Bureau of Statistics, since 2004, total investment in fixed assets has not included investment in acquiring minor items.
b) State-owned units include state-owned enterprises, state-owned associated enterprises and wholly state-owned enterprises.
c) Collectively-owned units include collectively-owned enterprises and collectively-owned associated enterprises.

5-3 按产业分全社会固定资产投资(1978-2015年)
INVESTMENT IN FIXED ASSETS BY INDUSTRY (1978-2015)

单位：亿元 (100 million yuan)

年份 Year	全社会固定资产投资 Total Investment in Fixed Assets	第一产业 Primary Industry	第二产业 Secondary Industry	第三产业 Tertiary Industry
1978	22.6	1.4	10.8	10.4
1979	26.5	1.0	12.0	13.5
1980	33.2	0.7	15.7	16.8
1981-1985	**286.8**	**5.9**	**98.1**	**130.4**
1981	36.6	0.6	13.6	17.2
1982	38.6	1.2	15.4	17.9
1983	51.3	1.2	16.4	20.9
1984	66.3	1.3	20.3	30.6
1985	94.0	1.6	32.4	43.8
1986-1990	**724.1**	**9.4**	**218.8**	**384.2**
1986	106.2	1.5	41.4	51.6
1987	136.2	1.6	46.9	72.9
1988	163.0	2.0	48.8	87.9
1989	139.5	1.9	38.4	81.9
1990	179.2	2.4	43.3	89.9
1991-1995	**2358.7**	**15.5**	**624.1**	**973.5**
1991	192.0	2.7	51.3	90.4
1992	266.0	3.9	82.9	114.2
1993	410.4	2.1	150.4	165.7
1994	648.8	3.7	185.8	318.4
1995	841.5	3.1	153.7	284.8
1996-2000	**5461.7**	**9.9**	**914.3**	**2160.2**
1996	876.9	2.8	174.9	319.7
1997	961.2	0.9	201.1	380.1
1998	1155.6	1.5	201.7	479.7
1999	1170.6	1.7	179.4	470.4
2000	1297.4	3.0	157.2	510.3
2001-2005	**10857.4**	**63.4**	**1410.6**	**9383.4**
2001	1530.5	8.4	154.2	1367.9
2002	1814.3	7.5	185.0	1621.8
2003	2157.1	21.0	260.7	1875.4
2004	2528.3	14.6	401.0	2112.7
2005	2827.2	11.9	409.7	2405.6
2006-2010	**21538.5**	**159.9**	**2172.8**	**19205.8**
2006	3371.5	14.5	363.2	2993.8
2007	3966.6	16.7	484.1	3465.8
2008	3848.5	28.1	386.0	3434.4
2009	4858.4	57.4	411.4	4389.5
2010	5493.5	43.2	528.1	4922.3
2011-2015	**34958.8**	**643.0**	**3630.9**	**30684.9**
2011	5910.6	47.2	762.2	5101.3
2012	6462.8	145.4	719.8	5597.5
2013	7032.2	175.5	755.0	6101.7
2014	7562.3	163.9	716.8	6681.6
2015	7990.9	111.0	677.1	7202.8

注：1. 根据国家统计局有关规定，从2004年起，全社会固定资产投资中不包括零星购置投资。
2. 2000年及以前按产业划分中，不含房地产开发投资及农村投资。2000年以后含房地产开发投资及农村固定资产投资。
3. 自2012年起，三次产业划分执行国家统计局《三次产业划分规定》(国统字〔2012〕108号)。

Note: a) According to related regulations of National Bureau of Statistics, since 2004, total investment in fixed assets has not included investment in acquiring minor items.
b) Data of investment in fixed assets grouped by industry excluded investment in real estate development and rural investment in 2000 and before. After 2000, data of investment in fixed assets included investment in real estate development and rural fixed assets.
c) Since 2012, the three industries have been classified according to the Regulations on the Classification of the Three Industries (G.T.Z. [2012] No. 108) issued by National Bureau of Statistics.

5-4 全社会固定资产投资资金来源情况(1978-2015年)
TOTAL INVESTMENT IN FIXED ASSETS BY SOURCE OF FUNDS (1978-2015)

单位：亿元 (100 million yuan)

年 份 Year	上年末结余资金 Surplus Funds by the End of the Previous Year	本年资金来源小计 Subtotal of Funds at Current Year	国家预算内资金 State Budgets	国内贷款 Domestic Loans	债券 Bonds	利用外资 Foreign Investment	自筹资金 Self-raised Funds	其他资金 Others
1978		22.5	16.9					
1979		26.5	19.2					
1980		33.2	18.5					
1981		31.4	15.4					
1982		34.5	14.1					
1983		38.5	16.0					
1984		52.2	22.5					
1985		77.8	30.4					
1986		94.5	33.0					
1987		126.2	43.1					
1988		149.4	37.4					
1989		123.1	35.0	12.8		18.2	44.5	12.6
1990		136.2	34.4	22.8		15.2	52.3	11.5
1991		151.1	35.5	28.2		13.9	65.5	8.0
1992		216.7	42.2	40.1		14.9	109.9	9.6
1993	54.3	425.2	47.1	79.2	1.6	28.0	205.2	64.1
1994	71.1	695.7	64.1	91.5	0.8	96.9	331.2	111.2
1995	200.8	915.8	70.3	122.7	1.1	187.3	339.8	194.6
1996	204.9	926.1	76.7	152.8	1.0	161.2	330.5	203.9
1997	183.1	1016.7	86.3	194.3		139.2	383.4	213.5
1998	207.1	1140.1	98.4	223.8	17.0	132.1	450.2	218.6
1999	212.1	1183.8	136.2	262.2	1.4	82.7	461.3	240.0
2000	293.1	1439.1	107.0	373.8	0.6	51.5	505.6	400.6
2001	325.5	1796.8	136.7	429.4	2.5	35.6	595.6	597.0
2002	433.2	2075.3	108.5	543.8	1.9	41.5	672.8	706.8
2003	542.7	2674.0	78.4	755.2		52.6	887.9	899.9
2004	654.6	3712.8	118.6	804.7		120.5	1245.7	1423.3
2005	924.4	4553.7	128.8	1055.8		70.9	1452.8	1845.4
2006	1043.8	4927.3	126.4	1347.5	32.7	76.2	1532.2	1812.3
2007	1202.2	6193.0	102.2	1513.3	22.4	82.8	2195.6	2276.7
2008	1469.5	5184.7	104.2	1394.2	35.5	80.0	2016.4	1554.5
2009	1321.7	8702.2	118.1	3038.5	17.5	39.3	2441.3	3047.4
2010	2109.1	8327.8	99.5	2218.7	4.3	43.8	3209.1	2752.4
2011	2341.4	8235.4	71.7	1853.6	85.4	29.8	3588.6	2606.3
2012	2830.7	9156.0	156.1	2186.3	12.7	24.9	3478.4	3297.6
2013	3133.1	10580.3	159.6	2554.1	0.8	23.5	4295.2	3547.2
2014	3586.5	10208.7	161.7	2841.0	8.0	33.3	4347.9	2816.8
2015	4238.6	10773.9	184.9	2390.1	10.6	13.2	4853.6	3321.5

注：1978-1992年不含房地产开发和农村投资；1993-2003年不含农村投资。

Note: Figures from 1978 to 1992 did not include investment in real estate development and rural investment; figures from 1993 to 2003 did not include rural investment.

5-5 全社会基础设施投资(1978-2015年)

单位：亿元

年 份 Year	基础设施投资 Infrastructure Investment	#能 源 Energy	电 力 Electricity	供 热 Heating	供 气 Gas	供 水 Water	#公共服务业 Public Services	#园林绿化 Landscaping	#环境卫生 Environmental Sanitation	#市政工程管理 Municipal Project Management
1978	5.4	1.4	0.7				0.6			
1979	5.8	1.1	0.4				1.3			
1980	6.0	0.9	0.6				2.3			
1981-1985	**40.6**	**9.4**	**5.4**				**11.2**			
1981	5.8	1.3	0.6				2.0			
1982	6.1	1.4	0.9				1.9			
1983	6.7	1.5	0.9				1.9			
1984	8.8	1.4	0.7				3.0			
1985	13.2	3.8	2.3				2.5			
1986-1990	**117.9**	**39.8**	**21.1**				**25.3**			
1986	14.5	4.8	2.3				2.1			
1987	22.1	8.0	4.1				3.1			
1988	23.2	8.8	4.1				5.3			
1989	26.5	9.2	5.2				6.6			
1990	31.6	9.0	5.3				8.3			
1991-1995	**494.9**	**134.1**	**84.6**	**12.3**	**15.2**	**22.0**	**62.9**	**2.9**		**57.3**
1991	35.2	12.4	6.4	2.0	1.3	2.7	7.5	0.3		6.8
1992	58.8	17.7	9.0	4.0	2.6	2.1	8.2	0.4		7.2
1993	91.4	19.3	11.4	1.4	2.6	3.9	4.1	1.6		1.7
1994	153.4	38.0	22.7	2.5	5.0	7.8	27.2	0.3		26.5
1995	156.1	46.7	35.1	2.4	3.7	5.5	15.9	0.3		15.1
1996-2000	**1382.1**	**363.4**	**239.7**	**45.2**	**41.4**	**37.1**	**321.0**	**14.2**	**27.1**	**275.9**
1996	188.8	59.2	48.2	3.4	4.1	3.5	29.1	2.3	0.1	25.4
1997	218.3	75.6	52.1	10.3	7.8	5.4	24.3	1.7	2.8	19.8
1998	320.4	85.1	54.2	14.2	6.7	10.0	38.0	3.0	1.9	33.1
1999	302.7	90.3	58.6	11.2	10.3	10.2	75.0	5.4	2.9	64.7
2000	351.9	53.2	26.6	6.1	12.5	8.0	154.6	1.8	19.4	132.9
2001-2005	**2260.0**	**301.7**	**165.2**	**52.7**	**53.9**	**29.9**	**668.6**	**23.1**	**79.9**	**511.4**
2001	356.4	40.8	19.3	7.2	11.0	3.3	114.6	6.7	22.4	85.4
2002	411.9	49.5	26.0	7.2	13.2	3.0	101.6	3.5	17.0	81.1
2003	417.8	36.1	10.6	11.3	10.8	3.4	152.8	1.9	17.0	103.6
2004	463.2	73.0	39.3	14.8	6.9	12.0	139.3	5.5	16.3	100.8
2005	610.7	102.3	70.0	12.2	12.0	8.1	160.3	5.5	7.2	140.6
2006-2010	**6137.3**	**780.3**	**443.6**	**176.9**	**57.6**	**102.1**	**1640.0**	**44.8**	**349.4**	**1117.7**
2006	935.3	113.4	72.8	18.7	11.0	10.9	265.3	3.4	55.4	194.8
2007	1175.8	200.2	121.0	43.0	11.2	25.0	289.5	8.0	75.7	187.3
2008	1160.7	144.1	88.4	25.9	8.1	21.7	291.6	8.0	82.2	188.7
2009	1462.0	165.4	88.9	40.1	10.5	25.8	434.5	15.9	77.7	314.0
2010	1403.5	157.2	72.5	49.2	16.8	18.7	359.1	9.5	58.4	232.9
2011-2015	**9167.7**	**1323.2**	**611.2**	**264.0**	**119.9**	**328.3**	**2335.7**	**125.6**	**236.9**	**1668.6**
2011	1400.2	171.1	90.1	25.3	17.0	38.8	379.4	8.1	40.5	267.8
2012	1789.2	231.9	106.3	64.8	27.3	33.5	508.1	22.0	23.5	361.6
2013	1785.7	270.2	133.7	53.6	38.1	44.8	451.3	18.2	53.6	318.3
2014	2018.1	352.7	149.1	81.4	21.3	100.9	502.5	67.7	35.9	366.6
2015	2174.5	297.3	132.0	38.9	16.2	110.3	494.4	9.6	83.4	354.3

注：2004年及以后基础设施投资包括农村基础设施投资。

TOTAL INVESTMENT IN INFRASTRUCTURE (1978-2015)

(100 million yuan)

#交通运输 Transportation	#铁路 Railway	#公路 Road	#城市公共交通业 Urban Public Transportation	#航空 Aviation	#邮政电信 Post & Telecommunications	邮政 Post	电信 Telecommunications	基础设施投资占全社会固定资产投资比重(%) Infrastructure Investment as Percentage of Total Investment in Fixed Assets (%)
1.7	0.8	0.4		0.5	0.4			23.9
1.7	0.4	0.4		0.8	0.4			21.9
2.3	1.1	0.7		0.5	0.5			17.9
11.1	**3.9**	**5.5**		**1.7**	**5.2**			
1.8	0.6	0.9		0.3	0.4			15.8
1.9	0.8	0.8		0.3	0.4			15.8
2.6	1.2	1.0		0.4	0.6			13.1
2.3	0.7	1.3		0.3	1.1			13.3
2.6	0.7	1.6		0.4	2.7			14.0
28.3	**5.0**	**19.3**		**4.0**	**20.3**			
3.1	1.0	1.5		0.6	3.5			13.7
6.6	1.2	4.0		1.3	3.2			16.2
4.7	1.4	3.0		0.4	3.0			14.2
5.2	0.7	3.9		0.6	5.2			19.0
8.7	0.7	6.9		1.1	5.4			17.6
123.0	**50.8**	**30.6**	**22.4**	**4.6**	**137.3**	**9.5**	**127.8**	
9.3	0.8	5.6	2.3	0.5	5.8	5.0	0.8	18.3
20.1	4.7	10.7	4.0	0.7	12.3	1.1	11.2	22.1
29.4	11.2	4.7	4.7	1.1	24.2	1.7	22.5	22.3
30.0	13.6	3.6	5.7	1.0	48.6	0.9	47.7	23.6
34.2	20.5	6.0	5.7	1.3	46.4	0.8	45.6	18.6
337.4	**26.0**	**131.3**	**80.0**	**3.2**	**299.6**	**6.0**	**293.6**	
54.0	11.7	15.8	6.0	1.2	44.1	0.9	43.2	21.5
51.2	6.0	11.1	9.1	0.2	60.3	2.1	58.2	22.7
104.6	8.0	42.1	24.4		77.5	1.8	75.7	27.7
63.0		30.1	20.7		54.0	0.4	53.6	25.9
64.6	0.3	32.2	19.8	1.8	63.7	0.8	62.9	27.1
766.2	**23.2**	**294.0**	**302.8**	**137.6**	**384.0**	**6.2**	**377.9**	
104.4	1.5	52.8	45.1	2.0	84.8	2.2	82.6	23.3
159.7	1.4	107.0	44.6	1.4	78.7	1.6	77.1	22.7
129.2	9.3	55.3	48.8	15.8	82.2	0.9	81.3	19.4
148.8	7.2	38.2	51.1	52.3	68.5	1.0	67.5	18.3
224.1	3.9	40.7	113.2	66.2	69.9	0.5	69.4	21.6
3010.9	**358.7**	**732.8**	**1456.7**	**457.7**	**462.9**	**8.2**	**454.4**	
439.6	25.1	140.6	201.0	72.2	72.3	1.2	71.1	27.7
548.0	65.7	189.6	202.4	87.5	84.8	…	84.7	29.6
604.2	75.9	170.5	215.8	141.8	86.7	0.3	86.3	30.2
698.6	114.9	134.8	426.7	21.9	124.9	3.3	121.5	30.1
720.5	77.1	97.3	410.8	134.3	94.2	3.4	90.8	25.5
3640.7	**191.8**	**506.8**	**1918.9**	**987.9**	**636.8**	**12.5**	**624.2**	
680.7	43.6	107.7	351.3	176.6	82.3	2.7	79.6	23.7
712.0	43.0	98.2	391.0	178.1	122.0	4.6	117.4	27.7
664.5	36.9	127.5	310.9	162.5	132.9	3.5	129.4	25.4
756.5	9.0	84.6	491.6	166.0	127.3	0.1	127.2	26.7
827.0	59.3	88.8	374.1	304.7	172.3	1.6	170.6	27.2

Note: Investment in infrastructure in and after 2004 includes that in rural infrastructure investment.

5-6 全社会基础设施投资(2015年)
TOTAL INVESTMENT IN INFRASTRUCTURE (2015)

项　目	Item	投资额(万元) Investment (10000 yuan) 全市 Beijing Municipality	#城镇 Urban	比重(%) Percentage (%) 全市 Beijing Municipality	#城镇 Urban
合　计	**Total**	**21745336**	**17687387**	**100.0**	**100.0**
能　源	**Energy**	**2973351**	**2761663**	**13.7**	**15.6**
电　力	Electricity	1319641	1196836	6.1	6.8
供　热	Heating	388541	365249	1.8	2.1
供　气	Gas	161946	145580	0.7	0.8
供　水	Water	1103223	1053998	5.1	6.0
公共服务业	**Public Services**	**4944126**	**4075058**	**22.7**	**23.0**
园林绿化	Landscaping	95761	63574	0.4	0.4
环境卫生	Environmental Sanitation	834366	618158	3.8	3.5
市政工程管理	Municipal Project Management	3542561	3267334	16.3	18.5
其他公共服务业	Others	471438	125992	2.2	0.7
交通运输	**Transportation**	**8270235**	**8027729**	**38.0**	**45.4**
铁　路	Railway	593345	590995	2.7	3.3
公　路	Road	888231	663098	4.1	3.7
管道运输	Pipeline				
城市公共交通业	Urban Public Transportation	3740962	3732319	17.2	21.1
#公交电汽车客运	Buses and Electirc Cars	336531	336531	1.5	1.9
出租汽车	Taxis	69781	61138	0.3	0.3
航　空	Aviation	3047467	3041317	14.0	17.2
其　他	Others	230			
邮政电信	**Post and Telecommunications**	**1722505**	**1722505**	**7.9**	**9.7**
邮　政	Post	16163	16163	0.1	0.1
电　信	Telecommunications	1706342	1706342	7.8	9.6
其　他	**Others**	**3835119**	**1100432**	**17.6**	**6.3**
#水　利	Water Conservancy	1399831	822768	6.4	4.7

5-7 全社会固定资产投资及新增固定资产(按行业分)(2015年)
TOTAL INVESTMENT IN FIXED ASSETS AND ITS INCREMENTAL FIXED ASSETS (GROUPED BY SECTOR) (2015)

单位：万元 (10000 yuan)

项目	Item	投资额 Investment			新增固定资产 Incremental Fixed Assets		
		合计 Total	中央 Central	地方 Local	合计 Total	中央 Central	地方 Local
合计	**Total**	**79909435**	**8958965**	**70950470**	**39931826**	**6794941**	**33136885**
农、林、牧、渔业	**Agriculture, Forestry, Animal Production and Hunting, Fishing**	**1093546**		**1093546**	**1001095**		**1001095**
农业	Agriculture	134186		134186	129259		129259
林业	Forestry	877671		877671	774806		774806
畜牧业	Animal Production and Hunting	25321		25321	53070		53070
渔业	Fishing	6732		6732	5600		5600
农、林、牧、渔服务业	Service Activities for Agriculture, Forestry, Animal Production and Hunting, Fishing	49636		49636	38360		38360
采矿业	**Mining and Quarrying**	**25705**		**25705**	**28912**		**28912**
煤炭开采和洗选业	Mining and Washing of Coal	1244		1244	466		466
黑色金属矿采选业	Mining of Ferrous Metal Ores	24461		24461	28446		28446
制造业	**Manufacturing**	**3682945**	**357778**	**3325167**	**4670083**	**235715**	**4434368**
农副食品加工业	Processing of Food from Agricultural Products	17902		17902	41506		41506
食品制造业	Manufacture of Foods	102591		102591	140740		140740
酒、饮料和精制茶制造业	Manufacture of Wines, Beverage and Refined Tea	38114		38114	43550		43550
烟草制品业	Manufacture of Cigarettes and Tobacco	5826	5826		29341	29341	
纺织业	Manufacture of Textile	1129		1129			
纺织服装、服饰业	Manufacture of Textile Wearing Apparel and Ornament	50607		50607	22740		22740
皮革、毛皮、羽毛及其制品和制鞋业	Manufacture of Leather, Fur, Feather and Its Products, and Footwear						
木材加工及木、竹藤、棕、草制品	Processing of Timbers, Manufacture of Wood, Bamboo, Rattan, Palm and Straw Products						
家具制造业	Manufacture of Furniture	17226		17226	6281		6281
造纸及纸制品业	Manufacture of Paper and Paper Products	24507		24507	32267		32267
印刷和记录媒介复制业	Printing, Reproduction of Recording Media	27953	6148	21805	30135	6948	23187
文教、工美、体育和娱乐用品制造业	Manufacture of Articles for Culture, Education, Artwork, Sport and Entertainment Activities	37926		37926	57748		57748
石油加工、炼焦及核燃料加工业	Processing of Petroleum, Coking, Processing of Nucleus Fuel	10117	59	10058	52		52
化学原料及化学制品制造业	Manufacture of Chemical Raw Materials and Chemical Products	231216	152879	78337	235492	106682	128810
医药制造业	Manufacture of Medicines	397914	38283	359631	135908	925	134983
化学纤维制造业	Manufacture of Chemical Fibers	1500		1500	19795		19795
橡胶和塑料制品业	Manufacture of Rubber and Plastic Products	29381		29381	9717		9717
非金属矿物制品业	Manufacture of Non-metallic Mineral Products	20125	1067	19058	54021	1151	52870
黑色金属冶炼及压延加工业	Manufacture and Pressing of Ferrous Metals	1100		1100	53937		53937
有色金属冶炼及压延加工业	Manufacture and Pressing of Non-ferrous Metals	11719	8361	3358	4815	4815	
金属制品业	Manufacture of Fabricated Metal Products	36200	55	36145	25153	6577	18576
通用设备制造业	Manufacture of General-Purpose Machinery	54016	17413	36603	25670		25670

注：1. 本表分行业数据不含农户投资。
2. 行业划分执行2011年国民经济行业分类标准(GB/T 4754-2011)。

Note: a) The figures of grouping exclude investment of rural households.
b) Sectors are classified in accordance with the Standard for Classification of National Economic Sectors 2011 (GB/T 4754-2011).

5-7 续表 1 Continued 1

单位：万元 (10000 yuan)

项目	Item	投资额 Investment			新增固定资产 Incremental Fixed Assets		
		合计 Total	中央 Central	地方 Local	合计 Total	中央 Central	地方 Local
专用设备制造业	Manufacture of Special-Purpose Machinery	191991	10399	181592	76542	12658	63884
汽车制造业	Manufacture of Motor Vehicles	1410188	46385	1363803	2918211	46385	2871826
铁路、船舶、航空航天和其他运输设备制造业	Manufacture of Railway Locomotives, Building of Ships and Boats, Manufacture of Air and Spacecrafts and Other Transportation Equipment	103087	55966	47121	60618	13878	46740
电气机械及器材制造业	Manufacture of Electrical Machinery and Equipment	154326	1983	152343	80796	2028	78768
计算机、通信和其他电子设备制造业	Manufacture of Computer, Communication Equipment and Other Electronic Equipment	639092	9871	629221	523910	177	523733
仪器仪表制造业	Manufacture of Measuring Instrument and Meter	57923		57923	36903		36903
其他制造业	Other Manufacturing	6869	3083	3786	4235	4150	85
废弃资源综合利用业	Waste Recycling and Recovery	2400		2400			
金属制品、机械和设备修理业	Repair of Fabricated Metal Products, Machinery and Equipment						
电力、热力、燃气及水生产和供应业	**Production and Distribution of Electricity, Heating Power, Gas and Water**	**3003873**	**135323**	**2868550**	**1689439**	**341071**	**1348368**
电力、热力的生产和供应业	Production and Supply of Electric Power and Heat Power	1709303	133816	1575487	1423379	341071	1082308
燃气生产和供应业	Production and Distribution of Gas	161946		161946	162998		162998
水的生产和供应业	Production and Distribution of Water	1132624	1507	1131117	103062		103062
建筑业	**Construction**	**55606**	**19187**	**36419**	**58764**	**19187**	**39577**
房屋建筑业	Construction of Building	28427		28427	9593		9593
土木工程建筑业	Civil Engineering Construction	23071	19187	3884	48326	19187	29139
建筑安装业	Construction Installation	2980		2980	845		845
建筑装饰和其他建筑业	Building Completion, Finishing and Other Construction	1128		1128			
批发和零售业	**Wholesale and Retail Trade**	**581537**	**25687**	**555850**	**251018**	**1730**	**249288**
批发业	Wholesale	275447	25687	249760	202586	1730	200856
零售业	Retail Trade	306090		306090	48432		48432
交通运输、仓储和邮政业	**Transport, Storage and Post**	**8495520**	**3393629**	**5101891**	**3334205**	**2017995**	**1316210**
铁路运输业	Transport via Railway	593345	590995	2350	525970	525970	
道路运输业	Transport via Road	4633217	8975	4624242	977900	8975	968925
水上运输业	Water Transport						
航空运输业	Air Transport	3053738	2733176	320562	1791442	1480666	310776
管道运输业	Transport via Pipeline						
装卸搬运和运输代理业	Loading, Unloading, Portage and Other Transport Services	2278		2278	2048		2048
仓储业	Storage	189781	60270	129511	11513		11513
邮政业	Post	23161	213	22948	25332	2384	22948
住宿和餐饮业	**Accommodation and Restaurants**	**406372**	**59330**	**347042**	**529821**	**93804**	**436017**
住宿业	Accommodation	392441	59330	333111	524117	93804	430313
餐饮业	Restaurants	13931		13931	5704		5704
信息传输、软件和信息技术服务业	**Information Transmission, Software and Information Technology Services**	**2427489**	**440352**	**1987137**	**2357112**	**389082**	**1968030**
电信、广播电视和卫星传输服务	Telecommunications, Broadcasting, Television and Satellite Transmission Services	1238962	215344	1023618	1456100	355857	1100243
互联网和相关服务	Internet and Related Services	468030	3103	464927	487216	3103	484113
软件和信息技术服务业	Software and Information Technology Services	720497	221905	498592	413796	30122	383674
金融业	**Finance**	**733086**	**522797**	**210289**	**366473**	**169215**	**197258**
货币金融服务	Monetary Financial Services	373312	351880	21432	179931	159285	20646
资本市场服务	Capital Market Services	11952		11952			
保险业	Insurance	332722	160337	172385	41495		41495
其他金融业	Other Financial Services	15100	10580	4520	145047	9930	135117

5-7 续表 2 Continued 2

单位：万元 (10000 yuan)

项 目	Item	投资额 Investment			新增固定资产 Incremental Fixed Assets		
		合计 Total	中央 Central	地方 Local	合计 Total	中央 Central	地方 Local
房地产业	**Real Estate**	**47130574**	**2261117**	**44869457**	**17748610**	**1866339**	**15882271**
租赁和商务服务业	**Renting and Leasing Activities Business Services**	**645392**	**73123**	**572269**	**882858**	**41891**	**840967**
租赁业	Renting and Leasing Activities	152652	42942	109710	140214	22789	117425
商务服务业	Business Services	492740	30181	462559	742644	19102	723542
科学研究和技术服务业	**Scientific Research and Ddevelopment, Technical Services**	**988713**	**551122**	**437591**	**665677**	**459662**	**206015**
研究与试验发展	Research and Experimental Development	482572	345002	137570	290609	163591	127018
专业技术服务业	Professional Technique Services	206265	95582	110683	47686	15685	32001
科技推广和应用服务业	Technique Generalization and Application Services	299876	110538	189338	327382	280386	46996
水利、环境和公共设施管理业	**Management of Water Conservancy, Environment and Public Facilities**	**5863032**	**169591**	**5693441**	**2728921**	**187860**	**2541061**
水利管理业	Management of Water Conservancy	1414751		1414751	591942		591942
生态保护和环境治理业	Ecological Protection and Environmental Control	228295		228295	116982		116982
公共设施管理业	Management of Public Facilities	4219986	169591	4050395	2019997	187860	1832137
居民服务、修理和其他服务业	**Resident Services, Repair and Other Services**	**217074**		**217074**	**93782**		**93782**
居民服务业	Resident Services	14033		14033	14033		14033
机动车、电子产品和日用产品修理业	Repair of Motor Vehicles, Electronics and Household Applicances	1450		1450	2000		2000
其他服务业	Other Services	201591		201591	77749		77749
教 育	**Education**	**1421810**	**627165**	**794645**	**972748**	**300526**	**672222**
卫生和社会工作	**Health Care and Social Works**	**662820**	**69246**	**593574**	**703947**	**305857**	**398090**
卫 生	Health Care	615496	69246	546250	665594	305857	359737
社会工作	Social Work activities	47324		47324	38353		38353
文化、体育和娱乐业	**Culture, Sports and Entertainment**	**1382049**	**204140**	**1177909**	**777580**	**249690**	**527890**
新闻出版业	Journalism and Publishing	41026	41026		187169	187169	
广播、电视、电影和影视录音制作业	Radio Broadcasting, Television,Movies, Videos and Sound Recording	168137	77452	90685	240416	39822	200594
文化艺术业	Culture and Arts	737191	82391	654800	258919	18430	240489
体 育	Sports Activities	36486	3271	33215	79563	4269	75294
娱乐业	Entertainment	399209		399209	11513		11513
公共管理、社会保障和社会组织	**Public Management, Social Security and Social Organizations**	**592556**	**49378**	**543178**	**587807**	**115317**	**472490**
中国共产党机关	Organs of Communist Party of China	27537	27537		6107	6107	
国家机构	Organs of State	509482	15981	493501	570710	109210	461500
社会保障	Social Security	4464	472	3992			
群众团体、社会团体和其他成员组织	Mass Communities, Social Organizations and Other Membership Organizations	45080	5388	39692	5150		5150
基层群众自治组织	Grass Roots Self-government Organizations	5993		5993	5840		5840

5-8 全社会房屋建筑施工及竣工面积(1978-2015年)
FLOOR SPACE OF BUILDINGS UNDER CONSTRUCTION AND COMPLETED (1978-2015)

单位：万平方米 (10000 sq.m)

年份 Year	施工面积 Floor Space of Buildings under Construction	#住宅 Residential Buildings	竣工面积 Floor Space of Buildings Completed	#住宅 Residential Buildings	中央 Central	地方 Local
1978	956.3	456.8	407.0	190.4	158.7	248.3
1979	1340.6	780.2	537.6	304.9	235.2	302.4
1980	1704.1	1037.0	648.4	396.9	315.8	332.6
1981-1985			**3941.6**	**2383.4**	**1723.2**	**2218.4**
1981	1875.8	1189.9	726.9	462.6	327.2	399.7
1982	1938.6	1210.1	728.3	463.8	303.7	424.6
1983	1952.1	1163.6	775.5	514.0	312.3	463.2
1984	2351.9	1327.1	818.7	437.6	352.7	466.0
1985	2802.7	1599.2	892.2	505.4	427.3	464.9
1986-1990			**5142.4**	**2939.9**	**2635.1**	**2507.3**
1986	2760.7	1557.4	906.5	532.7	424.5	482.0
1987	2578.0	1273.2	1042.2	608.9	507.8	534.4
1988	2642.2	1226.2	1065.6	623.5	499.6	566.0
1989	2450.8	1167.8	1046.9	601.8	565.8	481.1
1990	2864.9	1561.9	1081.2	573.0	637.4	443.8
1991-1995			**6206.7**	**3707.2**	**1869.2**	**4337.5**
1991	2818.0	1612.0	1036.4	601.8	396.2	640.2
1992	3126.8	1784.7	1111.4	681.2	399.3	712.1
1993	3607.5	1866.4	1158.0	654.8	320.5	837.5
1994	4460.9	2315.1	1370.7	832.1	366.8	1003.9
1995	5524.3	2897.6	1530.2	937.3	386.4	1143.8
1996-2000			**9644.3**	**5979.9**	**2726.7**	**6917.6**
1996	5633.2	2696.9	1517.5	870.4	452.0	1065.5
1997	5819.4	2881.3	1625.7	996.8	492.2	1133.5
1998	6496.1	3473.7	1821.5	1093.1	508.4	1313.1
1999	6556.5	3754.8	2321.4	1519.9	655.3	1666.1
2000	6995.9	4083.3	2358.2	1499.7	618.8	1739.4
2001-2005			**17781.6**	**11992.2**	**1733.0**	**16048.6**
2001	8203.3	5226.4	2554.6	1804.9	490.6	2064.0
2002	9697.7	6193.3	3121.8	2191.4	441.8	2680.0
2003	11262.2	7011.3	3222.8	2322.3	242.1	2980.7
2004	13121.9	7513.1	4203.2	2649.5	301.9	3901.3
2005	14096.2	8043.2	4679.2	3024.1	256.6	4422.6
2006-2010			**20059.1**	**10993.8**	**2002.6**	**18056.4**
2006	14069.2	7113.0	4191.0	2391.6	388.6	3802.4
2007	14146.7	6788.8	3866.4	2098.0	399.6	3466.8
2008	14145.3	6656.3	3840.7	1871.1	496.8	3343.9
2009	14380.6	7058.4	4252.6	2369.6	388.4	3864.2
2010	15572.1	7932.9	3908.4	2263.5	329.2	3579.1
2011-2015			**20883.8**	**10717.4**	**1919.2**	**18964.5**
2011	18065.2	8817.1	4032.9	2121.8	425.5	3607.4
2012	20045.4	9217.8	3723.5	1992.5	216.9	3506.6
2013	21526.0	9469.0	3989.7	2154.8	255.2	3734.4
2014	21677.7	8978.3	4967.5	2547.6	541.4	4426.1
2015	20009.1	7962.3	4170.2	1900.7	480.2	3690.0

注：2007年及以前，表中数据不包含农村农户房屋施工和竣工面积。

Note: Figures in and before 2007 excluded floor space of buildings under construction and completed in rural areas.

5-9 全社会房屋建筑施工及竣工面积
FLOOR SPACE OF BUILDINGS UNDER CONSTRUCTION AND COMPLETED

单位：万平方米 (10000 sq.m)

项 目	Item	2015	2014	占竣工面积比重(%) Proportion in Completed Floor Space (%)	
				2015	2014
施工总面积	**Floor Space of Buildings under Construction**	**20009.1**	**21677.7**		
竣工总面积	**Floor Space of Buildings Completed**	**4170.2**	**4967.5**	**100.0**	**100.0**
按隶属关系分	**By Affiliation**				
中 央	Central	480.2	541.4	11.5	10.9
地 方	Local	3690.0	4426.1	88.5	89.1
#国 有	State-owned	696.7	764.5	16.7	15.4
集 体	Collectively-owned	191.7	234.8	4.6	4.7
按功能区分	**By Functional Zone**				
首都功能核心区	Core Functional Area of the Capital	195.0	94.4	4.7	1.9
城市功能拓展区	Urban Function Extension Area	1064.3	1831.4	25.5	36.9
城市发展新区	New Area of Urban Development	2302.0	2380.8	55.2	47.9
生态涵养发展区	Ecological Conservation Area	609.0	661.0	14.6	13.3

5-10 房地产开发面积(1990-2015年)

单位：万平方米

年份 Year	商品房施工面积 Floor Space of Commercial Buildings under Construction	#本年新开工面积 Floor Space of Buildings Newly Started Construction in Current Year	住宅 Residential Houses	#经济适用房 Affordable Houses	#公寓别墅 Apartments & Villas	办公楼(写字楼) Office Buildings	商业、非公益用房及其他 Buildings for Commercial Use, Non-public Buildings and Others	商品房竣工面积 Floor Space of Commercial Buildings Completed	住宅 Residential Houses	#经济适用房 Affordable Houses	#公寓别墅 Apartments & Villas
1990	774.0	249.1	643.4			17.4	41.2	271.6	226.5		
1991	815.1	317.6	692.1			2.1	57.6	275.2	240.4		
1992	1021.1	508.6	865.4			7.6	54.8	331.4	300.8		
1993	1262.0	524.8	887.6					356.4	280.6		
1994	1593.2	659.4	1107.6					445.7	385.6		
1995	2810.2	1012.2	1728.7		334.8	462.7	252.6	653.0	506.3		55.6
1996	2824.6	578.7	1520.7		316.8	638.7	283.9	663.4	470.8		43.3
1997	2869.6	848.4	1541.1		335.7	637.7	260.8	682.3	478.3		99.8
1998	3499.1	1193.4	2107.2		368.3	590.7	297.7	842.8	588.7		57.0
1999	3784.0	1061.8	2447.9	301.4	390.7	484.4	281.3	1208.5	908.3	114.1	93.2
2000	4455.0	1676.9	2971.6	296.6	537.8	449.1	281.3	1365.6	1013.7	184.9	164.2
2001	5966.7	2789.8	4349.6	563.1	494.4	495.5	330.6	1707.4	1393.4	214.0	150.8
2002	7510.7	3206.0	5397.5	660.2	550.8	672.5	400.3	2384.4	1926.2	228.4	161.9
2003	9070.7	3433.8	6352.9	802.5	705.0	901.3	557.7	2593.7	2080.8	322.8	127.9
2004	9931.3	3054.3	6759.4	793.2	776.0	1122.4	641.8	3067.0	2343.9	298.8	153.2
2005	10748.5	2965.9	7283.4	783.4	1023.5	1209.8	809.2	3770.9	2841.4	325.6	342.7
2006	10483.5	3179.4	6311.3	551.9	913.8	1245.8	1403.0	3193.9	2193.3	270.1	255.6
2007	10438.6	2557.4	5914.5	440.1	1009.2	1364.6	1482.1	2891.7	1854.0	188.6	239.6
2008	10014.3	2337.2	5538.2	544.9	954.7	1287.2	1429.8	2558.0	1399.3	101.1	233.0
2009	9719.1	2246.6	5551.9	628.7	840.9	1132.2	1323.4	2678.6	1613.2	98.2	213.7
2010	10300.9	2974.2	6176.0	572.7	830.0	1054.8	1229.3	2386.7	1498.5	144.6	183.2
2011	12065.4	4246.1	7168.1	444.8	754.8	1422.7	1187.5	2245.2	1316.1	74.6	133.0
2012	13122.5	3224.2	7510.4	435.1	642.2	1711.9	1236.9	2390.9	1522.7	188.5	135.1
2013	13886.9	3577.5	7406.9	310.5	530.1	2114.1	4365.9	2666.4	1692.0	95.7	133.5
2014	13641.5	2502.8	6999.7	328.0	485.4	2277.1	4364.7	3054.1	1804.3	101.4	52.5
2015	13095.0	2790.2	6314.6	150.0	508.5	2426.8	4353.6	2631.5	1378.2	17.0	92.5

注：1. 2005年及以前的商品房销售面积为竣工后的全部商品房销售面积，2006年及以后为期房与现房销售面积之和。
2. 2010年起，商品房销售面积中包含定向安置房数据。
3. 2012年及以前商业、非公益用房及其他只包括商业及服务性等营业性用房。自2013年起包括：厂房、仓库、商业营业用房、服务业用房、教育用房、文化体育用房、医疗用房、科研用房及其他用房。

STATISTICS FOR FLOOR SPACE OF REAL ESTATE DEVELOPENT (1990−2015)

(10000 sq.m)

办公楼(写字楼) Office Buildings	商业、非公益用房及其他 Buildings for Commercial Use, Non-public Buildings and Others	商品房销售面积 Floor Space of Commercial Buildings Sold	住宅 Residential Houses	#经济适用房 Affordable Houses	#公寓别墅 Apartments & Villas	办公楼(写字楼) Office Buildings	商业、非公益用房及其他 Buildings for Commercial Use, Non-public Buildings and Others	年末商品房待售面积 Floor Space of Vacant Commercial Buildings at the Year End	#住宅 Residential Houses	#一年以内 Less than One Year	#三年以上 Over Three Years
9.7	13.3	142.2									
0.9	10.9	154.0	152.5								
2.7	8.3	159.1	153.0								
		182.0	182.0								
		168.6	149.0			17.2	1.1				
27.9	43.5	191.9	180.0		16.7	4.0	4.5	81.5			
79.0	38.3	215.3	183.1		24.9	13.7	14.4	214.8	179.6		
80.9	42.4	290.9	256.2		53.5	18.8	8.0	298.3	258.9		
92.3	69.8	409.2	377.0		40.0	23.2	7.0	334.8	262.9		
108.8	43.1	544.4	484.7	45.8	55.1	48.0	6.8	624.3	529.1		
97.2	48.7	956.9	898.2	166.5	107.6	41.2	6.1	627.4	515.1		
98.0	48.2	1205.0	1127.5	185.2	120.8	49.8	17.4	774.0	634.1	429.4	84.6
97.4	82.9	1708.3	1604.4	220.7	153.6	44.0	32.9	919.0	763.2	557.9	96.4
94.0	117.5	1895.8	1771.1	320.0	131.9	38.1	50.8	1123.4	896.9	745.5	109.8
153.9	225.3	2472.0	2285.8	306.3	172.7	92.5	60.2	1044.1	723.8	744.4	72.9
287.8	180.9	2803.2	2566.0	304.0	302.1	131.2	66.9	1374.2	799.7	993.5	75.8
304.4	289.2	2607.6	2205.0	176.3	276.9	260.3	108.6	1039.7	494.1	628.3	106.9
314.8	315.1	2176.6	1731.5	100.1	319.3	265.7	134.8	1136.2	411.8	697.2	203.1
364.6	313.1	1335.4	1031.4	108.3	164.6	139.4	112.4	1438.3	522.7	945.1	209.8
316.6	322.4	2362.3	1880.5	82.2	339.8	255.8	157.1	1351.4	426.8	768.0	229.9
198.4	271.9	1639.5	1201.4	49.5	175.9	208.1	142.1	1482.7	511.9	810.4	239.7
245.2	232.4	1440.0	1035.0	39.4	93.3	211.4	108.7	1792.6	699.8	1021.5	298.3
226.8	240.1	1943.7	1483.4	85.9	116.9	253.5	114.0	1911.8	789.5	958.7	309.0
273.1	701.3	1903.1	1363.7	106.6	87.8	317.9	221.5	1861.4	829.3	922.3	337.7
387.5	862.3	1459.0	1141.3	56.2	48.2	136.8	180.9	2065.7	864.8	1121.4	374.2
385.4	867.8	1554.7	1127.3	37.7	72.0	243.0	184.4	2168.1	867.7	1151.7	436.9

Note: a) Floor space of commercial buildings sold in 2005 and before was the floor space of completed commercial buildings, and after 2006, the figure is the sum of completed commercial buildings and those under construction.

b) Since 2010, the floor space of completed commercial buildings has included figures of targeted resettlement buildings.

c) In and Before 2012, buildings for commercial use, non-public buildings and others only included business and commercial buildings. Since 2013, it has included: factory buildings, warehouses, commercial buildings, buildings for service industy, education buildings, cultural and sports buildings, medical buildings, scientific research buildings and others.

5-11 房地产开发情况(1990-2015年)
STATISTICS FOR REAL ESTATE DEVELOPENT (1990-2015)

年 份 Year	房地产开发企业个数(个) Number of Real Estate Development Enterprises (unit)	房地产开发投资额(亿元) Investment in Real Estate Development (100 million yuan)		按用途分 By Purpose of Investment			按投资构成分 By Investment Structure	
			#土地购置费 Land Purchase Cost	住 宅 Residential Buildings	写字楼(办公楼) Office Buildings	商业、非公益用房及其他 Buildings for Commercial Use, Non-public Buildings and Others	#建筑安装工程 Construction and Installation Projects	#设备工器具购置 Purchase of Equipment, Tools and Devices
1990		22.5		12.3			18.4	
1991-1995		**568.4**		**264.8**			**341.9**	
1991	40	24.0		14.0			16.8	
1992	42	33.7		20.0			20.7	
1993	74	58.4	2.5	38.1			43.4	0.4
1994	81	99.5	4.0	50.3			69.3	0.9
1995	623	352.8	52.4	142.4	71.5	35.2	191.7	8.4
1996-2000		**1979.5**	**161.5**	**950.7**	**351.5**	**161.3**	**1280.6**	**95.5**
1996	554	328.2	15.0	124.9	84.2	35.2	222.0	17.0
1997	601	330.3	23.9	132.9	91.1	29.2	208.0	19.8
1998	585	377.4	28.4	168.0	78.5	36.1	250.7	20.7
1999	716	421.5	36.6	236.6	52.5	30.2	278.6	16.8
2000	893	522.1	57.6	288.3	45.2	30.6	321.3	21.2
2001-2005		**5974.0**	**993.6**	**3239.5**	**696.1**	**368.3**	**3498.9**	**137.8**
2001	1142	783.8	115.6	464.2	72.0	41.7	438.0	22.3
2002	1508	989.4	149.2	586.7	97.3	57.6	572.7	31.5
2003	1546	1202.5	213.2	633.0	142.7	61.3	716.2	24.3
2004	2704	1473.3	275.8	776.0	187.9	94.8	872.1	35.4
2005	3123	1525.0	239.8	779.5	196.2	112.9	881.8	42.3
2006-2010		**10863.2**	**3642.0**	**5211.5**	**1055.2**	**1270.8**	**4550.5**	**255.0**
2006	2882	1719.9	477.9	863.6	216.7	226.0	953.2	55.5
2007	2688	1995.8	644.7	991.7	242.2	267.4	1015.3	58.9
2008	3433	1908.7	639.0	940.6	170.5	240.4	829.6	48.6
2009	3171	2337.7	587.7	906.6	166.7	200.7	841.6	45.7
2010	3190	2901.1	1292.7	1509.0	259.1	336.3	910.8	46.3
2011-2015		**17810.7**	**7264.1**	**9055.6**	**3017.1**	**4275.8**	**7037.8**	**227.5**
2011	3069	3036.3	1301.2	1778.3	363.8	296.7	1235.1	38.5
2012	2960	3153.4	1102.7	1628.0	384.8	275.9	1383.1	65.7
2013	2927	3483.4	1159.5	1724.6	611.7	1147.1	1510.0	53.0
2014	2810	3911.3	1561.2	1962.0	750.2	1199.1	1601.9	47.3
2015	2780	4226.3	2139.5	1962.7	906.6	1357.0	1307.7	23.0

注：2012年及以前商业、非公益用房及其他只包括商业及服务性等营业性用房。自2013年起包括：厂房、仓库、商业营业用房、服务业用房、教育用房、文化体育用房、医疗用房、科研用房及其他用房。

Note: In and Before 2012, buildings for commercial use, non-public buildings and others only included business and commercial buildings. Since 2013, it has included: factory buildings, warehouses, commercial buildings, buildings for service industy, education buildings, cultural and sports buildings, medical buildings, scientific research buildings and others.

5-12 房地产开发企业经营情况(2015年)
REAL ESTATE DEVELOPMENT ENTERPRISES (2015)

项 目	Item	企业单位个数(个) Number of Enterprises (unit)	实收资本合计(万元) Paid-in Capital (10000 yuan)	资产总计(万元) Total Assets (10000 yuan)	主营业务收入(万元) Main Business Income (10000 yuan)	利润总额(万元) Total Profits (10000 yuan)	年末从业人员(人) Number of Staff at the Year End (person)
合 计	**Total**	**2780**	**65106792**	**505420025**	**38274800**	**7502079**	**89246**
按企业登记注册类型分	**By Registration Type**						
内资企业	Domestically-Funded Enterprises	2542	53571276	444034097	35698116	6994284	77581
国有企业	State-owned Enterprises	60	4514744	14026317	631019	160312	5623
集体企业	Collectively-owned Enterprises	16	65260	1765670	36877	24954	309
私营企业	Private Enterprises	533	2861535	25986636	1989048	-39223	8862
股份合作企业	Joint-equity Cooperative Enterprises	***	***	***	***	***	51
股份有限公司	Companies Limited by Shares	51	4881232	40419516	1572769	707857	3323
有限责任公司	Limited Liability Companies	1881	41243505	361824082	31468404	6142291	59413
港澳台商投资企业	Hong Kong, Macao and Taiwan-invested Enterprises	141	7591021	37696481	1642362	279398	7253
港澳台合资经营	Joint Ventures	49	2418000	9390406	637034	293226	1897
港澳台合作经营	Cooperative	52	1298086	8110462	438409	-31502	2703
港澳台商独资企业	Solely-funded Enterprises	40	3874935	20195613	566920	17673	2653
港澳台商投资股份有限公司	Companies Limited by Shares						
外商投资企业	Foreign-invested Enterprises	97	3944495	23689448	934322	228398	4412
中外合资经营	Joint Ventures	43	2003004	12198622	188613	165888	1545
中外合作经营	Cooperative	34	602745	3959931	453244	79547	1463
外资(独资)企业	Solely-funded Enterprises	18	1201209	6367346	256230	-14121	1037
外商投资股份有限公司	Companies Limited by Shares	***	***	***	***	***	367
按隶属关系分	**By Affiliation**						
中 央	Central	110	5675464	36848049	3374175	958562	4314
地 方	Local	2670	59431329	468571976	34900625	6543517	84932
按资质等级分	**By Qualification Grade**						
一 级	First-grade	108	9429112	108279932	5892501	2178691	12056
二 级	Second-grade	175	6981163	63444189	4791403	1046637	11930
三 级	Third-grade	220	3973507	38750225	3446552	357518	7871
四 级	Fourth-grade	1197	18047333	152668906	12669319	1650192	32528
暂 定	Provisional	574	15016594	97239799	9908002	1666752	15076
其 他	Others	506	11659083	45036975	1567023	602289	9785
按营业状况分	**By Operating Condition**						
营 业	Operating	2620	64381558	500792410	38098793	7448342	88055
停 业	Closed	140	572203	2937030	114962	34424	433
筹 建	In Preparation						
当年关闭	Closed in the Current Year	5	5000	6457		226	
当年破产	Bankrupted in the Current Year	1					
其 他	Others	14	148032	1684128	61045	19088	758

5-13 房地产开发企业开发建设情况(2015年)
DEVELOPMENT OF REAL ESTATE ENTERPRISES (2015)

单位：万元、平方米 (10000 yuan,sq.m)

项目	Item	全市合计 Total	#国有企业 State-owned	#三资企业 Foreign Funded	按隶属关系分 By Affiliation 中央 Central	地方 Local
计划总投资	**Total Planned Investment**	**235058222**	**14934646**	**15091725**	**14244037**	**220814185**
开始建设至本年度累计	**Accumulative Investment Completed**					
完成投资	**from Beginning to the End of This Year**	**181817209**	**11749108**	**12023539**	**12082014**	**169735195**
本年完成投资合计	**Investment Completed in the Current Year**	**42263473**	**2225039**	**1856192**	**1890657**	**40372816**
#土地购置费	Land Purchase Cost	21394689	852383	580908	862187	20532502
本年完成投资按用途分	**Grouped by Purpose of Investment**					
住宅	Residential Buildings	19626850	1150207	532902	1176936	18449914
办公楼(写字楼)	Office Buildings	9066311	165514	559142	165606	8900705
商业、非公益用房及其他	Buildings for Commercial Use, Non-public Buildings and Others	13570312	909318	764148	548115	13022197
本年购置土地面积	**Land Space Purchased in Current Year**	**3909562**	**118590**	**91051**	**157866**	**3751696**

5-14 保障性安居工程建设情况
CONSTRUCTION OF GOVERNMENT-SUBSIDIZED HOUSING PROJECTS

单位：亿元、万平方米 (100 million yuan,10000 sq.m)

项 目	Item	2015	2014	2015年为2014年% 2015 as % of 2014
完成投资额	**Investment Completed**	**824.0**	**639.0**	**129.0**
经济适用房	Affordable Houses	24.5	36.7	66.8
限价房	Price-capped Houses	303.4	131.9	230.1
公租(廉租)房	Public Rental (Low-rent) Houses	73.6	85.0	86.6
定向安置房	Targeted Resettlement Houses	422.5	385.4	109.6
施工面积	**Floor Space Under Construction**	**3870.5**	**4368.0**	**88.6**
经济适用房	Affordable Housing	200.7	328.0	61.2
限价房	Price-capped Housing	578.3	607.6	95.2
公租(廉租)房	Public Rental (Low-rent) Housing	395.5	381.7	103.6
定向安置房	Resettlement Housing	2696.0	3050.8	88.4
竣工面积	**Floor Space Completed**	**881.8**	**1201.6**	**73.4**
经济适用房	Affordable Houses	23.8	116.4	20.4
限价房	Price-capped Houses	164.6	217.7	75.6
公租(廉租)房	Public Rental (Low-rent) Houses	35.8	55.7	64.3
定向安置房	Targeted Resettlement Houses	657.6	811.9	81.0
本年新开工面积	**Floor Space Newly Started in the Year**	**636.6**	**509.5**	**124.9**
经济适用房	Affordable Houses	18.9	56.5	33.5
限价房	Price-capped Houses	183.3	177.4	103.3
公租(廉租)房	Public Rental (Low-rent) Houses	63.3	75.9	83.4
定向安置房	Targeted Resettlement Houses	371.0	199.8	185.7

主要统计指标解释

全社会固定资产投资 包括城镇固定资产投资（含房地产开发投资）和农村固定资产投资。

城镇固定资产投资 是指城镇各种登记注册类型的企业、事业、行政单位及个体户进行的计划总投资在500万元及以上的建设项目投资。镇及镇以上各级政府及主管部门直接领导、管理的建设项目和企事业单位的投资均为城镇固定资产投资。

农村固定资产投资 农村投资统计以投资项目建设地址所在的地域为界定农村投资统计的范围，即农村投资是指各种投资主体建设的建设项目地址在农村区域范围内的、以满足农村居民生产、生活需要为主要目的的各种投资活动。农村固定资产投资包括农户和非农户固定资产投资。

新增固定资产投资 是指报告期内交付使用的固定资产价值。包括本年内建成投入生产或交付使用的工程投资和达到固定资产标准的设备、工具、器具的投资及有关应摊入的费用。属于增加固定资产价值的其他建设费用，应随同交付使用的工程一并计入新增固定资产。

基础设施投资 是指能够为企业提供作为中间投入用于生产的基本需求；能够为消费者提供所需的基本消费服务；能够为社区提供用于改善不利的外部环境的服务等建设的投资，包括固定资产投资中用于市政工程、电信工程、公共设施和水利环保等建设的投资。

上年末结余资金 是指上年资金来源中没有形成固定资产投资额而结余的资金。包括尚未用到工程上去的材料价值、未开始安装的需要安装设备价值及结存的现金和银行存款等。

本年资金来源小计 是指固定资产投资单位在报告期收到的，用于固定资产投资的各种货币资金。包括国家预算内资金、国内贷款、债券、利用外资、自筹资金和其他资金。

国家预算内资金 分为财政拨款和财政安排的贷款两部分。包括中央财政的基本建设基金(分经营性基金和非经营性基金两部分)、专项支出(如煤代油专项等)、收回再贷、贴息资金，财政安排的挖潜改造和新产品试制支出、城建支出、商业部门简易建筑支出、不发达地区发展基金等资金中用于固定资产投资的资金；地方财政中由国家统筹安排的资金等。

国内贷款 是指报告期固定资产投资项目单位向银行及非银行金融机构借入的用于固定资产投资的各种国内借款，包括银行利用自有资金及吸收存款发放的贷款、上级主管部门拨入的国内贷款、国家专项贷款(包括煤代油贷款、劳改煤矿专项贷款等)，地方财政专项资金安排的贷款、国内储备贷款、周转贷款等。

利用外资 是指报告期收到的用于固定资产建造和购置投资的境外资金(包括设备、材料、技术在内)。包括外商直接投资、对外借款(外国政府贷款、国际金融组织贷款、出口信贷、外国银行商业贷款、对外发行债券和股票)及外商其他投资(包括利用外商投资收益在国内进行固定资产再投资活动的资金)。不包括我国自有外汇资金(包括国家外汇、地方外汇、留成外汇、调剂外汇和国内银行自有资金发行的外汇贷款等)。

自筹资金 指固定资产投资单位报告期收到的，由各地区、各部门及企业、事业单位筹集用于固定资产投资的预算外资金，包括中央各部门、各级地方和企业、事业单位的自有资金。

其他资金来源 是指在报告期收到的除以上各种资金之外其他用于固定资产投资的资金。包括社会集资、个人资金、无偿捐赠的资金及其他单位拨入的资金等。

住宅建设投资 是指专供居住使用的房屋，包括职工家属宿舍、职工单身宿舍、学生宿舍和经济适用房等房屋建造的投资，不包括购置的商品住宅。

建筑安装工程投资（建筑安装工作量） 是指各种房屋、建筑物的建造工程，各种设备、装置的安装工程，又称建筑安装工作量。建筑工程投资必须经过兴工动料，通过施工活动才能实现。在安装工程中，不包括被安装设备本身价值。

设备工器具购置 是指建设单位或企、事业单位购置或自制的，达到固定资产标准的设备、工具、器具的价值。

房地产开发投资 指从本年1月1日起至本年最后一天止完成的全部用于房屋建设工程和土地开发工程的投资额，以及公益性建筑和土地购置费等投资。

土地购置费 通过各种方式取得土地使用权而支付的费用（包括开发补偿费）。土地购置费包括：(1)通过“划拨”方式取得的土地使用权所支付的土地补偿费、附着物和青苗补偿费、安置补偿费及土地征收管理费等；竣工后计入新增固定资产。(2)通过“出让”方式（包括协议出让、招、拍、挂出让）取得的土地使用权所支付的费用；竣工后不计入新增固定资产。土地购置费按当期实际发生额计入投资。土地购置费为分期付款的，应分期计入投资。

经济适用住房 指政府提供政策优惠，限定套型面积和销售价格，按照合理标准建设，面向城镇低收入住房困难家庭供应的具有保障性质的政策性住房。

限价商品住房（限价房） 指政府控制土地出让价格，限定销售价格和套型面积，向城镇中等收入家庭供应的普通商品住房。

公共租赁住房（公租房） 指政府提供财政投入和政策支持，限定套型建筑面积标准，按照合理标准组织建设，或通过长期租赁等方式筹集，按照当地政府规定的供应标准，面向城镇中等偏下收入住房困难家庭、新就业职工和有稳定职业并在城镇居住一定年限的外来务工人员供应的保障性住房。

廉租住房（廉租房） 指政府提供财政投入和政策支持，限定套型建筑面积标准，按照合理标准组织建设，或通过购买、改建和租赁等方式筹集，按照当地政府规定的供应标准，面向城镇低收入住房困难家庭供应的具有保障性质的住房。

房屋施工面积 是指报告期内施工的全部房屋建筑面积。包括本期新开工的面积和上年开工跨入本期继续施工房屋面积，以及上期已停建在本期恢复施工的房屋面积。本期竣工和本期施工后又停建、缓建的房屋面积仍包括在施工面积中，多层建筑应填各层建筑面积之和。

房屋竣工面积 是指报告期内房屋建筑按照设计要求已全部完工，达到住人和使用条件，经验收鉴定合格（或达到竣工验收标准），可正式移交使用的各栋房屋建筑面积的总和。

待售面积 指报告期末已竣工的可供销售或出租的商品房屋建筑面积中，尚未销售或出租的商品房屋建筑面积，包括以前年度竣工和本期竣工的房屋面积，但不包括报告期已竣工的拆迁还建，统建代建，公共配套建筑、房地产公司自用及周转房等不可销售或出租的房屋面积。

Explanatory Notes on Main Statistical Indicators

Total Investment in Fixed Assets includes urban investment in fixed assets (including the investment in real estate development) and rural investment in fixed assets.

Investment in Urban Fixed Assets refers to investment in construction projects with a total planned investment over RMB 5,000,000 (inclusive) by enterprises with various types of registration, institutions, administrative units and individuals in urban areas. The investment in construction projects under the direct leadership and management of government agencies at and above town levels and investment by enterprises and public institutions are also calculated in investment in urban fixed assets.

Investment in Rural Fixed Assets refers to all investment activities that are conducted in rural areas to meet the production and living needs of the rural residents. Investment in rural fixed assets consists of investment in fixed assets by rural and non-rural households.

Incremental Fixed Assets Investment means the value of fixed assets put into use in the reporting period, including investment in projects completed and put into use within the year, and investment in equipment, tools and appliances that reach the standard of fixed assets, together with expenses incurred in these activities. Other construction costs adding value to fixed assets shall be calculated in the incremental fixed assets together with the projects put into use.

Infrastructure Investment refers to investment that provides intermediate inputs for enterprise to meet their basic production needs, provides consumers with basic consumer services needed, or provides communities with services for improving external environment, which includes the investment in municipal projects, telecom projects, public facilities, water conservancy and environmental protection.

Surplus Funds by the Year End of the Previous Year refers to the fund in the previous year that was not included in the investment in fixed assets, including the value of materials not yet used for projects, value of equipment to be installed, and balance of cash and bank deposits.

Subtotal of Funds at Current Year refers to monetary capital received by investors that was used for investment in fixed assets, including funds from state budgetary funds, domestic loans, bonds, foreign investment, self-raised funds and other funds.

State Budgets consists of budgetary appropriation and government loans. More specifically, it consists of infrastructure fund from the central government (operating fund and non-operating fund), earmarked expenditures (e.g. expenditures on replacing oil with coal), refinancing, discount interest funds, expenditures on technical updates, transformation and new products promotion, expenses on urban construction, expenses on temporary construction from business departments, development funds for less developed areas, as well as local budgetary funds transferred from the central budget.

Domestic Loans refer to loans of various forms borrowed by fixed assets investment project entities from banks and non-bank financial institutions for the purpose of investment in fixed assets during the reporting period, including loans issued by banks from their equity funds and deposits, loans appropriated by higher authorities, special loans allocated by the central government (including loans for replacing oil with coal, and special loans for labor camp coal mines), loans arranged by local government from special funds, domestic reserve loans and revolving loans.

Foreign Investment refers to foreign funds received during the reporting period for the investment in construction and purchase of fixed assets (including equipment, materials and technologies), including foreign direct investment, foreign loans (loans from foreign governments and international financial institutions, export credit, commercial loans from foreign banks, issued bonds and stocks overseas), and other foreign investments (including funds for domestic re-investment in fixed assets by earnings from foreign investment). It does not include foreign exchanges owned by China (foreign exchanges owned by the central and local governments, foreign exchanges retained, foreign exchange swap, loans in foreign exchanges issued by the domestic banks with their own funds, etc.).

Self-raised Funds refer to non-budgetary funds for investment in fixed assets received during the reporting period by different regions, departments, enterprises and public institutions, including self-owned funds of central departments, local authorities, enterprises and public institutions.

Other Funds refer to funds for investment in fixed assets received from sources other than those listed above, including social funds, personal funds, donated funds and funds transferred from other institutions.

Investment in Construction of Residential Buildings refer to the investment in houses specially used for residence, including employee family's dormitories, single employees' dormitories, student dormitories, and affordable houses, excluding purchased commercial residences.

Construction and Installation Investment (Workload of Construction and Installation) refers to the investment in construction projects of various houses and buildings, and installation projects of various equipment and devices, also known as the workload of construction and installation. It can only be realized through construction work and consumption of materials. For installation projects, the value of equipment installed is not included.

Purchase of Equipment, Tools and Devices refers to the

value of equipment, tools and devices purchased or made by construction companies, enterprises or public institutions, which reach the specified amount of fixed assets.

Real Estate Development Investment refers to all investment used for housing projects and land development projects, together with public welfare buildings and land purchase costs spent from January 1st to the last day of the year.

Land Purchase Cost refers to expenses on acquiring the land use right, including development compensation. It includes: (1) Expenses on land use right by allocation, including land compensation fees, compensation fees for its attached objects and crops; after completion, these expanses will be included in incremental fixed assets. (2) Expenses on land use right by transfer, including fees for agreement transfer, bid invitation, auction and listing; after completion, these expanses will not be included in incremental fixed assets. Land purchase expense shall be accounted according to actual amount paid. If paid by installment, it should be included in investment by stages.

Affordable Houses refer to government-subsidized houses that are supplied to urban low-income households and built in line with reasonable standards, limited size and fixed pricing.

Price-capped Houses refer to ordinary commercial houses with limited size and fixed pricing that are supplied to middle-income urban households, and their land transfer price is controlled by the government.

Public Rental Houses refer to government-subsidized houses that are built in line with reasonable standards and limited size, and can be rented by lower middle-income urban households with housing difficulties, new employees and migrant workers with stable jobs and have lived in the urban area for a certain period.

Low-rent Houses refer to government-subsidized houses that are built in line with reasonable standards and limited size, with funds raised by purchasing, reconstruction or leasing, and can be rented by low-income urban households with housing difficulties.

Floor Space of Buildings under Construction refers to the total floor space of all houses and buildings under construction during the reference period, including floor space of newly started buildings in current period, floor space of construction extended from the previous period to the current period, and floor space of construction suspended during the previous period and resumed in the current period. Floor space of construction completed in the current period, and floor space of construction started and then suspended in the current period are also included in the floor space under construction. For multi-storey buildings, the sum of floor space of all floors shall be calculated.

Floor Space of Buildings Completed refers to the total floor space of all houses and buildings fully completed as required in the design plan during the reference period, which have been examined as qualified for living and use, and can be handed over and put into use.

Floor Space of Vacant Commercial Buildings refers to total floor space of commercial buildings for sale or for renting by the end of the reference period. It consists of the floor space of completed buildings in previous years and in the current year, but does not include relocated houses or buildings of unified construction or agent contract, as well as houses not for sale or renting such as public facilities, houses used by real estate companies and temporary houses.

06

北京统计年鉴2016　　BEIJING STATISTICAL YEARBOOK

财政与税收
GOVERNMENT FINANCE AND TAX REVENUES

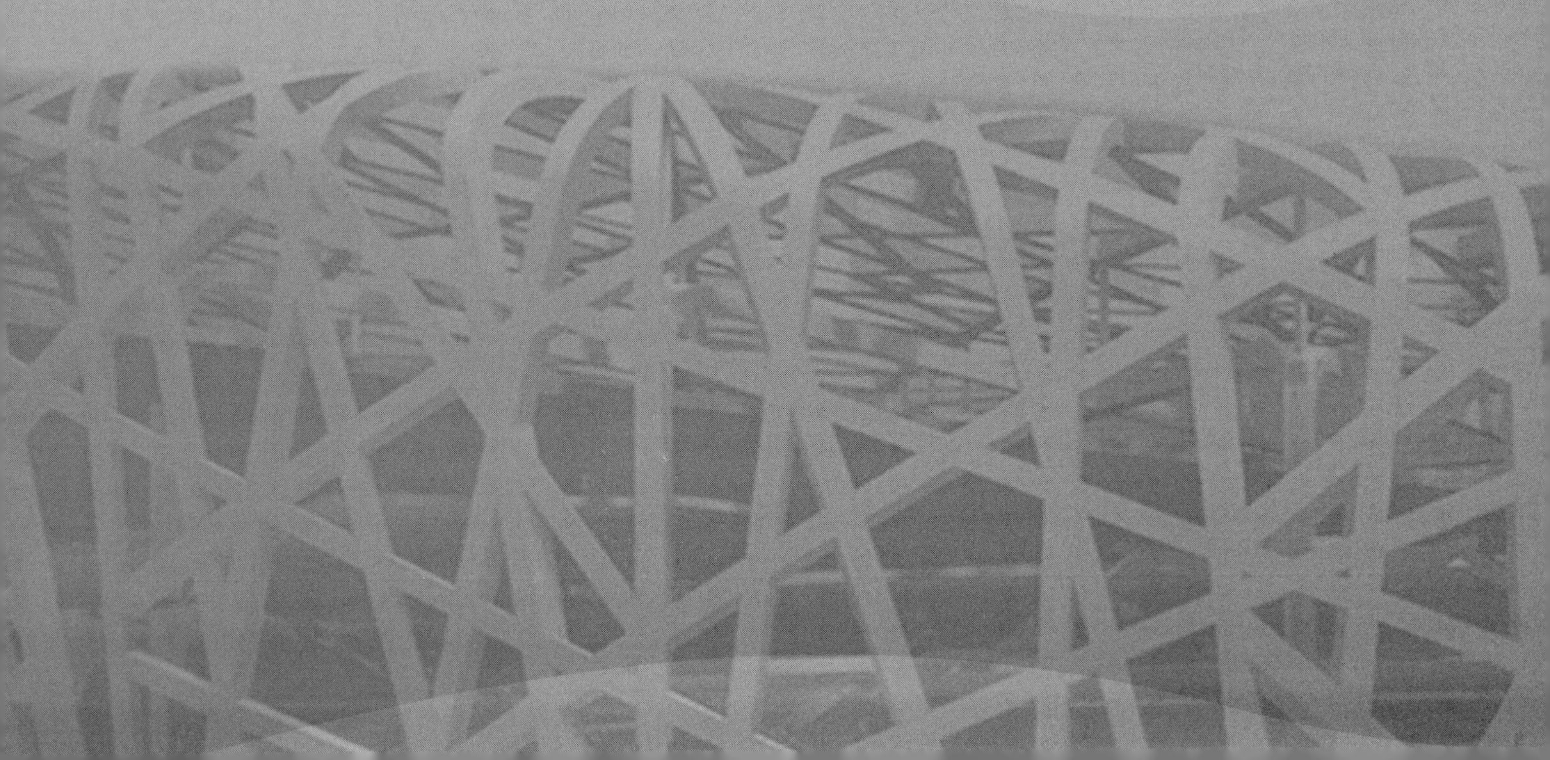

简要说明

一、本章资料的主要内容

本章资料包括北京市财政收支情况，北京市国税、地税税收(费)收入情况。其中财政收支包括历年财政收入、支出及相当于地区生产总值比例等情况；税收（费）收入包括国税、地税税收（费）收入分组情况。

二、本章资料的数据来源

本章财政收支数据由北京市财政局提供；税收（费）数据由北京市国家税务局、北京市地方税务局提供。

Brief Introduction

I. Main Content

Statistics in this chapter include fiscal revenues and expenditures, and state and local tax revenues of Beijing Municipality. Figures of fiscal revenues and expenditures include fiscal revenues, expenditures and their proportions to GDP of Beijing in previous years; figures of tax revenues include the grouped figures of state and local tax revenues.

II. Source of Data

Data of fiscal revenues and expenditures are from Beijing Municipal Bureau of Finance; data of tax revenues are from Beijing Municipal Bureau of State Tax and Beijing Municipal Bureau of Local Tax.

6-1 地方财政收支(1978-2015年)
LOCAL FINANCIAL REVENUE AND EXPENDITURE (1978-2015)

单位：亿元 (100 million yuan)

年份 Year	地方财政收入 Local Financial Revenue	#一般公共预算收入 Local Public Budgetary Revenue	税收收入 Tax Revenue	#增值税 Value-added Tax	#营业税 Operation Tax	#个人所得税 Individual Income Tax	#企业所得税 Company Income Tax	#城市维护建设税 Urban Maintenance and Construction Tax	非税收入 Non-tax Revenue	#政府性基金预算收入 Governmental Fund Budgetary Revenue
1978	50.46		18.25							
1979	47.75		19.41							
1980	51.29		21.22							
1981-1985	**234.27**		**191.96**	**8.34**	**11.46**	**0.61**	**43.77**	**2.16**		
1981	49.12		24.22			0.02	1.76			
1982	47.25		25.81	0.05		0.05	1.43			
1983	39.84		38.03	1.30		0.07	11.70			
1984	45.62		43.91	2.20	1.23	0.13	12.70			
1985	52.44		59.99	4.79	10.23	0.34	16.18	2.16		
1986-1990	**337.13**		**397.96**	**65.02**	**103.00**	**7.29**	**116.89**	**16.67**		
1986	60.34		60.83	7.61	13.19	0.97	20.46	2.51		
1987	63.62		67.77	9.09	15.42	1.54	21.87	2.70		
1988	68.11		84.04	15.10	21.11	1.23	27.70	3.37		
1989	71.05		91.09	16.75	25.33	1.53	24.31	3.74		
1990	74.01		94.23	16.47	27.95	2.02	22.55	4.35		
1991-1995	**456.48**		**643.24**	**136.88**	**228.80**	**35.46**	**105.24**	**34.07**		
1991	77.02		100.58	19.53	30.78	2.56	20.59	4.77		
1992	80.25		110.54	22.29	35.86	3.15	19.08	5.13		
1993	84.10		148.19	42.30	52.07	4.30	14.20	6.57		
1994	99.85		120.53	25.54	45.63	9.24	21.70	7.18		
1995	115.26		163.40	27.22	64.46	16.21	29.67	10.42		
1996-2000	**1341.65**		**1397.26**	**185.46**	**570.06**	**190.18**	**223.71**	**70.84**		
1996	150.90		201.32	29.53	81.61	22.67	37.22	11.36		
1997	209.91	182.32	235.82	32.67	97.54	28.76	41.05	12.74	-53.50	27.59
1998	262.01	229.45	272.23	37.58	113.00	36.49	41.42	14.12	-42.78	32.56
1999	320.44	281.37	315.10	39.72	128.86	45.88	45.99	15.27	-33.74	39.07
2000	398.39	345.00	372.79	45.96	149.05	56.38	58.03	17.35	-27.79	53.39
2001-2005	**3611.96**	**3244.40**	**3216.46**	**367.43**	**1389.75**	**355.88**	**566.23**	**147.84**	**27.94**	**367.57**
2001	507.68	454.17	475.00	59.00	181.35	79.52	86.07	20.53	-20.83	53.51
2002	600.96	533.99	539.87	66.69	227.79	61.29	100.00	24.91	-5.88	66.97
2003	665.94	592.54	588.96	75.26	263.69	57.21	93.70	28.85	3.58	73.40
2004	830.03	744.49	726.50	68.88	333.16	73.34	121.70	34.72	17.99	85.55
2005	1007.35	919.21	886.13	97.60	383.76	84.52	164.76	38.83	33.08	88.14
2006-2010	**11889.54**	**8827.85**	**8453.62**	**800.72**	**3321.83**	**801.97**	**1965.28**	**317.03**	**374.23**	**3061.69**
2006	1235.78	1117.15	1076.82	117.80	460.99	102.28	213.86	45.17	40.33	118.63
2007	1882.04	1492.64	1435.67	134.84	601.06	135.20	309.34	56.63	56.97	389.40
2008	2282.04	1837.32	1775.58	158.34	651.78	171.33	497.52	63.95	61.75	444.71
2009	2678.77	2026.81	1913.97	179.73	752.60	177.84	430.42	71.28	112.84	651.96
2010	3810.91	2353.93	2251.59	210.01	855.40	215.33	513.09	80.00	102.34	1456.98
2011-2015	**30334.19**	**18733.34**	**17619.09**	**2489.47**	**5513.81**	**1749.87**	**4178.87**	**875.00**	**1114.25**	**12074.97**
2011	4359.10	3006.28	2854.63	237.76	1071.51	272.90	683.71	145.65	151.65	1352.82
2012	4573.72	3314.93	3124.75	314.00	1152.74	281.49	752.47	160.34	190.18	1197.92
2013	5566.08	3661.11	3514.52	574.89	1034.79	333.84	802.12	177.41	146.59	1841.76
2014	7214.54	4027.16	3861.29	646.69	1068.64	383.52	915.84	187.24	165.87	3122.91
2015	6813.84	4723.86	4263.91	716.12	1186.13	478.12	1024.73	204.36	459.95	2028.37

注：1. 地方财政收支数为决算数。
2. 从2015年开始，原指标“地方公共财政预算收入”和“地方公共财政预算支出”调整为“一般公共预算收入”和“一般公共预算支出”(下同)。
3. 自2012年开始，地方财政收支包含三部分内容，即地方财政公共预算收支、政府性基金预算收支和国有资本经营预算收支(下同)，此前仅包含前两部分内容。

资料来源：北京市财政局。

Note: a) Local government revenue and expenditures are final accounts.
b) Since 2015, "local public financial budgetary revenue" and "local public financial budgetary expenditure" are renamed as "local general public budgetary revenue" and "local general public budgetary expenditure" (the same below).
c) Since 2012, local financial revenue and expenditure have included three parts: local public financial budgetary revenue and expenditure, governmental fund budgetary revenue and expenditure and budgetary revenue and expenditure of state-owned capital operation (the same below). And data before 2012 only includes the first two parts.

Source: Beijing Municipal Bureau of Finance.

6-1 续表

单位：亿元

年 份 Year	地 方 财政支出 Local Financial Expenditures	#一般公共 预算支出 Local Public Budgetary Expenditures	#一般公共 服 务 General Public Service	#教 育 Education	#科 学 技 术 Science and Technology	#文化体育 与传媒 Culture, Sports and Media	#社会保障 和就业 Social Security and Employ-ment
1978	20.38						
1979	20.06						
1980	14.87						
1981-1985	**111.40**						
1981	14.85						
1982	16.80						
1983	19.61						
1984	27.15						
1985	32.99						
1986-1990	**272.89**						
1986	44.27						
1987	49.67						
1988	52.93						
1989	59.50						
1990	66.52						
1991-1995	**473.64**						
1991	67.98						
1992	71.74						
1993	80.99						
1994	98.53						
1995	154.40						
1996-2000	**1646.07**						
1996	187.45						
1997	262.20	236.39					
1998	307.55	280.68					
1999	398.53	355.19					
2000	490.34	443.00					
2001-2005	**4219.74**	**3878.85**					
2001	614.92	559.11					
2002	683.98	628.35					
2003	809.39	734.80					
2004	974.17	898.28					
2005	1137.28	1058.31					
2006-2010	**12765.99**	**9942.31**	**987.56**	**1604.40**	**578.30**	**309.36**	**1048.02**
2006	1411.58	1296.84	159.95	209.21	70.14	40.51	149.22
2007	2067.65	1649.50	179.56	263.00	90.74	53.62	179.28
2008	2400.93	1959.29	196.27	316.30	112.19	61.11	209.33
2009	2820.86	2319.37	212.21	365.67	126.31	74.75	234.29
2010	4064.97	2717.32	239.57	450.22	178.92	79.36	275.90
2011-2015	**32263.13**	**21366.56**	**1417.42**	**3427.63**	**1188.20**	**735.49**	**2457.82**
2011	4574.94	3245.23	261.38	520.08	183.07	87.01	354.88
2012	4866.43	3685.31	286.57	628.65	199.94	141.37	424.31
2013	6039.42	4173.66	297.12	681.18	234.67	154.71	469.13
2014	7147.75	4524.67	272.23	742.05	282.71	163.90	509.01
2015	8080.71	5737.70	300.12	855.67	287.80	188.50	700.48

6-1 continued

(100 million yuan)

#医疗卫生与计划生育 Healthcare	#节能环保 Energy Conservation and Environmental Protection	#交通运输 Transportation	#城乡社区事务 Urban and Rural Community Affairs	#农林水 Agriculture, Forestry and Water Conservancy	#政府性基金预算支出 Governmental Fund Budgetary Expenditure
718.40	**199.77**	**422.53**	**1182.65**	**613.55**	**2823.69**
100.95	20.14	7.05	153.26	88.62	114.74
118.95	29.27	33.09	187.43	102.51	418.15
145.05	35.47	80.35	199.84	121.77	441.64
166.63	54.04	147.07	347.82	142.01	501.50
186.82	60.85	154.99	294.30	158.64	1347.65
1450.49	**862.83**	**1184.86**	**2843.48**	**1476.10**	**10637.82**
225.49	94.51	199.12	339.27	187.34	1329.71
256.06	113.54	243.76	430.76	222.69	1118.45
276.13	138.17	231.79	510.67	297.62	1798.81
322.29	213.36	214.55	567.40	343.67	2559.09
370.52	303.26	295.63	995.39	424.78	2281.30

6-2 地方财政收支增长速度情况(1978-2015年)
GROWTH RATE OF LOCAL FINANCIAL REVENUE AND EXPENDITURES (1978-2015)

单位：% (%)

年 份	增长速度(上年=100) Growth Rate (Previous Year=100)			
	地方财政收入 Local Financial Revenue	#一般公共预算收入 Local Public Budgetary Revenue	地方财政支出 Local Financial Expenditures	#一般公共预算支出 Local Public Budgetary Expenditures
1978	18.0		27.6	
1979	-5.4		-1.6	
1980	7.4		-25.9	
1981-1985				
1981	-4.2		-0.1	
1982	-3.8		13.1	
1983	-15.7		16.7	
1984	14.5		38.4	
1985	14.9		21.5	
1986-1990				
1986	15.1		34.2	
1987	5.4		12.2	
1988	7.1		6.6	
1989	4.3		12.4	
1990	4.2		11.8	
1991-1995				
1991	4.1		2.2	
1992	4.2		5.5	
1993	4.8		12.9	
1994	9.9		21.7	
1995	21.8		56.7	
1996-2000				
1996	30.9		21.4	
1997	25.5		39.9	
1998	24.8	20.0	17.4	18.7
1999	22.3	22.6	29.6	26.5
2000	24.3	22.7	23.0	24.7
2001-2005				
2001	27.4	31.6	25.4	26.2
2002	25.8	25.9	11.2	12.4
2003	17.2	18.2	18.3	16.9
2004	28.3	29.7	20.4	22.3
2005	21.4	23.5	16.7	17.8
2006-2010				
2006	22.7	21.5	24.1	22.5
2007	52.3	33.6	46.5	27.2
2008	21.3	23.1	16.1	18.8
2009	17.4	10.3	17.5	18.4
2010	42.3	16.1	44.1	17.2
2011-2015				
2011	14.4	27.7	12.5	19.4
2012	4.9	10.3	6.4	13.6
2013	21.7	10.4	24.1	13.3
2014	29.6	10.0	18.4	8.4
2015	-5.6	17.3	13.1	26.8

注：2002-2004年地方财政收入增长速度按可比口径计算。
资料来源：北京市财政局。
Note: The growth rate of local government revenue in 2002-2004 is calculated at comparable figures.
Source: Beijing Municipal Bureau of Finance.

6-3 地方财政收入
LOCAL FINANCIAL REVENUE

项目	Item	绝对数(万元) Absolute Value (10000 yuan) 2015	2014	2015年为2014年% 2015 as % of 2014	构成(%) Composition (%) 2015	2014
合计	**Total**	**68138373**	**72145371**	**94.4**	**100.0**	**100.0**
一般公共预算收入	**Local Public Budgetary Revenue**	**47238597**	**40271609**	**117.3**	**69.3**	**55.8**
#增值税	Value-added Tax	7161226	6466927	110.7	10.5	9.0
营业税	Business Tax	11861272	10686441	111.0	17.4	14.8
个人所得税	Personal Income Tax	4781200	3835236	124.7	7.0	5.3
城市维护建设税	Urban Maintenance and Construction Tax	2043646	1872354	109.1	3.0	2.6
耕地占用税	Arable Land Occupation Tax	45350	46892	96.7	0.1	0.1
企业所得税	Company Income Tax	10247332	9158440	111.9	15.0	12.7
国有资本经营收入	Operation Income of State-owned Assets	-649927	-947864			
罚没收入	Income of Fines and Confiscations	557809	386713	144.2	0.8	0.5
行政事业性收费收入	Administrative Fees	643842	538976	119.5	0.9	0.7
政府性基金预算收入	**Government Fund Budgetary Revenue**	**20283742**	**31229135**	**65.0**	**29.8**	**43.3**
国有资本经营预算收入	**Budgetary Revenue of State-owned Capital Operation**	**616034**	**644627**	**95.6**	**0.9**	**0.9**

资料来源：北京市财政局。
Source: Beijing Finance Bureau.

6-4 地方财政支出
LOCAL FINANCIAL EXPENDITURE

项目	Item	绝对数(万元) Absolute Value (10000 yuan) 2015	2014	2015年为2014年% 2015 as % of 2014	构成(%) Composition (%) 2015	2014
合计	**Total**	**80807129**	**71477458**	**113.1**	**100.0**	**100.0**
一般公共预算支出	**Local Public Budgetary Expenditures**	**57377011**	**45246690**	**126.8**	**71.0**	**63.3**
#一般公共服务	General Public Service	3001224	2722329	110.2	3.7	3.8
教育	Education	8556654	7420541	115.3	10.6	10.4
科学技术	Science and Technology	2877956	2827117	101.8	3.6	4.0
文化体育与传媒	Culture, Sports and Media	1884976	1639031	115.0	2.3	2.3
社会保障和就业	Social Security and Employment	7004823	5090079	137.6	8.7	7.1
医疗卫生与计划生育	Healthcare	3705234	3222919	115.0	4.6	4.5
节能环保	Energy Conservation and Environmental Protection	3032612	2133553	142.1	3.8	3.0
交通运输	Transportation	2956316	2145513	137.8	3.7	3.0
城乡社区事务	Urban and Rural Community Affairs	9953866	5673982	175.4	12.3	7.9
农林水事务	Agriculture, Forestry and Water Conservancy	4247815	3436680	123.6	5.3	4.8
政府性基金支出合计	**Total Expenditures of Governmental Funds**	**22812951**	**25590902**	**89.1**	**28.2**	**35.8**
国有资本经营预算支出	**Budgetary Expenditure of State-owned Capital Operation**	**617167**	**639866**	**96.5**	**0.8**	**0.9**

资料来源：北京市财政局。
Source: Beijing Municipal Bureau of Finance.

6-5 地税税费收入分税种、分行业完成情况(2010-2015年)
LOCAL TAX REVENUE BY CATEGORY AND INDUSTRY (2010-2015)

单位：亿元 (100 million yuan)

项 目	Item	2010	2011	2012	2013	2014	2015
地税税费收入	**Local Tax Revenue**	**2104.89**	**2666.62**	**2865.25**	**3061.60**	**3387.80**	**3868.24**
按税种分	**By Category**						
#营业税	Business Tax	855.40	1071.51	1152.74	1032.35	1067.92	1186.13
企业所得税	Coporate Income Tax	173.18	210.52	221.02	258.07	333.91	374.10
个人所得税	Personal Income Tax	536.27	681.27	703.48	834.47	958.79	1195.28
按行业分	**By Sector**						
第一产业	Primary Industry	3.67	3.90	4.94	4.98	7.74	7.87
第二产业	Secondary Industry	235.20	303.14	326.20	348.54	388.51	408.74
#制造业	Manufacturing	101.75	138.36	150.45	160.70	179.36	206.27
电力、燃气及水的生产和供应业	Production and Distribution of Electricity, Gas and Water	15.69	19.37	21.18	25.20	28.94	29.17
建筑业	Construction	109.88	134.37	144.65	153.99	171.73	166.45
第三产业	Tertiary Industry	1866.00	2359.58	2534.11	2708.14	2991.56	3451.63
#交通、运输、仓储及邮政业	Transport, Storage and Post	51.41	63.95	60.58	38.14	40.47	46.37
信息传输、计算机服务和软件业	Information Transmission, Computer Servicesand Software	98.02	125.48	132.76	123.65	141.82	147.05
批发和零售业	Wholesale and Retail Trade	111.40	159.35	169.30	188.84	206.15	230.14
金融业	Finance	276.40	366.35	446.67	477.99	599.52	762.95
房地产业	Real Estate	437.40	520.36	525.44	659.25	734.16	745.68

资料来源：北京市地方税务局。
Source: Beijing Municipal Bureau of Local Taxation.

6-6 国税税收收入分税种、分行业完成情况(2010-2015年)
STATE TAX REVENUE BY CATEGORY AND INDUSTRY (2010-2015)

单位：亿元 (100 million yuan)

项 目	Item	2010	2011	2012	2013	2014	2015
国税税收收入	**State Tax Revenue**	**4346.8**	**5332.5**	**6339.4**	**7470.9**	**8325.2**	**8655.2**
按税种分	**By Category**						
#增值税	Value-added Tax	868.3	961.7	1096.0	1456.3	1659.8	1710.5
营业税	Business Tax	145.4	161.3	191.3	203.7	80.7	150.7
企业所得税	Corporate Income Tax	2642.0	3506.5	3609.4	5024.4	5757.3	5937.2
按行业分	**By Sector**						
第一产业	Primary Industry	5.8	0.7	0.3	2.6	0.9	2.5
第二产业	Secondary Industry	779.1	881.1	843.8	1069.3	1159.4	1182.2
#制造业	Manufacturing	623.2	709.2	764.6	832.0	889.5	963.1
电力、燃气及水的生产和供应业	Production and Distribution of Electricity, Gas and Water	105.2	103.5	131.0	261.4	194.1	171.1
建筑业	Construction	30.1	45.3	54.8	57.0	50.9	63.9
第三产业	Tertiary Industry	3561.9	4450.8	5495.3	6399.0	7164.8	7470.5
#交通、运输、仓储及邮政业	Transport, Storage and Post	157.9	209.2	212.1	245.1	242.6	242.6
信息传输、计算机服务和软件业	Information Transmission, Computer Services and Software	30.8	105.9	245.9	373.2	296.2	285.0
批发和零售业	Wholesale and Retail Trade	1081.6	1410.8	1314.6	1451.0	1474.0	1420.6
金融业	Finance	1831.2	2158.0	3034.0	3500.2	4153.2	4401.4
房地产业	Real Estate	107.6	122.3	111.6	157.0	156.9	104.3

资料来源：北京市国家税务局。
Source: Beijing Municipal Bureau of State Taxation.

主要统计指标解释

财政部分

地方财政收入 指国家财政参与社会产品分配所得的收入，是实现国家职能的财力保证。包括地方公共财政预算收入、政府性基金预算收入和国有资本经营预算收入。

一般公共预算收入 是通过一定的形式和程序，由各级财政部门组织并纳入预算管理的各项收入。

政府性基金预算收入 是按规定收取，转入或通过当年财政安排，由财政管理并具有指定用途的政府性基金预算收入等。

国有资本经营预算 是指国家以所有者身份取得国有资本收益，并对所得收益进行分配而发生的各项收支预算，是政府预算的重要组成部分。

税收收入 包括增值税、营业税、企业所得税、个人所得税、资源税、城市维护建设税、房产税、印花税、城镇土地使用税、土地增值税、车船税、耕地占用税、契税等。

非税收收入 包括专项收入、行政事业性收费、罚没收入和其他收入。

地方财政支出 是以国家为主体，以财政的事权为依据进行的一种财政资金分配活动，集中反映了国家的职能活动范围及其所发生的耗费，包括地方公共财政预算支出和基金预算支出。

一般公共预算支出 是各级财政部门对集中的一般预算收入有计划地分配和使用而安排的支出。

政府性基金预算支出 是各级财政部门用基金预算收入安排的支出。

一般公共服务支出 指政府提供基本公共管理与服务的支出，包括人大事务、政协事务、政府办公厅（室)及相关机构事务、发展与改革事务、统计信息事务、财政事务、税收事务、审计事务、海关事务、人力资源事务、纪检监察事务、人口与计划生育事务、 商贸事务、知识产权事务、工商行政管理事务、国土资源事务、 海洋管理事务、 测绘事务、地震事务、气象事务、民族事务、宗教事务、港澳台侨事务、档案事务、共产党事务、民主党派事务及工商联事务、群众团体事务、彩票事务等。

教育支出 指政府教育事务支出，包括教育行政管理、学前教育、小学教育、初中教育、普通高中教育、普通高等教育、初等职业教育、中专教育、技校教育、职业高中教育、高等职业教育、广播电视教育、留学生教育、特殊教育、干部继续教育、教育机关服务等。

科学技术支出 指用于科学技术方面的支出，包括科学技术管理事务、基础研究、应用研究、技术研究与开发、科技条件与服务、社会科学、科学技术普及、科技交流与合作等。

文化教育与传媒支出 指政府在文化、文物、体育、广播影视、新闻出版等方面的支出。

社会保障和就业支出 指政府在社会保障与就业方面的支出，包括社会保障和就业管理事务、民政管理事务、财政对社会保险基金的补助、补充全国社会保障基金、行政事业单位离退休、企业改革补助、就业补助、抚恤、退役安置、社会福利、残疾人事业、城市居民最低生活保障、其他城镇社会救济、农村社会救济、自然灾害生活救助、红十字事务等。

医疗卫生与计划生育支出 指政府医疗卫生与计划生育管理方面的支出。

节能环保支出 指政府环境保护支出，包括环境保护管理事务支出、环境监测与监察支出、污染治理支出、自然生态保护支出、天然林保护工程支出、退耕还林支出、风沙荒漠治理支出、退牧还草支出、已垦草原退耕还草、能源节约利用、污染减排、可再生能源和资源综合利用等支出。

交通运输支出 指政府交通运输和邮政业方面的支出，包括公路运输支出、水路运输支出、铁路运输支出、民用航空运输支出、邮政业支出等。

城乡社区事务支出 指政府城乡社区事务支出，包括城乡社区管理事务支出、城乡社区规划与管理支出、城乡社区公共设施支出、城乡社区住宅支出、城乡社区环境卫生支出、建设市场管理与监督支出等。

农林水事务支出 指政府农林水事务支出，包括农业支出、林业支出、水利支出、扶贫支出、农业综合开发支出等。

税收部分

税费收入 指由各级地方税务局征缴的各项税收收入和罚没收入。包括营业税、企业所得税、个人所得税、资源税、房产税、契税、城市维护建设税等。

税收收入 指由各级国家税务局征缴的各项税收收入。包括增值税、消费税、营业税、企业所得税、个人所得税、城市维护建设税等。

营业税 是对在中华人民共和国境内提供应税劳务、转让无形资产或者销售不动产的单位和个人，就其取得营业额征收的一种税。

企业所得税 是对中国境内全部企业的生产经营所得和其他所得征收的一种税。

增值税 指以商品或劳务销售额为计税依据并实行扣除已征税款制度的一种流转税。

个人所得税 是对个人（自然人）取得的各项应税所得征收的一种税。

Explanatory Notes on Main Statistical Indicators

Finance

Local Financial Revenue refers to the revenue for the national finance through participating in the distribution of social products. It is the financial guarantee to ensure the functions and powers of the government. The local financial revenue includes local public budgetary revenue, governmental fund budgetary revenue and budget of state-owned capital operation.

Local Public Budgetary Revenue refers to the revenue organized by finance authorities at all levels in certain form and through certain procedures and involved in budgetary management.

Governmental Fund Budgetary Revenue refers to governmental fund budgetary revenues collected, transferred or allocated by government finance in the current year in accordance with regulations, and regulated by government finance and used for specific purpose.

Budget of State-owned Capital Operation refers to the state-owned capital income of the country as the owner and all kinds of income and expenditure budgets resulted from the allocation of the income. It is an important part of governmental budget.

Tax Revenue includes value-added tax, business tax, corporate income tax, individual income tax, resource tax, urban maintenance and construction tax, house property tax, stamp tax, urban land use tax, land appreciation tax, tax on vehicles and boat operation, farm land occupation tax, deed tax, etc.

Non-tax Revenue includes special program receipts, charge of administrative and institutional units, income of fines and confiscation, and other non-tax revenues.

Local Financial Expenditure refers to the allocation of financial funds by the state based on the financial administration, which demonstrates the scope of government functioning and the expenditures incurred. It includes local public budgetary expenditure and fund budgetary expenditure.

Local Public Budgetary Expenditure refers to the expenditure arranged by finance authorities at all levels from the general budgetary revenue according to the planned distribution .

Governmental Fund Budgetary Expenditure refers to the expenditure arranged by finance authorities at all levels according to the fund budget revenue.

Expenditure for General Public Services refers to the spending on the basic public management and services provided by the government, including the expenses on affairs of Beijing Municipal People's Congress, CPC Beijing Municipal Committee, General Office of Beijing Municipal Government and relative institutions, development and reform, statistical information, finance, taxation, audit, customs, human resources, discipline inspection and supervision, population and family planning, commerce and trade, intellectual property, administration for industry and commerce, land and resources, oceanic administration, surveying and mapping, earthquake, weather, ethnics, religions, Hong Kong, Macao, Taiwan, and Overseas Chinese, archive administration, Chinese Communist Party, democratic parties, federation of industry and commerce, mass organizations, and lottery, etc.

Expenditure for Education refers to the spending of government on education, including the expenses on the administration of education, pre-school education, primary education, junior high school education, senior high school education, general higher education, primary vocational education, secondary vocational education, technical school education, vocational senior high school education and higher vocational education, radio and television education, overseas student education, special education, continuing education for management personnel, and services for education authorities, etc.

Expenditure for Science and Technology refers to the spending on science and technology (S&T), including the expense on the administration of S&T, basic research, applied research, research and development, conditions and services of S&T, popularization of social science and S&T, exchanges and cooperation of S&T, etc.

Expenditure for Cultural Education and Media refers to the spending on culture, cultural relics, sports, radio, films, television, press and publication, etc.

Expenditure for Social Security and Employment refers to the spending on social security and employment, including the expenses on social security and employment administration affairs, civil affairs, budgetary subsidy on the social insurance funds, subsidy on National Social Security Fund, subsidy on retirees of administrative and institutional units, subsidy on enterprise reform, subsidy on employment, pension, reemployment of ex-serviceman, social welfare, the handicapped undertakings, subsistence allowances for urban residents, other urban social relief, rural social relief, relief for natural disasters, affairs of Red Cross, etc.

Expenditure for Health Care and Family Planning refers to the spending of government on health care and family planning.

Expenditure for Energy Conservation and Environmental Protection refers to the spending of government on environmental protection, including the expenses on administration of environmental protection, environment monitoring and supervision, pollution control, natural and ecological protection, projects of natural forest protection, reforestation, control of sand storms, returning pasture and grazing land to grassland, energy conservation and utilization, emission reduction, comprehensive utilization of renewable energy and resources, etc.

Expenditure for Transportation refers to the spending of government on transportation and postal services, including the expenses on highway transportation, waterway transportation, railway transportation, civil aviation transportation and postal services, etc.

Expenditure for Urban and Rural Community Affairs refers to the spending of government on urban and rural community affairs, including the expenses on administration of urban and rural communities, planning and management of urban and rural communities, public facilities in urban and rural communities, residential houses in urban and rural communities, sanitation in urban and rural communities, management and supervision of construction markets, etc.

Expenditure for Agriculture, Forestry and Water Conservancy Affairs refers to the spending of government on agriculture affairs, forestry affairs, water conservancy affairs, poverty alleviation and comprehensive agricultural development, etc.

Taxes

Local Tax Revenue refers to the revenue of taxes, fines and confiscations levied and collected by local tax bureaus at all levels, including business tax, corporate income tax, personal income tax, resource tax, house property tax, deed tax, urban maintenance and construction tax, etc.

State Tax Revenue refers to the revenue of taxes levied and collected by state tax bureaus at all levels, including value-added tax, excise tax, business tax, corporate income tax, individual income tax, urban maintenance and construction tax, etc.

Business Tax is a kind of tax levied against the business income of entities and individuals providing taxable labor services, transferring intangible assets or selling real estate within the territory of PRC.

Corporate Income Tax is a sort of tax levied against income of China domestic enterprises from their production and operation and other income.

Value-Added Tax is a sort of commodity turnover tax based on commodity and service sales, with a system of deduction of tax levied.

Personal Income Tax is a sort of tax levied against taxable income earned by individuals (natural persons).

北京统计年鉴2016　BEIJING STATISTICAL YEARBOOK

价格指数
PRICE INDEX

简要说明

一、本章资料的主要内容

本章价格指数资料，反映生产、流通、消费与投资的价格变动趋势和变动幅度。主要包括居民消费价格指数；商品零售价格指数；农产品生产者价格指数；工业生产者出厂价格指数；工业生产者购进价格指数；固定资产投资价格指数；住宅销售价格指数。

二、本章资料的数据来源

本章资料由国家统计局北京调查总队、北京市统计局提供。

三、调查方法

（一）居民消费价格指数和商品零售价格指数

编制居民消费价格指数、商品零售价格指数的资料采用抽样调查和重点调查相结合的方法取得，即在全市选择不同的区域，按照布局合理的原则抽选价格调查点，由国家确定调查商品和服务项目，在此基础上按照消费量大、价格变动趋势有较强代表性的原则选择调查样本，对其市场价格进行定期调查，以样本推算总体。现将指数编制过程按下列几个步骤进行说明。

抽选价格调查点。按照布局合理等原则，将不同区域各种类型的商场、农贸市场、服务网点分别按销售额、成交额和经营规模为标志，从高到低排队，依据所需调查点的数量进行等距抽样。

选择代表规格品。代表商品和服务项目由国家确定，代表规格品由各省市按照有关原则选择。选择原则：（1）消费量较大；（2）价格变动趋势和变动程度有较强的代表性，即选中规格品的价格变动特征与未选中规格品之间价格变动的相关性愈高愈好；（3）选中的规格品之间，性质相隔愈远愈好，价格变动特征的相关性愈低愈好；选中的工业消费品必须是合格产品，产品包装上有注册商标、产地、规格等级等标识。

目前，居民消费价格调查按用途划分为 8 大类，262 个基本分类，国家规定大城市调查规格品数量应在 600 种左右，北京市由于编制分收入层居民消费价格指数，代表规格品数量增加到 1728 种。商品零售价格指数划分为 16 个大类，229 个基本分类，北京市代表规格品数量为 1297 种。

价格资料的采集。采取定人、定点、定时直接调查的方法采集价格资料。

权数资料来源与计算。居民消费价格指数的权数根据城市居民家庭生活消费支出调查资料整理计算。商品零售价格指数的权数根据商业统计中社会消费品零售总额计算。

（二）工业生产者出厂价格指数和工业生产者购进价格指数

工业生产者出厂价格是工业品第一次出售时的出厂价格。该项调查采用重点调查与典型调查相结合的调查方法。重点调查对象为选中的全年主营业务收入 2000 万元及以上的工业法人样本单位及部分生产特定产品的全年主营业务收入 2000 万元以下的工业法人样本单位。

工业生产者购进价格是工业企业作为中间投入的价格。调查对象从填报工业生产者出厂价格的企业中选择。

选择代表企业的原则：（1）按工业行业选择调查企业，各中类行业原则上都要有调查企业；（2）大型（或占相当大比重）企业应尽量都选作调查企业；（3）选择生产正常、稳定的企业作为调查对象；（4）选择企业时要兼顾不同所有制形式。

选择代表产品的原则：（1）按工业行业选择代表产品；（2）选择对国计民生影响大的产品；（3）选择生产较为稳定的产品；（4）选择有发展前景的产品；（5）选择具有地方特色的产品。

除了以上原则及方法外，工业生产者购进价格调查还要考虑到特殊性，即调查企业要填报其生产中消耗的主要原材料、燃料、动力，不填报消耗较少、在生产投入中比重较小的原材料、燃料、动力。

权数的确定。编制工业生产者出厂价格小类及以上的权数资料来源于工业统计中分行业工业销售产值数据资料；基本分类的权数资料来源于独立的工业企业产品权数调查。购进价格权数资料主要来源于独立的工业企业产品权数调查，中类及以上的权数还要参考分行业的投入产出数据资料和相应行业的出厂权数资料。权数五年更换一次。

（三）固定资产投资价格指数

固定资产投资价格调查采用重点调查与典型调查相结合的方法。固定资产投资价格调查所涉及的价格是构成固定资产投资额实体的实际购进价格（或结算价格）。调查的内容包括构成当年建筑工程实体的钢材、木材、水泥、地方建筑材料、电料、化工材料等主要建筑材料价格，投入的劳动力价格（单位工资）和各种施工机械使用费用；设备工器具购置和其他费用投资价格。

选择建筑安装工程调查点的原则：（1）样本单位应具有一定覆盖面；（2）投资经济活动代表性强；（3）兼顾不同经济类型；（4）选择重点工程；（5）兼顾不同工程类别。

选择其他费用调查点的原则：在选择其他费用调查点时，所遵循的原则与建筑安装工程调查点的原则基本相同，特别是要注意选择那些投资额大的工程。但由于其他费用不易取得，所以在实际操作过程中，应同时在建设单位、施工单位开展重点调查，并辅以典型调查（从有关管理部门取得资料）。

权数的确定。固定资产投资价格指数的计算权数是建筑安装工程、设备工器具购置和其他费用三者前三年投资完成额的平均比重。

（四）住宅销售价格指数是反映住宅销售价格总水平变动趋势和程度的相对数。包括新建住宅销售价格指数和二手住宅销售价格指数。

新建住宅销售价格的调查方法：目前我国住宅销售价格调查在 70 个大中城市开展。新建住宅销售价格、面积、金额等资料直接采用当地房地产管理部门的网签数据。新建住宅的网签数据内容主要包括：住宅在建项目（楼盘）名称、项目地址、幢号、总层数、所在层数、住宅结构、建筑面积、成交总价（合同金额）、签约时间等。

二手住宅销售价格的调查方法：二手住宅销售价格调查为非全面调查，采用重点调查与典型调查相结合的方法，按照房地产经纪机构上报、房地产管理部门提供与调查员实地调查相结合的方式收集基础数据。

（五）农产品生产者价格指数

农产品生产者价格调查采取抽样调查和重点调查相结合的调查方法。抽取 300 个农产品生产和出售的农业生产经营单位及行政村作为调查对象。对一些区域性比较强的农产品采取在主产区主观选样的方法选择农业生产经营单位及行政村作为调查对象。

被调查单位及行政村在辅助调查员的指导下将在报告期出售的农产品的名称、出售数量、价格、金额即时记入农产品生产者价格调查台账，并上报，由市级超级汇总。

由于北京市林业产品（树苗）产值比重较少，不足 1%，根据国家统计局统计制度要求，不需要进行林业产品生产者价格调查。

Brief Introduction

I. Main Content

Price indexes in this chapter reflect the trend and rate of changes in prices of production, circulation, consumption and investment, mainly consisting of consumer price index (CPI), retail price index (RPI), producer price index for farm products, producer price index for industrial products (PPI); purchasing price index for industrial products; price index for investment in fixed assets; and selling price index for residential houses.

II. Source of Statistics

Statistics in this chapter are from NBS Survey Office in Beijing and Beijing Municipal Bureau of Statistics.

III. Survey Methods

1. Consumer Price Index (CPI) and Retail Price Index (RPI)

Data for compilation of the consumer price index and retail price index are collected through a combination of sample surveys and surveys of key units. Different areas are selected across the city as the sample areas and representative commodities with large amount of consumption and price changes are selected as the sample commodities in reasonable layout. Commodity and service items are identified by the central government. Regular surveys are conducted to collect data on their market prices. General indexes are inferred on the basis of the sample data. The process of CPI development is described as the following steps.

The selection of price survey sites: By adopting the principle of reasonable layout, an equidistant sampling is conducted for department stores, agricultural product trade markets and service outlets in different types and in different areas by their sales value, transaction value and operational scale, which will be ranked in a descending order based on the number of survey sites required.

The selection of representative commodities: Representative commodity and service items are determined by the country. Representative commodities are selected by provinces and cities according to relevant principles. Principles for selection: (1) large quantity of consumption; (2) strongly representative trend and extent of price changes, which means the characteristics of price changes of selected commodities shall be highly correlated with price changes of those that are not selected; (3) selected commodities shall be different in their nature and least correlated in the characteristics of price changes between each other; the selected industrial products must be qualified products, with registered trademark, origin, specifications, grade and other marks on the their package.

At present, data are collected over 600 specifications each month under 262 basic headings in 8 categories in the consumer price surveys. In Beijing, due to the development of CPI by income class, representative commodities have increased to 1728 specifications. Retail price index consists of 16 categories, 229 basic headings and 1297 specifications of representative commodities.

Method of data collection: Price data are collected through direct surveys by designated personnel at designated sites on periodic basis.

Source and calculation of the weights: CPI weights are calculated according to survey information on living expenditures of urban residents. RPI weights are calculated according to the total retail sales of commodities.

2. Producer Price Index for Industrial Products (PPI); Purchasing Price Index for Industrial Products

The producer price index for industrial products refers to the producer's price of industrial products when sold for the first time. The survey program is a combination of the key units' survey and typical units' survey methods. Key units refer to industrial enterprises with annual turnover from primary activities at and above RMB 20 million. Typical units refer to the industrial enterprises with annual revenue from the primary activities below RMB 20 million.

Purchasing price for Industrial Products refers to the price of intermediate inputs of industrial enterprise. Enterprises for survey are selected among those that have submitted the ex-factory prices of industrial products.

Principles for selecting the representative enterprises: (1) enterprises to be covered in the survey are selected by industrial sectors. In principle, every branch should have enterprises selected; (2) Large-sized enterprises (or enterprises accounting for large proportion) should be selected; (3) enterprises selected should be those with normal and stable production; (4) enterprises selected should include those with different ownerships.

Principles for selecting representative products: (1) representative products are be selected by industrial sectors; (2) the selected products should have significant impact on the national economy and people's livelihood; (3) the production of the goods selected should be relatively more stable; (4) the prospects of the goods selected should be promising; (5) the products selected shall represent the localities.

In addition to the above-mentioned principles, a special condition shall be taken into account in the survey of producer price index for industrial products. Namely, enterprises under survey shall report main raw materials, fuel and power consumed in production.

Determination of weights: Materials of weights used for compiling producer price index for industrial products (PPI) of small class and above come from data of industrial sales value collected by sectors in industrial statistics. Materials of weights in basic classification come from independent survey on industrial enterprise product weights. Materials of purchase price weights mainly come from independent survey on industrial enterprise product weights. Weights of medium class and above shall also take reference to input and output data collected by sectors and materials of factory weights in relevant sectors. The weights are changed every five years.

3. Price Index for Investment in Fixed Assets

A combined method of key survey and typical survey is used for the collection of data on prices of investment in fixed assets. The prices collected in the surveys of investment in fixed assets are the actual purchasing prices (or settlement prices) of entities of investment in fixed assets. The survey covers the prices of main construction materials that constitute the architectural engineering entities in the year, such as steel, timber, cement, local construction materials, electric parts and chemical materials in construction projects; prices of labor input (wages) and costs of use of construction machines; purchasing price of equipment, tools and devices as well as other expenditures.

Principles for selecting survey sites of construction and installation projects: (1) the sample unit shall have certain coverage; (2) the economic activity of investment should have strong representativeness; (3) different types of registration should be considered; (4) key projects shall be selected; (5) attention should be given to various types of projects.

Principles for selecting survey sites of other expenditures: in the selection of survey sites of other expenditures, the same principles shall be followed as in the selection of survey sites of building and installation projects. Especially projects with larger amount of investment shall be selected. Since it is not easy to obtain data on other expenditures, during the actual data operations, survey on key builders and construction units is to be conducted concurrently with survey on typical units (with information from administration units).

Determination of weights. Weights used for calculating the fixed assets investment price index are determined according to the average proportion of investment amount of construction and installation projects, purchase of equipment, tools and instruments and other expenditures completed in the previous three years.

4. Selling Price Index for Residential Houses is a relative number reflecting the trend and extent of overall level of house selling prices. It includes selling price index for new houses and second-hand houses.

Survey method of new house selling price:

At present, real estate price survey is conducted in 70 medium and large-sized cities across the country. For new houses, selling price, area, amount and other data are taken directly from the online data recorded by local real estate authorities. Online data of new house transaction mainly consist of the name of construction project in process, project location, building number, total number of floors, floor number, house structure, building area, total price of transaction (contractual amount), and date of contract signing, etc.

Survey method of second-hand house selling price: Survey of second-house selling price is incomplete survey conducted with the combined method of key survey and typical survey. Basic data are collected in a combined manner of reporting by real estate broker agencies, providing by real estate authorities and field survey by investigators.

5. Producer Price Index for Farm Products

A combined method of sample survey and key survey was used for the survey of producer prices of farm products. 300 entities and administrative villages producing and selling agricultural products are sampled. For some regional agricultural products, data on farm entities and administrative villages are collected with the method of subjective sampling in main production areas.

Under the instruction of assistant investigators, the surveyed entities and administrative villages will record the name, quantity, price and amount of farm products sold during the reporting period onto the log book and report them for summarization at the municipal level.

As the production of forestry products (saplings) in Beijing is relatively small, taking no more than 1%, so no survey on producer price for forestry products is conducted according to statistical requirements of National Bureau of Statistics.

7-1 各种价格指数(1978-2015年)
PRICE INDEXES (1978-2015)

(上年=100) (preceding year=100)

年份 Year	居民消费价格指数 Consumer Price Index	商品零售价格指数 Retail Price Index	农产品生产者价格指数 Producer Price Index for Farm Products	工业生产者出厂价格指数 Producer Price Index for Industrial Products (PPI)	工业生产者购进价格指数 Purchasing Price Index for Industrial Products	固定资产投资价格指数 Price Index for Investment in Fixed Assets
1978	100.6	100.6				
1979	101.8	101.8	109.5			
1980	106.0	106.7	105.5			
1981	101.3	101.4	109.4			
1982	101.8	102.0	101.9			
1983	100.5	100.6	101.8			
1984	102.2	102.1	102.3			
1985	117.6	118.6	117.6			
1986	106.8	106.7	108.1			
1987	108.6	108.7	116.1			
1988	120.4	121.9	123.2			
1989	117.2	118.5	106.8			
1990	105.4	104.1	101.9	107.9	114.8	
1991	111.9	108.5	101.7	105.8	111.7	107.3
1992	109.9	108.3	102.4	100.9	103.3	112.2
1993	119.0	116.9	107.0	121.8	133.2	126.6
1994	124.9	117.9	133.4	112.9	118.7	116.2
1995	117.3	112.6	130.6	107.3	106.7	113.9
1996	111.6	107.3	101.5	100.7	100.3	108.2
1997	105.3	103.8	92.8	101.1	103.4	102.7
1998	102.4	98.3	93.6	95.1	98.1	100.8
1999	100.6	98.8	97.5	97.7	95.8	99.9
2000	103.5	98.9	95.0	102.5	100.0	101.0
2001	103.1	98.8	102.0	99.4	100.5	100.6
2002	98.2	98.4	92.4	96.6	97.1	100.4
2003	100.2	98.2	102.5	101.5	104.7	102.2
2004	101.0	99.2	106.2	103.0	114.2	104.3
2005	101.5	99.7	102.9	101.3	111.4	100.7
2006	100.9	100.2	99.1	99.1	105.5	100.4
2007	102.4	100.8	114.4	99.7	105.0	102.8
2008	105.1	104.4	112.3	103.3	115.8	107.8
2009	98.5	97.8	98.3	94.4	88.6	97.1
2010	102.4	100.4	106.5	102.2	110.5	102.5
2011	105.6	103.2	110.7	102.3	108.4	105.7
2012	103.3	100.6	104.7	98.4	98.7	101.3
2013	103.3	99.8	104.7	97.4	97.8	99.9
2014	101.6	99.1	99.7	99.1	98.8	100.0
2015	101.8	98.5	99.8	96.9	93.7	97.6

注：1. 从2011年开始"工业品出厂价格指数"更名为工业生产者出厂价格指数，"原材料、燃料、动力购进价格指数"更名为工业生产者购进价格指数"(下同)。

2. 从2013年起，农产品生产价格指数调整为农产品生产者价格指数。

Note: a) From 2011, the "Ex-factory Price Index for Manufactured Products" has been renamed as "Producer Price Index for Industrial Products (PPI), and the "Purchasing Price Index for Raw Materials, Fuels and Power" has been renamed as "Purchasing Price Index for Industrial Products" (the same below).

b) From 2013, the "Producer Price Index For Agricultural Products" has been renamed as "Producer Price Index For Farm Products".

7-2 各种价格定基指数(1978-2015年)
FIXED-BASE PRICE INDEXES (1978-2015)

年 份 Year	居 民 消费价格 指 数 Consumer Price Index (1978=100)	商 品 零售价格 指 数 Retail Price Index (1978=100)	工业生产者 出 厂 价格指数 Producer Price Index for Industrial Products (1990=100)	工业生产者 购 进 价格指数 Purchasing Price Index for Industrial Products (1990=100)	固定资产 投 资 价格指数 Price Index for Investment in Fixed Assets (1990=100)
1978	100.0	100.0			
1979	101.8	101.8			
1980	107.9	108.6			
1981	109.3	110.1			
1982	111.3	112.3			
1983	111.8	113.0			
1984	114.3	115.4			
1985	134.4	136.8			
1986	143.5	145.9			
1987	155.8	158.6			
1988	187.6	193.3			
1989	219.9	229.1			
1990	231.8	238.5	100.0	100.0	100.0
1991	259.4	258.8	105.8	111.7	107.3
1992	285.1	280.3	106.8	115.4	120.4
1993	339.3	327.7	130.0	153.7	152.4
1994	423.8	386.4	146.8	182.4	177.1
1995	497.1	435.1	157.5	194.7	201.7
1996	554.8	466.9	158.6	195.2	218.3
1997	584.2	484.6	160.4	201.9	224.2
1998	598.2	476.4	152.5	198.0	226.0
1999	601.8	470.7	149.0	189.7	225.7
2000	622.9	465.5	152.7	189.7	228.0
2001	642.2	459.9	151.8	190.7	229.4
2002	630.6	452.5	146.6	185.1	230.3
2003	631.9	444.4	148.8	193.8	235.3
2004	638.2	440.8	153.3	221.4	245.5
2005	647.8	439.5	155.3	246.6	247.2
2006	653.6	440.4	153.9	260.2	248.2
2007	669.3	443.9	153.5	273.3	255.1
2008	703.4	463.4	158.6	316.3	275.0
2009	692.8	453.2	149.8	280.3	266.9
2010	709.4	455.0	153.1	309.7	273.6
2011	749.1	469.6	156.6	335.7	289.2
2012	773.8	472.4	154.1	331.3	293.0
2013	799.3	471.5	150.1	324.0	292.7
2014	812.1	467.3	148.7	320.1	292.7
2015	826.7	460.3	144.1	299.9	285.7

7-3 八大类居民消费价格指数(1978-2015年)

(上年=100)

年 份 Year	居民消费价格指数 Consumer Price Index	#服务项目价格指数 Price Index of Services	食品 Food	#粮食 Grain	#油脂 Oil or Fat	#肉禽及其制品 Meat, Poultry and Their Processed Products	#水产品 Aquatic Products
1978	100.6	100.0	101.2	100.0	100.0		100.6
1979	101.8	101.2	102.2	100.0	100.0		107.2
1980	106.0	95.5	108.2	100.0	100.0		131.3
1981	101.3	100.4	102.9	100.0	100.0		100.0
1982	101.8	100.1	104.2	100.0	100.0		100.0
1983	100.5	100.3	101.5	100.0	100.0		100.0
1984	102.2	103.1	102.8	99.3	100.6		106.6
1985	117.6	108.1	126.6	104.6	116.3		235.3
1986	106.8	107.9	109.6	103.6	132.4		129.7
1987	108.6	107.6	111.3	104.6	103.5		116.1
1988	120.4	106.0	123.9	114.4	120.7		144.9
1989	117.2	104.6	112.5	109.5	129.2		114.5
1990	105.4	118.2	103.7	104.5	101.9		101.7
1991	111.9	142.9	111.2	132.2	137.4		102.0
1992	109.9	122.8	111.5	134.3	110.9		101.8
1993	119.0	133.8	120.7	134.6	111.8		109.3
1994	124.9	136.1	126.7	144.0	133.8	138.2	125.6
1995	117.3	128.3	121.1	135.2	109.0	123.2	111.1
1996	111.6	120.0	107.7	112.2	90.8	101.5	104.5
1997	105.3	117.5	102.2	96.8	100.7	107.0	109.7
1998	102.4	121.3	97.1	96.4	103.3	93.2	94.8
1999	100.6	107.9	97.7	97.9	99.4	92.3	95.5
2000	103.5	116.2	97.9	91.4	85.8	98.4	107.3
2001	103.1	115.9	101.5	95.0	87.5	102.6	96.9
2002	98.2	99.4	98.0	98.5	94.7	98.9	95.7
2003	100.2	100.7	103.2	99.1	114.1	100.9	102.5
2004	101.0	101.8	104.8	120.6	117.0	110.1	107.1
2005	101.5	101.3	104.9	104.6	98.0	103.8	104.7
2006	100.9	101.2	102.8	101.6	101.5	99.4	101.9
2007	102.4	101.3	109.2	107.4	117.3	128.7	108.8
2008	105.1	99.9	116.1	108.9	121.3	125.1	120.1
2009	98.5	94.8	102.4	105.6	83.9	95.2	104.5
2010	102.4	103.7	105.5	109.6	100.9	101.2	110.6
2011	105.6	106.4	110.6	110.8	114.2	121.8	109.5
2012	103.3	104.2	106.6	102.6	104.5	106.7	104.8
2013	103.3	105.5	104.7	104.4	99.8	106.7	103.4
2014	101.6	102.5	103.2	102.2	96.9	99.9	106.1
2015	101.8	104.2	101.6	101.5	96.9	102.7	101.9

CONSUMER PRICE INDEX FOR EIGHT CATEGORIES (1978-2015)

(preceding year=100)

#鲜菜 Fresh Vegetables	#鲜果 Fresh Fruits	烟酒及用品 Tobacco, Liquor and Related Articles	衣着 Clothing	家庭设备用品及维修服务 Household Facilities, Articles and Repair Services	医疗保健和个人用品 Healthcare and Personal Articles	交通和通信 Transportation and Communication	娱乐教育文化用品及服务 Recreational, Educational, Cultural Articles and Services	居住 Residence
114.5	101.6		100.0		100.4		100.1	
100.2	99.5		99.3		103.7		104.5	
114.1	106.7		99.5		101.5		100.8	
111.4	100.8		99.4		101.4		100.3	
104.7	94.3		96.7		101.4		100.1	
104.9	119.1		97.0		103.0		98.1	
106.8	112.1		101.2		107.4		100.0	
162.0	148.6		103.0		106.5		101.6	
106.7	121.4		101.3		102.2		100.8	
118.4	124.0		104.0		103.1		103.5	
133.5	124.4		125.1		131.5		114.4	
105.1	112.0		126.2		119.5		133.1	
107.1	98.6		110.3		111.0		93.5	
118.4	111.1		105.7		105.0		94.4	
115.1	104.6		103.3		114.8		92.8	
114.5	109.2		109.2		115.1		99.7	
128.5	114.9		124.7	112.7	113.2	104.9	118.7	124.1
124.3	129.5		117.5	108.3	102.6	100.3	100.8	113.2
113.7	104.6		119.1	104.6	110.1	102.1	110.1	129.2
95.0	94.0		102.9	105.4	105.2	100.3	98.1	121.2
93.9	89.5		105.9	97.5	108.6	99.0	97.8	104.7
106.2	101.4		99.4	96.5	115.8	98.3	98.8	101.0
98.4	88.4		102.6	96.3	113.5	92.3	97.8	117.9
100.2	101.5	101.5	100.4	97.0	98.7	100.8	114.2	104.2
84.7	94.5	100.6	95.9	97.0	100.2	99.5	96.6	101.9
145.4	111.4	100.2	97.1	97.7	100.1	97.8	98.3	101.6
95.0	104.1	101.2	98.9	96.9	99.2	95.7	101.5	101.4
111.9	111.0	100.0	100.1	99.7	98.0	97.5	99.7	105.9
112.8	112.0	99.9	99.7	101.2	101.1	99.3	98.7	101.4
109.9	100.8	101.8	100.0	100.4	100.3	95.7	99.2	103.5
108.1	112.9	106.0	99.1	104.4	102.0	97.6	98.0	103.0
111.9	109.4	102.2	98.4	100.3	99.9	95.9	97.6	89.8
124.0	112.3	101.1	98.4	99.4	101.5	100.8	99.4	105.0
97.3	112.1	102.5	102.7	104.2	103.7	101.5	99.7	108.5
114.5	101.6	102.2	100.9	102.8	101.5	99.1	102.3	103.9
108.7	107.2	100.1	101.5	101.7	100.2	99.0	103.9	105.6
94.4	117.1	99.7	100.4	100.3	99.9	99.2	103.2	101.4
108.8	89.7	102.0	103.6	99.9	100.2	102.8	100.8	102.6

7-4 多基期居民消费价格指数(2015年)
CONSUMER PRICE INDEX WITH MULTIPLE BASE PERIODS (2015)

项目	Item	1978=100	1980=100	1990=100	2000=100	2005=100	2010=100
居民消费价格指数	**Consumer Price Index**	**826.7**	**766.0**	**356.5**	**132.7**	**127.7**	**116.6**
#服务项目价格指数	**Price Index of Services**	**3276.7**	**3268.2**	**1407.0**	**150.5**	**125.8**	**124.9**
食品	**Food**	**1331.8**	**1205.9**	**483.0**	**205.8**	**182.3**	**129.4**
#粮食	Grain	1274.3	1274.3	863.3	198.2	169.4	123.1
油脂	Oil and Fat	755.8	755.8	296.9	148.3	136.8	111.8
肉禽及其制品	Meat, Poultry and Their Processed Products	1604.9	1298.6	557.5	256.6	219.3	142.3
水产品	Aquatic Products	3326.6	2363.0	371.2	210.1	197.6	128.3
菜	Vegetables	3338.3	2953.4	812.5	290.1	228.7	125.2
#鲜菜	Fresh Vegetables	3682.2	3222.8	800.8	303.2	231.2	124.4
干菜及菜制品	Dried Vegetables and Vegetable Products	957.3	922.3	443.5	186.1	198.0	142.6
调味品	Flavoring	1070.9	1102.5	543.1	155.0	147.2	119.0
干鲜瓜果	Dried and Fresh Melons and Fruits	1386.7	1295.9	355.6	219.1	184.8	122.9
烟酒及用品	**Tobacco, Liquor and Related Articles**	**460.5**	**460.5**	**210.2**	**123.1**	**118.8**	**106.7**
衣着	**Clothing**	**367.4**	**375.8**	**224.8**	**96.9**	**104.6**	**109.4**
#服装	Garments	381.7	393.8	231.1	97.2	104.9	108.8
衣着材料	Clothing Materials	317.9	319.1	224.8	121.6	129.6	125.1
鞋袜帽	Footwear, Hosiery and Hats	387.1	392.8	229.5	92.7	102.1	109.8
家庭设备用品及维修服务	**Household Facilities, Articles and Repair Services**	**302.3**	**300.6**	**158.3**	**102.5**	**115.5**	**109.1**
医疗保健和个人用品	**Healthcare and Personal Articles**	**676.8**	**622.1**	**276.0**	**106.6**	**110.6**	**105.6**
交通和通信	**Transportation and Communication**	**107.3**	**107.3**	**90.5**	**83.4**	**91.0**	**101.6**
娱乐教育文化用品及服务	**Recreational, Educational, Cultural Commodities and Services**	**236.6**	**231.0**	**121.9**	**112.6**	**102.4**	**110.3**
居住	**Residence**	**749.2**	**1007.1**	**738.2**	**146.1**	**126.2**	**123.8**
#住房租金	House Rent	2078.6	3286.6	3260.5	166.7	145.8	127.4
水、电、燃料	Water, Electricity, and Fuels	790.1	790.1	651.5	173.3	117.1	110.0

7-5 居民消费价格分类指数(2015年)
CONSUMER PRICE INDEX BY CATEGORY (2015)

项　目	Item	2014 =100
居民消费价格指数	**Consumer Price Index**	**101.8**
#非食品价格指数	Non-food Price Index	**101.9**
#服务项目价格指数	Price Index for Services	**104.2**
#消费品价格指数	Price Index for Consumer Goods	**100.3**
食　品	**Food**	**101.6**
粮　食	Grain	101.5
淀粉及制品	Starches and Their Processed Products	102.4
干豆类及豆制品	Beans and Their Processed Products	103.6
油　脂	Oil and Fat	96.9
肉禽及其制品	Meat, Poultry and Their Processed Products	102.7
蛋	Eggs	93.6
水产品	Aquatic Products	101.9
菜	Vegetables	107.9
调味品	Flavoring	102.8
糖	Sugar	100.6
茶及饮料	Tea and Beverages	102.3
干鲜瓜果	Dried and Fresh Melons and Fruits	92.1
糕点饼干面包	Cake, Biscuits and Bread	102.6
液体乳及乳制品	Liquid Milk and Dairy Products	98.8
在外用膳食品	Foods Eaten Externally	103.9
其他食品	Other Foods	99.7
烟酒及用品	**Tobacco, Liquor and Related Articles**	**102.0**
烟　草	Tobacco	103.9
酒	Liquor	100.1
衣　着	**Clothing**	**103.6**
服　装	Garments	103.2
衣着材料	Clothing Materials	100.4
鞋袜帽	Footwear, Hosiery and Hats	104.7
衣着加工服务费	Clothing Processing Services	102.8
家庭设备用品及维修服务	**Households Facilities, Articles and Repairing Services**	**99.9**
耐用消费品	Durable Consumer Goods	98.6
室内装饰品	Interior Decorations	100.5
床上用品	Bedding	96.9
家庭日用杂品	Daily Groceries for Households	99.9
家庭服务及加工维修服务	Households Services and Maintenance Services	105.7
医疗保健和个人用品	**Healthcare and Personal Articles**	**100.2**
医疗保健	Health Care	101.1
医疗器具及用品	Medical Apparatus and Supplies	100.6
中药材及中成药	Traditional Chinese Medicial Materials and Chinese Patent Drugs	102.0
西　药	Western Medicines	101.3
保健器具及用品	Healthcare Appliances and Articles	101.8
医疗保健服务	Healthcare Services	100.0
个人用品及服务	Personal Articles and Services	98.3
化妆美容用品	Cosmetics	98.1
清洁类化妆品	Cosmetics for Cleaning	100.7
个人饰品	Personal Accessories	92.4
个人服务	Personal Services	104.2
交通和通信	**Transportation and Communication**	**102.8**
交　通	Transportation	104.6
交通工具	Vehicles	97.2
车用燃料及零配件	Fuels and Vehicle Parts	82.3
车辆使用及维修费	Fees for Use and Maintenance of Vehicles	102.5
市区公共交通费	Incity Public Traffic	172.3
城市间交通费	Intercity Traffic	104.3
通　信	Communication	98.4
通信工具	Communication Devices	81.7
通信服务	Communication Services	99.9
娱乐教育文化用品及服务	**Recreational, Educational, Cultural Articles and Related Services**	**100.8**
文娱用耐用消费品及服务	Durable Consumer Goods for Cultural and Recreation Use and Services	95.0
教　育	Education	104.5
文化娱乐类	Culture and Entertainment	101.8
旅　游	Tourism	94.2
居　住	**Residence**	**102.6**
建房及装修材料	Building and Decoration Materials	100.3
住房租金	House Rent	103.8
自有住房	Private Housing	103.1
水、电、燃料	Water, Electricity and Fuels	101.2

7-6 商品零售价格分类指数(2015年) RETAIL PRICE INDEX BY CATEGORY (2015)

项目	Item	2014 =100	项目	Item	2014 =100
商品零售价格指数	**Retail Price Index**	**98.5**	床上用品	Bedding	96.8
食品	**Food**	**101.6**	**家用电器及音像器材**	**Household Appliances, and Audio Equipment**	**96.2**
粮食	Grain	101.5	家庭设备	Household Appliances	95.8
淀粉及制品	Starches and Their Processed Products	102.4	文娱用耐用消费品	Durable Consumer Goods for Cultural and Recreation Use	94.6
干豆类及豆制品	Beans and Their Processed Products	103.6	专业音响器材	Professional Audio Equipment	99.4
油脂	Oil and Fat	96.9	**文化办公用品**	**Cultural and Office Ariticles**	**98.3**
肉禽及其制品	Meat, Poultry and Their Processed Products	102.7	**日用品**	**Domestic Commodities**	**99.1**
食用畜肉及副产品	Meat and Sideline Products	104.5	日用百货	General Merchandise	99.7
禽	Pourtry	99.5	日用杂品	Groceries for Daily Use	97.7
加工肉禽	Processed Meat and Poultry	99.0	洗涤用品	Washing Products	98.8
蛋	Eggs	93.6	其他日用品	Other Domestic Commodities	99.3
水产品	Aquatic Products	101.9	**体育娱乐用品**	**Sports and Entertainment Articles**	**99.8**
鱼	Fish	102.0	体育用品	Sports Articles	99.4
其他水产品	Other Aquatic Products	101.8	娱乐用品	Entertainment Articles	101.8
菜	Vegetables	107.9	**交通、通信用品**	**Transportation and Communication Articles**	**96.1**
调味品	Flavoring	102.8	交通运输机械	Transportation Machinery	97.4
糖	Sugar	100.6	通信器材	Communication Devices	84.5
干鲜瓜果	Dried and Fresh Melons and Fruits	92.1	**家具**	**Furnitures**	**101.7**
糕点饼干面包	Cake, Biscuits and Bread	102.6	**化妆品**	**Cosmetics**	**99.9**
液体乳及乳制品	Liquid Milk and Dairy Products	98.8	**金银珠宝**	**Gold, Silver and Jewelry**	**91.6**
在外用膳食品	Foods Eaten Externally	103.9	**中西药品及医疗保健用品**	**Traditional Chinese and Western Medicines and Healthcare Articles**	**101.6**
其他食品	Other Foods	99.7	医疗器具及用品	Medical Apparatus and Articles	100.6
饮料、烟酒	**Beverages, Tobacco and Liquor**	**102.2**	中药材及中成药	Traditional Chinese Medicial Materials and Chinese Patent Drugs	102.0
茶及饮料	Tea and Beverages	102.3	西药	Western Medicines	101.3
茶叶	Tea	103.9	保健器具及用品	Healthcare Apparatus and Articles	101.8
饮料	Beverages	101.1	**书报杂志及电子出版物**	**Books, Newspapers, Magazines and Electronic Publications**	**102.6**
烟草	Tobacco	103.9	教材及参考书	Teaching Materials and Reference Books	100.5
酒	Liquor	100.1	书报杂志	Books and Magazines	106.2
服装、鞋帽	**Garments, Footwear, and Hats**	**103.6**	电子音像制品	Electronic Publications	99.9
服装	Garments	103.2	**燃料**	**Fuels**	**85.7**
男式服装	Clothing for Men	101.5	煤炭及制品	Coal and Coal Products	91.9
女式服装	Clothing for Women	104.3	石油及制品	Petroleum and Related Products	85.1
儿童服装	Clothing for Children	104.2	**建筑材料及五金电料**	**Building Materials and Hardware**	**99.3**
鞋袜帽	Footwear, Hosiery and Hats	104.7	建筑装璜材料	Building and Decoration Materials	99.2
鞋	Shoes	105.2	五金电料	Hardware	101.0
袜子	Hosiery	98.2			
帽子	Hats	100.7			
其他	Others	97.0			
纺织品	**Textiles**	**97.3**			
衣着材料	Clothing Materials	100.4			

7-7 农产品生产者价格指数
PRODUCER PRICE INDEX FOR FARM PRODUCTS

(上年=100) (preceding year=100)

项　　目	Item	2015	2014
总 指 数	**General Index**	**99.8**	**99.7**
农业产品	Agricultural Products	97.5	100.1
#粮　食	Grain	92.4	102.3
蔬菜及食用菌	Vegetable and Edible Fungus	101.9	97.1
林业产品	Forestry Products		
畜牧业产品	Animal Husbandry Products	101.9	99.5
#肉　牛	Beef Cattle	100.7	104.2
肉　羊	Mutton Sheep	90.4	100.8
奶产品	Milk Products	90.7	110.6
猪	Hogs	111.2	89.9
肉禽(毛重)	Poultry (Gross Weight)	100.4	100.8
禽　蛋	Eggs	99.3	106.6
渔业产品	Fishing	101.0	97.5

7-8 工业生产者出厂价格及购进价格指数(2000-2015年)

(上年=100)

年份 Year	工业生产者出厂价格指数 Producer Price Index for Industrial Products (PPI)	轻工业 Light Industry	重工业 Heavy Industry	生产资料 Means of Production	生活资料 Comsumer Goods	工业生产者购进价格指数 Purchasing Price Index for Industrial Products	燃料、动力类 Fuels and Power
2000	102.5	98.0	104.2	103.4	98.8	100.0	104.3
2001	99.4	99.6	99.4	99.4	99.6	100.5	101.7
2002	96.6	97.6	96.4	96.4	97.9	97.1	102.3
2003	101.5	98.0	104.5	102.2	99.1	104.7	109.6
2004	103.0	100.2	105.3	103.7	100.6	114.2	120.0
2005	101.3	98.7	103.3	101.9	99.1	111.4	117.1
2006	99.1	97.9	99.6	99.0	99.3	105.5	113.1
2007	99.7	100.7	99.2	99.3	101.3	105.0	105.1
2008	103.3	101.8	104.0	103.8	101.3	115.8	132.3
2009	94.4	96.2	93.6	93.3	99.1	88.6	85.1
2010	102.2	98.7	103.8	102.7	100.3	110.5	121.3
2011	102.3	104.6	102.0	102.5	101.6	108.4	117.8
2012	98.4	101.1	98.0	97.8	101.0	98.7	99.0
2013	97.4	100.7	96.9	96.7	100.5	97.8	96.4
2014	99.1	100.8	98.8	98.7	100.9	98.8	99.4
2015	96.9	100.0	96.4	96.1	99.9	93.7	85.6

PRODUCER PRICE INDEX AND PURCHASING PRICE INDEX FOR INDUSTRIAL PRODUCTS (2000-2015)

(preceding year=100)

黑色金属材料类 Ferrous Metal Materials	有色金属材料和电线类 Nonferrous Metal Materials and Electric Wires	化工原料类 Chemical Raw Materials	木材及纸浆类 Timber and Paper Pulp	建筑材料及非金属矿类 Construction Materials and Nonmetal Ores	其他工业原材料及半成品类 Other Industrial Materials and Semi-finished Products	农副产品类 Agricultural Products	纺织原料类 Textile Raw Materials
100.5	106.9	103.4	94.8	101.9	98.4	94.5	91.5
100.3	97.9	97.6	98.3	99.5	98.8	103.5	100.6
96.4	96.1	99.3	102.5	97.6	92.3	93.6	97.8
110.9	101.4	107.3	100.6	99.0	95.2	114.3	98.1
124.5	120.9	111.1	100.7	105.8	103.8	122.3	102.8
108.3	123.3	114.9	103.6	101.8	102.8	96.3	106.2
96.7	138.3	104.1	100.3	99.4	98.0	101.3	100.9
115.6	112.2	106.7	101.7	103.5	95.3	138.6	99.2
128.5	97.9	108.3	108.5	115.2	94.9	132.6	101.5
79.8	81.1	82.3	97.0	99.4	95.3	88.2	97.6
115.4	121.6	111.7	104.2	102.7	99.0	106.6	102.8
112.7	115.2	112.7	105.7	103.0	98.9	128.8	108.2
92.2	96.7	102.5	99.0	93.9	98.8	98.5	100.8
94.6	92.1	98.6	98.4	94.2	98.9	102.2	99.6
95.3	95.3	99.2	99.9	96.8	98.9	97.5	100.7
87.2	93.7	94.1	99.0	95.7	98.4	103.1	99.8

7-9 工业生产者出厂价格指数
PRODUCER PRICE INDEX FOR INDUSTRIAL PRODUCTS

(上年=100) (preceding year=100)

项　　目	Item	2015	2014
总指数	**General Index**	**96.9**	**99.1**
按轻、重工业分	**By Light Industry and Heavy Industry**		
轻工业	Light Industry	100.0	100.8
以农产品为原料	Using Farming Products as Raw Materials	100.3	101.4
以非农产品为原料	Using Non-agricultural Products as Raw Materials	99.6	100.1
重工业	Heavy Industry	96.4	98.8
采　掘	Excavation	88.5	84.3
原　料	Raw Materials	95.8	104.6
加　工	Processing	97.0	97.3
按生产、生活资料分	**By Capital Goods and Living Goods**		
生产资料	Means of Production	96.1	98.7
采　掘	Excavation	88.5	84.3
原　料	Raw Materials	95.8	104.6
加　工	Processing	96.8	97.0
生活资料	Living Goods	99.9	100.9
食　品	Foods	101.8	103.7
衣　着	Clothing	100.1	98.2
一般日用品	Articles for Daily Use	100.0	100.4
耐用消费品	Durable Consumer Goods	97.9	99.3

7-10 工业生产者出厂价格指数(按行业分)
PRODUCER PRICE INDEX FOR INDUSTRIAL PRODUCTS (BY SECTOR)

(上年=100) (preceding year=100)

项　　目	Item	2015	2014
总 指 数	**General Index**	**96.9**	**99.1**
煤炭开采和洗选业	Mining and Washing of Coal	89.7	84.5
黑色金属矿采选业	Mining and Processing of Ferrous Metal Ores	64.8	77.4
非金属矿采选业	Mining and Processing of Nonmetal Ores	114.0	104.4
农副食品加工业	Processing of Food from Agriculture Products	101.5	100.0
食品制造业	Manufacture of Foods	99.0	104.5
酒、饮料和精制茶制造业	Manufacture of Wines, Beverage and Refined Tea	101.7	103.2
烟草制品业	Manufacture of Cigarettes and Tobacco	100.0	109.7
纺织业	Manufacture of Textile	99.4	96.7
纺织服装、服饰业	Manufacture of Textile Wearing Apparel and Ornament	100.4	99.8
皮革、毛皮、羽毛及其制品和制鞋业	Manufacture of Leather, Fur, Feather and Its Products, and Footwear	100.3	100.5
木材加工和木、竹、藤、棕、草制品业	Processing of Timbers, Manufacture of Wood, Bamboo, Rattan, Palm and Straw Products	98.3	99.8
家具制造业	Manufacture of Furniture	99.5	101.1
造纸和纸制品业	Manufacture of Paper and Paper Products	96.8	96.7
印刷和记录媒介复制业	Printing, Reproduction of Recording Media	100.2	99.6
文教、工美、体育和娱乐用品制造业	Manufacture of Articles for Culture, Education, Artwork, Sports and Entertainment Activity	100.1	100.1
石油加工、炼焦和核燃料加工业	Processing of Petroleum, Coking, Processing of Nucleus Fuel	84.8	97.5
化学原料和化学制品制造业	Manufacture of Chemical Raw Material and Chemical Products	91.9	98.6
医药制造业	Manufacture of Medicines	102.0	103.5
化学纤维制造业	Manufacture of Chemical Fibres	99.9	100.1
橡胶和塑料制品业	Manufacture of Rubber and Plastics Products	97.8	99.1
非金属矿物制品业	Manufacture of Non-Metallic Mineral Products	97.8	98.8
黑色金属冶炼和压延加工业	Manufacture and Processing of Ferrous Metals	81.5	94.1
有色金属冶炼和压延加工业	Manufacture and processing of Non-Ferrous Metals	90.8	96.8
金属制品业	Manufacture of Fabricated Metal Products	97.2	96.2
通用设备制造业	Manufacture of General-Purpose Machinery	99.1	99.2
专用设备制造业	Manufacture of Special-Purpose Machinery	99.0	98.9
汽车制造业	Manufacture of Motor Vehicles	98.4	99.8
铁路、船舶、航空航天和其他运输设备制造业	Manufacture of Railway Locomotives, Building of Ships and Boats, Manufacture of Air and Spacecrafts and Other Transportation Equipments	99.6	97.7
电气机械和器材制造业	Manufacture of Electrical Machinery and Equipment	99.5	99.6
计算机、通信和其他电子设备制造业	Manufacture of Computer, Communication Equipment and Other Electronic Equipment	95.5	93.8
仪器仪表制造业	Manufacture of Measuring Instrument and Meter	100.3	99.8
其他制造业	Other Manufacturing	99.9	100.3
废弃资源综合利用业	Waste Recycling and Recovery	97.4	86.8
金属制品、机械和设备修理业	Repair of Fabricated Metal Products, Machinery and Equipment	100.9	101.5
电力、热力生产和供应业	Production and Supply of Electricity and Heating Power	101.1	108.9
燃气生产和供应业	Production and Distribution of Gas	106.3	108.8
水的生产和供应业	Production and Distribution of Water	105.1	109.8

注：根据国家统计局规定，2012年起执行2011年国民经济行业分类标准(GB/T 4754-2011)。

Note: According to provisions of the National Bureau of Statistics, since 2012, sectors have been classified in accordance with the Standard for Classification of National Economic Sectors 2011(GB/T 4754-2011).

7-11 工业生产者购进价格指数
PURCHASING PRICE INDEX FOR INDUSTRIAL PRODUCTS

(上年=100) (preceding year=100)

项目	Item	2015	2014
总指数	**General Index**	**93.7**	**98.8**
燃料、动力类	Fuels and Power	85.6	99.4
黑色金属材料类	Ferrous Metal Materials	87.2	95.3
#钢材	Steel Products	85.4	94.7
其他	Others	94.2	97.6
有色金属材料和电线类	Nonferrous Metal Materials and Electric Wires	93.7	95.3
化工原料类	Chemical Raw Materials	94.1	99.2
木材及纸浆类	Timber and Paper Pulp	99.0	99.9
建筑材料及非金属矿类	Construction Materials and Nonmetal Ores	95.7	96.8
其他工业原材料及半成品类	Other Industrial Materials and Semi-finished Products	98.4	98.9
农副产品类	Agricultural Products	103.1	97.5
纺织原料类	Textile Raw Materials	99.8	100.7

7-12 固定资产投资价格指数(2015年)
PRICE INDEX FOR INVESTMENT IN FIXED ASSETS (2015)

项目	Item	1992 =100	1993 =100	1994 =100	2000 =100	2004 =100	2005 =100	2006 =100	2007 =100	2008 =100	2009 =100	2010 =100	2011 =100	2012 =100	2013 =100	2014 =100
总指数	**General Index**	**237.3**	**187.6**	**161.3**	**125.2**	**116.4**	**115.6**	**115.2**	**112.0**	**103.9**	**107.0**	**104.4**	**98.8**	**97.5**	**97.6**	**97.6**
建筑安装、装饰工程	Construction, Installation and Decoration Projects	278.1	212.0	176.9	129.6	112.4	111.8	112.2	107.7	96.4	102.2	98.3	89.6	90.5	93.0	94.4
人工费	Labor Cost	1074.9	760.0	525.3	230.6	198.4	190.8	183.3	172.7	158.3	151.9	142.8	127.9	116.6	109.6	104.1
材料费	Cost of Materials	213.2	158.1	134.4	115.7	99.1	99.3	100.7	96.9	85.7	93.4	90.0	81.8	84.8	89.1	91.9
机械使用费	Cost of Machinery Use				125.1	121.6	121.6	120.0	118.1	112.3	111.4	109.6	106.0	102.8	101.5	100.6
设备、工器具购置	Purchase of Equipment, Tools and Instruments	103.0	89.6	87.8	70.3	84.9	86.2	86.6	87.5	89.2	92.2	93.1	94.1	96.6	98.9	99.5
其他费用	Others	212.9	174.4	141.2	133.6	129.8	127.4	125.2	122.5	116.9	115.9	113.8	109.4	105.2	102.2	100.5

7-13 住宅销售价格指数(2015年各月)
SELLING PRICE INDEX OF RESIDENTIAL HOUSES (EACH MONTH OF 2015)

(上年同月=100) (same month of previous year=100)

项目	Item	1月 Jan.	2月 Feb.	3月 Mar.	4月 Apr.	5月 May	6月 Jun.
新建住宅	**New Residential Houses**	**96.8**	**96.4**	**96.3**	**96.8**	**97.7**	**98.9**
#新建商品住宅	New Commercial Residential Houses	96.0	95.5	95.3	96.0	97.1	98.6
90平方米及以下	90sq.m and below	93.0	91.9	91.6	91.2	91.9	92.5
90-144平方米	90-144sq.m	94.4	94.0	93.8	94.7	95.9	97.7
144平方米以上	Above 144sq.m	99.7	99.5	99.5	100.8	102.2	104.0
二手住宅	**Second-hand Residential Houses**	**96.0**	**95.9**	**96.2**	**98.4**	**103.5**	**107.2**
90平方米及以下	90sq.m and below	96.0	96.0	96.3	98.4	103.5	107.3
90-144平方米	90-144sq.m	95.7	95.8	96.2	98.3	103.3	107.1
144平方米以上	Above 144sq.m	96.3	95.9	96.1	98.3	103.8	107.3

7-13 续表 Continued

(上年同月=100) (same month of previous year=100)

项目	Item	7月 Jul.	8月 Aug.	9月 Sep.	10月 Oct.	11月 Nov.	12月 Dec.
新建住宅	**New Residential Houses**	**101.0**	**103.0**	**104.7**	**106.5**	**107.7**	**108.3**
#新建商品住宅	New Commercial Residential Houses	101.2	103.7	105.9	108.1	109.6	110.4
90平方米及以下	90sq.m and below	94.8	96.4	98.6	99.6	99.4	97.9
90-144平方米	90-144sq.m	100.9	103.6	105.9	109.0	110.4	113.2
144平方米以上	Above 144sq.m	106.4	109.3	111.3	113.7	116.5	117.0
二手住宅	**Second-hand Residential Houses**	**110.9**	**114.1**	**117.3**	**118.4**	**119.1**	**120.8**
90平方米及以下	90sq.m and below	110.8	114.2	117.4	118.5	119.1	120.8
90-144平方米	90-144sq.m	110.9	113.9	117.3	118.2	119.0	120.7
144平方米以上	Above 144sq.m	111.2	113.9	117.4	118.3	119.1	121.0

主要统计指标解释

居民消费价格指数 是度量消费商品及服务项目价格水平随着时间而变动的相对数，反映居民家庭购买的消费品及服务价格水平的变动情况。居民消费价格指数变动率通常被用来作为反映通货膨胀（或紧缩）程度的指标。

商品零售价格指数 是度量工业、商业、餐饮业和其他零售企业向城乡居民、机关团体出售生活消费品和办公用品价格水平随着时间而变动的相对数，反映市场商品零售价格的变动程度。

工业生产者出厂价格指数 是反映全部工业产品出厂价格总水平变动程度的相对数。其中包括工业企业售给商业、外贸、物资部门的产品，还包括售给工业和其他部门的生产资料以及直接售给居民的生活消费品。通过工业生产者价格指数能观察工业产品出厂价格变动对工业总产值的影响。

工业生产者购进价格指数 是反映全部工业原材料、燃料、动力购进价格总水平变动程度的相对数。用其可以观察和研究工业企业原材料价格变动对生产的影响，以及企业对原材料涨价的消化能力和承受能力，为制定价格政策提供依据。

固定资产投资价格指数 是反映固定资产投资额价格变动程度的相对数。固定资产投资额由建筑安装装饰工程投资完成额，设备、工器具购置投资完成额和其他费用投资完成额三部分组成。编制固定资产投资价格指数可以准确地反映固定资产投资中涉及的各类商品和取费项目价格变动幅度，消除按现价计算的固定资产投资指标中的价格变动因素，真实地反映固定资产投资的规模、速度、结构和效益，为国家科学地制定、检查固定资产投资计划，提高宏观调控水平，为完善国民经济核算体系提供科学、可靠的依据。

住宅销售价格指数 是反映住宅销售价格总水平变动趋势和程度的相对数。包括新建住宅销售价格指数和二手住宅销售价格指数。

农产品生产者价格指数 是指农产品生产者价格总水平变动程度的相对数。农产品生产者价格是指农产品生产者第一次出售其产品时的单位产品价格。

Explanatory Notes on Main Statistical Indicators

Consumer Price Index (CPI) is a relative number measuring the changes in prices of consumer goods and service purchased by consumers over time. CPI is usually used for reflecting the level of inflation (or deflation).

Retail Price Index is a relative number measuring the changes in prices of consumer goods and office supplies provided by industrial, commercial, restaurants and other retail businesses over time. It reflects the extent of changes in retail prices of commodities in the market.

Producer Price Index for Industrial Products (PPI) is a relative number reflecting the degree of changes in general producer prices of all industrial products, including products sold by industrial enterprises to commercial, foreign trade and materials companies, as well as production materials sold to industrial and other enterprises, and consumer goods directly sold to consumers. It can be used to analyze the impact of producer prices of industrial products on gross industrial output value.

Purchasing Price Index for Industrial Products is a relative number reflecting the degree of changes in the overall level of prices of all industrial materials, fuels and power. It can be used to observe and analyze the effect of changes in prices of raw materials in industrial enterprises on their production, as well as the enterprises' capacity of digesting and bearing the rising prices of raw materials, thus providing basis for formulating price policies.

Price Index for Investment in Fixed Assets is a relative number reflecting the degree of changes in prices of investment in fixed assets. The investment in fixed assets consists of three components, i.e. the investment in construction and installation, the investment in purchasing equipment and instrument, and the investment in other items. Removing the factor of price change in the aggregates of investment at current prices, this indicator shows the changes in the prices of commodities and fees involved in the investment of fixed assets, and can be used to observe the actual size, growth, structure, and efficiency of investment in fixed assets and provides reliable and scientific basis for government planning on and examination of fixed assets investment, thus to improve overall adjustment and controlling skill, and further improve the national accounting system.

Selling Price Index of Residential Houses is a relative number reflecting the trend and degree of changes in the overall level of house selling prices, including newly built residential house selling price index and second-hand house selling price index.

Producer Price Index for Farm **Products** is a relative number reflecting the degree of changes in the overall production prices of farm products. Producer price of farm products refers to the price of unit product at which the producers of farm products sell their products for the first time.

北京统计年鉴2016　BEIJING STATISTICAL YEARBOOK

人民生活
PEOPLE'S LIFE

简要说明

一、本章资料的主要内容

本章资料反映北京市居民生活现状及变化情况，分为全市居民生活、城镇居民生活和农村居民生活三部分。调查内容主要包括家庭基本情况、家庭收入和消费支出情况、主要商品购买数量及支出金额、居住状况和耐用消费品拥有量等。

二、本章资料的数据来源

城乡居民生活状况的数据来源于国家统计局北京调查总队、北京市统计局。

三、本章资料的调查方法

城乡居民生活状况调查方法和方案由国家统计局统一制定，采用抽样调查的方法，按对全市及分区居民主要收支指标有代表性的原则在全市城乡住户中抽取样本，并按一定的周期对样本进行轮换以保证其代表性。对抽中的住户采用日记账和问卷相结合的方式采集数据。

四、本章资料的调查范围

城镇住户调查的口径范围：2000-2003 年为 1000 户城市居民，覆盖城八区；2004-2006 年为 2000 户城市居民，覆盖城八区；2007 年为 3000 户城镇居民，覆盖所有区县；2008-2012 年为 5000 户城镇居民，覆盖所有区县。

农村住户调查的口径范围：2000-2002 年为 2710 户，覆盖 14 个郊区县；2003 年为 2670 户（石景山区全部农民转居民，40 个样本取消），覆盖 13 个郊区县；2004-2012 年为 3000 户，覆盖 13 个郊区县。

城乡住户调查一体化：2013 年，根据国家统计局实施城乡住户调查一体化改革的要求和《住户收支与生活状况调查方案》的有关规定，国家统计局北京调查总队、北京市统计局对全市城乡住户进行了统一的样本抽取，城乡住户调查样本量共计 10000 户。

按照国家统计局要求，自 2015 年起，我市按照改革后的新口径发布全市和分城乡的居民收支数据。与老口径相比，新口径的差异主要体现在三个方面：一是对居民收支指标口径进行了调整，将反映居民收入的核心指标由原来的城镇居民“人均可支配收入”和农村居民“人均纯收入”统一为“人均可支配收入”；二是按照国家城乡划分标准，将城镇地区的村委会由原来的农村划入城镇进行统计；三是在分城乡的居民收支数据基础上，增加了全体居民的人均可支配收入、人均消费支出数据。

五、五等分组的含义

要客观的反映不同收入层次家庭的收支及生活状况，必须按不同收入水平进行分组来观察和分析。“五等分组”即住户按人均可支配收入从低到高排队分别分成五等份，即低收入组、中低收入组、中等收入组、中高收入组和高收入组五部分，各组的户数均占总户数的 20%。通过对调查户的分组，分别加权后计算各组人均可支配收入、消费支出的情况，以观察不同收入组之间的差距和存在的问题。

Brief Introduction

I. Main Content

Statistics in this chapter reflect the living conditions of residents in Beijing and their changes, consisting of three parts, including the living conditions of the residents of the whole city, urban residents and rural residents. Figures include the basic family situation, household income and expenditures in cash, purchase quantity and expenditures of main commodities, housing conditions and number of durable consumer goods in possession.

II. Source of Statistics

Statistics on the living conditions of urban and rural residents are from NBS Survey Office in Beijing, and Beijing Municipal Bureau of Statistics.

III. Method of Survey

Methods and plans of survey for living conditions of urban and rural residents are designated by National Bureau of Statistics. The method of sampling survey is adopted to take samples across Beijing Municipality following the principle of selecting representative residents in terms of major income and expenditure indicators. Samples are changed in certain periods to ensure their representativeness. For selected residents, statistics are gathered through journals and questionnaires.

IV. Scope of Survey

Scope of survey for urban residents: In 2000-2003, the survey covered 1,000 urban households in 8 urban districts; in 2004-2006, covered 2,000 urban households in 8 urban districts; in 2007 covered 3,000 urban households in all districts and counties; in 2008-2012, covered 5,000 households in all districts and counties.

Scope of survey for rural residents: In 2000-2002, the survey covered 2,710 households in 14 suburban districts and counties; in 2003, covered 2,670 households (All rural residents became urban residents in Shijingshan District, so 40 samples were cancelled.) in 13 suburban districts and counties; in 2004-2012 covered 3,000 households in 13 suburban districts and counties.

Integration of survey on urban and rural residents: in 2013, according to the requirements of the National Bureau of Statistics on carrying out integrated reforms of urban and rural resident survey, and *Survey Plan on Income and Expenditure, and Living Conditions of Households*, the NBS Survey Office in Beijing and Beijing Municipal Bureau of Statistics took a total of 10,000 samples of urban and rural residents in an integrated way.

According to requirements of National Bureau of Statistics, since 2015, Beijing has started to issue data on income and expense of residents in the city and residents in urban and rural areas according to new standards after the reform. As compared with former standards, the new standards mainly show differences in the following 3 aspects: first, according to national standards on division of urban and rural areas, village committees in urban areas that were classified into rural areas are now classified into urban areas; second, standards on resident income and expense indicators are adjusted. Core indicators reflecting resident income are unified from original "per capita disposable income" of urban residents and "per capita net income" of rural residents to "per capita disposable income"; third, based on data on resident income and expense in urban and rural areas, data on per capita disposable income and per capita consumption expense of residents in Beijing are added.

V. Meaning of Five-level Grouping

It is necessary to have groups at different income levels for observation and analysis to objectively reflect the income and expenditure and living conditions of households at different income levels. "Five-level grouping" means that households are divided into five groups in a low-to-high order regarding the per capita disposable income. These five groups are the low-income, middle-low-income, middle-income, middle-high-income and high-income groups. The number of households in each group accounts for 20% of the total. Through grouping of the households under survey, we can calculate the per capita income and consumption expenditures of each group respectively so as to observe the differences between different income groups and existing problems.

8-1 全市居民家庭生活基本情况(2015年)
BASIC LIVING CONDITIONS OF THE WHOLE HOUSEHOLDS (2015)

单位：元 (yuan)

项　目	Item	2015	2015年为2014年% 2015 as % of 2014
全市居民家庭生活基本情况	**Basic Living Conditions of Residents**		
人均可支配收入	Per capita disposable income	48458	108.9
人均消费支出	Per capita consumption expenditure	33803	108.7
居民家庭恩格尔系数(%)	Engel's coefficient of households (%)	22.4	
人均住房建筑面积(平方米)	Per capita floor space of houses (sq.m)	33.23	101.0
城镇居民家庭生活基本情况	**Basic Living Conditions of Urban Households**		
人均可支配收入	Per capita disposable income	52859	108.9
人均消费支出	Per capita consumption expenditure	36642	108.7
居民家庭恩格尔系数(%)	Engel's coefficient of households (%)	22.1	
人均住房建筑面积(平方米)	Per capita floor space of houses (sq.m)	31.69	100.3
农村居民家庭生活基本情况	**Basic Living Conditions of Rural Households**		
人均可支配收入	Per capita disposable income	20569	109.0
人均消费支出	Per capita consumption expenditure	15811	108.8
居民家庭恩格尔系数(%)	Engel's coefficient of households (%)	27.7	
人均住房建筑面积(平方米)	Per capita floor space of houses (sq.m)	43.03	104.7

注：按照国家统计局要求，自2015年起北京按照改革后新口径发布全市和分城乡的居民收支数据，增长速度为同口径增速(下表同)。
Note: According to the requirements of National Bureau of Statistics, Beijing released data on income and expenses of urban and rural residents based on the reformed standard since 2015 and the growth rate was calculated under the same standard (the same to the follows).

8-2 全市居民家庭基本情况(按收入水平分)(2015年)
BASIC DATA ON URBAN HOUSEHOLDS(BY INCOME LEVEL) (2015)

项　目	Item	全市平均 Average	低收入户20% Low Income 20%	中低收入户20% Medium-Low Income 20%	中等收入户20% Medium Income 20%	中高收入户20% Medium-High Income 20%	高收入户20% High Income 20%
平均每户常住人口 (人)	Permanent Population Per Household (person)	2.8	3.1	3.0	2.7	2.6	2.4
平均每户就业人口数 (人)	Average Employee Per Household (person)	1.4	1.6	1.7	1.4	1.2	1.3
平均每一就业者负担人数 (人)	Dependents Per Employee (person)	1.6	1.9	1.6	1.5	1.4	1.2
平均每人年可支配收入 (元)	Per Capita Annual Disposable Income (yuan)	48458	18343	32968	45239	60627	99621
平均每人年消费支出 (元)	Per Capita Annual Consumption Expend (yuan)	33803	16549	23309	30554	42533	64857

8-3 全市居民家庭人均可支配收入(2015年)

单位：元

项目	Item	全市平均 Average
可支配收入	**Disposable Income**	**48458**
工资性收入	**Wage Income**	**30241**
工 资	Wage	27711
实物福利	Benefit in Kind	144
其 他	Other Income from Work	2386
经营净收入	**Net Income from Operations**	**1421**
第一产业经营净收入	Net Income from Operations in the Primary Industry	80
第二产业经营净收入	Net Income from Operations in the Secondary Industry	100
第三产业经营净收入	Net Income from Operations in the Tertiary Industry	1241
财产净收入	**Net Property Income**	**7499**
利息净收入	Net Interest Income	59
红利收入	Dividend Income	208
集体分配的红利	Dividend Distributed by the Collective	172
其他红利收入	Other Dividend Income	36
储蓄性保险净收益	Net Income from Saving Insurance	8
转让承包土地经营权租金净收入	Net Rent from Transfer of Contracted Land Management Right	39
出租房屋净收入	Net Income from House Rent	1031
出租机械专利版权等资产的收入	Income from Lease of Assets such as Mechanical Patent Copyright	2
其他财产净收入	Other Net Property Income	-1
自有住房折算净租金	Converted Net Rent from Owner-Occupied Housing	6153
转移净收入	**Net Transfer Income**	**9297**
转移性收入	Transfer Income	12623
养老金或离退休金	Pensions or Retirement Payments	11816
社会救济和补助	Social Relief and Subsidies	40
政策性生活补贴	Policy-type Living Allowances	63
报销医疗费	Reimbursement of Medical Fees	456
家庭外出从业人员寄回带回收入	Income from Family Members Going out for a Job	22
赡养收入	Alimony Income	89
其他经常转移收入	Other Current Transfer Income	109
从政府和组织得到的实物产品和服务折价	Converted Income from Physical Products and Services Obtained from the Government and Organizations	17
现金政策性惠农补贴	Subsidies Benefiting Peasants under Cash Policy	11
转移性支出	Transfer Expenditures	3326

注：全市居民人均可支配收入实际增长7.0%。
Note: Real growth rate of the per capita annual disposable income is 7.0%.

PER DISPOSABLE INCOME OF THE WHOLE HOUSEHOLDS (2015)

(yuan)

低收入户 20% Low Income 20%	中低收入户 20% Medium-Low Income 20%	中等收入户 20% Medium Income 20%	中高收入户 20% Medium-High Income 20%	高收入户 20% High Income 20%	2015年为2014年% 2015 as % of 2014
18343	**32968**	**45239**	**60627**	**99621**	**108.9**
13000	**21158**	**26538**	**32681**	**67106**	**109.7**
12342	19877	24445	29495	60640	109.8
57	161	115	74	354	125.2
601	1120	1978	3112	6112	108.1
1220	**1217**	**1013**	**1281**	**2600**	**97.9**
188	121	53			101.3
120	130	11	1	252	80.0
912	966	949	1280	2348	99.4
2069	**4770**	**7217**	**10417**	**15473**	**107.1**
7	5	-9	-18	367	95.2
283	212	182	165	180	100.0
282	196	176	137	26	120.3
1	16	6	28	154	55.4
3		11	20	6	88.9
79	64	14	16	9	102.6
475	1195	1559	919	1089	131.8
5	4				18.2
20	3	-1	-11	-28	8.3
1197	3287	5461	9326	13850	104.2
2054	**5823**	**10471**	**16248**	**14442**	**109.6**
3477	7892	13102	19985	22340	113.8
2739	7175	12513	19215	21021	112.9
85	83	10	2	1	102.6
117	73	36	26	52	190.9
135	269	358	585	1104	142.5
38	30	13	25		244.4
147	71	53	84	81	91.8
142	169	103	39	73	113.5
38	13	15	9	7	54.8
36	9	1		1	220.0
1423	2069	2631	3737	7898	127.2

8-4 全市居民家庭人均总支出(2015年)

单位：元

项 目	Item	全市平均 Average
家庭总支出	**Total Expenditures of Households**	**44497**
消费支出	**Consumption Expenditures**	**33803**
生产经营费用支出	**Expenditures of Production and Operating Costs**	**423**
第一产业经营费用支出	Operating Cost Expenditures in the Primary Industry	103
第二产业经营费用支出	Operating Cost Expenditures in the Secondary Industry	51
第三产业经营费用支出	Operating Cost Expenditures in the Tertiary Industry	269
财产性支出	**Property Expenditures**	**123**
转移性支出	**Transfer Expenditures**	**3326**
个人所得税	Individual Income Tax	555
社会保障支出	Social Security Expenditures	2387
个人缴纳的养老保险	Pensions Paid by Individual	1790
个人缴纳的医疗保险	Medical Funds Paid by Individual	544
个人缴纳的失业保险	Unemployment Funds Paid by Individual	48
其他社会保障支出	Other Social Security Expenditures	5
外来从业人员寄给家人的支出	Expenditures of Outside Employees for Their Family	69
赡养支出	Alimony Expenditures	258
其他转移性支出	Other Transfer Expenditures	57
部分商业保险支出	**Partially Commercial Insurance Expenditures**	**191**
意外伤害保险	Accident Insurance	22
商业医疗保险(含大病保险)	Commercial Medical Insurance (including Critical Illness Insurance)	95
其他非储蓄性商业保险	Other Non-saving Commercial Insurance	5
其他储蓄性商业保险	Other Saving Commercial Insurance	69
购置资产及非经常性转移支出	**Expenditures of Acquisition Assets and Non-recurrent Transfer**	**4679**
购置资产支出	Acquisition Asset Expenditures	3430
#建造住房支出	Expenditures of Building Houses	129
购买住房支出	Expenditures of Purchasing Houses	3076
非经常性转移支出	Non-recurrent Transfer Expenditures	1249
#一次性馈赠支出	Disposable Donation Expenditures	523
借贷性支出	**Credit Expenditures**	**1952**
#存入储蓄款	Saving Deposits	1191
归还借款	Repayment of Loans	67
购买有价证券	Purchase of Securities	67
归还住房贷款	Repayment of Housing Loan	510
归还汽车贷款	Repayment of Automobile Loans	32

PER CAPITA ANNUAL EXPENDITURES OF URBAN HOUSEHOLDS (2015)

(yuan)

低收入户 20% Low Income 20%	中低收入户 20% Medium-Low Income 20%	中等收入户 20% Medium Income 20%	中高收入户 20% Medium-High Income 20%	高收入户 20% High Income 20%	2015年为2014年% 2015 as % of 2014
22237	**29099**	**37583**	**51504**	**94938**	**115.6**
16549	**23309**	**30554**	**42533**	**64857**	**108.7**
1332	**255**	**199**	**60**	**62**	**70.1**
362	78	13	…	…	52.0
215	7	…	1		65.4
755	170	186	59	62	82.3
33	**64**	**73**	**151**	**349**	**183.6**
1423	**2070**	**2630**	**3737**	**7897**	**127.2**
13	71	198	588	2298	138.4
1056	1704	2142	2790	4917	127.9
742	1223	1599	2113	3812	130.0
293	439	491	617	1002	123.1
19	35	44	57	99	123.1
2	7	8	3	4	62.5
83	164	45	25	9	81.2
252	95	170	261	576	131.0
19	36	75	73	97	89.1
96	**135**	**156**	**194**	**431**	**164.7**
11	11	18	19	57	169.2
66	90	69	87	182	215.9
3	2	6	3	15	31.3
16	32	63	85	177	156.8
1977	**2367**	**2585**	**2894**	**15819**	**260.5**
964	1192	1339	1557	14247	638.7
434	102	2	5	37	94.2
256	1061	1317	1225	13682	852.1
1013	1175	1246	1337	1572	99.2
272	421	557	633	832	120.8
827	**899**	**1386**	**1935**	**5523**	**88.9**
533	662	784	1057	3400	63.4
33	33	10	83	205	139.6
97	19	23	52	156	257.6
86	150	511	567	1487	245.2
1	8	22	30	119	640.0

8-5 全市居民家庭人均消费支出(2015年)
PER CAPITA CONSUMPTION EXPENDITURES OF THE WHOLE HOUSEHOLDS (2015)

单位：元 (yuan)

项目	Item	全市平均 Average	低收入户20% Low Income 20%	中低收入户20% Medium-Low Income 20%	中等收入户20% Medium Income 20%	中高收入户20% Medium-High Income 20%	高收入户20% High Income 20%	2015年为2014年% 2015 as % of 2014
人均消费支出	**Per Capita Consumption Expenditures**	**33803**	**16549**	**23309**	**30554**	**42533**	**64857**	**108.7**
食品烟酒支出	Expenditures of Foods, Tobacco and Liquor	7584	4669	6331	7835	8815	11498	101.6
衣着支出	Clothing Expenditures	2426	1130	1703	2292	3021	4612	102.8
居住支出	Housing Expenditures	10350	4559	6424	8720	13750	21398	109.0
生活用品及服务支出	Expenditures of Living Articles and Services	2098	996	1403	1901	2545	4227	102.8
交通和通信支出	Expenditures of Transportation and Communication	4490	2061	3148	3621	5901	8973	125.5
教育、文化和娱乐支出	Educational, Cultural and Recreational Expenditures	3635	1623	2268	3231	4559	7571	111.2
医疗保健支出	Healthcare Expenditures	2229	1249	1517	2084	2716	4101	116.5
其他用品及服务支出	Expenditures of Other Goods and Services	991	262	515	870	1226	2477	101.6

注：全市居民人均消费支出实际增长6.8%。
Note: Real growth rate of the per capita consumption expenditures of the whole residents is 6.8%.

8-6 全市居民家庭人均消费支出构成(2015年)
COMPOSITION OF PER CAPITA CONSUMPTION EXPENDITURES OF THE WHOLE HOUSEHOLDS (2015)

单位：% (%)

项目	Item	全市平均 Average	低收入户20% Low Income 20%	中低收入户20% Medium-Low Income 20%	中等收入户20% Medium Income 20%	中高收入户20% Medium-High Income 20%	高收入户20% High Income 20%
人均消费支出	**Per Capita Consumption Expenditures**	**100.0**	**100.0**	**100.0**	**100.0**	**100.0**	**100.0**
食品烟酒支出(恩格尔系数)	Expenditures of Foods, Tobacco and Liquor (Engel Coefficient)	22.4	28.2	27.2	25.6	20.7	17.7
衣着支出	Clothing Expenditures	7.2	6.8	7.3	7.5	7.1	7.1
居住支出	Housing Expenditures	30.6	27.6	27.6	28.5	32.3	33.0
生活用品及服务支出	Expenditures of Living Articles and Services	6.2	6.0	6.0	6.2	6.0	6.5
交通和通信支出	Expenditures of Transportation and Communication	13.3	12.5	13.5	11.9	13.9	13.9
教育、文化和娱乐支出	Educational, Cultural and Recreational Expenditures	10.8	9.8	9.7	10.6	10.7	11.7
医疗保健支出	Healthcare Expenditures	6.6	7.5	6.5	6.8	6.4	6.3
其他用品及服务支出	Expenditures of Other Goods and Services	2.9	1.6	2.2	2.9	2.9	3.8

8-7 全市居民家庭人均食品烟酒支出(2015年) PER CAPITA EXPENDITURES ON FOODS, TOBACCO AND LIQUOR OF THE WHOLE HOUSEHOLDS (2015)

单位：元 (yuan)

项目	Item	全市平均 Average	低收入户20% Low Income 20%	中低收入户20% Medium-Low Income 20%	中等收入户20% Medium Income 20%	中高收入户20% Medium-High Income 20%	高收入户20% High Income 20%
食品烟酒支出	**Expenditures of Foods, Tobacco and Liquor**	**7584**	**4669**	**6331**	**7835**	**8815**	**11498**
食品	Foods	4644	3189	4088	4957	5365	6166
谷物	Grain	578	485	532	579	527	821
薯类	Potatoes	55	42	54	60	66	57
豆类	Beans	57	46	53	60	67	68
食用油	Edible Oil	233	169	204	248	274	294
蔬菜和食用菌	Vegetables and Edible Mushrooms	544	400	497	577	636	656
肉类	Meat	920	682	866	1010	1055	1057
禽类	Poultry	147	103	137	164	163	182
水产品	Aquatic Products	318	155	245	352	414	484
蛋类	Eggs	152	116	138	157	172	189
奶类	Milk	388	240	319	424	472	543
干鲜瓜果类	Nuts, Fresh Melons and Fruits	746	449	611	803	913	1070
糖果糕点类	Sweets and Cakes	253	129	205	264	315	399
其他食品	Other Foods	253	173	227	259	291	346
烟酒	Tobacco and Liquor	647	512	600	650	694	839
烟草	Tobacco	363	317	339	360	377	448
酒类	Liquor	284	195	261	290	317	391
饮料	Beverages	367	198	311	390	445	554
饮食服务	Catering Services	1926	770	1332	1838	2311	3939

8-8 全市居民家庭人均衣着、居住支出(2015年)

PER CAPITA ANNUAL EXPENDIATURES ON CLOTHING AND HOUSING OF URBAN HOUSEHOLDS (2015)

单位：元 (yuan)

项 目	Item	全市平均 Average	低收入户20% Low Income 20%	中低收入户20% Medium-Low Income 20%	中等收入户20% Medium Income 20%	中高收入户20% Medium-High Income 20%	高收入户20% High Income 20%
衣着支出	**Clothing Expenditures**	**2426**	**1130**	**1703**	**2292**	**3021**	**4612**
衣 类	Clothes	1760	772	1221	1644	2207	3432
服 装	Garments	1652	724	1146	1535	2070	3229
服装材料	Clothing Materials	10	5	8	11	12	15
其他衣类及配件	Other Clothes and Accessories	92	42	63	91	117	176
衣着加工服务费	Service Fees for Clothing Processing	6	1	4	7	8	12
鞋 类	Footwear	666	358	482	648	814	1180
居住支出	**Housing Expenditures**	**10350**	**4559**	**6424**	**8720**	**13750**	**21398**
租赁房房租	House Rent	465	263	466	374	493	819
住房维修及管理	Housing Maintenance and Management	861	457	397	467	1012	2304
#住房装潢	Housing Decoration	601	267	244	275	690	1801
住房维修	Housing Maintenance	126	163	105	106	138	108
物业管理费	Property Management Fees	125	15	44	78	171	383
水电燃料及其他	Water, Electricity, Fuels and Others	1122	1068	1067	1123	1077	1314
#水 费	Water	118	51	92	122	163	192
电 费	Electricity	366	366	358	375	362	368
燃 料	Fuels	293	495	315	276	157	163
自有住房折算租金	Converted Rent from Owner-Occupied Housing	7902	2771	4494	6756	11168	16961

8-9 全市居民家庭人均生活用品及服务、交通和通信支出(2015年)
PER CAPITA EXPENDITURE ON LIVING ARTICLES AND SERVICES, TRANSPORTATION AND COMMUNICATION OF THE WHOLE HOUSEHOLDS (2015)

单位：元 (yuan)

项目	Item	全市平均 Average	低收入户20% Low Income 20%	中低收入户20% Medium-Low Income 20%	中等收入户20% Medium Income 20%	中高收入户20% Medium-High Income 20%	高收入户20% High Income 20%
生活用品及服务支出	**Expenditures of Living Articles and Services**	**2098**	**996**	**1403**	**1901**	**2545**	**4227**
家具及室内装饰品	Furniture and Interior Decorations	402	180	229	301	490	946
家具	Furniture	338	155	193	251	412	791
家具材料	Furniture Materials	8	5	6	4	5	25
室内装饰品	Interior Decorations	56	20	30	46	73	130
家用器具	Household Appliances	465	252	309	432	590	859
耐用消费品	Durable Consumer Goods	352	208	233	320	445	637
小家电	Small Appliance	113	44	76	112	145	222
家用纺织品	Household Textile	178	75	125	169	218	351
#床上用品	Bedding	152	63	99	151	199	291
家庭日用杂品	Daily Groceries for Households	491	283	387	496	580	801
个人用品	Personal Articles	414	173	282	417	502	810
家庭服务	Domestic Services	148	33	71	86	165	460
交通和通信支出	**Expenditures of Transportation and Communication**	**4490**	**2061**	**3148**	**3621**	**5901**	**8973**
交通	Transportation	3291	1322	2173	2436	4504	7063
#交通工具	Vehicles	1156	390	691	580	1901	2644
交通费	Transportation Expenses	754	227	454	669	935	1756
通信	Communication	1199	739	975	1185	1397	1910
通信工具	Communication Devices	395	181	297	394	471	729
通信服务	Communication Services	804	558	678	791	926	1181

8-10 全市居民家庭人均教育文化和娱乐、医疗保健、其他用品及服务支出(2015年)

PER CAPITA EXPENDITURES ON EDUCATION, CULTURE, RECREATION, HEALTHCARE, OTHER GOODS AND SERVICES OF THE WHOLE HOUSEHOLDS (2015)

单位：元 (yuan)

项目	Item	全市平均 Average	低收入户 20% Low Income 20%	中低收入户 20% Medium-Low Income 20%	中等收入户 20% Medium Income 20%	中高收入户 20% Medium-High Income 20%	高收入户 20% High Income 20%
教育、文化和娱乐支出	**Educational, Cultural and Recreational Expenditures**	**3635**	**1623**	**2268**	**3231**	**4559**	**7571**
教育	Education	1043	892	889	1041	1039	1450
#学杂费	Tuition for Compulsory Education	241	240	262	226	213	264
培训费	Training Fees	425	222	237	437	522	820
一揽子教育服务（含食宿）	A Package of Education Services (including Accommodation)	280	343	315	298	204	216
学前教育	Pre-school Education	329	212	296	353	323	512
小学教育	Primary Education	169	113	132	190	170	265
初中教育	Junior Secondary Education	68	82	51	59	54	98
高中教育	Senior Secondary Education	100	138	74	79	105	102
中专职高教育	Secondary Vocational Education	12	38	12	2		1
大专及以上教育	Education for Junior College and Above	212	252	250	256	146	128
成人教育	Adult Education	153	57	74	102	241	344
文化和娱乐	Culture and Recreation	2592	731	1379	2190	3520	6121
文娱耐用消费品	Durable Consumer Goods for Cultural Recreation	397	169	296	339	453	845
其他文娱用品	Other Cultural and Recreational Articles	400	172	260	394	499	785
文化娱乐服务	Cultural and Recreational Services	1795	390	823	1457	2568	4491
医疗保健支出	**Healthcare Expenditures**	**2229**	**1249**	**1517**	**2084**	**2716**	**4101**
医疗器具及药品	Medical Apparatus and Medicine	819	486	554	713	1082	1444
药品	Medicine	497	410	404	446	626	660
滋补保健品	Nutritious Healthcare Products	267	62	120	205	362	702
医疗卫生器具	Medical and Hygienic Apparatus	26	9	15	26	37	49
保健器具	Healthcare Apparatus	29	5	15	36	57	33
医疗服务	Medical Services	1410	763	963	1371	1634	2657
其他用品及服务支出	**Expenditures of Other Goods and Services**	**991**	**262**	**515**	**870**	**1226**	**2477**
其他用品	Other Goods	554	151	297	491	626	1425
其他服务	Services	437	111	218	379	600	1052

8-11 全市居民家庭每百户主要耐用消费品拥有量(2015年)
NUMBER OF MAIN DURABLE CONSUMER GOODS PER 100 URBAN HOUSEHOLDS (2015)

项目		Item		全市平均 Average	低收入户 20% Low Income 20%	中低收入户 20% Medium-Low Income 20%	中等收入户 20% Medium Income 20%	中高收入户 20% Medium-High Income 20%	高收入户 20% High Income 20%
家用汽车	（辆）	Household Cars	(unit)	45	32	39	38	52	63
摩托车	（辆）	Motorcycles	(unit)	4	8	5	2	3	2
助力车	（台）	Powered Bicycles	(unit)	25	49	28	19	15	12
洗衣机	（台）	Washing Machines	(unit)	95	93	90	93	99	101
电冰箱（柜）	（台）	Refrigerators	(unit)	98	99	93	96	100	101
微波炉	（台）	Microwave Ovens	(unit)	77	58	70	79	89	91
彩色电视机	（台）	Color TV Sets	(unit)	130	126	122	128	135	139
#接入有线电视网络的电视机	（台）	TV Sets Accessed to Cable TV Network	(unit)	115	112	110	112	118	123
空调	（台）	Air Conditioners	(unit)	156	123	138	154	173	189
热水器	（台）	Water Heaters	(unit)	93	92	90	89	96	97
消毒碗柜	（台）	Disinfection cabinets	(unit)	4	2	2	2	5	7
洗碗机	（台）	Dishwashers	(unit)	1		1	1	2	2
移动电话	（部）	Mobile Phones	(unit)	221	228	223	216	226	212
#接入互联网的移动电话	（部）	Mobile Phones Accessed to the Internet	(unit)	133	109	126	134	144	152
计算机	（台）	Computers	(unit)	102	80	91	95	112	132
#接入互联网的计算机	（台）	Computers Accessed to the Internet	(unit)	92	69	82	86	102	119
摄像机	（台）	Video Cameras	(unit)	18	4	11	17	25	35
照相机	（台）	Cameras	(unit)	59	27	48	59	72	90
中高档乐器	（架）	ents of Middle and High-grade	(unit)	7	2	3	5	11	13
健身器材	（台）	Fitness Equipment	(unit)	7	3	4	7	8	12
组合音响	（套）	Audio Systems	(set)	7	4	4	6	7	12

8-12 全市居民家庭居住构成情况(2015)
COMPOSITION OF HOUSING CONDITIONS FOR URBAN HOUSEHOLDS (2015)

单位：% (%)

项目	Item	全市居民 Residents	城镇居民 Urban Residents	农村居民 Rural Residents
居住空间样式	**Style of Living Space**	**100.0**	**100.0**	**100.0**
单栋楼房占比重	Individual Storied Buildings	2.0	1.6	4.7
单栋平房占比重	Individual Single-storey Buildings	21.9	13.5	80.7
四居室及以上单元房占比重	Four-bedroom and above Flat	1.6	1.9	
三居室单元房占比重	Three-bedroom Flat	17.1	19.2	2.2
二居室单元房占比重	Two-bedroom Flat	38.7	44.0	1.6
一居室单元房占比重	One-bedroom Flat	7.7	8.7	0.1
筒子楼或连片平房占比重	Tube-shaped Apartment or Closely Grouped Single-storey Buildings	11.0	11.0	10.7
其他占比重	Others	…	0.1	
房屋来源	**Housing Property Right**	**100.0**	**100.0**	**100.0**
租赁公房占比重	Public Houses Rented	6.7	7.6	0.1
租赁私房占比重	Private Houses Rented	8.6	9.3	3.8
自建住房占比重	Self-building Houses	23.5	14.8	84.4
购买商品房占比重	Purchased Commercial Houses	25.7	29.0	2.3
购买房改住房占比重	Purchased Houses from Housing Reform	21.2	24.0	1.2
购买保障性住房占比重	Purchase of Indemnificatory Housing	4.4	5.1	
拆迁安置房占比重	Resettlement Housing	5.9	6.7	0.6
继承或获赠住房占比重	Housing under Inheritance or Donation	0.4	0.4	0.3
免费借用房占比重	Free Borrowed Houses	1.4	1.5	1.1
雇主提供免费住房占比重	Free Housing Supplied by Employers	2.1	1.5	6.2
其他来源占比重	Others	0.1	0.1	
住宅有管道供水情况	**Water Supply Conditions of Housing with Pipes**	**100.0**	**100.0**	**100.0**
管道供水入户	Water Supply to Households through Pipes	97.8	98.3	94.8
管道供水至公共取水点	Water Supply to Public Water-taking Location through Pipes	2.2	1.7	5.2
没有管道设施	Without Pipelines	…		…
饮用水来源情况	**Source of Drinking Water**	**100.0**	**100.0**	**100.0**
经过净化处理的自来水占比重	Tap Water via Purification Treatment	91.9	92.5	88.0
受保护的井水和泉水占比重	Protected Well Water and Spring Water	5.3	4.5	11.4
不受保护的井水和泉水占比重	Unprotected Well Water and Spring Water	…		0.1

8-12 续表 continued

单位：% (%)

项 目	Item	全市居民 Residents	城镇居民 Urban Residents	农村居民 Rural Residents
江河湖泊水占比重	Water from Rivers and Lakes			
收集雨水占比重	Collecting Rainwater			
桶装水占比重	Barreled Water	2.8	3.0	0.5
其他占比重	Others			
住户厕所类型	**Toilet Type of Households**	**100.0**	**100.0**	**100.0**
水冲式卫生厕所占比重	Water-flushing Sanitary Toilets	89.7	91.7	75.6
水冲式非卫生厕所占比重	Water-flushing Non-sanitary Toilets	0.5	0.3	1.9
卫生旱厕占比重	Sanitary Pit Toilet	2.9	2.3	7.6
普通旱厕占比重	Common Pit Toilet	4.1	2.6	14.6
无厕所占比重	Households Without Toilet	2.8	3.1	0.3
住户厕所使用情况	**Toilet Use Conditions of Households**	**100.0**	**100.0**	**100.0**
本住户独用占比重	Exclusive Use by One Household	88.1	88.0	89.3
几户合用占比重	One Toilet Shared by Several Households	2.3	1.7	6.1
公用厕所占比重	Communal Toilet	9.6	10.3	4.6
主要炊用能源状况	**Main Cooking Energy Conditions**	**100.0**	**100.0**	**100.0**
柴草占比重	Firewood	0.2		1.8
煤炭占比重	Coal	0.2	0.1	0.6
罐装液化石油气占比重	Bottled LPG	32.4	24.8	85.9
管道液化石油气占比重	Pipeline LPG	0.4	0.5	
管道煤气占比重	Pipeline Gas			
管道天然气占比重	Pipeline Natural Gas	63.0	71.6	2.6
电占比重	Electricity	2.0	1.8	3.1
燃料用油占比重	Oil Used in Fuel			
沼气占比重	Marsh Gas	0.2	0.2	0.6
其他占比重	Others			
无炊用行为占比重	Non-cooking Behaviors	1.6	1.0	5.4
住宅外道路路面状况	**Pavement Conditions of Roads Outside Houses**	**100.0**	**100.0**	**100.0**
水泥或柏油路面的户数占比重	Cement or Tar-coated Surface	94.9	94.9	94.6
沙石或石板等硬质路面的户数占比重	Hard Surface Paved with Sand and Stones or Slates	4.5	4.4	5.4
其它路面的户数占比重	Other Pavements	0.6	0.7	

8-13 城镇居民家庭生活基本情况(1978-2015年)
BASIC LIVING CONDITIONS OF URBAN HOUSEHOLDS (1978-2015)

年份 Year	人均家庭总收入(元) Per Capita Total Income (Yuan)	人均可支配收入(元) Per Capita Disposable Income (Yuan)	人均可支配收入实际增长(%) Actual Growth Rate of Per Capita Disposable Income (%)	人均消费支出(元) Per Capita Living Expenditures (Yuan)	#食品烟酒 Foods Tobacco and Liquor	城镇居民家庭恩格尔系数(%) Engel Coefficient of Urban Households (%)	每一城镇就业者负担人数(人) Dependents Per Urban Employee (person)	城镇居民人均住房建筑面积(平方米) Per Capita Floor Space of Houses in Urban Areas (sq.m)
1978	450.2	365.4		359.9	211.2	58.7	1.86	
1979	491.5	415.0	11.6	408.7	236.7	57.9	1.83	
1980	599.4	501.4	14.0	490.4	271.0	55.3	1.80	
1981	619.6	514.1	1.2	511.4	295.1	57.7	1.72	
1982	668.1	561.1	7.2	534.8	317.6	59.3	1.66	
1983	716.6	590.5	4.7	574.1	337.7	58.8	1.65	
1984	837.7	693.7	15.0	666.8	379.1	56.8	1.63	
1985	1158.8	907.7	11.3	923.3	466.9	50.6	1.66	
1986	1317.3	1067.5	10.1	1067.4	543.4	50.9	1.66	
1987	1413.2	1181.9	1.9	1147.6	605.0	52.7	1.65	
1988	1767.7	1437.0	1.0	1455.6	743.4	51.1	1.71	
1989	1899.6	1597.1	-5.2	1520.4	841.3	55.3	1.52	
1990	2067.3	1787.1	6.2	1646.1	892.2	54.2	1.52	
1991	2359.9	2040.4	2.1	1860.2	1016.8	54.7	1.47	
1992	2813.1	2363.7	5.4	2134.7	1126.3	52.8	1.43	
1993	3935.4	3296.0	17.1	2939.6	1404.7	47.8	1.42	
1994	5585.9	4731.2	14.9	4134.1	1919.0	46.4	1.41	
1995	6748.7	5868.4	5.7	5019.8	2436.5	48.5	1.41	
1996	7945.8	6885.5	5.1	5729.5	2671.5	46.6	1.41	
1997	8741.7	7813.1	7.8	6531.8	2854.4	43.7	1.43	
1998	10098.2	8472.0	5.9	6970.8	2865.7	41.1	1.40	
1999	10654.8	9182.8	7.8	7498.5	2959.2	39.5	1.41	
2000	12560.3	10349.7	8.9	8493.5	3083.4	36.3	1.41	
2001	13768.8	11577.8	8.5	8922.7	3229.3	36.2	1.39	
2002	13253.3	12463.9	15.6	10285.8	3472.5	33.8	1.41	19.22
2003	14959.3	13882.6	11.2	11123.8	3522.7	31.7	1.39	19.71
2004	17116.5	15637.8	11.5	12200.4	3925.5	32.2	1.44	21.49
2005	19533.3	17653.0	11.2	13244.2	4215.6	31.8	1.39	22.03
2006	22417.0	19978.0	12.2	14825.0	4561.0	30.8	1.40	23.65
2007	24576.0	21989.0	11.2	15330.0	4934.0	32.2	1.40	24.77
2008	27678.0	24725.0	7.0	16460.0	5562.0	33.8	1.40	26.90
2009	30674.0	26738.0	9.7	17893.0	5936.0	33.2	1.40	27.69
2010	33360.0	29073.0	6.2	19934.0	6393.0	32.1	1.40	28.94
2011	37124.0	32903.0	7.2	21984.0	6905.0	31.4	1.50	29.38
2012	41103.0	36469.0	7.3	24046.0	7535.0	31.3	1.40	29.26
2013	45274.0	40321.0	7.1	26275.0	8170.0	31.1	1.50	31.31
2014	49730.0	43910.0	7.2	28009.0	8632.0	30.8	1.50	31.54
2015		52859.0	7.0	36642.0	8091.0	22.1	1.50	31.69

8-14 城镇居民家庭基本情况(按收入水平分)(2015年) BASIC DATA ON URBAN HOUSEHOLDS (BY INCOME LEVEL) (2015)

项 目	Item	全市平均 Average	低收入户20% Low Income 20%	中低收入户20% Medium-Low Income 20%	中等收入户20% Medium Income 20%	中高收入户20% Medium-High Income 20%	高收入户20% High Income 20%
平均每户常住人口 (人)	Permanent Population Per Household (person)	2.7	3.1	2.9	2.7	2.5	2.3
平均每户就业人口数 (人)	Average Employee Per Household (person)	1.3	1.5	1.4	1.2	1.2	1.3
平均每一就业者负担人数 (人)	Dependents Per Employee (person)	1.5	1.9	1.6	1.5	1.3	1.2
平均每人年可支配收入 (元)	Per Capita Annual Disposable Income (yuan)	52859	23442	37709	49314	64206	103748
平均每人年消费支出 (元)	Per Capita Annual Consumption Expend (yuan)	36642	19489	26703	33186	45498	66840

8-15 城镇居民家庭人均可支配收入(2015年)

单位：元

项　目	Item	全市平均 Average
可支配收入	**Disposable Income**	**52859**
工资性收入	**Wage Income**	**32568**
工资	Wage	29781
实物福利	Benefit in Kind	140
其他	Other Income from Work	2647
经营净收入	**Net Income from Operations**	**1337**
第一产业经营净收入	Net Income from Operations in the Primary Industry	6
第二产业经营净收入	Net Income from Operations in the Secondary Industry	103
第三产业经营净收入	Net Income from Operations in the Tertiary Industry	1228
财产净收入	**Net Property Income**	**8492**
利息净收入	Net Interest Income	63
红利收入	Dividend Income	177
储蓄性保险净收益	Net Income from Saving Insurance	9
转让承包土地经营权租金净收入	Net Rent from Transfer of Contracted Land Management Right	18
出租房屋净收入	Net Income from House Rent	1107
出租机械专利版权等资产的收入	Income from Lease of Assets such as Mechanical Patent Copyright	1
其他财产净收入	Other Net Property Income	-7
自有住房折算净租金	Converted Net Rent from Owner-Occupied Housing	7124
转移净收入	**Net Transfer Income**	**10462**
转移性收入	Transfer Income	14066
#养老金或离退休金	Pensions or Retirement Payments	13297
社会救济和补助	Social Relief and Subsidies	30
赡养收入	Alimony Income	82
其他经常转移收入	Other Current Transfer Income	99
#失业保险金	Unemployment Insurance Benefits	4
经常性捐赠收入	Recurrent Donation Income	2
其他转移性收入	Other Transfer Income	93
转移性支出	Transfer Expenditures	3604
非收入所得	**Non-revenue Proceeds**	**1969**
出售资产所得	Proceeds from assets sales	632
#出售住房本金所得	Proceeds from Selling Housing Principal	
出售住房溢价所得(含亏损)	Proceeds from Selling Housing Premium (including losses)	
出售其他财物和收回其他投资本金所得	Proceeds from Property Sales and Taking other Investment Principal back	26
非经常性转移所得	Non-recurrent Transfer Proceeds	1312
#提取住房公积金	Withdrawing Public Reserve Fund for Housing	212
调查补贴	Survey Subsidy	653
其他非收入所得	Other Non-revenue Proceeds	25
借贷性所得	**Loan Proceeds**	**3339**

注：城镇居民人均可支配收入实际增长7.0%。
Note: Real growth rate of the per capita annual disposable income is 7.0%.

PER CAPITA DISPOSABLE INCOME OF URBAN HOUSEHOLDS (2015)

(yuan)

低 收 入 户 20% Low Income 20%	中 低 收入户 20% Medium- Low Income 20%	中 等 收入户 20% Medium Income 20%	中 高 收入户 20% Medium- High Income 20%	高 收 入 户 20% High Income 20%	2015年为 2014年% 2015 as % of 2014
23442	**37709**	**49314**	**64206**	**103748**	**108.9**
15761	**22340**	**27452**	**36380**	**70258**	**109.8**
14953	20820	25084	32866	63483	109.8
61	126	85	109	366	126.1
747	1394	2283	3405	6409	109.4
1017	**988**	**1202**	**817**	**2952**	**96.3**
4	11	15			300.0
162	69	10	1	290	85.8
851	908	1177	816	2662	96.9
3583	6205	7845	10988	16076	106.5
-6	-4	-13	9	393	94.0
195	160	189	136	206	87.6
2	3	9	23	8	90.0
44	11	3	15	10	163.6
797	1509	1233	936	1070	130.4
4	2				10.0
9	-4	-1	-14	-31	…
2538	4528	6425	9883	14420	104.2
3081	**8176**	**12815**	**16021**	**14462**	**110.0**
4754	10375	15692	20132	22774	113.9
4103	9822	15042	19407	21381	113.2
105	21	6	2	1	96.8
120	52	61	96	77	89.1
154	165	48	27	83	111.2
10	1	3	3	3	133.3
1			2	11	33.3
143	164	45	22	69	117.7
1673	2199	2877	4111	8312	126.9
1552	**1249**	**1235**	**1905**	**4385**	**159.6**
576	77	126	200	2486	299.5
34	7	13	14	66	
968	1150	1102	1681	1824	325.0
21	102	94	416	524	186.0
563	615	661	682	779	103.5
8	22	7	24	75	357.1
1406	**1561**	**1398**	**1757**	**12286**	**141.4**

8-16 城镇居民家庭人均总支出(2015年)

单位：元

项　　目	Item	全市平均 Average
家庭总支出	**Total Expenditures of Households**	**47917**
消费支出	**Consumption Expenditures**	**36642**
#车辆保险支出	Expenditures of Automotive Insurance	165
生产经营费用支出	**Expenditures of Production and Operating Costs**	**189**
第一产业经营费用支出	Operating Cost Expenditures in the Primary Industry	6
第二产业经营费用支出	Operating Cost Expenditures in the Secondary Industry	8
第三产业经营费用支出	Operating Cost Expenditures in the Tertiary Industry	175
财产性支出	**Property Expenditures**	**140**
转移性支出	**Transfer Expenditures**	**3604**
个人所得税	Individual Income Tax	638
社会保障支出	Social Security Expenditures	2588
个人缴纳的养老保险	Pensions Paid by Individual	1948
个人缴纳的医疗保险	Medical Funds Paid by Individual	583
个人缴纳的失业保险	Unemployment Funds Paid by Individual	53
其他社会保障支出	Other Social Security Expenditures	4
外来从业人员寄给家人的支出	Expenditures of Outside Employees for Their Family	34
赡养支出	Alimony Expenditures	282
其他转移性支出	Other Transfer Expenditures	62
部分商业保险支出	**Partially Commercial Insurance Expenditures**	**208**
意外伤害保险	Accident Insurance	23
商业医疗保险(含大病保险)	Commercial Medical Insurance (including Critical Illness Insurance)	101
其他非储蓄性商业保险	Other Non-saving Commercial Insurance	6
其他储蓄性商业保险	Other Saving Commercial Insurance	78
购置资产及非经常性转移支出	**Expenditures of Acquisition Assets and Non-recurrent Transfer**	**4956**
购置资产支出	Acquisition Asset Expenditures	3758
#建造住房支出	Expenditures of Building Houses	93
购买住房支出	Expenditures of Purchasing Houses	3420
非经常性转移支出	Non-recurrent Transfer Expenditures	1198
#一次性馈赠支出	Disposable Donation Expenditures	544
借贷性支出	**Credit Expenditures**	**2178**
#存入储蓄款	Saving Deposits	1313
归还借款	Repayment of Loans	67
购买有价证券	Purchase of Securities	77
归还住房贷款	Repayment of Housing Loan	587
归还汽车贷款	Repayment of Automobile Loans	37

PER CAPITA ANNUAL EXPENDITURES OF URBAN HOUSEHOLDS (2015)

(yuan)

低收入户 20% Low Income 20%	中低收入户 20% Medium-Low Income 20%	中等收入户 20% Medium Income 20%	中高收入户 20% Medium-High Income 20%	高收入户 20% High Income 20%	2015年为2014年% 2015 as % of 2014
24270	**32869**	**40724**	**54958**	**99893**	**116.4**
19489	**26703**	**33186**	**45498**	**66840**	**108.7**
86	142	143	181	308	147.3
481	**93**	**206**	**43**	**54**	**64.9**
22	4	3	…	…	10.6
35	…		1		29.6
424	89	203	42	54	87.9
49	**75**	**79**	**163**	**392**	**209.0**
1673	**2199**	**2877**	**4111**	**8312**	**126.9**
34	96	258	716	2511	138.1
1319	1823	2327	3032	5098	126.6
935	1323	1743	2310	3958	128.9
353	458	529	658	1033	121.0
28	37	48	61	102	123.3
3	5	7	3	5	57.1
33	72	46	3	10	56.7
268	128	180	304	592	136.9
19	80	66	56	101	91.2
91	**178**	**165**	**211**	**454**	**163.8**
9	20	11	23	58	176.9
62	113	62	95	192	219.6
3	4	5	3	17	33.3
17	41	87	90	187	159.2
1448	**2498**	**2666**	**2902**	**17862**	**275.8**
642	1410	1441	1383	16379	659.3
368		3	38	2	76.9
	1386	1424	965	15771	826.1
806	1088	1225	1519	1483	97.6
251	486	565	708	809	119.6
1039	**1123**	**1545**	**2030**	**5979**	**93.3**
654	833	788	1172	3601	65.9
28	3	21	85	236	152.3
111	20	49	71	139	256.7
149	232	567	548	1703	248.7
9		30	30	137	925.0

8-17 城镇居民家庭人均消费支出(2015年)
PER CAPITA CONSUMPTION EXPENDITURES OF URBAN HOUSEHOLDS (2015)

单位：元 (yuan)

项目	Item	全市平均 Average	低收入户20% Low Income 20%	中低收入户20% Medium-Low Income 20%	中等收入户20% Medium Income 20%	中高收入户20% Medium-High Income 20%	高收入户20% High Income 20%	2015年为2014年% 2015 as % of 2014
人均消费支出	**Per Capita Consumption Expenditures**	**36642**	**19489**	**26703**	**33186**	**45498**	**66840**	**108.7**
食品烟酒支出	Expenditures of Foods, Tobacco and Liquor	8091	5479	7080	8209	9070	11712	101.0
衣着支出	Clothing Expenditures	2651	1457	1979	2406	3207	4801	102.5
居住支出	Housing Expenditures	11252	5224	7404	9714	14673	22350	109.2
生活用品及服务支出	Expenditures of Living Articles and Services	2273	1157	1661	1982	2748	4383	103.0
交通和通信支出	Expenditures of Transportation and Communication	4860	2415	3379	3964	6682	9099	126.0
教育、文化和娱乐支出	Educational, Cultural and Recreational Expenditures	4028	2118	2770	3479	5075	7704	111.5
医疗保健支出	Healthcare Expenditures	2370	1245	1733	2545	2632	4209	115.9
其他用品及服务支出	Expenditures of Other Goods and Services	1117	394	697	887	1411	2582	102.0

注：城镇居民人均消费支出实际增长6.8%。
Note: Real growth rate of the per capita consumption expenditures of urban residents is 6.8%.

8-18 城镇居民家庭人均消费支出构成(2015年)
COMPOSITION OF PER CAPITA CONSUMPTION EXPENDITURES OF URBAN HOUSEHOLDS (2015)

单位：% (%)

项目	Item	全市平均 Average	低收入户20% Low Income 20%	中低收入户20% Medium-Low Income 20%	中等收入户20% Medium Income 20%	中高收入户20% Medium-High Income 20%	高收入户20% High Income 20%
人均消费支出	**Per Capita Consumption Expenditures**	**100.0**	**100.0**	**100.0**	**100.0**	**100.0**	**100.0**
食品烟酒支出（恩格尔系数）	Expenditures of Foods, Tobacco and Liquor (Engel Coefficient)	22.1	28.1	26.5	24.7	19.9	17.5
衣着支出	Clothing Expenditures	7.2	7.5	7.4	7.3	7.0	7.2
居住支出	Housing Expenditures	30.7	26.8	27.7	29.3	32.2	33.4
生活用品及服务支出	Expenditures of Living Articles and Services	6.2	5.9	6.2	6.0	6.0	6.6
交通和通信支出	Expenditures of Transportation and Communication	13.3	12.4	12.7	11.9	14.7	13.6
教育、文化和娱乐支出	Educational, Cultural and Recreational Expenditures	11.0	10.9	10.4	10.5	11.2	11.5
医疗保健支出	Healthcare Expenditures	6.5	6.4	6.5	7.7	5.8	6.3
其他用品及服务支出	Expenditures of Other Goods and Services	3.0	2.0	2.6	2.6	3.2	3.9

8-19 城镇居民家庭人均食品烟酒支出(2015年)
PER CAPITA EXPENDITURES ON FOODS, TOBACCO AND LIQUOR OF URBAN HOUSEHOLDS (2015)

单位：元 (yuan)

项目	Item	全市平均 Average	低收入户20% Low Income 20%	中低收入户20% Medium-Low Income 20%	中等收入户20% Medium Income 20%	中高收入户20% Medium-High Income 20%	高收入户20% High Income 20%
食品烟酒支出	**Expenditures of Foods, Tobacco and Liquor**	**8091**	**5479**	**7080**	**8209**	**9070**	**11712**
食品	Foods	4912	3663	4534	5149	5408	6264
谷物	Grain	595	542	517	582	535	849
薯类	Potatoes	58	47	56	65	62	57
豆类	Beans	60	46	57	64	64	69
食用油	Edible Oil	246	193	236	238	282	299
蔬菜和食用菌	Vegetables and Edible Mushrooms	572	453	550	603	630	662
肉类	Meat	957	748	939	1053	1040	1062
禽类	Poultry	157	124	155	168	163	185
水产品	Aquatic Products	349	204	310	366	425	492
蛋类	Eggs	157	126	147	163	171	192
奶类	Milk	417	277	385	432	488	553
干鲜瓜果类	Nuts, Fresh Melons and Fruits	800	525	707	854	926	1090
糖果糕点类	Sweets and Cakes	275	172	231	284	328	403
食糖	Sugar	9	7	8	11	10	10
糖果	Sweets	26	17	20	26	30	42
糕点	Cakes	153	96	131	159	187	211
其他糖果糕点	Other Sweets and Cakes	87	52	72	88	101	140
其他食品	Other Foods	269	206	244	277	294	351
#调味品	Flavoring	137	100	133	145	158	161
烟酒	Tobacco and Liquor	658	515	630	656	711	833
烟草	Tobacco	363	299	356	359	390	436
酒类	Liquor	295	216	274	297	321	397
饮料	Beverages	395	256	344	400	471	561
饮食服务	Catering Services	2126	1045	1572	2004	2480	4054

8-20 城镇居民家庭人均衣着、居住支出(2015年)
PER CAPITA EXPENDITURES ON FOODS, TOBACCO AND LIQUOR OF URBAN HOUSEHOLDS (2015)

单位：元 (yuan)

项目	Item	全市平均 Average	低收入户20% Low Income 20%	中低收入户20% Medium-Low Income 20%	中等收入户20% Medium Income 20%	中高收入户20% Medium-High Income 20%	高收入户20% High Income 20%
衣着支出	**Clothing Expenditures**	**2651**	**1457**	**1979**	**2406**	**3207**	**4801**
衣类	Clothes	1929	1028	1409	1735	2353	3574
服装	Garments	1811	970	1315	1624	2213	3360
服装材料	Clothing Materials	11	6	9	12	12	16
其他衣类及配件	Other Clothes and Accessories	100	50	79	92	119	184
衣着加工服务费	Service Fees for Clothing Processing	7	2	6	7	9	14
鞋类	Footwear	722	429	570	671	854	1227
居住支出	**Housing Expenditures**	**11252**	**5224**	**7404**	**9714**	**14673**	**22350**
租赁房房租	House Rent	520	509	372	419	472	895
住房维修及管理	Housing Maintenance and Management	917	402	423	495	1148	2486
#住房装潢	Housing Decoration	655	267	258	294	784	1969
住房维修	Housing Maintenance	110	101	100	88	160	104
物业管理费	Property Management Fees	144	26	60	102	197	400
水电燃料及其他	Water, Electricity, Fuels and Others	1103	997	1081	1050	1142	1295
#水费	Water	135	85	109	145	163	194
电费	Electricity	357	353	350	352	376	357
燃料	Fuels	232	328	271	211	160	156
自有住房折算租金	Converted Rent from Owner-Occupied Housing	8712	3316	5528	7750	11911	17674

8-21 城镇居民家庭人均生活用品及服务、交通和通信支出(2015年)
PER CAPITA EXPENDITURES ON LIVING ARTICLES AND SERVICES, TRANSPORTATION AND COMMUNICATION OF URBAN HOUSEHOLDS (2015)

单位：元 (yuan)

项目	Item	全市平均 Average	低收入户20% Low Income 20%	中低收入户20% Medium-Low Income 20%	中等收入户20% Medium Income 20%	中高收入户20% Medium-High Income 20%	高收入户20% High Income 20%
生活用品及服务支出	**Expenditures of Living Articles and Services**	**2273**	**1157**	**1661**	**1982**	**2748**	**4383**
家具及室内装饰品	Furniture and Interior Decorations	439	198	297	321	517	999
家具	Furniture	368	172	242	273	428	838
家具材料	Furniture Materials	9	3	7	5	12	20
室内装饰品	Interior Decorations	62	23	48	43	77	141
家用器具	Household Appliances	492	253	369	431	649	870
耐用消费品	Durable Consumer Goods	367	193	271	322	492	640
小家电	Small Appliance	125	60	98	109	157	230
家用纺织品	Household Textile	193	91	147	180	236	357
#床上用品	Bedding	167	82	120	163	212	295
家庭日用杂品	Daily Groceries for Households	524	332	423	533	611	808
个人用品	Personal Articles	458	243	342	426	536	847
家庭服务	Domestic Services	167	40	83	91	199	502
交通和通信支出	**Expenditures of Transportation and Communication**	**4860**	**2415**	**3379**	**3964**	**6682**	**9099**
交通	Transportation	3584	1540	2306	2754	5250	7116
#交通工具	Vehicles	1274	451	655	752	2389	2552
交通费	Transportation Expenses	844	336	553	721	1049	1823
通信	Communication	1276	875	1073	1210	1432	1983
通信工具	Communication Devices	433	268	338	377	491	777
通信服务	Communication Services	843	607	735	833	941	1206

8-22 城镇居民家庭人均教育文化和娱乐、医疗保健、其他用品及服务支出(2015年)

PER CAPITA EXPENDITURES ON EDUCATION, CULTURE, RECREATION, HEALTHCARE, OTHER GOODS AND SERVICES OF URBAN HOUSEHOLDS (2015)

单位：元 (yuan)

项目	Item	全市平均 Average	低收入户20% Low Income 20%	中低收入户20% Medium-Low Income 20%	中等收入户20% Medium Income 20%	中高收入户20% Medium-High Income 20%	高收入户20% High Income 20%
教育、文化和娱乐支出	**Educational, Cultural and Recreational Expenditures**	**4028**	**2118**	**2770**	**3479**	**5075**	**7704**
教育	**Education**	**1101**	**1052**	**1013**	**973**	**1126**	**1403**
#学杂费	Tuition for Compulsory Education	251	313	246	217	203	265
培训费	Training Fees	474	275	335	450	617	788
一揽子教育服务(含食宿)	A Package of Education Services (including Accommodation)	274	370	344	227	179	218
学前教育	Pre-school Education	365	332	337	343	347	492
小学教育	Primary Education	186	151	166	175	219	237
初中教育	Junior Secondary Education	70	71	75	45	75	87
高中教育	Senior Secondary Education	96	111	72	75	132	87
中专职高教育	Secondary Vocational Education	8	24	11	…		…
大专及以上教育	Education for Junior College and Above	207	296	272	176	118	138
成人教育	Adult Education	169	67	80	159	235	362
文化和娱乐	Culture and Recreation	2927	1066	1757	2506	3949	6301
文娱耐用消费品	Durable Consumer Goods for Cultural Recreation	439	248	306	395	478	876
其他文娱用品	Other Cultural and Recreational Articles	443	220	334	417	552	790
文化娱乐服务	Cultural and Recreational Services	2045	598	1117	1694	2919	4635
医疗保健支出	**Healthcare Expenditures**	**2370**	**1245**	**1733**	**2545**	**2632**	**4209**
医疗器具及药品	Medical Apparatus and Medicine	870	532	549	972	1017	1452
药品	Medicine	507	399	386	572	571	668
滋补保健品	Nutritious Healthcare Products	302	107	124	311	376	697
医疗卫生器具	Medical and Hygienic Apparatus	29	13	15	31	41	51
保健器具	Healthcare Apparatus	32	13	24	58	29	36
医疗服务	Medical Services	1500	713	1184	1573	1615	2757
其他用品及服务支出	**Expenditures of Other Goods and Services**	**1117**	**394**	**697**	**887**	**1411**	**2582**
其他用品	Other Goods	623	233	387	495	732	1488
其他服务	Services	494	161	310	392	679	1094

8-23 城镇居民家庭每百户主要耐用消费品拥有量(1978-2015年)
NUMBER OF MAIN DURABLE CONSUMER GOODS PER 100 URBAN HOUSEHOLDS (1978-2015)

年 份 Year	热水器 (台) Water Heaters (unit)	洗衣机 (台) Washing Machines (unit)	彩 色 电视机 (台) Color TV Sets (unit)	电冰箱 (台) Refrige-rators (unit)	照相机 (台) Cameras (unit)	空调器 (台) Air Conditioners (unit)	计算机 (台) Computers (unit)	移动电话 (部) Mobile Phones (unit)	家用汽车 (辆) Household Cars (unit)
1978					8				
1979		…			10				
1980		2		…	11				
1981		12	2	2	13				
1982		19	2	3	17				
1983		29	4	7	21				
1984		42	8	15	29				
1985		58	32	42	35				
1986		76	51	62	47				
1987		83	58	72	56				
1988		86	70	81	60				
1989		90	81	89	62				
1990		93	91	96	67				
1991		93	97	102	73	…			
1992	17	96	101	101	77	1			
1993	23	100	107	101	82	2			
1994	39	103	112	104	85	5			
1995	45	100	114	104	87	12			
1996	52	101	119	105	87	14			
1997	58	101	124	104	88	27	12	1	1
1998	65	102	133	105	95	34	15	3	1
1999	67	100	141	103	95	50	24	13	3
2000	74	103	146	107	96	70	32	28	3
2001	78	102	149	107	101	90	45	62	3
2002	84	99	148	102	100	107	56	94	4
2003	85	99	147	100	103	119	68	134	7
2004	94	102	151	103	100	136	79	165	13
2005	97	105	153	104	109	147	89	190	14
2006	98	107	155	105	113	157	96	206	18
2007	99	102	147	108	99	157	92	207	20
2008	95	99	134	103	82	152	86	191	23
2009	98	100	138	104	89	163	97	213	30
2010	98	100	140	103	92	169	104	221	34
2011	97	100	138	103	85	171	104	215	38
2012	99	101	141	103	90	179	112	226	42
2013	99	100	140	103	85	180	110	225	43
2014	99	101	141	104	88	186	114	229	45
2015	93	96	130	98	65	161	107	220	47

8-24 城镇居民家庭每百户主要耐用消费品拥有量(2015年) NUMBER OF MAIN DURABLE CONSUMER GOODS PER 100 URBAN HOUSEHOLDS (2015)

项目	Item	全市平均 Average	低收入户20% Low Income 20%	中低收入户20% Medium-Low Income 20%	中等收入户20% Medium Income 20%	中高收入户20% Medium-High Income 20%	高收入户20% High Income 20%
家用汽车（辆）	Household Cars (unit)	47	35	40	41	55	64
摩托车（辆）	Motorcycles (unit)	3	4	3	3	2	2
助力车（台）	Powered Bicycles (unit)	19	29	23	14	16	12
洗衣机（台）	Washing Machines (unit)	96	92	91	95	99	102
电冰箱（柜）（台）	Refrigerators (unit)	98	99	93	98	101	101
微波炉（台）	Microwave Ovens (unit)	81	67	75	82	90	91
彩色电视机（台）	Color TV Sets (unit)	130	119	125	129	136	141
#接入有线电视网络的电视机（台）	TV Sets Accessed to Cable TV Network (unit)	115	106	112	112	119	123
空调（台）	Air Conditioners (unit)	161	129	148	159	175	193
热水器（台）	Water Heaters (unit)	93	90	88	92	95	97
消毒碗柜（台）	Disinfection cabinets (unit)	4	2	3	2	7	7
洗碗机（台）	Dishwashers (unit)	1	1	1	1	3	2
移动电话（部）	Mobile Phones (unit)	220	223	221	218	227	210
#接入互联网的移动电话（部）	Mobile Phones Accessed to the Internet (unit)	138	119	138	130	149	152
计算机（台）	Computers (unit)	107	91	93	101	114	134
#接入互联网的计算机（台）	Computers Accessed to the Internet (unit)	96	80	86	92	103	121
摄像机（台）	Video Cameras (unit)	20	6	16	18	28	35
照相机（台）	Cameras (unit)	65	39	56	62	76	92
中高档乐器（架）	Musical Instruments of Middle and High-grade (unit)	8	3	5	6	12	12
健身器材（台）	Fitness Equipment (unit)	8	5	4	8	8	14
组合音响（套）	Audio Systems (set)	7	3	5	7	7	12

8-25 农村居民家庭基本情况(1978-2015年)
BASIC LIVING CONDITIONS OF RURAL HOUSEHOLDS (1978-2015)

年份 Year	人均可支配收入(元) Per Capita Disposable Income (yuan)	人均可支配收入实际增长(%) Actual Growth Rate of Per Capita Disposable Income (%)	人均总支出(元) Per Capita Total Expen-ditures (yuan)	人均消费支出(元) Per Capita Consumption Expen-ditures (yuan)	#食品烟酒 Foods Tobacco and Liquor	农村居民家庭恩格尔系数(%) Engel Coefficient of Rural Households (%)	每一农村劳动力负担人数(人) Dependents Per Rural Labor Force (person)	农村居民人均住房面积(平方米) Per Capita Living Space of Rural Residents (sq.m)
1978	224.8		219.0	185.4	116.7	63.2	2.15	9.20
1979	250.0	10.9	235.0	204.7	131.1	63.9	2.16	9.67
1980	308.1	22.1	290.0	256.8	140.2	54.1	2.13	10.09
1981	361.4	17.1	350.5	307.2	160.6	52.3	2.14	12.35
1982	430.2	17.3	411.2	345.5	181.1	52.4	1.97	13.01
1983	519.5	20.9	498.5	384.4	193.8	50.4	1.82	14.24
1984	664.2	25.7	559.3	435.0	222.5	51.1	1.79	14.22
1985	775.1	14.5	726.0	510.0	240.5	47.1	1.64	16.48
1986	823.1	3.7	857.0	645.3	292.4	45.3	1.66	17.41
1987	916.4	6.5	943.0	705.5	340.9	48.3	1.64	18.38
1988	1062.6	3.1	1246.0	883.3	407.9	46.2	1.63	19.23
1989	1230.7	2.2	1356.0	976.3	484.3	49.6	1.62	20.09
1990	1297.1	2.1	1372.0	980.7	497.0	50.7	1.61	20.62
1991	1422.3	1.7	1585.0	1100.1	537.0	48.8	1.59	21.92
1992	1568.8	2.0	1684.0	1179.0	573.8	48.7	1.58	22.67
1993	1854.8	5.1	1714.0	1308.9	611.7	46.8	1.51	23.70
1994	2422.1	9.1	2175.0	1676.5	824.8	49.2	1.49	24.42
1995	3208.5	6.3	3080.0	2433.0	1206.0	49.6	1.47	24.74
1996	3562.7	4.8	3272.0	2655.5	1233.1	46.4	1.45	25.74
1997	3762.4	5.1	3379.0	2795.4	1248.4	44.7	1.48	27.39
1998	4028.9	6.7	3617.0	2945.5	1241.9	42.2	1.44	27.64
1999	4316.4	7.2	3938.0	3132.5	1253.5	40.0	1.43	28.65
2000	4687.0	7.3	4517.9	3441.4	1263.6	36.7	1.51	28.91
2001	5274.3	8.7	5098.8	3871.5	1353.2	34.9	1.52	31.01
2002	5880.1	12.3	5548.7	4206.0	1386.6	33.0	1.48	32.58
2003	6496.3	11.5	5886.6	4655.3	1475.6	31.7	1.45	33.95
2004	7172.1	9.2	6275.2	4886.4	1592.3	32.6	1.46	34.21
2005	7860.0	8.1	7181.2	5515.0	1807.0	32.8	1.45	36.94
2006	8620.0	8.7	7935.0	6061.0	1937.0	32.0	1.42	39.10
2007	9559.0	8.2	8866.0	6828.0	2190.0	32.1	1.40	39.54
2008	10747.0	6.5	10166.0	7656.0	2629.0	34.3	1.40	39.40
2009	11986.0	13.4	11814.0	9141.0	2961.0	32.4	1.39	39.42
2010	13262.0	8.1	12805.0	10109.0	3121.0	30.9	1.39	40.62
2011	14736.0	7.6	14503.0	11078.0	3593.0	32.4	1.38	48.63
2012	16476.0	8.2	15196.0	11879.0	3945.0	33.2	1.40	49.08
2013	18337.0	7.7	16994.0	13553.0	4696.0	34.6	1.49	51.35
2014	20226.0	8.6	18011.0	14529.0	5043.0	34.7	1.50	52.42
2015	20569.0	7.1	22823.0	15811.0	4372.0	27.7	1.60	43.03

注：2015年开始，根据国家统计局城乡居民统计新口径要求，“农村居民人均纯收入”统一改为“人均可支配收入”。

Note: According to the requirements of the National Bureau of Statistics on the new statistical range for urban and rural residents, "per capita net income of rural residents" shall be modified as "per capita disposable income" since 2015.

8-26 农村居民家庭基本情况(按收入水平分)(2015年)
BASIC DATA ON RURAL HOUSEHOLDS (BY INCOME LEVEL) (2015)

项目	Item	全市平均 Average	低收入户20% Low Income 20%	中低收入户20% Medium-Low Income 20%	中等收入户20% Medium Income 20%	中高收入户20% Medium-High Income 20%	高收入户20% High Income 20%
平均每户常住人口（人）	Permanent Population Per Household (person)	2.9	3.0	3.1	3.1	2.9	2.5
平均每户整半劳动力（个）	Full/Semi Labor Force Per Household (person)	2.3	2.2	2.4	2.5	2.4	2.2
平均每一劳动力负担人口（人）	Dependents Per Labor Force (person)	1.6	2.1	1.7	1.6	1.5	1.3
人均住房面积（平方米）	Per Capita Living Space (sq.m)	43.03	41.83	42.55	41.09	43.09	47.59
人均可支配收入（元）	Per Capita Disposable Income (yuan)	20569	8494	15589	20177	25735	36534
人均消费支出（元）	Per Capita Consumption Expenditures (yuan)	15811	11649	14343	15022	17581	21847
农村居民家庭恩格尔系数（%）	Engel Coefficient of Rural Households (%)	27.7	28.4	26.4	28.0	28.5	27.1

8-27 农村居民家庭人均可支配收入(2015年)

单位：元

项　　目	Item	全市平均 Average
人均可支配收入	**Per Capita Disposable Income**	**20569**
生产性收入	**Productive Income**	**17450**
工资性收入	**Wage Income**	**15491**
工　资	Wage	14594
实物福利	Benefit in Kind	164
其　他	Other Income from Work	733
经营净收入	**Net Income from Operations**	**1959**
第一产业净收入	Net Income from the Primary Industry	546
#农业收入	Agricultural Income	430
牧业收入	Animal Husbandry Income	91
第二产业净收入	Net Income from the Secondary Industry	80
#工业收入	Industrial Income	19
第三产业净收入	Net Income from the Tertiary Industry	1333
#交通运输业收入	Transportation Income	638
非生产性收入	**Non-productive Income**	**3119**
财产净收入	**Net Property Income**	**1204**
利息净收入	Net Interest Income	34
红利收入	Dividend Income	402
#集体分配的红利	Dividend Distributed by the Collective	402
储蓄性保险净收益	Net Income from Saving Insurance	2
转让承包土地经营权租金净收入	Net Rent from Transfer of Contracted Land Management Right	175
出租房屋净收入	Net Income from House Rent	551
出租机械专利版权等资产的收入	Income from Lease of Assets such as Mechanical Patent Copyright	8
其他财产净收入	Other Net Property Income	32
自有住房折算净租金	Converted Net Rent from Owner-Occupied Housing	
转移净收入	**Net Transfer Income**	**1915**
转移性收入	**Transfer Income**	**3477**
#养老金或离退休金	Pensions or Retirement Payments	2429
家庭外出从业人员寄回带回收入	Income from Family Members Going out for a Job	133
其他经常转移收入	Other Current Transfer Income	169
#经常性捐赠收入	Recurrent Donation Income	…
现金政策性惠农补贴	Subsidies Benefiting Peasants under Cash Policy	66
转移性支出	**Transfer Expenditures**	**1562**

注：农村居民人均可支配收入实际增长7.1%。
Note: Real growth rate of the per capita disposable income of rural residents is 7.1%.

PER CAPITA DISPOSABLE INCOME OF RURAL HOUSEHOLDS (2015)

(yuan)

低 收 入 户 20% Low Income 20%	中 低 收入户 20% Medium-Low Income 20%	中 等 收入户 20% Medium Income 20%	中 高 收入户 20% Medium-High Income 20%	高 收 入 户 20% High Income 20%	2015年为 2014年% 2015 as % of 2014
8494	**15589**	**20177**	**25735**	**36534**	**109.0**
6670	**13486**	**17118**	**21768**	**31395**	**108.3**
5919	**11580**	**15171**	**20105**	**27515**	**108.6**
5567	10871	14401	19086	25676	110.1
22	42	71	280	485	114.7
330	667	699	739	1354	85.0
751	**1906**	**1947**	**1663**	**3880**	**105.7**
111	545	433	568	1209	96.5
284	389	390	464	680	96.2
-63	135	46	107	264	77.1
-32	146	3	156	143	50.6
-44	20		104	21	105.6
672	1215	1511	939	2528	118.0
598	539	932	330	795	140.8
1824	**2103**	**3059**	**3967**	**5139**	**113.0**
543	**621**	**1207**	**1952**	**1911**	**147.2**
19	41	23	24	70	
288	263	371	622	511	162.5
288	263	365	622	511	162.8
9					66.7
93	110	154	270	279	85.0
117	154	628	943	1049	154.3
	11	5	25		57.1
17	42	26	68	2	
1281	**1482**	**1852**	**2015**	**3228**	**99.0**
2305	**2470**	**3090**	**4220**	**5875**	**111.6**
1525	1500	2303	3066	4177	102.4
	77	48	240	356	214.5
77	161	182	184	263	119.9
		…			
102	75	39	69	39	275.0
1024	**988**	**1238**	**2205**	**2647**	**132.3**

8-28 农村居民家庭人均消费支出(2015年)
PER CAPITA CONSUMPTION EXPENDITURE OF RURAL HOUSEHOLDS (2015)

单位：元 (Yuan)

项目	Item	全市平均 Average	低收入户20% Low Income 20%	中低收入户20% Medium-Low Income 20%	中等收入户20% Medium Income 20%	中高收入户20% Medium-High Income 20%	高收入户20% High Income 20%	2015年为2014年% 2015 as % of 2014
人均消费支出	**Per Capita Consumption Expenditures**	**15811**	**11649**	**14343**	**15022**	**17581**	**21847**	**108.8**
食品烟酒支出	Expenditures of Foods, Tobacco and Liquor	4372	3304	3783	4215	5013	5921	108.0
衣着支出	Clothing Expenditures	996	576	823	951	1249	1507	108.5
居住支出	Housing Expenditures	4636	3737	4590	4176	4744	6277	106.3
生活用品及服务支出	Expenditures of Living Articles and Services	993	629	839	1000	1015	1610	99.9
交通和通信支出	Expenditures of Transportation and Communication	2140	1186	1841	2133	2638	3146	118.0
教育、文化和娱乐支出	Educational, Cultural and Recreational Expenditures	1145	1023	1102	1185	1075	1379	104.4
医疗保健支出	Healthcare Expenditures	1336	1094	1216	1168	1622	1679	122.7
其他用品及服务支出	Expenditures of Other Goods and Services	193	100	149	194	225	328	89.8

注：农村居民人均消费支出实际增长6.9%。
Note: Real growth rate of the per capita consumption expenditures of rural residents is 6.9%.

8-29 农村居民家庭人均消费支出构成(2015年)
COMPOSITION OF PER CAPITA CONSUMPTION EXPENDITURES OF RURAL HOUSEHOLDS (2015)

单位：% (%)

项目	Item	全市平均 Average	低收入户20% Low Income 20%	中低收入户20% Medium-Low Income 20%	中等收入户20% Medium Income 20%	中高收入户20% Medium-High Income 20%	高收入户20% High Income 20%
人均消费支出	**Per Capita Consumption Expenditures**	**100.0**	**100.0**	**100.0**	**100.0**	**100.0**	**100.0**
食品烟酒支出(恩格尔系数)	Expenditures of Foods, Tobacco and Liquor (Engel Coefficient)	27.7	28.4	26.4	28.0	28.5	27.1
衣着支出	Clothing Expenditures	6.3	4.9	5.7	6.3	7.1	6.9
居住支出	Housing Expenditures	29.3	32.1	32.0	27.8	27.0	28.7
生活用品及服务支出	Expenditures of Living Articles and Services	6.3	5.4	5.8	6.7	5.8	7.4
交通和通信支出	Expenditures of Transportation and Communication	13.5	10.2	12.8	14.2	15.0	14.4
教育、文化和娱乐支出	Educational, Cultural and Recreational Expenditures	7.2	8.8	7.7	7.9	6.1	6.3
医疗保健支出	Healthcare Expenditures	8.5	9.4	8.5	7.8	9.2	7.7
其他用品及服务支出	Expenditures of Other Goods and Services	1.2	0.8	1.1	1.3	1.3	1.5

8-30 农村居民家庭人均食品烟酒、衣着支出(2015年)
PER CAPITA EXPENDITURES ON FOOD, TOBACCO, LIQUOR AND CLOTHING OF RURAL HOUSEHOLDS (2015)

单位：元 (yuan)

项　　目	Item	全市平均 Average	低收入户20% Low Income 20%	中低收入户20% Medium-Low Income 20%	中等收入户20% Medium Income 20%	中高收入户20% Medium-High Income 20%	高收入户20% High Income 20%
食品烟酒支出	**Expenditures of Foods, Tobacco and Liquor**	**4372**	**3304**	**3783**	**4215**	**5013**	**5921**
食　品	Foods	2949	2444	2640	2851	3286	3712
谷　物	Grain	469	410	406	408	486	683
薯　类	Potatoes	43	42	42	42	44	41
豆　类	Beans	50	52	44	44	54	53
食用油	Edible Oil	153	142	148	152	157	171
蔬菜和食用菌	Vegetables and Edible Mushrooms	362	299	341	368	411	405
肉　类	Meat	684	576	594	694	746	848
禽　类	Poultry	84	71	74	89	85	106
水产品	Aquatic Products	119	88	104	117	141	155
蛋　类	Eggs	115	110	110	113	117	132
奶　类	Milk	206	127	183	190	298	249
干鲜瓜果类	Nuts, Fresh Melons and Fruits	403	317	351	391	458	530
糖果糕点类	Sweets and Cakes	109	82	104	100	129	137
其他食品	Other Foods	152	128	139	143	160	202
烟　酒	Tobacco and Liquor	581	423	492	580	648	817
烟　草	Tobacco	365	266	315	357	391	533
酒　类	Liquor	216	157	177	223	257	284
饮　料	Beverages	185	131	171	163	202	277
饮食服务	Catering Services	657	306	480	621	877	1115
#其他在外饮食	Other Meals at a Restaurant	561	253	383	520	755	999
衣着支出	**Clothing Expenditures**	**996**	**576**	**823**	**951**	**1249**	**1507**
衣　类	Clothes	682	381	545	637	862	1081
服　装	Garments	639	353	505	597	812	1018
服装材料	Clothing Materials	5	4	7	5	7	5
其他衣类及配件	Other Clothes and Accessories	36	23	32	33	41	56
衣着加工服务费	Service Fees for Clothing Processing	2	1	1	2	2	2
鞋　类	Footwear	314	195	278	314	387	426

8-31 农村居民家庭人均居住、生活用品及服务、交通和通信支出(2015年)

PER CAPITA EXPENDITURES ON HOUSING, LIVING ARTICLES AND SERVICES, TRANSPORTATION AND COMMUNICATION OF RURAL HOUSEHOLDS (2015)

单位：元 (yuan)

项目	Item	全市平均 Average	低收入户20% Low Income 20%	中低收入户20% Medium-Low Income 20%	中等收入户20% Medium Income 20%	中高收入户20% Medium-High Income 20%	高收入户20% High Income 20%
居住支出	**Housing Expenditures**	**4636**	**3737**	**4590**	**4176**	**4744**	**6277**
租赁房房租	House Rent	118	60	85	94	149	230
住房维修及管理	Housing Maintenance and Management	507	349	583	406	482	763
#住房装潢	Housing Decoration	259	146	272	213	275	422
住房维修	Housing Maintenance	226	194	295	162	197	296
物业管理费	Property Management Fees	5	1	5	1	8	13
水电燃料及其他	Water, Electricity, Fuels and Others	1240	1100	1118	1229	1392	1410
#水费	Water	12	8	10	12	11	17
电费	Electricity	420	399	380	405	476	454
燃料	Fuels	684	627	676	711	724	688
#生活用煤	Living Coals	528	468	512	562	570	530
自有住房折算租金	Converted Rent from Owner-Occupied Housing	2771	2228	2804	2447	2721	3874
生活用品及服务支出	**Expenditures of Living Articles and Services**	**993**	**629**	**839**	**1000**	**1015**	**1610**
家具及室内装饰品	Furniture and Interior Decorations	167	94	117	148	124	394
家具	Furniture	147	77	94	137	107	360
家具材料	Furniture Materials	6	11	8	2	5	1
室内装饰品	Interior Decorations	14	6	15	9	12	33
家用器具	Household Appliances	301	174	265	343	303	449
耐用消费品	Durable Consumer Goods	259	145	234	296	262	385
小家电	Small Appliance	42	29	31	47	41	64
家用纺织品	Household Textile	80	46	66	79	87	132
#床上用品	Bedding	59	35	46	60	69	94
家庭日用杂品	Daily Groceries for Households	278	226	248	275	296	364
个人用品	Personal Articles	136	75	110	129	180	208
家庭服务	Domestic Services	31	14	33	26	25	63
交通和通信支出	**Expenditures of Transportation and Communication**	**2140**	**1186**	**1841**	**2133**	**2638**	**3146**
交通	Transportation	1428	640	1202	1408	1859	2224
#交通工具	Vehicles	408	76	322	448	485	788
交通费	Transportation Expenses	182	115	160	165	211	286
通信	Communication	712	546	639	725	779	922
通讯工具	Communication Devices	157	111	103	188	176	227
通信服务	Communication Services	555	435	536	537	603	695

8-32 农村居民家庭人均教育文化和娱乐、医疗保健、其他用品及服务支出(2015年)

PER CAPITA EXPENDITURES ON EDUCATION, CULTURE, RECREATION, HEALTHCARE, OTHER GOODS AND SERVICES OF RURAL HOUSEHOLDS (2015)

单位：元 (yuan)

项目	Item	全市平均 Average	低收入户20% Low Income 20%	中低收入户20% Medium-Low Income 20%	中等收入户20% Medium Income 20%	中高收入户20% Medium-High Income 20%	高收入户20% High Income 20%
教育、文化和娱乐支出	**Educational, Cultural and Recreational Expenditures**	**1145**	**1023**	**1102**	**1185**	**1075**	**1379**
教育	Education	671	756	735	703	550	577
学杂费	Tuition for Compulsory Education	176	191	197	215	133	129
培训费	Training Fees	117	62	117	83	157	181
一揽子教育服务(含食宿)	A Package of Education Services (including Accommodation)	316	450	358	331	197	211
学前教育	Pre-school Education	101	109	110	127	85	66
小学教育	Primary Education	60	56	46	39	107	53
初中教育	Junior Secondary Education	57	51	93	46	49	41
高中教育	Senior Secondary Education	130	134	158	135	68	157
中专职高教育	Secondary Vocational Education	36	63	47	47	9	3
大专及以上教育	Education for Junior College and Above	241	319	252	265	171	179
成人教育	Adult Education	46	24	29	44	61	78
文化和娱乐	Cultural and Recreational Articles	474	267	367	482	525	802
文娱耐用消费品	Durable Consumer Goods for Cultural Recreation	131	80	105	163	103	222
其他文娱用品	Other Cultural and Recreational Articles	129	86	109	123	166	173
文化娱乐服务	Cultural and Recreational Services	214	101	153	196	256	407
#团体旅游	Group Tour	102	25	55	91	119	255
医疗保健支出	**Healthcare Expenditures**	**1336**	**1094**	**1216**	**1168**	**1622**	**1679**
医疗器具及药品	Medical Apparatus and Medicine	495	472	489	504	463	557
药品	Medicine	435	454	449	455	393	416
滋补保健品	Nutritious Healthcare Products	46	13	25	40	47	122
医疗卫生器具	Medical and Hygienic Apparatus	7	5	8	7	7	10
保健器具	Healthcare Apparatus	7		7	2	16	9
医疗服务	Medical Services	841	622	727	664	1159	1122
其他用品及服务支出	**Expenditures of Other Goods and Services**	**193**	**100**	**149**	**194**	**225**	**328**
其他用品	Other Goods	112	59	91	111	107	212
其他服务	Services	81	41	58	83	118	116

8-33 农村居民家庭人均粮食收支情况(2015年)
PER CAPITA GRAIN BALANCE OF RURAL HOUSEHOLDS (2015)

单位：公斤 (kg)

项目	Item	全市平均 Average	低收入户20% Low Income 20%	中低收入户20% Medium-Low Income 20%	中等收入户20% Medium Income 20%	中高收入户20% Medium-High Income 20%	高收入户20% High Income 20%
年内粮食收入实物量	**Grain Collected in the Year**	**226.9**	**313.3**	**263.9**	**195.9**	**192.9**	**150.8**
家庭经营生产	Household-based Production	139.6	227.0	174.4	113.0	101.8	63.8
购买	Purchased	87.3	86.3	89.5	82.9	91.1	87.0
年内粮食消费量	**Grain Consumed in the Year**	**105.6**	**107.7**	**108.5**	**99.0**	**108.6**	**104.5**
#稻谷	Rice	33.4	32.7	34.4	32.7	33.2	34.2
小麦	Wheat	57.3	58.3	60.3	52.1	60.3	55.6
年内粮食出售量	**Grain Sold in the Year**	**99.6**	**143.5**	**151.3**	**83.7**	**61.5**	**42.5**
出售谷物	Cereal Sold	99.1	143.5	151.2	81.9	61.5	42.3
#小麦	Wheat	19.8	23.8	28.2	16.3	16.4	12.4

8-34 农村居民家庭主要食品人均消费量(2015年)
PER CAPITA CONSUMPTION OF MAJOR FOODS OF RURAL HOUSEHOLDS (2015)

单位：公斤 (kg)

项目	Item	全市平均 Average	低收入户20% Low Income 20%	中低收入户20% Medium-Low Income 20%	中等收入户20% Medium Income 20%	中高收入户20% Medium-High Income 20%	高收入户20% High Income 20%
粮食	Grain	105.6	107.7	108.5	99.0	108.6	104.5
豆类	Beans	7.4	7.8	6.8	6.8	7.9	8.0
蔬菜及菜制品	Vegetables and Vegetable Products	91.0	84.8	89.6	89.8	96.5	95.6
植物油	Vegetable Oil	9.4	9.3	9.3	9.5	9.0	10.0
猪肉	Pork	15.3	13.4	14.6	15.7	16.2	16.9
牛羊肉	Beef and Mutton	4.1	3.2	3.2	4.0	4.6	5.7
禽类	Poultry	4.2	3.7	4.0	4.4	4.2	4.8
蛋类及其制品	Eggs and Egg Products	11.7	11.3	11.3	11.6	11.9	12.8
奶及奶制品	Milk and Dairy Products	13.9	10.7	13.2	13.5	15.4	17.6
水产品	Aquatic Products	5.6	4.6	5.1	5.6	6.3	6.8
食糖	Sugar	1.0	1.1	1.1	0.9	1.0	1.0
酒类	Liquor	17.4	15.7	15.1	18.9	17.8	20.4
茶叶	Tea	0.5	0.4	0.5	0.5	0.5	0.7
干鲜瓜果类	Nuts, Fresh Melons and Fruits	52.1	45.5	48.7	50.5	54.8	63.7

8-35 农村居民家庭每百户主要耐用消费品拥有量(1985-2015年)
NUMBER OF MAIN DURABLE CONSUMER GOODS PER 100 RURAL HOUSEHOLDS (1985-2015)

年份 Year	移动电话 (部) Mobile Phones (unit)	空调机 (台) Air Conditioners (unit)	彩色电视机 (台) Color TV Sets (unit)	家用计算机 (台) Computers (unit)	照相机 (架) Cameras (unit)	洗衣机 (台) Washing Machines (unit)	电冰箱 (台) Refrigerators (unit)	家用汽车 (辆) Household Cars (unit)
1985			7		2	23	2	
1986			12		4	39	5	
1987			15		5	48	9	
1988			20		7	56	14	
1989			25		8	61	19	
1990			29		8	63	23	
1991			42		11	69	36	
1992			46		14	73	40	
1993			56		15	76	47	
1994		1	65		17	80	53	
1995		2	74		21	81	63	
1996		2	79		21	83	67	
1997		3	85		25	84	72	
1998		5	92		26	85	75	
1999		9	101		29	86	81	
2000	14	20	107	7	26	85	84	3
2001	30	27	112	12	29	91	86	5
2002	52	35	116	16	32	94	91	6
2003	77	39	116	22	32	94	94	6
2004	102	47	119	27	35	96	96	8
2005	139	63	129	36	37	97	100	10
2006	161	72	131	41	38	97	100	10
2007	182	78	134	46	37	99	104	11
2008	201	89	137	52	39	101	104	12
2009	212	98	138	58	42	101	105	12
2010	224	107	139	64	42	103	107	16
2011	231	108	134	63	37	99	104	19
2012	235	113	136	67	37	99	103	21
2013	221	123	132	74	32	95	102	34
2014	222	127	132	75	32	97	103	35
2015	230	118	131	69	21	90	95	32

8-36 农村居民家庭每百户主要耐用消费品拥有量(2015年)
NUMBER OF MAIN DURABLE CONSUMER GOODS PER 100 RURAL HOUSEHOLDS (2015)

项目	Item	全市平均 Average	低收入户20% Low Income 20%	中低收入户20% Low-Medium Income 20%	中等收入户20% Medium Income 20%	中高收入户20% Medium-High Income 20%	高收入户20% High Income 20%
家用汽车 （辆）	Household Cars (unit)	32	22	33	35	38	33
摩托车 （辆）	Motorcycles (unit)	12	10	14	15	12	9
助力车 （台）	Powered Bicycles (unit)	64	62	77	71	60	52
洗衣机 （台）	Washing Machines (unit)	90	92	100	93	86	81
电冰箱（柜） （台）	Refrigerators (unit)	95	100	101	97	90	85
微波炉 （台）	Microwave Ovens (unit)	50	37	52	53	55	56
彩色电视机 （台）	Color TV Sets (unit)	131	125	139	134	132	125
#接入有线电视网络的电视机 （台）	TV Sets Accessed to Cable TV Network (unit)	117	116	126	114	121	110
空　调 （台）	Air Conditioners (unit)	118	90	121	120	130	131
热水器 （台）	Water Heaters (unit)	93	90	101	96	88	88
消毒碗柜 （台）	Disinfection Cabinets (unit)	1	1	2	1	1	2
洗碗机 （台）	Dishwashers (unit)	1	1	1	1		1
移动电话 （部）	Mobile Phones (unit)	230	219	244	241	227	218
#接入互联网的移动电话 （部）	Mobile Phones Accessed to the Internet (unit)	99	82	99	109	103	105
计算机 （台）	Computers (unit)	69	56	71	72	74	74
#接入互联网的计算机 （台）	Computers Accessed to the Internet (unit)	60	49	56	64	64	65
摄像机 （台）	Video Cameras (unit)	3	1	2	3	5	3
照相机 （台）	Cameras (unit)	21	12	17	20	28	26
中高档乐器 （架）	Musical Instruments of Middle and High-grade (set)	1	1	2	2	1	1
健身器材 （台）	Fitness Equipment (set)	2	1	2	3	3	4
组合音响 （套）	Audio Systems (set)	6	6	6	7	7	6

主要统计指标解释

按照国家统计局要求，自2015年起，我市按照改革后的新口径发布全市和分城乡的居民收支数据。与老口径相比，新口径的差异主要体现在三个方面：一是按照国家城乡划分标准，将城镇地区的村委会由原来的农村划入城镇进行统计；二是对居民收支指标口径进行了调整，将反映居民收入的核心指标由原来的城镇居民“人均可支配收入”和农村居民“人均纯收入”统一为“人均可支配收入”；三是在分城乡的居民收支数据基础上，增加了全体居民的人均可支配收入、人均消费支出数据。

可支配收入 指调查户在调查期内获得的、可用于最终消费支出和储蓄的总和，即调查户可以用来自由支配的收入。可支配收入既包括现金，也包括实物收入。按照收入的来源，可支配收入包含四项，分别为：工资性收入、经营净收入、财产净收入和转移净收入。计算公式为：

可支配收入＝工资性收入+经营净收入+财产净收入+转移净收入

其中：经营净收入=经营收入-经营费用-生产性固定资产折旧-生产税

财产净收入=财产性收入-财产性支出

转移净收入=转移性收入-转移性支出。

工资性收入 指就业人员通过各种途径得到的全部劳动报酬和各种福利，包括受雇于单位或个人、从事各种自由职业、兼职和零星劳动得到的全部劳动报酬和福利。

工资 指就业人员通过劳动从单位或雇主获取的各种现金报酬。

实物福利 指单位或雇主免费或低价提供给员工的各种实物产品和服务折价。

其他 指就业人员获取的、除工资以外的其他现金劳动报酬以及单位缴纳的各种社会保障费。

经营净收入 指住户或住户成员从事生产经营活动所获得的净收入，是全部经营收入中扣除经营费用、生产性固定资产折旧和生产税之后得到的净收入。计算公式为：

经营净收入=经营收入-经营费用-生产性固定资产折旧-生产税

财产净收入 指住户或住户成员将其所拥有的金融资产、住房等非金融资产和自然资源交由其他机构单位、住户或个人支配而获得的回报并扣除相关的费用之后得到的净收入。财产净收入不包括转让资产所有权的溢价所得，计入“非收入所得”。

红利收入 指住户或个人作为股东将其资金交由公司支配或处置而有权获得的收益。包括股票发行公司按入股数量定期分配的股息、年终分红以及从集体财产入股或其他投资分配得到的股息和红利。股票买卖结算后获得的收益（含亏损）不包含在内，计入“非收入所得”。

储蓄性保险净收益 指住户或住户成员参加商业性的储蓄性保险，扣除缴纳的保险本金及相关费用后所获得的保险净收益。不包括保险责任人对保险受益人给予的保险理赔收入。

转移性收入 指国家、单位、社会团体对住户的各种经常性转移支付和住户之间的经常性收入转移。包括养老金或退休金、社会救济和补助、政策性生产补贴、政策性生活补贴、救灾款、经常性捐赠和赔偿、报销医疗费、住户之间的赡养收入，以及本住户非常住成员寄回带回的收入等。转移性收入不包括住户之间的实物馈赠。

其他经常转移收入 指住户从除上述各项转移性收入以外得到的其他经常性转移收入。如经常性捐赠收入、经常性赔偿收入、失业保险金、亲友搭伙费等。

转移净收入 指国家、单位、社会团体对住户的各种经常性转移支付和住户之间的经常性收入转移，在扣减调查户对国家、单位、住户或者个人的经常性或义务性转移支付后的净收入。

计算公式为：转移净收入=转移性收入-转移性支出。

转移性支出 指调查户对国家、单位、住户或个人的经常性或义务性转移支付。包括缴纳的税款、各项社会保障支出、赡养支出、经常性捐赠和赔偿支出以及其他经常转移支出等。

出售资产所得 指调查户出售家庭财物所得到的收入。由于出售财物是家庭财产从实物形态转为货币形态，家庭财产总量不变，因此不计入可支配收入中。

记账补贴 指调查户因承担记账工作从统计部门、工作单位和其他途径所得到的现金和实物折价收入。

借贷性所得 指家庭资产不发生增减的周转性非生产经营性收入。包括提取银行存款、借入款、收回借出款等。

家庭总支出 指包括借贷性支出的全部实际支出。包括消费支出、生产经营费用支出、财产性支出、转移性支出、部分商业保险支出、购置资产及非经常性转移支出、借贷性支出。

消费支出 指住户用于满足家庭日常生活消费需要的全部支出，包括用于消费品的支出和用于服务性消费的支出。根据用途不同，消费支出可划分为食品烟酒、衣着、居住、生活用品及服务、交通和通信、教育文化娱乐、医疗保健、其他用品及服务八大类。根据来源不同，消费支出可划分为现金消费支出、实物消费支出（含自产自用、来自单位或雇主、来自政府和其他社会组织）。

生产经营费用支出 包括农业生产经营费用和非农业生产经营费用。

财产性支出 指家庭购买或维护财产所支付的利息等有关费用。

转移性支出 指调查户对国家、单位、住户或个人的经常性或义务性转移支付。包括缴纳的税款、各项社会保障支出、赡养支出、经常性捐赠和赔偿支出以及其他经常转移支出等。

部分商业保险支出 包括意外伤害保险、商业医疗保险（含大病保险）、其他非储蓄性商业保险、其他储蓄性商业保险。

购置资产及非经常性转移支出 购置资产支出包括建造住房、购买住房的全部支出，以及购建生产性固定资产支出；非经常性转移支出包括博采支出、婚丧嫁娶（礼金、宴请等）支出、一次性赔偿支出、一次性馈赠支出等。

借贷性支出 指包括所有权没有变化的周转性非生产经营性支付，如存入储蓄款、借出款；资金归还，如归还借款、归还各类贷款等。

平均每一劳动力负担人口 是由调查户常住人口除以整半劳动力计算得到的。计算公式为：

$$平均每一劳动力负担人口=\frac{调查户常住人口}{整半劳动力}$$

农村居民家庭整半劳动力 指农村常住居民家庭成员中有劳动能力并经常参加实际劳动的人员。是生产的基本要素指标之一，是发展生产增加农民家庭收入的重要源泉。按规定，农村男18周岁至50周岁、女18周岁至45周岁为整劳动力；男16周岁至17周岁、51周岁到60周岁，女16周岁到17周岁、46周岁至55周岁为半劳动力。农民家庭整半劳动力既包括在上述规定劳动年龄内和在劳动年龄以外有劳动能力并经常参加实际劳动的男女整半劳动力，也包括农民家庭常住人员中属于职工的劳动力。但不包括在劳动年龄内已丧失劳动能力的人员。

现住房总建筑面积 指调查户现住房的总建筑面积。现住房计算总建筑面积时以房屋产权证或租赁证为准，建筑面积也可按使用面积 × 1.333计算得出。应扣除住房中专门用于出租的建筑面积。

恩格尔系数 随着家庭和个人收入增加，收入中用于食品方面的支出比例将逐渐减小，这一定律被称为恩格尔定律，反映这一定律的系数被称为恩格尔系数。计算公式为：

$$恩格尔系数=\frac{食品支出总额}{家庭或个人消费支出总额}\times 100\%$$

Explanatory Notes on Main Statistical Indicators

According to requirements of National Bureau of Statistics, since 2015, Beijing has started to issue data on income and expense of residents in the city and residents in urban and rural areas according to new standards after the reform. As compared with former standards, the new standards mainly show differences in the following 3 aspects: first, according to national standards on division of urban and rural areas, village committees in urban areas that were classified into rural areas are now classified into urban areas; second, standards on resident income and expense indicators are adjusted. Core indicators reflecting resident income are unified from original "per capita disposable income" of urban residents and "per capita net income" of rural residents to "per capita disposable income"; third, based on data on resident income and expense in urban and rural areas, data on per capita disposable income and per capita consumption expense of residents in Beijing are added.

Disposable Income refers to the total income at the disposal of sampled households gained during the survey, which can be used for final consumption expenditures and savings. Disposable income includes cash and income in kind. By income source, disposable income can be divided into 4 types, namely wage income, net business income, net property income and net transfer income. The following formula is used:

Disposable Income = wage income + net business income + net property income + net transfer income

Of which: Net business income = business income - business expense - depreciation of productive fixed assets - production tax

Net property income = property income - property expenditure

Net transfer income = transfer income - transfer expenditure

Wage Income refers to all payments of labour and various welfares earned by employed persons through all channels, including all payments of labour and welfare gained from institutional or individual employers, various freelance work, part-time job, and scattered work.

Wages refer to all cash rewards received by an employee from institutional or individual employer.

Physical Welfare refers to various physical products and service discounts provided by an institutional or individual employer to the employee for free or at a low price.

Other Income from Work refers to other cash compensation gained by an employed person except wages and various social security benefits paid by the employer.

Net Business Income refers to the net income of a family or family members from productive and operating activities. It is the net income of all operating income deducting business cost, depreciation of productive fixed assets and production tax. The following formula is used:

Net business income = business income - business cost - depreciation of productive fixed assets - production tax

Net Property Income refers to the net income of a family or family members earned by deducting relevant expenses from returns of their financial assets, non-financial assets (such as house) and natural resource delivered to other institutions, families or individuals for management. Net property income does not include income from premium of property ownership transfer and it shall be regarded as "non-revenue proceeds".

Dividend Income refers to legal benefits of households or individuals who deliver their capitals as shareholders to the company for management or disposal. It includes stock dividend regularly distributed by stock issuance company according to share amount, annual bonus and stock dividend and bonus gained from shares in collective properties or other investments. Benefits (including losses) gained from stock trading settlement are not included and shall be regarded as "non-revenue proceeds".

Net Proceeds from Saving Insurance refer to the net proceeds of insurance gained by households or members for participating in commercial saving insurance after the paid insurance principal and relevant fees are deducted, excluding the income of insurance claim paid by the responsible person to insurance beneficiary.

Transfer Income refers to various recurrent transfer payment from the nation, institutions and social groups to households, along with recurrent income transfer among households, including retirement pension, social relief and allowance, policy production subsidiary, policy living subsidiary, disaster relief fund, recurrent donation and compensations, medical expense reimbursement, alimony income among households and income mailed or brought by non-permanent members of such household, etc. Transfer income does not include physical donation among households.

Other Recurrent Transfer Income refers to other recurrent transfer income of households excluding the various transfer income stated above. It includes recurrent donation income, recurrent compensation income, unemployment insurance benefits and relative boarding expense, etc.

Net Transfer Income refers to net income after deducting recurrent or compulsory transfer payment of sampled households to the nation, institutions, households or individuals from various recurrent transfer payments by the nation, institutions, social groups to households and recurrent income transfer among households.

Net Transfer Income the following formula is used: Net transfer income = transfer income - transfer expenditure

Transfer Expenditure refers to the recurrent or

compulsory transfer payment made by the sampled households to the nation, institutions, households or individuals, including tax payment, various social security expenditures, alimony expenditure, recurrent donation and compensation expenditure and other recurrent transfer expenditure, etc.

Income from Asset Sales refers to the income received by the sampled household for selling any household properties. As the sale of household property is a conversion of physical form of household property to monetary form, and the total amount of household properties remains unchanged, the income from selling property is not included in the disposable income.

Account Subsidy refers to the cash paid by authorities of statistics, employers and other channels to the sampled household for its responsibility of accounts keeping, excluding any allowance in kind.

Loan Proceeds refer to the non-productive and non-operating income which causes no change in the amount of household asset, including withdrawal of bank deposits, borrowings and lending repaid, etc.

Total Household Expenditures refer to all actual expenditures including credit expenditures. It includes consumption expenditure, production and operation expenditure, properties expenditure, transfer expenditure, partial commercial insurance expenditure, property purchase and non-recurrent transfer expenditure, and loan expenditure.

Consumption Expenditure refers to total expenditures of households for consumption in daily life, including expenditures on consumer goods and services. By usage, it includes 8 categories, i.e. expenditures on food, tobacco and liquor, clothing, housing, living articles and services, transportation and communication, educational, cultural and recreational services, healthcare and medical services, and other goods and services. By source, it includes cash consumption and physical consumption (including self-produced and self-used products and those from institutions or employers, government and other social organizations).

Production and Operation Expenditure includes expenditure for agricultural production and operation and for non-agricultural production and operation.

Property Expenditure refers to relevant costs including interest paid by the sampled households for purchasing or maintaining properties.

Transfer Expenditure refers to the recurrent or compulsory transfer payment made by the sampled households to the nation, institutions, households or individuals, including tax payment, various social security expenditures, alimony expenditure, recurrent donation and compensation expenditure and other recurrent transfer expenditure, etc.

Partial Commercial Insurance Expenditure includes accident insurance, commercial medical insurance (including critical illness insurance), other non-saving commercial insurance and other saving commercial insurance.

Expenditures for Asset Purchase and Non-recurrent Transfer Payment Asset purchase expenditure refers to all expenditures for building and purchasing houses and expenditure on purchase and construction of productive fixed assets; non-recurrent transfer expenditure includes gaming expense, weddings and funerals (cash gift and entertaining, etc.) expense, lump-sum compensation and lump-sum gifting, etc.

Loan Expenditure refers to the revolving non-productive and non-operating expenditure which causes no change in ownership, including saving deposits, borrowings; capitals repayment, such as repayment of borrowings and various loans, etc.

Dependents Per Labour Force refers to the number of permanent population in the sampled household divided by the number of full/semi labourers. The following formula is used:

Dependents Per Laborer = Number of Permanent Population in the Sampled Households / Number of Full/Semi laborers

Full/Semi Labour Force in Rural Households refers to persons among permanent family members in rural households who are capable of working and work frequently. This is one of the indicators for basic production elements, and an important source for production development and increase of farmer's household income. As stated in regulations, rural males aged 18-50 and females aged 18-45 are full labours. Males aged 16-17 and 51-60 and females aged 16-17 and 46-55 are semi labor force. Full/Semi Labour Force in Rural Households includes the male and female full/semi labour force within the above-mentioned range age as well as those beyond such range of ages who are capable of working and work frequently; also include labourers among permanent members in rural households who are employees. But it excludes persons who are within the range of labour age but incapable of working.

Total Building Area of Current Houses refers to the total building area of house resided by the surveyed households, which is calculated on the basis of the property ownership certificate or lease certificate. The building area can also be calculated as the usable floor space multiplied by 1.333, which shall deduct the building area of the house specially used for lease.

Engel's Coefficient Along with the increase in household and personal income, a gradually smaller proportion of income is used for purchase of food. This law is called Engel's law, and the coefficient reflecting such law is called Engel's Coefficient. The following formula is used:

$$\text{Engels Coefficient} = \frac{\text{expenditure on food}}{\text{total consumption expenditure}} \times 100\%$$

09

北京统计年鉴2016　BEIJING STATISTICAL YEARBOOK

城市公用事业
PUBLIC UTILITIES

简要说明

一、本章资料的主要内容

本章资料反映北京市城市公用事业的综合水平，主要内容包括四部分：

1. 历年城市公用事业基本情况；
2. 水、气、热等供应及消费情况；
3. 城市公交、出租车情况；
4. 市政主要设施情况。

二、本章资料的数据来源

本章城市供热、供气情况由北京市市政市容管理委员会提供；自来水情况由北京市水务局提供；城市公交、出租车情况由北京市交通委员会提供；道路及市政主要设施情况由北京市交通委员会、北京市公安交通管理局、北京市路灯管理中心提供。

Brief Introduction

I. Main Content

Statistics in this chapter show the overall level of urban public utilities in Beijing, which consist of four parts:

1. Basic statistics for urban public utilities in previous years;
2. Water, gas and heating supply and consumption;
3. Urban public transport and taxi services;
4. Main public facilities.

II. Source of Data

Data on urban heating and gas supply were provided by Beijing Municipal Commission of City Administration and Environment; data on tap water were provided by Beijing Water Authority; data on urban public transport and taxi services were provided by Beijing Municipal Commission of Transport; data on roads and main public facilities were provided by Beijing Municipal Commission of Transport, Beijing Traffic Management Bureau and Street Lighting Administration Center Of Beijing.

9-1 公路、城市道路及桥梁(1978-2015年)
HIGHWAYS, URBAN ROADS AND BRIDGES (1978-2015)

年份 Year	境内道路总里程(公里) Total Length of Highways and Roads (km)	公路里程(公里) Total Length of Highways (km)	#高速公路 Express-ways	城市道路里程(公里) Length of Urban Roads (km)	#快速路 Rapid Roads	#主干路 Trunk Roads	城市道路面积(万平方米) Area of Urban Roads (10000 sq.m)	城市道路桥梁(座) Number of Bridges (unit)	#立交桥 Overpasses
1978		6562		2078			1611	351	2
1979		7278		2131			1618	348	2
1980		7487		2185			1664	351	6
1981		7566		2234			1742	342	8
1982		7683		2671			2098	408	9
1983		8058		2820			2265	431	10
1984		8271		2928			2393	440	11
1985		8482		2979			2485	460	16
1986		8995		3038			2559	479	16
1987		9103		3087			2631	510	22
1988		9124		3151			2701	522	23
1989		9371		3235			2815	552	27
1990		9648	35	3276			2905	562	33
1991		10259	63	3308			3134	569	40
1992		10827	71	3189			3212	595	55
1993		11260	99	3285			3398	596	64
1994		11532	112	3316			3470	616	75
1995		11811	113	3194			3494	582	84
1996		12084	114	3665			3807	646	133
1997		12306	144	3637			4061	693	140
1998		12498	190	3721			4214	715	138
1999		12825	230	3753			4353	787	141
2000		13600	268	4126			4921	834	149
2001		13891	335	4312			6062	891	160
2002		14359	463	5444			7645	1051	180
2003	18942	14453	499	3055			5345	848	119
2004	19010	14630	525	4067	219	834	6417	949	271
2005	19015	14696	548	4073	239	922	7437	964	304
2006	25377	20503	625	4419	232	955	7258	1079	376
2007	25765	20754	628	4460	236	960	7632	1230	377
2008	26921	20340	777	6186	242	755	8941	1738	381
2009	27436	20755	884	6247	242	805	9179	1765	393
2010	27907	21114	903	6355	263	874	9395	1855	411
2011	28446	21347	912	6258	263	861	9164	1885	418
2012	28585	21492	923	6271	263	865	9236	1950	413
2013	28808	21673	923	6295	269	953	9611	1998	414
2014	29209	21849	982	6426	383	965	10002	2042	422
2015	29069	21885	982	6423	383	969	10029	2069	427

注：1. 境内道路总里程为全市道路和公路里程之和(剔除道路、公路交叉重复部分)。
2. 道路及桥梁1978年-1981年统计范围为城八区及通县；1982年-2002年统计范围为城八区及14个县城；2003年-2010年统计范围为城八区和北京经济技术开发区。2011年起城市道路及其附属设施统计范围为城六区。
3. 2008年道路数据为北京市城市道路普查数据。

资料来源：北京市交通委员会。

Note: a) Total length of highways and roads means the sum of roads and highways across the city (excluding intersections of roads and highways)
b) Statistics for roads and bridges covered 8 urban districts and Tongzhou County in 1978-1981; the coverage was extended to 8 urban districts and 14 counties in 1982-2002; in 2003-2010, the coverage included 8 central urban districts and Beijing Economic-Technological Development Zone; since 2011, statistics for urban roads and the auxiliary facilities have been confined to 6 urban districts.
c) Statistics for roads and highways in 2008 were from Beijing Urban Road Census.

Source: Beijing Municipal Commission of Transport.

9-2 城市公共交通(1978-2015年)

年 份 Year	公共交通运营线路条数(条) Number of Operating Public Transport Routes (line)	公共电汽车 Buses and Trolley Buses	轨道交通 Rail Transit	公共交通运营线路长度(公里) Length of Operating Public Transport Lines (km)	公共电汽车 Buses and Trolley Buses	轨道交通 Rail Transit	公共交通运营车辆(辆) Number of Operating Public Transport Vehicles in Operation (vehicle)
1978	119	118	1	1427	1403	24	2743
1979	121	120	1	1469	1446	24	2997
1980	123	122	1	1479	1455	24	3113
1981	127	126	1	1525	1501	24	3375
1982	139	138	1	1678	1654	24	3620
1983	151	150	1	1820	1797	24	3907
1984	164	162	2	1939	1899	40	4221
1985	191	189	2	2312	2272	40	4583
1986	200	198	2	2574	2534	40	4576
1987	194	192	2	2382	2342	40	4776
1988	199	197	2	2445	2405	40	4787
1989	207	205	2	2525	2485	40	4890
1990	216	214	2	2654	2614	40	5160
1991	223	221	2	2755	2715	40	5182
1992	262	260	2	3379	3338	42	5223
1993	268	266	2	3532	3491	42	5213
1994	284	282	2	4117	4075	42	5319
1995	300	298	2	4538	4497	42	5367
1996	399	397	2	7317	7276	42	6828
1997	667	665	2	14011	13969	42	10479
1998	690	688	2	14929	14888	42	10819
1999	750	748	2	16566	16513	54	12509
2000	682	680	2	15639	15585	54	14191
2001	555	553	2	13180	13126	54	15420
2002	592	589	3	15835	15760	75	17580
2003	620	616	4	16131	16017	114	17445
2004	621	617	4	15247	15133	114	19343
2005	626	622	4	18328	18214	114	19471
2006	624	620	4	18582	18468	114	20489
2007	649	644	5	17495	17353	142	20525
2008	679	671	8	18057	17857	200	23221
2009	701	692	9	18498	18270	228	23730
2010	727	713	14	19079	18743	336	24011
2011	764	749	15	19832	19460	372	24478
2012	795	779	16	19989	19547	442	25831
2013	830	813	17	20153	19688	465	27590
2014	895	877	18	20776	20249	527	28331
2015	894	876	18	20740	20186	554	28311

注：自2006年5月1日起，公共电汽车、轨道交通售票采取刷卡方式，并陆续进行了票制票价改革，客运量统计口径方法相应调整，因此与历史数据不可比。

资料来源：本表2005年及以后数据来源于北京市交通委员会。

URBAN PUBLIC TRANSPORT (1978-2015)

		公共交通			出租小汽车 Taxis Service	
公共电汽车 Buses and Trolley Buses	轨道交通 Rail Transit	客运量（万人次） Passengers Carried by Public Transport (10000 person-times)	公共电汽车 Buses and Trolley Buses	轨道交通 Rail Transit	运营车辆（辆） Operating Vehicles (vehicle)	客运量（万人次） Passenger Traffic (10000 persons)
2627	116	172559	169465	3094		
2889	108	205703	200918	4785		
3001	112	236998	231477	5521		
3259	116	263944	257478	6466		
3500	120	284175	276922	7253		
3753	154	302501	294301	8200		
4037	184	324437	314132	10305		
4398	185	335227	321264	13963		
4371	205	328770	312990	15780		
4524	252	330417	311190	19227		
4535	252	337094	306396	30698		
4587	303	306435	275383	31052		
4857	303	334673	296495	38178		
4877	305	344525	307438	37087		
4900	323	348770	305959	42811		
4890	323	335378	286268	49110		
4984	335	353289	299993	53296		
4984	383	371579	315777	55802		
6427	401	349847	305433	44414		
10044	435	391182	346676	44507		
10382	437	418825	372494	46331		
12018	491	426706	378483	48223		
13604	587	406691	363213	43478		
14803	617	449720	402850	46870		
16939	641	492122	443880	48242		
16753	692	426628	379380	47248		
18451	892	499830	439130	60700		
18503	968	517769	449793	67976	66000	65000
19522	967	468225	397919	70306	66646	64121
19395	1130	488138	422645	65493	66646	64111
21507	1714	592523	470863	121660	66646	69000
21716	2014	658785	516517	142268	66646	68000
21548	2463	689788	505144	184645	66646	69000
21628	2850	722552	503272	219280	66646	69600
22146	3685	761578	515416	246162	66646	69862
23592	3998	804775	484306	320469	67046	69946
23667	4664	815849	477180	338668	67546	66828
23287	5024	738384	406003	332381	68284	58750

Note: Since May 1, 2006, buses, trolley buses and rail transit tickets were sold by card swiping. Ticket system and prices were also reformed successively. The statistical coverage and methods for passenger traffic were adjusted accordingly, so these figures were incomparable with historical data.

Source: Since 2005, data in this table were provided by Beijing Municipal Commission of Transport.

9-3 城市供水、供气及供热(1978-2015年)
URBAN WATER SUPPLY, GAS SUPPLY AND HEAT SUPPLY (1978-2015)

年 份 Year	全市集中供热管道长度(公里) Total Length of Pipelines for Centralized Heating (km)	全市集中供热面积(万平方米) Centralized Heating Area in Beijing (10000 sq.m)	#住 宅 Residence	煤 气销售量(万立方米) Sales Volume of Coal Gas (10000 cu.m)	液化石油气销 售 量(吨) Sales Volume of Liquefied Petroleum Gas (ton)	天然气销售量(万立方米) Sales Volume of Natural Gas (10000 cu.m)
1978				32687	97255	
1979				32113	114350	
1980				34935	128990	
1981				36309	134771	
1982				36748	149805	
1983				37319	150058	
1984				38710	156421	
1985				41678	169720	
1986				44542	182239	
1987				47594	178205	
1988				49595	177112	287
1989				56056	175814	1805
1990		3702		59508	172688	3544
1991		4560		66111	174326	5062
1992		5281		73615	174694	6040
1993		5730		80163	177065	6702
1994		7056		80409	173105	7623
1995		7537		85201	177637	11003
1996		7838		88356	185304	13504
1997		8399		76429	172879	16565
1998		9102		68998	174464	32619
1999		9992		61846	188450	64833
2000		10860		46719	190571	95919
2001		14729		33960	182188	150585
2002		18172		21077	234680	176504
2003		25108		23991	311657	208837
2004		28150	18962	17714	431660	250326
2005	6272	31736	22218	16776	356551	294279
2006	7013	34977	23158	9763	415268	389202
2007	10424	37203	23697		319631	441327
2008	11948	42501	26738		289576	578626
2009	12156	44240	27694		332693	645356
2010	12224	46715	32305		299392	677009
2011	11734	50794	34563		394437	726229
2012	11031	52555	35104		379371	883385
2013	11192	54591	36806		453546	956852
2014	12038	56786	38085		531556	1088999
2015	12207	58465	39031		523391	1400441

注：1. 2006年6月开始全市煤气家庭用户已全部置换为天然气用户，因此2007年以后煤气销售量无数据。
2. 自2012年起，自来水数据口径调整为城镇公共供水。
资料来源：北京市市政市容管理委员会、北京市水务局。
Note: a) Since June 2006, all households using coal gas have started to use natual gas. Therefore, there are no data on coal gas sales volume since 2007
b) Since 2012, Relevant figures of tap water were changed to cover urban public water supply.
Source: Beijing Municipal Commission of City Administration and Environment and Beijing Water Authority.

9-3 续表 Continued

年 份 Year	居 民 燃气用户 (万户) Gas Using Households (10000 households)	自来水综合 生产能力 (万立方米/日) Gereral Production Capacity of Tap Water (10000 cu.m/day)	自来水供水 管线长度 (公里) Length of Tap Water Supply Pipelines (km)	自 来 水 销售总量 (万立方米) Total Sales Volume of Tap Water (10000 cu.m)
1978	65.2	134	2926	32664
1979	76.7	151	3083	36232
1980	80.3	163	3272	38933
1981	85.1	167	3435	41634
1982	88.0	164	4216	41136
1983	90.9	166	4452	42778
1984	96.9	167	4622	43716
1985	102.3	176	4927	45601
1986	153.6	188	5079	46695
1987	160.9	185	5257	47680
1988	165.4	189	5550	50059
1989	172.6	206	5647	50145
1990	176.1	215	5770	52718
1991	184.7	221	5947	56107
1992	192.4	226	6130	58704
1993	197.5	234	6367	60794
1994	210.3	242	6727	67977
1995	219.8	264	6907	67877
1996	188.1	266	6907	69684
1997	243.0	302	6339	79046
1998	254.4	330	6989	75969
1999	259.8	357	7179	78098
2000	291.9	367	7610	75364
2001	310.0	371	8146	69807
2002	336.4	428	8555	79322
2003	406.0	429	9278	71583
2004	438.6	399	9981	82986
2005	462.6	348	9831	71600
2006	540.2	373	11899	74970
2007	556.4	391	13133	77778
2008	591.0	404	14118	80792
2009	600.0	424	14791	86881
2010	634.2	445	16144	89185
2011	644.1	473	16963	94622
2012	713.5	411	14029	93826
2013	737.4	444	14495	98178
2014	846.0	503	14994	103402
2015	885.7	506	15421	103950

9-4 全市集中供热
CENTRALIZED HEATING SUPPLY

项目	Item	2015	2014	2015年为2014年% 2015 as % of 2014
供热面积 （万平方米）	**Total Area of Heating Supply (10000 sq.m)**	**58465**	**56786**	**103.0**
#住宅	Residence	39031	38085	102.5
供热能力 （兆瓦）	**Heating Supply Capacity (megawatt)**	**41451**	**40445**	**102.5**
热电厂供热	Heating from Thermal Power Plants	7590	7509	101.1
锅炉房供热	Heating from Boiler Houses	33861	32936	102.8
供热总量 （万吉焦）	**Total Heating Supply (10000 giga joules)**	**35857**	**35300**	**101.6**
热电厂供热	Heating from Thermal Power Plants	5551	5518	100.6
锅炉房供热	Heating from Boiler Houses	30306	29782	101.8
供热管道长度 （公里）	**Length of Pipelines (km)**	**12207**	**12038**	**101.4**

资料来源：北京市市政市容管理委员会。
Source: Beijing Municipal Commission of City Administration and Environment.

9-5 液化石油气及天然气
LIQUEFIED PETROLEUM GAS AND NATURAL GAS

项目	Item	2015	2014	2015年为2014年% 2015 as % of 2014
液化石油气	**Liquefied Petroleum Gas**			
供气总量 (吨)	Gas Supply (ton)	576306	546293	105.5
销售气量 (吨)	Gas Sales (ton)	523391	531556	98.5
#家庭用量 (吨)	Domestic Consumption (ton)	189188	234779	80.6
家庭用户 (万户)	Domestic Consumers (10000 households)	296.9	278.2	106.7
天然气	**Natural Gas**			
供气总量 (万立方米)	Gas Supply (10000 cu.m)	1417557	1136874	124.7
销售气量 (万立方米)	Gas Sales (10000 cu.m)	1400441	1088999	128.6
#家庭用量 (万立方米)	Domestic Consumption (10000 cu.m)	137199	126503	108.5
家庭用户 (万户)	Domestic Consumers (10000 households)	588.8	567.8	103.7
居民燃气用户 (万户)	**Household Gas Users (10000 households)**	**885.7**	**846.0**	**104.7**

注：本表天然气、液化石油气用量中包含燕山石化用气量。
资料来源：北京市市政市容管理委员会、中国石化集团北京燕山石化有限公司。
Note: Data on natural gas consumption and liquefied petroleum gas consumption in this table include the consumption of Yanshan Petrochemical.
Source: Beijing Municipal Commission of City Administration and Environment, and SINOPEC Beijing Yanshan Petrochemical Co., Ltd.

9-6 自来水及自备水源
TAP WATER AND SELF-PROVIDED SOURCES OF WATER

项目		Item		2015	2014
自来水		**Tap Water**			
综合生产能力	(万立方米/日)	General Production Capacity	(10000cu.m/day)	506.0	502.9
供水管道长度	(公里)	Length of Water Supply Pipelines	(km)	15421	14994
销售总量	(万立方米)	Total Sales Volume	(10000 cu.m)	103950	103402
#生产运营用	(万立方米)	For Production Use	(10000 cu.m)	12831	12661
公共服务用	(万立方米)	For Public Service Use	(10000 cu.m)	37145	37865
居民家庭用	(万立方米)	For Domestic Use	(10000 cu.m)	50902	51739
自备井水		**Self-provided Well Water**			
用水量	(万立方米)	Consumption	(10000 cu.m)	58110	59373
#生产运营用	(万立方米)	For Production Use	(10000 cu.m)	15103	14811
公共服务用	(万立方米)	For Public Service Use	(10000 cu.m)	17202	18130
居民家庭用	(万立方米)	For Domestic Use	(10000 cu.m)	18779	19378

注：自来水数据口径为城镇公共供水。2013年起自备井水相关数据的填报范围调整为市区、卫星城、中心镇、一般建制镇，不含农业。
资料来源：北京市水务局。
Note: Statistical basis for tap water is urban public water supply. Since 2013, statistical scope for the data on self-provided well water were changed to cover urban area, satellite city, central town, town with general organizational structure, except agriculture.
Source: Beijing Water Authority.

9-7 公共交通及客运出租小轿车
PUBLIC TRANSPORT AND TAXI SERVICES

项目		Item		2015	2014
公共交通		**Public Transportation**			
运营车辆	(辆)	Operating Vehicles	(unit)	28311	28331
公共电汽车	(辆)	Buses and Trolley Buses	(unit)	23287	23667
轨道交通	(辆)	Rail Transit	(unit)	5024	4664
运营线路条数	(条)	Number of Operating Routes	(line)	894	895
公共电汽车	(条)	Buses and Trolley Buses	(line)	876	877
轨道交通	(条)	Rail Transit	(line)	18	18
运营线路长度	(公里)	Length of Operating Routes	(km)	20740	20776
公共电汽车	(公里)	Buses and Trolley Buses	(km)	20186	20249
轨道交通	(公里)	Rail Transit	(km)	554	527
客运量	(万人次)	Passenger Traffic	(10000 person-times)	738384	815849
公共电汽车	(万人次)	Buses and Trolley Buses	(10000 person-times)	406003	477180
轨道交通	(万人次)	Rail Transit	(10000 person-times)	332381	338668
客运出租小轿车		**Taxi Services**			
年末运营车辆	(辆)	Vehicles in Operation (year-end)	(unit)	68284	67546
客运量	(万人次)	Passenger Traffic	(10000 person-times)	58750	66828

资料来源：北京市交通委员会。
Source: Beijing Municipal Commission of Transport.

9-8 市政设施情况
BASIC STATISTICS FOR MUNICIPAL FACILITIES

项　　目		Item		2015	2014
境内道路总里程	（公里）	Total Length of Highways and Roads	(km)	29069	29209
高速公路里程	（公里）	Length of Expressways	(km)	982	982
城市道路里程	（公里）	Length of Urban Roads	(km)	6423	6426
#快速路	（公里）	Rapid Roads	(km)	383	383
#主干路	（公里）	Trunk Roads	(km)	969	965
城市道路面积	（万平方米）	Coverage of Urban Roads	(10000 sq.m)	10029	10002
#铺装步道	（万平方米）	Paved Roads	(10000 sq.m)	1676	1667
城市道路立交桥数	（座）	Number of Overpasses in City	(unit)	427	422
城市过街天桥数	（座）	Number of Pedestrain Overpasses in City	(unit)	531	528
城市地下通道数	（座）	Number of Underpasses in City	(unit)	213	211
备案停车场个数	（个）	Number of Parking Lots Recorded	(unit)	6690	6448
备案停车场车位总数	（个）	Total Capacity of Parking Lots Recorded	(unit)	1905949	1757718
路口电视监视点位	（台）	TV Monitors at Crossings	(unit)	1224	1235
城六区照明线路长度	（公里）	Length of Lighting Lines in 6 Urban Districl	(km)	6500	6407

注：1．本表统计范围为城六区。

2．表中“备案停车场个数”和“备案停车场车位总数”为原指标“经营性停车场个数”和“经营性停车场车位总数”。

资料来源：北京市交通委员会、北京市公安交通管理局、北京市路灯管理中心。

Note: a) Data in this table covers 6 urban districts .

b) In the table, the "Parking Lots Recorded" and "Total Capacity of Parking Lots Recorded" are the original indicators "Operational Parking Lots" and "Total Capacity of Operational Parking Lots".

Source: Beijing Municipal Communission of Transport, Beijing Traffic Management Bureau., Beijing Street Lamp Administration Center.

主要统计指标解释

自来水综合生产能力　指按供水设施取水、净化、送水、出厂输水干管等环节实际测定计算的综合生产能力。不包括供水高峰阶段，超负荷增加的生产能力。计算时，以四个环节中最薄弱的环节为主确定能力。

自来水供水管道长度　指从送水泵至用户水表之间所有管道的长度。不包括新安装尚未使用的管道。

生产运营用水　指在城市范围内生产、运营的农、林、牧、渔业、工业、建筑业、交通运输业等单位在生产、运营过程中的用水。

公共服务用水　指为城市社会公共生活服务的用水。包括行政事业单位、部队营区和公共设施服务、社会服务业、批发零售贸易业、旅馆饮食业以及社会服务业等单位的用水。

居民家庭用水　指城市范围内所有居民家庭的日常生活用水。包括城市居民家庭、农民家庭、公共供水站用水。

公共交通年末运营车辆　指公交企业（单位）用于运营业务的全部车辆数。

运营线路总长度　指全部运营线路长度之和。计算公式:

$$\text{运营线路长度}=\sum\text{各条运营线路长度}$$

$$=\sum\left[\begin{pmatrix}\text{上行起点至终点里程}+\text{下行起点至终点里程}\\ +\text{上下行终点掉头里程}\end{pmatrix}\right]$$

公路里程　指公路的长度，凡达到《公路工程技术标准（JTGB01-2003）》规定的技术等级的公路，均统计公路里程，包括大、中城市的郊区公路里程，公路通过城镇（指县城、集镇）街道的里程和公路桥梁长度、隧道长度、渡口的宽度以及分期修建的公路已验收交付使用的里程。国道、省道、县道、乡道和专用公路中新增的人工修建的、路基宽度在4.5米以上的等外路里程也纳入公路里程统计。按技术等级公路可分为高速公路、一级公路、二级公路、三级公路、四级公路和等外公路。

道路里程　指道路长度和与道路相通的桥梁、隧道的长度，按车行道中心线计算。城市道路由车行道和人行道两部分组成。在统计时只统计路面宽度在3.5米（含3.5米）以上的各种铺装道路，包括开放型工业区和住宅区道路在内。

道路面积　指道路面积和与道路相通的广场、桥梁、隧道的面积（统计时，将人行道面积单独统计）。人行道面积按道路两侧面积相加计算。包括步行街和广场，不含人车混行的道路。

Explanatory Notes on Main Statistical Indicators

General Production Capacity of Tap Water means the comprehensive production capacity of water facilities calculated by on-site measurement, including capacity of the water in-taking, treatment, transmission and delivery; while overloaded capacity during water supply peak hours are not included. Calculation of the capacity was mainly dependent upon the weakest link of the whole production process.

Length of Tap Water Supply Pipelines means the length of all pipes linking between the water outlet pumps and users' water meters, excluding the ones newly installed and not yet put into use.

Water for Production Use means the water used for production and operation of business entities within the city, covering sectors including agriculture, forestry, animal production and hunting, fishing, industry, construction, transportation, etc.

Water for Public Service Use means the water used for urban public services, including water supply for administrative and public institutions, military units, public facilities, social services, wholesale and retail trades, hotels and catering, and social service organizations.

Water for Domestic Use means the water used for daily life of all households in urban area, including the water used for urban residents, rural households, and public water supply stations.

Year-end Public Transport Vehicles in Operation means the number of all vehicles used for operational businesses in public transit enterprises (institutions).

Total Length of Public Transport Routes means the sum of all lines in operation. It is calculated with the formula:

Length of Public Transit Lines = ∑ Length of all lines in operation = ∑ [(mileage from the upward starting point to the end point + mileage from the downward starting point to the end point + mileage of double back from upward and downward end points)]

Total Length of Highways means the length of highways. Such statistics apply for any highway reaching the technical grade stated in *Highway Engineering Technical Standards (JTGB01-2003)*, including the mileage of highways in suburbs of middle and large cities, mileage of highways passing through streets in towns (counties and townships), length of highway bridges, length of tunnels, width of ferries, and mileage of highways constructed in several phases and put into use. The mileage of non-graded new highways built manually onto national highways, provincial highways, county highways, township highways and special highways, with roadbed width of 4.5m and above, are also incorporated. In terms of technical grade, highways fall into expressways, first-grade highways, second-grade highways, third-grade highways, fourth-grade highways, and non-graded highways.

Length of Highways and Roads means the length of roads and bridges and tunnels connecting with roads, calculated by the central lines of carriage ways. Urban roads consist of carriageways and sidewalks. Statistics only cover paved roads with width of pavement above 3.5m (including 3.5m), roads in open industrial zones and residential zones included.

Area of Roads means the area of roads and the area of squares, bridges and tunnels connecting to the roads (the area of sidewalks is calculated separately). The area of sidewalks is the sum of area on both sides of roads, including pedestrian streets and squares, excluding roads passable for both pedestrians and vehicles.

北京统计年鉴2016　BEIJING STATISTICAL YEARBOOK

农业及农村经济
AGRICULTURE AND RURAL ECONOMY

简要说明

一、本章资料的主要内容

本章资料反映北京市农业生产和农村经济基本情况，主要包括农村基层组织情况、农村地区人口、从业人员、耕地、农林牧渔业产值及主要农产品生产情况、设施农业、农业观光园、民俗旅游、农村固定资产投资、乡镇企业情况、农村经济收入与分配情况等。

二、本章资料的统计范围

农林牧渔业统计范围包括辖区内全部农林牧渔业生产单位、非农行业单位附属的农林牧渔业生产活动单位以及农户的农业生产活动。军委系统的农林牧渔业生产（除军马外）也应包括在内，但不包括农业科学试验机构进行的农业生产。

1. 农业：指各种农作物的种植活动。包括谷物、豆类、薯类、棉花、油料、糖料、麻类、烟叶、蔬菜、食用菌及花卉盆景园艺产品、水果、坚果、饲料和香料作物、药材及其它作物的种植。

2. 林业：包括林木的栽培(不包括茶园、桑园和果园的栽培、管理和收获等活动)、木材和竹材的采运、林产品的采集。

3. 畜牧业：包括牲畜饲养和放牧、家禽饲养以及野生动物的捕猎和饲养。

4. 渔业：分为淡水养殖和海水养殖，包括水生动物和海藻类植物的养殖和捕捞。

农村社会经济统计范围包括所有乡镇辖区内的社会经济活动。

三、本章资料的数据来源

乡镇企业数据由北京市经济和信息化委员会提供。农村经济收入分配数据由北京市农村经济研究中心农村合作经济经营管理站提供，耕地数据由北京市国土资源局提供，林业数据由北京市园林绿化局提供，水产品数据由北京市农业局提供，农村基层组织资料由北京市民政局提供。其余资料均由北京市统计局、国家统计局北京调查总队提供。

四、本章资料的调查方法和核算方法

根据农业生产特点，农林牧渔业总产值的核算采用“产品法”计算，即用产品产量乘以价格求出各种产品的产值，按产品产值类别分别汇总，计算出农林牧渔各业的产值，各业相加为农林牧渔业总产值。

(1)农业：包括谷物和其他作物；蔬菜、食用菌及花卉盆景园艺产品；水果、坚果、饲料、香料；中药材。

(2)林业：包括林木的培育和种植；木材、竹材采运；林产品的采集。

(3)牧业：包括除渔业养殖以外的一切动物饲养和放牧以及野生动物的捕猎和饲养。

(4)渔业：包括水生动物和海藻类植物的养殖和捕捞。

(5)服务业：产值等于农林牧渔服务业营业收入。

1957 年以前的农业总产值中包括了厩肥和农民自给性手工业（如农民自制衣服、鞋、袜，自己从事粮食初步加工等）。1958 年及以后的林业产值中增加了村及村以下竹木采伐产值；牧业中取消了厩肥产值；副业中取消了农民自给性手工业产值；渔业中增加了海洋捕捞水产品产值。1980 年及以后的农业总产值，在副业中增加了农民家庭兼营工业商品部分的产值。从 1984 年起村及村以下办工业产值划归工业。从 1993 年起，取消副业，将野生动物的捕猎划入牧业，野生植物采集和农民家庭兼营商品性工业划归农业。从 2003 年起按照新的《国民经济行业分类》标准取消了“其它农业”；将农林牧渔服务业产值纳入农林牧渔业总产值中；从农林牧渔业总产值中取消了“家庭兼营商品性工业”；将村以上木材和竹材的采运划入了林业；产值计算采用生产者价格，即生产者第一次出售农产品的价格。2004 年国家统计局报表制度规定农林牧渔业总产值增加按可比价计算的产值及发展速度（计算方法：用现价产值的中类数据除以中类缩减指数求得各中类的可比价产值，各中类相加得大类的可比价产值，最后用大类数据相加得农业可比价总产值，可比价产值除以上年现价产值得发展速度）。从 2005 年起，取消了按 1990 年价格计算的农业产值。由于 2006 年农业普查后对农业生产历史数据进行了修订，新修订的农业产值数据只到大类，如果按大类缩减计算农业可比价总产值不符合国家报表制度要求，故 2005 年及以前年度没有按可比价计算的发展速度。2010 年起，根据新的《统计用产品分类目录》将原林业产值中的核桃、栗子、白果、松子等干果产值调整至农业产值中，为同口径对比，将 2009 年年报数据也作了相应调整。

主要粮食播种面积数据通过卫星遥感测量方法取得，粮食产量数据通过抽样调查方法取得。农林牧渔业生产统计采取全面调查方法，村级起报。

五、本章中关于历史数据调整的问题

根据 2006 年第二次农业普查结果，北京市统计局、国家统计局北京调查总队按照国务院农普办要求，依照国际通用做法，已对 1997—2005 年的相关指标历史数据进行了修订。

Brief Introduction

I. Main Content

Statistics in this chapter show basic situation of agricultural production and rural economy in Beijing, mainly consisting of statistics for rural grass-root organizations, population and employment, arable land, output of agriculture, forestry, animal production and hunting, fishing, production of main agricultural products, facility agriculture, agricultural sightseeing gardens, folk-custom tourism, investment in fixed assets in rural areas, township enterprises, income and distribution of rural economy.

II. Scope of Statistics

Statistics on agriculture, forestry, animal production and hunting, fishing cover all related producing entities, producers affiliated to non-agricultural departments, as well as farmers' agricultural production activities. Production by the military commission system shall also be included (except for army horse breeding), but the production by scientific testing agencies is not included.

1. Agriculture: It refers to the growing of various agricultural crops, including grains, beans, potatoes, cotton, oil plants, sugar plants, fiber plants, tobacco leaves, vegetables, edible fungus, flower bonsai and gardening products, fruits, nuts, feedstuff, and spice crops, herbs, and other crops.

2. Forestry: It includes tree planting (except for the cultivation, management and harvest of tea gardens, mulberry fields, and orchards), the logging of timber and bamboo, and the collection of forestry products.

3. Animal production and hunting: It includes the breeding and grazing of livestock, poultry agriculture, as well as hunting and breeding of wildlife.

4. Fishing: It falls into two parts: freshwater agriculture and mariculture, including the cultivation and fishing for aquatic animals and algae.

Statistics for social and economic development in rural areas cover social and economic activities of all villages and towns within the jurisdiction.

III. Source of Statistics

Statistics on township enterprises were provided by Beijing Municipal Commission of Economy and Information Technology. Statistics on income distribution in rural economy were provided by the Operation and Management Station of Rural Cooperative Economy, Beijing Research Center for Rural Economy. Statistics on arable land were provided by Beijing Municipal Bureau of Land and Resources. Forestry statistics were provided by Beijing Municipal Bureau of Landscape and Forestry. Statistics on aquatic products were provided by Beijing Municipal Bureau of Agriculture. Statistics on rural basic organization were provided by Beijing Municipal Bureau of civil Affairs. All other statistics were provided by Beijing Municipal Bureau of Statistics and National Bureau of Statistics Survey Office in Beijing.

IV. Method for Survey and Counting

Based on agricultural production characteristics, the gross output value of agriculture, forestry, animal production and hunting, fishing was calculated by the "product approach"--that is to multiply production volume by the unit price, so as to get output value of each product, then sum it up by category, namely agriculture, forestry, animal production and hunting, fishing; and the sum total of these categories will be gross output value of the whole sector.

(1) Agriculture: including cereal and other crops; vegetables, edible mushrooms, flower bonsai and gardening products; fruits, nuts, beverage, spices, and herbs.

(2) Forestry: including the cultivation and planting of forest trees; logging of timber and bamboo; and collection of forestry products.

(3) Animal production and hunting: including the breeding and grazing of animals other than fish breeding, as well as hunting and breeding of wildlife.

(4) Fishing: including cultivation and catching of aquatic animals and seaweed plants.

(5) Service: the output value equals the operating income of services in support of agriculture, forestry, animal production and hunting, fishing.

Prior to 1957, China's gross agricultural output value included the output of barnyard manure and handicraft products for self-consumption (e.g. clothes, shoes, socks, and primary grain processing by peasants). Since 1958, output value of bamboo and timber logging by villages and units subordinated to villages has been included in the statistics of forestry; output value of barnyard manure has been excluded from animal production and hunting statistics; subsistence handicrafts has been excluded from sideline products output value; and the output value of aquatic products by marine fishing has been added to fishing. Since 1980, the output value of industrial commodities operated by rural households has been included in the output value of sideline products. Since 1984, industrial output value produced by villages and units subordinated to villages has been added in the sector of industry. In 1993, the group "sideline products" was cancelled; the hunting of wild animals has been classified as animal production and hunting, and the gathering of wild plants and commercial industrial businesses run by rural households have been included in agriculture. A new Standard for *Classification of National Economic Sectors* was introduced in 2003. According to the new classification, the group "other agricultural activities" was cancelled; the output value of services in support of agriculture, forestry, animal production and hunting, fishing is included in the gross output value of agriculture; the value of industrial output by households is excluded; output value of wood and bamboo logging is included in forestry statistics; the output value is calculated at the producer's price, namely the price at which producers sell their agricultural products for the first time; the 2004 Reporting System of National Bureau of Statistics states that, for incremental gross output value of agriculture, forestry, animal production and hunting, fishing, the output value and growth rate shall be calculated at comparable prices (calculation method: use the output value of groups at present prices to divide the groups' deflator, so as to get the output value at comparable prices; then add up the groups' output value to get the whole division's output value at comparable prices; in the end, add up all divisions' output value to get the gross output value at comparable prices for agriculture sector and divide the output value at comparable prices by the output value at current prices in the previous year to get the growth rate). Since 2005, the practice of using prices of 1990 as reference numbers to calculate agricultural output value has been cancelled. As historical data of agricultural production were revised after the agricultural census in 2006, revised agricultural production output value figures were presented only in divisions; and it does not meet the requirements of national reporting system to calculate the gross agricultural output value at comparable prices by divisions' deflator. Therefore, there were no figures of growth rate at comparable prices in and prior to 2005. Since 2010, the output value of nuts such as walnuts, chestnuts, gingkoes and pine nuts formerly included in forestry has been added in the output value of framing according to the new *Catalog on Statistical Product Classification*. In order to conduct same-caliber comparison, data in the 2009 annual report have also been adjusted accordingly.

Data on the sown area of major grain were collected by satellite remote sensing; data on grain yield were gathered through sampling survey; and the production figures on agriculture, forestry, animal production and hunting, fishing sectors were added up by complete survey, starting from the village level.

V. Adjustments to Historical Statistics

Based on results of the second agricultural census 2006, Beijing Municipal Bureau of Statistics and NBS Survey Office in Beijing revised related historical statistics during 1997-2005 as required by the Agricultural Census Office of the State Council and in accordance with the international practice.

10-1 农村基本情况(1978-2015年)
BASIC STATISTICS FOR RURAL AREAS (1978-2015)

年份 Year	乡政府 (个) Township Governments (unit)	镇政府 (个) Town Governments (unit)	村民委员会 (个) Villagers' Committees (unit)	乡镇及行政村常住户数 (万户) Number of Permanent Households in Towns and Administrative Villages (10000 households)	乡镇及行政村常住人口 (万人) Permanent Population in Towns and Administrative Villages (10000 persons)	乡镇及行政村从业人员 (万人) Employed Persons in Towns and Administrative Villages (10000 persons)
1978				91.9	382.1	165.3
1979				92.9	374.7	165.1
1980				95.0	374.3	167.4
1981				98.9	377.6	172.9
1982				103.2	381.8	179.4
1983				106.6	384.0	184.6
1984				108.9	385.6	188.9
1985	350	15	4394	111.8	387.2	190.0
1986	327	15	4400	113.1	386.9	189.5
1987	324	14	4326	115.7	388.9	189.8
1988	321	13	4111	118.6	389.6	189.2
1989	322	14	4483	121.5	390.0	186.1
1990	252	77	4481	124.5	392.0	184.3
1991	209	77	4480	125.5	390.7	182.1
1992	209	77	4229	126.2	387.6	178.7
1993	192	81	4476	126.5	382.4	176.0
1994	174	92	4464	124.9	376.0	171.6
1995	166	100	4355	125.0	371.5	163.6
1996	166	100	4357	124.6	368.9	164.2
1997	132	108	4348	124.6	365.3	161.2
1998	126	105	4032	125.9	364.4	161.0
1999	125	103	4040	125.9	363.9	165.3
2000	70	142	4039	126.8	363.7	165.8
2001	52	139	4010	127.6	361.6	165.3
2002	51	141	4005	128.0	357.6	165.6
2003	45	142	3985	131.1	360.6	169.6
2004	42	142	3985	132.8	359.9	171.4
2005	43	142	3953	142.2	381.8	184.0
2006	41	142	3957	143.6	501.6	316.9
2007	41	142	3955	176.9	510.0	313.4
2008	40	142	3951	189.8	547.4	321.3
2009	40	142	3950	203.8	572.5	338.7
2010	40	142	3943	216.0	589.4	347.8
2011	38	144	3941	212.4	574.8	338.3
2012	38	144	3940	215.2	582.5	341.7
2013	38	144	3938	221.9	599.5	353.5
2014	38	144	3937	225.2	606.9	357.0
2015	38	144	3936	221.4	593.5	348.0

注：1. 从业人员指标1998年以前为乡村劳动力。
2. 乡政府个数、镇政府个数、村民委员会个数由北京市民政局提供。
3. 2006年乡镇及行政村人口和从业人员为农业普查数据；2007年以后乡镇及行政村人口和从业人员为农业普查口径，包含居住半年以上外来人口。
4. 2006年乡镇及行政村户数为农业普查数据，为自然户口径；2007年以后为居住一年以上的户口径。

Note: a) Employed persons before 1998 were rural labor force.
b) Numbers of township governments, town governments, villagers' committees are provided by Beijing Municipal Bureau of Civil Affairs.
c) Population and employed persons in towns and administrative villages were agriculture census data in 2006.
Statistical range of agriculture census data have covered population and employed persons in towns and administrative villages since 2007 including migrant population residing for over 6 months.
d) Number of households in towns and administrative villages in 2006 was from agricultural census, using natural households as the caliber; since 2007, the caliber was changed into households residing for over a year.

10-2 农业生产条件(1978-2015年)
CONDITIONS FOR AGRICULTURAL PRODUCTION (1978-2015)

年份 Year	年末实有耕地面积(万公顷) Actual Area of Arable Land (year-end) (10000 hectares)	农业机械总动力(万千瓦) Total Power of Agricultural Machinery (10000 kw)	农村用电量(万千瓦小时) Rural Electricity Consumption (10000 kwh)	化肥施用量(万吨) Consumption of Chemical Fertilizers (10000 tons)
1978	42.9	189.4	58802	11.6
1979	42.7	212.2	63124	11.3
1980	42.6	234.6	76753	12.3
1981	42.5	244.8	91844	11.2
1982	42.4	242.2	96961	12.0
1983	42.3	261.8	104608	12.0
1984	42.2	290.8	119289	10.7
1985	42.1	320.4	126830	8.2
1986	41.9	345.5	180640	9.1
1987	41.8	388.4	159450	10.0
1988	41.6	399.7	163986	10.6
1989	41.4	423.9	128414	11.8
1990	41.3	416.2	122711	14.4
1991	41.1	384.8	111347	14.4
1992	40.9	399.8	143963	14.4
1993	40.6	450.5	169911	14.9
1994	40.2	459.2	172042	19.8
1995	39.4	468.1	201731	18.8
1996	34.4	468.4	275871	18.9
1997	34.2	433.2	301655	19.7
1998	34.1	415.5	290859	19.3
1999	33.8	410.4	330069	19.0
2000	32.9	399.2	572257	17.9
2001	29.2	394.9	619806	15.7
2002	27.5	381.8	414248	14.9
2003	26.0	366.9	427266	14.3
2004	23.6	340.3	383954	14.5
2005	23.3	337.7	421680	14.8
2006	23.3	325.5	416459	14.8
2007	23.2	300.5	411238	14.0
2008	23.2	267.0	427377	13.6
2009	22.7	271.5	439099	13.8
2010	22.4	276.0	443774	13.7
2011	22.2	265.2	454009	13.8
2012	22.1	241.1	473121	13.7
2013	22.1	207.7	485320	12.8
2014	22.0	195.8	505559	11.6
2015		185.9	516705	10.5

注：1. 化肥施用量为折纯量。
2. 2003年以前农村用电量由原北京市供电局提供。
3. 农业机械总动力数据由北京市农业局提供。

Note: a) Data on consumption of chemical fertilizers were net amount.
b) Figures of rural electricity consumption before 2003 were provided by the former Beijing Electric Power Supply Bureau.
c) Figures of total power of agricultural machinery were provided by Beijing Municipal Bureau of Agriculture.

10-3 农作物播种面积和造林面积(1978-2015年)
SOWN AND AFFORESTATION AREA (1978-2015)

年 份 Year	农作物播种面积(万公顷) Sown Area (10000 hectares)	#粮食作物 Grain Crops	#玉米 Corn	#小麦 Wheat	#油料 Oil-bearing Crops	#蔬菜及食用菌 Vegetables and Edible Mushrooms	#瓜类及草莓 Melons & Strawberries	#饲料 Forage	造林面积(万公顷) Afforestation Area (10000 hectares)
1978	69.1	56.1	16.9	19.2	3.3	5.6	0.2	2.0	1.4
1979	67.7	56.0	18.2	19.7	3.0	5.4	0.3	2.0	1.6
1980	65.7	54.9	19.7	18.8	2.8	5.1	0.4	1.8	2.4
1981	64.4	53.0	19.8	18.4	2.7	5.5	0.6	1.7	2.7
1982	64.2	52.7	19.7	18.1	2.4	5.9	0.8	1.6	2.8
1983	63.8	53.0	20.1	18.7	1.9	5.7	0.5	1.5	3.3
1984	63.3	52.3	20.6	19.5	1.8	5.8	0.7	1.5	3.2
1985	61.8	51.1	21.7	19.1	2.0	5.4	0.9	1.3	3.0
1986	60.5	49.9	21.6	18.5	2.0	5.8	1.1	1.0	1.5
1987	59.8	49.5	22.3	18.3	1.6	6.0	0.9	1.1	2.0
1988	59.5	48.8	22.2	18.6	1.5	6.3	1.0	1.2	1.6
1989	58.9	48.3	21.9	18.5	1.3	6.8	0.8	1.1	0.8
1990	59.0	48.4	22.4	18.8	1.2	7.0	0.6	1.1	1.3
1991	59.0	48.3	22.3	19.2	1.2	7.3	0.5	1.0	1.5
1992	58.5	47.7	22.4	19.2	1.2	7.5	0.5	0.8	1.5
1993	56.5	45.6	21.8	17.8	1.3	7.8	0.5	0.7	4.8
1994	55.1	43.0	20.6	16.4	1.2	9.1	0.6	0.6	5.5
1995	55.3	43.4	20.8	17.2	1.2	9.1	0.5		4.7
1996	53.8	42.7	20.8	17.1	1.1	8.8	0.5	0.5	4.0
1997	53.6	42.5	20.6	17.1	1.0	8.9	0.5	0.5	3.8
1998	53.5	42.3	20.8	17.1	1.0	9.0	0.5	0.5	3.7
1999	52.6	41.0	19.8	16.8	1.0	9.2	0.5	0.5	3.0
2000	45.4	30.8	13.6	12.2	1.5	10.4	0.8	1.2	2.6
2001	38.0	21.4	10.0	7.3	1.4	11.3	0.9	1.9	3.2
2002	33.5	16.9	8.7	4.7	1.6	11.5	0.9	1.8	4.8
2003	30.1	14.1	7.5	3.6	1.4	10.8	0.9	1.9	4.7
2004	30.4	15.4	9.4	3.9	1.1	9.1	0.8	2.8	3.2
2005	30.8	19.2	12.0	5.3	0.9	7.9	0.8	1.5	1.2
2006	32.0	22.0	13.6	6.3	0.7	7.1	0.9	0.6	1.3
2007	29.5	19.7	13.9	4.1	0.7	7.0	0.9	0.4	1.1
2008	32.2	22.6	14.6	6.4	0.7	6.8	0.8	0.4	0.9
2009	32.0	22.6	15.1	6.1	0.6	6.8	0.8	0.4	1.8
2010	31.7	22.3	15.0	6.2	0.5	6.8	0.8	0.5	1.4
2011	30.3	20.9	14.1	5.8	0.5	6.7	0.8	0.5	2.1
2012	28.3	19.4	13.2	5.2	0.5	6.4	0.8	0.3	3.6
2013	24.2	15.9	11.4	3.6	0.3	6.2	0.7	0.2	4.4
2014	20.0	12.0	8.9	2.4	0.3	5.7	0.6	0.3	2.3
2015	17.7	10.4	7.6	2.1	0.2	5.4	0.5	0.2	0.8

注：1. 蔬菜播种面积2006年为农业普查衔接数据，1997年-2005年为历史修订数据。
2. 造林面积2009年以前为人工造林面积，2009年起调整为荒山荒(沙)地造林面积，包括人工造林、无林地和疏林地新封面积。

Note: a) Figures of vegetable sown area in 2006 were from agricultural census, and figures in 1997-2005 were historically revised data.
b) Afforestation area before 2009 was artificial afforestation area, and after 2009 it became barren mountains and barren (sand) afforestation area, including the area of artificial forests, non-forest land and newly enclosed forest land.

10-4 农林牧渔业总产值(1978-2015年)
GROSS OUTPUT VALUE OF AGRICULTURE, FORESTRY, ANIMAL PRODUCTION AND HUNTING, FISHING (1978-2015)

年份 Year	农林牧渔业总产值(亿元) Gross Output Value of Agriculture, Forestry, Animal Production and Hunting, Fishing (100 million yuan)						农林牧渔业总产值比上年增长(%) Growth Rate (%)	
		农业 Agriculture	林业 Forestry	牧业 Animal Production and Hunting	渔业 Fishing	农林牧渔服务业 Related Service Industry	按现价计算 Calculated at Current Price	按可比价计算 Calculated at Comparable Price
1978	11.5	8.9	0.2	2.4	0.01			
1979	12.3	8.8	0.2	3.3	0.02		7.0	
1980	14.3	9.8	0.5	3.9	0.05		16.3	
1981-1985	**99.4**	**64.6**	**3.9**	**30.1**	**0.8**			
1981	14.9	10.1	0.7	4.1	0.05		4.2	
1982	16.8	11.3	0.7	4.7	0.05		12.8	
1983	19.6	12.7	0.8	6.0	0.1		16.7	
1984	22.2	14.4	0.9	6.7	0.2		13.3	
1985	25.9	16.1	0.8	8.6	0.4		16.7	
1986-1990	**245.7**	**142.1**	**4.1**	**91.6**	**7.9**			
1986	28.1	17.2	0.8	9.4	0.7		8.5	
1987	34.4	20.3	0.8	12.3	1.0		22.4	
1988	52.6	31.4	0.9	18.6	1.7		52.9	
1989	60.4	34.2	0.7	23.3	2.2		14.8	
1990	70.2	39.0	0.9	28.0	2.3		16.2	
1991-1995	**570.1**	**293.2**	**11.2**	**244.6**	**21.1**			
1991	76.5	39.6	1.5	32.8	2.6		9.0	
1992	84.5	43.2	1.6	36.3	3.4		10.5	
1993	100.4	51.1	2.3	42.7	4.3		18.8	
1994	144.3	72.5	3.1	64.0	4.7		43.7	
1995	164.4	86.8	2.7	68.8	6.1		13.9	
1996-2000	**883.4**	**441.8**	**18.2**	**388.5**	**34.9**			
1996	168.9	89.2	2.8	71.1	5.8		2.7	
1997	170.5	86.8	2.9	74.6	6.2		0.9	
1998	174.8	88.3	3.2	75.8	7.5		2.5	
1999	180.6	89.4	4.1	79.5	7.6		3.3	
2000	188.6	88.1	5.2	87.5	7.8		4.4	
2001-2005	**1114.6**	**423.2**	**57.0**	**567.3**	**45.6**			
2001	202.2	84.7	9.0	99.3	9.2		7.2	
2002	213.5	83.5	11.9	108.6	9.5		5.6	
2003	224.7	80.9	12.3	114.3	9.3	7.9	5.2	
2004	234.9	83.1	11.4	124.3	8.9	7.2	4.5	
2005	239.3	91.0	12.4	120.8	8.7	6.4	1.9	
2006-2010	**1459.4**	**648.4**	**87.1**	**643.7**	**51.5**	**28.7**		
2006	240.2	104.5	14.8	105.1	9.8	6.0	0.4	0.9
2007	272.3	115.5	17.8	122.4	10.1	6.5	13.4	0.8
2008	303.9	128.1	20.5	140.5	9.8	5.0	11.6	0.8
2009	315.0	146.1	17.2	136.1	10.3	5.3	3.6	5.5
2010	328.0	154.2	16.8	139.6	11.5	5.9	4.1	-1.7
2011-2015	**1968.9**	**809.7**	**297.6**	**760.2**	**62.4**	**39.2**		
2011	363.1	163.4	18.9	162.7	11.5	6.6	10.7	0.9
2012	395.7	166.3	54.8	154.2	13.0	7.5	9.0	2.9
2013	421.8	170.4	75.9	154.8	12.8	8.0	6.6	2.1
2014	420.1	155.1	90.7	152.7	13.2	8.4	-0.4	…
2015	368.2	154.5	57.3	135.9	11.9	8.7	-12.3	-11.7

注：1.农林牧渔业总产值绝对数按现价计算，从2003年起执行新《国民经济行业分类标准》，农林牧渔业总产值中含农林牧渔服务业产值。
2.2003年以后，计算农林牧渔业总产值使用的价格从农产品综合平均价调整为农产品生产价格。
3.2006年为与农业普查衔接的数据，1997-2005年为历史修订数据。
4.2010年按照新的《统计用产品分类目录》，将原归属林业产值的核桃、板栗等林产品调整至农业产值，并对2009年数据作了调整。

Note: a) The absolute number of agricultural gross output value are calculated at current prices. In the year of 2003, new Standard for Classification of National Economic Sectors was implemented, and gross output value of agriculture, forestry, animal production and hunting, fishing has included the output value of services for agriculture, forestry, animal production and hunting, fishing.

b) After 2003, the prices used for calculating the output value of agriculture, forestry, animal production and hunting, fishing have been changed from comprehensive average price of agricultural products to production price of agricultural products.

c) Figures for 2006 were from agricultural census, and figures in 1997-2005 were historically revised data.

d) Output value of forestry productions such as walnuts and chestnuts was transferred to that of the agriculture sector in 2010 according to the new Catalog of Product Classification Used for Statistics. Figures of 2009 were adjusted accordingly.

10-5 主要农业产品产量(1978-2015年)
OUTPUT OF MAJOR AGRICULTURAL PRODUCTS (1978-2015)

单位：万吨 (10000 tons)

年 份 Year	粮 食 Grain	油 料 Oil-bearing Crops	蔬菜及食用菌 Vegetables and Edible Mushroom	干鲜果品 Nuts and Fresh Fruits	牛 奶 Milk	肉 类 Meat	#猪牛羊肉 Pork, Beef and Mutton	禽蛋产量 Poultry and Eggs	水产品 Aquatic Products
1978	186.0	2.6	164.5	17.5	5.4	11.9	11.9	2.1	0.2
1979	172.8	2.6	181.3	15.8	6.0	13.1	13.1	3.1	0.3
1980	186.0	3.1	175.9	15.9	6.8	15.1	15.1	3.4	0.4
1981-1985	**1004.8**	**13.1**	**1002.2**	**86.7**	**53.3**	**69.0**	**69.0**	**44.3**	**4.0**
1981	180.7	2.2	172.8	15.6	7.6	13.2	13.2	3.7	0.4
1982	185.5	2.3	208.3	13.8	8.9	13.9	13.9	5.4	0.4
1983	201.5	2.1	199.1	18.2	10.6	14.9	14.9	8.9	0.6
1984	217.4	2.6	218.0	20.2	12.6	13.4	13.4	12.2	1.0
1985	219.7	3.9	204.0	18.9	13.5	13.6	13.6	14.1	1.6
1986-1990	**1181.9**	**15.2**	**1422.2**	**119.3**	**89.7**	**90.8**	**78.3**	**103.8**	**18.8**
1986	216.5	3.0	222.7	18.7	14.6	13.3	13.3	14.7	2.2
1987	227.0	3.3	241.1	22.5	15.5	12.9	12.9	16.8	3.0
1988	234.6	3.0	271.3	23.8	18.0	14.5	14.5	21.8	3.9
1989	239.2	2.8	331.0	26.7	19.9	23.3	17.2	24.7	4.6
1990	264.6	3.1	356.1	27.6	21.7	26.8	20.4	25.8	5.1
1991-1995	**1354.7**	**17.6**	**1915.9**	**198.5**	**113.7**	**180.7**	**134.0**	**139.3**	**34.7**
1991	279.7	3.3	368.4	29.3	23.9	33.9	24.8	27.9	5.6
1992	281.9	3.4	381.4	34.0	24.5	35.9	27.3	30.0	6.4
1993	284.1	3.8	418.8	39.6	22.5	36.7	28.2	31.4	7.0
1994	249.2	3.8	350.0	48.8	22.2	34.4	24.8	31.2	7.6
1995	259.8	3.3	397.3	46.8	20.6	39.8	28.9	28.5	8.1
1996-2000	**1059.4**	**15.0**	**2101.9**	**291.8**	**120.2**	**218.1**	**146.5**	**98.2**	**38.2**
1996	237.4	2.9	403.2	51.3	21.0	38.2	27.3	24.7	7.8
1997	237.5	2.7	408.8	54.8	22.2	39.9	27.8	23.8	7.7
1998	239.3	2.8	403.8	59.5	22.7	43.4	30.3	17.9	7.6
1999	201.0	2.8	419.8	60.2	24.0	46.1	30.2	15.8	7.6
2000	144.2	3.8	466.3	66.0	30.3	50.5	30.9	16.0	7.5
2001-2005	**410.3**	**18.5**	**2302.3**	**419.5**	**295.5**	**287.8**	**169.1**	**78.9**	**35.0**
2001	104.9	4.3	491.0	71.9	42.9	55.9	33.0	15.6	7.4
2002	82.3	4.6	507.4	78.7	55.1	60.9	35.2	15.2	7.4
2003	58.0	3.3	486.7	84.1	63.3	60.6	35.2	16.2	7.1
2004	70.2	2.9	444.1	90.9	70.0	57.4	34.0	15.9	6.7
2005	94.9	2.5	373.1	93.9	64.2	53.3	31.7	16.0	6.4
2006-2010	**577.3**	**10.0**	**1622.7**	**445.3**	**322.1**	**231.7**	**135.0**	**76.5**	**29.6**
2006	109.2	2.2	341.2	88.7	61.9	45.3	26.9	15.2	5.4
2007	102.1	2.2	340.1	91.1	62.2	47.9	27.1	15.6	6.0
2008	125.5	2.2	321.3	89.8	66.4	45.1	25.9	15.2	6.1
2009	124.8	1.8	317.1	90.3	67.4	47.2	27.6	15.4	5.8
2010	115.7	1.6	303.0	85.4	64.1	46.3	27.5	15.1	6.3
2011-2015	**458.3**	**4.9**	**1285.0**	**397.5**	**307.3**	**205.1**	**134.9**	**87.1**	**33.9**
2011	121.8	1.4	296.9	87.8	64.0	44.4	27.6	15.1	6.1
2012	113.8	1.3	279.9	84.3	65.1	43.2	27.3	15.2	6.4
2013	96.1	1.0	266.9	79.5	61.5	41.8	27.9	17.5	6.4
2014	63.9	0.7	236.2	74.5	59.5	39.3	26.9	19.7	6.8
2015	62.6	0.6	205.1	71.4	57.2	36.4	25.2	19.6	8.2

注：1. 蔬菜、干鲜果品、猪牛羊肉产量2006年为农业普查衔接数据，1997年-2005年为历史修订数据。
2. 肉类产量1988年及以前为猪牛羊肉产量。
3. 2006年及以前水产品产量为淡水鱼产量，2007年以后含远洋捕捞量。水产品数据由北京市农业局提供。

Note: a) Figures of output for vegetables, nuts and fresh fruits, pork, beef and mutton in 2006 were from agricultural census, and figures in 1997-2005 were historically revised data.
b) Output of meat in and before 1988 was the output of pork, beef and mutton.
c) Output of aquatic products was output of fresh water fish in and before 2006, and long-range fishing has been included since 2007. Figures of aquatic products were provided by Beijing Municipal Bureau of Agriculture.

10-6 平均每一从业人员创造农、林、牧、渔业产值(1990-2015年)
AVERAGE OUTPUT VALUE OF AGRICULTURE, FORESTRY, ANIMAL PRODUCTION AND HUNTING, FISHING CREATED BY EACH PERSON (1990-2015)

单位：元 (Yuan)

年 份 Year	农林牧渔业总产值 Total Output Value of Agriculture, Forestry, Animal Production and Hunting, Fishing	#农 业 Agriculture	#林 业 Forestry	#畜牧业 Animal Production and Hunting	#渔 业 Fishing
1990	8507	5537	1540	54837	22729
1991	9523	5722	2807	68268	26442
1992	11329	6678	3826	78905	33689
1993	13859	8271	4558	92901	39518
1994	21002	12461	6507	139136	39182
1995	25110	15760	5750	156332	47266
1996	25250	15504	6741	173404	53133
1997	26101	15605	6886	169541	56211
1998	25817	15653	7724	124279	68379
1999	25396	15621	8398	101869	63684
2000	27061	16454	8416	99481	65223
2001	29772	16838	12287	109151	76321
2002	33313	18193	15209	116799	86784
2003	37770	19579	14634	129862	92879
2004	40569	20934	12376	153518	98619
2005	40834	22700	12496	156911	96184
2006	36559	21147	17398	166889	195867
2007	44276	25892	19324	177359	126998
2008	49175	28405	22031	212910	122318
2009	51750	33061	18507	215008	128750
2010	54579	35130	17886	228814	164441
2011	62556	38613	20344	285988	155637
2012	70258	40585	59852	282916	175234
2013	77516	43643	81323	294659	179937
2014	81816	42790	98094	313314	199704
2015	74570	45000	60007	292513	183929

注：1. 2006年从业人员为农业普查数据，2007年以后为农业普查口径，含居住半年以上的外来人口。
2. 2006年农林牧渔业总产值及分行业产值为与农业普查衔接的数据，1997-2005年为历史修订数据。
3. 2010年按照新的《统计用产品分类目录》，将原归属林业产值的核桃、板栗等林产品调整至农业产值，并对2009年数据作了调整。

Note: a) Figures of employed persons in 2006 were from agriculture census. These figures are from agriculture census and include migrant population who have resided for over half a year since 2007.

b) Figures of output value for agriculture, forestry, animal production and hunting, fishing in 2006 were from agricultural census, and figures in 1997-2005 were historically revised data.

c) Output value of forestry, such as walnuts and chestnuts, was transferred to the agriculture sector in 2010 according to the new Catalog of Product Classification Used for Statistics. Figures in 2009 were adjusted accordingly.

10-7 耕地面积(2009-2014年)
ARABLE LAND AREA (2009-2014)

单位：公顷 (hectare)

项目	Item	2009	2010	2011	2012	2013	2014
年初耕地总资源	**Total Arable Land Resources at the Beginning of the Year**		**227170.4**	**223779.4**	**221956.2**	**220856.2**	**221157.3**
年内增加	**Increase in the Year**		**11.1**	**521.5**	**545.4**	**1776.4**	**53.5**
土地整理	Land Consolidation				429.6	1748.7	42.1
土地复垦	Land Rehabilitation						
土地开发	Land Development			4.8			
农业结构调整	Agricultural Structure Adjustment			489.8	42.8		9.1
其　他	Others		11.1	26.9	73.1	27.6	2.4
年内减少	**Decrease in the Year**		**3402.1**	**2344.7**	**1645.4**	**1475.2**	**1262.1**
建设占用	Occupied by Construction		3038.2	1917.0	1302.3	1310.6	911.6
灾害损毁	Disaster Damage				172.9	1.3	
生态退耕	Farmland Converted for EcologicalPreservation						
农业结构调整	Agricultural Structure Adjustment		321.0	412.7	83.6	163.4	350.4
其　他	Others		43.0	15.0	86.7		
年末耕地面积	**Total Arable Land Resources at the End of the Year**	**227170.43**	**223779.4**	**221956.2**	**220856.2**	**221157.3**	**219948.8**
水　田	Paddy Field	2240.49	2207.9	2155.2	2121.1	2059.7	1992.8
水浇地	Irrigable Land	171983.18	169205.7	167694.0	166562.7	167208.6	166347.2
其　他	Others	52946.76	52365.7	52107.0	52172.4	51889.0	51608.8

注：表中2009年耕地面积相关数据为第二次全国土地调查数据，2010年以后为各年土地变更调查数据。

资料来源：北京市国土资源局。

Note: Related statistics for Arable land area in 2009 were from the 2nd National Land Survey, and statistics after 2010 were survey data of land changed.

Source: Beijing Municipal Bureau of Land and Resources.

10-8 农业观光园、民俗旅游、种业和设施农业(2005-2015年)

项目	Item	2005	2006
农业观光园	**Agricultural Sightseeing Gardens**		
农业观光园个数 (个)	Number of Agricultural Sightseeing Gardens (unit)	1012	1230
高峰期从业人员 (人)	Employed Persons in Peak Production Period (person)	40729	52828
接待人次 (万人次)	Visits Received (10000 person-times)	892.5	1210.6
经营总收入 (亿元)	Total Operating Income (100 million yuan)	7.88	10.49
民俗旅游	**Folk-Custom Tourism Receiption**		
从事民俗旅游实际经营接待户 (户)	Number of Actual Operating Households in Folk-Custom Tourism Receiption (household)	7268	8726
高峰期从业人员 (人)	Employed Persons in Peak Production Period of the Term (person)	14070	18253
民俗旅游接待人次 (万人次)	Number of Visits Received by Folk-Custom Tourism (10000 person-times)	758.9	982.5
民俗旅游总收入 (亿元)	Total Income of Folk-Custom Tourism (100 million yuan)	3.14	3.65
种　业	**Seed Industry**		
种业收入 (亿元)	Income (100 million yuan)	5.94	7.75
#销往外埠收入 (亿元)	Sales to Other Areas (100 million yuan)		
#牧业收入 (亿元)	Income from Animal Production and Hunting (100 million yuan)		
设施农业	**Facility Agriculture**		
设施农业实际利用占地面积 (公顷)	Actual Area Utilized by Facility Agriculture (hectare)	15645	17832
设施农业播种面积 (公顷)	Sown Area of Facility Agriculture (hectare)		
设施农业收入 (亿元)	Income of Facility Agriculture (100 million yuan)	18.62	21.11

AGRICULTURAL SIGHTSEEING GARDENS, FOLK-CUSTOM TOURISM, BREEDING OF SEEDS AND FACILITY AGRICULTURE (2005-2015)

2007	2008	2009	2010	2011	2012	2013	2014	2015
1302	1332	1294	1303	1300	1283	1299	1301	1328
51392	49366	49504	42561	46038	48906	50406	47088	42617
1446.8	1498.2	1597.4	1774.9	1842.9	1939.9	1944.4	1911.2	1903.3
13.15	13.58	15.24	17.80	21.72	26.88	27.36	24.92	26.31
10323	9151	8705	7979	8396	8367	8530	8863	8941
20750	19421	19790	16856	18232	18705	19578	21493	22313
1167.6	1205.6	1393.1	1553.6	1668.9	1695.8	1806.5	1914.2	2139.7
4.96	5.29	6.09	7.35	8.68	9.05	10.20	11.25	12.86
9.91	10.93	12.84	14.57	18.12	16.09	13.98	14.04	12.67
3.99	5.78	7.28	8.05	11.68	9.70	8.23	7.95	6.64
8.27	9.27	10.56	12.13	15.09	13.63	12.59	12.51	11.23
18022	17051	18762	18323	18616	19059	18852	18232	17397
30331	33889	36203	36811	38006	37797	38763	38115	41088
28.12	28.17	33.91	40.72	45.58	51.98	57.32	51.27	55.50

10-9 农业生产条件
PRODUCTIVE CONDITIONS OF AGRICULTURE

项目		Item		2015	2014	2015年为2014年% 2015 as % of 2014
主要农业机械拥有量		**Possession of Major Agricultural Machinery**				
农业机械总动力	(万千瓦)	Total Power of Agricultural Machinery	(10000 kW)	185.9	195.8	95.0
大中型拖拉机	(混合台)	Large and Medium-sized Tractors	(unit)	6998	6649	105.2
小型拖拉机	(台)	Mini Tractors	(unit)	1445	1973	73.2
机引农具	(台)	Tractor-propelled Farm Tools	(unit)	12348	13451	91.8
机动喷雾器	(部)	Motorized Sprayers	(unit)	19946	20884	95.5
联合收割机	(台)	Combine Harvesters	(unit)	1783	2088	85.4
机动脱粒机	(台)	Motorized Shellers	(unit)	3947	3941	100.2
米面加工机	(台)	Processing Machines of Rice and Flour	(unit)	3762	4158	90.5
机动挤奶器	(台)	Motorized Milkers	(unit)	1873	2056	91.1
饲料粉碎机	(台)	Fodder Grinders	(unit)	3796	3869	98.1
载重汽车	(辆)	Motor Trucks	(unit)	1527	1696	90.0
农业机械作业面积		**Operation Area of Agricultural Machinery**				
机耕面积	(公顷)	Cultivated Area by Machinery	(hectare)	12553	13007	96.5
占全部耕地面积比重	(%)	Share in the Total Arable Land	(%)	89.6	89.9	-
机播面积	(公顷)	Sown Area by Machinery	(hectare)	94229	112854	83.5
占播种面积比重	(%)	Share in the Total Sown Area	(%)	93.8	94.2	-
机收面积	(公顷)	Harvest Area by Machinery	(hectare)	80979	94636	85.6
占收获面积比重	(%)	Share in the Total Harvest Area	(%)	78.9	77.8	-
农村用电量		**Rural Electricity Consumption and Small Hydropower Stations**				
农村用电量	(万千瓦小时)	Rural Electricity Consumption	(10000 kWh)	516705	505559	102.2
农田水利		**Irrigation and Water Conservancy**				
排灌用动力机械	(台)	Irrigation Machinery	(unit)	39449	40024	98.6
排灌用动力机械动力	(万千瓦)	Power of Irrigation Machinery	(10000 kW)	45.6	45.1	101.2
机(电)井	(眼)	Motor-pumped Wells	(unit)	32586	32586	100.0
#已配套	(眼)	Completed Sets	(unit)	30645	30645	100.0
扬水站(固定机电排灌站)	(处)	Pumping Stations (Drainage and Irrigation Stations with Fixed Machinery)	(unit)	1573	1573	100.0
化肥施用量(折纯)		**Consumption of Chemical Fertilizers (converted into net amount)**				
化肥施用量	(吨)	Consumption of Chemical Fertilizers	(ton)	105284	116398	90.5
#氮　肥	(吨)	Nitrogenous Fertilizers	(ton)	48524	53678	90.4
磷　肥	(吨)	Phosphate Fertilizers	(ton)	5981	6673	89.6
钾　肥	(吨)	Potash Fertilizers	(ton)	5373	6026	89.2

注：1. 农村小水电站是指乡村两级小水电站实有数。
2. 主要农业机械拥有量、农业机械作业面积、排灌动力机械数据由北京市农业局提供。
3. 机(电)井、扬水站数据由北京市水务局提供。

Note: a) Figures of rural small hydropower stations refer to actual number of small hydropower stations at township and village level.
b) Figures of possession of major agricultural machinery, operation area of agricultural machinery and irrigation machinery are provided by Beijing Municipal Bureau of Agriculture.
c) Figures of motor-pumped wells and pumping stations are provided by Beijing Water Authority.

10-10 农林牧渔业总产值
GROSS OUTPUT VALUE OF AGRICULTURE, FORESTRY, ANIMAL PRODUCTION AND HUNTING, FISHING

单位：万元 (10000 yuan)

项目	Item	总产值 Gross Output Value 2015	2014	2015年为2014年% 2015 as % of 2014
合 计	**Total**	**3682372.2**	**4200672.4**	**87.7**
农 业	**Agriclture**	**1544776.6**	**1551014.9**	**99.6**
谷 物	Cereal	124551.0	138057.6	90.2
豆 类	Beans	4645.7	4043.5	114.9
经济作物	Cash Crops	5021.8	5988.4	83.9
蔬菜、食用菌	Vegetables and Edible Mushromms	709806.4	650456.8	109.1
水果（含瓜果类）	Fruits (including melons)	506714.3	551942.2	91.8
其 他	Others	194037.4	200526.4	96.8
林 业	**Forestry**	**573278.6**	**906852.3**	**63.2**
牧 业	**Animal Production and Hunting**	**1358578.1**	**1526589.6**	**89.0**
牲畜饲养	Animal Breeding	392526.8	455134.6	86.2
养 猪	Hogs	465125.5	475438.7	97.8
家禽饲养	Poultry	463283.6	517795.8	89.5
#禽 蛋	Poultry Eggs	248813.5	273770.1	90.9
其 他	Others	37642.2	78220.5	48.1
渔 业	**Fishing**	**118689.5**	**132024.0**	**89.9**
农林牧渔服务业	**Services for Farming, Forestry, Animal Production and Hunting, Fishing**	**87049.4**	**84191.6**	**103.4**

10-11 主要农作物播种面积及产量
SOWN AREA AND OUTPUT OF MAJOR CROPS

项目	Item	2015 播种面积（公顷） Sown Areas (hectare)	2015 单产（公斤／公顷） Output Per Unit (kg/hectare)	2015 总产量（吨） Total Output (ton)	2014 播种面积（公顷） Sown Areas (hectare)	2014 单产（公斤／公顷） Output Per Unit (kg/hectare)	2014 总产量（吨） Total Output (ton)
粮 食	**Grain**	**104453.5**	**5996.6**	**626362.4**	**120174.1**	**5320.4**	**639369.1**
按季节分	By Season						
夏 粮	Summer Grain	20863.9	5343.1	111478.3	23614.8	5174.5	122195.7
秋 粮	Autumn Grain	83589.5	6159.7	514884.1	96559.3	5356.0	517173.4
按品种分	Grouped by Variety						
稻 谷	Rice	199.6	6971.4	1391.5	182.8	6943.1	1269.2
冬小麦	Winter Wheat	20697.6	5356.8	110872.9	23550.6	5177.7	121937.9
玉 米	Corn	76290.0	6481.7	494485.1	88619.0	5646.5	500382.8
薯 类	Tubers	1404.9	5952.6	8362.9	1306.3	5220.6	6819.5
大 豆	Soybeans	3477.6	1877.2	6528.3	4143.1	1457.6	6039.0
棉 花	**Cotton**	**96.2**	**1044.7**	**100.5**	**104.3**	**1026.5**	**107.1**
油 料	**Oil-bearing Crops**	**2115.7**	**2674.3**	**5657.9**	**2590.6**	**2597.7**	**6729.6**
#花 生	Peanuts	1779.1	2904.5	5167.3	2198.7	2767.4	6084.7
药 材	**Medical Materials**	**2252.7**	**1047.9**	**2360.6**	**2741.9**	**639.2**	**1752.6**
蔬菜及食用菌	**Vegetables and Edible Mushrooms**	**54270.7**	**37800.2**	**2051446.8**	**57481.9**	**41084.9**	**2361634.5**
瓜类及草莓	**Melons & Strawberries**	**5203.3**	**39427.5**	**205154.6**	**6476.1**	**38855.8**	**251632.9**
#西 瓜	Watermelons	4355.4	42886.5	186787.7	5607.8	40894.1	229326.0
饲 料	**Forage**	**2250.5**			**3359.9**		
#牧 草	Forage Grass	366.9			301.4		
花 卉	**Flowers**	**2825.1**			**3813.7**		

10-12 林业及干鲜果品生产
FORESTRY, NUTS AND FRESH FRUIT PRODUCTION

项目		Item		2015	2014	2015年为2014年% 2015 as % of 2014
林业生产		**Forestry**				
造林面积	(公顷)	Afforestation Area	(hectare)	8133	22937	35.5
#人工造林面积	(公顷)	Artificial Afforestation Area	(hectare)	8133	22937	35.5
#平原造林面积	(公顷)	Afforestation Area on the Plain	(hectare)	7585	23600	32.1
育苗面积	(公顷)	Seedling Growing Area	(hectare)	15161	13052	116.2
#本年新育	(公顷)	Newly Growing in the Current Year	(hectare)		2600	
果类生产		**Fruits**				
干鲜果总产量	(吨)	Output of Nuts and Fresh Fruit	(ton)	713827	745147	95.8
干　果	(吨)	Nuts	(ton)	39558	32250	122.7
#核　桃	(吨)	Walnuts	(ton)	10473	9280	112.8
板　栗	(吨)	Chinese Chestnuts	(ton)	25220	19853	127.0
鲜　果	(吨)	Fresh Fruits	(ton)	674270	712897	94.6
#苹　果	(吨)	Apples	(ton)	80357	75015	107.1
梨	(吨)	Pears	(ton)	126637	132822	95.3
葡　萄	(吨)	Grapes	(ton)	32697	34360	95.2
柿　子	(吨)	Persimmons	(ton)	35541	41613	85.4
桃	(吨)	Peaches	(ton)	340771	367617	92.7
年末实有果园面积	**(公顷)**	**Actual Orchard Area (year-end)**	**(hectare)**	**57137**	**57524**	**99.3**

资料来源：林业生产数据由北京市园林绿化局提供。
Source: Figures of forestry are from Beijing Municipal Bureau of Landscape and Forestry.

10-13 牲畜饲养及畜产品产量
LIVESTOCK BREEDING AND OUTPUT

项目		Item		2015	2014	2015年为2014年% 2015 as % of 2014
畜禽存栏		**Amount of Livestock and Poultry on Hand**				
大牲畜	(万头)	Large Animals	(10000 heads)	18.08	20.32	89.0
#牛	(万头)	Cattle and Buffaloes	(10000 heads)	17.48	19.68	88.8
猪	(万头)	Hogs	(10000 heads)	165.61	179.60	92.2
羊	(万只)	Sheep	(10000 units)	69.35	68.35	101.5
山　羊	(万只)	Goats	(10000 units)	18.97	17.19	110.4
绵　羊	(万只)	Sheep	(10000 units)	50.38	51.16	98.5
家　禽	(万只)	Poultry	(10000 units)	2128.44	2544.58	83.6
#产蛋鸡	(万只)	Hens	(10000 units)	1533.80	1678.44	91.4
肉　鸡	(万只)	Chickens	(10000 units)	420.43	584.64	71.9
鸭	(万只)	Ducks	(10000 units)	163.35	273.48	59.7
兔	(万只)	Rabbits	(10000 units)	4.32	4.28	100.8
畜禽出栏		**Amount of Livestock and Poultry Marketed**				
牛	(万头)	Cattle	(10000 heads)	8.44	9.20	91.7
猪	(万头)	Hogs	(10000 heads)	284.42	305.76	93.0
羊	(万只)	Sheep	(10000 units)	70.99	68.67	103.4
畜禽产品产量		**Output of Livestock and Poultry Products**				
肉类产量	(万吨)	Output of Meat	(10000 tons)	36.42	39.32	92.6
#猪　肉	(万吨)	Pork	(10000 tons)	22.48	24.01	93.6
牛　肉	(万吨)	Beef	(10000 tons)	1.55	1.70	90.9
羊　肉	(万吨)	Mutton	(10000 tons)	1.20	1.17	102.2
牛奶产量	(万吨)	Output of Milk	(10000 tons)	57.22	59.48	96.2
禽　蛋	(万吨)	Poultry Eggs	(10000 tons)	19.58	19.65	99.6
#鸡　蛋	(万吨)	Eggs	(10000 tons)	19.28	19.32	99.8
蜂　蜜	(吨)	Honey	(ton)	1631.30	2321	70.3

10-14 水产品生产
AQUATIC PRODUCTS

项　　目	Item	2015	2014	2015年为2014年% 2015 as % of 2014
渔业水域面积　（公顷）	**Area of Fishery Waters (hectare)**	**24986**	**25463**	**98.1**
#淡水养殖面积　（公顷）	Freshwater Agriculture (hectare)	3633	3924	92.6
#池　塘　（公顷）	Puddles and Ponds (hectare)	3563	3850	92.5
水产品产量　（吨）	**Output of Aquatic Products (ton)**	**82480**	**68184**	**121.0**
#淡水鱼产量　（吨）	Output of Freshwater Fish (ton)	65813	54962	119.7
#大水库　（吨）	Large Reservoirs (ton)	2405	2339	102.8
中、小水库　（吨）	Medium and Small Reservoirs (ton)	1699	1752	97.0
池　塘　（吨）	Puddles and Ponds (ton)	39728	44181	89.9

资料来源：北京市农业局。
Source: Beijing Municipal Bureau of Agriculture.

10-15 农业观光园
STATISTICS FOR AGRICULTURAL SIGHTSEEING GARDENS

项　　目	Item	2015	2014	2015年为2014年% 2015 as % of 2014
农业观光园个数　（个）	Number of Agricultural Sightseeing Gardens (unit)	1328	1301	102.1
高峰期从业人员　（人）	Employed Persons in Peak Production Period (person)	42617	47088	90.5
接待人次　（万人次）	Visits Received (10000 person-times)	1903.3	1911.2	99.6
经营总收入　（万元）	Total Operating Income (10000 yuan)	263138.9	249154.7	105.6

10-16 民俗旅游
STATISTICS FOR FOLK-CUSTOM TOURISM

项目	Item	2015	2014	2015年为2014年% 2015 as % of 2014
从事民俗旅游实际经营接待户 (户)	Number of Actual Operating Households in Folk-Custom Tourism Receiption (household)	8941	8863	100.9
高峰期从业人员 (人)	Number of Employed Persons at the End of the Term (person)	22313	21493	103.8
民俗旅游接待人次 (万人次)	Number of Visits Received by Folk-Custom Tourism (10000 person-times)	2139.7	1914.2	111.8
民俗旅游总收入 (万元)	Total Income of Folk-Custom Tourism (10000 yuan)	128550.1	112543.0	114.2

注：从2014年起，将民俗旅游中期末从业人员调整为高峰期从业人员。
Note: From 2014, employed persons of folk-custom tourism in late period are changed as the persons in peak production period.

10-17 种业生产
STATISTICS FOR PRODUCTION OF SEED INDUSTRY

项目	Item	产量 Output			收入(万元) Income (10000 yuan)		
		2015	2014	2015年为2014年% 2015 as % of 2014	2015	2014	2015年为2014年% 2015 as % of 2014
合计	**Total**				**126733.7**	**140354.0**	**90.3**
农业	**Agriculture**				**6825.5**	**6429.2**	**106.2**
#小麦种 (公斤)	Wheat Seeds (kg)	1197400	1470993	81.4	294.0	429.7	68.4
玉米种 (公斤)	Corn Seeds (kg)	542838	493627	110.0	384.6	339.4	113.3
蔬菜种 (公斤)	Vegetable Seeds (kg)	241020	165130	146.0	1382.1	1642.2	84.2
林业	**Forestry**				**3270.3**	**5925.7**	**55.2**
#树苗 (百株)	Saplings (100 units)	6082.0	9274.0	65.6	3240.2	5925.6	54.7
牧业	**Animal Production and Hunting**				**112331.3**	**125111.4**	**89.8**
#种猪 (头)	Boars (head)	134832	210746	64.0	29022.0	45354.3	64.0
种雏禽 (万只)	Breeding Birds (10000 units)	2830.3	2903.9	97.5	19672.2	20618.6	95.4
种蛋 (万枚)	Breeding Eggs (10000 units)	39311.4	43720.6	89.9	53502.1	49008.1	109.2
渔业	**Fishing**				**4306.6**	**2887.7**	**149.1**
#种鱼苗 (万尾)	Breeding Fish Fry (10000 units)	9155.0	7048.8	129.9	3560.6	2552.7	139.5

10-18 设施农业(2015年)
FACILITY AGRICULTURE (2015)

项 目	Item	设施农业播种面积（公顷）Sown Area of Facility Agriculture (hectare)	设施农业产量（吨）Output of Facility Agriculture (ton)	设施农业收入（万元）Income of Facility Agriculture (10000 yuan)
合 计	**Total**	**41088**		**555012.1**
温 室	**Greenhousse**	**23651**		**396448.1**
蔬菜及食用菌	Vegetables and Edible Mushrooms	21141	758625	299481.1
花卉苗木	Flowers and Saplings	1024		32578.4
#切 花	Cut Flowers	208	2978	5207.3
盆 花	Potted Flowers	781	8276	27208.9
瓜果类	Melons	805	19681	45188.9
园林水果	Fruits	556	5234	13407.6
其 它	Others	125		5792.1
大 棚	**Greenhouse Garden**	**14452**		**136992.0**
蔬菜及食用菌	Vegetables and Edible Mushrooms	11237	404606	101567.8
花卉苗木	Flowers and Sapling	227		7095.6
#切 花	Cut Flowers	35	784	816.7
盆 花	Potted Flowers	167	1583	6199.9
瓜果类	Melons	2553	113798	24571.7
园林水果	Fruits	334	1428	1839.1
其 它	Other	102		1917.8
中小棚	**Medium and Small Shed**	**2985**		**21572.0**
蔬菜及食用菌	Vegetables and Edible Mushrooms	1735	55668	13661.6
花卉苗木	Flowers and Sapling	60		1108.1
#切 花	Cut Flowers	8	13	67.7
盆 花	Potted Flowers	32	435	855.4
瓜果类	Melons	1150	43907	6269.1
园林水果	Fruits	14	9	29.0
其 它	Other	27		504.2

注：切花产量的计量单位是万枝，盆花产量的计量单位是万盆。
Note: Cut flowers output are measured in 10000 ones; and potted flowers, 10000 pots.

10-19 乡镇企业各业基本情况(2015年)
BASIC STATISTICS FOR TOWN AND TOWNSHIP ENTERPRISES IN DIFFERENT SECTORS (2015)

项目	Item	企业个数(个) Number of Enterprises (unit)		从业人员(人) Employed Persons (person)		总收入(万元) Total Income (10000 yuan)		利润总额(万元) Total Profits (10000 yuan)	
		数量 Number	构成(%) Composition (%)	数量 Number	构成(%) Composition (%)	数量 Number	构成(%) Composition (%)	数量 Number	构成(%) Composition (%)
合计	**Total**	**128854**	**100.0**	**984986**	**100.0**	**49244991**	**100.0**	**2887248**	**100.0**
农业	Agriculture	2748	2.1	9856	1.0	373734	0.8	31970	1.1
工业	Industry	62439	48.5	578162	58.7	27722757	56.3	1625775	56.3
建筑业	Construction	5142	4.0	79493	8.1	5083087	10.3	197569	6.8
交通运输业	Transportation	7125	5.5	33349	3.4	1824348	3.7	150148	5.2
批发零售业	Wholesale and Retail Trade	18318	14.2	61165	6.2	7782700	15.8	281132	9.7
住宿及餐饮业	Lodging and Catering Services	7607	5.9	47637	4.8	613616	1.2	34234	1.2
居民服务、其它服务和娱乐业	Household Services, Other Services and Entertainment	23805	18.5	132222	13.4	3526584	7.2	396625	13.7
其他	Others	1670	1.3	43102	4.4	2318165	4.7	169795	5.9

资料来源：北京市经济和信息化委员会。
Source: Beijing Municipal Commission of Economy and Information Technology.

10-20 农村经济收入与分配
INCOME AND DISTRIBUTION OF RURAL ECONOMY

单位：万元 (10000 yuan)

项　　目	Item	2015	2014	2015年为2014年% 2015 as % of 2014
营业收入	**Operation Income**	**56147281.1**	**54363139.5**	**103.3**
农　业	Agriculture	1176236.9	1145991.6	102.6
#粮　食	Grain	263299.5	267984.7	98.3
林　业	Forestry	240935.5	269242.3	89.5
牧　业	Animal Production and Hunting	1294755.9	1248455.6	103.7
渔　业	Fishing	108356.5	112345.1	96.4
工　业	Industry	14564095.1	15098140.0	96.5
建筑业	Construction	7140149.2	6663592.5	107.2
交通运输业	Transportation	3352646.7	3110454.1	107.8
商业、饮食业	Commerce and Catering	11407147.0	10976478.2	103.9
服务业	Services	12410963.8	11557852.0	107.4
其　他	Others	4451994.5	4180588.1	106.5
营业成本	**Operation Costs**	**50072515.8**	**48312777.2**	**103.6**
农　业	Agriculture	1152135.1	1126818.9	102.2
#粮　食	Grain	262342.3	265478.3	98.8
林　业	Forestry	238641.6	266010.2	89.7
牧　业	Animal Production and Hunting	1278921.2	1235995.5	103.5
渔　业	Fishing	106325.2	108983.3	97.6
工　业	Industry	12830992.9	13299656.1	96.5
建筑业	Construction	6397942.2	5957220.8	107.4
交通运输业	Transportation	3216146.4	3003249.9	107.1
商业、饮食业	Commerce and Catering	10552010.0	9910009.5	106.5
服务业	Services	10383251.1	9739446.0	106.6
其　他	Others	3916150.1	3665387.0	106.8
营业利润	**Operating Profits**	**1509389.8**	**1347589.5**	**112.0**
利润总额	**Total Profits**	**2135137.8**	**1975759.0**	**108.1**
税后利润	**After-tax Profits**	**1879561.4**	**1711218.4**	**109.8**
可供分配的利润	**Profits Available for Distribution**	**2270482.9**	**2207386.9**	**102.9**
未分配利润	**Undistributed Profits**	**1605023.0**	**1520704.5**	**105.5**

资料来源：北京市农村经济研究中心农村合作经济经营管理站。
Source: Operation and Management Station for Rural Cooperative Economy of Beijing Rural Economy Research Center.

10-21 乡镇企业出口供货情况
GOODS SUPPLIES FOR EXPORT OF TOWN AND TOWNSHIP ENTERPRISES

单位：万元 (10000 yuan)

项　　目	Item	2015	2014
合　计	**Total**	**931928**	**1138012**
化　工	Chemical Products	43923	53636
机　械	Machinery	15689	19159
矿　产	Mineral Products	8687	10610
轻　工	Light Industry	140915	172077
食　品	Food	101018	123357
土产畜产	Local and Livestock Products	21744	26552
纺织服装	Textile and Garments	316837	386901
工艺品	Artworks	22734	27761
其　他	Others	260380	317959

资料来源：北京市经济和信息化委员会。
Source: Beijing Municipal Commission of Economy and Information Technology.

主要统计指标解释

农林牧渔业总产值 是以货币表现的农林牧渔业的全部产品总量和对农林牧渔业生产活动进行的各种支持性服务活动的价值。

耕地 指种植农作物的土地，包括熟地，新开发、复垦、整理地，休闲地（含轮歇地、轮作地）；以种植农作物（含蔬菜）为主，间有零星果树、桑树或其他树木的土地；平均每年能保证收获一季的已垦滩地和海涂。耕地中包括南方宽度<1.0米、北方宽度<小于2.0米固定的沟、渠、路和地坎（埂）；临时种植药材、草皮、花卉、苗木等的耕地，以及其他临时改变用途的耕地。

农作物播种面积 指实际播种或移植有农作物的面积。凡是实际种植有农作物的面积，不论种植在耕地上还是种植在非耕地上，均包括在农作物播种面积中。在播种季节基本结束后，因遭灾而重新改种和补种的农作物面积，也包括在内。

设施农业 指以工厂化生产方式，建造人工设施，改变气候条件，提高农作物抵御自然灾害的能力，改良生物特性，使作物实现错季或反季节生产，达到农作物均衡生产的目的。

农业机械总动力 指主要用于农、林、牧、渔业的各种动力机械的动力总和。包括耕作机械、排灌机械、收获机械、农用运输机械、植物保护机械、牧业机械、渔业机械和其他农用机械[内燃机按引擎马力折成瓦（特）计算，电动机按功率折成瓦（特）计算]。不包括专门用于乡、镇、村、组办工业、基本建设、非农业运输、科学实验和教学等非农业生产方面用的动力机械与作业机械。

农村用电量 指本年度内，扣除在农村中的国有经济工业交通、基建等单位的用电量以后的农村生产和生活的全年用电总量（计量单位千瓦小时，按全年累计数统计），即包括国家电网供电，也包括农村自办电站供电量。

农用化肥施用量 指本年度内实际用于农业生产的化学肥料数量，包括氮肥、磷肥、钾肥和复合肥。施用量要求按折纯量计算数量，即各类化学肥料的实际施用数量按其含氮、含五氧化二磷、含氧化钾的比例折成百分之百计算。

折纯量＝实物量 × 某种化肥有效成份含量的百分比

乡镇及行政村单位常住户数 指长期（一年以上）居住在乡镇（不包括城关镇）行政管理区域内的住户，还包括居住在城关镇所辖行政村范围内的农村住户。户口不在本地而在本地居住一年及以上的住户也包括在本地农村住户内；有本地户口，但举家外出谋生一年以上的住户，无论是否保留承包耕地都不包括在本地农村住户范围内。不包括乡村地区内的国有经济的机关、团体、学校、企业、事业单位的集体户。

乡镇及行政村常住人口 指乡村地区常住居民户数中的常住人口数，即经常在家或在家居住6个月以上，而且经济和生活与本户连成一体的人口。外出从业人员在外居住时间虽然在6个月以上，但收入主要带回家中，经济与本户连为一体，仍视为家庭常住人口；在家居住，生活和本户连成一体的国家职工、退休人员也为家庭常住人口。但是现役军人、中专及以上（走读生除外）的在校学生、以及常年在外（不包括探亲、看病等）且已有稳定的职业与居住场所的外出从业人员，不应当作家庭常住人口。

乡镇及行政村从业人员 指全部乡镇及行政村人口中16岁以上实际参加生产经营活动并取得实物或货币收入的人员，既包括劳动年龄内经常参加劳动的人员，也包括超过劳动年龄但经常参加劳动的人员。但不包括户口在家的在外学生、现役军人和丧失劳动能力的人，也不包括待业人员和家务劳动者。从业人员按从事主业时间最长（时间相同按收入）分为农业从业人员，工业从业人员，建筑业从业人员，交通运输仓储及邮政业从业人员，信息传输、计算机服务和软件业，批发与零售业从业人员，住宿和餐饮业从业人员，其它从业人员。

Explanatory Notes on Main Statistical Indicators

Gross Output Value of Agriculture, Forestry, Animal Production and Hunting, Fishing refers to the monetary value of all products of agriculture, forestry, animal production and hunting, fishing, as well as the monetary value of services provided in support of all the above-mentioned sectors.

Arable Land refers to the land suitable for growing crops, including cultivated land; any land newly opened up, reclaimed and cultivated; fallow land (including swidden and rotated land); land mostly for growing crops (including vegetables), supplemented by mulberry trees, fruit trees, and other trees; cultivated bottomland and shallows that can secure an average of one harvest annually. Arable land includes furrows, ditches, paths and field ridges less than 1m wide in the southern part of China, or less than 2m wide in the northern part. It also covers arable land that is temporarily for growing medicinal materials, turf, flowers, nursery stock and other uses.

Sown Area refers to the area of all lands actually sown or transplanted with crops, including both the cultivated and non-cultivated land. Area of lands re-planted after seedtime has passed due to natural disasters is also included.

Facility Agriculture means to produce in an industrialized manner, put in place facilities of manual intervention, change climate conditions, increase the crops' capability to resist natural disasters, and improve the crops' biological property, so as to stagger harvest seasons, create anti-season production, and achieve balanced production of crops.

Total Power of Agricultural Machinery refers to the total power of motive power machines used in agriculture, forestry, animal production and hunting, fishing sectors, including machinery for ploughing, irrigation and drainage, harvesting, agricultural transport, plant protection, animal production and hunting, fishing and other farm machinery (The horsepower of internal combustion engines is converted into watts, and the output of electric motors is also converted into watts). Motive power machines and operating machines exclusively used for non-agricultural production activities, such as industrial operations run by counties, towns, villages and teams, capital construction, non-agricultural transport, scientific experiments and teaching, are not included.

Rural Electricity Consumption refers to the total rural production and rural residents' electricity consumption in the whole year (unit of measurement: kilowatt-hour; the data representing accumulative usage of the year), deducting the consumption by entities like state-owned industry, transport, and infrastructure construction. The data cover both power supplies by the State Grid and by the rural self-run power stations.

Consumption of Chemical Fertilizers refers to the total quantity of chemical fertilizers applied in agricultural production within the year, including nitrogenous fertilizer, phosphate fertilizer, potash fertilizer, and compound fertilizer. The amount of chemical fertilizers applied is calculated in terms of net amount, that is, to use the gross weight of the respective fertilizers in calculating the quantity of effective ingredients (e.g. nitrogen content in nitrogenous fertilizer, phosphorous pent oxide content in phosphate fertilizer, and potassium oxide content in potash fertilizer).

Net Amount = Physical Quantity× Content (%) of Effective Ingredients in Certain Chemical Fertilizer

Number of Resident Households in Towns and Administrative Villages refers to households living in the administrative areas of towns and villages (excluding township government premises) on a long-term basis (more than one year), including those living in administrative villages within township government premises. Households with non-local household registration but having been living locally for more than one year are also counted as local rural households; while households with local household registration but left to make a living elsewhere for more than one year, with or without contract lands, are not counted as local rural households. Collective households of state-owned organs, groups, schools, enterprises, and public institutions, as well as households living in grouped commercial residential quarters in rural areas are not included.

Permanent Population in Towns and Administrative Villages refers to the population of permanent households in rural areas, namely those who stay home regularly or live at home for more than 6 months with their economic life and livelihood incorporated into the household. Migrant workers who live away from home for more than 6 months but taking most of their earnings back home, with their economic life still incorporated into the household, are also counted as permanent population of the household; state employees and retirees who live locally with their life incorporated into the household are also considered permanent population. But soldiers in active service, enrolled students (externs excluded) in technical secondary schools or above, as well as migrant workers who lived away from home for years (excluding those who travel to visit their families or to seek medical care) with a stable job and residence elsewhere, are not regarded as permanent population.

Employ Persons in Towns and Administrative Villages refer to persons aged above 16 in all towns and administrative villages, who actually participate in productive and operating activities and earn incomes in kind or cash, including persons within the range of labor age and regularly participating in labor, and persons beyond the range of labor age but regularly participating in labor; while local registered students who left home for education, soldiers in active service, and people who lost the ability to work are not included, neither are the people waiting for employment or domestic workers. In terms of the length of employment period (or in terms of income if the employment periods are identical), employment falls into the following categories: agriculture, industry, construction, transportation, storage and post, information transmission, software and information technology services, wholesale and retail trade, accommodation and restaurants, and other sectors.

11

北京统计年鉴2016　　BEIJING STATISTICAL YEARBOOK

工 业
INDUSTRY

简要说明

一、本章统计的主要内容

本章资料反映北京市工业方面的基本情况，主要包括按登记注册类型、轻重工业、企业规模、工业行业大类等分组的主要经济指标数据，还包括国有控股工业企业、股份制工业企业、港澳台及外商投资工业企业、大中型工业企业的主要经济指标数据。

具体指标包括单位数、工业总产值、工业增加值、资产总计、负债合计、主营业务收入、主营业务成本、主营业务税金及附加、利润总额、应交增值税、总资产贡献率、资产负债率、成本费用利润率、主要工业产品产量等。

二、本章资料的统计范围

1984 年以前农村的村及村以下办工业归属农业，1984 年以后划归工业。

1999 年以前，工业的统计范围按隶属关系划分为乡及乡以上独立核算工业企业和非独立核算生产单位、村办工业、城镇合作工业、农村合作工业、城镇个体工业、农村个体工业六大部分（1984 年以前村办工业不在工业统计范围内）。

2000 年-2006 年，工业统计调查范围由按隶属关系划分，改变为按企业规模划分。2000 年至 2006 年，分为全部国有及年主营业务收入在 500 万元及以上非国有工业企业（简称“规模以上”）和年主营业务收入在 500 万元以下非国有工业企业和全部个体经营工业单位（简称“规模以下”）两部分。

2007 年-2010 年，分为年主营业务收入在 500 万元及以上法人工业企业（简称“规模以上”）和年主营业务收入在 500 万元以下法人工业企业和全部个体经营工业单位（简称“规模以下”）两部分。

2011 年及以后，分为年主营业务收入在 2000 万元及以上法人工业企业（简称“规模以上”）和年主营业务收入在 2000 万元以下法人工业企业和全部个体经营工业单位（简称“规模以下”）两部分。

三、数据来源和调查方法

本章工业企业统计数据来源于北京市统计局、国家统计局北京调查总队。其中，规模以上数据为全面调查，规模以下数据为抽样调查。

四、有关统计标准的变化说明

（一）关于行业划分：本章资料中工业行业分类 2002-2011 年期间执行 2002 年《国民经济行业分类标准》(GB/T 4754-2002)划分标准，2012 年开始执行 2011 年《国民经济行业分类》(GB/T 4754-2011)划分标准。

（二）关于企业标准划分：2010 年以前企业大中小型划分执行《统计上大中小型企业划分办法（暂行）》标准，自 2011 年开始，大中小微型企业划分标准执行国家统计局《关于统计上大中小微型企业划分办法》（国统字[2011]75 号）。

五、本章中关于历史数据调整的问题

1993-2003 年规模以上工业总产值及增加值历史资料根据“北京市第一次全国经济普查”的结果采用“趋势离差法”进行了修正，2004 年为第一次经济普查数据，2008 年为第二次经济普查数据，2013 年为第三次经济普查数据。

Brief Introduction

I. Main Content

Data in this chapter show the basic situation of industry in Beijing, including: major economic indicators grouped by type of registration, light or heavy industry, enterprise scale, and industrial sector. and also includes main economic indicators for state-holding industrial enterprises, industrial enterprises limited by shares, Hong Kong, Macao, Taiwan and foreign-invested enterprises, and the large and medium-sized industrial enterprises.

Indicators include: unit number, gross industrial output value, industrial added value, total assets, total liabilities, main business income, main business cost, main business tax and surtax, total profits, payable VAT, contribution rate to total assets, asset-liability ratio, cost-profit ratio, and output of main industrial products, etc.

II. Scope of Statistics

Prior to 1984, the rural industrial production run by villages and units subordinated to villages was classified as agriculture. Since 1984, it has been grouped into industry.

Before 1999, industrial statistics coverage was divided into six parts by registration type, i.e. industrial enterprises at the township-level and above with and without independent accounting, village-run industry, urban cooperative industry, rural cooperative industry, urban individual operated industry, and rural individual operated industry (village-run industry was not included in the industrial statistics before 1984).

2000-2006, the scope of industrial statistics was grouped by enterprise scale instead of registration type. From 2000 to 2006, industrial enterprises fell into two classes. One class includes all state-owned enterprises and non-state-owned ones with annual main business income of RMB 5 million and above ("above designated size"), while the other class covers all individual operations and non-state-owned enterprises with annual main business income below RMB 5 million ("below designated size").

2007-2010, industrial enterprises fell into two classes. One includes corporate industrial enterprises with main business income of RMB 5 million and above ("above designated size"), the other includes corporate industrial enterprises with main business income below RMB 5 million and all individual operations ("below designated size").

In and after 2011, industrial enterprises fell into two classes. One includes corporate industrial enterprises with main business income of RMB 20 million and above ("above designated size"), the other includes corporate industrial enterprises with main business income below RMB 20 million and all individual operations ("below designated size").

III. Source of Data and Methods of Survey

Data on industrial enterprises in this chapter were provided by Beijing Municipal Bureau of Statistics and NBS Survey Office in Beijing. Data on industrial enterprises above designated size were gathered through complete survey, and data on those below designated size were obtained through sampling survey.

IV. Changes in Relevant Statistical Standards

(I) Classification of Industrial Sectors: In this chapter, classification of industrial sectors during 2002-2011 was based on the *Standard for Classification of National Economic Sectors 2002* (GB/T 4754-2002). *Standard for Classification of National Economic Sectors 2011* (GB/T 4754-2011) began to be enforced in 2012;

(II) Classification of Enterprises: Before 2010, small, medium and large-sized enterprises were classified by standards of *Measures for Statistical Classification of Small, Medium and Large-sized Enterprises (Temporary)*. Since 2011, the classification of micro, small, medium and large-sized enterprises has been in line with standards of Circular by National Bureau of Statistics on Printing and Issuing the *Measures for Statistical Classification of Micro, Small, Medium and Large-sized Enterprises* (G.T.Z. [2011] No. 75).

V. About the Adjustment to Historical Data

In accordance with the unified requirements and methods of the National Bureau of Statistics, data on total output value and added value of industrial enterprises above designated size were based on results from the "first national economic census in Beijing" after revision through the "trend deviation method". The time span of the revised data is from 1993 to 2003. The first economic census was carried out in 2004 and the second in 2008, and the third in 2013.

11-1 规模以上工业总产值(1984-2015年)
GROSS OUTPUT VALUE OF INDUSTRY ABOVE DESIGNATED SIZE (1984-2015)

单位：亿元 (100 million yuan)

年 份 Year	合 计 Total	轻工业 Light Industry	重工业 Heavy Industry	#大中型工业 Medium and Large-sized Industry
1984	276.2	118.0	158.2	178.7
1985	324.2	135.8	188.4	213.7
1986-1990	**2448.3**	**1039.7**	**1408.6**	**1691.2**
1986	336.5	140.8	195.7	231.6
1987	387.6	160.1	227.5	272.1
1988	495.6	212.5	283.1	345.4
1989	602.7	264.1	338.6	408.3
1990	625.9	262.2	363.7	433.8
1991-1995	**5826.7**	**1936.6**	**3890.1**	**3770.8**
1991	730.2	298.1	432.1	507.4
1992	860.0	306.5	553.5	587.4
1993	1166.6	361.9	804.7	747.6
1994	1576.6	497.9	1078.7	990.7
1995	1493.3	472.2	1021.1	937.7
1996-2000	**10382.8**	**3026.2**	**7356.6**	**5765.7**
1996	1590.6	509.1	1081.5	962.3
1997	1819.7	577.8	1241.9	999.6
1998	1947.0	598.2	1348.8	1059.8
1999	2183.5	621.8	1561.7	1090.9
2000	2842.0	719.3	2122.7	1653.1
2001-2005	**23980.6**	**4911.1**	**19069.5**	**16858.4**
2001	3270.1	842.4	2427.7	2298.4
2002	3620.2	882.4	2737.8	2434.7
2003	4410.8	936.7	3474.1	3183.9
2004	5733.3	1084.7	4648.6	3699.3
2005	6946.2	1164.9	5781.3	5242.1
2006-2010	**53010.4**	**8204.7**	**44805.7**	**40357.2**
2006	8210.0	1258.2	6951.8	6237.9
2007	9648.4	1505.5	8142.9	7365.9
2008	10413.1	1674.3	8738.8	7898.9
2009	11039.1	1766.7	9272.4	8349.3
2010	13699.8	2000.0	11699.8	10505.3
2011-2015	**83383.2**	**12349.7**	**71033.5**	**66759.9**
2011	14513.6	2227.2	12286.4	11289.3
2012	15596.2	2402.1	13194.1	12239.6
2013	17370.9	2541.5	14829.4	13941.3
2014	18452.9	2568.0	15884.9	15039.5
2015	17449.6	2610.8	14838.8	14250.3

注：1. 工业总产值按现价计算。
2. 规模以上工业：2000年以前各年为乡及乡以上工业口径；2000-2006年调整为全部国有及年主营业务收入在500万元及以上非国有工业口径；2007年-2010年调整为年主营业务收入500万元及以上的全部法人工业企业；2011年及以后调整为年主营业务收入2000万元及以上的全部法人工业企业(下同)。
3. 自2011年开始，大中型企业划分标准执行国家统计局《关于统计上大中小微型企业划分办法》(国统字[2011]75号)(下同)。

Note: a) Gross output value is calculated at current prices.
b) Data on industry above designated size covered enterprises at and above the township level before 2000, 2000-2006 covered all State-owned enterprises and non-State-owned enterprises with main business income of over RMB 5 million annually, 2007-2010 covered all corporate industrial enterprises with main business income of over RMB 5 million annually, and from 2011 covered all corporate industrial enterprises with main business income over RMB 20 million (the same below).
c) Since 2011, Division standards of medium and large-sized enterprises complies with Statistical Division Standards of Micro, Small, Medium and Large-sized Enterprises issued by National Bureau of Statistics (G.T.Z. [2011] No. 75) (the same below).

11-2 规模以上工业企业主要指标(1978-2015年)
MAIN INDICATORS FOR INDUSTRIAL ENTERPRISES ABOVE DESIGNATED SIZE (1978-2015)

年 份 Year	企业单位个数(个) Number of Enterprises (unit)	从业人员平均人数(万人) Average Number of Employed Persons (10000 persons)	资产总计(万元) Total Assets (10000 yuan)	负债合计(万元) Total Liabilities (10000 yuan)	固定资产原价(万元) Original Value of Fixed Assets (10000 yuan)	主营业务收入(万元) Main Business Income (10000 yuan)	利润总额(万元) Total Profits (10000 yuan)	利税总额(万元) Total Taxes & Profits (10000 yuan)
1978	4225	114.79			1305271	1098279	370551	501588
1979	3746	116.79	1417223		1371335	1186497	414344	554895
1980	3733	140.91	1547267		1495083	1987967	453147	604241
1981-1985						**12561630**	**2404751**	**3383077**
1981	3778	152.90	1650869		1622035	2054862	440753	599452
1982	3867	158.70	1748915		1750727	2183458	440000	604372
1983	4011	161.98	1846698		1886857	2408893	469364	642437
1984	4291	165.50	2003625		2045344	2728866	505249	707360
1985	4458	165.63	2338194		2337082	3175551	549385	829456
1986-1990						**24054442**	**2924045**	**4825016**
1986	5461	169.85	2720485		2627346	3385055	523961	813979
1987	5746	170.52	3147157		3008917	3935004	570760	885303
1988	5932	170.54	3607173		3412765	5032042	701574	1081370
1989	6175		4343353		3890267	5597829	638385	1087017
1990	6272	173.46	4982746		4382462	6104512	489365	957347
1991-1995						**57731437**	**4241285**	**8051832**
1991	6344	172.39	5672894		5052285	7271529	583381	1106009
1992	6205	175.48	6409037		5754181	8526860	748098	1347058
1993	10320	167.90	15209851		9986886	12822058	1095165	1811556
1994	10889	179.50	19692285		9648050	13207344	961715	1857476
1995	10712	176.16	25826309	15287699	13900296	15903646	852926	1929733
1996-2000						**103617473**	**3188809**	**8655552**
1996	16905	166.63	28755517	17220941	16319878	15801389	330539	1225314
1997	19387	157.52	34083006	20496564	18503218	17070867	405129	1405499
1998	18089	167.11	40129028	24839166	22213387	20345380	484460	1617338
1999	19682	161.10	42540707	25863159	23121446	22186280	697807	1846310
2000	16027	145.60	46127325	26763977	25316408	28213557	1270874	2561091
2001-2005						**233471075**	**13486920**	**23453788**
2001	4356	108.02	44482243	24595592	25036546	30068965	1369794	2795203
2002	4551	107.56	47429487	25278299	26554117	31827790	1655153	3219863
2003	4019	100.81	51779832	27511740	27559571	38856527	2352909	4189859
2004	6872	113.60	120495094	41430793	39221838	59926564	3974076	6417537
2005	6301	117.06	128298350	47067350	44340413	72791229	4134988	6831326
2006-2010						**576103251**	**35550064**	**57599572**
2006	6400	117.36	142444009	55423362	50306165	89141630	5311453	8479249
2007	6398	119.25	162155043	65083476	58148433	104401683	6956067	10552194
2008	7206	123.38	168024206	80850104	65745860	112758173	5569968	9379138
2009	6891	120.41	195407033	98746128	70836396	121730618	7429216	12699472
2010	6885	124.15	227505774	115480740	79360648	148071147	10283360	16489519
2011-2015						**899886856**	**67937345**	**108777212**
2011	3740	117.87	253217462	126486073	86208174	157533565	11294991	18061726
2012	3692	120.15	286131557	148372202	102771932	169051357	12678868	20104385
2013	3641	116.14	308007299	162079598	107885887	186886314	12828840	21252443
2014	3686	116.55	335570497	171375654	115329380	197766666	15157524	24078630
2015	3548	110.44	386097637	181024377	122654798	188648954	15977122	25280028

11-3 规模以上工业增加值(1993-2015年)

单位：亿元

年 份 Year	增加值 Added Value of Industry	轻工业 Light Industry	重工业 Heavy Industry	#计算机、通信和其他电子设备制造业 Manufacture of Computers, Communication Equipment and Other Electronic Equipment	#汽车制造业 Manufacture of Motor Vehicles	#电力、热力生产和供应业 Production and Supply of Electricity and Heating Power	#铁路、船舶、航空航天和其他运输设备制造业 Manufacture of Railway Locomotives, Building of Ships Manufacture Air and Spacecrafts and Other Transportation Equipment
1993	304.1	98.3	205.8	22.6	28.4	4.6	
1994	374.6	138.0	236.6	30.9	29.7	9.5	
1995	473.1	112.3	360.8	46.7	44.4	33.0	
1996-2000	**3058.8**	**981.7**	**2077.1**	**622.0**	**180.7**	**170.4**	
1996	500.2	168.8	331.4	66.6	38.1	-12.1	
1997	558.0	170.1	387.9	75.7	58.0	45.8	
1998	588.2	197.2	391.0	133.8	30.0	41.5	
1999	636.5	200.6	435.9	154.5	25.6	45.4	
2000	776.0	245.0	531.0	191.4	29.0	49.8	
2001-2005	**6153.4**	**1549.4**	**4604.0**	**1078.7**	**505.4**	**564.2**	
2001	866.3	265.2	601.0	203.6	39.0	52.4	
2002	960.7	306.6	654.1	177.8	54.8	66.6	
2003	1174.7	304.8	869.9	228.3	126.0	78.3	
2004	1524.7	332.6	1192.1	197.5	144.2	174.4	
2005	1627.0	340.2	1286.8	271.5	141.4	192.5	
2006-2010	**11071.1**	**2366.2**	**8704.9**	**1423.7**	**1329.5**	**1705.0**	
2006	1840.2	370.1	1470.1	329.7	155.1	254.6	
2007	2159.4	427.6	1731.9	363.6	194.9	355.2	
2008	2037.6	482.3	1555.3	289.4	211.1	358.4	
2009	2282.2	529.4	1752.8	201.2	310.6	327.3	
2010	2751.7	556.8	2194.8	239.8	457.8	409.5	
2011-2015	**16653.2**	**3591.0**	**13062.1**	**1342.0**	**3333.2**	**2931.3**	
2011	2899.1	619.2	2279.9	204.5	562.1	448.8	
2012	3033.3	681.3	2352.0	243.6	512.6	536.0	53.5
2013	3432.1	749.7	2682.4	304.4	732.3	602.3	71.7
2014	3612.0	766.6	2845.3	305.1	726.2	682.0	96.9
2015	3676.6	774.2	2902.5	284.4	799.9	662.1	97.5

注：1. 本表增加值均按生产法计算，2004年以前数据为根据全国第一次经济普查数据调整后的数据。
2. 2012年开始行业划分执行2011年国民经济行业分类标准(GB/T 4754-2011)；表中2012年前，汽车制造业为原“交通运输设备制造业”数据，计算机、通信和其它电子设备制造业为原“通信设备、计算机及其他电子设备制造业”的数据。

ADDED VALUE OF INDUSTRY ABOVE DESIGNATED SIZE (1993-2015)

(100 million yuan)

#化学原料和化学制品制造业 Manufacture of Chemical Raw Materials and Chemical Products	#通用设备制造业 Manufacture of General-Purpose Machinery	#专用设备制造业 Manufacture of Special-Purpose Machinery	#电气机械和器材制造业 Manufacture of Electrical Machinery and Equipment	#仪器仪表制造业 Manufacture of Measuring Instruments and Meters	#医药制造业 Manufacture of Medicines	#非金属矿物制品业 Manufacture of Non-Metallic Mineral Products	#石油加工、炼焦和核燃料加工业 Processing of Petroleum, Coking, Processing of Nuclear Fuel
15.5	13.0	10.0	10.1	3.2	5.5	14.8	12.5
19.7	15.9	26.4	11.6	4.5	5.3	21.2	14.2
28.9	17.2	12.1	9.8	9.0	7.5	17.7	45.9
136.2	**73.1**	**114.5**	**99.5**	**52.6**	**90.3**	**139.4**	**194.5**
26.0	18.1	16.9	15.4	10.6	11.8	28.4	37.9
21.4	13.2	19.3	17.3	7.5	15.6	25.7	42.3
25.3	17.5	22.9	21.0	10.9	12.6	30.9	31.4
24.0	8.2	22.9	19.0	11.1	22.7	19.6	42.3
39.5	16.1	32.5	26.8	12.4	27.6	34.8	40.6
381.2	**200.8**	**263.7**	**257.8**	**142.2**	**225.4**	**230.1**	**215.6**
44.1	25.7	29.2	36.5	17.0	31.0	34.4	35.8
55.3	25.5	56.3	38.7	19.0	47.2	47.2	53.9
76.3	36.6	49.8	54.9	21.6	53.2	48.5	29.6
141.8	56.5	67.7	65.1	38.3	44.7	52.0	19.7
63.7	56.5	60.7	62.6	46.4	49.3	48.0	76.6
331.2	**495.2**	**526.7**	**497.0**	**313.6**	**543.0**	**333.5**	**461.6**
56.9	72.6	86.6	57.1	57.2	57.0	53.5	49.6
72.6	84.7	84.7	85.8	70.6	81.6	52.7	56.9
60.5	99.1	111.9	92.9	58.7	115.3	55.2	-2.3
57.1	97.4	112.3	126.4	61.0	135.8	85.8	172.5
84.1	141.4	131.2	134.8	66.1	153.3	86.3	184.9
322.6	**685.2**	**708.1**	**692.5**	**332.9**	**1246.0**	**383.0**	**680.0**
77.7	153.1	139.8	137.1	63.6	184.2	80.7	122.8
56.1	130.2	130.4	124.8	59.6	222.2	79.5	126.2
55.8	125.0	158.1	135.4	64.9	254.2	80.5	98.2
62.3	147.3	132.6	145.5	68.2	283.1	75.0	151.3
70.6	129.6	147.3	149.7	76.7	302.3	67.3	181.5

Note: a) Added value in this table is calculated with production method. Figures before 2004 are adjusted according to the national first economic census.

b) The Standard for Classification of National Economic Sectors 2011 (GB/T 4754-2011) became effective in 2012; in this table,figures of "manufacture of motor vehicles" in 2012 were figures of the former "manufacture of transportation equipment", and figures of "manufacture of computers, communication equipment and other electronic equipment" were figures of the former "manufacture of communication equipment, computers and other electronic equipment".

11-4 规模以上工业产品产量(1978-2015年)
OUTPUT OF INDUSTRIAL PRODUCTS ABOVE DESIGNATED SIZE (1978-2015)

年份 Year	布 (万米) Cloth (10000 m)	机制纸及纸板 (万吨) Machine-made Paper and Paperboard (10000 tons)	饮料酒 (万千升) Alcoholic Beverage (10000 kl)	乳制品 (万吨) Dairy Products (10000 tons)	家用电冰箱 (万台) Household Refrigerators (10000 units)	照相机 (万台) Camera (10000 units)	家具 (万件) Furniture (10000 pieces)	原煤 (万吨) Raw Coal (10000 tons)	原油加工量 (万吨) Crude Oil Processed (10000 tons)	乙稀 (万吨) Ethylene (10000 tons)	发电量 (万千瓦时) Electricity Generation (10000 kwh)
1978	25436	12.1	8.4			0.5	137.8	818.7			990750
1979	27297	13.9	9.9		2.0	0.7	171.3	711.1			1042870
1980	28940	14.0	11.6		2.6	1.0	200.2	791.0	591.1		1065060
1981-1985	**142080**	**86.9**	**87.3**	**2.0**	**41.6**	**25.7**	**1348.4**	**4269.1**	**2811.3**	**132.3**	**5101356**
1981	28635	14.5	13.4		3.1	4.2	217.7	788.7	533.5	24.7	993071
1982	29758	15.8	14.9	0.2	4.5	0.9	243.5	811.3	533.5	25.6	1003446
1983	30068	17.1	17.4	0.3	6.4	2.8	254.2	840.5	563.8	27.3	1028826
1984	27621	18.9	20.3	0.6	10.3	5.3	297.9	884.3	589.4	26.9	1038842
1985	25998	20.6	21.3	0.9	17.3	12.5	335.1	944.3	591.1	27.8	1037171
1986-1990	**153032**	**120.5**	**131.4**	**4.7**	**96.4**	**74.6**	**2096.6**	**4745.3**	**3210.5**	**141.8**	**5656282**
1986	27503	21.9	21.5	0.7	18.1	15.9	303.8	917.2	619.0	25.3	1043208
1987	29738	24.1	22.7	0.8	19.4	16.5	283.0	899.8	640.2	27.0	1057493
1988	32262	23.3	23.9	1.0	23.6	15.8	347.1	906.0	645.0	30.3	1110758
1989	32271	25.8	28.7	1.0	24.7	13.5	572.1	1016.8	651.9	29.1	1191269
1990	31258	25.4	34.6	1.2	10.7	12.9	590.6	1005.5	654.4	30.1	1253554
1991-1995	**133994**	**116.5**	**347.3**	**5.9**	**27.0**	**450.8**	**3261.0**	**4851.0**	**3269.9**	**172.2**	**6772732**
1991	31497	27.2	43.8	1.3	7.1	5.4	602.0	996.5	653.4	31.1	1318000
1992	29717	22.6	56.6	1.2	9.1	4.2	570.0	1015.2	662.5	32.8	1423000
1993	26816	19.1	72.6	1.6	4.2	39.3	729.0	835.4	664.0	27.2	1410900
1994	21440	21.0	83.1	0.3	6.6	158.8	605.0	1008.5	642.0	28.1	1298718
1995	24524	26.6	91.2	1.5		243.1	755.0	995.4	648.0	53.0	1322114
1996-2000	**96005**	**70.0**	**436.6**	**7.3**	**15.9**	**706.5**	**1986.8**	**4360.0**	**3336.5**	**306.0**	**7330814**
1996	22585	15.3	102.2	1.2	6.3	234.3	510.6	1013.7	633.6	57.5	1415555
1997	25185	18.1	…	1.7	…	157.7	469.4	1011.7	657.0	58.0	1464302
1998	21299	13.1		0.9	0.3	177.7	348.5	989.5	602.3	57.0	1566621
1999	14753	13.0	148.8	1.4	5.8	81.6	386.2	792.1	701.9	68.0	1431772
2000	12183	10.6	185.6	2.1	3.6	55.2	272.1	553.0	741.7	65.5	1452564
2001-2005	**38411**	**59.5**	**700.9**	**119.7**	**189.7**	**685.0**	**2036.9**	**4359.5**	**3624.5**	**430.7**	**8369923**
2001	11353	8.8	135.8	3.7	5.9	61.3	370.6	690.2	647.9	54.3	1326588
2002	10314	6.2	138.7	1.4	16.2	220.7	368.3	880.9	695.2	90.4	1419754
2003	8393	7.9	132.8	1.3	22.8	238.3	323.8	822.6	701.1	88.8	1451197
2004	4081	19.6	148.0	56.4	63.1	116.8	567.7	1067.9	783.4	98.2	2038933
2005	4270	17.0	145.6	56.9	81.7	47.9	406.5	897.9	796.9	99.0	2133451
2006-2010	**4508**	**64.0**	**906.9**	**270.8**	**447.0**	**189.1**	**3765.4**	**2971.5**	**5143.2**	**455.6**	**11960020**
2006	930	14.0	170.8	63.5	74.1	49.2	893.4	629.2	828.9	99.1	2136918
2007	536	10.4	189.1	57.9	73.1	34.7	638.8	633.3	915.0	90.9	2278658
2008	1583	14.9	180.0	44.9	79.0	49.0	690.9	567.7	1114.6	85.4	2431255
2009	965	14.1	181.1	52.2	128.7	27.1	719.4	641.3	1161.3	84.1	2424839
2010	495	10.6	185.8	52.3	92.1	29.2	822.8	500.0	1123.4	96.2	2688350
2011-2015	**1586**	**42.9**	**931.2**	**296.4**	**237.6**	**70.9**	**3841.4**	**2400.9**	**5110.9**	**402.1**	**16408207**
2011	339	10.0	187.0	58.6	73.5	26.6	750.2	500.1	1103.1	89.6	2628331
2012	351	11.3	191.7	56.6	80.4	18.2	720.1	493.1	1075.0	84.0	2908214
2013	361	10.0	198.0	58.5	83.7	17.9	995.9	500.1	881.6	72.3	3312116
2014	361	6.6	187.4	60.6		6.6	674.7	457.5	1051.1	77.6	3385699
2015	174	5.0	167.1	62.1		1.6	700.5	450.1	1000.1	78.6	4173847

11-4 续表 Continued

年 份 Year	粗 钢 (万吨) Crude Steel (10000 tons)	钢 材 (万吨) Rolled Steel (10000 tons)	水 泥 (万吨) Cement (10000 tons)	交 流 电动机 (万千瓦) Alternator (10000 kw)	汽 车 (万辆) Motor Vehicles (10000 units)	#轿 车 Sedan Cars	移动通信手持机 (万台) Mobile Phones (10000 units)	微型计算机设 备 (万台) Micro-Computers (10000 units)	数控金属切削机床 (台) CNC Metal Cutting Lathe (unit)	显示器 (万台) Displays (10000 units)	集 成 电 路 (亿块) IC (100 million units)
1978	191.0	116.8	191.5	152.5	1.8						
1979	196.5	137.5	196.9	179.7	2.4						
1980	200.9	152.1	217.4	142.7	2.8						
1981-1985	**1114.2**	**907.9**	**1355.7**	**713.0**	**17.2**			**2.0**			
1981	190.3	149.5	225.7	104.0	2.7						
1982	200.4	159.4	249.1	123.3	2.8						
1983	214.1	177.9	270.8	148.3	3.1			0.3			
1984	241.7	200.1	291.6	165.4	3.6			1.2			
1985	267.7	221.0	318.5	172.0	5.0			0.5			
1986-1990	**1837.8**	**1556.7**	**1649.3**	**889.7**	**39.5**			**6.9**			
1986	303.6	255.5	310.5	178.4	5.8			0.5			
1987	335.5	283.4	319.6	196.4	7.4			0.9			
1988	369.0	314.9	334.3	199.5	9.0			3.0			
1989	386.0	327.9	345.9	163.8	8.5			1.3			
1990	443.7	375.0	339.0	151.6	8.8			1.2			
1991-1995	**3411.0**	**2613.9**	**2364.7**	**824.3**	**70.8**			**32.3**			
1991	499.7	402.9	377.6	156.7	11.0			1.7			
1992	575.0	438.3	403.0	174.9	13.8			3.0			
1993	702.7	525.3	477.9	162.3	13.4			4.1			
1994	828.7	617.6	531.7	165.0	14.7			4.3			
1995	804.9	629.8	574.2	165.4	17.9			19.2			
1996-2000	**3937.5**	**3343.3**	**3758.9**	**753.3**	**57.7**			**686.6**	**2238**		**5.4**
1996	794.7	654.3	666.0	151.9	13.4			28.1	326		0.5
1997	801.7	652.4	700.9	148.7	11.0			59.8	433		0.6
1998	803.2	676.1	762.0	149.7	8.5			160.9	430		0.6
1999	734.5	663.8	803.0	142.0	12.3	1.0		180.0	481		1.3
2000	803.4	696.7	827.0	161.0	12.5	0.5	1549.6	257.8	568		2.4
2001-2005	**4113.3**	**4096.9**	**4963.3**	**1169.8**	**179.6**	**45.7**	**21081.2**	**2407.0**	**5783**		**33.0**
2001	824.9	727.3	809.0	175.1	14.3	0.5	2163.4	339.7	1004		2.1
2002	816.9	750.0	884.0	199.3	18.1	0.7	2280.1	415.7	912		2.5
2003	816.4	785.0	882.0	253.1	34.7	7.3	3334.5	469.3	1188		4.7
2004	827.5	868.3	1204.5	279.4	53.9	15.0	4172.1	532.7	1024		11.1
2005	827.6	966.3	1183.8	262.9	58.6	22.2	9131.1	649.6	1655		12.6
2006-2010	**2988.1**	**4267.1**	**5443.8**	**1160.6**	**492.9**	**191.6**	**106256.6**	**4052.3**	**23256**	**3205.7**	**90.2**
2006	818.1	1016.3	1269.4	269.0	68.3	27.0	14068.0	736.1	1875	680.7	11.8
2007	810.8	1030.4	1167.3	281.9	70.7	20.3	22719.9	843.3	2382	513.6	15.7
2008	466.8	656.8	880.8	259.7	76.6	28.3	20725.5	691.7	3108	478.1	19.1
2009	464.9	769.6	1077.4	159.0	127.1	53.8	21355.3	842.7	6125	655.6	18.3
2010	427.5	794.0	1049.0	191.1	150.3	62.2	27388.0	938.6	9766	877.8	25.3
2011-2015	**11.4**	**1132.6**	**3911.0**	**563.8**	**959.9**	**477.6**	**92219.5**	**5166.3**	**59213**	**3020.7**	**219.3**
2011	2.9	287.0	911.5	146.0	150.5	67.1	25962.3	1083.7	12537	851.4	32.0
2012	2.6	253.8	874.5	117.1	167.0	78.5	19949.3	1074.5	13332	796.9	31.9
2013	2.3	221.8	868.4	145.4	203.8	94.5	18783.4	1106.9	6983	305.3	38.4
2014	2.1	195.0	703.1	115.0	216.7	118.6	17983.6	1015.6	13890	548.1	54.3
2015	1.5	175.0	553.5	40.3	221.9	118.9	9540.8	885.6	12471	519.0	62.7

11-5 规模以上工业企业主要经济指标(2015年)

单位：万元

项　　目	Item	企业单位个数(个) Number of Enterprises (unit)	#亏损企业 Loss-Suffering Enterprises	工业总产值(当年价格) Gross Output Value of Industry (at current year's prices)	工业增加值 Added Value of Industry	工业销售产值(当年价格) Sales Value of Industry (at current)	#出口交货值 Delivery Value of Exports
合　　计	**Total**	**3548**	**757**	**174496269**	**36766396**	**172792712**	**10783871**
按隶属关系分组	**By Affiliation**						
中央企业	Central Enterprises	239	45	59074616	12713407	58964367	381516
地方企业	Local Enterprises	3309	712	115421653	24052989	113828345	10402355
按登记注册类型分组	**By Registration Type**						
内资企业	Domestially-Invested Enterprises	2745	546	103904167	21974112	102750804	3307703
国有企业	State-owned Enterprises	72	9	34301682	6062255	34311957	19739
集体企业	Collectively-owned Enterprises	40	13	246729	67921	252956	5569
股份合作企业	Joint-equity Cooperative Enterprises	58	10	718110	115324	713728	15628
有限责任公司	Limited Liability Companies	1236	292	37915629	8191700	37471166	1821015
股份有限公司	Companies Limited by Shares	245	50	21229171	5267639	20833319	892054
私营企业	Private Enterprises	1093	172	9490314	2268777	9165334	553698
其他企业	Others	***	***	***	***	***	***
港澳台商投资企业	Hong Kong, Macao and Taiwan-invested Enterprises	195	52	18669714	2187609	18147896	1802905
港澳台合资经营	Joint Ventures	96	22	4445251	1188288	4498589	902669
港澳台合作经营	Cooperatives	***	***	***	***	***	***
港澳台商独资企业	Solely-funded Enterprises	85	28	13597360	1012356	13054808	835631
港澳台商投资股份有限公司	Companies Limited by Shares	11	2	604316	-26175	574525	64605
外商投资企业	Foreign-invested Enterprises	608	159	51922388	12604675	51894012	5673263
中外合资经营	Joint Ventures	230	54	32871811	8723426	32780280	3239531
中外合作经营	Cooperatives	10	4	207889	92652	196387	29583
外资(独资)企业	Solely-funded Enterprises	356	99	18195584	3642722	18254769	2349780
外商投资股份有限公司	Companies Limited by Shares	12	2	647104	145875	662575	54370
按城乡分组	**By urban and rural regions**						
#农村企业	Rural Enterprises	24	9	170871	25617	171498	1408
按控股类型分组	**By holding types**						
#国有控股	State-holding Enterprises	745	177	100613752	22282119	100264121	2663959
集体控股	Collectively-holding Enterprises	112	23	3604958	744226	3477034	177009
私人控股	Private-holding Enterprises	1984	365	24464063	5833947	23700735	1185332
港澳台控股	Hong Kong, Macao, and Taiwan-holding Enterprises	145	40	15990208	1436067	15497902	1253171
外商控股	Foreign-Investor-holding Enterprises	528	144	29209094	6303291	29242346	5486984
按轻重工业分组	**By light and heavy industries**						
轻工业	Light Industry	1231	252	26108405	7741606	25607631	1498985
重工业	Heavy Industry	2317	505	148387864	29024789	147185081	9284886
按规模分组	**By size**						
#大中型企业	Medium and Large-sized Enterprises	694	144	142502541	29864755	141230251	9072499

注：1. 工业增加值按生产法计算(下表同)。
2. 应交税金合计包括应交增值税、所得税费用、营业税金及附加和管理费用中的税金，计算应交增值税时企业应交增值税为负数的按实际计算(下表同)。

MAIN ECONOMIC INDICATORS OF INDUSTRIAL ENTERPRISES ABOVE DESIGNATED SIZE (2015)

(10000 yuan)

平均用工人数(人) Average Number of Employed Persons (person)	资产负债 Assets and Liabilities						
	资产总计 Total Assets	流动资产合计 Total Current Assets	#存货 Inventories	#产成品 Finished Products	#应收账款 Accounts Receivable (Net)	固定资产合计 Total Fixed Assets	固定资产原价 Total Original Value of Fixed Assets
1104384	**386097637**	**152214302**	**22771594**	**7779401**	**38304001**	**66601836**	**122654798**
184961	182462044	40286277	4548156	1025069	7735996	29938666	62839509
919423	203635593	111928025	18223438	6754332	30568005	36663170	59815289
734778	309652392	105697307	14852815	4919861	26249963	52757858	97341610
46801	147562244	24311328	1188252	138610	2624961	19178332	40942715
6477	377506	267620	67225	32602	50336	78124	155350
8079	635521	467747	118436	60730	139076	94850	160314
364460	97233635	45434068	7134383	2403071	13440185	26045224	43136189
163128	49399081	24962109	3789923	1244256	6523715	5410463	9948935
145803	14441412	10252059	2553384	1040498	3471518	1950261	2997435
30	***	***	***	***	***	***	***
91971	22232519	14145824	2496148	987309	3698830	3486514	6652194
39693	5646850	3575255	632392	195953	1097657	1244515	3407128
366	***	***	***	***	***	***	***
46475	13102413	8224693	1344211	740012	1772252	2157586	3057326
5437	3449060	2316247	514964	48081	816034	81356	180635
277635	54212726	32371171	5422632	1872232	8355207	10357464	18660994
133870	31237912	18289195	2739946	824339	3551840	6346265	9883964
6252	318945	251165	-18123	5712	59431	48780	129785
128083	17639922	12327561	2637697	1016800	4594865	3637375	7882663
9430	5015946	1503251	63112	25382	149072	325045	764582
4040	243995	195441	69709	30093	70190	40615	82784
469045	283001704	85234274	9850665	2893950	16483014	53244124	98957267
26467	4450877	3417146	721493	180874	1476372	431415	709318
324745	51684737	32107586	6406992	2396531	10326080	5036877	7795095
68549	17826582	11353659	1881785	850407	2901043	2660769	4032930
206738	27870375	19150134	3779106	1401071	6905862	5140318	10994536
346919	41164814	24329026	5651661	2500062	5150276	7322890	13470453
757465	344932823	127885276	17119933	5279339	33153725	59278946	109184345
758731	324419998	113959365	14208259	4960472	26137946	57468112	107856174

Note: a) Added value of industry is calculated with production method (the same to the following tables).

b) Total tax payable mainly includes VAT payable, income tax expense, business tax and surtax, and tax in management expenses. The negative VAT payable of enterprises should be calculated by the actual value when calculating the VAT payable (the same to the following tables).

11-5 续表

单位：万元

项目	Item	资产负债 Assets and Liabilities 负债合计 Total Liabilities	#流动负债合计 Total Current Liabilities	#应付账款 Accounts Receivable	所有者权益合计 Total Owner's Equity	#实收资本 Paid-up Capital
合计	**Total**	**181024377**	**122281820**	**40062346**	**204801933**	**108089475**
按隶属关系分组	**By Affiliation**					
中央企业	Central Enterprises	74535633	37042446	9214986	107912844	65707343
地方企业	Local Enterprises	106488743	85239374	30847360	96889089	42382132
按登记注册类型分组	**By Registration Type**					
内资企业	Domestially-Invested Enterprises	139722845	85537160	24217117	169742554	91717472
国有企业	State-owned Enterprises	54873733	20673764	3412037	92688511	56397540
集体企业	Collectively-owned Enterprises	233285	198208	51485	144221	34896
股份合作企业	Joint-equity Cooperative Enterprises	373179	356371	173452	262343	128848
有限责任公司	Limited Liability Companies	55624245	40773315	12581664	41554309	24261430
股份有限公司	Companies Limited by Shares	20678215	16128826	5080242	28639122	7967195
私营企业	Private Enterprises	7937936	7404946	2917936	6453309	2927271
其他企业	Others	***	***	***	***	***
港澳台商投资企业	Hong Kong, Macao and Taiwan-invested Enterprises	13008282	12034611	5104197	9209305	4141290
港澳台合资经营	Joint Ventures	2549023	2397004	822897	3084731	1715920
港澳台合作经营	Cooperatives	***	***	***	***	***
港澳台商独资企业	Solely-funded Enterprises	8456041	7941061	3680228	4644536	1481993
港澳台商投资股份有限公司	Companies Limited by Shares	1998050	1691377	598981	1451010	936709
外商投资企业	Foreign-invested Enterprises	28293249	24710049	10741032	25850074	12230713
中外合资经营	Joint Ventures	16729500	14957142	6339991	14461433	6085686
中外合作经营	Cooperatives	169749	137554	57435	153221	166564
外资(独资)企业	Solely-funded Enterprises	9538214	8457160	4230376	8075260	4563465
外商投资股份有限公司	Companies Limited by Shares	1855787	1158193	113230	3160159	1414997
按城乡分组	**By urban and rural regions**					
#农村企业	Rural Enterprises	151397	117519	38373	92597	48834
按控股类型分组	**By holding types**					
#国有控股	State-holding Enterprises	127433648	74185273	20012764	155533518	87998470
集体控股	Collectively-holding Enterprises	2521334	2349681	935870	1929543	656184
私人控股	Private-holding Enterprises	24257783	21308574	7822813	27278441	9645144
港澳台控股	Hong Kong, Macao, and Taiwan-holding Enterprises	11164469	10414688	4642594	6647181	2812795
外商控股	Foreign-Investor-holding Enterprises	14916082	13316561	6407798	12880949	6763445
按轻重工业分组	**By light and heavy industries**					
轻工业	Light Industry	19391117	16586242	4709045	21730085	9139482
重工业	Heavy Industry	161633260	105695578	35353301	183071848	98949992
按规模分组	**By size**					
#大中型企业	Medium and Large-sized Enterprises	149082379	94269495	29361555	175297341	94109525

11-5 Continued

(10000 yuan)

损益 Profits and Losses											
营业收入 Business Income	#主营业务收入 Main Business Income	营业成本 Business Cost	#主营业务成本 Main Business Cost	销售费用 Sales Expenses	管理费用 Management Expenses	财务费用 Financial Expenses	利润总额 Total Profits	应交税金合计 Total Tax	#营业税金及附加 Business Tax and Surtax	#主营业务税金及附加 Main Business Tax and Surtax	#应交增值税 Value Added Tax Payable
192561382	**188648954**	**159984640**	**157109677**	**9252530**	**9566087**	**2116560**	**15977122**	**11791045**	**3337157**	**3318066**	**5693787**
61274462	60498421	54362698	53738244	423870	1622549	809302	6388664	4029629	1533464	1527098	1791308
131286920	128150533	105621943	103371433	8828660	7943538	1307258	9588458	7761416	1803693	1790968	3902478
112876506	110910248	96212198	94743143	3455258	5997096	1608615	10124452	6622223	1959319	1941298	3265021
34578558	34474366	31598990	31540314	140325	348801	575892	4960527	1817638	429674	427115	979728
267103	257178	227966	223940	13951	26344	-328	9745	20724	3042	2789	14600
789367	784666	699337	696418	35473	37521	3250	27274	23900	2114	2109	16688
42974608	42089595	37459975	36809636	1301316	2902043	619347	2403724	1798581	190442	179998	1035305
23918114	23132565	18325117	17683859	1254534	1676142	324035	2019621	2477913	1285220	1281239	911055
10346412	10169534	7898792	7786956	709618	1006093	86390	703465	483460	48821	48042	307644
***	***	***	***	***	***	***	***	***	***	***	***
23334763	22770940	20185565	19829491	1413691	965342	151101	828417	627356	65490	64805	354160
4853448	4712211	3751724	3632257	280393	286296	34590	519856	307643	33674	33490	149278
***	***	***	***	***	***	***	***	***	***	***	***
17619173	17340153	15728157	15632991	998423	593664	86080	415613	282260	24828	24327	183979
833601	690496	686544	545426	133351	80831	30463	-110021	34783	6759	6759	18970
56350113	54967765	43586878	42537043	4383581	2603649	356844	5024253	4541466	1312348	1311963	2074605
34038929	33420122	26277006	25839274	2050239	1423824	117784	3655432	3390205	1211809	1211773	1370485
380216	373596	305125	298979	47314	19222	-3404	9441	17394	1412	1412	12532
21137566	20456542	16454835	15886452	2200948	1070711	177092	1166570	1082554	93892	93744	657437
793402	717506	549912	512338	85081	89891	65372	192810	51313	5234	5034	34151
181077	176702	165085	162187	3414	16416	2434	-3876	7135	655	633	5260
106890324	105076838	91732041	90392792	2642276	4144589	1402191	10790099	7797308	2966140	2951366	3208512
3674520	3631179	3035018	3014336	224522	247185	14633	195536	188538	21733	20229	134663
26866127	26342289	19948582	19586540	2076915	2588281	370156	2286028	1423250	147388	145380	900260
20510076	20044891	18103634	17834390	1240722	769894	121752	296979	425125	42965	42458	254862
33923570	32894814	26630090	25779441	3019409	1752860	201287	2360917	1918289	155443	155276	1169773
30714503	29854348	20671591	20057506	4669948	2431183	274169	2638987	2603073	590685	587428	1455392
161846879	158794606	139313049	137052171	4582583	7134904	1842391	13338135	9187972	2746472	2730638	4238395
155709992	152709160	130025958	127770795	7551113	6439044	1787383	13542466	10117314	3163661	3149262	4701650

11-6 规模以上工业企业主要经济指标(按行业分)(2015年)

单位：万元

项目	Item	企业单位个数(个) Number of Enterprises (unit)	#亏损企业 Loss-Suffering Enterprises	工业总产值(当年价格) Gross Output Value of Industry (at current year's prices)	工业增加值 Added Value of Industry
合计	**Total**	**3548**	**757**	**174496269**	**36766396**
煤炭开采和洗选业	Mining and Washing of Coal	***	***	***	***
石油和天然气开采业	Extraction of Petroleum and Natural Gas	***	***	***	***
黑色金属矿采选业	Mining and Processing of Ferrous Metal Ores	7	5	809254	18155
非金属矿采选业	Mining and Processing of Nonmetal Ores	***	***	***	***
开采辅助活动	Mining Support Service Activities	6	3	1708288	965972
农副食品加工业	Processing of Food from Agricultural Products	138	37	3569659	500501
食品制造业	Manufacture of Foods	130	25	2832664	359054
酒、饮料和精制茶制造业	Manufacture of Wines, Beverage and Refined Tea	43	15	1746545	546465
烟草制品业	Manufacture of Cigarettes and Tobacco	***	***	***	***
纺织业	Manufacture of Textile	23	8	122962	21749
纺织服装、服饰业	Manufacture of Textile Wearing Apparel and Ornament	128	32	1198539	480420
皮革、毛皮、羽毛及其制品和制鞋业	Manufacture of Leather, Fur, Feather and Its Products, and Footwear	12	1	101321	17191
木材加工和木、竹、藤、棕、草制品业	Processing of Timbers, Manufacture of Wood, Bamboo, Rattan, Palm, and Straw Products	16	3	161671	29402
家具制造业	Manufacture of Furniture	65	9	850216	189985
造纸和纸制品业	Manufacture of Paper and Paper Products	40	11	614707	214529
印刷和记录媒介复制业	Printing, Reproduction of Recording Media	113	29	1118314	438891
文教、工美、体育和娱乐用品制造业	Manufacture of Articles for Culture, Education, Artwork, Sport and Entertainment Activities	34	7	1194121	75009
石油加工、炼焦和核燃料加工业	Processing of Petroleum, Coking, Processing of Mucleus Fuels	20		5911246	1814962
化学原料和化学制品制造业	Manufacture of Chemical Raw Materials and Chemical Products	204	41	3192888	706438
医药制造业	Manufacture of Medicines	201	31	7330183	3022914
化学纤维制造业	Manufacture of Chemical Fibres	***	***	***	***
橡胶和塑料制品业	Manufacture of Rubber and Plastics Products	112	23	920551	205086
非金属矿物制品业	Manufacture of Non-metallic Mineral Products	237	80	3921585	673490
黑色金属冶炼和压延加工业	Manufacture and Pressing of Ferrous Metals	23	4	1022759	23229
有色金属冶炼和压延加工业	Manufacture and Pressing of Non-ferrous Metals	36	7	637682	84447
金属制品业	Manufacture of Fabricated Metal Products	203	47	2934154	747192
通用设备制造业	Manufacture of General-purpose Machinery	238	58	4879508	1296132
专用设备制造业	Manufacture of Special-purpose Machinery	319	58	5437411	1472561
汽车制造业	Manufacture of Motor Vehicles	232	48	38828644	7999090
铁路、船舶、航空航天和其他运输设备制造业	Manufacture of Railway Locomotives, Building of Ships and Boats, Manufacture of Air and Spacecrafts and Other Transportation Equipment	74	8	3844651	974773
电气机械和器材制造业	Manufacture of Electrical Machinery and Equipment	261	54	7861668	1496527
计算机、通信和其他电子设备制造业	Manufacture of Computers, Communication Equipment and Other Electronic Equipment	293	69	21102026	2843549
仪器仪表制造业	Manufacture of Measuring Instruments and Meters	163	17	2576995	766685
其他制造业	Other Manufacturing	31	4	786317	264750
废弃资源综合利用业	Waste Recycling and Recovery	10	3	57638	10222
金属制品、机械和设备修理业	Repair of Fabricated Metal Products, Machinery and Equipment	15	1	662359	250132
电力、热力生产和供应业	Production and Distribution of Electricity and Heating Power	68	13	40855582	6621453
燃气生产和供应业	Production and Distribution of Gas	21	1	4077637	550170
水的生产和供应业	Production and Distribution of Water	23	3	654867	330061

MAIN ECONOMIC INDICATORS OF INDUSTRIAL ENTERPRISES ABOVE DESIGNATED SIZE (BY SECTOR) (2015)

(10000 yuan)

工业销售产值(当年价格) Sales Value of Industry (at current year's prices)	#出口交货值 Delivery Value of Exports	平均用工人数(人) Average Number of Employed Persons (person)	资产负债 Assets and Liabilities						
			资产总计 Total Assets	流动资产合计 Total Current Assets	#存货 Inventories	#产成品 Finished Products	#应收账款 Accounts Receivable	固定资产合计 Total Fixed Assets	固定资产原价 Total Original Value of Fixed Assets
172792712	**10783871**	**1104384**	**386097637**	**152214302**	**22771594**	**7779401**	**38304001**	**66601836**	**122654798**
***	***	10523	***	***	***	***	***	***	***
***	***	1999	***	***	***			***	***
803083		23602	23625156	8277938	248665	38467	1619393	3959845	5734462
***	***	342	***	***	***	***	***	***	***
1708288	125601	19926	5446628	2755494	245696	14946	1097496	1160040	2621768
3541484	78622	33072	4281103	2875030	478503	262266	427326	508719	822432
2817705	140185	51457	4087473	2437512	446986	213678	530343	779626	1393846
1833987	14832	27114	4162432	1546938	251344	70972	115890	620633	1379763
***	***	916	***	***	***	***	***	***	***
130139	19405	3528	474360	288752	39666	21954	60538	79480	135642
1154095	193797	40452	1735478	1329319	601647	361139	206003	227201	373930
101101	13513	1862	101135	83155	44221	21546	24067	8348	16382
161434	13538	3021	168882	105989	26534	6771	32749	45411	93531
845591	55727	14274	1031772	697917	199157	83790	175504	169088	263080
619619	47949	5320	553339	347390	96795	31372	92762	150295	348427
1130762	13911	24438	2165324	1211908	256833	91039	240935	608036	1507376
1219881	50868	6313	817503	651557	325541	189505	122072	79843	148438
5921386		11686	2742770	1136616	680843	109754	204163	1166420	3166156
3082059	127834	34001	4559508	2857338	569730	255676	703599	992517	2490055
6894001	119177	73562	11514980	6925587	1850442	800118	1713071	1890757	2772290
***	***	128	***	***	***	***	***	***	***
919995	94401	18505	1165345	756869	164323	75758	261217	269675	504233
3919902	94574	48894	9564887	6965828	902499	222630	3346511	963715	1944812
1016352	74172	5571	1105620	449917	189783	67084	153760	482848	816987
642091	101610	5555	796670	489993	136538	44684	147727	99672	176410
2959594	238997	37714	5895571	3641036	822946	344668	840367	827793	1429124
4802417	852540	54921	10040202	7283470	1899172	587563	1750166	1104318	2029029
5408563	692214	66800	16672118	10764108	1799397	553378	3159403	1135535	1911737
38753657	622825	141680	37160912	19836298	2508304	1015396	5475450	8071430	11427077
3739397	44635	36773	6504453	4701178	1518665	214171	1645193	856539	1363507
7678286	486177	55308	12215581	9278512	1612088	431318	4127202	751552	1369147
20422464	6052959	116198	30657310	18833366	3317379	1338001	4541281	4258216	9064299
2561099	144256	31738	5024413	3811126	886056	185641	1276050	400921	653878
750665	113875	8173	1442170	858052	188492	51909	275833	308377	542174
57140	1093	960	207233	48407	3309	2003	3542	90674	113053
658433	49592	10615	717844	445929	158797	4029	174864	207809	383063
40846775		53820	161836943	24677707	127164	9551	2801115	28688304	57068354
4077637		12116	4913252	1380682	14719	7061	344959	1677124	2338183
654405		11507	9321727	3411553	15903	426	527907	3379359	5316593

11-6 续表

单位：万元

项目	Item	资产负债 Assets and Liabilities 负债合计 Total Liabilities	#流动负债合计 Total Current Liabilities	#应付账款 Accounts Payable	所有者权益合计 Total Owner's Equity
合计	**Total**	**181024377**	**122281820**	**40062346**	**204801933**
煤炭开采和洗选业	Mining and Washing of Coal	***	***	***	***
石油和天然气开采业	Extraction of Petroleum and Natural Gas	***	***	***	***
黑色金属矿采选业	Mining and Processing of Ferrous Metal Ores	13239660	7705348	848036	10385496
非金属矿采选业	Mining and Processing of Nonmetal Ores	***	***	***	***
开采辅助活动	Mining Support Service Activities	2177926	2064430	661531	3268703
农副食品加工业	Processing of Food from Agricultural Products	2417275	1955781	336530	1859497
食品制造业	Manufacture of Foods	2243668	2133628	675943	1840296
酒、饮料和精制茶制造业	Manufacture of Wines, Beverage and Refined Tea	1640717	1473637	350827	2521716
烟草制品业	Manufacture of Cigarettes and Tobacco	***	***	***	***
纺织业	Manufacture of Textile	242145	146776	27678	226694
纺织服装、服饰业	Manufacture of Textile Wearing Apparel and Ornament	1034845	930528	280005	697515
皮革、毛皮、羽毛及其制品和制鞋业	Manufacture of Leather, Fur, Feather and Its Products, and Footwear	61136	59837	14747	39999
木材加工和木、竹、藤、棕、草制品业	Processing of Timbers, Manufacture of Wood, Bamboo, Rattan, Palm, and Straw Products	103645	100840	24742	65238
家具制造业	Manufacture of Furniture	556970	526057	129324	474802
造纸和纸制品业	Manufacture of Paper and Paper Products	294179	266815	86191	259796
印刷和记录媒介复制业	Printing, Reproduction of Recording Media	872783	754174	269208	1292541
文教、工美、体育和娱乐用品制造业	Manufacture of Articles for Culture, Education, Artwork, Sport and Entertainment Activities	490567	458860	195729	326936
石油加工、炼焦和核燃料加工业	Processing of Petroleum, Coking, Processing of Mucleus Fuels	1531982	1491158	380294	1210787
化学原料和化学制品制造业	Manufacture of Chemical Raw Materials and Chemical Products	2446661	2188282	629854	2079237
医药制造业	Manufacture of Medicines	4768626	4080514	1280683	6745119
化学纤维制造业	Manufacture of Chemical Fibres	***	***	***	***
橡胶和塑料制品业	Manufacture of Rubber and Plastics Products	622206	549423	193862	580770
非金属矿物制品业	Manufacture of Non-metallic Mineral Products	5866508	5383944	2464604	3639811
黑色金属冶炼和压延加工业	Manufacture and Pressing of Ferrous Metals	1028147	471670	291331	73521
有色金属冶炼和压延加工业	Manufacture and Pressing of Non-ferrous Metals	347573	298557	143936	449098
金属制品业	Manufacture of Fabricated Metal Products	3196369	2723860	914422	2699532
通用设备制造业	Manufacture of General-purpose Machinery	4525385	4085782	1189595	5491898
专用设备制造业	Manufacture of Special-purpose Machinery	8643623	7079573	2252679	8010971
汽车制造业	Manufacture of Motor Vehicles	21484166	18836725	9321140	15663424
铁路、船舶、航空航天和其他运输设备制造业	Manufacture of Railway Locomotives, Building of Ships and Boats, Manufacture of Air and Spacecrafts and Other Transportation Equipment	4032725	3644758	1271429	2471728
电气机械和器材制造业	Manufacture of Electrical Machinery and Equipment	7224096	6762558	2687561	4964780
计算机、通信和其他电子设备制造业	Manufacture of Computers, Communication Equipment and Other Electronic Equipment	16022092	13967423	6098348	14526240
仪器仪表制造业	Manufacture of Measuring Instruments and Meters	2344775	2200550	914910	2679638
其他制造业	Other Manufacturing	574148	451538	192958	868022
废弃资源综合利用业	Waste Recycling and Recovery	135059	91113	43444	72175
金属制品、机械和设备修理业	Repair of Fabricated Metal Products, Machinery and Equipment	392616	362807	98303	325227
电力、热力生产和供应业	Production and Distribution of Electricity and Heating Power	63230539	25961823	5219864	98599775
燃气生产和供应业	Production and Distribution of Gas	1494605	1140395	195597	3418647
水的生产和供应业	Production and Distribution of Water	4226408	1261160	232444	5095319

11-6 Continued

(10000 yuan)

	损 益 Profits and Losses											
#实收资本 Paid-up Capital	营业收入 Business Income	#主营业务收入 Main Business Income	营业成本 Business Cost	#主营业务成本 Main Business Cost	销售费用 Sales Expenses	管理费用 Management Expenses	财务费用 Financial Expenses	利润总额 Total Profits	应交税金合计 Total Tax Payable	#营业税金及附加 Business Tax and Surtax	#主营业务税金及附加 Main Business Tax and Surtax	#应交增值税 Value Added Tax Payable
108089475	**192561382**	**188648954**	**159984640**	**157109677**	**9252530**	**9566087**	**2116560**	**15977122**	**11791045**	**3337157**	**3318066**	**5693787**
***	***	***	***	***	***	***	***	***	***	***	***	***
***	***	***	***	***	***	***	***	***	***	***	***	***
2902434	2284506	2177087	2273607	2136715	8915	141721	157584	164593	67546	9633	8916	49473
***	***	***	***	***	***	***	***	***	***	***	***	***
2835903	1643593	1639009	1459822	1456891	5931	75237	8933	102947	59458	14942	14856	21051
757160	4166191	4132307	3442539	3424815	289163	201464	43624	141882	193201	102724	102669	54859
1190203	5126585	5008278	3364551	3253233	1242087	267732	14506	242635	356014	30713	30613	264280
837020	2063262	1948075	1476246	1382117	315604	140488	2584	68443	215247	69746	69359	110041
***	***	***	***	***	***	***	***	***	***	***	***	***
191707	262692	255154	217120	214471	5605	28660	5656	237	10504	1869	1669	5393
296760	1328218	1290206	876576	847828	231269	135603	9566	82182	99552	9430	9285	73451
12092	126453	123141	106141	103544	4967	6789	707	7607	5578	461	460	3058
70097	165925	164903	139719	139042	12668	12453	723	-1352	6542	527	526	5286
248964	834925	818542	648143	637362	75454	70989	6522	44563	39365	3668	3545	25843
173291	649720	634497	506727	496038	24021	33761	524	83782	51691	3071	2931	22971
712838	1351611	1292699	1063818	1033258	44204	164510	128	78873	105130	10101	9519	69855
227885	1347260	1325709	1262777	1256544	24282	46871	4944	8236	15987	2846	1934	9490
51127	6487665	6261057	4982675	4758944	57255	162236	23732	291885	1321114	961585	960630	282064
1742945	3625013	3536944	2848186	2780628	305735	289047	54721	124078	198457	21988	21727	130758
2048724	7417223	7156774	3524727	3305706	1914759	714292	133930	1318805	827126	65448	65344	541881
***	***	***	***	***	***	***	***	***	***	***	***	***
329528	1134104	1089417	974432	940968	39778	95174	5911	22013	41269	4676	4567	26880
1754714	4632706	4511276	3981063	3877602	198904	361296	60550	148218	171086	27100	26332	107218
341252	1078096	1067566	1066212	1058155	40392	31451	17684	-80252	20197	1692	1610	9318
151115	874864	706299	794416	633561	11222	45776	2685	19417	16231	3274	3220	9147
1270743	3535912	3366224	2931418	2807206	106839	272333	36547	256056	135487	20461	19787	75183
2099811	5465491	5376044	4152068	4108805	328679	494727	38465	580920	304887	29509	29222	172895
2942750	6420871	6206021	4640524	4531915	394089	746854	146775	537460	412238	45437	44594	267968
6483248	40418573	39540177	33439419	32813664	1541905	1482282	169620	3497269	3195539	1291704	1290960	1162406
1034425	4074530	4038416	3281051	3254220	67199	342595	35592	384189	181928	13917	13418	101879
3011762	8630331	8383325	6882431	6659689	540803	588774	50950	331992	405646	34472	33800	239472
6983705	25676915	25197910	22410803	22159030	1089976	1487077	197534	637603	625286	77930	75822	368217
884335	3128786	3073819	2200428	2174080	225907	352745	11241	391925	220616	20717	19878	136655
357938	794899	787869	578507	575396	27046	82998	224	114056	39436	3842	3836	18509
55881	60540	59794	54495	53829	442	8621	1436	3070	3060	263	240	2211
255571	728560	675117	594413	545409	6678	104637	9571	33592	44456	3666	3645	29931
60415347	41166038	41026529	38945339	38870548	10535	246583	801329	5582442	1748319	166229	162617	1081367
826363	4125649	4082592	3763132	3736362	33890	147482	17226	391703	127441	12372	11463	84800
4139835	817432	801823	644535	636972	3817	67981	20519	277052	129443	5095	3531	16739

11-7 规模以上工业企业主要经济效益指标(2015年)

单位: %

项目	Item	工业经济效益综合指数 Aggregate Index of Industrial Economic Efficiency	企业亏损面 Loss-Suffering Enterprises as % of Total	总资产贡献率 Contribution Rate of Total Assets	资产保值增值率 Rate of Assets Preservation and Appreciation
合 计	**Total**	**302.38**	**21.34**	**6.79**	**124.95**
按隶属关系分组	**By Affiliation**				
中央企业	Central Enterprises	528.57	18.83	5.49	142.95
地方企业	Local Enterprises	254.17	21.52	7.95	109.60
按登记注册类型分组	**By Registration Type**				
内资企业	Domestically-funded Enterprises	279.93	19.89	5.28	129.30
国有企业	State-owned Enterprises	910.72	12.50	4.37	154.73
集体企业	Collectively-Owned Enterprises	138.48	32.50	7.13	90.87
股份合作企业	Joint-equity Cooperative Enterprises	173.06	17.24	7.78	124.42
有限责任公司	Limited Liability Companies	215.16	23.62	4.29	110.50
股份有限公司	Company Limited by Shares	296.61	20.41	9.12	103.33
私营企业	Private Enterprises	186.61	15.74	7.89	113.67
其他企业	Others	172.88		4.45	103.59
港澳台商投资企业	Hong Kong, Macao and Taiwan-invested Enterprises	224.16	26.67	5.82	104.32
港澳台合资经营	Joint Ventures	305.30	22.92	12.92	116.50
港澳台合作经营	Cooperatives	325.83		14.88	19.44
港澳台商独资企业	Solely-funded Enterprises	210.23	32.94	4.68	107.48
港澳台商投资股份有限公司	Companies Limited by Shares	-37.01	18.18	-1.59	84.90
外商投资企业	Foreign-invested Enterprises	399.16	26.15	15.84	108.66
中外合资经营	Joint Ventures	535.74	23.48	20.25	96.85
中外合作经营	Cooperatives	165.95	40.00	6.10	115.33
外资(独资)企业	Solely-funded Enterprises	271.87	27.81	11.03	107.37
外商投资股份有限公司	Companies Limited by Shares	262.93	16.67	5.91	262.22
按城乡分组	**By urban and rural regions**				
#农村企业	Rural Enterprises	79.46	37.50	1.80	80.33
按控股类型分组	**By holding types**				
#国有控股	State-holding Enterprises	395.54	23.76	6.29	129.64
集体控股	Collectively-holding Enterprises	257.57	20.54	8.25	113.01
私人控股	Private-holding Enterprises	205.75	18.40	7.02	118.62
港澳台控股	Hong Kong, Macao, and Taiwan-holding Enterprises	196.88	27.59	3.42	112.38
外商控股	Foreign-Investor-holding Enterprises	294.27	27.27	13.35	99.94
按轻重工业分组	**By light and heavy industries**				
轻工业	Light Industry	245.57	20.47	11.73	113.78
重工业	Heavy Industry	331.55	21.80	6.20	126.44
按规模分组	**By size**				
#大中型企业	Medium and Large-sized Enterprises	342.13	20.75	6.89	125.26

MAIN INDICATORS OF ECONOMIC BENEFITS OF INDUSTRIAL ENTERPRISES ABOVE DESIGNATED SIZE (2015)

(%)

资产负债率 Assets-Liabilities Ratio	流动资产周转率(次) Turnover of Current Assets (times)	成本费用利润率 Ratio of Profits to Costs	全员劳动生产率(元/人) Overall Labor Productivity (yuan/person)	产品销售率 Sales Rate of Products	增加值率 Value-added Rate	人均销售收入(元/人) Sales Revenue Per Capita (yuan)	流动比率(倍) Liquidity Ratio (times)	速动比率(倍) Quick Ratio (times)
46.89	**1.27**	**8.83**	**332913**	**99.02**	**21.07**	**1708183**	**1.24**	**1.06**
40.85	1.52	11.17	687356	99.81	21.52	3270874	1.09	0.96
52.29	1.17	7.75	261610	98.62	20.84	1393815	1.31	1.10
45.12	1.07	9.44	299058	98.89	21.15	1509439	1.24	1.06
37.19	1.42	15.19	1295326	100.03	17.67	7366160	1.18	1.12
61.80	1.00	3.64	104865	102.52	27.53	397063	1.35	1.01
58.72	1.69	3.52	142746	99.39	16.06	971241	1.31	0.98
57.21	0.95	5.68	224763	98.83	21.61	1154848	1.11	0.94
41.86	0.96	9.36	322914	98.14	24.81	1418062	1.55	1.31
54.97	1.01	7.25	155606	96.58	23.91	697485	1.38	1.04
75.30	0.99	4.31	165286	92.61	19.59	781500	1.37	0.67
58.51	1.65	3.65	237859	97.21	11.72	2475883	1.18	0.97
45.14	1.36	11.94	299370	101.20	26.73	1187164	1.49	1.23
15.11	0.96	11.79	359026	87.65	57.66	767208	5.73	4.85
64.54	2.14	2.39	217828	96.01	7.45	3731071	1.04	0.87
57.93	0.36	-11.82	-48143	95.07	-4.33	1269995	1.37	1.06
52.19	1.74	9.86	454002	99.95	24.28	1979857	1.31	1.09
53.56	1.86	12.24	651634	99.72	26.54	2496461	1.22	1.04
53.22	1.51	2.56	148196	94.47	44.57	597563	1.83	1.96
54.07	1.71	5.86	284403	100.33	20.02	1597132	1.46	1.15
37.00	0.53	24.40	154692	102.39	22.54	760875	1.30	1.24
62.05	0.93	-2.07	63409	100.37	14.99	437382	1.66	1.07
45.03	1.25	10.80	475053	99.65	22.15	2240229	1.15	1.02
56.65	1.08	5.55	281190	96.45	20.64	1371965	1.45	1.15
46.93	0.84	9.15	179647	96.88	23.85	811168	1.51	1.21
62.63	1.81	1.47	209495	96.92	8.98	2924170	1.09	0.91
53.52	1.77	7.47	304893	100.11	21.58	1591135	1.44	1.15
47.11	1.26	9.41	223153	98.08	29.65	860557	1.47	1.13
46.86	1.27	8.72	383183	99.19	19.56	2096395	1.21	1.05
45.95	1.37	9.29	393615	99.11	20.96	2012692	1.21	1.06

11-8 规模以上国有控股工业企业主要经济指标(2015年)

单位：万元

项目	Item	企业单位个数(个) Number of Enterprises (unit)	#亏损企业 Loss-Suffering Enterprises	工业总产值(当年价格) Gross Output Value of Industry (at current year's prices)	工业增加值 Added Value of Industry	工业销售产值(当年价格) Sales Value of Industry (at current year's prices)
合　计	**Total**	**745**	**177**	**100613752**	**22282119**	**100264121**
按隶属关系分组	**By Affiliation**					
中央企业	Central Enterprises	233	44	58914274	12695626	58795704
地方企业	Local Enterprises	512	133	41699479	9586493	41468417
按轻重工业分组	**By light and heavy industries**					
轻工业	Light Industry	185	47	6811904	2438082	6692482
重工业	Heavy Industry	560	130	93801849	19844037	93571639
按规模分组	**By size**					
#大中型企业	Medium and Large-sized Enterprises	240	59	90399281	20201574	90164146

11-8 续表

单位：万元

项目	Item	资产负债 Assets and Liabilities					营业收入 Business Income
		负债合计 Total Liabilities	#流动负债合计 Total Current Liabilities	#应付账款 Accounts Payable	所有者权益合计 Total Owner's Equity	#实收资本 Paid-up Capital	
合　计	**Total**	**127433648**	**74185273**	**20012764**	**155533518**	**87998470**	**106890324**
按隶属关系分组	**By Affiliation**						
中央企业	Central Enterprises	73929765	36583034	9113142	107517395	65615410	60957992
地方企业	Local Enterprises	53503882	37602238	10899621	48016123	22383060	45932332
按轻重工业分组	**By light and heavy industries**						
轻工业	Light Industry	6465930	4623153	946148	9422465	3329449	7833273
重工业	Heavy Industry	120967717	69562120	19066616	146111054	84669021	99057051
按规模分组	**By size**						
#大中型企业	Medium and Large-sized Enterprises	114395378	63807500	16617003	145961953	82527785	95007943

MAIN ECONOMIC INDICATORS OF STATE-HOLDING INDUSTRIAL ENTERPRISES ABOVE DESIGNATED SIZE (2015)

(10000 yuan)

#出口交货值 Delivery Value of Exports	平均用工人数(人) Average Number of Employed Persons (person)	资产负债 Assets and Liabilities: 资产总计 Total Assets	流动资产合计 Total Current Assets	#存货 Inventories	#产成品 Finished Products	#应收账款 Accounts Receivable	固定资产合计 Total Fixed Assets	固定资产原价 Total Original Value of Fixed Assets
2663959	**469045**	**283001704**	**85234274**	**9850665**	**2893950**	**16483014**	**53244124**	**98957267**
370301	181792	181460727	39771593	4508364	1006120	7642592	29897393	62751920
2293658	287253	101540977	45462682	5342301	1887830	8840422	23346732	36205347
90189	88983	15898238	8195644	1757366	705227	1265264	3125777	6199762
2573769	380062	267103466	77038631	8093299	2188723	15217749	50118347	92757505
2512317	374686	260357331	72532054	6936103	2203481	12797995	48567859	91945390

11-8 Continued

(10000 yuan)

损益 Profits and Losses: #主营业务收入 Main Business Income	营业成本 Business Cost	#主营业务成本 Main Business Cost	销售费用 Sales Expenses	管理费用 Management Expenses	财务费用 Financial Expenses	利润总额 Total Profits	应交税金合计 Total Tax Payable	#营业税金及附加 Business Tax and Surtax	#主营业务税金及附加 Main Business Tax and Surtax	#应交增值税 Value Added Tax Payable
105076838	**91732041**	**90392792**	**2642276**	**4144589**	**1402191**	**10790099**	**7797308**	**2966140**	**2951366**	**3208512**
60225479	54091129	53505671	410652	1592384	795377	6369621	4014967	1532226	1525860	1781916
44851359	37640913	36887121	2231624	2552205	606814	4420478	3782342	1433915	1425506	1426596
7653852	5554520	5450837	676952	668108	48497	690848	962000	442891	441234	374871
97422986	86177522	84941955	1965324	3476481	1353695	10099252	6835308	2523249	2510132	2833641
93528088	81582939	80438326	2367553	3204628	1246791	9846032	7376912	2918301	2906453	3010556

11-9 规模以上国有控股工业企业主要经济指标(按行业分)(2015年)

单位：万元

项目	Item	企业单位个数(个) Number of Enterprises (unit)	#亏损企业 Loss-Suffering Enterprises	工业总产值(当年价格) Gross Output Value of Industry (at current year's prices)	工业增加值 Added Value of Industry
合计	**Total**	**745**	**177**	**100613752**	**22282119**
煤炭开采和洗选业	Mining and Washing of Coal	***	***	***	***
石油和天然气开采业	Extraction of Petroleum and Natural Gas	***	***	***	***
黑色金属矿采选业	Mining and Processing of Ferrous Metal Ores	4	2	767749	4278
非金属矿采选业	Mining and processing of nonmetal ores	***	***	***	***
开采辅助活动	Mining Support Service Activities	***	***	***	***
农副食品加工业	Processing of Food from Agricultural Products	24	9	1750266	276626
食品制造业	Manufacture of Foods	16	4	553743	116657
酒、饮料和精制茶制造业	Manufacture of Wines, Beverage and Refined Tea	8	4	542869	229664
烟草制品业	Manufacture of Cigarettes and Tobacco	***	***	***	***
纺织业	Manufacture of Textile	10	4	33880	4835
纺织服装、服饰业	Manufacture of Textile Wearing Apparel and Ornament	6		48387	8948
皮革、毛皮、羽毛及其制品和制鞋业	Manufacture of Leather, Fur, Feather and Its Products, and Footwear	***	***	***	***
木材加工和木、竹、藤、棕、草制品业	Processing of Timbers, Manufacture of Wood, Bamboo, Rattan, Palm, and Straw Products				
家具制造业	Manufacture of Furniture	***	***	***	***
造纸和纸制品业	Manufacture of Paper and Paper Products	***	***	***	***
印刷和记录媒介复制业	Printing, Reproduction of Recording Media	33	11	532369	230559
文教、工美、体育和娱乐用品制造业	Manufacture of Articles for Culture, Education, Artwork, Sport and Entertainment Activities	7	2	122459	18039
石油加工、炼焦和核燃料加工业	Processing of Petroleum, Coking, Processing of Mucleus Fuels	8		5315235	1722655
化学原料和化学制品制造业	Manufacture of Chemical Raw Materials and Chemical Products	38	13	1268168	121467
医药制造业	Manufacture of Medicines	31	5	1586684	721777
化学纤维制造业	Manufacture of Chemical Fibres	***	***	***	***
橡胶和塑料制品业	Manufacture of Rubber and Plastics Products	9	1	97893	38853
非金属矿物制品业	Manufacture of Non-metallic Mineral Products	56	28	1175826	177087
黑色金属冶炼和压延加工业	Manufacture and Pressing of Ferrous Metals	4	3	561490	-49250
有色金属冶炼和压延加工业	Manufacture and Pressing of Non-ferrous Metals	8	2	283924	26873
金属制品业	Manufacture of Fabricated Metal Products	33	10	1167584	297190
通用设备制造业	Manufacture of General-purpose Machinery	43	15	905475	222740
专用设备制造业	Manufacture of Special-purpose Machinery	59	11	1470136	358780
汽车制造业	Manufacture of Motor Vehicles	40	6	26743916	6316481
铁路、船舶、航空航天和其他运输设备制造业	Manufacture of Railway Locomotives, Building of Ships and Boats, Manufacture of Air and Spacecrafts and Other Transportation Equipment	35	6	3236400	763336
电气机械和器材制造业	Manufacture of Electrical Machinery and Equipment	31	6	1479578	183871
计算机、通信和其他电子设备制造业	Manufacture of Computers, Communication Equipment and Other Electronic Equipment	74	15	4384781	1102549
仪器仪表制造业	Manufacture of Measuring Instruments and Meters	49	5	821578	191707
其他制造业	Other Manufacturing	12		595588	241003
废弃资源综合利用业	Waste Recycling and Recovery	***	***	***	***
金属制品、机械和设备修理业	Repair of Fabricated Metal Products, Machinery and Equipment	4		598346	218374
电力、热力生产和供应业	Production and Distribution of Electricity and Heating Power	53	8	40673347	6627587
燃气生产和供应业	Production and Distribution of Gas	13	1	586990	81684
水的生产和供应业	Production and Distribution of Water	19	1	615316	312749

MAIN ECONOMIC INDICATORS OF STATE-OWNED AND STATE-CONTROLLED INDUSTIRAL ENTERPRISES ABOVE DESIGNATED SIZE (BY SECTOR) (2015)

(10000 yuan)

工业销售产值(当年价格) Sales Value of Industry (at current year's prices)	#出口交货值 Delivery Value of Exports	平均用工人数(人) Average Number of Employed Persons (person)	资产负债 Assets and Liabilities						
			资产总计 Total Assets	流动资产合计 Total Current Assets	#存货 Inventories	#产成品 Finished Products	#应收账款 Accounts Receivable	固定资产合计 Total Fixed Assets	固定资产原价 Total Original Value of Fixed Assets
100264121	**2663959**	**469045**	**283001704**	**85234274**	**9850665**	**2893950**	**16483014**	**53244124**	**98957267**
***	***	10523	***	***	***	***	***	***	***
***	***	1999	***	***	***	***	***	***	***
762783		22445	23552310	8242833	240342	36217	1614657	3925944	5677980
***	***	81	***	***	***	***	***	***	***
***	***	18849	***	***	***	***	***	***	***
1737478	6501	11977	2160134	1602952	247941	176198	142813	214361	325703
575788	6149	9262	1080680	551956	59048	22481	111058	143216	239064
539320	4437	11566	2565219	890705	115880	20010	40114	205372	542989
***	***	916	***	***	***	***	***	***	***
40212	2052	1726	343216	193737	18967	13008	20411	55209	75222
48392	19245	1318	73045	49771	26975	12115	11443	16041	26851
***	***	436	***	***	***	***	***	***	***
***	***	1505	***	***	***	***	***	***	***
***	***	288	***	***	***	***	***	***	***
546778	239	11750	1190166	629008	113168	50240	122046	313990	880028
157158	4421	1877	397614	314753	180791	111776	84116	35571	60765
5325872		10231	2574958	1005697	640976	100329	166357	1147660	3126072
1189782	17645	10806	1919425	1122814	244956	134191	218447	472365	1533688
1425025	4621	19098	3620264	1920262	651223	225555	409472	631095	995629
***	***	86	***	***	***	***	***	***	***
104092	31469	3599	211682	134995	23256	11233	29980	45830	76765
1172169	21778	18598	3734387	2628858	194515	74679	1093354	485890	945547
559254	40143	1855	719859	144040	77310	37596	39649	437922	686095
292319	65785	2325	434992	277335	78093	18173	61284	59130	102753
1190728	96671	13342	2519234	1264601	224777	63842	250847	467080	737881
927018	52017	14723	2551651	1858916	670014	144424	400603	228487	499305
1481811	22423	21628	4024701	2946183	770677	275957	1017358	474441	804632
26694146	337347	82820	27919683	13806542	1605293	669265	2078173	6246804	8460001
3135209	38524	30965	5294999	3888926	1361758	170613	1306104	787642	1241622
1477907	16784	8490	2623777	1845303	254306	28928	936272	154941	290187
4313499	1563142	32917	10811377	6242571	952191	303430	1286395	2218553	4482726
838355	8422	9572	1251476	997870	294028	68687	287045	101399	182564
569176	16445	6339	1181920	672870	149151	37393	214553	268580	480253
***	***	254	***	***	***	***	***	***	***
594689	47455	9809	581465	341156	142465	253	143785	189360	350287
40672664		50490	161493011	24489292	101320	8801	2765357	28587572	56931409
586990		3762	601291	341765	12367	6749	33085	226652	349409
614926		10818	9204080	3356120	9527		519760	3359358	5284224

11-9 续表

单位：万元

项目	Item	资产负债 Assets and Liabilities 负债合计 Total Liabilities	#流动负债合计 Total Current Liabilities	#应付账款 Accounts Payable	所有者权益合计 Total Owner's Equity
合计	**Total**	**127433648**	**74185273**	**20012764**	**155533518**
煤炭开采和洗选业	Mining and Washing of Coal	***	***	***	***
石油和天然气开采业	Extraction of Petroleum and Natural Gas	***	***	***	***
黑色金属矿采选业	Mining and Processing of Ferrous Metal Ores	13198323	7666589	843329	10353987
非金属矿采选业	Mining and processing of nonmetal ores	***	***	***	***
开采辅助活动	Mining Support Service Activities	***	***	***	***
农副食品加工业	Processing of Food from Agricultural Products	1350968	988943	95174	809166
食品制造业	Manufacture of Foods	400945	342361	119860	676097
酒、饮料和精制茶制造业	Manufacture of Wines, Beverage and Refined Tea	695462	583011	31240	1869757
烟草制品业	Manufacture of Cigarettes and Tobacco	***	***	***	***
纺织业	Manufacture of Textile	173896	79910	4491	163799
纺织服装、服饰业	Manufacture of Textile Wearing Apparel and Ornament	54830	40091	17644	18215
皮革、毛皮、羽毛及其制品和制鞋业	Manufacture of Leather, Fur, Feather and Its Products, and Footwear	1524	1524	706	827
木材加工和木、竹、藤、棕、草制品业	Processing of Timbers, Manufacture of Wood, Bamboo, Rattan, Palm, and Straw Products				
家具制造业	Manufacture of Furniture	***	***	***	***
造纸和纸制品业	Manufacture of Paper and Paper Products	***	***	***	***
印刷和记录媒介复制业	Printing, Reproduction of Recording Media	393195	334010	99791	796971
文教、工美、体育和娱乐用品制造业	Manufacture of Articles for Culture, Education, Artwork, Sport and Entertainment Activities	256532	229440	139283	141082
石油加工、炼焦和核燃料加工业	Processing of Petroleum, Coking, Processing of Mucleus Fuels	1467066	1426346	345490	1107892
化学原料和化学制品制造业	Manufacture of Chemical Raw Materials and Chemical Products	1305219	1129117	327820	597561
医药制造业	Manufacture of Medicines	1079761	764172	198691	2539268
化学纤维制造业	Manufacture of Chemical Fibres	***	***	***	***
橡胶和塑料制品业	Manufacture of Rubber and Plastics Products	113207	67881	17871	136106
非金属矿物制品业	Manufacture of Non-metallic Mineral Products	2155292	2035419	749132	1546833
黑色金属冶炼和压延加工业	Manufacture and Pressing of Ferrous Metals	811113	268527	189570	-91254
有色金属冶炼和压延加工业	Manufacture and Pressing of Non-ferrous Metals	123485	84098	42360	311507
金属制品业	Manufacture of Fabricated Metal Products	1301740	1088400	395960	1217494
通用设备制造业	Manufacture of General-purpose Machinery	1552293	1459277	325781	999359
专用设备制造业	Manufacture of Special-purpose Machinery	2613803	2150420	766882	1410898
汽车制造业	Manufacture of Motor Vehicles	15962449	13804488	6016635	11950360
铁路、船舶、航空航天和其他运输设备制造业	Manufacture of Railway Locomotives, Building of Ships and Boats, Manufacture of Air and Spacecrafts and Other Transportation Equipment	3514476	3166527	1045138	1780523
电气机械和器材制造业	Manufacture of Electrical Machinery and Equipment	1875091	1736209	629091	748686
计算机、通信和其他电子设备制造业	Manufacture of Computers, Communication Equipment and Other Electronic Equipment	4776248	3886610	1030400	6035129
仪器仪表制造业	Manufacture of Measuring Instruments and Meters	713998	619041	212454	537478
其他制造业	Other Manufacturing	426497	307699	134804	755423
废弃资源综合利用业	Waste Recycling and Recovery	***	***	***	***
金属制品、机械和设备修理业	Repair of Fabricated Metal Products, Machinery and Equipment	346291	316782	81432	235174
电力、热力生产和供应业	Production and Distribution of Electricity and Heating Power	62954687	25749432	5152119	98531696
燃气生产和供应业	Production and Distribution of Gas	301567	263511	46555	299724
水的生产和供应业	Production and Distribution of Water	4176214	1222240	211856	5027866

11-9 Continued

(10000 yuan)

#实收资本 Paid-up Capital	损益 Profits and Losses								应交税金合计 Total Tax Payable	#营业税金及附加 Business Tax and Surtax	#主营业务税金及附加 Main Business Tax and Surtax	#应交增值税 Value Added Tax Payable
	营业收入 Business Income	#主营业务收入 Main Business Income	营业成本 Business Cost	#主营业务成本 Main Business Cost	销售费用 Sales Expenses	管理费用 Management Expenses	财务费用 Financial Expenses	利润总额 Total Profits				
87998470	**106890324**	**105076838**	**91732041**	**90392792**	**2642276**	**4144589**	**1402191**	**10790099**	**7797308**	**2966140**	**2951366**	**3208512**
***	***	***	***	***	***	***	***	***	***	***	***	***
***	***	***	***	***	***	***	***	***	***	***	***	***
2900369	2243856	2147435	2238172	2109659	7654	135725	156812	168519	63305	8230	7512	46732
***	***	***	***	***	***	***	***	***	***	***	***	***
***	***	***	***	***	***	***	***	***	***	***	***	***
208097	2161351	2153069	1749207	1746562	171213	74757	16139	69075	167252	100920	100881	46483
281487	684755	660777	502155	476052	114978	38373	934	27385	37621	3000	3000	29215
146635	640268	608237	450866	429055	69017	39228	-6027	41066	104167	54010	53805	38745
***	***	***	***	***	***	***	***	***	***	***	***	***
145559	133488	128906	107915	106801	1758	20829	4110	-6094	4921	1330	1133	1968
49305	73148	71877	65335	64671	1859	6958	1176	13967	1735	280	256	1034
1019	10314	10033	9168	8905	331	638	-73	184	211	76	76	66
***	***	***	***	***	***	***	***	***	***	***	***	***
***	***	***	***	***	***	***	***	***	***	***	***	***
458595	705742	665922	541393	524574	13889	107843	-3161	49325	59975	6221	5640	36724
137839	176759	170103	147046	144845	9257	14045	5127	2090	5923	798	652	3902
29586	5805240	5581359	4380128	4157565	36216	144039	23003	257683	1292430	956233	955277	267568
1066094	1309213	1263734	1167686	1130954	31458	125394	35878	-47576	31801	3303	3154	24711
694308	1513437	1491909	814060	804664	237757	176701	16023	314278	180319	15138	15065	114509
***	***	***	***	***	***	***	***	***	***	***	***	***
56422	179993	164462	152287	142326	5831	22875	-244	1058	10506	1182	1134	6621
812354	1627940	1566788	1434163	1384583	65083	144902	23233	80607	63240	8526	7767	40943
264086	586772	578064	637265	629890	26512	13068	13376	-105019	3302	360	303	113
74044	472345	309920	437582	281828	4874	22408	-145	3990	5546	2263	2230	2379
596666	1399615	1327959	1221186	1177242	22532	98229	8604	82508	33259	6571	6421	15869
573369	1128095	1104223	933060	917195	34679	121719	10453	22397	68426	8096	7855	52811
843247	1823411	1777844	1415092	1396020	73086	209708	19468	86508	81626	12355	11602	47470
4998182	27280221	26797832	21712010	21432114	1337716	1007651	89286	2853952	2746669	1263547	1262956	903187
827875	3388869	3355847	2825199	2798963	33720	266650	24385	254152	124098	10349	9850	71507
695691	1555116	1541264	1323782	1318102	71211	96654	26127	27790	38199	5724	5646	23429
3567287	4893069	4783448	3893946	3806647	167978	487311	86810	358648	200297	32971	31185	111705
230461	959734	943445	766292	756759	36191	105545	2767	50726	44676	4996	4729	31397
273285	593225	588930	408769	406780	13690	67966	-1033	113183	37151	3221	3216	17980
***	***	***	***	***	***	***	***	***	***	***	***	***
226742	653850	601734	549057	500469	3269	91259	8956	10167	31113	2711	2690	22400
60377117	40958927	40822017	38739195	38666262	6044	228522	798601	5570443	1745337	165847	162234	1081228
195807	616266	587014	582304	567571	5842	36141	-4614	33777	29916	2719	2129	16921
4099012	777547	762462	619228	611735	1922	60460	19970	272292	126249	4553	2989	14705

11-10 规模以上股份制工业企业主要经济指标(2015年)

单位：万元

项目	Item	企业单位个数(个) Number of Enterprises (unit)	#亏损企业 Loss-Suffering Enterprises	工业总产值(当年价格) Gross Output Value of Industry (at current year's prices)	工业增加值 Added Value of Industry	工业销售产值(当年价格) Sales Value of Industry (at current year's prices)	#出口交货值 Delivery Value of Exports
合 计	**Total**	**1481**	**342**	**59144800**	**13459338**	**58304485**	**2713069**
按隶属关系分组	**By Affiliation**						
中央企业	Central Enterprises	188	38	24553027	6334741	24475096	308238
地方企业	Local Enterprises	1293	304	34591774	7124598	33829389	2404831
按轻重工业分组	**By Light and Heavy Industries**						
轻工业	Light Industry	447	90	10088651	3126991	9722129	170307
重工业	Heavy Industry	1034	252	49056150	10332347	48582356	2542762
按规模分组	**By Size**						
#大中型企业	Medium and Large-sized Enterprises	321	76	43963104	10293515	43449074	2296571

11-10 续表

单位：万元

项目	Item	资产负债 Assets and Liabilities					
		固定资产原价 Total Original Value of Fixed Assets	负债合计 Total Liabilities	#流动负债合计 Total Current Liabilities	#应付账款 Accounts Payable	所有者权益合计 Total Owner's Equity	#实收资本 Paid-up Capital
合 计	**Total**	**53085123**	**76302460**	**56902140**	**17661905**	**70193431**	**32228625**
按隶属关系分组	**By Affiliation**						
中央企业	Central Enterprises	21285929	19863650	16432939	5766537	16046711	8616759
地方企业	Local Enterprises	31799194	56438809	40469202	11895369	54146720	23611866
按轻重工业分组	**By Light and Heavy Industries**						
轻工业	Light Industry	6761066	9050428	7202768	1647868	10652644	4428972
重工业	Heavy Industry	46324057	67252031	49699373	16014038	59540787	27799653
按规模分组	**By Size**						
#大中型企业	Medium and Large-sized Enterprises	45150910	59156719	41907854	11937228	53314418	24621746

MAIN ECONOMIC INDICATORS OF SHARE-HOLDING INDUSTRIAL ENTERPRISES ABOVE DESIGNATED SIZE (2015)

(10000 yuan)

平均用工人数(人) Average Number of Employed Persons (person)	资产负债 Assets and Liabilities: 资产总计 Total Assets	流动资产合计 Total Current Assets	#存货 Inventories	#产成品 Finished Products	#应收账款 Accounts Receivable	固定资产合计 Total Fixed Assets
527588	**146632716**	**70396177**	**10924306**	**3647327**	**19963900**	**31455687**
141938	35923928	16548255	3328714	886806	4954248	10752797
385650	110708788	53847922	7595592	2760521	15009652	20702889
131556	19712832	11264721	2477496	1138160	2123005	3778890
396032	126919884	59131456	8446810	2509167	17840895	27676797
369894	112489514	50418480	6647516	2255190	13403797	26251384

11-10 Continued

(10000 yuan)

损益 Profits and Losses: 营业收入 Business Income	#主营业务收入 Main Business Income	营业成本 Business Cost	#主营业务成本 Main Business Cost	销售费用 Sales Expenses	管理费用 Management Expenses	财务费用 Financial Expenses	利润总额 Total Profits	应交税金合计 Total Tax Payable	#营业税金及附加 Business Tax and Surtax	#主营业务税金及附加 Main Business Tax and Surtax	#应交增值税 Value Added Tax Payable
66892722	**65222160**	**55785092**	**54493494**	**2555851**	**4578185**	**943381**	**4423345**	**4276494**	**1475662**	**1461236**	**1946360**
26375678	25778531	22628310	22132188	345222	1227841	206839	1277949	2171512	1129166	1125023	789653
40517044	39443629	33156782	32361307	2210629	3350344	736542	3145395	2104983	346496	336213	1156707
11161963	10949739	7898216	7783457	1124325	988513	96942	1320943	872200	180996	178429	477523
55730759	54272421	47886876	46710037	1431526	3589673	846439	3102402	3404295	1294666	1282807	1468837
49311656	48075904	41263373	40251938	1933316	3036720	787341	3200227	3590339	1398825	1387683	1575377

11-11 规模以上股份制工业企业主要经济指标(按行业分)(2015年)

单位：万元

项目	Item	企业单位个数(个) Number of Enterprises (unit)	#亏损企业 Loss-Suffering Enterprises	工业总产值(当年价格) Gross Output Value of Industry (at current year's prices)	工业增加值 Added Value of Industry
合计	**Total**	**1481**	**342**	**59144800**	**13459338**
煤炭开采和洗选业	Mining and Washing of Coal	***	***	***	***
石油和天然气开采业	Extraction of Petroleum and Natural Gas	***	***	***	***
黑色金属矿采选业	Mining and Processing of Ferrous Metal Ores	5	3	788193	10371
非金属矿采选业	Mining and Processing of Nonmetal Ores	***	***	***	***
开采辅助活动	Mining Support Service Activities	***	***	***	***
农副食品加工业	Processing of Food from Agricultural Products	62	19	2101043	373716
食品制造业	Manufacture of Foods	37	9	538420	141111
酒、饮料和精制茶制造业	Manufacture of Wines, Beverage and Refined Tea	12	6	134867	59732
纺织业	Manufacture of Textile	13	4	50039	7255
纺织服装、服饰业	Manufacture of Textile Wearing Apparel and Ornament	33	8	442932	201281
皮革、毛皮、羽毛及其制品和制鞋业	Manufacture of Leather, Fur, Feather and Its Products, and Footwear	***	***	***	***
木材加工和木、竹、藤、棕、草制品业	Processing of Timbers, Manufacture of Wood, Bamboo, Rattan, Palm, and Straw Products	5	2	32967	8750
家具制造业	Manufacture of Furniture	17	3	131636	33462
造纸和纸制品业	Manufacture of Paper and Paper Products	16	4	84523	15909
印刷和记录媒介复制业	Printing, Reproduction of Recording Media	39	8	580872	244075
文教、工美、体育和娱乐用品制造业	Manufacture of Articles for Culture, Education, Artwork, Sport and Entertainment Activities	15	2	1093064	52734
石油加工、炼焦和核燃料加工业	Processing of Petroleum, Coking, Processing of Mucleus Fuels	11		5265835	1715439
化学原料和化学制品制造业	Manufacture of Chemical Raw Materials and Chemical Products	82	21	1425156	219532
医药制造业	Manufacture of Medicines	94	12	2981875	1368618
化学纤维制造业	Manufacture of Chemical Fibres	***	***	***	***
橡胶和塑料制品业	Manufacture of Rubber and Plastics Products	30	10	209161	43801
非金属矿物制品业	Manufacture of Non-metallic Mineral Products	120	49	2568396	349065
黑色金属冶炼和压延加工业	Manufacture and Pressing of Ferrous Metals	12	4	637118	-24524
有色金属冶炼和压延加工业	Manufacture and Pressing of Non-ferrous Metals	16	3	470326	65249
金属制品业	Manufacture of Fabricated Metal Products	75	19	1603275	416416
通用设备制造业	Manufacture of General-purpose Machinery	84	27	1039169	252024
专用设备制造业	Manufacture of Special-purpose Machinery	136	25	3297719	889148
汽车制造业	Manufacture of Motor Vehicles	67	18	6815771	782218
铁路、船舶、航空航天和其他运输设备制造业	Manufacture of Railway Locomotives, Building of Ships and Boats, Manufacture of Air and Spacecrafts and Other Transportation Equipment	43	6	2063056	513133
电气机械和器材制造业	Manufacture of Electrical Machinery and Equipment	114	21	4489451	786727
计算机、通信和其他电子设备制造业	Manufacture of Computers, Communication Equipment and Other Electronic Equipment	146	33	5681322	1059252
仪器仪表制造业	Manufacture of Measuring Instruments and Meters	83	9	1444549	478020
其他制造业	Other Manufacturing	17	1	645636	244835
废弃资源综合利用业	Waste Recycling and Recovery	4	1	38978	6803
金属制品、机械和设备修理业	Repair of Fabricated Metal Products, Machinery and Equipment	7		56008	15088
电力、热力生产和供应业	Production and Distribution of Electricity and Heating Power	45	8	9273810	1475500
燃气生产和供应业	Production and Distribution of Gas	12	1	441102	64917
水的生产和供应业	Production and Distribution of Water	17	2	590464	292635

MAIN ECONOMIC INDICATORS OF SHARE-HOLDING INDUSTRIAL ENTERPRISES ABOVE DESIGNATED SIZE (BY SECTOR) (2015)

(10000 yuan)

工业销售产值(当年价格) Sales Value of Industry (at current year's prices)	#出口交货值 Delivery Value of Exports	平均用工人数(人) Average Number of Employed Persons (person)	资产负债 Assets and Liabilities: 资产总计 Total Assets	流动资产合计 Total Current Assets	#存货 Inventories	#产成品 Finished Products	#应收账款 Accounts Receivable	固定资产合计 Total Fixed Assets
58304485	**2713069**	**527588**	**146632716**	**70396177**	**10924306**	**3647327**	**19963900**	**31455687**
***	***	10523	***	***	***	***	***	***
***	***	10523	***	***	***	***	***	***
781315		22711	23580943	8256766	243327	37182	1615212	3937176
***	***	214	***	***	***	***	***	***
***	***	18849	***	***	***	***	***	***
2047377	4709	15998	3341257	2259427	286381	187302	256009	285033
529782	38533	11322	863447	517383	115154	43078	122083	138401
129211	1987	3132	394302	192557	75778	36937	40981	106874
55328	2411	2058	376578	225021	25069	14601	32797	56799
435751	33788	13996	772373	537233	241443	166126	91325	119021
***	***	226	***	***	***	***	***	***
32655		694	48203	35077	9454	3016	12180	8717
135728	3525	3215	254481	159438	59496	33044	26244	48294
81676	1821	1695	101794	48199	17284	9164	18082	30407
588820	5648	11516	1123347	656108	137391	43075	126455	326008
1109333	7582	3690	635450	497563	268210	155765	93745	65185
5277253		10269	2542651	998368	625219	91602	169318	1127035
1338959	26187	15751	2279947	1492494	341696	166576	322279	427233
2758688	17955	35492	6417385	3573894	823819	307542	759037	1079879
***	***	86	***	***	***	***	***	***
212758	30726	5476	433819	260390	54742	28966	63823	106625
2588996	50830	32167	7001559	5129012	512192	147561	2482012	680327
636015	45681	3824	832245	212500	114556	53325	55809	471195
475397	79322	3823	648667	376065	106808	34213	106049	79443
1618862	100407	18999	3304068	1825894	426233	117038	425311	537979
1007622	90834	18999	3942969	2570941	547034	194171	639956	364383
3221934	218887	37111	11507552	7190733	1207662	411185	1989608	732385
6778992	322829	51290	9770194	4361479	662664	317967	1427755	1918923
2003513	40278	23706	4161471	3079249	700135	131330	1363082	438183
4357928	41398	27819	7022160	5137188	761612	173928	2743484	460748
5561852	1268704	44554	16713351	8214350	1472307	524956	1992891	2323970
1422029	35370	17695	2815878	2114314	539685	118324	587455	217902
613380	18663	6689	1299614	754759	170591	45505	241645	274682
39575	1093	566	191221	41064	1949	1097	2408	82799
60317		1114	144346	72022	31158	644	22686	24741
9264993		37865	16772720	2885219	58734	1547	524229	9990177
441102		2235	358656	210392	4419	275	33115	118210
590538		10220	9132411	3315502	9037		519676	3318931

11-11 续表

单位：万元

项 目	Item	资产负债 Assets and Liabilities 固定资产原价 Total Original Value of Fixed Assets	负债合计 Total Liabilities	#流动负债合计 Total Current Liabilities	#应付账款 Accounts Payable	所有者权益合计 Total Owner's Equity
合 计	**Total**	**53085123**	**76302460**	**56902140**	**17661905**	**70193431**
煤炭开采和洗选业	Mining and Washing of Coal	***	***	***	***	***
石油和天然气开采业	Extraction of Petroleum and Natural Gas	***	***	***	***	***
黑色金属矿采选业	Mining and Processing of Ferrous Metal Ores	5694177	13210659	7678922	843635	10370284
非金属矿采选业	Mining and Processing of Nonmetal Ores	***	***	***	***	***
开采辅助活动	Mining Support Service Activities	***	***	***	***	***
农副食品加工业	Processing of Food from Agricultural Products	432583	1791534	1368777	169284	1549722
食品制造业	Manufacture of Foods	212635	611268	581960	104278	248541
酒、饮料和精制茶制造业	Manufacture of Wines, Beverage and Refined Tea	163497	220194	210001	18023	174108
纺织业	Manufacture of Textile	79775	188434	94449	16097	182622
纺织服装、服饰业	Manufacture of Textile Wearing Apparel and Ornament					
皮革、毛皮、羽毛及其制品和制鞋业	Manufacture of Leather, Fur, Feather and Its Products, and Footwear	***	***	***	***	***
木材加工和木、竹、藤、棕、草制品业	Processing of Timbers, Manufacture of Wood, Bamboo, Rattan, Palm, and Straw Products	18555	26767	26762	7057	21436
家具制造业	Manufacture of Furniture	76442	141190	117933	31684	113291
造纸和纸制品业	Manufacture of Paper and Paper Products	39739	73306	58507	21263	29124
印刷和记录媒介复制业	Printing, Reproduction of Recording Media	812441	425209	383225	134416	698137
文教、工美、体育和娱乐用品制造业	Manufacture of Articles for Culture, Education, Artwork, Sport and Entertainment Activities	121397	392389	361938	163735	243061
石油加工、炼焦和核燃料加工业	Processing of Petroleum, Coking, Processing of Mucleus Fuels	3105198	1457294	1416470	342854	1085357
化学原料和化学制品制造业	Manufacture of Chemical Raw Materials and Chemical Products	1452847	1397045	1250625	278797	860558
医药制造业	Manufacture of Medicines	1636057	2196815	1871490	498732	4219336
化学纤维制造业	Manufacture of Chemical Fibres	***	***	***	***	***
橡胶和塑料制品业	Manufacture of Rubber and Plastics Products	171980	249366	193442	42093	222084
非金属矿物制品业	Manufacture of Non-metallic Mineral Products	1292298	4290332	3949336	1726590	2660274
黑色金属冶炼和压延加工业	Manufacture and Pressing of Ferrous Metals	761712	884415	341116	206929	-52170
有色金属冶炼和压延加工业	Manufacture and Pressing of Non-ferrous Metals	138366	261385	214256	103202	387282
金属制品业	Manufacture of Fabricated Metal Products	858480	1677937	1450667	524784	1626131
通用设备制造业	Manufacture of General-purpose Machinery	656904	1742944	1528526	373673	2199007
专用设备制造业	Manufacture of Special-purpose Machinery	1157426	5866699	4590568	1491785	5637240
汽车制造业	Manufacture of Motor Vehicles	2467888	6047053	4993655	2313334	3716267
铁路、船舶、航空航天和其他运输设备制造业	Manufacture of Railway Locomotives, Building of Ships and Boats, Manufacture of Air and Spacecrafts and Other Transportation Equipment	787717	2520194	2389307	973724	1641277
电气机械和器材制造业	Manufacture of Electrical Machinery and Equipment	735890	4510133	4225449	1653068	2512027
计算机、通信和其他电子设备制造业	Manufacture of Computers, Communication Equipment and Other Electronic Equipment	3936585	6662541	5426445	1781092	9977544
仪器仪表制造业	Manufacture of Measuring Instruments and Meters	352407	1142084	1076432	402798	1673794
其他制造业	Other Manufacturing	489510	491471	372415	158329	808143
废弃资源综合利用业	Waste Recycling and Recovery	101903	125455	81530	39616	65766
金属制品、机械和设备修理业	Repair of Fabricated Metal Products, Machinery and Equipment	36636	53294	52835	27884	91052
电力、热力生产和供应业	Production and Distribution of Electricity and Heating	16535601	9685050	6534906	2105438	7081043
燃气生产和供应业	Production and Distribution of Gas	155336	223496	213560	51528	135160
水的生产和供应业	Production and Distribution of Water	5202146	4178724	1233558	226544	4953688

11-11 Continued

(10000 yuan)

	损益 Profits and Losses								应交税金合计 Total Tax Payable			
#实收资本 Paid-up Capital	营业收入 Business Income	#主营业务收入 Main Business Income	营业成本 Business Cost	#主营业务成本 Main Business Cost	销售费用 Sales Expenses	管理费用 Management Expenses	财务费用 Financial Expenses	利润总额 Total Profits	应交税金合计 Total Tax Payable	#营业税金及附加 Business Tax and Surtax	#主营业务税金及附加 Main Business Tax and Surtax	#应交增值税 Value Added Tax Payable
32228625	**66892722**	**65222160**	**55785092**	**54493494**	**2555851**	**4578185**	**943381**	**4423345**	**4276494**	**1475662**	**1461236**	**1946360**
***	***	***	***	***	***	***	***	***	***	***	***	***
***	***	***	***	***	***	***	***	***	***	***	***	***
2901824	2262737	2158563	2253980	2119402	8138	138324	157278	167511	64751	8939	8222	47430
***	***	***	***	***	***	***	***	***	***	***	***	***
***	***	***	***	***	***	***	***	***	***	***	***	***
534384	2496998	2476159	1983514	1974452	184953	125503	29886	124410	172279	101029	101010	46485
173629	628470	611662	441781	422801	84566	44097	8301	49212	51430	3904	3804	33125
118767	204448	198975	158284	155272	11926	15682	2150	-3518	33642	21621	21523	8388
161239	154926	149938	125937	124456	2424	23093	4108	-5552	5777	1406	1205	2621
***	***	***	***	***	***	***	***	***	***	***	***	***
16000	32346	31777	25276	24968	1129	3558	282	555	1703	139	139	1262
59312	154424	151424	117733	116918	19258	12008	1266	5660	10484	1043	920	7056
24516	98705	94912	87953	84364	2686	7774	873	-308	2409	203	203	1741
406592	691291	658550	530782	516383	18210	90117	-2173	48770	56601	5177	4674	37157
200041	1233694	1212818	1172016	1166105	15518	35844	3942	6059	12750	2203	1292	7786
8426	5746989	5522194	4328966	4106059	34728	142532	22267	255870	1287383	954568	953613	264995
1123277	1634270	1592849	1373474	1341068	79946	156965	35093	-8754	45710	5671	5482	30689
1181766	2869720	2816577	1375660	1344064	530945	337221	14877	816073	347090	26784	26696	217658
***	***	***	***	***	***	***	***	***	***	***	***	***
128804	334613	314268	299613	285836	10142	33391	1601	-4384	12017	1347	1242	7872
1225876	3240151	3136882	2853540	2762194	124904	255362	44336	78319	96982	19516	18756	58491
276675	669560	659572	701916	694002	28205	21786	15407	-100147	8389	883	801	3811
108028	678602	513567	614749	455422	8756	35010	2218	16402	13187	2771	2716	7436
736544	1772733	1705061	1497944	1461801	33365	132514	16953	129321	57017	9966	9816	29557
990639	1258604	1222932	977261	954929	69621	159448	24743	47251	57956	7584	7327	38117
2121713	3659373	3583190	2702162	2651683	192399	374990	111539	283883	238233	28076	27287	164832
1755585	7929112	7655782	7078545	6912412	184909	467585	30216	353563	311965	123936	123358	132105
865912	2265212	2237400	1874629	1854594	43365	194794	18568	171126	100871	7788	7289	64860
1456212	4741547	4679506	3839538	3792793	275204	318622	41340	264829	186692	19329	18657	128088
4078141	6529376	6409295	5235082	5140634	333668	700311	127507	269061	256839	38533	36727	143485
516607	1604362	1573535	1104818	1086699	94566	206469	2082	231049	121001	11137	10433	76226
306914	646727	642338	448451	446443	18402	73489	-241	114881	37289	3455	3449	17604
51976	42361	42057	36989	36501	374	7090	1138	1434	1696	138	138	1185
55504	73071	70800	48972	48518	4866	12159	643	9366	7074	513	492	5416
3246825	9537965	9461557	9493786	9440140	7195	183231	177643	605201	355936	30353	28899	227961
117253	463811	440480	422285	410127	4608	19635	-2506	20308	21539	1929	1529	13686
4062506	753445	740495	605950	600277	196	54307	20243	269414	124540	4410	2845	13869

11-12 规模以上港澳台及外商投资工业企业主要经济指标(2015年)

单位：万元

项目	Item	企业单位个数(个) Number of Enterprises (unit)	#亏损企业 Loss-Suffering Enterprises	工业总产值(当年价格) Gross Output Value of Industry (at current year's prices)	工业增加值 Added Value of Industry	工业销售产值(当年价格) Sales Value of Industry (at current year's prices)	#出口交货值 Delivery Value of Exports
合　计	**Total**	**803**	**211**	**70592102**	**14792284**	**70041908**	**7476168**
按隶属关系分组	**By Affiliation**						
中央企业	Central Enterprises	11		1359089	520750	1355414	58523
地方企业	Local Enterprises	792	211	69233013	14271534	68686494	7417645
按轻重工业分组	**By Light and Heavy Industries**						
轻工业	Light Industry	296	87	10942237	2998426	10860265	1137485
重工业	Heavy Industry	507	124	59649865	11793858	59181643	6338683
按规模分组	**By Size**						
#大中型企业	Medium and Large-sized Enterprises	246	50	62348476	12930490	61716557	6453279

11-12 续表

单位：万元

项目	Item	固定资产原价 Total Original Value of Fixed Assets	资产负债 Assets and Liabilities: 负债合计 Total Liabilities	#流动负债合计 Total Current Liabilities	#应付账款 Accounts Payable	所有者权益合计 Total Owner's Equity	#实收资本 Paid-up Capital
合　计	**Total**	**25313188**	**41301531**	**36744660**	**15845229**	**35059379**	**16372003**
按隶属关系分组	**By Affiliation**						
中央企业	Central Enterprises	1829906	1105556	926779	204477	1661979	959066
地方企业	Local Enterprises	23483282	40195976	35817881	15640751	33397400	15412937
按轻重工业分组	**By Light and Heavy Industries**						
轻工业	Light Industry	4204527	6562481	6037438	2203650	6623412	3480391
重工业	Heavy Industry	21108661	34739050	30707222	13641579	28435967	12891612
按规模分组	**By Size**						
#大中型企业	Medium and Large-sized Enterprises	21651571	34454311	30856533	13517580	27845486	12616011

MAIN ECONOMIC INDICATORS OF HONGKONG, MACAO, TAIWAN AND FOREIGN-INVESTED INDUSTRIAL ENTERPRISES ABOVE DESIGNATED SIZE (2015)

(10000 yuan)

平均用工人数(人) Average Number of Employed Persons	资产负债 Assets and Liabilities					
	资产总计 Total Assets	流动资产合计 Total Current Assets	#存货 Inventories	#产成品 Finished Products	#应收账款 Accounts Receivable	固定资产合计 Total Fixed Assets
369606	**76445245**	**46516995**	**7918779**	**2859541**	**12054038**	**13843978**
14046	2767534	1004196	172907	30323	340323	645318
355560	73677711	45512798	7745873	2829218	11713715	13198660
128198	13212425	8504919	1959149	925650	2102700	2156442
241408	63232820	38012076	5959631	1933890	9951338	11687536
298994	62299796	37668677	6249060	2274401	9317596	11951991

11-12 Continued

(10000 yuan)

损益 Profits and Losses								应交税金合计 Total Tax Payable	#营业税金及附加 Business Tax and Surtax	#主营业务税金及附加 Main Business Tax and Surtax	#应交增值税 Value Added Tax Payable
营业收入 Business Income	#主营业务收入 Main Business Income	营业成本 Business Cost	#主营业务成本 Main Business Cost	销售费用 Sales Expenses	管理费用 Management Expenses	财务费用 Financial Expenses	利润总额 Total Profits				
79684876	**77738706**	**63772442**	**62366534**	**5797272**	**3568991**	**507945**	**5852669**	**5168822**	**1377838**	**1376768**	**2428766**
1600292	1466612	1225991	1124056	17025	149365	24808	232857	133376	8589	8589	62446
78084584	76272093	62546451	61242477	5780247	3419626	483137	5619812	5035447	1369250	1368180	2366319
14047357	13497867	8871530	8431785	3068425	957373	147023	966669	1097145	103901	103592	725226
65637519	64240838	54900912	53934749	2728848	2611618	360922	4886000	4071677	1273937	1273177	1703540
69779346	68145695	55873826	54706792	5187474	2828930	411996	5125486	4558604	1323250	1322605	2043869

11-13 规模以上港澳台及外商投资工业企业主要经济指标(按行业分)(2015年)

单位：万元

项目	Item	企业单位个数(个) Number of Enterprises (unit)	#亏损企业 Loss-Suffering Enterprises	工业总产值(当年价格) Gross Output Value of Industry (at current year's prices)	工业增加值 Added Value of Industry
合计	**Total**	**803**	**211**	**70592102**	**14792284**
开采辅助活动	Mining Support Service Activities	***	***	***	***
农副食品加工业	Processing of Food from Agricultural Products	23	13	637852	77538
食品制造业	Manufacture of Foods	43	7	1905886	117056
酒、饮料和精制茶制造业	Manufacture of Wines, Beverage and Refined Tea	24	8	1166409	309548
纺织业	Manufacture of Textile	***	***	***	***
纺织服装、服饰业	Manufacture of Textile Wearing Apparel and Ornament	24	10	243788	77386
皮革、毛皮、羽毛及其制品和制鞋业	Manufacture of Leather, Fur, Feather and Its Products, and Footwear	***	***	***	***
木材加工和木、竹、藤、棕、草制品业	Processing of Timbers, Manufacture of Wood, Bamboo, Rattan, Palm, and Straw Products	***	***	***	***
家具制造业	Manufacture of Furniture	10	2	364855	62997
造纸和纸制品业	Manufacture of Paper and Paper Products	14	6	480799	191417
印刷和记录媒介复制业	Printing, Reproduction of Recording Media	17	7	201512	74506
文教、工美、体育和娱乐用品制造业	Manufacture of Articles for Culture, Education, Artwork, Sport and Entertainment Activities	10	3	50724	11254
石油加工、炼焦和核燃料加工业	Processing of Petroleum, Coking, Processing of Mucleus Fuels	***	***	***	***
化学原料和化学制品制造业	Manufacture of Chemical Raw Materials and Chemical Products	39	8	1008928	337924
医药制造业	Manufacture of Medicines	38	7	3596035	1402163
橡胶和塑料制品业	Manufacture of Rubber and Plastics Products	23	5	355284	105469
非金属矿物制品业	Manufacture of Non-metallic Mineral Products	24	9	467018	169820
黑色金属冶炼和压延加工业	Manufacture and Pressing of Ferrous Metals	4		350428	43170
有色金属冶炼和压延加工业	Manufacture and Pressing of Non-ferrous Metals	***	***	***	***
金属制品业	Manufacture of Fabricated Metal Products	35	9	575938	185907
通用设备制造业	Manufacture of General-purpose Machinery	82	20	2928655	729206
专用设备制造业	Manufacture of Special-purpose Machinery	82	22	1420186	332365
汽车制造业	Manufacture of Motor Vehicles	113	22	31524189	7129359
铁路、船舶、航空航天和其他运输设备制造业	Manufacture of Railway Locomotives, Building of Ships and Boats, Manufacture of Air and Spacecrafts and Other Transportation Equipment	7		231477	82969
电气机械和器材制造业	Manufacture of Electrical Machinery and Equipment	47	16	2482424	542581
计算机、通信和其他电子设备制造业	Manufacture of Computers, Communication Equipment and Other Electronic Equipment	69	26	14560281	1516505
仪器仪表制造业	Manufacture of Measuring Instruments and Meters	34	1	750439	187268
其他制造业	Other Manufacturing	8	2	124010	16627
废弃资源综合利用业	Waste recycling and recovery	***	***	***	***
金属制品、机械和设备修理业	Repair of Fabricated Metal Products, Machinery and Equipment	5	1	590350	227317
电力、热力生产和供应业	Production and Distribution of Electricity and Heating Power	4		664232	246415
燃气生产和供应业	Production and Distribution of Gas	6		3474244	469431
水的生产和供应业	Production and Distribution of Water	***	***	***	***

FOREIGN-INVESTED INDUSTRIAL ENTERPRISES ABOVE DESIGNATED SIZE (BY SECTOR) (2015)

(10000 yuan)

工业销售产值(当年价格) Sales Value of Industry (at current year's prices)	#出口交货值 Delivery Value of Exports	平均用工人数(人) Average Number of Employed Persons (person)	资产负债 Assets and Liabilities: 资产总计 Total Assets	流动资产合计 Total Current Assets	#存货 Inventories	#产成品 Finished Products	#应收账款 Accounts Receivable	固定资产合计 Total Fixed Assets
70041908	**7476168**	**369606**	**76445245**	**46516995**	**7918779**	**2859541**	**12054038**	**13843978**
***	***	1077	***	***	***	***	***	***
628272	56864	8221	460795	285289	99272	31574	89984	124253
1907489	96679	31815	2816890	1660580	229983	143048	347297	544236
1268571	10321	15018	1499129	636112	99888	27251	60631	351151
***	***	750	***	***	***	***	***	***
224123	129912	9630	258441	222782	102828	48014	33441	20274
***	***	864	***	***	***	***	***	***
***	***	151	38655	8620	3041	1047	3755	29946
357851	32102	3882	257755	184124	67345	30110	58367	43233
488389	45897	2941	389124	259888	70034	17314	65309	98934
199638	8263	4268	293652	191915	34433	18490	50837	86281
61838	34341	1643	120270	109034	45191	28955	14538	8525
***	***	1096	***	***	***	***	***	***
989839	55500	9180	1283682	757706	103329	39351	184474	370270
3411917	92972	27580	3933038	2721033	873625	452776	715440	507176
356043	54771	7703	400025	267824	50343	18752	108883	97563
461619	26838	6891	817686	559128	196974	20238	187854	130339
345764	24258	1251	243307	213556	67563	11414	88990	7133
***	***	299	***	***	***	***	***	***
596309	46601	6704	1425661	918087	125058	36954	201406	161374
2945195	618816	25068	4811146	3788413	1068972	260978	803236	583236
1461832	409553	16021	3473911	2312567	337323	75108	689652	262111
31532035	286541	84200	26883357	15125559	1765036	657677	3904741	6049376
235454	150	830	192670	180445	37620	9227	73282	9576
2506821	432547	15018	3571372	2907355	527889	114414	1008480	176620
14036382	4742124	60227	12311316	9433425	1610010	742617	2172138	1814151
749328	98876	6920	1203415	992953	188410	35124	422525	68666
119717	93384	999	79708	58853	13106	4225	23789	17390
***	***	118	***	***	***	***	***	***
582116	49592	9325	550671	354346	123601	3384	144546	180806
664232		1317	3955460	754805	6796	6076	119233	553226
3474244		8212	4285822	1029385	3431	211	310875	1445156
***	***	387	***	***	***	***	***	***

11-13 续表

单位：万元

项目	Item	资产负债 Assets and Liabilities 固定资产原价 Total Original Value of Fixed Assets	负债合计 Total Liabilities	#流动负债合计 Total Current Liabilities	#应付账款 Accounts Payable	所有者权益合计 Total Owner's Equity
合 计	**Total**	**25313188**	**41301531**	**36744660**	**15845229**	**35059379**
开采辅助活动	Mining Support Service Activities	***	***	***	***	***
农副食品加工业	Processing of Food from Agricultural Products	243843	331677	319699	105643	129118
食品制造业	Manufacture of Foods	1041956	1405140	1342734	489686	1411750
酒、饮料和精制茶制造业	Manufacture of Wines, Beverage and Refined Tea	771292	880495	829943	306212	618634
纺织业	Manufacture of Textile	***	***	***	***	***
纺织服装、服饰业	Manufacture of Textile Wearing Apparel and Ornament	55476	176063	171989	41798	82378
皮革、毛皮、羽毛及其制品和制鞋业	Manufacture of Leather, Fur, Feather and Its Products, and Footwear	7876	20881	19582	14221	25742
木材加工和木、竹、藤、棕、草制品业	Processing of Timbers, Manufacture of Wood, Bamboo, Rattan, Palm, and Straw Products	64582	9727	9727	7083	28928
家具制造业	Manufacture of Furniture	66969	163146	160044	32898	94609
造纸和纸制品业	Manufacture of Paper and Paper Products	279238	177678	174632	55585	211447
印刷和记录媒介复制业	Printing, Reproduction of Recording Media	216060	98300	86704	31121	195352
文教、工美、体育和娱乐用品制造业	Manufacture of Articles for Culture, Education, Artwork, Sport and Entertainment Activities	17129	57019	56903	21991	63251
石油加工、炼焦和核燃料加工业	Processing of Petroleum, Coking, Processing of Mucleus Fuels	30580	23718	23718	9993	84945
化学原料和化学制品制造业	Manufacture of Chemical Raw Materials and Chemical Products	696800	566236	488549	206570	706180
医药制造业	Manufacture of Medicines	736463	1900278	1634131	612189	2032759
橡胶和塑料制品业	Manufacture of Rubber and Plastics Products	221590	176114	163460	69701	223911
非金属矿物制品业	Manufacture of Non-metallic Mineral Products	336818	455662	424933	126098	363351
黑色金属冶炼和压延加工业	Manufacture and Pressing of Ferrous Metals	47704	124659	111480	80829	114697
有色金属冶炼和压延加工业	Manufacture and Pressing of Non-ferrous Metals	***	***	***	***	***
金属制品业	Manufacture of Fabricated Metal Products	354159	728864	526296	102408	696798
通用设备制造业	Manufacture of General-purpose Machinery	1141098	2194401	2005482	601089	2616745
专用设备制造业	Manufacture of Special-purpose Machinery	486163	1993016	1771935	538556	1479059
汽车制造业	Manufacture of Motor Vehicles	8808372	15090223	13527294	6852699	11786687
铁路、船舶、航空航天和其他运输设备制造业	Manufacture of Railway Locomotives, Building of Ships and Boats, Manufacture of Air and Spacecrafts and Other Transportation Equipment	20812	121188	121161	51030	71482
电气机械和器材制造业	Manufacture of Electrical Machinery and Equipment	449608	1852614	1696935	736223	1692310
计算机、通信和其他电子设备制造业	Manufacture of Computers, Communication Equipment and Other Electronic Equipment	4959231	8672280	7884927	4034438	3603324
仪器仪表制造业	Manufacture of Measuring Instruments and Meters	153856	700722	684201	338021	502693
其他制造业	Other Manufacturing	31820	37166	37163	29909	42542
废弃资源综合利用业	Waste recycling and recovery	***	***	***	***	***
金属制品、机械和设备修理业	Repair of Fabricated Metal Products, Machinery and Equipment	342626	331661	302310	66992	219010
电力、热力生产和供应业	Production and Distribution of Electricity and Heating Power	1603910	1337710	847934	48972	2617749
燃气生产和供应业	Production and Distribution of Gas	1982367	1182812	866658	141855	3103010
水的生产和供应业	Production and Distribution of Water	***	***	***	***	***

11-13 Continued

(10000 yuan)

	损 益 Profits and Losses											
#实收资本 Paid-up Capital	营业收入 Business Income	#主营业务收入 Main Business Income	营业成本 Business Cost	#主营业务成本 Main Business Cost	销售费用 Sales Expenses	管理费用 Manage-ment Expenses	财务费用 Financial Expenses	利润总额 Total Profits	应交税金合计 Total Tax Payable	#营业税金及附加 Business Tax and Surtax	#主营业务税金及附加 Main Business Tax and Surtax	#应交增值税 Value Added Tax Payable
16372003	**79684876**	**77738706**	**63772442**	**62366534**	**5797272**	**3568991**	**507945**	**5852669**	**5168822**	**1377838**	**1376768**	**2428766**
***	***	***	***	***	***	***	***	***	***	***	***	***
149390	731555	722064	638974	631019	54699	39969	7974	-14287	7610	1056	1056	2730
916060	4060534	3961570	2580682	2489734	1120948	192762	3579	167927	279512	24923	24923	213659
701377	1384961	1306247	999247	929489	241689	95447	8377	24470	110295	17032	16850	70334
***	***	***	***	***	***	***	***	***	***	***	***	***
55175	276301	250901	221425	197480	29299	25964	1375	182	9618	1166	1054	7158
3442	73502	70479	62204	59613	1035	3238	163	6677	4174	281	281	2125
44987	26983	26897	27207	27187	2342	1325	31	-3612	1368	140	140	1190
30857	283142	271167	203200	193830	40360	25702	2322	11270	8217	954	954	5499
138206	497379	487336	371763	364663	20686	22801	-1259	82215	47552	2629	2629	20225
121914	230264	226177	184567	182528	12279	20030	-184	14856	18463	1618	1618	12801
10824	66287	65885	55191	54975	4376	5290	-227	1418	1654	442	442	472
11173	289005	287639	214340	213891	19099	15872	287	33886	27289	5043	5043	13532
415033	1051832	1033553	687641	673897	179212	64937	13386	98318	115285	13169	13168	72818
684586	3812956	3611760	1718616	1535124	1271712	276041	111941	422235	420887	34015	34004	282547
121064	413915	393807	329218	312199	19789	41654	1962	19010	20507	2188	2184	13130
201293	493246	483146	378950	372765	21748	39880	6231	43513	39708	3932	3932	24654
56774	372084	371995	331654	331546	10360	8166	1961	19441	10778	679	679	4726
***	***	***	***	***	***	***	***	***	***	***	***	***
310878	778142	720578	619354	562714	38389	66798	14836	70039	47589	4346	4345	30893
929133	3279257	3249182	2559886	2548981	193755	237877	8682	397146	192847	16536	16536	107894
489896	1894148	1771190	1361720	1307606	130274	250922	28483	163348	111608	10009	10002	63370
4665424	32025549	31432246	25968912	25518376	1343005	979628	136756	3120592	2866257	1166286	1166266	1019445
19563	259566	259200	180190	180184	9774	11310	6349	50140	29776	1436	1436	13824
1058314	2963465	2787138	2330190	2158968	205708	174326	-2467	12587	175834	11380	11380	82162
2591707	18217087	17876270	16541439	16394323	688649	628439	62423	276848	313043	33358	33210	190909
210120	1046386	1034538	776673	772915	97098	71234	4746	106115	68395	6172	6171	39868
40558	127925	126190	115735	115294	6177	4596	74	1123	817	234	234	111
***	***	***	***	***	***	***	***	***	***	***	***	***
198167	638877	587704	535953	487403	1352	90369	8857	19880	34772	2811	2811	22910
1389603	714348	664226	474010	459754		36219	52745	331385	97876	5222	5025	35239
620496	3492042	3476367	3163787	3150726	26911	111266	21436	359146	97806	9633	9247	67867
***	***	***	***	***	***	***	***	***	***	***	***	***

11-14 大中型工业企业主要经济指标(2015年)

单位：万元

项目	Item	企业单位个数(个) Number of Enterprises (unit)	#亏损企业 Loss-Suffering Enterprises	工业总产值(当年价格) Gross Output Value of Industry (at current year's prices)	工业增加值 Added Value of Industry
合计	**Total**	**694**	**144**	**142502541**	**29864755**
按隶属关系分组	**By Affiliation**				
中央工业	Central Enterprises	86	15	54467808	11522857
地方工业	Local Enterprises	608	129	88034733	18341898
按登记注册类型分组	**By Registration Type**				
内资企业	Domestially-Invested Enterprises	448	94	80154065	16934265
国有企业	State-owned Enterprises	28	3	33156954	5691815
集体企业	Collectively-owned Enterprises	4	1	75686	39379
股份合作企业	Joint-equity Cooperative Enterprises	***	***	***	***
有限责任公司	Limited Liability Companies	223	61	24769262	5541814
股份有限公司	Companies Limited by Shares	98	15	19193842	4751701
私营企业	Private Enterprises	93	13	2885731	861926
港澳台商投资企业	Hong Kong, Macao and Taiwan-invested Enterprises	61	17	16551927	1792739
港澳台合资经营	Joint Ventures	33	8	3602974	958797
港澳台合作经营	Cooperatives				
港澳台商独资企业	Solely-funded Enterprises	22	7	12420790	872665
港澳台商投资股份有限公司	Companies Limited by Shares	6	2	528163	-38724
外商投资企业	Foreign-invested Enterprises	185	33	45796549	11137752
中外合资经营	Joint Ventures	76	8	30901054	8128656
中外合作经营	Cooperatives	4	2	183404	82815
外资(独资)企业	Solely-funded Enterprises	99	22	14119567	2759963
外商投资股份有限公司	Companies Limited by Shares	6	1	592524	166318
按城乡分组	**By Urban and Rural Regions**				
#农村企业	Rural Enterprises	***	***	***	***
按轻重工业分组	**By Light and Heavy Industries**				
轻工业	Light Industry	262	56	17624224	5558688
重工业	Heavy Industry	432	88	124878317	24306067
按规模分组	**By Size**				
#大型企业	Medium and Large-sized Enterprises	139	23	112335775	22775547

MAIN ECONOMIC INDICATORS OF LOCAL MEDIUM AND LARGE-SIZED INDUSTRIAL ENTERPRISES (2015)

(10000 yuan)

工业销售产值(当年价格) Sales Value of Industry (at current year's prices)	#出口交货值 Delivery Value of Exports	平均用工人数(人) Average Number of Employed Persons (person)	资产负债 Assets and Liabilities: 资产总计 Total Assets	流动资产合计 Total Current Assets	#存货 Inventories	#产成品 Finished Products	#应收账款 Accounts Receivable	固定资产合计 Total Fixed Assets
141230251	**9072499**	**758731**	**324419998**	**113959365**	**14208259**	**4960472**	**26137946**	**57468112**
54492869	324395	141147	173122326	34100233	2720857	678516	6089878	28381982
86737382	8748104	617584	151297672	79859132	11487402	4281956	20048067	29086130
79513694	2619220	459737	262120202	76290688	7959199	2686071	16820350	45516121
33171331	16915	32868	144935470	22830666	557392	96564	2421743	18519716
80212		2759	101883	73281	13837	3761	10401	22563
***	***	2387	***	***	***	***	***	***
24583533	1569710	229412	73339968	29688384	3530807	1237077	8200512	21363114
18865542	726862	140482	39149546	20730097	3116709	1018113	5203285	4888271
2733766	300269	51829	4463811	2870051	715214	312190	967633	695293
16001830	1570674	73899	18473748	11460747	2032481	791624	2961652	3055495
3608709	765855	30558	3868492	2279887	451441	113006	740563	1031508
11886814	741733	38664	11479019	7083958	1118385	633702	1485013	1954838
506307	63086	4677	3126237	2096902	462656	44916	736077	69150
45714728	4882605	225095	43826048	26207930	4216579	1482778	6355944	8896496
30774820	3026346	114224	28016610	15957175	2285208	663240	2907979	5811318
173949	24349	5635	268988	221389	-26980	2308	52489	42516
14155563	1785003	96701	13301117	9164776	1910174	796990	3273423	2845317
610396	46907	8535	2239333	864590	48178	20240	122053	197346
***	***	1570	***	***	***	***	***	***
17220932	867707	229922	27567750	15392299	3350945	1533908	2845484	4939351
124009320	8204792	528809	296852248	98567066	10857314	3426564	23292461	52528761
111228285	6968280	451869	271397840	82278165	8457867	3219686	16021070	49058924

11-14 续表

单位：万元

项　目	Item	资产负债 Assets and Liabilities 固定资产原价 Total Original Value of Fixed Assets	负债合计 Total Liabilities	#流动负债合计 Total Current Liabilities	#应付账款 Accounts Payable	所有者权益合计 Total Owner's Equity	#实收资本 Paid-up Capital
合　计	**Total**	**107856174**	**149082379**	**94269495**	**29361555**	**175297341**	**94109525**
按隶属关系分组	**By Affiliation**						
中央工业	Central Enterprises	60222164	68801780	32212484	7681830	104320546	64109105
地方工业	Local Enterprises	47634010	80280599	62057011	21679725	70976795	30000420
按登记注册类型分组	**By Registration Type**						
内资企业	Domestially-Invested Enterprises	86204603	114628068	63412962	15843975	147451855	81493514
国有企业	State-owned Enterprises	39927250	53240667	19470019	3242762	91694803	56093270
集体企业	Collectively-owned Enterprises	66232	35323	32748	5693	66560	12880
股份合作企业	Joint-equity Cooperative Enterprises	***	***	***	***	***	***
有限责任公司	Limited Liability Companies	36018016	40967699	27948743	7518820	32353892	18625916
股份有限公司	Companies Limited by Shares	9132894	18189020	13959111	4418409	20960526	5995831
私营企业	Private Enterprises	1018691	2151706	1962144	637672	2290203	751618
港澳台商投资企业	Hong Kong, Macao and Taiwan-invested Enterprises	5810682	11212635	10371119	4419751	7261113	3233970
港澳台合资经营	Joint Ventures	2975391	1773459	1673948	628546	2095033	1309333
港澳台合作经营	Cooperatives						
港澳台商独资企业	Solely-funded Enterprises	2676262	7647030	7210198	3292831	3831989	1061650
港澳台商投资股份有限公司	Companies Limited by Shares	159029	1792146	1486973	498374	1334091	862987
外商投资企业	Foreign-invested Enterprises	15840889	23241675	20485414	9097829	20584373	9382041
中外合资经营	Joint Ventures	8828568	15027672	13414742	5777458	12988938	5142288
中外合作经营	Cooperatives	115491	135426	125752	51170	133562	157446
外资(独资)企业	Solely-funded Enterprises	6313973	7411661	6480491	3169208	5889456	3381603
外商投资股份有限公司	Companies Limited by Shares	582858	666917	464428	99993	1572416	700704
按城乡分组	**By Urban and Rural Regions**						
#农村企业	Rural Enterprises	***	***	***	***	***	***
按轻重工业分组	**By Light and Heavy Industries**						
轻工业	Light Industry	9211615	12646140	10512063	2741839	14921610	5386693
重工业	Heavy Industry	98644559	136436239	83757432	26619716	160375731	88722832
按规模分组	**By Size**						
#大型企业	Medium and Large-sized Enterprises	92177471	122155121	72270057	21597243	149242720	82338939

11-14 Continued

(10000 yuan)

损益 Profits and Losses								应交税金合计 Total Tax Payable			
营业收入 Business Income	#主营业务收入 Main Business Income	营业成本 Business Cost	#主营业务成本 Main Business Cost	销售费用 Sales Expenses	管理费用 Manage-ment Expenses	财务费用 Financial Expenses	利润总额 Total Profits	应交税金合计 Total Tax Payable	#营业税金及附加 Business Tax and Surtax	#主营业务税金及附加 Main Business Tax and Surtax	#应交增值税 Value Added Tax Payable
155709992	**152709160**	**130025958**	**127770795**	**7551113**	**6439044**	**1787383**	**13542466**	**10117314**	**3163661**	**3149262**	**4701650**
56022058	55370461	50013863	49454173	327824	1192781	773391	5985015	3899836	1511363	1506102	1742182
99687934	97338699	80012095	78316622	7223289	5246263	1013991	7557451	6217479	1652299	1643160	2959467
85930646	84563465	74152132	73064003	2363639	3610114	1375387	8416980	5558711	1840411	1826657	2657781
33333827	33266622	30613718	30572238	101868	221298	568160	4861385	1775588	422851	420486	964180
81106	76967	60965	58090	5512	11019	-733	3864	10993	1467	1467	8575
***	***	***	***	***	***	***	***	***	***	***	***
27869291	27338282	24783317	24354285	833447	1675893	493009	1392448	1235285	130177	122806	737303
21442366	20737622	16480056	15897653	1099869	1360826	294333	1807779	2355053	1268648	1264877	838074
3117490	3058178	2169166	2136917	303819	331169	20473	339546	173430	16586	16340	103178
20641981	20106419	18130379	17791217	1174738	758610	131508	622086	472128	51595	50982	259449
3844622	3717062	3019932	2909907	198508	188679	29783	394445	238117	27660	27549	110955
16061138	15795888	14494628	14406445	852128	498446	73517	344527	204821	17700	17198	133581
736221	593470	615820	474866	124102	71485	28208	-116886	29191	6235	6235	14913
49137365	48039276	37743448	36915575	4012736	2070320	280488	4503401	4086475	1271655	1271623	1784420
31679877	31182273	24389648	24056932	1922382	1238501	111311	3525383	3183893	1191181	1191152	1223620
357624	351542	287124	281488	46498	14696	-3736	8861	16108	1296	1296	11701
16376892	15846028	12551902	12099392	1963298	743578	158916	896528	845006	74632	74631	520307
722971	659433	514774	477763	80558	73545	13997	72629	41468	4547	4544	28792
***	***	***	***	***	***	***	***	***	***	***	***
20922257	20247879	13251043	12757477	3888875	1563148	204537	1938522	2054734	539474	537091	1117482
134787735	132461281	116774916	115013318	3662238	4875896	1582846	11603944	8062580	2624187	2612171	3584167
120187580	118388557	102247832	100904648	5331315	3803718	1328163	10553950	7800808	2721589	2711355	3507295

11-15 大中型工业企业主要经济指标(按行业分)(2015年)

单位：万元

项目	Item	企业单位个数(个) Number of Enterprises (unit)	#亏损企业 Loss-Suffering Enterprises	工业总产值(当年价格) Gross Output Value of Industry (at current year's prices)	工业增加值 Added Value of Industry
合计	**Total**	**694**	**144**	**142502541**	**29864755**
煤炭开采和洗选业	Mining and Washing of Coal	***	***	***	***
石油和天然气开采业	Extraction of Petroleum and Natural Gas	***	***	***	***
黑色金属矿采选业	Mining and Processing of Ferrous Metal Ores	5	3	783004	10492
开采辅助活动	Mining Support Service Activities	4	2	1672744	951510
农副食品加工业	Processing of Food from Agricultural Products	27	8	2214446	391609
食品制造业	Manufacture of Foods	41	9	2047901	197724
酒、饮料和精制茶制造业	Manufacture of Wines, Beverage and Refined Tea	16	6	1575650	489993
烟草制品业	Manufacture of Cigarettes and Tobacco	***	***	***	***
纺织业	Manufacture of Textile	***	***	***	***
纺织服装、服饰业	Manufacture of Textile Wearing Apparel and Ornament	34	12	731557	364304
皮革、毛皮、羽毛及其制品和制鞋业	Manufacture of Leather, Fur, Feather and Its Products, and Footwear	***	***	***	***
木材加工和木、竹、藤、棕、草制品业	Processing of Timbers, Manufacture of Wood, Bamboo, Rattan, Palm, and Straw Products	***	***	***	***
家具制造业	Manufacture of Furniture	10		548309	127174
造纸和纸制品业	Manufacture of Paper and Paper Products	6	1	411053	169105
印刷和记录媒介复制业	Printing, Reproduction of Recording Media	17	7	575034	233791
文教、工美、体育和娱乐用品制造业	Manufacture of Articles for Culture, Education, Artwork, Sport and Entertainment Activities	4	1	943732	31293
石油加工、炼焦和核燃料加工业	Processing of Petroleum, Coking, Processing of Mucleus Fuels	4		5404830	1782228
化学原料和化学制品制造业	Manufacture of Chemical Raw Materials and Chemical Products	23	4	1313536	297188
医药制造业	Manufacture of Medicines	51	6	5788860	2408004
化学纤维制造业	Manufacture of Chemical fibres				
橡胶和塑料制品业	Manufacture of Rubber and Plastics Products	12		324282	88778
非金属矿物制品业	Manufacture of Non-metallic Mineral Products	32	12	2226231	392621
黑色金属冶炼和压延加工业	Manufacture and Pressing of Ferrous Metals	5	1	643054	-25570
有色金属冶炼和压延加工业	Manufacture and Pressing of Non-ferrous Metals	6	2	243003	37315
金属制品业	Manufacture of Fabricated Metal Products	21	5	886090	271899
通用设备制造业	Manufacture of General-purpose Machinery	40	8	3333559	926505
专用设备制造业	Manufacture of Special-purpose Machinery	51	12	3216121	850147
汽车制造业	Manufacture of Motor Vehicles	71	10	35785219	7491075
铁路、船舶、航空航天和其他运输设备制造业	Manufacture of Railway Locomotives, Building of Ships and Boats, Manufacture of Air and Spacecrafts and Other Transportation Equipment	15	4	1836139	405540
电气机械和器材制造业	Manufacture of Electrical Machinery and Equipment	44	7	5545118	1005294
计算机、通信和其他电子设备制造业	Manufacture of Computers, Communication Equipment and Other Electronic Equipment	75	16	17906024	2071808
仪器仪表制造业	Manufacture of Measuring Instrument and Meter	25	1	1122877	415840
其他制造业	Other Manufacturing	4		246175	144546
金属制品、机械和设备修理业	Repair of Fabricated Metal Products, Machinery and Equipment	***	***	***	***
电力、热力生产和供应业	Production and Distribution of Electricity and Heating Power	29	6	39410128	6607361
燃气生产和供应业	Production and Distribution of Gas	***	***	***	***
水的生产和供应业	Production and Distribution of Water	5		504323	245021

MAIN ECONOMIC INDICATORS OF MEDIUM AND LARGE-SIZED INDUSTRIAL ENTERPRISES (BY SECTOR) (2015)

(10000 yuan)

工业销售产值(当年价格) Sales Value of Industry (at current year's prices)	#出口交货值 Delivery Value of Exports	平均用工人数(人) Average Number of Employed Persons (person)	资产负债 Assets and Liabilities 资产总计 Total Assets	流动资产合计 Total Current Assets	#存货 Inventories	#产成品 Finished Products	#应收账款 Accounts Receivable	固定资产合计 Total Fixed Assets	固定资产原价 Total Original Value of Fixed Assets
141230251	**9072499**	**758731**	**324419998**	**113959365**	**14208259**	**4960472**	**26137946**	**57468112**	**107856174**
***	***	10523	***	***	***	***	***	***	***
***	***	1999	***	***	***	***	***	***	***
778167		23017	23583185	8259095	243436	37104	1618838	3940449	5702115
1672744	125601	19640	5374846	2716986	244758	14130	1064761	1131112	2581310
2190687	21928	21401	3375075	2260148	292938	186291	263559	325655	513848
2040660	95185	41151	2786632	1558603	258350	142396	337895	572272	1007285
1672493	14519	24034	3579432	1301985	185293	35748	65589	465667	1129943
***	***	916	***	***	***	***	***	***	***
***	***	1442	***	***	***	***	***	***	***
700682	127911	27354	890571	642376	273065	186194	106315	139690	215132
***	***	1164	***	***	***	***	***	***	***
***	***	1593	***	***	***	***	***	***	***
552462	32539	8575	599367	368007	88673	39689	96096	120728	176166
415472	19443	2463	273204	178842	60826	14623	39235	62927	197095
597215	7907	12849	1100056	547588	106348	45429	75934	327757	846694
930902	11865	2496	242666	167037	70075	33381	19085	45940	86821
5416407		10825	2601197	1036118	625003	91588	183668	1135332	3115768
1273070	51990	19001	1753000	1100939	164153	71335	174607	380837	1489268
5422722	80620	52631	8868384	5191810	1493338	693060	1262998	1407218	1993239
324203	68200	7997	312249	196733	38992	16246	89957	84056	174148
2242998	50272	27800	6057100	4222502	568200	113014	1911870	575030	1120726
642188	60905	3754	829652	204436	109480	46880	64488	464002	758156
251136	64582	2926	430981	270144	77560	23494	55219	49895	89784
913694	182899	12228	2284421	1264770	237658	83708	261703	335861	516003
3216416	647305	31849	5992307	4470028	1277086	413126	1013500	696297	1345552
3208812	488407	36759	11689588	7153355	1058590	349215	1811610	713858	1241769
35754454	546218	121843	34540010	17827019	2054799	833017	4591730	7668334	10807707
1805511	15849	14834	2204108	1711482	488761	148180	736261	266653	500810
5406772	394441	32972	7864347	6016865	886903	165737	2895050	408509	830667
17319827	5736260	88226	21277330	14358880	2447132	989657	3402794	3814471	8314916
1097964	54964	13725	2154190	1665821	371465	82016	543391	161689	278921
221341	12431	1957	390095	239830	62718	27950	36698	84072	159020
***	***	9620	***	***	***	***	***	***	***
39401972		49918	156418972	23401499	95723	9551	2445313	26758937	54452181
***	***	10535	***	***	***	***	***	***	***
504323		8714	8395574	2941552	8170		402700	3072050	4813144

11-15 续表

单位：万元

项　目	Item	资产负债 Assets and Liabilities			
		负债合计 Total Liabilities	#流动负债合计 Total Current Liabilities	#应付账款 Accounts Payable	所有者权益合计 Total Owner's Equity
合计	**Total**	**149082379**	**94269495**	**29361555**	**175297341**
煤炭开采和洗选业	Mining and Washing of Coal	***	***	***	***
石油和天然气开采业	Extraction of Petroleum and Natural Gas	***	***	***	***
黑色金属矿采选业	Mining and Processing of Ferrous Metal Ores	13215161	7680852	845085	10368024
开采辅助活动	Mining Support Service Activities	2145216	2044097	655581	3229630
农副食品加工业	Processing of Food from Agricultural Products	1812087	1391328	164306	1562988
食品制造业	Manufacture of Foods	1592411	1518047	529999	1194221
酒、饮料和精制茶制造业	Manufacture of Wines, Beverage and Refined Tea	1369521	1221290	304870	2209911
烟草制品业	Manufacture of Cigarettes and Tobacco	***	***	***	***
纺织业	Manufacture of Textile	***	***	***	***
纺织服装、服饰业	Manufacture of Textile Wearing Apparel and Ornament	435467	411609	147596	455104
皮革、毛皮、羽毛及其制品和制鞋业	Manufacture of Leather, Fur, Feather and Its Products, and Footwear	***	***	***	***
木材加工和木、竹、藤、棕、草制品业	Processing of Timbers, Manufacture of Wood, Bamboo, Rattan, Palm, and Straw Products	***	***	***	***
家具制造业	Manufacture of Furniture	307394	280424	62762	291973
造纸和纸制品业	Manufacture of Paper and Paper Products	153251	152864	48802	119953
印刷和记录媒介复制业	Printing, Reproduction of Recording Media	337913	299233	105214	762143
文教、工美、体育和娱乐用品制造业	Manufacture of Articles for Culture, Education, Artwork, Sport and Entertainment Activities	142777	115556	29992	99889
石油加工、炼焦和核燃料加工业	Processing of Petroleum, Coking, Processing of Mucleus Fuels	1460026	1419306	348752	1141171
化学原料和化学制品制造业	Manufacture of Chemical Raw Materials and Chemical Products	926334	880561	116196	826667
医药制造业	Manufacture of Medicines	3791542	3224822	957167	5076841
化学纤维制造业	Manufacture of Chemical fibres				
橡胶和塑料制品业	Manufacture of Rubber and Plastics Products	158851	141636	58079	153398
非金属矿物制品业	Manufacture of Non-metallic Mineral Products	3395185	3052644	1193503	2643539
黑色金属冶炼和压延加工业	Manufacture and Pressing of Ferrous Metals	864531	321715	208212	-34879
有色金属冶炼和压延加工业	Manufacture and Pressing of Non-ferrous Metals	128082	89415	38788	302899
金属制品业	Manufacture of Fabricated Metal Products	1100485	792994	224513	1183935
通用设备制造业	Manufacture of General-purpose Machinery	2591653	2360737	692528	3378752
专用设备制造业	Manufacture of Special-purpose Machinery	5867788	4644038	1386500	5821800
汽车制造业	Manufacture of Motor Vehicles	19804165	17236208	8312955	14735845
铁路、船舶、航空航天和其他运输设备制造业	Manufacture of Railway Locomotives, Building of Ships and Boats, Manufacture of Air and Spacecrafts and Other Transportation Equipment	1352356	1295762	628509	851752
电气机械和器材制造业	Manufacture of Electrical Machinery and Equipment	4809730	4532642	1634465	3054617
计算机、通信和其他电子设备制造业	Manufacture of Computers, Communication Equipment and Other Electronic Equipment	12940232	11117784	5045439	8337098
仪器仪表制造业	Manufacture of Measuring Instrument and Meter	872139	827395	340858	1282052
其他制造业	Other Manufacturing	75441	65934	14997	314654
金属制品、机械和设备修理业	Repair of Fabricated Metal Products, Machinery and Equipment	***	***	***	***
电力、热力生产和供应业	Production and Distribution of Electricity and Heating Power	60199178	24132120	4714564	96219794
燃气生产和供应业	Production and Distribution of Gas	***	***	***	***
水的生产和供应业	Production and Distribution of Water	4011529	1081179	184119	4384045

11-15 Continued

(10000 yuan)

#实收资本 Paid-up Capital	损益 Profits and Losses: 营业收入 Business Income	#主营业务收入 Main Business Income	营业成本 Business Cost	#主营业务成本 Main Business Cost	销售费用 Sales Expenses	管理费用 Management Expenses	财务费用 Financial Expenses	利润总额 Total Profits	应交税金合计 Total Tax Payable	#营业税金及附加 Business Tax and Surtax	#主营业务税金及附加 Main Business Tax and Surtax	#应交增值税 Value Added Tax Payable
94109525	**155709992**	**152709160**	**130025958**	**127770795**	**7551113**	**6439044**	**1787383**	**13542466**	**10117314**	**3163661**	**3149262**	**4701650**
***	***	***	***	***	***	***	***	***	***	***	***	***
***	***	***	***	***	***	***	***	***	***	***	***	***
2900719	2259240	2159574	2249733	2118906	8430	138918	157114	167634	65733	8891	8174	48447
2797616	1608049	1603465	1434661	1431729	5197	68553	8020	101222	57080	14659	14573	18882
590187	2564703	2547367	1986586	1981402	222360	131580	30423	136143	178664	101625	101614	48153
754097	4131117	4022632	2693520	2589315	1084658	187353	7043	158758	270585	23482	23382	205473
576464	1814846	1706612	1278331	1186956	294825	117834	1381	62430	200214	65208	64854	104298
***	***	***	***	***	***	***	***	***	***	***	***	***
***	***	***	***	***	***	***	***	***	***	***	***	***
153726	788803	756260	448623	423494	174044	86518	2889	83457	75737	6884	6772	54895
***	***	***	***	***	***	***	***	***	***	***	***	***
***	***	***	***	***	***	***	***	***	***	***	***	***
105680	483794	470965	355708	345758	57825	43029	3940	33312	25387	2391	2300	16696
54088	423539	411317	306858	297154	19562	19086	-369	77760	43883	2435	2435	18847
409671	695657	666292	565738	550591	20823	89685	-1511	18262	54567	5270	4845	40810
70123	1028295	1014009	998161	996104	6019	23394	1773	-923	6045	1379	666	3224
11444	5892275	5667845	4413917	4191572	52516	150614	21925	287007	1308819	957924	956969	275257
978808	1442272	1415507	1069747	1049200	209040	138496	22846	-9098	95258	13069	12977	69291
1329634	5880218	5641581	2698923	2494795	1665543	518503	127370	1057696	671029	53898	53795	442433
61091	372784	359183	304678	293893	15413	35743	1831	15019	14364	1906	1906	9139
1059897	2856599	2755710	2439090	2350756	113247	213268	40629	153447	112161	20343	19670	68169
311352	688805	680170	711463	703704	35263	22597	16998	-106700	7758	972	947	4070
67198	404645	277262	366893	243658	4612	21866	1	6873	6833	2341	2308	3292
504300	1122387	1051653	862136	797613	43079	105714	22222	118343	57809	7873	7601	33503
1102238	3521459	3463820	2651743	2621652	216130	263704	15748	498562	205594	19841	19769	106827
1856265	3740240	3582791	2753569	2671754	208802	397222	128055	287596	248345	24110	23795	171393
6090410	37006748	36261861	30469538	29951954	1470002	1314665	155754	3309467	3072798	1283184	1282600	1088057
553794	1891375	1882711	1482353	1477238	39730	159521	20201	198893	137835	9802	9710	85575
1843047	5933129	5760075	4683972	4522734	444272	347816	23503	198330	293375	23504	22909	169373
5379892	21887787	21522439	19390625	19227340	942098	1088730	193371	409816	410239	53078	51375	221939
380462	1318761	1307091	858420	853123	113266	139802	3644	238767	122414	10349	10007	71038
93296	228251	226029	116428	115410	13483	25209	-2652	78580	29523	2427	2427	15835
***	***	***	***	***	***	***	***	***	***	***	***	***
59116650	39690798	39568366	37453908	37381430	8126	192894	707877	5241250	1681995	162874	159462	1077744
***	***	***	***	***	***	***	***	***	***	***	***	***
3544341	687339	676492	535655	531322	1431	47393	23656	258345	121658	4178	2715	13954

11-16 规模以上工业企业主要工业产品生产能力
PRODUCTION CAPACITY OF MAIN INDUSTRIAL PRODUCTS IN INDUSTRIAL ENTERPRISES ABOVE DESIGNATED SIZE

主要工业产品名称		Name of Main Industrial Products		2015	2014
原油加工能力	(吨)	Crude Oil Processing Capacity	(ton)	11500000	11500000
硅酸盐水泥熟料	(吨)	Portland Cement Chamotte	(ton)	5870000	6266000
发电设备容量总计	(万千瓦)	Total Capacity of Power Generation Equipment	(10000 kW)	1122	1555
火电设备容量	(万千瓦)	Capacity of Thermal Power Equipment	(10000 kW)	983	782
水电设备容量	(万千瓦)	Capacity of Hydropower Equipment	(10000 kW)	98	98
风电设备容量	(万千瓦)	Capacity of Wind Power Equipment	(10000 kW)	15	15
原煤	(吨)	Raw Coal	(ton)	5200000	5200000
卷烟	(万支)	Cigarette	(10000 units)	3996000	4185000
气流纺锭	(头)	Air Spinning Spindles (Rotating-cup Spinning)	(unit)	1656	1656
棉布织机	(台)	Cotton Cloth Weaver	(unit)	66	66
水泥	(吨)	Cement	(ton)	7350000	8350000
钢材	(吨)	Rolled Steel	(ton)	1758410	1764694
金属切削机床	(台)	Metal-Cutting Machine Tools	(unit)	21995	24524
汽车	(辆)	Motor Vehicles	(unit)	2266600	2277500
#基本型乘用车(轿车	(辆)	Basic-type Passenger Vehicles (Sedans)	(unit)	1142000	1069000
移动通信手持机(手机)	(台)	Mobile Communication Handsets (Mobile Phones	(unit)	25093019	63540000
微型计算机设备	(台)	Micro-computers	(unit)	20068000	20138300

11-17 主要工业产品产量
OUTPUT OF MAIN INDUSTRIAL PRODUCTS

工业产品名称		Name of Main Industrial Product		2015	2014
单晶硅	(千克)	Monocrystalline Silicon	(kg)	90872.0	122372.8
中成药	(万吨)	Finished Traditional Chinese Herbal Medicines	(10000 tons)	4.6	4.4
沥青和改性沥青防水卷材	(万平方米)	Asphalt and Modified Asphalt Waterproof Roll Materials	(10000 sq.m)	5063.6	6653.6
纤维增强塑料制品	(万吨)	Fiber-reinforced Plastic Products	(10000 tons)	3.5	3.2
耐火材料制品	(万吨)	Products Made from Fire-resistant Materials	(10000 tons)	48.7	50.3
冷轧薄宽钢带	(万吨)	Cold-rolled Thin Broad Steel Bands	(10000 tons)	92.5	106.4
单一稀土金属	(千克)	Single Rare Earth Metals	(kg)	120729.0	272553.0
发动机	(万千瓦)	Engines	(10000 kW)	15065.1	12616.3
气动元件	(万件)	Pneumatic Components	(10000 units)	22427.3	20645.6
数控金属切削机床	(台)	Digital Metal Cutting Tools	(unit)	12471	13890
机床数控装置	(套)	CNC Units of Lathe	(unit)	39187	61072
工业电炉	(台)	Industrial Electric Cookers	(unit)	40	161
环境污染防治专用设备	(台套)	Special Equipment for Prevention and Control of Environmental Pollution	(set)	109378	79645
汽车	(万辆)	Automobiles	(10000 units)	221.9	216.7
#基本型成用车(轿车)	(万辆)	Including: Basic-type Passenger Vehicles (Sedans)	(10000 units)	118.9	118.6
运动型多用途乘用车(SUV)	(万辆)	Sport Utility Vehicles (SUV)	(10000 units)	42.1	33.4
载货汽车	(万辆)	Freight Trucks	(10000 units)	42.1	51.2
改装汽车	(万辆)	Refitted Automobiles	(10000 units)	1.3	1.9
风力发电机组	(万千瓦)	Wind Power Generator Units	(10000 kW)	421.9	439.4
锂离子电池	(万只)	Lithiums Ion Batteries	(10000 units)	2305.3	5509.6
移动通信手持机(手机)	(万台)	Mobile Communication Handsets (Mobile Phones)	(10000 units)	9540.8	17983.6
微型计算机设备	(万台)	Micro-computer Equipment	(10000 units)	885.6	1015.6
服务器	(台)	Servers	(unit)	259353	164099
液晶显示模组	(万套)	Liquid Crystal Display Modules	(10000 sets)	6510.6	7616.5
显示器	(万台)	Displays	(10000 units)	519.0	548.1
集成电路	(亿块)	Integrated Circuits	(100 million pieces)	62.7	54.3
彩色电视机	(万台)	Color TV Sets	(10000 units)	222.4	193.6

11-18 规模以上高技术制造业主要经济指标(2015年)
MAIN ECONOMIC INDICATORS OF HIGH-TECH MANUFACTURING ENTERPRISES ABOVE DESIGNATED SIZE (2015)

单位：亿元 (100 million yuan)

项 目	Item	工业总产值 Gross Output Value of Industry	主营业务收入 Main Business Income	利润总额 Total Profits	应交税金 Tax Payable
合 计	**Total**	**3499.4**	**3967.9**	**263.0**	**177.9**
按登记注册类型分组	**By Registration Type**				
内 资	Domestially-Invested Enterprises	1444.8	1549.0	171.4	90.4
国 有	State-owned Enterprises	74.9	76.4	6.3	1.5
集 体	Collectively-owned Enterprises	1.1	1.2	0.0	0.1
股份合作企业	Joint-equity Cooperative Enterprises	5.0	5.1	0.1	0.2
有限责任公司	Limited Liability Companies	844.7	888.3	78.3	43.1
股份有限公司	Companies Limited by Shares	313.7	359.3	61.8	30.8
私营企业	Private Enterprises	205.4	218.7	24.8	14.7
其 他	Others				
港澳台商投资	Hong Kong, Macao and Taiwan-invested Enterprises	1093.1	1418.4	20.9	15.6
外商投资	Foreign-invested Enterprises	961.6	1000.5	70.7	71.9
按高技术领域分组	**By Field of High Technology**				
信息化学品制造	Information Chemical Manufacturing	8.1	16.8	-0.2	-0.5
医药制造业	Manufacture of Medicines	702.3	686.4	126.6	78.8
航空、航天器及设备制造业	Manufacture of Aircrafts and Spacecrafts	233.8	241.5	13.6	5.1
电子及通信设备制造业	Manufacture of Electronic Equipment and Communication Equipment	1805.1	1866.0	54.3	52.6
计算机及办公设备制造业	Manufacture of Computers and Office Equipments	375.5	729.6	10.2	11.5
医疗仪器设备及仪器仪表制造业	Manufacture of Medical Equipments and Meters	374.7	427.5	58.4	30.5

11-19 工业企业战略性新兴产业总产值
TOTAL OUTPUT VALUE OF STRATEGIC EMERGING INDUSTRIES AMONG INDUSTRIAL ENTERPRISES

单位：万元 (10000 yuan)

项目	Item	2015	2014
战略性新兴产业工业总产值	**Total industrial output value of strategic emerging industries**	**358715883**	**353475571**
节能环保产业	Energy conservation and environmental protection industry	33211056	37564663
新一代信息技术产业	New generation IT industry	158908990	160158565
生物产业	Bioindustry	68167942	64250942
高端装备制造业	High-end equipment manufacturing	40948381	38899292
新能源产业	New energy industry	18974166	13489092
新材料产业	New material industry	28204283	32597043
新能源汽车	New energy automobiles	10301065	6515974

11-20 规模以下工业主要指标(2015年)
MAJOR INDICATORS FOR INDUSTRIAL ENTERPRISES BELOW DESIGNATED SIZE (2015)

项目	Item	单位个数 (个) Number of Enterprises (unit)	从业人员平均人数 (人) Average Number of Employed Persons (person)	工业总产值 (当年价格，万元) Gross Output Value (at year's current prices, 10000 yuan)
合计	**Total**	**22705**	**229678**	**5499215**
法人工业企业	Corporate Industrial Enterprises	18109	208588	5213535
个体经营工业单位	Individual Operated Business	4596	21090	285680

注：规模以下工业企业指年主营业务收入2000万元以下的法人工业企业和全部个体经营工业单位。

Note: Industrial enterprises below designed size refers to corperate industrial enterprises with main business income below RMB 20 million and all individual operated business.

主要统计指标解释

工业 指从事自然资源的开采，对采掘品和农产品进行加工和再加工的物质生产部门。具体包括：（1）对自然资源的开采，如采矿、晒盐、森林采伐等（但不包括禽兽捕猎和水产捕捞）；（2）对农副产品的加工、再加工，如粮油加工、食品加工、扎花、纺织、制革等；（3）对采掘品的加工、再加工，如炼铁、炼钢、化工生产、石油加工、机器制造、木材加工等，以及电力、自来水、煤气的生产和供应等；（4）对工业品的修理、翻新，如机器设备的修理。

轻工业 指主要提供生活消费品和制作手工工具的工业。按其所使用的原料不同，可分为两大类：（1）以农业为原料的轻工业，是指直接或间接以农产品为基本原料的轻工业。主要包括食品制造、饮料制造、烟草加工、纺织、缝纫、皮革和毛皮制作、造纸以及印刷等工业；（2）以非农产品为原料的轻工业，是指以工业品为原料的轻工业。主要包括文教体育用品、化学药品制造、合成纤维制造、日用化学制品、日用玻璃制品、日用金属制品、手工工具制造、医疗器械制造、文化和办公用机械制造等工业。

重工业 是指为国民经济各部门提供物质技术基础的主要生产资料的工业。按其生产性质和产品用途，可以分为下列三类：（1）采掘（伐）工业，是指对自然资源的开采，包括石油开采、煤炭开采、金属矿开采、非金属矿开采和木材采伐等工业；（2）原材料工业，指向国民经济各部门提供基本材料、动力和燃料的工业。包括金属冶炼及加工、炼焦及焦炭化学、化工原料、水泥、人造板以及电力、石油和煤炭加工等工业；（3）加工工业，是指对工业原材料进行再加工制造的工业。包括装备国民经济各部门的机械设备制造工业、金属结构、水泥制品等工业，以及为农业提供的生产资料如化肥、农药等工业。

根据上述划分原则，修理业中以重工业产品为修理作业对象的划为重工业，反之划为轻工业。

工业总产值 指工业企业在报告期内生产的以货币形式表现的工业最终产品和提供工业劳务活动的总价值量。它包括：在本企业内不再进行加工，经检验、包装入库（规定不需包装的产品除外）的成品价值，对外加工费收入，自制半成品、在制品期末期初差额价值。工业总产值采用“工厂法”计算，即以工业企业作为一个整体，按企业生产活动的最终成果来计算。

工业增加值 是指工业企业在报告期内以货币形式表现的工业生产活动的最终成果，反映企业生产过程中新创造的价值。

工业销售产值 是以货币形式表现的，工业企业在报告期内销售的本企业生产的工业产品或提供工业性劳务价值的总价值量。包括企业在报告期内实际销售（包括本期生产和非本期生产）的全部成品、半成品的总价值，报告期内完成的对外承接的工业品加工的加工费收入，对外工业品修理作业可获取的加工费收入和对内非工业部门提供的加工修理、设备安装等收入。已销售的成品、半成品不论是本期生产的、还是非本期生产的，只要是本期销售出去的均包括在内。企业为本单位基本建设部门、生活福利部门等提供的产品和工业性作业及自制设备也应视同销售，这部分也应作为销售统计。

资产总计 指企业过去的交易或者事项形成的、由企业拥有或者控制的、预期会给企业带来经济利益的资源。资产一般按流动性分为流动资产和非流动资产。其中流动资产可分为货币资金、交易性金融资产、应收票据、应收账款、预付款项、其他应收款、存货等；非流动资产可分为长期股权投资、固定资产、无形资产及其他非流动资产等。

（1）流动资产合计 资产满足以下条件之一应归为流动资产：①预计在一个正常营业周期中变现、出售或耗用，主要包括存货、应收账款等；②主要为交易目的而持有；③预计在资产负债表日起一年内（含一年）变现；④自资产负债表日起一年内，交换其他资产或清偿负债的能力不受限制的现金或现金等价物。包括货币资金、应收票据、应收账款、存货等项目。

（2）固定资产合计 指企业为生产商品、提供劳务、出租或经营管理而持有的，使用寿命超过一个会计年度的有形资产。包括使用期限超过一年的房屋、建筑物、机器、机械、运输工具以及其他与生产、经营有关的设备、器具、工具等。固定资产合计是时点指标，表示固定资产经过扣减折旧、减值准备等后的期末余额。

负债合计 指企业过去的交易或者事项形成的，预期会导致经济利益流出企业的现时义务。负债一般按偿还期长短分为流动负债和非流动负债。

（1）流动负债合计 负债满足下列条件之一的应归为流动负债：①预计在一个正常营业周期中清偿；②主要为交易目的而持有；③自资产负债表日起一年内到期应予清偿；④企业无权自主地将清偿推迟至资产负债表日后一年以上。包括短期借款、应付票据、应付账款、应付职工薪酬、应交税费等项目。

（2）非流动负债合计 指流动负债之外的负债。包括长期借款、应付债券等。

所有者权益合计 指企业资产扣除负债后由所有者享有的剩余权益。公司的所有者权益又称股东权益。包括实收资本、资本公积、盈余公积、未分配利润等。

实收资本 指企业各投资者实际投入的资本（或股本）总额，包括货币、实物、无形资产等各种形式的投入。实收资本按投资主体可分为国家资本、集体资本、法人资本、个人资本、港澳台资本和外商资本。

主营业务收入 指企业确认的销售商品、提供劳务等主营业务的收入。

主营业务成本 指企业经营主要业务所发生的成本总额。

主营业务税金及附加 指企业经营主要业务应负担的营业税、消费税、城市维护建设税、教育费附加等。

营业利润 指企业从事生产经营活动所取得的利润。

利润总额 指企业在一定会计期间的经营成果，是生产经营过程中各种收入扣除各种耗费后的盈余，反映企业在报告期内实现的亏盈总额。

应交增值税 指企业按税法规定，从事货物销售或提供加工、修理修配劳务等增加货物价值的活动本期应交纳的税金。

应交增值税=销项税额-（进项税额-进项税额转出）-出口抵减内销产品应纳税额-减免税款+出口退税

应交增值税不含期初未抵扣税额。

工业产品销售率 指报告期工业销售产值与工业总产值之比。计算公式:

$$\text{工业产品销售率}(\%)=\frac{\text{报告期现价工业销售产值}}{\text{报告期现价工业总产值}}\times 100\%$$

工业增加值率 指报告期工业增加值占工业总产值的比重，反映降低中间消耗的经济效益。计算公式:

$$\text{工业增加率}(\%)=\frac{\text{报告期现价工业增加值}}{\text{报告期现价工业总产值}}\times 100\%$$

工业成本费用利润率 指在一定时期内实现的利润与成本费用之比，是反映工业生产成本及费用投入的经济效益指标，同时也是反映降低成本的经济效益的指标。计算公式:

$$\text{工业成本费用利润率}(\%)=\frac{\text{利润总额}}{\text{成本费用总额}}\times 100\%$$

工业全员劳动生产率 指根据产品的价值量指标计算的平均每一个职工在单位时间内创造的工业生产最终成果。是考核企业经济活动的重要指标，是企业生产技术水平、经济管理水平、职工技术熟练程度和劳动积极性的综合表现。

$$\text{工业全员劳动生产率（元／人）}=\frac{\text{工业增加值（现价）}}{\text{平均用工人数}}$$

平均用工人数 指报告期企业平均实际拥有的、参与本企业生产经营活动的人员数。

流动资产周转次数 指在一定时期内流动资产完成的周转次数，反映流动资产的周转速度。计算公式:

$$\text{流动资产周转次数(次)}=\frac{\text{产品销售收入}}{\text{流动资产平均余额}}$$

流动比率 是反映企业每百元流动负债中，有多少元流动资产作后盾。计算公式:

$$\text{流动比率(倍)}=\frac{\text{流动资产总额}}{\text{流动负债总额}}$$

速动比率 是衡量企业流动资产中可以立即用于偿付流动负债的能力。计算公式:

$$\text{速动比率(倍)}=\frac{\text{流动资产总额}-\text{存货}}{\text{流动负债总额}}$$

资产负债率 反映在企业资产总额中有多少资产是通过借债而得的，也可以用于衡量企业利用债权人提供资金进行经营活动的能力以及企业在清算时保护债权人利益的程度。计算公式:

$$\text{资产负债率}=\frac{\text{负债总额}}{\text{资产总额}}\times 100\%$$

总资产贡献率 反映企业全部资产的获利能力，是企业经营业绩和管理水平的集中体现，是评价和考核企业盈利能力的核心指标。计算公式为:

$$\text{总资产贡献率}=\left(\text{利润总额}+\text{税金总额}+\text{利息支出}\right)\div\text{平均资产总额}\times 100\%$$

其中：税金总额为主营业务税金及附加、管理费用中的税金与应交增值税之和；平均资产总额为期初期末资产总计的算术平均值。

资本保值增值率 反映企业净资产的变动状况，是企业发展能力的集中体现。计算公式为:

$$\text{资本保值增值率}=\frac{\text{报告期期末所有者权益}}{\text{上年同期期末所有者权益}}\times 100\%$$

高技术制造业 是指国民经济行业中 R&D 投入强度相对较高的制造业行业，根据国家统计局《高技术产业（制造业）分类（2013)》标准界定。

Explanatory Notes on Main Statistical Indicators

Industry refers to the material production sector which is engaged in extraction of natural resources and processing and reprocessing of minerals and agricultural products, including (1) extraction of natural resources, such as mining, salt production, logging (but not including animal hunting and fishing); (2) processing and reprocessing of agricultural products, such as grain and oil processing, food processing, embroidery, textile manufacturing and leather making; (3) processing and reprocessing of mining products, such as iron making, steel making, chemical production, petroleum processing, machine building, timber processing; and production and supply of electric power, tap water and gas; (4) repair and refurbishment of industrial products, such as the repair of machinery equipment.

Light Industry refers to the industries that produce consumer goods and hand tools. It falls into two categories, based on different raw materials:

(1) Industries basing the raw materials on agriculture, which directly or indirectly use farm products as basic raw materials, mainly include the manufacture of foods and beverages, tobacco processing, textile manufacturing, tailoring, fur and leather manufacturing, paper making, printing, etc.

(2) Industries using non-agricultural products as raw materials, which means the manufactured goods are used as raw materials, mainly include the manufacture of cultural, educational articles and sports goods, chemical medicines, synthetic fiber, daily chemical products, glass products for daily use, metal products for daily use, hand tools, medical appliances and instruments, as well as stationery and office machinery.

Heavy Industry refers to the industries that provide material and technical foundation as key means of production for various sectors of the national economy. It falls into the following three categories according to the purpose of production or the use of products:

(1) Mining, quarrying and logging industry refers to the industry that extracts natural resources, including the extraction of petroleum, coal, metal and non-metal ores and logging.

(2) Raw material industry refers to the industry that provides various sectors of the national economy with basic materials, fuels and power. It includes smelting and processing of metals, coking and coke chemistry, chemical materials, cement, artificial boards, as well as power generation, petroleum refining and coal processing.

(3) Processing industry refers to the industry that reprocesses raw materials. It includes machine manufacturing, which equips various sectors of the national economy, metal structure, cement products, and chemical fertilizer and pesticide industry that provide means of production for agriculture.

According to the above principle of classification, the repair services for products of heavy industry are classified as heavy industry, while the repair services for products of light industry are classified as light industry.

Gross Output Value of Industry is the total value in monetary terms for final industrial products and industrial labor service provided by industrial enterprises during the reporting period. It includes the value of the finished products, which will not be further processed in the enterprises and have been inspected, packed and put in storage (except for products required not to be packed), the revenue from processing products for others, the value of semi-finished products, and the price spread between the finished products and products at the initial stage. The gross industrial output value is calculated with "factory method"; that is, to take an industrial enterprise as a whole. It calculates the final products created by the enterprise.

Added Value of Industry refers to the final results of industrial production by industrial enterprises in monetary terms during the reporting period. It shows the newly created value generated in production by the enterprises.

Sales Value of Industry refers to the total value of industrial products sold or labor service provided by an industrial enterprise during the reporting period in monetary terms. It includes the total value of all finished and semi-finished products actually sold by the enterprise (including products produced in current period and noncurrent period), revenue from processing products for others, repairing industrial products for others, as well as processing, repairing, and installing equipment for internal non-industrial departments in the reporting period. All finished and semi-finished products sold in the current period will be counted, regardless of whether they were produced in the current period or not. The value of products, industrial work and home-built equipment provided by the enterprise for its capital construction department and welfare department will also be included in the industrial sales value.

Total Assets refer to resources formed by previous transactions or matters of an enterprise, owned or controlled by the enterprise, and expected to bring economic benefits to the enterprise. Classified by the liquidity, assets fall into current assets and non-current assets. Current assets include monetary capital, tradable financial assets, notes receivable, accounts receivable, prepayment, other receivables, and inventory, etc.; while non-current assets include long-term equity investment, fixed assets, intangible assets, and other non-current assets, etc.

(1) Total Current Assets Assets that meet any of the following requirements are considered current assets: a. assets expected to be cashed in, sold or consumed in a normal operating cycle, which mainly includes inventory and accounts receivable, etc.; b. assets held mainly for transaction; c. assets expected to be cashed in within one year (including one year) from the balance sheet date; d. cash or cash equivalents with unrestricted capacity of exchanging for other assets or paying off debts within one year from the balance sheet date, which include monetary capital, notes receivable, accounts receivable, inventory, etc.

(2) Total Fixed Assets refer to tangible assets held by an enterprise for producing commodities, rendering labor services, leasing or management, with service life exceeding one fiscal year, which include houses and buildings, apparatus, machinery, means of transport, as well as other equipment, instruments and tools related to production and operation, which have a service life exceeding one year. Total Fixed Assets is a time point indicator, showing the ending balance of fixed assets after deduction and discount, and impairment provision, etc.

Total Liabilities refer to the present obligations formed by previous transactions or matters of an enterprise, expected to lead the flow of economic benefits out of the enterprise. By the term of payment, liabilities generally include current liabilities and non-current liabilities.

(1) Total Current liabilities Liabilities that meet any of the following requirements are considered current liabilities: a. assets expected to be paid off within one normal operating cycle; b. assets held mostly for the purpose of transaction; c. assets expected to be due and paid off within one year from the balance sheet date; d. assets that the enterprise has no right to delay the payment to more than one year after the balance sheet date on its own. They include short-term loans, notes payable, accounts payable, wages payable, taxes and fees payable, etc.

(2) Total Non-current Liabilities refer to liabilities other than current liabilities, including long-term borrowings and bonds payable, etc.

Total Owner's Equity refers to the remaining equity of assets in an enterprise held by owners after deducting the liabilities. Owner's equity of a company is also called shareholders' equity, including paid-up capital, capital reserves, operating surplus reserves and non-distributed profits, etc.

Paid-up Capital refers to the total capital (or equity) actually contributed by investors to an enterprise, including input in various forms, such as monetary investment, physical investment and intangible assets. Categorized by investors, paid-up capital includes state capital, collective capital, legal person's capital, personal capital, capital from Hong Kong, Macao and Taiwan, and foreign capital.

Main Business Income refers to the income from main business of selling commodities and rendering services recognized by the enterprise.

Main Business Cost refers to the total cost incurred by the enterprise during its operation of main business.

Main Business Tax and Surtax refers to the business tax, excise tax, urban maintenance and construction tax, educational surcharge to be levied against the main business operated by an enterprise.

Operating Profits refer to the profits reaped by an enterprise from its productive and operating activities.

Total Profits refer to the operating results of an enterprise during certain accounting period, representing the surplus of various incomes from production and operation deducting various expenses, reflecting the total gains and losses realized by the enterprise during the reporting period.

VAT Payable refer to the tax payable by an enterprise in current period according to provisions in Law of Tax for its activities of adding value to goods, such as selling the goods, providing labor service for processing, repair and replacement.

VAT Payable = Output Tax – (Input Tax – Transfer-out of Input Tax) – Tax Payable Deducted by Export from Output Tax of Domestically Sold Products – Tax Concession + Export Rebate

VAT Payable excludes the taxes not deducted at the beginning of the period.

Sales Rate of Industrial Products refers to the ratio of industrial sales output to the gross output value of industry during the reporting period. The following formula is used:

Sales Rate of Industrial Products (%) = Sales Value of Industry at Present Value During the Reporting Period / Gross Output Value of Industry at Present Value During the Reporting Period × 100%

Rate of Industrial Added Value refers to the ratio of added value of industry to the gross output value of industry during the reporting period. It indicates the economic benefits from reduction of intermediate consumption. The following formula is used:

Rate of Industrial Added Value = Added Value of Industry at Present Value During the Reporting Period / Gross Output Value of Industry at Present Value During the Reporting Period × 100%

Rate of Profits to Total Industrial Costs refers to the ratio of profits realized in a given period to the total costs in the same period, which reflects the economic efficiency of industrial production input. The following formula is used:

Rate of Profits to Total Industrial Cost (%) = (Total Profits/ Total Costs) ×100%

Overall Labor Productivity of Industry refers to the average final result of industrial production created by each employee within a unit time, measured with the value of products. It is an important indicator evaluating the economic activities of an enterprise, and it reflects the level of production technology and economic management of the enterprise, employees' skills, as well as enthusiasm for work.

Overall Labor Productivity of Industry (RMB/person) = Added Value of Industry (at present value) / Average Number of Employees

Turnover of Current Assets refer to the number of times for current assets turnover within a given period of time. It reflects the turnover velocity of current assets. The following formula is used:

Turnover of Current Assets (No. of times) = Product Sales Income / Average Balance of Current Assets

Liquidity Ratio reflects how many current assets are backing up every RMB 100 of current liabilities in an enterprise. The following formula is used:

Liquidity Ratio (times) = Total Current Assets / Total Current Liabilities

Quick Ratio indicates the capacity of an enterprise's current assets for paying off current liabilities immediately. The following formula is used:

Quick Ratio (times) = (Total Current Assets – Inventory) / Total Current Liabilities

Assets-liabilities Ratio reflects how many assets—out of the total assets of the enterprise, are obtained by borrowing. It can be used to evaluate the enterprise's capability of operating by using the funds provided by creditors, and to what extent the enterprise will be able to protect the creditors' interests in the case of liquidation. The following formula is used:

Assets-liabilities Ratio = Total Liabilities / Total Assets × 100%

Contribution Rate of Total Assets indicates the profitability of all assets in an enterprise, reflecting the operating performance and management of the enterprise. It serves as a core indicator evaluating the enterprise's profitability. The following formula is used:

Total Assets Contribution rate = (Total Profit + Total Tax + Total Interest Expenses) / Average Total Assets × 100%

Note: the total tax is the sum of main business tax and surtax, tax in management expenses, and VAT payable; average total assets are represented by the arithmetic average of total assets at the beginning and the end of the period.

Rate of Assets Preservation and Appreciation reflects the changes in the net assets of an enterprise. It reflects the growth potential of the enterprise. The following formula is used:

Capital Preservation and Appreciation Rate = Owner's Equity at the End of the Reporting Period / Owner's Equity at the End of the Same Period in the Previous Year × 100%

High-tech Manufacturing Sector refers to all sectors in the high-tech industry other than software development.

北京统计年鉴2016　BEIJING STATISTICAL YEARBOOK

建筑业
CONSTRUCTION

简要说明

一、本章资料的主要内容

本章资料主要反映北京市建筑业企业基本情况和生产经营情况。主要指标包括企业个数、从业人员、建筑业总产值、建筑业企业房屋建筑面积、利润、税金等。

二、本章资料的统计范围

建筑业统计范围从 2004 年起，由原具有建筑业资质等级四级及四级以上的独立核算的建筑业企业调整为具有施工总承包、专业承包资质的所有法人建筑业企业。

三、本章资料的数据来源及调查方法

本章建筑业企业统计数据根据国家统计局制定的《建筑业统计报表制度》整理汇总。建筑业统计数据采取全面调查的方法。资料由北京市统计局、国家统计局北京调查总队提供。

四、有关统计标准的变化说明

本章资料中建筑业行业分类 2002-2011 年期间执行 2002 年《国民经济行业分类标准》(GB/T 4754-2002)划分标准，2012 年开始执行 2011 年《国民经济行业分类》(GB/T 4754-2011)划分标准。

五、本章中关于历史数据调整的问题

由于 2004 年开展了“北京市第一次全国经济普查”，按照国家统计局统一要求和统一方法，历史资料要根据普查结果进行修正。本章中 1993 至 2003 年的建筑业总产值数据采用“趋势离差法”进行了调整，2004 年为第一次经济普查数据，2008 年为第二次经济普查数据，2013 年为第三次经济普查数据。

Brief Introduction

I. Main Content

Data in this chapter reflect the basic situation and operation of construction enterprises in Beijing. Main indicators include number of enterprises, employees, total output value of the construction sector, as well as floor space, profits, and tax of construction enterprises.

II. Scope of Statistics

Since 2004, data on construction sector, which previously covered construction enterprises with independent accounting at or above Level-4 in construction qualifications, have been adjusted to cover all construction enterprises with qualifications of general and specialized contracting.

III. Source of Data and Methods of Survey

Data on construction enterprises in this chapter were gathered based on *Statistical Statement System for Construction Sector* developed by the National Bureau of Statistics. The figures were gained through complete survey, and were provided by Beijing Municipal Bureau of Statistics and NBS Survey Office in Beijing.

IV. Changes in Relevant Statistical Standards

In this chapter, classification of construction sectors during 2002-2011 was based on the *Standard for Classification of National Economic Sectors 2002* (GB/T 4754-2002). *Standard for Classification of National Economic Sectors 2011* (GB/T 4754-2011) began to be enforced in 2012.

V. About the Adjustment to Historical Data

As “The First National Economic Census in Beijing” was conducted in 2004, in accordance with the principles of unified requirements and methods by the National Bureau of Statistics, historical data must be revised on basis of the census result. Data of total output value of construction sector during 1993-2003 were revised by “trend deviation method”. The first economic census was in 2004, and the second was in 2008, and the third was in 2013.

12-1 建筑业企业基本情况(1978-2015年)
BASIC STATISTICS FOR ENTERPRISES IN THE CONSTRUCTION INDUSTRY (1978-2015)

年份 Year	建筑施工企业单位数(个) Construction Enterprises (unit)	建筑施工企业年末从业人员(万人) Employed Persons (year-end) (10000 persons)	建筑施工企业总产值(亿元) Gross Output Value (100 million yuan)	主营业务收入(亿元) Main Business Income (100 million yuan)	建筑施工企业利润总额(亿元) Total Profits (100 million yuan)	建筑施工企业房屋建筑面积(万平方米) Floor Space of Buildings (10000 sq.m)	
						施工面积 Floor Space under Construction	竣工面积 Floor Space Completed
1978	64	25.4	10.5		0.7		
1979	70	26.4	12.7		0.9		
1980	71	27.8	14.7		1.5		
1981	71	27.0	14.5		1.6		
1982	91	30.7	17.3		1.7		
1983	116	37.2	22.6		2.5		
1984	2765	53.0	33.4		3.2		
1985	2549	63.9	43.9		3.9		
1986	2361	61.3	51.3		3.3		
1987	2292	64.4	67.0		4.1		
1988	1659	64.2	81.6		3.9		
1989	1545	60.0	89.0		3.8		
1990	994	60.2	94.7		3.4		
1991	922	60.3	99.6		2.8	2495	1172
1992	976	62.7	122.6		3.1	2774	1227
1993	1098	75.9	215.5	205.5	6.1	3499	1428
1994	1259	73.4	336.0	289.4	9.4	4035	1437
1995	1332	82.6	426.6	337.6	7.8	4602	1593
1996	1292	82.5	494.7	431.3	8.9	5328	1967
1997	1297	80.3	556.4	481.1	10.4	5801	2117
1998	1482	75.6	678.6	579.3	12.4	6525	2225
1999	1588	62.0	750.6	645.8	13.6	6824	2632
2000	1697	56.6	812.5	706.8	16.4	7247	2809
2001	1811	57.8	1055.4	906.9	18.7	8919	3198
2002	2122	57.0	1211.3	1094.0	24.7	10241	3827
2003	2419	59.1	1521.2	1329.9	31.5	12160	4486
2004	2623	51.2	1659.8	1936.0	40.0	14424	5258
2005	2752	67.2	1894.0	2206.9	67.3	15418	4862
2006	2800	66.9	2167.9	2666.2	112.8	16202	4786
2007	2845	51.7	2576.8	3351.3	115.7	18225	4946
2008	3527	47.0	3066.2	3856.8	84.5	19537	4803
2009	3556	56.2	4059.7	5081.1	217.4	22721	5225
2010	3594	59.9	5196.0	6545.0	265.2	29440	5933
2011	3667	49.6	6046.3	7565.9	219.6	36507	6456
2012	3572	49.2	6588.3	8125.2	293.0	41660	8414
2013	3522	49.3	7459.6	9404.3	385.8	49259	8950
2014	3426	51.0	8209.8	10492.2	473.2	56477	9275
2015	3369	59.0	8436.7	11018.5	520.1	59777	9886

注：1. 1996-2003年全部指标的统计口径为四级及四级以上的法人建筑施工企业。
2. 2004年开始全部指标的统计口径为建筑施工总承包、专业承包的建筑业企业。
3. 建筑施工企业房屋建筑面积包括在本市和外省完成的施工、竣工面积。

Note: a) Data from 1996 to 2003 covers the corporate construction enterprises at Grade IV and above.
b) Data from 2004 covers general contracting and specialized contracting construction enterprises.
c) Data on floor space covers buildings under construction and completed in Beijing and other provinces.and outside the city.

12-2 建筑业施工企业基本情况(2015年)
BASIC STATISTICS FOR CONSTRUCTION ENTERPRISES (2015)

项目	Item	总产值 (万元) Gross Output Value (10000 yuan)	年末从业人员 (人) Employed Persons (year-end) (person)	签订合同额 (万元) Value of Contract Signed (10000 yuan)	竣工产值 (万元) Output Value of Completion (10000 yuan)
合　计	**Total**	**84367296**	**590288**	**232301131**	**42870708**
按企业登记注册类型分	**By Registration Type**				
内资企业	Domestically-funded Enterprises	83403258	577825	229196284	42342740
国有企业	State-owned Enterprises	2559311	39945	7716722	2015786
集体企业	Collectively-owned Enterprises	1003363	13051	1811605	621802
股份合作企业	Joint-equity Cooperative Enterprises	365201	7437	453803	261544
联营企业	Associate Enterprises	69	2	69	69
有限责任公司	Limited Liability Companies	68056023	388942	191980544	34224283
股份有限公司	Companies Limited by Shares	5427836	19264	18275153	996674
私营企业	Private Enterprises	5991455	109184	8958389	4222581
港、澳、台商投资企业	Hong Kong, Macao and Taiwan-invested Enterprises	562622	6255	1273999	396424
外商投资企业	Foreign-invested Enterprises	401417	6208	1830848	131544
按隶属关系分	**By Affiliation**				
中　央	Central	49775725	236050	158396199	20477910
地　方	Local	34591571	354238	73904933	22392798
按行业分	**By Sector**				
房屋建筑业	Construction of Buildings	43310355	234246	133675603	26391051
土木工程建筑业	Civil Engineering Construction	27548537	176150	75907935	8995463
建筑安装业	Construction Installation	6674436	88746	13194504	3108408
建筑装饰和其他建筑业	Building Decoration and Other Construction	6833969	91146	9523089	4375786

注：1. 统计范围为施工总承包、专业承包的法人建筑业企业（下表同)。
2. 行业划分执行2011年国民经济行业分类标准(GB/T 4754-2011)。

Note: a) Statistics covers general contracting and specialized contracting corporate construction enterprises(same as the following table).
b) Sectors in this table are classified in accordance with the Standard for Classification of National Economic Sectors in 2011(GB/T 4754-2011).

12-3 建筑业施工企业主要财务指标(2015年)

单位：万元

项目	Item	企业单位个数(个) Number of Enterprises (unit)	资产负债 Assets and Liabilities 资产总计 Total Assets	流动资产合计 Total Current Assets	#应收账款 Accounts Receivable	固定资产合计 Total Fixed Assets	固定资产原价 Total Original Value of Fixed Assets	负债合计 Total Liabilities	#流动负债合计 Total Current Liabilities
合　计	**Total**	**3369**	**200743808**	**136434741**	**30335907**	**5254583**	**8828621**	**135951250**	**120422215**
按企业登记注册类型分	**By Registration Type**								
内资企业	Domestically-funded Enterprises	3287	198788867	134684019	29769157	5191647	8709199	134448095	118951366
国有企业	State-owned Enterprises	82	9480325	7321862	1215532	349744	704707	5940926	5609014
集体企业	Collectively-owned Enterprises	101	1991105	1636192	217583	73867	146872	1601812	1594375
股份合作企业	Joint-Equity Cooperative Enterprises	61	518238	462790	55618	33657	68802	342260	341413
联营企业	Associate Enterprises	***	***	***	***	***	***	***	***
有限责任公司	Limited Liability Companies	1179	118838142	95453633	23579977	3688450	6245178	95498512	88701474
股份有限公司	Companies Limited by Shares	53	57467389	20922843	1973777	426848	580223	24317521	16198222
私营企业	Private Enterprises	1810	10492882	8885914	2726045	619080	963380	6746761	6506564
港、澳、台商投资企业	Hong Kong, Macao and Taiwan- invested Enterprises	41	999450	917779	242606	18111	39876	836392	817959
外商投资企业	Foreign-invested Enterprises	41	955490	832943	324145	44825	79547	666762	652891
按隶属关系分	**By Affiliation**								
中　央	Central	193	142652870	87805770	16932172	2630397	4678754	91809559	78751278
地　方	Local	3176	58090938	48628972	13403735	2624186	4149867	44141691	41670937
按国民经济行业分	**By Sector**								
房屋建筑业	Construction of Buildings	619	84296825	62896869	16901125	2074085	3397826	62282220	55366205
土木工程建筑业	Civil Engineering Construction	570	94538416	55101230	8042756	1783138	3405914	57809303	49703118
建筑安装业	Construction Installation	815	11600368	9831639	2514937	517955	846113	8497951	8266239
建筑装饰和其他建筑业	Building Decoration and Other Construction	1365	10308198	8605003	2877089	879404	1178768	7361776	7086653

注：1. 行业划分执行2011年国民经济行业分类标准(GB/T 4754-2011)。
2. 应交税金合计包括应交增值税、应交所得税、营业税金及附加和管理费用中的税金。

MAIN FINANCIAL INDICATORS OF CONSTRUCTION ENTERPRISES (2015)

(10000 yuan)

			损益 Profits and Loss							应交		
#应付账款 Accounts Payable	所有者权益合计 Total Owner's Equity	#实收资本 Paid-up Capital	营业收入 Business Income	#主营业务收入 Main Business Income	营业成本 Business Cost	#主营业务成本 Main Business Cost	管理费用 Management Expenses	财务费用 Financial Expenses	利润总额 Total Profits	税金合计 Total Taxes Payable	#营业税金及附加 Business Tax and Surtax	#主营业务税金及附加 Main Business Tax and Surtax
44694061	**64770511**	**28356000**	**110819201**	**110184657**	**100698972**	**100308785**	**4161790**	**840782**	**5200983**	**3691672**	**2523415**	**2508832**
44166244	64318585	28053959	109063008	108452713	99151523	98775437	4063933	834804	5158297	3625916	2483549	2469162
1721695	3537119	1541612	5404997	5373043	5003104	4984151	192132	-10684	236909	180337	92002	91289
405923	389293	192743	1296747	1288580	1124518	1113224	91484	-2669	56872	56758	38829	37982
52473	175978	106837	474464	444847	421099	394257	21386	998	2789	18620	14298	14144
***	***	***	***	***	***	***	***	***	***	***	***	***
37971057	23326362	14574653	86463712	86055979	78951825	78693979	2901174	598306	2705982	2844660	2025154	2015328
1554703	33149868	8664073	7222520	7183438	6615773	6607933	279557	216347	2022281	213690	71109	69321
2460387	3739483	2973541	8200500	8106758	7035171	6981861	578164	32507	133466	311849	242156	241095
209681	163058	136701	859029	843977	764318	754175	47473	3115	18785	32172	20526	20469
318136	288868	165340	897164	887967	783132	779172	50384	2863	23902	33583	19339	19202
30119588	50840071	19231244	67712171	67471798	62256063	62108407	2073780	508028	4249534	2164458	1333976	1327346
14574473	13930440	9124755	43107030	42712859	38442909	38200378	2088010	332754	951450	1527214	1189438	1181486
25645325	22012605	10467111	52031738	51848789	47821143	47715889	1478351	539383	2223086	1669329	1165753	1160175
13517431	36726435	13821063	39237130	39003775	35707839	35568265	1601813	244570	2458537	1321497	842624	836976
2990582	3100421	1989283	10604420	10473327	9424408	9316038	563998	16996	325333	354903	264619	262487
2540724	2931050	2078543	8945913	8858766	7745583	7708593	517628	39832	194027	345944	250419	249194

Note: a) Sectors in this table are classified in accordance with the Standard for Classification of National Economic Sectors 2011 (GB/T 4754-2011).
b) Total tax payable mainly includes VAT payable, income tax payable, business tax and surtax, and tax in management expenses.

12-3 续表 Continued

项 目	Item	#应交所得税 Income Tax Payable (10000 yuan)	#应交增值税 Value Added Tax Payable	流动比率(倍) Current Ratio (times)	速动比率(倍) Quick Ratio (times)	资产负债率(%) Assets-Liabilities Ratio (%)	资本金利润率(%) Capital-Profit Ratio (%)
合 计	**Total**	**791856**	**316097**	**1.13**	**0.96**	**67.7**	**18.3**
按企业登记注册类型分	**By Registration Type**						
内资企业	Domestically-funded Enterprises	778886	304431	1.13	0.96	67.6	18.4
国有企业	State-owned Enterprises	51199	33143	1.31	1.00	62.7	15.4
集体企业	Collectively-owned Enterprises	14630	1520	1.03	0.72	80.4	29.5
股份合作企业	Joint-Equity Cooperative Enterprises	3836	271	1.36	0.96	66.0	2.6
联营企业	Associate Enterprises			2.58	2.40	38.6	-0.2
有限责任公司	Limited Liability Companies	543401	236856	1.08	0.89	80.4	18.6
股份有限公司	Companies Limited by Shares	122293	15450	1.29	1.23	42.3	23.3
私营企业	Private Enterprises	43528	17191	1.37	1.19	64.3	4.5
港、澳、台商投资企业	Hong Kong, Macao and Taiwan-invested Enterprises	4390	6513	1.12	0.80	83.7	13.7
外商投资企业	Foreign-invested Enterprises	8579	5153	1.28	1.06	69.8	14.5
按隶属关系分	**By Affiliation**						
中 央	Central	555617	249497	1.11	0.97	64.4	22.1
地 方	Local	236239	66600	1.17	0.95	76.0	10.4
按国民经济行业分	**Grouped by Sector**						
房屋建筑业	Construction of Buildings	408276	70738	1.14	0.92	73.9	21.2
土木工程建筑业	Civil Engineering Construction	274166	184848	1.11	0.97	61.1	17.8
建筑安装业	Construction Installation	56679	25413	1.19	1.01	73.3	16.4
建筑装饰和其他建筑业	Building Decoration and Other Construction	52736	35097	1.21	1.07	71.4	9.3

12-4 建筑业施工企业竣工率
PROJECT COMPLETION RATE OF CONSTRUCTION ENTERPRISES

单位：% (%)

项 目	Item	产值竣工率 Completion Rate by Output Value		面积竣工率 Completion Rate by Floor Space	
		2015	2014	2015	2014
合 计	**Total**	**50.8**	**49.4**	**16.5**	**16.4**
按企业登记注册类型分	**By Registration Type**				
内资企业	Domestically-funded Enterprises	50.8	49.2	16.6	16.4
国有企业	State-owned Enterprises	78.8	108.8	20.7	26.1
集体企业	Collectively-owned Enterprises	62.0	69.9	15.2	32.1
股份合作企业	Joint-equity Cooperative Enterprises	71.6	92.5	31.3	49.5
联营企业	Associate Enterprises	100.0			
有限责任公司	Limited Liability Companies	50.3	46.9		
股份有限公司	Companies Limited by Shares	18.4	29.1	33.2	12.2
私营企业	Private Enterprises	70.5	59.4		
港、澳、台商投资企业	Hong Kong, Macao and Taiwan-invested Enterprises	70.5	74.6	3.0	8.9
外商投资企业	Foreign-invested Enterprises	32.8	48.5	8.2	20.5
按隶属关系分	**By Affiliation Relationship**				
中 央	Central	41.1	43.1	14.1	13.5
地 方	Local	64.7	57.0	21.9	22.2
按国民经济行业分	**By Sector**				
房屋建筑业	Construction of Buildings	60.9	54.1	16.8	16.2
土木工程建筑业	Civil Engineering Construction	32.7	42.6	11.5	23.3
建筑安装业	Construction Installation	46.6	40.3	13.4	15.2
建筑装饰和其他建筑业	Building Completion, Finishing and Other Construction	64.0	54.4	333.0	0.1

注：行业划分执行2011年国民经济行业分类标准(GB/T 4754-2011)。
Note: Sectors in this table are classified in accordance with the Standard for Classification of National Economic Sectors in 2011 (GB/T 4754-2011).

主要统计指标解释

建筑业总产值 是以货币表现的建筑业企业在一定时期内生产的建筑产品和服务的总和。它包括建筑工程产值、设备安装工程产值、其他产值三部分内容。

(1)**建筑工程产值** 指列入建筑工程预(概)算内的各种工程价值。

(2)**安装工程产值** 指为设备安装而发生的安装工程费用，在设备安装产值中，不得包括被安装设备本身价值。

(3)**其他产值** 建筑业总产值中除建筑工程、安装工程以外的产值，包括房屋构筑物修理产值、非标准设备制造产值、总包企业向分包企业收取的管理费，以及不能明确划分的施工活动所完成的产值。

年末从业人员 指年末最后一日24小时在本单位工作，并取得工资或其他形式劳动报酬的人员数。该指标为时点指标，不包括最后一日当天及以前与单位解除劳动合同关系的人员，是在岗职工、劳务派遣人员及其他从业人员之和。

房屋施工面积 指报告期内施过工的全部房屋建筑面积，包括：本期新开工的房屋面积、上期施工跨入本期继续施工的房屋面积、上期停缓建本期复工的房屋面积、本期开工又停缓建和本期竣工的房屋面积。

房屋竣工面积 指在报告期内房屋建筑按照设计要求已全部完工，达到了住人和使用条件，经检查验收鉴定合格或达到竣工验收标准，可正式移交使用的房屋建筑面积。

签订合同额 指建筑业企业在报告期直接同建设单位签订合同的总价款和以前年度同建设单位签定合同的未完工程跨入本年度继续施工工程合同的总价款余额。

主营业务收入 指企业确认的销售商品、提供劳务等主营业务的收入。

主营业务成本 指企业经营主要业务所发生的成本总额。

主营业务税金及附加 指企业经营主要业务应负担的营业税、消费税、城市维护建设税、教育费附加等。

利润总额 指企业在一定会计期间的经营成果，是生产经营过程中各种收入扣除各种耗费后的盈余，反映企业在报告期内实现的亏盈总额。

Explanatory Notes on Main Statistical Indicators

Gross Output Value of Construction refers to total of construction products and services, expressed in money terms, completed by construction and installation enterprises during a given period of time. It includes: output value of construction works, output value of installation works and other output value.

(1) Output Value of Construction Works means the value of works involved in project budgets.

(2) Output Value of Installation Works means the costs of installation works incurred for equipment installation. Output value of equipment installation does not include the value of installed equipment itself.

(3) Other Output Value means, of the total output value of construction, the output value other than that of construction and installations works. It includes the repair output value of houses and structures, manufacturing output value of non-standard equipment, management charges collected by general contracting enterprises from subcontracting enterprises, as well as the output value of construction activities falling in no specific categories.

Year-end Employed Persons refers to the number of employed persons who work during the 24 hours of the last day in a year and acquire wage or other forms of labor income. This time-spot index, which does not include persons who terminate their labor contracts at or before the last day of the year, is the sum of fully employed persons, dispatched personnel of labor service and other employed persons.

House Construction Area means the building area of all houses in the reporting period, including: the area of houses newly started in current period, area of houses built in the previous period and continued in current period, area of houses suspended in the previous period and restarted in current period, area of houses started and suspended in current period, and area of houses completed in current period.

Area of Houses Completed means the area of houses and buildings entirely completed in line with requirements of design, meeting conditions of living and use, satisfactorily accepted by relevant authorities or reaching standards for completion inspection and officially delivered and used in the reporting period.

Value of Signed Contracts means total price of contracts signed directly between construction and installation enterprises and builders in the reporting period and the balance of total price of contracts signed with builders in previous year and continued the implementation in the current year.

Main Business Income means the income recognized by an enterprise from main business such as sale of commodities and rendering of service.

Main Business Cost means the total cost incurred in an enterprise for the operation of main business.

Main Business Tax and Surtax means the sales tax, excise, urban maintenance and construction tax, educational surcharge, etc. to be paid by an enterprise for the operation of main business.

Total Profits mean the operating result of an enterprise in certain accounting period. It is the surplus of all revenues deducting all costs in its production and operation, reflecting its total profit and loss realized in the reporting period.

北京统计年鉴2016 BEIJING STATISTICAL YEARBOOK

交通运输邮电

TRANSPORT, POST AND TELECOMMUNICATON SERVICES

简要说明

一、本章资料的主要内容

本章资料反映北京市交通运输业和邮政电信业发展的基本状况。

交通运输业资料主要包括：铁路、公路、民航、管道四种运输方式的线路条数、里程、总运量及周转量、主要技术经济指标（不含管道）；机动车拥有情况。

邮政电信业资料主要包括：邮电业务完成情况、邮政电信发展水平等资料。

二、各部分资料的调查范围及数据来源

1．铁路资料：主要是国家铁路运营情况，不含地方铁路、合资铁路和军用铁路及由厂矿企事业单位自建的铁路专用线和专用铁道，资料来源于北京铁路局。

2．公路资料：(1)公路里程为年末通车里程数，不含在建和未正式投入使用的公路里程；(2)公路运输统计范围包括在北京市注册从事公路货运的全部企事业单位和私人(包括个体联户)，资料来源于北京市交通委员会。

3．管道运输资料：包括输送原油、成品油、天然气以及其他气体的管线长度、输送能力及完成的运输量。管道运输统计数据主要来源于中石油北京天然气管道有限公司和中国石油化工股份有限公司北京燕山分公司所属的管道运输企业，由两家集团公司分别负责收集审核本部门统计数据。

4．民航运输资料：不包括在京运输飞行的外省市及外国航空公司。统计范围为各航空公司从事国内运输、港澳台运输、国际运输的定期航班航线条数及里程、运输量等。2009年及以前数据主要来源于中国国际航空公司、新华航空有限责任公司，2010年起为北京地区的民航运输法人单位。

5．邮政电信资料：包括邮政和电信运营企业为社会公众提供的各类邮政和电信服务，不含专用网业务资料。邮电业务量按业务种类分为邮政业务量和电信业务量。数据主要来源于北京市邮政公司、中国联合网络通信有限公司北京市分公司、中国移动通信集团北京有限公司、中国铁通集团有限公司北京分公司、中国电信股份有限公司北京分公司。

6．民用汽车拥有量资料：民用汽车指在公安交通管理部门已注册登记领有民用车辆牌照的全部汽车数量。民用汽车根据汽车结构分为载客汽车、载货汽车及其他汽车；根据汽车所有者不同分为私人汽车、单位汽车。民用汽车数据来自于北京市公安局公安交通管理局。

Brief Introduction

I. Main Content

Figures in this chapter show the basic situation of development of transport, post and telecommunication in Beijing.

Transportation statistics include the number of lines, mileage, total volume of transport, turnover and main technological and economic indicators (excluding pipelines) for four transport modes, i.e. railway, highway, civil aviation, and pipeline,; and number of motor vehicles.

Post and telecommunication statistics include: performance of post and telecom services, development level of post and telecommunication sector, and so on.

II. Scope of Survey and Source of Data

1. Data on railways: including the operation of national railways, excluding local railways, railways built by joint ventures, military railways, and dedicated lines and railways built by factories, mines, enterprises and public institutions. These data are from Beijing Railway Bureau.

2. Data on highways: (1) highway mileage covers highways open to traffic at the year end, excluding those under construction and not put into use; (2) highway transport statistics cover all enterprises and public institutions as well as individuals (including self-employed) registered in Beijing for highway cargo transportation. These data are from Beijing Municipal Commission of Transport.

3. Data on pipeline transport: including the length, capacity and completed traffic of pipelines for transport of crude oil, refined oil, natural gas, and other gases. These data are mainly from Beijing Natural Gas Pipelines Co., Ltd. of Sinopec and CNPC. Statistical data on the pipelines transportation business affiliated to Beijing Yanshan Branch were collected and reviewed by the two corporations mentioned above respectively.

4. Data on civil aviation: excluding non-local and foreign airlines flying and operating in Beijing. Statistics consist of the number, mileage, and traffic volume of regular flight lines for domestic transport, transport from and to Hong Kong, Macao and Taiwan, and international transport. Data for 2009 and earlier are sourced from Air China and Xinhua Airline; from 2010, from corporate entities of civil aviation transport in Beijing area.

5. Data on post and telecommunication: including those on postal and telecom services offered by post and telecom operators, excluding data on services of dedicated networks. Business volume falls into two categories, namely postal service and telecommunication service. Data are mainly sourced from Beijing Post and Telecom Company, Beijing Branch of China Unicom, China Mobile Beijing Company, Beijing Branch of China Tietong, and Beijing Branch of China Telecom.

6. Data on number of civil automobiles: civil automobiles refer to all vehicles registered with traffic administration and granted license plates. In terms of automobile structure, civil automobiles consist of passenger automobiles, cargo automobiles, and so on; in terms of ownership, they include private and company ones. These data are sourced from Beijing Traffic Management Bureau.

13-1 交通运输邮电业基本情况(1978-2015年)
TRANSPORT, POST AND TELECOMMUNICATION (1978-2015)

年份 Year	铁路里程(公里) Railway Mileage (km)	公路里程(公里) Highway Mileage (km)	客运量(万人) Passenger Traffic (10000 persons)				货运量(万吨) Freight Traffic (10000 tons)				
				铁路 Railway	公路 Highway	民航 Civil Aviation		铁路 Railway	公路 Highway	民航 Civil Aviation	管道 Pipeline
1978	699	6562	4431	2264	2120	47	7394	3370	4023	1	
1979	700	7278	4777	2504	2220	53	7764	3485	4277	2	
1980	707	7487	5285	2762	2465	58	7571	3356	4213	2	
1981-1985			**33230**	**17688**	**15058**	**484**	**45456**	**15425**	**29063**	**14**	**954**
1981	858	7566	5877	2982	2824	71	8546	3046	5498	2	
1982	858	7683	6215	3205	2931	79	9097	3065	5812	2	218
1983	860	8058	6662	3546	3038	78	9403	3152	6016	3	232
1984	864	8271	7273	3877	3287	109	9671	3133	6301	3	234
1985	876	8482	7203	4078	2978	147	8739	3029	5436	4	270
1986-1990			**38506**	**21290**	**16160**	**1056**	**121771**	**15518**	**104929**	**41**	**1283**
1986	876	8995	7337	4106	3059	172	22121	3030	18794	6	291
1987	876	9103	7763	4418	3117	228	23068	3125	19734	8	201
1988	876	9124	8491	4782	3460	249	24749	3168	21308	9	264
1989	876	9371	7434	4214	3034	186	25184	3144	21767	8	265
1990	876	9648	7480	3770	3490	220	26648	3051	23326	10	262
1991-1995			**40918**	**20615**	**18010**	**2292**	**147385**	**14923**	**131956**	**79**	**427**
1991	876	10259	7704	4036	3378	289	26804	2983	23739	11	71
1992	875	10827	8158	4196	3593	369	27707	2912	24700	14	80
1993	875	11260	7607	4374	2781	452	29865	3048	26730	17	70
1994	875	11532	8537	3992	4008	537	30825	3006	27700	19	99
1995	875	11811	8913	4017	4250	646	32184	2974	29087	17	106
1996-2000			**62554**	**19683**	**38888**	**3983**	**154376**	**13491**	**140455**	**125**	**304**
1996	922	12084	8801	3650	4395	756	32907	2851	29960	18	78
1997	924	12306	9263	3613	4902	748	32351	2883	29360	20	87
1998	924	12498	11228	3762	6704	762	30127	2563	27490	22	52
1999	997	12825	14866	4201	9878	788	28275	2583	25635	30	27
2000	997	13600	18396	4458	13009	929	30717	2612	28010	35	60
2001-2005			**191964**	**25350**	**157061**	**9553**	**156702**	**11053**	**144049**	**277**	**1323**
2001	987	13891	22469	4750	16630	1090	30607	2505	28007	38	57
2002	987	14359	28384	5032	22103	1249	30961	2348	28375	44	194
2003	964	14453	30520	4352	24940	1228	30925	2265	28361	45	254
2004	964	14630	49750	5437	41463	2850	31700	1959	29256	73	412
2005	966	14696	60841	5779	51925	3137	32509	1976	30050	77	406
2006-2010			**435377**	**37892**	**376377**	**21107**	**121931**	**8820**	**106451**	**508**	**6151**
2006	962	20503	12276	6269	2482	3525	33547	1956	30953	89	549
2007	962	20754	20040	6915	9275	3850	20770	1925	17872	98	875
2008	956	20340	128525	7644	117118	3763	21885	1733	18689	93	1369
2009	956	20755	133872	8161	121373	4339	22017	1635	18753	98	1531
2010	956	21114	140663	8903	126130	5630	23712	1572	20184	130	1827
2011-2015			**507504**	**57086**	**417017**	**33402**	**136546**	**5826**	**117312**	**709**	**12700**
2011	1067	21347	145773	9755	129918	6100	26849	1380	23276	132	2061
2012	1115	21492	149037	10315	132333	6389	28650	1232	24925	134	2359
2013	1116	21673	71056	11588	52481	6988	28294	1078	24651	136	2429
2014	1124	21849	71715	12609	52354	6752	29518	1132	25416	149	2821
2015	1124	21885	69924	12821	49931	7172	23236	1004	19044	158	3030

注：1. 铁路数据为北京市市辖范围，2005年以前取自北京铁路分局，2005年及以后取自北京铁路局。

2. 从2006年开始，公路里程包括村道数据。

3. 2006-2007年公路客运量为持有道路运输经营许可证的客运车辆发生的旅客运输量；从2008年开始，公路客运量根据交通运输部《公路水路运输量专项调查方案》调整旅客运输量统计口径,调整后包括旅游客运、省际客运企业、郊区客运和市郊公交的运输量。2013年公路客运量、公路旅客周转量按照《交通运输部办公厅关于印发公路水路运输量统计试行方案(2014)的通知》，统计范围调整为省际客运、旅游客运和郊区客运，市郊公交不再纳入客运量统计。

4. 从2007年开始,公路货物运输为营业性运量。

5. 民航统计范围为北京地区的民航运输法人单位，不包括在京运输飞行的外省市及外国航空公司。

Note: a) Railway figures are statistics within Beijing's jurisdiction. Figures for years before 2005 were from Beijing Railway Branch, those in and after 2005 were from Beijing Railway Bureau.

b) From 2006, road mileage includes figures of rural roads.

c) In 2006 and 2007, highway passenger traffic refered to numbers of passengers traveled by vehicles with road transportation permit ; From 2008, highway passenger traffic refers to passengers travelled for tourism, cross-provincial, suburban and peri-urban purposes, in line with the adjustments made in Special Survey Program for Highway and Water Way Transportation Volume by the Ministry of Traffic and Transportation. In 2013, according to the Notice by the General Office of the Ministry of Transport on Printing and Issuing Provisional Plan for Counting Highway and Water Way Transportation Volume,the statistical scope of highway passenger traffic and highway passenger turnover was changed to inter-provincial, tourist and suburban transport, and suburban buses are no longer counted.

d) From 2007, highway freight traffic refers to freight for operational purpose.

e) Civil aviation covers legal entities of civil aviation registered in Beijing, excluding airlines of other provinces and other countries with transport and flight in Beijing.

13-1 续表 1 Continued 1

年 份 Year	旅客周转量(万人公里) Total Passenger Turnover (10000 passengers-km)	铁 路 Railway	公 路 Highway	民 航 Civil Aviation	货物周转量(万吨公里) Total Freight Turnover (10000 ton-km)	铁 路 Railway	公 路 Highway	民 航 Civil Aviation	管 道 Pipeline
1978			59367				92247		
1979			64033				97616		
1980			73692				93899		
1981-1985			**498768**				**540035**		
1981			81879				93254		
1982	755815	641550	90092	24173	3451037	3329450	106767	13530	1290
1983	853655	723200	103742	26713	3794223	3666600	110118	16099	1406
1984	968481	821431	113871	33179	4309798	4171789	115740	20896	1373
1985	1089919	936300	109184	44435	4719663	4576400	114156	27437	1670
1986-1990	**6333894**	**2608550**	**649210**	**3076133**	**13703344**	**11007906**	**2496086**	**191715**	**7637**
1986	1133620	496288	119065	518267	2569579	2133836	405645	28281	1817
1987	1281763	534720	133735	613308	2792589	2282106	471393	37966	1124
1988	1503508	588947	141625	772936	2887270	2344684	498391	42612	1583
1989	1216981	521263	122435	573283	2765660	2179878	546022	38194	1566
1990	1198022	467332	132350	598339	2688246	2067402	574635	44662	1547
1991-1995	**8690001**	**2645880**	**842807**	**5201314**	**15220745**	**11382191**	**3488944**	**346841**	**2769**
1991	1383465	506431	139041	737993	2799731	2153176	591187	54929	439
1992	1666810	531574	161735	973501	2938746	2230406	642200	65614	527
1993	1656130	551392	127461	977277	3143512	2301941	767790	73216	565
1994	1906718	547488	180030	1179200	3107722	2303265	725740	78142	575
1995	2076879	508995	234540	1333344	3231034	2393403	762027	74940	663
1996-2000	**12752549**	**2649587**	**1744526**	**8358436**	**14987253**	**10458031**	**3918017**	**609517**	**1688**
1996	2219196	459514	250488	1509194	3176234	2311011	784888	79983	352
1997	2272177	477538	261204	1533435	3129097	2263274	769190	96202	431
1998	2419787	505554	304592	1609641	2846652	1952602	783237	110470	343
1999	2701471	579759	400597	1721115	2838857	1929269	754264	155171	153
2000	3139918	627222	527645	1985051	2996414	2001875	826438	167691	410
2001-2005	**27318106**	**3454437**	**5282581**	**18581088**	**18786284**	**12470145**	**4130198**	**1121536**	**1064404**
2001	3462571	677146	529776	2255649	3159848	2167201	826437	165832	378
2002	3961623	642676	603510	2715437	3405498	2213728	835873	195792	160105
2003	3933077	619631	693100	2620346	3620777	2409620	789952	208058	213147
2004	7580057	738956	1582441	5258660	4022791	2571459	822992	270182	358158
2005	8380778	776028	1873754	5730996	4577370	3108137	854944	281672	332617
2006-2010	**53738139**	**4632513**	**10259436**	**38846188**	**22812698**	**12714298**	**4414583**	**1906235**	**3777583**
2006	8254536	890691	791947	6571898	4231243	2625719	885991	335693	383840
2007	9603464	908438	1474249	7220776	4490390	2684862	792883	376074	636572
2008	10419977	902281	2409604	7108091	4542168	2535249	840878	356744	809297
2009	11464758	935596	2677144	7852018	4412317	2293902	878887	355257	884271
2010	13995404	995507	2906492	10093405	5136580	2574567	1015944	482467	1063602
2011-2015	**79736122**	**6279416**	**10129420**	**63327285**	**32326572**	**14512331**	**7498424**	**2647241**	**7668576**
2011	15286501	1086609	3036655	11163237	6169272	3113203	1323259	474856	1257955
2012	15957877	1163833	3047757	11746287	6383052	3076143	1397736	489845	1419328
2013	14987719	1179555	1360831	12447333	6809063	3231824	1561929	491861	1523448
2014	16027249	1356313	1382967	13287969	6728238	2843623	1651938	553661	1679016
2015	17476775	1493106	1301210	14682459	6236947	2247538	1563562	637018	1788829

13-1 续表 2 Continued 2

年 份 Year	机动车拥有量 (万辆) Possession of Motor Vehicles (10000 units)	#民用汽车拥有量 Possession of Civil Motor Vehicles	#私人 Private	邮电业务总量 (万元) Business Volume of Post and Telecommunications Service (10000 yuan)	年末固定电话用户数 (万户) Number of Fixed Telephone Subscribers (10000 subscribers)	年末移动电话用户数 (万户) Number of Mobile Phone Subscribers (10000 subscribers)	固定电话主线普及率 (线/百人) Popularization Rate of Landline Telephones (lines/100 persons)	移动电话普及率 (户/百人) Popularization Rate of Mobile Phones (subscribers/100 persons)	互联网宽带接入用户数 (万户) Subscribers of Broad Band Internet (10000 subscribers)
1978		6.1		24114	7.3		0.8		
1979		7.0		26724	7.8		0.9		
1980		8.1		30047	8.4		0.9		
1981-1985				**204839**					
1981		8.9		31907	9.2		1.0		
1982		9.3		34777	9.8		1.1		
1983		9.8		38525	10.9		1.2		
1984		12.1		45629	12.1		1.3		
1985		16.0		54002	13.6		1.4		
1986-1990				**434582**					
1986		18.6		62079	16.5		1.6		
1987		19.3	0.7	71152	19.5		1.9		
1988		22.2	1.3	84331	23.8		2.2		
1989		24.8	2.4	98124	27.8		2.6		
1990		27.1	2.8	118896	33.3	0.3	3.1	0.03	
1991-1995				**1664508**					
1991		29.7	3.5	157418	39.5	0.7	3.6	0.1	
1992		34.1	4.9	215769	48.0	1.2	4.4	0.1	
1993		41.6	6.7	311251	66.5	3.2	6.0	0.3	
1994		48.1	8.5	418774	100.4	7.7	8.9	0.7	
1995		58.9	12.8	561296	150.5	16.9	12.0	1.4	
1996-2000				**6756754**					
1996		62.2	17.4	729022	195.7	31.0	15.5	2.5	
1997		78.4	29.8	930137	251.2	62.0	20.3	5.0	
1998		89.8	40.7	1290967	313.3	104.2	25.1	8.4	
1999		95.1	44.7	1659133	376.3	186.2	29.9	14.8	
2000	157.8	104.1	49.4	2147496	451.2	347.2	33.1	25.5	
2001-2005				**15331552**					
2001	169.9	114.5	62.4	2182782	525.7	629.4	38.0	45.4	
2002	189.9	133.9	81.1	2540454	585.5	919.5	41.1	64.6	
2003	212.4	163.1	107.1	3040327	682.7	1109.0	46.9	76.1	
2004	229.6	187.1	129.8	3438376	847.8	1340.9	56.8	89.8	
2005	258.3	214.6	154.0	4129614	943.5	1459.8	61.3	94.9	228.9
2006-2010				**40044606**					
2006	287.6	244.1	181.0	5046014	905.2	1571.1	56.5	98.1	281.2
2007	312.8	277.8	212.1	6726273	914.5	1598.3	54.6	95.4	347.2
2008	350.4	318.1	248.3	8008147	884.9	1616.2	50.0	91.3	382.7
2009	401.9	372.1	300.3	9175072	893.1	1825.4	48.0	98.1	451.7
2010	480.9	452.9	374.4	11089100	885.6	2129.8	45.1	108.6	545.6
				(4284217)					
2011-2015				**34291472**					
2011	498.3	473.2	389.7	4878792	883.9	2575.9	43.8	127.6	523.4
2012	520.0	495.7	407.5	5464681	883.1	3168.0	42.7	153.1	572.0
2013	543.7	518.9	426.5	6524689	867.6	3373.8	41.0	159.5	534.7
2014	559.1	532.4	437.2	7511309	831.1	4076.2	38.6	189.4	552.7
2015	561.9	535.0	440.3	9912001	784.7	4051.6	36.2	186.7	491.7

注：1. 邮电业务总量2000年及以前按1990年不变价格计算，2001-2010年按2000年不变价格计算，2011年开始按2010年不变价格计算。表内2010年邮电业务总量是按2000年价格计算,()内数据是按2010年价格计算。

2. 2006-2010年主线普及率和移动电话普及率根据第六次人口普查数据进行了调整。

Note: a) Business volume of post and telecommunications before 2000 was calculated at 1990's constant prices; that of 2001-2010 was calculated at 2000's constant prices; and from 2011, the volume was calculated at 2010's constant prices. In this table, the volume of post and telecommunication service in 2010 was calculated at 2000's price, and figures in () were calculated at 2010's price.

b) Data of popularization rate of landline telephones and mobile phones for 2006-2010 were adjusted based on the results from the 6th population census.

13-2 社会客货运总量(换算周转量)
PASSENGER AND FREIGHT TRAFFIC (CONVERTED TURNOVER)

单位：万吨公里 (10000 tons-km)

项　目	Item	2015	2014	2015年为2014年% 2015 as % of 2014	构　成(%) Composition(%)	
					2015	2014
运输总量	**Total**	**9158904.0**	**9399252.6**	**97.4**	**100.0**	**100.0**
铁　路	Railway	3740643.9	4199936.8	89.1	40.8	44.7
公　路	Highway	1693683.0	1790234.7	94.6	18.5	19.0
民　航	Civil Aviation	1935748.1	1730065.0	111.9	21.1	18.4
管　道	Pipeline	1788829.1	1679016.1	106.5	19.5	17.9

13-3 运输线路
TRANSPORTATION ROUTES

项　目	Item	条　数（条） Number (line)		长　度（公里） Length (km)	
		2015	2014	2015	2014
铁　路	Railway	56	56	1123.6	1123.6
公　路	Highway	9853	10372	21885	21848.8
民　航	Civil Aviation				
#中国国际航空公司	Air China	360	322		
中国新华航空有限责任公司	China Xinhua Airlines	396	370		
管　道	Pipeline	18	17	4058.9	3825.5

注：铁路长度为营业里程，管道长度为管输里程。

Note: Railway length refers to operating mileage, and pipeline length refers to transportation mileage.

13-4 铁路、民航主要技术经济指标
MAIN TECHNICAL AND ECONOMIC INDICATORS OF RAILWAY AND CIVIL AVIATION

项　　目	Item	2015	2014	2015年为2014年% 2015 as % of 2014
铁　路	**Railway**			
内燃机车每万吨公里耗柴油 (千克)	Diesel Consumption of Diesel Locomotives per 10 000 Ton-km (kg)	36.4	34.4	105.8
电力机车每万吨公里耗电 (千瓦小时)	Electricity Consumption of Electric Locomotives per 10000 Ton-km (kWh)	106.5	100.3	106.2
民　航	**Civil Aviation**			
每吨公里耗航空油 (千克)	Aviation-oil Consumption per Ton-km (kg)	0.28	0.29	97.7

13-5 机动车拥有量
NUMBER OF CIVIL MOTOR VEHICLES

单位：万辆 (10000 units)

项　　目	Item	2015	2014	2015年为2014年% 2015 as % of 2014
机动车	**Motor Vehicles**	**561.9**	**559.1**	**100.5**
#民用汽车	Civil Automobiles	535.0	532.4	100.5
#载货汽车	Trucks	30.6	28.9	105.9
载客汽车	Passanger Vehicles	498.1	496.9	100.2
#私人汽车	Private Cars	440.3	437.2	100.7
#轿　车	Sedans	316.5	316.5	100.0

资料来源：北京市公安局公安交通管理局。
Source: Beijing Traffic Management Bureau.

13-6 邮电业务主要指标
MAIN INDICATORS OF POST AND TELECOMMUNICATION SERVICE

项目	Item	2015	2014	2015年为2014年% 2015 as % of 2014
邮电业务总量 (万元)	**Business Volume of Post and Telecommunications (10000 yuan)**	**9912001.3**	**7511308.7**	**132.0**
邮政业务量	Post	678364.7	637602.2	106.4
电信业务量	Telecommunications	9233636.6	6873706.5	134.3
邮电业务	**Total Amount of Post and Telecommunication Businesses**			
函　件 (万件)	Letters (10000 pcs)	61139.6	66090.9	92.5
包　件 (万件)	Parcels (10000 pcs)	670.4	499.9	134.1
特快专递业务量 (万件)	Express Mail Services (10000 pcs)	141447.3	111011.9	127.4
汇　票 (万件)	Money Orders (10000 pcs)	286.7	439.7	65.2
订销报纸(累计) (万份)	Newspapers Subscribed (10000 copies)	70901.5	72504.2	97.8
订销杂志(累计) (万份)	Magazines Subscribed (10000 copies)	3526.7	3857.6	91.4
邮政储蓄期末余额 (亿元)	Post Savings Deposit Balance (100 million yuan)	746.9	764.1	97.8
长途电话通话量(固定) (亿分钟)	Long-distance Calls (Fixed-line Telephon (100 million minutes)	44.9	42.4	105.7
本地电话通话量(固定) (亿分钟)	Local Calls (Fixed-line Telephone) (100 million times)	117.4	135.8	86.4
移动电话通话量 (亿分钟)	Calls of Mobile Phones (100 million minutes)	1558.7	1587.5	98.2
移动短信业务量 (亿条)	Short Message Services (100 million messages)	517.2	453.4	114.1
年末移动电话用户 (万户)	Mobile Phone Subscribers (10000 subscribers)	4051.6	4076.2	99.4
#3G移动电话用户数 (万户)	3G Mobile Phone Subscribers (10000 subscribers)	1451.1	1928.8	75.2
年末固定电话用户 (万户)	Fixed Telephone Subscribers (10000 subscribers)	784.7	831.1	94.4
#住宅电话用户 (万户)	Household Telephone Subscribers (10000 subscribers)	417.6	501.0	83.4
长途光缆纤芯长度 (芯公里)	Fiber Core Length of Long-distance Optic Cables (core-km)	198183.0	180670.0	109.7
长途电话交换机容量 (万路端)	Capacity of Long-distance Telephone Exchanges (10000 roadheads)	48.7	53.8	90.5
局用交换机容量 (万门)	Capacity of Office Telephone Exchanges (10000 units)	1587.4	1514.5	104.8
移动电话交换机容量 (万户)	Capacity of Mobile Phone Exchanges (10000 subscribers)	5102.0	4910	103.9
固定电话主线普及率 (线/百人)	Popularization Rate of Fixed-line Telephones (lines/100 persons)	36.2	38.6	93.7
移动电话普及率 (户/百人)	Popularization Rate of Mobile Phones (subscribers/100 persons)	186.7	189.4	98.6
固定互联网宽带接入用户数 (万户)	Subscribers of Broad Band Internet (10000 subscribers)	491.7	552.7	89.0
互联网上网人数 (万人)	Number of Internet Users (10000 persons)	1647.0	1593.0	103.4

注：1. 邮电业务总量为2010年不变价计算。
2. "互联网上网人数"来源于中国互联网络信息中心（CNNIC)发布的《中国互联网络发展状况统计报告》。
3. 从2013年开始，特快专递业务量填报范围扩大为取得快递业务经营许可企业及其备案分支机构。

Note: a) Business volume of post and telecommunications is calculated based on constant price in 2010.
b) "Number of Internet Users" was sourced from the Statistical Report on Internet Development in China issued by CNNIC.
c) Since 2013, enterprises permitted to conduct express delivery businesses and their filed branches are required to submit the business volume of Express Mail Services.

主要统计指标解释

货（客）运量 指在一定时期内，各种运输工具实际运送的货物（旅客）数量。是反映运输业为国民经济和人民生活服务的数量指标，也是制定和检查运输生产计划，研究运输发展规模和速度的重要指标。货运按吨计算，客运按人计算。货物不论运输距离长短，货物类别，均按实际重量统计；旅客不论行程远近或票价多少，均按一人一次作为客运量统计。半价票、小孩票也按一人统计。

货物（旅客）周转量 指在一定时期内，由各种运输工具运送的货物（旅客）数量与其相应运输距离的乘积之总和，是反映运输业生产总成果的重要指标，也是编制和检查运输生产计划、计算运输效率、劳动生产率以及核算运输单位的主要基础资料。计算货物周转量通常按发出站与到达站之间的最短距离，也就是计费距离计算。

邮电业务总量 是以货币形式表示的邮政电信企业为社会提供各类邮政通信服务的总数量。计算公式为：

$$邮电业务总量 = \sum\left(\begin{array}{l}各类邮政通信业务量 \times 不变\\单价\end{array}\right) + 出租代维及其他业务收入$$

函件 是指邮政部门为用户传递以书面信息为主的邮件，包括信件、印刷品和邮送广告。

包件 指符合包裹准寄范围，通过邮政渠道寄递的物品。包括国内普通包裹、国内快递包裹、国际及港澳台包裹。

长途电话交换机容量 是指用于接入长途电话网的电话交换机的设备额定容量。

局用交换机容量 是指安装在本地电信企业内用于接续本地固定电话的电话交换机容量。包括现用和备用的人工或自动交换机（含远端模块）的全部容量，包括接入网设备容量。

移动电话交换机容量 分为 GSM、CDMA 两种。指移动电话交换机根据一定话务模型和交换机处理能力计算出来的最大同时服务用户的数量。

固定电话主线普及率 是指报告期行政区域常住人口中，平均每百人拥有的固定电话主线数。计算公式为：

$$固定电话主线普及率 = \frac{电话主线数(本地电话用户)}{行政区域常住人口数}$$

移动电话普及率 是指报告期行政区域常住人口中，平均每百人拥有的移动电话的用户数。计算公式为：

$$移动电话普及率 = \frac{移动电话用户总数}{行政区域常住人口数}$$

固定互联网宽带接入用户数 指报告期末在电信企业登记注册，通过 xDSL、FTTx+LAN 以及其他宽带接入方式和普通专线接入公众互联网的用户。

Explanatory Notes on Main Statistical Indicators

Freight (Passenger) Traffic refers to the volume of freight (passenger) transported with various means during a certain period of time. It is a quantitative measure to show how the transport industry serves the national economy and people's life, and is also an important indicator for preparing and reviewing transport plan and studying the development scale and speed of the transport industry. Freight transport is calculated in tons and passenger traffic is calculated in the number of persons. Regardless of the types or traveling distance of freight, freight transport is calculated in the actual weight of goods: and regardless of the traveling distance or ticket price, passenger traffic is calculated following the principle that one person can be counted only once in one travel. The passenger who travels with a half-price ticket or a child ticket is also calculated as one person.

Freight (Passenger) Turnover refers to the sum of the transported cargo (passengers) multiplied by the transport distance during a certain period of time. This is an important indicator to show the total results of the transport industry, and also serves as main basic data for preparing and reviewing transport plans and measuring transport efficiency, labor productivity and the transport unit. Freight Turnover is usually calculated by the shortest distance between the departure station and the arrival station, namely the charging distance.

Business Volume of Post and Telecommunications refers to the total amount of post and telecommunication services, expressed in monetary terms, provided by the post and telecommunication sectors for the society. The formula is as follows:

Business Volume of Post and Telecommunications= ∑(Transactions of Post and Telecommunication Service x Constant Price) + Income from Leasing, Maintenance and other Services

Correspondences mean mails mainly in the form of written information delivered by postal authorities, including letters, prints and delivered advertisements.

Parcels means articles permitted for mailing, and mailed through postal channels, including domestic express parcels, international parcels, and parcels from and to Hong Kong, Macao and Taiwan.

Capacity of Long-distance Phone Exchanges means the rated capacity of phone exchangers used for connecting to the long-distance phone network.

Capacity of Local Exchanges means the capacity of phone exchangers installed in local telecom businesses and used for linking local fixed telephones. It is the sum of all capacity of existing and backup manual or automatic exchangers (with far-end modules), including the capacity of network access equipment.

Capacity of Mobile Phone Exchanges, divided into GSM and CDMA, means the maximum number of users receiving services simultaneously from mobile phone exchangers, calculated from certain traffic model and exchanger processing capacity.

Popularization Rate of Fixed-line Telephones means the average number of main lines of fixed-line telephones owned per one hundred persons of permanent population in administrative areas in the reporting period. It is calculated with the following formula:

Popularization Rate of Landline= Number of Main Lines of Telephone (Local Phone Users) / Number of Permanent Population in Administrative Areas

Popularization Rate of Mobile Phones means the average number of mobile phones owned per 100 persons among permanent population in administrative areas in the reporting period. It is calculated with the following formula:

Popularization Rate of Mobile Phones = Total Number of Mobile Phone Users / Permanent Population in Administrative Areas

Subscribers of Broadband Internet means subscribers registered at telecom companies to connect with public Internet through xDSL, FTTx+LAN as well as other broadband connections and general special lines at the end of reporting period.

北京统计年鉴2016 BEIJING STATISTICAL YEARBOOK

批发和零售业、住宿和餐饮业
WHOLESALE AND RETAIL TRADE, ACCOMMODATION AND RESTAURANTS

简要说明

一、本章资料的主要内容

本章资料反映北京市商品流通市场发展及批发和零售业、住宿和餐饮业经营情况。主要内容有社会消费品零售总额；批发和零售业商品购进、销售、库存总值、商品分类销售情况及主要商品销售情况；住宿业和餐饮业经营情况；机动车销售情况；限额以上批发和零售业、住宿业和餐饮业财务状况；连锁企业基本情况；商品交易市场基本情况、成交额；北京消费者信心指数。

二、本章的统计范围

社会消费品零售总额指标于 1993 年、1997 年和 2003 年做了较大调整。1993 年起不再包括对农民的农业生产资料；1997 年起不再包括居民购买住房；2003 年起不再包括由各种经济类型的制造业法人企业、产业活动单位直接售给城乡居民（包括本企业职工）和社会集团的商品以及农民对非农业居民的零售额。

限额以上批发和零售业、住宿业和餐饮业统计限额标准：2008 年以前，批发业为年销售额 2000 万元及以上；零售业为年销售额 500 万元及以上；住宿业为星级饭店和星级以外年营业收入 500 万元及以上；餐饮业为年营业额 200 万元及以上。2008 年调整后，批发业为年主营业务收入 2000 万元及以上；零售业为年主营收入 500 万元及以上；住宿业为星级饭店和星级以外年主营业务收入 200 万元及以上；餐饮业为年主营业务收入 200 万元及以上。

北京消费者信心指数调查范围覆盖全市 16 个区。

三、本章的资料来源

本章资料中所有资料均由北京市统计局、国家统计局北京调查总队提供。

四、本章的统计调查方法

限额以上批发和零售业、住宿和餐饮业单位采用全面调查；连锁企业、商品交易市场采取全数调查；限额以下批发和零售业、住宿和餐饮业法人单位及个体户采用抽样调查。

北京消费者信心指数调查采用计算机辅助电话方式调查，调查对象为居住在北京市半年以上 18-65 周岁的城乡居民。

五、有关统计标准的变化说明

2010 年以前企业大中小型划分执行 2003 年《统计上大中小型企业划分办法（暂行）》标准；自 2011 年开始，大中小微型企业划分标准执行国家统计局《关于统计上大中小微型企业划分办法》（国统字[2011]75 号）。

六、本章中关于历史数据调整的问题

按照国家统计局统一要求和统一方法，本章中 1978 年至 2003 年的社会消费品零售总额数据，根据第一次经济普查结果，采用“速度推算法”进行了修正，2004 年数据为第一次经济普查数据；2005-2007 年数据根据第二次经济普查结果，采用“趋势离差法”进行了修正，2008 年数据为第二次经济普查数据；2009-2012 年数据根据第三次经济普查结果进行了修正，2013 年数据为第三次经济普查数据。

Brief Introduction

I. Main Content

Statistics in this chapter show the development of commodity circulation market and the operations of wholesale and retail trades, accommodation and restaurants. Figures mainly include retail sales of consumer goods, total value of commodity purchase, sales and inventory in wholesale and retail trades, sales of commodities by category, and sales of main commodities; operation situation of accommodation and restaurants; sales of mobile vehicles; financial status of wholesale, retail, accommodation and restaurants enterprises above designated size; basic situation of chain businesses; basic situation and turnover of commodity transaction markets, and trading volume of main commodities; and settlement of consumer complaints; and consumer confidence index.

II. Scope of Statistics

Major adjustments were made to the indicators of Retail Sales of Consumer Goods for 1993, 1997 and 2003. From 1993, the indicator did not cover agricultural means of production for farmers any longer; from 1997, it did not cover houses bought by residents any longer; from 2003, it did not cover goods sold by corporate manufacturing enterprises and industrial activity entities of various economic types to urban and rural residents (including enterprises' own employees) and social groups as well as retail sales by farmers to non-agricultural residents any longer.

As for standards for wholesale and retail trades, accommodation and restaurants above designated size, before 2008, for wholesale trades, the standard was annual sales of RMB 20 million and above; for retail trades, annual sales of RMB 5 million and above; for accommodation, star-rated hotels and non-star-rated hotels with annual turnover of RMB 5 million and above; for restaurants, annual turnover of RMB 2 million and above. After adjustments were made in 2008, the designated size is, for whole sale trades, annual sales of RMB 20 million and above; for retail trades, annual sales of RMB 5 million and above; for accommodation, star-rated hotels and non-star-rated hotels with annual main business income of RMB 2 million and above; for restaurants, annual main business income of RMB 2 million and above.

Survey of consumer confidence index covers 16 districts in the City.

III. Source of Data

Data in settlement are all sourced from Beijing Municipal Bureau of Statistics and NBS Survey Office in Beijing.

IV. Survey Methodology

The method of comprehensive survey was used for statistics of wholesale and retail trades, accommodation, and restaurants service enterprises above designated size; complete enumeration was used for chain businesses, and commodity trading markets; sample survey was used for wholesale and retail trades, accommodation, and restaurants corporate enterprises below designated size as well as self-employed businesses.

Statistics on consumer confidence index were obtained through computer-aided phone calls to urban and rural residents at 18-65 who have been living in Beijing for more than half a year.

V. Changes in Relevant Statistical Standards

Before 2010，the classification of small, medium and large-sized enterprises should comply with the standard of *Measures for Statistical Classification of Small, Medium and Large-sized Enterprises (Temporary)* 2003. Since 2011, the classification of micro, small, medium and large-sized enterprises has been in line with standards of Circular by National Bureau of Statistics on Printing and Issuing the *Measures for Statistical Classification of Micro, Small, Medium and Large-sized Enterprises* (G.T.Z. [2011] No. 75).

VI. Adjustment to Historical Data

In accordance with the unified requirements and methods put forward by the National Bureau of Statistics, data for 1978-2003 on retail sales of consumer goods were adjusted with the “speed calculation method” according to the first economic census results in 2004. Data for 2004 are gathered from the first economic census. Data for 2005-2007 were revised with the “trend deviation method” in accordance with the second economic census results in 2008. Data for 2008 are gathered from the second economic census. Data for 2009-2012 were revised with the “trend deviation method” in accordance with the third economic census results in 2013. Data for 2013 were gathered from the third economic census.

14-1 历年社会消费品零售总额(1978-2015年)
TOTAL RETAIL SALES OF CONSUMER GOODS (1978-2015)

单位：亿元 (100 million yuan)

年 份 Year	社会消费品零售总额 Total Retail Sales of Consumer Goods	按商品类别分 By Category of Commodity			
		吃类商品 Food	穿类商品 Clothing	用类商品 Daily Supplies	烧类商品 Fuels
1978	44.2	18.0	8.9	16.0	1.3
1979	53.3	20.8	11.3	19.7	1.5
1980	62.8	24.9	13.4	22.9	1.6
1981-1985	**472.7**	**180.9**	**85.1**	**196.2**	**10.5**
1981	70.7	28.0	14.5	26.5	1.7
1982	75.4	29.7	13.7	30.3	1.7
1983	86.4	34.0	15.7	34.8	1.9
1984	105.8	39.6	18.7	45.2	2.3
1985	134.4	49.6	22.5	59.4	2.9
1986-1990	**1239.8**	**494.9**	**166.7**	**551.8**	**26.4**
1986	155.0	60.7	22.8	68.0	3.5
1987	188.9	77.4	27.4	80.2	3.9
1988	256.0	100.6	36.0	114.9	4.5
1989	294.8	119.4	34.9	134.1	6.4
1990	345.1	136.8	45.6	154.6	8.1
1991-1995	**3239.5**	**1261.4**	**481.3**	**1422.2**	**74.6**
1991	408.3	158.2	53.7	187.6	8.8
1992	503.0	193.6	66.9	230.5	12.0
1993	611.2	220.7	96.5	277.6	16.4
1994	766.6	283.2	125.3	338.6	19.5
1995	950.4	405.7	138.9	387.9	17.9
1996-2000	**6811.7**	**2177.0**	**858.9**	**3576.5**	**199.3**
1996	1061.6	427.5	152.5	461.8	19.8
1997	1208.5	447.9	161.6	565.6	33.4
1998	1373.6	399.8	167.2	764.2	42.4
1999	1509.3	430.4	178.8	852.9	47.2
2000	1658.7	471.4	198.8	932.0	56.5
2001-2005	**11671.8**	**3061.2**	**1218.6**	**6722.7**	**669.3**
2001	1831.4	528.7	221.9	1016.9	63.9
2002	2005.2	540.2	219.9	1167.4	77.7
2003	2296.9	596.4	252.3	1356.4	91.8
2004	2626.6	644.9	242.1	1538.3	201.3
2005	2911.7	751.0	282.4	1643.7	234.6
2006-2010	**23503.8**	**5388.2**	**2126.1**	**14130.0**	**1859.5**
2006	3295.3	818.8	314.7	1852.6	309.2
2007	3835.2	940.4	359.3	2205.2	330.3
2008	4645.5	1073.3	411.7	2799.4	361.1
2009	5387.5	1201.0	482.2	3319.6	384.7
2010	6340.3	1354.7	558.2	3953.2	474.2
2011-2015	**44193.8**	**9029.0**	**3785.2**	**28590.4**	**2789.2**
2011	7222.2	1636.6	712.7	4310.0	562.9
2012	8123.5	1759.9	769.3	4999.5	594.8
2013	8872.1	1804.7	777.1	5711.1	579.2
2014	9638.0	1860.5	783.3	6413.5	580.7
2015	10338.0	1967.3	742.8	7156.3	471.6

注：1978-2003年社会消费品零售额按2004年第一次经济普查数据进行了修订，2004年为第一次经济普查数据，2005-2007年数据按第二次经济普查进行了修订，2008年数据为第二次经济普查数据；2009-2012年数据根据第三次全国经济普查数据进行了修订，2013年数据为第三次全国经济普查数据。

Note: Retail sales of consumer goods for 1978-2003 were revised according to the first economic cencus in 2004. Figures for 2004 were gathered from the first economic census. Figures for 2005-2007 were revised based on the results of the second economic census. Figures for 2008 were gathered from the second economic census.Data for 2009-2012 were revised acording to the third national economic census; and data for 2013 were collected from the third national economic census.

14-2 社会消费品零售总额(2010-2015年)
TOTAL RETAIL SALES OF CONSUMER GOODS (2010-2015)

单位：亿元 (100 million yuan)

项 目	Item	2010	2011	2012	2013	2014	2015	2015年为2014年% 2015 as % of 2014
社会消费品零售总额	**Total Retail Sales of Consumer Goods**	**6340.3**	**7222.2**	**8123.5**	**8872.1**	**9638.0**	**10338.0**	**107.3**
按商品类别分	**By Category of Commodity**							
吃类商品	Food	1354.7	1636.6	1759.9	1804.7	1860.5	1967.3	109.2
穿类商品	Clothing	558.2	712.7	769.3	777.1	783.3	742.8	100.9
用类商品	Daily Supplies	3953.2	4310.0	4999.5	5711.1	6413.5	7156.3	109.4
烧类商品	Fuels	474.2	562.9	594.8	579.2	580.7	471.6	84.3
按销售单位所在地分	**By Location of Seller**							
城 镇	Urban	6238.0	7106.1	7995.1	8721.0	9471.5	10162.8	107.3
农 村	Rural	102.3	116.1	128.4	151.1	166.5	175.2	105.7
按消费品形态分	**By Form of Consumer Goods**							
餐饮收入	Food and Beverage Income	678.5	817.8	880.2	836.1	829.7	846.8	103.3
商品零售	Retail Sales of Commodities	5661.8	6404.4	7243.3	8036.0	8808.3	9491.2	107.6

注：1.2010年-2012年数据根据第三次全国经济普查进行了修订，2013年数据为第三次全国经济普查数据。
2.2015年为2014年发展速度指标是按可比口径计算的数据。

Note: a)Data for 2010-2012 were revised acording to the third national economic census; and data for 2013 were collected from the third national economic census.
b) Growth rates of 2015 as present of 2014 are calculated in comparable terms.

14-3 按登记注册类型分限额以上批发和零售企业商品零售额(2015年)
RETAIL SALES OF GOODS IN WHOLESALE AND RETAIL ENTERPRISES ABOVE DESIGNATED SIZE BY REGISTRATION TYPE (2015)

单位：万元 (10000 yuan)

项 目	Item	合 计 Total Sales	批发业 Wholesale	零售业 Retail Trade
总 计	**Total**	**75358303**	**5608851**	**69749452**
内资企业	Domestic Funded Enterprises	60782433	4592305	56190128
#国 有	State-owned Enterprises	1091376	71165	1020211
集 体	Collectively-owned Enterprises	391856	3653	388203
股份有限公司	Companies Limited by Shares	8708038	1196810	7511228
港澳台商投资企业	Hong Kong, Macao and Taiwan-invested Enterprises	4554317	417355	4136962
外商投资企业	Foreign-invested Enterprises	10021553	599190	9422362

注：本表统计范围为限额以上批发和零售业法人单位、产业活动单位和个体经营户。

Note: Figures in this table cover legal entities in wholesale and retail trade above designated size, activity entities and individual entities .

14-4 批发和零售业商品购进、销售、库存情况
TOTAL VALUE OF PURCHASES, SALES AND INVENTORY OF COMMODITIES IN WHOLESALE AND RETAIL TRADE

单位：万元 (10000 yuan)

项目	Item	2015	2014	2015年为2014年% 2015 as % of 2014
商品购进额	**Total Purchases of Commodities**	**559845370**	**598222733**	**93.6**
市内购进	In the City	158465858	146762720	108.0
市外购进	From Outside Beijing	326307060	357719468	91.2
进　口	Imported	75072452	93740545	80.1
商品销售额	**Total Sales of Commodities**	**607250902**	**665129727**	**91.3**
批发额	**Wholesale**	**513897910**	**577053329**	**89.1**
市内批发	In the City	163838171	146860106	111.6
市外批发	To Outside Beijing	326633659	403390728	81.0
出　口	Exported	23426080	26802495	87.4
零售额	**Retail**	**93352992**	**88076398**	**106.0**
期末商品库存额	**Inventory (Year-end)**	**57443661**	**56129381**	**102.3**

注：本表统计范围为批发和零售业法人单位、产业活动单位和个体经营。
Note: Figures in this table cover legal entities in wholesale and retail trade above designated size, activity entities and individual entities.

14-5 限额以上批发和零售业商品购进、销售、库存情况(2015年)
TOTAL VALUE OF PURCHASES, SALES AND INVENTORY IN WHOLESALE AND RETAIL ENTERPRISES ABOVE DESIGNATED SIZE (2015)

单位：万元 (10000 yuan)

项目	Item	合计 Total Sales	批发业 Wholesale	零售业 Retail
商品购进额	**Total Purchases of Commodities**	**484090954**	**409842967**	**74247987**
市内购进	In the City	117939922	78146420	39793502
市外购进	From Outside Beijing	290671555	257893443	32778112
进　口	Imported	75466734	73790361	1676373
商品销售额	**Total Sales of Commodities**	**518112598**	**436249524**	**81863074**
批发额	**Wholesale**	**442754295**	**430640673**	**12113622**
市内批发	In the City	123186976	116515778	6671199
市外批发	To Outside Beijing	296438068	291324552	5113516
出　口	Exported	23114398	22785491	328907
零售额	**Retail**	**75358303**	**5608851**	**69749452**
期末商品库存额	**Inventory (Year-end)**	**56173397**	**49695778**	**6477620**

注：本表统计范围为限额以上批发和零售业法人单位、产业活动单位和个体经营户。
Note: Figures in this table cover legal entities in wholesale and retail trade above designated size, activity entities and individual entities.

14-6 限额以上批发和零售业商品销售类值(2015年)
SALES BY CATEGORY FOR WHOLESALE AND RETAIL ENTERPRISES ABOVE DESIGNATED SIZE (2015)

单位：万元 (10000 yuan)

项　　目	Item	商品销售额 Total Sales	批发额 Wholesale	零售额 Retail
合　计	**Total**	**518112598**	**442754295**	**75358303**
粮油、食品类	Cereal, Oil and Food	22313750	16391482	5922267
#粮油类	Cereal and Oil	10504464	9588584	915880
肉禽蛋类	Meat, Poultry and Eggs	2088006	1285884	802122
饮料类	Beverages	4562623	3823023	739600
烟酒类	Tobacco and Liquor	10297187	9001058	1296129
服装鞋帽、针、纺织品类	Clothing, Shoes, Hats and Textiles	11344548	5030628	6313919
服装类	Clothing	7242835	2374627	4868208
鞋帽类	Shoes and Hats	2327211	1243473	1083738
针、纺织品类	Knitwear and Textiles	1728057	1400944	327114
化妆品类	Cosmetics	2792574	1085647	1706926
金银珠宝类	Gold, Silver and Jewelry	12349125	9127334	3221792
日用品类	Articles for Daily Use	8832295	4812273	4020022
#儿童玩具类	Children's Toys	206756	69023	137733
五金、电料类	Hardware and Electrical Materials	1124104	1000824	123280
体育、娱乐用品类	Sports and Recreation Goods	6177503	5204868	972635
书报、杂志类	Newspapers and Magazines	1940890	1110428	830461
电子出版物及音像制品类	E-Journals and Video Products	533139	269177	263963
家用电器和音像器材类	Household Appliances and Audiovisual Products	17560824	13438658	4122166
中西药品类	Traditional Chinese and Western Medicines	18121719	14215183	3906535
#西药类	Western Medicines	12959890	10108106	2851784
中草药及中成药类	Chinese Herbal Medicines and Chinese Patent Medicines	3142449	2197185	945264
文化、办公用品类	Cultural and Office Goods	26375083	20929727	5445356
家具类	Furniture	1014589	139347	875242
通讯器材类	Communication Devices	50700721	39551576	11149146
煤炭及制品类	Coal and Coal Products	21231443	21210590	20853
木材及制品类	Wood and Wooden Products	2987069	2987069	
石油及制品类	Petroleum and Its Products	51591553	47065064	4526490
化工材料及制品类	Raw Chemical Materials	55732163	55732163	
#化肥类	Fertilizer	11487953	11487953	
金属材料类	Metal Materials	66243031	66243031	
建筑及装潢材料类	Building and Decoration Materials	3271256	3034290	236965
机电产品及设备类	Electric-mechanic Products and Equipment	24238953	23748367	490586
#农机类	Agricultural Machinery	205608	205608	
汽车类	Automobiles	73288613	55206706	18081907
种子饲料类	Seed and Feedstuff	1907340	1907340	
棉麻类	Cotton and Hemp	2119364	2118741	623
其他类	Others	19461141	18369700	1091441

注：本表统计范围为限额以上批发和零售业法人单位、产业活动单位和个体经营户。
Note: Figures in this table cover legal entities in wholesale and retail trade above designated size, activity entities and individual entities .

14-7 限额以上批发和零售业商品销售情况(2015年)
COMMODITY SALES OF WHOLESALE AND RETAIL ENTERPRISES ABOVE DESIGNATED SIZE (2015)

项目	Item	商品销售量 Total Sales	批发量 Wholesale Volume	零售量 Retail Volume
大米(稻米) (百公斤)	Rice (100 kg)	25998644	23939633	2059011
白面(小麦面) (百公斤)	Flour (Wheat Flour) (100 kg)	3843124	3099860	743264
杂粮 (百公斤)	Coarse Cereals (100 kg)	54766135	54418308	347826
食用植物油 (百公斤)	Edible Vegetable Oil (100 kg)	64635417	63488466	1146951
猪肉 (百公斤)	Pork (100 kg)	2908217	2092441	815777
牛肉 (百公斤)	Beef (100 kg)	800820	657098	143723
羊肉 (百公斤)	Mutton (100 kg)	220906	128281	92625
禽肉 (百公斤)	Poultry (100 kg)	2776653	2504466	272187
鲜蛋 (百公斤)	Fresh Eggs (100 kg)	752398	225940	526458
鲜菜 (百公斤)	Fresh Vegetable (100 kg)	6892350	2866130	4026220
鲜瓜果 (百公斤)	Fresh Melons and Fruits (100 kg)	5046670	1869570	3177100
水产品 (百公斤)	Aquatic Products (100 kg)	3531990	3040780	491210
食糖 (百公斤)	Sugar (100 kg)	45856650	44843390	1013260
卷烟 (万支)	Cigarettes (10000 units)	10200395	9769858	430538
酒 (百升)	Wine (100 liter)	64270048	62329411	1940637
#白酒 (百升)	Distillate Spirit (100 liter)	5138147	4024242	1113905
啤酒 (百升)	Beer (100 liter)	58332167	57805222	526945
茶叶 (百公斤)	Tea (100 kg)	85600	49630	35970
各种服装 (百件)	Clothing (100 units)	5012523	3265945	1746578
鞋 (百双)	Shoes (100 pairs)	1304128	908793	395335
数码照相机 (台)	Digital Cameras (unit)	14862849	13741715	1121134
自行车 (辆)	Bicycles (unit)	572970	453109	119861
彩色电视机 (台)	Color TV Sets (unit)	10384008	7020321	3363687
数码摄像机 (台)	Digital Video Cameras (unit)	1596231	1559471	36760
家用电风扇 (台)	Household Electrical Fans (unit)	1593269	1320537	272732
电冰箱（家用电冰箱） (台)	Household Refrigerators (unit)	4238136	3335743	902393
洗衣机（家用洗衣机） (台)	Household Washing Machines (unit)	7311570	6430294	881276
家用空调器（房间空调器） (台)	Household Air Conditioners (Room Air Conditioners) (unit)	10086875	8846760	1240115
微波炉 (台)	Microwave Ovens (unit)	1347073	992632	354441
热水淋浴器 (台)	Showers (unit)	1645780	1076928	568852
吸尘器 (台)	Vacuum Cleaners (unit)	2127279	1772159	355120
抽油烟机 (台)	Range Hoods (unit)	603892	266394	337498
电脑（微型计算机） (台)	Computers (Micro Computers) (unit)	33412851	25468387	7944464
移动电话机 (部)	Mobile Phones (unit)	292937359	223117935	69819424
钢材 (吨)	Steel Products (ton)	115050184	115046006	4178
水泥 (吨)	Cement (ton)	36403781	36366101	37680
汽车 (辆)	Motor Vehicles (unit)	2820551	1998661	821890
#轿车 (辆)	Sedan Cars (unit)	1578332	897717	680615
化学肥料 (吨)	Chemical Fertilizers (ton)	80112235	80085995	26240
化学农药 (吨)	Chemical Pesticides (ton)	316237	316237	
铜 (吨)	Copper (ton)	3787144	3786994	150
铝 (吨)	Aluminium (ton)	6383830	6383830	

注：本表统计范围为限额以上批发和零售业法人单位、产业活动单位和个体经营户。

Note: Figures in this table cover legal entities in wholesale and retail trade above designated size, activity entities and individual entities .

14-8 机动车销售情况(2001-2015年)
SALES OF MOTOR VEHICLES (2001-2015)

单位：万辆 (10000 units)

项目	Item	2001	2002	2003	2004	2005	2006	2007	2008	2009	2010	2011	2012	2013	2014	2015
机动车销售量	**Sales of Motor Vehicles**	**22.9**	**26.0**	**40.8**	**44.7**	**57.0**	**71.4**	**79.8**	**87.8**	**114.8**	**143.2**	**79.7**	**128.5**	**128.2**	**127.5**	**114.8**
#轿　车	Sedan Cars	11.4	15.1	25.2	27.2	38.0	46.2	52.7	54.5	70.6	92.4	49.0	83.2	80.5	74.2	69.1
新　车	**New Vehicles**	**16.4**	**17.7**	**29.3**	**30.4**	**37.2**	**39.1**	**44.3**	**49.3**	**70.2**	**91.6**	**40.0**	**58.6**	**58.5**	**54.2**	**46.1**
#轿　车	Sedan Cars	10.0	12.0	19.7	20.6	27.7	30.3	34.8	34.9	50.6	66.6	26.2	39.4	37.9	32.0	26.9
旧　车	**Second-hand Vehicles**	**6.6**	**8.3**	**11.5**	**14.3**	**19.8**	**32.3**	**35.5**	**38.5**	**44.6**	**51.6**	**39.7**	**69.9**	**69.7**	**73.3**	**68.7**
#轿　车	Sedan Cars	1.4	3.0	5.6	6.6	10.2	15.9	17.9	19.5	19.9	25.8	22.8	43.8	42.6	42.2	42.2

资料来源：北京市工商行政管理局。
Source: Beijing Administration For Industry & Commerce.

14-9 限额以上住宿和餐饮业经营情况(2015年)
STATISTICS FOR ACCOMMODATION AND RESTAURANTS ABOVE DESIGNATED SIZE (2015)

项目	Item	合计 Total	住宿业 Accommodation Industry	餐饮业 Catering Industry
客房数 (间)	**Number of Rooms (room)**	**234894**	**228672**	**6222**
床位数 (个)	**Number of Beds (unit)**	**387033**	**376212**	**10821**
餐位数 (位)	**Number of Tables (table)**	**1389356**	**336986**	**1052370**
营业额 (万元)	**Turnover (10000 yuan)**	**9739279**	**4271088**	**5468191**
客房收入	Income from Rooms	2336571	2299671	36900
餐费收入	Income from Money	6405270	1169783	5235488
商品销售额	Sales of Commodities	115180	43012	72168
其他收入	Other Incomes	882258	758622	123636

注：本表统计范围为限额以上住宿和餐饮业法人单位、产业活动单位和个体经营户。
Note:This table covers legal entities in accommodation and restaurants above designated size, activity entities and individual entities .

14-10 限额以上批发和零售企业财务状况(2015年)

单位：万元

项　目	Item	企业单位个数(个) Number of Enterprises (unit)	资产总计 Total Assets	流动资产合计 Total Current Assets
合　计	**Total**	**6216**	**361283997**	**261767766**
按隶属关系分	**By Affiliation**			
中　央	Central	449	150086690	100463703
地　方	Local	5767	211197307	161304064
按企业登记注册类型分	**By Registration Type**			
内　资	Domestically-invested Enterprises	5726	287773959	205039134
国　有	State-owned Enterprises	229	30046615	22083394
集　体	Collectively-owned Enterprises	65	1226933	749285
股份合作	Joint-equity Cooperative Enterprises	45	163251	109737
联　营	Associate Enterprises	4	18914	17998
有限责任公司	Limited Liability Companies	2221	184583842	135243699
股份有限公司	Companies Limited by Shares	119	43317070	22747614
私　营	Private Enterprises	3042	28416623	24087091
其　他	Other	***	***	***
港澳台商投资	Hong Kong, Macao and Taiwan-invested Enterprises	181	15083311	11612712
外商投资	Foreign-invested Enterprises	309	58426727	45115921
按国民经济行业分	**By Sector**			
批发业	**Wholesale**	**4256**	**319162344**	**231035868**
农、林、牧产品批发	Wholesale of Agriculture, Forestry and Animal Production and Hunting Products	91	17499288	8434519
食品、饮料及烟草制品批发	Wholesale of Foods, Beverage and Tobaccos	335	14325562	11166755
纺织、服装及家庭日用品批发	Wholesale of Textile, Clothes and Household Commodities	370	16285984	12240172
文化、体育用品及器材批发	Wholesale of Cultural and Sports Goods and Equipment	187	9264883	6486427
医药及医疗器材批发	Wholesale of Medicine and Medical Devices	572	14024906	10999435
矿产品、建材及化工产品批发	Wholesale of Mineral Products, Building Materials, and Chemical Products	1364	137863431	97663778
机械设备、五金交电及电子产品批发	Wholesale of Mechanical Equipment, Hardware and Electronic Products	1189	84172085	64300338
贸易经纪与代理	Trade Broker and Agent	68	16940227	14843074
其他批发	Others	80	8785979	4901370
零售业	**Retail**	**1960**	**42121653**	**30731898**
综合零售	Integrated Retail	207	13051155	8007099
食品、饮料及烟草制品专门零售	Special Retails of Foods, Beverage and Tobacoos	88	956921	717483
纺织、服装及日用品专门零售	Special Retail of Textile, Clothing and Domestic Commodities	155	1779466	1397244
文化、体育用品及器材专门零售	Special Retail of Cultural and Sports Goods and Equipment	135	3382424	2714237
医药及医疗器材专门零售	Special Retail of Medicine and Medical Devices	97	3160557	1804343
汽车、摩托车、燃料及零配件专门零售	Special Retail of Automobiles, Motorcycles, Fuels and Their Accessories	785	9767267	7631457
家用电器及电子产品专门零售	Special Retail of Household Electrical Appliances and Electronic Products	291	7979962	6824900
五金、家具及室内装修材料专门零售	Special Retail of Hardware, Furniture and Indoor Decoration Materials	66	550096	417423
货摊、无店铺及其他零售业	Stand Retail, Retail Without Shops and Other Retail	136	1493806	1217713
按规模划分	**By Size**			
#大中型企业	Medium-and Large-sized Enterprises	3096	308850840	220146889

注：1. 限额以上批发和零售企业是指年主营业务收入2000万元及以上批发业和年主营业务收入500万元及以上的零售业法人企业。
2. 行业划分执行2011年国民经济行业分类标准(GB/T 4754-2011)。
3. 自2011年开始，大中型企业划分标准执行国家统计局《关于统计上大中小微型企业划分办法》(国统字[2011]75号)(下同)。

FINANCIAL STATUS OF WHOLESALE AND RETAIL ENTERPRISES ABOVE DESIGNATED SIZE (2015)

(10000 yuan)

资产负债 Assets and Liabilities							
#应收账款 Accounts Receivable	固定资产合计 Total Fixed Assets	固定资产原价 Total Original Value of Fixed Assets	负债合计 Total Liabilities	#流动负债合计 Total Current Liabilities	#应付账款 Accounts Payable	所有者权益合计 Total Owner's Equity	#实收资本 Paid-up Capital
44948753	**9778884**	**15813337**	**257995921**	**223826076**	**58579057**	**103288075**	**53958122**
20055788	2378533	3757488	107780381	91062092	19924815	42306309	22919299
24892966	7400351	12055850	150215540	132763984	38654242	60981766	31038823
38198034	8176744	12671388	212886769	181057397	44791976	74887189	43587792
3658361	889476	1382688	20086169	17378459	2894778	9960447	4107939
221453	99461	157720	979886	753100	292846	247047	78036
14417	33812	45621	134689	134173	21016	28562	35941
1457	916	1914	16878	16878	12252	2035	1373
24915141	5330022	7956578	143559797	124549925	32813858	41024044	29967309
2957713	1031962	1816563	25573881	16578033	2780028	17743189	5349426
6429380	790701	1309911	22534114	21645473	5977036	5882509	4047769
***	***	***	***	***	***	***	***
1709625	515489	862459	10654127	9780507	4107265	4429184	2673588
5041095	1086651	2279490	34455025	32988173	9679816	23971702	7696742
41926723	**6535935**	**10301774**	**225828161**	**193934158**	**51825200**	**93334183**	**47840059**
553639	266984	378148	11125592	8963772	1031184	6373696	2758300
1322763	503592	833206	10629720	10200919	2689234	3695843	1884511
1289758	442568	632770	10500678	10155693	4131610	5785306	2957211
1266366	273922	462552	6305809	4619146	749767	2959074	1505103
4174057	278131	529427	9909694	9302221	4245774	4115212	1767006
17224404	3064269	4471485	100391188	82181661	20279774	37472243	24447876
9816486	1450158	2614348	54973625	50480446	12571041	29198461	10486307
5194727	163574	236672	14211545	13632822	5245680	2728682	1620460
1084524	92738	143165	7780311	4397478	881138	1005667	413285
3022030	**3242949**	**5511563**	**32167760**	**29891918**	**6753857**	**9953893**	**6118063**
360776	1623214	2736748	9304860	7826818	1877731	3746295	1879436
34506	145978	248614	471659	460668	144180	485261	158165
307377	132119	243455	1516784	1362371	618351	262682	410834
150127	139282	198863	2426101	2266333	637461	956322	366928
451950	32994	66532	2617330	2516680	464074	543228	184815
393268	955856	1620914	7799420	7550208	592239	1967847	1781603
1048264	84686	169125	5230514	5161289	1007979	2749448	833626
97066	76278	127330	476592	462785	75167	73504	144384
178698	52543	99984	2324499	2284764	1336676	-830694	358273
38471537	7656264	12950142	218129564	188909073	49864701	90721276	42078698

Note: a) Wholesale and retail enterprises above designated size refer to wholesale enterprises with an annual main business income of RMB 20 million or above and retail enterprises of RMB 5 million or above.

b) Sectors in this table are classified in accordance with the Standard for Classification of National Economic Sectors 2011 (GB/T 4754-2011).

c) Since 2011, Division standards of medium and large-sized enterprises complies with Statistical Division Standards of Micro, Small, Medium and Large-sized Enterprises issued by National Bureau of Statistics (G.T.Z. [2011] No. 75) (the same below).

14-10 续表

单位：万元

项目	Item	损益 营业收入 Business Income	#主营业务收入 Main Business Income	营业成本 Business Cost	#主营业务成本 Main Business Cost
合计	**Total**	**449009712**	**439639699**	**413826075**	**407726832**
按隶属关系分	**By Affiliation**				
中央	Central	154681885	149855448	147755321	143450397
地方	Local	294327827	289784250	266070754	264276436
按企业登记注册类型分	**By Registration Type**				
内资	Domestically-invested Enterprises	338177015	330914433	317723240	312649379
国有	State-owned Enterprises	36945547	36784918	34810748	34779226
集体	Collectively-owned Enterprises	1365867	1327128	1295177	1283535
股份合作	Joint-equity Cooperative Enterprises	403838	402403	382035	381848
联营	Associate Enterprises	41849	41823	37685	37685
有限责任公司	Limited Liability Companies	223602666	217466918	211090069	206268532
股份有限公司	Companies Limited by Shares	30094414	29541700	27998799	27880283
私营	Private Enterprises	45719907	45346616	42105841	42015382
其他	Other	***	***	***	***
港澳台商投资	Hong Kong, Macao and Taiwan-invested Enterprises	33196151	32960100	30040016	29985573
外商投资	Foreign-invested Enterprises	77636546	75765166	66062820	65091881
按国民经济行业分	**By Sector**				
批发业	**Wholesale**	**377106016**	**369482410**	**350884999**	**345059974**
农、林、牧产品批发	Wholesale of Agriculture, Forestry and Animal Poduction and Hunting Products	10862682	10790679	10393419	10375226
食品、饮料及烟草制品批发	Wholesale of Foods, Beverage and Tobaccos	19271781	18483035	16488286	15826378
纺织、服装及家庭日用品批发	Wholesale of Textile, Clothes and Household Commodities	32614520	32374073	29088067	28946484
文化、体育用品及器材批发	Wholesale of Cultural and Sports Goods and Equipment	12149474	11974354	11167668	11092882
医药及医疗器材批发	Wholesale of Medicine and Medical Devices	18599632	18325788	16133234	16044910
矿产品、建材及化工产品批发	Wholesale of Mineral Products, Building Materials, and Chemical Products	168096030	167373857	163563608	163031952
机械设备、五金交电及电子产品批发	Wholesale of Mechanical Equipment, Hardware and Electronic Products	104024618	98822639	93716803	89416517
贸易经纪与代理	Trade Broker and Agent	5882099	5749917	5289268	5284799
其他批发	Others	5605180	5588068	5044646	5040825
零售业	**Retail**	**71903697**	**70157289**	**62941077**	**62666859**
综合零售	Integrated Retail	15467709	14494513	12371870	12331818
食品、饮料及烟草制品专门零售	Special Retails of Foods, Beverage and Tobacoos	1262896	1230307	813124	803947
纺织、服装及日用品专门零售	Special Retail of Textile, Clothing and Domestic Commodities	2653458	2591037	1691072	1686105
文化、体育用品及器材专门零售	Special Retail of Cultural and Sports Goods and Equipment	2824807	2781051	2353728	2340598
医药及医疗器材专门零售	Special Retail of Medicine and Medical Devices	2287109	2261405	2037194	2026911
汽车、摩托车、燃料及零配件专门零售	Special Retail of Automobiles, Motorcycles, Fuels and Their Accessories	22916513	22525167	21304838	21161774
家用电器及电子产品专门零售	Special Retail of Household Electrical Appliances and Electronic Products	20756103	20623641	19259428	19220378
五金、家具及室内装修材料专门零售	Special Retail of Hardware, Furniture and Indoor Decoration Materials	660684	647233	410268	405906
货摊、无店铺及其他零售业	Stand Retail, Retail Without Shops and Other Retail	3074419	3002936	2699556	2689424
按规模划分	**By Size**				
#大中型企业	Medium-and Large-sized Enterprises	392752547	383927211	360038694	354296800

注：应交税金合计包括应交增值税、应交所得税、营业税金及附加和管理费用中的税金。

14-10 Continued

(10000 yuan)

Profits and Losses				应交税金合计 Total Tax Payable				
销售费用 Sales Expenses	管理费用 Management Expenses	财务费用 Financial Expenses	利润总额 Total Profits		#营业税金及附加 Business Tax and Surcharges	#主营业务税金及附加 Business Tax and Surtax	#应交增值税 Value Added Tax Payable	#应交所得税 Income Tax Payable
18870035	**8346627**	**3131100**	**8740829**	**7563239**	**1064514**	**1011526**	**4159129**	**2339596**
2503762	1636557	1174569	3183897	1921405	317886	303405	806028	797490
16366273	6710070	1956530	5556932	5811974	746628	708121	3353101	1542106
10053998	5119276	2954892	4136489	4365078	763430	717022	2286724	1314924
522967	445363	234497	1100481	759634	268804	265628	232144	258687
29827	31030	17903	-1073	8648	2467	1842	5402	779
9419	13062	2911	-2007	3644	446	413	2806	392
2818	927	88	270	1535	123	122	1337	67
6286679	2884404	2100738	2217900	2679268	322176	302144	1351144	901702
1181377	510020	362285	662429	339750	88648	69750	207834	43267
2020410	1234460	236471	158689	692091	80765	77123	486057	110031
***	***	***	***	***	***	***	***	***
2223817	684902	210632	118930	599328	73985	69795	424056	101287
6592221	2542449	-34424	4485411	2598834	227099	224710	1448349	923385
13090652	**6124584**	**2805023**	**7198713**	**5991765**	**784933**	**757231**	**3174828**	**2032005**
148922	203195	211669	448311	99880	11480	10021	47237	41162
1756041	373280	87717	823551	825167	290681	289865	393072	141414
2457696	708531	39073	508314	599312	59460	58631	421589	118263
408244	241876	99193	332743	247896	20973	20799	137034	89888
1240018	529856	91829	659760	546703	47890	46817	350595	148217
1768843	1229134	1710527	425335	943342	133434	118582	440659	369248
5000606	2586701	222509	3626674	2487809	197050	189066	1306260	984499
142974	140090	287112	106928	127124	16941	16652	35046	75138
167309	111921	55395	267098	114533	7024	6799	43335	64175
5779383	**2222043**	**326077**	**1542116**	**1571474**	**279581**	**254295**	**984302**	**307591**
1931459	742216	101208	456378	520006	135230	118108	261807	122970
311213	80044	3897	47589	110525	10197	9798	77825	22504
729488	185886	13128	17562	169319	22613	20979	132064	14642
262568	140099	20520	55085	64514	11151	10791	36995	16368
132913	66141	66523	44911	49892	5726	5465	40892	3273
809531	520194	145112	116393	323902	40587	36338	225501	57813
1077981	298212	-40711	911485	227689	38905	38356	137009	51774
138801	51278	3263	49247	47928	8499	7904	25837	13593
385429	137972	13138	-156534	57699	6673	6555	46372	4654
17680800	7555819	2362482	8786809	7165749	985364	933974	3846525	2109427

Note: Total tax payable mainly includes VAT payable, income tax payable, business tax and surtax, and tax in management expenses.

14-11 限额以上住宿业企业财务状况(2015年)

单位：万元

项　目	Item	企业单位个数(个) Number of Enterprises (unit)	资产总计 Total Assets	流动资产合计 Total Current Assets
合　计	**Total**	**984**	**13457707**	**4763144**
按隶属关系分	**By Affiliation**			
中　央	Central	170	2042311	606808
地　方	Local	814	11415395	4156336
按登记注册类型分	**By Registration Type**			
内　资	Domestically-invested Enterprises	917	9530901	3443411
国　有	State-owned Enterprises	213	2569427	619819
集　体	Collectively-owned Enterprises	36	245772	59495
股份合作	Joint-equity Cooperative Enterprises	22	87896	31954
联　营	Associate Enterprises	***	***	***
有限责任公司	Limited Liability Companies	370	5285689	1969238
股份有限公司	Companies Limited by Shares	7	324936	157372
私　营	Private Enterprises	267	1012741	601683
港澳台商投资	Hong Kong, Macao and Taiwan-invested Enterprises	38	2445399	815314
外商投资	Foreign-invested Enterprises	29	1481407	504420
按行业类别分	**By Sector Type**			
旅游饭店	Tourism Hotels	591	11088076	3662705
一般旅馆	Common Inns	366	1788948	744243
其他住宿服务	Other Accomodation Services	27	580682	356196

注：1. 限额以上住宿业企业是指年主营业务收入200万元及以上的住宿业法人企业。
2. 应交税金合计包括应交增值税、应交所得税、营业税金及附加和管理费用中的税金。

FINANCIAL STATUS OF ACCOMMODATION ENTERPRISES ABOVE DESIGNATED SIZE (2015)

(10000 yuan)

资产负债 Assets and Liabilities							
#应收账款 Accounts Receivable	固定资产合计 Total Fixed Assets	固定资产原价 Total Original Value of Fixed Assets	负债合计 Total Liabilities	#流动负债合计 Total Current Liabilities	#应付账款 Accounts Payable	所有者权益合计 Total Owner's Equity	#实收资本 Paid-up Capital
89074	**5033045**	**8540209**	**10174554**	**6931286**	**434088**	**3283153**	**3893213**
27008	1027223	1861035	1127904	818507	56062	914408	836995
62067	4005822	6679174	9046650	6112779	378026	2368745	3056217
60664	3799721	5817918	7799499	5648076	359095	1731402	2655434
23706	1473918	2013938	1808693	1185710	59260	760734	860821
1284	158355	268951	168579	74578	6835	77194	29289
1932	24013	59734	69374	54423	4198	18523	12504
***	***	***	***	***	***	***	***
-7483	1853600	3023580	4373139	3288573	173607	912551	1500896
2143	67825	111741	292629	207514	19589	32307	42830
39631	221482	335369	1079311	829603	94886	-66570	205173
20446	805508	1737072	1600452	920970	51958	844946	879987
7964	427815	985219	774602	362240	23034	706805	357791
25017	4617488	7849511	8524890	5846871	323532	2563186	3123973
60915	311219	530589	1098759	947444	100110	690189	697258
3142	104338	160109	550905	136971	10446	29777	71982

Note: a) Accommodation enterprises above designated size refer to corporate enterprises with an annual main business income of RMB 2 million or above.

b) Total tax payable mainly includes VAT payable, income tax payable, business tax and surtax, and tax in management expenses.

14-11 续表

单位：万元

项目	Item	损益 营业收入 Business Income	#主营业务收入 Main Business Income	营业成本 Business Cost	#主营业务成本 Main Business Cost
合计	**Total**	**3473702**	**3436774**	**921887**	**915402**
按隶属关系分	**By Affiliation**				
中央	Central	702139	697275	199215	197868
地方	Local	2771563	2739498	722672	717534
按登记注册类型分	**By Registration Type**				
内资	Domestically-invested Enterprises	2498645	2465269	646952	641459
国有	State-owned Enterprises	705961	697989	193689	192224
集体	Collectively-owned Enterprises	89991	89663	13657	13643
股份合作	Joint-equity Cooperative Enterprises	33106	33062	9637	9635
联营	Associate Enterprises	***	***	***	***
有限责任公司	Limited Liability Companies	1267481	1245863	313275	309572
股份有限公司	Companies Limited by Shares	38238	36488	26092	26091
私营	Private Enterprises	358965	357301	89248	88939
港澳台商投资	Hong Kong, Macao and Taiwan-invested Enterprises	644076	643021	202171	201991
外商投资	Foreign-invested Enterprises	330980	328483	72763	71952
按行业类别分	**By Sector Type**				
旅游饭店	Tourism Hotels	2763533	2740277	722444	718448
一般旅馆	Common Inns	616224	603084	182731	180270
其他住宿服务	Other Accomodation Services	93945	93413	16712	16684

14-11 continued

(10000 yuan)

Profits and Losses				应交税金合计				
销售费用 Sales Expenses	管理费用 Management Expenses	财务费用 Financial Expenses	利润总额 Total Profits	Total Tax Payable	营业税金及附加 Business Tax and Surcharges	#主营业务税金及附加 Main Business Tax and Surtax	#应交增值税 Value Added Tax Payable	#应交所得税 Income Tax Payable
1085531	**1214394**	**207756**	**-43715**	**329867**	**191314**	**190663**	**878**	**56628**
198957	253708	3353	18174	66160	38280	38158	679	12077
886574	960685	204403	-61890	263708	153034	152504	199	44551
879300	902680	134378	-124640	221173	137267	136616	1285	27675
222730	281742	19744	-8946	61537	38315	38050	864	8480
42868	25735	149	2905	8825	5020	5016	11	1298
11631	9936	344	26	2541	1815	1815	23	362
***	***	***	***	***	***	***	***	***
442369	463665	90976	-83479	120617	69778	69447	445	15780
4940	7759	7127	-9192	3360	2147	2147	3	194
153723	111493	16025	-25782	23982	19882	19831	-60	1562
136614	200115	53260	39439	66308	35584	35584	526	14575
69617	111599	20118	41485	42386	18463	18463	-933	14378
852404	1006311	175456	-53374	273141	152261	151815	399	46762
205549	175891	12732	16860	49183	34144	33944	204	9097
27577	32192	19568	-7201	7543	4910	4903	275	769

14-12 限额以上餐饮业企业财务状况(2015年)

单位：万元

项目	Item	企业单位个数(个) Number of Enterprises (unit)	资产总计 Total Assets	流动资产合计 Total Current Assets
合计	**Total**	**1399**	**3953281**	**2315364**
按隶属关系分	**By Affiliation**			
中央	Central	11	82112	66392
地方	Local	1388	3871170	2248972
按登记注册类型分	**By Registration Type**			
内资	Domestically-invested Enterprises	1276	2784091	1735271
国有	State-owned Enterprises	27	46572	31624
集体	Collectively-owned Enterprises	16	11708	3717
股份合作	Joint-equity Cooperative Enterprise	23	21143	15968
有限责任公司	Limited Liability Companies	396	1201252	713278
股份有限公司	Companies Limited by Shares	15	473239	325798
私营	Private Enterprises	799	1030177	644887
港澳台商投资	Hong Kong, Macao and Taiwan-invested Enterprises	55	568079	384667
外商投资	Foreign-invested Enterprises	68	601111	195426
按行业类别分	**By Sector Type**			
正餐	Dinner	1206	2985909	1785273
快餐	Fast Food	111	674095	320156
饮料及冷饮	Beverage and Cold Drink	24	136935	78398
其他餐饮业	Others	58	156343	131536

注：1. 限额以上餐饮业企业是指年主营业务收入200万元及以上的餐饮业法人企业。
2. 应交税金合计包括应交增值税、应交所得税、营业税金及附加和管理费用中的税金。

FINANCIAL STATUS OF RESTAURANTS ENTERPRISES ABOVE DESIGNATED SIZE (2015)

(10000 yuan)

资产负债 Assets and Liabilities							
#应收账款 Accounts Receiv-able	固定资产合计 Total Fixed Assets	固定资产原价 Total Original Value of Fixed Assets	负债合计 Total Liabilities	#流动负债合计 Total Current Liabilities	#应付账款 Accounts Payable	所有者权益合计 Total Owner's Equity	#实收资本 Paid-up Capital
125476	**575910**	**1192863**	**3316488**	**3116297**	**605944**	**636794**	**764069**
5712	8888	18897	56856	56848	17551	25256	9342
119764	567023	1173966	3259632	3059449	588393	611537	754727
106279	383356	795772	2527261	2373465	485490	256830	491381
1735	6931	18299	30334	24365	4565	16238	7494
751	3702	6452	12017	11858	983	-309	626
509	1736	5245	20068	18953	1820	1075	1359
45815	204236	398233	1116048	1039969	190947	85205	248945
3408	51300	101380	301996	300798	98604	171243	48589
54060	115451	266163	1046798	977522	188570	-16621	184368
6350	65405	126487	329149	308978	49239	238930	123492
12847	127149	270604	460078	433854	71216	141034	149196
92888	420076	863939	2629477	2468968	482359	356432	564199
14965	125328	265797	425092	400777	91921	249003	152686
4870	16868	33689	90528	85418	4370	46406	18143
12753	13639	29437	171391	161134	27293	-15048	29041

Note: a) Restaurants enterprises above designated size refer to corporate enterprises with an annual main business income of RMB 2 million or above.
b)Total tax payable mainly includes VAT payable, income tax payable, business tax and surtax, and tax in management expenses.

14-12 续表

单位：万元

项目	Item	损益			
		营业收入 Business Income	#主营业务收入 Main Business Income	营业成本 Business Cost	#主营业务成本 Main Business Cost
合计	**Total**	**5453105**	**5394774**	**2241702**	**2222225**
按隶属关系分	**By Affiliation**				
中央	Central	95799	91457	39909	36698
地方	Local	5357306	5303318	2201793	2185527
按登记注册类型分	**By Registration Type**				
内资	Domestically-invested Enterprises	3265699	3223226	1366083	1354310
国有	State-owned Enterprises	56838	49872	26024	22813
集体	Collectively-owned Enterprises	16408	16387	8982	8982
股份合作	Joint-equity Cooperative Enterprise	28774	28700	14901	14901
有限责任公司	Limited Liability Companies	1465604	1446161	574386	567355
股份有限公司	Companies Limited by Shares	140018	134255	44723	44522
私营	Private Enterprises	1558058	1547852	697067	695737
港澳台商投资	Hong Kong, Macao and Taiwan-invested Enterprises	792490	791325	262746	262161
外商投资	Foreign-invested Enterprises	1394917	1380223	612873	605754
按行业类别分	**By Sector Type**				
正餐	Dinner	3525063	3490816	1461740	1450419
快餐	Fast Food	1452473	1429400	577013	569148
饮料及冷饮	Beverage and Cold Drink	228060	227464	61419	61419
其他餐饮业	Others	247509	247094	141531	141239

14-12 continued

(10000 yuan)

Profits and Losses				应交税金合计 Total Tax Payable				
销售费用 Sales Expenses	管理费用 Management Expenses	财务费用 Financial Expenses	利润总额 Total Profits		#营业税金及附加 Business Tax and Surtax	#主营业务税金及附加 Main Business Tax and Surcharges	#应交增值税 Value Added Tax Payable	#应交所得税 Income Tax Payable
2225883	**645152**	**50825**	**24599**	**353079**	**287762**	**286353**	**11104**	**45924**
24778	21957	-409	4577	6982	5267	4992	91	1527
2201105	623195	51235	20022	346097	282495	281362	11013	44397
1308200	431137	44016	-36219	210998	175313	174013	4956	23546
17857	9513	77	1854	4115	2984	2598	248	597
4660	1912	58	27	1026	922	922		93
10802	1647	131	-298	1739	1592	1592	9	68
610371	198144	13382	-1268	98352	78446	77887	2600	14186
61262	20468	11674	5287	11266	7013	7013	458	2892
603249	199454	18693	-41822	94500	84356	84002	1643	5710
366843	74160	3400	50075	59220	41292	41292	2014	15336
550840	139856	3409	10743	82861	71157	71049	4134	7042
1405518	465398	43404	-20235	228498	191740	191041	3525	26057
631144	137674	4802	29005	90028	73449	72741	4378	11406
114252	19143	740	20106	20155	11771	11770	814	7515
74969	22937	1879	-4277	14398	10803	10802	2388	946

14-13 连锁企业基本情况(2001-2015年)
STATISTICS FOR CHAIN ENTERPRISES (2001-2015)

年份 Year	连锁总店(个) Number of General Chain Stores (unit)	门店总数(个) Number of Chain Stores (unit)	从业人员年末人数(人) Number of Employed Persons Year-end (person)	营业面积(平方米) Operational Area (sq.m)	商品销售总额(营业额)(万元) Total Sales of Commodities (Turnover) (10000 yuan)	#零售额 Retail Sales
2001	129	2123	139470	1605808	4831168	2186540
2002	146	3523	109089	2356266	6621975	6487185
2003	153	4519	132030	3405562	8404232	7601221
2004	196	5432	153942	3783507	8603560	8337829
2005	188	5973	166598	4376383	10612658	9507168
2006	205	6730	170007	5546003	11229026	9514297
2007	210	7645	185114	6677266	13890913	11573838
2008	240	8611	223954	6745802	15720473	12954839
2009	240	8928	218024	6995047	17366414	13816796
2010	234	9299	228292	7268786	21329783	16255496
2011	233	9845	280798	7953891	25742536	19507890
2012	220	10014	287975	8339674	26758403	20140433
2013	241	11111	299445	9026207	27834646	21495798
2014	243	11433	279567	9252645	28173728	21100845
2015	238	11942	279596	9238023	30453838	24508274

14-14 连锁企业基本情况(按登记注册类型、经营业态分)(2015年)

STATISTICS FOR CHAIN ENTERPRISES (BY REGISTRATION TYPE OF ENTERPRISES AND OPERATION FORMS) (2015)

项目	Item	门店总数(个) Number of Chain Stores (unit)	从业人员年末人数(人) Year-end Employed Persons (person)	营业面积(平方米) Operational Area (sq.m)	商品销售额(营业额)(万元) Total sales of Commodities (10000 yuan)	#零售额 Retail Sales
合　计	**Total**	**11942**	**279596**	**9238023**	**30453838**	**24508274**
按登记注册类型分	**By Registration Type**					
内　资	Domestically-invested Enterprises	7745	177046	7031135	21960670	16469716
国　有	State-owned Enterprises	79	1414	20296	50629	44156
集　体	Collectively-owned Enterprises	296	1087	86590	91926	86242
股份合作	Joint-equity Cooperative Enterprises	6	158	4310	2979	2979
联　营	Associate Enterprises	5	30	928	836	836
有限责任公司	Limited Liability Companies	3596	91367	3528258	9177626	7260789
股份有限公司	Companies Limited by Shares	1742	51623	2657204	11413409	7891775
私　营	Private Enterprises	2021	31367	733549	1223265	1182941
其　他	Others					
港、澳、台商投资	Hong Kong, Macao and Taiwan-invested Enterprises	1760	33662	526562	1314098	1109499
外商投资	Foreign-invested Enterprises	2437	68888	1680326	7179071	6929058
按经营业态分	**By Operation Form**					
零售业态	**Retail**	**7577**	**156584**	**7481651**	**27332756**	**21510312**
便利店	Convenient Stores	1064	5731	133342	309119	302371
折扣店	Discount Stores	8	659	89792	147485	147485
超　市	Supermarkets	1424	50325	2169146	5237771	3654965
大型超市	Large Supermarkets	232	27435	1297506	2652804	2453472
仓储会员店	Warehouse Club Stores	7	2235	134877	342486	342486
百货店	Department Stores	68	14219	1650907	2925088	2921855
专业店	Specialty Stores	2272	28143	1195532	5648562	4659983
加油站	Gas Stations	702	6600	356521	5889517	2975273
专卖店	Boutiques	1789	20237	370516	3954530	3827029
家居建材商店	Furniture and Building Material Stores	11	1000	83512	225395	225395
餐饮业态	**Chain Catering Enterprises**	**4239**	**119584**	**1748606**	**3019896**	**2994537**
中式正餐	Chinese Dinner	746	51548	973813	1079949	1069831
中式快餐	Chinese Fast Food	1250	19316	282740	529029	518139
外国风味正餐	Exotic Dinner	682	16765	59105	459573	457269
外国风味快餐	Exotic Fast Food	1039	26788	344417	734698	732651
茶　馆	Teahouses	9	40	910	291	291
咖啡店	Cafés	485	4547	84564	203065	203065
其　他	Others	28	580	3057	13291	13291
住宿业态	**Chain Accomodation Enterprises**	**126**	**3428**	**7766**	**101186**	**3425**
旅游饭店	Tourism Hotels	59	1770	3196	52277	514
一般旅馆	Common Inns	67	1658	4570	48910	2911

14-15 商品交易市场基本情况(2015年)
STATISTICS FOR COMMODITY TRANSACTION MARKETS (2015)

项 目	Item	市场数量(个) Number of Markets (unit)	总摊位数(个) Number of Booths (unit)	成交额(亿元) Turnover (100 million yuan)
全市合计	**Total**	**719**	**243883**	**3604.7**
按经营方式分	**By Business Practice**			
批发市场	Wholesale Market	120	87130	2212.6
零售市场	Retail Market	599	156753	1392.1
按经营环境分	**By Business Environment**			
露天式	Open-air	138	54741	1497.8
封闭式	Closed	548	174052	1772.5
其 他	Others	33	15090	334.4
按市场地理环境分	**By Market Place**			
二环以内	Inside the Second Ring Road	44	17412	57.4
二环至三环以内	Between the Second and Third Ring Road	91	31987	81.0
三环到四环以内	Between the Third and Fourth Ring Road	108	48658	1249.6
四环至五环以内	Between the Fourth and Fifth Ring Road	94	34065	1259.6
五环至六环以内	Between the Fifth and Sixth Ring Road	167	43959	642.5
六环以外	Outside the Sixth Ring Road	215	67802	314.6
按功能区分	**By Functional Area**			
首都功能核心区	Core Functional Area of the Capital	73	32660	108.0
城市功能拓展区	Urban Function Extension Area	309	115080	2738.9
城市发展新区	New Area of Urban Development	242	68181	662.6
生态涵养发展区	Ecological Conservation Area	95	27962	95.1

14-16 亿元及以上商品交易市场基本情况(2015年)
STATISTICS FOR COMMODITY TRANSACTION MARKETS OVER RMB 100 MILLION (2015)

项 目	Item	市场数量(个) Number of markets (unit)	总摊位数(个) Number of Booths (unit)	#出租摊位数 Number of Booths on Lease	成交额(亿元) Turnover (100 million yuan)
全市合计	**Total**	**125**	**113312**	**97157**	**3482.5**
按经营方式分	**By Business Practice**				
批发市场	Wholesale Market	56	67769	54634	2191.6
零售市场	Retail Market	69	45543	42523	1290.9
按经营环境分	**By Business Environment**				
露天式	Open-air	19	21156	11495	1473.0
封闭式	Closed	99	82312	76347	1680.6
其 他	Others	7	9844	9315	328.9
按市场地理环境分	**By Market Place**				
二环以内	Inside the Second Ring Road	7	12425	11567	50.5
二环至三环以内	Between the Second and Third Ring Road	11	10138	9984	63.4
三环到四环以内	Between the Third and Fourth Ring Road	32	31508	30146	1227.6
四环至五环以内	Between the Fourth and Fifth Ring Road	21	18452	16701	1246.1
五环至六环以内	Between the Fifth and Sixth Ring Road	25	15511	14298	615.6
六环以外	Outside the Sixth Ring Road	29	25278	14461	279.3
按功能区分	**By Functional Area**				
首都功能核心区	Core Functional Area of the Capital	13	20332	19372	96.4
城市功能拓展区	Urban Function Extension Area	69	60930	56948	2685.8
城市发展新区	New Area of Urban Development	26	20919	13199	620.7
生态涵养发展区	Ecological Conservation Area	17	11131	7638	79.6

14-17 商品交易市场经营情况(2015年)
STATISTICS FOR COMMODITY TRANSACTION MARKETS (2015)

项目	Item	市场数量(个) Number of Markets (unit)	出租摊位数(个) Number of Booths (unit)	营业面积(万平方米) Operating Area (10,000 sq.m)	成交额(亿元) Turnover (100 million yuan)
合 计	**Total**	**719**	**201530**	**1221.8**	**3604.7**
综合市场	**Comprehensive Markets**	**333**	**93005**	**539.0**	**1821.0**
生产资料综合市场	Comprehensive Market of Capital Goods	1	310	1.3	0.1
工业消费品综合市场	Comprehensive Market of Industrial Consumer Goods	56	24356	64.9	94.8
农产品综合市场	Comprehensive Market of Agricultural Products	193	46526	344.8	1530.0
其他综合市场	Other Comprehensive Markets	83	21813	128.2	196.1
专业市场	**Specialized Markets**	**386**	**108525**	**682.6**	**1783.7**
生产资料市场	**Market of Capital Goods**	**51**	**8973**	**84.1**	**77.8**
木材市场	Timber Market	1	60	6.0	…
建材市场	Building Material Market	44	7948	61.0	54.0
化工材料及制品市场	Chemical Material and Product Market				
金属材料市场	Metal Material Market	4	433	11.7	4.0
机械设备市场	Mechanical Equipment Market	1	262	3.3	9.2
其他生产资料市场	Other Markets of Capital Goods	1	270	2.1	10.6
农产品市场	**Agricultural Product Market**	**64**	**13681**	**90.3**	**344.6**
粮油市场	Foodstuff and Oil Market	7	2083	19.0	185.6
肉禽蛋市场	Meat, Poultry and Egg Market	4	729	1.2	5.7
水产品市场	Aquatic Product Market	4	2128	8.2	101.4
蔬菜市场	Vegetable Market	24	3349	21.6	17.8
干鲜果品市场	Dried and Fresh Fruit Market	4	588	26.8	15.4
其他农产品市场	Other Agricultural Product Markets	21	4804	13.5	18.7
食品、饮料及烟酒市场	**Food, Beverage, Tobacco and Wine Market**	**13**	**1730**	**8.5**	**6.1**
食品饮料市场	Food and Beverage Market	3	213	0.3	0.5
茶叶市场	Tea Market	6	994	6.1	5.4
其他食品饮料及烟酒市场	Other Food, Beverage, Tobacco and Wine Markets	4	523	2.1	0.1
纺织、服装、鞋帽市场	**Textile, Costume, Shoe and Hat Market**	**70**	**36278**	**111.3**	**63.2**
布料及纺织品市场	Cloth and Textile Market	6	1717	6.2	2.5
服装市场	Clothing Market	53	30037	88.8	52.8
鞋帽市场	Shoe and Hat Market	2	1020	6.2	1.2
其他纺织服装鞋帽市场	Other Textile, Costume, Shoe and Cap Markets	9	3504	10.1	6.7
日用品及文化用品市场	**Domestic Commodity and Cultural Article Market**	**13**	**5932**	**14.1**	**44.9**
小商品市场	Small Commodity Market	5	3793	4.9	25.5

14-17 续表 Continued

项　目	Item	市场数量(个) Number of Markets (unit)	出租摊位数(个) Number of Booths (unit)	营业面积(万平方米) Operating Area (10000 sq.m)	成交额(亿元) Turnover (100 million yuan)
文具市场	Stationary Market	1	828	4.3	15.7
图书、报刊杂志市场	Book, Newspaper, and Magazine Market	1	180	1.2	2.2
其他日用品及文化用品市场	Other Domestic Commodity and Cultural Article Market	6	1131	3.7	1.5
黄金、珠宝、玉器等首饰市场	**Market of Gold, Jewelry, and Jade**	**13**	**3205**	**13.1**	**17.2**
电器、通讯器材、电子设备市场	**Market of Electrical Appliances, Communication Devices, and Electronic Equipment**	**16**	**4437**	**11.7**	**67.8**
家电市场	Household Appliance Market	2	81	0.2	0.2
通讯器材市场	Communication Device Market	3	707	1.8	1.6
照相、摄像器材市场	Photographic and Camera Shooting Equipment Market	2	327	1.5	3.6
计算机及辅助设备市场	Computer and Supporting Equipment Market	6	2475	6.2	50.1
其他电器、通讯器材、电子设	Other Electrical Appliance, Communication Device	3	847	2.0	12.3
家具、五金及装饰材料市场	**Furniture, Hardware, and Decoration Material Market**	**72**	**15405**	**179.3**	**165.3**
家具市场	Furniture Market	32	6114	100.2	63.7
装饰材料市场	Decoration Materials Market	18	4819	46.0	69.3
灯具市场	Lamp and Lantern Market	4	719	9.8	2.7
五金材料市场	Hardware Market	12	2603	14.3	26.9
其他装修市场	Other Decoration Market	6	1150	9.1	2.7
汽车、摩托车及零配件市场	**Automobile, Autobike, and Part and Fitting Market**	**24**	**5831**	**107.4**	**978.0**
汽车市场	Automobile Market	10	1473	66.0	918.0
机动车零配件市场	Automobile Part and Fitting Market	14	4358	41.4	60.0
花、鸟、鱼、虫市场	**Flower, Bird, Fish and Insect Market**	**18**	**3855**	**14.1**	**5.3**
花卉市场	Flower Market	15	3243	10.3	4.7
观赏鱼市场	Fish Market	1	105	1.8	0.3
其他花鸟鱼虫市场	Other Flower, Bird, Fish and Insect Market	2	507	2.0	0.2
旧货市场	**Secondhand Goods Market**	**12**	**7071**	**13.6**	**7.0**
古玩、古董、字画市场	Curio, Antique, Calligraphy and Painting Market	5	1076	6.6	0.8
邮票、硬币市场	Stamp and Coin Market	2	933	0.8	0.8
其他旧货市场	Other Secondhand Goods Market	5	5062	6.2	5.4
其他专业市场	**Other Specialized Markets**	**20**	**2127**	**35.2**	**6.5**

14-18 北京消费者信心指数(2015年)
BEIJING CONSUMER CONFIDENCE INDEX (2015)

项　目	Item	一季度 First Quarter	二季度 Second Quarter	三季度 Third Quarter	四季度 Fourth Quarter
消费者信心指数	**Consumer Confidence Index**	**107.9**	**107.8**	**108.1**	**107.9**
消费者满意指数	**Consumer Satisfaction Index**	**108.7**	**109.0**	**109.5**	**109.8**
就业状况满意指数	Index of Satisfaction with Employment Status	122.9	122.2	123.1	123.3
家庭收入状况满意指数	Index of Satisfaction with Household Income Status	99.9	100.0	100.3	100.7
耐用消费品购买时机满意指数	Index of Satisfaction with Durable Consumer Goods	103.3	104.9	105.2	105.5
消费者预期指数	**Consumer Expectation Index**	**107.4**	**107.0**	**107.2**	**106.7**
就业状况预期指数	Index of Expectation for Employment Status	112.3	112.0	112.6	112.4
家庭收入状况预期指数	Index of Expectation for Household Income Status	102.4	102.0	101.8	100.9

主要统计指标解释

社会消费品零售总额 指企业（单位、个体户）通过交易直接售给个人、社会集团非生产、非经营用的实物商品金额，以及提供餐饮服务所取得的收入金额。个人包括城乡居民和入境人员，社会集团包括机关、社会团体、部队、学校、企事业单位、居委会或村委会等。

批发和零售业单位 指在流通环节从事商品批发活动和零售活动的单位。

商品购进额 指从本企业（单位）以外的单位和个人购进(包括从国外直接进口)作为转卖或加工后转卖的商品金额（含增值税）。本指标反映批发和零售业从国内外市场上购进商品的总量。

商品销售额 指对本企业以外的单位和个人出售的商品金额（包括售给本单位消费用的商品，含增值税）。本指标反映批发和零售业在国内市场上销售商品以及出口商品的总量。

期末商品库存额 对于批发和零售业法人企业和个体经营户，是指取得所有权的全部商品金额（含增值税）；对于批发和零售业产业活动单位，是指期末实际在库且归属法人具有所有权的全部商品金额（含增值税）。这个指标反映批发和零售业的商品库存情况，以及对市场商品供应的保证程度。

连锁总店（总部） 负责连锁企业资源（商号、商誉、经营模式、服务标准、管理模式等）的开发、配置、控制或使用等功能的企业核心管理机构。连锁经营是指经营同类商品或服务，使用统一商号的若干店铺，在同一总店（总部）的管理下，采取统一采购或特许经营等方式,实现规模效益的组织形式，包括直营连锁、特许连锁和自愿连锁三种形式。直营连锁是指连锁店铺由连锁公司全资或控股开设，在总部的直接控制下，开展统一经营的连锁经营形式；特许连锁是指拥有注册商标、企业标志、专利、专有技术等经营资源的企业（特许人），以合同形式将其拥有的经营资源许可其他经营者（被特许人）使用，被特许人按合同约定在统一的经营模式下开展经营，并向特许人支付特许经营费用的连锁经营形式；自愿连锁是指若干个店铺或企业自愿组合起来，在不改变各自资产所有权关系的情况下，以同一个品牌形象面对消费者，以共同进货为纽带开展的连锁经营形式。

连锁门店 在连锁企业经营管理的基础上，按照总店（总部）的指示和服务规范要求，承担日常销售业务的店铺，称连锁门店，包括直营店（控股店）和加盟店。

（1）直营店（控股店） 是指由连锁企业总部投资开设，按连锁经营管理模式，由总部统一管理的店铺。

（2）加盟店 是指在特许连锁中，被特许人获得特许人授权后，使用其商标、商号、经营模式、专利和专有技术等经营资源建立的店铺，也包括自愿连锁的成员店。

门店总数 指该连锁企业所拥有的全部门店（包括直营店和加盟店）数量。其中，总店（如果总公司有门店的话）作为一个直营店处理。此外，有的地区分出控股店，控股店按直营店统计。

餐饮业企业 指在一定场所，专门从事对食物进行现场烹饪、调制，并出售给顾客主要供现场消费服务活动的企业。如各种饭馆、中西餐厅、酒馆、茶馆和火车餐车、车站食堂、飞机场餐厅等。

住宿业企业 指有偿为顾客提供临时住宿服务活动的单位。如旅游饭店、宾馆、酒店和旅馆、旅店等。

商品交易市场 指经有关部门和组织批准设立，有固定场所、设施，有经营管理部门和监管人员，若干市场经营者入内，常年或实际开业三个月以上，集中、公开、独立地进行生活消费品、生产资料等现货商品交易以及提供相关服务的交易场所，包括各类消费品市场，生产资料市场等。

消费者信心指数 是综合反映并量化消费者对当前经济形势评价和对经济前景、收入水平、收入预期以及消费心理状态的主观感受，是预测经济走势和消费趋向的一个先行指标，是监测经济周期变化不可缺少的依据。消费者信心指数由消费者满意指数和消费者预期指数构成。其中消费者满意指数反映了消费者对当前经济生活的评价；消费者预期指数反映了消费者对未来一段时期经济发展变化的预期。

指数值的含义 指数取值介于 0 和 200 之间，100 为指数强弱临界点。指数超过 100，表明消费者信心处于强信心区，数值由 100 趋近 200，表明消费者信心逐渐增强；反之，指数小于 100 时，表示消费者信心处于弱信心区，数值由 100 趋近 0，表明消费者信心逐渐减弱。

Explanatory Notes on Main Statistical Indicators

Total Retail Sales of Consumer Goods refer to the total prices of physical commodities sold by enterprises (entities or self-employed businesses) through transaction directly to individuals and social groups to be used for non-productive and non-operating purposes, combined with the amount of income from provision of food and beverage services. Individuals include urban and rural residents and persons entering China. Social groups include government agencies, social organizations, armies, schools, enterprises and public institutions, residents' committee or villagers' committee, and so on.

Wholesale and Retail Entities refer to entities engaged in commodity wholesale and retail activities in circulation.

Total Purchases of Commodities refer to the total value (including value added tax) of purchases (including direct imports from foreign countries) of commodities by the enterprises (entities) from other entities or individuals for the purpose of re-selling, either with or without further processing of the commodities purchased. This indicator is used to show the total value of purchases of retail and wholesale commodities from domestic and overseas markets.

Total Sales of Commodities refer to value of commodities sold by the enterprises to other entities and individuals (including the commodities consumed by the enterprises themselves, including value added tax). This indicator is used to show the total value of wholesale and retail commodities sold in domestic markets and exported.

Inventory (year-end) refers to, for wholesale and retail enterprises and self-employed businesses, the value of all commodities with ownership gained (VAT included); for wholesale and retail entities, refer to the value of all commodities with ownership, actually in storage at the end of a period, and owned by the legal person (VAT included). This indicator shows the commodity inventory in wholesale and retail trades, and to what extent the commodities will be supplied to the market.

General Chain Store (Headquarters) means the core management organization in an enterprise, responsible for the development, deployment, control or use of resources (trade name, goodwill, operating model, service standards and management model, etc.) of the chain enterprise. Chain operation means an organization form in which several stores using unified trade name merchandise the same commodities or provide the same services through uniform purchase or franchise operation under the management of the same general store (headquarters) to achieve benefits of scale. Chain operation falls into direct-sale chain, franchised chain and voluntary chain. Direct-sale chain is a form of chain operation that chain stores are wholly funded or controlled by chain companies, carrying out uniform operation under the direct control of headquarters; franchised chain is a form of chain operation that any enterprise (the franchiser) owning operating resources, such as trademarks, logos, patents and proprietary technologies, authorize such operating resources to any other operator (the franchisee) by contract, and the franchisee operates under uniform operating model as stated in the contract, and pays franchise fees to the franchiser; voluntary chain is a form of chain operation that several stores or enterprises combine together voluntarily to face consumers with the same brand image without changing their own asset ownership relations, and link together through joint purchase.

Chain Stores Based on the operation and management of chain enterprises, stores carrying out daily sales business by following the general store's (headquarters) instruction and required service standards are called chained stores. They include direct-sale stores (controlled stores) and franchise stores.

(1) Direct-sale Stores (Controlled Stores) refer to stores opened with funds from the headquarters of chain enterprises, using the chain operation and management model, and under the uniform management of the headquarters.

(2) Franchised Stores refer to, in franchise chains, stores established after the franchisee is authorized by the franchiser to use its trademark, trade name, operating mode, patent and proprietary technologies and other operating resources. Voluntary chain members are also included.

Total Number of Stores refers to the number of all stores owned by the chain enterprises (including direct-sale stores and franchised stores). The general store (if the parent company has stores) is regarded as a direct-sale store. In addition, controlled stores are considered separately in some areas, which are regarded as direct-sale stores.

Restaurants Enterprises refer to enterprises specialized in cooking and seasoning food which is sold to clients for on-site consumption at a specific site, such as various restaurants, Chinese food and Western food restaurants, pubs, teahouses, dining compartments on trains, canteens at railway stations, and restaurants at airports.

Accommodation Enterprises refer to entities providing clients with temporary accommodation services, such as tourist hotels, guesthouses, rest houses and inns.

Commodity Transaction Markets refer to transaction sites approved by competent authorities and organizations, with fixed places and facilities. There are operation management departments and regulating personnel in the markets, where several operators stay over years or open for over three months, conducting transactions of on-hand commodities such as living consumables and capital goods, and offering relevant services in a concentrated, open and independent manner.

Commodity transaction markets include various markets of consumer goods and capital good market, etc.

Consumer Confidence Index is an indicator reflecting and quantifying the consumers' evaluation on current economic situation, and their personal feeling about the economic prospects, income level, income expectation, and psychological state of consumption. It serves as a leading indicator predicting the trend of economy tendency of consumption, and an essential basis for monitoring the changes in economic cycle and other conditions as well as expectation on the economic prospects in the future. Consumer Confidence Index consists of consumer satisfaction index and consumer expectation index, and the latter one reflects consumers' evaluation on current economic life; consumer expectation index reflects consumers' expectation on the development and changes in the economic prospect in the future.

Indexes range from 0 to 200. 100 represents a critical point between strong and weak confidence. An index greater than 100 indicates the consumers' confidence is strong. An index going toward 200 from 100 shows the consumers' confidence is becoming gradually strong; in contrary, an index smaller than 100 means the consumers' confidence is weak. When the indexes go toward 0 from 100, it means the consumers' confidence is weakening gradually.

北京统计年鉴2016　BEIJING STATISTICAL YEARBOOK

对外经济贸易
FOREIGN ECONOMY AND TRADE

简要说明

一、本章资料的主要内容

本章资料主要反映北京市对外经济贸易的发展状况，包括对外贸易、利用外资、对外经济合作的历年概况，以及对外友好交往情况。

二、本章资料的统计范围和数据来源

1.对外贸易情况

对外贸易统计的范围是凡能引起北京市海关境内物质资源存量增加或减少的进出口货物，除制度另有规定者外，均列入该项统计，调查方法采用全面调查。主要内容包括北京地区进出口总值；主要产品进出口数量等。数据来源于中华人民共和国北京海关。

2.口岸运营情况

口岸运营情况的统计范围是北京首都国际机场空港口岸、北京丰台货运口岸、北京朝阳口岸、北京西站铁路口岸、北京平谷国际陆港、北京天竺综合保税区。主要内容包括旅客吞吐量、货邮吞吐量、监管货物的数量、征收关税等。数据来源于北京市人民政府口岸办公室。

3.利用外资情况

利用外资情况的统计范围是凡经工商行政管理机关核准登记，在中华人民共和国北京地域内所有使用外资（包括港澳台地区投资）的单位和部门，经批准设立的中外合资经营企业、合作经营企业、外资企业、外商投资股份制企业、合作开发项目等具有法人资格的独立核算企业(包括港澳台地区投资企业)，在华从事经营活动的外国及港澳台地区企业及外国公司在中国境内设立的分支机构。主要内容包括实际利用外商直接投资，外商投资企业经营情况，调查方法采用全面调查。数据来源于北京市商务委员会(原北京市商务局)和北京市统计局。

4.对外经济合作

对外经济合作的统计范围是经各级商务部门批准的从事对外承包、劳务合作和设计咨询业务并具有法人资格的对外承包劳务企业；调查方法采用全面调查。主要内容包括对外承包工程、劳务合作和设计咨询。数据来源于北京市商务委员会(原北京市商务局)。

5.友好城市

主要内容包括与北京市建立友好关系的城市名录。数据来源于北京市人民政府外事办公室。

Brief Introduction

I. Main Content

Data in this chapter show the development of foreign economic relations and trade in Beijing, including foreign trade, foreign capital utilization, and foreign economic cooperation in Beijing over the years, as well as friendly exchanges.

II. Scope of Statistical and Source of Data

1. Foreign trade

Foreign trade statistics apply for: any imports and exports that lead to increase or decrease in the stock of physical resources at Beijing customs, except for those otherwise stated in regulations, and were obtained through comprehensive survey. Foreign trade data include: total volume of import and export in Beijing, and quantity of main import and export products, and so on.. Foreign trade data are from Beijing Customs, P.R.C..

2. Statistics for Port Operation

The statistical scope of port operation covers the Port of Beijing Capital International Airport, Beijing Fengtai Cargo Transport Port, Beijing Chaoyang Transport Port, Railway Port at Beijing West Railway Station, Beijing Pinggu International Land Port, and Beijing Tianzhu Comprehensive Bonded Zone. Statistics in this chapter, which is sourced from Port Administration Office of the People's Government of Beijing Municipality, mainly include passenger throughput, cargo throughput, cargos under customs regulation and duties levied.

3. Foreign capital utilization

Scope of statistics: all entities and organizations registered with administration for industry and commerce upon approval, and using foreign capital (including investment from Hong Kong, Macao and Taiwan region) within the jurisdiction of Beijing, P.R.C, enterprises with legal person statues and independent accounting system (including enterprises invested by companies from Hong Kong, Macao and Taiwan region), including joint ventures, cooperative enterprises and foreign-invested enterprises, foreign-invested joint-stock enterprises, and cooperative development projects, and enterprises of foreign countries and Hong Kong, Macao and Taiwan region conducting operations in China as well as branch offices opened by foreign companies in China. Foreign capital utilization data include foreign direct investment, operation of foreign-invested enterprises, and were obtained through comprehensive survey. Data are sourced from Beijing Municipal Commission of Commerce (former Beijing Municipal Bureau of Commerce) and Beijing Municipal Bureau of Statistics.

4. Foreign economic cooperation

Statistics cover foreign labor service enterprises with legal person statues that are engaged in foreign contracting, labor service cooperation and design consulting with approval from departments of commerce at different levels. Comprehensive survey was used. Foreign economic cooperation statistics apply for: foreign contracting projects, labor service cooperation and design consulting. Data are sourced from Beijing Municipal Commission of Commerce (former Beijing Municipal Bureau of Commerce).

5. Sister cities

Data showing the detailed list of sister cities of Beijing are from Foreign Affairs Office of the People's Government of Beijing Municipality.

15-1 北京地区对外经济贸易(1980-2015年)
FOREIGN ECONOMIC RELATIONS AND TRADE (1980-2015)

年 份 Year	进出口总值(万美元) Total Value of Imports and Exports (USD 10000)	出 口 Exports	#高新技术产品 High-tech Products	#机电产品 Mechanical and Electrical Products	进 口 Imports	#高新技术产品 High-tech Products	#机电产品 Mechanical and Electrical Products
1980							
1981-1985							
1981							
1982							
1983	3059926	1468740			1591186		
1984	3559284	1751704			1807580		
1985	3254341	437398			2816943		
1986-1990	**13945243**	**1865234**			**12080009**		
1986	3060236	371282			2688954		
1987	2670466	354374			2316092		
1988	2988576	395887			2592689		
1989	2861489	302343			2559146		
1990	2364476	441348			1923128		
1991-1995	**14305670**	**3547263**			**10758405**		
1991	2424137	457114			1967023		
1992	2498241	561037		157835	1937204	271005	731359
1993	2791700	669930		151133	2121769	302965	885074
1994	2888079	834205		194937	2053873	421071	1121082
1995	3703513	1024977		281810	2678536	407176	1225200
1996-2000	**17397285**	**5011639**		**1609152**	**12385646**	**2242338**	**5049210**
1996	2931833	811975		254450	2119858	240903	733641
1997	3038852	961103		271119	2077749	346166	766288
1998	3050608	1051293		325390	1999315	347556	909222
1999	3435951	990352		320852	2445599	567687	1213857
2000	4940041	1196916	226549	437341	3743125	740026	1426202
2001-2005	**39258570**	**9270820**	**2525916**	**4291246**	**29987748**	**5318558**	**10501427**
2001	5149809	1177236	263382	477568	3972572	992797	1883151
2002	5250529	1261386	314174	570971	3989142	916363	1701504
2003	6850017	1688682	396489	715359	5161335	990357	1949077
2004	9457572	2056926	580929	970117	7400647	1053395	2271805
2005	12550643	3086590	970942	1557231	9464052	1365646	2695890
2006-2010	**113918161**	**24817747**	**8781469**	**14861935**	**89100414**	**11589524**	**25107110**
2006	15803663	3795398	1388925	2170700	12008265	1704997	3786847
2007	19299976	4892639	1797751	2862301	14407337	2360093	4477646
2008	27169290	5749961	1906381	3354179	21419329	2417936	4987666
2009	21479103	4835807	1751571	3080447	16643296	2357239	5194072
2010	30166129	5543942	1936840	3394308	24622187	2749258	6660878
2011-2015	**196258645**	**29872913**	**9027650**	**18089490**	**166385732**	**14606903**	**36430695**
2011	38958314	5899770	1811744	3523452	33058544	3145224	7667795
2012	40810735	5963212	1901750	3737918	34847523	2987939	7217809
2013	42994169	6309757	2035695	3894782	36684413	2923787	7167539
2014	41553810	6233597	1874973	3789748	35320213	2937309	7785199
2015	31941616	5466577	1403488	3143590	26475039	2612644	6592353

注：进出口总值为海关统计的北京地区进出口数据(包括中央单位)。
资料来源：北京市商务委员会、中华人民共和国北京海关。
Note: Figures of "total value of imports and exports" were imports and exports of Beijing counted by Beijing Customs (including central entities).
Source: Beijing Municipal Commission of Commerce and Beijing Customs of People's Republic of China.

15-1 续表 Continued

年 份 Year	外商直接投资项目(合同)个数 (个) Number of Foreign Direct Investment Projects (Contracts) (unit)	实际利用外商直接投资额 (万美元) Actal Use of Foreign Direct Investment (USD10000)
1980	4	
1981-1985	**124**	
1981	3	
1982	4	
1983	5	
1984	29	
1985	83	
1986-1990	**709**	
1986	63	
1987	72	9534
1988	148	50278
1989	185	31846
1990	241	27696
1991-1995	**10912**	**410896**
1991	724	24482
1992	2208	34984
1993	3753	66693
1994	2675	144460
1995	1552	140277
1996-2000	**4100**	**989794**
1996	868	155290
1997	790	159286
1998	651	206415
1999	644	223004
2000	1147	245799
2001-2005	**7821**	**1231631**
2001	1147	177000
2002	1370	178964
2003	1362	214675
2004	1806	308354
2005	2136	352638
2006-2010	**9232**	**2818387**
2006	2106	455191
2007	2177	506572
2008	1897	608172
2009	1423	612094
2010	1629	636358
2011-2015	**6599**	**4565745**
2011	1345	705447
2012	1360	804160
2013	1190	852418
2014	1318	904085
2015	1386	1299635

15-2 北京地区海关进出口贸易总值(按登记注册类型、贸易方式分)
TOTAL VALUE OF IMPORTS AND EXPORTS AT BEIJING CUSTOMS (BY REGISTRATION TYPE AND COMPOSITION)

项目	Item	金额(万美元) Value (USD 10000) 2015	2014	2015年为2014年% 2015as % of 2014	构成(%) Composition(%) 2015	2014
出口	**Local Exports**	**5466577**	**6233597**	**87.7**	**100.00**	**100.00**
按登记注册类型分	**By Registration Type**					
内资企业	Domestically-invested Enterprises	3991004	4159533	95.9	73.01	66.73
国有企业	State-owned Enterprises	3023535	3371995	89.7	55.31	54.09
集体企业	Collectively-owned Enterprises	3211	8397	38.2	0.06	0.13
其他	Others	964258	779141	123.8	17.64	12.50
外商投资企业	Foreign-invested Enterprises	1475573	2074064	71.1	26.99	33.27
中外合资	Joint Ventures	668911	1223146	54.7	12.24	19.62
中外合作	Cooperatives	4571	5661	80.7	0.08	0.09
外商独资	Solely-funded Enterprises	802091	845258	94.9	14.67	13.56
按贸易方式分	**By Composition**					
#一般贸易	General Trade	2994745	2837416	105.5	54.78	45.52
来料加工装配贸易	Trade of Processing & Assembling Supplied Materials	597712	722020	82.8	10.93	11.58
进料加工贸易	Trade of Processing Imported Materials	931221	1511197	61.6	17.03	24.24
对外承包工程货物	Contracted Foreign Goods and Projects	630388	801066	78.7	11.53	12.85
出料加工贸易	Trade of Processing Exported Materials	2416	3719	65.0	0.04	0.06
进口	**Imports**	**26475039**	**35320213**	**75.0**	**100.00**	**100.00**
按登记注册类型分	**By Registration Type**					
内资企业	Domestically-invested Enterprises	21434297	29458492	72.8	80.96	83.40
国有企业	State-owned Enterprises	19863530	24493991	81.1	75.03	69.35
集体企业	Collectively-owned Enterprises	98113	95276	103.0	0.37	0.27
其他	Other	1472653	4869226	30.2	5.56	13.79
外商投资企业	Foreign-invested Enterprises	5040742	5861721	86.0	19.04	16.60
中外合资	Joint Ventures	1011323	1208553	83.7	3.82	3.42
中外合作	Cooperatives	5405	7420	72.8	0.02	0.02
外商独资	Solely-funded Enterprises	4024014	4645748	86.6	15.20	13.15
按贸易方式分	**By Composition**					
#一般贸易	General Trade	22696536	30509017	74.4	85.73	86.38
来料加工装配贸易	Trade of Processing and Assembling Supplied Materials	1563598	1854276	84.3	5.91	5.25
进料加工贸易	Trade of Processing Imported Materials	468247	653396	71.7	1.77	1.85
外商投资企业进口设备、物品	Equipment and Goods Imported by Foreign-invested Enterprises	5823	28924	20.1	0.02	0.08
租赁贸易	Leasing Trade	160431	190810	84.1	0.61	0.54

资料来源：中华人民共和国北京海关。
Source: Beijing Customs of People's Republic of China.

15-3 北京地区海关进出口贸易总值(按国别、地区分)
TOTAL VALUE OF IMPORTS AND EXPORTS AT BEIJING CUSTOMS (BY COUNTRY AND REGION)

项目	Item	金额(万美元) Value (USD 10000)		2015年为2014年% 2015 as % of 2014	构成(%) Composition(%)	
		2015	2014		2015	2014
出口合计	**Total Exports**	**5466577**	**6233597**	**87.7**	**100.00**	**100.00**
按国别(地区)分	**By Country (Region)**					
#中国香港	Hong Kong, China	486582	507876	95.8	8.90	8.15
中国澳门	Macao, China	28654	36609	78.3	0.52	0.59
中国台湾	Taiwan, China	125470	133640	93.9	2.30	2.14
日　本	Japan	449913	470331	95.7	8.23	7.55
新加坡	Singapore	190938	192497	99.2	3.49	3.09
韩　国	Korea	207698	242991	85.5	3.80	3.90
越　南	Vietnam	191578	259906	73.7	3.50	4.17
伊　朗	Iran	162444	188560	86.1	2.97	3.02
印　度	India	197150	219417	89.9	3.61	3.52
印度尼西亚	Indonesia	108460	165677	65.5	1.98	2.66
英　国	United Kingdom	120832	117014	103.3	2.21	1.88
德　国	Germany	112499	133478	84.3	2.06	2.14
法　国	France	59704	80779	73.9	1.09	1.30
意大利	Italy	42467	52090	81.5	0.78	0.84
匈牙利	Hungary	7840	42505	18.4	0.14	0.68
俄罗斯联邦	Russian Federation	126334	161754	78.1	2.31	2.59
美　国	United States	495661	578246	85.7	9.07	9.28
澳大利亚	Australia	119496	73470	162.6	2.19	1.18
进口合计	**Total Imports**	**26475039**	**35320213**	**75.0**	**100.00**	**100.00**
按国别(地区)分	**By Country (Region)**					
#中国香港	Hong Kong, China	184397	143940	128.1	0.70	0.41
日　本	Japan	957100	1278859	74.8	3.62	3.62
新加坡	Singapore	203079	200064	101.5	0.77	0.57
韩　国	Korea	923731	1142957	80.8	3.49	3.24
沙特阿拉伯	Saudi Arabia	1477198	2723621	54.2	5.58	7.71
英　国	United Kingdom	359137	424411	84.6	1.36	1.20
德　国	Germany	1916550	2246743	85.3	7.24	6.36
法　国	France	299372	293808	101.9	1.13	0.83
意大利	Italy	200815	211268	95.1	0.76	0.60
瑞　士	Switzerland	1679705	1874212	89.6	6.34	5.31
比利时	Belgium	72970	82918	88.0	0.28	0.23
俄罗斯联邦	Russian Federation	1099626	1275884	86.2	4.15	3.61
加拿大	Canada	922538	638306	144.5	3.48	1.81
美　国	United States	2686606	2908354	92.4	10.15	8.23
澳大利亚	Australia	1120257	1281957	87.4	4.23	3.63
阿　曼	Oman	882155	1530101	57.7	3.33	4.33
安哥拉	Angola	1379771	2503663	55.1	5.21	7.09

资料来源：中华人民共和国北京海关。
Source: Beijing Customs of People's Republic of China.

15-4 北京地区海关主要商品进口量及金额(2015年)
VOLUME & VALUE OF MAJOR COMMODITIES IMPORTED AT BEIJING CUSTOMS (2015)

项　目		Item		进口数量 Import Volume	进口金额 (万美元) Import Value (USD 10000)
粮　食	(万吨)	Grain	(10000 tons)	1679	623360
食用植物油	(万吨)	Edible Vegetable Oil	(10000 tons)	108	93714
食　糖	(万吨)	Sugar	(10000 tons)	105	43211
酒　类	(万升)	Alcohol	(10000 liters)	26050	40736
合成橡胶(包括胶乳)	(万吨)	Synthetic Rubber (Including Latex)	(10000 tons)	3	5349
纸　浆	(万吨)	Paper Pulp	(10000 tons)	100	60489
羊　毛	(万吨)	Wool	(10000 tons)	5	28813
棉　花	(万吨)	Cotton	(10000 tons)	23	37362
纺织用合成纤维	(万吨)	Synthetic Fiber for Textile	(10000 tons)	2	3449
铁矿砂及其精矿	(万吨)	Iron Sand and Iron Ore Concentrates	(10000 tons)	12139	710886
原　油	(万吨)	Crude Oil	(10000 tons)	23457	9407787
成品油	(万吨)	Product Oil	(10000 tons)	920	432396
医药品	(万吨)	Medicines	(10000 tons)	2	465380
肥　料	(万吨)	Fertilizers	(10000 tons)	653	206936
非泡沫塑料的板、片、膜、箔	(万吨)	Non-foam Plastic Plates, Sheets, Films and Foils	(10000 tons)	2	12696
纸及纸板(未切成形的)	(万吨)	Paper and Pressboard (Not Shaped by Cutting)	(10000 tons)	18	27909
纺织纱线、织物及制品		Textile Yarn, Fabric and Products			97110
服装及衣着附件		Clothes and Clothing Accessories			37232
钢　材	(万吨)	Steel Products	(10000 tons)	30	77301
建筑及采矿用机械及零件		Building and Mining Machinery and Parts			20522
印刷、装订机械及零件		Printing and Binding Machinery and Parts			83572
自动数据处理设备及其部件		Automatic Data Processing Equipment and Their Components			159913
电动机及发电机	(万台)	Electromotors and Generators	(10000 sets)	759	33194
变压、整流、电感器及零件		Voltage Transformer, Rectifier, Inductor and Parts			94682
电视摄像机、数字照相机及视频摄录一体机	(万台)	Television Cameras, Digital Cameras and Integrated Video Cameras and Recorders	(10000 sets)	251	112996
印刷电路	(万块)	Printed Circuits	(10000 pieces)	145381	6753
集成电路	(万个)	Integrated Circuits	(10000 units)	859980	256817
电线和电缆	(万吨)	Wires and Cables	(10000 tons)	1	17280
汽　车		Automobiles			2309097
汽车零件		Auto Parts			406046
飞　机		Aircrafts			270512
船　舶		Ships and Boats			4766
医疗仪器及器械		Medical Instruments and Devices			195423
计量检测分析自控仪器及器具		Automatically-controlled Measuring, Testing and Analyzing Instruments			480922

资料来源：中华人民共和国北京海关。
Source: Beijing Customs of People's Republic of China.

15-5 北京地区海关主要商品出口量及金额(2015年)
VOLUME & VALUE OF MAIN COMMODITIES EXPORTED AT BEIJING CUSTOMS (2015)

项目		Item		出口数量 Export Volume	出口金额 Export Value (万美元) (USD 10000)
粮 食	(万吨)	Grain	(10000 tons)	19	16369
果蔬汁	(万吨)	Fruit and Vegetable Juice	(10000 tons)	10	10863
肥 料	(万吨)	Fertilizers	(10000 tons)	553	164943
煤	(万吨)	Coal	(10000 tons)	89	9243
焦炭、半焦炭	(万吨)	Coke and Semi-coke	(10000 tons)	241	37238
成品油	(万吨)	Product Oil	(10000 tons)	1280	713910
医药品	(万吨)	Medicines	(10000 tons)	1	41687
纺织纱线、织物及制品		Textile Yarn, Fabric and Products			67670
铁合金	(万吨)	Ferroalloy	(10000 tons)	2	16492
钢 材	(万吨)	Steel Products	(10000 tons)	570	347852
未锻造的铝及铝材	(万吨)	Non-forged Aluminum and Aluminum Products	(10000 tons)	4	12753
纺织机械及零件		Textile Machinery and Parts			17446
金属加工机床	(万台)	Metal Processing Lathe	(10000 sets)	2	14625
自动数据处理设备及其部件		Automatic Data Processing Equipment and Their Components			58478
液晶显示板	(万个)	LCD Plates	(10000 units)	1320	71256
电动机及发电机	(万台)	Electromotors and Generators	(10000 sets)	220	9738
变压器	(万个)	Voltage Transformers	(10000 units)	50	24186
蓄电池	(万个)	Storage Cells	(10000 units)	1182	6301
电话机	(万台)	Telephone Sets	(10000 sets)	2601	429374
二极管及类似半导体器件	(万个)	Diode and Similar Semiconductor Devices	(10000 units)	98996	14485
集成电路	(万个)	Integrated Circuits	(10000 units)	706522	176254
电线和电缆	(万吨)	Wires and Cables	(10000 tons)	5	53651
汽车(包括整套散件)	(万辆)	Automobiles (Including Complete Sets of Spare Parts	(10000 sets)	5	112008
汽车零件		Auto Parts			184738
船 舶		Boats and Ships			126335
医疗仪器及器械		Medical Instruments and Devices			61620
家具及其零件		Furnitures and Their Parts			19171
服装及衣着附件		Clothes and Clothing Accessories			254784
鞋 类	(万吨)	Footwear	(10000 tons)	2	18848
塑料制品	(万吨)	Plastic Products	(10000 tons)	5	28220

资料来源：中华人民共和国北京海关。
Source: Beijing Customs of People's Republic of China.

15-6 北京口岸运营情况
STATISTICS FOR PORT OPERATION IN BEIJING

项　　目		Item		2015	2014	2015年为2014年% 2015 as % of 2014
北京首都国际机场空港口岸		**Port of Beijing Capital International Airport**				
旅客吞吐量	(万人次)	Passenger Throughput	(10000 person-times)	8994	8613	104.4
进出境人员	(万人次)	Inbound/Outbound Visitors	(10000 person-times)	2323	2205	105.4
#外籍人员进出境	(万人次)	Inbound/Outbound Foreign Visitors	(10000 person-times)	712	790	90.1
货邮吞吐量	(万吨)	Cargos Carried	(10000 tons)	189	185	102.2
飞机起降	(架次)	Takeoff and Landing of Airplanes	(unit)	590169	581953	101.4
#进出境飞机起降	(架次)	Takeoff and Landing of Airplanes Inbound/Outbound	(unit)	132613	125760	105.4
海关监管货物	(万吨)	Cargos under Customs Regulation	(10000 tons)	4159.73	1960.77	212.1
海关征收关税及代征税	(万元)	Duties Levied and Collected by Customs	(10000 yuan)	3259276	3347288	97.4
北京丰台货运口岸		**Beijing Fengtai Cargo Transport Port**				
海关监管货物	(吨)	Cargos under Customs Regulation	(ton)	17767	17336	102.5
海关征收关税及代征税	(万元)	Duties Levied and Collected by Customs	(10000 yuan)	9872	9699	101.8
北京朝阳口岸		**Beijing Chaoyang Transport Port**				
海关监管货物	(标箱)	Cargos under Customs Regulation	(standard container)	116050	114251	101.6
海关监管货物	(吨)	Cargos under Customs Regulation	(ton)	937912	1193909	78.6
海关征收关税及代征税	(万元)	Duties Levied and Collected by Customs	(10000 yuan)	1205137	1258514	95.8
北京西站铁路口岸		**Railway Port at Beijing West Railway Station**				
进出境人员	(人次)	Inbound/Outbound Visitors	(person-times)	66548	91996	72.3
#外籍人员进出境	(人次)	Inbound/Outbound Foreign Visitors	(person-times)	4196	5535	75.8
北京平谷国际陆港		**Beijing Pinggu International Land Port**				
海关监管货物	(标箱)	Cargos under Customs Regulation	(standard container)	30709	31142	98.6
海关监管货物	(吨)	Cargos under Customs Regulation	(ton)	189997	198586	95.7
海关征收关税及代征税	(万元)	Duties Levied and Collected by Customs	(10000 yuan)	202582	211451	95.8
北京天竺综合保税区		**Beijing Tianzhu Comprehensive Bonded Zone**				
实际进出货物	(吨)	Cargos under Customs Regulation	(ton)	62133	49592	125.3
海关征收关税及代征税	(万元)	Duties Levied and Collected by Customs	(10000 yuan)	748313	662750	112.9

资料来源：北京市人民政府口岸办公室。
Source: Port Administration Office of the People's Government of Beijing Municipality.

15-7 外商投资企业实际利用外资情况(2006-2015年)

单位：万美元

项目	Item	2006	2007
实际利用外商直接投资额	**Actual Use of Foreign Direct Investment**	**455191**	**506572**
按登记注册类型分	**By Registration Type**		
合资经营	Joint Ventures	80570	77887
合作经营	Cooperatives	33039	18037
独资经营	Solely-funded Enterprises	341367	408754
外商投资股份制	Companies Limited by Shares	215	1894
按产业分	**By Industry**		
第一产业	Primary Industry	544	4774
第二产业	Secondary Industry	109380	93391
第三产业	Tertiary Industry	345267	408407
按行业分	**By Sector**		
农、林、牧、渔业	Agriculture, Forestry, Animal Production and Hunting, Fishing	544	4774
制造业	Manufacturing	105590	89618
建筑业	Construction	1254	878
信息传输、计算机服务和软件业	Information Transmission, Computer Services and Software	44341	78470
批发与零售业	Wholesale and Retail Trade	24378	33318
住宿和餐饮业	Accommodation and Restaurants	1882	5824
房地产业	Real Estate	72242	119476
租赁和商务服务业	Renting and Leasing Activities, Business Services	174342	92896
其他行业	Other Sectors	30618	81318
按外商国别(地区)分	**By Country (Region) of Foreign Investors**		
#中国香港	Hongkong,China	86600	149291
英属维尔京群岛	Virgin Islands	78445	104154
开曼群岛	Cayman Islands	27596	68646
日　本	Japan	67580	30386
韩　国	Korea	35357	24420
美　国	United States	20043	18280
新加坡	Singapore	17616	15328
巴巴多斯	Barbados	7278	13789
德　国	Germany	47797	11476
毛里求斯	Mauritius	10166	8068
百慕大	Bermuda	1658	7540
萨摩亚	Samoan	1483	6189
荷　兰	Netherlands	4610	4876
法　国	France	3578	3824
英　国	United Kingdom	2977	3304

资料来源：北京市商务委员会。
Source: Beijing Municipal Commission of Commerce.

ACTUAL USE OF FOREIGN CAPITAL BY FOREIGN INVESTED ENTERPRISES (2006-2015)

(USD 10000)

2008	2009	2010	2011	2012	2013	2014	2015
608172	**612094**	**636358**	**705447**	**804160**	**852418**	**904085**	**1299635**
90916	91049	91335	78983	191944	190667	154808	268500
21372	32249	22890	15068	14184	22887	5166	202
490252	448912	516766	594890	592310	593258	704367	995202
5632	39884	5367	16506	5722	45606	39744	35731
2032	3833	1246	214	733	1717	13947	7620
162515	88536	71899	80798	112326	149687	97254	59528
443625	519725	563213	624435	691101	701014	792884	1232487
2032	3833	1246	214	733	1717	13947	7620
150056	75364	68496	63303	86378	106848	84226	59397
1715	2493	411	2343	383	193	703	131
105396	94752	95453	109246	135121	119547	115292	48611
34677	55411	66032	115437	74311	92739	54792	242167
3357	8427	3525	1705	2877	1822	2047	549
78787	79682	141728	112539	87739	148057	136822	27541
132541	225888	175580	190363	161595	171079	339759	71199
99611	66244	83887	110297	255023	210416	156497	842420
173292	270295	312863	323041	440357	360481	541495	993199
125045	123201	76255	112981	28882	51111	37592	189644
75463	41389	45209	35982	59320	43982	36835	5774
47174	23905	40692	77196	59022	44781	31125	12193
27841	17601	14725	22372	70959	21029	18584	8143
17888	18628	21370	30221	21097	38882	15634	3677
10520	12600	24888	12898	31656	19383	35631	16468
15803	2384	941	821	200	2839	3000	3
26654	14308	22344	17939	25763	107467	99968	35761
7780	5615	7179	1311	1392	3297	3586	275
1699	4441	4860	813	1483	265	2005	
2468	1310	1705	893	1163	589	311	1463
28520	4906	10639	3677	8542	14619	12119	508
2583	6349	3700	6642	2286	1409	6284	16054
4897	4242	1120	6245	3828	2387	1738	2010

15-8 外商投资企业基本情况

项 目	Item	企业单位数（个） Number of Enterprises (unit) 2015	2014
合 计	**Total**	**3835**	**4107**
按登记注册类型分	**By Registration Type**		
港澳台商投资企业	Hong Kong, Macao and Taiwan-invested Enterprises	1481	1564
与港澳台商合资	Joint Ventures	467	491
与港澳台商合作	Cooperatives	104	119
港澳台商独资	Solely-funded Enterprises	879	922
港澳台商投资股份有限公司	Companies Limited by Shares	30	31
其他港澳台投资企业	Others	***	***
外商投资企业	Foreign-invested Enterprises	2354	2543
中外合资	Joint Ventures	689	743
中外合作	Cooperatives	97	104
外商独资	Solely-funded Enterprises	1521	1657
外商投资股份有限公司	Companies Limited by Shares	38	36
其他外商投资企业	Others	9	3
按国民经济行业分	**By Sector**		
农、林、牧、渔业	Agriculture, Forestry, Animal Production and Hunting, Fishing		
制造业	Manufacturing	789	838
建筑业	Construction	82	83
批发与零售业	Wholesale and Retail Trade	490	596
住宿和餐饮业	Accommodation and Restaurants	190	212
信息传输、软件和信息技术服务业	Information Transmission, Software and Information Technology Services	522	532
房地产业	Real Estate	381	394
租赁和商务服务业	Renting and Leasing Activities, Business Services	589	627
其他行业	Other Sectors	792	825
按三次产业分	**By Industry**		
第一产业	Primary Industry		
第二产业	Secondary Industry	877	928
第三产业	Tertiary Industry	2958	3179

注：1. 本表统计范围为限额以上法人企业。
2. 行业划分执行2011年国民经济行业分类标准(GB/T 4754-2011)。

STATISTICS FOR FOREIGN-INVESTED ENTERPRISES

从业人员平均人数(人) Average Number of Persons Employed (person)		主营业务收入(万元) Revenue from Main Businesses (10000 yuan)		利润总额(万元) Total Profits (10000 yuan)		应交税金合计(万元) Total Taxes Paid (10000 yuan)	
2015	2014	2015	2014	2015	2014	2015	2014
1354764	**1355156**	**258960457**	**258975400**	**37024049**	**32236919**	**9134588**	**8909118**
556649	524962	92266827	74163799	8320533	9131162	2340965	2337891
140317	148350	14670402	14026110	2800611	2242179	648346	697805
18554	19324	1617303	1574471	238192	281993	156906	144474
336678	294757	66802264	49034042	4384180	5977075	1506092	1463291
56511	58178	8881942	9246811	843905	568441	15577	19490
4589	4353	***	***	***	***	***	***
798115	830194	166693631	184811601	28703516	23105757	6793623	6571227
281641	289432	57082878	60652611	8113541	7408245	3391631	3009711
17361	18438	1626346	1670099	158371	150736	126468	135494
471914	496025	106781150	121303047	19998067	15221937	3189767	3349544
25982	26008	1058275	1182391	396681	324977	76029	75333
1217	***	144982	***	36855	***	9728	***
354557	377470	73467769	75733923	5149087	5453339	3794873	3428240
11175	12189	1731944	2052475	42687	36114	52786	54039
206262	211082	108725266	110247069	4604341	5220950	2242543	2358084
102159	100346	3143053	2984229	141742	119170	199444	196744
243850	226801	24385008	21365567	12750113	8501618	891656	941568
62677	64851	4665419	5848543	909663	1295147	511314	712169
120820	115361	16932333	16263818	4005597	3152276	468248	491769
253264	247056	25909665	24479776	9420821	8458306	973724	726506
368969	393088	78771509	80702840	5865349	6068379	3942968	3643803
985795	962068	180188949	178272560	31158701	26168541	5191619	5265315

Note: a) Statistics in this table cover corporate enterprises above designated size.

b) Sectors in this table are classified in accordance with the Standard for Classification of National Economic Sectors 2011 (GB/T 4754-2011).

15-9 境外投资情况(2003-2014年)
STATISTICS FOR OVERSEAS INVESTMENT (2003-2014)

单位：万美元 (USD 10000)

年 份 Year	中方投资额 Amount of Investment by China	截至到各年期末直接投资存量 Diret Investment Stock by the Year End
2003	30054	44844
2004	15739	70086
2005	11306	92940
2006	5612	91873
2007	15295	159195
2008	47299	251019
2009	45185	375865
2010	76614	480882
2011	117503	603380
2012	168900	757800
2013	413010	1276456
2014	727353	2848870

资料来源：北京市商务委员会。
Source: Beijing Municipal Commission of Commerce.

15-10 对外经济合作(1984-2015年)
STATISTICS FOR FOREIGN ECONOMIC COOPERATION (1984-2015)

年份 Year	合同数(份) Number of Contracts (unit)	#对外承包工程 Foreign Contracted Works	合同额(万美元) Contract Value (USD 10000)	#对外承包工程 Foreign Contracted Works	完成营业额(万美元) Turnover (USD 10000)	#对外承包工程 Foreign Contracted Works	年末在外人数(人) Year-end Workers Staying Abroad (person)	对外承包工程 Foreign Contracted Works	对外劳务合作 Foreign Labor Service Cooperation
1984	9	2	2801	2768	502	331	541	163	378
1985	12	2	852	736	2083	355	2401	18	2383
1986	30	7	446	319	1535	90	837	71	766
1987	37	5	547	354	696	186	690	20	670
1988	46	5	885	344	802	281	819	104	715
1989	111	7	1685	235	1018	459	600	83	517
1990	105	16	3756	2253	1056	625	336	25	311
1991	114	9	3202	1671	1897	1469	980	306	674
1992	130	16	8889	7762	3140	2543	952	264	688
1993	143	48	29397	27625	9748	8871	1555	532	1023
1994	114	34	15715	15089	18783	17822	2720	1694	1026
1995	116	35	15613	14014	12789	12156	2604	1297	1307
1996	116	49	67689	62945	43057	38124	2516	1559	957
1997	107	37	35640	23374	29629	17945	3122	1993	1129
1998	180	48	25526	19292	31009	24930	3647	2239	1408
1999	90	28	25232	18715	26167	19690	3476	2199	1277
2000	104	54	16285	9936	19799	13543	3205	1660	1545
2001	105	54	21439	14758	18628	11680	3494	2141	1353
2002	73	42	27949	19376	23160	14453	2134	1112	1022
2003	117	99	48271	30761	34926	17334	2097	1270	827
2004	128	116	81185	51136	59630	29241	2552	1629	923
2005	272	238	93732	56709	71281	35554	4424	2528	1896
2006	232	166	176752	160328	83518	70062	8962	6760	2202
2007	317	143	236881	211560	94077	71727	11299	7060	4239
2008	486	197	558714	520973	168416	131686	11422	6366	5056
2009	190	182	336223	296851	226893	185017	17121	11805	5316
2010	199	170	286179	251114	259794	222514	22499	17145	5354
2011	229	229	264019	262078	252951	249146	17821	12393	5428
2012	340	340	405885	403475	295639	289902	16747	12143	4604
2013	349	349	564383	562440	341046	335854	21036	16549	4487
2014	283	283	437463	429369	365358	357432	29457	21683	7774
2015	208	208	471988	464808	370880	354868	34183	19287	14896

注：1984-2008年，对外承包工程统计中含对外设计咨询统计数据。
资料来源：北京市商务委员会。
Note: In 1984-2008, statistics for foreign contracted projects included statistics for consultation on foreign design.
Source: Beijing Municipal Commission of Commerce.

15-11 北京市市级友好城市
MUNICIPAL-LEVEL SISTER CITIES OF BEIJING

顺序 No.	城市	City	所在国家	Contury	所属洲	Continent	缔结日期 Date of Conclusion
1	东京都	Tokyo	日本	Japan	亚洲	Asia	1979.03.14
2	纽约市	New York	美国	USA	北美洲	North America	1980.02.25
3	贝尔格莱德市	Belgrade	塞尔维亚	Serbia	欧洲	Europe	1980.10.14
4	利马市	Lima	秘鲁	Peru	南美洲	South America	1983.11.21
5	华盛顿特区	Washington, DC	美国	USA	北美洲	North America	1984.05.15
6	马德里市	Madrid	西班牙	Spain	欧洲	Europe	1985.09.16
7	里约热内卢市	Rio De Janeiro	巴西	Brazil	南美洲	South America	1986.11.24
8	巴黎大区	Greater Parisian Region	法国	France	欧洲	Europe	1987.07.02
9	科隆市	Cologne	德国	Germany	欧洲	Europe	1987.09.14
10	安卡拉市	Ankara	土耳其	Turkey	亚洲	Asia	1990.06.20
11	开罗省	Cairo	埃及	Egypt	非洲	Africa	1990.10.28
12	雅加达省	Jakarta	印度尼西亚	Indonesia	亚洲	Asia	1992.08.04
13	伊斯兰堡市	Islamabad	巴基斯坦	Pakistan	亚洲	Asia	1992.10.08
14	曼谷市	Bangkok	泰国	Thailand	亚洲	Asia	1993.05.26
15	布宜诺斯艾利斯市	Buenos Aires	阿根廷	Argentina	南美洲	South America	1993.07.13
16	首尔特别市	Seoul Special City	韩国	South Korea	亚洲	Asia	1993.10.23
17	基辅市	Kiev	乌克兰	Ukraine	欧洲	Europe	1993.12.13
18	柏林市	Berlin	德国	Germany	欧洲	Europe	1994.04.05
19	布鲁塞尔大区	Greater Brussels Region	比利时	Belgium	欧洲	Europe	1994.09.22
20	河内市	Hanoi	越南	Viet Nam	亚洲	Asia	1994.10.06
21	阿姆斯特丹市	Amsterdam	荷兰	Holland	欧洲	Europe	1994.10.29
22	莫斯科市	Moscow	俄罗斯	Russia	欧洲	Europe	1995.05.16
23	巴黎市	Paris	法国	France	欧洲	Europe	1997.10.23
24	罗马市	Rome	意大利	Italy	欧洲	Europe	1998.05.28
25	豪登省	Gauteng	南非	South Africa	非洲	Africa	1998.12.06
26	渥太华市	Ottawa	加拿大	Canada	北美洲	North America	1999.10.18
27	首都地区	The Capital Region	澳大利亚	Australia	大洋洲	Oceania	2000.09.14
28	马德里自治区	Madrid Autonomous Region	西班牙	Spain	欧洲	Europe	2005.01.17
29	雅典市	Athens	希腊	Greece	欧洲	Europe	2005.05.10
30	布达佩斯市	Budapest	匈牙利	Hungary	欧洲	Europe	2005.06.16
31	布加勒斯特市	Bucharest	罗马尼亚	Rumania	欧洲	Europe	2005.06.21
32	哈瓦那市	Havana	古巴	Cuba	南美洲	South America	2005.09.24
33	马尼拉市	Manila	菲律宾	Philippines	亚洲	Asia	2005.11.14
34	伦敦市	London	英国	UK	欧洲	Europe	2006.04.11
35	亚的斯亚贝巴市	Addis Abeba	埃塞俄比亚	Ethiopia	非洲	Africa	2006.04.17
36	惠灵顿市	Wellington	新西兰	New Zealand	大洋洲	Oceania	2006.05.10
37	赫尔辛基市	Helsinki	芬兰	Finland	欧洲	Europe	2006.07.14
38	阿斯塔纳市	Astana	哈萨克斯坦	Kazakstan	亚洲	Asia	2006.11.16
39	特拉维夫市	Tel Aviv	以色列	Israel	亚洲	Asia	2006.11.21
40	首都大区	The Greater Capital Region	智利	Chile	南美洲	South America	2007.08.06
41	里斯本市	Lisbon	葡萄牙	Portugal	欧洲	Europe	2007.10.22
42	地拉那市	Tirana	阿尔巴尼亚	Albania	欧洲	Europe	2008.03.21
43	多哈市	Doha	卡塔尔	Qatar	亚洲	Asia	2008.06.23
44	圣何塞市	San Jose	哥斯达黎加	Costarica	北美洲	North America	2009.10.17
45	墨西哥城	Mexican City	墨西哥	Mexico	北美洲	North America	2009.10.19
46	都柏林市	Dublin	爱尔兰	Ireland	欧洲	Europe	2011.06.02
47	哥本哈根市	Copenhagen	丹麦	Denmark	欧洲	Europe	2012.06.28
48	新南威尔士州	New South Wales	澳大利亚	Australia	大洋洲	Oceania	2012.08.03
49	德里邦	Delhi	印度	India	亚洲	Asia	2013.10.23
50	德黑兰	Teheran	伊朗	Iran	亚洲	Asia	2014.02.27
51	乌兰巴托	Ulaanbaatar	蒙古国	Mongolia	亚洲	Asia	2014.08.17
52	万象市	Vientiane	老挝	Laos	亚洲	Asia	2015.04.24

资料来源：北京市人民政府外事办公室。
Sourse: Foreign Affairs Office of the People's Government of Beijing Municipality.

主要统计指标解释

进出口总值 指实际进、出我国海关并能引起我国境内物质资源增加或减少的进出口货物总金额。包括我国境内法人和其他组织以一般贸易、易货贸易、加工贸易、补偿贸易、寄售代销贸易等方式进出口的货物、租赁期一年及以上的租赁进出口货物、边境小额贸易货物、国际援助物资或捐赠品、保税区和保税仓库进出口货物等的金额合计。进出口总值用以观察一个国家在对外贸易方面的总规模。我国规定出口货物按离岸价格统计，进口货物按到岸价格统计。

一般贸易 指我国境内有进出口经营权的企业单边进口或单边出口的货物。

来料加工装配贸易 指由外商提供全部或部分原材料、辅料、零部件、元器件、配套件和包装物料，必要时提供设备，由我方按对方的要求进行加工装配，成品交对方销售，我方收取工缴费；或对方提供的作价设备价款，我方用工缴费偿还的交易形式。

进料加工贸易 指我方用外汇购买进口的原料、材料、辅料、元器件、零部件、配套件和包装物料，加工成品或半成品后再外销出口的交易形式。

旅客吞吐量 指经乘航班进出北京民用运输机场的中国公民、港澳台同胞、华侨及外国人等旅客数量的总和。

货邮吞吐量 指通过民用运输机场的航班运输的货物、邮寄物品和随身携带的行李物品重量总和。

飞机起降架次 指进出民用运输机场的正常航班架次，不包括包机和其他非正常航班。

海关征收关税 指进出口商品在经过国家关境时，由政府设置的海关向进出口国所征收的税收。

批准外商直接投资企业项目个数 指外商直接投资中批准设立的外商投资企业个数、批准的合作开发项目个数。

实际利用外商直接投资额 指批准的合同外资金额的实际执行数，外国投资者根据批准外商投资企业的合同（章程）的规定实际缴付的出资额和企业投资总额内外国投资者以自己的境外自有资金实际直接向企业提供的贷款。

对外承包工程 指企业按照国际通行做法，在国（境）外承揽和实施各类工程项目的经济活动。企业承揽的我国对外经济援助项目、我国驻外使（领）馆等建设项目视同对外承包工程项目。

对外劳务合作 指企业按照与国（境）外政府有关机构、团体、企业、私人雇主所签合同规定，向国（境）外派遣各类劳务人员的经济活动。企业自带设备以提供技术服务的形式在国（境）外承揽的项目视同对外劳务合作项目。

对外设计咨询 指企业在国（境）外承揽的工程设计、工程监理、技术咨询和人员培训等经济活动。

Explanatory Notes on Main Statistical Indicators

Total Value of Imports and Exports refer to the total value of goods actually imported and exported at China's customs, which lead to increase or decrease in the physical resources in China, including goods imported/exported by China domestic legal persons and other organizations in such manners as general trade, barter trade, processing trade, compensation trade, commission-based sales trade, leasing imports/exports with a lease period of one year and more, small-sum border trade goods, international aid goods and donations, imports/exports in bonded zones and bonded warehouses. The indicator of the Total Value of Imports and Exports can be used to observe the total size of foreign trade in a country. In accordance with the stipulation of the Chinese government, imports are calculated at CIF, while exports are calculated at FOB.

General Trade means goods imported and exported unilaterally by domestic enterprises with import/export rights.

Trade of Processing and Assembling Supplied Materials is a form of transaction in which all or part of raw materials, auxiliary materials, parts and components, elements, fittings, and packaging materials, and equipment if necessary are provided by the foreign party, processed or assemble by Chinese party according to requirements of the foreign party, and the finished products are sold by the foreign party. The Chinese party charges processing fees and pays back the money of priced equipment provided by the foreign party with processing charges.

Trade of Processing Imported Materials is a form of transaction in which the Chinese party purchases raw materials, auxiliary materials, parts and components, elements, fittings, and packaging materials with foreign exchange, processing them into finished or semi-finished products and export them.

Passenger Throughput means the total number of Chinese citizens, compatriots form Hong Kong, Macao and Taiwan, oversea Chinese and foreigners that take off and land at civil airports in Beijing by flights.

Cargos Throughput means the sum of goods, mailed articles and luggage transported by flights taking off from and landing at civil airports in Beijing.

Takeoff and Landing of Airplanes means the number of regular flights taking off from and landing at civil airports in Beijing, excluding chartered flights and other non-regular flights.

Duties Levied and Collected by Customs mean the sum of duties actually levied from the imported and exported by customs established by the government when imported and exported goods are going through national borders.

Number of Direct Foreign-invested Enterprises Approved means the number of foreign-invested enterprises and joint development projects approved in foreign direct investment (FDI).

Actual Use of Foreign Capital means the value of approved contractual foreign investment actually used, the amount of actual capital contribution by foreign investors according to the contract (articles of incorporation) of the foreign-invested enterprise approved and, in the total investment of an enterprise, the amount of loans provided directly by foreign investor with its own overseas money.

Foreign Contracted Projects refer to economic activities in which enterprises undertake and implement various projects in foreign (overseas) countries in line with international practices. Foreign economic aid projects and construction projects of Chinese Embassies (Consulates) undertaken by enterprises are deemed as foreign contracted projects.

Foreign Labor Service Cooperation means any economic activity in which enterprises dispatch labors to foreign (overseas) countries as stated in contracts signed with foreign (overseas) government agencies, groups, enterprises, and private employers. Projects undertaken by enterprises in foreign (overseas) countries in a manner of providing technical service with their own equipment are deemed as foreign labor service cooperation projects.

Foreign Design Consulting means any economic activity of project design, project supervision, technical consulting and personnel training undertaken in foreign (overseas) countries by enterprises.

旅游业
TOURISM

简要说明

一、本章资料的主要内容和统计范围

本章内容主要包括来京旅游者人数及其在京花费情况、星级饭店经营及接待住宿者情况、旅行社接待及出境旅游情况、A级及以上重点旅游景区活动情况等。

统计范围包括国际旅游和国内旅游。

二、本章资料的数据来源

本章中的旅游外汇收入、国内旅游者人数、国内旅游收入、在京旅游花费情况资料来源于北京市旅游发展委员会。入境旅游者人数根据北京市统计局的星级饭店、限额以上非星级饭店全面调查、限额以下饭店抽样调查，以及北京市旅游发展委员会的其他住宿设施抽样调查结果汇总得出。星级饭店、旅行社、A级及以上和重点旅游景区有关数据通过全面调查取得，由北京市统计局、国家统计局北京调查总队提供。

Brief Introduction

I. Main Content and Scope of Statistics

This chapter includes statistics for the number and cost of tourists to Beijing, operation and reception of star-rated hotels, reception and outbound tours made through travel agencies, activities at Level A-or-above key scenic spots, and so on.

Statistics include international and domestic tours.

II. Source of Data

Data of foreign exchange income from tourism, number of domestic tourists, domestic tourism income, and cost of tourists in Beijing are sourced from Beijing Municipal Commission of Tourism Development. The number of inbound tourists is summed from the results of comprehensive survey of star-rated hotels and non-star-rated hotels above designated size, sample survey of hotels below designated size conducted by Beijing Municipal Bureau of Statistics, as well as the results of sample survey of other accommodation facilities conducted by Beijing Municipal Commission of Tourism Development. Data concerning star-rated hotels, travel agencies, Level A-or-above key scenic spots were obtained through comprehensive survey, and provided by Beijing Municipal Bureau of Statistics and NBS Survey Office in Beijing.

16-1 国际、国内旅游情况(1978-2015年)
STATISTICS FOR INTERNATIONAL AND DOMESTIC TOURISM (1978-2015)

年份 Year	来京旅游者人数(万人次) Number of Tourists to Beijing (10000 person-times)	入境旅游者人数 Inbound Tourists	国内旅游者人数 Domestic Tourists	旅游外汇收入总额(万美元) Foreign Exchange Earnings of Tourism (USD 10000)	国内旅游收入(亿元) Revenue from Domestic Tourism (100 million yuan)
1978		18.7		10000	
1979		25.2		9000	
1980		28.6		12000	
1981-1985		**295.4**		**94000**	
1981		39.4		12000	
1982		45.7		13000	
1983		50.9		14000	
1984		65.7		23000	
1985		93.7		32000	
1986-1990		**492.0**		**280901**	
1986		99.0		46000	
1987		108.1		55000	
1988		120.4		67000	
1989		64.5		47195	
1990		100.0		65706	
1991-1995		**919.6**		**735519**	
1991		132.0		85001	
1992		174.8		107286	
1993		202.8		124128	
1994	6913.0	203.0	6710.0	200904	298.0
1995	6527.0	207.0	6320.0	218200	352.6
1996-2000	**45284.7**	**1203.3**	**44081.4**	**1214800**	**2388.4**
1996	7901.9	218.9	7683.0	225200	359.6
1997	8450.8	229.8	8221.0	224800	391.3
1998	8951.5	220.1	8731.4	238400	424.5
1999	9512.4	252.4	9260.0	249600	530.0
2000	10468.1	282.1	10186.0	276800	683.0
2001-2005	**57116.7**	**1459.7**	**55657.0**	**1475000**	**4968.7**
2001	11292.8	285.8	11007.0	295000	887.7
2002	11810.4	310.4	11500.0	311000	930.0
2003	8885.1	185.1	8700.0	190000	706.0
2004	12265.5	315.5	11950.0	317000	1145.0
2005	12862.9	362.9	12500.0	362000	1300.0
2006-2010	**77925.4**	**2107.4**	**75818.0**	**2247000**	**9712.9**
2006	13590.3	390.3	13200.0	402600	1482.7
2007	14715.5	435.5	14280.0	458000	1753.6
2008	14560.0	379.0	14181.0	446000	1907.0
2009	16669.5	412.5	16257.0	436000	2144.5
2010	18390.1	490.1	17900.0	504400	2425.1
2011-2015	**123156.6**	**2318.8**	**120837.7**	**2457238**	**18148.8**
2011	21404.4	520.4	20884.0	541600	2864.3
2012	23134.6	500.9	22633.7	514900	3301.3
2013	25189.0	450.1	24738.8	479468	3666.3
2014	26149.7	427.5	25722.2	460770	3997.0
2015	27279.0	420.0	26859.0	460500	4320.0

资料来源：旅游外汇收入总额、国内旅游者人数、国内旅游收入来源于北京市旅游发展委员会。

Source: Data of "Foreign Exchange Earnings of Tourism, Number of Domestic Tourists, Revenue from Domestic Tourism" were provided by Beijing Municipal Commission of Tourism Development.

16-2 按客源地分入境旅游者人数(1978-2015年)
NUMBER OF INBOUND TOURISTS BY COUNTRY/REGION (1978-2015)

单位：万人次 (10000 person-times)

年 份 Year	入境旅游者人数 Number of Inbound Tourists	港澳台同胞 Hong Kong, Macao and Taiwan Tourists	外国人 Foreigner	#中国香港 Hong Kong, China	#日 本 Japan	#韩 国 Korea	#美 国 United States	#英 国 United Kingdom	#法 国 France	#德 国 Germany	#俄罗斯 Russia
1978	18.7	3.3	15.4								
1979	25.2	4.1	21.1								
1980	28.6	5.8	21.7		6.0		3.7	1.3	0.9	0.9	
1981-1985	**295.4**	**47.5**	**233.0**		**68.3**		**47.1**	**10.1**	**9.2**	**10.6**	
1981	39.4	6.8	31.3		5.3		3.8	1.1	1.1	1.0	
1982	45.7	8.2	35.9		8.2		6.6	1.3	1.3	1.4	
1983	50.9	8.9	39.7		10.0		9.4	1.5	1.5	1.7	0.1
1984	65.7	10.0	52.1		17.2		12.5	2.3	2.1	2.5	0.1
1985	93.7	13.6	74.0		27.6		14.8	3.9	3.2	4.0	0.2
1986-1990	**492.0**	**117.7**	**357.0**		**110.0**		**63.8**	**18.1**	**15.7**	**22.4**	**3.8**
1986	99.0	15.8	79.0		25.5		14.7	4.1	3.1	4.6	0.3
1987	108.1	21.8	81.7		26.3		16.5	4.5	4.3	5.1	0.3
1988	120.4	28.8	86.5		27.8		16.7	4.2	4.2	5.4	0.7
1989	64.5	16.6	46.0		12.2		7.3	2.4	2.1	3.3	1.0
1990	100.0	34.7	63.8	11.4	18.2		8.6	2.9	2.0	4.0	1.5
1991-1995	**919.6**	**217.9**	**683.4**	**122.7**	**188.0**	**47.2**	**68.9**	**25.2**	**30.1**	**45.9**	**27.4**
1991	132.0	38.2	91.4	17.6	27.6	4.3	9.5	4.3	3.7	6.0	3.5
1992	174.8	51.2	120.5	24.6	37.6	5.6	12.3	4.4	6.6	9.4	5.1
1993	202.8	52.8	145.0	29.4	39.3	7.3	14.3	5.3	6.9	12.0	7.7
1994	203.0	39.4	160.0	25.7	41.1	12.7	15.4	5.4	6.7	9.7	4.9
1995	207.0	36.3	166.5	25.4	42.4	17.3	17.4	5.8	6.2	8.8	6.2
1996-2000	**1203.3**	**206.2**	**984.3**	**128.3**	**229.4**	**92.6**	**118.6**	**43.8**	**37.5**	**53.0**	**28.1**
1996	218.9	38.6	176.2	25.5	43.0	18.0	18.5	7.5	6.6	10.0	6.9
1997	229.8	40.3	186.9	26.3	43.0	19.4	21.7	9.0	6.5	9.1	6.5
1998	220.1	39.1	178.2	25.0	43.5	8.2	23.2	8.8	6.9	11.3	6.2
1999	252.4	44.1	205.0	26.5	45.6	19.2	24.1	8.8	7.9	10.5	4.6
2000	282.1	44.1	238.0	25.0	54.3	27.8	31.1	9.7	9.6	12.1	3.9
2001-2005	**1459.7**	**220.9**	**1238.8**	**133.2**	**233.7**	**182.9**	**173.8**	**57.8**	**51.7**	**56.9**	**33.2**
2001	285.8	45.9	239.9	26.9	50.7	32.7	33.1	11.1	10.2	12.3	4.9
2002	310.4	43.9	266.5	25.5	56.5	38.0	37.4	12.9	11.3	12.2	5.2
2003	185.1	32.4	152.7	21.7	29.2	24.5	19.4	8.1	5.5	6.3	5.2
2004	315.5	47.4	268.1	27.7	52.3	42.4	37.4	11.8	11.1	11.5	8.2
2005	362.9	51.3	311.6	31.4	45.0	45.3	46.5	13.9	13.6	14.6	9.7
2006-2010	**2107.4**	**286.2**	**1821.1**	**174.4**	**248.2**	**207.9**	**291.8**	**82.4**	**72.3**	**85.7**	**85.2**
2006	390.3	52.0	338.3	30.3	50.6	42.4	49.8	14.8	14.2	15.3	15.0
2007	435.5	52.9	382.6	31.3	58.8	44.4	60.3	17.0	16.4	17.5	18.3
2008	379.0	43.3	335.7	28.1	40.0	35.3	53.8	17.5	14.5	16.0	17.9
2009	412.5	69.6	342.9	44.4	46.2	35.2	57.9	16.3	12.9	16.8	15.0
2010	490.1	68.4	421.6	40.3	52.6	50.6	70.0	16.8	14.3	20.1	19.0
2011-2015	**2318.9**	**326.4**	**1992.5**	**185.5**	**170.3**	**215.6**	**369.6**	**88.9**	**72.2**	**113.5**	**81.2**
2011	520.4	73.0	447.4	43.4	51.0	53.4	78.9	18.8	15.0	22.2	20.5
2012	500.9	66.5	434.4	37.6	43.7	44.2	75.1	18.5	15.1	24.5	20.0
2013	450.1	62.5	387.6	35.4	24.9	37.7	74.7	17.5	13.4	23.0	16.7
2014	427.5	62.0	365.5	34.2	24.9	38.7	71.5	16.9	13.4	22.6	13.7
2015	420.0	62.4	357.6	34.9	25.8	41.6	69.4	17.2	15.3	21.2	10.3

注：1．1980-1999年的入境旅游者人数由外国游客、港澳台游客、华侨三部分组成。
2．1990-1999年香港游客人数为香港、澳门合计。

Note: a) "Number of inbound tourists" in 1980-1999 consisted of foreign visitors, visitors from Hong Kong, Macao and Taiwan,and overseas Chinese.
b) Tourists from Hong Kong in 1990-1999 were the total number of tourists from Hong Kong and Macao.

16-3 来京旅游者人数
NUMBER OF TOURISTS TO BEIJING

单位：万人次 (10000 person-times)

项　　目	Item	2015	2014	2015年为2014年% 2015 as % of 2014
合　　计	**Total**	**27279.0**	**26149.7**	**104.3**
国内旅游人数	**Number of Domestic Tourists**	**26859.0**	**25722.2**	**104.4**
外地来京旅游者人数	Number of Tourists to Beijing from Outside Beijing	16253.0	15615.8	104.1
市民在京游人数	Number of Beijing Citizens Touring in Beijing	10606.0	10106.4	104.9
入境旅游者人数	**Number of Inbound Tourists**	**420.0**	**427.5**	**98.3**
港澳台同胞	Hong Kong, Macao and Taiwan Tourists	62.4	62.0	100.7
中国香港	Hong Kong, China	34.9	34.2	102.1
中国澳门	Macao, China	2.1	2.2	95.0
中国台湾	Taiwan, China	25.4	25.6	99.2
外国人	Foreigners	357.6	365.5	97.8
亚　洲	Asia	133.1	130.4	102.1
#日　本	Japan	25.8	24.9	103.9
韩　国	Korea	41.6	38.7	107.5
菲律宾	Philippines	2.3	1.9	120.3
印度尼西亚	Indonesia	4.9	5.4	89.9
马来西亚	Malaysia	7.8	8.1	95.8
新加坡	Singapore	11.0	11.6	94.6
泰　国	Thailand	5.0	5.3	94.6
印　度	India	8.0	6.9	116.9
蒙　古	Mongolia	4.4	5.5	80.1
美　洲	America	91.6	94.8	96.7
#美　国	United States	69.4	71.5	97.1
加拿大	Canada	13.0	14.0	93.1
欧　洲	Europe	106.9	112.8	94.8
#英　国	United Kingdom	17.2	16.9	101.7
法　国	France	15.3	13.4	114.2
德　国	Germany	21.2	22.6	93.7
意大利	Italy	6.2	6.4	96.7
西班牙	Spain	4.4	4.5	98.4
瑞　典	Sweden	3.8	4.6	83.0
瑞　士	Switzerland	2.9	3.5	82.9
俄罗斯	Russia	10.3	13.7	75.1
大洋洲	Oceania	16.3	17.5	93.0
#澳大利亚	Australia	13.6	14.6	93.0
新西兰	New Zealand	2.1	2.0	106.3
非　洲	Africa	8.9	9.2	96.5
其　他	Others	0.7	0.7	101.4

资料来源：表中“国内旅游人数”的相关资料来自北京市旅游发展委员会。
Source: Data related to "Number of Domestic Tourists" in this table were provided by Beijing Municipal Commission of Tourism Development.

16-4 在京旅游花费构成情况(2005-2015年)
COMPOSITION OF EXPENDITURES FOR TOURISM IN BEIJING (2005-2015)

单位：% (%)

项 目	Item	2005	2006	2007	2008	2009	2010	2011	2012	2013	2014	2015
入境旅游者花费构成	**Compositition of Expenditures for Inbound Tourists**	**100.0**	**100.0**	**100.0**	**100.0**	**100.0**	**100.0**	**100.0**	**100.0**	**100.0**	**100.0**	**100.0**
长途交通费	Long-distance Transportation Expenses	35.3	30.0	29.0	31.1	37.4	28.1	26.4	28.0	26.9	27.0	36.8
民 航	Air	30.9	29.6	24.4	25.3	27.1	19.8	20.5	22.3	21.2	21.4	30.8
铁 路	Railway	1.1	0.3	3.0	3.6	5.5	5.3	3.4	3.3	3.7	3.6	3.2
公 路	Highway	3.3	0.1	1.6	2.2	4.8	3.0	2.5	2.4	2.0	2.0	2.7
市内交通费	Local Transportation Expenses	1.1	1.7	2.6	2.4	2.7	3.4	3.5	3.5	2.5	2.6	2.4
住 宿	Accommodation	17.3	32.0	16.9	16.4	14.5	14.4	15.5	16.5	16.9	16.7	12.8
餐 饮	Restaurants	9.2	11.7	8.7	8.7	7.5	8.7	6.8	7.4	7.3	7.4	6.2
购 物	Shopping	19.9	15.9	22.5	19.1	20.4	25.1	25.3	23.5	27.6	26.7	19.9
邮电通讯	Post and Telecommunications	3.4	0.8	2.7	3.8	2.7	3.2	2.0	2.2	1.7	1.7	2.4
景区游览	Scenic Spot Sightseeing	4.7	2.3	4.2	4.8	3.9	4.7	4.2	5.0	4.2	4.3	3.3
文化娱乐	Culture and Entertainment	4.6	3.2	5.0	4.5	4.6	5.0	6.0	5.4	3.8	4.0	4.2
其 他	Others	4.5	2.4	8.4	9.2	6.3	7.4	10.3	8.5	9.1	9.6	12.1
外地来京游客花费构成	**Compositition of Expenditures for Tourists from Outside Beijing**	**100.0**	**100.0**	**100.0**	**100.0**	**100.0**	**100.0**	**100.0**	**100.0**	**100.0**	**100.0**	**100.0**
长途交通费	Long-distance Transportation Expenses	12.8	15.1	16.3	15.4	12.9	12.8	13.5	15.5	17.0	17.6	17.0
民 航	Air		8.0	9.2	9.1	6.6	6.0	6.2	7.7	7.5	7.1	7.4
铁 路	Railway		6.1	6.4	4.5	1.3	5.8	6.9	7.5	9.1	10.2	9.3
公 路	Highway		1.1	0.7	1.8	5.0	1.0	0.3	0.3	0.4	0.3	0.3
市内交通费	Local Transportation Expenses	5.7	5.1	5.5	5.6	4.9	5.0	4.5	4.0	3.8	3.8	4.0
住 宿	Accommodation	17.2	14.9	17.3	15.1	17.7	19.6	20.0	19.8	19.5	20.2	18.7
餐 饮	Restaurants	19.8	18.7	20.5	23.2	21.8	20.2	20.9	21.4	21.4	22.1	22.1
购 物	Shopping	24.1	22.2	25.8	32.7	34.5	34.5	34.3	32.1	30.9	28.2	30.2
邮电通讯	Post and Telecommunications	1.0	1.2	1.8	1.0	0.6	0.5	0.3	0.2	0.2	0.3	0.3
景区游览	Scenic Spot Sightseeing	9.1	9.5	7.2	4.5	6.1	6.2	5.7	6.1	6.6	6.5	6.2
文化娱乐	Culture and Entertainment	3.1	2.5	1.9	1.6	1.2	1.0	0.8	0.7	0.5	0.6	0.7
其 他	Others	7.1	10.8	3.7	0.9	0.3	0.2	0.1	0.1	0.1	0.7	0.8

资料来源：北京市旅游发展委员会。
Source: Beijing Municipal Commission of Tourism Development.

16-5 旅游服务设施情况(1978-2015年)
TOURISM SERVICE FACILITIES (1978-2015)

年份 Year	饭店个数(个) Number of Hotels (unit)	五星 5-star	四星 4-star	三星 3-star	二星 2-star	一星 1-star	饭店客房数(万间) Number of Hotel Guest Rooms (10,000 rooms)	旅行社家数(个) Number of Travel Agencies (unit)	#国际社 International Travel Agencies	A级及以上景区个数(个) Number of Scenic Spots at Grade-A and Above (unit)	5A	4A	3A	2A	1A
1978	11						0.39								
1979	13						0.44								
1980	20						0.49								
1981	35						0.69								
1982	39						1.00								
1983	41						1.03								
1984	50						1.30								
1985	63						1.66								
1986	80						2.10								
1987	97						2.40								
1988	96						2.80	30							
1989	101						3.50	77							
1990	122						3.95	77							
1991	213						4.40	69							
1992	226						5.20	69							
1993	226						5.20	55							
1994	175	14	20	32	72	37	5.40	297	113						
1995	197	15	25	43	79	35	5.90	310	125						
1996	204	15	25	46	82	36	6.10	349	128						
1997	248	16	26	60	109	37	6.80	350	130						
1998	258	16	32	65	113	32	7.00	380	135						
1999	268	17	32	71	117	31	7.20	419	144						
2000	409	21	34	132	176	46	8.40	456	150						
2001	506	21	43	154	230	58	9.30	490	160	47		17	4	22	4
2002	572	26	56	175	252	63	10.30	505	161	86		25	9	43	9
2003	614	30	62	195	267	60	10.90	530	165	93		28	9	46	10
2004	613	34	70	207	260	42	9.10	585	170	93		28	9	46	10
2005	652	36	79	224	267	46	10.97	714	196	124		36	26	50	12
2006	700	37	91	228	292	52	11.20	790	212	124		36	26	50	12
2007	806	42	114	257	338	55	13.00	844	239	154	4	41	35	54	20
2008	836	52	127	272	334	51	13.40	860	266	158	4	44	36	54	20
2009	757	54	129	268	269	37	12.95	888	265	179	4	55	53	51	16
2010	729	64	139	262	237	27	13.05	819		201	4	66	72	44	15
2011	598	63	127	207	181	20	11.64	919		211	6	63	80	46	16
2012	612	62	130	207	191	22	11.71	1021		203	8	64	78	40	13
2013	614	62	131	207	193	21	11.64	1147		213	8	67	86	42	10
2014	581	65	133	205	165	13	11.38	1243		221	8	69	89	45	10
2015	528	63	127	193	135	10	10.86	1238		227	8	72	95	44	8

注：1. 1993年及以前饭店数为涉外饭店口径,1994年以后为星级饭店口径。

2. 1994-1996年国际旅行社为一、二类旅行社合计。从2010年起，旅行社不再按国际旅行社和国内旅行社分组。

资料来源：北京市旅游发展委员会。

Note: a) Number of hotels in 1993 and before was the number of hotels for foreign tourists, and after 1994,the number of star-rated hotels.

b) International travel agencies were the total number of travel agencies of categories I and II after 1994-1996. From 2010, statistics of travel agencies were no more grouped into international and domestic angencies.

Source: Beijing Municipal Commission of Tourism Development.

16-6 星级饭店接待及经营情况(1995-2015年)
RECEPTION AND OPERATION OF STAR-RATED HOTELS (1995-2015)

年份 Year	企业个数(个) Number of Enterprises (unit)	接待住宿人数(万人次) Tourists Received (10000 person-time)	接待住宿人天数(万人天) Persons-Day Received (10000 person-day)	出租率(%) Renting Rate (%)	平均房价(元/间天) Average Prices (yuan/room.day)	营业收入(万元) Business Income (10000 yuan)	利润总额(万元) Total Profits (10000 yuan)	从业人员平均人数(人) Average Number of Employed Persons (person)
1995	191	484.6	1843.4	67.0	491	1136136	188095	98535
1996-2000		**3168.1**	**10110.0**			**5388348**	**286868**	
1996	207	485.3	1691.6	63.0	483	1132827	153145	94352
1997	235	541.8	1801.4	59.0	463	1145884	104918	103255
1998	262	605.0	1867.7	55.0	397	1038991	-24239	104391
1999	263	681.5	1918.6	57.0	352	970907	22383	103827
2000	294	854.5	2830.6	61.0	394	1099739	30661	96115
2001-2005		**5931.5**	**14152.9**			**7243160**	**316031**	
2001	363	1038.5	3191.7	62.0	384	1202746	50466	105792
2002	390	1071.2	2437.6	62.0	392	1307094	27212	107091
2003	441	1007.4	2497.2	52.0	389	1227956	-33471	105994
2004	464	1270.8	2798.9	65.0	409	1654198	117541	107386
2005	594	1543.6	3227.5	62.0	425	1851166	154283	126817
2006-2010		**8761.5**	**17721.0**			**11799293**	**650440**	
2006	597	1578.5	3284.5	61.3	460	2055300	194460	126430
2007	638	1664.2	3403.6	60.2	494	2369964	219891	129523
2008	694	1566.1	3206.6	52.0	605	2504849	232746	130609
2009	815	1827.3	3652.8	49.2	430	2261411	-76121	134159
2010	729	2125.4	4173.5	56.4	450	2607769	79464	130050
2010-2015		**10119.8**	**19429.6**			**13756636**	**518904**	
2011	598	2111.1	4119.6	59.9	482	2853358	162374	128609
2012	612	2101.0	4085.2	60.0	523	3031116	179495	122379
2013	614	1958.8	3769.5	58.4	530	2727974	111669	112512
2014	581	1940.3	3664.6	57.6	513	2568185	12499	99258
2015	528	2008.6	3790.7	60.6	520	2576003	52866	92606

注：1. 表中企业个数为全市星级宾馆饭店数，其余指标1995-1999年为涉外饭店数据，2000年及以后为星级宾馆饭店数据。
2. 从2011年开始北京市旅游发展委员会每年对全市星级饭店进行重新评定，对未达标饭店取消星级。

Note: a) Number of Enterprises refer to the number of star-rated hotels in Beijing, Other indicators covered hotels for foreign tourists for 1995-1999, and star-rated hotels after 2000.

b) From 2011, Beijing Municipal Tourism Development Commission reevalutaed star-rated hotels across the city , and cancelled the rating of hotels that did not meet the standard.

16-7 星级饭店经营情况
OPERATION OF STAR-RATED HOTELS

项目	Item	企业个数(个) Number of Enterprises (unit)		出租率(%) Renting Rate (%)		平均房价(元/间天) Average Prices (yuan/room.day)	
		2015	2014	2015	2014	2015	2014
合计	**Total**	**528**	**581**	**60.6**	**57.6**	**520**	**513**
四星、五星合计	**Hotels of 4 and 5 Star Grade**	**190**	**198**	**62.5**	**60.2**	**640**	**630**
五星	5-Star	63	65	64.0	63.0	821	802
四星	4-Star	127	133	61.4	58.1	491	489
一星至三星合计	**Hotels of 1 to 3-Star Grade**	**338**	**383**	**57.8**	**54.0**	**331**	**330**
三星	3-Star	193	205	57.6	54.6	361	357
二星	2-Star	135	165	58.8	54.0	253	268
一星	1-Star	10	13	42.9	27.6	204	181

16-7 续表 Continued

项目	Item	营业收入(万元) Business Income (10000 yuan)		利润总额(万元) Total Profits (10000 yuan)		从业人员平均人数(人) Average Number of Employed Persons (person)	
		2015	2014	2015	2014	2015	2014
合计	**Total**	**2576003**	**2568185**	**52866**	**12499**	**92606**	**99258**
四星、五星合计	**Hotels of 4 and 5 Star Grade**	**1986642**	**1937983**	**64208**	**32711**	**63294**	**67168**
五星	5-Star	1180293	1120181	65453	42689	30995	32265
四星	4-Star	806349	817802	-1244	-9978	32299	34903
一星至三星合计	**Hotels of 1 to 3-Star Grade**	**589361**	**630202**	**-11342**	**-20212**	**29312**	**32090**
三星	3-Star	491043	507979	-14208	-22091	24108	25497
二星	2-Star	98097	120237	2778	1872	5183	6404
一星	1-Star	222	1986	88	7	21	189

16-8 星级饭店接待住宿者情况(按住宿者类别分)
TOURSITS RECEIVED BY STAR-RATED HOTELS (BY TYPE OF TOURISTS)

项　目	Item	2015 接待量 Tourists Received	2015 构　成(%) Composition (%)	2014 接待量 Tourists Received	2014 构　成(%) Composition (%)	2015年为2014年% 2015 as % of 2014
接待住宿人数　（万人次）	**Tourists Received　(10000 person-times)**	**2008.6**	**100.0**	**1940.3**	**100.0**	**103.5**
国内住宿者	Domestic Tourists	1775.7	88.4	1693.8	87.3	104.8
外国人	Foreigners	200.9	10.0	215.5	11.1	93.2
香港同胞	Compatriots from Hong Kong, China	18.5	0.9	17.1	0.9	108.1
澳门同胞	Compatriots from Macao, China	0.9	…	0.8	…	111.2
台湾同胞	Compatriots from Taiwan, China	12.6	0.6	13.0	0.7	96.5
接待住宿人天数　（万人天）	**Persons-day Received (10000 persons-day)**	**3790.7**	**100.0**	**3664.6**	**100.0**	**103.4**
国内住宿者	Domestic Tourists	3298.3	87.0	3127.5	85.3	105.5
外国人	Foreigners	425.0	11.2	469.3	12.8	90.6
香港同胞	Compatriots from Hong Kong, China	37.3	1.0	35.8	1.0	104.1
澳门同胞	Compatriots from Macao, China	2.2	0.1	2.2	0.1	101.4
台湾同胞	Compatriots from Taiwan, China	27.8	0.7	29.8	0.8	93.4

16-9 星级饭店接待住宿者情况(按饭店星级分)
TOURSITS RECEIVED BY STAR-RATED HOTELS (BY STAR RATING)

单位：万人次　　(10000 person-times)

项　目	Item	2015 接待量 Tourists Received	2015 构　成(%) Composition (%)	2014 接待量 Tourists Received	2014 构　成(%) Composition (%)	2015年为2014年% 2015 as % of 2014
接待住宿人数	**Tourists Received**	**2008.6**	**100.0**	**1940.3**	**100.0**	**103.5**
五星级	5-Star	550.9	27.4	516.9	26.6	106.6
四星级	4-Star	670.4	33.4	623.3	32.1	107.6
三星级	3-Star	556.9	27.7	541.7	27.9	102.8
二星级	2-Star	225.8	11.2	249.4	12.9	90.5
一星级	1-Star	4.6	0.2	9.0	0.5	51.0
接待入境住宿人数	**Inbound Tourists Received**	**232.9**	**100.0**	**246.5**	**100.0**	**94.5**
五星级	5-Star	131.1	56.3	139.5	56.6	94.0
四星级	4-Star	83.2	35.7	85.4	34.6	97.5
三星级	3-Star	14.1	6.0	16.1	6.5	87.4
二星级	2-Star	4.4	1.9	5.5	2.2	81.0
一星级	1-Star	…	…	…	…	90.1

16-10 旅行社接待及经营情况(1990-2015年)
RECEPTION AND OPERATION OF TRAVEL AGENCIES (1990-2015)

年 份 Year	企 业 个 数 (个) Number of Enterprises (unit)	外联(组团) 人 数 (万人次) Number of Inbound Tourists (Organized) (10000 person-times)	接 待 人 数 (万人次) Tourists Received (10000 person-times)	国内居民 出境人数 (万人次) Number of Outbound Chinese Tourists (10000 person-times)	营 业 收 入 (万元) Business Income (10000 yuan)	利 润 总 额 (万元) Total Profits (10000 yuan)	从业人员 平均人数 (人) Average Number of Employed Persons (person)
1990		32.5	54.7				
1991-1995		**355.6**	**451.7**				
1991		53.3	69.1				
1992		61.2	100.7				
1993		71.3	103.6				
1994		84.1	91.0	1.0			
1995	100	85.7	87.4	1.2	290987.9	107654.6	
1996-2000		**487.1**	**417.5**	**37.9**	**2187374.9**	**106167.0**	
1996	105	88.0	78.6	2.7	351634.7	13520.8	
1997	110	87.3	76.0	3.8	386254.1	16009.6	
1998	131	85.0	69.0	6.6	387562.7	21319.9	
1999	120	103.1	92.9	11.1	485678.8	26572.0	
2000	127	123.7	101.0	13.7	576244.6	28744.7	6280
2001-2005		**986.2**	**919.6**	**185.4**	**4453919.0**	**51899.5**	
2001	140	143.4	130.1	21.9	700529.0	18682.5	8259
2002	151	179.4	176.3	28.5	823551.0	23362.0	9350
2003	147	80.2	82.4	31.9	553787.0	-11829.0	8382
2004	147	274.8	252.6	51.4	1059989.0	11444.0	7760
2005	147	308.4	278.2	51.7	1316063.0	10240.0	8752
2006-2010		**2036.3**	**1852.4**	**515.9**	**11530195.8**	**82083.6**	
2006	147	343.9	315.7	79.2	1610265.0	7012.0	8659
2007	189	424.1	377.9	100.2	2101874.5	28409.2	11597
2008	245	359.6	310.1	102.0	2166898.1	18121.6	14369
2009	265	370.6	306.6	84.9	2134058.8	5904.6	15262
2010	819	538.1	542.2	149.6	3517099.4	22636.2	21454
2011-2015		**3223.2**	**2408.0**	**1731.1**	**31300961.3**	**131080.7**	
2011	919	593.9	552.3	184.3	4436713.3	20879.2	23871
2012	1021	684.5	519.1	272.5	5415692.9	35274.4	28022
2013	1147	661.3	441.6	331.0	6103603.4	64177.5	31694
2014	1243	628.0	427.0	410.2	6989125.4	27881.7	33591
2015	1238	655.5	468.0	533.1	8355826.3	-17132.1	37780

注：1. 本表2009年及以前为国际旅行社口径，从2010年起调整为全部旅行社口径。
2. 国内居民出境人数为旅行社组织出境游客的实际人次数，不重复统计。

Note: a) Figures in this table refer to international travel agencies in and before 2009, and all travel agencies after 2010.
b) Number of outbound Chinese visitors is the actual number of tourists going abroad that were organized by travel agencies, which has not been calculated repeatedly.

16-11 旅行社外联(组团)及接待情况
TOURISTS GROUPED (ORGANIZED) AND RECEIVED BY TRAVEL AGENCIES

项目	Item	2015	2014	2015年为2014年% 2015 as % of 2014
外联(组团)人数 (万人次)	**Tourists Grouped (Organized) (10000 person-times)**	**655.5**	**628.0**	**104.4**
国内旅游者	Domestic Tourists	515.0	457.2	112.6
港澳同胞	Compatriots from Hong Kong and Macao, China	6.3	4.2	150.0
台湾同胞	Compatriots from Taiwan, China	5.1	4.3	118.6
外国人	Foreigners	129.1	162.2	79.6
接待人数 (万人次)	**Tourists Received (10000 person-times)**	**468.0**	**427.0**	**109.6**
国内旅游者	Domestic Tourists	344.0	317.2	108.4
港澳同胞	Compatriots from Hong Kong and Macao, China	8.7	8.5	102.4
台湾同胞	Compatriots from Taiwan, China	3.8	3.6	105.6
外国人	Foreigners	111.5	97.7	114.1
外联(组团)人天数(万人天)	**Persons-day of Tourists Grouped (Organized) (10000 persons-day)**	**2687.7**	**2469.6**	**108.8**
国内旅游者	Domestic Tourists	2009.2	1693.0	118.7
港澳同胞	Compatriots from Hong Kong and Macao, China	27.2	17.6	154.6
台湾同胞	Compatriots from Taiwan, China	26.5	23.5	112.7
外国人	Foreigners	624.8	735.5	85.0
接待人天数 (万人天)	**Persons-day of Tourists Received (10000 persons-day)**	**1935.8**	**1656.8**	**116.8**
国内旅游者	Domestic Tourists	1371.7	1137.3	120.6
港澳同胞	Compatriots from Hong Kong and Macao, China	43.1	41.7	103.3
台湾同胞	Compatriots from Taiwan, China	21.4	19.1	112.1
外国人	Foreigners	499.7	458.7	108.9

16-12 旅行社组织国内居民出境旅游情况
OUTBOUND CHINESE TOURISTS ORGANIZED BY TRAVEL AGENCIES

单位：万人次 (10000 person-times)

项目	Item	2015	2014	2015年为2014年% 2015 as % of 2014
旅行社个数(个)	**Number of Travel Agencies (unit)**	**400**	**367**	**109.0**
国内居民出境人数	**Number of Outbound Chinese Tourists**	**533.1**	**410.2**	**130.0**
前往国别及地区	**Countries and Regions of Destination**			
#中国香港	Hong Kong, China	21.5	26.3	81.6
中国澳门	Macao, China	15.1	13.3	113.5
中国台湾	Taiwan, China	30.1	27.1	111.0
泰　国	Thailand	93.4	47.1	198.3
新加坡	Singapore	14.7	10.6	138.7
马来西亚	Malaysia	10.7	9.4	113.6
菲律宾	Philippines	2.5	3.5	72.2
韩　国	Korea	68.0	73.7	92.3
日　本	Japan	89.7	43.5	206.3
澳大利亚	Australia	12.7	11.2	113.2
新西兰	New Zealand	7.9	5.4	145.8

注：1. 本表统计范围为有特许经营出境旅游业务权的旅行社。
2. 国内居民出境人数为旅行社组织出境游客的实际人次数，不重复统计。
3. 前往国别及地区统计中，游客一次出境旅游去往多个国家及地区的，分别计入前往国家及地区。

Note: a) Figures in this table cover the travel agencies that are franchised to operate outbound travelling business.
b) Number of outbound Chinese tourists is the actual number of tourists going abroad who were organized by travel agencies,which has not been calculated repeatedly.
c) In the statistics for "countries and regions of destination", if a tourist went to several countries and regions, he/she would be included in each country and region.

16-13 旅行社经营情况
OPERATION OF TRAVEL SERVICES

单位：万元 (10000 yuan)

项目	Item	2015	2014	2015年为2014年% 2015 as % of 2014
企业个数 (个)	Number of Enterprises (unit)	1238	1243	99.6
营业收入	Business Income	8355826.3	6989125.4	119.6
主营业务成本	Main Business Cost	6969927.9	6514223.8	107.0
营业费用	Business Expenses	326021.3	244497.5	133.3
主营业务税金及附加	Main Business Tax and Surtax	29739.4	28120.7	105.8
主营业务利润	Main Business Profits	436187.4	437225.4	99.8
管理费用	Management Expenses	251488.1	213697.3	117.7
营业利润	Business Profits	-24962.0	20062.7	
利润总额	Total Profits	-17132.1	27881.7	
从业人员平均人数 (人)	Average Number of Employed Persons (person)	37780	33591	112.5

16-14 A级及以上和重点旅游景区活动情况
STATISTICS FOR KEY SIGHT SPOTS ABOVE GRADE A

项目	Item	2015	2014	2015年为2014年% 2015 as % of 2014
A级及以上和重点旅游景区数 (个)	Number of Key Sight Spots Above Grade (unit)	248	221	112.2
收入合计 (万元)	Total Income (10000 yuan)	728568	656909	110.9
门票收入	Ticket Income	462318	417698	110.7
商品销售收入	Commodity Sales	19299	16750	115.2
其他收入	Other Income	246951	222462	111.0
接待人数 (万人次)	Tourists Received (10000 person-times)	29405	28685	102.5
#入境旅游者人数	Inbound Tourists	844	897	94.1

主要统计指标解释

入境旅游者 指来中国（大陆）观光、度假、探亲访友、就医疗养、购物、参加会议或从事经济、文化、体育、宗教活动，且在中国（大陆）的旅游住宿设施内至少停留一夜的外国人、港澳台同胞等游客。入境旅游者不包括以下人员：（1）应邀来华访问的政府部长以上官员及其随行人员；（2）外国驻华使领馆官员、外交人员以及随行的家庭服务人员和受赡养者；（3）常住中国（大陆）一年以上的外国专家、留学生、记者、商务机构人员等；（4）乘坐国际航班过境不需要通过护照检查进入中国（大陆）口岸的中转旅客；（5）边境地区往来的边民；（6）回大陆定居的港澳台同胞；（7）已在中国（大陆）定居的外国人和原已出境又返回在中国（大陆）定居的外国侨民；（8）归国的中国（大陆）出国人员。

国内旅游者 指中国（大陆）居民离开惯常居住地在境内其他地方的旅游住宿设施内至少停留一夜，最长不超过12个月的国内游客。

旅游外汇收入 指入境游客在中国（大陆）境内旅行、游览过程中用于交通、参观游览、住宿、餐饮、购物、娱乐等全部花费。

国内旅游收入 指国内游客在国内旅行、游览过程中用于交通、参观游览、住宿、餐饮、购物、娱乐等全部花费。

外联（组团）入境旅游者人数 指报告期内旅行社自组外联的入境旅游者人数，反映旅行社对外招徕的能力。旅行社按以下要求统计外联人数：入境游客不论其停留时间多少、旅游线路长短，只统计一次；旅行社只统计本社自组外联团的实到人数，不包括非本社外联、仅由本社接受委托办理签证的人数。

接待入境旅游者人数 指报告期内本旅行社派地陪接待的入境人数。

出境旅游总人数 指中国（大陆）公民因公或因私出境前往其他国家、中国香港特别行政区、澳门特别行政区和台湾省观光、度假、探亲访友、就医疗养、购物、参加会议或从事经济、文化、体育、宗教活动的人数。统计时，出境游客按每出境一次统计1人次。

Explanatory Notes on Main Statistical Indicators

Inbound Tourists refer to tourists from foreign countries, Hong Kong, Macao and Taiwan to (mainland of) China for sightseeing, holidays, visiting relatives and friends, medical service and rehabilitation, shopping, conferences, or economic, cultural, sports and religious activities, and staying in a tour accommodation facility in (the mainland of) China for at least one night. They do not include: (1) officials above the rank of governmental ministers, and their accompanying persons who visit China upon invitation; (2) officials in foreign embassies and consulates in Beijing, diplomatic personnel, and their accompanying family service personnel and dependents; (3) foreign experts, students, reporters, and personnel in business institutions who have been in (the mainland of) China for more than one year; (4) transit passengers via (the mainland of) China by international flights without passport checking; (5) people living on the frontiers who pass through borders; (6) compatriots from Hong Kong, Macao and Taiwan who settle down in the mainland of China; (7) Foreigners that have settled down in China and foreign nationals that have left the country and then come back to settle down in (the mainland of) China; (8) Chinese (Mainland) people who have gone abroad and returned to China.

Domestic Tourists refer to domestic visitors as residents in (the mainland of) China who leave their regular dwelling places to stay at least one night and at most 12 months in a travel accommodation facility of other domestic places.

Foreign Exchange Earnings of Tourism means the total spending of international tourists on traffic, tour, accommodation, restaurants, shopping, entertainment and so on during their tour and travel in (the mainland of) China.

Revenue from Domestic Tourism means the total spending of domestic tourists on traffic, tour, accommodation, restaurants, shopping and entertainment, and so on during their tour and travel in China.

Number of Inbound Tourists Organized by Travel Agencies means the number of inbound tourists organized by travel agencies in the reporting period. It shows the capacity of travel agencies in attracting inbound tourists; travel agencies shall count the tourists organized as follows: an inbound tourist is regarded as one visit regardless of the duration and distance of the tour; only the actual tourists organized by travel agencies are included. Those organized by other travel agencies or those who have visa submitted by the travel agencies are not included.

Number of Inbound Tourists Received means the number of inbound tourists received by local guides dispatched by travel agencies in the reporting period.

Total Number of Outbound Tourists means the number of citizens from (the mainland of) China who visit other countries, Hong Kong Special Administrative Region of PRC, Macao Special Administrative Region of PRC, and Taiwan for sightseeing, holiday, visiting relatives and friends, medical service and rehabilitation, shopping, conferences, or economic, cultural, sport and religious activities for official or private purpose. One visit is calculated as one person-time.

17

北京统计年鉴2016　BEIJING STATISTICAL YEARBOOK

金融和保险
FINANCE AND INSURANCE

简要说明

一、本章资料的主要内容

本章反映北京地区金融业发展情况。主要包括以下四个部分:

1. 金融机构信贷收支情况;
2. 证券市场交易情况;
3. 保险业务情况;
4. 上市公司基本情况。

二、本章资料的数据来源

1. 信贷收支数据来源于中国人民银行营业管理部。
2. 证券市场交易量数据来源于北京市统计局。
3. 银行、保险系统机构及人员数据来源于北京市统计局。
4. 保险业务数据来源于中国保险监督管理委员会北京监管局。
5. 上市公司数据来源于中国证券监督管理委员会北京证监局。

Brief Introduction

I. Main Content

This chapter reflects the development of the financial industry in Beijing, mainly consisting of four parts:

1. Balance of credit for financial institutions;
2. Transactions in securities market;
3. Insurance business;
4. Basic information of listed companies.

II. Source of Data

1. Figures of balance of credit are gathered from the Banking Management Department of the People's Bank of China.
2. Data of transactions in securities market are gathered from Beijing Municipal Bureau of Statistics.
3. Data of banks, insurance institutions and personnel are gathered from Beijing Municipal Bureau of Statistics.
4. Data of insurance business are gathered from Beijing Bureau of China Insurance Regulatory Commission.
5. Data of basic information of listed companies are gathered from Beijing Securities Regulatory Bureau of China Securities Regulatory Commission.

17-1 北京市金融机构(含外资)存贷款余额(1978-2015年)
DEPOSIT AND LOAN BALANCE OF FINANCIAL INSTITUTIONS (INCLUDING FOREIGN BANKS) (1978-2015)

单位：亿元 (100 million yuan)

年份 Year	金融机构本外币存款 Balance of Savings Deposit in Domestic and Foreign Currencies in Financial Institutions	#人民币存款 RMB Deposits	金融机构本外币存款 Deposits in Domestic and Foreign Currencies in Financial Institutions					
			中资金融机构 Chinese Financial Institutions			外资银行 Foreign-funded Financial Bank		
			存款合计 Total Deposits	人民币存款 RMB Deposits	外汇(亿美元) Foreign Exchange (USD 100 million)	存款合计 Total Deposits	人民币存款 RMB Deposits	外汇(亿美元) Foreign Exchange (USD 100 million)
1978				114.7				
1979				139.1				
1980				168.0				
1981				220.5				
1982				279.2				
1983				321.3				
1984				375.5				
1985				411.0				
1986				508.8				
1987				610.8				
1988				609.9				
1989				717.6				
1990				893.9				
1991				1244.1				
1992				1528.3				
1993				1873.1				
1994				2677.3				
1995				3527.2				
1996				4378.9				
1997				5228.0				
1998				6666.8				
1999				8267.2				
2000	11526.0			9759.8	205.6			…
2001	14109.2		14042.1	12223.4	219.8			7.3
2002	17438.4		17369.9	15392.7	238.9			8.3
2003	20476.0		20398.2	18321.9	250.9			9.4
2004	23781.3	21625.9	23679.3	21625.9	248.1			12.3
2005	28969.9	26785.9	28800.9	26731.3	256.4		54.6	14.2
2006	33793.3	31313.8	33484.1	31179.2	295.2		134.5	22.4
2007	37700.3	35369.7	37087.5	35014.1	283.8		355.6	35.2
2008	43980.7	42107.6	43094.4	41500.0	233.3	886.3	607.5	40.8
2009	56960.1	54275.5	55804.8	53428.8	348.0	1155.3	846.6	45.2
2010	66584.6	64453.9	64897.6	63025.2	282.7	1687.0	1428.7	39.0
2011	75001.9	72655.4	73018.9	70985.1	322.8	1983.1	1670.3	49.6
2012	84837.3	81389.6	82615.9	79620.6	476.5	2221.4	1769.1	72.0
2013	91660.5	87990.6	89187.4	85897.2	539.6	2473.1	2093.4	62.3
2014	100095.5	95370.5	97645.9	93326.0	706.0	2449.6	2044.5	66.2
2015	128573.0	123767.4	126164.8	121878.9	660.0	2461.0	1941.3	80.0

资料来源：中国人民银行营业管理部。
Source: Operations Office of People's Bank of China.

17-1 续表 Continued

单位：亿元 (100 million yuan)

年 份 Year	金融机构本外币贷款余额 Balance of Loans in Domestic and Foreign Currencies in Financial Institutions	#人民币贷 款 RMB Loans	#中长期贷 款 Medium-term &Long-term Loans	金融机构本外币贷款 Loans in Domestic and Foreign Currencies in Financial Institutions 中资金融机构 Chinese Financial Institutions 贷款合计 Total Loans	 人民币贷 款 RMB Loans	 外 汇(亿美元) Foreign Exchange (USD 100 million)	 外资银行 Foreign-funded Financial Bank 贷款合计 Total Loans	 人民币贷 款 RMB Loans	 外 汇(亿美元) Foreign Exchange (USD 100 million)
1978					53.9				
1979					74.2				
1980					87.3				
1981					91.3				
1982					109.1				
1983					149.5				
1984					174.3				
1985					249.8				
1986					299.2				
1987					346.1				
1988					415.7				
1989					487.1				
1990					573.1				
1991					735.8				
1992					894.7				
1993					1128.1				
1994					1429.0				
1995					1779.1				
1996					2082.8				
1997					2720.7				
1998					3326.6				
1999					4007.8				
2000	6407.9		3106.7	6306.3	6008.2	27.7			9.0
2001	7612.2		3797.3	7514.9	7202.9	37.4			10.8
2002	9704.3		5026.9	9602.6	9230.8	44.9			12.1
2003	12057.7		6352.0	11884.4	11314.7	68.8			20.9
2004	13577.7		7506.4	13312.3	12600.2	86.0			32.0
2005	15335.5		8632.4	14996.6	13792.2	149.2		42.3	36.8
2006	18131.6	15632.7	11142.8	17631.7	15486.9	274.7		145.8	45.4
2007	19861.5	17812.5	12217.6	19053.9	17360.2	231.9	807.5	452.3	48.6
2008	23010.7	19985.0	14688.9	22160.5	19431.1	399.4	850.2	554.0	43.3
2009	31052.9	25421.8	21163.8	30151.6	24805.1	783.0	901.3	616.7	41.7
2010	36479.6	29563.8	26180.2	35352.0	28748.1	997.2	1127.6	815.6	47.1
2011	39660.5	33367.0	24886.3	38410.3	32434.6	948.4	1250.2	932.5	50.4
2012	43189.5	36441.3	26333.5	41839.8	35441.7	1017.9	1349.7	999.6	55.7
2013	47880.9	40506.7	28171.7	46539.5	39557.5	1145.2	1341.4	949.2	64.3
2014	53650.6	45458.7	30882.3	52254.3	44438.8	1277.3	1396.2	1019.9	61.5
2015	58559.4	50559.5	33671.3	57281.2	49530.8	1193.6	1994.3	1676.9	48.9

资料来源：中国人民银行营业管理部。
Source: Operations Office of People's Bank of China.

17-2 北京市金融机构(含外资)本外币信贷收支表

BALANCE OF CREIT IN DOMESTIC AND FOREIGN CURRENCIES FOR FINANCIAL INSTITUTIONS (INCLUDE FOREIGN BANKS)

单位：万元，汇率：6.4936 (10000 yuan ,at an exchange rate of 6.4936)

项目	Item	余额 Balance	比年初增减额(+、-) Increase or Decrease than the Beginning of the Year
各项存款	**Total Deposits**	**1285729650**	**152486837**
#人民币存款	RMB Deposits	1237673673	153282599
境内存款	Domestic deposits	1274954835	154848202
住户存款	Resident deposits	277038603	16772275
非金融企业存款	Non-financial corporate deposits	463369641	50088880
广义政府存款	General government deposits	266417355	26925921
#财政性存款	Fiscal deposits	14551492	-7351802
非银行业金融机构存款	Deposits of non-banking financial institutions	268129236	61061127
境外存款	Overseas deposits	10774815	-2361365
各项贷款	**Total Loans**	**585594023**	**48220604**
#人民币贷款	RMB Loans	505595179	50212476
境内贷款	Domestic Loans	547070542	40756598
住户贷款	Resident loans	111817261	17836470
非金融企业及机关团体贷款	Loans of non-financial companies and organizations	430824572	19115160
非银行业金融机构贷款	Loans of non-banking financial institutions	4428709	3804968
境外贷款	Overseas Loans	38523482	7464006

资料来源：中国人民银行营业管理部。
Source: Operations Office of People's Bank of China.

17-3 北京市中资金融机构本外币信贷收支表

BALANCE OF CREDIT IN DOMESTIC AND FOREIGN CURRENCIES FOR DOMESTICALLY-FUNDED FINANCIAL INSTITUTIONS

单位：万元，汇率：6.4936 (10000 yuan ,at an exchange rate of 6.4936)

项目	Item	余额 Balance	比年初增减额(+、-) Increase or Decrease than Year-beginning
各项存款	**Total Deposits**	**1261648055**	**153115804**
#人民币存款	RMB Deposits	1218788556	154982621
境内存款	Domestic deposits	1252768689	155591848
住户存款	Resident deposits	275095443	16802374
非金融企业存款	Non-financial corporate deposits	444986602	51259197
广义政府存款	General government deposits	266412648	26945238
#财政性存款	Fiscal deposits	14551492	-7351802
非银行业金融机构存款	Deposits of non-banking financial institutions	266273996	60585040
境外存款	Overseas deposits	8879367	-2476044
各项贷款	**Total Loans**	**572812468**	**49823429**
#人民币贷款	RMB Loans	495307508	50473492
境内贷款	Domestic Loans	535033049	42413459
住户贷款	Resident loans	110379221	17542758
非金融企业及机关团体贷款	Loans of non-financial companies and organizations	420325120	20785138
非银行业金融机构贷款	Loans of non-banking financial institutions	4328709	4085563
境外贷款	Overseas Loans	37779418	7409970

资料来源：中国人民银行营业管理部。
Source: Operations Office of People's Bank of China.

17-4 银行、保险系统机构及人员(2015年)
INSTITUTIONS AND PERSONNEL OF BANKING AND INSURANCE SYSTEMS (2015)

项 目	Item	银行系统 Banking System		保险系统 Insurance System	
		机 构(个) Institutions (unit)	人 员(人) Personnel (person)	机 构(个) Institutions (unit)	人 员(人) Personnel (person)
全 市	**Total**	**4206**	**190652**	**664**	**143923**
首都功能核心区	Core Functional Area of the Capital	752	94866	164	49605
城市功能拓展区	Urban Function Extension Area	2171	75668	224	60541
城市发展新区	New Area of Urban Development	887	14570	187	23968
生态涵养发展区	Ecological Conservation Area	396	5548	89	9809

注：1. 本表口径为在北京地区经营的银行、保险公司的总行(总公司)、分行(分公司)及所属分支机构。
2. 保险系统人员构成中含营销员。

Note: a) Figures in this table cover the headquarters (head offices), branches banks (branch companies) and subsidiaries of banks and insurance companies operating in Beijing.
b) Personnel of insurance system includes marketing personnel.

17-5 上市公司基本情况(1993-2015年)
LISTED COMPANIES (1993-2015)

年 份 Year	年末上市公司(家) Companies Listed by Year-end (unit)	上市公司总股本(万股) Total Equity of Listed Companies (10000 Shares)	股票首发数量(万股) Initial Public Offering Shares (10000 Shares)	首发募集资金(亿元) Funds Raised Through IPO (10000 yuan)	增发募集资金(亿元) Funds Raised Through Right Offerings (10000 yuan)	配股募集资金(亿元) Funds Raised Through Seasoned Equity Offerings (10000 yuan)
1993	3	24592	3924	58.0		28.8
1994	7	124038	20300	11.7		0.5
1995	7	133309				3.8
1996-2000			**439955**	**304.4**	**33.0**	**85.8**
1996	13	198956	29763	12.8		1.9
1997	26	470026	80200	52.2		7.0
1998	33	723561	52750	32.9		20.2
1999	43	1439894	121242	63.0	10.8	10.7
2000	54	2015049	156000	143.5	22.2	46.0
2001-2005			**764200**	**413.8**	**49.2**	**26.3**
2001	63	9764783	345500	191.6		17.0
2002	68	11929954	23800	16.8	14.9	
2003	74	11493598	373600	188.7	2.8	2.2
2004	83	12553074	21300	16.7	28.4	7.1
2005	83	13159721			3.1	
2006-2010			**11456582**	**6506.1**	**1665.5**	**852.8**
2006	92	58156652	2667911	1073.4	79.4	
2007	104	86151941	2428976	2433.3	304.7	12.1
2008	109	90486962	698853	546.9	502.0	63.8
2009	126	97911881	2179290	1154.2	430.7	
2010	165	137726461	3481552	1298.3	348.7	777.0
2011-2015			**1232164**	**1040.8**	**4024.0**	**282.1**
2011	194	143088054	420483	462.0	661.7	175.6
2012	217	146788089	211752	191.4	436.2	69.1
2013	219	151694399			183.9	32.5
2014	235	214359521	67787	74.9	1319.0	4.9
2015	264	225020500	532142	312.5	1423.3	

注：1. 此表数据统计口径为注册地统计。
2. 1995年、2005年和2013年没有新股发行。
资料来源：中国证券监督管理委员会北京证监局。

Note: a) Statistics in this table are counted in terms of registered area.
b) There were no shares issued in 1995, 2005 and 2013.
Source: Beijing Regulatory Bureau of China Securities Regulatory Commission.

17-6 证券市场交易额情况(1994-2015年)
TRADE VOLUME OF STOCK MARKETS (1994-2015)

单位：亿元 (100 million yuan)

年份 Year	证券市场交易额 Trading Volume of Stock Market	#股票交易 Stock Trading	#基金交易 Fund Trading	#债券交易 Bond Trading	年末证券市场累计资金账户开户数(万户) Accumulative Capital Accounts in Stock Market (year-end) (10000 Accounts)
1994	183.3	135.5		47.8	
1995	1619.0	520.5		152.3	
1996	5224.8	2900.6		2324.1	
1997	7934.4	3900.9		3844.8	
1998	10241.5	3426.4	187.0	6435.4	
1999	10694.5	5268.2	341.7	5005.5	88.9
2000	14457.0	9136.5	346.0	4825.9	115.2
2001	12596.5	5339.6	400.6	6729.7	149.0
2002	12565.9	3788.2	485.8	8216.5	155.0
2003	23369.8	5041.4	110.5	18048.4	162.4
2004	18512.9	7247.7	78.9	10928.9	166.2
2005	9322.5	4343.7	91.3	4567.3	169.8
2006	19557.1	14851.5	298.3	2075.2	189.4
2007	97978.7	77487.8	1535.0	2060.1	314.9
2008	62773.6	46231.3	1389.4	4052.5	373.6
2009	92148.0	78339.5	2253.5	1791.3	426.1
2010	87575.4	79843.1	1714.9	3384.3	475.1
2011	79103.1	61743.2	1494.8	15275.3	521.5
2012	85412.9	44993.4	2355.9	37388.6	551.5
2013	145932.7	61596.3	4104.8	69625.4	563.6
2014	232318.6	85714.5	7311.7	110657.5	587.5
2015	597169.7	305252.9	24054.2	182495.0	758.8

注：2015年起“年末证券市场累计开户数”指标改为“年末证券市场累计资金账户开户数”。

Note: The indicator of "accumulative accounts in stock market (year-end)" modified as "accumulative capital accounts in stock market (year-end)"since 2015.

17-7 证券市场交易额情况
TRADE VOLUME OF STOCK MARKETS

项　目	Item	2015	2014	2015年为2014年% 2015 as % of 2014
成交额合计 （亿元）	**Total Trade Volume (100 million yuan)**	**597169.7**	**232318.6**	**257.0**
股票交易	Stock Trading	305252.9	85714.5	356.1
债券交易	Bond Trading	182495.0	110657.5	164.9
债券现货	Bonds in Stock	3559.6	2867.5	124.1
债券回购	Bond Repurchasing	178394.4	107790.0	165.5
募集资金交易	Trading of Funds Raised	3258.2	345.5	943.0
基金交易	Fun Trading	24054.2	7311.7	329.0
其他交易	Other Tradings	82109.4	28289.3	290.2
年末证券市场累计开户数 （万户）	**Accumulative Capital Accounts in Stock Market (year-end) (10000 Accounts)**	**758.8**	**587.5**	**129.2**

注：2015年起“年末证券市场累计开户数”指标改为“年末证券市场累计资金账户开户数”。
Note: The indicator of "accumulative accounts in stock market (year-end)" modified as "accumulative capital accounts in stock market (year-end)"since 2015.

17-8 保险业务情况(1997-2015年)
INSURANCE BUSINESS (1997-2015)

单位：亿元 (100 million yuan)

年份 Year	原保险保费收入 Premium Income of Original Insurance	人身险 Life Insurance	财产险 Property Insurance	赔付支出 Compensation Expenses	人身险 Life Insurance	财产险 Property Insurance
1997	102.5					
1998	88.6					
1999	91.8			29.9		
2000	93.4			28.4		
2001	141.3			32.0		
2002	234.1			46.9		
2003	282.5			48.0		
2004	279.3			55.3		
2005	498.2			75.4		
2006	411.5	327.2	84.4	84.0	45.1	38.9
2007	498.1	386.3	111.8	135.4	85.7	49.7
2008	585.9	451.8	134.1	188.9	121.0	67.9
2009	697.6	533.2	164.4	196.0	110.6	85.4
2010	966.5	754.2	212.3	199.7	105.9	93.7
2011	820.9	588.4	232.6	232.8	113.8	119.0
2012	923.1	656.1	267.0	286.2	133.9	152.3
2013	994.4	706.4	288.0	318.2	152.9	165.3
2014	1207.2	892.5	314.8	407.2	224.6	182.7
2015	1403.9	1059.2	344.7	506.6	300.0	206.6

资料来源：中国保险监督管理委员会北京监管局。
Source: Beijing Regulatory Bureau of China Insurance Regulatory Commission.

17-9 保险业务情况
STATISTICS FOR INSURANCE BUSINESS

单位：亿元 (100 million yuan)

项　　目	Item	原保险保费收入 Premium Income of Original Insurance		赔付支出 Compensation Expenses	
		2015	2014	2015	2014
合　计	**Total**	**1403.9**	**1207.2**	**506.6**	**407.2**
人身险业务小计	**Subtotal of Life Insurance**	**1059.2**	**892.5**	**300.0**	**224.6**
人寿保险	Life Insurance	778.2	708.7	231.7	164.7
非分红产品	Non-participating Products	350.0	246.5	22.6	17.1
分红产品	Participating Products	424.0	457.9	207.8	146.6
投资连接产品	Investment-linked Products	0.5	0.5	0.3	0.1
万能产品	Universal Products	3.7	3.8	1.0	1.0
意外伤害保险	Accident Insurance	37.7	34.6	11.5	9.2
健康保险	Health Insurance	243.3	149.2	56.8	50.7
财产险业务小计	**Subtotal of Property Insurance**	**344.7**	**314.8**	**206.6**	**182.7**
#企业财产保险	Enterprise Property Insurance	34.9	34.0	30.6	25.1
家庭财产保险	Household Property Insurance	1.6	0.9	0.4	0.3
机动车辆及第三者责任保险	Motor Vehicle and Third Party Liability Insurance	243.6	224.1	143.0	135.0
货物运输保险	Freight Transport Insurance	9.9	11.0	5.2	4.0
责任保险	Liability Insurance	24.7	18.8	11.5	6.6
工程险	Construction Insurance	7.8	7.8	3.0	2.4

资料来源：中国保险监督管理委员会北京监管局。
Source: Beijing Regulatory Bureau of China Insurance Regulatory Commission.

主要统计指标解释

存款 企业、机关、团体或居民根据可以收回的原则，把货币资金存入银行或其他信用机构保管并取得一定利息的一种信用活动形式。根据存款对象的不同可划分为企业存款、财政存款、机关团体存款、储蓄存款、农业存款等科目。它是银行信贷资金的主要来源。

贷款 银行或其他信用机构根据必须归还的原则，按一定利率，为企业、个人等提供资金的一种信用活动形式。我国银行贷款分为短期贷款、中长期贷款、委托及信托类贷款、其他类贷款等。

原保险保费收入 是指保险企业确认的原保险合同保费收入。是投保人根据保险合同的有关规定，为被保险人取得因约定危险事故发生所造成的经济损失补偿（或给付）权利，付给保险人的代价。包括财产险和人身险收入。

保险赔付支出 公司按保险合同约定支付给被保险人（或受益人）的赔款、保险金、给付等。包括赔款支出、死伤医疗给付、满期给付和年金给付。

股票交易额 指报告期投资者在各类证券交易场所进行股票买卖交易活动的金额。包括A股、B股、股份转让等。不含申购新股及申购中签交易额，也不含配股、分红、送股及转增交易额。

基金交易额 指报告期投资者在各类证券交易场所进行基金买卖交易活动的金额。包括封闭式基金、开放式基金中的ＥＴＦ、LOF等。填报时，不在交易所挂牌交易的开放式基金的交易额不计在内。

债券交易额 指报告期投资者在各类证券交易场所进行债券买卖交易活动的金额。包括国债、地方政府债、金融债、企业债、公司债、分离债、可转债、私募债、资产支持类债券等。

债券现货交易额 指报告期投资者在各类证券交易场所进行债券买卖交易活动现货成交金额。

Explanatory Notes on Main Statistical Indicators

Deposit is a form of credit activity that enterprises, public institutions, groups or residents save their money, on a reclaimable basis, in banks or other credit institutions and receive certain interest. In terms of depositors, there are enterprise deposit, fiscal deposit, government agency deposit, savings deposit, agricultural deposit and so on, which constitute a main source of bank funds for extending credit..

Loan is a form of credit activity that banks or other credit institutions provide funds which must be repaid for enterprise and individuals at a given interest rate,. In China, bank loans are classified as short-,, medium-, and long-term loans, entrusted and trust loans, and others.

Premium Income means the income of insurance premium of original insurance contracts confirmed by insurance companies. It is the price paid by policy holders to the insurer for the right to receive compensation (claim settlement) for any economic loss caused by agreed dangerous accidents pursuant to relevant provisions in the insurance contract. There are property insurance and life insurance incomes.

Insurance Indemnity Payments refer to indemnity, insurance money, and claim settlement, etc. paid by the insurance company to the insurant (or beneficiary) as agreed in the insurance contract, including indemnity payment, claim settlement for medical costs of death and injury, maturity payment and annuity payment.

Stock Market Turnover means the value of shares traded by investors in various securities exchanges, including: A share, B share and share transfer, etc., excluding turnover related to IPO subscription, IPO lot-winning, allotment, dividend, share-granting and capital reserve converted into share capital.

Funds Turnover means the value of funds traded by investors in various securities exchanges during the reporting period, including ETF and LOF, etc. in the closed-end funds and open-end funds. The turnover of open-end funds not listed and traded in exchanges shall not be included in the funds turnover reported.

Bonds Turnover means the value of bonds traded by investors in various securities exchanges during the reporting period, including treasury bonds, local government bonds, financial bonds, enterprise bonds, corporate bonds, convertible bonds, warrants bonds, private placement bonds and asset-backed bonds.

Bonds Spot Turnover means the spot turnover of bonds traded by investors in various securities exchanges during the reporting period.

18

教育、文化
EDUCATION AND CULTURE

简要说明

一、教育部分的主要内容和资料来源

教育统计资料包括高等教育（研究生教育、普通本专科教育、成人本专科教育、其他各类高等学历教育）、中等教育(高中阶段、初中阶段)、小学教育、学前教育、特殊教育(盲聋哑和弱智儿童学校等)、工读学校等资料。主要指标包括学校数、在校学生数、招生数、毕业生数、教职工数、专任教师数等内容。

除技工学校数据来源于北京市人力资源和社会保障局外，其他教育统计资料均由北京市教育委员会提供。

二、文化部分的主要内容和资料来源

文化部分主要包括专业艺术剧团、公共图书馆、博物馆、文化馆、档案馆、文化站、广播、电影、电视以及新闻等文化单位的机构、人员和业务活动情况。

文化部分数据中，专业艺术剧团、公共图书馆和群众文化活动的资料主要来自北京市文化局；档案馆资料来自北京市档案局；博物馆资料来自北京市文物局；广播、电影和电视，报纸、期刊、图书出版资料来自北京市新闻出版广电局。

Brief Introduction

I. Main Content and Sources of Data for the Part of Education

Educational statistics include those for higher education (postgraduate education, undergraduate and junior college education, undergraduate and junior college education for adults, and other kinds of higher education for diplomas); secondary education (senior high school, junior high school); primary education; preschool education; special education (schools for the blind, deaf and mute, and mentally handicapped children, etc.); work-study schools for delinquent children. Main indicators include the number of schools, student enrollment, , number of new enrollment, number of teachers and staff, and number of full-time teachers, etc.

Date of Technician Training Schools from Beijing Municipal Bureau of Human Resources and Social Security, the other educational data were provided by Beijing Municipal Commission of Education.

II. Main Content and Sources of Data for the Part of Culture

Cultural statistics include the number, personnel and activities of professional art troupes, public libraries, museums, cultural centers, archives, broadcast, films, television and press, and other cultural organizations.

In Cultural data, figures of art, libraries, and mass culture are from Beijing Municipal Bureau of Culture; data of archives are from Beijing Municipal Bureau of Archives; data of museums are from Beijing Municipal Administration of Cultural Heritage; radio, film and television, newspaper, magazine and book publications data are from Beijing Municipal Administration of Press, Publication, Radio, Film and Television.

18-1 教育基本情况(1978-2015年)
BASIC STATISTICS FOR EDUCATION (1978-2015)

年份 Year	全市各类学校数(个) Total Number of Various Schools (unit)	#普通高等学校 General Institutions of Higher Education	#普通中等学校 General Middle Schools	#高中 Senior Middle Schools	#小学 Primary Schools	全市各类学校在校学生数(人) Enrolled Students in Various Schools (person)	#普通高等学校 General Institutions of Higher Education	#普通中等学校 General Middle Schools	#高中 Senior Middle Schools	#小学 Primary Schools
1978		35			4666		48618		415612	937336
1979		48			4534		55073		299974	968723
1980		50			4485		83032		312188	951763
1981		51			4445		98044		175180	900350
1982		51			4381		93878		92401	854516
1983		54			4269		90894		88657	838078
1984		57			4168		102962		110916	763204
1985		61			4059		122791		119876	733605
1986		66			3995		129647		109862	749101
1987		67			3875		136694		109023	777982
1988		67			3793		145134		108106	850577
1989		67			3703		141625		110745	934696
1990		67			3611		139646		100669	995831
1991	8496	67	1168	282	3482	2142085	136940	565357	93728	1013268
1992	8052	67	1150	279	3306	2194268	139978	617847	82894	1001762
1993	7789	66	1145	280	3190	2266932	158906	679821	78261	1022166
1994	7574	67	1150	280	3035	2348406	175203	758310	86584	1024503
1995	7158	65	1170	286	2867	2380096	182173	834903	102522	1007301
1996	7121	65	1189	296	2780	2388002	189953	881912	118476	999740
1997	6858	65	1181	288	2696	2361438	195842	887644	133461	977323
1998	6456	63	1190	282	2511	2325043	212984	895042	145966	919531
1999	5807	64	1182	275	2352	2297673	234033	931029	161473	836655
2000	5458	59	1159	302	2169	2299433	282585	972930	179002	743109
2001	4873	61	1111	289	1960	2297107	340284	988985	194283	664443
2002	4447	62	998	325	1824	2294947	398573	984117	220667	594241
2003	4158	74	977	329	1652	2299416	458898	968035	250959	546530
2004	3971	77	945	338	1504	2291594	500245	919178	274803	516042
2005	3782	79	917	335	1403	2264004	536724	859132	278358	494482
2006	3751	82	888	335	1310	2910228	554702	799074	259414	473275
2007	3593	83	863	328	1235	3195763	567875	839038	243818	666617
2008	3508	82	838	325	1202	3208704	575639	782866	219163	659500
2009	3425	88	804	305	1160	3214354	577154	740396	203477	647101
2010	3330	89	779	289	1104	3299555	577828	727741	198415	653255
2011	3367	89	769	290	1090	3426025	578633	711130	195072	680457
2012	3314	91	760	289	1081	3568273	581844	732224	193505	718655
2013	3439	89	757	291	1093	3736003	589234	706713	187586	789276
2014	3437	89	766	306	1040	3774868	594614	651443	177554	821152
2015	3454	90	768	306	996	3734245	593448	587112	169412	850321

注：1. 从2007年开始，普通中学、小学、工读学校、特殊教育、学前教育在校学生数包括外省市户口借读学生。
2. 1991-2005年，普通中等学校包括普通中专、技工学校、职业中学、普通中学和工读学校。2006年及以后普通中等学校为中等教育口径，包括普通中专、成人中专、技工学校、职业高中和普通中学。

资料来源：北京市教育委员会。

Note: a) From 2007, enrolled students in general high schools, primary schools, work-study schools for delinquent children, special education schools, and pre-school education included those from outside Beijing and studying in Beijing on temporary basis.

b) In 1991-2005, general middle schools included technical secondary schools, technician training schools, vocational schools, general high schools, and work-study schools. In and after 2006, middle schools included technical secondary schools, technical secondary schools for adults, technician training schools, vocational senior high schools and general high schools.

Source: Beijing Municipal Commission of Education.

18-1 续表 1 Continued 1

年份 Year	全市各类学校招生数(人) New Enrollment in Various Schools (person)	#普通高等学校 General Institutions of Higher Education	#普通中等学校 General Middle Schools	#高中 Senior Middle Schools	#小学 Primary Schools	全市各类学校毕业生数(人) Number of Graduates in Various Schools (person)	#普通高等学校 General Institutions of Higher Education
1978		17445		161288	199076		10881
1979		15848		160340	154809		8585
1980		17972		131961	138751		8233
1981		17921		54296	121744		2289
1982		21936		35212	104357		25753
1983		27988		40282	96028		31009
1984		31805		47068	103482		20110
1985		40670		35265	135048		21442
1986		35390		27863	160513		26953
1987		41163		41186	156954		34894
1988		42187		35429	184516		33066
1989		33557		33254	184609		35863
1990		36275		30596	161742		36171
1991	571685	37700	205107	28589	148300	487740	37702
1992	622142	41517	232765	25790	157145	520787	37075
1993	651729	52205	242274	26275	175853	526982	32888
1994	704933	51884	287642	34704	186315	528199	34855
1995	691972	52868	308786	40803	168903	554690	45094
1996	628772	55269	289612	42603	156898	575969	46471
1997	581091	56884	289719	49566	124231	584120	49973
1998	581786	62264	308157	52956	100415	600662	49322
1999	603332	78354	320731	56998	94358	603027	49936
2000	635328	99397	324862	65890	92002	604900	51556
2001	641432	116344	313257	69195	91230	617889	55831
2002	671956	128320	326835	84679	86406	624329	67621
2003	662877	143483	302071	94894	82631	610826	83816
2004	635842	147298	271396	93519	73577	614137	99637
2005	630515	156124	259133	88605	71020	622974	117367
2006	851808	154969	234524	76375	73138	787596	132488
2007	927144	156222	252709	71590	109203	851126	138834
2008	938891	157238	236714	68397	110440	832585	149459
2009	962648	158992	240937	65983	102414	865025	152336
2010	1002141	155228	238954	65649	113728	834340	150156
2011	1050131	157543	243754	64146	132719	838521	151277
2012	1108574	162042	254790	63381	141738	881804	152980
2013	1182301	163081	239010	59983	165807	923050	148689
2014	1113688	160056	202434	55184	153249	937209	147023
2015	1091756	152741	186517	56743	145876	961180	152118

18-1 续表 2 Continued 2

年 份 Year	#普通中等学校 General Middle Schools	#高 中 Senior Middle Schools	#小 学 Primary Schools	学龄儿童入学率(%) Enrollment Rate of Children at School-age (%)	专任教师数(人) Full-time Teachers (person)	平均每一专任教师负担学生数(人) Average Number of Students Instructed by a Full-time Teacher(person) 普通中学 General Middle Schools	小 学 Primary Schools
1978		174899	151950	99.00		19.9	20.7
1979		239813	114047	98.50		16.1	21.3
1980		145501	144025	98.70		14.8	21.7
1981		170992	162306	98.90		13.4	19.7
1982		111153	135562	98.90		12.3	19.5
1983			95919	99.10		11.5	19.6
1984		24498	169251	99.30		13.2	18.2
1985		24720	156035	99.10		13.9	17.4
1986		36942	138350	99.50		14.1	17.3
1987		43589	121599	99.50		12.8	16.8
1988		36127	105948	99.50		11.4	17.6
1989		29267	97208	99.70		11.0	19.1
1990		40369	102782	99.50		10.1	18.6
1991		34428	132544	99.17	168485	10.5	18.0
1992		32471	156306	99.65	169249	11.3	17.4
1993		27428	157838	99.88	170361	12.1	17.4
1994		24112	184566	99.92	175025	13.1	16.9
1995		23353	183894	99.93	176591	13.6	16.5
1996		25170	162030	99.93	178006	13.7	16.1
1997		33010	146023	99.95	179080	13.2	15.7
1998		39683	156194	99.96	178210	12.8	14.9
1999		40660	175656	99.95	175496	13.2	13.7
2000		47569	185059	99.95	167040	14.1	12.8
2001		51263	167076	99.62	168080	14.3	12.1
2002		51180	156683	99.63	166490	14.2	11.2
2003		56601	123580	99.95	166510	13.7	11.0
2004		66556	100139	99.92	172055	12.9	10.6
2005		73260	93486	99.90	174589	11.8	10.3
2006	290047	78037	90799	99.96	191365	10.8	9.8
2007	272651	78408	112332	100.00	195568	11.5	13.8
2008	262871	78468	112268	100.00	199114	10.9	13.5
2009	253067	70132	110730	100.00	203825	10.0	13.0
2010	233837	62305	102971	99.96	206602	10.2	13.2
2011	223955	58275	101678	99.99	199789	9.8	13.4
2012	224938	55657	109492	99.99	204812	9.7	13.7
2013	240225	58072	111839	99.99	216463	9.5	14.4
2014	229640	57773	112819	100.00	225165	9.0	14.4
2015	205795	57738	103893	100.00	226043	8.4	14.3

18-2 幼儿园基本情况(1978-2015年)
BASIC STATISTICS FOR KINDERGARTENS (1978-2015)

单位：人 (person)

年份 Year	园数(所) Number of Kindergartens (unit)	班数(个) Number of Classes (unit)	离园人数 Children Leaving	入园人数 Children Entering	在园人数 Children Enrollment	教职工数 Teachers and Staff	#专任教师 Full-time Teachers
1978	5074				235923	39982	8369
1979	4623				237037	40424	8777
1980	3991				219407	38475	7765
1981	3888				233089	38832	8814
1982	3849				254458	42663	9271
1983	1999				306975	48666	8234
1984	3682				295427	47721	9499
1985	2955				316024	47033	10523
1986	3503				342824	52654	12690
1987	3732				364011	54211	14449
1988	3563				354367	52105	14705
1989	3509				344394	50280	17208
1990	3798				372555	49587	17972
1991	3761		133788	172884	402699	49472	18788
1992	3510		158740	181299	404779	48007	18513
1993	3369		165963	170580	372368	44741	18114
1994	3301		113652	167267	352979	42118	17413
1995	3024		103355	148272	315277	38549	16084
1996	3056		135376	112449	271752	33586	14792
1997	2892		110345	95140	253478	32811	14596
1998	2662		99279	93819	245046	30362	13841
1999	2180		91996	89463	237055	29367	13216
2000	2047		85301	91724	229012	27257	12595
2001	1719	8259	85842	87892	217521	26106	12479
2002	1540	8494	79447	91092	213794	25402	12127
2003	1430	7733	76879	86465	199390	26324	13056
2004	1422	8087	71677	86672	205532	28326	14208
2005	1358	8148	71926	83485	202301	28026	14813
2006	1361	8051	70400	68299	197546	28958	15632
2007	1306	8132	70681	83969	214423	30465	17013
2008	1266	8382	72119	85938	226681	32535	18176
2009	1253	9036	65684	89761	247778	34973	17952
2010	1245	9883	68135	105048	276994	37227	21677
2011	1305	11213	76790	115539	311417	44458	24170
2012	1266	11882	79131	115248	331524	48080	26330
2013	1384	12580	88322	128106	348681	53049	28806
2014	1426	13245	96478	133977	364954	57950	31692
2015	1487	14098	101928	149042	394121	61903	34040

资料来源：北京市教育委员会。
Source: Beijing Municipal Commission of Education.

18-3 各类学校基本情况
BASIC STATISTICS FOR VARIOUS SCHOOLS

单位：人 (person)

项目	Item	校数(所) Number of Schools (unit) 2015	2014	教职工数 Teachers and Staff 2015	2014	#专任教师 Full-time Teachers 2015	2014
合计	**Total**	**3454**	**3437**	**366571**	**365318**	**226043**	**225165**
高等教育	**Higher Education**	**175**	**177**	**146318**	**148930**	**68506**	**71079**
研究生培养机构(不计校数)	Institutions Providing Postgraduate Programs (Number of Schools Not Counted)	(138)	(136)			(54481)	(51415)
高等学校	Institutions of Higer Education	(58)	(56)			(44391)	(41648)
科研机构	Research Institutes	(80)	(80)			(10090)	(9767)
普通高等学校	General Institutions of Higher Education	90	89	138396	140685	65230	67549
成人高等学校	Adult Institutions of Higher Education	19	19	3332	3273	1542	1551
民办的其他高等教育机构	Privately-funded Institutions of Higher Education	66	69	4590	4972	1734	1979
中等教育	**Secondary Education**	**768**	**766**	**98479**	**98766**	**72265**	**71799**
高中阶段教育	Senior Secondary Education	428	429	98479	98766	50794	51105
普通高中	General Middle Schools	306	306	83970	82224	41920	40349
中等职业教育	Secondary Vocational Schools	122	123	14509	16542	8874	10756
普通中专	General Technical Secondary Schools	31	31	3514	3614	1963	2002
成人中专	Technical Secondary Schools for Adults	11	11	618	565	340	308
职业高中	Vocational Senior High Schools	51	52	7098	7495	4745	4889
技工学校	Technician Training Schools	29	29	3279	4868	1826	3557
初中阶段教育	Junior Secondary Education	340	337			21471	20694
小学教育	**Primary Schools**	**996**	**1040**	**58308**	**58108**	**50053**	**49434**
工读学校	**Work-Study Schools for Delinquent Children**	**6**	**6**	**287**	**286**	**200**	**195**
特殊教育	**Special Education**	**22**	**22**	**1276**	**1278**	**979**	**966**
学前教育	**Pre-school Education**	**1487**	**1426**	**61903**	**57950**	**34040**	**31692**

注：1. 普通高中的教职工数中包含普通初中的教职工数。
2. 表中带()数据不计入"校数"的合计数据中。
资料来源：技工学校数据来源于北京市人力资源和社会保障局，其他数据均来源于北京市教育委员会。
Note: a) Number of "Teachers and Staff" in general senior high schools includes those in general junior high schools.
b) In this table data with () were not be calculated in the total number of schools.
Source:Date of Technician Training Schools from Beijing Municipal Bureau of Human Resources and Social Security, the others all from Beijing Municipal Commission of Education.

18-3 续表 Continued

单位：人 (person)

项目	Item	毕业生数 Graduates 2015	毕业生数 Graduates 2014	招生数 New Enrollment 2015	招生数 New Enrollment 2014	在校学生数 Total Enrollment 2015	在校学生数 Total Enrollment 2014
合 计	**Total**	**961180**	**937209**	**1091756**	**1113688**	**3734245**	**3774868**
高等教育	**Higher Education**	**547403**	**495945**	**609060**	**622602**	**1894894**	**1928977**
研究生	Postgraduates	79699	77442	95087	92776	283831	274443
高等学校	Institutions of Higher Education	74840	72706	89545	87040	265888	257231
科研机构	Scientific Research Institutions	4859	4736	5542	5736	17943	17212
普通本专科	General Undergraduates and College Students	152118	147023	152741	160056	593448	594614
中央部委属高校	Under Central Ministries and Commissions	73588	72740	78780	79067	310399	307689
市属高校	Under Municipal Government	78530	74283	79093	80989	283049	286925
公办高校	Public Colleges and Universities	58189	56959	61410	62109	215939	218608
民办高校	Privately-funded Colleges and Universities	20341	17324	17683	18880	67110	68317
成人本专科	Adult Undergraduates and College Students	95277	93874	74980	88282	204311	237644
成人高等学校	Adult Institutions of Higher Education	7999	8964	7287	7923	18413	20412
普通高等学校	General Institutions of Higher Education	87278	84910	67693	80359	185898	217232
在职人员攻读硕士学位	Employees Enrolled in Graduate Programes Leading to Master Degrees			14794	21974	83022	87157
网络本专科生	Students Enrolled in Internet-based Courses	220309	177606	271458	259514	730282	735119
中等教育	**Secondary Education**	**205795**	**229640**	**186517**	**202434**	**587112**	**651443**
高中阶段教育	Senior Secondary	113022	139500	97365	99741	303746	344654
普通高中	General Middle Schools	57738	57773	56743	55184	169412	177554
#北京市户籍	Registered Residents of Beijing	52337	53315	52387	50787	154455	158951
中等职业教育	Secondary Vocational Schools	55284	81727	40622	44557	134334	167100
普通中专	General Technical Secondary Schools	14644	16394	12129	12319	47465	51296
成人中专	Technical Secondary Schools for Adults	10042	33778	9948	11861	30412	40568
职业高中	Vocational High Schools	16715	16792	5031	5585	18400	34155
技工学校	Technical Schools	13883	14763	13514	14792	38057	41081
初中阶段教育	Junior Secondary Education	92773	90140	89152	102693	283366	306789
#北京市户籍	Registered Residents of Beijing	70924	67667	55754	65722	188608	204451
小学教育	**Primary Education**	**103893**	**112819**	**145876**	**153249**	**850321**	**821152**
#北京市户籍	Registered Residents of Beijing	55878	65555	99685	98016	496523	452651
工读学校	**Work-study School for Delinquent Children**	**375**	**330**	**331**	**316**	**661**	**600**
特殊教育	**Special Education Schools**	**1786**	**1997**	**930**	**1110**	**7136**	**7742**
学前教育	**Preschool Education**	**101928**	**96478**	**149042**	**133977**	**394121**	**364954**

18-4 全市高等教育学生情况(2015年)
STATISTICS FOR STUDENTS IN INSTITUTIONS OF HIGHER EDUCATION (2015)

单位：人 (person)

项　　目	Item	毕(结)业生人数 Number of Graduates	招生数 New Enrollment	在校学生数 Total Enrollment
普通本科、专科生	General Undergraduates and Junior College Students	**152118**	**157873**	**593448**
专　科	Enrolled in Specialized Courses Education	36798	31218	97883
本　科	Enrolled in Full Undergraduate Courses	115320	126655	495565
成人本科、专科生	Adult Undergraduates and Junior College Students	95277	74980	204311
专　科	Enrolled in Specialized Courses Education	40996	31733	78182
本　科	Enrolled in Full Undergraduate Courses	54281	43247	126129
网络本科、专科生	Students Enrolled in Internet-based Courses	220309	271458	730282
专　科	Enrolled in Specialized Courses	134996	161845	392079
本　科	Enrolled in Full Undergraduate Courses	85313	109613	338203
研究生	Postgraduates	79699	95087	283831
硕　士	Master Degree	65519	76131	203857
博　士	Doctor Degree	14180	18956	79974
在职人员攻读硕士学位	Employees Enrolled in Graduate Programes Leading to Master Degrees		14794	83022
自考助学班	Classes for Self-Learning Programs	592		1036
普通预科生	College Preparatory Courses			1438
研究生课程进修班	Postgraduate Courses for Advanced Study	7569		13891
进修及培训	In-Service Training Courses	866325		735477
留学生	Overseas Students	25335	28081	39459

资料来源：北京市教育委员会。
Source: Beijing Municipal Commission of Education.

18-5 普通高等学校本专科基本情况(2015年)
BASIC STATISTICS FOR GENERAL INSTITUTIONS OF HIGHER EDUCATION (2015)

单位：人 (person)

项　　目	Item	校数(所) Number of Schools (unit)	毕业生数 Graduates	招生数 New Enrollment	在校学生数 Total Enrollment	教职工数 Teachers and Staff	#专任教师 Full-time Teachers
合　计	**Total**	**90**	**152118**	**157873**	**593448**	**138396**	**65230**
#女　性	Females		79297	81050	306282	68504	30032
综合大学	Comprehensive Universities	5	20389	19862	74042	23437	10325
理工院校	Science and Engineering	30	62569	65053	245127	52629	26450
农业院校	Agriculture	3	6231	6207	22926	4818	2531
林业院校	Forestry	1	3178	3292	13324	1871	1192
医药院校	Medicine	4	3138	4211	15031	17771	3380
师范院校	Teacher Training	2	4777	5713	21406	5712	3529
语文院校	Literature	9	11138	11838	43149	7170	4073
财经院校	Finance and Economics	16	21941	20677	81135	10917	6401
政法院校	Politics and Law	8	10036	11408	39738	6662	2972
体育院校	Physical Culture	3	2666	3131	11954	1678	1050
艺术院校	Art	8	3395	3689	14256	3731	2115
民族院校	Minorities Colleges	1	2660	2792	11360	2000	1212

资料来源：北京市教育委员会。
Source: Beijing Municipal Commission of Education.

18-6 全市分学科研究生情况(2015年)
BASIC STATISTICS FOR POSTGRADUATES BY SUBJECT OF STUDY (2015)

单位：人 (person)

项 目	Item	毕业生 Graduates			招生数 New Enrollment			在校学生数 Student Enrollment		
		合计 Total	硕士 Master Degree	博士 Doctor Degree	合计 Total	硕士 Master Degree	博士 Doctor Degree	合计 Total	硕士 Master Degree	博士 Doctor Degree
合 计	**Total**	**74840**	**61852**	**12988**	**89545**	**72268**	**17277**	**265888**	**192324**	**73564**
#女 性	Females	37530	32422	5108	45275	38281	6994	127573	99442	28131
学术型学位	**Academic Degree**	**49187**	**36828**	**12359**	**56115**	**39465**	**16650**	**183014**	**111718**	**71296**
哲 学	Philosophy	551	396	155	605	410	195	2050	1196	854
经济学	Economics	3403	2900	503	3308	2595	713	9943	6651	3292
法 学	Law	4276	3507	769	4658	3679	979	14467	10008	4459
教育学	Education	1545	1263	282	1665	1269	396	5532	4004	1528
文 学	Literature	3295	2789	506	3563	2891	672	11403	8473	2930
历史学	History	494	348	146	552	376	176	1861	1106	755
理 学	Science	6523	3593	2930	9327	5156	4171	30441	14355	16086
工 学	Engineering	18942	14301	4641	21781	15330	6451	73439	44232	29207
农 学	Agriculture	1400	938	462	1363	893	470	4087	2181	1906
医 学	Medicine	2866	1999	867	3435	2412	1023	9711	6355	3356
军事学	Military	36	26	10	19	13	6	82	47	35
管理学	Management	4334	3453	881	4492	3372	1120	15333	9509	5824
艺术学	Art	1522	1315	207	1347	1069	278	4665	3601	1064

资料来源：北京市教育委员会。
Source: Beijing Municipal Commission of Education.

18-7 高等教育外国留学生情况(2015年)
STATISTICS FOR FOREIGN STUDENTS STUDYING IN BEIJING FOR HIGHER EDUCATION (2015)

单位：人 (person)

项 目	Item	毕(结)业生数 Graduates	授予学位人数 Number of Students Conferred with Degree	招生数 New Enrollment	在校学生数 Total Enrollment
合 计	**Total**	**24535**	**4830**	**27227**	**39017**
#女 性	Females	12096	2245	13509	18021
按学历划分	**By Educational Background**				
专 科	Enrolled in Specialized Courses	54		136	200
本 科	Enrolled in Full Undergraduate Courses	3906	2827	4078	15025
硕 士	Master Degree	1968	1715	2831	5842
博 士	Doctor Degree	341	288	823	2838
培 训	Training	18266		19359	15112
按地区划分	**By Region**				
亚 洲	Asia	13266	3430	14703	25121
非 洲	Africa	1155	448	1671	3140
欧 洲	Europe	5904	526	6517	6689
北美洲	North America	3276	287	3329	2929
南美洲	South America	561	87	634	710
大洋洲	Oceania	373	52	373	428
按经费来源	**By Source of Funds**				
国际组织资助	From International Organizations	78	14	93	223
中国政府资助	From Chinese Government	3305	1336	4985	8699
本国政府资助	From the Government of the Students' Home Country	199	84	273	824
学校间交换	Interscholastic Exchange	2935	128	3448	2866
自 费	Self Funding	18018	3268	18428	26405

资料来源：北京市教育委员会。
Source: Beijing Municipal Commission of Education.

18-8 普通中专分科情况(2015年)
BASIC STATISTICS FOR SPECIALIZED SECONDARY SCHOOLS BY MAJOR (2015)

单位：人 (person)

项　　目	Item	毕业生数 Graduates	招生数 New Enrollment	在校学生数 Total Enrollment
合　计	**Total**	**14644**	**12129**	**47465**
#女　生	Females	7185	5311	21413
按类别分	**By Category**			
农林牧渔类	Agriculture, Forestry, Animal Production and Hunting, Fishing	165	150	598
资源环境类	Resources and Environment	117	71	276
能源与新能源类	Energy and New Energy	288	92	348
土木水利类	Construction and Water Conservancy	879	600	2527
加工制造类	Processing and Manufacturing	1502	1038	3828
石油化工类	Petroleum and Chemicals	36		
轻纺食品类	Light Industry, Textile and Foods	124	155	388
交通运输类	Transportation	2376	2486	9726
信息技术类	IT	1127	858	3122
医药卫生类	Medicine and Health	3207	2050	9282
休闲保健类	Recreation and Healthcare			
财经商贸类	Finance, Business and Trade	1633	1391	4660
旅游服务类	Tourism Services	178	258	708
文化艺术类	Culture and Arts	1558	1471	7435
体育与健身	Sports and Fitness	508	422	1429
教育类	Education	424	280	991
司法服务类	Judicial Services	156	294	600
公共管理与服务类	Public Management and Services	185	230	811
其　他	Others	181	283	736

资料来源：北京市教育委员会。
Source: Beijing Municipal Commission of Education.

18-9 职业高中分科情况(2015年)
BASIC STATISTICS FOR VOCATIONAL SCHOOLS BY MAJOR (2015)

单位：人 (person)

项　　目	Item	毕业生数 Graduates	招生数 New Enrollment	在校学生数 Total Enrollment
合　计	**Total**	**16715**	**5031**	**18400**
#女　生	Females	8146	2478	9278
按类别分	**By Category**			
农林牧渔类	Agriculture, Forestry, Animal Production and Hunting, Fishing	266	96	343
资源环境类	Resources and Environment			
能源与新能源类	Energy and New Energy	1		
土木水利类	Construction and Water Conservancy	105	24	114
加工制造类	Processing and Manufacturing	933	120	617
石油化工类	Petroleum and Chemicals			
轻纺食品类	Light Industry, Textile and Foods	112	20	117
交通运输类	Transportation	1933	731	2647
信息技术类	IT	2420	749	2394
医药卫生类	Medicine and Health	357	100	389
休闲保健类	Recreation and Healthcare	545	68	224
财经商贸类	Finance, Business and Trade	2695	644	2668
旅游服务类	Tourism Services	1799	672	1983
文化艺术类	Culture and Arts	2152	560	3347
体育与健身	Sports and Fitness	300	13	47
教育类	Education	2561	1099	3083
司法服务类	Judicial Services	214	26	55
公共管理与服务类	Public Management and Services	322	79	330
其　他	Others		30	42

资料来源：北京市教育委员会。
Source: Beijing Municipal Commission of Education.

18-10 校外教育情况(2015年)
STATISTICS FOR AFTER-SCHOOL EDUCATION (2015)

单位：人 (person)

项 目	Item	单位数(个) Number of Organizations(unit)	活动小组数(个) Activity Groups(unit)	参加小组学生数 Participating Students	教职工人数 Teachers and Staff	#专职辅导员 Full-time Coaches	兼职辅导员 Part-time Coaches
合 计	**Total**	**705**	**9609**	**277966**	**4504**	**1783**	**2571**
少年宫	Children's Palaces	22	5789	112955	1478	780	821
少年科技馆	Children's Scientific Museums	8	956	55012	260	194	179
少年之家	Children's Homes	34	1580	61927	561	303	447
少年活动站	Children's Clubs	641	1284	48072	2205	506	1124

资料来源：北京市教育委员会。
Source: Beijing Municipal Commission of Education.

18-11 幼儿园基本情况(2015年)
STATISTICS FOR KINDERGARTENS (2015)

单位：人 (person)

项 目	Item	总 计 Total	#女 Females	城 区 In City	镇 区 In Counties and Towns	乡 村 In Villages
园 数 (所)	Number of Kindergartens (unit)	1487		1082	197	208
班 数 (个)	Number of Classes (unit)	14098		11502	1590	1006
在园幼儿数	Children Enrollment	394121	188977	324586	44339	25196
教职工数	Teachers and Staff	61903	56673	52695	6188	3020
#园 长	Headmasters	2242	2151	1764	279	199
专任教师	Full-time Teachers	34040	33269	28532	3619	1889
保健医	Health Workers	2517	2489	2193	222	102

资料来源：北京市教育委员会。
Source: Beijing Municipal Commission of Education.

18-12 高等教育自学考试情况
STATISTICS FOR HIGHER EDUCATION SELF-STUDY EXAMINATION

项目	Item	2015	2014
报考人次 (人次)	Number of Registered Person-times (person-time)	144357	148711
报考科次 (科次)	Number of Registered Subject-times (person-time)	475744	439767
发出专科毕业证书 (个)	Number of Junior College Diplomas Issued (unit)	3103	2449
发出本科毕业证书 (个)	Number of General College Diplomas Issued (unit)	4362	3816
开考专业 (个)	Number of Majors Examined (unit)	99	106

资料来源：北京市教育委员会。
Source: Beijing Municipal Commission of Education.

18-13 特殊教育情况(2015年)
STATISTICS FOR SPECIAL EDUCATION (2015)

单位：人 (person)

项目	Item	毕业生 Graduates	招生数 New Enrollment	在校学生数 Total Enrollment
合计	**Total**	**1786**	**930**	**7136**
#女性	Females	626	350	2581
特殊教育学校	Special Education Schools	436	289	2560
小学附设特教班	Special Classes Attached to Primary Schools	10	9	137
小学随班就读	Studying in Primary Schools	526	157	2474
普通(职业)初中随班就读	Studying in General Junior Secondary (Vocational) Classes	814	475	1965

资料来源：北京市教育委员会。
Source: Beijing Municipal Commission of Education.

18-14 职业技术培训机构基本情况(2015年)
BASIC STATISTICS FOR VOCATIONAL AND TECHNICAL TRAINING INSTITUTIONS(2015)

项 目	Item	学校数(所) Schools (unit)	教学班(点、个) Teaching Classes (site,unit)	结业生数(人次) Students Completing Courses (person-time)	#女 性 Females
合 计	**Total**	**3659**	**44359**	**2836998**	**1480519**
#少数民族	National Miniorities			21918	9937
按培训机构分	**By Training Institution**				
职工技术培训学校(机构)	**Technical Training Schools (Institutions) for Employees**	**26**	**489**	**43274**	**18903**
教育部门和集体办	Run by Education Authorities and Collectively-run	1	117	5790	3353
其他部门办	Run by Other Authorities	6	344	34955	14335
民 办	Privately-funded	19	28	2529	1215
农村成人文化技术培训学校(机构)	**Cultural and Technical Training Schools (Institutions) for Rural Adults**	**2280**	**12023**	**951233**	**555124**
#教育部门和集体办	Run by Education Authorities and Collectively-run	2193	8935	862147	501327
县 办	Run by Counties	13	397	67674	35044
乡 办	Run by Townships	147	4791	452802	263762
村 办	Run by Villages	2033	3747	341671	202521
其他培训机构(含社会培训机构)	**Other Training Institutions (Including Social Training Institutions)**	**1353**	**31847**	**1842491**	**906492**
教育部门和集体办	Run by Education Authorities and Collectively-run	65		76934	38741
其他部门办	Run by Other Authorities	152		685047	287249
民 办	Privately-funded	1136	31847	1080510	580502
按培训时间分	**By Training Duration**				
一个月以内	within 1 month			1481037	813835
一个月至三个月以内	1-3 months			427813	221573
三个月至半年以内	3-6 months			542104	248121
半年至一年以内	6 months to 1 year			277649	129355
一年及以上	over 1 year			108395	67635
按培训形式分	**Group by Form of Training**				
#资格证书培训	Qualification Certificate Training			390890	207875
岗位证书培训	Job Post Certificate Training			290432	138502

资料来源：北京市教育委员会。
Source: Beijing Municipal Commission of Education.

18-14 续表 Continued

单位：人 (person)

项目	Item	注册学生数 Student Enrollment 合计 Total	#女性 Females	教职工数 Teachers and Staff 合计 Total	#专任教师 Full-time Teachers	聘请校外教师 External Teachers Retained
合计	**Total**	**2767429**	**1381244**	**57950**	**24637**	**17568**
#少数民族	National Miniorities	22724	10409	134	71	61
按培训机构分	**By Training Institution**					
职工技术培训学校(机构)	**Technical Training Schools (Institutions) for Employees**	**38618**	**16856**	**383**	**274**	**126**
教育部门和集体办	Run by Education Authorities and Collectively-run	8551	4821	82	69	63
其他部门办	Run by Other Authorities	27552	10868	179	108	61
民办	Privately-funded	2515	1167	122	97	2
农村成人文化技术培训学校(机构)	**Cultural and Technical Training Schools (Institutions) for Rural Adults**	**825106**	**476564**	**3114**	**1525**	**3636**
#教育部门和集体办	Run by Education Authorities and Collectively-run	718722	416738	1430	790	2887
县办	Run by Counties	67625	34932	94	44	223
乡办	Run by Townships	397712	222666	681	424	1506
村办	Run by Villages	253385	159140	655	322	1158
其他培训机构(含社会培训机构)	**Other Training Institutions (Including Social Training Institutions)**	**1903705**	**887824**	**54453**	**22838**	**13806**
教育部门和集体办	Run by Education Authorities and Collectively-run	84562	75517	2746	1273	984
其他部门办	Run by Other Authorities	711846	207290	20542	6845	5347
民办	Privately-funded	1107297	605017	31165	14720	7475
按培训时间分	**By Training Duration**					
一个月以内	within 1 month	1351557	680794			
一个月至三个月以内	1-3 months	381971	190916			
三个月至半年以内	3-6 months	546230	254907			
半年至一年以内	6 months to 1 year	340150	159097			
一年及以上	over 1 year	147521	95530			
按培训形式分	**Group by Form of Training**					
#资格证书培训	Qualification Certificate Training	422538	229588			
岗位证书培训	Job Post Certificate Training	192375	86940			

18-15 民办教育基本情况(2015年)
STATSTICS FOR PRIVATELY-FUNDED EDUCATION (2015)

单位：人 (person)

项目	Item	校数(所) Number of Schools (unit)	毕业生数 Graduates	招生数 New Enrollment	在校学生数 Total Enrollment	教职工数 Teachers and Staff	#专任教师 Full-time Teachers	聘请校外教师数 External Teachers Retained
合计	**Total**	**830**	**81163**	**87586**	**313147**	**50772**	**26733**	**3738**
民办高等教育	**Privately-funded Higher Education**	**81**	**20341**	**17683**	**67110**	**10759**	**5001**	**3314**
普通高校	General Institutions of Higher Education	15	20341	17683	67110	6169	3267	1739
民办高等教育机构	Other Privately-funded Higher Education Institutions	66				4590	1734	1575
民办中等教育	**Privately-funded Secondary Education**	**115**	**15872**	**11051**	**39143**	**11445**	**7077**	**310**
高中阶段教育	Senior High School Education	90	7752	3234	14752	11445	7077	310
民办普通高中	Privately-funded Senior High Schools	68	5972	2871	12323	10299	6466	49
民办中等职业教育	Privately-funded Secondary Vocational Education	22	1780	363	2429	1146	611	261
初中阶段教育	Junior High School Education	25	8120	7817	24391			
民办小学	**Privately-funded Primary Schools**	**60**	**10306**	**7386**	**67258**	**2453**	**1808**	**2**
民办幼儿园	**Privately-funded Kindergartens**	**574**	**34644**	**51466**	**139636**	**26115**	**12847**	**112**

注：普通中学教职工数、专任教师及聘请校外教师数为初中高中合计数。
资料来源：北京市教育委员会。
Note: Number of teachers,staff,full-time teachers,substitutive and part-time teachers in regular secondary schools includes those in junior and senior middle schools.
Source: Beijing Municipal Commission of Education.

18-16 高校办学条件(2015年)
SCHOOL CONDITIONS OF HIGHER EDUCATION INSTITUTIONS (2015)

项目		Item		合计 Total	中央 Central	市属市管 Municipal
普通高校		**General Institutions of Higher Education**				
校舍建筑面积	(平方米)	Building Area	(sq.m)	36780907	25100555	11680352
占地面积	(平方米)	Floor Space	(sq.m)	44571890	28580577	15991313
图书	(万册)	Books	(10000 volumes)	11204	7197	4007
电子图书藏量	(千兆字节)	E-books Collections	(Gigabyte)	6979774	6690324	289450
拥有教学用计算机	(台)	Computers for Teaching	(unit)	420364	219957	200407
成人高校		**Institutions of Higher Education for Adults**				
校舍建筑面积	(平方米)	Building Area	(sq.m)	899622	270974	628648
占地面积	(平方米)	Floor Space	(sq.m)	1294800	322805	971995
图书	(万册)	Books	(10000 volumes)	223	45.3	177.7
电子图书藏量	(千兆字节)	E-books Collections	(Gigabyte)	123086	115605	7481
拥有教学用计算机	(台)	Computers for Teaching	(unit)	10767	1345	9422

资料来源：北京市教育委员会。
Source: Beijing Municipal Commission of Education.

18-17 基础教育办学条件(2015年)
SCHOOL CONDITIONS OF BASIC EDUCATION (2015)

单位：平方米 (sq.m)

项　　目	Item	普通中学 General Middle Schools	小　学 Primary Schools
学校占地面积	Floor Space	23495925	14013946
校舍建筑面积	Building Area	13303553	6807295
#当年新增	Newly Added in the Year	438353	171909
#危房面积	Area of Dangerous Buildings		
教学及辅助用房	Teaching and Auxiliary Houses	4989549	3168853
普通教室	Classrooms	2921311	2475695
实验室	Laboratories	849533	208657
图书室	Libraries	365649	162564
微机室	Computer Rooms	212598	139092
语音室	Language Labs	34133	14294
体育馆	Gymnasiums	606325	168550
行政办公用房	Administrative Houses	1474241	789180
生活用房	Houses for Life (Residencial Houses)	3716320	1161864
其他用房	Houses for Other Purposes	3123443	1687398
计算机　(台)	Computers　(unit)	280820	228925
图书藏量　(册)	Books Collections　(volume)	29584585	28298944
电子图书藏量（千兆字节）	E-book Collections　(Gigabyte)	218629.17	135203.41

资料来源：北京市教育委员会。
Source: Beijing Municipal Commission of Education.

18-18 非本市户籍、外国籍学生情况(2015年)
STATISTICS FOR STUDENTS FROM OTHER PROVINCES, MUNICIPALITIES AND AUTONOMOUS REGIONS ALONG WITH OTHER COUNTRIES (2015)

单位：人 (person)

项　　目	Item	非本市户籍学生数 Students from Other Provinces, Municipalities and Autonomous Regions	#民办学校 Privately-funded Schools	外国籍学生数 Overseas Students	#民办学校 Privately-funded Education
合　　计	**Total**	**605820**	**128096**	**5922**	**2262**
普通中学	General Middle Schools	109715	15742	2056	538
初　中	Junior Secondary Schools	94758	13220	883	243
高　中	Senior Secondary Schools	14957	2522	1173	295
中等职业教育	Vocational Secondary Schools	36818	2300	113	
小　学	Primary Schools	353798	56672	2427	774
特殊教育	Special Education Schools	590	10	7	
幼儿园	Kindergartens	104899	53372	1319	950

资料来源：北京市教育委员会。
Source: Beijing Municipal Commission of Education.

18-19 图书馆、文化馆、档案馆情况(1978-2015年) LIBRARIES, CULTURAL CENTERS AND ARCHIVES (1978-2015)

年 份 Year	公共图书馆 Public Libraries				群众艺术馆、文化馆 Mass Art Centers, Cultural Centers		档案馆 Archiving Institutions			
	个 数 (个) Number (unit)	总藏数 (万册、万件) Total Collections (10000 volumes)	建筑面积 (万平方米) Building Area (10000 sq.m)	书刊文献外借人次 (万人次) Person-times Borrowing Books, Magazines, and Documents (10000 person-times)	个 数 (个) Number (unit)	组织文艺活动 (次) Art Activities Organized (times)	个 数 (个) Number (unit)	建筑面积 (平方米) Building Area (10000 sq.m)	利用档案资料人次 (万人次) Persons of Using Files (10000 person-times)	案 卷 (万卷件) Records (10000 rolls)
1978	18	1423		168.5	19	516				
1979	21	1502		173.7	19	1033				
1980	20	1606	1.8	210.4	19	778				
1981	21	1614	1.9	211.0	19	1131				
1982	21	1676	2.0	228.4	20	1334				
1983	21	1733	1.9	243.0	20	1015				
1984	22	1824	2.3	223.7	22	489				
1985	22	1860	3.0	219.9	23	469				
1986	23	1874	6.0	219.9	23	883				
1987	23	1959	20.6	169.8	23	1067	20	10695	1.30	86.13
1988	23	2050	23.4	300.4	23	647	20	21472	1.46	115.98
1989	23	2128	24.5		23	1411	20	31280	1.48	156.28
1990	23	2205	25.0		23	1429	20	23618	2.51	167.37
1991	23	2281	25.3		23	1128	20	33491	3.24	177.45
1992	23	2397	25.4	147.0	23	978	20	35950	2.64	181.31
1993	23	2461	25.5	212.0	23	764	20	37650	1.73	192.39
1994	23	2548	23.8	383.8	23	1034	20	42641	1.50	192.35
1995	23	2629	24.1	139.3	23	1127	20	65489	1.42	204.06
1996	22	2652	25.3	145.6	23	2277	20	62994	3.03	223.70
1997	23	2789	25.7	188.0	23	1875	20	64147	2.69	227.42
1998	24	2848	25.6	189.0	23	2554	20	67759	2.71	240.78
1999	24	2934	26.4	607.0	23	1490	20	72597	2.52	259.50
2000	26	3020	27.0	283.0	23	1809	20	72596	3.01	278.29
2001	26	3133	31.4	287.7	23	1822	20	72730	4.17	297.02
2002	26	3248	30.7	337.5	20	1817	20	72946	4.53	328.42
2003	26	3355	30.9	334.8	20	2023	20	81519	6.27	358.95
2004	26	3451	30.9	405.0	22	1826	20	83162	7.03	379.13
2005	26	3626	31.7	480.0	22	3697	20	84656	6.97	404.69
2006	25	3776	31.0	515.0	21	2200	20	93773	10.59	436.70
2007	25	3940	31.5	479.0	21	4752	20	93463	9.51	461.67
2008	25	4100	33.4	450.0	20	3007	20	97605	9.00	495.70
2009	25	4368	41.9	471.0	20	3470	20	97605	9.88	523.84
2010	25	4613	42.4	441.0	20	3564	18	97611	13.45	557.99
2011	25	5049	42.1	333.0	20	3401	18	97976	12.30	582.92
2012	25	5556	47.6	317.0	20	3848	18	98879	12.37	602.54
2013	25	5316	48.4	325.0	20	4769	18	101896	23.85	636.10
2014	25	5601	52.7	407.0	20	2158	18	98220	22.18	697.90
2015	25	5943	52.4	438.0	20	2587	18	96256	14.90	733.23

注：1978-1981年，群众艺术馆、文化馆数据不包括群众艺术馆。

资料来源：北京市文化局、国家图书馆、北京市档案局。

Note: In 1978-1981, the data of mass art centers and cultural centers didn't include those of mass art centers.

Source: Beijing Municipal Bureau of Culture, National Library of China, and Beijing Municipal Bureau of Archives.

18-20 博物馆情况(1982-2015年)
STATISTICS FOR MUSEUMS (1982-2015)

年份 Year	北京地区博物馆数 (个) Number of Museums in Beijing (unit)	文物藏品数 (万件) Cultural Relic Collections (10000 units)	博物馆及其他文物保护机构(文物局系统内) Museums and Other Cultural Relic Protection and Administration Organizations (under the jurisdiction of Beijing Municipal Administration of Cultural Heritage)				
			个数 (个) Number (unit)	#博物馆 Museums	文物藏品数 (万件) Cultural Relic Collections (10000 units)	#一级品 (件) Grade-I Collections (unit)	参观人次 (万人次) Visitors (10000 person-times)
1982			28		8.4	294	9.7
1983			29		4.0		58.0
1984							
1985			32		9.0		20.0
1986			39	7	21.0		905.0
1987							
1988			42	11	21.0		1098.0
1989			46	12	14.0		992.0
1990							
1991			46	12	11.7	2901	6629.1
1992							
1993			50	16	17.4	479	2423.4
1994			51	17	16.7	447	955.0
1995			51	17	16.7	447	2100.3
1996			51	17	18.0	443	2009.3
1997			54	24	18.2	443	935.8
1998			56	26	18.3	387	697.8
1999			54	26	18.5	374	5641.8
2000			53	25	18.2	367	702.7
2001			58	26	17.3	366	99.1
2002			48	27	20.1	716	170.8
2003			55	27	112.4	716	119.2
2004			66	31	370.4	656	599.9
2005			73	34	115.1	620	1370.9
2006			70	33	115.5	643	1416.7
2007			69	34	113.5	439	1493.0
2008	148	331	71	37	116.0	678	1368.4
2009	151	331	76	40	117.0	722	1647.9
2010	156	332	79	41	117.0	725	1712.1
2011	162	430	78	41	117.0	852	1373.4
2012	165	430	78	41	117.0	903	1887.9
2013	167	430	78	41	117.0	903	1760.0
2014	171	430	78	41	128.0	891	1848.0
2015	173	430	77	40	126.0	931	2069.1

资料来源：北京市文物局。
Source: Beijing Municipal Administration of Cultural Heritage.

18-21 博物馆及其他文物保护管理机构情况(2015年)
STATISTICS FOR MUSEUMS AND OTHER CULTURAL RELIC PROTECTION AND ADMINISTRATION ORGANIZATIONS (2015)

项目	Item	合计 Total	市属 Under the Jurisdiction of the City	区县属 Under the Jurisdiction of a District/County
全市按行业管理登记的博物馆	**Museums Registered by Industry Administration**			
博物馆数 (个)	Museums (unit)	**173**	**43**	**44**
#免费开放的博物馆数 (个)	Museums Open for Free (unit)	80	24	24
文物藏品数 (万件)	Cultural Relic Collections (10000 units)	430		
参观人次 (万人次)	Visitors (10000 person-times)	3600		
文物古迹个数 (处)	Cultural Relics and Historical Sites (unit)	3840		
文物拍卖机构数 (个)	Organizations of Cultural Relic Auctions (unit)	156		
举办文物艺术品拍卖场次 (场)	Cultural Relic Auctions (time)	243		
文物拍卖标的数 (件、套)	Auction Targets (unit)	170843		
文物拍卖标的成交金额 (万元)	Turnover of Cultural Relic Auctions (10000 yuan)	1774840.37		
文物局系统内博物馆及文物保护管理机构 (个)	**Museums and Cultural Relic Protection and Administration Organizations under the Municipal Administration of Cultural Heritage (unit)**	**77**	**30**	**47**
#博物馆 (个)	Museums (unit)	40	16	24
博物馆按类别分	Grouped by Category			
综合性 (个)	Comprehensive (unit)	11	2	9
历史性 (个)	Historical (unit)	17	7	10
艺术性 (个)	Art (unit)	6	5	1
自然科技类 (个)	Natural Science (unit)	2	1	1
其他类 (个)	Others (unit)	5	2	3
从业人员 (人)	Employment (person)	4602	1174	
文物藏品数 (万件)	Cultural Relic Collections (10000 units)	126	121	
#一级品 (件)	Grade-I Collections (unit)	931	670	
参观人次 (万人次)	Visitors (10000 person-times)	2069	363	1706
本年收入 (万元)	Revenues in the Year (10000 yuan)	380957	95566	285391
#财政收入 (万元)	Fiscal Revenue (10000 yuan)	295471	61379	234092
门票收入 (万元)	Ticket Revenue (10000 yuan)	43345	2007	41338
本年支出 (万元)	Expenditures in the Year (10000 yuan)	390710	103739	286971

注：全市博物馆数为北京地区按行业管理登记的博物馆数。

资料来源：北京市文物局。

Note: Number of museums in the city means the number of museums registered by industrial administration in Beijing.

Source: Beijing Municipal Administration of Cultural Heritage.

18-22 公共图书馆(2015年)
PUBLIC LIBRARIES (2015)

项目		Item		合计 Total	中央属 Under Central Jurisdiction	市属 Under the Jurisdiction of the City	区县属 Under the Jurisdiction of a District/County
个数	(个)	Number	(unit)	25	1	1	23
从业人员	(人)	Employed Persons	(person)	2842	1579	365	898
总藏数	(万册、万件)	Total Collections	(10000 volumes)	5943	3518	771	1654
#图书	(万册、万件)	Books	(10000 volumes)	3397	1262	630	1505
建筑面积	(万平方米)	Building Area	(10000 sq.m)	52.4	27.8	9.4	15.2
阅览座席	(个)	Seating Capacity of Reading Rooms	(unit)	20772	5303	2924	12545
总流通人次	(万人次)	Total Number of Visitors	(10000 person-times)	1652	388	514	750
#书刊文献外借人次	(万人次)	Person-times Borrowing Books, Magazines and Documents	(10000 person-times)	438	44	58	336
#书刊文献外借册次	(万册次)	Volume-times of Borrowed Books, Magazines and Documents	(10000 volunme-times)	1006	66	252	688

资料来源：北京市文化局、国家图书馆。
Source: Beijing Municipal Bureau of Culture, and National Library of China.

18-23 群众艺术馆、文化馆和文化站情况(2015年)
STATISTICS FOR MASS ART CENTERS, CULTURAL CENTERS AND CULTURAL STATIONS(2015)

项目		Item		合计 Total	群众艺术馆 Mass Art Centers	文化馆 Cultural Centers	文化站 Cultural Stations
个数	(个)	Number	(unit)	349	1	19	329
从业人员	(人)	Employed Persons	(person)	2602	55	766	1781
举办展览个数	(个)	Exhibitions Held	(unit)	1992	10	197	1785
组织文艺活动	(次)	Art Activities Organized	(times)	27175	16	2571	24588

资料来源：北京市文化局。
Source: Beijing Municipal Bureau of Culture.

18-24 档案事业基本情况(2015年)
STATISTICS FOR ARCHIVING INSTITUTIONS (2015)

项 目		Item		合 计 Total	市 属 Under the Jurisdiction of the City	区 属 Under the Jurisdiction of a District/County
档案馆个数	**（个）**	**Number of Archives**	**(unit)**	**18**	**2**	**16**
建筑面积	**（平方米）**	**Building Areas**	**(sq.m)**	**99220**	**30962**	**68258**
馆藏档案情况		**Files Colllected in Archives**				
全 宗	（个）	Full Archives	(unit)	3131	885	2246
案 卷	（万卷件）	Records	(10000 rolls)	733.23	308.85	424.38
建国前档案	（万卷件）	Files Prior to the Foundation of PRC	(10000 rolls)	100.49	98.84	1.64
建国后档案	（万卷件）	Files After the Foundation of PRC	(10000 rolls)	632.86	210.01	422.85
录音、录像、影片档案	（盘）	Tape, Video, and Film Files	(piece)	38278	33303	4975
照片档案	（张）	Photo Files	(disc)	669954	356407	313547
缩微胶片		Microfiches				
平片、开窗卡	（张）	Flat and Window-open Microfiches	(disc)	289048	289048	
卷 片	（万幅）	Rolled Microfiches	(10000 rolls)	5426	5376	50.0
档案利用情况		**File Utilization**				
本年利用档案人次	（人次）	Person-times Using Files in the Year	(person-times)	148405	12623	135782
本年利用档案	（万卷件次）	Files Used in the Year	(10000 roll.times)	21	5	16
本年利用资料册次	（册次）	Data Books Used in the Year	(volume-times)	1963	246	1717
本年利用资料人次	（人次）	Person-times Using Data in the Year	(person-times)	586	92	494
本年编研档案、资料	（万字）	Files and Data Edited and Studied in the Year	(10000 Chinese characters)	916	462	454
档案馆网站来访IP次数	**（万次）**	**IPs Visiting Archive Websites**	**(10000 times)**	**119**	**75**	**44**

资料来源：北京市档案局。
Source: Beijing Municipal Bureau of Archives.

18-25 电影、电视、广播电台情况(1978-2015年)

年 份 Year	电影 Films			电视 TVs		
	放映场次 (万场次) Show Times (10000 Times)	观众人次 (万人次) Audience (10000 Person-times)	票房收入 (亿元) Ticket Revenue (100 million yuan)	电视节目套数 (套) Number of TV Programs (unit)	平均每日电视节目播出时间 (小时) Daily Show Hours of TV Programs (hour)	电视综合覆盖率 (%) Comprehensive Coverage Rate of TVs (%)
1978	31.9	29924.1				
1979	35.5	34626.0				
1980	33.1	31189.5		1	4.25	
1981	31.9	30067.0		1	5.46	100.00
1982	32.8	28743.5		1	6.85	91.00
1983	30.1	27345.5		1	7.07	90.00
1984	27.8	23966.7		1	7.15	98.00
1985	23.0	18875.0		1	7.54	98.00
1986	20.6	15904.4		2	19.07	98.00
1987	19.0	13517.7		2	13.64	98.00
1988	19.2	13269.4		2	19.39	98.00
1989	21.5	14492.6		4	25.43	98.00
1990	20.7	12771.2		4	29.43	98.00
1991	21.3	12558.3		4	27.79	98.00
1992	22.1	11587.4		6	45.02	98.00
1993	11.9	5369.8		7	58.18	98.00
1994	10.6	2166.5	0.51	9	77.79	98.30
1995	9.2	1598.6	0.93	12	98.36	98.30
1996	11.5	1644.1	1.07	12	101.01	98.81
1997	12.6	1742.3	1.17	12	111.00	99.12
1998	12.3	1443.5	1.28	12	110.68	99.60
1999	11.7	964.7		12	118.36	99.80
2000	12.2	873.2		12	122.45	99.80
2001	12.6	804.7	0.92	16	200.15	99.91
2002	12.3	827.4	1.09	18	329.40	99.82
2003	11.8	683.0	1.35	19	259.32	99.90
2004	18.1	814.4	1.86	24	244.17	99.50
2005	22.6	873.8	2.29	25	329.81	99.99
2006	28.0	1221.0	3.02	25	294.23	99.99
2007	38.0	1711.0	3.70	25	309.12	99.99
2008	46.8	1767.3	5.37	24	309.06	99.99
2009	62.4	2451.5	8.19	26	319.13	99.99
2010	74.3	2923.3	11.81	26	319.24	99.99
2011	97.4	3235.9	13.52	25	334.22	100.00
2012	120.0	3954.6	16.23	26	343.68	100.00
2013	137.8	4288.5	18.60	26	347.89	100.00
2014	162.8	5281.31	22.90	26	344.02	100.00
2015	198.1	7212.65	31.56	26	351.08	100.00

资料来源：北京市新闻出版广电局。

STATISTICS FOR FILMS, TELEVISIONS, AND BROADCASTING STATIONS (1978-2015)

电视 TVs				广播电台 Broadcasting Stations			
农村电视综合覆盖率 (%) Comprehensive Coverage Rate of TVs in Rural Area (%)	无线电视综合覆盖率 (%) Comprehensive Coverage Rate of Wireless TVs (%)	有线电视注册用户数 (万户) Subscnbers of Cable Televisions (10000 households)	有线广播电视入户率 (%) Access Rate of Cable Televisions (%)	广播节目套数 (套) Number of Radio Programs (unit)	平均每日广播节目播出时间 (小时) Daily Show Hours of Radio Programs (hour)	广播综合覆盖率 (%) Comprehensive Coverage Rate of Broadcast (%)	广告收入 (万元) Advertising Income (10000 yuan)
				4	56.08		
				4	57.22	100.00	139
				4	59.37	98.00	166
				5	61.97	98.00	117
				5	73.67	98.00	668
				5	65.87	98.00	645
				5	66.17	98.00	555
				6	68.75	98.00	771
				6	76.33	98.00	964
				7	78.67	98.00	1668
				7	77.87	98.00	2885
				7	77.87	98.00	5115
				10	94.75	98.00	9680
				12	134.75	98.00	15225
		52.71		12	134.85	98.00	26480
		82.21		13	148.25	91.00	45398
		182.97		13	150.25	96.97	93428
		202.75		15	156.05	98.44	100546
		230.97		16	174.67	99.98	106773
		165.78	43.24	16	178.20	99.96	115072
		175.71	45.80	16	188.90	97.7	149661
		205.95	51.76	16	192.43	99.91	136451
		231.24	57.05	16	197.43	99.88	154317
		243.00	58.39	16	197.86	99.91	157210
	97.57	265.50	62.09	16	229.55	100.00	212091
	99.99	282.00	64.12	17	281.88	100.00	236334
99.97	94.90	319.58	70.75	17	282.88	100.00	240146
99.97	93.13	345.06	74.43	17	288.92	99.98	317437
99.97	93.19	383.13	81.00	17	297.40	99.98	385231
99.97	94.38	413.50	85.90	18	316.58	99.99	453932
99.97	98.72	448.12	91.68	18	324.82	99.99	613672
100.00	99.74	475.92	95.90	18	329.56	100.00	796113
100.00	99.75	495.70	99.13	25	471.69	100.00	1081857
100.00	99.75	524.59	103.00	25	473.62	100.00	1689443
100.00	99.75	551.57	106.85	25	472.61	100.00	1753933
100.00	99.75	569.13	108.88	25	470.42	100.00	2153546

Source: Beijing Municipal Administration of Press, Publication, Radio, Film and Television.

18-26 电影、电视剧制作情况
STATISTICS FOR PRODUCTION OF FILMS AND TV PLAYS

项目		Item		2015			2014		
				全国 National Total	北京 Beijing	占全国比重(%) As % of National Total	全国 National Total	北京 Beijing	占全国比重(%) As % of National Total
生产故事片	(部)	Feature Films	(Piece)	888	291	32.8	618	270	43.7
制作电视剧	(部)	TV Plays	(Piece)	394	75	19.0	429	86	20.0
	(集)		(Episode)	16540	2878	17.4	15983	3129	19.6
电视剧出口量部	(部)	TV Plays Exported	(Piece)	381	53	13.9	296	47	15.9
	(集)		(Episode)	15902	2116	13.3	13824	1754	12.7
电视剧出口额	(万元)	Value of TV Plays Exported	(10000 yuan)	37705	6211	16.5	20795	5084	24.4

资料来源：北京市新闻出版广电局。
Source: Beijing Municipal Administration of Press, Publication, Radio, Film and Television.

18-27 电影放映单位情况(2015年)
STATISTICS FOR MOVIE PROJECTION ORGANIZATIONS (2015)

项目	Item	放映单位数(个) Number of Projection Organizations (unit)	总银幕数(块) Total Screens (Piece)	#3D银幕数 3D Screens	#IMAX巨幕数 IMAX Large Screens	放映场次(万场次) Show Times (10000 Times)	观影人次(万人次) Audience (10000 Person-times)	票房收入(亿元) Ticket Revenues (100 million yuan)
合计	**Total**	**182**	**1050**	**951**	**14**	**198.14**	**7212.65**	**31.56**
院线影院	Cinema Chains	182	1050	951	14	197.98	7164.21	31.51
二级市场	Secondary Market					0.16	48.44	0.05

资料来源：北京市新闻出版广电局。
Source: Beijing Municipal Administration of Press, Publication, Radio, Film and Television.

18-28 电视台情况
STATISTICS FOR TELEVISION STATIONS

项　　目	Item	2015 中央 Central	2015 地方 Local	2014 中央 Central	2014 地方 Local
基本情况	**Basic Statistics**				
电视台 (座)	Television Stations (unit)	1	1	1	1
公共节目套数 (套)	Number of Public Programs (unit)	43	26	35	26
全年公共节目播出时间 (小时)	Annual Broadcast Time of Public Programs (hour)	359898.6	128143.5	291462	125569
播放节目情况	**Shows of TV Programs**				
新闻咨询类节目 (小时)	News and Consulting Programs (hour)	75766	22792	80249	22905
专题服务类节目 (小时)	Special Service Programs (hour)	90699	49656	85482	48160
综艺益智类节目 (小时)	Entertainment and Education Programs (hour)	41613	10007	41140	9284
影视剧类节目 (小时)	Movie and TV Play Programs (hour)	73926	26981	69645	28373
广告类节目 (小时)	Commercial Programs (hour)	5666	9270	5020	9782
其他类节目 (小时)	Other Programs (hour)	72228	9437	9927	7065

注：电视台数不包括区县电视台。
资料来源：北京市新闻出版广电局。
Note: Number of television stations excludes TV stations of districts and counties.
Source: Beijing Municipal Administration of Press, Publication, Radio, Film and Television.

18-29 广播电台情况
STATISTICS FOR BROADCASTING STATIONS

项　　目	Item	2015 中央 Central	2015 地方 Local	2014 中央 Central	2014 地方 Local
基本情况	**Basic Statistics**				
电台数 (座)	Number of Broadcasting Stations (unit)	2	1	2	1
公共节目套数 (套)	Number of Public Programs (unit)	23	25	22	25
全年公共节目播出时间 (小时)	Annual Broadcast Time of Public Programs (hour)	262963	171702	342365	172503
播放节目情况	**Shows of Radio Programs**				
新闻咨询类节目 (小时)	News and Consulting Programs (hour)	68043	19811	107856	18874
专题服务类节目 (小时)	Special Service Programs (hour)	99244	39010	135643	42422
综艺类节目 (小时)	Entertainment and Education Programs (hour)	65204	82092	58311	82288
广播剧类节目 (小时)	Radio Plays (hour)	8170	11519	10454	10738
广告类节目 (小时)	Commercial Programs (hour)	12851	12308	14555	11835
其他类节目 (小时)	Other Programs (hour)	9451	6963	15545	6346

注：1. 广播电台数不包括区县电台。
　　2. 公共节目套数中含县级广播电视台的广播节目套数。
资料来源：北京市新闻出版广电局。
Note: a) Number of broadcasting stations excluded those of districts and counties.
　　b) Public programs included broadcast programs of radio stations at county levels.
Source: Beijing Municipal Administration of Press, Publication, Radio, Film and Television.

18-30 广播电视综合覆盖率(2015年)
COMPREHENSIVE COVERAGE RATE OF BROADCASTS AND TELEVISIONS (2015)

项 目		Item		2015
广播综合覆盖率	(%)	Comprehensive Coverage Rate of Broadcasts	(%)	100.0
农村广播综合覆盖率	(%)	Comprehensive Coverage Rate of Broadcasts in Rural Areas	(%)	100.0
无线广播综合覆盖率	(%)	Comprehensive Coverage Rate of Radios	(%)	100.0
电视综合覆盖率	(%)	Comprehensive Coverage Rate of Televisions	(%)	100.0
农村电视综合覆盖率	(%)	Comprehensive Coverage Rate of Televisions in Rural Areas	(%)	100.0
无线电视综合覆盖率	(%)	Comprehensive Coverage Rate of Wireless Televisions	(%)	99.75
有线电视入户率	(%)	Access Rate of Wire Broadcasting and Cable TVs	(%)	108.88
有线电视注册用户数	(万户)	Registered Subscribers of Cable TVs	(10000 households)	569.13
#高清交互数字电视用户数	(万户)	Subscribers of High-definition Interactive Digital Televisions	(10000 households)	460.00
付费电视用户数	(万户)	Subscribers of Pay TVs	(10000 households)	61.34
农村有线广播电视用户数	(万户)	Subscribers of Wire Broadcasting and Cable TVs in Rural Areas	(10000 households)	79.07

资料来源：北京市新闻出版广电局。

Source: Beijing Municipal Administration of Press, Publication, Radio, Film and Television.

18-31 报纸、期刊、图书出版情况(1978-2014年)
NEWSPAPER, JOURNAL AND BOOK PUBLICATIONS (1978-2014)

年份 Year	报纸出版 Newspaper Publications				期刊出版 Journal Publications				图书出版 Books Publications		
	种数(种) Types (kind)	平均期印数(万份) Average Printed Copies Per Issue (10000 copies)	总印数(亿份) Total Printed Copies (100 million copies)	总印张(亿印张) Total Sheets Printed (100 million pieces)	种数(种) Types (kind)	平均期印数(万册) Average Printed Copies Per Issue (10000 copies)	总印数(亿册) Total Printed Copies (100 million copies)	总印张(亿印张) Total Sheets Printed (100 million pieces)	种数(种) Types (kind)	总印数(亿册、亿张) Total Sheets Printed (100 million copies)	总印张(亿印张) Total Sheets Printed (100 million pieces)
1978	11		68.50		468		4.50		5253	5.12	
1979	16		81.60		697		5.92		6723	5.91	
1980	41		84.50		839		5.80		9534	6.28	
1981	55		83.10		886		6.69		11139	7.84	
1982	57		78.30		882		6.67		13862	8.71	
1983	61		79.90		940		6.84		14384	8.49	
1984	73		83.00		987		7.89		15636	8.43	
1985	99		86.00		1098		8.21		17178	9.01	
1986	126		82.00		1206		7.95		19362	5.82	
1987	129		86.00		1409		8.24		21843	6.94	
1988	151		87.00		1514		8.23		23689	7.28	
1989	161		66.00		1580		6.24		25980	6.31	
1990	148		68.00		1415		5.90		27345	6.17	
1991	157		76.70		1499		6.83		29609	7.05	
1992	164	3886	81.38	88.39	1594	6043	7.79	22.30	31320	7.83	58.67
1993	170	3965	81.70	87.71	1597	6037	7.80	22.36	34393	8.60	70.96
1994	233	3759	69.98	92.59	1854	5328	6.29	19.11	38498	8.28	71.71
1995	240	3823	72.92	108.32	1884	5018	6.38	19.62	38819	8.33	70.15
1996	242		70.52		2129		6.13		41572	9.45	
1997	242	3624	71.80	122.17	2162	5396	6.61	22.87	45775	9.93	78.62
1998	247	3561	71.70	130.01	2274	5797	7.28	26.54	50155	10.95	86.05
1999	247	3520	71.65	144.65	2273	6116	8.04	35.18	54783	11.34	93.38
2000	240	3343	68.67	149.58	2352	5909	7.91	32.96	57821	9.63	92.98
2001	243	3339	69.35	153.22	2374	5761	8.09	32.61	63928	10.27	105.06
2002	247	3364	71.02	169.87	2377	5708	8.23	34.34	73836	12.16	127.48
2003	250	3393	72.45	190.35	2382	5702	8.18	34.25	85244	13.82	140.77
2004	253	3405	70.40	206.53	2791	5233	7.97	35.53	98312	15.22	157.17
2005	255	3169	66.16	227.22	2809	4957	7.72	40.80	108152	17.07	180.51
2006	256	3651	74.01	240.39	2809	5077	8.29	47.39	113232	17.19	186.10
2007	256	3454	73.09	218.55	2809	5340	9.17	54.21	125412	18.68	195.30
2008	259	3328	73.21	241.27	2898	5392	9.36	55.39	136284	20.78	220.00
2009	260	3232	71.63	232.50	3030	5373	9.70	59.35	144211	21.04	220.21
2010	262	3406	77.54	275.62	3063	5519	10.03	69.61	155209	21.45	251.18
2011	254	3453	83.07	293.72	3044	5991	10.19	76.74	167942	22.60	243.05
2012	257	3725	89.49	300.17	3064	5940	10.31	76.68	179634	22.54	250.70
2013	254	3737	91.72	298.20	3053	6094	10.36	78.02	192137	24.01	269.54
2014	256	3550	89.90	289.30	3123	5867	9.95	74.04	194259	23.56	258.65

注：1991年及以前，报纸、期刊、图书为出版数；1992年及以后均为总印数。

资料来源：北京市新闻出版广电局。

Note: Figures on newspaper, journals and books in and before 1991 were figures of publications; after 1992, they were total sheet printed.

Source: Beijing Municipal Administration of Press, Publication, Radio, Film and Television.

18-32 报纸出版情况
NEWSPAPER PUBLICATION

项 目	Item	种数(种) Types of Publications (kind)		平均期印数(万份) Average Printed Copies Per Issue (10000 copies)		总印数(亿份) Total Printed Copies (100 million copies)		总印张(亿印张) Total Sheets Printed (100 million pieces)	
		2014	2013	2014	2013	2014	2013	2014	2013
合 计	**Total**	**256**	**254**	**3550**	**3737**	**89.9**	**91.7**	**289.3**	**298.2**
综合报	Comprehensive	30	30	1337	1436	45.8	47.2	169.5	177.3
专业报	Professional	226	224	2213	2301	44.1	44.5	119.8	120.9

资料来源：北京市新闻出版广电局。
Source: Beijing Municipal Administration of Press, Publication, Radio, Film and Television.

18-33 期刊出版情况
JOURNAL PUBLICATION

项 目	Item	种 数(种) Types of Publications (kind)		平均期印数(万册) Average Printed Copies Per Issue (10000 copies)		总 印 数(亿册) Total Printed Copies (100 million copies)		总 印 张(亿印张) Total Sheets Printed (100 million pieces)	
		2014	2013	2014	2013	2014	2013	2014	2013
合 计	**Total**	**3123**	**3053**	**5867**	**6094**	**9.95**	**10.36**	**74.04**	**78.02**
综 合	Comprehensive	68	70	123	150	0.30	0.37	2.09	2.67
哲学、社会科学	Philosophy and Social Sciences	939	906	3705	3759	6.33	6.43	34.57	34.61
自然科学技术	Natural Sciences and Technology	1595	1568	1151	1280	1.58	1.79	18.10	20.40
文化、教育	Culture and Education	373	368	705	712	1.34	1.37	16.57	17.46
文学、艺术	Literature and Art	148	141	183	194	0.40	0.40	2.71	2.87

资料来源：北京市新闻出版广电局。
Source: Beijing Municipal Administration of Press, Publication, Radio, Film and Television.

18-34 图书出版情况
BOOK PUBLICATION

项目	Item	出版图书种数合计(种) Types of Publications (kind)		#新书 New Publications		总印数 (万册、万张) Total Printed Copies (10000 volumes, 10000 pieces)		总印张 (万印张) Total Sheets Printed (10000 print sheets)	
		2014	2013	2014	2013	2014	2013	2014	2013
合　计	**Total**	**194259**	**192137**	**113605**	**111865**	**235632**	**240142**	**2586544**	**2695355**
书籍合计	**Books**	**194189**	**192047**	**113565**	**111789**	**233165**	**238106**	**2575153**	**2683793**
马列主义、毛泽东思想	Maxism, Leninism, Mao Zedong Thought	516	426	321	297	1737	1175	29666	23225
哲　学	Philosophy	4820	5183	3197	3599	3288	3172	48599	47664
社会科学总论	General Social Sciences	3477	3287	2175	2019	1743	1845	29952	32873
政治、法律	Politics and Law	13470	13180	9914	10122	14877	13550	169374	182810
军　事	Military Science	975	986	810	802	448	540	7099	7919
经　济	Economics	22224	21520	13741	13488	10886	10875	187999	189657
文化、科学、教育、体育	Culture,Science,Education and Sports	37775	38084	19067	18644	129651	126301	1049900	1010837
语言、文字	Languages	11891	12706	5644	5906	11875	21447	211571	322320
文　学	Literature	15731	15512	11844	11761	14619	14450	180654	191311
艺　术	Art	8858	8051	6250	5560	5433	4861	50653	46411
历史、地理	History and Geography	8637	8263	6194	5936	8097	8461	93850	93373
自然科学总论	General Natural Sciences	342	381	220	257	175	252	2442	2849
数学科学、化学	Mathematics and Chemistry	5232	5326	1925	2001	2620	3016	46562	49736
天文学、物理科学	Astronomy and Physics	1561	1608	1091	1129	588	555	6593	7253
生物科学	Biology	1580	1629	858	917	799	871	11131	12581
医药、卫生	Medicine and Healthcare	11484	11687	6532	6726	6590	7019	124175	132823
农业科学	Agricultural Sciences	3327	3269	2037	1931	1298	1316	14327	16174
工业技术	Industrial Technologies	35286	34462	17649	16911	14231	14657	252816	261873
交通运输	Transportation	4014	3892	1893	1982	2567	2588	35004	35118
航空、航天	Aeronautics and Aerospace	319	305	240	236	85	107	1339	1545
环境科学	Environmental Sciences	1443	1289	1032	868	497	456	6051	6257
综合性图书	General Books	1227	1001	931	697	1060	593	15394	9181
图片及小件印品合计	**Pictures and Small Printed Publications**	**70**	**90**	**40**	**76**	**2467**	**2036**	**11392**	**11563**

资料来源：北京市新闻出版广电局。
Source: Beijing Municipal Administration of Press, Publication, Radio, Film and Television.

18-35 录音制品出版情况
PUBLICATION OF AUDIO PRODUCTS

项 目 Item	录音带 Audio-tapes				激光唱盘 CDs				高密度激光唱盘 DVDs-A			
	种数(种) Types (kind)		数量(万盒) Number (10000 cassettes)		种数(种) Types (kind)		数量(万张) Number (10000 pieces)		种数(种) Types (kind)		数量(万张) Number (10000 pieces)	
	2014	2013	2014	2013	2014	2013	2014	2013	2014	2013	2014	2013
合 计 Total	**1095**	**1310**	**12366.6**	**15243.3**	**1654**	**2128**	**2657.8**	**2345.1**	**1069**	**917**	**830.4**	**738.7**
#市 属 Municipal	78	69	6.2	7.8	192	64	157.3	60.6	31	10	89.1	2.4

资料来源：北京市新闻出版广电局。
Source: Beijing Municipal Administration of Press, Publication, Radio, Film and Television.

18-36 录像制品出版情况
PUBLICATION OF VIDEO PRODUCTS

项 目 Item	录像带 Videotapes				激光视盘 VCDs				高密度激光视盘 DVD-Vs			
	种数(种) Types (kind)		数量(万盒) Number (10000 cassettes)		种数(种) Kind (kind)		数量(万张) Number (10000 pieces)		种数(种) Types (kind)		数量(万张) Number (10000 pieces)	
	2014	2013	2014	2013	2014	2013	2014	2013	2014	2013	2014	2013
合 计 Total	**93**	**117**	**18.5**	**49.8**	**523**	**1003**	**1456.7**	**2590.7**	**1799**	**2703**	**2669.8**	**3459.7**
#市 属 Municipal		5		38.5		1			54	83	287.0	201.1

资料来源：北京市新闻出版广电局。
Source: Beijing Municipal Administration of Press, Publication, Radio, Film and Television.

18-37 电子出版物出版情况(2014年)
PUBLICATION OF E-PUBLICATIONS (2014)

项 目	Item	只读光盘 CD-ROMs 种数(种) Types (kind)	只读光盘 CD-ROMs 数量(万盒) Number (10000 cassettes)	交互式光盘 CD-Is 种数(种) Types (kind)	交互式光盘 CD-Is 数量(万张) Number (10000 pieces)	高密度只读光盘 DVD-ROMs 种数(种) Types (kind)	高密度只读光盘 DVD-ROMs 数量(万张) Number (10000 pieces)
合 计	**Total**	**4203**	**23122.94**	**939**	**1466.55**	**2582**	**2027.15**
#市 属	Municipal	27	13.09	19	1.60	46	13.23

资料来源：北京市新闻出版广电局。
Source: Beijing Municipal Administration of Press, Publication, Radio, Film and Television.

18-38 引进版权量情况
NUMBER OF IMPORTED COPYRIGHTS

项 目	Item	2014	2013
引进版权量 （件）	**Number of Imported Copyrights (set)**	**8647**	**9391**
软件和电子出版物 (件)	Softwares and E-Publications (set)	92	176
图 书 (件)	Books (set)	8555	9215

注：2012年引进图书版权量含期刊。
资料来源：北京市新闻出版广电局。
Note: Data on number of imported copyrights in 2012 includes journals.
Source: Beijing Municipal Administration of Press, Publication, Radio, Film and Television.

主要统计指标解释

教　育

研究生培养机构　指经国家批准按国家计划招收和培养硕士、博士和其他研究生的高等学校和科学研究机构。

普通高等学校　指按国家规定的设置标准和审批程序批准举办的，通过国家统一招生考试，招收高中毕业生为主要培养对象，实施高等教育的全日制大学、独立设置的学院和高等专科学校、短期职业大学。

成人高等学校　指按国家规定的设置标准和审批程序批准举办的，通过全国成人高等教育统一招生考试，招收具有高中毕业或同等学历的人员为主要培养对象，利用函授、业余、脱产等多种形式对其实施高等学历教育的学校。包括:职工高等学校、农民高等学校、管理干部学院、教育学院、独立函授学院、广播电视大学和其他机构。

高等教育机构　指经省、自治区、直辖市教育行政部门审批并颁发办学许可证，不具有颁发学历文凭资格的实施高等教育的单位。

民办学校　指经有关主管部门批准，公民个人、社会团体及其他社会组织等利用非国家财政性教育经费，面向社会举办的学校及其他教育机构。

学历文凭考试机构　经教育行政部门专门批准，进行全日制高等教育的民办其他高等教育机构。

专科教育　应当使学生掌握本专业必备的基础理论、专门应用技术知识，具有从事本专业实际工作的基本技能和技术应用能力。全日制专科教育的基本修业年限为二至三年。

本科教育　应当使学生比较系统地掌握本学科、专业必需的基础理论、基本知识，掌握本专业必要的基本技能、方法和相关知识，具有从事本专业实际工作和研究工作的初步能力。全日制本科教育的基本修业年限为四至五年。

硕士研究生教育　应当使学生掌握本学科坚实的基础理论、系统的专业知识，掌握相应的技能、方法和相关知识，具有从事本专业实际工作和科学研究工作的能力。硕士研究生教育的基本修业年限为二至三年。

博士研究生教育　应当使学生掌握本学科坚实宽广的基础理论、系统深入的专业知识、相应的技能和方法，具有独立从事本学科创造性科学研究工作和实际工作的能力。博士研究生教育的基本修业年限为三至四年。

网络学生　指经教育部批准的现代远程教育试点学校设立的网络教育学院，基于互联网上实施高等学历教育所招收的普通和成人本科、专科学生。

在职人员攻读博士、硕士学位学生　指经国务院学位委员会批准的，为提高在职人员业务水平，通过攻读博士、硕士学位入学全国联考所招收的学生。培养的学生只有学位没有学历。

证书教育　指由各类高等教育机构举办的，招收具有高中毕业文化程度，从事专业技术工作或专业性较强的管理工作人员，经过学校学习及考试合格，取得达到岗位要求的专业知识水平证明的非学历教育。证书教育形式包括单科班和专业证书班。

单科班　指学生在学校只学一个科目中的一门或几门课程，考试合格可获得单科结业证书。

专业证书班　学生在学校学习 8 至 10 门课程，考试合格可获得岗位要求的大专层次专业知识水平的证书。

岗位培训　指由各类高等教育机构举办的，以提高本职工作能力为目的的非学历教育和培训活动。接受培训的各类人员按要求经考核合格，颁发岗位合格证书和上岗任职聘任书。岗位培训形式包括资格性培训和适应性培训。

资格性培训　指学生按照岗位规范要求取得上岗(在岗)、转岗、晋升等资格的培训。

适应性培训　指学生根据本岗位工作的发展需要而进行各种适应性的培训。

进修及培训　指对具有大学专科以上学历和中级以上职称的专业人员和管理人员进行扩展知识，提高技能的非学历教育。

外国留学生　指接受来中国学习的外籍学生。

毕业生数　指上学年度内，具有学籍的学生学完教学计划规定的全部课程，考试及格，取得毕业证书，实际毕业的学生数。不包括结业生和肄业生数。

招生数　指新学年开始时，按照国家计划实际招收入学的新生数。不包括留级生和复读学生数。

在校学生数　指学年初开学以后，具有学籍的注册学生数。

结业生数　指具有学籍的学生学习期满，有一门以上主要课程(包括毕业论文或毕业设计)不及格或其他方面不合格，未予毕业而发给结业证书的学生数。不包括短训班和单科结业学生。

教职工数　指在学校(机构)工作并由学校(机构)支付工资的教职工人数。教职工数包括校本部教职工、科研机构人员、校办企业职工、其他附设机构人员。

专任教师　指主要从事教育工作的人员。包括临时（一年以内）调去帮助做其他工作的教学人员。不包括调离教学岗位，担任行政领导工作或其他工作的原教学人员；不包括兼任教师和代课教师。

特殊教育学校 指招收盲聋哑青少年进行初中等教育的学校。

校舍建筑面积 指产权归学校所有，已经使用的各种用房的建筑面积。不包括尚未竣工的在建工程和借用、租用的房舍或临时搭用的棚舍。

危房面积 指年久失修、结构构件受到严重损坏，有倒塌危险，经房管部门鉴定属于危房的面积。

学校占地面积 指学校校园内的土地面积，不包括校园外学校拥有的农场、林场及校办工厂等的土地面积。

文　化

公共图书馆藏书 指各级文化部门举办的面向社会服务的独立的图书馆（不包括文化馆的图书室，也不包括文化系统以外的图书馆）藏书数量。

广播综合覆盖率 根据国家广电总局制定的《广播电视人口覆盖率统计技术标准和方法》进行统计调查的，在对象区内能接收到广播节目的覆盖人口数占本行政区域内人口总数的比率。

农村广播综合覆盖率 根据国家广电总局制定的《广播电视人口覆盖率统计技术标准和方法》进行统计调查的，在对象区内能接收到广播节目的农村人口数占本行政区域内农村人口总数的比率。农村是指经国家批准设立的乡镇人民政府的乡和农村建制镇所辖区，不包括县政府驻地镇。

无线广播综合覆盖率 根据国家广电总局制定的《广播电视人口覆盖率统计技术标准和方法》进行统计调查的，在对象区内能接收到用中、短波、调频等无线传输技术发射转播的广播节目的人口数占本行政区域内人口总数的比率。包括中央、省、地市、县四级无线广播综合覆盖人口。

电视综合覆盖率 根据国家广电总局制定的《广播电视人口覆盖率统计技术标准和方法》进行统计调查的，在对象区内能接收到电视节目的人口数占本行政区域内人口总数的比率，包括中央、省、地市、县电视节目综合覆盖人口。

农村电视综合覆盖率 根据国家广电总局制定的《广播电视人口覆盖率统计技术标准和方法》进行统计调查的，在对象区内能接收到电视节目的农村人口数占本行政区域内农村人口总数的比率，包括中央、省、地市、县电视节目综合覆盖农村人口。农村是指经国家批准设立的乡镇人民政府的乡和农村建制镇所辖区，不包括县政府驻地镇。

无线电视综合覆盖率 根据国家广电总局制定的《广播电视人口覆盖率统计技术标准和方法》进行统计调查的，在对象区内能接收到用中、短波、调频等无线传输技术发射转播的电视节目的人口数占本行政区域内人口总数的比率。包括中央、省、地市、县四级无线电视综合覆盖人口。

有线电视入户率 指通过广播电视有线传输网收看电视节目的家庭用户数（包括接收模拟信号和接收数字信号的有线电视用户数，不包括宾馆、单位、写字楼等集体用户）与本行政区域内总户数的比率。

数字电视用户数 指通过广播电视有线传输网收看数字信号电视节目的家庭用户数。

付费电视用户数 指通过广播电视有线传输网收看数字信号的电视节目，并交纳收看费的有线电视家庭用户数。

Explanatory Notes on Main Statistical Indicators

Education

Institutions Providing Postgraduate Programs refer to colleges and universities, research institutions recruiting and educating postgraduates of master's degree, doctor's degree and other degree upon approval by the government and under the State Plan.

Regular Institutions of Higher Education refer to educational establishments set up according to the government evaluation and approval procedures, recruiting graduates from senior secondary schools as the main target by National Matriculation Test. They include full-time universities, independent colleges and higher professional schools, short-term vocational colleges.

Adult Institutions of Higher Education refer to educational establishments, set up in line with relevant rules approved by the government, recruiting personnel with senior high school or equivalent educational diploma through national college entrance test for adults, and providing higher education courses in many forms of correspondence, spare-time, or full-time teaching for adults. Institutions of higher learning for adults include schools of higher education for staff and workers, schools of higher education for farmers, colleges for management cadres, pedagogical colleges, independent correspondence colleges, Radio and TV universities and other educational establishments.

Higher Education Institutions refer to institutions offering higher education upon examination and approval by administrative departments in charge of education in provinces, autonomous regions and municipalities, with an education license, which are not eligible for conferring diploma.

Civilian-run Schools refer to schools and other educational institutions run by individuals, social groups and other social organizations upon approval by relevant competent authorities, by using educational funds not from state revenues.

Diploma Test Institutions refer to other civilian-run higher education institutions offering full-time higher education upon special approval by educational administration.

Secondary Technical Education shall enable students to understand necessary basic theories and special knowledge on applied technologies of a specialty, have basic skills and technical application ability for practice of the specialty. Full-time secondary technically education offers a basic study term of 2-3 years.

Undergraduate Education shall enable students to understand necessary basic theories and knowledge of a subject or specialty, have necessary basic skills, methodology and relevant knowledge of the specialty, and have preliminary skills for practical work and research of the specialty. Full-time undergraduate education offers a basic study term of 4-5 years.

Master's-degree Postgraduate Education shall enable students to understand solid basic theories, systematic professional knowledge of a subject, have relevant skills, methodology and relevant knowledge of the specialty, and have preliminary skills for practical work and research of the specialty. Master's-degree postgraduate education offers a basic study term of 2-3 years.

Doctor's-degree Postgraduate Education shall enable students to understand solid and extensive basic theories, systematic and in-depth professional knowledge, relevant skills and methodology of a subject, have relevant skills, methodology and relevant knowledge of the specialty, and have preliminary skills for independent creative research and practical work of the specialty. Doctor's-degree postgraduate education offers a basic study term of 3-4 years.

Online Students refer to students for Internet-based general higher courses, undergraduate courses for adults, and secondary technical courses recruited in online education colleges opened in schools as modern remote education pilots approved by the Ministry of Education.

Employees Enrolled in Graduate Programs refer to students recruited through national joint test for studies of Doctor's and Master's degrees approved by the Academic Degree Commission of the State Council, in order to improve the practical skills of on-the-job personnel. Graduated students will be conferred academic degree only, without academic credentials.

Certificate Education refers to education not for academic credentials, run by various higher education institutions that recruit management personnel who are graduated from senior high schools and engaged in professional technical work or strongly professional management work, and receive a certificate for professional knowledge level meeting the requirements of their job position after studying in the school and pass the test. It consists of single-subject program and professional certificate program.

Single-subject Program means that students study only one or more courses of one subject, and will be awarded a certificate of completion of single subject.

Professional Certificate Program means that students study 8-10 courses in the school, and will be awarded a certificate for professional knowledge at junior college level required for their job.

Occupational Training refers to educational and

training activities not for academic credentials, aiming to improve the competence, run by various higher education institutions. Various trainees will be awarded Occupational Incumbency Certification and Engagement Certification. The occupational training is in the form of qualification training and adaptability training.

Qualification Training means any training for students to become qualified for being employed (reemployed) on a job, transfer of job, and promotion as required by job criterion.

Adaptability Training means that students receive training for adaptability in line with needs of their own job.

Advanced Studies and Trainings means education not for academic credentials, offered for professional and managers with educational background of college and above, and technical title above middle rank, to expand their knowledge and improve their skill.

Foreign Students Studying in China refers to foreign students who study in China.

Number of Graduated Students means the number of enrolled students who are actually graduated after passing all exams and receiving a diploma upon completing all courses stated in the teaching plan within the last academic year. This does not include the number of students completing all courses with any one course not passed, and students not completing all courses or discontinuing their schooling.

Number of New Students refers to the number of students actually recruited at the beginning of an academic year in line with State plan, excluding the number of students failing to go up to the next grade and those resuming their interrupted studies.

Number of Enrolled Students means the number of students enrolled at the beginning of a new academic year.

Number of Students Completing Courses means the number of enrolled students completing their schooling with one and more courses not passed (including the graduation paper or graduation design) or other aspects not passed, who are not granted for graduation and awarded a certificate of completion, excluding the number of students completing short-term training courses and single-subject programs.

Faculty Number means the number of faculty working in and paid by schools (institutions). It includes the number of teachers and workers in the principal campus, in research institutions, school-run enterprises and other subsidiaries.

Full-time Teachers refer to personnel mainly engaged in teaching, including persons temporarily (within one year) transferred to other jobs, excluding persons transferred from teaching to administrative leadership or other jobs; excluding part-time teachers and teachers taking over a class for absent teachers.

Schools for Special Education mean schools recruiting blind, deaf and mute teenagers for primary and secondary education.

Floor Space of Schoolhouse refers to the building area of various houses of which the property right is owned by the school and which have been used, excluding houses not completed and under construction, borrowed and rented, or temporarily built sheds and houses.

Area of Dilapidated Houses refers to the area of those houses that have not been repaired for many years, have seriously damaged components, are at the risk of collapse, and are identified by the house administration authority as dilapidated houses.

Area of Land Occupied by School means the area of land within campus, excluding the area of land for farms and forest land outside schools and school-run factories.

Culture

Collection of Books in Public Libraries means the number of books collected in independent libraries open to the public and run by all-level cultural bodies (excluding book rooms in culture centers, and books collected in libraries not included in the cultural system).

Comprehensive Coverage Rate of Broadcast means the share of population who can receive broadcasting programs in the target area, calculated in line with *Statistical Standard and Method on Television and Radio Coverage of Population* established by the State Administration of Broadcasting, Film and Television, of the total population in the administrative area.

Comprehensive Coverage Rate of Broadcast in Rural Area means the share of rural population who can receive broadcasting programs in the target area, calculated in line with *Statistical Standard and Method on Television and Radio Coverage of Population* established by the National Administration of Broadcasting, Film and Television, of the total rural population in the administrative area. Rural area means villages of towns with people's governments approved by the State and areas under the jurisdiction of rural towns with organizational system, excluding towns where people's governments of counties are located.

Comprehensive Coverage Rate of Radio means the share of population who can receive broadcasting programs transmitted with short-wave, medium-wave, FM and other radio transmission technologies in the target area, calculated in line with *Statistical Standard and Method on Television and Radio Coverage of Population* established by the National Administration of Broadcasting, Film and Television, of the total population in the administrative area, including the population covered by broadcasting programs from central, provincial, prefectural cities and county radio stations.

Comprehensive Coverage Rate of TV means the share of population who can receive TV programs in the target area, calculated in line with *Statistical Standard and Method on Television and Radio Coverage of Population* established by the National Administration of Broadcasting, Film and Television, of the total population in the administrative area, including the population covered by TV programs from central, provincial, prefectural cities and county TV stations.

Comprehensive Coverage Rate of TV in Rural Area means the share of rural population who can receive TV programs in the target area, calculated in line with *Statistical Standard and Method on Television and Radio Coverage of*

Population established by the National Administration of Broadcasting, Film and Television, of the total rural population in the administrative area, including the population covered by TV programs from central, provincial, prefectural cities and county TV stations. Rural area means villages of towns with people's governments approved by the State and areas under the jurisdiction of rural towns with organizational system, excluding towns where people's governments of counties are located.

Comprehensive Coverage Rate of Wireless TV means the share of population who can receive TV programs transmitted with short-wave, medium-wave, FM and other radio transmission technologies in the target area, calculated in line with *Statistical Standard and Method on Television and Radio Coverage of Population* established by the National Administration of Broadcasting, Film and Television, of the total population in the administrative area, including the population covered by radio television programs from central, provincial, prefectural cities and county TV stations.

Access Rate of CATV refers to the percentage of households which can watch television programs by cable broadcasting and television transmission network (including cable TV households receiving analog signals and digital signals, excluding collective subscribers such as hotels, companies and entities, office buildings), to the total households in the administrative area).

Number of Digital Broadcast/TV Subscribers means the number of households watching digital-signal TV programs through the TV and radio cable transmission network.

Number of Pay TV Subscribers means the number of cable TV households watching digital-signal TV programs through the TV and radio cable transmission network and paying fees for watching.

19

科 技
SCIENCE AND TECHNOLOGY

简要说明

一、本章资料的主要内容

本章主要包括：研究与试验发展（R&D）人员情况，研究与试验发展（R&D）经费情况，研究与试验发展（R&D）项目（课题）情况，研究机构情况，规模以上工业企业R&D活动基本情况，限额以上信息传输、软件和信息技术服务业企业研究与试验发展(R&D)活动基本情况，规模以上高技术制造业主要科技指标，高等学校科技活动情况、研究与开发机构研发活动、专利申请及授权情况等。

二、本章资料的统计范围

国民经济中研究与试验发展（R&D）活动相对密集行业的法人单位，主要数据包括：农、林、牧、渔业，采矿业，制造业，电力、热力、燃气及水的生产和供应业，建筑业，交通运输、仓储和邮政业，信息传输、软件和信息技术服务业，金融业，租赁和商务服务业，科学研究和技术服务业，水利、环境和公共设施管理业，教育，卫生和社会工作，文化、体育和娱乐业，公共管理、社会保障和社会组织等。

三、本章资料的数据来源

本章由北京市统计局、北京市科学技术委员会、北京市教育委员会、北京市经济和信息化委员会、北京市人力资源和社会保障局、北京市知识产权局、北京市科学技术协会、北京技术市场管理办公室等部门提供。

四、有关统计标准的变化说明

（一）关于行业划分。根据国家统计局规定，自2012年开始执行《国民经济行业分类》(GB/T 4754-2011）标准。

（二）关于三次产业划分。根据国家统计局《三次产业划分规定》(国统字[2012]108号)，该规定对三次产业的范围进行了调整。其中第一产业是指农、林、牧、渔业（不含农、林、牧、渔服务业）；第二产业是指采矿业（不含开采辅助活动），制造业（不含金属制品、机械和设备修理业），电力、热力、燃气及水生产和供应业，建筑业；第三产业是指除第一产业、第二产业以外的其他行业。自2012年开始执行此规定。

（三）关于高技术制造业。根据国家统计局《关于印发高技术产业（制造业）分类（2013）的通知》(国统字〔2013〕55号)，本分类在《高技术产业统计分类目录》(国统字〔2002〕33号）的基础上修订完成，采用了原分类的基本结构框架。自2013年开始执行此标准。

Brief Introduction

I. Main Content

Data in this chapter reflect the situation of scientific and technological activities and patents, R&D personnel, R&D funds, R&D projects (tasks), research institutions, basic information on R&D of industrial enterprises above the designated size, basic information on R&D of information transmission, software and information technology service enterprises, scientific and technological activities of colleges and universities, R&D of research institutions and personnel, patent application and licensing, etc.

II. Scope of Statistics

Included in this chapter are the corporate entities in sectors with relatively intensive R&D activities in national economy, such as agriculture, forestry, animal production and hunting, fishing, mining, manufacturing, generation and distribution of electricity, heating, gas and water, construction, transport, storage and post, scientific research and development, technology services, information transmission, software and information technology services, finance, renting and leasing activities and business services, management of water conservancy, environment and public facilities, education, healthcare and social works, culture, sports and entertainment, public administration, social security and social organizations, etc.

III. Source of Data

Data in this chapter are from Beijing Municipal Bureau of Statistics, Beijing Municipal Science & Technology Commission, Beijing Municipal Commission of Education, Beijing Municipal Commission of Economy and Information Technology, Beijing Municipal Bureau of Human Resources and Social Security, Beijing Intellectual Property Bureau, Beijing Municipal Association of Science and Technology, and Beijing Technical Market Management Office, etc.

IV. Changes in Relevant Statistical Standards

(I) Classification of Sectors. According to relevant provisions of National Bureau of Statistics, the Standard for *Classification of National Economic Sectors* (GB/T4754-2011) became effective in 2012.

(II) Classification of Primary, Secondary, and Tertiary Industries. According to the *Provision of Classification of Three Industries* (G.T.Z. [2012] No. 108) issued by National Bureau of Statistics, the scope of three industries has changed. The primary industry includes agriculture, forestry, animal production and hunting, fishing (excluding agricultural, forestry, animal production and hunting, fishing services); the secondary industry includes mining (excluding mining support activities), manufacturing (excluding metal products, machinery and equipment repairing), production and distribution of electricity, heating, natural gas and water and construction industry; the tertiary industry means industries other than the primary and secondary industries. The *Provisions of Classification of Three Industries* (G.T.Z. [2012] No. 108) came into effect in 2012.

(III) High-tech Manufacturing. According to the *Circular of National Bureau of Statistics on Printing and Issuing the Classification of High-tech Industry (Manufacturing) 2013* (G.T.Z. [2013] No. 55). This Classification is revised on the basis of *Classified Catalog of High-tech Industry Statistics* (G.T.Z. [2002] No. 33), following the structure of the original classification. The standard has been put in place since 2013.

19-1 科技活动及专利情况(1985-2015年)
SCIENCE AND TECHNOLOGY ACTIVITIES AND PATENTS (1985-2015)

年 份 Year	科技活动人员(人) Personnel Engaged in Science and Technology Activities (person)	研究与试验发展(R&D)人员折合全时当量(人年) Full-time Equivalent of R&D Professionals (person-year)	研究与试验发展(R&D)经费内部支出(万元) Internal R&D Expenditures (10000 yuan)	研究与试验发展(R&D)经费内部支出相当于地区生产总值比例(%) Internal R&D Expenditures as Percentage of GDP (%)
1985				
1986-1990				
1986				
1987				
1988				
1989				
1990				
1991-1995				
1991	228167			
1992	247525			
1993	252811			
1994	240386			
1995	252232			
1996-2000			**4307457**	
1996	265552	84793	418614	2.34
1997	273161	84913	532257	2.56
1998	237127	86602	861138	3.62
1999	229584	85740	938437	3.50
2000	261113	98723	1557011	4.92
2001-2005			**13434129**	
2001	240609	95255	1711696	4.62
2002	257326	114919	2195402	5.09
2003	270921	110358	2562518	5.12
2004	301202	152132	3169064	5.25
2005	383153	177765	3795450	5.45
2006-2010			**30706037**	
2006	382756	168875	4329878	5.33
2007	450331	204668	5270591	5.35
2008	450147	200080	6200983	5.58
2009	529985	191779	6686351	5.50
2010	529811	193718	8218234	5.82
2011-2015			**58378733**	
2011	605980	217255	9366440	5.76
2012	651003	235493	10633640	5.95
2013	681346	242175	11850469	5.98
2014	726792	245384	12687953	5.95
2015	747461	245728	13840231	6.01

资料来源：北京市统计局、北京市科学技术委员会、北京市教育委员会、北京市经济和信息化委员会、北京市知识产权局。
Source: Beijing Municipal Bureau of Statistics, Beijing Municipal Science & Technology Commission, Beijing Municipal Commission of Education, Beijing Municipal Commission of Economy and Information Technology, Beijing Intellectual Property Office.

19-1 续表 Continued

年份 Year	专利申请量（件） Patent Applications (unit)	发明 Inventions	实用新型 Utility Models	外观设计 Industrial Designs	专利授权量（件） Patents Granted (unit)	发明 Inventions	实用新型 Utility Models	外观设计 Industrial Designs
1985	1540	754	720	66				
1986-1990	**15087**	**3332**	**11003**	**752**	**6700**	**737**	**5614**	**349**
1986	1692	535	1091	66	491	43	408	40
1987	2425	523	1796	106	776	102	630	44
1988	3342	702	2494	146	1376	169	1147	60
1989	3344	742	2408	194	1789	207	1497	85
1990	4284	830	3214	240	2268	216	1932	120
1991-1995	**31126**	**6604**	**21787**	**2736**	**19379**	**1801**	**15835**	**1743**
1991	4624	1023	3324	277	2369	263	1917	189
1992	6316	1340	4493	483	3265	312	2724	229
1993	6972	1483	4931	558	5806	530	4780	496
1994	6852	1506	4666	680	3914	368	3245	301
1995	6362	1252	4372	738	4025	328	3169	528
1996-2000	**37296**	**10344**	**20395**	**6557**	**22156**	**2483**	**14836**	**4837**
1996	6595	1441	4255	899	3295	246	2563	486
1997	6313	1678	3667	968	3327	281	2340	706
1998	6321	1754	3444	1123	3800	309	2522	969
1999	7723	2062	4045	1616	5829	573	3948	1308
2000	10344	3409	4984	1951	5905	1074	3463	1368
2001-2005	**83993**	**39312**	**30960**	**13721**	**39944**	**10960**	**20019**	**8965**
2001	12174	4984	5114	2076	6246	946	3600	1700
2002	13842	5785	5920	2137	6345	1061	3721	1563
2003	17003	7833	6665	2505	8248	2261	4244	1743
2004	18402	8608	6321	3473	9005	3216	3956	1833
2005	22572	12102	6940	3530	10100	3476	4498	2126
2006-2010	**209275**	**124175**	**62237**	**22863**	**100371**	**35532**	**48350**	**16489**
2006	26555	14226	8200	4129	11238	3864	5490	1884
2007	31680	18763	8819	4098	14954	4824	7364	2766
2008	43508	28394	11157	3957	17747	6478	8776	2493
2009	50236	29326	15424	5486	22921	9157	10141	3623
2010	57296	33466	18637	5193	33511	11209	16579	5723
2011-2015	**588019**	**332390**	**208281**	**47348**	**322762**	**115260**	**170445**	**37057**
2011	77955	45057	26615	6283	40888	15880	19628	5380
2012	92305	52720	32609	6976	50511	20140	24672	5699
2013	123336	67554	47586	8196	62671	20695	36301	5675
2014	138111	78129	48228	11754	74661	23237	44071	7353
2015	156312	88930	53243	14139	94031	35308	45773	12950

19-2 研究与试验发展(R&D)活动人员情况

项目	Item	研究与试验发展(R&D)人员(人) R&D Personnel (person) 2015	2014	#本科及以上学历 Bachelor Degree or above 2015	2014
合计	**Total**	**350721**	**343165**	**246741**	**231650**
按执行部门分	**By Executive Department**				
企业	Enterprises	146896	145430	66173	58903
工业企业	Industrial Enterprises	72802	79915	28613	29171
非工业企业	Non-industrial Enterprises	74094	65515	37560	29732
科研机构	Scientific Research Institutions	111272	109363	99291	95511
高等学校	Institutions of Higher Education	80744	77255	75311	71892
事业单位	Public Institutions	11809	11117	5966	5344
按隶属关系分	**By Affiliation**				
中央	Central	208503	204527	172781	164052
地方	Local	142218	138638	73960	67598
按行业门类分	**By Sector**				
#制造业	Manufacturing	69756	76427	27412	28133
信息传输、软件和信息技术服务业	Information Transmission, Software and Information Technology Services	34590	31872	10994	9425
科学研究和技术服务业	Scientific Research and Development, Technical Services	142575	133074	127945	116972
教育	Education	80744	77255	75311	71892

注：行业划分执行2011年国民经济行业分类标准(GB/T 4754-2011)。

资料来源：北京市统计局、北京市科学技术委员会、北京市教育委员会、北京市经济和信息化委员会。

RESEARCH AND EXPERIMENTAL DEVELOPMENT PERSONNEL

研究与试验发展(R&D)人员折合全时当量(人年) Full-time Equivalent of R&D Professionals (person-year)		基础研究 Basic Research		应用研究 Applied Research		试验发展 Experimental Development	
2015	2014	2015	2014	2015	2014	2015	2014
245728	**245384**	**41324**	**39042**	**61644**	**59082**	**142763**	**147263**
106625	108612	535	403	4614	3029	101478	105182
50773	57761	17	27	878	578	49879	57156
55852	50851	519	376	3737	2451	51599	48026
97988	97130	26121	24731	34857	34277	37010	38122
34460	33557	13690	13058	19989	19651	781	847
6655	6086	977	850	2184	2125	3495	3112
151047	149620	36405	34336	50183	48495	64460	66790
94681	95764	4919	4706	11461	10588	78303	80473
48385	55090	6	25	865	559	47514	54506
26322	25264	25		1231	943	25066	24322
122751	117007	27055	25391	37802	36428	57894	55188
34460	33557	13690	13058	19989	19651	781	847

Note: Sectors in this table are classified in accordance with the Standard for Classification of National Economic Sectors 2011 (GB/T 4754-2011).

Source: Beijing Municipal Bureau of Statistics, Beijing Municipal Science & Technology Commission, Beijing Municipal Commission of Education, Beijing Municipal Commission of Economy and Information Technology.

19-3 研究与试验发展(R&D)经费情况

单位：万元

项目	Item	研究与试验发展(R&D)经费内部支出 Internal R&D Expenditures 2015	2014	按活动类型分 Group by Type of Activity: 基础研究 Basic Research 2015	2014	应用研究 Applied Research 2015	2014
合计	**Total**	**13840231**	**12687953**	**1909930**	**1594874**	**3182637**	**2749447**
按执行部门分	**By Executive Department**						
企业	Enterprises	4964801	4634972	26790	32777	249601	193078
工业企业	Industrial Enterprises	2440875	2335010	1170	243	30272	27751
非工业企业	Non-industrial Enterprises	2523927	2299962	25620	32534	219329	165327
科研机构	Scientific Research Institutions	7027642	6409252	1232527	992537	1940278	1669940
高等学校	Institutions of Higher Education	1626476	1456552	622028	546908	932921	836295
事业单位	Public Institutions	221312	187177	28585	22651	59837	50134
按隶属关系分	**By Affiliation**						
中央	Central	9888233	9128156	1806243	1489670	2835007	2454637
地方	Local	3951998	3559797	103687	105204	347630	294810
按行业门类分	**By Sector**						
#制造业	Manufacturing	2365034	2247003	76	175	29065	27151
信息传输、软件和信息技术服务业	Information Transmission, Software and Information Technology Services	1181114	1121101	545		90853	67197
科学研究和技术服务业	Scientific Research and Development, Technical Services	8260041	7432375	1279558	1040824	2092820	1795065
教育	Education	1626476	1456552	622028	546908	932921	836295

注：行业划分执行2011年国民经济行业分类标准(GB/T 4754-2011)。
资料来源：北京市统计局、北京市科学技术委员会、北京市教育委员会、北京市经济和信息化委员会。

RESEARCH AND EXPERIMENTAL DEVELOPMENT FUNDS

(10000 yuan)

		按支出用途分 Group by Purpose of Payment							
试验发展 Experimental Development		日常性支出 Routine Expenses		#人员劳务费 Labor Cost		资产性支出 Expenditures for Assets		#仪器和设备 Instruments and Equipment	
2015	2014	2015	2014	2015	2014	2015	2014	2015	2014
8747665	**8343632**	**11677460**	**10738643**	**3889660**	**3535287**	**2162771**	**1949310**	**1639922**	**1356112**
4688410	4409116	4514413	4309758	2320791	2173860	450389	325213	420826	303662
2409432	2307016	2212021	2237692	969877	930509	228853	97319	226534	93892
2278978	2102100	2302392	2072067	1350914	1243351	221535	227895	194292	209770
3854837	3746776	5597785	5037747	1277295	1106064	1429857	1371506	972218	829442
71528	73349	1380680	1243993	216615	197902	245796	212560	221517	183833
132890	114391	184583	147146	74959	57461	36729	40031	25360	39175
5246984	5183850	8109519	7441103	1983695	1769122	1778715	1687054	1279604	1120926
3500681	3159782	3567941	3297541	1905965	1766165	384056	262256	360318	235186
2335892	2219677	2139398	2152902	940664	895355	225636	94101	223427	90875
1089716	1053904	1129526	1041285	827693	791157	51589	79816	50086	79548
4887663	4596486	6668450	5918857	1739215	1479613	1591591	1513518	1098061	954003
71528	73349	1380680	1243993	216615	197902	245796	212560	221517	183833

Note: Sectors in this table are classified in accordance with the Standard for Classification of National Economic Sectors 2011 (GB/T 4754-2011).

Source: Beijing Municipal Bureau of Statistics, Beijing Municipal Science & Technology Commission, Beijing Municipal Commission of Education, Beijing Municipal Commission of Economy and Information Technology.

19-3 续表 Continued

单位：万元 (10000 yuan)

项目	Item	按资金来源分 Group by Fund Source							
		政府资金 Governmental Funds		企业资金 Enterprise Funds		国外资金 Foreign Funds		其他资金 Others	
		2015	2014	2015	2014	2015	2014	2015	2014
合计	**Total**	**7916391**	**7000675**	**4722359**	**4346862**	**403247**	**405612**	**798234**	**934803**
按执行部门分	**By Executive Department**								
企业	Enterprises	412517	391766	4117110	3789590	356319	358482	78855	95134
工业企业	Industrial Enterprises	244291	222348	2097799	2022384	41929	18128	56856	72150
非工业企业	Non-industrial Enterprises	168227	169418	2019312	1767206	314390	340355	21999	22984
科研机构	Scientific Research Institutions	6196676	5471283	150103	124089	20088	18421	660775	795459
高等学校	Institutions of Higher Education	1132410	974566	448191	427589	25868	27232	20007	27165
事业单位	Public Institutions	174788	163060	6955	5594	972	1477	38597	17046
按隶属关系分	**By Affiliation**								
中央	Central	7330742	6550678	1766315	1651777	49041	49496	742136	876205
地方	Local	585649	449997	2956044	2695085	354207	356116	56098	58599
按行业门类分	**By Sector**								
#制造业	Manufacturing	237717	215678	2028532	1945073	41929	18128	56856	68124
信息传输、软件和信息技术服务业	Information Transmission, Software and Information Technology Services	27242	19577	914137	843023	232148	247891	7588	10609
科学研究和技术服务业	Scientific Research and Development, Technical Services	6484699	5754802	961873	746623	101687	108369	711781	822581
教育	Education	1132410	974566	448191	427589	25868	27232	20007	27165

19-4　单位内部办研发机构情况
STATISTICS FOR IN-HOUSE RESEARCH AND DEVELOPMENT INSTITUTIONS

项　目	Item	机构数 (个) Number of Institutions (unit)		机构研究与试验发展(R&D)人员 (人) R&D Personnel (Person)		机构研究与试验发展(R&D)经费支出 (万元) R&D Expenditures (10000 yuan)	
		2015	2014	2015	2014	2015	2014
合　计	**Total**	**2658**	**2601**	**191232**	**181967**	**10317729**	**8991229**
按机构所属学科分	**By Subject of Institution**						
自然科学	Natural Science	156	152	29114	27779	1299660	1226659
农业科学	Agricultural Science	93	79	6361	5910	274982	237400
医药科学	Medical Science	128	106	12911	10270	427325	316804
工程与技术科学	Engineering and Techical Science	1942	1897	131710	126696	8105250	7014381
人文与社会科学	Humanities and Social Science	339	367	11136	11312	210512	195985
按机构组成类型分	**By Institution Composition**						
政府部门办	Run by Government Agency	528	558	116031	121240	7106379	6922877
与国内高校合办	Jointly Run with Domestic Colleges and Universities	43	31	804	586	41670	40411
与国内独立研究机构合办	Jointly Run with Domestic Independent Research Institutions	9	10	144	188	824	741
与境外机构合办	Jointly Run with Overseas Institutions	5	9	65	107	531	979
与境内注册外商独资企业合办	Jointly Run with Solely Foreign-invseted Enterprises Registered in China						
与境内注册其他企业合办	Jointly Run with Other Enterprises Registered in China	68	62	1314	1304	45113	50323
单位自办	Self Run	2001	1928	72784	58451	3122802	1975627
其　他	Others	4	3	90	91	411	271

资料来源：北京市统计局、北京市科学技术委员会、北京市教育委员会、北京市经济和信息化委员会。
Source: Beijing Municipal Bureau of Statistics, Beijing Municipal Science & Technology Commission, Beijing Municipal Commission of Education, Beijing Municipal Commission of Economy and Information Technology.

19-5 研究与试验发展(R&D)项目(课题)情况
RESEARCH AND EXPERIMENTAL DEVELOPMENT PROJECTS (TASKS)

项目	Item	项目(课题)数 (项) Number of Projects (Tasks) (unit)		项目(课题)人员折合全时当量 (人年) Full-time Equivalent of Project (Task) Personnel (person-year)		项目(课题)经费内部支出 (万元) Internal Project (Task) Expenditures (10000 yuan)	
		2015	2014	2015	2014	2015	2014
合　计	**Total**	**136969**	**128179**	**223637**	**231280**	**10497955**	**9647685**
按项目(课题)来源分	**By Source**						
国家科技项目	National Science and Technology Projects	57827	54619	97296	95925	5272977	4782961
地方科技项目	Local Science and Technology Projects	13978	12524	11491	10972	223341	209303
企业委托科技项目	Science and Technology Projects Entrusted by Enterprises	32496	29679	20877	21866	872256	812070
自选科技项目	Self-chosen Science and Technology Projects	26534	25476	71166	79581	2872489	2706193
来自国外的科技项目	Science and Technology Projects from Foreign Countries	2127	2037	9925	8632	492927	470541
其它科技项目	Other Science and Technology Projects	4006	3843	12881	14304	763965	666617
按项目(课题)合作形式分	**By Form of Cooperation**						
与境外机构合作	Cooperating with Overseas Institutions	1745	1706	6324	5774	297178	326880
与国内高校合作	Cooperating with Domestic Colleges and Universities	7253	6894	10387	11806	431168	431616
与国内独立研究机构合作	Cooperating with Domestic Independent Research Institutions	8853	8443	18319	18681	1045808	788032
与境内注册外商独资企业合作	Cooperating with solely Foreign-invested Enterprises Registered in China	207	239	160	386	7669	15779
与境内注册其他企业合作	Cooperating with Other Enterprises Registered in China	7371	6262	11164	10732	597067	538965
独立完成	Independent	108368	101611	170151	176254	7831323	7237575
其　他	Others	3171	3023	7133	7647	287743	308838
按项目(课题)活动类型分	**By Type of Project (Task) Activity**						
基础研究	Basic Research	47864	43529	39086	36326	1322954	1084606
应用研究	Applied Research	68234	61997	58459	56256	2295658	2018892
试验发展	Experimental Development	20871	22653	126092	138698	6879344	6544187
按项目(课题)社会经济目标分	**By Social and Economic Objective**						
#环境保护及污染防治	Environmental Protection and Pollution Prevention and Control	6983	6404	7137	7724	263796	263147
促进能源的生产、分配和合理利用	Promotion of Production, Allocation and Reasonable Utilization of Energy	10686	8636	13600	15560	613675	649328
促进卫生事业的发展	Promotion of Public Health	9992	9161	17279	16763	298404	262895
促进教育事业的发展	Promotion of Education	11488	10910	3008	3074	57053	58540
基础设施以及城市和农村规划	Infrastructure,Urban and Rural Planning	7053	6916	9344	10040	299837	337616

资料来源：北京市统计局、北京市科学技术委员会、北京市教育委员会、北京市经济和信息化委员会。

Source: Beijing Municipal Bureau of Statistics, Beijing Municipal Science & Technology Commission, Beijing Municipal Commission of Education, Beijing Municipal Commission of Economy and Information Technology.

19-5 续表 Continued

项目	Item	项目(课题)数(项) Number of Projects (Tasks) (unit) 2015	2014	项目(课题)人员折合全时当量(人年) Full-time Equivalent of Project (Task) Personnel (person-year) 2015	2014	项目(课题)经费内部支出(万元) Internal Project (Task) Expenditures (10000 yuan) 2015	2014
社会发展和社会服务	Social Development and Social Service	16078	14535	10656	9057	274831	215249
地球和大气层的探索和利用	Exploration and Exploitation of Earth and Aerosphere	3325	3427	4812	5369	167354	158387
民用空间的探测及开发	Exploration and Exploitation of Civil Space	1018	861	3293	1229	239263	100983
促进农林牧渔业发展	Promotion of Agriculture, Forestry, Animal Production and Hunting, Fishing	8190	6329	7151	7009	240186	211719
促进工商业发展	Promotion of Industry and Commerce	22877	23518	82554	86119	3555276	3257025
非定向研究	Non-oriented Research	30365	28097	24204	23029	864724	772025
按项目(课题)服务的国民经济行业分	**By Sector of National Economy Served**						
农、林、牧、渔业	Agriculture, Forestry, Animal Production and Hunting, Fishing	8799	6735	6491	6082	224657	195991
采矿业	Mining and Quarrying	3187	3322	4727	6361	231829	284711
制造业	Manufacturing	25352	23772	73081	61970	3740985	2425426
电力、热力、燃气及水生产和供应业	Production and Distribution of Electricity, Heating Power, Gas, Water	2577	2325	3083	2660	124741	112133
建筑业	Construction	2972	3015	6547	6569	195989	208059
批发和零售业	Wholesale and Retail Trade	185	183	53	68	3894	2822
交通运输、仓储和邮政业	Transport, Storage and Post	2491	3089	2565	2849	77773	68978
住宿和餐饮业	Accommodation and Restaurants	279	99	117	32	6298	1289
信息传输、软件和信息技术服务业	Information Transmission,Software and Information Technology Services	5309	5047	26159	26670	1143231	1115301
金融业	Finance	1201	1087	300	299	4844	4423
房地产业	Real Estate	133	134	35	37	532	1077
租赁和商务服务业	Renting and Leasing Activities and Business Services	2746	2242	1960	1984	75368	83924
科学研究和技术服务业	Scientific Research and Development, Technical Services	46885	44579	72035	88560	4123470	4612744
水利、环境和公共设施管理业	Management of Water Conservancy, Environment and Public Falicities	3566	3909	4283	5693	155874	194051
居民服务、修理和其他服务业	Resident Services, Repair and Other Services	1065	2217	339	504	15809	13604
教　育	Education	10664	8035	2965	2877	71080	65701
卫生和社会工作	Healthcare and Social Works	8360	6506	13139	12218	204276	171674
文化、体育和娱乐业	Culture, Sports and Entertainment	5314	4875	3521	3739	35203	35384
公共管理、社会保障和社会组织	Public Management, Social Security and Social Organizations	5744	4198	2196	2078	61385	49887
国际组织	International Organizations	140	106	42	33	719	506

注：行业划分执行2011年国民经济行业分类标准(GB/T 4754-2011)。
Note: Sectors in this table are classified in accordance with the Standard for Classification of National Economic Sectors 2011 (GB/T 4754-2011).

19-6 规模以上工业企业研究与试验发展(R&D)活动基本情况(2015年)

项目	Item	企业数(个) Number of Enterprises (unit)	#有研究与试验发展(R&D)活动的企业数 Enterprises with R&D Activities	研究与试验发展(R&D)人员(人) R&D Personnel (person)	研究与试验发展(R&D)人员折合全时当量(人年) Full-time Equivalent of R&D Personnel (person-year)	研究与试验发展(R&D)经费内部支出(万元) Internal R&D Expenditures (10000 yuan)
合计	**Total**	**3548**	**1141**	**72802**	**50773**	**2440875**
按企业规模分	**By Size of Enterprise**					
#大中型企业	Medium and Large-sized	714	366	53860	37494	1981446
按隶属关系分	**By Affiliation**					
中央	Central	239	137	13850	10714	476507
地方	Local	3309	1004	58952	40059	1964367
按登记注册类型分	**By Registration Type**					
内资企业	Domestically-invested Enterprises	2745	931	55515	37890	1477549
#国有企业	State-owned Enterprises	72	22	3231	2385	96951
港澳台商投资企业	Hong Kong, Macao and Taiwan-invested Enterprises	195	62	5386	4073	283109
外商投资企业	Foreign-invested Enterprises	608	148	11901	8810	680217
按重点产业分	**By Key Sector**					
#高技术制造业	High-tech Manufacturing	804	450	29698	22344	1202250
#现代制造业	Modern Manufacturing	1452	646	45508	32171	1840198

BASIC INFORMATION ON RESEARCH AND EXPERIMENTAL DEVELOPMENT ACTIVITIES OF INDUSTRIAL ENTERPRISES ABOVE DESIGNATED SIZE (2015)

政府资金 Governmental Funds	企业资金 Enterprise Funds	国外资金 Foreign Funds	其他资金 Others	专利申请数(件) Patent Applications (unit)	#发明专利 Inventions	新产品产值(万元) Output Value of New Products (10000 yuan)	新产品销售收入(万元) Sales Income of New Products (10000 yuan)	#出口 Exports
244291	**2097799**	**41929**	**56856**	**20024**	**10281**	**36478135**	**35640401**	**2438988**
215846	1673292	39667	52641	14921	8228	30022696	29242511	2021292
63179	367654	830	44845	4011	2181	4640560	4718528	85512
181112	1730145	41100	12011	16013	8100	31837575	30921873	2353476
137545	1285028	980	53997	14211	6936	19552067	19122728	739187
10570	85008		1373	826	457	1364452	1310330	2479
3564	246085	33011	450	3872	2877	10029870	9600994	874529
103182	566686	7939	2410	1941	468	6896199	6916679	825271
205027	910599	33522	53102	7837	5305	16636861	15978092	1400824
186818	1557020	41895	54465	13679	7547	28157124	27166608	1721560

19-7 规模以上工业企业研究与试验发展(R&D)活动基本情况(按行业分)(2015年)

项目	Item	企业数(个) Number of Enterprises (unit)	#有研究与试验发展(R&D)活动的企业数 Enterprises with R&D Activities	研究与试验发展(R&D)人员(人) R&D Personnel (person)
合计	**Total**	**3548**	**1141**	**72802**
采矿业	**Mining and Quarrying**	**19**	**9**	**1761**
煤炭开采和洗选业	Mining and Washing of Coal	1	1	614
石油和天然气开采业	Extraction of Petroleum and Natural Gas	2	2	178
黑色金属矿采选业	Mining and Processing of Ferrous Metal Ores	7	1	439
有色金属矿采选业	Mining and Processing of Non-Ferrous Metal Ores			
非金属矿采选业	Mining and Processing of Nonmetal Ores	3		
开采辅助活动	Mining Support Service Activities	6	5	530
其他采矿业	Mining of Other Ores			
制造业	**Manufacturing**	**3417**	**1118**	**69756**
农副食品加工业	Processing of Food from Agriculture Products	138	25	697
食品制造业	Manufacture of Foods	130	19	995
酒、饮料和精制茶制造业	Manufacture of Wine, Beverage and Refined Tea	43	3	851
烟草制品业	Manufacture of Cigarettes and Tobacco	1	1	37
纺织业	Manufacture of Textile	23	7	82
纺织服装、服饰业	Manufacture of Textile Wearing Apparel and Ornament	127	6	278
皮革、毛皮、羽毛及其制品和制鞋业	Manufacture of Leather, Fur, Feather and Its Products, and Footwear	12		
木材加工和木、竹、藤、棕、草制品业	Processing of Timbers, Manufacture of Wood, Bamboo, Rattan, Palm, and Straw Products	16	1	11
家具制造业	Manufacture of Furniture	65	3	481
造纸和纸制品业	Manufacture of Paper and Paper Products	40	2	99
印刷和记录媒介复制业	Printing, Reproduction of Recording Media	113	13	631
文教、工美、体育和娱乐用品制造业	Manufacture of Articles for Culture,Education, Artwork, Sport and Entertainment Activities	34	6	160
石油加工、炼焦和核燃料加工业	Processing of Petroleum, Coking, Processing of Nuclear Fuel	20	2	46
化学原料和化学制品制造业	Manufacture of Raw Chemical Materials and Chemical Products	203	80	2196
医药制造业	Manufacture of Medicines	200	111	6024
化学纤维制造业	Manufacture of Chemical Fibers	2	2	12
橡胶和塑料制品业	Manufacture of Rubber and Plastics Products	112	16	547
非金属矿物制品业	Manufacture of Non-Metallic Mineral Products	237	53	2774
黑色金属冶炼和压延加工业	Smelting and Pressing of Ferrous Metals	23	5	212
有色金属冶炼和压延加工业	Smelting and Pressing of Non-Ferrous Metals	36	15	902
金属制品业	Manufacture of Fabricated Metal Products	203	32	1545
通用设备制造业	Manufacture of General-Purpose Machinery	238	106	6121
专用设备制造业	Manufacture of Special-Purpose Machinery	319	148	6678
汽车制造业	Manufacture of Motor Vehicles	232	44	8703
铁路、船舶、航空航天和其他运输设备制造业	Manufacture of Railway Locomotives, Building of Ships and Boats, Manufacture of Air and Spacecrafts and Other Transportation Equipment	74	41	4937
电气机械和器材制造业	Manufacture of Electrical Machinery and Equipment	261	102	5622
计算机、通信和其他电子设备制造业	Manufacture of Computers, Communication Equipment and Other Electronic Equipment	293	158	13378
仪器仪表制造业	Manufacture of Measuring Instruments and Meters	163	98	3879
其他制造业	Other Manufacturing	34	12	1284
废弃资源综合利用业	Recycling and Disposal of Waste	10	2	25
金属制品、机械和设备修理业	Repair of Fabricated Metal Products, Machinery and Equipment	15	5	549
电力、热力、燃气及水的生产和供应业	**Production and Distribution of Electricity, Heating Power, Gas and Water**	**112**	**14**	**1285**
电力、热力生产和供应业	Production and Distribution of Electricity and Heating Power	68	8	464
燃气生产和供应业	Production and Distribution of Gas	21	1	537
水的生产和供应业	Production and Distribution of Water	23	5	284

注：行业划分执行2011年国民经济行业分类标准(GB/T 4754-2011)。
Note: Sectors in this table are classified in accordance with the Standard for Classification of National Economic Sectors 2011 (GB/T 4754-2011).

BASIC INFORMATION ON RESEARCH AND EXPERIMENTAL DEVELOPMENT ACTIVITIES OF INDUSTRIAL ENTERPRISES ABOVE ESIGNATED SIZE (BY SECTOR) (2015)

研究与试验发展(R&D)人员折合全时当量(人年) Full-time Equivalent of R&D Personnel (person-year)	研究与试验发展(R&D)经费内部支出(万元) Internal R&D Expenditures (10000 yuan)	政府资金 Governmental Funds	企业资金 Enterprise Funds	国外资金 Foreign Funds	其他资金 Others	专利申请数(件) Applications Patents (unit)	#发明专利 Inventions	新产品产值(万元) Output Value of New Products (10000 yuan)	新产品销售收入(万元) Sales Income of New Products (10000 yuan)	#出口 Exports
50772	**2440875**	**244291**	**2097799**	**41929**	**56856**	**20024**	**10281**	**36478135**	**35640401**	**2438988**
1394	**56064**	**5028**	**51036**			**393**	**204**	**9804**	**9804**	
353	7054		7054			36	2			
144	5349	3776	1573			19	10			
439	11600	348	11252			176	129			
458	32060	904	31156			162	63	9804	9804	
48385	**2365034**	**237717**	**2028532**	**41929**	**56856**	**18204**	**9449**	**36456153**	**35620680**	**2438988**
541	20957	876	19825		255	193	137	258145	255631	5365
717	25839	1001	24752		87	116	57	191895	198232	2860
635	16012		16012			16	10	251559	293222	3667
37	1653		1653					506	496	
36	1093	259	834			49	29	20138	26839	2498
117	7800	253	7547			42	9	190141	196432	164
						8				
1	70		70			1		381	381	
250	4298		4298			277	62	116763	106769	
68	1250		1250			31	22	62305	62825	15327
290	7366	98	6818		449	51	13	187319	193399	1197
66	2852		2852			39	6	24274	28318	220
11	340	96	244			9	7	148255	276111	
1696	40846	507	40339			354	319	678021	645209	69853
4220	183821	11434	169574	9	2804	414	288	1704698	1535064	16685
12	176		176			1	1	3204	3684	
328	9916	18	9898			71	11	127883	134985	2598
1682	64326	3948	60378			961	284	1528344	1598580	30170
78	2986	423	2562			39	15	76167	76416	1766
623	21955	3171	18708		76	165	113	323549	330910	75324
1082	27468	887	26420	9	153	440	161	594824	588516	85353
4299	135695	6696	128533	39	426	741	292	2152447	2209892	606306
4731	194710	9423	184670	25	592	2382	1267	2357114	2177466	368867
4513	411978	5829	405971		177	3233	957	6007396	5991493	25312
4271	198756	26816	126314	443	45183	792	423	1517237	1469764	4795
4209	182555	1458	172671	8333	92	1464	598	3863811	3785858	114768
9967	677271	150828	491745	31357	3342	5489	3976	12459283	11846590	953000
2802	93978	10633	78705	1713	2927	658	300	1289855	1310545	52628
945	21754	3042	18419		293	129	70	301120	256796	
5	664		664			9	8	14241	15987	265
153	6652	22	6630			30	14	5276	4272	
993	**19777**	**1546**	**18231**			**1427**	**628**	**12178**	**9917**	
374	8803	1316	7487			1351	594			
375	6486	139	6346			43	24			
244	4489	92	4397			33	10	12178	9917	

19-8 规模以上高技术制造业主要科技指标

项　目	Item	R&D人员折合全时当量（人年）Full-time Equivalent of R&D Personnel (person-year)	
		2015	2014
高技术制造业	**High-tech Manufacturing**	**22344**	**23741**
医药制造业	Manufacture of Medicines	4220	5459
#化学药品制造	Manufacture of Chemical Medicine	1850	2290
生物药品制造	Manufacture of Biological Medicine and Biochemical Chemical Products	1625	1475
航空、航天器及设备制造业	Manufacture of Aircrafts and Spacecrafts	3258	3291
#航空航天器修理	Repair of Air and Spacecrafts	146	367
电子及通信设备制造业	Manufacture of Electronic Equipment and Communication Equipment	8591	8303
#通信设备制造	Manufacture of Communication Equipment	4382	2951
电子器件制造	Manufacture of Electronic Appliances	1480	2604
电子元件制造	Manufacture of Electronic Components	478	797
其他电子设备制造	Manufacture of Other Electronic Equipment	1408	1131
计算机及办公设备制造业	Manufacture of Computers and Office Equipments	1687	1880
#计算机整机制造	Manufacture of Entired Computer	1048	1328
医疗仪器设备及仪器仪表制造业	Manufacture of Medical Equipments and Meters	4383	4809
医疗仪器设备及器械制造	Manufacture of Medical Equipment and Appliances	1581	1449
仪器仪表制造	Manufacture of Measuring Instrument and Meter	2802	3360

注：本表高技术行业中不包括信息化学品制造业。
Note: Photographic equipment manufacturing is not included in the high-tech sector stated in this table.

MAJOR SCIENCE AND TECHNOLOGY INDICATORS OF HIGH-TECH MANUFACTURING ABOVE DESIGNATER SIZE

R&D经费支出 (亿元) R&D Expenditures (100 million yuan)		新产品销售收入 (亿元) Sales Income of New Products (100 million yuan)		专利申请数 (件) Patent Applications (unit)		#发明专利 Inventions	
2015	2014	2015	2014	2015	2014	2015	2014
120.2	**110.8**	**1597.8**	**1865.1**	**7837**	**8906**	**5305**	**5845**
18.4	17.1	153.5	164.4	414	479	288	364
8.4	8.3	50.1	51.8	146	211	116	170
7.9	5.3	49.7	47.9	162	118	113	90
15.0	23.8	37.9	33.5	368	385	251	236
0.6	1.1			9	10	7	1
50.9	40.2	925.9	1210.9	2549	3463	1711	2114
17.0	13.6	612.5	906.1	978	688	824	553
21.8	18.6	171.2	190.4	825	1813	415	897
1.9	1.7	25.4	25.2	81	96	42	28
7.1	4.0	59.3	46.9	473	601	311	500
18.3	15.2	303.0	327.4	3038	3456	2336	2642
15.9	13.2	222.3	248.7	2741	3065	2206	2482
17.4	14.5	171.3	128.9	1388	1123	642	489
8.0	5.7	40.3	17.8	730	499	342	253
9.4	8.8	131.1	111.1	658	624	300	236

19-9 限额以上信息传输、软件和信息技术服务业企业研究与试验发展(R&D)活动基本情况(2015年)

项目	Item	企业数(个) Number of Enterprises (unit)	#有研究与试验发展(R&D)活动的企业数 Enterprises with R&D Activities	研究与试验发展(R&D)人员(人) R&D Personnel (person)	研究与试验发展(R&D)人员折合全时当量(人年) Full-time Equivalent of R&D Personnel (person-year)
合计	**Total**	**2787**	**332**	**34590**	**26322**
按隶属关系分	**By Affiliation**				
中央	Central	144	34	2630	1835
地方	Local	2643	298	31960	24487
按登记注册类型分	**By Registration Type**				
内资企业	Domestically-invested Enterprises	2267	293	20006	13411
#国有企业	State-owned Enterprises	22	5	527	356
港澳台商投资企业	Hong Kong, Macao and Taiwan-invested Enterprises	196	13	3576	2836
外商投资企业	Foreign-invested Enterprises	324	26	11008	10075
按行业分	**By Sector**				
电信、广播电视和卫星传输服务	Telecommunications, Broadcasting, Television and Satellite Transmission services	200	25	5969	5746
互联网和相关服务	Internet and Related Services	278	21	5744	5052
软件和信息技术服务业	Software and Information Technology Services	2309	286	22877	15524

注：行业划分执行2011年国民经济行业分类标准(GB/T 4754-2011)。
Note: Sectors in this table are classified in accordance with the Standard for Classification of National Economic Sectors 2011 (GB/T 4754-2011).

BASIC INFORMATION ON R&D ACTIVITIES OF INFORMATION TRANSMISSIOM, SOFTWARE AND INFORMATION TECHNICIAL SERVICE ENTERPRISES ABOVE DESIGNATED SIZE (2015)

研究与试验发展(R&D)经费内部支出(万元) Internal R&D Expenditures (10000 yuan)	政府资金 Govern-mental Funds	企业资金 Enterprise Funds	国外资金 Foreign Funds	其他资金 Others	专利申请数(件) Patent Applications (unit)	#发明专利 Inventions
1181114	**27242**	**914137**	**232148**	**7588**	**17008**	**13876**
102084	4759	95714		1611	2847	2596
1079031	22483	818423	232148	5977	14161	11280
471148	25898	437662		7588	12352	10846
24607	976	23631			1330	1253
128446		123395	5051		812	531
581520	1343	353081	227096		3844	2499
242572	1365	157303	82329	1574	1797	1659
260553	191	260362			5395	4495
677989	25685	496472	149819	6014	9816	7722

19-10 研究与开发机构研发活动情况(2007-2015年)

项　目		Item		2007
研究与开发机构基本情况		**Basic Information on R&D Institutions**		
机构数	(个)	Number	(unit)	265
中　央	(个)	Central	(unit)	221
地　方	(个)	Local	(unit)	44
研究与试验发展(R&D)投入情况		**R&D Input**		
R&D人员	(万人)	R&D Personnel	(10000 persons)	4.6
按隶属关系分		By Affiliation		
中　央	(万人)	Central	(10000 persons)	4.4
地　方	(万人)	Local	(10000 persons)	0.2
R&D人员折合全时当量	(万人年)	Full-time Equivalent of R&D Personnel	(10000 persons-year)	3.8
基础研究	(万人年)	Basic Research	(10000 persons-year)	1.2
应用研究	(万人年)	Applied Research	(10000 persons-year)	1.6
试验发展	(万人年)	Experimental Development	(10000 persons-year)	1.0
R&D经费内部支出	(亿元)	Internal R&D Expenditures	(100 million yuan)	103.1
按隶属关系分		By Affiliation		
中　央	(亿元)	Central	(100 million yuan)	99.0
地　方	(亿元)	Local	(100 million yuan)	4.1
按活动类型分		By Type of Activity		
基础研究	(亿元)	Basic Research	(100 million yuan)	26.4
应用研究	(亿元)	Applied Research	(100 million yuan)	45.2
试验发展	(亿元)	Experimental Development	(100 million yuan)	31.5
按资金来源分		By Source of Funds		
政府资金	(亿元)	Governmental Funds	(100 million yuan)	88.6
企业资金	(亿元)	Enterprise Funds	(100 million yuan)	3.2
境外资金	(亿元)	Foreign Funds	(100 million yuan)	1.3
其他资金	(亿元)	Others	(100 million yuan)	10.0
研究与试验发展(R&D)项目(课题)情况		**R&D Projects (Tasks)**		
R&D项目(课题)数	(项)	Number of R&D Projects (Tasks)	(unit)	15079
R&D项目(课题)人员折合全时当量	(万人年)	Full-time Equivalent of R&D Personnel	(10000 persons-year)	2.2
R&D项目(课题)经费内部支出	(亿元)	Internal R&D Expenditures	(100 million yuan)	57.1
科技产出及成果情况		**Science & Technology Output and Achievement**		
发表科技论文	(篇)	Published Articles on Science and Technology	(unit)	37232
#国外发表	(篇)	Published Abroad	(unit)	9005
出版科技著作	(种)	Published Writings on Science and Technology	(Sort)	1489
专利申请数	(件)	Number of Patents Applications	(unit)	1993
#发明专利	(件)	Invention Patents	(unit)	1784
专利授权数	(件)	Number of Patents Granted	(unit)	985
#发明专利	(件)	Invention Patents	(unit)	752

注：研究与开发机构范围是北京市政府部门属的科学研究与技术开发机构、科技情报与文献机构。
资料来源：北京市科学技术委员会。

STATISTICS FOR R&D ACTIVITIES IN RESEARCH AND DEVELOPMENT INSTITUTIONS (2007-2015)

2008	2009	2010	2011	2012	2013	2014	2015
266	275	281	280	288	287	299	296
225	228	231	231	238	237	248	245
41	47	50	49	50	50	51	51
4.8	5.2	5.7	5.9	6.3	6.6	6.6	6.8
4.5	4.9	5.4	5.6	5.9	6.2	6.2	6.3
0.3	0.3	0.3	0.3	0.4	0.4	0.4	0.5
3.9	4.2	4.6	4.7	5.3	5.5	5.5	5.6
1.3	1.4	1.5	1.6	1.8	1.9	2.0	2.1
1.6	1.7	2.0	2.1	2.2	2.3	2.3	2.2
1.0	1.1	1.1	1.0	1.3	1.3	1.2	1.3
123.8	150.3	187.0	195.1	222.0	246.8	271.2	295.6
117.4	143.9	178.9	185.1	211.5	236.3	253.6	277.0
6.4	6.4	8.1	10.0	10.5	10.5	17.6	18.6
28.3	39.2	49.9	58.5	65.1	73.6	86.5	96.8
49.0	61.5	78.0	84.0	92.0	102.2	108.9	120.5
46.5	49.6	59.1	52.6	64.9	71.0	75.8	78.3
106.6	126.3	164.4	168.0	192.6	220.0	244.6	266.3
4.0	4.4	3.6	6.6	6.5	8.2	8.2	12.1
1.8	2.0	1.5	2.5	1.5	1.9	1.8	2.0
11.4	17.6	17.5	18.0	21.4	16.7	16.6	15.2
16383	17816	19545	20333	22842	23949	25550	26762
2.3	3.8	4.1	4.3	4.9	5.0	5.0	5.0
70.9	87.1	107.2	115.0	142.7	156.8	161.0	173.5
37149	39380	39384	41442	44218	45509	48040	48734
9184	12011	11696	13361	14003	17216	17905	18915
1636	1873	1601	1828	1670	1921	2058	2261
2488	3182	3879	4880	5456	6192	6004	6464
2119	2772	3450	4373	4798	5144	5115	5164
1146	1574	1879	2260	3251	3646	3932	4702
922	1299	1455	1756	2635	2763	3001	3529

Note: R&D institutions cover scientific research and technological development institutions, scientific and technological information institutions subordinate to government authorities of Beijing.

Source: Beijing Municipal Science & Technology Commission.

19-11 高等学校研发活动情况
STATISTICS FOR R&D ACTIVITIES IN COLLEGES & UNIVERSITIES

项　　目		Item		2015	2014
高等学校基本情况		**Basic Information of Colleges & Universities**			
学校数	(个)	Number of Colleges and Universities	(unit)	115	99
#理工农医	(个)	Colleges & Universities of Science, Engineeri Agriculture, Medical Science	(unit)	72	69
#人文社科	(个)	Colleges & Universities of Arts and Social Sciences	(unit)	90	66
研究与试验发展(R&D)机构数	(个)	Number of R&D Institutions	(unit)	863	833
研究与试验发展(R&D)投入情况		**R&D Input**			
R&D人员	(万人)	R&D Personnel	(10000 person)	8.07	7.73
R&D人员折合全时当量	(万人年)	Full-time Equivalent of R&D Personnel	(10000 persons-year)	3.45	3.36
基础研究	(万人年)	Basic Research	(10000 persons-year)	1.37	1.31
应用研究	(万人年)	Applied Research	(10000 persons-year)	2.00	1.97
试验发展	(万人年)	Experimental Development	(10000 persons-year)	0.08	0.08
R&D经费内部支出	(亿元)	Internal R&D Expenditures	(100 million yuan)	162.65	145.66
按活动类型分		By Type of Activity			
基础研究	(亿元)	Basic Research	(100 million yuan)	62.20	54.69
应用研究	(亿元)	Applied Research	(100 million yuan)	93.29	83.63
试验发展	(亿元)	Experimental Development	(100 million yuan)	7.15	7.34
按资金来源分		By Source of Funds			
#政府资金	(亿元)	Governmental Funds	(100 million yuan)	113.24	97.46
企业资金	(亿元)	Enterprise Funds	(100 million yuan)	44.82	42.76
研究与试验发展(R&D)项目(课题)情况		**R&D Projects (Tasks)**			
R&D项目(课题)数	(项)	Number of R&D Projects (Tasks)	(unit)	92243	83455
R&D项目(课题)人员折合全时当量	(万人年)	Full-time Equivalent of R&D Personnel	(10000 persons-year)	3.44	3.35
R&D项目(课题)经费内部支出	(亿元)	Internal R&D Expenditures	(100 million yuan)	125.17	118.94
科技产出及成果情况		**Science & Technology Output and Achievement**			
发表科技论文	(篇)	Published Articles on Science and Technology	(unit)	118985	115143
#国外发表	(篇)	Published Abroad	(unit)		
出版科技著作	(种)	Published Writings on Science and Technolog	(Sort)	5225	5357
专利申请数	(件)	Number of Patent Applications	(unit)	13363	11503
#发明专利	(件)	Invention Patents	(unit)	10795	10025
专利授权数	(件)	Number of Patents Granted	(unit)	9212	7279
#发明专利	(件)	Invention Patents	(unit)	7161	5829

资料来源：北京市教育委员会。
Source: Beijing Municipal Commission of Education.

19-12 科学技术协会及所属学会工作情况(2015年)
STATISTICS FOR SCIENCE AND TECHNOLOGY ASSOCIATION AND SUBORDINATE INSTITUTES (2015)

项 目		Item		合 计 Total	市科协 Municipal Science and Technology Association	市级学会 Institutes at Municipal Level
基本情况		**Basic Information**				
机构数	(个)	Number of Institutions	(unit)	179	1	178
机构从业人员	(人)	Number of Employed Persons in the Institutions	(person)	999	48	951
学术交流活动		**Academic Exchange Activities**				
国内学术会议	(次)	Domestic Academic Meetings	(time)	1192	1	1191
参加人数	(人次)	Number of Participants	(person-time)	405989	120	405869
交流论文	(篇)	Number of Papers Exchagned	(unit)	19195	18	19177
境内国际学术会议	(次)	Domestically-held International Academic Meetings	(time)	76		76
参加人数	(人次)	Number of Participants	(person-time)	14509		14509
交流论文	(篇)	Number of Papers Exchagned	(unit)	2217		2217
港澳台地区学术会议	(次)	Academic Meetings Held in Kong Kong, Macao and Taiwan	(time)	11		11
参加人数	(人次)	Number of Participants	(person-time)	995		995
交流论文	(篇)	Number of Papers Exchagned	(unit)	253		253
科技期刊		**Science and Technology Journals**				
主办科技期刊种数	(种)	Types of Science and Technology Journals Sponsored	(sort)	33	1	32
科技期刊总印数	(万册)	Number of Total Printings of Science and Technology Journals	(10000 copies)	106.19	2.40	103.79
科技期刊发表论文数	(篇)	Papers Published on Science and Technology Journals	(unit)	2900	17	2883
科普活动		**Activities to Popularize Scientific Knowledge**				
举办科普宣讲活动	(次)	Scientific Knowledge Lectures	(time)	6530	1745	4785
播放科技广播、影视节目	(分钟)	Playing Radio, Films and TV Programs on Science and Technology	(minute)	5611	1309	4302
举办实用技术培训	(次)	Holding Practical Technology Trainings	(time)	1063	642	421
推广新技术、新品种	(项)	Promoting New Technologies and New Varieties	(unit)	358		358
参加活动科技人员总数	(人次)	Participating in Science and Technology Personnel	(person-time)	55213	17285	37928
参加活动的学会、协会、研究会	(个次)	Participating in Socieities, Associations and Research Institutes	(unit-time)	1576	1015	561
科技传播		**Science and Technology Dissemination**				
主办科技报纸种数	(种)	Types of Science and Technology Newspaper Sponsored	(sort)	1	1	
制作科普挂图种数	(种)	Types of Scientific Knowlede Flip Charts Produced	(sort)	236	27	209
制作科技广播、影视节目套数	(套)	Science and Technology Raido, Films and TV Programs Produced	(unit)	31		31
制作科技光盘种数	(种)	Types of Science and Technology CDs Produced	(sort)	94	38	56
制作科普动漫作品套数	(套)	Scientific Knowledge Animation Works Produced	(unit)	27	10	17
主办科技网站	(个)	Science and Technology Websites Sponsored	(unit)	60	10	50
科技开放与交流		**Science and Technology Opening-up and Exchange**				
加入国际民间科技组织	(个)	International Cilvilian Science and Technology Organizations Joined	(unit)	9		9
促成科技合作项目	(项)	Scientific and Technological Cooperation Projects Facilitated	(unit)	11		11
参加国外科技活动人数	(人次)	Number of Persons Participating in Foreign Science and Technology Activities	(person-time)	521	135	386
参加港澳台地区科技活动人数	(人次)	Number of Persons Participating in Science and Technology Activities in Hong Kong, Macao and Taiwan	(person-time)	338	61	277
接待国外专家学者	(人次)	Foreign Experts and Scholars Received	(person-time)	970	373	597
接待港澳台地区专家学者	(人次)	Experts and Scholars from Kong Kong, Macao and Taiwan Received	(person-time)	270	41	229
科技服务		**Science and Technology Service**				
提供决策咨询报告	(篇)	Providing Policy-making Consulting Reports	(unit)	206	70	136
举办决策咨询活动	(次)	Holding Policy-making Consulting Activities	(time)	216	38	178

注：本表统计范围是北京市科学技术协会所属学会、研究会。
资料来源：北京市科学技术协会。
Note: Figures in this table cover societies and research institutes affiliated with Beijing Association for Science & Technology.
Source: Beijing Association for Science & Technology.

19-13 公有经济企事业单位专业技术人员(2015年)
NUMBER OF PORFESSIONAL TECHNICAL PERSONNEL IN PUBLIC ENTERPRISES AND INSTITUTIONS (2015)

单位：人 (person)

项目	Item	合计 Total	#高级 Senior	#中级 Intermediate	#初级 Junior
合计	**Total**	**524089**	**68014**	**173728**	**193887**
#工程技术人员	Engineering Technicians	127201	13704	32214	40537
农业技术人员	Agricultural Technicians	4470	535	1243	2002
科学研究人员	Science Research Personnel	7739	1904	3051	1178
卫生技术人员	Medical Technicians	96800	12016	33241	48014
教学人员	Teaching Personnel	171514	31879	75395	61246
经济人员	Economic Personnel	63236	3474	13920	17672
会计人员	Accountants	26867	1535	6346	12755
统计人员	Statisticians	3073	102	659	1345

注：公有经济是指北京市属国有和集体企事业单位,不包含在京中央属企事业单位。

资料来源：北京市人力资源和社会保障局。

Note: Public sector means state-owned and collectively-owned enterprises and institutions in Beijing, excluding central enterprises and institutions located in Beijing.

Source: Beijing Municipal Bureau of Human Resources and Social Security.

19-14 技术合同成交情况(1990-2015年)
STATISTICS FOR CONCLUSION OF TECHNOLOGICAL CONTRACTS (1990-2015)

年 份 Year	合同数 (项) Number of Contracts (unit)	技术合同成交总额 (亿元) Total Volume of Transaction of Technological Contracts Concluded (100 million yuan)	#技术交易额 Total Volume of Transaction of Technology	#流向外省市技术合同额 Amount of Transaction Flowing to Other Provinces and Municipalities	实现合同总金额 (亿元) Total Volume of Transaction Achieved in Contracts (100 million yuan)	#技术交易实现金额 Amount of Technological Transactions Achieved
1990	18588	20.3	10.5		15.4	8.4
1991-1995	**93970**	**167.7**	**120.0**		**115.4**	**83.8**
1991	18547	22.4	13.1		15.3	9.1
1992	23395	31.3	22.2		20.0	14.4
1993	20461	35.6	25.6		24.9	17.6
1994	15220	37.2	26.9		26.9	20.4
1995	16347	41.2	32.2		28.4	22.3
1996-2000	**91421**	**414.2**	**375.9**		**206.7**	**188.1**
1996	14850	45.8	39.2		29.6	25.4
1997	13866	54.3	48.1		31.1	27.8
1998	20724	81.6	73.9		42.1	37.6
1999	20711	92.2	88.5		43.6	41.0
2000	21270	140.3	126.3	65.5	60.3	56.3
2001-2005	**156114**	**1443.8**	**1217.2**	**688.9**	**669.5**	**628.1**
2001	23921	191.0	164.8	85.4	97.6	93.0
2002	27037	221.1	181.0	100.4	101.9	97.2
2003	32173	265.5	226.8	132.4	119.9	113.9
2004	35478	331.8	294.3	165.8	148.7	143.4
2005	37505	434.4	350.4	204.9	201.4	180.6
2006-2010	**256074**	**5422.8**	**3984.7**	**2372.7**	**2226.7**	**2006.7**
2006	51575	697.3	572.6	325.3	349.5	319.7
2007	50972	882.6	660.3	407.4	418.1	353.5
2008	52742	1027.2	778.1	487.0	406.2	375.0
2009	49938	1236.2	906.9	498.2	516.8	452.9
2010	50847	1579.5	1066.7	654.8	536.0	505.6
2011-2015	**315814**	**13788.6**	**10868.6**	**7237.5**	**3942.1**	**3811.6**
2011	53552	1890.3	1268.3	635.9	580.4	563.3
2012	59969	2458.5	2048.6	1385.0	739.8	707.0
2013	62743	2851.2	2252.4	1615.9	684.0	659.3
2014	67278	3136.0	2531.5	1722.0	708.2	675.1
2015	72272	3452.6	2767.8	1878.7	1229.7	1206.9

资料来源：北京技术市场管理办公室。
Source: Beijing Technical Market Management Office.

19-15 技术合同成交情况
CONCLUSION OF TECHNICAL CONTRACTS

项　目	Item	合同数(项) Number of Contracts (unit)		成交额(万元) Volume of Transaction (10000 yuan)	
		2015	2014	2015	2014
合　计	**Total**	**72272**	**67278**	**34525661.6**	**31359985.3**
按合同类别分类	**By Type of Contract**				
技术开发合同	Technological Development	27886	24938	6479482.5	6833184.3
技术转让合同	Technology Transfer	1338	1296	607524.9	647595.2
技术咨询合同	Technical Consultation	4907	4302	536515.7	395252.3
技术服务合同	Technical Service	38141	36742	26902138.4	23483953.5
按合同卖方类别分类	**By Type of Seller**				
机关法人	Government Organisations	22	21	2606.3	5017.4
事业法人	Public Institutions	13918	11122	1503626.3	1098148.6
社团法人	Mass Organisations	14	15	572.5	1095.5
企业法人	Enterprises	57727	56069	30713014.6	30233204.0
自然人	Natural Persons	27	28	8240.1	6573.7
其他组织	Other Organizations	564	23	2297601.7	15946.2
按合同买方类别分类	**By Type of Buyer**				
机关法人	Government Organisations	5570	5280	4953626.5	1787487.3
事业法人	Public Institutions	15274	12066	2097516.8	1643707.5
社团法人	Mass Organisations	473	313	20373.1	24959.3
企业法人	Enterprises	49678	48527	26613959.4	25230280.1
自然人	Natural Persons	336	404	42918.8	102228.4
其他组织	Other Organizations	941	688	797267.0	2571322.7
按服务社会经济目标分类	**By Social and Economic Service Objectives**				
环境保护、生态建设及污染防治	Environmental Protection, Ecological Development and Pollution Control	2857	3386	4743858.5	3660854
能源生产、分配和合理利用	Energy Production, Allocation and Reasonable Utilization	4463	5420	3605908.6	5647012.1
卫生事业发展	Health Services	2236	1950	786368.9	352179.8
教育事业发展	Education Development	2388	1864	216182.7	272018.45
基础设施以及城市和农村规划	Infrastructure and Rural and Urban Planning	4018	7563	6249296.6	8565501.5
社会发展和社会服务	Social Development and Social Services	32962	24763	11121994.1	6934936.6
地球和大气层的探索与利用	Exploration and Utilization Of The Earth and Atmosphere	71	167	34369.0	473492.8
民用空间探测及开发	Private Space Exploration and Development	481	700	97514.8	108175.8
农林牧渔业发展	Development in Agriculture, Forestry, Animal Production and Hunting, Fishing	1778	1926	104089.0	297670.6
工商业发展	Industrial and Commercial Development	3326	3185	841931.8	754497.35
非定向研究	Non-Directional Research	2880	1590	2157559.0	666005.6
其他民用目标	Other Cvilian Target	9624	11741	3494623.2	3069743.1
国防	National Defense	5188	3023	1071965.3	557897.6
按技术流向分类	**By Spread Area of Technology**				
流向本市	To Beijing	33514	28830	6250403.1	7172432.0
流向外省市	To Other Provinces and Municipalities	37447	37212	18786775.4	17219865.4
技术出口	Exports	1311	1236	9488483.1	6967687.9

资料来源：北京技术市场管理办公室。
Source: Beijing Technical Market Management Office.

19-16　科技成果及获奖情况(2001-2015年)
STATISTICS FOR SCIENTIFIC AND TECHNOLOGICAL ACHIEVEMENTS AND AWARDS (2001-2015)

单位：项 (unit)

年　份 Year	科技成果登记数 Registered Number of Scientific and Technological Achievements	#国家技术发明奖 National Awards of Technical Invention	#国家科学技术进步奖 National Awards of Scientific and Technological Advancement
2001-2005	**3063**	**25**	**233**
2001	326	1	38
2002	275	5	48
2003	468	5	52
2004	976	6	43
2005	1018	8	52
2006-2010	**5081**	**56**	**257**
2006	1002	12	64
2007	1010	9	44
2008	1016	13	42
2009	1023	11	54
2010	1030	11	53
2011-2015	**5205**	**78**	**238**
2011	1035	5	56
2012	1040	22	53
2013	1043	19	38
2014	1042	15	49
2015	1045	17	42

资料来源：北京市科学技术委员会。
Source: Beijing Municipal Science & Technology Commission.

19-17 专利申请及授权情况
APPLICATIONS AND GRANTING OF PATENTS

单位：件 (unit)

项目	Item	申请量 Patent Applications		授权量 Patents Granted	
		2015	2014	2015	2014
合计	**Total**	**156312**	**138111**	**94031**	**74661**
按种类分	**By Type**				
发明	Inventions	88930	78129	35308	23237
实用新型	Utility Models	53243	48228	45773	44071
外观设计	Industrial Designs	14139	11754	12950	7353
按对象分	**By Applicant**				
工矿企业	Industrial and Mining Enterprises	107921	94998	66007	52181
大专院校	Universities & Colleges	14887	13574	8700	6823
科研单位	Scientific Research Institutes	14779	12884	8692	7165
机关团体	Government Organizations	2296	1556	1309	777
个人	Individuals	16429	15099	9323	7715

资料来源：北京市知识产权局。
Source: Beijing Intellectual Property Office.

19-18 有效发明专利情况
STATISTICS FOR VALID INVENTION PATENTS

单位：件 (unit)

项目	Item	2015	2014
合计	**Total**	**133040**	**103638**
按对象分	**By Applicant**		
工矿企业	Industrial and Mininig Enterprises	74594	54574
大专院校	Universities & Colleges	25698	22069
科研单位	Scientific Research Institutes	24907	20090
机关团体	Government Organizations	1476	1086
个人	Individuals	6365	5819

资料来源：北京市知识产权局。
Source: Beijing Intellectual Property Office.

主要统计指标解释

科技活动人员 指报告年度调查单位直接从事科技活动、以及从事科技活动管理和为科技活动提供直接服务的人员。直接从事科技活动人员包括：在单位办的研究室、实验室、技术开发中心及中试车间（基地）等机构中从事科技活动的人员；虽不在上述机构工作，但编入科技活动项目（课题）组的人员等。从事科技活动管理和为科技活动提供直接服务的人员包括：与科技活动相关的行政管理人员，以及直接为科技活动提供资料文献、材料供应、设备维护等服务的人员。

研究与试验发展（R&D） 指在科学技术领域，为增加知识总量、以及运用这些知识去创造新的应用而进行的系统的创造性的活动，包括基础研究、应用研究、试验发展三类活动。

研究与试验发展（R&D）人员 指单位内部从事基础研究、应用研究和试验发展三类活动的人员。包括直接参加上述三类项目活动的人员以及这三类项目的管理人员和直接服务人员。为研发活动提供直接服务的人员包括直接为研发活动提供资料文献、材料供应、设备维护等服务的人员。

研究与试验发展（R&D）人员折合全时当量 是国际上通用的、用于比较科技人力投入的指标。指 R&D 全时人员（全年从事 R&D 活动累积工作时间占全部工作时间的 90% 及以上人员）工作量与非全时人员按实际工作时间折算的工作量之和。

研究与试验发展（R&D）内部支出 指调查单位在报告年度用于内部开展 R&D 活动（基础研究、应用研究和试验发展）的实际支出。包括用于 R&D 项目（课题）活动的直接支出，以及间接用于 R&D 活动的管理费、服务费、与 R&D 有关的基本建设支出以及外协加工费等，不包括生产性活动支出、归还贷款支出以及与外单位合作或委托外单位进行 R&D 活动而转拨给对方的经费支出。

专业技术人员 指从事专业技术工作的人员以及从事专业技术管理工作且已在 1983 年以前评定了专业技术职称或在 1984 年以后聘任了专业技术职务的人员。从事专业技术工作的人员具体指工程技术人员，农业技术人员，科学研究人员（含自然科学研究及实验技术人员），卫生技术人员，教学人员（含高等院校、中等专业学校、技工学校、中学、小学），民用航空飞行技术人员，船舶技术人员，经济专业人员，会计人员，统计人员，翻译人员，图书资料、档案、文博人员，新闻、出版人员，律师、公证人员，广播电视播音人员，工艺美术人员，体育人员，艺术人员及企业政治思想工作人员。从事专业技术管理工作的人员是指企业、事业单位领导；企业、事业单位下设的职能机构、企业的生产车间的辅助车间（或附属辅助生产单位）中从事生产、技术、经济管理和政治工作的人员；按照公务员管理或参照公务员管理的人员不统计为专业技术人员。

专利 是专利权的简称，是对发明人的发明创造经审查合格后，由专利局依据专利法授予发明人和设计人对该项发明创造享有的专有权。包括发明、实用新型和外观设计。

发明专利 指专利法及其实施细则所称的发明，指对产品、方法或者改进所提出的新的技术方案。

实用新型专利 指专利法及其实施细则所称的实用新型，指对产品的形状、构造或者其结合所提出的适于实用的新的技术方案。

外观设计专利 指专利法及其实施细则所称的外观设计，指对产品的形状、图案、色彩或者其结合所做出的富有美感并适于工业上应用的新设计。

Explanatory Notes on Main Statistical Indicators

Personnel Engaged in Science and Technology Activities refer to persons directly engaged in science and technology activities as well as persons engaged in science and technology management and persons offering direct services to science and technology activities in the surveyed entities in the reporting year. Persons directly engaged in science and technology activities include: persons engaged in science and technology activities in such institutions as research labs of entities, laboratories, technical development centers and middle-stage test workshops (bases); persons not working in the above-mentioned institutions but included in the science and technology activity project (task) team, etc. Persons engaged in science and technology management and persons offering direct services for science and technology activities include administrative staff related to science and technology activities, as well as persons directly providing information and literature, supply of materials, equipment maintenance and other services.

R&D refers to systematic and creative activities in the field of science and technology to increase the total knowledge, and apply such knowledge to create new applications, including three kinds of activities, i.e. basic research, applied research, and experimental development.

R&D Personnel refer to persons in the surveyed entities who are engaged in three kinds of activities, i.e. basic research, applied research and experimental development. They include those who participate in the above-mentioned three kinds of activities directly, research management personnel and persons directly serving these activities. Persons providing direct services include those who provide information and literature, supply of materials, equipment maintenance and other services.

Full-Time Equivalent of R&D Personnel is an indicator globally used to compare input of scientific talents. It refers to the sum of workload of full-time R&D personnel (the personnel whose accumulative annual working time involved in R&D activities takes 90% and above of the whole working time) plus the workload of non-full time personnel that is equivalent of the actual working time.

Internal R&D Expenditure means the actual disbursement of investigated entities on internal R&D activities (basic research, applied research, and experimental development) in the reporting year, including direct spending on R&D project (task) activities, and management expenses and service fees indirectly spent on R&D activities, R&D related basic construction expense and external assisting processing charges, etc., excluding production-based activity expense, loan repayment expense and fund transferred to external institution cooperated or entrusted to conduct R&D activities.

Professional Technical Personnel refer to persons engaged in professional technological work and professional technological management whose professional technological titles were assessed and granted before 1983 or who have been retained at professional technological positions after 1984. Persons engaged in professional technological work refer to engineering technicians, agricultural technicians, research personnel (including natural science research and experiment technicians), medical technicians, teaching staff (including those in colleges and universities, technical secondary schools, vocational schools, high schools, and elementary schools), civil aviation flight technicians, watercraft technicians, economics professionals, accountants, statisticians, translators and interpreters, librarians, archivists, cultural expo personnel, journalists, publishers , lawyers, notaries, TV and radio broadcasters, industrial arts staff, sportspersons, artists, as well as personnel responsible for political ideology work in enterprises.. The professional technological management refer to leaders of enterprises and public institutions; persons engaged in management of production, technology and economy as well as political work in functional organs under enterprises and public institutions, auxiliary workplaces (or affiliated auxiliary production entities) of production workplaces of enterprises; persons managed as civil servants or with reference to civil servants are not counted as professional technicians.

Patent is the abbreviation of patent right, referring to the exclusive right granted by patent authorities upon examination and approval of inventions and creations to the inventors and designers with regard to the invention, including inventions, utility models and industrial designs.

Invention means the invention mentioned in the Patent Law and its detailed rules for implementation, i.e. the new technological solutions presented for the product, methodology, or improvement.

Utility Model means the utility model mentioned in the Patent Law and its detailed rules for implementation, i.e. the new practical technological solutions presented for the product shape, structure, color or combination.

Industrial Design means the industrial design mentioned in the Patent Law and its detailed rules for implementation, i.e. new designs of product shape, pattern, color or combination which are aesthetic and suitable for industrial applications.

北京统计年鉴2016 BEIJING STATISTICAL YEARBOOK

卫生、体育
HEALTH CARE AND SPORTS

简 要 说 明

一、本章资料的主要内容

本章主要反映卫生、体育的发展情况。

卫生部分主要内容包括卫生总费用、卫生机构、卫生技术人员、床位数，医院诊疗人次及入院人数，主要疾病死亡原因及构成，全市主要健康指标等情况。体育部分主要包括群众体育活动情况、体育场地情况、运动员获奖情况、体育彩票情况等。

二、本章资料的数据来源

卫生部分的资料由北京市卫生和计划生育委员会提供，体育部分的资料由北京市体育局提供。

Brief Introduction

I. Main Content

This chapter mainly reflects the development of health and sports.

Health statistics include the total health expenditures, the number of health institutions, health technicians, ward beds, patients treated and hospitalized persons, major causes of death and composition, main health indicators of Beijing, and so on. Sports statistics include public sports and sports venues, awards received by athletes, and sports lottery tickets, etc.

II. Source of Data

Health data are from Beijing Municipal Commission of Health and Family Planning. Sports data are from Beijing Municipal Bureau of Sports.

20-1 卫生事业基本情况(1978-2015年)
BASIC STATISTICS ON HEALTH CARE (1978-2015)

年 份 Year	卫生机构(个) Healthcare Institutions (unit)	#医 院 Hospitals	#疾病预防控制中心(防疫站) Centers for Disease Control and Prevention	#妇幼保健院(所、站) Maternity and Child Care Centers (Stations)	#社区卫生服务中心(站) Community Health Services Centers (Stations)
1978	3263		22	15	
1979	3614		22	17	
1980	3818		22	19	
1981	4135		22	19	
1982	4389		22	18	
1983	4312		22	19	
1984	4173		22	18	
1985	4248		22	18	
1986	4483		22	20	
1987	4744		22	19	
1988	4342		22	17	
1989	4398		22	17	
1990	4953		22	17	
1991	4970	337	22	17	
1992	4868	345	22	16	
1993	4962	364	32	16	
1994	4958	387	33	16	
1995	4955	387	33	15	
1996	6470	405	33	13	
1997	6577	435	33	13	
1998	5723	449	32	11	
1999	5990	460	32	8	
2000	6176	458	30	8	
2001	5969	458	30	9	
2002	4998	461	24	19	35
2003	5075	459	29	19	36
2004	4835	503	29	19	43
2005	4818	519	28	18	93
2006	4878	541	28	18	90
2007	6189	535	31	18	1126
2008	6523	537	31	19	1282
2009	6603	522	31	19	1395
2010	6539	550	31	19	1587
2011	9699	569	32	19	1744
2012	9974	608	32	19	1897
2013	10141	647	32	19	1926
2014	10265	672	32	19	1958
2015	10425	701	30	19	1979

注：1. 2010年及以前，本表中所有数据都不包含村卫生室及驻京部队医院情况。2011年开始，包含村卫生室情况。 2012年开始，除床位数外均包含驻京部队医院数据(下表同)。
2. 2010年开始，原卫生院数据并入到社区卫生服务中心(站)等其他卫生机构。

资料来源：北京市卫生和计划生育委员会。

Note: a) In and before 2010, figures in this table did not include village health clinics and hospitals of troops stationed in Beijing. From 2011, figures included village health clinics. From 2012,figures in this table include troops stationed in Beijing with the bed number excluded. stationed in Beijing (the same to the follow tables).

b) From 2010, data on health centers were incorporated into other health institutions such as community health service centers (stations).

Source: Beijing Municipal Commission of Health and Family Planning.

20-1 续表 Continued

年 份 Year	卫生机构人员(人) Employed Persons in Healthcare Institutions (person)	#卫生技术人员 Medical Technical Personnel	#执业(助理)医师 Certified (Assistant) Physicians	#注册护士 Registered Nurses	实有床位数(张) Beds (unit)	#医院 Hospitals	每千户籍人口执业(助理)医师数(人) Certified Physicians Per 1000 Persons (person)	每千户籍人口注册护士数(人) Registered Nurses Per 1000 Persons (person)	每千户籍人口医院床位数(张) Beds Per 1000 Persons (unit)
1978	90174	65943	28435	16085	29767		3.35	1.89	3.11
1979	97942	72131	31842	17398	30231		3.66	1.87	3.08
1980	102601	74753	34365	17492	32453		3.88	1.97	3.22
1981	110774	81183	37886	20025	33666		4.20	2.20	3.30
1982	114420	83843	39385	20389	34574		4.30	2.23	3.40
1983	119222	86593	41216	21181	35987		4.40	2.26	3.50
1984	124664	89362	42112	22286	38580		4.40	2.33	3.70
1985	127771	90831	42216	23782	41603		4.44	2.48	3.99
1986	132865	94433	43403	25383	43956		4.47	3.72	4.21
1987	142556	101829	46007	27786	47538		4.66	2.81	4.49
1988	145362	105237	48216	30250	53078		4.82	3.02	4.87
1989	150062	108108	49361	32056	55623		4.83	3.14	5.08
1990	156304	111614	50934	34565	59036		4.93	3.35	5.37
1991	161103	114342	52309	35714	61744	54888	5.03	3.44	5.65
1992	164213	115825	53254	36768	63230	55858	5.10	3.52	5.73
1993	165170	116173	53906	36687	65621	58605	5.13	3.49	5.93
1994	164867	116818	53865	36608	67112	60661	5.07	3.45	6.07
1995	164436	115967	54114	36719	66925	60337	5.06	3.43	6.00
1996	164981	116849	54091	37712	66760	60997	5.02	3.50	6.02
1997	167090	119256	54909	38630	67946	61865	5.06	3.56	6.06
1998	162609	115976	51902	38883	69095	63144	4.76	3.56	6.13
1999	161823	116597	52646	39625	69465	63660	4.79	3.60	6.15
2000	160258	115510	51570	39900	71245	65138	4.66	3.60	6.25
2001	158185	115935	52100	40537	73053	66537	4.64	3.61	6.31
2002	144021	109564	47236	38879	75188	67750	4.18	3.44	6.46
2003	148406	112212	47887	39912	74298	66990	4.21	3.51	5.89
2004	153154	116610	48988	41547	77359	69850	4.25	3.60	6.54
2005	157133	119874	50617	42897	79067	72329	4.32	3.66	6.65
2006	166278	126904	52795	45647	81440	74762	4.41	3.84	6.77
2007	182475	139275	54989	50890	83736	76915	4.53	4.19	6.34
2008	193799	149916	58773	55349	86196	79089	4.78	4.50	6.43
2009	208156	160435	62348	61604	90100	82471	5.00	4.94	6.62
2010	219762	171093	65954	67308	92871	85935	5.24	5.35	6.83
2011	235708	181938	69749	72812	94735	87596	5.46	5.70	6.85
2012	276654	219714	82192	95202	100167	92610	6.33	7.34	7.14
2013	294012	229720	85819	100652	104034	96558	6.52	7.65	8.76
2014	304990	242923	89590	106167	109789	102851	6.72	7.96	7.71
2015	321151	256531	96445	114294	111555	104644	7.17	8.50	7.76

注：表中每千户籍人口执业(助理)医师数、每千户籍人口注册护士数、每千户籍人口医院床位数均按年末户籍人口计算。2015年上述指标按年末常住人口计算分别为4.44人、5.27人和5.14张。

Note:The data of "Certified Physicians per 1000 Persons", "Registered Nurses per 1000 Persons", "Beds per 1000 Persons" were calculated by year-end registered population. These indicators for 2014 calculated by year-end permanent population were 4.44 persons, 5.27 persons and 4.82 units.

20-2 卫生总费用(2000-2014年)
TOTAL HEALTH EXPENDITURES (2000-2014)

年份 Year	卫生总费用(亿元) Total Health Expenditures (100 million yuan)	政府卫生支出 Health Expenditures by Governments		社会卫生支出 Social Health Expenditures		个人现金卫生支出 Health Expenditures in Cash by Individuals		相当于地区生产总值比例(%) Total Health Expenditure as % of GDP Total (%)
		绝对数(亿元) Absolute Number (100 million yuan)	占卫生总费用比重(%) As % of Total (%)	绝对数(亿元) Absolute Number (100 million yuan)	占卫生总费用比重(%) As % of Total (%)	绝对数(亿元) Absolute Number (100 million yuan)	占卫生总费用比重(%) As % of Total (%)	
2000	166.72	34.70	20.81	61.78	37.05	70.25	42.13	5.27
2001	201.12	45.28	22.52	73.18	36.39	82.65	41.10	5.42
2002	262.36	48.51	18.49	99.61	37.97	114.23	43.54	6.08
2003	314.16	65.80	20.94	132.04	42.03	116.33	37.03	6.27
2004	357.19	69.35	19.41	150.72	42.20	137.12	38.39	5.92
2005	432.80	85.73	19.81	187.84	43.40	159.22	36.79	6.21
2006	497.41	115.89	23.30	208.00	41.82	173.52	34.88	6.13
2007	523.20	142.03	27.15	212.00	40.52	169.17	32.33	5.31
2008	668.52	180.01	26.93	271.26	40.58	217.25	32.50	6.01
2009	689.60	201.14	29.17	296.25	42.96	192.21	27.87	5.67
2010	814.74	226.84	27.84	385.10	47.27	202.80	24.89	5.77
2011	977.26	275.48	28.19	453.16	46.37	248.62	25.44	6.01
2012	1190.01	320.40	26.92	600.96	50.50	268.65	22.58	6.66
2013	1349.62	356.42	26.41	717.75	53.18	275.45	20.41	6.92
2014	1594.64	394.38	24.73	890.57	55.85	309.69	19.42	7.48

资料来源：北京市卫生和计划生育委员会。
Source: Beijing Municipal Commission of Health and Family Planning.

20-3 卫生机构基本情况
BASIC STATISTICS FOR HEALTH CARE INSTITUTIONS

项目	Item	2015	2014	构成 (%) Composition (%) 2015	构成 (%) Composition (%) 2014
卫生机构 （个）	**Health Care Institutions (unit)**	**10425**	**10265**	**100.0**	**100.0**
#医院	Hospitals	701	672	6.7	6.5
社区卫生服务中心(站)	Health Service Centers (Stations) for Community	1979	1958	19.0	19.1
门诊部	Outpatient Departments	1070	1016	10.3	9.9
妇幼保健院(所、站)	Maternity and Child Care Hospitals	19	19	0.2	0.2
疾病预防控制中心(防疫站)	Disease Prevention and Control Center (Epidemic Prevention Station)	30	32	0.3	0.3
专科疾病防治院(所、站)	Specific Disease Prevention and Cure Centers	25	27	0.2	0.3
诊所、卫生所、医务室、护理站	Clinics, Health Centers, Infirmaries, Nursing Stations	3630	3529	34.8	34.3
床位 （张）	**Beds (unit)**	**111555**	**109789**	**100.0**	**100.0**
#医院	Hospitals	104644	102851	93.8	93.7
社区卫生服务中心(站)	Health Service Centers (Stations) for Community	4412	4515	4.0	4.1
妇幼保健院(所、站)	Maternity and Child Care Hospitals	1935	1939	1.7	1.8
专科疾病防治院(所、站)	Specific Disease Prevention and Cure Centers	534	484	0.5	0.4
卫生技术人员 （人）	**Medical Technical Personnel (person)**	**256531**	**242923**	**100.0**	**100.0**
#医院	Hospitals	194203	182567	75.7	75.2
社区卫生服务中心(站)	Health Service Centers (Stations) for Community	26193	25561	10.2	10.5
妇幼保健院(所、站)	Maternity and Child Care Hospitals	5135	5000	2.0	2.1
专科疾病防治院(所、站)	Specific Disease Prevention and Cure Centers	550	588	0.2	0.2
#执业(助理)医师	Certified Doctors	96445	89590	37.6	36.9
注册护士	Registered Nurses	114294	106167	44.6	43.7

注：本表数据除床位数外均包含驻京部队医院数据。
资料来源：北京市卫生和计划生育委员会。
Note: Figures in this table include troops stationed in Beijing with the bed number excluded.
Source: Beijing Municipal Commission of Health and Family Planning.

20-4 全市医院基本情况(2015年)
BASIC STATISTICS ON HOSPITALS (2015)

项目	Item	医院数 (个) Hospitals (unit)	床位数 (张) Beds (unit)	职工人数 (人) Employed Persons (person)	#卫生技术人员 Medical Technical Personnel	#执业医师 Certified Doctors	#中医 Doctors of Traditional Chinese Medicine
合计	**Total**	**701**	**104644**	**239155**	**194203**	**66667**	**9811**
按隶属关系分	**By Affiliation**						
#市级	Municipal	30	21634	46475	37561	12284	835
区	Districts and Counties	99	29941	55288	44990	15593	3118
按专业分	**By Specialty**						
综合医院	General Hospitals	337	62005	160434	134708	46227	2310
中医医院	Hospital Specialized in Traditional Chinese Medicine	158	13276	26555	21191	8458	5934
中西医结合医院	Hospitals Combining Western Medicine with Traditional Chinese Medicine	26	6287	8425	6869	2532	1008
民族医院	Nationality Hospitals	3	247	523	291	94	47
口腔医院	Stomatology Hospitals	18	384	4323	3444	1339	4
眼科医院	Ophthalmology Hospitals	9	436	752	446	152	10
肿瘤医院	Tumor Hospitals	9	3176	5749	4152	1208	54
心血管病医院	Hospitals for Cardiovascular Diseases	2	1298	3193	2693	656	4
胸科医院	Thorax Hospitals	1	533	821	634	161	1
妇(产)科医院	Hospitals for Gynecology and Obstetrics	14	1018	3852	2479	719	27
儿童医院	Children's Hospitals	11	2001	5061	4102	1382	66
精神病医院	Psychiatric Hospital	22	7388	5787	4207	945	59
传染病医院	Infectious Disease Hospitals	3	1416	3258	2501	776	40
骨科医院	Hospitals of Orthopedics	8	898	1307	954	285	61
整形外科医院	Orthopaedics Hospitals	1	328	753	534	165	
其他专科医院	Other Specialized Hospitals	72	3853	8299	4958	1554	182
护理院	Nursing Hospitals	7	100	63	40	14	4

注：本表数据除床位数外均包括驻京部队数据。
资料来源：北京市卫生和计划生育委员会。
Note: Figures in this table include troops stationed in Beijing with the bed number excluded.
Source: Beijing Municipal Commission of Health and Family Planning.

20-4 续表 Continued

单位：人 (person)

项 目	Item	#执业助理医师 Certified Assistant Doctors	#中医 Doctors of Traditional Chinese Medicine	#注册护士 Registered Nurses	#药师(士) Pharmacists (Assistant Pharmacists)	#技师(士) Technicians (Assistant Technicians)	#检验师(士) Laboratorians (Assistant Laboratorians)
合 计	**Total**	**1517**	**317**	**95895**	**8687**	**8016**	**5149**
按隶属关系分	**By Affiliation**						
#市 级	Municipal	117	4	18322	1784	1966	1259
区	Districts and Counties	527	74	20680	2632	2084	
按专业分	**By Specialty**						
综合医院	General Hospitals	771	106	69243	5008	5026	3169
中医医院	Hospital Specialized in Traditional Chinese Medicine	299	149	7983	1978	1021	667
中西医结合医院	Hospitals Combining Western Medicine with Traditional Chinese Medicine	102	28	3005	419	286	201
民族医院	Nationality Hospitals	11	3	120	20	17	10
口腔医院	Stomatology Hospitals	24		1529	41	91	26
眼科医院	Ophthalmology Hospitals	17	1	217	23	19	14
肿瘤医院	Tumor Hospitals	9	1	2064	187	261	120
心血管病医院	Hospitals for Cardiovascular Diseases	1		1502	61	71	48
胸科医院	Thorax Hospitals			370	30	53	24
妇(产)科医院	Hospitals for Gynecology and Obstetrics	14	2	1347	96	166	130
儿童医院	Children's Hospitals	13	5	1835	222	345	276
精神病医院	Psychiatric Hospitals	73	5	2357	205	146	117
传染病医院	Infectious Disease Hospitals	7		1297	125	168	131
骨科医院	Hospitals of Orthopedics	24	5	417	37	51	31
整形外科医院	Orthopaedics Hospitals			260	13	16	9
其他专科医院	Other Specialized Hospitals	151	11	2334	219	276	174
护理院	Nursing Hospitals	1	1	15	3	3	2

资料来源：北京市卫生和计划生育委员会。
Source: Beijing Municipal Commission of Health and Family Planning.

20-5 医院工作情况(2015年)
WORKS OF HOSPITALS (2015)

项 目	Item	诊疗人次数（千人次） Patients Treated (1000 person times)	#门诊 Out-patients	健康检查人数（千人次） Health Check (1000 person times)	平均开放病床数（张） Beds in Use (unit)	入院人数（千人次） In-patients (1000 person times)	出院人数（千人次） Discharged Patients (1000 person times)
合 计	**Total**	**163497.9**	**136284.0**	**3446.0**	**101936**	**2657.6**	**3275.2**
综合医院	General Hospitals	109711.5	84619.0	2632.8	60744	1803.1	2428.8
中医医院	Hospital Specialized in Traditional Chinese Medicine	30358.2	29446.6	341.5	12978	253.1	250.4
中西医结合医院	Hospitals Combining Western Medicine with Traditional Chinese Medicine	6203.4	5813.2	282.8	6244	81.8	81.4
民族医院	Nationality Hospitals	185.6	185.6	5.2	219	2.4	2.3
口腔医院	Stomatology Hospitals	2499.3	2403.8	1.8	366	9.4	9.4
眼科医院	Ophthalmology Hospitals	255.3	255.3	30.7	432	11.5	11.5
肿瘤医院	Tumor Hospitals	1422.1	1403.5	78.8	3103	114.6	114.6
心血管病医院	Hospitals for Cardiovascular Diseases	684.7	657.5	3.5	1102	58.6	58.5
胸科医院	Thorax Hospitals	268.2	263.4		533	11.8	11.8
妇(产)科医院	Hospitals for Gynecology and Obstetrics	1605.0	1571.6	6.2	931	46.2	45.6
儿童医院	Children's Hospitals	6123.3	5654.7	16.8	1839	111.7	108.8
精神病医院	Psychiatric Hospitals	1242.5	1227.3	5.8	7291	20.4	20.4
传染病医院	Infectious Disease Hospitals	1267.6	1196.2		1382	46.1	46.1
骨科医院	Hospitals of Orthopedics	384.4	367.6	22.5	889	20.0	19.4
整形外科医院	Orthopaedics Hospitals	135.6	130.5	0.2	328	13.1	13.0
其他专科医院	Other Specialized Hospitals	1150.3	1087.1	17.0	3455	53.9	53.1
护理院	Nursing Centers	0.8	0.8	0.3	100		

资料来源：北京市卫生和计划生育委员会。
Source: Beijing Municipal Commission of Health and Family Planning.

20-5 续表 Continued

项　目	Item	病死率 (%) Case Fatality Rate (%)	病床周转次数 (次) Turnover Beds (time)	病床使用率 (%) Utilization Rate of Beds (%)	出院者平均住院日 (日) Average Hospitalization Period (day)
合　计	**Total**	**1.08**	**32.1**	**80.58**	**10.1**
综合医院	General Hospitals	1.12	40.0	80.73	9.8
中医医院	Hospital Specialized in Traditional Chinese Medicine	1.36	19.3	71.78	13.1
中西医结合医院	Hospitals Combining Western Medicine with Traditional Chinese Medicine	2.67	13.0	75.37	18.3
民族医院	Nationality Hospitals	1.21	10.6	52.27	17.5
口腔医院	Stomatology Hospitals		25.7	57.19	8.1
眼科医院	Ophthalmology Hospitals		26.7	63.82	7.1
肿瘤医院	Tumor Hospitals	0.44	36.9	88.07	8.7
心血管病医院	Hospitals for Cardiovascular Diseases	0.22	53.1	104.79	7.2
胸科医院	Thorax Hospitals	1.28	22.2	99.99	16.5
妇(产)科医院	Hospitals for Gynecology and Obstetrics	0.00	48.9	66.43	4.7
儿童医院	Children's Hospitals	0.09	59.1	100.86	6.0
精神病医院	Psychiatric Hospital	0.78	2.8	98.24	114.0
传染病医院	Infectious Disease Hospitals	1.95	33.4	105.07	11.5
骨科医院	Hospitals of Orthopedics	0.37	21.8	92.81	15.3
整形外科医院	Orthopaedics Hospitals		39.8	66.33	6.1
其他专科医院	Other Specialized Hospitals	1.27	15.4	55.97	12.7
护理院	Nursing Centers				

20-6 全市居民前十位死因顺位、死亡率及构成(2015年)
DEATH RATE AND COMPOSITION OF 10 MAJOR DISEASES (2015)

顺位 No.	死因名称	Cause of Death	死亡率(1/10万) Death Rate (1/100 thousands)	构 成(%) Composition (%)
	全 市	**Total**		
1	恶性肿瘤	Malignant Tumour	176.12	27.43
2	心脏病	Heart Disease	165.21	25.73
3	脑血管病	Cerebrovasular Disease	125.57	19.55
4	呼吸系统疾病	Disease of the Respiratory System	65.04	10.13
5	损伤和中毒	Trauma and Toxicosis	23.03	3.59
6	内分泌、营养、代谢及免疫疾病	Endocrine, Nutrition, Metabolite and Immunity Disease	19.12	2.98
7	消化系统疾病	Disease of the Gigestive System	16.84	2.62
8	神经系统疾病	Neurological Disease	7.65	1.19
9	泌尿生殖系统疾病	Disease of the Genitourinary System	6.00	0.93
10	传染病	Infectious Disease	4.70	0.73
	男 性	**Male**		
1	恶性肿瘤	Malignant Tumour	211.11	29.27
2	心脏病	Heart Disease	175.04	24.27
3	脑血管病	Cerebrovasular Disease	139.49	19.34
4	呼吸系统疾病	Disease of the Respiratory System	74.33	10.30
5	损伤和中毒	Trauma and Toxicosis	27.21	3.77
6	内分泌、营养、代谢及免疫疾病	Endocrine, Nutrition, Metabolite and Immunity Disease	19.25	2.67
7	消化系统疾病	Disease of the Gigestive System	19.22	2.66
8	神经系统疾病	Neurological Disease	8.27	1.15
9	传染病	Infectious Disease	6.23	0.86
10	泌尿生殖系统疾病	Disease of the Genitourinary System	6.16	0.85
	女 性	**Female**		
1	心脏病	Heart Disease	155.35	27.60
2	恶性肿瘤	Malignant Tumour	141.01	25.06
3	脑血管病	Cerebrovasular Disease	111.60	19.83
4	呼吸系统疾病	Disease of the Respiratory System	55.72	9.90
5	内分泌、营养、代谢及免疫疾病	Endocrine, Nutrition, Metabolite and Immunity Disease	19.00	3.38
6	损伤和中毒	Trauma and Toxicosis	18.85	3.35
7	消化系统疾病	Disease of the Gigestive System	14.45	2.57
8	神经系统疾病	Neurological Disease	7.03	1.25
9	泌尿生殖系统疾病	Disease of the Genitourinary System	5.85	1.04
10	传染病	Infectious Disease	3.17	0.56

资料来源：北京市卫生和计划生育委员会。
Source: Beijing Municipal Commission of Health and Family Planning.

20-7 全市主要健康指标情况(1978-2015年)
MAJOR HEALTH INDICATIONS OF BEIJING (1978-2015)

年 份 Year	婴 儿 死亡率 (‰) Infant Mortality (‰)	城 郊 Suburban Districts	远 县 Counties	新生儿 死亡率 (‰) Newborn Baby Mortality (‰)	城 郊 Suburban Districts	远 县 Counties	孕产妇 死亡率 (1/10万) Pregnant & Lying-in Women Mortality (1/100000)	城 郊 Suburban Districts	远 县 Counties	甲乙类传染病发病率 (1/10万) Incidence Rate of Catogory A and B Epidemics (1/100000)
1978	17.11	10.34	21.15	12.21	7.35	15.60	31.00	5.00	53.00	
1979	16.97	12.81	19.43	10.08	8.00	12.77	34.70	13.10	41.30	1584.25
1980	14.79	10.40	17.73	10.24	7.12	12.81	26.30	12.50	34.60	2165.23
1981	13.84	9.69	17.26	9.22	6.00	11.85	48.50	18.70	76.10	2225.71
1982	12.97	9.95	15.19	8.02	6.20	9.76	24.50	21.70	32.60	2193.16
1983	13.79	10.54	17.24	8.78	6.22	11.84	28.10	24.30	45.10	1904.55
1984	10.98	10.33	12.49	7.78	6.72	9.20	16.80	11.40	41.50	1666.68
1985	13.94	10.02	18.85	10.41	6.40	15.97	22.90	24.30	35.10	1335.23
1986	16.05	13.42	19.24	12.13	8.97	15.41	30.50	22.90	43.10	1120.19
1987	15.56	12.63	18.23	11.08	8.01	14.02	26.60	14.80	33.30	826.51
1988	14.98	11.71	17.92	10.48	7.96	13.20	24.80	25.40	32.40	640.98
1989	14.96	11.59	18.30	10.53	8.08	13.23	34.50	3.90	55.80	547.61
1990	11.66	10.12	12.55	8.49	7.43	9.38	25.00	13.00	30.50	509.55
1991	12.46	11.94	13.11	8.56	7.83	9.47	24.00	23.80	24.20	448.23
1992	12.12	10.81	14.43	8.93	7.72	11.18	30.10	30.20	29.80	385.98
1993	10.38	10.68	9.93	7.21	7.28	7.10	16.50	21.10	9.60	356.66
1994	10.93	12.09	9.43	7.29	7.57	6.94	18.94	21.02	16.26	374.31
1995	11.45	14.23	8.20	7.52	8.91	5.90	22.27	23.89	20.36	309.99
1996	10.05	11.57	8.13	6.97	7.61	6.17	15.32	11.45	20.19	340.24
1997	9.45	10.49	8.05	6.36	6.75	5.83	23.69	25.25	21.60	294.41
1998	7.58	9.07	5.75	5.53	6.46	4.39	10.46	10.87	9.97	306.37
1999	7.95	7.78	8.38	5.94	5.74	6.45	17.53	15.69	22.06	308.10
2000	5.36	6.29	4.05	3.70	4.26	2.91	9.70	7.10	13.38	301.19
2001	6.01	6.26	5.62	4.05	4.16	3.89	11.71	13.85	8.45	276.85
2002	5.56	5.57	5.54	3.70	3.65	3.77	15.12	16.24	13.29	282.95
2003	5.89	5.91	5.83	3.83	3.56	4.33	15.60	6.92	31.35	228.00
2004	4.61	4.51	4.79	3.49	3.42	3.62	15.19	17.69	10.66	408.03
2005	4.35	4.08	4.84	3.29	3.03	3.79	15.91	7.33	31.95	445.91
2006	4.66	3.96	6.04	3.42	2.99	4.26	7.87	7.12	9.36	448.70
2007	3.89	3.50	4.72	2.65	2.31	3.39	16.74	18.92	12.10	421.02
2008	3.70	3.49	4.21	2.45	2.41	2.52	18.52	15.86	24.76	312.99
2009	3.49	3.28	4.02	2.47	2.37	2.73	14.55	12.56	19.49	339.89
2010	3.29	2.95	4.25	2.06	1.94	2.42	12.14	8.95	21.23	268.99
2011	2.84	2.62	3.43	1.88	1.77	2.17	9.09	9.99	6.67	226.76
2012	2.87	2.48	3.87	1.91	1.65	2.60	6.05	4.20	10.82	174.45
2013	2.33	2.19	2.69	1.52	1.48	1.63	9.45	6.51	17.20	155.87
2014	2.33	2.23	2.57	1.46	1.46	1.58	7.19	5.53	11.27	165.49
2015	2.42	2.11	3.26	1.52	1.33	2.02	8.69	7.61	11.54	150.86

注：城郊包括东城区、西城区、朝阳区、丰台区、石景山区、海淀区、门头沟区、房山区；远县包括通州区、昌平区、顺义区、大兴区、怀柔区、平谷区、密云区、延庆区。

资料来源：北京市卫生和计划生育委员会。

Note: Suburban districts include Dongcheng, Xicheng, Chaoyang, Fengtai, Shijingshan, Haidian, Mentougou, and Fangshan Districts. Counties include Tongzhou, Changping, Shunyi, and Daxing Districts, Huairou, Pinggu, Miyun and Yanqing Counties.

Source: Beijing Municipal Commission of Health and Family Planning.

20-8 主要年份体育场地情况
SITUATION OF THE GYMNASIUMS AND STADIUMS IN MAIN YEARS

单位：个 (unit)

年 份 Year	合 计 Total	#体育场 Stadiums	#体育馆 Gymnasiums	#游泳场馆 Natatoriums	#室 内 Indoor	#各种训练房 Exercise Rooms
1950	19	1				2
1955	61	1		2	2	10
1960	124	2		4	3	19
1970	188	2	2	8	3	24
1975	234	3	2	11	4	28
1980	293	3	2	12	4	32
1985	405	4	2	20	8	54
1990	780	12	12	49	26	153
1995	1381	18	18	88	56	291
2000	2815	35	24	214	161	863
2001	3500	42	27	283	216	1101
2002	4176	57	33	334	263	1358
2003	6100	93	36	443	371	1729
2004	6104	93	36	443	371	1729
2005	6112	93	36	446	374	1731
2006	6122	93	36	446	374	1734
2007	6146	94	37	446	374	1736
2008	6149	94	37	446	374	1739
2009	6149	94	37	446	374	1739
2010	6151	94	37	446	374	1741
2011	6151	94	37	446	374	1741
2012	6156	94	37	447	375	1742
2013	20075	131	70	590	548	2836
2014	20075	131	70	590	548	2836
2015	20075	131	70	590	548	2836

注：本表2013年以后数据口径为第六次全国体育场地普查数据资料，此次普查时点为2013年12月31日。

资料来源：北京市体育局。

Note: The data in the table after 2013 werr collected according to the sixth national census on gymnasiums and stadiums. The date of this census is December 31st, 2013.

Source: Beijing Municipal Bureau of Sports.

20-9 群众体育活动情况
ACTIVITIES OF MASS SPORTS

项目	Item	2015	2014
晨晚练辅导站 (个)	Instruction Stations of Morning and Evening Exercises (unit)	8990	7981
青少年体育俱乐部数 (个)	Number of Teenager Sport Clubs (unit)	200	211
社会体育指导员 (人)	Social Sport Instructors (person)	48858	45522
社区健身俱乐部 (个)	Community Fitness Clubs (unit)	154	144
体育生活化社区 (个)	Life-oriented Sports Communities (unit)	2778	2113

资料来源：北京市体育局。
Source: Beijing Municipal Bureau of Sports.

20-10 运动员、裁判员情况
ATHLETES AND REFEREES

单位：人 (person)

项目	Item	2015	#女性 Females	2014	#女性 Females
分等级运动员发展人数	**Number of Graded Athletes**	**1449**	**588**	**1826**	**793**
国际级运动健将	World-class Athletes	15	9	12	3
国家级运动健将	National Grade Athletes	118	62	93	38
一级	First Grade Athletes	374	155	528	274
二级	Second Grade Athletes	942	362	1193	478
分等级裁判员发展人数	**Number of Graded Referees**	**1790**	**438**	**1468**	**437**
国家级	National Grade Referees			36	9
一级	First Grade Referees	320	91	282	112
二级	Second Grade Referees	1470	347	1150	316

资料来源：北京市体育局。
Source: Beijing Municipal Bureau of Sports.

20-11 运动员获奖牌情况(2015年) STATISTICS FOR MEDALS WON (2015)

单位：块 (piece)

项目	Item	金牌 Gold	银牌 Silver	铜牌 Copper
合计	**Total**	**66**	**49**	**36**
国际比赛	International Competitions	11	7	2
国内比赛	Domestic Competitions	55	42	34

资料来源：北京市体育局。
Source: Beijing Municipal Bureau of Sports.

20-12 体育彩票 SPORTS LOTTERY

项目	Item	2015	2014
电脑体育彩票销售个数 (个)	Number of Computer Sports Lottery Tickets Sold (unit)	2680	2420
体育彩票发行额 (万元)	Circulation of Sports Lottery (10000 yuan)	502981	624258
体育彩票公益金提取额 (万元)	Public Welfare Funds Drawn from Sports Lottery (10000 yuan)	133204	153617

资料来源：北京市体育局。
Source: Beijing Municipal Bureau of Sports.

主要统计指标解释

卫 生

卫生机构 指从卫生行政部门取得《医疗机构执业许可证》，或从民政、工商行政、机构编制管理部门取得法人单位登记证书，为社会提供医疗保健、疾病控制、卫生监督服务或从事医学科研和医学在职培训等工作的单位。

卫生技术人员 指由卫生机构支付工资的全部固定职工和合同制职工中现任职务为卫生技术工作的专业人员，不包括从事管理工作的人员。

执业医师和注册护士 指领取医师执业证书和注册护士证书的人员，不包括从事管理工作的医师和护士。

死亡率（死因死亡率） 是指某种原因（如疾病）所致的死亡人数占户籍人口比重。

婴儿死亡率 指某地区一年内每 1000 名活产婴儿与未满 1 岁的婴儿死亡人数之比。婴儿死亡率可以衡量一个国家或地区经济文化、居民健康状况和卫生保健事业发展情况，同时也是人口平均期望寿命研究的重要内容。

5岁以下儿童死亡率 指某地区一年内每1000名活产婴儿与未满 5 岁儿童死亡人数之比。5 岁以下儿童死亡率是目前国际上公认的反映儿童生存状况的重要指标。

孕产妇死亡率 指某年某地每十万活产中的孕产妇死亡比例。同婴儿死亡率一样，孕产妇死亡率是评价某一地区社会发展状况的重要指标，它的高低与社会经济状况、孕产妇社会环境及卫生保健服务有直接的联系。

体 育

体育场地 指专门用于体育训练、比赛和健身活动的，有一定投资的公益性或经营性体育建筑设施，包括必要的附属功能用房。

晨晚练辅导站 是指本市公民自愿参加，在本市体育场馆、公园、街道、街心花园等公共场所设立的，利用早晚时间，以开展健身活动为目的的群众体育健身场所。

青少年体育俱乐部数 指创建单位利用自己所拥有的体育场馆、人才等资源建立起来的具有社会公益性的新型社会化青少年体育组织。

社会体育指导员 指在竞技体育、学校体育、部队体育以外的群众性体育活动中从事技能传授、锻炼指导和组织管理的工作人员。

专项球类活动场地 为满足不同人群特别是青少年的健身需求，而建设的专项球类活动场地，分篮球广场、笼式多功能球场、乒乓球长廊三种类型。

社区健身俱乐部 指“城市社区居民根据共同的目的和兴趣自愿组成的，以辖区内特定的体育场地设施为依托，经常开展体育活动，且隶属于街道办事处或社区居委会的公益性群众体育组织。”

等级运动员人数 指经考核正式批准授予等级运动员称号的人数。运动员等级分为国际级运动健将、国家级运动健将、一级运动员、二级运动员、三级运动员、少年级运动员。

等级裁判员人数 指经考核正式批准授予等级裁判员称号的人数。裁判员等级分为国际级裁判、国家级裁判、一级裁判、二级裁判、三级裁判。

运动员获奖牌情况 指当年北京市运动员在世界比赛、亚洲比赛、全国比赛中获得金、银、铜牌的数量。

Explanatory Notes on Main Statistical Indicators

Health

Healthcare Institutions refer to institutions granted with *License for Medical Institution* by the health administration authority, or granted with certificate of corporate unit by the civil affair, administration for industry and commerce, management authority of institutional organization, and providing medical service and healthcare, disease control, health supervision service or carrying out medical research and education, and so on.

Medical Technical Personnel refer to all fixed employees and of contract-based employees, professional personnel in health technology, who receive pays from health institutions, excluding personnel engaged in management.

Certified Doctors and Registered Nurses refer to personnel who have received a physician practicing certificate and certified nurse certificate, excluding physicians and nurses engaged in management.

Mortality (Cause-specific Death Rate) means the proportion of persons dead due to certain cause (such as disease) in the permanent population.

Infant Mortality means the rate of dead infants under 1 year old to 1,000 live infants in an area in a year. Infant death rate measures the development of economy, culture, citizen health and health care in a country or region. It is also an important component of study on average life expectancy of population.

Mortality of Children under 5 means the rate of dead children under 5 years old to 1,000 live infants in an area in a year. This is an important indicator now internationally recognized to reflect the survival status of children.

Pregnant and Lying-in Women Mortality refers to the rate of dead pregnant and lying-in women to 100,000 live pregnant and lying-in women in an area in a year. This is an important indicator to evaluate the social development status in an area. The figure of this indicator is directly related to the social and economic status, social environment and health care service for pregnant and lying-in women.

Sports

Sports Venues refer to sports building facilities for public welfare or operating purpose, specially used for sports training, games and fitness activities, and with certain investment.

Instruction Station of Morning and Evening Exercise refer to public sports and fitness sites located in sports gyms and stadiums, parks, streets, street parks and other public sites in a city, where the citizens in the city participate in voluntarily fitness activities in the morning or evening.

Number of Teenager Sports Clubs means the number of new-type social sports organizations for teenagers in the nature of socialistic public welfare, which are established by the builder with its own resources such as sports gyms and stadiums and human resource.

Social Sports Instructors refer to working personnel who carry out skill teaching, exercise instruction, organization and management in mass sports activities other than athletic sports, school sports and army sports.

Special Ball Game Venue and Facilities are special venues for ball activities built to meet the fitness need of different population, especially teenagers, consisting of three types, i.e. basketball squares, multi-purpose cage-shaped courts, and table tennis corridors.

Community Fitness Clubs refer to "mass sports organizations in the nature of public welfare, which are formed by residents in urban communities voluntarily according to their common purpose and interest, based on specific sports venue facilities in the jurisdiction, for frequent sports activities, and under the jurisdiction of sub-district administrative office or community neighborhood committee."

Number of Graded Athletes means the number of athletes formally granted with the title of graded athlete upon examination. Grades of athletes include international master sportsman, national maser sportsman, grade-I athlete, grade-II athlete, grade-III athlete and juvenile athlete.

Number of Graded Referees means the number of referees formally granted with the title of graded referees upon examination. Grades of referees include international referee, national referee, grade-I referee, grade-II referee and grade-III referee.

Medals Won by Athletes mean the number of gold, silver and copper medals won by athletes of Beijing in world games, Asian games and national games.

21

北京统计年鉴2016　BEIJING STATISTICAL YEARBOOK

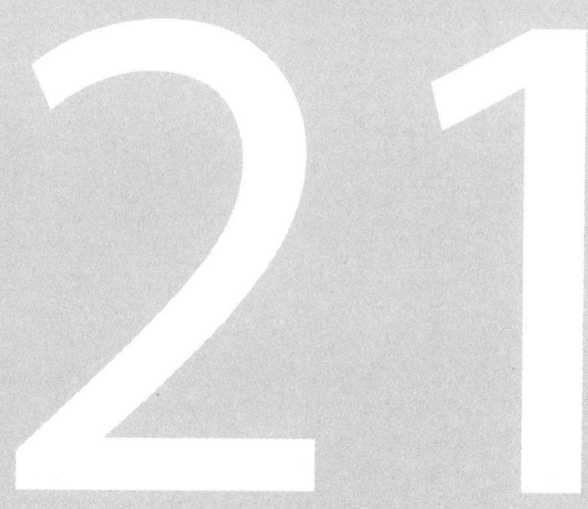

社会福利、社区、政法及其他
SOCIAL WELFARE, COMMUNITY, LAW AND OTHERS

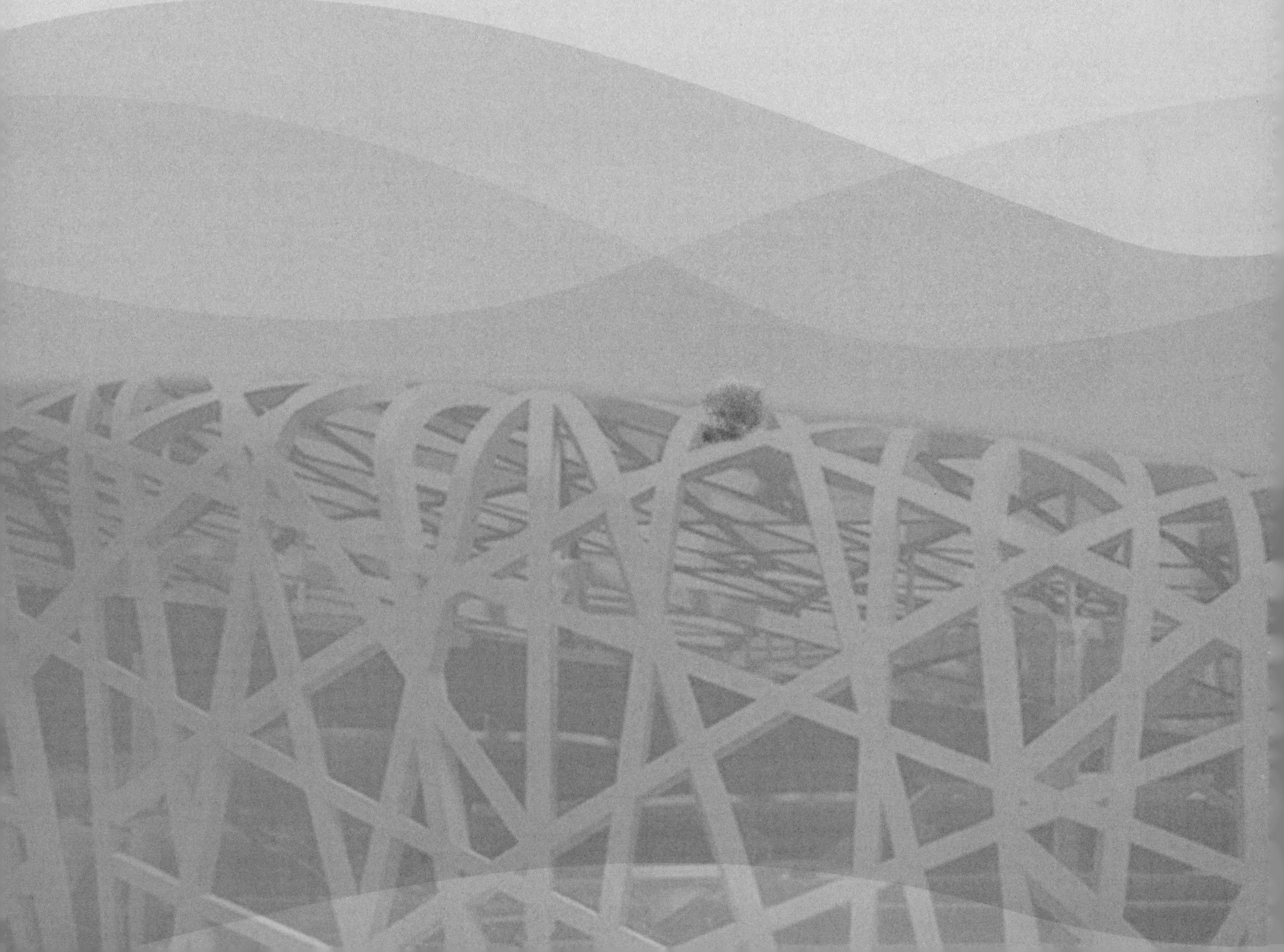

简要说明

一、本章资料的主要内容

本章资料主要包括社会活动参与、公检法司、民政事业、劳动保障、残疾人事业、妇女及儿童发展规划监测情况等内容。

二、本章资料的数据来源

1.社会活动参与的内容主要包括历届北京市人大代表和政协委员人数及议案情况、妇联组织和工会组织情况等。资料分别由北京市人民代表大会常务委员会、中国人民政治协商会议北京市委员会、北京市妇女联合会和北京市总工会提供。

2.公检法司的资料主要包括公安机关的刑事案件立案情况和治安案件查处情况，交通、火灾事故情况，检察机关的办案情况，人民法院审理案件和收结案情况，以及司法局提供的律师、公证、调解工作等情况。资料分别由北京市公安局、北京市高级人民法院、北京市人民检察院和北京市司法局提供。

3.民政事业和劳动保障统计资料主要包括社会福利企事业机构、人员、优抚和社会救济情况、婚姻登记情况。资料分别由北京市民政局、北京市人力资源和社会保障局提供。

4.残疾人资料主要包括残疾人康复、教育、就业、扶贫和残联组织建设等情况。资料由北京市残疾人联合会提供。

5.妇女与儿童发展规划监测资料主要包括妇女参与决策和管理、就业、教育、健康、法律保护等情况；儿童的健康、教育、法律保护社会生活环境等情况。资料由北京市统计局依据部门统计报表资料整理提供。

6.安全生产情况由北京市行政工商管理局、北京市食品药品监督管理局、北京市公安交通管理局、北京市安全生产监督管理局提供。

Brief Introduction

I. Main Content

This chapter consists of statistics for social activity participation, public security institutions, procuratorates, courts, judicial authorities, civil affairs, labor security, undertakings for disabled people, women and children development planning and monitoring.

II. Data Sources

1. Statistics for social activity participation consist of the numbers of deputies and proposals at people's congress and political consulting conferences of Beijing in previous years, women's federation and organizations, and labor unions. Data were provided respectively by the Standing Committee of Beijing Municipal People's Congress, Beijing Committee of CPPCC, Beijing Women's Federation, and Beijing Federation of Labor Unions.

2. Statistics for public security institutions, procuratorates, courts, and judicial authorities cover criminal cases put on the record of public security organs as well as public security investigation and punishments, traffic accidents and fires, case settlements in procuratorates, cases accepted and settled by people's courts, information on lawyers, notary, mediation provided by juridical bureaus. Data were provided by Beijing Municipal Bureau of Public Security, People's High Court of Beijing, People's Procuratorate of Beijing, and Beijing Municipal Bureau of Justice.

3. Statistics for civil affairs and labor security mainly consist of social welfare institutions, personnel, social relief, special care, and marriage registration. Data were provided by Beijing Municipal Bureau of Civil Affairs, and Beijing Municipal Bureau of Human Resources and Social Security.

4. Statistics for disabled persons mainly include information on rehabilitation, education, employment and poverty reduction, and building of federations for disabled persons, etc. Data were provided by Beijing Disabled Persons' Federation.

5. Supervision data on women and children development are composed of women's participation in decision making and management, employment, education, health, legal protection, and so on; children's health, education, legal protection, social living environment, etc. Data were provided respectively by Beijing Municipal Bureau of Statistics in accordance with statistic reporting system of different departments.

6. Safe production data were provided by Beijing Administration for Industry and Commerce, Beijing Municipal Food and Drug Administration, Beijing Municipal Bureau of Traffic Management, Beijing Administration of Work Safety.

21-1 北京市历年社会保障相关待遇标准(1994-2015年)
HISTORICAL LEVEL ON SOCIAL WELFARE IN BEIJING (1994-2015)

单位：元/月 (yuan/month)

年份 Year	标准 Standard	职工最低工资 Minimum Wages of Employed Persons	失业保险金最低标准 Minimum Unemployment Insurance	城市居民最低生活保障标准 Minimum Subsistence for Allowance Urban Residents	企业退休人员基本养老金最低标准 Minimum of Basic Pensions for Retired Persons	企业退职人员基本养老金最低标准 Minimum of Basic Pensions for Resigned Persons	企业退养人员基本养老金最低标准 Minimum of Basic Pensions for Early-retired Persons
1994		210					
1995		240	174				
1996		270	189	170	263	202	170
1997		290	203	190	293	232	200
1998		310	217	200	336	265	233
1999年第一次	First-time in 1999	320	224	210			
1999年第二次	Second-time in 1999	400	291	273	396	335	288
2000		412	300	280	421	360	308
2001		435	305	285	441	380	317
2002		465	326	290	466	405	367
2003		465	326	290	466	405	367
2004年第一次	First-time in 2004	495					
2004年第二次	Second-time in 2004	545	347	290	510	443	402
2005		580	382	300	563	488	443
2006		640	392	310	620	537	487
2007		730	422	330	675	592	527
2008		800	502	390	775	682	607
2009		800	562	410	900	800	700
2010		960	632	430	1000	900	800
2011		1160	782	500	1100	1000	900
2012		1260	842	520	1210	1100	1000
2013		1400	892	580	1330	1210	1100
2014		1560	1012	650	1463	1331	1210
2015		1720	1122	710	1609	1464	1331

资料来源：城市居民最低生活保障标准由北京市民政局提供，本表其他资料由北京市人力资源和社会保障局提供。

Source: Data on minimum subsistence allowance for urban residents was provided by Beijing Municipal Bureau of Civil Affairs,others were provided by Beijing Municipal Bureau of Human Resources and Social Security.

21-2 北京市历年参加社会保障情况(1995-2015年)

单位：万人

年 份 Year	参加职工基本养老保险人数 Employed Persons Participating in Basic Pension Insurance	参加职工基本医疗保险人数 Staff and Workers Participating in Basic Medical Care Insurance	参加失业保险人数 Employed Persons Participating in Unemployment Insurance	参加工伤保险人数 Employed Persons Participating in Work-related Injury Insurance	参加生育保险人数 Employed Persons Participating in Maternity Insurance
1995	261.1		219.8		
1996	252.0		214.5		
1997	264.3		214.0		
1998	359.2		222.9		
1999	379.0		289.0		
2000	391.6		287.8	212.0	
2001	425.9	210.2	287.2	212.7	
2002	436.2	353.8	299.5	221.0	
2003	448.5	436.1	306.6	242.9	
2004	460.0	484.0	308.0	259.0	
2005	520.0	574.8	394.6	328.9	226.1
2006	604.1	679.5	482.2	465.3	263.3
2007	671.7	783.0	535.3	609.2	290.6
2008	758.1	871.0	614.3	666.5	324.1
2009	827.7	938.4	675.7	747.1	346.8
2010	982.5	1063.7	774.2	823.8	372.2
2011	1091.9	1188.0	881.0	862.4	395.3
2012	1206.4	1279.7	1006.7	897.2	844.7
2013	1311.3	1354.8	1025.1	920.3	883.2
2014	1392.6	1431.3	1057.1	961.0	915.6
2015	1424.2	1475.7	1082.3	1020.1	941.6

注：1. 2001年开始设置基本医疗保险指标，以前年份称为大病统筹，2000年参加大病统筹人数为232.6万人。
2. 2005年7月1日《北京市企业职工生育保险规定》开始实施。全市农村社会养老保险1992年试点，1996年全市正式实施。
3. 从2006年起，农村最低生活保障人数不含农村五保供养人员。
4. 农村居民参加城乡居民养老保险人数在2007年及以前为参加农村社会养老保险人数口径；2008年为参加新型农村社会养老保险人数；2009年及以后为参加城乡居民养老保险人数中农村参保人数。

资料来源：城乡居民享受最低生活保障人数来源于北京市民政局；参加新型农村合作医疗人数和参合率来源于北京市卫生和计划生育委员会；其他资料来源于北京市人力资源和社会保障局。

SOCIAL SECURITY PARTICIPATION IN BEIJING (1995-2015)

(10000 persons)

参加城乡居民基本养老保险人数 Residents Participating in Basic Pension Insurance	#农村居民 Rural Residents	参加城镇居民基本医疗保险人数 Residents Participating in Basic Urban Medical Insurance	参加新型农村合作医疗人数 Residents Participating in New-type Rural Cooperative Medicare	城市居民最低生活保障人数 Persons Receiving Subsistence Allowances in Urban Areas	农村最低生活保障人数 Persons Receiving Subsistence Allowances in Rural Areas	新型农村合作医疗参合率 (%) Percentage of Persons Participating in New-type Rural Cooperative Medicare
	29.2			0.9		
	37.4			0.9		
	41.2			2.8		
	34.4			4.3	1.2	
	38.5			6.7	1.6	
	34.7			7.6	1.8	
	32.0			12.0	5.4	
	33.6			16.1	6.7	
	36.8		234.0	16.1	7.5	71.9
	40.6		250.4	15.5	7.8	80.3
	44.8		261.0	15.2	7.6	86.9
	49.1		268.5	14.8	7.8	88.9
	127.5		272.5	14.5	7.9	92.9
	153.9		274.9	14.7	8.0	95.7
168.5	159.3	143.7	278.5	13.7	7.7	96.7
173.4	163.7	159.8	276.8	11.7	7.0	97.7
177.3	167.0	151.9	267.5	11.0	6.3	98.1
180.1	168.7	160.1	254.4	10.4	6.0	98.0
186.2	173.4	173.0	242.6	8.9	5.1	99.6
187.6	174.0	181.0	223.9	8.5	4.9	99.3

Note: a) The basic medicare indicator was set from 2001. Before that it was called general healthcare program for major diseases which covered 2.326 million people in 2000.

b) Regulations of Beijing on Maternity Insurance for Enterprise Employed Persons became effective from July 1st, 2005. Pilots were made for social pension program in rural area of Beijing in 1992. The program was formally effective in 1996 across the city.

c) Rural persons receiving minimum subsistence allowance excluded rural persons enjoying five guarantees from 2006.

d) In and before 2007, the number of rural people participating in urban and rural pension insurance covered the people participating in rural social pension insurance; in 2008, this figure covered the people participating in new-type rural social pension insurance; since 2009, this figure covered the rural people of those participating in the urban and rural pension insurance.

Source: Figures on persons receiving subsistence allowances in urban and rural areas are from Beijing Municipal Bureau of Civil Affairs; Figures on persons participating in new-type rural medicare and percentage of these persons are from Beijing Municipal Commission of Health and Family Planning; other data are from Beijing Municipal Bureau of Human Resources and Social Security.

21-3 城镇职工参加社会保险情况(2015年)
PARTICIPATION OF EMPLOYED PERSONS FOR SOCIAL SECURITY INSURANCE PROGRAMS IN THE URBAN AREA (2015)

项目	Item	职工基本养老保险 Basic Pension Insurance		职工基本医疗保险 Basic Medical Insurance	
		单位个数(个) Number of Entities (unit)	人数(人) Number of Persons (person)	单位个数(个) Number of Entities (unit)	人数(人) Number of Persons (person)
合计	**Total**	**412187**	**14242483**	**398401**	**14756583**
按登记注册类型分	**By Registration Type**				
国有	State-owned	6622	1994261	5502	1899323
集体	Collectively-owned	6148	254774	5148	248010
其他	Others	399417	11993448	387751	12609250
按隶属关系划分	**By Affiliation**				
中央单位	Central	7155	1862890	6510	1798642
地方单位	Local	405032	12379593	391891	12957941

资料来源：北京市人力资源和社会保障局。
Source: Beijing Municipal Bureau of Human Resources and Social Security.

21-3 续表 Continued

项目	Item	失业保险 Unemployment Insurance		工伤保险 Industrial Injury Insurance		生育保险 Maternity Insurance	
		单位个数(个) Number of Entities (unit)	人数(人) Number of Persons (person)	单位个数(个) Number of Entities (unit)	人数(人) Number of Persons (person)	单位个数(个) Number of Entities (unit)	人数(人) Number of Persons (person)
合计	**Total**	**409600**	**10822872**	**422375**	**10200565**	**406643**	**9416495**
按登记注册类型分	**By Registration Type**						
国有	State-owned	5960	996293	6136	1013654	5999	955312
集体	Collectively-owned	5588	129743	5790	133513	5551	117599
其他	Others	398052	9696836	410449	9053398	395093	8343584
按隶属关系划分	**By Affiliation**						
中央单位	Central	6865	1456453	7199	1405252	6865	1194285
地方单位	Local	402735	9366419	415176	8795313	399778	8222210

资料来源：北京市人力资源和社会保障局。
Source: Beijing Municipal Bureau of Human Resources and Social Security.

21-4 城乡居民参加社会保险情况(2010-2015年)
PARTICIPATION OF RURAL AND URBAN RESIDENTS FOR SOCIAL SECURITY INSURANCE PROGRAMS (2010-2015)

单位：万人 (10000 persons)

年 份 Year	城乡居民基本养老保险人数 Basic Pension Insurance		城镇居民基本医疗保险人数 Basic Medical Care Insurance			
	合 计 Total	#农村居民 Rural Residents	合 计 Total	学生儿童 Students and Children	无保障老人 Unguaranteed Aged Persons	无业居民 Unemployed Residents
2010	168.5	159.3	143.7	121.3	17.7	4.7
2011	173.4	163.7	159.8	135.5	19.1	5.3
2012	177.3	167.0	151.9	128.6	18.5	4.8
2013	180.1	168.7	160.1	137.5	18.8	3.7
2014	186.2	173.4	173.0	149.8	19.7	3.6
2015	187.6	174.0	181.0	157.7	19.8	3.4

资料来源：北京市人力资源和社会保障局。
Source: Beijing Municipal Bureau of Human Resources and Social Security.

21-5 优抚及主要救助对象情况
STATISTICS FOR PERSONS RECEIVING SPECIAL CARE AND RELIEF

单位：人 (person)

项 目	Item	人 数 Number of Persons		2015年为2014年% 2015 as % of 2014
		2015	2014	
抚恤、补助优抚对象总人数	**Total Number of Persons Receiving Pensions, Subsidies, and Special Care Treatment**	**44391**	**44537**	**99.7**
定期抚恤人数	Number of Persons Receiving Regular Pensions	1572	1708	92.0
定期补助人数	Number of Persons Receiving Regular Subsidies	31107	31392	99.1
伤残人数	Total Number of Disabled Persons	11712	11437	102.4
医疗救助人次数	**Total Number of Persons Receiving Medical Assistance**	**97698**	**88873**	**109.9**
社会救助对象总人数	**Total Number of Persons Receiving Social Relief**	**138161**	**144653**	**95.5**
城市居民最低生活保障人数	Number of Persons Receiving Subsistence Allowances in Urban Areas	84860	89135	95.2
农村居民最低生活保障人数	Number of Persons Receiving Subsistence Allowances in Rural Areas	48850	51324	95.2
农村五保供养人数	Rural Residents Enjoying Five Guarantees	4451	4194	106.1
农村集中五保供养人数	Collective Rural Residents Enjoying Five Guarantees	1837	1964	93.5
农村分散五保供养人数	Scattered Rural Residents Enjoying Five Guarantees	2614	2230	117.2

注：“农村居民最低生活保障人数”不含“农村五保供养人数”。
资料来源：北京市民政局。
Note: Number of persons receiving subsistence allowances in rural areas excludes "Rural Residents Enjoying the Five Guarantees".
Source: Beijing Municipal Bureau of Civil Affairs.

21-6 社会福利事业、社区情况情况
STATISTICS FOR SOCIAL WELFARE AND COMMUNITY

项目		Item		2015	2014	2015年为2014年% 2015 as % of 2014
社区服务机构数	(个)	Number of Service Facilities in Urban Communities	(unit)	11528	11134	103.5
#社区服务中心	(个)	Community Service Centers	(unit)	199	193	103.1
社区服务志愿者组织数	(个)	Number of Community Service Volunteer Organizations	(unit)	11801	10253	115.1
城市便民利民服务网点数	(个)	Number of Urban Convenient Service Outlets	(unit)	5247	10372	50.6
社会福利企业单位数	(个)	Number of Social Welfare Enterprises	(unit)	528	574	92.0
社会福利企业年末职工人数	(人)	Year-end Employed Persons in Social Welfare Enterprise	(person)	23936	26179	91.4
#残疾职工	(人)	Disabled Employed Persons	(person)	9649	10443	92.4

资料来源：北京市民政局。
Source: Beijing Municipal Buresu of Civil Affairs.

21-7 收养性单位情况(2015年)
STATISTICS ON ADOPTING INSTITUTIONS (2015)

项目		Item		合计	#光荣院 Homes for Disabled Veterans	#社会福利院 Social Welfare Institutions	#儿童福利院 Children's Welfare Institutions	#福利类精神病院和医院 Welfare Mental Hospitals and Hospitals	#城市养老服务机构 Urban Elderly Care Agencies	#农村养老服务机构 Rural Elderly Care Agencies
单位数	(个)	Institutions	(unit)	470	10	9	10	1	167	273
职工人数	(人)	Employed Persons	(person)	12884	185	1090	485	171	5580	5373
床位数	(张)	Beds	(unit)	92244	662	3078	1460	150	33829	53065
年末在院人数	(人)	Persons Received	(person)	36523	138	2882	1174	27	14529	17773
#自费	(人)	Self-supported	(person)	31034	24	2023	104	27	13446	15410

资料来源：北京市民政局。
Source: Beijing Municipal Buresu of Civil Affairs.

21-8 离婚、青少年刑事案犯情况
STATISTICS FOR DIVORCE AND JUVENILE CRIMINAL CASES

项目		Item		2015	2014
婚姻家庭纠纷案件数(结案)	(件)	Marriage and Family Disputes (Closed)	(case)	33694	30542
#离婚案件数	(件)	Divorce Cases	(case)	21799	20159
#调离案件数	(件)	Cases of Divorce Reconciled	(case)	6113	6464
#判离案件数	(件)	Cases of Divorce Judged	(case)	3082	2971
建立少年法庭个数	(个)	Juvenile Courts Established	(unit)	20	20
青少年罪犯人数	(人)	Teenager Offenders	(person)	5215	6372
14周岁以上不满16周岁罪犯人数	(人)	Teenager Offenders 14-16	(person)	29	73
16周岁以上不满18周岁罪犯人数	(人)	Teenager Offenders 16-18	(person)	444	772
18周岁以上不满25周岁罪犯人数	(人)	Teenager Offenders 18-25	(person)	4742	5527
青少年刑事案犯占全部刑事案犯的比重	(%)	Teenager Criminal Offenders as % of Total Criminal Offenders	(%)	22.06	24.64

资料来源：北京市高级人民法院。
Source: The People's High Court of Beijing.

21-9 婚姻登记(1981-2015年)
BASIC STATISTICS FOR MARRIAGE AND DIVORCE REGISTRATIONS (1981-2015)

年份 Year	结婚对数(对) Registered Marriages (couple)	#涉外及华侨、港澳台居民登记结婚对数 Registered Marriages Involving Foreigners and Citizens of Hong Kong, Macao and Taiwan	初婚总人数(人) First Marriages (person)	离婚对数(对) Registered Divorces (couple)	#民政部门登记离婚对数 Divorces Registered in the Civil Affair Department (couple)
1981	200352		392855	5170	1780
1982	141253		265834	5359	1581
1983	117976			5322	1465
1984	113362		218009	5654	1387
1985	134462		258256	5874	1746
1986	143105		273634	7541	2474
1987	149952		285803	8916	3218
1988	113333		212070	10664	4198
1989	103829		190978	12515	5174
1990	92988		168304	14748	5791
1991	91979		166579	15287	6483
1992	89095		159588	15567	6477
1993	89938		160127	17829	7589
1994	90379		161972	19928	8327
1995	85511		149878	20160	8096
1996	86803		147855	20716	8225
1997	84208		145099	22257	8628
1998	85534		148026	23708	9381
1999	83312		141740	23922	8502
2000	80212		135620	26616	6384
2001	79385	873	133259	27683	5425
2002	76136	606	126371	27691	5810
2003	93526	761	158729	30637	10142
2004	126436	974	214443	32657	21013
2005	96596	937	158736	34244	23991
2006	171286	1172	294223	35505	24954
2007	117926	991	193387	36622	26432
2008	147516	1165	246309	37619	27277
2009	181771	1176	305803	41299	29998
2010	138104	1085	222269	43970	32595
2011	173238	1260	288406	43521	32999
2012	174114	1242	287436	48575	38243
2013	163676	1070	251636	64610	54536
2014	170027	1149	253774	65627	56192
2015	166018	1018	229546	82195	73000

注：离婚对数包括在民政部门登记的对数和经法院调离和判离的对数。
资料来源：北京市民政局、北京市高级人民法院。
Note: Registered divorces include those registered in the civil affair department and those mediated and judged in courts.
Source: Beijing Municipal Bureau of Civil Affairs, and The People's High Court of Beijing.

21-10 婚姻登记情况
BASIC STATISTICS ON MARRIAGE AND DIVORCE REGISTRATIONS

项　目		Item		2015	2014	2015年为2014年% 2015 as % of 2014
登记结婚对数	**（对）**	**Registered Marriages**	**(couple)**	**166018**	**170027**	**97.6**
按婚前状况分		**By Pre-marriage Status**				
初婚人数	（人）	First Marriages	(person)	229546	253774	90.5
再婚人数	（人）	Remarriages	(person)	102490	86280	118.8
#女　性	（人）	Females	(person)	49274	41213	119.6
按居住地分		**By Place of Residence**				
内地居民登记结婚对数	（对）	Registered Marriages in Mainland	(couple)	165000	168878	97.7
涉外及华侨、港澳台居民登记结婚对数	（对）	Registered Marriages with involving Foreigner and the Citizens of Hong Kong, Macao and Taiwan	(couple)	1018	1149	88.6
内地居民	（人）	Mainland Residents	(person)	933	1052	88.7
#女　性	（人）	Females	(person)	664	733	90.6
香港居民	（人）	Hong Kong Residents	(person)	68	45	151.1
澳门居民	（人）	Macao Residents	(person)	5	4	125.0
台湾居民	（人）	Taiwan Residents	(person)	143	158	90.5
华　侨	（人）	Overseas Chinese	(person)	18	40	45.0
外国人	（人）	Foreigners	(person)	869	999	87.0
离婚登记对数	**（对）**	**Registered Divorces**	**(couple)**	**73000**	**56192**	**129.9**
内地居民登记离婚对数	（对）	Mainland Residents	(couple)	72746	55989	129.9
涉外及华侨、港澳台居民登记离婚对数	（对）	Overseas Chinese,Hongkong,Macao, Taiwan Residents	(couple)	254	203	125.1

注：离婚对数不含法院判离数。
资料来源：北京市民政局。
Note: Number of registered divorces excludes the divorces ruled by courts.
Source: Beijing Municipal Bureau of Civil Affairs.

21-11 残疾人事业基本情况
BASIC INFORMATION OF UNDERTAKINGS FOR DISABLED PERSONS

项目		Item		2015	2014
康复		**Rehabilitation**			
0-6岁残疾儿童享受康复政策人数	(人)	Number of Disabled Children of 0 to 6 Years Old Enjoying Rehabilitation Policies	(person)	977	813
7-15岁残疾儿童少年享受康复政策人数	(人)	Number of Disabled Children and Teenagers of 7 to15 Years Old Enjoying Rehabilitation Policies	(person)	960	908
残疾人接受辅助器具服务人数	(人)	Number of Disabled Persons With Assistive Devices	(person)	8596	15778
精神残疾人接受免费服药人数	(人)	Number of Mentally Disabled Persons Receiving Free Drug Treatment	(person)	12047	22000
贫困白内障患者接受减免费复明手术人数	(人)	Number of Poor Cataract Patients Receiving Free Cataract Surgery or That of Preferential Price	(person)	2947	1626
盲人接受定向行走训练人数	(人)	Number of Blind Persons Receiving Mobility and Orientation Training	(person)	1422	835
肢残人在社区接受康复训练人数	(人)	Number of The Physical Disabled Receiving Rehabilitation Training In Communities	(person)	7677	7425
智障人在社区接受康复训练人数	(人)	Number of Retarded Persons Receiving Rehabilitation Training In Communities	(person)	6476	7269
精神残疾人在社区接受康复训练人数	(人)	Number of Mentally Disabled Persons Receiving Rehabilitation Training In Communities	(person)	3485	3341
家庭康复培训残疾人亲友、家属总人数	(人)	Total Number of Family Members and Friends of Disabled Persons Receiving Family Rehabilitation Training	(person)	44169	50000
教育		**Education**			
未入学适龄残疾儿童少年	(人)	School-age Disabled Children Without Schooling	(person)	31	76
培训		**Training**			
职业教育与培训机构数(残联认定)	(个)	Number of Vocational Education and Training Institutions (recognized by China Disabled Persons' Federation)	(unit)	62	64
职业技能培训人数	(人次)	Number of Persons Receiving Vocational Skill Training	(person-time)	12374	9260
就业		**Employment**			
城镇残疾人就业状况		Employment of Urban Disabled Persons			
当年安排就业人数	(人)	Persons Employed by Arrangement in the Year	(person)	3541	4285
#按比例就业人数	(人)	Employed by Quota Scheme	(person)	1388	1805
集中就业人数	(人)	Disabled Persons Employed in Concentrated Way	(person)	228	190
个体就业人数	(人)	Self-employed	(person)	1336	1918
残疾人就业服务机构数	(个)	Employment Placement Service Facilities for Disabled Jobseekers	(unit)	17	17
盲人按摩		Massage by Persons with Visual Disability			
保健按摩机构	(家)	Healthcare Massage Institutions	(unit)	458	396
医疗按摩机构	(家)	Medical Massage Institutions	(unit)	4	4
保健按摩员培训人次	(人次)	Massage Therapists Training	(person-time)	389	1491
医疗按摩员培训人次	(人次)	Keep-fit Massager Training	(person-time)	124	279
扶贫		**Poverty Alleviation**			
享受城镇廉租住房的残疾人户数	(户)	Number of Households with Disabled Persons Enjoying Low-cost Urban House Leasing	(household)	1654	1629
扶持农村残疾人数	(人)	Number of Disabled Persons Supported in Rural Areas	(person)	2398	3824
社会保障		**Social Security**			
城镇		Urban Areas			
已纳入最低生活保障范围人数	(人)	Covered by the Basic Living System	(person)	19082	20875
享受失业且无稳定收入生活补助重残人数	(人)	Number of Severely Disabled Persons Enjoying Allowance For Unemployment and Unsteady Income	(person)	14428	13908
享受失业且无稳定收入生活补助非重残人数	(人)	Number of Non-Severely Disabled Persons Enjoying Allowance For Unemployment and Unsteady Income	(person)	7882	8408
参加城乡居民养老保险残疾人数	(人)	Number of Disabled Persons Insured by Urban Resident Pension Insurance	(person)	26551	26817
参加城镇居民医疗保险残疾人数	(人)	Number of Disabled Persons Insured by Urban Resident Medical Insurance	(person)	43226	45000
其他救助救济人数	(人)	Number of Other Persons Assisted and Supported	(person)	10204	14516
农村		Rural Areas			
已纳入最低生活保障范围人数	(人)	Covered by The Basic Living System	(person)	17665	20416
享受失业且无稳定收入生活补助重残人数	(人)	Number of Severely Disabled Persons Enjoying Allowance For Unemployment and Unsteady Income	(person)	24746	23555
享受失业且无稳定收入生活补助非重残人数	(人)	Number of Non-severely Disabled Persons Enjoying Allowance For Unemployment and Unsteady Income	(person)	29827	30452
参加城乡居民养老保险残疾人数	(人)	Number of Disabled Persons Insured by Urban Resident Pension Insurance	(person)	66398	71413
参加新型农村合作医疗保险残疾人数	(人)	Number of Disabled Persons Insured by New Rural Cooperative Medical Service	(person)	141912	121977
其他救助救济人数	(人)	Number of Other Persons Assisted and Supported	(person)	15914	14226
残联组织建设		**Organization Building of Disabled Persons' Federation**			
残疾人工作者数	(人)	Workers for Disabled Persons	(person)	1255	1214

资料来源：北京市残疾人联合会。
Source: Beijing Disabled Persons' Federation.

21-12 残疾人就业、维权援助情况
STATISTICS FOR EMPLOYMENT AND AID FOR RIGHT PROTECTION OF DISABLED PERSONS

项　　目		Item		2015	2014
残疾人职业培训人数	(人)	Number of Disabled Persons Trained for Employment	(person)	13817	16283
#女　性	(人)	Females	(person)	6460	6918
新安置残疾人员就业人数	(人)	New Employment of Disabled Persons	(person)	4622	3812
#女　性	(人)	Females	(peoson)	2106	2566
维权信访咨询件数	(件)	Right Protection Letters, Visits and Consulting	(case)	22055	23066
维权法律服务件数	(件)	Right Protection Legal Aid	(case)	2568	2840

资料来源：北京市残疾人联合会。
Source: Beijing Disabled Persons Federation.

21-13 律师工作
STATISTICS FOR LAWYERS

项　　目		Item		2015	2014	2015年为2014年% 2015 as % of 2014
律师事务所	(个)	Law Firms	(unit)	2100	1924	109.1
执业律师	(人)	Number of Practicing Lawyers	(person)	25542	24467	104.4
专职律师	(人)	Full-time Lawyers	(person)	24163	23067	104.8
兼职律师	(人)	Part-time Lawyers	(person)	943	928	101.6
公司律师	(人)	Company Lawyers	(person)	325	345	94.2
公职律师	(人)	Government Lawyers	(person)	111	127	87.4
担任法律顾问	(家)	Legal Counsel	(unit)	25366	22872	110.9
民事诉讼代理	(件)	Civil Case Litigation Agencies	(case)	94480	90115	104.8
行政诉讼代理	(件)	Administrative Case Litigation Agencies	(case)	6614	4384	150.9
刑事诉讼辩护及代理	(件)	Criminal Case Litigation Agencies	(case)	26976	25144	107.3
非诉讼法律事务	(件)	Off-court Cases	(case)	89638	86884	103.2

资料来源：北京市司法局。
Source: Beijing Municipal Bureau of Justice.

21-14 调解工作
MEDIATION

项　　目		Item		2015	2014	2015年为2014年% 2015 as % of 2014
人民调解委员会个数	(个)	People's Mediation Committees	(unit)	7850	7722	101.7
调解员人数	(万人)	Mediators	(10000 persons)	7.68	8.22	93.4
调解各类纠纷件数	(万件)	Disputes Mediated	(10000 cases)	18.56	19.41	95.6
#调解各类纠纷成功件数	(万件)	Succeed Disputes Mediated	(10000 cases)	17.8	18.86	94.4
防止民间纠纷激化件数	(件)	Civil Disputes Prevented from Intensifi	(case)	1251	1627	76.9
防止民间纠纷激化人数	(人次)	Persons Involved in Civil Disputes Prev	(person)	9970	15092	66.1

资料来源：北京市司法局。
Source: Beijing Municipal Bureau of Justice.

21-15 公证工作
NOTARIZATIONS

项　　目		Item		2015	2014	2015年为2014年% 2015 as % of 2014
公证机构个数	(个)	Notary Offices	(unit)	25	25	100.0
执业公证员人数	(人)	Certified Notaries	(person)	310	327	94.8
总办证数	(件)	Certificates Issued	(case)	1077217	940373	114.6
国内公证业务	(件)	Domestic Notarial Services	(case)	570486	431105	132.3
涉外公证业务	(件)	Foreign-Relatesd Notarial Docummemts	(case)	500956	501173	100.0
涉港澳公证业务	(件)	Hongkong,Macao affairs	(case)	2810	4598	61.1
涉台公证业务	(件)	Naiwan Notarial Services	(case)	2965	3497	84.8

资料来源：北京市司法局。
Source: Beijing Municipal Bureau of Justice.

21-16 法律援助工作情况
STATISTICS FOR LEGAL AID

项目		Item		2015	2014	2015年为2014年% 2015 as % of 2014
法律援助机构个数	(个)	Number of Legal Aid Agencies	(unit)	29	25	116.0
法律援助机构人员数	(人)	Number of Legal Aid Persons	(person)	215	286	75.2
承办民事法律援助案件数	(件)	Civil Cases Aided	(case)	18229	15420	118.2
承办刑事法律援助案件数	(件)	Criminal Cases Aided	(case)	3256	2822	115.4
承办行政法律援助案件数	(件)	Administrative Cases Aided	(case)	47	31	151.6
法律援助机构接待咨询人次	(万人次)	Consultations by Legal Aid Agencies	(10000 person-times)	16.8	13.2	127.3
得到法律援助机构援助的妇女人数	(人次)	Females Receiving Aids from Legal Aid Agencies	(person-times)	6247	6132	101.9
得到法律援助机构援助的儿童人数	(人次)	Children Receiving Aids from Legal Aid Agencies	(person-times)	1505	2111	71.3

资料来源：北京市司法局。

Source: Beijing Municiapl Bureau of Justice.

21-17 司法鉴定工作情况
STATISTICS FOR JUDICIAL APPRAISAL

项目		Item		2015	2014
司法鉴定机构个数	(个)	Judicial Appraisal Organizations	(unit)	109	108
司法鉴定人员数	(人)	Judicial Appraisal Personnel	(person)	1691	1680
司法鉴定业务量	(件)	Judicial Appraisal Cases Proceeded	(case)	78686	71157

注：本表中司法鉴定机构数为“北京市司法局审核登记的全部司法鉴定机构”个数。

资料来源：北京市司法局。

Note: In the table, the number of judicial appraisal organizations is the number of "all judicial appraisal organizations approved by and registered with Beijing Municipal Bureau of Justice".

Source: Beijing Municipal Bureau of Justice.

21-18 公安、法院、检察院收案、结案情况(2005-2015年)
CASES ACCEPTED AND SETTLED BY PUBLIC SECURITY DEPARTMENTS, COURTS AND PROCURATORATES (2005-2015)

项目		Item		2005	2006	2007	2008	2009
公安部门侦破刑事案件		**Criminal Cases Detected by Public Security Departments**						
立案	(起)	Cases Put on File	(case)	107988	120554	127446	90045	98750
破案	(起)	Cases Settled	(case)	59035	66399	74232	63294	71950
法院刑事案件收、结案情况		**Criminal Cases Accepted and Settled in Courts**						
收案	(件)	Cases Accepted	(case)	17488	17725	19592	20024	18819
结案	(件)	Cases Settled	(case)	17624	17701	19536	20004	18773
法院婚姻家庭、继承纠纷案件收、结案情况		**Marriage and Inheritance Dispute Cases Accepted and Settled in Courts**						
收案	(件)	Cases Accepted	(case)	26739	27860	28089	30402	33056
结案	(件)	Cases Settled	(case)	27002	27845	27916	29499	32902
法院合同纠纷案件收、结案情况		**Contract Dispute Cases Accepted and Settled in Courts**						
收案	(件)	Cases Accepted	(case)	133534	141485	135099	144948	153766
结案	(件)	Cases Settled	(case)	135612	141439	134829	140512	152128
法院权属、侵权纠纷及其他民事案件收、结案情况		**Ownership, Infringement Dispute and Other Civil Cases Accepted and Settled in Courts**						
收案	(件)	Cases Accepted	(case)	42690	44890	46892	53864	58057
结案	(件)	Cases Settled	(case)	43166	45005	46372	51668	57135
检察机关查办反贪污贿赂案件		**Anti-Corruption and Bribery Cases Handled by Procuratorates**						
受案	(件)	Cases Accepted	(case)	1202	1330	1276	1060	1113
立案		Cases Put on File						
件数	(件)	Number of Cases	(case)	292	321	322	282	319
人数	(人)	Number of Persons Involved	(person)	356	363	372	333	369
挽回经济损失	(万元)	Economic Losses Redeemed	(10000 yuan)	30701	29545	14703	21148	62542
检察机关办理渎职侵权案件		**Misconduct and Infringement Cases Handled by Procuratorates**						
受案	(件)	Cases Accepted	(case)	218	162	205	150	206
立案		Cases Put on File						
件数	(件)	Number of Cases	(case)	37	30	34	29	48
人数	(人)	Number of Persons Involved	(person)	38	31	36	31	53
挽回经济损失	(万元)	Economic Losses Redeemed	(10000 yuan)	1320	458	71	3019	25

资料来源：北京市公安局、北京市人民检察院、北京市高级人民法院。
Source: Beijing Municipal Bureau of Public Security, the People's Procuratorate of Beijing, and the People's High Court of Beijing.

21-18 续表 Continued

项 目	Item	2010	2011	2012	2013	2014	2015
公安部门侦破刑事案件	**Criminal Cases Detected by Public Security Departments**						
立 案 (起)	Cases Put on File (case)	104327	142835	145724	140498	153334	174374
破 案 (起)	Cases Settled (case)	80401	89156	101776	112594	122383	115807
法院刑事案件收、结案情况	**Criminal Cases Accepted and Settled in Courts**						
收 案 (件)	Cases Accepted (case)	19824	19574	22168	19109	20556	19980
结 案 (件)	Cases Settled (case)	19870	19423	22084	19012	20357	19667
法院婚姻家庭、继承纠纷案件收、结案情况	**Marriage and Inheritance Dispute Cases Accepted and Settled in Courts**						
收 案 (件)	Cases Accepted (case)	36799	35251	35418	37347	39390	43869
结 案 (件)	Cases Settled (case)	37160	35149	35201	35296	38565	40436
法院合同纠纷案件收、结案情况	**Contract Dispute Cases Accepted and Settled in Courts**						
收 案 (件)	Cases Accepted (case)	148655	144433	145017	149237	162893	237850
结 案 (件)	Cases Settled (case)	153130	144766	143153	141642	155472	207012
法院权属、侵权纠纷及其他民事案件收、结案情况	**Ownership, Infringement Dispute and Other Civil Cases Accepted and Settled in Courts**						
收 案 (件)	Cases Accepted (case)	64379	65972	62736	64747	69541	85554
结 案 (件)	Cases Settled (case)	65763	66405	62235	61688	67444	76644
检察机关查办贪污贿赂案件	**Anti-Corruption and Bribery Cases Handled by Procuratorates**						
受 案 (件)	Cases Accepted (case)	1138	988	1070	871	1087	880
立 案	Cases Put on File						
件 数 (件)	Number of Cases (case)	356	343	379	299	382	312
人 数 (人)	Number of Persons Involved (person)	418	425	459	357	429	339
挽回经济损失 (万元)	Economic Losses Redeemed (10000 yuan)	14634	36469	29955	16171	9050	30435
检察机关办理渎职侵权案件	**Misconduct and Infringement Cases Handled by Procuratorates**						
受 案 (件)	Cases Accepted (case)	213	193	351	443	291	104
立 案	Cases Put on File						
件 数 (件)	Number of Cases (case)	57	55	77	74	75	46
人 数 (人)	Number of Persons Involved (person)	60	66	94	81	78	49
挽回经济损失 (万元)	Economic Losses Redeemed (10000 yuan)	16	58	735	962	210	919

21-19 法院行政案件收、结案情况(2015年)
STATISTICS FOR ADMINISTRATIVE CASES ACCEPTED AND SETTLED BY COURT (2015)

单位：件 (case)

项目	Item	收案 Cases Accepted	结案 Cases Settled	#判决 Judgment	#裁定 Mediation
合计	**Total**	**18747**	**18378**	**11523**	**7052**
公安	Public Security	884	720	289	435
资源	Resources	291	266	77	190
城建	City Construction	1481	1270	449	823
工商	Industry and Commerce	297	189	80	109
专利	Patents	1371	480	395	86
劳动和社会保障	Labor and Social Security	175	141	80	62
教育	Education	106	95	8	87
其他	Others	14142	15217	10145	5260

资料来源：北京市高级人民法院。
Source: The People's High Court of Beijing.

21-20 法院刑事案件收、结案情况(2015年)
STATISTICS FOR CRIMINAL CASES ACCEPTED AND SETTLED BY COURT (2015)

项目	Item	收案(件) Cases Accepted (case)	结案(件) Cases Settled (case)	判决发生法律效力 Judgment with Legal Forces	
				件数(件) Number of Cases (case)	人数(人) Number of Persons (person)
合计	**Total**	**19980**	**19667**	**19660**	**23640**
#危害公共安全罪	Offences against Public Security	3084	3070	2927	3019
破坏社会主义市场经济秩序罪	Offences against the Socialist Market Economy Order	2101	2071	2140	2703
侵犯公民人身权利、民主权利罪	Offences against Civil Personal Rights and Democratic Rights	3995	3923	3798	4416
侵犯财产罪	Offences against Property	6004	5946	6024	7243
妨害社会管理秩序罪	Offences against Social Administration	4436	4387	4481	5926
危害国防利益罪	Offences against National Defense Interest	17	19	11	21
贪污贿赂罪	Crimes of Corruption and Bribery	304	213	242	279
渎职罪	Crimes of Misconduct in Office	31	32	27	29

资料来源：北京市高级人民法院。
Source: The People's High Court of Beijing.

21-21 法院婚姻家庭、继承纠纷案件收、结案情况(2015年)
STATISTICS FOR MARRIAGE AND FAMILY AND INHERITANCE DISPUTE CASES ACCEPTED AND SETTLED BY COURT (2015)

单位：件 (case)

项　目	Item	收　案 Cases Accepted	结　案 Cases Settled	#判　决 Judgment	#调　解 Mediation
合　计	**Total**	**43869**	**40436**	**12130**	**16150**
婚姻家庭纠纷	**Marriage and Family Disputes**				
离　婚	Divorces	21799	20282	7099	6367
解除非法同居关系	Relieving the Relation of Illicit Cohabitation	372	346	101	150
抚养、扶养关系纠纷	Child-support Disputes	1233	1198	280	585
抚育费纠纷	Child-support Payment Disputes	1237	1146	473	382
赡养纠纷	Support Disputes	1211	1146	543	255
分家析产	Family Property Division	4736	4298	634	2573
其　他	Others	3106	2887	982	815
继承纠纷	**Inheritance Disputes**				
法定继承	Legal Inheritance	6339	5838	1008	3578
遗嘱继承	Testamentary Inheritance	1193	1032	405	391
继承权确认纠纷	Inheritance Right Dispute				
其　他	Others	2643	2263	605	1054

资料来源：北京市高级人民法院。
Source: The People's High Court of Beijing.

21-22 法院合同纠纷案件收、结案情况(2015年)
STATISTICS FOR CONTRACT CASES ACCEPTED AND SETTLED BY COURT (2015)

单位：件 (case)

项　目	Item	收　案 Cases Accepted	结　案 Cases Settled	#判　决 Judgment	#调　解 Mediation
合　计	**Total**	**237850**	**207012**	**74714**	**33432**
#买卖合同纠纷	Trade Contracts	28581	22429	8208	4578
房地产开发经营合同纠纷	Real Estate Development & Operation Contracts	8292	7809	4095	1513
供用电、水、气、热力合同纠纷	Electricity, Water, Gas, Heating Supply contracts	19524	18794	2398	3472
借款合同纠纷	Loan Contracts	42594	32997	14469	5394
租赁合同纠纷	Lease Contracts	16046	13717	5825	2061
建设工程合同纠纷	Construction Contracts	5594	4705	1934	934
承揽合同纠纷	Contracts for Hire of Work	3535	2925	1033	636
运输合同纠纷	Transportation Contracts	876	817	421	148
经营合同纠纷	Management Contracts	2251	1871	749	257
农村承包合同纠纷	Rural Contracts	61	68	44	
劳动争议	Labor Disputes	24812	22565	11283	5128

资料来源：北京市高级人民法院。
Source: The People's High Court of Beijing.

21-23 法院权属、侵权纠纷及其他民事案件收、结案情况(2015年)
STATISTICS FOR OWNERSHIP, TORTIOUS DISPUTES AND OTHER CIVIL CASES ACCEPTED AND SETTLED BY COURT (2015)

单位：件 (case)

项目	Item	收案 Cases Accepted	结案 Cases Settled	#判决 Judgment	#调解 Mediation
合计	**Total**	**85554**	**76644**	**31453**	**14692**
所有权及与所有权相关权利纠纷	Ownership and Related Rights	23181	20996	7157	5669
票据、证券权益纠纷	Bill and Securities Rights	446	389	141	54
股东权纠纷	Shareholder's Rights	1643	1339	589	82
不正当竞争纠纷	Unfair Competition	532	266	93	17
人身权纠纷	Personal Rights	13443	11700	5893	2469
特殊侵权纠纷	Special Infringements	22664	20638	11644	5075
适用特别程序案件	Special-poceeding Cases	9002	8635	3095	
其他	Others	14643	12681	2841	1326

资料来源：北京市高级人民法院。
Source: The People's High Court of Beijing.

21-24 检察机关办理各类案件情况(2015年)
STATISTICS FOR CASES HANDLED BY PROCURATORIAL ORGANS (2015)

项目	Item	受案(受理) Cases Accepted		审结案合计 Cases Settled	
		件 Case	人 Person	件 Case	人 Person
审查逮捕	**Arrests to Be Examined and Approved**	**14880**	**18722**	**14840**	**18692**
批准逮捕	Approved			10762	12913
不批准逮捕	Disapproved			4078	5779
审查起诉	**Prosecution to Be Reviewed and Made**	**20181**	**24468**	**19935**	**24367**
起诉	Prosecuted			18171	21878
不起诉	Non-prosecution			1674	2365
附条件不起诉	Conditional Non-prosecution			90	124
举报案件	**Reported Cases**	**2875**		**2484**	
控告案件	**Complaints**	**4330**		**4299**	
申诉案件	**Appeal Cases**	**4008**		**3534**	
民事检察案件	**Civil Cases**	**1552**		**1445**	
行政检察案件	**Administrative Cases**	**342**		**266**	

资料来源：北京市人民检察院。
Source: The People's Procuratorate of Beijing.

21-25 查办贪污贿赂、渎职侵权案件情况(2015年)
STATISTICS FOR CORRUPTION, BRIBERY, MALPRACTICE AND INFRINGEMENT CASES (2015)

项目		Item		查办贪污贿赂案件 Corruption and Bribery Cases	贪污案 Corruption Cases	贿赂案 Bribery Cases	挪用公款案 Misappropriation of Public Funds	其他 Others	渎职侵权案件 Malpractice and Infringement Cases
受案	**(件)**	**Cases Accepted**	**(case)**	**880**	**278**	**546**	**35**	**21**	**104**
立案		**Cases Registered**							
件数	(件)	Number of Cases	(case)	312	78	213	19	2	46
人数	(人)	Persons involved	(person)	339	91	226	20	2	49
大案	**(件)**	**Major Cases**	**(case)**	**297**	**76**	**203**	**18**		**22**
按查办贪污贿赂案件类型分		**By Type of Corruption and Bribery Case**							
5万至10万元(不含)	(件)	50000-100000 Yuan	(case)	31	9	22			
10万至50万元(不含)	(件)	100000-500000 Yuan	(case)	100	30	66	4		
50万至100万元(不含)	(件)	500000-1000000 Yuan	(case)	55	9	43	3		
100万至1000万元(不含)	(件)	1000000-10000000 Yuan	(case)	92	17	66	9		
1000万元及以上	(件)	Above 10000000 Yuan	(case)	19	11	6	2		
按查办渎职侵权案件类型分		**By Type of Malpractice and Infringement Case**							
重大	(件)	Serious Cases	(case)						11
特大	(件)	Extraordinary Serious Cas	(case)						11
要案	**(人)**	**Important Cases**	**(person)**	**117**	**29**	**85**	**3**		**11**
县处级	(人)	County Level	(person)	69	19	47	3		6
地厅级	(人)	Departmental Level	(person)	45	10	35			5
省部级以上	(人)	Above Provincial Level	(person)	3		3			
侦结		**Cases Closed**							
件数	(件)	Number of Cases	(case)	307	70	218	17	2	23
人数	(人)	Number of Persons	(person)	348	86	242	17	3	24
#移送起诉		Handed over to Law Suit							
件数	(件)	Number of Cases	(case)	303	69	215	17	2	22
人数	(人)	Number of Persons	(person)	342	84	238	17	3	23
#移送不起诉		Handed over yet Immunity from Suit							
件数	(件)	Number of Cases	(case)	2		2			
人数	(人)	Number of Persons	(person)	2		2			
挽回经济损失	**(万元)**	**Economic Losses Redeemed**	**(10000 yuan)**	**30435**	**10207**	**19962**	**266**		**919**

资料来源：北京市人民检察院。
Source: The People's Procuratorate of Beijing.

21-26 刑事案件情况
STATISTICS FOR CRIMINAL CASES

单位：起 (case)

项　　目	Item	2015	2014	2015年为2014年% 2015 as % of 2014
刑事案件	**Criminal Cases**			
立　案	Cases Registered	174374	153334	113.7
破　案	Cases Settled	115807	122383	94.6

资料来源：北京市公安局。
Source: Beijing Municipal Bureau of Public Security.

21-27 消防建设情况(1996-2015年)
STATISTICS FOR FIRECONTROL (1996-2015)

年　份 Year	公安消防队数 (支) Number of Fire Brigades of Public Security (unit)	公安消防车辆 (辆) Number of Fire-fighting Vehicles of Public Security (unit)	企业专职消防队队数 (支) Number of Full-time Fire Brigades in Enterprises (unit)	企业专职消防队人数 (人) Persons of Full-time Fire-fighters in Enterprises (person)
1996	36	180	101	1865
1997	38	190	104	1885
1998	41	210	108	1993
1999	44	236	120	2447
2000	47	259	120	2447
2001	50	266	120	2447
2002	52	296	112	2228
2003	56	303	112	2147
2004	57	381	120	2477
2005	57	342	120	2477
2006	64	357	109	2269
2007	69	401	109	2269
2008	77	558	109	2269
2009	86	572	109	2269
2010	91	664	109	2269
2011	98	604	87	1766
2012	107	670	76	1405
2013	122	735	76	1405
2014	125	799	76	1405
2015	134	858	78	1410

资料来源：北京市公安局消防局。
Source: Fire Department of Beijing Municipal Bureau of Public Security.

21-28 火灾及损失
FIRE ACCIDENTS AND LOSSES

项目	Item	数量 Number 2015	数量 Number 2014	直接经济损失(万元) Direct Economic Losses (10000 yuan) 2015	直接经济损失(万元) Direct Economic Losses (10000 yuan) 2014
火灾起数 （起）	**Fire Accidents (case)**	**3769**	**4480**	**6104.0**	**7833.7**
特别重大火灾	Extraordinarily Serious				
重大火灾	Serious				
较大火灾	Big Fire	2		62.6	
一般火灾	Relatively Big Fire	3767	4480	6041.3	7833.7
起火原因	**Cause of Fire**				
电　气	Electricity and Gas	1244	1322	2982.5	4292.8
生产作业	Violation of Operation	113	115	260.0	1431.5
生活用火不慎	Carelessness in Fire Use	511	704	289.1	611.0
吸　烟	Smoking	103	100	69.7	43.5
玩　火	Fire Playing	59	47	435.7	30.3
自　燃	Spontaneous Combustion	93	117	78.3	344.7
雷　击	Thunderstroke	4	3	0.0	2.8
静　电	Static	5	2	10.6	2.5
放　火	Incendiarism	78	107	294.8	119.5
其　他	Others	1559	1963	1683.4	955.0
受伤人数 （人）	**Number of Injuries (person)**	**23**	**15**		
死亡人数 （人）	**Number of Deaths (person)**	**48**	**51**		

资料来源：北京市公安局消防局。
Source: Fire Department of Beijing Municipal Bureau of Public Security.

21-29 安全生产情况
STATISTICS FOR SAFE PRODUCTION

项目	Item	2015	2014
亿元地区生产总值安全生产事故死亡率 (人/亿元)	Death Rate of Work Accidents Per 100 million yuan GDP (person/100 million yuan)	0.045	0.051
工矿商贸企业从业人员10万人生产安全事故死亡率 (人/10万人)	Death Rate of Work Accidents in the Mining, Commercial and Trade Industries Per 100,000 Persons (1/100000)	0.43	0.94
煤矿百万吨死亡率 (人/百万吨)	The Death Rate of Coal Mines Per Million Tons (Person/million tons)	0.22	0.91
道路交通万车死亡率 (人/万车)	Road Traffic Death Rate Per 10000 Vehicles (person/10000 vehicles)	1.64	1.65
65大类食品检验合格率 (%)	Up-to -standard Rate in Inspection on 65 Categories of Food (%)	97.60	97.46
#重点食品安全监测抽检合格率 (%)	Up-to-standard Rate of Key Foods Security Monitor Spot Checks (%)	98.42	98.39
药品抽验合格率 (%)	Up-to-standard Rate of Drug Spot Checks (%)	99.71	99.88

数据来源：北京市食品药品监督管理局、北京市公安交通管理局、北京市安全生产监督管理局。
Source: Beijing Municipal Food and Drug Administration, Beijing Municipal Bureau of Traffic Management, Beijing Administration of Work Safety.

21-30 交通事故及损失
STATISTICS FOR TRAFFIC ACCIDENTS AND LOSSES

项　　目		Item		2015	2014	2015年为2014年% 2015 as % of 2014
交通事故		**Traffic Accidents**				
交通事故发生数	(起)	Number of Traffic Accidents	(case)	2639	3268	80.8
受伤人数	(人)	Number of Injuries	(person)	2619	3362	77.9
死亡人数	(人)	Number of Deaths	(person)	921	923	99.8
机动车事故		**Motor Vehicle Accidents**				
机动车事故发生数	(起)	Number of Motor Vehicle Accidents	(case)	2187	2753	79.4
受伤人数	(人)	Number of Injuries	(person)	2222	2885	77.0
死亡人数	(人)	Number of Deaths	(person)	792	824	96.1
直接经济损失	**(万元)**	**Direct Economic Losses**	**(10000 yuan)**	**2089.6**	**3129.2**	**66.8**
每万辆机动车死亡人数	**(人)**	**Persons Died Per 10,000 Motor Vehicles**	**(person)**	**1.64**	**1.65**	**99.4**

资料来源：北京市公安局公安交通管理局。
Source: Beijing Municipal Bureau of Traffic Management.

21-31 地震应急避难场所情况
EMERGENT EARTHQUAKE REFUGES

项　　目		Item		2015	2014
地震应急避难场所累计个数	(个)	Total Number of Emergent Earthquake Refuges	(unit)	106	94
地震应急避难场所累计面积	(万平方米)	Total Area of Emergent Earthquake Refuges	(10000 sq.m)	2809	1644

资料来源：北京市地震局。
Source: Beijing Municipal Bureau of Earthquake.

21-32 妇联组织状况
STATISTICS FOR WOMEN'S FEDERATIONS AND ORGANIZATIONS

单位：个，人　　(unit,person)

项　　目	Item	2015	2014	2015年为2014年% 2015 as % of 2014
妇联组织状况	**Status of Women's Federations and Organizations**			
区妇联数	Number of Women's Federations in Districts	16	14	114.3
县妇联数	Number of Women's Federations in Counties		2	
乡、镇妇联组织数	Number of Women's Federations in Townships	182	182	100.0
街道妇联组织数	Number of Women's Federations in Subdistricts	147	145	101.4
妇联干部状况	**Status of Cadres in Women's Federation**			
区妇联干部数	Cadres in Women's Federations in Districts	295	250	118.0
县妇联干部数	Cadres in Women's Federations in Counties		33	
乡、镇、街道妇联干部数	Cadres in Women's Federations in Townships, Towns and Subdistricts	333	327	101.8
妇联基层妇代会组织个数	**Number of Grass-root Women Congresses of Women's Federations**			
城　市	Urban	2903	2951	98.4
农　村	Rural	3936	3709	106.1
各类妇女联谊组织数	**Women's Sodalities**	**31**	**31**	**100.0**

资料来源：北京市妇女联合会。
Source: Beijing Women's Federation.

21-33 工会组织建设情况(2015年)
STATISTICS FOR LABOR UNIONS (2015)

项 目	Item	基层工会组织(个) Grassroot Labor Unions (unit)	职工人数(人) Number of Employed Persons (person)	会员人数(人) Number of Members (person)
合 计	**Total**	**31583**	**4721949**	**4212372**
按单位类别划分	**By Registration Type**			
国有企业	State-owned Enterprises	1494	705203	680283
集体企业	Collectively-owned Enterprises	1654	136700	122010
股份合作企业	Joint-equity Cooperative Enterprises	551	83757	71690
联营企业	Associated Enterprises	29	1428	1294
国有独资公司	Solely State-owned Enterprises	373	157712	151125
其他有限责任公司	Other Limited-Liability Companies	8468	995156	796064
国有控股公司	State-holding Companies	439	329671	315120
其他股份有限公司	Other Holding Companies	1039	212726	172805
私营企业	Private Enterprises	6798	486741	380496
其他内资企业	Other Domestically-invested Enterprises	61	4604	3768
港澳台商投资企业	Hong Kong, Macao and Taiwan-invested Enterprises	276	72844	63162
外商投资企业	Foreign-invested Enterprises	652	269253	249979
事业单位	Public Institutions	4265	643173	613493
机 关	Governmental Agencies and Organizations	1711	272950	260320
其 他	Others	3773	350031	330763
按系统分	**By System**			
工业国防工会	Labor Unions for Industry and National Defence	720	390659	377518
工 业	Industry	703	367838	354841
国 防	National Defence	17	22821	22677
建筑工会	Construction	1893	846408	625514
本 市	Local	488	244087	229505
市 外	Non-local	1405	602321	396009
服务业工会	Services	751	258711	240869
交通运输工会	Transportation	246	336222	329784
机关事业部	Governmental Institutions	293	112239	109763
教育工会	Education	97	162980	151479
金融工会	Finance	78	127911	122233
市直机关工会	Institutions under Direct Municipal Leadership	489	55840	53347
区县工会	Labor Unions in Districts and Counties	27016	2430979	2201865

资料来源：北京市总工会。
Source: Beijing Federation of Labor Unions.

21-34 北京市妇女发展规划监测统计资料
SUPERVISORY STATISTICS ON WOMEN DEVELOPMENT PROGRAMS OF BEIJING

项目		Item		2015	2014
城镇单位就业人员数	(万人)	Employed Persons in Urban Entites	(10000 persons)	777.3	755.9
#女性		Females		314.8	303.3
城镇登记失业人员总数	(万人)	Urban Registered Unemployment	(10000 persons)	24.0	25.2
#女性		Females		9.6	10.2
城镇登记失业人员就业人数	(万人)	Employed Persons from Urban Registered Unemployment	(10000 persons)	15.3	16.9
#女性		Females		6.1	6.9
参加基本养老保险人数	(万人)	Number of Participants in Basic Pension Insurance	(10000 persons)	1424.2	1392.6
#女性		Females		647.1	633.2
参加基本医疗保险人数	(万人)	Number of Participants in Basic Medical Insurance	(10000 persons)	1475.7	1431.3
#女性		Females		680.7	660.8
参加失业保险人数	(万人)	Number of Participants in Unemployment Insurance	(10000 persons)	1082.3	1057.1
#女性		Females		474.5	464.4
参加工伤保险人数	(万人)	Number of Participants in Work Injury Insurance	(10000 persons)	1020.1	961.0
#女性		Females		435.7	407.7
城乡居民养老保险参保人数	(万人)	Number of Urban and Rural Residents Participating in Basic Pension Insurance for Urban and Rural Residents	(10000 persons)	187.6	186.2
#女性		Females		97.3	96.7
市人大女代表领衔提出的议案数	(件)	Number of Proposals Put Forward by Women Deputies of Beijing Municipal People's Congress(BMPC)	(case)	84	19
市政协女委员提出的提案数	(件)	Number of Proposals Put Forward by Women Deputies of Beijing Committee of Chinese People's Political Consultative Conference	(case)	429	401
普通高校在校学生人数	(万人)	Enrollment in Institutions of Higher Education	(10000 persons)	59.3	59.5
#女性		Females		30.6	30.6
在读研究生人数	(万人)	Number of Enrolled Postgraduates	(10000 persons)	28.4	27.4
#女性		Females		13.5	12.9
成人本专科在校生人数	(万人)	Enrollment of Technical Higher and Secondary Education for Adults	(10000 persons)	20.4	23.8
#女性		Females		11.2	13.2
妇科病普查率	(%)	Rate of Gynaopathy General Surveys	(%)	54.2	50.7
高危孕产妇住院分娩率	(%)	Birth-giving Rate of High-risk Lying-in Women in Hospitals	(%)	100.0	100.0
已婚育龄妇女综合避孕率	(%)	Practising Contraception Rate of Married Women of Child Bearing Age	(%)	83.8	77.3
抓获刑事作案成员中女性比例	(%)	Share of Females in Criminal Suspects Captured	(%)	20.1	18.5
得到法律援助机构援助的妇女人数	(人)	Number of Women Receiving Aids from Law Aid Institutions	(person)	6247	6132

21-35 北京市儿童发展规划监测统计资料
SUPERVISORY STATISTICS FOR CHILDREN DEVELOPMENT IN BEIJING

项　目		Item		2015	2014
婚前医学检查率	(%)	Rate of Premarital Medical Checks	(%)	9.4	6.8
新生儿遗传代谢性疾病筛查率	(%)	Screening Rate of Genic Metabolic Diseases for Newborn	(%)	100.0	98.6
出生缺陷监测率	(%)	Monitoring Rate of Birth Deficiencies	(%)	100.0	100.0
新生儿听力筛查率	(%)	Screening Rate of Hearing for Newborns	(%)	96.92	96.54
出生缺陷发生率	(‰)	Rate of Birth Deficiencies	(‰)	16.37	14.02
7岁以下儿童保健管理率	(%)	Rate of Health Management for Children Under 7 Years Old	(%)	98.02	97.88
0-6个月婴儿纯母乳喂养率	(%)	Rate of Exclusive Breast Breeding for Infants of 0-6 Months	(%)	70.33	71.22
婴儿死亡率	(‰)	Mortality Rate of Infants	(‰)	2.33	2.33
5岁以下儿童死亡率	(‰)	Mortality Rate of Children below 5 Years Old	(‰)	3.02	2.89
儿童肥胖率(0-6岁)	(%)	Rate of Obesity for Children of 0-6 Years Old	(%)	3.95	3.79
儿童龋齿率(0-6岁)	(%)	Rate of Decayed Teeth for Children of 0-6 Years Old	(%)	17.30	18.01
卡介苗疫苗接种率	(%)	Rate of Inoculation of BCG Vaccines	(%)	99.94	99.86
脊髓灰质炎疫苗接种率	(%)	Rate of Inoculation of Poliomyelities Polio Vaccines	(%)	99.73	99.55
百白破疫苗接种率	(%)	Rate of Inoculation of Pertussis, Diphtheria and Tetanus Vaccines	(%)	99.94	99.55
含麻疹成分疫苗接种率	(%)	Rate of Inoculation of Vaccines with Measle Ingredients	(%)	99.88	99.64
孕产妇系统管理率	(%)	Rate of Systematic Management for Pregnant and Lying-in	(%)	97.27	97.43
城　市		Urban		97.15	96.99
农　村		Rural		97.53	98.26
孕产妇健康教育普及率	(%)	Popularization Rate of Health Education for Pregnant and Lying-in Women	(%)	99.98	99.97
孕产妇住院分娩率	(%)	Birth-giving Rate of Pregnant and Lying-in Women in Hospital	(%)	100.0	100.0
孕产妇死亡率	(1/10万)	Mortality Rate of Pregnant and Lying-in Women	(1/100000)	8.69	7.19

21-36 北京市历届人代会代表人数性别构成及议案、建议数
NUMBER AND SEX COMPOSITION OF DEPUTIES、NUMBERS OF PROPOSALS AND SUGGESTIONS AT PREVIOUS SESSIONS OF PEOPLE'S CONGRESS OF BEIJING

单位：人、%、件 (person,%,case)

项目 Item	代表人数 Number of Deputies			性别比例 Sex Percentage		议案立案数 Number of Proposals on Record	建议数 Suggestions
	合计 Total	女性 Females	男性 Males	女性 Females	男性 Males		
第一届 1st	564	106	458	18.8	81.2		
第二届 2nd	619	142	477	22.9	77.1		
第三届 3rd	618	162	456	26.2	73.8		
第四届 4th	745	202	543	27.1	72.9		
第五届 5th	751	203	548	27.0	73.0		
第七届 7th	1195	325	870	27.1	72.9		
第八届 8th	973	252	721	25.9	74.1	55	6644
第九届 9th	880	217	663	24.7	75.3	86	7921
第十届 10th	885	224	661	25.3	74.7	156	7281
第十一届 11th	763	197	566	25.8	74.2	166	9717
第十二届 12th	762	235	527	30.8	69.2	276	9859
第十三届 13th	779	237	542	30.4	69.6	153	7576
第十四届 14th	771	257	514	33.3	66.7	148	3674

注：1. 北京市人大常委会是经北京市七届三次人民代表大会选举成立的，故一至七届人代会无议案及建议数。
2. 代表人数为届首选举数，议案及建议数均是本届五年会上及平时议案及建议的合计数。
3. 第十四届议案立案及建议数截止到2015年12月底。

资料来源：北京市人民代表大会常务委员会。

Note: a) Standing Committee of Beijing People's Congress was established upon election at the 3rd Session of Beijing 7th People's Congress. As a result, there were no proposals and suggestions at the 1st-7th People's Congresses.
b) Deputies were those first elected for that term. Proposals and suggestions at other terms of Congress included those at the meeting of the term and/or at ordinary times.
c) Data of proposals and suggestions of 14th Congress was counted by the end of december of 2014.

Source: Standing Committee of Beijing Municipal People's Congress (BMPC).

21-37 北京市历届政协会委员人数及提案立案数
NUMBER OF MEMBERS AND PROPOSALS AT HISTORICAL BEIJING CPPCC

单位：人、件 (person,case)

届别 Term	起止年月 Beginning-ending Month	委员人数 Number of Members			提案立案数 Number of Proposals on Record
		合计 Total	女性 Females	男性 Males	
第一届 1st	1955.04-1959.09	270	40	230	37
第二届 2nd	1959.09-1962.12	463	84	379	13
第三届 3rd	1962.12-1965.09	519	92	427	884
第四届 4th	1965.09-1977.11	529	88	441	23
第五届 5th	1977.11-1983.03	779	161	618	1610
第六届 6th	1983.03-1988.01	766	168	598	3122
第七届 7th	1988.01-1993.01	703	179	524	4276
第八届 8th	1993.01-1998.01	740	185	555	4975
第九届 9th	1998.01-2003.01	782	203	579	6240
第十届 10th	2003.01-2008.01	824	226	598	6871
第十一届 11th	2008.01-2013.01	737	233	504	5354
第十二届 12th	2013.01-2015.12	758	236	522	2812

资料来源：中国人民政治协商会议北京市委员会。

Source: The Chinese People's Political Consultative Conference Beijing Committe.

主要统计指标解释

优抚对象 依照法律和政策的规定，享受国家、社会和群众抚恤优待的人员，包括中国人民解放军（包括中国人民武装警察部队）现役军人、革命伤残人员、复员退伍军人、革命烈士家属、因公牺牲军人家属、病故军人家属、现役军人家属。

社会救助对象总人数 指在报告期末生活在当地规定的最低生活保障线以下的家庭人员及国家规定由民政部门救济的特殊人员和60年代精简退职老职工救济人员等。

城市居民最低生活保障人数 指报告期末家庭平均收入在当地规定的最低生活保障线以下的城镇居民数。包括“三无”对象、失业人员和在职、下岗、退休人员等。

农村居民最低生活保障人数 指报告期末在建立农村最低生活保障制度的地区，得到当地政府或集体给予最低生活保障的农业人口家庭人数。

参加基本养老保险人数 指报告期末按照国家法律、法规和有关政策规定参加基本养老保险并在社保经办机构已建立缴费记录档案的职工人数，包括中断缴费但未终止养老保险关系的职工人数和参加基本养老保险的离休、退休和退职人员的人数。不包括只登记未建立缴费记录档案的人数。

参加基本医疗保险人数 指报告期末按国家有关规定参加基本医疗保险的人数。包括参加保险的职工人数和退休人员数。

参加失业保险人数 指报告期末按照国家法律、法规和有关政策规定参加了失业保险的城镇企业事业单位的职工及地方政府规定参加失业保险的其他人员的人数。参加失业保险人数为参加失业保险的职工人数。

参加工伤保险人数 指报告期末参加工伤保险的职工人数。

参加生育保险人数 指报告期末参加生育保险的职工人数。

农村居民参加城乡居民养老保险人数 指截止报告期末参加城乡居民养老保险的农村居民人数。

参加农村新型合作医疗人数 指截止报告期末乡镇已参加农村新型合作医疗的总人数。农村新型合作医疗制度是由政府组织、引导、支持，农民自愿参加，集体、个人和政府多方筹资，以大病统筹为主的农民医疗互助共济制度。

社区服务机构数 指报告期末社区服务站、社区服务中心、其它社区服务设施的总和。

律师 指受聘参加律师事务所工作，提任法律顾问、刑（民）事代理人、刑事辩护人，办理非诉讼事件、解答法律询问，代写法律事务文书等主要从事律师业务的专职法律工作者和兼职律师。

公证人员 指在国家公证机关依法办理公证事务的司法人员。包括公证员、助理公证员和在公证处工作的其他人员。

办理公证文书 指公证处在一定时期内办结的公证文书件数。公证文书系按司法部规定或批准的格式制作。

调解人员 指人民调解委员会担负调解民间一般民事纠纷和轻微违法行为所引起的纠纷的工作人员。包括调解委员会的委员和调解小组调解员。

调解民间纠纷 指调解委员会依照法律规定，根据自愿原则，用说服教育的方法调解民间发生的有关民事权利和义务的争执，促成当事双方达到协议和谅解，解决纠纷。包括婚姻家庭纠纷，财产权益纠纷等。不包括法院受理调解的民事案件数。

地震应急避难场所 指适用于地震等自然灾害，也适用于其他事件应急状态下，供居民紧急疏散的公园、公共绿地、城市广场、体育场、学校运动场等场地数量。

Explanatory Notes on Main Statistical Indicators

Persons Receiving Special Care refer to persons receiving special treatment from the country, society and the public in accordance with provisions in laws and policies, including active servicemen of PLA (including the People's Armed Policy Army), persons wounded and disabled due to revolution, veterans, military dependents of revolutionary martyrs, military dependents of servicemen who sacrificed on duty, military dependents of servicemen who died of illness, military dependents of active servicemen.

Total Number of Persons Receiving Social Relief refer to the number of family members living under the minimum living standard provided by local governments, special persons receiving relief by civil affair authorities in line with national regulations, as well as employed persons retired because of streamlining in the 1960s, at the end of the reporting period.

Number of Persons Receiving Subsistence Allowances in Urban Areas refers to the number of urban residents whose average family income is below locally provided minimum living standard, including elderly persons, minors, psychotic patients and disables who have no statutory guardian, no fixed pocketbook, no labor ability, unemployed persons, on-the-job persons, laid-off persons, and retired persons, etc.

Number of Persons Receiving Subsistence Allowances in Rural Areas refers to the number of persons in agricultural families covered by subsistence allowances of local government or collective entities in an area where rural minimum living standard guarantee system is established, at the end of reporting period.

Number of People Participating in Basic Pension Insurance refers to the number of employed persons participating in basic pension insurance and keeping insurance premium payment records with social security organizations in accordance with provisions in national laws, rules and relevant policies at the end of reporting period, including the number of employed persons suspending the payment of insurance premium without terminating the pension insurance relation as well as retired employed persons participating in basic endowment insurance, excluding the number of persons only registered but having no insurance premium payment records.

Number of People Participating in Basic Medical Insurance refers to the number of persons participating in medical insurance programs at the end of the reporting period in accordance with relevant national regulations, including the number of employed persons and retired persons participating in the insurance.

Number of People Participating in Unemployment Insurance refers to the number of employed persons in urban enterprises and public institutions participating in unemployment insurance programs at the end of the reporting period in accordance with provisions in national laws, rules and relevant policies, as well as other persons specified by local governments to participate in unemployment insurance. The number of persons participating in unemployment insurance program is the number of employees who participate in unemployment insurance.

Number of People Participating in Work-related Injury Insurance refers to the number of persons participating in work injury insurance programs at the end of the reporting period.

Number of People Participating in Maternity Insurance refers to the number of persons participating in maternity insurance programs at the end of the reporting period.

Number of People Participating in Rural Basic Pension Insurance refers to the number of rural residents who had participated in urban and rural pension insurance programs by the end of the reporting period.

Number of People Participating in New-type Rural Cooperative Medicare refers to the total number of persons who had participated in the rural new-type cooperative medical service by the end of reporting period. The rural new-type cooperative medical service system is a mutual aid medical system for farmers, focusing on general health care programs for major diseases, organized, guided and supported by government, with farmers' voluntary participation.

Number of Service Facilities in Urban Communities refers to the total number of community service stations, service centers, and other service facilities, by the end of reporting period.

Lawyer refers to a full-time legal worker and part-time lawyer joining a law firm, serving as a legal consultant, criminal (civil) proxy, criminal counsel, handling non-lawsuit events, answering legal questions, writing legal documents for others, and other lawyer business.

Notary refers to any judicial person handling notarization matters in national notarization agencies according to laws, including notaries, assistant notaries, and other personnel working in notarization offices.

Notarization Documents Executed refers to the number of notarization documents executed at notarization offices within a given period of time. Notarization documents are prepared in the format specified or approved by the Ministry of Justice.

Mediator refer to working personnel responsible for mediating general civil disputes as well as disputes caused by slightly illegal acts in any people's mediation committee, including members of people's mediation committees and mediators of mediation teams.

Mediation of Civil Disputes refers to the mediation of disputes against civil rights and obligations by mediation committees on voluntary basis and in accordance with provisions in laws in order to urge both parties to reach an agreement and understanding to resolve the dispute, including marriage and family disputes, property rights and interest disputes, etc., excluding the number of civil cases accepted by courts.

Emergent Earthquake Refuges refer to the number of parks, public green land, city squares, gyms, school playgrounds for residents' emergent evacuation in the event of natural disasters such as earthquake, and under the condition of other emergent events.

22

北京统计年鉴2016　BEIJING STATISTICAL YEARBOOK

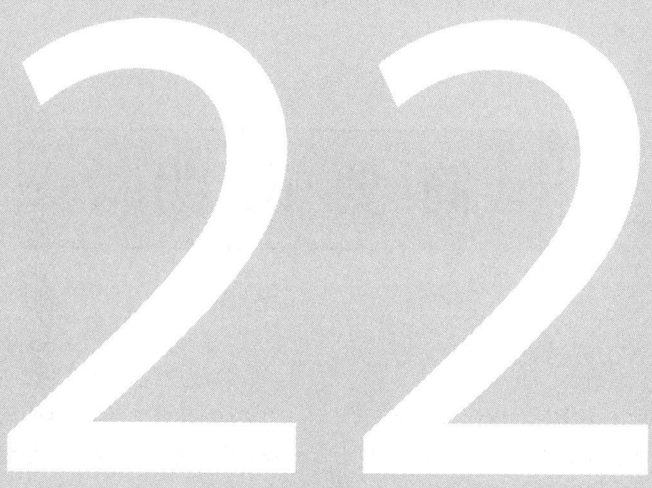

第三产业
TERTIARY INDUSTRY

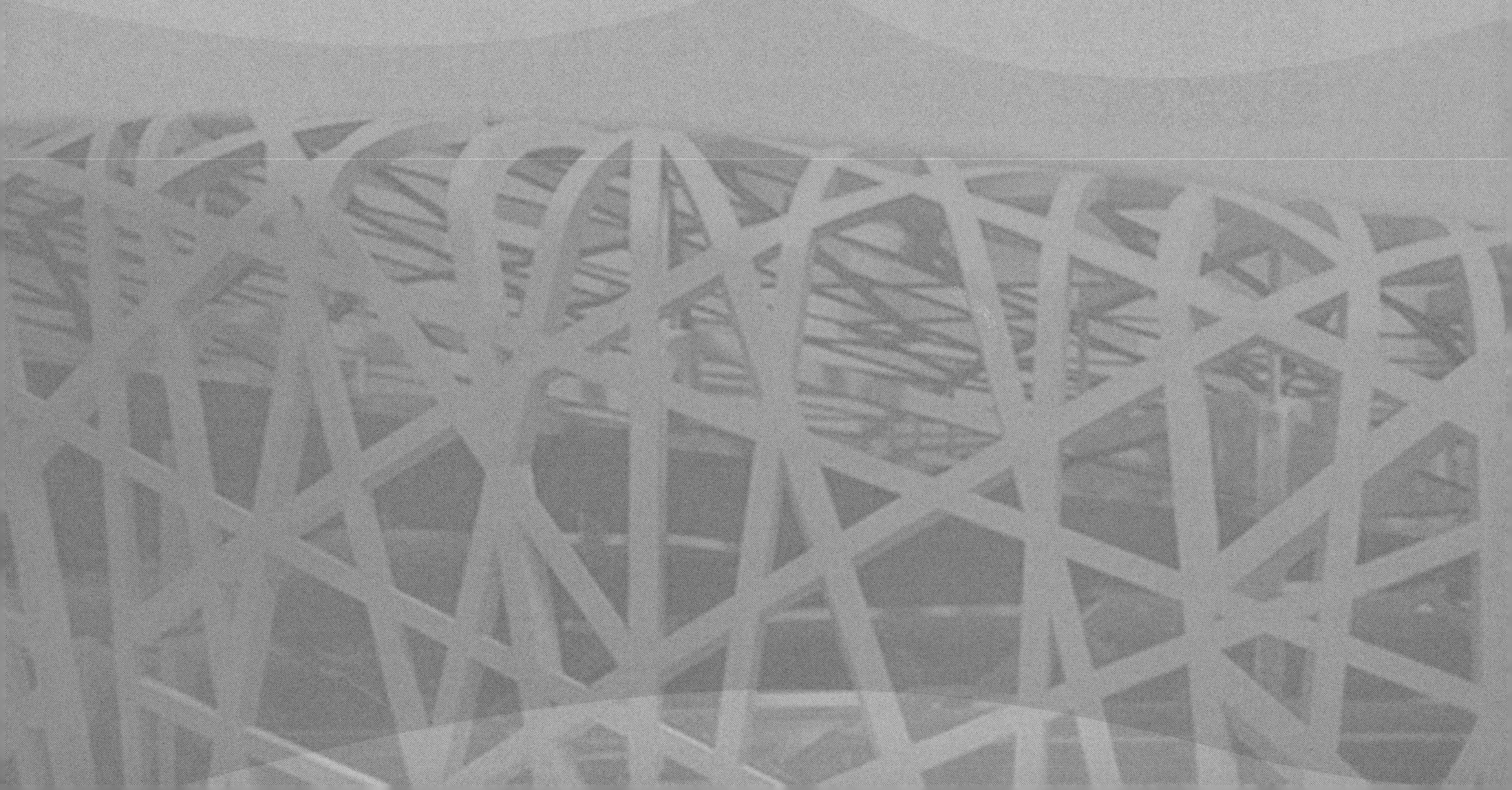

简要说明

一、本章资料的主要内容

本章主要内容包括第三产业主要指标、规模以上第三产业主要指标、规模以上第三产业企业财务状况、北京地区服务贸易、文化创意产业、物流业、会展活动和体育及相关产业活动情况等。

二、本章资料的数据来源

本章除北京地区服务贸易情况由北京市商务委员会提供外，其他资料由北京市统计局、国家统计局北京调查总队提供。

三、本章资料的统计范围

本章规模以上第三产业是指除国际组织以外的各行业限额以上的法人单位。具体为：房地产开发业的全部法人单位；金融业为全部金融监管法人单位及年营业收入500万元及以上的非金融监管的金融业法人单位；批发业为年主营业务收入2000万元及以上的企业；零售业为年主营业务收入500万元及以上的企业；住宿业为星级饭店和星级以外年主营业务收入200万元及以上企业；餐饮业为年主营业务收入200万元及以上的企业；居民服务、修理和其他服务业，文化、体育和娱乐业为年营业收入500万元及以上或从业人员期末人数50人及以上的企业；其余行业为年营业收入1000万元及以上或从业人员期末人数50人及以上的企业；执行行政事业、民间非营利组织会计制度收入合计1000万元及以上的法人单位。

文化创意产业资料根据文化创意产业法人单位的统计年报等有关资料测算取得。

物流业统计范围主要涉及铁路运输业、道路运输业、水上运输业、航空运输业、管道运输业、装卸搬运和运输代理业、仓储业、邮政业、包装服务业、批发业、零售业和工业企业。

会展业统计对象涉及会展活动的举办服务单位和接待单位。具体包括限额以上住宿业法人单位、从事各种会展活动的场馆、大型会展活动的举办单位（名单主要由北京市公安局提供）以及为会展活动提供各类专业服务的规模以上单位和旅行社。由于每年的统计对象单位范围不完全相同（有新增或撤销单位），为保持数据的可比性，同时列出统计对象本年和上年数据。

体育及相关产业情况根据体育及相关产业单位的统计年报等有关资料汇总计算，执行2008年国家体育总局、国家统计局颁布的《体育及相关产业分类（试行)》标准。

四、有关统计标准的变化说明

（一）关于行业划分。根据国家统计局规定，自2012年开始执行《国民经济行业分类》GB/T 4754-2011标准。

（二）关于三次产业划分。根据国家统计局《三次产业划分规定》(国统字[2012]108号)，该规定对三次产业的范围进行了调整。其中第一产业是指农、林、牧、渔业（不含农、林、牧、渔服务业)；第二产业是指采矿业（不含开采辅助活动)，制造业（不含金属制品、机械和设备修理业)，电力、热力、燃气及水生产和供应业，建筑业；第三产业是指除第一产业、第二产业以外的其他行业。自2012年开始执行此规定。

Brief Introduction

I. Main Content

This chapter includes: main indicators for tertiary industry, main indicators for tertiary industry above designated size, financial status of tertiary industry above designated size, service trade, cultural and creative industry, logistics industry, exhibition activities, sports and activities in related sectors in Beijing.

II. Date Source

Except for the data on service trade in Beijing, which are acquired from Beijing Municipal Commission of Commerce, other data are provided by Beijing Municipal Bureau of Statistics, and NBS Survey Office in Beijing.

III. Scope of Statistics

In this chapter, the tertiary industry above designated size refers to corporate enterprises above designated size other than international organizations. It includes all corporate enterprises in real estate development sectors, all corporate enterprises under financial regulation and the ones without financial regulation whose annual business income hitting RMB 5 million and more in finance, enterprises with annual main business income of RMB 20 million and more in wholesale trade, enterprises with annual main business income of RMB 5 million and more in retail trade, star-level hotels and non-star-level enterprises with annual main business income of RMB 2 million and more in accommodation, enterprises with annual main business income of RMB 2 million and more in restaurants, enterprises with annual business income of RMB 5 million and above or with period-end employees of 50 and above in resident service, repair, other services, culture, sports and entertainment, enterprises with annual business income of RMB 10 million and above or with period-end employees of 50 and above in other sectors, and corporate enterprises with total income of RMB 10 million and more following accounting system designed for administrative institutions and non-profit private organizations.

Data on cultural and creative industry were calculated based on annual statistical reports and other related materials of corporate enterprises in cultural and creative sector.

The statistical scope of logistics include enterprises in railway transport, road transport, water transport, air transport, transport via pipelines, loading, unloading, portage, storage, post, packaging services, wholesale trade, retail trade and industrial enterprises above designated size.

Statistical scope of MICE industry covers service companies and reception companies holding the exhibitions, in details, including: star-level hotels and those hotels with annual main business income of RMB 2 million and more; venues for exhibitions; sponsors of large exhibitions (with the list provided by Beijing Municipal Bureau of Public Security) together with organizations providing various professional services to exhibitions. Statistics for MICE in 2013 are calculated after collecting data from annual statistical report and relevant departments. As the scope of companies under survey is not completely the same (there are companies newly added and phasing out), data in both the current year and previous year are collected from the surveyed companies to keep the data comparable.

Data on sports and related industry were calculated according to the data in annual statistical reports and other related materials. As for the scope of statistics, the standards in the *Classification of Sports and Related Industry (Temporary)* issued by the State Administration for Sports and National Bureau of Statistics were applied.

Ⅳ. Changes in Relevant Statistical Standards

(I) Classification of Sectors. According to relevant provisions of National Bureau of Statistics, the *Standard for Classification of National Economic Sectors* (GB/T4754-2011) became effective in 2012.

(II) Classification of Three Industries. According to the Provisions of the National Bureau of Statistics on *Classification of Three Industries* (GTZ [2012] No. 108), the scope of three industries was changed. The primary industry refers to agriculture, forestry, animal production and hunting, fishing (excluding service for agriculture, forestry, animal production and hunting, fishing); the secondary industry refers to mining and quarrying (excluding mining support activities), manufacturing (excluding metal products, machinery and equipment repair), production and distribution of electricity, heating power, gas and water, and construction; the tertiary industry refers to sectors other than the primary and secondary industries. the Provisions of the National Bureau of Statistics on *Classification of Three Industries* (GTZ [2012] No. 108) came into effect in 2012.

22-1 第三产业主要指标及占全市比重(2000-2015年)

项 目	Item	2000	2001	2002	2003
增加值 (亿元)	Value Added (100 million yuan)	2055.1	2492.3	2988.8	3443.0
占全市比重 (%)	Percentage of the Total (%)	65.0	67.2	69.2	68.8
劳动生产率 (元/人)	Overall Labor Productivity (yuan/person)	61705	73303	83242	87043
相当于全市比例 (%)	Percentage of the Total (%)	120.8	123.4	126.2	120.2
从业人员年末人数 (万人)	Year-end Employed Persons (10000 persons)	338.2	341.8	376.3	414.8
占全市比重 (%)	Percentage of the Total (%)	54.6	54.4	55.4	59.0
固定资产投资 (亿元)	Investment in Fixed Assets (100 million yuan)	510.3	1367.9	1621.8	1875.4
占全市比重 (%)	Percentage of the Total (%)	39.3	89.3	89.4	86.9
实际利用外资金额 (亿美元)	Actual Use of Foreign Capital (USD 100 million)	22.2	12.8	12.5	14.0
占全市比重 (%)	Percentage of the Total (%)	90.5	72.4	69.8	65.3
能源消费总量 (万吨标准煤)	Energy Consumption (10000 tons of SCE)	1080.9	1196.2	1334.5	1391.0
占全市比重 (%)	Percentage of the Total (%)	26.1	28.3	30.1	29.9

MAIN INDICATORS OF THE TERTIARY INDUSTRY AND THEIR PERCENTAGES OF BEIJING'S TOTAL (2000-2015)

2004	2005	2006	2007	2008	2009	2010	2011	2012	2013	2014	2015
4102.4	4866.1	5854.5	7253.5	8410.7	9232.0	10665.2	12439.5	13768.7	15348.6	16627.0	18331.7
68.0	69.9	72.1	73.7	75.7	75.9	75.5	76.6	77.0	77.5	77.9	79.7
84186	85035	96078	112658	123306	127602	141824	159593	169066	179296	187973	200414
108.7	105.7	106.4	106.5	106.7	103.9	102.0	103.2	102.9	101.8	101.2	102.0
559.8	584.7	634.0	653.7	710.5	736.5	767.5	791.4	837.4	874.7	894.4	935.0
65.5	66.6	68.9	69.3	72.4	73.8	74.4	74.0	75.6	76.7	77.3	78.8
2112.7	2405.6	2993.8	3465.8	3434.4	4389.5	4922.3	5101.3	5597.5	6101.7	6681.6	7202.8
83.6	85.1	88.8	87.4	89.2	90.3	89.6	86.3	86.6	86.8	88.4	90.1
19.2	23.0	34.5	40.8	44.4	52.0	56.3	62.4	69.1	70.1	79.3	123.2
62.4	65.2	75.9	80.6	72.9	84.9	88.5	88.5	85.9	82.2	87.7	94.8
1638.0	1771.7	1962.8	2198.4	2394.3	2527.3	2654.4	2818.9	2967	3109.1	3236.5	3312.6
31.9	35.1	36.4	38.2	41.4	42.1	41.7	44.1	45.2	46.2	47.4	48.3

22-2 北京地区服务贸易情况(2015)
STATISTICS FOR SERVICE TRADE IN BEIJING (2015)

单位：亿美元 (USD 100000000)

项　目	Item	进出口总额 Total export-import volume	出口额 Export volume	进口额 Import volume	差额 Balance
合　计	**Total**	**1302.78**	**490.67**	**812.11**	**-321.44**
旅　行	Tourism	471.91	84.53	387.38	-302.85
运输服务	Transportation	189.94	51.50	138.44	-86.93
专业和管理咨询服务	Professional and management consulting services	111.85	83.75	28.10	55.65
电信、计算机和信息服务	Telecommunications, computer and information services	120.09	65.98	54.12	11.86
建筑服务	Construction services	141.71	88.37	53.35	35.02
技术服务	Technical services	38.03	21.98	16.05	5.92
知识产权使用费	Charge for use of intellectual properties	36.22	2.27	33.95	-31.69
保险服务	Insurance services	64.96	27.38	37.58	-10.20
金融服务	Financial services	9.98	1.55	8.43	-6.89
文化和娱乐服务	Cultural and recreational services	10.52	2.72	7.81	-5.09
其他服务	Other services	107.57	60.66	46.90	13.76

注：2015年根据商务部服务贸易项目统计口径调整要求，北京地区服务贸易情况相应进行调整。

资料来源：北京市商务委员会。

Note: The service trade in Beijing was correspondingly adjusted in 2015 according to the statistical range adjustment requirements of the Ministry of Commerce for service trade.

Source: Beijing Municipal Commission of Commerce .

22-3 规模以上第三产业主要指标(2004-2015年)
MAIN INDICATORS FOR TERTIARY INDUSTRY ENTERPRISES ABOVE DESIGNATED SIZE (2004-2015)

项　目	Item	2004	2005	2006	2007	2008
单位数 (个)	Number of Enterprises (unit)	25725	23661	24921	25651	34820
从业人员平均人数 (万人)	Average Number of Employed Persons (10000 persons)	301.4	323.3	340.4	373.5	443.6
资产总计 (亿元)	Total Assets (100 million yuan)	184985.5	274180.3	336485.9	422458.7	579095.5
收入合计 (亿元)	Income (100 million yuan)	21467.2	24444.6	29468.7	38361.8	47524.3
应交税金合计 (亿元)	Total Tax Payable (100 million yuan)	908.1	1004.0	1376.0	2360.9	1855.2
企业利润总额 (亿元)	Total Profits (100 million yuan)	1544.8	2696.1	2967.2	4511.2	4577.6

注：应交税金合计主要包括应交增值税、应交所得税、营业税金及附加和管理费用中的税金等。

Note: Total tax payable mainly includes VAT payable, income tax payable, business tax and surtax, and tax in management expenses, etc.

22-3 续表 Continued

项目	Item	2009	2010	2011	2012	2013	2014	2015
单位数 (个)	Number of Enterprises (unit)	36177	36064	36102	36616	36504	36361	32698
从业人员平均人数 (万人)	Average Number of Employed Persons (10000 persons)	472.1	487.9	509.9	545.0	565.2	586.6	616.9
资产总计 (亿元)	Total Assets (100 million yuan)	712313.4	798485.4	909953.5	1022850	1093973.1	1242344.8	1397969.4
收入合计 (亿元)	Total Income (100 million yuan)	55390.3	69106.8	79246.0	92138.2	103398.8	110308.2	110154.4
应交税金合计 (亿元)	Total Tax Payable (100 million yuan)	2560.8	3122.4	4018.9	4652.8	5415.4	5998.0	6725.2
企业利润总额 (亿元)	Total Profits (100 million yuan)	10540.8	10236.3	11413.1	14248.4	18410.6	20601.7	24752.9

22-4 规模以上第三产业单位主要经济指标(2015年)
MAIN INDICATORS FOR TERTIARY INDUSTRY ENTERPRISES ABOVE DESIGNATED SIZE (2015)

项 目	Item	单位数 (个) Enter -prises (unit)	从业人员平均人数 (万人) Average Number of Employed Persons (10000 persons)	资产总计 (亿元) Total Assets (100 million yuan)	收入合计 (亿元) Total Incomes (100 million yuan)	应交税金合计 (亿元) Total Tax (100 million yuan)	利润总额 (亿元) Total Profits (100 million yuan)
合 计	**Total**	**32698**	**616.9**	**1397969.4**	**110154.4**	**6725.2**	**24752.9**
按隶属关系分	**By Affiliation**						
中 央	Central	3966	129.4	1094072.3	46556.6	3723.0	17860.5
地 方	Local	28732	487.5	303897.1	63597.8	3002.2	6892.4
按行业分	**By Sector**						
批发和零售业	Wholesale and Retail Trade	6216	69.3	36128.4	44901.0	779.6	874.1
交通运输、仓储和邮政业	Transport, Storage and Post	989	60.8	14956.3	4158.1	360.3	422.2
住宿和餐饮业	Accommodation and Restaurants	2383	35.1	1741.1	892.7	68.3	-1.9
信息传输、软件和信息技术服务业	Information Transmission,Software and Information Technology Services	2858	74.0	30425.2	6757.1	369.7	2159.9
金融业	Financial Intermediation	1887	44.7	1123216.9	21932.6	3601.6	14725.0
房地产业	Real Estate	4271	44.8	56013.3	4997.7	732.1	893.6
租赁和商务服务业	Leasing and Business Services	4833	92.7	98921.1	8369.1	466.2	5052.4
科学研究和技术服务业	Scientific Research and Technical Services	3274	59.2	18636.7	7989.3	224.5	455.9
水利、环境和公共设施管理业	Management of Water Conservancy, Environment and Public Facilities	532	9.8	1975.1	550.4	17.3	36.0
居民服务、修理和其他服务业	Resident Services, Repair and Other Services	419	8.6	173.3	166.3	9.0	0.7
教 育	Education	1488	39.3	4340.3	1827.5	19.8	22.0
卫生和社会工作	Health Care and Social Works	680	24.5	1501.6	1665.0	2.7	-4.4
文化、体育和娱乐业	Culture, Sports and Entertainment	1194	15.7	4284.1	1525.0	70.8	117.4
公共管理、社会保障和社会组织	Pulic Administration,Social Security and Social Organizations	1674	38.3	5656.0	4422.7	3.4	
按登记注册类型分	**By Registration Type**						
内 资	Domestic Investment Economy	29747	520.4	1343300.0	90468.5	5828.1	21629.0
国 有	State-owned Units	5954	158.2	321578.0	17757.3	579.0	3982.3
集 体	Collective-owned Units	466	5.9	1590.8	322.5	11.6	15.9
股份合作	Share Holding	258	2.7	572.0	112.0	4.7	3.2
联 营	Joint Ownership Units	24	0.2	85.4	17.0	0.9	5.2
有限责任公司	Limited-Liability Corporations	11352	183.8	232667.5	44871.8	1873.9	9384.2
股份有限公司	Share Holding Corporations Ltd.	966	60.2	773082.4	17975.2	3041.2	7936.2
私 营	Private Units	10319	103.0	12826.0	8927.9	311.7	294.5
其 他	Others	408	6.5	897.9	484.8	5.2	7.5
港澳台商投资	Hong Kong, Macao and Taiwan-invested Enterprises	1245	45.4	18866.0	7317.0	352.6	750.5
外商投资	Foreign Funded Units	1706	51.0	35803.4	12369.0	544.4	2373.4

注：1. 行业划分执行2011年国民经济行业分类标准(GB/T 4754-2011)。
2. 应交税金合计主要包括应交增值税、应交所得税、营业税金及附加和管理费用中的税金等。

Note: a) Sectors in this table are classified in accordance with the Standard for Classification of National Economic Sectors 2011 (GB/T 4754-2011).
b) Total Tax mainly includes payable VAT,payable income tax, business tax and surtax, and tax in management expenses, etc.

22-5 规模以上第三产业企业财务状况(按登记注册类型分)(2015年)

单位：万元

项 目	Item	企业单位个数(个) Number of Enterprises (unit)	资产负债		
			资产总计 Total Assets	流动资产合计 Total Current Assets	#应收账款 Accounts Receivable
合 计	**Total**	**27777**	**11790354536**	**1300759812**	**118491451**
按隶属关系分	**By Affiliation**				
中 央	Central	2538	8819089431	418923025	37921725
地 方	Local	25239	2971265105	881836787	80569726
按登记注册类型分	**By Registration Type**				
内资企业	Domestically-invested Enterprises	24829	11243697295	1115889586	92728337
国有企业	State-owned Enterprises	1498	1035514985	154400031	8423562
集体企业	Collectively-owned Enterprises	397	14788909	9428577	636577
股份合作企业	Joint-equity Cooperative Enterprises	252	5697588	3667842	389553
联营企业	Associated Enterprises	20	810783	584124	2857
有限责任公司	Limited-Liability Companies	11348	2326660745	680642340	54963614
股份有限公司	Companies Limited by Shares	966	7730824237	173122307	12628138
私营企业	Private Enterprises	10285	128088340	93067439	15672064
其他企业	Others	63	1311709	976925	11971
港澳台商投资企业	Hong Kong, Macao and Taiwan-invested Enterprises	1245	188659847	73542406	8580850
外商投资企业	Foreign-invested Enterprises	1703	357997394	111327820	17182263

注：1. 行业划分执行2011年国民经济行业分类标准(GB/T 4754-2011)。
2. 应交税金合计主要包括应交增值税、应交所得税、营业税金及附加和管理费用中的税金。
3. 执行《2006年会计准则》的银行、证券、保险业企业，其"主营营业税金及附加"用"营业税金及附加"代替，"营业成本"和"主营业务成本"用"营业支出-营业税金及附加"代替。

FINANCIAL STATUS OF TERTIARY INDUSTRY ENTERPRISES ABOVE DESIGNATED SIZE(BY REGISTRATION TYPE) (2015)

(10000 yuan)

Assets and Liabilites						
固定资产合计 Total Fixed Assets	固定资产原价 Total Original Value of Fixed Assets	负债合计 Total Liabilities	#流动负债合计 Total Current Liabilities	#应付账款 Accounts Payable	所有者权益合计 Total Owner's Equity	#实收资本 Paid-up Capital
178777700	**259376402**	**8898882619**	**1010958894**	**146098682**	**2891471917**	**1259934140**
74070783	110985109	6661372567	365660503	49963862	2157716864	913900440
104706918	148391293	2237510053	645298391	96134820	733755053	346033700
144408632	200024522	8596850702	877205851	113718352	2646846593	1165627015
30354891	44478281	624965689	123940928	9333137	410549296	239205600
2002605	2827540	10711986	8030857	521116	4076923	1054874
720489	1047835	3949891	3429767	283464	1747696	456097
47282	93332	191382	113173	15160	619401	609900
67487348	93192126	1249561019	531444047	76209832	1077099726	550477523
37541205	48912938	6615405008	129287338	13077814	1115419229	348155628
5981484	9114109	91310122	80233684	14119683	36778218	25603940
273327	358361	755605	726056	158146	556104	63454
27446244	46456170	106933742	52811960	13335398	81726105	55057017
6922825	12895710	195098176	80941084	19044933	162899219	39250108

Note:a) Sectors in this table are classified in accordance with the Standard for Classification of National Economic Sectors in 2011(GB/T 4754-2011).

b) Total taxes payable mainly include VAT payable, income tax payable, business tax and surtax, and tax in management expenses, etc.

c) For banks, security and insurance enterprises implementing 2006 Standard of Accounting System, the indicator of "Main Business Tax and Surtax" is replaced with "Business Tax and Surtax" and indicators of "Business Cost" and "Main Business Cost" are replaced with "Business Cost-Busniess Tax and Surtax".

22-5 续表

单位：万元

项　目	Item	损益及分配 营业收入 Revenue from Main Businesses	#主营业务收入 Main Business Income	营业成本 Business Cost	#主营业务成本 Main Business Cost
合　计	**Total**	**994734665**	**977971075**	**713141732**	**703959440**
按隶属关系分	**By Affiliation**				
中　央	Central	409224974	401111096	263691297	258203242
地　方	Local	585509691	576859979	449450435	445756198
按登记注册类型分	**By Registration Type**				
内资企业	Domestically-invested Enterprises	797903357	784398537	566357910	558619700
国有企业	State-owned Enterprises	75787439	73587701	65470209	64910014
集体企业	Collectively-owned Enterprises	2545025	2399735	1867283	1818575
股份合作企业	Joint-equity Cooperative Enterprises	1091876	1074019	719170	713284
联营企业	Associated Enterprises	158159	156035	93589	92884
有限责任公司	Limited-Liability Companies	448705177	439665441	333664045	327520334
股份有限公司	Companies Limited by Shares	179751596	178688892	94741958	94360774
私营企业	Private Enterprises	89144377	88117771	69434162	68841584
其他企业	Others	719708	708944	367494	362252
港澳台商投资企业	Hong Kong, Macao and Taiwan-invested Enterprises	73169591	72316306	52477532	52118861
外商投资企业	Foreign-invested Enterprises	123661717	121256233	94306291	93220880

22-5 continued

(10000 yuan)

Profits and Losses							
销售费用 Sales Expenses	管理费用 Management Expenses	财务费用 Financial Expenses	利润总额 Total Profits	应交税金合计 Total Tax Payable	#营业税金及附加 Business Tax and Surtax	#主营业务税金及附加 Business Tax and Surtax	#应交所得税 Income Tax Payable
45998686	**51529634**	**16298481**	**247529028**	**66747622**	**14900384**	**14411090**	**39550733**
5530712	11304072	6256148	178604859	36801344	5111297	4839182	27330984
40467974	40225562	10042333	68924169	29946277	9789087	9571908	12219749
27992672	36551871	14186685	216290025	57777284	13166132	12706687	35763831
1395327	5117273	1654434	39822651	5311132	1333259	1166307	1509087
139139	367018	25284	159165	113999	51176	48000	37768
111005	229100	5349	31890	46789	20164	19996	13127
9784	21837	-717	51853	7926	3085	1365	1472
14687775	18255714	9127885	93842053	18738350	5844350	5620597	9005209
3020390	4144255	2525736	79362426	30411785	4981936	4942309	24426565
8505018	8253135	872234	2945394	3115642	913341	889467	762963
124234	163538	-23520	74593	31662	18821	18647	7641
6936886	6046902	1542920	7505411	3526259	715588	702866	1654836
11069128	8930861	568877	23733592	5444078	1018664	1001537	2132066

22-6 规模以上第三产业企业财务状况(按行业分)(2015年)

单位：万元

项目	Item	企业单位个数(个) Number of Enterprises (unit)	资产负债 资产总计 Total Assets	流动资产合计 Total Current Assets
合计	**Total**	**27777**	**11790354536**	**1300759812**
批发和零售业	**Wholesale and Retail Trade**	**6216**	**361283997**	**261767766**
批发业	Wholesale	4256	319162344	231035868
零售业	Retail Trade	1960	42121653	30731898
交通运输、仓储和邮政业	**Transport, Storage and Post**	**989**	**149562712**	**40915688**
铁路运输业	Railway Transport	16	55808446	7760250
道路运输业	Road Transport	479	21113894	5488354
水上运输业	Water Transport	5	56481	18927
航空运输业	Air Transport	22	26227496	5033318
管道运输业	Transport Via Pipelines	2	9510975	36221
装卸搬运和运输代理业	Loading, Unloading, Portage and Other Transport Services	325	6915478	4256988
仓储业	Storage	110	25368329	15803602
邮政业	Post	30	4561613	2518029
住宿和餐饮业	**Accommodation and Restaurants**	**2383**	**17410988**	**7078507**
住宿业	Accommodation	984	13457707	4763144
餐饮业	Restaurants	1399	3953281	2315364
信息传输、软件和信息技术服务业	**Information Transmission, Software and Information Technology Services**	**2810**	**302018337**	**100616900**
电信、广播电视和卫星传输服务	Telecommunications, Broadcasting, Television and Satellite Transmission Services	200	211766393	37395059
互联网和相关服务	Internet and Related Services	281	17737222	12748239
软件和信息技术服务业	Software and Information Technology Services	2329	72514722	50473601
金融业	**Finance**	**1863**	**9241408480**	**61094624**
货币金融服务	Monetary Financial Services	498	7571294991	9727099
资本市场服务	Capital Market Services	535	332695589	14940465
保险业	Insurance	396	453872116	935730
其他金融业	Other Financial Services	434	883545783	35491329

FINANCIAL STATUS OF TERTIARY INDUSTRY ENTERPRISES ABOVE DESIGNATED SIZE(BY SECTOR) (2015)

(10000 yuan)

Assets and Liabilites							
	固定资产合计	固定资产原价	负债合计			所有者权益合计	
#应收账款 Accounts Receivable	Total Fixed Assets	Total Original Value of Fixed Assets	Total Liabilities	#流动负债合计 Total Current Liabilities	#应付账款 Accounts Payable	Total Owner's Equity	#实收资本 Paid-up Capital
118491451	**178777700**	**259376402**	**8898882619**	**1010958894**	**146098682**	**2891471917**	**1259934140**
44948753	**9778884**	**15813337**	**257995921**	**223826076**	**58579057**	**103288075**	**53958122**
41926723	6535935	10301774	225828161	193934158	51825200	93334183	47840059
3022030	3242949	5511563	32167760	29891918	6753857	9953893	6118063
4760680	**69952101**	**94704658**	**77461722**	**52048138**	**8577344**	**72100990**	**55623842**
1307202	32159867	41884270	18206790	10783090	3121934	37601656	40665390
814303	12592044	16482568	12456984	6142628	1328919	8656911	5639212
2597	35755	73596	30143	19293	3313	26338	12088
1018680	15078324	22402187	16555891	6051254	2637228	9671605	3405569
26019	8678319	11408872	605225	445225	326651	8905750	1522200
1045864	483984	855354	3336942	3058057	944817	3578537	1874731
121537	488254	697768	24516678	24127192	32819	851652	415413
424479	435554	900043	1753071	1421400	181664	2808542	2089238
214550	**5608955**	**9733072**	**13491041**	**10047583**	**1040032**	**3919947**	**4657281**
89074	5033045	8540209	10174554	6931286	434088	3283153	3893213
125476	575910	1192863	3316488	3116297	605944	636794	764069
21478707	**15067019**	**32758152**	**99095428**	**73585169**	**17997846**	**202922909**	**120855774**
6075742	8914612	21374270	55310013	33679310	8094859	156456380	102956163
1531526	1968276	3606919	9335826	8304227	1729636	8401396	2106145
13871439	4184131	7776963	34449589	31601631	8173351	38065134	15793466
3556167	**19602083**	**25664512**	**7513255323**	**47061773**	**2118174**	**1728153157**	**652098101**
1246129	13939466	19474254	6758730629	10220351	219605	812564363	233272977
951180	967705	1345709	180773600	11057401	757357	151921989	50628687
139613	3636759	3147650	300368036	340611	110740	153504081	49748126
1219245	1058154	1696899	273383059	25443410	1030471	610162724	318448310

22-6 续表 1

单位：万元

项　目	Item	损益及分配 营业收入 Business Income	#主营业务收入 Revenue from Main Business	营业成本 Business Cost
合　计	**Total**	**994734665**	**977971075**	**713141732**
批发和零售业	**Wholesale and Retail Trade**	**449009712**	**439639699**	**413826075**
批发业	Wholesale	377106016	369482410	350884999
零售业	Retail Trade	71903697	70157289	62941077
交通运输、仓储和邮政业	**Transport, Storage and Post**	**41580767**	**40628244**	**34137459**
铁路运输业	Railway Transport	10147403	9783403	8966004
道路运输业	Road Transport	5807595	5702231	6133209
水上运输业	Water Transport	31977	31977	19697
航空运输业	Air Transport	11130394	10771345	8570442
管道运输业	Transport Via Pipelines	2750659	2696249	1101637
装卸搬运和运输代理业	Loading, Unloading, Portage and Other Transport Services	7832682	7801896	6743471
仓储业	Storage	1003756	990955	742534
邮政业	Post	2876302	2850190	1860467
住宿和餐饮业	**Accommodation and Restaurants**	**8926807**	**8831548**	**3163589**
住宿业	Accommodation	3473702	3436774	921887
餐饮业	Restaurants	5453105	5394774	2241702
信息传输、软件和信息技术服务业	**Information Transmission, Software and Information Technology Services**	**66829767**	**66156373**	**40902065**
电信、广播电视和卫星传输服务	Telecommunications, Broadcasting, Television and Satellite Transmission Services	12584792	12369812	8496420
互联网和相关服务	Internet and Related Services	11128895	11106006	5685471
软件和信息技术服务业	Software and Information Technology Services	43116079	42680555	26720175
金融业	**Finance**	**218892281**	**218669136**	**67584979**
货币金融服务	Monetary Financial Services	80917811	80904670	26538404
资本市场服务	Capital Market Services	11054633	10981003	4676021
保险业	Insurance	59391850	59382386	29450703
其他金融业	Other Financial Services	67527987	67401077	6919852

22-6 continued 1

(10000 yuan)

Profits and Losses								
#主营业务成本 Main Business Cost	销售费用 Sales Expenses	管理费用 Manage-ment Expenses	财务费用 Financial Expenses	利润总额 Total Profits	应交税金合计 Total Tax Payable	#营业税金及附加 Business Tax and Surtax	#主营业务税金及附加 Business Tax and Surtax	#应交所得税 Income Tax Payable
703959440	**45998686**	**51529634**	**16298481**	**247529028**	**66747622**	**14900384**	**14411090**	**39550733**
407726832	**18870035**	**8346627**	**3131100**	**8740829**	**7795901**	**1064514**	**1011526**	**2339596**
345059974	13090652	6124584	2805023	7198713	6166241	784933	757231	2032005
62666859	5779383	2222043	326077	1542116	1629661	279581	254295	307591
33505334	**1651799**	**2434799**	**1517328**	**4222263**	**3602637**	**184053**	**164818**	**994814**
8602675	5282	396941	375215	365309	431567	38532	27560	180101
6086238	193222	575135	338441	262632	238305	63550	59289	64282
19697	2611	5413	879	3643	1433	19	19	1242
8396873	660362	370691	779092	1043711	229443	31152	29770	221515
1060176	27166	74067	10000	1653389	612726	27988	26557	343180
6741468	309482	527464	-6503	527251	150915	11035	10337	90912
739561	82282	95930	13345	108361	1807747	5382	5108	7574
1858648	371393	389160	6859	257968	130501	6393	6177	86008
3137628	**3311414**	**1859546**	**258581**	**-19116**	**682946**	**479076**	**477016**	**102552**
915402	1085531	1214394	207756	-43715	329867	191314	190663	56628
2222225	2225883	645152	50825	24599	353079	287762	286353	45924
40461981	**9286828**	**11175714**	**-32421**	**21599370**	**3691717**	**481639**	**462581**	**1147190**
8337421	1550234	1693746	12739	15136814	417596	67887	51218	48593
5623527	2342851	1760205	-189795	1633965	686630	146996	146616	278175
26501034	5393743	7721763	144634	4828591	2587491	266756	264747	820422
67536778	**656315**	**2141776**	**657464**	**147250417**	**36015090**	**6281159**	**6216579**	**29347708**
26530736	61749	197774	193830	50566291	26103871	3973393	3973245	21902703
4664039	61405	817064	191188	6568076	3032821	703023	688507	2286932
29449225	72974	180684	-2045	28639275	3754488	1161996	1161412	2551935
6892778	460187	946254	274491	61476775	3123911	442746	393414	2606138

22-6 续表 2

单位：万元

项目	Item	企业单位个数(个) Number of Enterprises (unit)	资产负债 资产总计 Total Assets
房地产业	**Real Estate**	**4252**	**559863089**
租赁和商务服务业	**Renting and Leasing Activities, Business Services**	**4577**	**982375789**
租赁业	Renting and Leasing	103	8250666
商务服务业	Business Services	4474	974125123
科学研究和技术服务业	**Scientific Research and Development, Technical Services**	**2696**	**130156363**
研究和试验发展	Research and Experimental Development	261	20280660
专业技术服务业	Professional Technical Services	1303	78521441
科技推广和应用服务业	Technique Generalization and Application Services	1132	31354261
水利、环境和公共设施管理业	**Management of Water Conservancy, Environment and Public Facilities**	**321**	**17261298**
水利管理业	Management of Water Conservancy	11	703279
生态保护和环境治理业	Ecological Protection and Environmental Control	46	3012058
公共设施管理业	Management of Public Facilities	264	13545961
居民服务、修理和其他服务业	**Resident Services, Repair and Other Services**	**379**	**1381977**
居民服务业	Resident Services	101	583910
机动车、电子产品和日用产品修理业	Repair of Motor Vehicles, Electronics and Household Appliances	133	569679
其他服务业	Other Services	145	228389
教　育	**Education**	**185**	**2972784**
卫生和社会工作	**Healthcare and Social Works**	**190**	**1647124**
卫　生	Healthcare	183	1594016
社会工作	Social Works	7	53109
文化、体育和娱乐业	**Culture, Sports and Entertainment**	**916**	**23011597**
新闻和出版业	Journalism and Publishing	414	11398328
广播、电视、电影和影视录音制作业	Radio Broadcasting, Television, Movies, Videos and Sound Recording	201	8262684
文化艺术业	Culture and Arts	111	895505
体　育	Sports Activities	131	1653863
娱乐业	Entertainment	59	801218

22-6 Continued 2

(10000 yuan)

Assets and Liabilites								
流动资产合计 Total Current Assets	#应收账款 Accounts Receivable	固定资产合计 Total Fixed Assets	固定资产原价 Total Original Value of Fixed Assets	负债合计 Total Liabilities	#流动负债合计 Total Current Liabilities	#应付账款 Accounts Payable	所有者权益合计 Total Owner's Equity	#实收资本 Paid-up Capital
422635377	**8521551**	**19759174**	**26016102**	**428632266**	**288608138**	**19321839**	**131230824**	**77866990**
300785188	**16106955**	**23618115**	**32196573**	**407398881**	**233884985**	**14808017**	**574976909**	**263243734**
2794803	704318	3262208	4003969	5548624	1764531	350764	2702042	2011532
297990385	15402637	20355907	28192604	401850257	232120454	14457253	572274866	261232201
81191541	**15453391**	**6943224**	**11155587**	**77394651**	**65782852**	**19535144**	**52761711**	**23432592**
14639373	1157192	1852824	2763130	13269108	10480000	3083456	7011552	3200315
46671004	9674764	3028944	5263419	44774936	38860206	11333626	33746505	12556533
19881164	4621436	2061456	3129038	19350607	16442647	5118062	12003654	7675744
6397097	**1559362**	**4875215**	**5502122**	**10235064**	**4378994**	**1473225**	**7026234**	**2100913**
171182	18353	103822	196156	349563	157721	5097	353716	203373
1892971	752146	559603	680875	1785313	1303267	591311	1226745	732429
4332943	788863	4211791	4625091	8100188	2918006	876817	5445773	1165112
1033329	**149197**	**138979**	**287603**	**1092869**	**955838**	**138011**	**289109**	**351781**
411309	14382	61796	129330	559377	435182	31143	24533	73985
427957	78231	57920	116442	377268	364721	69105	192411	214106
194064	56584	19263	41831	156224	155935	37762	72165	63690
2076573	**65976**	**375191**	**667118**	**1894613**	**1824993**	**216112**	**1078172**	**372446**
884738	**113463**	**489421**	**764312**	**1167059**	**923372**	**281251**	**480065**	**372239**
851938	112835	471290	723587	1127611	884356	274469	466405	370553
32801	627	18131	40725	39448	39016	6782	13661	1685
14282484	**1562699**	**2569341**	**4113255**	**9767782**	**8030985**	**2012631**	**13243815**	**5000328**
7594883	556969	1399463	2084240	3995138	3279050	785079	7403191	2473195
4812971	863754	482288	841357	3063340	2561131	982955	5199344	1835011
543978	81956	113097	191411	473975	429053	88634	421530	218929
774296	43317	469857	835462	1638669	1285883	112145	15194	363189
556358	16702	104636	160785	596661	475867	43818	204557	110004

22-6 续表 3

单位：万元

项 目	Item	损益及分配 营业收入 Business Income	#主营业务收入 Revenue from Business Income
房地产业	**Real Estate**	**49918779**	**48676734**
租赁和商务服务业	**Renting and Leasing Activities, Business Services**	**81838442**	**78580575**
租赁业	Renting and Leasing	1498832	1467419
商务服务业	Business Services	80339610	77113157
科学研究和技术服务业	**Scientific Research and Development, Technical Services**	**60257008**	**59777002**
研究和试验发展	Research and Experimental Development	3678407	3548680
专业技术服务业	Professional Technical Services	41775956	41593789
科技推广和应用服务业	Technique Generalization and Application Services	14802646	14634533
水利、环境和公共设施管理业	**Management of Water Conservancy, Environment and Public Facilities**	**3665864**	**3632147**
水利管理业	Management of Water Conservancy	48206	44775
生态保护和环境治理业	Ecological Protection and Environmental Control	1150110	1145740
公共设施管理业	Management of Public Facilities	2467548	2441632
居民服务、修理和其他服务业	**Resident Services, Repair and Other Services**	**1455490**	**1417587**
居民服务业	Resident Services	375739	368879
机动车、电子产品和日用产品修理业	Repair of Motor Vehicles, Electronics and Household Appliances	696344	670284
其他服务业	Other Services	383407	378424
教 育	**Education**	**1775374**	**1753252**
卫生和社会工作	**Healthcare and Social Works**	**1474820**	**1469095**
卫 生	Healthcare	1462390	1458066
社会工作	Social Works	12429	11030
文化、体育和娱乐业	**Culture, Sports and Entertainment**	**9109554**	**8739684**
新闻和出版业	Journalism and Publishing	4182168	3889671
广播、电视、电影和影视录音制作业	Radio Broadcasting, Television, Movies, Videos and Sound Recording	3680260	3624237
文化艺术业	Culture and Arts	468959	464952
体 育	Sports Activities	537119	520552
娱乐业	Entertainment	241048	240272

22-6 continued 3

(10000 yuan)

Profits and Losses									
营业成本 Business Cost	#主营业务成本 Main Business Cost	销售费用 Sales Expenses	管理费用 Management Expenses	财务费用 Financial Expenses	利润总额 Total Profits	应交税金合计 Total Taxes Payable	#营业税金及附加 Business Tax and Surtax	#主营业务税金及附加 Main Business Tax and Surtax	#应交所得税 Income Tax Payable
30470980	**29973565**	**2067857**	**4806742**	**3211057**	**8935625**	**7319958**	**4642334**	**4536897**	**2308643**
61631891	**60673762**	**6154699**	**12222347**	**7342898**	**50524420**	**4619942**	**1092864**	**889199**	**2332369**
974638	968262	54245	197548	67963	230327	98352	10165	10073	62908
60657253	59705500	6100454	12024799	7274936	50294093	4521590	1082699	879125	2269461
49759666	**49487675**	**2137943**	**5548128**	**181927**	**4558986**	**2091194**	**397346**	**383711**	**691132**
2682741	2600033	143729	806249	-35834	459679	210055	24771	20350	71017
35445184	35374025	819449	3045682	148711	3594371	1331235	276063	268298	454305
11631741	11513616	1174764	1696197	69050	504936	549904	96512	95063	165810
2740889	**2726217**	**126438**	**396715**	**64441**	**359636**	**164242**	**86881**	**82816**	**62271**
20178	19618	462	32404	10164	40341	15933	3681	285	11839
855734	854745	37043	82183	23209	168830	39075	11590	11470	23226
1864977	1851854	88932	282127	31067	150465	109235	71609	71060	27206
860269	**847867**	**322606**	**226171**	**6219**	**6564**	**88246**	**38350**	**37417**	**17331**
142212	140836	141142	80946	2306	-6308	25118	12580	12467	8142
487333	480643	113623	79801	3526	6653	40894	6676	6041	7185
230724	226388	67841	65424	387	6218	22234	19094	18910	2003
849738	**840005**	**330173**	**385772**	**-27395**	**219898**	**105544**	**51592**	**51453**	**39847**
1043774	**1042195**	**149142**	**342742**	**18682**	**-43902**	**20774**	**1805**	**1698**	**16706**
1033939	1032360	149002	337175	18788	-42932	20439	1791	1685	16692
9835	9835	140	5567	-106	-970	335	14	14	15
6170358	**5999601**	**933436**	**1642555**	**-31399**	**1174041**	**549430**	**98774**	**95381**	**150576**
2458351	2321879	528598	970765	-58150	755331	315332	41677	40235	53993
2974880	2947604	203967	377314	15414	424516	144840	15627	14107	75620
292824	290025	51711	96742	159	36862	28441	7415	7366	8426
297833	293889	116493	160487	10930	-62342	42697	24704	24350	8325
146469	146203	32669	37247	248	19674	18120	9351	9323	4213

22-7 文化创意产业活动单位基本情况
STATISTICS FOR CULTURAL AND CREATIVE INDUSTRY

单位：亿元 (100 million yuan)

项　目	Item	资产总计 Total Assets		收入合计 Total Income		从业人员平均人数（万人） Average Number of Employed Persons (10000 persons)	
		2015	2014	2015	2014	2015	2014
合　计	**Total**	**31893.9**	**26441.8**	**15877.8**	**13982.0**	**202.3**	**191.6**
文化艺术	Culture and Arts	1497.8	1284.4	421.8	410.1	12.6	11.2
新闻出版	Journalism and Publications	2453.3	2257.3	1026.4	1034.8	15.2	15.7
广播、电视、电影	Radios, Televisions amd Movies	2934.2	2433.1	917.4	859.4	7.4	7.2
软件、网络及计算机服务	Software, Network & Computer Services	13719.4	11143.7	6442.2	5380.0	101.4	90.8
广告会展	Advertisements & Exhibitions	2462.2	1922.5	2178.4	1835.0	16.8	17.3
艺术品交易	Transaction of Artworks	978.5	892.8	1021.8	1094.5	2.5	2.7
设计服务	Design Services	1116.9	1053.6	563.6	576.1	16.6	16.7
旅游、休闲娱乐	Tourism and Enterainment	1947.6	1678.8	1207.0	1054.7	13.1	13.0
其他辅助服务	Other Auxiliary Services	4783.9	3775.5	2099.2	1737.5	16.7	17.0

22-8 物流业活动情况
STATISTICS FOR LOGISTICS

项目	Item	2015	2014	2015年为2014年% 2015 as % of 2014
物流业务收入 (亿元)	**Business Income of Logistics Sector (100 million yuan)**	**2409**	**2482.5**	**97.0**
运输收入	Transportation Income	1712.9	1757.9	97.4
保管收入	Storage Income	633.2	659.2	96.1
一体化物流业务收入	Integrated Logistics Income	63	65.3	96.5
社会物流总额 (亿元)	**Total Amount of Social Logistics (100 million yuan)**	**67648.7**	**75923.6**	**89.1**
农产品	Agricultural Products	312.8	358.2	87.3
工业品	Industrial Products	17829.2	17911.6	99.5
进口货物	Imported Goods	16442.6	21695.5	75.8
再生资源	Renewable Resources	131.5	201.7	65.2
外省市流入物品	Goods from Other Provinces and Cities	32691.8	35508.4	92.1
单位与居民物品	Entities and Residents' Goods	240.8	248.2	97.0
物流业从业人员平均人数 (万人)	**Employment in Logistics Sector (10000 persons)**	**50.3**	**50.8**	**99.0**
交通运输、邮政、仓储业	Transportation, Post, Storage	35.7	35.2	101.4
采掘业、制造业、批发和零售业	Excavation, Manufacturing, Wholesale and Retail Trade	14.6	15.6	93.6

22-9 会展业活动情况
STATISTICS FOR MICE INDUSTRY IN BEIJING

项目		Item		2015	2014	2015年为2014% 2015 as % of 2014
人员情况		**Employed Persons**				
从业人员平均人数	(万人)	Year-end Employed Persons	(10000 person)	19.9	20.3	98.0
接待设施情况		**Facilities**				
接待场所会议室个数	(个)	Number of Meeting Rooms	(unit)	5041	4908	102.7
#座位数超过500座的会议室	(个)	Number of Meeting Rooms with More Than 500 Seats	(unit)	177	174	101.7
接待场所会议室使用面积	(万平方米)	Usable Area of Meeting Rooms	(10000 sq.m)	74.1	72.4	102.3
接待场所会议室可容纳人数	(万人)	Capacity of Meeting Rooms	(10000 person)	45.3	43.9	103.2
会议情况		**Meetings**				
接待会议个数	(万个)	Number of Meetings Held in Beijing	(10000 unit)	20.9	20.4	102.7
#国际会议	(万个)	International Meetings	(10000 unit)	0.5	0.6	92.1
接待会议人数	(万人次)	Number of Meeting Participants	(10000 person-times)	1527.6	1418.6	107.7
#国际会议	(万人次)	International Meeting Participants	(10000 person-times)	59.4	62.2	95.5
展览情况		**Exhibitions**				
接待展览个数	(个)	Number of Exhibitions Held in Beijing	(unit)	789	723	109.1
#国际展览	(个)	International Exhibitions	(unit)	173	201	86.1
#展览面积1万(不含)平方米以下的展览个数	(个)	Number of Exhibitions with Exhibition Area under 10,000 sq.m (10,000 sq.m excluded)	(unit)	596	532	112.0
展览面积1万平方米及以上的展览个数	(个)	Number of Exhibitions with Exhibition Area of 10,000 sq.m and over	(unit)	193	191	101.0
接待展览累计面积(含室外展览面积)	(万平方米)	Total Exhibition Area (including outdoor exhibition area)	(10000 sq.m)	612.6	675.2	90.7
#国际展览累计面积	(万平方米)	International Exhibition Area	(10000 sq.m)	325.8	410.6	79.4
接待展览观众人数	(万人次)	Number of Exhibition Visitors	(10000 person-times)	772.8	911.6	84.8
#国际展览观众人数	(万人次)	International Exhibition Visitors	(10000 person-times)	259.1	373.2	69.4
奖励旅游情况		**Incentives**				
服务奖励旅游人数	(万人次)	Number of Incentive Tourists	(10000 person-times)	19.5	26.7	73.0
收入情况		**Revenues**				
会展收入	(亿元)	Total Revenues from MICE Industry	(100 million yuan)	218.5	210.3	103.9
会议收入	(亿元)	Revenues from Meetings	(100 million yuan)	97.1	96.6	100.5
#国际会议收入	(亿元)	Revenues from International Meetings	(100 million yuan)	6.7	8.9	75.3
展览收入	(亿元)	Revenues from Exhibitions	(100 million yuan)	110.5	105.6	104.7
#国际展览收入	(亿元)	Revenues from International Exhibitions	(100 million yuan)	34.3	36.8	93.1
奖励旅游收入	(亿元)	Revenues from Incentives	(100 million yuan)	10.9	8.1	134.1

注：会展业统计范围包括会展场馆、限额以上住宿业法人单位、会展举办单位以及规模以上会议及展览服务业法人单位和旅行社等。由于统计范围内的单位名录每年均有变化,为保证数据的可比性，需要调整上年同期数据以计算可比增速。

Note: Statistical scope in MICE industry includes MICE venue, star-level hotel and main organizer of MICE, etc. As items in the said statistical scope change every year, so in order to ensure figure comparability, figures of the same period in the previous year need to be adjusted to calculate comparable growth rate.

22-10 体育及相关产业情况
STATISTICS FOR SPORTS AND RELEVANT INDUSTRY

项 目	Item	收入合计 (亿元) Total Income (100 million yuan)		从业人员平均人数（万人） Average Number of Employed Persons (10000 persons)	
		2014	2013	2014	2013
合 计	**Total**	**1055.7**	**961.7**	**14.1**	**13.8**
体育管理活动	Sports Management Activities	29.3	26.7	0.3	0.2
体育竞赛表演活动	Sports Contests and Performance Activities	76.1	68.3	1.3	1.0
体育健身休闲活动	Sports, Body Building and Entertainment Activities	38.3	40.6	3.3	3.6
体育场馆服务	Sports Venues Service	17.7	21.0	0.6	0.7
体育中介服务	Sports Agency Service	32.6	23.6	0.4	0.3
体育培训与教育	Sports Training and Education	16.5	14.8	0.6	0.5
体育传媒与信息服务	Sports Media and Information Service	82.8	79.6	0.6	0.7
其他与体育相关服务	Other Service Related to Sports	99.9	107.3	1.0	0.8
体育用品及相关产品制造	Manufacture of Sports Goods and Related Products	60	68.1	0.8	1.1
体育用品及相关产品销售、	Sales of Sports Goods and Related Products				
贸易代理与出租	Trade Agency and Rent	578.1	499.1	5.0	4.8
体育场地设施建设	Construction of Sports Venues and Facilities	24.3	12.6	0.1	0.1

注：2015年9月，国家统计局修订了原有体育产业分类，发布《体育产业统计分类(2015)》标准，据此分类，需要重新对2014年和2013年数据进行测算。另外，国家体育总局将在2016年开展体育产业专项调查工作，2015年度数据测算将根据国家统一要求延后，故今年暂不出2015年数据，而是按新标准测算2014年度及2013年度数据。

Note: The National Bureau of Statistics of the Peoples' Republic of China revised the original classification of sports industry and issued the standard for Statistical Classification of Sports Industry (2015) in September 2015. According to the above standard, it is necessary to re-measure and re-calculate the data in 2014 and 2013. Moreover, General Administration of Sport of China plans to conduct a special investigation on sports industry in 2016, and the data measurement and calculation work of 2015 will be postponed in accordance with the unified requirement of the state, therefore, no data of 2015 is available this year and the data measurement and calculation work of 2014 and 2013 will be conducted according to the new standard.

主要统计指标解释

物流业务收入 指通过物流业务活动取得的收入。包括企业完成运输、存储、装卸、搬运、包装、流通加工、配送、信息等物流业务取得的收入之和。反映物流相关行业物流活动的总规模。

物流业从业人员 指企业中直接或间接从事物流活动的人数。直接从事物流活动的人员包括在企业中从事运输、配送、装卸搬运、仓储保管等物流活动并取得劳动报酬的从业人员；间接从事物流活动的人员包括在企业中从事物流管理活动并取得劳动报酬的从业人员，包括采购、销售部门的主管人员，但不包括采购、销售部门内部办事人员。

社会物流总额 指第一次进入市内需求领域，产生从供应地向接受地实体流动的物品的价值总额。包括六个方面的内容：进入需求领域的农产品物流总额、工业品物流总额、进口货物物流总额、外省市调入物品物流总额、再生资源物流总额、单位与居民物品物流总额。.

接待会议个数 指报告期内，接待的各种类型会议的个数。包括国际会议和国内会议。

接待国际会议个数 指报告期内，接待的国际会议的个数。国际会议是指在我国境内举办的，与会者来自3个或3个以上中国大陆以外国家和地区（含港、澳、台地区）的会议、论坛、研讨会、报告会、交流会等。

接待展览个数 指报告期内，接待的各种类型展览的个数。包括国际展览和国内展览。

接待国际展览个数 指报告期内，接待的国际展览的个数。国际展览指中国大陆以外国家和地区（含港、澳、台地区）的参展商参展面积达到该次展出面积20%以上的展览个数。

服务奖励旅游人数 指报告期内，服务的奖励旅游人数的总和（含接待）。

服务贸易 服务贸易包括跨境提供、境外消费、商业存在和自然人移动等内容。

体育组织管理活动 指专门为社会公众提供比赛、训练、辅导和管理的组织的活动，如群众性体育组织、专项性体育管理组织的活动。

体育场馆管理活动 指为社会公众提供观赏比赛和专业训练的体育场馆管理活动，如综合性体育场馆，训练用场地的管理活动。

体育健身休闲活动 指社会公众提供的可供参与和选择的各种健身休闲活动场所的管理活动。

体育中介活动 指为社会公众提供的体育中介活动，如各种体育商务代理、经纪、咨询活动。

其他体育活动 指为社会公众提供的其他体育服务活动。包括体育培训服务、体育科研服务、体育彩票服务、体育传媒服务、体育展览服务、体育市场管理服务、体育场馆设计服务、体育场所保洁服务和体育文物及文化保护服务。

体育用品、服装、鞋帽及相关体育产品的制造 指提供体育服务所必须的体育用品、服装、鞋帽及相关体育产品的制造活动。

体育用品、服装、鞋帽及相关体育产品的销售 指提供体育服务所必须的体育用品、服装、鞋帽及相关体育产品的销售活动。

体育场馆管理活动 指提供体育服务所必须的体育场馆建筑活动。

Explanatory Notes on Main Statistical Indicators

Business Income of Logistics Sector refers to the income earned from logistics business activities, which is equal to the sum of incomes from such logistics operations completed by enterprises as transportation, storage, loading and unloading, handling, package, circulation and processing, delivery, and information. It reflects the overall scale of logistics activities in logistics related sector.

Employees in Logistics Sector refers to the number of persons directly and indirectly engaged in logistics activities in enterprises. Persons directly engaging in logistics activities are those engaging in logistics activities such as transportation, delivery, loading and unloading, handling, storage and warehouse keeping in enterprises and receiving labor remuneration; persons indirectly engaging in logistics activities are those engaging in management activities in enterprises and receiving labor remuneration, including executives in purchase and sales departments, but excluding clerks in purchase and sales departments.

Total Amount of Social Logistics refers to the total value of goods entering the demand area in the city for the first time and having physical flow from the supply place to the receiving place, consisting of value on six aspects: total logistics amount of agricultural products, total logistics amount of industrial products, total logistics amount of imported goods, total logistics amount of goods transferred from other provinces and cities, total logistics amount of recycled resources, and total logistics amount of corporate and household supplies entering the demand field.

Number of Meeting Held in Beijing refers to the number of various types of conference held in Beijing in the reporting period, including international and domestic conferences.

Number of International Meeting refers to the number of international conferences held in Beijing in the reporting period. International conference means any conference, forum, seminar, report conference, and workshops, etc. held in our country, with participants coming from 3 or more countries and regions (including Hong Kong, Macao and Taiwan) outside Chinese mainland.

Number of Exhibitions Held in Beijing refers to the number of various types of exhibitions held in Beijing in the reporting period, including international and domestic exhibitions.

Number of International Exhibitions Received refers to the number of international exhibitions received in the reporting period. International exhibition means any exhibition with participants from countries and regions (including Hong Kong, Macao and Taiwan) outside Chinese mainland whose exhibition floorage accounts for more than 20% of the exhibition.

Number of Incentive Tourists refers to the sum of persons of incentive tour served in the reporting period.

Service Trade includes overseas provision, overseas consumption, commercial existence, movement of natural persons, and so on.

Overseas Provision refers to any service provider provides service within China for service consumers in any other country or region, and any service provider provides service in any other country or region to service consumers within China.

Gym Management Activities mean management activities in gym providing games for view and special trainings for the public, such as management activities in comprehensive sports venues and training fields and courts.

Sports, Body Building and Entertainment Activities mean management activities provided for the public at Sports bodybuilding and entertainment sites, which are to be participated in and chosen.

Sports Agency Activities refer to sport agency activities provided for the public, such as various sports business agency, broker and consulting activities.

Other Sports Activities refer to activities of other sports service provided for the public, including sports training service, sports research service, sports lottery service, sports communication service, sports exhibition service, sports market management service, sports venue design service, sports site cleaning service, sports cultural relics and cultural protection service.

Manufacturing of Sports Supplies, Clothes, Shoes and Caps, and Related Sports Products refers to manufacturing of sports supplies, clothes, shoes and caps, and related sports products necessary for provision of sports service.

Sales of Sports Supplies, Clothes, Shoes and Caps, and Related Sports Products refers to sales of sports supplies, clothes, shoes and caps, and related sports products necessary for provision of sports service.

Gymnasium Building Activities refer to activities of construction of sports venues necessary for provision of sports service.

23

北京统计年鉴2016　BEIJING STATISTICAL YEARBOOK

开发区
DEVELOPMENT ZONES

简要说明

一、本章资料的主要内容

本章资料主要反映北京市开发区的基本情况，招商、入资，企业生产经营、财务、研发活动和人力资源情况，重点介绍了北京经济技术开发区、中关村国家自主创新示范区及北京天竺综合保税区的主要情况。其中，中关村国家自主创新示范区亦庄园在中关村国家自主创新示范区与北京经济技术开发区中为重叠部分。

二、本章资料的数据来源

本章中关村国家自主创新示范区的统计资料由北京市统计局提供；其他各开发区中涉及招商、土地、投资的统计资料由各开发区管委会提供，财务资料由北京市统计局提供；北京经济技术开发区的统计资料由北京经济技术开发区统计局、调查队提供；北京天竺综合保税区中涉及招商、土地、投资等方面的统计资料由北京天竺综合保税区管委会提供，财务资料由北京市统计局提供。

三、本章的有关变化说明

根据 2012 年《国务院关于同意调整中关村国家自主创新示范区空间规模和布局的批复》，自 2013 年起，中关村国家自主创新示范区的统计范围在原有的海淀园、丰台园、昌平园、电子城科技园、亦庄园、德胜园、雍和园、石景山园、通州园和大兴生物医药产业基地的基础上，增加了平谷园、门头沟园、顺义园、房山园、密云园、怀柔园和延庆园七个园区。同时，“电子城科技园”更名为“朝阳园”；“德胜园”更名为“西城园”；“雍和园”更名为“东城园”。

Brief Introduction

I. Main Content

Data in this chapter mainly shows the basic condition of development zones in Beijing, business invitation, investment, production and operation of enterprises, financial status, scientific and technological activities, and human resources. This chapter mainly focuses on the situation of Beijing Economic-Technological Development Area, Zhongguancun National Innovation Demonstration Zone and Beijing Tianzhu Bonded Zone. Data of Zhongguancun Yizhuang Sub-park is counted in both Zhongguancun National Innovation Demonstration Zone and Beijing Economic-Technological Development Area.

II. Source of Data

Data of Zhongguancun National Innovation Demonstration Zone in this chapter are sourced from Beijing Municipal Bureau of Statistics; statistics for other development zones in terms of business innovation, land and investment are gathered and provided by Beijing Municipal Commission of Economy and Information Technology and financial data are provided by Beijing Municipal Bureau of Statistics; data for Beijing Economic- Technological Development Area are from the Statistics Bureau and Survey Team of Beijing Economic-Technological Development Area; data for business invitation and land in Beijing Tianzhu Bonded Zone are provided by the Administrative Committee of the Bonded Zone, while other data are from Beijing Municipal Bureau of Statistics.

III. Notes on Changes in This Chapter

According to the *Official Reply of the State Council on Approving the Adjustment of Spatial Scale and Layout of Zhongguancun National Innovation Demonstration Area* issued in 2012, the statistic scope of Zhongguancun Area has been enlarged to include Pinggu Sub-park, Mentougou Sub-park, Shunyi Sub-park, Fangshan Sub-park, Miyun Sub-park, Huairou Sub-park and Yanqing Sub-park to supplement Haidian Sub-park, Fengtai Sub-park, Changping Sub-park, Electronic Park, Yizhuang Sub-park, Deshengyuan Sub-park, Yonghe Sub-park, Shijingshan Sub-park, Tongzhou Sub-park and Daxing Ecological Sub-park Pharmaceutical Base. At the same time, Electronic Park is changed into Chaoyang Sub-park, Deshengyuan Sub-park into Xicheng Sub-park and Yonghe Sub-park into Dongcheng Sub-park.

23-1 开发区基本情况(2015年)
STATISTICS ON DEVELOPMENT ZONES (2015)

项　目		Item		国家级 National	市　级 Municipal
开发区个数	(个)	Number of Development Zones	(unit)	3	16
区规划总面积	(公顷)	Total Planned Area of Development Zones	(hectare)	45395.9	9252.6
累计已开发土地面积	(公顷)	Accumulated Area of Developed Land	(hectare)	30324.4	6488.1
累计已供应土地面积	(公顷)	Accumulated Area of Supplied Land	(hectare)	27934.9	5255.1
累计已建成城镇建设用地面积	(公顷)	Accumulated Area of Land for Urban Development	(hectare)	24595.5	5151.9
累计招商项目企业个数	(个)	Accumulated Number of Enterprises of Business Inviting Programs	(unit)	52574	18888
累计招商项目总投资	(亿元)	Accumulative Total Investment of Business Inviting	(100 million yuan)	18194.1	3254.1
累计招商项目注册资本	(亿元)	Accumulative Registered Capital of Business Inviting Programs	(100 million yuan)	16108.4	2265.2
#三资企业	(亿元)	Three Kinds of Foreign-funded Enterprises	(100 million yuan)	2267.1	332.6
累计招商项目合同外资金额	(亿美元)	Accumulative Contracted Foreign Capital of Business Inviting Programs	(USD 100 million)	291.1	54.2
累计招商项目外商实际投资	(亿美元)	Accumulated Actual Foreign Investment of Business Inviting Programs	(USD 100 million)	225.3	60.3
固定资产投资	(亿元)	Investment in Fixed Assets	(100 million yuan)	925.5	169.5
总收入	(亿元)	Total Revenue	(100 million yuan)	43785.1	4907.0
工业总产值(当年价格)	(亿元)	Gross Output Value Of Industry (at current prices)	(100 million yuan)	9802.3	1335.9
工业销售产值(当年价格)	(亿元)	Sales Value of Industry (at current prices)	(100 million yuan)	9215.4	1316.1
利润总额	(亿元)	Total Profits	(100 million yuan)	3492.8	250.5
应缴税金	(亿元)	Total Taxes Payable	(100 million yuan)	2081.8	178.6

注：1. 本表所指开发区包括北京市级及国家级开发区情况。
2. 表内“累计”指自开始至年末的累计数。
3. 本表“总收入”、“工业总产值(当年价格)”、“工业销售产值”(当年价格)、“利润总额”和“应缴税金”数据的统计范围为注册在开发区内的规模(限额)以上法人单位。

Note: a) Development zones in this table include those at Beijing municipal level and national level.
b) Accumulative data in this table refer to the accumulation from the beginning to the end of this year.
c) The statistical scope of total revenue, gross output value of industry (at current prices), sales value of industry (at current prices), total profits and total taxes payable in this table cover legal entities above designated size that are registered in the development zones.

23-2 开发区土地开发情况(2015年)
LAND EXPLOITATION OF DEVELOPMENT ZONES(2015)

单位：公顷 (hectare)

名　　称	Item	规划总面积 Total Planned Area	累计已开发土地面积 Accumulated Area of Developed Land	累计已供应土地面积 Accumulated Area of Supplied Land	累计已建成城镇建设用地 Accumulated Area of Land for Urban Development
国家级开发区	**State-level Development Zone**	**45395.9**	**30324.4**	**27934.9**	**24595.5**
北京经济技术开发区	Beijing Economic-Technological Development Area	4680.0	3700.0	3886.5	3700.0
中关村国家自主创新示范区	Zhongguancun National Independent Demonstration Zone	42799.5	28779.0	23700.4	23367.4
中关村示范区海淀园	Zhongguancun Haidian Sub-park	17430.6	13764.1	13624.6	13324.3
中关村示范区丰台园	Zhongguancun Fengtai Sub-park	1763.0	330.7	237.4	181.7
中关村示范区昌平园	Zhongguancun Changping Sub-park	5140.0	2209.7	2017.4	1868.6
中关村示范区朝阳园	Zhongguancun Chaoyang Sub-park	2610.0	1471.9	1447.1	1036.6
中关村示范区亦庄园	Zhongguancun Yizhuang Sub-park	2678.0	2678.0		2678.0
中关村示范区西城园	Zhongguancun Xicheng Sub-park	1000.0	1000.0	1000.0	
中关村示范区东城园	Zhongguancun Dongcheng Sub-park	603.0	288.8		288.8
中关村示范区石景山园	Zhongguancun Shijingshan Sub-park	1334.0	127.6	58.3	127.6
中关村示范区通州园	Zhongguancun Tongzhou Sub-park	3434.6	2387.2	1910.4	1709.8
中关村示范区大兴园	Zhongguancun Daxing Sub-park	1124.7	710.2	559.0	298.2
中关村示范区平谷园	Zhongguancun PingGu Sub-park	508.0	329.0	103.4	85.2
中关村示范区门头沟园	Zhongguancun MenTouGou Sub-park	189.0	120.0	120.0	
中关村示范区房山园	Zhongguancun FangShan Sub-park	1573.0	1214.0	1038.4	695.4
中关村示范区顺义园	Zhongguancun ShunYi Sub-park	1208.5	912.4	562.5	402.4
中关村示范区密云园	Zhongguancun MiYun Sub-park	1000.8	699.3	607.0	462.4
中关村示范区怀柔园	Zhongguancun HuaiRou Sub-park	711.0	266.3	165.3	17.9
中关村示范区延庆园	Zhongguancun YanQing Sub-park	491.2	270.0	249.6	190.6
北京天竺综合保税区	Beijing Tianzhu Bonded Area	594.4	523.4	348.0	206.2
市级开发区	**Municipal-level Development Zone**	**9252.6**	**6488.1**	**5255.1**	**5151.9**
北京石龙经济开发区	Shilong Economic Development Zone	189.0	120.0	120.0	
北京良乡经济开发区	Liangxiang Economic Development Zone	240.9	136.1	132.7	110.7
北京大兴经济开发区	Daxing Economic Development Zone	414.8	289.9	278.0	257.8
北京通州经济开发区	Tongzhou Economic Development Zone	1947.6	772.6	752.4	637.3
北京雁栖经济开发区	Yanqi Economic Development Zone	1096.0	942.4	712.9	659.5
北京兴谷经济开发区	Xinggu Economic Development Zone	503.2	571.7	409.0	586.0
北京密云经济开发区	Miyun Economic Development Zone	1249.5	1249.5	1000.4	910.0
北京林河经济开发区	Linhe Economic Development Zone	416.0	385.0	260.0	349.0
北京天竺空港经济开发区	Tianzhu Economic Development Zone	660.0	660.0	449.0	402.1
北京八达岭经济开发区	Badaling Economic Development Zone	480.8	318.6	209.6	295.1
北京永乐经济开发区	Yongle Economic Development Zone	459.8	219.3	137.1	137.1
北京延庆经济开发区	Yanqing Economic Development Zone	418.6	173.2	143.0	221.0
北京昌平小汤山工业园区	Changping Xiaotangshan Industrial Park	257.3	14.3	23.5	45.3
北京采育经济开发区	Caiyu Economic Development Zone	355.0	327.1	319.7	306.9
北京房山工业园区	Fangshan Industrial Park	218.5	159.5	159.5	122.8
北京马坊工业园区	Mafang Bonded Area Industrial Park	345.6	149.0	148.4	111.5

注：1. 本表所指开发区包括北京市级及国家级开发区情况。
2. 中关村国家自主创新示范区亦庄园数据在中关村国家自主创新示范区与北京经济技术开发区中为重叠部分。
3. 自2013年起，平谷园、门头沟园、房山园、顺义园、密云园、怀柔园和延庆园七个园区纳入中关村国家自主创新示范区统计范围，后表同(详见简要说明)。
4. 除中关村国家自主创新示范区海淀园外，中关村国家自主创新示范区各园"规划总面积"指标均填报批复土地面积，范围较2012年有所变化。
5. 表内"累计"指自开始至年末的累计数。

Note: a) Development zones in this table include those at Beijing municipal level and national level.
b) Data on Yizhuang Sub-park of Zhongguancun Demonstration Zone are overlapped in Zhongguancun National Innovation Demonstration Zone and Beijing Economic and Technological Development Area.
c) Since 2013, the Pinggu Sub-park, Mentougou Sub-park, Fangshan Sub-park, Shunyi Sub-park, Huairou Sub-park and Yanqing Sub-park are incorporated into the statistical scope of Zhongguancun National Independent Innovation Demonstration Zone (the same in the following tables). (For details, please refer to the Brief Introduction to this chapter.)
d) Apart from Haidian Sub-park, the total planned area of all sub-parks of Zhongguancun National Independent Innovation Demonstration Zone refers to the approved area of land. The statistical scope is slightly different from that of 2012.
e) "Accumulated" in this table refers to the accumlation from the beginning to the end of the year.

23-3 开发区招商、入资情况(2015年)

名 称	Item	招商项目企业个数(个) Number of Enterprises Involved in Business Inviting Programs (unit)
国家级开发区	**State-level Development Zone**	**52574**
北京经济技术开发区	Beijing Economic-Technological Development Area	12722
中关村国家自主创新示范区	Zhongguancun National Independent Innovation Demonstration Zone	40443
中关村示范区海淀园	Zhongguancun Haidian Sub-park	22051
中关村示范区丰台园	Zhongguancun Fengtai Sub-park	6863
中关村示范区昌平园	Zhongguancun Changping Sub-park	3246
中关村示范区朝阳园	Zhongguancun Chaoyang Sub-park	1463
中关村示范区亦庄园	Zhongguancun Yizhuang Sub-park	852
中关村示范区西城园	Zhongguancun Xicheng Sub-park	523
中关村示范区东城园	Zhongguancun Dongcheng Sub-park	1912
中关村示范区石景山园	Zhongguancun Shijingshan Sub-park	2487
中关村示范区通州园	Zhongguancun Tongzhou Sub-park	250
中关村示范区大兴园	Zhongguancun Daxing Sub-park	89
中关村示范区平谷园	Zhongguancun PingGu Sub-park	37
中关村示范区门头沟园	Zhongguancun MenTouGou Sub-park	100
中关村示范区房山园	Zhongguancun FangShan Sub-park	120
中关村示范区顺义园	Zhongguancun ShunYi Sub-park	251
中关村示范区密云园	Zhongguancun MiYun Sub-park	120
中关村示范区怀柔园	Zhongguancun HuaiRou Sub-park	41
中关村示范区延庆园	Zhongguancun YanQing Sub-park	38
北京天竺综合保税区	Beijing Tianzhu Bonded Area	261
市级开发区	**Municipal-level Development Zone**	**18888**
北京石龙经济开发区	Shilong Economic Development Zone	10265
北京良乡经济开发区	Liangxiang Economic Development Zone	83
北京大兴经济开发区	Daxing Economic Development Zone	2451
北京通州经济开发区	Tongzhou Economic Development Zone	79
北京雁栖经济开发区	Yanqi Economic Development Zone	1707
北京兴谷经济开发区	Xinggu Economic Development Zone	198
北京密云经济开发区	Miyun Economic Development Zone	251
北京林河经济开发区	Linhe Economic Development Zone	292
北京天竺空港经济开发区	Tianzhu Economic Development Zone	751
北京八达岭经济开发区	Badaling Economic Development Zone	1386
北京永乐经济开发区	Yongle Economic Development Zone	26
北京延庆经济开发区	Yanqing Economic Development Zone	1184
北京昌平小汤山工业园区	Changping Xiaotangshan Industrial Park	78
大兴采育经济开发区	Caiyu Economic Development Zone	54
北京房山工业园区	Fangshan Industrial Park	23
北京马坊工业园区	Mafang Industrial Park	60

注：中关村国家自主创新示范区亦庄园数据在中关村国家自主创新示范区与北京经济技术开发区中为重叠部分。

STATISTICS FOR BUSINESS INVITATION AND INVESTMENT IN DEVELOPMENT ZONES (2015)

自开始至报告期累计 Accumulative Number from Beginning				
项目总投资 (万元) Total Investment (10000 yuan)	注册资本 (万元) Registered Capital (10000 yuan)	#三资企业 Foreign-funded Enterprises	合同外资金额 (万美元) Contracted Foreign Capital (USD 10000)	外商实际投资 (万美元) Actual Foreign Investment (USD 10000)
181940961	**161084230**	**22670778**	**2910847**	**2253156**
50330270	42046517	8376568	927701	703016
145564747	127213537	18214479	2202166	1760695
57377660	47897546	9198933	1341962	895909
17647845	17647845	227253	26905	33239
22552785	22342269	1163864	85912	85912
9906380	9906380	1334112	110633	110633
17213168	9480050	4549670	365887	357421
7774996	7774996	30219	97578	97578
2093000	2093000	101275	3293	3142
2919449	2926591	203505	31308	34210
1844603	1099160	304082	16395	16395
233304	225500	16000	5200	4750
100987	100987	11500	2129	2129
973270	973270	10372	1019	319
32684	976545	222823	75	1451
3476293	3055458	800190	109749	111489
657000	582808	38055	3759	5732
715665	79857			
45658	51275	2626	363	386
3259112	1304226	629401	146866	146866
32541041	**22651612**	**3326269**	**541527**	**602769**
3671137	3671137	41465	8028	6454
328651	138091	12057	1532	1532
478512	1176237	151535	10675	9491
2827846	656915	213306	44370	41208
3303258	939172	460489	240471	252780
799886	315676	233643	48109	58506
2946471	541267	131210	24807	53601
905300	591402	94562	12612	7879
5567894	3829889	1950961	142283	161842
664745	824896	19991	60	60
193769	47139	1000		1487
9661968	9392479		5857	6494
52800	34731	6242	989	655
690041	158792	9808	1735	780
209822	94848			
238941	238941			

Note: Data on Yizhuang Sub-park of Zhongguancun Demonstration Zone are overlapped in Zhongguancun National Innovation Demonstration Zone and Beijing Economic and Technological Development Area.

23-4 开发区投资、生产情况(2015年)
INVESTMENT AND PRODUCTION OF DEVELOPMENT ZONES (2015)

名称	Item	自年初累计 Accumulative Number from Year-beginning		
		固定资产投资(万元) Investment in Fixed Assets (10000 yuan)	总收入(万元) Total Revenue (10000 yuan)	利润总额(万元) Total Profits (10000 yuan)
国家级开发区	**State-level Development Zone**	**9254708**	**437850730**	**34928303**
北京经济技术开发区	Beijing Economic-Technological Development Area	3976205	66707451	3845651
中关村国家自主创新示范区	Zhongguancun National Independent Innovation Demonstration Zone	6721912	408119156	34045288
中关村示范区海淀园	Zhongguancun Haidian Sub-park	1368417	163573321	11807509
中关村示范区丰台园	Zhongguancun Fengtai Sub-park	831000	40041748	2992449
中关村示范区昌平园	Zhongguancun Changping Sub-park	298368	33816229	2590676
中关村示范区朝阳园	Zhongguancun Chaoyang Sub-park	300000	42256585	4474515
中关村示范区亦庄园	Zhongguancun Yizhuang Sub-park	1577409	38810670	3182688
中关村示范区西城园	Zhongguancun Xicheng Sub-park	32750	25751554	2451345
中关村示范区东城园	Zhongguancun Dongcheng Sub-park	269492	16703702	1827994
中关村示范区石景山园	Zhongguancun Shijingshan Sub-park	54532	16324566	2437407
中关村示范区通州园	Zhongguancun Tongzhou Sub-park	963840	5976446	449299
中关村示范区大兴园	Zhongguancun Daxing Sub-park	200999	4079480	284148
中关村示范区平谷园	Zhongguancun PingGu Sub-park	45720	997035	54303
中关村示范区门头沟园	Zhongguancun MenTouGou Sub-park	29616	1309775	75658
中关村示范区房山园	Zhongguancun FangShan Sub-park	409200	2183593	118698
中关村示范区顺义园	Zhongguancun ShunYi Sub-park	164004	10397049	869070
中关村示范区密云园	Zhongguancun MiYun Sub-park	32356	1901008	156583
中关村示范区怀柔园	Zhongguancun HuaiRou Sub-park	119213	2898388	195862
中关村示范区延庆园	Zhongguancun YanQing Sub-park	24996	1098007	77083
北京天竺综合保税区	Beijing Tianzhu Bonded Area	134000	1834793	220051
市级开发区	**Municipal-level Development Zone**	**1694612**	**49070250**	**2505266**
北京石龙经济开发区	Shilong Economic Development Zone	29616	7913192	-292861
北京良乡经济开发区	Liangxiang Economic Development Zone	11925	2020028	-697
北京大兴经济开发区	Daxing Economic Development Zone	74395	2266631	27183
北京通州经济开发区	Tongzhou Economic Development Zone	141322	1177231	312591
北京雁栖经济开发区	Yanqi Economic Development Zone	119213	3685540	283542
北京兴谷经济开发区	Xinggu Economic Development Zone	123490	2245375	96420
北京密云经济开发区	Miyun Economic Development Zone	77877	3347449	154222
北京林河经济开发区	Linhe Economic Development Zone	116997	1829856	62869
北京天竺空港经济开发区	Tianzhu Economic Development Zone	851628	20184970	1618795
北京八达岭经济开发区	Badaling Economic Development Zone	24996	1411368	209749
北京永乐经济开发区	Yongle Economic Development Zone	36436	72441	9004
北京延庆经济开发区	Yanqing Economic Development Zone	2033	1235541	25842
北京昌平小汤山工业园区	Changping Xiaotangshan Industrial Park		4457	4
大兴采育经济开发区	Caiyu Economic Development Zone	15950	1175579	38002
北京房山工业园区	Fangshan Industrial Park	36686	208566	-37451
北京马坊工业园区	Mafang Industrial Park	32048	292025	-1949

注：1.中关村国家自主创新示范区亦庄园数据在中关村国家自主创新示范区与北京经济技术开发区中为重叠部分。
2.北京经济技术开发区、市级各开发区"总收入"、"利润总额"指标的统计范围为规模(限额)以上法人单位。

Note: a) Data on Yizhuang Sub-park of Zhongguancun Demonstration Zone are overlapped in Zhongguancun National Innovation Demonstration Zone and Beijing Economic and Technological Development Area.

b) The statistical scope of total revenue and total profits for Beijing Economic-Technological Development Area and other municipal-level development zones covers legal entities above designated size.

23-5 北京经济技术开发区主要经济指标
MAIN ECONOMIC INDICATORS FOR BEIJING ECONOMIC-TECHNOLOGICAL DEVELOPMENT AREA

项 目		Item		2015	2014	2015年为2014年% 2015 as % of 2014
规划面积	(公顷)	Area Planned	(hectare)	4680.0	4680.0	100.0
开发区生产总值	(亿元)	Gross Output Value	(100 million yuan)	1081.4	997.4	108.4
工业总产值	(亿元)	Gross Output Value of Industry	(100 million yuan)	2555.5	2421.0	105.6
(当年价格)		(at current prices)				
#高新技术企业	(亿元)	High and New Technology Enterprises	(100 million yuan)	2333.2	2201.7	106.0
销售(营业)收入	(亿元)	Sales(Business)Revenue	(100 million yuan)	6670.7	5589.9	119.3
利润总额	(亿元)	Total Profits	(100 million yuan)	384.6	249.2	154.3
进出口总值	(亿美元)	Total Value of Imports and Exports	(USD 100 million)	146.6	190.0	77.2
出 口	(亿美元)	Exports	(USD 100 million)	52.6	88.6	59.4
进 口	(亿美元)	Imports	(USD 100 million)	94.0	101.4	92.7
公共财政预算收入	(亿元)	Local Public Finance Budget Revenue	(100 million yuan)	134.9	120.0	112.4
公共财政预算支出	(亿元)	Local Public Finance Budget Expenditure	(100 million yuan)	145.4	112.1	129.7
批准企业个数	(个)	Number of Enterprises Ratified	(unit)	3197	2736	116.8
入区企业投资额	(亿美元)	Investment of Enterprises Entering the Area	(USD 100 million)	192.6	119.5	161.2
注册资本	(亿美元)	Registered Capital	(USD 100 million)	169.7	113.5	149.5
合同外资金额	(亿美元)	Contracted Foreign Capital	(USD 100 million)	9.2	5.0	184.3
实际利用外资	(亿美元)	Actual Use of Foreign Capital	(USD 100 million)	3.0	6.4	47.5
固定资产投资	(亿元)	Investment in Fixed Assets	(100 million yuan)	397.6	391.0	101.7
从业人员期末人数	(人)	Number of Employed Persons	(person)	314059	286133	109.8
从业人员工资总额	(万元)	Total Wages of Employed Persons	(10000 yuan)	3140220	2885362	108.8

注：工业总产值(当年价格)、销售(营业)收入和利润总额指标的统计范围是规模(限额)以上法人单位。

资料来源：北京经济技术开发区统计局、调查队。

Note: The statistical scope of gross output value of industry (at current prices), sales (business) revenue and total profits covers legal entities above designated size.

Source: Statistics Bureau and Survey Team of Beijing Economic-Technological Development Area.

23-6 中关村国家自主创新示范区企业经营及科技活动情况(2008-2015年) OPERATING ACTIVITIES AND SCIENCE ACTIVITIES OF ENTERPRISES IN ZHONGGUANCUN NATIONAL INNOVATION DEMONSTRATION ZONE (2008-2015)

项目	Item	2008	2009	2010	2011	2012	2013	2014	2015
总收入 (亿元)	**Total Revenue (100 million yuan)**	**10222.4**	**13004.6**	**15940.2**	**19646.0**	**25025.0**	**30497.4**	**36057.6**	**40811.9**
技术收入 (亿元)	Technological Revenue (100 million yuan)	1693.4	2093.6	2478.3	2845.9	3403.1	4032.4	4837.7	6623.6
产品销售收入 (亿元)	Products Sales Revenue (100 million yuan)	5229.2	5923.6	6889.6	7809.4	8741.2	10788.4	12474.2	13300.0
#新产品销售收入 (亿元)	Sales Revenue of New Products (100 million yuan)	3327.0	3203.7	3949.2	3405.1	3352.1	4070.4	4614.8	4397.5
商品销售收入 (亿元)	Commodity Sales Revenue (100 million yuan)	2398.9	3689.4	5032.2	7161.9	10077.4	11339.6	12832.6	13339.5
其他收入 (亿元)	Other Revenues (100 million yuan)	900.9	1298.0	1540.1	1828.9	2803.4	4337.0	5913.1	7548.9
出口总额 (亿美元)	Total Exports (USD 100 million)	207.4	208.2	227.4	237.3	261.7	336.2	337.3	299.4
实缴税费总额 (亿元)	Total Tax Paid (100 million yuan)	504.0	658.7	767.2	925.8	1445.8	1506.6	1857.6	2038.1
利润总额 (亿元)	Total Profits (100 million yuan)	726.3	1122.4	1298.9	1533.9	1788.6	2264.8	3031.5	3404.5
获奖成果情况	**Statistics on Prize-winning Achievements**								
获奖成果个数 (个)	Number of Prize-winning Achievements (unit)	1448	1909	1811	2329	2509	2852	2636	3577
#国家级 (个)	National (unit)	282	276	256	323	377	450	364	358
省部级 (个)	Provincial (unit)	641	1044	1015	1351	1318	1652	1522	2219
专利情况	**Statistics on Patents**								
专利申请数 (件)	Number of Patents Applied (unit)	17219	17226	18515	24894	34192	44275	55009	68944
拥有有效发明专利数(件)	Number of Patents in Force (unit)	9836	11611	13988	15232	23198	35000	44870	63171
专利授权数 (件)	Number of Patents Licensed (unit)	9050	10512	13151	12951	17969	22308	25065	32327

23-7 中关村国家自主创新示范区企业经营活动情况 OPERATING ACTIVITIES OF ENTERPRISES IN ZHONGGUANCUN NATIONAL INNOVATION DEMONSTRATION ZONE

单位：亿元 (100 million yuan)

项目	Item	2015	2014
工业总产值(当年价格)	Gross Output Value of Industry (at current prices)	9561.7	9289.0
工业销售产值(当年价格)	Sales Value of Industry (at current prices)	8972.4	9102.0
#出口交货值	Delivery Value of Exports	720.1	963.2
总收入	Total Revenue	40811.9	36057.6
技术收入	Technological Revenue	6623.6	4837.7
产品销售收入	Products Sales Revenue	13300.0	12474.2
#新产品销售收入	Sales Revenue of New Products	4397.5	4614.8
#出口收入	Export Revenue	854.8	1023.7
商品销售收入	Commodity Sales Revenue	13339.5	12832.6
其他收入	Other Revenues	7548.9	5913.1
利润总额	Total Profits	3404.5	3031.5
实缴税费总额	Total Tax Paid	2038.1	1857.6
#增值税	Value Added Tax	904.5	830.2
营业税	Business Tax	166.4	138.7
所得税	Corporate Income Tax	534.3	493.4
本年实缴关税	Duties Paid in the Year	196.4	184.1
减免税总额	Reduced and Exempted Tax	359.8	315.0
#增值税	Value Added Tax	159.8	105.6
营业税	Business Tax	4.2	1.2
所得税	Corporate Income Tax	188.0	202.2
应交增值税	Value Added Tax Payable	764.6	647.8
出口总额 (亿美元)	Foreign Exchange Created by Export (USD100 million)	299.4	337.3

23-8 中关村国家自主创新示范区企业研发活动情况
SCIENTIFIC ACTIVITIES OF ENTERPRISES IN ZHONGGUANCUN NATIONAL INNOVATION DEMONSTRATION ZONE

项 目		Item		2015	2014
研发活动情况		**Statistics on Scientific and Technological Activities**			
研发人员合计	(人)	Total Number of Personnel Engaged in Scientific and Technological Activities	(person)	604816	531609
#全职人员		Full-time Personnel		557124	476858
企业内部的日常研发经费支出	(亿元)	Total Expenditures on Research Activities Inside Enterprises	(100 million yuan)	1522.6	1224.1
#人员人工费(包括各种补贴)		Labor Cost (Including Various Subsidies)		836.1	662.0
原材料费		Cost of Raw Materials		261.0	215.3
委托外单位开展研发的经费支出	(亿元)	Expenditures on Scientific and Technological Activities Institutions Conducted by External Institutes Entrusted	(100 million yuan)	149.5	131.9
#对境内研究机构及高等学校的支出		Spending on Domestic Research Institutes and of Higher Education		69.7	92.3
对境外支出		Overseas Spending		7.4	6.1
企业科技活动产出情况		**Scientific and Technological Output**			
获奖成果情况		**Statistics on Prize-winning Achievements**			
获奖成果个数	(个)	Number of Prize-winning Achievements	(unit)	3577	2636
#国家级	(个)	National	(unit)	358	364
省部级	(个)	Provincial	(unit)	2219	1522
地市级	(个)	Prefecture and City-level	(unit)	1000	750
专利情况		**Statistics on Patents**			
当年专利申请受理数	(件)	Number of Patents Applied	(case)	68944	55009
#发明专利	(件)	Invention Patents	(case)	45939	34523
期末拥有有效发明专利数	(件)	Number of Patents in Force	(case)	63171	44870
当年专利授权数	(件)	Number of Patent Licensed	(case)	32327	25065
论文、著作情况		**Statistics on Papers and Writings**			
发表科技论文	(篇)	Number of Published Scientific Papers	(unit)	16693	14744
技术改造和技术获取情况		**Technical Rennovation and Acquisition**			
技术改造经费支出	(亿元)	Expenditures on Technical Rennovation	(100 million yuan)	24.1	37.9
引进境外技术经费支出	(亿元)	Expenditures on Introduction of Foreign Technologies	(100 million yuan)	20.7	13.4
引进技术的消化吸收经费支出	(亿元)	Expenditures on Absorption of Imported Technologies	(100 million yuan)	7.6	7.7
购买境内技术经费支出	(亿元)	Expenditures on Purchasing Domestic Technologies	(100 million yuan)	13.3	9.7

23-9 中关村国家自主创新示范区企业人力资源情况 HUMAN RESOURCES OF ENTERPRISES IN ZHONGGUANCUN NATIONAL INNOVATION DEMONSTRATION ZONE

单位：人 (person)

项目	Item	2015	2014
企业人力资源情况	**Statistics on Human Resource**		
从业人员年末人数	**Number of Employeed Persons at the Year End**	**2316372**	**2010448**
#工程技术人员	Engineering Technician	673046	572664
#留学归国人员	Returned Students Studying Abroad	27435	21521
#在岗长期职工	On-the-post Long-term Employed Persons	2125468	1835847
按文化程度分	**By Educational Background**		
博士及以上	Doctor Degree and Above	23492	19774
#留学归国人员	Returned Students Studying Abroad	2782	2237
硕　士	Masters	238324	198237
#留学归国人员	Returned Students Studying Abroad	18864	14363
大　本	Undergraduates	944733	810731
大　专	Junior College	499736	433752
按技术职称分	**By Technical Post**		
高　级	Senior	140654	122111
中　级	Middle	249076	223465
初　级	Junior	262349	240694
按年龄分	**By Age**		
#29岁及以下	Age 29 and Below	1024651	899410
30-39岁	30-39	814472	690093
40-49岁	40-49	320017	282530
从业人员平均人数	**Average Number of Empolyed Persons**	**2298503**	**1972084**
在岗职工参加社会保险人数	**Number of Employees Covered by the Social Insurance**	**1996831**	**1761881**

23-10 中关村国家自主创新示范区企业财务状况 FINANCIAL STATUS OF ENTERPRISES IN ZHONGGUANCUN NATIONAL INNOVATION DEMONSTRATION ZONE

单位：亿元 (100 million yuan)

项目	Item	2015	2014
资产总计	Total Assets	79917.4	64770.8
流动资产合计	Total Current Assets	57221.4	35648.9
固定资产合计	Total Fixed Assets	7745.4	7495.2
固定资产原价	Original Value of Fixed Assets	11861.8	10997.0
累计折旧	Accumulative Depreciation	4350.3	3731.0
负债合计	Total Liabilities	43795.3	36105.7
所有者权益合计	Total Owner's Equity	36122.1	28665.1
实收资本	Paid-up Capital	16264.7	15010.2
主营业务收入	Operating Income	38991.2	34857.1
主营业务成本	Main Business Cost	31627.8	28601.9
主营业务税金及附加	Main Business Tax and Surtax	338.7	283.5
利润总额	Total Profits	3404.5	3031.5

主要统计指标解释

已开发土地面积 指在规划范围内达到“七通一平”标准的，具备进行房屋建筑物施工或出让条件的土地面积。

已供应土地面积 指开发区内通过各种方式获得土地使用权的土地面积，包括出让、划拨、租赁等。

已建成城镇建设用地面积 截至报告期，已经建设并通过竣工验收的国有建设用地。包括已建成的住宅用地、工矿仓储用地、多功能用地、交通运输用地、商服用地、公共管理与公共服务用地，以及其他城镇建设用地等。海关特殊监管区域的已建成城镇建设用地包括现状围网范围内已建成的城镇建设用地，及开发区四至范围与围网范围间的海关专属办公用地。

累计招商项目企业个数 指自开始至报告期末累计招商入区，并经工商管理机关注册取得法人营业执照的企业个数。

累计招商项目总投资 指自开始至报告期末累计批准的合同（章程）规定的投资总额。

累计招商项目注册资本 指自开始至报告期末累计为设立经营企业在工商行政管理机关注册的资本总额。

累计招商项目合同外资金额 指自开始至报告期末累计批准的合同（章程）中，外商和港、澳、台商的出资额。

累计招商项目外商实际投资 指自开始至报告期末累计按合同规定的外方和港、澳、台方以现金、实物、工业产权及专有技术的计价实缴资本投资额。

总收入 指企业全年的生产产品销售收入、技术性收入和与本企业产品相关的商品的销售收入、其它收入等各种收入的总和，总收入等于主营业务收入加上其他业务收入。总收入应按不含增值税的价格计算，不包括补贴收入、营业外收入、投资收益。

出口总额 指出售给外贸部门或直接出售给外商的产品、商品、技术或服务的总金额。包括来料加工装配出口，境外技术合同实现金额及在国内以外汇计价的商品出售和技术服务的总额等。以千美元计价。

留学归国人员 指出国学习，取得学位的归国人员。

Explanatory Notes on Main Statistical Indicators

Area of Developed Land refers to the area of land that meets the standard of "seven connections and one leveling" and is qualified for construction or sale.

Area of Supplied Land refers to the area of land whose right of use is acquired in the development zones by various means including sale, transfer, and lease.

Area of Land for Urban Development refers to state-owned construction land that has already gone through construction and acceptance check by the end of the reporting period. It includes land for complete residential buildings, land for industrial, mining and storage use, multi-functional land, land for transportation, land for commercial services, land for public administration and services and other lands for urban development. Land for urban development under special administration of customs includes urban development land completed inside the current seine and land for office buildings of customs inside the development zones and between the seines.

Accumulated Number of Enterprises Involved in Business Inviting Programs refers to the total number of enterprises invited to development zones and awarded with business licenses for legal persons from the administration for industry and commerce from the beginning to the end of the reporting period.

Accumulative Investment of Business Inviting Programs refers to the total investment of contracts (articles of incorporation) approved from the beginning to the end of the reporting period.

Accumulative Registered Capital of Business Inviting Programs refers to the total capital registered with the administration for industry and commerce for the purpose of establishment of operating enterprises from the beginning to the end of the reporting period.

Accumulative Contracted Foreign Capital of Business Inviting Programs refers to the cumulative capital contribution of investors from foreign countries, Hong Kong, Macao and Taiwan as approved in contracts (articles of incorporation) from the beginning to the end of the reporting period.

Accumulative Actual Foreign Investment of Business Inviting Programs refers to the cumulative amount of paid-up capital investment from foreign countries, Hong Kong, Macao and Taiwan made in cash, in physical material, industrial property right and proprietary technology, as stated in contracts, from the beginning to the end of the reporting period.

Total Revenue refers to the sum of income earned by enterprises from sales of their own products, technological income, and income from selling commodities related to their own products, and other income. Total revenue is the sum of main business income and other business income. Total revenue shall be calculated at VAT-excluded prices, and exclude subsidies, non-operating income and return on investment across the year.

Total Exports refers to the total amount of products or commodities sold to foreign trade organizations or directly sold to foreign traders. It includes the value of export of investor's raw materials processed, the value of technical contracts completed at home and abroad, and the total value of domestic commodity sales and technical services measured in foreign currency.

Returned Students Studying Abroad refer to persons who have come home after studying abroad and been conferred with academic degrees.